The Handbook of
SOCIAL WORK DIRECT PRACTICE

The Handbook of
SOCIAL WORK DIRECT PRACTICE

Edited by

Paula Allen-Meares
Charles Garvin

Sage Publications, Inc.
International Educational and Professional Publisher
Thousand Oaks ▪ London ▪ New Delhi

For information:

 Sage Publications, Inc.
2455 Teller Road
Thousand Oaks, California 91320
E-mail: order@sagepub.com

Sage Publications Ltd.
6 Bonhill Street
London EC2A 4PU
United Kingdom

Sage Publications India Pvt. Ltd.
M-32 Market
Greater Kailash I
New Delhi 110 048 India

Printed in the United States of America

Library of Congress Cataloging-in-Publication Data

Main entry under title:
The handbook of social work direct practice / edited by Paula
Allen-Meares and Charles Garvin.
    p. cm.
Includes bibliographical references and index.
  ISBN 0-7619-1499-4 (cloth: alk. paper) — ISBN 0-7619-1500-1
(pbk. : alk. paper)
  1. Social service. 2. Social service—United States. I.
Allen-Meares, Paula, 1948- II. Garvin, Charles D.
  HV40 .H2827 2000
    361.3'0973—dc21   00-008074

00 01 02 03 10 9 8 7 6 5 4 3 2 1

Acquiring Editor:	Nancy Hale
Editorial Assistant:	Heidi Van Middlesworth
Production Editors:	Diana E. Axelsen/Elly Korn
Editorial Assistant:	Cindy Bear
Designer:	Marion Warren
Typesetter:	Danielle Dillahunt
Indexer:	Virgil Diodato
Cover Designer:	Michelle Lee

Contents

Acknowledgements   ix

Introduction   xi

PART I: THE CONTEXT OF PRACTICE   I

1. The Context of Social Work Practice   5
   Robert Fisher and Howard Jacob Karger

2. Legal Issues in Practice   23
   Robert G. Madden

3. The Role of Critical Thinking in Evidence-Based Social Work   43
   Eileen Gambrill

4. The Concept of Levels and Systems in Social Work   65
   John E. Tropman and Katherine E. Richards-Schuster

PART II: FRAMEWORKS FOR PRACTICE   85

5. Prevention: A Risk and Resilience Perspective   89
   Mark W. Fraser, Karen A. Randolph, and M. Daniel Bennett

6. Empowerment-Oriented Practice: From Practice Value
    to Practice Model   113
    Enid O. Cox and Ruth J. Parsons

7. Multicultural Perspectives on Direct Practice in Social Work   131
    Michael Spencer, Edith Lewis, and Lorraine Gutiérrez

8. Feminist Social Work Practice: Womanly Warrior
    or Damsel in Distress?   151
    Mary Bricker-Jenkins

PART III: APPROACHES TO CHANGE   171

9. Thinking Differently: The Cognitive-Integrative Approach
    to Changing a Mind   175
    Sharon B. Berlin and Jane E. Barden

10. Approaches to Behavioral Change   197
    Bruce A. Thyer and Laura L. Myers

11. Affective Change: Depression and Anxiety Disorders   217
    Joseph A. Himle

12. Adult Change   241
    William J. Reid and Elizabeth Misener

13. Individual Change in Children and Direct Social Work Practice 261
    Kathleen Coulborn Faller

14. Change in Groups   281
    David E. Pollio, Aaron M. Brower, and Maeda J. Galinsky

15. Advances in Family Therapy: Theory and Practice   301
    Froma Walsh and Carmen Crosser

16. Crisis Intervention Practices in Social Work Settings   327
    Albert R. Roberts and Jacqui Corcoran

17. Coping   349
    Paula S. Nurius

18. Social Work in the Social Environment:
    Integrated Practice—An Empowerment/Structural Approach   373
    Marie Weil

PART IV: FIELDS OF PRACTICE   411

19. Direct Practice in Fields Related to Developmental Tasks:
    A Life-Span Perspective   415
    Edith M. Freeman

20. The New World of Practice in Physical and Mental Health:
    Comorbidity, Cultural Competence, and Managed Care   437
    Lonnie R. Snowden

21. The Juvenile Justice System in Crisis: Challenges and
    Opportunities for Social Workers   451
    Rosemary C. Sarri

22. Social Work Practice With Lesbians and Gay Men   477
    John F. Longres and Karen I. Fredriksen

23. Practice in the World of Work: Promise Unrealized   499
    Sheila H. Akabas

24. Social Work Practice Issues Related to Poverty and Homelessness   519
    Elizabeth A. Segal and Layne K. Stromwall

PART V: RESEARCH AND EMPIRICAL ISSUES   533

25. Pragmatic Applications of Single-Case and Group Designs
    in Social Work Practice Evaluation and Research   535
    Neil Abell and Walter W. Hudson

26. Assessment and Measurement Issues in Direct Practice
    in Social Work   551
    Betty Blythe and Anita Reithoffer

27. Computer-Mediated Communications in Direct Social
    Work Practice   565
    Marilyn Flynn

PART VI: PROFESSIONAL ISSUES   585

28. Ethical Issues in Direct Practice   589
    Frederic G. Reamer

29. Supervision Standards of Practice in an Era of
    Societal Restructuring   611
    Carlton E. Munson

30. International Perspectives on Social Work Practice   633
    Doreen Elliott and Nazneen S. Mayadas

31. Fund-Raising for the Direct Services   651
    Armand Lauffer

Conclusion   667

Author Index   669

Subject Index   699

About the Editors   727

About the Contributors   729

Acknowledgments

In the early planning of this book, we benefited from the advice of a group of colleagues at the University of Michigan, consisting of Professors Siri Jayarante, Kris Siefert, Kathleen Faller, David Tucker, Richard Tolman, and Berit Ingersoll-Dayton. In addition, we consulted with many faculty from other institutions. This list would be too long to include here. We wish to extend our gratitude to Professors Rino Patti and James Midgley, the editors of other volumes of this Handbook series, for their thoughtful feedback and critiques of our prospectus. We are deeply indebted to Jim Nageotte, formerly the Social Work Editor at Sage, and his staff, for inspiring this series and continuing to nurture it. A special thank-you is also extended to Sharon Moskwiak, Executive Secretary to Paula Allen-Meares, who spent countless hours contacting authors and organizing the final document.

We appreciate that Walter Hudson worked diligently on a chapter for this book, virtually until the day of his untimely death. Walter will always be remembered for his dedication to the profession of social work and for his unique contributions to the scholarship and research required for us to continue to move forward.

Finally, we as editors have found the work on this project to be an exciting and stimulating activity made more so by the numerous opportunities it gave us to get to know each other better, to increase our respect for each other, and to learn from each other. It is impossible to say anything so mundane as who did what or how much with respect to the final project, and this is reflected in our decision to list ourselves alphabetically.

PAULA ALLEN-MEARES
University of Michigan

CHARLES GARVIN
University of Michigan

Introduction

The Handbook of Social Work Direct Practice is one of four volumes that describe the major issues confronting social work today, summarize the most recent and advanced ideas about how these issues are addressed, and predict directions this field will take in the next century. The other volumes deal with social welfare administration, social policy, social work research, and community organization. These books take advantage of the attention being paid to the start of a new millenium by creating an agenda for the evolution of social work practice, theory, and research for the next century.

The purpose of this volume is to focus on the issues confronting direct practice; direct practice is typically defined as the methods used by social workers to serve individuals, one at a time or in families and groups. Although this volume does deal with these methods, we, as its editors, have a broader concept of direct practice. We accept the classical definition that social work attends to the ways individuals, singly as well as collectively, enhance their lives and solve social problems as they interact with their environments. Social workers, consequently, work to bring about changes in the ways people cope with these environments as well as in the environments themselves.

We see direct practitioners as people and environmental change agents. First, they help people change environmental conditions that oppress them, and second, they bring about environmental changes that have this effect. We see a major difference between the roles of direct and macro practitioners in that the former focus on specific environments and policies that affect the individuals, families, and groups they serve and the latter focus on environments that have an impact on classes of individuals, such as those in poverty or those who suffer from mental illness. Thus, macro practitioners may target specific agencies and organizations, communities, whole societies, or even global circumstances. They may seek to alter structural circumstances, policies, belief systems, or institutional goals. They may do this through such processes as planning, program development, advocacy, coordination, conflict mediation, and data collection and analysis.

The chapters in this book seek to offer a contextualized view of both the field of social work and the many social conditions targeted by this profession. One chapter focuses on the meaning of contextualized practice, and all authors were asked to consider how their separate topics relate to environmental contexts. The concept of environment includes physical environments, cultures, political forces, ethical considerations, relations among social groups, forces of social and economic exploitation and oppression, and the media.

To carry out the purpose of this volume, we asked the authors to indicate how their topics relate to five themes. There are differences, however, in how the authors considered these themes due to their own ideologies and the nature of their specific topics. One such theme is the recognition that the phenomena of concern to social workers take place in a socially and culturally diverse world and that many societies, such as the United States, Great Britain, Canada, Russia, and China—to name a few—are themselves highly culturally diverse. We see, therefore, that the issues of diversity within a country and among countries are related. We also maintain that the world should be seen as a global community in which events that happen in one country or region have wide reverberations, sometimes worldwide. This is, on the one hand, one of the contextual realities to which we have just referred. It is also a demand that social work practices be relevant to and useful for a *progressive* practice with members of the social group to which they are applied. By a progressive practice, we mean one in which sources of disadvantage, wherever they originate, are confronted and in which human growth to reach human potential is promoted.

Another theme, related to the first, is that of social and economic justice. We see many of the problems experienced by the people served by the profession as resulting from a lack of such justice. This occurs when individuals are discriminated against because of their color, ethnicity, spiritual beliefs, gender, national origin, sexual orientation, age, disability, and so forth. This discrimination may take the form of inferior education, lack of job opportunity, unavailability of housing, exposure to violence, denial of opportunity to participate in democratic processes, and attributions of inferiority. Every social work method should incorporate ways that social justice may be achieved.

A third theme is the principle that social work practice should be grounded in scientific evidence. Practice assertions include those about reality (e.g., the majority of the residents in a community are poor), about the causes of behavior or other events (e.g., an individual's rebellious behavior is caused by the punishment he receives), or about the validity of a practice prescription (e.g., exposure therapy should be used to help a client with an anxiety disorder). Scientific evidence means that relevant data have been collected and analyzed in ways that can be replicated by others, concepts have been carefully defined, and assumptions have been made explicit. When relevant to do so, data collection and analysis have been guided by clear hypotheses.

We also assert that the next generation of knowledge for social work will even be more interdisciplinary in nature and that social workers will have to evaluate and use carefully knowledge from disciplines such as the social sciences, the humanities, and the biological sciences, as well as from other professions such as psychiatry, nursing, law, public health, social administration, and public policy. The phenomena with which social workers deal are complex, and everything is to be gained by integrating knowledge and expertise from the disciplines.

The fourth theme is that social workers should think systemically and critically in view of the complexity of the relationships among the variables practitioners must take into consideration. We view all social events as occurring in social systems. A social system is an entity with boundaries, internal structures, goals, a means of maintaining order within the boundaries, and a means of relating to the larger system in which the system is embedded. The system, itself, may incorporate still smaller systems. Thus, a family is a system embedded in a community and may incorporate a smaller system composed of the adults in the family. We are particularly concerned in this volume with how the individuals, families, and groups with whom direct practice social workers interact are affected by and in turn affect such larger systems as communities, organizations, political states, and ultimately the whole earth.

The fifth theme is that of prevention. Practitioners often view direct social work practice as rehabilitation of people who are dysfunctional or who suffer from severe problem situations. In public health terms, this is conceptualized as tertiary prevention. This is a costly approach to the promotion of functional behavior or, if you will, mental health. It is consistent with our previous discussion of social justice, an appreciation of diversity, and an understanding of systems to urge the field of social work to pay more attention to primary prevention—both to help people enhance their ability to cope with social systems and to work for the amelioration of social conditions that place people at risk of developing serious problems.

We have asked the authors of the chapters in this volume to consider how these themes relate to their separate topics. In addition, we have commissioned a number of chapters to deal in depth with these themes. These include separate chapters on multiculturalism and diversity issues, multiculturalism in an international framework, empowerment, feminism, and change in the social environment. The scientific basis for direct practice is dealt with in all of the chapters of Part V, where research and empirical issues are analyzed. Systemic thinking is described in one chapter and reinforced in a chapter on environmental change. Finally, prevention issues underlie the content of two chapters, one on coping with stress and the other on prevention, itself viewed broadly.

We will clarify further how these and other issues blend together as we introduce each of the sections of this book. The section organization itself represents our approach to the complex and demanding task of representing the multifaceted nature of direct practice. Part I presents a series of issues that underlie all of the facets of direct practice: its contexts, its legal base, its requirement for critical thinking, and its systemic nature. Part II presents a series of conceptual frameworks that should help in the choice of theories and models. These frameworks are those of prevention, empowerment, multiculturalism, and feminism. Part III offers chapters that discuss theories and modalities that are drawn on when change is sought in different aspects of individual behavior or in systems of different levels of complexity (individual, family, group, environmental systems). The chapters in Part IV discuss approaches that re- late to selected fields of practice such as those serving people who have physical or mental health problems, who live in poverty, or who are identified with sexual minorities. Part V deals with research and knowledge development activities. Part VI analyzes a series of professional concerns, with a focus on direct practice, such as ethics and values, education, and the acquisition of new forms of financial support for services.

PART I

The Context of Practice

As we stated in the introduction to this book, we believe that social work direct practice cannot be adequately described or developed without attention to a series of contextual forces. One type of force is exerted by the economic, political, and cultural environment within which the practice takes place. Practitioners must understand how these forces determine the selection of change goals, interventions, and targets, as well as how outcomes are evaluated.

Fisher and Karger, in Chapter 1, address the changing context of social work—in a world that is in dynamic transition, as a consequence of the global economy, new communications technology,

and worldwide reactionary political climate. They argue that these changes will produce new opportunities for social workers to engage in social change. They further argue that to engage in social change one must contextualize practice within the new context created by these dynamic forces. The social change perspective of social work practice is advocated to prevent the privatization and the erosion of what is best for the public good. The authors identify a list of elements we can draw on to contextualize practice—for example, establishing macro social work analysis and practice as the base of social work practice and including a social change ideology into social work practice.

Another set of forces is provided by the legal system. This system determines what kinds of practice are permitted, what kinds of protection the laws provide to both practitioners and recipients of service, what is legal or illegal for clients to do, and what is regarded as ethical or unethical. At times, practitioners must interact with the legal system, including lawyers, the police, and the courts, and they must have the skills to do so in ways that benefit the practice of social work as well as the rights of clients.

The intersections of law and social work will take on increasing importance as we move into the next century. This should not be surprising, given what has occurred in the last few decades of the 20th century. As Madden points out in Chapter 2, social justice can be "realized through careful use of the legal system in addressing class issues such as poverty, unemployment, and discrimination" (p. 24). From the beginning of the profession, we have challenged unfair policies, discriminatory practices, and societal conditions on behalf of disempowered and/or disadvantaged groups who did not have equal access to power, influence, and legal representation. In an attempt to provide the reader with an introduction to legal content/terms/definitions, Madden also explores some important legal issues arising from rapid social and technological advances and what social workers must consider to minimize legal exposure.

Another type of contextual issue is how practitioners think and communicate their thoughts. An understanding of these mental activities not only draws from such social sciences as psychology and linguistics but from many of the humanities—for example, communication studies—as well as logic and other branches of philosophy. It is to some degree because of this aspect of professional action that the Council on Social Work Education in the United States has insisted on a liberal arts foundation for social work.

Gambrill discusses the call for critical thinking and evidence-based social work in Chapter 3. Critical thinking involves questioning what others take for granted, and asking "What's the evidence for this?" (p. 44).

During the late 1960s and early 1970s, we were inundated with social work literature that urged us to become more accountable, to evaluate our practice, to test and replicate different interventions, and, in general, to become more analytical about our professional behavior and thinking. If the last few decades of the 20th century are indicators of what the new millennium will bring in terms of social issues, complicated social problems, ethical issues, and new client and service system issues, we will need enhanced critical thinking and better evidence to achieve our professional goals.

Another issue that goes straight to the core of contextual thinking is how systems are understood. All practice activities take place within a set of systems that are often conceived of as concentric circles surrounding the practice. And some practice situations themselves constitute complex systems enclosing smaller systems. Most ideas about the transactions between clients and environments make use of one or another approach to understanding systems. Practitioners need a means of planning interventions that have effects at different systemic levels.

In Chapter 4, Tropman and Richards-Schuster contribute theory and conceptual undergirding to the discussion of systems and levels by examining more fully the different systems/contexts within which practice occurs. For example, one system in which social workers practice is the child welfare system. Another illustrative example is the community. A level, on the other hand, can be defined as the echelon, or step, on which a system organizes itself. What becomes very explicit in this chapter is that practitioners must understand and become more knowledgeable about these concepts—systems and levels and their usefulness for developing intervention strategies to achieve social work goals and objectives. Social service systems are growing in complexity as public and private systems contract, merge, and consolidate. Analytical frameworks, like the systems and levels discussion, will be invaluable.

Thus, this section makes the case that social workers need to adapt and/or to contextualize their practice, given new social problems, social forces, and the intersections of knowledge from other disciplines and professions. In the 20th century, social workers were taught to start "where the client is." In the 21st century, another directive will be added to this important phrase: Contextualize your practice.

CHAPTER ONE

The Context of Social Work Practice

ROBERT FISHER

HOWARD JACOB KARGER

This is an important and challenging time to be practicing social work. The world is in a dynamic state of transition, responding to changes rooted in the global economy, new communication technologies, and a worldwide reactionary political climate. Events in places as distant from each other as Russia, Sudan, Bosnia, and urban America make it seem that society is disintegrating; the attacks of neoconservative politicians on social welfare policy and the diminution of governmental responsibility reinforce this perception. The barriers to progressive change seem immense. For-tunately, new contexts produce new openings for social change. To fully exploit the opportunities provided by this contemporary transition, social workers and clients must understand the nature of the new conditions and how to use them for progressive social change.

To advance social change, we argue for the importance of context in social work. By context, we are referring to knowing and understanding the connection between daily social work practice and the structural dynamics of society—its history, economy, politics, and social and cultural dimensions. Contextualization

AUTHORS' NOTE: This chapter is based on material in *Social Work and Community in a Private World: Getting Out in Public* (Fisher & Karger, 1997).

assumes that individual, family, and community problems are always tied to larger structural factors. At the heart of a critical contextualization is an analysis of power and inequality, as well as a social change ideology that translates this critical analysis into action.

This chapter offers an analysis of contemporary life and proposes a model for contextualizing social work practice. Specifically, the chapter examines the idea of public and private worlds and looks at the privatization of social life. The chapter also examines the substitution of a public for a private life. In effect, the authors investigate the transformation of the political into the personal and its social impact. In that vein, the chapter looks at how privatization changes citizens' sense of the proper role of government and how it leads to new forms of social life and social organization. The chapter also discusses why, in the final analysis, privatized market economies are limited in their impact on social welfare activities. Building on this analysis, the authors examine the effects of privatization on social work practice by focusing on the three primary factors that promote the privatization of private life: economic globalization, the neoconservative response to it, and the absence of effective grassroots challenges to the new global economy. Finally, because contexts are multiple and multilayered (e.g., they extend across time from the past to the present and across space from the individual to the global), this chapter examines varied contexts for practice and their impact on social work practice. It also investigates the components required for an integrated social work practice that builds on micro and macro practice understandings. By emphasizing the need for social workers to expand public life and promote a progressive understanding of the public good,

we hope to challenge the profession to move beyond its current emphasis on a depoliticized and decontextualized personal and family therapy that reinforces the conservative context (Fisher & Karger, 1997).

As social work practice confronts the challenges of a new millennium, it is essential for practitioners to understand the larger context. The world in which social workers live and work is increasingly moving away from the public, away from the social, and toward a preoccupation with the private. Shifts in context and their impact on practice are not unexpected in social work. "Perhaps more than any other profession, social work is affected by the times in which it is practiced," begins Leon Ginsburg in his introduction to the 1987 edition of the *Encyclopedia of Social Work*. "Each decade of post-World War II America has clearly changed the content and extent of social work services and practice modes" (p. xxiii). In this new and challenging context for social work, important questions arise. For example, how do we practice *social* work in a world increasingly antagonistic to the social, that is, the public sphere? How do we create empowered public citizens in a social world that increasingly values independent and autonomous private consumers, workers, and family members?

We find ourselves increasingly in a private as opposed to a public world, with profound implications for social work practice. As the societal context becomes more asocial—focused on private needs and institutions and divorced from social concerns—public life falls into a state of decline and the concept of a public good becomes more conservative and exclusionary. Ryan (1992) argues that a public world encourages "open, inclusive, and effective deliberation about matters of common and critical concern"

(p. 259). Habermas (1989) notes that the public world represents what is open to all, as opposed to what is exclusive or closed. Or what is public is tied to the state, such as a public building, which is not necessarily open to all but which does house the government and is fundamentally about "promoting the public or common welfare of its rightful members" (p. 2). The public realm is about the creation and maintenance of society and existence in a social world that is larger than one's self or one's family. Public life is life at work, at school, in communities, and through national and international citizenship. The public realm is the world of contact with acquaintances and strangers, including a broad diversity of people. It is the *social* in social work.

The privatization of our contemporary context has several central features: It reflects a society dominated by *a culture of private individuals, a physical world of private spaces,* and *a political economy of private institutions.* These developments are not new. American society has always been highly individualistic, and this is the core of the Lockean political theory on which our democratic civilization rests. In the 1830s, de Tocqueville (1988) found individualism to be the distinguishing feature of American life, especially when compared with the more collectivistic mentality of Europe. Indeed, American capitalism has almost always been characterized by a strong antagonism to public institutions helping the poor and oppressed and by a preference for private institutions such as business or private charity taking care of things. Because capitalism has been the engine that drives American society, what capitalism has done well, American society has done well. What it has done poorly, such as address the public and social needs that exist outside the world of profit, American society has done poorly (Bellah, Madsen, Sullivan, Swidler, & Tipton, 1985; Warner, 1968).

The new privatization of life, however, is occurring with a massive speed and grander reach than ever before. In the past generation, an extraordinary social, political, and economic transformation has dramatically accelerated and expanded the privatization process, profoundly reshaping the context in which social workers practice. Understanding the contemporary context—its barriers and opportunities—is a critical element in social work practice.

THE CONTEMPORARY CONTEXT

As noted earlier, the world in which we live and work is increasingly moving away from the public, away from the social, and toward a preoccupation with the private. The concept of privatization is viewed in this chapter through a big-picture lens; it is not narrowly defined as a specific set of policy responses, such as the privatization of welfare, education, or prisons. Instead, it is used here as a broad concept that captures the dominant trend in our contemporary world, of which policies to privatize welfare, education, and prisons are but small parts.

Of course, any overarching conceptualization simplifies contemporary reality to better explain it. For example, the concept of dualisms, such as public and private, underestimates the complex interaction between the two parts, not to mention the divergent uses of the terms. Private churches do public work; for years, public governments have been heavily influenced by the initiatives of private businesses or business groups; businesses go "public" when they become stock-issuing corporations.

Philosopher and critic Berman (1986) reminds us that individualism is essential to the open-minded public spaces. It is only when people are enjoying the private rights of citizens that they are free to walk in the public sun. Moreover, public and private are not static. Versailles was once the epitome of private space; now, it is a public park. These caveats aside, the new privatization of life is occurring with greater speed and impact than ever before, accelerating the three trends and posing serious challenges not only to those interested in addressing social problems but to society in general.

Culture of Private Individuals

Some social commentators argue that Americans, and people in much of the world, are becoming increasingly self-absorbed with the private and the personal. Putnam (1996) argues that people are increasingly moving away from a concern with the larger society, away from commitment to a public life. Bellah et al. (1985) see this vividly in the contemporary penchant for psychotherapy—the sharing of a "first language of individualism" and the goals of self-actualization—by large numbers of the citizenry across the political spectrum. Reality is explained through a lens of individual will, personal life, and personal morality. For example, even the U.S. Army, an organization that seeks to subvert the individual will of soldiers to its collective goals, has for years promised potential recruits an opportunity to "Be all you can be."

Sennett (1974) and Lasch (1978) see this penchant for the personal as a retreat from the world into narcissism. So did Hannah Arendt (quoted in Sennett, 1990), who said that the retreat into the personal, what she called "the fear

of making contact," reflects "a lack of the will to live in the world" (p. 135). Martin and O'Connor (1989) propose that the focus on individualism discourages Americans from clearly seeing the impact of the social context on their lives. As society appears more difficult, divided, and dangerous, the increasing fear of the social world causes people to turn inward to a preoccupation with themselves and their families.

A world that overemphasizes the culture of private individuals turns the private domains of self and family, of private intimate matters, into the *proper* arenas and concerns of life. If public life is the "open, inclusive, and effective deliberation about matters of common and critical concern" (Ryan, 1992, p. 259), in a private world, personal intimate issues become matters of public concern. Public life becomes all about private life. To verify this conclusion, one has only to watch television (and not simply the crudest talk shows), which engages millions daily in a discussion of the most intimate matters of personal life, in place of a public deliberation about common and critical concerns. The political becomes personal, and the personal gets more personal.

The dominant culture of private individualism makes social work and social change more difficult. To the extent that discourse remains focused on individuals, so do discussions of problems and solutions. Witness contemporary debates about the nature of problems such as poverty, homelessness, AIDS, and so forth. When government is not being blamed, the victims are cited for their alleged individual shortcomings. They are lazy, unintelligent, mentally unstable, promiscuous, or simply tied to a deviant culture (underclass, homosexual, homeless, etc.). The problem is personal and so, therefore, must be the solution: Work your way out of poverty; parents are responsible for kids not do-ing well in school; if society is too violent, indi-viduals should pack a handgun, as many states now allow with laws regarding concealed weap-ons. In short, no social problems would exist if everyone who had a problem solved it individu-ally. Likewise, viewing issues as collective prob-lems (poverty, sexism, racism, and so forth) and calling for collective solutions (government in-tervention, social policy, mass action, etc.) are regarded as increasingly inappropriate. Individ-uals help themselves or are helped by other in-dividuals. In social work, too many social prob-lems are treated as if both the cause and the solution rest within the individual.

Physical World of Private Spaces

Some commentators observe that in the new privatized context public space declines as pri-vate space increases. Boyte (1992) describes public spaces as "environments that are open, accessible, and involve a mix of different people and groups" (p. 6). They also are spaces, like city streets or public parks and beaches, that are "owned" by the people. They have a primarily public function, for people to gather, walk, jog, play, and talk *in public*. Private spaces, con-versely, are intentionally designed as limited-access, closed places that are restricted to ho-mogeneous groups. These can include the house or apartment where one lives, a suburban en-clave, or increasingly proliferating private spaces such as gated communities or shopping malls. In all private spaces, there is a desire to provide a controlled space of order and clarity, one removed from a more unpredictable and complex public space. "On the most physical level," Sennett (1974) writes, the private "envi-ronment prompts people to think of the public

domain as meaningless" (p. 12). Private spaces are also primarily designed to make money, as with malls or suburban developments, or to provide a closed, exclusive space, such as a downtown underground tunnel system or a re-stricted country club.

In *City of Quartz,* Mike Davis (1992) cap-tures the condition brilliantly:

> In Los Angeles, once-upon-a-time a demi-paradise of free beaches, luxurious parks, and "cruising strips," genuinely democratic space is all but ex-tinct. In a city of several million yearning immi-grants, public amenities are radically shrinking, parks are becoming derelict and beaches more segregated, libraries and playgrounds are closing, youth congregations of ordinary kinds are banned, and the streets are becoming more deso-late and dangerous. (p. 227)

As space disaggregates and people are sepa-rated by larger distances, the simple act of social workers' trying to bring people together physi-cally to build a sense of community, of public life, is made harder. To the extent that citizens and space are reduced to their market function (citizens as workers and consumers), the strug-gle to redefine citizenship in social terms be-comes more difficult. "Hanging out" at today's fancy suburban mall is not the same as "hanging out" decades ago on city streets. The privatiza-tion of space contributes to a decrease in the sense of social ownership. Moreover, the pri-vatization of space is often divisive—dividing city from suburb, neighborhood from neigh-borhood, residential compound from residen-tial compound. The privatization and partial-ization of space is also evident within families that can afford it. For example, if everyone has his or her own bedroom equipped with a televi-sion, VCR, and phone, the sense of social interaction is dramatically weakened. The American dream, as well as American society, has become an increasingly private place.

Political Economy of Private Institutions

One of the most significant international developments in the 1980s and early 1990s has been the rise of the privatization strategy. Throughout the world, the strictures are clear: Economic progress will not come unless we weaken the state, cut labor costs, undermine unions and social change organizations, cut the costs of capital investment, and make the prerogatives of business the same as society's. The context of privatization forces almost all social and political agendas away from social welfare conceptualizations toward laissez-faire ones. Social problems are ignored as much as possible as new corporate agendas of unfettered capitalism come to dominate global, national, and local decision making.

The argument is made that in the new global economy, nations or cities cannot afford costly social programs. The idea behind privatization is to diminish the power of the state as much as possible to reduce the imposition of "social costs" on the corporate sector and the affluent, those segments of the population assumed to be the engines of economic growth. As noted earlier, privatization is used here as a broad orientation toward this objective, which includes but is much more than a specific set of policy alternatives. Both neoconservatives and neoliberals take pride in curbing big government, ending "welfare as we know it," hammering at the costs of government, lowering taxes on the rich, undermining regulatory programs, and delegitimizing social welfare programs.

The act of undermining the citizenry's sense of the proper role of government in American life pushes problems and solutions out of public spaces into an asocial focus on the individual and the family and onto communities that lack the resources to address deep-rooted social problems. It is clear that the private sector does not have the funds at its disposal—given its primary responsibility to stockholders rather than the homeless or the unemployed—to effectively address social problems in more than a token way. The penchant for private charity produces, Schram (1993) argues, a mentality of "welfare by the bag." Massive collective problems like homelessness and hunger are expected to be addressed by private individuals giving a can of tuna fish or beans, producing a bag of goods to tide over the alms recipient. Moreover, the very idea that government is the problem and the marketplace is the solution to social problems poses a serious barrier to effectively addressing the problem. The "1,000 points of light" version of traditional charity did not work in the 19th century (which is why the welfare state developed throughout the industrial world), and it is not clear that it works any better for the poor today. As Wolpert (1993) proposes in *Patterns of Generosity in America,* "Theory suggests that government expenditures crowd out voluntary contributions and that less government involvement in social support would stimulate private giving. Yet, the evidence shows that public and private generosity are more generally complementary" (p. 6). In such a context, social work is reduced, like almost everything else, to the economic bottom line, and practicing good social work becomes increasingly difficult (Fabricant & Burghardt, 1992).

The policy of arresting or dismantling social service programs is not only harmful in its failure to address social problems, it undermines democracy. Proponents of privatization argue the opposite, that getting government off people's backs enhances democracy, as if the United States were the former Soviet Union. But dismantling the public sector in the United States makes it more difficult for social workers and clients to hold politicians (once known as public servants) accountable. "Where can citizens go in a privatized context to make claims and demands or to engage in democratic debate? Suffice it to say that privatization diminishes the public sphere—the sphere of public information, deliberation, and accountability" (Starr, 1987, p. 11).

Even in an increasingly private world, not all government disappears. As Piven and Cloward (1982) noted in *The New Class War*, not all of the victories of prior generations of working people, people of color, and women can be quickly unraveled or destroyed. The governments of nation-states, as well as of localities, remain central players in the new private world, but they do so more than before as active partners in business-initiated or business-enhancing programs. In a political economy of unchallenged private institutions, definitions of the public good become narrower, lessening the ability of social workers to help address social problems and individual needs.

Why has the private world accelerated with such force in the past generation? Communitarians such as Bellah (1991), Putnam (1996), and Etzioni (1993) have different views on the issue, but all see the decline of public life in the world of ideas, culture, and technology. Robert Bellah (1991) and Specht and Courtney (1994) argue that privatization is linked to the proliferation of psychotherapy. Putnam (1996), in a multivariate analysis that dispenses quickly

with such factors as "everyone is working much harder than before," declares that television is the culprit. Television is a highly private act that takes up hours of time that could be spent in public life. Neoconservatives like William Kristol (cited in Atlas, 1995) find causes in some people's culture and a general decline in traditional values and "civility." If people would just act nicer, be more accepting and polite, there would be a more favorable sense of public life. We disagree with such apolitical analyses. Instead, we find three primary and linked causal factors: contemporary economic globalization, the neoconservative political response to it, and the absence of effective grassroots challenges to the new global economy.

Global Capitalism and the Political Responses to It

Global capitalism includes a combination of features such as the rapid movement of capital and industrial jobs to areas of the world where wages and social costs are low, the dramatic centralization of power among global corporations that are increasingly unaccountable and uncontrollable by society, the accelerated impoverishment of global populations who at any given time and place do not fit into the upper echelons of global economic restructuring, and marked opposition to a progressive public sector, social welfare programs, or social change. What this ultimately means is a nearly complete distancing from the *social* at the very moment that these global entities are responsible for so much social change and damage worldwide.

At this stage, economic globalization is primarily the massing of private power on a global level. The concentration of wealth so evident in the United States in the 1980s and 1990s reflects these worldwide economic trends. In response to these global changes, the new reality is characterized by heightened poverty across the globe (including affluent nations like the United States) and a growing inequality between the winners and losers in the global transformation—the rising entrepreneurial class and the economically stagnant poor. As stateless megacompanies

> search the world for bargain labor, sell their stock on exchanges from London to Hong Kong, and pin more and more of their hopes on customers in the emerging markets, most of them in Asia, they are walking away from the enormous public problems their private decisions create for American society. (Barnet, 1994, p. 754)

Curiously, as capital and power centralize in the new global economy, the functions of implementing its tasks and cleaning up its mess are increasingly decentralized. This leads, paradoxically, to significant new forms of public life. Voluntary-sector social efforts proliferate worldwide to address problems as diverse as ecological disasters, inadequate public education, crime prevention, and AIDS. Total Quality Management (TQM) strategies spread in the workplace, part of the effort to decentralize decision making around work strategies and performance. Public schools increasingly have site autonomy to develop participatory decision structures that include administrators, teachers, parents, and business representatives. The voluntary sector expands exponentially, helping to address the needs of society through multitudinous nonprofit grassroots efforts. Social workers are in demand, but at the same time, their employment as autonomous professionals declines. This proliferation of voluntary and nonprofit organizations and groups is a mixed

blessing, for although the tasks in the new global economy are handled on a more decentralized basis, power to make the essential decisions regarding the allocation of resources and organizational objectives is increasingly centralized. "Decentralization of production" accompanies "concentration of control" (Montgomery, 1995, p. 461).

Economic globalization is filled with new opportunities for some (we are witnessing a massive concentration of wealth and economic power), fraught with pressures for most. Brecher and Costello's (1994) book on the subject is aptly called *Global Village or Global Pillage*. In response to the new global economy, the neoconservative response, fashioned in the early 1970s, primarily seeks to lower corporate costs, both labor costs and social costs associated with government and public life, such as taxes, regulations, and social programs. Under the new credo, most of society is reduced to the economic bottom line. A nation or city is measured not by the quality of life it provides for its citizens or its commitment to promoting the social good, but by how it could be made more attractive as a business site for new and existing investment. What this ultimately yields is a push away from the social—an overemphasis on the individual as the source of problems and the source of solutions, the similar restructuring of urban space throughout the world, and the end of public costs, as much as possible. Furthering this trend to privatization is the relative quietude and ineffectiveness of alternatives and challenges to the neoconservative vision of the new world order. The prerogatives of economic globalization dominate the world, neoconservative politics reinforces and implements its agenda, and resistance to it is relatively absent or focused on other matters such as culture, concerns that are usually not directly associated with political economy.

On a very significant level, the new private world of today, so singular in its view and so increasingly concentrated in its power and control, has greatly diminished our democratic experiment and the goals of social and economic justice. This is what underlies our discussion of public life, our emphasis on the importance of social workers' understanding the contemporary context, and our thoughts, which follow, on what social workers can do about it.

CONTEXTUALIZING SOCIAL WORK PRACTICE

How can social work help rebuild the public realm, relegitimize the social sphere, and promote social change? How can social workers help clients to rebuild communities while the privatized context in which they work makes problems worse and their jobs harder? In other words, what can social workers do to best serve the needs of those they assist, fight against the forces that cause misery for clients and communities, *and* help rebuild a sense of a progressive public life? This has always been the central dilemma for the social work profession. Some core elements of a contextualized practice framework for social work include the following:

1. Establishing an integrated social work practice
2. Refocusing social work education on power
3. Putting macro social work analysis and practice at the base of social work practice
4. Understanding the political nature of social work practice
5. Including a social change ideology in social work practice

6. Emphasizing collective processes and strategies in social work practice
7. Connecting community, class, and culture in social work practice

Establishing an Integrated Social Work Practice

In their provocative *Unfaithful Angels*, Specht and Courtney (1994) argue that the problem in meeting human need rests in the individualistic nature of society. This individualistic focus is replicated in social work by the nearly unanimous and uncritical adoption of psychotherapeutic belief systems, analyses, and interventive strategies. It is this same turn to humanistic psychology and its emphasis on individual improvement (and individual failing) that Bellah et al. (1985), Sennett (1974), and Lasch (1978) attack more broadly in the larger society. Specht and Courtney argue that psychotherapy's basic belief in the perfectibility of the individual conflicts with social work's belief in the perfectibility of society. According to the authors, over the past 60 years, social work has increasingly turned away from its social base toward humanistic psychology and private psychotherapeutic practice. They argue that this turning away from social problems, public work, and collective intervention complements the larger shift in society to privatism in all its forms. They call for social work to expel its micro component, arguing that the only true social work is community-based.

We disagree, proposing instead an argument for an integrated social work practice that combines levels of intervention from the individual to the global. Drawing a connection between the personal and the social is a smart strategy because intervention with individuals is the essence of most social work practice. Although community work and associations are essential to building public life in the contemporary context, turning away from individual work completely and adopting only macro practice as the true social work is both impractical and problematic. It certainly runs counter to building a progressive common good based on both collective material needs and personal autonomy (Doyal & Gough, 1991). Moreover, it runs counter to the trend in social work toward practice integration.

Refocusing Social Work Education on Power

Where can social workers gain knowledge of an integrated practice that links the individual and the social? Much of social work has always been about the link between cause and function, social change and social service. More recently, ecological theory and the person-in-the-environment conceptualization contributed to social work practice by seeking to link the individual and the social. Accordingly, ecological theory does not dichotomize social work narrowly into micro/individual adjustment, on the one hand, and macro/social change, on the other. Good person-in-the-environment theory sees the importance of context and the social change function of social work. At its best, it seeks to integrate the two levels of social work—micro and macro—into a more generalist approach (Compton & Galaway, 1994).

Although ecological theory is an important step in reconnecting the personal world to the social world, an integrated approach to social work that ties together the micro and the macro is not enough in the context of global privatization. Despite a concern for the social, narrow systems approaches contain a bias toward the "private troubles" of clients. In effect, they manage to separate—through both intervention strategies and inadequate critical contextualization—the personal and the social (Longres & McLeod, 1980). At the heart of an integrated practice must lie a critical contextualization that focuses on power. Power must be understood as potentially coercive *and* empowering, laden with the potential to both deny and support social change. The emphasis on the role of power is not found in most systems or ecological theories. For these systems, everything is out there, in "suprasystems" or in the environment beyond the individual. Rarely are elements of the environment weighted for power differentials or inequities. Easing individuals into a better fit with their environment does not mean that they or the social worker understand the contextual and structural factors that shape their problem and their world.

Empowerment theory does this only somewhat better. The concept of empowerment is today arguably the dominant theory in social work practice. Because of its salience to social service practitioners, its appeal to almost all client populations, and its adoption by activists across the political spectrum, empowerment has come to provide a coordinating theme for social work in the 1990s. However, the concept of empowerment is hotly contested political terrain outside of social work. Because of its overuse, empowerment has become almost a hackneyed phrase. Therapists use it to describe a form of active insight, progressives use it to describe social change, and even the Republican party used it in its *Contract with America*. Within social work, the term is less contested but often murky. Although Simon (1994) and other progressives see empowerment as an extension of the left/liberal tradition in social

work, other social workers see it as nearly synonymous with an individualistic, self-efficacy
or strengths perspective. For empowerment to
be useful in social change, it must be contextualized in a larger political framework that understands power differentials and collectivizes
issues and problems, thereby drawing micro
practice into the larger canvas of social change.

Putting Macro Social Work Analysis and Practice at the Base of Social Work Practice

To achieve the twin goals of integrating and
politicizing practice, empowerment must be
contextualized. The empowerment process is
largely seen as linear. It begins with an individual in need. It helps this person from a strengths
or self-efficacy perspective to stabilize and then
links the personal to the collective and political.
For example, a middle-aged woman who is
homeless drops by a shelter on a very cold
morning. She might receive extensive intake
procedures, short-term shelter and food, and
individual counseling. If the social worker is
committed to an empowerment-based practice
that connects the micro and macro, the woman
might be referred to a shelter's resident council
or a homeless advocacy effort once she is placed
in a longer-term shelter or is back on her feet.

The concept of putting a macro contextualization at the base of social work practice
proposes that the macro connection—the collective and political nature of the person's problem—should be included at the beginning of the
process rather than at the end. This is not to bias
micro practice in favor of macro practice but
rather to propose a truly integrated practice
that counters the current bias in social work toward a decontextualized micro practice. Micro

theory and practice will and should remain important to the profession. But to be effective, to
connect the individual to the larger problems
posed by the contemporary context, social
work education and practice must also be built
on a critical knowledge of macro analysis and
practice.

Understanding the Political Nature of Social Work Practice

A politicized social work begins with the recognition that social work is fundamentally
about power, public life, and social as well as
personal change (Abramovitz, 1993; Haynes &
Mickelson, 1991; Rees, 1991; Withorn, 1984).
Restoration of the public also means restoration
of the political: public involvement, discussion,
and action regarding public matters. Progressive and radical traditions in social work understand its political nature (Chambers, 1967; Davis, 1967; Wagner, 1990).

An integrated knowledge and practice base
has always been at the heart of the radical and
"critical theory" traditions in social work. According to Burghardt and Fabricant (1987),
"Radical practice begins with the fundamental
premise that the circumstances of at-risk populations can be traced to political or economic relationships that exist in the larger social order"
(p. 456). Those in the radical tradition perceive
from the outset that individual "dysfunction" is
almost always rooted in larger social factors
that pattern individual behavior. A battered
woman is seen as a victim of physical abuse
rooted in a patriarchal society. A homeless person is not seen primarily as a person with a behavioral dysfunction, but as someone who, although he or she might have psychological
problems, is homeless because of oppressive

work, family, and class structures (Wagner, 1993). This leads to a more integrated social work practice that opposes the dichotomization of practice into narrow skill or methodological specializations such as case work, group work, and community organization. The emphasis is on helping the person or group get to the root of the problem.

Including a Social Change Ideology in Social Work Practice

Social workers constantly learn about new problems and needs in society; thus, they are always expanding their knowledge of contextual factors. But how do social workers mobilize and put into practice this knowledge and critical analysis? Withorn (1984) and Hyde (1989) suggest that this occurs best through ties with a social movement. The division between social service and social change disappears when practice becomes part of a social movement, such as a feminist domestic violence center. Social movements are able to contextualize practice because they supply, among other things, a social justice ideology that includes a critical analysis of the workings of the larger society. They also tie this understanding to daily life and the need for social change.

Ideology offers a map that provides not only an analysis of the contemporary context but also a clear understanding of the problems people face and even a blueprint for action. It remains essential to

> move people to a set of ideas that critiques the current system, understands the importance of class and community, connects work to place and public to private spheres, and gets people to take risks and transcend what they thought was possi-

ble for themselves and their world. (Fisher & Kling, 1991, p. 82)

Ideological competence is essential to the creation of social work agencies and organizations able to articulate problems and help people reach a deeper understanding of the larger world that dominates daily life. Depending on the situation and within the bounds of good social work practice, social workers engaged in a collaborative practice with people should share their analysis, their values, and their visions of social change.

Emphasizing Collective Processes and Strategies in Social Work Practice

The framework we have proposed so far for contextualized practice reads as follows: Real empowerment practice is integrated, attentive to issues of power inequities, critically contextualized at the base, politicized, and mobilized by a social change ideology. To this, we now add "and facilitated by collectivization. Collectivization refers to the importance of collective settings, collective issues and problems, and collective solutions to empowerment.

Empowerment can occur on an individual or a collective basis. But according to Longres and McLeod (1980), when social workers deal with individuals and families separately, and when they separate clients from larger collectivities, "the weight is too strongly distributed in favor of working toward a resolution of private troubles" (p. 273). The key to effectively contextualizing problems is building groups of people with shared commonalities who may, with the help of a social change agent, reveal to each other the structural basis of their individual problems and the potential for collective and individual change.

Although individual intervention has its place—people can learn a great deal in one-to-one counseling—it is intervention in groups and in larger collective settings that more naturally contextualizes problems and connects people to an understanding of social change. A contextualized practice should lead practitioners to consider not only more collective processes but also collective as well as individual solutions.

Connecting Community, Class, and Culture in Social Work Practice

Community work is important as a natural site for collective cohesion, processes, strategies, and solutions. This is the goal of a communitarian movement that appears to be gaining adherents in intellectual circles (Elshtain, 1994; Etzioni, 1993). A number of recent studies in social work also point in this direction. Specht and Courtney (1994) call for a communitarian revival in social work focused on the delivery of community-based services. Fabricant and Burghardt (1992), although critical of a narrow communitarianism, agree that social service providers must become part of the communities they serve, and citizens and clients must be made part of the agencies in their communities. The organic connection between the building of community and the provision of social services must be renewed.

Admittedly, community organization and community work have changed in the past decades. The nature of urban life and the bonds that unite people are different in the post-industrial, postmodern city than they were in the industrial metropolis where community or-

ganizing began. Delgado (1994) argues that community work has gone "beyond the politics of place" to focus on the politics of culture. Locality is critical to community organizing but even more so are the bonds of race, gender, ethnicity, language, religion, and sexual orientation.

Critical issues of power need to be kept in mind if an equitable society is to be fashioned. These include challenging the absolute prerogative of private decisions, emphasizing social responsibilities as well as rights, refashioning the welfare state to better support basic human needs, and limiting the power and scope of corporations and global capital. The community is ultimately too narrow and too lacking in resources to perform such functions. Many applaud the focus on culture as an essential means of identity and a better collective gel in an era where working people no longer stick together through class identity. But culture by itself is not sufficient. Communities almost always need help from outside. Cultural issues, such as gender and race, need to be connected with those of class. Both objectives can be addressed in a renewed focus in social work practice against attacks on the welfare state and in support of cultural diversity. In this combined struggle, not only is the importance of class and the state reasserted, but these are tied to the contemporary identification around culture.

The task is not to find a single strategy to meet the challenges of global privatization; multiple strategies from multiple efforts are needed. Brecher and Costello (1994), Brecher, Childs, and Cutler (1993), and Amin (1990) suggest the importance of linking grassroots organizations worldwide. This linkage would connect community groups increasingly organized around culture in the northern hemisphere with those focused on issues of class in the southern hemisphere. Linking grassroots efforts worldwide also underscores the need for social change activists to link together issues of class and culture. This is not always easy. Based on a long history in the 20th century of deception and abandonment of cultural efforts for class-based ones, multiculturalists argue against the centrality of class issues because they tend to exclude cultural concerns (Rivera & Erlich, 1995). Some recent structuralists, however, seek to bridge the gap between the two by broadening the structural base to include not only economic but also cultural matters. Class becomes one identity, albeit an essential one, among many. Most important for social work, class is put back into the equation of social change.

The PIVOT Project: An Example of Contextualized Practice

One good example of contextualized practice is the PIVOT Project of AVDA (Aid to Victims of Domestic Abuse), a program for male batterers in Houston, Texas, started by feminist activist Toby Myers. Grounded in feminist ideology, PIVOT attempts to raise the consciousness of male batterers as an integral part of the program's work to address violence against women. It grounds the experience of the battering male in the larger social world of patriarchy and the violence it engenders. This program uses an integrated method, working with the men in large groups, small groups, and individual therapy. An understanding of power differentials and the misuse of power undergirds practice at PIVOT. Connections about power, violence, and patriarchy are drawn as early as the first orientation session. This orientation

session is an excellent example of putting macro contextualization at the base of practice. At this session some 50 to 100 men, and sometimes their female partners, listen and respond to a critical analysis of the extent, nature, and causes of male violence against women. The individual issues of each offender are viewed not only as personal problems, but as collective ones resting on a base of patriarchy and violence. The men, assigned to PIVOT by the court system, hear how their personal problem is also a social one. They hear how the roots of male battering rest both within the men who commit violence against women and in the larger society. During their extended work at PIVOT, the male batterers will participate primarily in small groups and individual counseling, getting at the roots of their problem and continuing the consciousness raising that begins at the first orientation session. But it is the macro contextualization of the mass orientation session, the critique of patriarchy and violence, that informs all work at every level of intervention; the understanding of male violence against women as a social as well as personal issue chiefly serves as the basis for a contextualized practice.

Myers came to this work through her political understanding and activism as a feminist in Houston. Feminist ideology and theory helped found PIVOT. It is social change ideology, specifically feminist theory, that continues to unmask oppression, fuel individual healing, and help sustain workers at PIVOT. Of course, no single effort can be expected to embody all aspects of contextualized practice as we have described it in this chapter. Every aspect of contextualized practice is not salient for all agencies and organizations. Issues of community and class are not as much a focus at PIVOT as they would be, for example, in a community organization such as an AIDS group trying to get beyond its initial constituency and reach out to the poor and people of color with AIDS. The bridging of community, cultural identity, and class would be more striking in an organization trying to mobilize African Americans in a struggle for a citywide minimum wage increase. But PIVOT is one splendid example of many aspects of contextualized practice. (For others, see Fisher, 1994; Gil, 1998; Hyde, 1992; Nowak, 1998; Withorn, 1984.)

CONCLUSION

American society is in a period of profound social transformation. As social problems mount and the ranks of the disenfranchised grow, Americans of all ilk become more alienated from and frightened by the very society they countenance. Much of the middle and upper classes have become so cynical about public life, not to mention the public sector, that they isolate themselves in barricaded neighborhoods that resemble mini nation-states. Walled off by high fences, private roads, private schools, private recreational areas, and strong deed restrictions, those who can afford it prefer to invest in private security services rather than in publicly sponsored law enforcement. This development is especially troubling because one of the few agreed-on principles among liberals and conservatives is the government's responsibility to ensure personal safety. Part of the problem is found in the retreat from a more inclusive vision of the public good.

Many of today's social problems have been exacerbated, if not created, by the centralization of power inherent in the global economy. The global economy has led to a shrinking tax base, more joblessness, greater insecurity in the workplace, higher numbers of people in poverty, and a climate in which the disparities between the overclass and the poor are growing. Corporations that once yielded to union pressure and provided workers with decent wages, job security, and benefits are being replaced by stateless corporations that repudiate any long-term obligations to their workforce, let alone to the United States or the common good of its people. The costs of this global economy are paid for not only by the poor and working class, but also by a middle class that, despite a decline in real wages, continues to identify more strongly with the politics of those at the top than with those at the bottom (Ehrenreich, 1990).

Instead of developing social policies to tame the negative features of the global economy, for almost 30 years, federal and state governments have shown scant commitment to improving community life. The state's retreat from progressive social policy is a retreat from social responsibility. Contrary to neoconservative dogma, the demands of the global economy require government to be more rather than less active in managing social affairs and redirecting fiscal and human resources. The guiding principle behind governmental action must be to advance an inclusive and egalitarian vision of the public good, especially because the state is the only institution capable of rebuilding America's neglected social and public infrastructure.

An important element in restoring public citizenship and government responsiveness to community life is the creation of a progressive view of the common good. The Civil Rights Movement teaches us that such a vision must address the economic, democratic, cultural, social, and spiritual dimensions of human existence. Any egalitarian framework for the common good must encompass human needs for both material security and individual autonomy. These include the need for adequate nutrition, health, suitable clothing and shelter, access to educational opportunities, and autonomy, freedom, self-determination, and self-expression (Doyal & Gough, 1991).

The concept of a public good has long been debated in American political life. Because of society's class, racial, gender, and cultural divisions, the question inevitably becomes "Whose public good?" In contrast to conservative dogma, advancing public life requires a stronger not a weaker national government. Only a strong federal government, pushed from the grassroots by progressive movements, organizations, and agencies, can reduce the growing disparity between the economic classes.

The social conflict we have described is occurring just as many professions are busying themselves with narrow professional concerns. Social workers are also guilty of pursuing narrow self-interests, including spending large amounts of time, money, and energy on licensure and third-party reimbursement for private practitioners. Like most professions, social work is deflecting its social justice mission onto narrower professional issues. This is unfortunately occurring just as the social work profession is being pressured from without and struggling from within to find its identity and its niche in a postindustrial welfare state. For social workers, this diversion is particularly problematic because it is the only profession that has the historical mandate to help and protect the poor and vulnerable.

Social workers have sometimes fallen victim to the belief that social change and the public good can be advanced only through individual moral reformation or by psychological insight.

This belief is based on the idea that real institutional change must be preceded by individual change. It is a message embedded in popular psychology and self-awareness movements from Esalen to biofeedback, from transpersonal psychology to Enneagram, and from crystal gazing to organizational and religious gurus. The personal search for "truth and wisdom" has led some social workers away from the inescapable truth that public life can be promoted only by redesigning institutions and by rethinking strategies for changing them. Social workers can play a major role in advancing public life and social change. More than members of other professions, social workers understand the relationship between the environmental and the psychological side of human existence. This is especially true because a core tenet of the profession is that human beings exist in the interconnection between the social and the personal.

The promotion of public activism and a vision of an inclusive and egalitarian public good are principles by which social work can be organized. To accomplish this, social work practice at all levels must be linked to the macro context. Once contextualized, the rigid boundaries between micro, mezzo, and macro social work practice become permeable. Social workers involved in advocacy, community organization, legislative activity, social planning, and social policy analysis are enhancing the individual good just as surely as micro-level practitioners. Conversely, direct service work with individuals contributes to the development of more effective citizens and public life. In that sense, the level at which social workers practice is incidental to working toward social change. Contextualized social work proposes that the causes of social problems and most individual ills cannot be addressed effectively without an analysis of the contemporary context and a practice strategy willing and able to deal with it.

REFERENCES

Abramovitz, M. (1993). Should all social workers be educated for social change? Pro. *Journal of Social Work Education, 29,* 6-11, 17-18.

Amin, S. (1990). *Transforming the revolution: Social movements and the world-system.* New York: Monthly Review Press.

Atlas, J. (1995, February 12). The counter counterculture. *The New York Times,* pp. 32-38, 54, 61-65.

Barnet, R. J. (1994, December 19). Lords of the global economy. *The Nation,* pp. 754-757.

Bellah, R. (1991). *The good society.* New York: Knopf.

Bellah, R., Madsen, R., Sullivan, W., Swidler, A., & Tipton, S. (1985). *Habits of the heart: Individualism and commitment in American life.* New York: Harper & Row.

Berman, M. (1986, Fall). Take it to the streets. *Dissent,* pp. 20-33.

Boyte, H. (1992). The pragmatic ends of popular politics. In R. Bellah, R. Madsen, W. Sullivan, R. Neelly, & A. Swidler (Eds.), *The good society* (pp. 109-135). New York: Knopf.

Brecher, J., Childs, J., & Cutler, J. (Eds.). (1993). *Global visions: Beyond the new world order.* Boston: South End Press.

Brecher, J., & Costello, T. (1994). *Global village or global pillage: Economic reconstruction from the bottom up.* Boston: South End Press.

Burghardt, S., & Fabricant, M. (1987). Radical social work. In *Encyclopedia of social work* (18th ed., Vol. 2, pp. 455-462). Silver Spring, MD: NASW Press.

Chambers, C. (1967). *Seedtime of reform: American social service and social action, 1918-1933.* Ann Arbor: University of Michigan Press.

Compton, B., & Galaway, B. (1994). *Social work processes.* Belmont, CA: Brooks/Cole.

Davis, A. (1967). *Spearheads for reform.* New York: Oxford University Press.

Davis, M. (1992). *City of quartz.* New York: Vintage.

de Tocqueville, A. (1988). *Democracy in America* (G. Lawrence, Trans., J. P. Mayer, Ed.). New York: HarperCollins.

Delgado, G. (1994). *Beyond the politics of place: New directions for community organizing in the 1990s.* Oakland, CA: Applied Research Center.

Doyal, L., & Gough, I. (1991). *A theory of human need.* New York: Guilford.

Ehrenreich, B. (1990). *Fear of falling: The inner life of the middle class.* New York: Harper.

Elshtain, J. (1994). *Democracy on trial.* New York: Basic Books.

Etzioni, A. (1993). *The spirit of community: Rights, responsibilities, and the communitarian agenda.* New York: Crown.

Fabricant, M., & Burghardt, S. (1992). *The welfare state crisis and the transformation of social service work.* Armonk, NY: M. E. Sharpe.

Fisher, R. (1994). *Let the people decide: Neighborhood organizing in America.* New York: Twayne.

Fisher, R., & Karger, H. (1997). *Social work and community in a private world: Getting out in public.* New York: Longman.

Fisher, R., & Kling, J. (1991, Winter). Popular mobilization in the 1990s: Prospects for the new social movements. *New Politics, 3,* 71-84.

Gil, D. (1998). *Confronting injustice and oppression.* New York: Columbia University Press.

Ginsburg, L. (1987). Economic, political, and social context. In *Encyclopedia of social work* (18th ed., Vol. 3, pp. 1974-1976). Silver Spring, MD: NASW Press.

Habermas, J. (1989). *The structural transformation of the public sphere.* Boston: Harvard University Press.

Haynes, K., & Mickelson, J. (1991). *Affecting change: Social workers in the political arena.* New York: Longman.

Hyde, C. (1989). A feminist model for macro-practice: Promises and problems. *Administration in Social Work, 13,* 145-181.

Hyde, C. (1992). The ideational system of social movement agencies: An examination of feminist health centers. In Y. Hasenfeld (Ed.), *Human services as complex organizations* (pp. 121-144). Newbury Park, CA: Sage.

Lasch, C. (1978). *The culture of narcissism.* New York: Norton.

Longres, J., & McLeod, E. (1980). Consciousness raising and social work practice. *Social Casework, 61,* 267-276.

Martin, P., & O'Connor, J. (1989). *The social environment.* New York: Longman.

Montgomery, D. (1995, April 3). What the world needs now. *The Nation,* pp. 461-463.

Nowak, B. (1998, March). *Micro/macro chasms: Helping students cross the bridge into contextualized social work practice.* Paper presented at the Council on Social Work Education, Annual Program Meeting, Orlando, FL.

Piven, F., & Cloward, R. (1982). *The new class war: Reagan's attack on the welfare state and its consequences.* New York: Pantheon.

Putnam, R. (1996 Winter). The strange disappearance of civic America. *American Prospect, 24,* pp. 22-38.

Rees, S. (1991). *Achieving power: Practice and policy in social welfare.* North Sydney, Australia: Allen & Unwin.

Rivera, F., & Erlich, J. (1995). *Community organizing in a diverse society* (2nd ed.). Boston: Allyn & Bacon.

Ryan, M. (1992). Gender and public access: Women's politics in nineteenth century America. In C. Calhoun (Ed.), *Habermas and the public sphere* (pp. 259-288). Boston: MIT Press.

Schram, P. (1993, June). *Inverting political economy: Looking at welfare from the bottom up.* Paper presented at the annual meeting of the American Political Science Association, Chicago, IL.

Sennett, R. (1974). *The fall of public man.* New York: Norton.

Sennett, R. (1990). *The conscience of the eye.* New York: Norton.

Simon, B. (1994). *The empowerment tradition in American social work: A history.* New York: Columbia University Press.

Specht, H., & Courtney, M. (1994). *Unfaithful angels: How social work has abandoned its mission.* New York: Free Press.

Starr, P. (1987). *The limits of privatization.* Washington, DC: Economic Policy Institute.

Wagner, D. (1990). *The quest for a radical profession: Social service careers and political ideology.* Lanham, MD: University Press of America.

Wagner, D. (1993). *Checkerboard square.* Boulder, CO: Westview.

Warner, S. (1968). *The private city: Philadelphia in three periods of growth.* Philadelphia: University of Pennsylvania Press.

Withorn, A. (1984). *Serving the people: Social services and social change.* New York: Columbia University Press.

Wolpert, J. (1993). *Patterns of generosity in America: Who's holding the safety net?* New York: Twentieth Century Fund Press.

CHAPTER TWO

Legal Issues in Practice

ROBERT G. MADDEN

In the preface to Louise Odencrantz's (1929) classic text, *The Social Worker in Family, Medical, and Psychiatric Social Work,* she lamented the difficulty of getting at the elements of the job of a social worker "who deals with such intangible things as human relationships in a field where there exist practically no methods of measuring results, and where few criteria have been set up to determine what constitutes good social work" (p. 2). In the 70 years since Odencrantz penned her reflections, the legal system has influenced the social work profession to develop more explicit and empirical standards for practice. Today, social workers must interact with the law on many levels, and competent practice now requires social workers to have a basic knowledge of legal issues.

This chapter introduces legal content significant to social work, seeks to demystify legal language and concepts, and provides an understanding of the purpose and functions of the legal system as it relates to social work practice. Legal issues for each stage of direct practice are discussed and analyzed. Rapid social and technological changes confronting social work at the start of the new millenium will result in emerging legal issues and new challenges and opportunities for the profession. As the boundaries of individual professions become more flexible to allow for cooperative practice environments in interdisciplinary settings, social workers must develop the knowledge and skills to be able to practice in legal settings and to assist clients who are dealing with legal issues while in treatment. Increased legal knowledge for social workers provides opportunities to influence the legal system toward more therapeutic results for clients and the development of acceptable standards for practice.

INTRODUCTION

For many professionals engaged in direct social work practice, the law is experienced as an interference—an indecipherable set of rules and expectations best dealt with by avoidance and denial. Social workers who are brought into legal situations wonder if their practice is worth the price paid in anxiety and stress. Subpoenas are received without clarity as to whether the social worker is required, or even allowed, to respond with records or testimony. Complaints are filed with state licensing boards or through various types of lawsuits alleging a violation of uncertain professional standards. Clients bring their legal problems into their interactions with social workers, who are unprepared to offer adequate information, support, and advocacy. This trend is certain to continue. Contemporary social workers must accept the inevitability of legal system involvement and develop the knowledge and skills to support competent practice.

Social workers have been slow to embrace the legal system. Perhaps, it is the historic sense of *invulnerability* developed from the romanticized service ideal in social work that suggests that clients will not sue because they know social workers care about them and are committed to meeting their needs (Jones & Alcabes, 1989). Writing in another context, Brookfield (1995) warns teachers that "the sincerity of their intention does not guarantee the purity of their practice" (p. 1). So it is in social work, where the development of fee-for-service and private practice models, along with the increased attention to standards of care in mental health practice, has created expectations that may transcend the goodwill of the practitioner.

The law intersects with direct social work practice in several ways. The context of direct practice is shaped by *legal structures,* such as state and professional licensing/certification systems that regulate practice; *legal rules,* detailing how a social worker handles such tasks as keeping records, releasing confidential information, and responding to subpoenas; and *legal expectations,* establishing standards for professional practice. In addition to these direct practice concerns, social workers frequently deal with the legal issues faced by clients, such as divorce, custody, commitment, guardianship, child abuse, and criminal charges. Social workers must play active roles in providing advocacy, support, and information to clients who may be overwhelmed by the legal system. Finally, some social workers practice directly in legal settings, such as family and juvenile courts, probation, legal clinics, and in forensic treatment and evaluation. In these settings, interprofessional practice skills must be developed to enable more effective practice with legal professionals.

FOUNDATIONS FOR EXAMINING LAW AND SOCIAL WORK

Values. The law has the capacity to support the core values of social work. In the section on ethical principles for social work, the *National Association of Social Workers Code of Ethics* (NASW, 1996a) calls on professionals to challenge social injustice (p. 5). Many of the people who seek social work services may not have access to, the protection of, or clout with the legal system. Social justice goals are realized through careful use of the legal system in addressing class issues such as poverty, unemployment, and discrimination. Social workers have used the law to challenge unjust or discriminatory practices, to fight for the human rights of groups of people who have little voice in the political process, and to challenge the way government services are designed and allocated.

The *Code of Ethics* forms the basis of legal expectations governing the behavior of social workers. As such, the law looks to the code when evaluating a complaint of malpractice or a violation of the standard of care. The code stresses the central importance of human relationships and spells out inappropriate boundary violations and the fundamental responsibility of protecting clients' privacy. Furthermore, the code requires social workers to behave ethically and to practice within their areas of competence (NASW, 1996a, p. 6). When a legal case examines the actions of a social worker, the professional community should be vigilant in monitoring and advocating for decisions that support the principles articulated in this code of ethics.

In addition to clarifying and enforcing standards, the law also has the capacity to distort and impede social work practice. A school social worker laments not being able to take a student out for an ice cream because of his fear of liability. A clinician in private practice declines a case when, during an initial phone call, the woman informs her that she is involved in a custody dispute and the clinician does not want to testify. How does the direct social work practitioner respond to the law? How does one maintain a commitment to social work ethical principles and core values while remaining within the expectations of the law? If a social worker overreacts to a high-profile case that finds a practitioner liable, or if an agency administration is hypersensitive to the possibility of a lawsuit, the result will be defensive practice and the abandonment of some values that make social work unique and effective. In addition, defensive

practice may put a social worker at greater risk by choosing interventions that prioritize self-interest over client interest.

If social workers are to become more comfortable with the law, it is important that the legal issues affecting practice are addressed directly and honestly. Because the number of lawsuits against social workers remains low compared with suits against other professions, much of the risk-phobia that has gripped the profession is unfounded. The law acts as a means of enforcing a set of expectations concerning the treatment of clients and the qualifications of the direct practice social worker. It is essential that social workers follow the maxim, "above all, do no harm." This requires social workers to routinely analyze whether any negative side effects result from practice (McKnight, 1989) and whether particular treatment approaches are effective (Granello & Witmer, 1998). The law has been an effective tool for protecting consumers from incompetent and unethical practice. Although there can never be a guarantee against the filing of legal complaints by angry or disturbed clients/family members based on negative outcomes to a treatment experience, those who practice social work in a manner consistent with basic practice standards will minimize potential liability.

Theoretical foundations. Many of the laws that affect practice are designed to provide restitution to people injured directly as a result of a social worker's actions or omissions. Other laws and regulations are designed to regulate poor practice and to remove incompetent social workers. Some laws do not directly affect practice but can have an enormous impact on the lives of social work clients when the judicial system is not attuned to the human costs of legal policies and procedures. Finally, law can be a weapon for social change when it is used creatively by social workers to address social problems (Schroeder, 1995). One of the problems for social workers has been finding a framework from which to understand legal issues across this broad range of areas. Because of the overwhelming scope of the law and its unfamiliar language and culture, insufficient study and limited interventions have been directed at changing the legal system.

Therapeutic jurisprudence is an interdisciplinary area of scholarship emanating from the field of mental health law; it recognizes that the law can be a therapeutic agent. It examines the therapeutic and antitherapeutic consequences that flow from legal rules, legal procedures, and legal actors (Stolle & Wexler, 1997). Therapeutic jurisprudence has yet to be applied extensively by social workers, even though the concepts fit well with ecological theory and the values of the profession. Examining legal situations from the perspective of therapeutic jurisprudence provides guidance as to the roles social workers can assume. Some examples are needed to clarify this point.

1. *In clinical practice,* social workers are expected to allow clients to review or receive copies of their treatment records. A state licensing board, unfamiliar with social work practice, issued a preliminary ruling finding a violation of practice standards based on a complaint that a social worker would not provide a client with a complete copy of her records. The social worker assessed the client as vulnerable and determined that providing her with the complete record would pose a risk of harm to the client. The state chapter of NASW informed the licensing board of the practice standard as detailed in the 1996 Code of Ethics (Sect. 1.08). This effort averted the antitherapeutic result that would have occurred from the preliminary ruling.

2. *In cases of sexual assault,* the criminal justice system often retraumatizes the victim of the assault. Social workers employed by crisis programs can be invaluable in reforming the manner in which legal evidence is collected so that the accused person's rights are protected while the person who has been assaulted is not further traumatized by the legal system.

3. *In the mental health field,* judges often make decisions to reject a proposed commitment of a person with mental illness on the grounds that it would violate the person's civil rights. Although this might be a legally correct decision, the unfettered release of the person may not be a therapeutic decision. Social workers are able to advocate for alternative levels of care and program options that protect the individual's rights and safety, as well as the interests of the public.

4. *In family law,* social workers frequently are involved in divorce and custody hearings. It is common to have judicial decisions that address the current situation but that have little relevance to the way the families may developmentally change, reconfigure, or relocate in the future (Babb, 1997). Legal professionals often have minimal training in issues such as the effects of domestic violence on children. Social workers can testify and serve as expert witnesses, educating the courts to improve decisions.

A therapeutic jurisprudence approach, by its nature, generates empirical questions (Wexler, 1996). Social workers, who have a unique understanding of the impact of a legal issue on individuals, families, communities, and professional practice, can inform legal professionals of empirical evidence to support particular issues in a case and to support legal reforms. This approach resonates with ecological theory in that it identifies the legal system as a possible locus for interventions rather than merely dealing with the adverse consequences of a legal decision. Therapeutic jurisprudence also reinforces the recent focus on the need to continue to develop empirically validated treatments (Myers & Thyer, 1997)

Social workers who engage in activities related to therapeutic jurisprudence can practice empowerment strategies. Advocating for civil rights and supporting legal cases brought by clients sometimes results in their voices being heard, their rights and property being protected, and their needs being met. Challenging legal policies in cases that involve professional issues and filing friend of the court (amicus curiae) briefs to support social work standards of practice can be an empowering experience for the practitioner and the profession. Legal policy does not just happen. It reflects value choices that are made by administrative, legislative, and judicial systems (Flynn, 1992). For practitioners, empowerment comes through knowledge of the legal system (Chapin, 1995) along with the skills to become active agents in the workings of the legal system.

The concept of applying the law therapeutically is far from self-executing (Stolle & Wexler, 1997). Social workers must make the commitment to have a significant influence on the legal system through education, advocacy, and proactive legal policy development. For a profession that historically has been a strong voice in hostile environments, social work has neglected opportunities to influence the legal system to improve its decisions for clients and

practitioners (Madden, in press). The legal system must become a target of social work interventions, much as the legislature has in recent years (Haynes & Mickelson, 1991).

TREATMENT ISSUES

Most of the practice standards for social work are expressed through policies and procedures. These fundamentals of professional practice guide social workers about expected behavior and help to inform clients about acceptable practice. Different issues surface as the treatment relationship progresses. This section discusses legal issues in the beginning, treatment, and ending phases of social work practice.

Beginning Stage Issues

Early in the social work relationship, a key issue is the development of trust between the client and worker. Trust is predicated on the expectation that the content of the work will remain private and that the professional will act in a competent and ethical manner. These may seem like obvious expectations, but many times, situations arise in which the social worker is faced with competing duties. Effective management of information and clear communication with clients are significant risk-reduction strategies (Madden, 1998). Many lawsuits and licensing board complaints arise from bad experiences, such as angry clients who leave treatment or family members who believe they have not been treated fairly. Clear practice policies, well-formulated and rigorously applied, can help the practitioner navigate through the dilemmas inherent in these complex situations.

Regulation of practice. The initial means for ensuring that clients receive competent social work services is to regulate who can be called a social worker and to sanction those whose practice violates professional standards. The following case illustrates some of the important issues in the regulation of social work practice.

> Paul was surprised when he received notice from the state licensing board that a complaint had been filed against him. His surprise turned to anger and fear when he read the complaint. It had been filed by the husband of one of his clients. The complaint claimed Paul had harassed him by contacting him at work and by writing unsubstantiated and untrue letters about him, even though he had never met Paul.

Any person, including consumers, family members, and colleagues, may bring complaints concerning a social worker to either the state licensing board or the National Association of Social Workers. A civil suit may also be filed against the practitioner, regardless of the outcome of other hearing processes. In fact, it is not uncommon for a licensing board complaint to be pursued by a client because of its low cost. The state collects evidence, conducts the investigation, and recommends disciplinary action.

States have developed different models for regulating the practice of social work. Most states have some form of licensing or certification of social workers (Saltzman & Proch, 1990). Some states regulate only clinical practitioners, whereas other states sanction various professional categories including practice at the bachelor of social work level. The regulations ensure a minimal level of education and supervised practice experience as well as an examination requirement. A license or certification may be revoked or suspended, and other sanctions,

ranging from mandatory supervision to participation in continuing education programs, may be required after a finding that a practitioner violated a practice standard.

Because licensing boards are designed from a consumer protection orientation, there is a bias toward finding professionals at fault. One danger of this orientation is that these findings of fault may be used to support a civil lawsuit against the practitioner. Also, a fault finding may result in higher malpractice insurance costs and possible exclusion from managed care preferred-provider panels. This is not to suggest that violations of practice standards should be minimized or ignored. The social work community needs to cooperate as partners with state administrative agencies to improve their level of familiarity with social work standards of care so that legitimate complaints result in appropriate sanctions.

> Paul had, indeed, called Mr. James at home and once at work in an effort to convince him to participate in marriage counseling sessions. Mr. James declined and belittled the idea of therapy. Over the ensuing months, Mr. James engaged in a pattern of emotional abuse and controlling behaviors with his wife. The abuse continued to escalate until the police were called to quell a disturbance at Mrs. James's workplace. Paul believed that Mr. James was attempting to get his wife fired from her job so that she would be increasingly dependent on him and unable to file for divorce. Mr. James also was a gun collector, and Paul worried that the emotional abuse might be a prelude to physical violence.
>
> At the request of Mrs. James, Paul wrote a letter to the court detailing his concerns. In the letter, he failed to identify the source of his information about the alleged abusive behaviors of Mr. James. The lawyer handling the licensing board case for the state sent the letter and Mr. James's complaint to a social work consultant to review for possible violations of

the standard of care. Not having the context of the whole family picture, the consultant suggested that Paul, in his letter, failed to attribute the source of the statements; the consultant also noted that the tone of the letter reflected a level of anger at Mr. James that was inappropriate in a professional communication.

Social workers who face a licensing board hearing are advised to seek consultation and legal representation to protect themselves and their practice. Paul responded to the initial complaint with minimal information. He was incredulous that a man who was abusive and controlling of his wife was given sanction by the state to use the same tactics with his wife's therapist. After receiving the consultant's report, Paul met with a lawyer and was able to submit additional evidence as to the abuse, Paul's fears for his client's safety, and the advocacy role in social work. The complaint eventually was dismissed.

The National Association of Social Workers (1994) has established procedures for peer review of grievances and alleged ethical violations involving its members. A violation generally results in disciplinary action such as requiring corrective actions or sanctions (Houston-Vega, Nuehring, & Daguio, 1997). The records of grievance hearings, unlike most state procedures, usually are not open and may not be used in subsequent court actions against the practitioner (*Swatch v. Treat,* 1996).

Confidentiality. Social workers have an ethical obligation to maintain the privacy of a client's participation in social work services. Confidentiality has been referred to as the foundation of the therapeutic relationship (Watkins, 1989). Because of the clearly worded language supporting confidentiality in the NASW Code of Ethics of 1996 (sect. 1.07), there is unquestionable legal significance to this obligation. The right to have social work communications remain confidential is rooted in the explicit and implied conditions of the social work contract. Because of the unique characteristics of the work, clients have an expectation that the process will remain strictly confidential. This expectation has been affirmed in many court decisions, but it is also well-established that confidentiality is not absolute.

Some authors express growing concern about the erosion of confidentiality in recent years (Bollas & Sundelson, 1995; Kopels & Kagle, 1994). The exceptions to the general requirement of confidentiality have their basis in legal mandates and court cases. These exceptions have become part of the accepted standard of practice and include breaking confidentiality to warn third parties of danger from clients (*Tarasoff v. Board of Regents of the University of California,* 1976) or to take actions to protect a potentially suicidal person (*Meier v. Ross General Hospital,* 1968). Confidentiality may also be waived when a parent legally consents to release information for a minor, or when a court-appointed guardian consents to release information for a person found by a court to be incompetent. Also, state abuse statutes usually require the reporting of suspected abuse of a minor, a person with a developmental disability, or a person who is elderly (Dickson, 1998; *Landeros v. Flood,* 1976).

It is important for practitioners to maintain a current state of knowledge concerning exceptions to confidentiality to properly inform clients of the limitations. For example, in group or family therapy, social workers can control only the information that flows from themselves. Group or family members may choose not to abide by the expectation of privacy. Children often seek guarantees from social workers "not to tell anyone," but this is a promise professionals may not be able to keep if the child communicates an abusive or otherwise dangerous situation. Because social workers cannot guarantee confidentiality, a clear disclosure of the limits of confidentiality should be reviewed with clients at the beginning of treatment. In this way, clients can make an informed decision as to whether to share certain information (Boback, Moore, Bloch, & Shelton, 1996; Dickson, 1998).

Privilege. In all 50 states, the professional obligation of maintaining confidentiality has been strengthened by the passage of privilege statutes for social workers and other psychotherapists (for a citation to each state's statutes, see *Jaffe v. Redmond,* 1996, p. 1929). Privilege is the client's right to keep certain communications private and not available as evidence in a legal proceeding (Polowy & Gorenberg, 1995). Generally, privilege statutes apply only to licensed professionals and social workers or students practicing under their direct supervision.

Trial lawyers and judges traditionally disapprove of the concept of privilege because it conflicts with the principle that justice requires courts to have access to all available evidence (Madden, 1998). As a result, privileges are construed narrowly by the courts, and social workers may need to advocate for the privilege to be upheld. In 1996, the U.S. Supreme Court defended the rationale for a psychotherapy privilege, calling confidentiality in mental health treatment "a public good of transcendent importance" (*Jaffe v. Redmond,* 1996).

Although the Supreme Court and most state courts have supported the concept of social work privilege, there is universal agreement that such privilege is not absolute (Baumoel, 1992). For example, when a child is the subject of a hearing regarding abuse or custody, the "best interests of the child" standard often takes precedence and courts may require social workers to testify. Similarly, in criminal cases, some states have found that an accused person's constitutional rights to a fair trial are sufficient to trump a privilege (*Michigan v. Stanaway* and *Michigan v. Caruso,* 1994). Although results in these cases vary across states, the general rule is that courts will require social workers to testify or produce records, despite the existence of privilege, when the public interest outweighs the violation of the client's privacy.

Privilege is limited by statutory language to information about direct practice situations that create an expectation of confidentiality in clients. When a social worker conducts a court-ordered evaluation or is otherwise not in a "treatment relationship" with a client, privilege does not attach to these communications. Privilege may also be forfeited by a client if otherwise-protected information is disclosed to other parties and thus is considered by a court to be no longer confidential. Finally, if a client raises personal mental health issues in a legal case, such as claiming to have sustained emotional harm, courts do not allow the use of privilege to block the opposing party's access to treatment records or testimony. Social workers have an obligation to assert a client's privilege until ordered by the court to provide information.

Release of information. The legal requirements for a valid release of information form have been well established, but many social workers and agencies are not rigorous in protecting the rights of clients to control the flow of confidential information. Stromberg et al. (1988) listed the components of a valid form. They include (a) identification of information about the parties, including the sending and receiving agencies and professionals; (b) the purpose for which the information is sought; (c) a checklist or description of the type of material to be released or received (e.g., psychosocial, treatment plan); (d) an expiration date and a statement that a client is free to revoke the permission at any time; (e) a notice prohibiting the receiving party from rereleasing the material; and (f) the client's signature, along with the signature of a witness.

Because some clients may not be able to read and understand the forms, social workers should always take the time to review the release to ensure there is true consent. If a release form is received that is invalid or inappropriate, social workers should not supply the information but should return the form, noting specific reasons for being unable to comply (Houston-Vega et al., 1997). In cases where a release form gives the social worker permission to engage in ongoing communications with another professional, a new release should be signed periodically (every 2 to 3 months) to confirm a client's continued consent.

Responding to subpoenas. Few occurrences in the practice of social work strike as much fear and anxiety as the receipt of a subpoena. Whether the subpoena arrives by mail or is delivered by a sheriff, a social worker should take certain procedural steps to safeguard clients, protect privileged information, and reduce the possibility of liability for the social worker. Let us consider the following case:

Polly was an experienced mental health clinician working in a Pennsylvania clinic. One of Polly's supervisees, who was unlicensed, began treatment with Sarah, a teenage girl. Sarah was having "psychological problems and severe headaches" following a head injury. She had suffered the injury in a fall at a local community center. In preparing a lawsuit against the community center, Sarah's mother spoke with Polly and signed a release requesting that the treatment records be sent to the family's attorney. Soon after, Polly received a subpoena in the mail from the attorney representing the community center. Polly subsequently provided a copy of the records to this attorney, as well. In response, Sarah's mother filed a complaint with the state licensing board for improper release of information.

Polly's defense to the complaint stressed that she had released the records pursuant to a legal subpoena. A court, reviewing the findings of a state licensing board, found that Polly had a duty to protect the confidentiality of her client's records. She should have known the basic procedures for responding to a subpoena so as to take appropriate actions either to contest the subpoena or to contact the client before sending out any records (*Rost v. State Board of Psychology*, 1995).

A subpoena is a legal requirement to appear, but it is not the same as being compelled to testify or provide records. It is important to understand that, in most states, a subpoena is prepared by an attorney seeking testimony or information in regard to a legal action. Although generally signed by a court clerk, there has been no ruling by a judge on the validity of the subpoena. A social worker who, as Polly did, releases confidential information without either a signed consent or a court order is potentially liable.

The following procedures provide an outline for social workers to follow in response to a subpoena. These procedures assume the social work treatment is covered by a privilege statute. Technically, privilege relates only to the question of admissibility of evidence in a civil or criminal trial. If there is no privilege, social workers should still seek to follow these guidelines to protect confidentiality as an ethical matter. Without privilege, there is a less powerful argument for a court to exclude confidential information.

Because the legal rules differ across jurisdictions, it is advised that professionals consult a local attorney to review the procedures and to assist with difficult issues. When a subpoena is received, observe the following procedures:

1. Check with the client to see if there is a signed consent to release information.
2. Scrutinize the records to determine if releasing them would violate the confidential information of third parties.
3. If there are concerns about the privilege of others, such as third-party information in the records or treatment that included other parties such as a spouse, the social worker should seek the permission of the client to discuss these issues with the attorney. Often, the interests of the social worker are consistent with the issues of the client.
4. If a social worker is unable to determine whether a client has consented, there is a duty to claim the privilege for the client. In other words, the privilege exists until the client waives it in writing.
5. In most states and in federal court, the privilege survives the death of the client (*Swidler & Berlin v. United States*, 1998). The executor of the estate has the legal authority to allow the release of information.

If the social worker has no written consent to release information, several steps are available to respond to the subpoena. First, it is possible to contest a subpoena by having an attorney file a motion to have the subpoena quashed (invalidated). In some jurisdictions, a letter to the pre-

siding judge may be sufficient to seek a ruling. If there is insufficient time to pursue these steps, the social worker can still act in a manner that safely and adequately responds to the subpoena.

A social worker may bring a sealed copy of the requested records to court on the date and time indicated on the subpoena. The validity of the subpoena will then need to be determined by the judge. If there is some evidence to suggest that the information the social worker is being asked to testify about is relevant and material to the case, and there are no other sources for this information, a judge may decide to conduct an *in camera* review. In this process, the judge examines the documents privately before ruling on the privilege issue. The judge may uphold privilege and excuse the social worker from testifying, require limited testimony on a specific issue, or allow more general testimony from the social worker.

At times, social workers are asked to provide testimony as expert witnesses. The purpose of an expert is to provide scientific, technical, or other specialized knowledge that will assist the judge and jury to understand the evidence or decide on a factual question (Melton, 1994). Some cases have challenged whether a social worker is qualified to serve as an expert and found that the individual's training and experience are the deciding factors (*America West Airlines Inc. v. Tope*, 1996). It is common for attorneys to seek to qualify the treating professional as an expert, but social workers who are testifying as evidence witnesses should resist assuming multiple roles in the same case.

Record keeping. In legal arenas, it is frequently repeated: That which is not documented is not done. Social work records are considered medical records in most states (Roach, Chernoff, & Esley, 1985). As such, specific statutory guidelines cover issues such as length of time to retain records as well as the structure and form of certain types of records; social workers should be knowledgeable about these guidelines.

Kagle (1991) lists three competing goals of record keeping: accountability, efficiency, and client privacy. The legal system is primarily concerned with the first and third of these goals. Social workers need to document their conduct and treatment decisions when their practice is questioned in relation to a client's complaint or when they provide testimony about evaluation or treatment. Records must be thorough and complete to fulfill the goal of accountability. This includes documentation to enable emergency treatment of a client when a social worker is unavailable and to communicate with other agency employees who may be involved in the treatment of a client (*Peck v. Counseling Service of Addison County,* 1985). However, the goal of client privacy need not be sacrificed in the process. It is important that social workers develop rigorous adherence to procedures that reduce the chance of an unauthorized release of confidential information.

Some social workers maintain a set of personal notes on active clients. Except in those states where protected by statute (see, e.g., *District of Columbia Mental Health Information Code,* 1996; *Illinois Mental Health & Developmental Disabilities Confidentiality Act,* 1996), personal notes are subject to subpoenas. Material in personal notes may be more subjective and speculative than data in an official file. Such notes may contain hypotheses or opinions that contradict the information in the official file. If these notes are subpoenaed, the credibility of

the social worker as witness can be severely compromised.

It is important to write records as though they may some day be made public in a court action (Barker, 1987). This means avoiding specific information about third parties not directly related to the treatment, noting the source of a statement about another party (e.g., Carl reported that he believed his father was using drugs again), and writing in a professional style at all times. Records should detail the purpose of the work (assessment and goal setting), the process of the work (intervention and treatment plan), and the impact of the treatment (evaluation and plans for completion of work.) Another professional should be able to read a case record and have a clear understanding of the case. This is particularly important in cases where an expert opinion is needed to assess whether a social worker practiced within acceptable professional standards.

A social worker should never change a record or falsify any information in a client's file. If a mistake is found in a case note, the record may be corrected in the margin with a notation as to the date of correction. A separate entry should be placed chronologically in the case file to document the timing of the change and avoid accusations of record tampering (Simon, 1992).

It is important to remember that although information in a file belongs to a client, the actual record belongs to the agency or practitioner. Clients have a right to review their files or receive a copy of the record. Social workers, however, have a duty to prevent possible harm by monitoring the client when reviewing a file and excising any information that would violate the privilege of third parties. In unusual situations, particularly if a social worker has reason to believe the information contained in the file would be harmful to the client, permission to see the file may be denied. The social worker may seek a legal representative or court-appointed guardian as the party to whom the record is released to protect the client while complying with the request.

Informed consent. Many social workers marginalize the involvement of clients in treatment decisions, providing little more than lip service to informed consent. The concept of informed consent fits well with the values and practice principles in social work, including self-determination, dignity and worth of the individual, and empowerment approaches to practice. Making certain that all clients understand the offer of service as well as the risks and alternatives to the treatment approach is an ethical duty but also has legal implications.

Informed consent involves two distinct levels of agreement (Madden, 1998). There is an initial consent reached in the beginning of treatment that involves the basic elements of the contract to provide services, including such matters as meeting times, payment options, and other practice policies. The second level of consent follows the assessment process. Clients should be informed about specific intervention strategies and techniques and the social worker's level of experience with the techniques. Information as to the advantages of the favored treatment approach should be balanced by a discussion of risks, including possible effects on health, emotions, and relationships. Clients should understand alternative treatments that may be available as well as the risks of refusing treatment. Finally, it is important to let clients know the anticipated duration and costs of treatment (Appelbaum, Lidz, & Meisel, 1987; Reamer, 1994; Regehr & Antle, 1997).

Treatment Stage Issues

Standard of care in direct social work practice. Black's Law Dictionary (1983) refers to the *standard of care* as a measure of professional competence. A social worker is expected to exercise the average degree of skill, care, and diligence exercised by other social workers, in light of the present state of professional knowledge and research. If a social worker presents as an expert in a field, the standard of care rises accordingly. Perhaps more than any other area of social work practice, the concept of standard of care has been ignored by the professional community. As a result, several outside forces, including legal cases, have unduly influenced the way social workers practice.

Granello and Witmer (1998) distinguish two distinct components of the standard of care that provide clarity to the concept. *Practice standards* are the behavioral expectations or the manner in which the professional conducts practice. The following duties are among the basic expectations: Social workers should keep adequate records, maintain confidentiality, obtain informed consent, arrange for client coverage when unavailable, refrain from dual relationships with clients, conduct business affairs honestly, arrange for regular supervision/consultation, and participate in ongoing professional development (Madden, 1998). These practice standards are drawn from professional literature (see, e.g., NASW guidelines on the private practice of clinical social work, 1991) and the social work code of ethics. They constitute a framework for appropriate professional conduct. In general, practice standards are well established so that courts and licensing boards are able to assess the validity of complaints in these areas.

The standard of care also includes *clinical standards,* which articulate the procedures used in the diagnosis and treatment of clients and the protocols to be followed for particular clinical situations (Granello & Witmer, 1998; Sanderson, 1998). Clinical standards have not been well defined and generate considerable controversy in the field. Some clinicians worry that treatment guidelines will impinge on creativity and eclectic approaches, but the absence of standards results in the interrelated dangers of poorly informed practitioners and increased liability.

Clinical standards should be developed from outcome-based research. Social workers are able to protect clients and avoid liability when they use empirically validated treatment guidelines. When a social worker is charged with malpractice, courts rely on the testimony of expert witnesses to articulate the standard of care and to opine whether the social worker violated the standard. In areas where standards are developed by a professional organization (see, e.g., NASW, 1998, treatment guidelines for emergency medical services for children; and NASW, 1996b, practice update on treatment of adults with the possibility of recovered memories of child sexual abuse), legal decisions are less likely to create new standards that may be antitherapeutic for clients or social workers.

Social workers have a duty to stay informed about developments in practice research. The managed care industry has used some practice outcome research to develop "preferred practice" approaches (Corcoran & Vandiver, 1996). These standards reflect the industry's interests in short-term, goal-oriented treatment approaches. Others have argued for an approach that uses empirical research to identify "best practices" (Steenbarger & Smith, 1996). If so-

cial work and other mental health professions follow the best practices approach, it will strengthen the ability of clinicians to challenge third-party payers to fully fund empirically validated treatments or face increased likelihood that managed care companies will be found liable for denying coverage (Granello & Witmer, 1998).

Reasonable Care in Risk Situations

Social workers should be knowledgeable about the standard of care in several practice situations where there is a heightened risk of liability. In some areas of practice, such as sexual relations with clients, the standard of care is unambiguous. In other areas, such as choosing among treatment approaches, there is little clarity to guide the social worker. However, the areas of practice that have generated the most risk have also generated the most specific standards of care.

Misdiagnosis/incorrect treatment cases. A social worker has a duty to diagnose/assess a condition correctly, but that does not mean that a diagnosis/assessment must be accurate (Mackie, 1994). The expectation is that social workers follow commonly accepted procedures such as obtaining supervision or consultation, making referrals for medical or diagnostic evaluations, and following up on information that suggests suicide intent or other potentially dangerous condition. If a social worker does not possess the knowledge or experience to handle a case situation, or if a social worker does not exercise reasonable care in managing a case, a client can establish the basis of a lawsuit for incorrect care, as long as there is evidence that the client suffered damages as a direct result.

Professional boundary issues: Managing transference. It is well established that social workers are forbidden from engaging in any form of sexual or romantic relationship with current or former clients (Youngren & Skorka, 1992). The prohibition is consistently enforced by the courts (*Simmons v. United States,* 1986), and several states have enacted legislation criminalizing such acts (Wisconsin Statutes Annotated, 1984). *Transference* involves the client's emotional reaction to the therapist, whereas *counter-transference* is the term for the therapist's feelings toward the client. The standard of care requires clinicians to manage the strong feelings that emerge in the treatment relationship (transference phenomenon). This duty is consistent with the expectation that social workers receive regular supervision.

Child sexual abuse/recovered memory cases. The debate surrounding the treatment of clients who seem to be struggling with traumatic memory symptoms has been political and rancorous (Madden & Parody, 1997). The clinical issues provide a useful example of the need for social work and other mental health professions to establish a standard of care rather than allow courts to rule on the basis of individual cases. Most of the vigorous debate concerning recovered memory treatment has emerged from legal cases in which the arguments about the possibility of robust repression of traumatic memories is necessarily polarized by the adversarial process.

Clients have filed suit or pressed criminal charges against their alleged perpetrators; third parties, such as parents, have sued therapists for causing harm to them by implanting false memories of sexual abuse in their children. Unfortunately, courts have not been uniform in handling these cases, and as a result, cases with similar factual situations have resulted in wildly contrasting results (e.g., compare *Shahzade v. Gregory,* 1996, with *Doe v. Maskill,* 1996).

In response to the confusion, many of the professional organizations have developed standards for work in the recovered memory arena (NASW, 1996b), and there is growing acceptance of the clinical standards in the professional literature (Gold & Brown, 1997; Madden & Parody, 1997). The standards cover the basic clinical and ethical principles governing the therapeutic relationship, evaluation, and treatment of adults with the possibility of recovered memories.

Social workers providing treatment have been urged to remain separate from the forensic issues involved with searching out corroboration and assuming an active role in legal actions initiated by clients (Madden & Parody, 1998). The standards further instruct social workers to remain empathic, nonjudgmental, and neutral while informing clients that their memories may or may not be historically accurate. Only experienced and specially trained social workers should use memory recovery techniques, and all social workers who encounter these cases should avail themselves of appropriate supervision (NASW, 1996b).

Dangerous clients/duty to warn or protect. Since the 1976 California Supreme Court decision in *Tarasoff v. Board of Regents of the University of California,* which found a duty on the part of a therapist to warn an intended victim, there has been an active debate within the mental health community about how to handle dangerous client situations. When a client in therapy threatens to do a violent act, what is the responsibility of the clinician? Does the duty change when the client threatens harm to a specific individual? What if the threat concerns suicide? Does the duty extend to the reporting of fantasies or the expression of angry impulses in treatment?

The initial difficulty in these situations is for the social worker to differentiate the threats that are real and likely to be carried out from those that are appropriate, therapy room, uninhibited, emotional expressions. The most widely accepted standard in the field today calls for a social worker to take some action to warn or protect when the following conditions are met: The threat is assessed as real and likely to be carried out by the client, and the intended victim is identified or identifiable. However, in some cases, therapist liability has been found in the absence of a clear victim (*Lipari v. Sears Roebuck & Co.,* 1980). Recently, a case that involved fantasy content concerning pedophilia, without a specific action or threat, was found to be sufficient to create a duty for the professional to take action (Bruni, 1998).

A social worker who determines that an intervention is required to reduce the risk of harm to the intended victim may be required to contact local police and the intended victim directly. If the client is in an inpatient facility, the duty is to control the individual by such means as extending the person's confinement. Clinical interventions, such as a referral to evaluate the need for medication or emergency hospitalization, are appropriate responses when clients are seen in outpatient settings.

The danger of imposing civil liability on social workers for failing to control the dangerous impulses of their clients goes far beyond the individual cases. If the promise of confidentiality is too casily waived, clients will be reluctant to enter treatment. They may be inhibited from sharing their most intimate thoughts and emotions. It is extremely difficult for clinicians to predict violence. When the liability costs of not breaching confidentiality become too high, social workers may predict violence too readily and will seek unnecessary commitments. This is an example of the legal system creating an antitherapeutic result for both clients and professionals.

Some cases have supported a "professional judgment" rule in which a court will not engage in second-guessing a clinician who has acted within the standard of care. This rule is based on a balancing of the need to protect victims with the rights of a client to good treatment, including the right to be free from unnecessary breaches of confidentiality (*Lorenzo v. Fuerst,* 1997). The professional judgment rule is an example of a therapeutic jurisprudence approach to deciding legal issues in mental health practice.

Supervisor liability. There is a growing trend in mental health law to hold supervisors legally liable for the practice of those they supervise. *Supervisor liability* is essentially a negligence claim in which the actions of the clinician that cause damages to a client are not the direct subject of the lawsuit. Instead, the argument is advanced that the supervisor assumed a duty of care to the clients of the worker to adequately monitor and evaluate the performance of the worker. Most of the claims involve incorrect diagnoses, confidentiality violations, misguided interventions, and other clinical issues such as mishandling of the transference phenomenon. As a result of inadequate performance of the supervision role, the supervisor breached the standard of care, the practitioner's actions were not corrected, and an injury to the client occurred.

A second legal theory relied on for supervisor liability is *respondeat superior* (let the master respond). This contract-based theory is relevant in agency settings and holds supervisors and agencies responsible for the actions of workers that occur within the scope of their job responsibilities. The rationale is to ensure that the legal entity not be able to avoid responsibility for actions done by employees by claiming that "it was the individual who was at fault."

Ending Stage Issues

The legal issues in the ending stage of service are related primarily to unplanned terminations, client disappointment with the results of treatment, billing disputes, and inappropriate referrals (Houston-Vega et al., 1997). Many of the risks can be reduced with consistent application of sound practice policies and clear communication with clients.

Abandonment and referral problems. The issue of client abandonment has received very little attention in the professional literature but is a source of potential liability for social workers. Many terminations occur outside the mutual decision-making process. When a worker initiates the termination as a result of a job change, relocation, or retirement, there is a duty to make sure the client has ready access to alternative services.

> Dr. Liptzin, a mental health clinician, had seen Wendell six times at the student health center. Wendell had been referred after disrupting his law school class by claiming to have evidence that he was telepathic. Dr. Liptzin prescribed medication, and Wendell improved. At the end of the term, Dr. Liptzin retired. Because of uncertainty as to where Wendell would spend the summer, Dr. Liptzin did not refer Wendell to another specific psychiatrist but did give instructions that he should continue being monitored by a doctor. Wendell went home, stopped taking his medication, developed psychotic symptoms, and, a few months later, opened fire with a rifle on a crowd of people. After being found not guilty by reason of insanity, Wendell sued Dr. Liptzin. He charged that the doctor had misdiagnosed his condition and failed to inform Wendell of the seriousness of his illness and the risks of not following up with medication and treatment. A jury agreed, finding Dr. Liptzin liable (*Williamson v. Liptzin*, 1998).

As in the example case above, providing general information to a client on termination may not be sufficient. A social worker has the legal duty to take reasonable steps to ensure that the client receives the necessary treatment (*Brandt v. Grubin*, 1974). These steps might include conjoint sessions with the new service provider, involvement of family members, and information concerning the risks of not receiving treatment.

Managed care denials. One of the most difficult issues in termination occurs when a client's insurance benefits have been depleted. Here is a relevant case.

> Nitai, a 16-year-old boy, was admitted to a community hospital after twice attempting suicide. The managed care company terminated the inpatient hospital care and required Nitai to be transferred to a residential treatment center that primarily treated substance abuse problems. While there, Nitai hanged himself. His father filed suit against the hospital, the treatment center, and the managed care company. In a landmark decision, a federal district court permitted a malpractice claim against the HMO to proceed (*Moscovitch v. Danbury Hospital*, 1998).

The social worker's duty is to provide all of the care that is necessary, irrespective of a managed care company's decision not to authorize payment for ongoing treatment. The decision to terminate services must be based on clinical evidence, not the availability of payment (Corcoran & Vandiver, 1996). The social worker has a duty to pursue all insurance appeals processes, to arrange for payment plans where feasible, or to refer to an agency that can provide free or reduced-fee services. It appears inevitable that managed care companies soon will be responsible for client injuries that flow from a denial of coverage for necessary services. Several cases are in the process of appellate review at the time of this writing including the *Moscovitch v. Danbury Hospital* (1998) case summarized above. A federal law historically has blocked such lawsuits, but several states have introduced legislation to allow clients to sue managed care companies ("Court Says," 1998). Currently, Texas is the only state that allows lawsuits against managed care companies for malpractice (Frisman, 1998). Ultimately, the prospect of HMO liability should result in improved protection for consumers and a return of decision making in mental health services to clients and clinicians.

EMERGING LEGAL ISSUES FOR THE 21ST CENTURY

At the beginning of the 21st century, emerging societal issues are creating new challenges for social work and new legal roles for practitioners. In the introduction to their book, *Social Work in the 21st Century,* Reisch and Gambrill (1997) reflect that, in the last century, economic, political, cultural, and technological events have all had an impact on the evolution of social work (p. 2). There is no reason to suspect that the next century will hold anything different. In the area of social work and the law, demographic trends, technological develop-ments, and structural changes in the legal system have produced new challenges and opportunities.

Demographic challenges. The two prominent demographic shifts that face the United States at the start of the new century are the aging of the population and its increasing racial and ethnic diversity (Ozawa, 1997, 1999). These demographic changes will require social workers to develop their knowledge of the legal protections for populations that are vulnerable. Increasing economic and social inequality is likely, along with pressure on existing resources. Social workers should prepare for expanded roles in legal arenas that involve guardianship and conservator processes; the guarantee of basic human needs through involvement in legal policy initiatives, such as children's rights and social security reform; immigration law; and the protection of the civil rights of all groups. As communication systems and the media increase access to reports of injustice and oppression from around the world, social workers must become committed to using international law and treaties to advocate for social justice across the globe.

Technological challenges. In an increasingly litigious environment, social workers must consider whether their practice policies adequately minimize their legal exposure. Gelman, Pollock, and Weiner (1999) have examined new challenges to confidentiality brought on by electronic records and communication. They argue that the changes in technology have outpaced the ability of social workers to adequately safeguard client information. As managed care has expanded, the number of people who have access to treatment records has grown.

Many agencies have made the shift to electronic records, raising concerns for the confidentiality of client records. Rock and Congress (1999) suggest specific strategies for safeguarding client information, such as instituting strict log-on procedures and installing firewalls and encryption technology. They list guidelines for promoting and protecting confidentiality in the technological age, stressing continuing education of staff, informed consent of clients, revised agency policies, and a commitment of the social work profession to advocacy to protect confidentiality. The continuing evolution of information technology will present new challenges to social workers in the future. The commitment to safeguarding confidentiality is both an ethical imperative and a legal mandate. To protect our clients and ourselves, social workers will need to be at the forefront of the movement to protect privacy as new threats arise.

Legal system challenges. Mason (1997) presents a compelling argument for social workers to participate more actively in a variety of legal settings. Courts are overcrowded, and many cases that directly affect people's lives take too long to reach a final decision. There is a growing skepticism about the ability of the traditional adversarial process to deal with complex problems such as child custody, domestic violence, mental illness, and victim services. New and expanded roles for social workers are emerging as mediators and quasi-judicial hearing officers in juvenile and family court cases (Mason, 1997). Social workers have an excellent knowledge base from which to assume these new legal roles, but the profession must claim these roles and expand the legal content in social work education and professional development to better prepare social workers for these new challenges.

The movement to treat juvenile offenders as adults is growing across the nation in response to well-publicized incidents of gang violence and school shootings. The focus on punishment rather than prevention, treatment, and rehabilitation has limited the roles of social workers in the juvenile justice system (Schwartz, 1997). Social work has an opportunity to lead reform efforts that separate political motives from development of policies that promote effective services.

The concerns for social justice that are at the core of social work require the profession to become involved in legal issues. The rights of individuals are protected by an increasingly complex system of laws including federal protections for people with disabilities, minority groups, special education students, and children in the child welfare system. Local and state laws have been enacted to protect the rights of people affected by domestic violence and AIDS. All of these laws affect clients and suggest the need for social workers to enhance their knowledge of the law so as to become more effective advocates.

SUMMARY

Social workers who engage in direct practice need to develop a sound base of knowledge about the law and the many ways it affects practice. If involvement in legal issues is accepted as an inevitable reality in today's practice environment, social workers can respond with informed, persuasive information that can influence legal decisions. When social workers understand the purpose of a proceeding, clarify the roles of attorneys and other professionals, and prepare themselves for the roles they are being asked to play, there will be opportunities to create a legacy of *therapeutic* decisions that will benefit clients and social workers.

REFERENCES

America West Airlines Inc. v. Tope, 1996 WL 663559 (Tex. App. Nov. 14, 1996).

Appelbaum, P. S., Lidz, C. W., & Meisel, A. (1987). *Informed consent: Legal theory and clinical practice.* New York: Oxford University Press.

Babb, B. A. (1997). An interdisciplinary approach to family law jurisprudence: Application of an ecological and therapeutic perspective. *Indiana Law Journal, 72,* 775-808.

Barker, R. (1987). To record or not to record: That is the question. *Journal of Independent Social Work, 2*(2), 1-5.

Baumoel, J. (1992). The beginning of the end for the psychotherapist-patient privilege. *University of Cincinnati Law Review, 60*(3), 797-826.

Black's Law Dictionary (Abridged 5th ed.). (1983). St. Paul, MI: West.

Boback, H. B., Moore, R. F., Bloch, F. S., & Shelton, M. (1996). Confidentiality in group psychotherapy: Empirical findings and the law. *International Journal of Group Psychotherapy, 46,* 117-135.

Bollas, C., & Sundelson, D. (1995). *The new informants: The betrayal of confidentiality in psychoanalysis and psychotherapy.* Northvale, NJ: Jason Aronson.

Brandt v. Grubin, 329 A.2d 82 (Sup. Ct. N.J. 1974).

Brookfield, S. D. (1995). *Becoming a critically reflective teacher.* San Francisco: Jossey-Bass.

Bruni, F. (1998, October 9). Jury finds psychiatrist was negligent in pedophile case. *The New York Times,* p. B4.

Chapin, R. K. (1995). Social policy development: The strengths perspective. *Social Work, 40,* 506-514.

Corcoran, K., & Vandiver, V. (1996). *Maneuvering the maze of managed care.* New York: Free Press.

Court says pay denied is care denied. (1998, July). *NASW News,* p. 10.

Dickson, D. T. (1998). *Confidentiality and privacy in social work: A guide to the law for practitioners and students.* New York: Free Press.

District of Columbia Mental Health Information Code, Sect. 6-2003 (1996).

Doe v. Maskill, 679 A.2d 1087 (Md. Ct. App. 1996).

Flynn, J. (1992). *Social agency policy* (2nd ed.). Chicago: Nelson-Hall.

Frisman, P. (1998, November 9). Measuring mental misery. *The Connecticut Law Tribune, 24*(45), 1, 12-14.

Gelman, S. R., Pollack, D., & Weiner, A. (1999). Confidentiality of social work records in the computer age. *Social Work, 44,* 243-252.

Gold, S. N., & Brown, L. S. (1997). Therapeutic responses to delayed recall: Beyond recovered memory. *Psychotherapy, 34,* 182-191.

Granello, P. F., & Witmer, J. M. (1998). Standards of care: Potential implications for the counseling profession. *Journal of Counseling & Development, 76,* 371-380.

Haynes, K. S., & Mickelson, J. S. (1991). *Affecting change: Social workers in the political arena* (2nd ed.). New York: Longman.

Houston-Vega, M. K., Nuehring, E. M., & Daguio, E. R. (1997). *Prudent practice: A guide for managing malpractice risk.* Washington, DC: NASW Press.

Illinois Mental Health & Developmental Disabilities Confidentiality Act, 740 ILCS 110 (1996).

Jaffe v. Redmond, 116 S.Ct. 1923 (1996).

Jones, J. A., & Alcabes, A. (1989). Clients don't sue: The invulnerable social worker. *Social Casework: Journal of Contemporary Social Work, 70,* 414-420.

Kagle, J. D. (1991). *Social work records* (2nd ed.). Belmont, CA: Wadsworth.

Kopels, S., & Kagle, J. D. (1994). Teaching confidentiality breaches as a form of discrimination. *Arete, 19*(1), 1-9.

Landeros v. Flood, 551 P.2d 389 (Cal., 1976).

Lipari v. Sears Roebuck & Co., 497 F.Supp. 185 (D. Neb. 1980).

Lorenzo v. Fuerst, 1997 Ohio App. LEXIS 12 (1997).

Mackie, S. A. (1994). Proof of psychotherapists negligence in diagnosing and treating a patient's mental condition. In *American Jurisprudence Proof of Facts 3d, 25* (pp. 117-187). Rochester, NY: Lawyers Cooperative.

Madden, R. G. (1998). *Legal issues in social work, counseling, and mental health: Guidelines for clinical practice in psychotherapy.* Thousand Oaks, CA: Sage.

Madden, R. G. (in press). Legal content in social work education: Preparing students for interprofessional practice. *Journal of Teaching in Social Work.*

Madden, R. G., & Parody, M. (1997). Between a legal rock and a practice hard place: Legal issues in "recovered memory" cases. *Clinical Social Work Journal, 25,* 223-247.

Madden, R. G., & Parody, M. (1998). Helping without harming: A reply to Feld and Fetkewicz. *Clinical Social Work Journal, 26,* 227-232.

Mason, M. A. (1997). Opportunities for social workers in the law? The jury is out. In M. Reisch & E. Gambrill (Eds.), *Social work in the 21st century* (pp. 219-225). Thousand Oaks, CA: Pine Forge.

McKnight, J. (1989). Do no harm: Policy options that meet human needs. *Social Policy, 20,* 5-15.

Meier v. Ross General Hospital, 445 P.2d 519 (Cal. 1968).

Melton, G. B. (1994). Expert opinions: "Not for cosmic understanding." In B. D. Sales & G. R. VandenBos (Eds.), *Psychology in litigation and legislation* (pp. 55-100). Washington, DC: American Psychological Association.

Michigan v. Stanaway & Michigan v. Caruso, 521 N.W.2d 557 (1994).

Moscovitch v. Danbury Hospital, 1998 U.S. Dist. LEXIS 17609 Dkt. No. 3:97cv1654 (CFD) (1998).

Myers, L. L., & Thyer, B. A. (1997). Should social work clients have the right to effective treatment? *Social Work, 42,* 288-289.

National Association of Social Workers. (1991). *NASW guidelines on the private practice of clinical social work.* Silver Spring, MD: Author.

National Association of Social Workers. (1994). *NASW procedures for the adjudication of grievances* (3rd ed.). Washington, DC: Author.

National Association of Social Workers. (1996a). *NASW Code of ethics.* Washington, DC: Author.

National Association of Social Workers. (1996b). *Practice update: Evaluation and treatment of adults with the possibility of recovered memories of child sexual abuse.* Washington, DC: Author.

National Association of Social Workers. (1998). *Emergency medical services for children guidelines.* Washington, DC: Author.

Odencrantz, L. C. (1929). *The social worker in family, medical, and psychiatric social work.* New York: Harper & Brothers.

Ozawa, M. N. (1997). Demographic changes and their implications. In M. Reisch & E. Gambrill (Eds.), *Social work in the 21st century* (pp. 8-27). Thousand Oaks, CA: Pine Forge.

Ozawa, M. N. (1999). The economic well-being of elderly people and children in a changing society. *Social Work, 44,* 9-19.

Peck v. Counseling Service of Addison County, 499 A.2d 422 (Vermont, 1985).

Polowy, C. I., & Gorenberg, C. (1995). *Office of General Counsel law notes: Client confidentiality and privileged communications.* Washington, DC: National Association of Social Workers.

Reamer, F. G. (1994). *Social work malpractice and liability: Strategies for prevention.* New York: Columbia University Press.

Regehr, C., & Antle, B. (1997). Coercive influences: Informed consent in court-mandated social work practice. *Social Work, 42,* 300-306.

Reisch, M., & Gambrill, E. (1997). *Social work in the 21st century.* Thousand Oaks, CA: Pine Forge.

Roach, W. H., Chernoff, S. N., & Esley, C. L. (1985). *Medical records and the law.* Rockville, MD: Aspen.

Rock, B., & Congress, E. (1999). The new confidentiality for the 21st century in a managed care environment. *Social Work, 44,* 253-262.

Rost v. State Board of Psychology, 659 A.2d 626 (Com. Ct. Pa. 1995).

Saltzman, A., & Proch, K. (1990). *Law in social work practice.* Chicago: Nelson-Hall.

Sanderson, W. C. (1998). The case for evidence-based psychotherapy treatment guidelines. *American Journal of Psychotherapy, 52,* 382-387.

Schroeder, L. O. (1995). *The legal environment of social work* (rev. ed.). Washington, DC: NASW Press.

Schwartz, I. M. (1997). Juvenile justice: Back to the future, or will we learn from the past. In M. Reisch & E. Gambrill (Eds.), *Social work in the 21st century* (pp. 120-126). Thousand Oaks, CA: Pine Forge.

Shahzade v. Gregory, 923 F. Supp. 286 (D. Mass. 1996).

Simmons v. United States, 805 F.2d 1363 (9th Cir. 1986).

Simon, R. I. (1992). *Clinical psychiatry and the law* (2nd ed.). Washington, DC: American Psychiatric Press.

Steenbarger, B. N., & Smith, H. B. (1996). Assessing the quality of counseling services: Developing accountable helping systems. *Journal of Counseling & Development, 75,* 145-150.

Stolle, D. P., & Wexler, D. B. (1997). Therapeutic jurisprudence and preventive law: A combined concentration to invigorate the everyday practice of law. *Arizona Law Review, 39,* 25-32.

Stromberg, C., Haggarty, D. J., Leibenluft, R. F., McMillan, M. H., Mishkin, B., Rubin, B. L., & Trillings, H. R. (1988). *The psychologist's legal handbook.* Washington, DC: Council for National Register of Health Service Providers in Psychology.

Swatch v. Treat, 671 N.E.2d 1004 (Mass. App. Ct. 1996).

Swidler & Berlin v. United States, 524 U.S. 399 (1998).

Tarasoff v. Board of Regents of the University of California, 17 Cal.3d 425, 551 P.2d 334 (1976).

Watkins, S. (1989). Confidentiality and privileged communications: Legal dilemmas for family therapists. *Social Work, 34,* 133-136.

Wexler, D. B. (1996). Therapeutic jurisprudence in clinical practice. *American Journal of Psychiatry, 153,* 453-455.

Williamson v. Liptzin, No. 97CVS690 (N.C. Super. Ct., Orange City. Sept. 21, 1998).

Wisconson Statutes Annotated. 940.22(2) (West Supp. 1984).

Witkin, S. L. (1998). Human rights and social work. *Social Work, 43,* 197-201.

Youngren, J. N., & Skorka, D. (1992). The non-therapeutic psychotherapy relationship. *Law and Psychology Review, 16,* 13-28.

CHAPTER THREE

The Role of Critical Thinking in Evidence-Based Social Work

EILEEN GAMBRILL

This chapter describes the role of critical thinking in social work and its relationship to evidence-based practice and ethical guidelines of the National Association of Social Workers (1996). This code advises social workers to "critically examine and keep current with emerging knowledge relevant to social work" and "fully use evaluation and research evidence in their professional practice" (Standard 5.02). Critical thinking is also relevant to Value 6 of the *NASW Code of Ethics,* which calls on social workers to "practice within their areas of competence and to develop and enhance their professional expertise" (NASW, 1996, p. 6). The Council on Social Work Education requires educational programs to train students in critical thinking skills.

WHAT IS CRITICAL THINKING?

Critical thinking involves the careful appraisal of beliefs and actions to arrive at well-reasoned ones that maximize the likelihood of helping clients and avoiding harm. It involves reasonable and reflective thinking focused on deciding what to believe or do (Dewey, 1933; Ennis, 1987). Viewed broadly, the process is part of problem solving. It requires clarity of expression, critical appraisal of evidence and reasons, and the consideration of alternative points of view. Critical thinkers question what others take for granted. They challenge accepted beliefs and ways of acting. They ask questions such as: Have there been any critical tests of this claim? Could there be another explanation?

Other questions include:

How do I know a claim is true?

Who presented it as accurate? How reliable are these sources?

Are the facts presented correct?

Have any facts been omitted?

Is there evidence a claim is true? How compelling is this?

What samples were used? How representative were these? Were studies relatively free of bias? Have results been replicated?

Are there other plausible explanations?

If correlations are presented, how strong are these?

Are weak appeals used, such as appeal to emotion or special interests?

Related Attitudes, Values, and Styles

Critical thinking involves more than the mere possession of related knowledge and skills. It requires using them in everyday situations and acting on the results of thinking carefully (Paul, 1992). It involves *accurately* presenting alternative perspectives and paying attention to the *process* of reasoning, not just the product. Strong-sense critical thinking involves a genuine fair-mindedness in which opposing views are accurately presented and there is a genuine effort to fairly critique both preferred and unpreferred views (Paul, 1992, p. 278). Critical thinking involves questioning what others take for granted, asking "What's the evidence for this?" even when professors, supervisors, or administrators would rather not consider such questions. It requires paying attention to gaps between our background knowledge (current beliefs and related evidence) and related research findings. Critical thinking and scientific reasoning are closely related. Both place value on clarity and the critical appraisal of claims.

Both share a commitment to fair mindedness and reliance on standards that are more likely than others to yield accurate answers to certain kinds of questions.

DOES IT MATTER?

Problem solving and decision making, whether explicit or implicit, are at the heart of social work. Decisions are made at many different levels of complexity. They involve collecting, integrating, and interpreting diverse sources of data. The judgments made are often difficult ones, requiring distinctions between causes and secondary effects, problems and the results of attempted solutions, personal and environmental contributors to complaints, and findings and evidence (links between assumptions and findings). The benefits and risks of different options must be considered and probabilities of success estimated in a context of inevitable uncertainty. The purpose of thinking critically about practice-related claims is to maximize services that are effective in achieving valued outcomes and to minimize ineffective and harmful services. Basing decisions on incomplete or inaccurate accounts may result in the use of ineffective or harmful methods. The history of the mental health industry reveals a long list of false causes for personal troubles and social problems, as well as harmful interventions to cure "mental illnesses" (e.g., see Breggin, 1991; Ofshe & Watters, 1994; Szasz, 1987, 1994; Valenstein, 1986). Inappropriate reliance on psychological levels of assessment and intervention masks environmental conditions related to many problems, including depression, substance abuse, and family violence. Errors in judgment may result in incorrect assumptions about the causes of problems and inaccurate predictions about suicidal potential, need for hospitalization, future recurrence of violent acts, or the results of a new service policy. Errors may occur both in structuring problems and in drawing inferences (e.g., see Munroe, 1996). Errors may result in (a) failing to offer help that could be provided and is desired by clients, (b) forcing clients to accept "help" they do not want, (c) offering help that is really not needed, or (d) selecting methods that aggravate rather than alleviate client concerns. Clients, as well as social workers, may feel more hopeless and helpless about ever achieving desired outcomes as a result of poor decisions.

Research regarding professional practice shows that a variety of biases come into play that dilute the quality of decisions (for related research, see Dawes, 1994; Gambrill, 1990; Gibbs & Gambrill, 1999; Levy, 1997; Skrabanek & McCormick, 1990). Examples include the *fundamental attribution error* (the tendency to attribute the cause of behaviors to personal characteristics of people and to overlook environmental factors) and the *behavioral confirmation bias* (the tendency to search for data that support favored positions and to ignore data that do not). We use different criteria to examine other points of view than we use to examine our own beliefs. We are influenced by the availability of material, including vivid case examples, which may be misleading rather than informative. Such biases have been found not only in the helping professions but in a wide range of other contexts as well (e.g., see Nisbett & Ross, 1980). The behavioral confirmation bias often results in overlooking contradictory data. Failing to ask "Is there an alternative account that is better?" and "What are problems with my view?" encourages rationalizing favored views rather than exploring alternative accounts. The emphasis on gathering evidence for and justifying one's own positions rather than on exploring alternative views gets in the way of discovering valuable options. Base-rate data are often ignored as these affect probabilities. A social worker who sees many parents who sexually abuse their children may "overdiagnose" this event because of her unique situation; she may overestimate the true prevalence of sexual abuse. Resemblance criteria (the extent to which a characteristic seems to resemble or be similar to another characteristic) can also lead us astray. We may assume that effects resemble their causes when in fact causes and effects may bear little or no resemblance to one another. Such representative thinking is an associative process in which the associations we have with a certain kind of person (such as child abuser) influence our judgments. A child welfare worker may have a stereotype of what a child abuser is like and incorrectly classify a client as a child abuser based on this stereotype. In misuse of representativeness, we rely on cues that do not accurately predict an outcome.

BENEFITS OF THINKING CRITICALLY ABOUT IMPORTANT PRACTICE DECISIONS

Good intentions are not enough if we want to maximize the likelihood of helping clients. Only if social workers are aware of common biases and develop skills to counter them can such biases be minimized. Critical thinking knowledge, skills, and values can help social workers to critically appraise claims and arguments, use language effectively, recognize affective influences on decisions, avoid cognitive biases that interfere with sound decision making, and spot pseudoscience and quackery and so help to avoid their influence. The term *pseudoscience* refers to material that makes sciencelike claims but provides no evidence for these claims. It is characterized by a casual approach to evidence; weak evidence is accepted as readily as strong evidence. Quackery refers to the promotion for profit of products and materials known to be false or which are untested (Pepper, 1984). Critical thinking skills increase the likelihood of discovering and closing gaps between our background knowledge and practice-related research findings. We will ask, "Are my assumptions compatible with what is known about the relationships between behavior and the environment?" For example, knowledge about behavioral principles would lead to the conclusion that programs such as family preservation services, in which intensive work with a family for a short time is followed by no contact, would probably fail, given data describing the common lack of generalization and maintenance of positive outcomes. Critical thinking will help social workers spot and avoid the effects of practice-related propaganda, including that published by professional organizations (e.g., glittering generalizations that sound good but are devoid of related evidence regarding their accuracy) and bandwagon appeals (everyone is doing it).

Critical thinking can help social workers to be evidence-based and so to honor their ethical obligations to clients (i.e., to inform them and offer competent services). Evidence-based practice is the conscientious, explicit, and judicious use of current best evidence in making decisions about the care of clients (Sackett, Richardson, Rosenberg, & Haynes, 1997, p. 2; see also Gray, 1997; Warren & Mosteller, 1993). It involves integrating individual practice exper-

tise with the best available external evidence from systematic research as well as considering the values and expectations of clients. External research findings related to problems are drawn on if they are available and they apply to a particular client. Involving clients as informed participants in a collaborative helping relationship is a hallmark of evidence-based practice. Clients are fully informed about the risks and benefits of recommended services as well as alternatives (including the alternative of doing nothing). If no external research findings are available showing that recommended methods help people with similar kinds of concerns, clients are so informed, and the theoretical rationale for recommended programs is described in clear terms that clients can understand.

The kind of evidence needed to answer a question depends on the question. Every research method is limited in the kinds of questions it can critically test. Some tests are more rigorous than others and so offer more information about what may be true or false. Compared with anecdotal reports, experimental tests are more severe tests of claims of effectiveness. Unlike anecdotal reports, they are carefully designed to rule out certain biases (for example, in sample selection) and so provide more opportunities to discover that a theory is not correct. The question raised will suggest the research method required to critically explore it. If our purpose is to communicate the emotional complexity of a certain kind of experience (e.g., the death of an infant), then qualitative methods may be needed (e.g., detailed case examples, thematic analyses of journal entries, openended interviews at different times). On the other hand, if we are concerned about the effects of a service method, we must use experimental studies. Failure to do so has resulted in

TABLE 3.1   Five Types of Answerable Questions

Effectiveness questions concern how effective an intervention might be for a particular client. For example, What method, if any, will most effectively forestall the onset of Alzheimer's disease among nursing home residents like those here at Lakeside? Which method has been most effective as a way to help interdisciplinary teams to work effectively?

Risk/prognosis questions concern the likelihood that a particular person will engage in a particular behavior or experience a particular event in a given period of time. For example, What is the likelihood that a sex offender like Joe will commit a new offense within 2 years of his parole? If I place sexually abused siblings in the same adoptive home, is it likely that they will abuse each other?

Description questions concern base-rate data (estimates of the frequency of a problem in a given population based on a sample of individuals from that population) or what has been found regarding similar clients. For example, What are the most common reasons for readmission to a hospital for aged people who were discharged to community support services? What is the base rate of teenage pregnancy in this city?

Assessment questions concern accurate descriptions of clients' problems, alternative competing behaviors, and their contexts. For example, Is there a reliable, valid measure of depression (substance abuse, parenting skills) that will be valuable with my client? What is the quickest, easiest to administer, least intrusive, and most accurate assessment tool to see whether a client here at Sacred Heart Hospital has an alcohol abuse problem?

Prevention questions concern the most effective way to prevent the initial occurrence of a problem or undesirable event. For example, What is it the most effective way to prevent teenage pregnancy among students at South Middle School? Which is the most effective way to teach kindergartners and first graders not to wander off with someone not authorized to take the child from school?

NOTE: Based on Gibbs and Gambrill (1999, pp. 236-237). See also Sackett et al. (1997).

harm to clients and significant others (e.g., see Jacobson, Mulick, & Schwartz, 1995). Answering other kinds of practice-related questions such as "What is the accuracy of this assessment measure?" requires other research methods. Kinds of important answerable practice questions are illustrated in Table 3.1. *Answerable* refers to questions of fact (not preferences or values). The influence of evidence-based practice is starting to make its way into social work (e.g., see Macdonald, 1998). A Center for Evidence-Based Social Services has been established at the University of Exeter in England. Courses and workshops designed to enhance practitioner skills in locating and critically appraising evidence related to important practice decisions have been offered in dentistry and medicine for many years (see Critical Appraisal Skills Pro-

gram). The term *evidence-based practice* is preferable to the term *empirical practice*. The latter term now seems to be applied to material that has been published, whether or not it is evidence-based. Such use represents an appeal to authority (not evidence).

Critical thinking skills can help social workers to avoid questionable grounds for accepting practice-related claims (e.g., about effectiveness) such as authority, tradition, popularity, newness, intuition, and manner of presentation (see Table 3.2). For example, critical appraisal skills and knowledge are of value in understanding what we can and cannot learn from intuition. Although intuition is an invaluable source of ideas about what may be true or false, it is not a sound guide for testing those beliefs. Attributing sound judgment to intuition de-

TABLE 3.2   Common Fallacies

Ad hominem appeals: Attacking (or praising) the person rather than examining the person's argument

Appeal to authority: Basing claims solely on a person's status; no evidence is provided to support or refute claims made

Influence by manner of presentation: Believing a claim because of the apparent sincerity, speaking voice, attractiveness, stage presence, likability, or other trait of a speaker

Appeal to numbers or popularity: Relying on number of people who use a method or who have a belief

Appeal to tradition: Accepting a practice solely because it has been used for a long time

Appeal to newness: Accepting a method simply because it is new

Appeal to anecdotal experience: Accepting or rejecting claims about the effectiveness of methods based on unsystematic personal experience

Appeal to good intentions: Assuming that good intentions reflect good results

Relying on testimonials: Claiming that a method is effective based on one's own experiences

Relying on case examples: Drawing conclusions about many clients based on one or a few unrepresentative individuals

Uncritical documentation: Assuming that because something is described in the literature it must be true; literature is cited, but no information is given about how the cited author arrived at a conclusion

After this, therefore on account of this—post hoc ergo propter hoc: The incorrect belief that if Event A (a service program) precedes Event B (a positive outcome), A has caused B

NOTE: For further description, see Gibbs and Gambrill (1999).

creases opportunities to teach helping skills (one has "it" but does not know how or why "it" works). Relying on intuition, on what "feels right," is not wise if it results in ignoring information about problems, causes, and remedies.

Critical thinking will help social workers appraise practice theories. Theories are conjectures (guesses) about what may be true. We always have theories. "There is no pure, disinterested, theory-free observation" (Popper, 1994, p. 8). Because our theories influence our decisions, they are important to examine. Many people accept a justificationist approach to knowledge development, focusing on gathering support for (justifying, confirming) claims and theories. Let's say that you see 3,000 swans, all of which are white. Does this mean that all swans are white? Can we generalize from the particular (seeing 3,000 swans, all of which are white) to the general, that all swans are white? Karl Popper (and others) contend that we cannot discover what is true by means of induction (making generalizations based on particular instances) because we may later discover exceptions (swans that are not white). (In fact, black swans are found in New Zealand.) Popper (1972) maintains that falsification (attempts to falsify, to discover the errors in our beliefs) by means of critical discussion and testing is the only sound way to develop knowledge. Confirmations of a theory can readily be found if we look for them. Thus, falsifiability is an important characteristic to look for in evaluating assertions. Some assertions are not falsifiable; there is no way to find out if they are false (e.g., Is there a God?). Theories differ in the extent to which they have been tested and in the rigor of the tests used. Although we can justify the selection of a theory by its having survived more risky tests concerning a wider variety of hypotheses (not been falsified) compared with other theories that have not been tested or that have been falsified, we can never accurately claim that this theory is "the truth." We can only eliminate false beliefs.

Critical thinking skills will help social workers to sort the wheat from the chaff in the multicultural literature (e.g., see Ortiz de Mantellano, 1991, 1992) and to consider the downside of an emphasis on particular groups. This can result in overlooking shared similarities, obscuring problems that many different groups confront, and missing opportunities to work together to address shared concerns (Webster, 1992, 1994). Chaff includes admonitions to act in certain ways with individuals in a particular group when this recommendation (e.g., "Consider the clients' pace") applies to all clients. Stereotypes created by inaccurate generalizations about a group may result in overlooking individual differences within groups.

Critical thinking skills and values will contribute to honoring ethical guidelines described in the 1996 *National Association of Social Workers Code of Ethics*. It could be argued that only with such skills and related values can the recommendations described in this code be honored. Consider informed consent. Evidence-informed client choice entails three criteria: (a) the decision involves which intervention a person will or will not receive; (b) the person is given research-based information about effectiveness (likely outcomes, risks and benefits) of at least two alternatives (which may include the option of doing nothing); and (c) the person provides input into the decision-making process (Entwistle, Sheldon, Sowden, & Watt, 1998). Only if social workers themselves are informed about research findings related to answerable questions concerning important practice decisions (e.g., Has this service method been found to help people like my client?) can they inform their clients about the risks and benefits of recommended methods as well as alternatives, as required by their code of ethics. Critical thinking skills will help social workers to ask answerable questions that allow them to critically appraise research findings, as well as the expertise and track records of potential consultants, trainers, or agencies from whom they may purchase services.

ENCOURAGE EVIDENCE-BASED ASSESSMENT

Assessment requires many decisions such as: (a) what data to collect to understand problems and their potential for resolution, (b) how to gather it (e.g., self-report of clients, observation), and (c) how to integrate different kinds of data. Concerns about validity and factors that influence this (e.g., reliability) are not confined to researchers. They are also relevant to everyday practice. If social workers rely on irrelevant or inaccurate measures, they may select ineffective or harmful plans because of faulty assumptions about the causes of client concerns. For example, if a social worker selects an inaccurate measure of social skills, she may assume incorrectly that a client has the skills required to succeed in certain situations when the client does not. This could result in punishing social reactions such as rejection and less willingness on the part of a client to try new options. Critical appraisal skills can help social workers to an-

swer important questions that arise during assessment such as the following:

> Is this assessment measure reliable? Does it provide
> consistent data by the same person at different
> times and over different practitioners?

> Is this assessment instrument valid? Does it mea-
> sure what it purports to measure? Does it ap-
> ply to my client?

> Are norms available for this measure that involve
> people like my client?

> What assumptions am I making? Can I provide
> evidence or a sound argument for them (e.g.,
> demonstrate compatibility with what is known
> about behavior)?

> Does my assessment have clear intervention guide-
> lines?

> Have I relied on valid sources of information?

> Are there alternative views for which there is a
> stronger argument?

> Have I paid attention to common errors in inte-
> grating data (e.g., focusing only on data that
> confirm my preferred views)?

> Have I considered the values and preferences of
> my clients and their significant others?

Critical thinking skills will be of value in spotting informal fallacies such as ad hominem attacks and diversion methods that dilute the
quality of decisions made during case conferences and will guide selection of group norms
that contribute to well-reasoned decisions (e.g.,
seeking alternative views).

Selecting an Assessment Framework

The question "Can this problem be minimized or resolved?" may be answerable only by
a sound assessment through which opportunities to pursue valued outcomes are discovered.
Thinking critically about assessment ap-

proaches will help social workers to describe accurately the extent to which different theories
have been critically evaluated and found to result in selection of services that help clients.
Critical thinking will help social workers to
identify key assumptions related to different
views of behavior and its consequences
(e.g., psychiatric views, constructional views)
and to spot and question the medicalization of
problems-in-living as psychiatric illness. Critical
thinking will help them to spot values (e.g.,
about how people should live) disguised as scientific findings. Assessment frameworks differ
in their vulnerability to certain kinds of errors.
Approaches that focus on alleged pathologies of
clients may result in overlooking valuable resources, such as caregiving skills. Such approaches can be contrasted with a constructional assessment that encourages a focus on
clients' strengths (e.g., available alternative behaviors that will compete successfully with disliked behaviors) and environmental resources
(e.g., see Gambrill, 1997; Goldiamond, 1984;
Meyer & Evans, 1989). Critical appraisal skills
will encourage a contextual understanding of
problems and their possibilities. Without this, it
is easy to fall into blaming others and focusing
on "changing them" or giving clients a rationale
for their plights rather than helping them to alter environmental conditions related to achieving outcomes they value. Discovering options
may require a multilevel contingency analysis
of agencies and residential settings, including
supervisory and administrative practices. This
will often reveal competing contingencies that
may interfere with offering evidence-based services to clients. *Contingencies* refers to associations among behaviors of interest and related
antecedents and consequences.

Selecting Sources of Assessment Data

No matter what their assessment framework, social workers have a limited number of options for collecting information: (a) various forms of self-report (e.g., what clients say, what significant others say, written measures), (b) self-monitoring, (c) observation in role-play or in real life, and (d) physiological measures (e.g., see Bergan & Kratochwill, 1990; Gambrill, 1997; Kozloff, 1994; Sulzer-Azaroff & Mayer, 1991). Case records contain information based on one or more of these sources. Each method has advantages and disadvantages and certain requisites (e.g., see Ceci & Bruck, 1995; Ofshe & Watters, 1994). Careful selection of assessment methods maximizes opportunities for accurate problem description including available alternative behaviors that may successfully compete with disturbing behaviors. Evidence-based selection of assessment methods requires skill in critically appraising the relevance and accuracy of different kinds of data. Let us say a parent tells you that she is a good parent and knows how to use positive methods to discipline her child. How can you find out if this is accurate? Or, let us say that your supervisor asks you to use the Zung Depression Inventory to assess a client's complaint of depression. What information do you need to judge for yourself whether this measure is a good choice (i.e, is it reliable, and does it provide an accurate account of depression for this client)?

Judging whether a certain source provides reliable and valid data requires access skills for discovering related research findings and critical appraisal skills for reviewing what is found. Critical appraisal skills allow social workers to judge the relevance and accuracy of measures *for themselves* based on critical appraisal of related research (e.g., regarding whether a measure actually measures what it is it supposed to measure). Considerable advances have been made in some areas in identifying problem-related contingencies. For example, assessment protocols have been developed to identify the cues and consequences related to self-injurious behavior of children (Luiselli, Matson, & Singh, 1992). This is truly "starting where the client is."

Integrating Assessment Data

Certain kinds of errors are common in this stage of assessment. For example, we are subject to the confirmation bias—looking only for data that support our preferred views and ignoring counter evidence. We may reject actuarial methods for combining data, which rely on statistical associations found among certain predictors and an outcome, in favor of clinical intuition, which is not as accurate (e.g., see Dawes, 1994; Dawes, Faust, & Meehl, 1983; Ruscio, 1998). Critical thinking skills encourage us to focus on relevant data and to be aware of vivid, misleading data. A few worthless items can dilute the effect of one helpful item. Consider the study in which social work graduate students were asked to estimate the likelihood that some people were child abusers. Being told that the person "fixes cars in his spare time" and "once ran away from home as a boy" decreased the effects of the description of this man as having "sadomasochistic sexual fantasies" (see Nisbett & Ross, 1980, p. 155). There is no research showing that people who fix cars in their spare time and once ran away from home as a boy are more (or less) likely to abuse their children. Irrelevant material about this person tended to make him less "similar" to someone who might abuse his child.

Critical thinking skills, knowledge, and values can increase the likelihood of avoiding common errors in problem definition, such as jumping to conclusions, stereotyping, and misapplying group data to individuals. Howitt (1992) describes the example of a social worker who assumed that because a parent was a stepfather, and because there is a correlation between being a stepfather and abuse of children, this particular stepfather was responsible for the abuse. (This was not true.) Critical appraisal skills can help social workers to evaluate popular classification systems such as the *Diagnostic and Statistical Manual of Mental Disorders* (*DSM-IV;* American Psychiatric Association, 1994). Kirk and Kutchins (1992), both social workers, document problems with the *DSM-IV,* such as the consensual nature of what is included (agreement among individuals is relied on rather than empirical criteria), lack of agreement about what label to assign clients (poor reliability), and lack of association between a diagnosis and indication of what plans will be effective. They discuss the role of political and economic considerations in the creation and "selling" of the *DSM.* (See also other critiques of psychiatric labels, such as Boyle, 1990; Szasz, 1994).

ENCOURAGE USE OF EVIDENCE-BASED SERVICE METHODS

Critical thinking skills can help social workers to fulfill requirements in the NASW Code of Ethics by considering related research findings when making important practice decisions.

Practice decisions include what service methods to use, what levels to offer (e.g., 5 or 10 parent training sessions), who will provide service, and how progress will be tracked to see if hoped-for outcomes are attained and to what degree. Key answerable questions that arise at this stage are: Is there any evidence that this service method will be effective in achieving hoped-for outcomes with this client with a minimum of harm? Have other methods been found to be more effective? What do results of systematic reviews reveal? (Oxman & Guyatt, 1993). Inflated claims about what works are the norm rather than the exception in the helping professions. This means that social workers, like master detectives, must sort the wheat (service methods that have been found to be effective in rigorous tests) from the chaff (recommendations that are based on authority or consensus—they have not been critically tested). Accountability to clients requires selection of service methods that are acceptable to clients and significant others and that are most likely to result in hoped-for outcomes in an efficient manner with a minimum of negative effects. To make such selections, social workers need ready access to computerized databases describing relevant external research findings, as well as skills in critically appraising what they find regarding questions such as: Will this parent training program help this parent to improve her parenting skills. Research related to a particular service method will indicate into which of the following categories a service method falls:

1. Beneficial forms of care demonstrated by clear evidence from controlled trials
2. Forms of care likely to be beneficial (The evidence in favor of these forms of care is not as firm as for those in Category 1.)

3. Forms of care with a trade-off between beneficial and adverse effects (Clients and significant others should weigh these effects according to individual circumstances and priorities.)

4. Forms of care of unknown effectiveness (There are insufficient or inadequate quality data on which to base a recommendation for practice.)

5. Forms of care unlikely to be beneficial (The evidence against these forms of care is not as firm as for those in Category 6.)

6. Forms of care likely to be ineffective or harmful (Ineffectiveness or harm demonstrated by clear evidence.) (Enkin, Keirse, Renfrew, & Neilson, 1995)

Implementing Services

Procedural fidelity refers to the match between how a method *should be* implemented for maximal effect and how it *is* implemented. A concern for accountability highlights the importance of attending to process (what was done) as well as outcome (what was achieved). Dilution effects are common. This refers to providing an intervention in a diluted form (e.g., offering 5 rather than the 10 sessions found to be effective or using an untrained provider rather than one who has attained criterion levels of performance). Thinking critically about implementation may result in a decision not to use a diluted form of a program that is likely to be ineffective.

Purchasing of Services

Critical appraisal skills can also help social workers to select wisely among service providers. For example, child welfare staff often contract out services to other providers. Critical appraisal encourages questions such as: What evidence is there that this agency helps clients?

Does the agency help clients like those I will send? Five different agencies in a community may offer treatment programs to clients whose alleged substance abuse is presumed to be related to the abuse or neglect of children. For each provider, we should ask, To what extent does the service include: (a) an individualized assessment of each client's concerns, including the extent to which particular circumstances or behaviors (e.g., substance abuse) are related to alleged child abuse or neglect; (b) a search for external research findings related to presenting problems and a judicious judgment about the extent to which they apply to a particular client; and (c) consideration of the values and expectations of clients. For each service purchased, we should ask, Is anything known about its effectiveness? If so, what? Do we know if a service

1. Does more good than harm?
2. Does more harm than good?
3. Is of unknown effect—not in research setting or in poor-quality research?
4. Is of unknown effect, but in good-quality research program? (Gray, 1997)

Services offered should maximize the likelihood of hoped-for outcomes. For each service provider, we should examine the gap between what is provided to referred clients and what could be provided, based on best current evidence.

Planning for Generalization and Maintenance

Lack of generalization of valued behaviors to real-life settings (such as the home) and lack of maintenance of valued outcomes over time are major problems. Maintenance programs will be required whenever reinforcement for new be-haviors will not be naturally provided in real-life settings or when it may decrease over time. Thinking carefully about the conditions re-quired for effective maintenance and general-ization may increase the likelihood of providing requisites.

EVALUATION

The *NASW Code of Ethics of 1996* calls on so-cial workers to "monitor and evaluate practices, the implementation of programs, and practice interventions" (5.02). Clients have a right to know whether services help or harm or are ir-relevant. Does parent training affect the fre-quency of child abuse? Critical thinking skills can help social workers at all levels to avoid fooling themselves and their clients about the results of service programs. Questions that arise here include:

Are desired outcomes clearly described?
Do progress measures accurately reflect the degree of change?
Are changes valued by clients and significant others?
Are progress indicators cost-effective?

Critical thinking skills can help social workers to avoid common biases that give misleading es-timates of progress, such as wishful thinking, looking only for data that show benefits, and failing to consider harmful effects. Ongoing monitoring based on valid progress measures allows timely case management decisions and offers opportunities to keep clients informed about their degree of progress. Such monitor-ing will help to avoid common sources of error such as overconfidence and hindsight bias, which result in inaccurate estimates of progress and the role of services.

Attending to Social Validity as well as Outcomes

Critical appraisal skills will help social work-ers to make effective use of social validity data as well as data regarding outcomes. Questions regarding social validity concern three areas (Wolf, 1978): (a) are the goals pursued impor-tant to clients and significant others and rele-vant to desired changes? (b) are the methods used acceptable to consumers and the commu-nity, or do they cost too much (e.g., in terms of effort, time, discomfort, etc.)? (c) are the con-sumers satisfied with the outcome, including predicted changes as well as unpredicted ef-fects? Social validity data provide an important supplement to clear, valid, reliable outcome measures. As Schwartz and Baer (1991) empha-size, the key purpose of such assessment is to an-ticipate the rejection of a program before that happens and, for this reason, assessment should include feedback from all relevant consumers of a program. Information gathered should be used to improve the acceptability of services; otherwise, as Schwartz and Baer note, such as-sessments are in some sense fraudulent. This emphasizes the value of information about so-cial *invalidity* (e.g., complaints about specific aspects of a program) as well as social validity. The point is to identify specific program aspects that are liked and disliked and to increase the former and minimize the latter.

CRITICAL THINKING AS A GUIDE FOR RECORDING AND SEEKING CONSULTATION

Standard 3.04(a) of the *NASW Code of Ethics* states that "social workers should take reasonable steps to ensure that documentation in records is accurate and reflects the services provided" (p. 20). Critical thinking skills will be of value in preparing clear, accurate records as well as in spotting deficiencies in case records that may get in the way of providing effective services as, for example, fuzzy goals, an emphasis on alleged client pathology, and a neglect of client assets (e.g., see Tallent, 1993). The *NASW Code of Ethics* calls on social workers to "refer clients to other professionals when the other professionals' specialized knowledge or expertise is needed to serve clients fully or when social workers believe that they are not being effective or making reasonable progress with clients and that additional service is required" (2.06, a); and "to seek consultation only from colleagues who have demonstrated knowledge, expertise, and competence related to the subject of the consultation" (2.05, b). Critical thinking skills can help social workers ask questions about other professionals that will help them to make sound decisions in this area (such as, What is your demonstrated track record of success in achieving outcomes sought by my client based on data you have gathered systematically and regularly?). We cannot assume that possessing a certain degree, or having certain training or experience, necessarily makes a person competent to offer services that maximize the likelihood of successful outcomes with clients.

THE ROLE OF CRITICAL APPRAISAL IN EVIDENCE-BASED ADMINISTRATION AND SUPERVISION

Clearly describing goals and selecting clear, valid progress indicators can help administrators and supervisors carry out required tasks. Clear performance standards allow staff at all levels to monitor the quality of their performance. Administrators have a responsibility to arrange for training programs that maintain staff at minimally acceptable competency levels in relation to practice-related knowledge and skills required to attain hoped-for outcomes. Competency-based, criterion-referenced training should be provided as needed. This refers to training based on what is known about how to achieve valued outcomes (what competencies are required) and which includes clearly defined intermediate steps and criteria levels that can be used to determine the skill level mastered. Familiarity with the fallacies described in Table 3.2 can be of value in critically appraising claims regarding training programs (e.g., the California parent training program results in behavior changes that enhance positive outcomes achieved with clients). Criteria such as participants' ratings of a training program or testimonials may not be associated with on-the-job changes in performance levels and are therefore not a sound guide to whether or not a training program results in improved services.

Administrators have a responsibility to cultivate a culture of thoughtfulness. Knowledge can grow only in an open environment in which staff are free to raise questions (express criticism) about current practices and policies and their outcomes. The *Code of Ethics for Child*

Welfare Professionals calls on administrators to "provide organization members with a working environment which permits frank discussion and criticism of agency operations and with an administrative means for dissent, assurance of due process, and safeguards against reprisal" (Office of the Inspector General, 1999, p. 15). Criticism provides information that may help to minimize avoidable mistakes. All professionals make mistakes. Many are unavoidable; they could not have been prevented by the most skilled of the skilled. Others are avoidable by better training, more effective audit procedures, or appropriate incentive systems (e.g., see Howitt, 1992; Munroe, 1996). Staff willingness to identify mistakes is influenced by agency culture. If reporting mistakes is punished, few will do it. On the other hand, if agency policy clearly recognizes that mistakes are inevitable, and staff are encouraged to discuss them with their supervisors at an early point, mistakes are less likely to result in further negative effects and more likely to provide an opportunity to learn how to avoid them in the future—if they are avoidable mistakes.

Administrators choose among methods that differ in the opportunities they provide to make transparent the quality of services offered to clients and, therefore, to enhance quality. Ethical decisions require an accurate estimate of the likelihood that certain services can meet client needs based on sound arguments and related research findings. The proof of the pudding concerning the effects of policies, programs, and plans is whether or not hoped-for outcomes result. No one really knows if a program is harming or helping clients or making no difference at all unless service outcomes are carefully explored. The more vague the assessment of progress, the greater the opportunities for the unrec-

ognized play of biases, such as overconfidence, that may limit opportunities to help clients. Berk and Rossi (1990) suggest the following questions of concern:

Is the program reaching the appropriate beneficiaries?

Is the program being properly delivered?

Are the funds being used appropriately?

Can effectiveness be estimated? (Are program goals clear? Is the program sufficiently clear and uniformly delivered? Are the requisite resources available?)

Did the program work? How good is good enough? Unless the size of the program effect required is clearly described, "evaluators are shooting at a moving target" (p. 76).

Was the program worth it? Answering this question requires comparing cost with effectiveness.

The "compared with what" question is critical. Is a program compared with the lack of a program or with two different programs, or is the effectiveness of different program levels explored (e.g., follow-up services for 6 months and 3 months)?

A candid recognition that resources are scarce and an open exploration of related ethical implications (not all people will get what they want) requires consideration of populations as well as individuals (e.g., see Eddy, 1996; Gray, 1997). That is, administrators and policy makers should consider what populations they are required to serve, what services they could provide, what the likely effect might be, based on related external evidence; they should also consider what populations they now serve, what kind of services they now provide, and with what effect. Only by thinking about populations as well as individuals are we likely to make ethical decisions about the distribution of scarce resources.

ENCOURAGING LIFELONG SELF-DIRECTED LEARNING

Critical appraisal values, skills, and knowledge will contribute to accurately appraising professional knowledge and skills in relation to what is needed to resolve concerns. It takes courage and a sincere interest in helping clients to candidly review the match between our values, knowledge, and skills and what is needed to help clients and avoid harm. Regular review will help social workers to spot learning opportunities. The following questions are helpful:

What skills would I like to acquire?

What evidence is there that acquiring certain skills would help me help my clients attain certain outcomes?

What exactly would I do (and not do) if I had this skill?

What approximations take me closer to my goal?

What criteria would most accurately reflect mastery of skills?

Is this skill of value in other situations?

What training programs would be most effective in helping me learn this skill?

BARRIERS

There are formidable barriers to thinking carefully about practice-related claims, arguments, and decisions (Gambrill, 1990). Perhaps the greatest is what Ellul (1965) refers to as *sociological propaganda:* "the penetration of an ideology by means of its sociological context" (p. 63) via economic, political, and sociological structures. Consider, for example, the in-

creased medicalization of personal conduct. Much is at stake in how problems are framed, and people with vested interests devote considerable time, money, and effort to influence what others believe. "Problem crusaders" (people with a particular interest in a particular view of a problem) put forward particular definitions. Problem definition is influenced by professionals' interest in maintaining and gaining power, status, and economic resources, as well as by differences of opinion about what makes one explanation better than another. Concerns about protecting vested interests (e.g., economic gain and power) may loom larger than concerns about helping clients and "telling the truth" (e.g., see Dawes, 1994; Lang, 1998). The mental health industry is big business resulting in inflated claims of success (e.g., see Gomory, 1998, 1999). Critical discussion is not in the interests of many groups because it would reveal the lack of evidence for claims made and policies recommended: Fuzzy thinking is the oppressor's friend. Thinking critically about the causes of problems such as poverty and substance abuse may call in question comfortable positions that protect special interests of the status quo. If you can no longer focus on the individual characteristics of clients as the source of problems, the obvious role of troubled and troubling environmental circumstances related to these problems may be revealed (e.g., lack of medical care, good schools, safe housing). Profit making is a key aim of for-profit and many (supposedly) not-for-profit service enterprises. There is also "the prophet motive"—the lure of being an insightful sage privy to special insights about behaviors and their causes (Jarvis, 1990).

We live in a society in which pseudoscience and quackery are rife and in which science and related critical thinking skills are often misrepresented. Misuses, nonuses, and misrepresentation of science pose barriers to critical thinking. Surveys show that most people do not understand the basic characteristics of the scientific method (Stevens, 1988). Social workers are not immune to this educational deficit, which is so common in our culture and which accounts in large part for the ready acceptance of proposed causal factors without any evidence that they are relevant. Misuses of science include labeling things as scientific when in fact there is nothing scientific about the enterprise (the trappings of science are used without the substance). The media, pop psychology, and professional journals often present incomplete accounts of problems that obscure the complexity of issues. We may read "Crack-addicted mother kills baby." The focus is on the mother's addiction. Little or nothing may be said about her impoverished life circumstances, both past and present, and related economic and political factors. Feelings and thoughts are often more vivid than environmental causes. It is easy to overlook environmental circumstances that contribute to these thoughts and feelings. Environments differ in the extent to which they encourage critical thinking. Administrators who wish to push through programs with little discussion may not welcome probing questions about proposed policies and practices. Critical thinkers may be dubbed troublemakers, and attempts may be made to marginalize or besmirch such individuals. We are gullible creatures, as any history of science, fashion, or just about anything else would testify (e.g., see Cialdini, 1993; Gilovich, 1991). Authority, rather than critical appraisal of arguments and related evidence, is often used as the criterion on which to base practice and policy decisions (Gambrill, 1999). This was a

key reason for starting the evidence-based movement in medicine.

The costs of critical thinking include forgoing the comfortable feeling of certainty and putting in the time and hard work required to think critically about popular ideas such as "mental illness" and to locate and critically review research related to important practice decisions. It requires confronting contradictions between what you want for yourself (e.g., informed physicians) and what you offer your clients (Gambrill & Gibbs, 1999). Access to practice-related research findings may be difficult because of busy schedules. Supervisors may not model the intellectual virtues associated with critical inquiry, such as selecting methods based on evidence of what is helpful in attaining outcomes clients value. Teachers may encourage a relativistic position, arguing that "all truths have the same evidentiary status." Professional ideology poses an obstacle if it interferes with the critical appraisal of claims. It takes courage to challenge accepted beliefs, especially when held by "authorities" who do not value a culture of thoughtfulness, in which alternative views are welcomed and arguments are critically evaluated. To those who uncritically embrace a "doing good ideology," asking that compassion and caring be accompanied by evidence of helping may seem disloyal or absurd. To the autocratic and powerful, raising questions threatens their power to simply "pronounce" what is and what is not, without taking responsibility for presenting well-reasoned arguments and related evidence and involving others in decisions. Even when you ask questions tactfully, people may feel threatened, and they may become defensive, hostile, or angry when you question what they say—even when you do so with courtesy and intellectual empathy. Socrates was sentenced to death because he questioned other people's beliefs (see Plato's *Apology*, p. 59). It takes courage to question our beliefs and candidly examine their accuracy, especially if we do not usually do so. Unless we have grown up in an environment in which critical thinking was valued and modeled, we may feel personally attacked when someone disagrees with or questions what we say.

REMEDIES

Although there are many barriers to evidence-based practice, there are also many remedies. Some are suggested in the section that follows.

Remember What Is at Stake

A key remedy is a dogged focus on helping clients to achieve outcomes they value with a minimum of coercion and a maximum of collaborative involvement as required by evidence-based practice and by the *NASW Code of Ethics*. A concern for involving clients in making decisions that affect their lives highlights the importance of informed (in contrast to uninformed or misinformed) consent. Concentrating on helping clients attain outcomes they value will give social workers the courage and focus they need to use critical thinking skills. This will help them not to take things personally and to keep their purpose clearly in view: to help clients achieve outcomes they value and to avoid harm. It will help social workers have the courage and take the time needed to question what should be questioned. Social workers should immunize themselves against excessive concern about social approval, which may inhibit them from raising important questions re-

lated to our profession's very own code of ethics. Such questions include: Has this client been fully informed? Does this agency provide evidence-based services to clients?

Recognize the Uncertainty Involved in Social Work

Social work, like other professional practice, is inherently uncertain. A key reason that social workers do not think critically about what they do and to what effect may be that they do not want to recognize the uncertainty involved in their everyday work. However, not recognizing it may result in doing more harm than good and prohibits fulfillment of key NASW ethical guidelines, such as informing clients. Clients have a right to know whether services recommended have been found to help people like them.

View Mistakes as Learning Opportunities

Feedback is an essential part of learning. If we are not making mistakes, we are probably not learning. The outcomes of our actions provide valuable feedback. Did we achieve what we hoped for? Only by making and recognizing our mistakes can we make better guesses about what difficulties we may have in solving a problem. Failure provides an opportunity to do better in the future. By criticizing our efforts, "we learn more and more about our problems: we learn where its difficulties lie" (Popper, 1994, p. 158).

Use Helpful Guidelines

Focus on service goals.
Seek out and critically appraise evidence against your favored point of view.

Seek practice-related research findings related to important practice decisions.

Look for material that is both accurate and relevant to important practice decisions.

Recognize the inherent uncertainty in everyday work.

Ask what is missing.

Distinguish between questions of fact and value.

Ask: Where did the sample come from? (This question will help you avoid decisions based on biased samples.)

Keep in Touch With Other Evidence-Based Professionals and Clients

The Internet provides many opportunities to keep in touch with evidence-based helpers and clients throughout the world (e.g., see websites in reference list). Take advantage of published material (e.g., see Silverman, 1998; *Skeptic; Skeptical Inquirer; Evidence-Based Medicine Website*).

Take Advantage of Electronic Databases

The Cochrane Collaboration is a worldwide network of centers designed to prepare, maintain, and disseminate high-quality systematic reviews of the effects of health care (Bero & Rennie, 1995; Chalmers, Sackett, & Silagy, 1997). Its organizational units include Cochrane Centers around the world and collaborative review groups. Reviews are entered on the Cochrane Database of Systematic Reviews, which is available by subscription. At this point, of course, it is still incomplete in relation to questions addressed. The United Kingdom's Cochrane Center is part of the National Health Service Research and Development information systems strategy. A notable feature of both evidence-based practice and the Cochrane Col-

laboration is the concern for client interests and the involvement of consumers of health services as active participants in health-related decision-making processes. Consumers have access to Cochrane Collaboration Internet communication networks, through which they can raise questions and give comments. Attention to the values and expectations of clients is a key hallmark of evidence-based practice (Sackett et al., 1997). This is also reflected in the attention given to the development of accessible, accountable, complaint procedures (e.g., National Association of Health Authorities, 1994).

SUMMARY

Critical thinking requires a careful examination of the evidence related to practice beliefs and a fair-minded consideration of alternative views. It requires an acceptance of well-reasoned conclusions even when they are not our preferred ones. Critical appraisal values, knowledge, and skills contribute to evidence-based practice, in which social workers make well-reasoned practice decisions based on related research findings and fully inform clients about the risks and benefits of recommended services as well as alternatives. Critical appraisal can help social workers to choose wisely among options—to select those that, compared with others, are most likely to help clients. It will help social workers to discover alternative views and avoid false prophets. Another benefit is reaching decisions in which the interests of all involved parties are considered in a context of informed consent. Many of the costs of not thinking carefully about beliefs and actions are hidden, such as false assumptions that may result in harming in the name of helping. Curiosity may languish when we accept vague, oversimplified accounts that obscure the complexity of issues and give the illusion of understanding but offer no guidelines for helping clients. Complaints may continue because causes remain hidden. Thinking critically about how problems are viewed is not an easy task, especially when views that are uncritically promoted in the profession match those that are daily proffered in the society at large (e.g., the transformation of problems-in-living into mental illnesses). Yet, being a professional requires that we critically appraise beliefs, especially when they affect our clients. A focus on helping clients will provide courage to question assumptions. We owe it to our clients *not* to depend on authority or consensus as criteria on which to judge the accuracy of claims. We owe it to our clients to go beyond *who* says so, or *how many* say so, to asking: What's the evidence? and critically appraising this evidence. In this way, we honor our code of ethics to inform clients and provide competent services.

REFERENCES

American Psychiatric Association. (1994). *Diagnostic and statistical manual of mental disorders* (4th ed.). Washington, DC: Author.

Bergan, J. R., & Kratochwill, T. R. (1990). *Behavioral consultation and therapy*. New York: Plenum.

Berk, R. A., & Rossi, P. H. (1990). *Thinking about program evaluation*. Newbury Park, CA: Sage.

Bero, L., & Rennie, D. (1995). The Cochrane Collaboration: Preparing, maintaining, and disseminating systematic reviews of the effects of health care. *Journal of the American Medical Association, 274,* 1935-1938.

Boyle, M. (1990). *Schizophrenia: A scientific delusion?* London: Routledge.

Breggin, P. R. (1991). *Toxic psychiatry*. New York: St. Martin's.

Ceci, S. J., & Bruck, M. (1995). *Jeopardy in the courtroom: A scientific analysis of children's testimony*. Washington, DC: American Psychological Association.

Center for Evidence-Based Social Services. Armory Bldg., University of Exeter, England, EX4 4RJ. FAX: 01392 263324. E-mail: S.E.Bosley@exeter.ac.uk. Director: Brian Sheldon.

Chalmers, I., Sackett, D., & Silagy, C. (1997). The Cochrane Collaboration. In A. Maynard & I. Chalmers (Eds.), *Non-random reflections on health services research: On the 25th anniversary of Archie Cochrane's effectiveness and efficiency* (pp. 231-249). London: BMJ.

Cialdini, R. B. (1993). *Influence: Science and practice* (3rd ed.). New York: Harper.

Cochrane Centre, UK. NHS R & D Program, Summertown Pavilion, Middle Way, oxford, OX2 7LG, U.K. E-mail address: general@cochrane.co.uk. FAX: +44—(0) 1865-516311. Telephone: +44—(0) 1865-516300.

Critical Appraisal Skills Program (CASP). P.O. Box 777, Oxford, England OX3 7LF. E-mail: casp@cix.co.uk. Website: http://www.ihs.ox.ac.uk/casp/

Dawes, R. M. (1994). *House of cards: Psychology and psychotherapy built on myth*. New York: Free Press.

Dawes, R. M., Faust, D., & Meehl, P. E. (1993). Statistical prediction versus clinical prediction: Improving what works. In G. Keren & C. Lewis (Eds.), *Handbook for data analysis in the behavioral sciences: Methodological issues*. Hillsdale, NJ: Lawrence Erlbaum.

Dewey, J. (1933). *How we think: A restatement of the relation of reflective thinking to the education process*. Boston: Heath.

Eddy, D. M. (1996). *Clinical decision making: From theory to practice*. Sudbury, MA: Jones & Bartlett.

Ellul, J. (1965). *Propaganda: The formation of men's attitudes*. New York: Vantage.

Enkin, M. W., Keirse, M. J. N. C., Renfrew, M. J., & Neilson, J. P. (1995). *A guide to effective care in pregnancy & childbirth* (2nd ed.). New York: Oxford University Press.

Ennis, R. H. (1987). A taxonomy of critical thinking dispositions and abilities. In J. B. Baron & R. J. Sternberg (Eds.), *Teaching thinking skills: Theory and practice* (pp. 9-26). New York: W. H. Freeman.

Entwistle, V. A., Sheldon, T. A., Sowden, A., & Watt, I. S. (1998). Evidence-informed patient choice: Practical issues of involving patients in decisions about health care technologies. *International Journal of Technology Assessment in Health Care, 14,* 212-225.

Evidence-Based Medicine Website. (See also Database of Abstracts and Reviews of Effectiveness [DARE], http://nhscrd.york.ac.uk; Medline; Grateful Med).

Gambrill, E. (1990). *Critical thinking in clinical practice: Improving the accuracy of judgments and decisions about clients.* San Francisco: Jossey-Bass.

Gambrill, E. (1997). *Social work practice: A critical thinker's guide.* New York: Oxford University Press.

Gambrill, E. (1999). Evidence-based practice: an alternative to authority-based practice. *Families in Society, 80,* 341-350.

Gambrill, E., & Gibbs, L. (1999). *Making practice decisions: Is what's good for the goose good for the gander?* Unpublished manuscript, University of California at Berkeley.

Gibbs, L., & Gambrill, E. (1999). *Critical thinking for social workers: Exercises for the helping professions* (2nd ed.). Thousand Oaks, CA: Pine Forge Press.

Gilovich, T. (1991). *How we know what isn't so: The fallibility of human reasoning in everyday life.* New York: Free Press.

Goldiamond, I. (1984). Training parent trainers and ethicists in nonlinear analysis of behavior. In R. F. Dangel & R. A. Polster (Eds.), *Parent training: Foundations of research and practice* (pp. 504-546). New York: Guilford.

Gomory, T. (1998). *Coercion justified—Evaluating the training in community living model—A conceptual and empirical critique.* Dissertation, School of Social Welfare, University of California at Berkeley, Spring 1991.

Gomory, T. (1999). Programs of assertive community treatment (PACT): A critical review. *Ethical Human Sciences and Services, 1,* 147-163.

Gray, J. A. M. (1997). *Evidence-based health care: How to make health policy and management decisions.* New York: Churchill Livingstone.

Howitt, D. (1992). *Child abuse errors: When good intentions go wrong.* New York: Harvester Wheatsheaf.

Jacobson, J. W., Mulick, J. A., & Schwartz, A. A. (1995). A history of facilitated communication: Science, pseudoscience, and antiscience (Science Working Group on Facilitated Communication). *American Psychologist, 50,* 750-765.

Jarvis, W. T. (1990). *Dubious dentistry: A dental continuing education course.* Loma Linda, CA: Loma Linda University School of Dentistry.

Kirk, S. A., & Kutchins, H. (1992). *The selling of DSM: The rhetoric of science in psychiatry.* New York: Aldine de Gruyter.

Kozloff, M. A. (1994). *Improving educational outcomes for children with disabilities: Principles for assessment, program planning, and evaluation.* Baltimore: Paul H. Brookes.

Lang, S. (1998). *Challenges.* New York: Springer-Verlag.

Levy, D. (1997). *Tools of critical thinking: Metathoughts for psychology.* Boston: Allyn & Bacon.

Luiselli, J. K., Matson, J. L., & Singh, N.H. (Eds.), (1992). *Self-injurious behavior: Analysis, assessment, and treatment.* New York: Springer-Verlag.

Macdonald, G. (1998). Promoting evidence-based practice in child protection. *Clinical Child Psychology and Psychiatry, 31,* 71-85.

Meyer, L. H., & Evans, I. N. (1989). *Nonaversive intervention for behavior problems: A manual for home and community.* Baltimore, MD: Paul H. Brookes.

Munroe, E. (1996). Avoidable and unavoidable mistakes in child protection work. *British Journal of Social Work, 26,* 793-808.

National Association of Health Authorities. (1994). *Complaints do matter: A consultive paper on future NHS [National Health Service] complaints arrangements.* London: Author.

National Association of Social Workers. (1996). *NASW code of ethics.* Washington, DC: Author.

Nisbett, R., & Ross, L. (1980). *Human inference: Strategies and shortcomings of social judgment.* Englewood Cliffs, NJ: Prentice Hall.

Office of the Inspector General. (1999). *Code of ethics for child welfare professionals.* Chicago: Illinois Department of Children and Family Services.

Ofshe, R., & Watters, E. (1994). *Making monsters: False memories, psychotherapy, and sexual hysteria.* New York: Charles Scribner's.

Ortiz de Montellano, B. (1991). Multicultural pseudoscience: Spreading scientific illiteracy among minorities, Part I. *Skeptical Inquirer, 16,* 46-50.

Ortiz de Montellano, B. (1992). Magic melanin: Spreading scientific illiteracy among minorities: Part II. *Skeptical Inquirer, 16,* 162-166.

Oxman, A. D., & Guyatt, G. H. (1993). The science of reviewing research. In K. S. Warren & F. Mosteller (Eds.), *Doing more good than harm: The evaluation of health care interventions* (pp. 125-133). New York: New York Academy of Sciences.

Paul, R. (1992). *Critical thinking: What every person needs to survive in a rapidly changing world* (2nd ed.). Sonoma, CA: Foundation for Critical Thinking.

Pepper, C. (1984). *Quackery: A $10 billion scandal* (Subcommittee on health and long-term care of the Select Committee on Aging, U. S. House of Representatives, No. 98-435). Washington, DC: Government Printing Office.

Plato. *The last days of Socrates.* Translated by H. Tredennick & H. Tarrant. (1993). New York: Penguin. (Original work published 1954)

Popper, K. R. (1972). *Conjectures and refutations: The growth of scientific knowledge* (4th ed.) London: Routledge & Kegan Paul.

Popper, K. R. (1994). *The myth of the framework: In defense of science and rationality* (M. A. Notturn, Ed.). New York: Routledge.

Ruscio, J. (1998). Information integration in child welfare cases: An introduction to statistical decision making. *Child Maltreatment, 3,* 143-156.

Sackett, D. L., Richardson, W. S., Rosenberg, W., & Haynes, R. B. (1997). *Evidence-based medicine: How to practice and teach EBM.* New York: Churchill Livingstone.

Schwartz, I. S., & Baer, D. M. (1991). Social validity assessments: Is current practice state of the art? *Journal of Applied Behavior Analysis, 24,* 189-204.

Silverman, W. A. (1998). *Where's the evidence? Debates in modern medicine.* Oxford, UK: Oxford University Press.

Skeptic. P.O. Box 338. Altadena, CA 91001 (818-794-3119).

Skeptical Inquirer. P.O. Box 229, Buffalo, NY 14215-9927.

Skrabanek, P., & McCormick, J. (1990). *Follies & fallacies in medicine.* Buffalo, NY: Prometheus.

Stevens, P., Jr. (1988). The appeal of the occult: Some thoughts on history, religion, and science. *Skeptical Inquirer, 12,* 376-385.

Sulzer-Azaroff, B., & Mayer, G. R. (1991). *Behavior analysis for lasting change.* Fort Worth, TX: Holt, Rinehart and Winston.

Szasz, T. S. (1987). *Insanity: The idea and its consequences.* New York: John Wiley.

Szasz, T. S. (1994). *Cruel compassion: Psychiatric control of society's unwanted.* New York: John Wiley.

Tallent, N. (1993). *Psychological report writing* (4th ed.). Englewood Cliffs, NJ: Prentice Hall.

Valenstein, E. S. (1986). *Great and desperate cues: The rise and decline of psychosurgery and other medical treatments for mental illness.* New York: Basic Books.

Warren, K. S., & Mosteller, F. (1993). *Doing more good than harm: The evaluation of health care interventions* (Vol. 703). New York: Academy of Science.

Webster, Y. O. (1992). *The racialization of America.* New York: St. Martin's.

Webster, Y. O. (1994). *Against the multicultural agenda: A critical thinking alternative.* Westport, CT: Praeger.

Wolf, M. M. (1978). Social validity: The case for subjective measurement or how applied behavior analysis is finding its heart. *Journal of Applied Behavior Analysis, 11,* 203-214.

CHAPTER FOUR

The Concept of Levels and Systems in Social Work

JOHN E. TROPMAN

KATHERINE E. RICHARDS-SCHUSTER

W hat do social workers do? Some social workers would say they work with the juvenile justice system, the medical system, or the school system. Still other social workers would say they work with individuals, they work with and in communities, they provide help to nonprofit organizations, and they advocate on behalf of the poor in the nation. Some of us work on interventions with systems—the justice system, the foster care system, the school system—and others work at various levels of intervention—the individual, the family, the organization, the community and so forth. Our field reflects both breath and depth—all very different—yet all very much social work. Understanding the concepts of systems and levels is crucial in helping social workers systematically think about our breath and our depth and their connection to each other.

This chapter helps provide a basic overview of systems and levels and their applicability to the field of social work. It is our hope that read-

AUTHORS' NOTE: This chapter builds on Chapter 4, "Choosing a System Level for Change," in Charles Garvin and John E. Tropman, *Social Work in Contemporary Society* (2nd ed.) (Boston: Allyn & Bacon, 1998).

ers will understand the concepts and begin to apply their new knowledge to their own work in the field.

SYSTEMS AND LEVELS

A Basic Definition of Systems and Levels

Although we may intuitively understand these terms, how are systems and levels viewed in social work? Anderson and Carter (1990) quote a discussion by Hearn (1969) on the vitality and importance of what they call the systems approach in social work.

> The general systems approach is based upon the assumption that matter, in all its forms, living and nonliving, can be regarded as systems and that systems, as systems, have certain discrete properties that are capable of being studied. Individuals, small groups—including families and organizations—and other complex human organizations such as neighborhoods and communities—in short, the entities with which social work is usually involved—can all be regarded as systems, with certain common properties. If the general systems approach could be used to order knowledge about the entities with which we work, perhaps it could also be used as a means of developing a fundamental conception of the social work process itself. (p. 2)

In the previous section, we introduced the terms *system* and *level*. A *system* can be thought of as an integrated group of interrelated and reciprocal functions. For example, one system in social work is the child welfare system. This system has an integrated group—foster care parents, case workers, social service providers, and judges—who perform interrelated and reciprocal functions. A *level,* on the other hand, can be defined as the echelon, or step, on which a system organizes itself. For example, Anderson and Carter (1990) discuss culture and society, communities and organizations, groups, families, and the person as appropriate levels for social work interest and intervention. In our foster care example, levels could be the individual's case, the foster care family, the county foster care system, the state foster care system, and the societal issue of foster care.

Although each of these terms is thought of distinctively, they are interrelated and together have special utility in social work. We are all aware that identifiable systems exist at recognized levels. We intuitively understand that these *system levels* are appropriate targets of intervention. But understanding the systems allows us to target our intervention on a specific component while at the same time emphasizing the interrelatedness of social elements that may affect a particular client. Therefore, although the intervention might be at the individual level—the child in foster care—a social worker must also be cognizant of the impact of the other elements in the system—the foster care parents, the caseworkers, and the like on the child and on the intervention.

Many other scholars have discussed the idea of systems levels. In his book, Mehr (1998) discusses micro environmental change and macro environmental change, a sort of two-level approach. Gilbert, Miller, and Specht (1980) discuss direct service intervention with individuals and groups and focus on the context of social work practices and indirect services dealing with the organization and the community. Friedlander and Apte's (1980) emphasis is on family, children, youth, and aging. And, finally, Skidmore and Thackeray (1988) concentrate on work with individuals, with groups, with the community, and in administration and related practices. Perhaps the most common overall division these scholars make is the one between *micro,* which focuses on the individual and perhaps the individual-in-small-group, and *macro,* which focuses on the larger-scale environment. For example, Rothman, Erlich, and Tropman (1995) attend to the micro relationships involved in macro practice.

The concepts of systems and levels, then, are fundamental to the social work enterprise, because systems and levels represent the fundamental units of the world in which we live. Everything and everyone can be situated in a system and in a level.

A Technical Look at Defining Systems

Let us think about some more technical approaches to the definition of systems and levels. We have noted that systems are a set of interrelated elements that perform reciprocal functions. According to Rapoport (1968b), systems have the following properties:

1. Something consisting of a set . . . of entities
2. among which a set of relations is specified [for example, cell organization, human interaction, grammar, culture]
3. so that deductions are possible from some relations to others. (p. 453)

To look at the definition in our terms, the entities could be cells, people, words, or beliefs and the relations could be cell organization, human interaction, grammar, social structure, or culture. As Anderson and Carter (1990) emphasize, quoting Walter Buckley (1967, p. 41), a system is "a complex element of components directly or indirectly related in a causal network, such that each component is related to at least some others in a more or less stable way within a particular period of time" (p. 3). Miller (1978) suggests that systems can be thought about "as entities some of which process matter or energy, some of which process information, and some of which process all three" (p. 1).

Systems, then, are complex sets of interconnections and, at their own level, function as wholes. Rapoport (1968a) suggests that "a whole which functions as a whole by virtue of the independence of its parts is called a system" (p. xvii). Levels, as we shall see in a moment, are kinds of wholes that fit together to form larger and more complex entities but function as well in their own right. Within the system level concept, a system is both a means and an end. It is a means to a larger system as individuals make up families, families in turn make up communities, and so on. But individuals and families, organizations and communities, are systems in and of themselves, as well.

There are, however, two components that need to be added to the definition of systems. One of them is history. Systems—families, individuals, countries—have pasts. What happens today or tomorrow depends in part at least on what has happened previously (Rapoport, 1968a).

The other component is "what lies ahead." Systems also have, in some ways, a future. Thinking systems can anticipate what might happen and adjust current behavior to take future expectations into account. As the economist Schelling (1972) points out, one can think of the individual person as two selves—a here-and-now self and a then-and-there self. Not only is the past prologue, the present is as well.

Examples of Systems

Based on our definition, one can find many examples of systems. In social work, our primary focal interest is on the human system (the individual) and the social system (the family, the group, the organization, the community, the society). We are also interested in the interaction between living and nonliving systems. Although not in our definition above, systems can be living or nonliving. For example, some social workers study the impact of the nonliving system of communication (e.g., verbal abuse) on the well-being of children (a human system). Other social workers might study the impact of the Internet (a nonliving system) on organizing community residents to create change (a social system). Hence, within system levels, there are subsystems—integrated entities that interact with other subsystems to assist the functioning of the total system. Intervention can occur within systems levels, within subsystems, or both.

Aspects of Systems

Every system, whether it is a system or subsystem, has two major aspects: One aspect can be thought of as the softer side of systems—ideas, values, norms, beliefs, attitudes. Scholars refer to this as the cultural system. The second aspect of systems is the action and the what-happens. Scholars call this aspect the social system. For our understanding, in a human system, this is "doing" and in social systems this is "action"—for example, laws, edicts, buildings, streets, and weapons. These distinctions have important implications for social work intervention. The social system is the interrelated pattern of actions, acts, and behaviors that are

characteristic of a human entity. Anderson and Carter (1990) quote Olsen (1968) as follows:

> Very briefly, a social system is a model of social organization that possesses a distinctive total unit beyond its component parts, that is distinguished from its environment by a clearly defined boundary, and whose subunits are at least partially interrelated within relatively stable patterns of social order. Put even more simply, *a social system is a bounded set of interrelated activities that together constitute a single entity* [italics in original]. (p. 4)

The cultural system is the interrelated set of beliefs, attitudes, norms, and thoughts that constitute the distinctive set of mental activities of a system. It is important to recognize that these systems are not mutually exclusive. Although we separate them for purposes of discussion and examination, neither system exists without the other. Thoughts, values, beliefs, and so on guide actions and acts in human systems, at least to some degree. Similarly, thoughts, values, beliefs, and attitudes are influenced by the actual patterns of behavior, the patterns of opportunities, and so on, although the influence may be dragged out, slowed, or in other ways lag. One might think of a sociocultural system as the daily operating combination of behaviors and norms.

The articulation of these two systems is, however, an important task for social work intervention. Social workers need to be able to tease apart systems to determine where interventions should occur when working with both human sociocultural systems. Cultural lag, a term developed by the sociologist W. F. Ogburn, is one example of when teasing apart cultural or social systems is helpful for intervention. Cultural lag occurs, in a human system, when the pattern of ideas, thoughts, and beliefs does not

develop as quickly as the pattern of actions and opportunities. For example, a new technological device is introduced into a village or tribe within a community development context. The tribe may not have the norms and values available to handle the increased production, wealth, and leisure that may result from the introduction of such a time-saving element. Social workers working with the tribe might target their intervention to focus on building the tribe's ability to handle the new way of life.

Similarly, there can be changes in culture, beliefs, values, and attitudes that are not mirrored at once by changes in the social structure or in patterns of behavior. This is a case of structural lag. It occurs when ideas about what to do get ahead of the ways available to do it. For example, a person's idea may be ahead of the current time, while the person herself is trapped in the current structure (an idea whose time has *not* come). In these cases, the social worker might help to procure the necessary technology or social structures to "catch up" to the already changed cultural view.

System Functioning

To determine the best intervention for any given case, it is essential to understand how a system functions. A system functions much like a factory—materials come in, products get made, and final products go out (are discharged). Structurally, systems have four major subsystems— three processing systems and one orchestrating system. Technically, the processing subsystems are an input subsystem, a throughput or processing subsystem, and an output subsystem. Linking them and orchestrating their activity is a so-called executive system.

Whether the system is processing units of energy, information, or materials, the unit must enter the system at the input subsystem. It must be processed, and it must be moved out. To better understand the subsystems, one could look at the example of a residential treatment center. Intake is that input subsystem through which clients are brought into the system. The throughput subsystem, or processing system, is the set of technologies that "works on" the clients in an attempt to achieve improvement and change. This is called treatment. Discharge is the output subsystem. The executive subsystem coordinates input, throughput, and output to assure a balanced and even flow and secures resources. Although this example is at the organizational level, any system could be understood by specifying its various functions.

Building on Systems Functioning Well

Increasingly, social workers are focusing on systems functioning well; we are looking at the strengths and assets of systems and building on what is right, not just what is wrong. For example, many social workers are studying nonprofit management to strengthen nonprofit organizations' ability to compete in the 21st century. Kretzmann and McKnight (1993) advocate looking at community assets and helping people to acknowledge and map the strengths and positive aspects of their community as a tool for creating community change. For years, enhancing the positive has been stressed as a virtue of the optimist. Corporations use "best practices" and benchmarking to figure out who does what really well and then try to replicate it.

The social sciences are also getting off the "what's wrong with this picture?" mind-set.

Ruark (1999), in a state-of-the-art article for the *Chronicle of Higher Education,* points out that "psychologists lead movement to shift scholars' attention away from societal ills and toward studying what works" (p. A13).

Repairing Systems Functioning Poorly

Although building on strengths is becoming more common in our field, traditionally and historically, social work has concerned itself when systems don't work well, when they are dysfunctioning or the underfunctioning systems. Domestic violence, abuse and neglect, and school dropouts are all examples of system dysfunctioning.

When the subsystems do not work well together in synchrony and sequence, problems in system function occur. For example, if intake is too great, the system becomes overloaded and cannot function. If intake is limited, the system begins to starve. If, on the other hand, output is too quick, the system also suffers and may starve; if output is too slow, the system begins to swell. If throughput does not work well, the processing that occurs is either ineffective (does not work) or counterproductive (produces results opposite to that intended), as in the case of some prison systems. Context—where do the inputs come from, where do they go—is also an essential element of the system to understand. Executive systems, therefore, not only deal with intrasystem articulation of the subsystems among each other but also seek to articulate the external environment with respect to input and output issues.

A county hospital is an example of a system not functioning well. Because the poor usually lack insurance, many county hospitals serve as their only source of health care. Emergency rooms are flooded with cases, from trauma to the common cold. The overflow of the input coupled with the lack of medical staff to meet the need lead to poor patient care. Thus, the throughput system is slow, may not treat the patient, and leaves both the staff and the patients frustrated. Without proper care or a proper understanding of their ailment, patients are discharged, only to return again shortly for follow-up care. Furthermore, the county, as the executive subsystem, often does not have enough money or resources to orchestrate the system well.

In general, problems occur, then, in processing (intra-subsystem activities, such as intake, the treatment itself, and the discharge/exiting process), in pace/rate (the pace at which activities occur—too fast, too slow, just right), in orchestrating the appropriate sequence and timing (do you get your ketchup when the fries are still hot, or many minutes later when you do not want/need it anymore), or in the executive function itself. Paralysis in the executive subsystem may create problems not only in the operation of the system but also in the direction and articulation of systems of components. Typically, executive functions deal with the following types of system problems:

Giving problems their proper weight and context

Taking problems at the right time

Taking problems in the right sequence

Establishing and shifting decision criteria

Acting as the coxswain (beating out the pace of decision action) (Sayles & Chandler, 1971)

In a particular organization, social workers may seek not only to improve the intake process, client processing, or the discharge process but also to improve the executive and decision-making process.

Analogous helping/improving activities may occur at all levels. As Rapoport (1968a) says,

> Human social aggregates (families, institutions, communities, nations) exhibit all the features of organized systems. The degree of organization varies, of course, as does the robustness and "viability" of these systems. When a system or subsystem works poorly, it therefore makes sense to speak of the "pathology" of such systems. (p. xxi)

This notion of pathology presents a challenge to the field of social work. Because social workers work with human lives and with human cultures, there is the possibility that ethnocentrism or some other "ism" might serve to define what is normal or OK and what is dysfunctional or not OK. It is probably always the case that power holders have a bit of their own bias in the definition, but it seems also possible to work toward some level of objectivity.

The notion of pathology has been well established at the level of the person, and one can even think of the pathological family. It is perhaps a little strange to think of the pathological organization, community, or society, but there are examples. The neurotic organization is one such example. The Holocaust, for example, certainly involves pathology of the social and cultural system, as do manifestations of racism and sexism within our own society.

Other examples of pathology are communities and organizations that are hostile and negative, depriving their members or clients of dignity, liberty, and meaning. Indeed, some of the major organizations that are designed to provide assistance to individuals may be in a state of pathological crisis today. It is frequently asserted, for example, that few of these large organizational systems work well. The schools do not teach. Mental hospitals do not heal. Prisons do not reform, and so on. Indeed, some even argue that pathology extends beyond lack of goal accomplishment into a paradoxically inverse counterproductivity. When one enters school, one's IQ drops. When one enters a mental health facility, one becomes more mentally ill. When one enters a prison, one becomes more criminal. If true, these would clearly be system dysfunctions/system pathologies, and social workers can intervene in these systems to make them right. Being harmed by systems created to help can be called the "law" of paradoxical counterproductivity.

Manifest and Latent Functions

As was clear in the discussion of the paradoxical law of counterproductivity, systems do not always function the way they are supposed to, or at least do not always produce the results they are supposed to. The terms *manifest function* and *latent function* (Merton, 1958) are used to describe the difference between what systems are created to do and what they actually do. For example, "out of wedlock" births (illegitimacy) function to signal the culturally determined inappropriateness of premarital sex; illegitimacy, however, also functions to provide a supply of infants to the childless.

A manifest function is the public, up-front purpose of the system. Prisons, hospitals, and schools are supposed to help. Often, they no doubt do. But take schools as a case in point. Perhaps, a latent function of the K-12 system is to give children an extended experience in a formal organization (with all its grunts and tweaks) to better prepare them for the large formal organizations they will work in as adults. That would be a latent function. We are not saying this is true in this case. Rather, it is a caution that what one sees in systems is often not always what one gets. In social work, for example, a medical social worker might be surprised and shocked (as a new social worker might be) when a mother pulled her son out of hospital care just as he was learning to accept responsibility for his medication. It takes experience to realize that an important latent function of the son's illness was that it brought *her* lots of attention and sympathy. As he became well, she became less the center of attention. Analysts and helpers, therefore, need to be alert for both manifest and latent functions and their causes.

Emergent Properties of System Levels

A unique feature of human systems is emergent properties. These are characteristics that emerge in the system that may have not been present in the original parts. For example, communities have a structure and a character that continues, as we mentioned, despite changes in their membership. Families have strengths and pathologies that seem to exist over historical time. Hence, as we noted, history is one of the unique features that emerges at each system level. The family history is different from the organizational history; the community history is different from the individual history; and these histories shape and direct activities and acts, thoughts and attitudes.

A second feature to emerge at different system levels is variety, range, and diversity. At any moment in time, an individual may have a temperature, but an individual cannot have a standard deviation. As Gerard (1968) says,

> Thus, higher level orgs (entities, units, parts) are likely to have a greater variety than lower order ones and they are more likely to depend on their particular past. They are more individual. But they are also less plentiful since several subordinate units contribute to each. (p. 53)

Gerard mentions history and variety, and he also introduces the notion of individuality and uniqueness. For this reason, social workers learn about each system level, because of the unique properties at each of the levels.

TRANSLATING THE CONCEPT OF SYSTEMS LEVELS TO SOCIAL WORK INTERVENTIONS

Up until now, this piece has focused on understanding system levels—their properties and their functions. We have asserted that system levels need to be understood as systems levels but that the compositional and contextual elements need to be understood as well. One should not make the mistake of assuming that all understanding comes from an understanding of the parts that are compositional elements of the whole. In other words, analyses of the behavior of larger, more complex wholes cannot be explained away by reducing those wholes to their component parts and explaining the behavior of the parts. This is called *reductionism.* Societies, for example, cannot be explained in terms of the sociology of communities and organizations that compose them or of the psychology of the families and individuals who are their members, any more than an individual can be explained by looking at molecular functioning. To give some practical examples from the social work field, we would question if someone said that organizational behavior is simply explainable in terms of the psychology of the individual members of the organization, or if a family pathology can be explained solely in terms of the individual psychological states of family members. These pieces of information are certainly important and fit into an overall picture of why the organization or family acts as it does, but they do not constitute a total explanation.

A similar caution is pointed out to those who might err on the other side and explain behaviors of particular wholes not in terms of parts but rather in terms of the elements that form their context. In this case, a social worker might assert that an individual's behavior was "determined by" his or her family, that a family's pathology is "completely the result of" the community in which its members live, or that an organization's actions were "without doubt the result of" social policies in the nation at the time. This perspective deprives the individual unit of integrity. It relocates reality away from the individual into the family, away from the family into the community, away from the organization into the society or whatever other contextual element is selected.

Hence, social workers will always encounter three aspects to an assessment. First, we must assess the functioning of the system level in question, the person-as-system, the family-as-system, the group-as-system, the organization-as-system, the community-as-system, the society-as-system. Second, we must look at compositional elements. In the case of the person, for example, we would be foolish not to consider possible biological and pharmacological conditions that might affect particular be-

haviors. Third, we also need to look at contextual elements in the case of the person, again, the family, the community, and the organization. And we needs to take care in making an assessment that we attend to all three while not at the same time slipping either into compositionalism or contextualism.

As we shall see presently, these three perspectives remain very important because they provide a way to conceptualize interventions. Sometimes, even though the problem occurs at an organizational level and we recognizes that this is so, an intervention through the group level might prove to be most efficacious and sensible in the particular case at hand. Similarly, even though a problem may occur at an individual level, intervention through a contextual element might be appropriate. There is also a fourth perspective that warrants attention when intervening in social systems—the relationships that form between clients and contacts across levels.

Systems Levels and Relationships

As system levels become more complex, the intensity of relationships decreases. Generally, we can think of social work as being concerned with three modes of relationship intensity: primary, secondary, and tertiary.

Primary relationships are those that characterize our most intimate associations including the association with ourselves, our family, and our dearest friends. They tend to be characterized by commitment, and these commitments exist over substantial time and space.

Secondary relationships are communal in nature and involve memberships in territorial groups (geographic communities), religious and ethnic associations (functional communities), and communities of work (organizations), among others. Communal relationships involve commitment and identification. However, they vary from patterns of daily association, which are very close to primary associations, to those that are much more distant and resemble tertiary relationships. A great deal of our daily life is spent in communal relationships, and they serve to balance the very intimate primary associations with the most distant and formalistic tertiary ones.

Tertiary relationships involve civic roles and responsibilities. They tend to be formal and contain common rights, duties, and obligations. For example, people are assured of free speech, not because they are nice or because they have been good to their mother, but rather because they are citizens of a particular nation or state in which free speech is emphasized.

Primary relationships occur for each individual with relatively few others and involve the small group and the family. Secondary relationships are much more numerous and more limited in their emotional depth than those within the family, but they are still very powerful. Secondary relationships are among the more enduring ties and identifications that humans experience. Tertiary relationships may be quite numerous—we are members of many civic associations and groups of that sort—but they are limited in emotional commitment.

In this sense, emotional commitment and number of relationships tend to be inversely related. As one ascends system levels, more relationships occur, but they have more limited emotional involvement and span. One kind of difficulty that can occur among system levels is the placement of emotional identifications and attachments at the wrong levels. When, for example, communal relationships become a substitute for primary relationships, that not only leaves a vacuum in the life of the individual, something that social work may wish to attend to by intervention, but also overburdens the communal level, requiring it to provide the kinds of gratifications that it is not prepared to provide and to experience the kinds of demands it is not prepared to meet.

Another problem that can occur is inadequate functioning of a particular level. In some nations, for example, civic relations are so weak that communal relations tend to substitute for them. The state and other large-scale civic associations are thereby further weakened. A converse situation can also occur in which secondary associations can become so weak that an entire society moves from primary to tertiary relationships. Tertiary relationships take on a communal quality, and the individual becomes overinvolved with the state as a source of meaning and identification. In terms of intervention, the use of self during a social work intervention will be quite different in primary, secondary, and tertiary types of relationships. Problems in primary relationships are best dealt with by clinical uses of self; problems in secondary relationships, by organizational uses of self; tertiary or civic type relationships, perhaps by intellectual uses of self involving the creation of new patterns and new policies.

The whole idea of system levels, however, is that problems at any relationship level may involve or be the result of either composition or context. Problems at the communal level—in the organization, territorial community, or subculture—may in part be a result of difficulties at the primary or tertiary relationship level. Hence, when assessments are made, there are always compositional or contextual elements to consider. This approach is elaborated in the next section.

SYSTEM LEVELS AND SOCIAL INTERVENTION

We have already mentioned that, for human systems, key levels are the individual, family and group, organization, community, and society. At each level, units can be considered wholes as well as parts for the next level. Hence, families and groups are made up of individuals. Organizations are made up of individuals and groups. Communities are made up of individuals, families and groups, and organizations. Societies are made up of individuals, families and groups, organizations, and communities.

As Miller (1978) suggested, however, the fit is not quite as neat as we would like especially in the areas of family and group and organization and community (family/group and organization/community). The individual can be seen to fit as a part into other levels (as a family member, community member, employee, or citizen). Similarly, all of the levels can be seen to fit into society, but in the middle, things broaden out a bit. Families and groups are often thought of together because they are both small groups, but it might make better sense to separate them, especially when there are family groups, organizational groups, work groups, and indeed, a whole range of groups that social workers deal with, which exist in a wide variety of settings apart from the family. In addition to that distinction, there are a number of purposes for such groups. The family group obviously has one set of purposes. A therapy group

has a different set. A Boy Scout group presumably has another purpose, and so on. Hence, the family and group "level" may actually be a band with a lot of groups of various types and locations in it.

In addition, some of the groups may indeed be on the primary association level with highly committed relationships. Others, like a Boy Scout group, may fit more into a communal or quasi-communal level, if we use relationships as a measure. Similarly, when we get to the level of organization and community, separation of these two becomes as much a problem as integration did at the family and group level. As social workers are well aware, *community* is not an unambiguous concept. Indeed, many think of the community level as involving three elements—the organizational, the territorial, and the subcultural (Tropman, Erlich, & Cox, 1977; Tropman & Johnson, 1979). Regarding geographical (territorial) areas as communities is perhaps the most common, or certainly a very common conception of communities; however, as we have previously mentioned, functional (subcultural) communities of identification, such as the Catholic community, the Jewish community, the Greek community, and the black community are also relatively common and may or may not have a specific geographic location for their members. Similarly, emphasis on the organization as a community has recently become more prominent with an emphasis on organizational culture (Schein, 1992). Hence, for our purposes here, we have decided to divide communal relationships into two areas, taking the view that organizations are components of communities but recognizing that organizations have communal aspects to them.

Composition and Context:
Parts and Wholes

Another challenge facing systems is in understanding the systems' composition and context. We often refer to this as the system's parts and wholes. What is a whole system? What is a part of a system? These are important questions for intervention. What is the boundary of a level? When does one approach the next level? The human social systems that social work addresses are open to some degree, but openness blurs the boundaries. Viewing the individual as a system is apparently relatively straightforward, at least in the physical sense. We can see the individual; each has a name, an address, and so on. And yet, we have often been surprised at how differently an individual behaves and thinks in different situations.

For the micro practitioner, families, groups, communities, organizations, and societies are often thought to be contexts. *Context* refers to the elements outside and above the target system in question. Hence, if the individual is the target, then the group and family, the community, the organization, and certainly the society and the world become the context. However, if the community is the target in question, and community change the goal to be achieved, then, the society and the world become the contexts. This use of the word *context* allows us to remember that there are always "bigger" systems influencing our change target, which may at some point become targets themselves, because a change in client context is sometimes needed to assist the client. Hence, the individual-in-context may vary considerably, as contexts vary.

Similarly, although the contexts may be relatively the same, the composition of the person-

system may differ (e.g., in genetics, history). These compositional elements exist inside and below a given system level. For example, when we work with an individual, there are biological elements, which are compositional in nature. The same is true for organizations; they are composed of individuals, groups, and so on.

Therefore, as context and composition change so too must the interventions change. Thus, we confront the difficult situation in which the individual we see as a system might function quite differently depending on the context. This is the case, even though the compositional subsystems (which make up the person) of the individual person may be relatively similar across people. The converse is also possible.

Then, there is the issue of relevant contexts and compositional elements. Consider the family. Which members compose "the family system?" What if there is a blended family? Does one include the former partners as well as current partners? What are the relevant parts of the family system?

In addition, all contextual elements are not of importance. Which ones are? That depends— the illustrative grid in Table 4.1 helps in the analysis.

Similar questions can be asked of communities, organizations, and nations. Parts and wholes are in a constant process of development and change. It is for this reason that the concept of the *open system,* or boundaryless system is useful. It suggests that elements in a system are not necessarily fixed and can change. Social work practice should be alert to the constant reconfiguration of parts and wholes within system levels. However, this fact of openness does not mean that any system level is less real than any other level. The fact that the organization, for example, changes clients, workers, directors, and location does not, by that fact alone, make the organization any less real. It has a history, a tradition, and a location in space-time, and these endure over the entry and exit of different workers, clients, and the like. Similarly, the family system may change memberships but retain its identity (with positive or negative consequences) for its members. The fact, then, that a particular system level is a part of another system is an important contextual aspect of that system level, but it does not detract from either the viability or importance of that system level in its own right. Thus, the concept of means and ends is a useful one to apply to parts and wholes. Each system level becomes a part of means for larger system levels.

An Illustrative Grid

One way to think about the whole problem and the issues of levels and their compositional and contextual elements is to place them in a matrix format (Table 4.1). This allows all the levels that we are discussing to be displayed simultaneously and points the way to potential interventions. Several features of the grid will now be discussed in some detail.

First, note that we have included biological and world system levels to give a more complete picture of the total range of complex system levels that might be available. Although social workers may not intervene to a great degree at the biological level, clearly, situations exist there, everything from illnesses to chronic conditions, that require social work assistance. Some problems, such as chemical dependency, have biological manifestations, and social workers may need to link up with other professionals to deal with aspects of this issue.

It is perhaps also true that social workers do not intervene much at the world level, although, as we have mentioned before, social work has a distinguished history in this area. It is also clear that social work concerns, unlike politics, do not stop at the water's edge. Problems of world conflict and configuration are of concern not only because of their human cost, but also because of their potential for infection around the world. Some problems, like international drug trafficking, require global cooperation. Although we will not focus much here on biological and world system levels, it is still important for us to be aware that, for the most part, we focus on certain levels because of our own history rather than because of any logical requirement.

The second point that should be stressed about the grid has already been implied in the previous discussion. A level can be seen either as the source of a particular problem—one that occurs, for example, at the organizational level—or it can be seen as a target of intervention, as Meyer, Litwak, Thomas, and Vinter (1967) suggest. This perspective should be a clarifying one for social work diagnosis and intervention.

Reading down the diagonal of Table 4.1 are boxes that we call direct intervention. Here, the intervention occurs at the level where the problem exists. Hence, if a problem occurs at the individual level, individual level interventions are decided on and carried out. Similarly, if the problem occurs on a biologic level, then, a biologic intervention is conceived and carried out, and so on. But a whole set of boxes exists off the diagonal. These we call indirect interventions; they are of two sorts, already noted in the previous discussion. To the right of the boldface boxes are systems that form the context of the problem system. Hence, if there is a problem at

TABLE 4.1 Target for Intervention

Issue		Biological Level	Individual Level	Family-Group Level	Organizational Level	Community Level	Society Level
Developmental disability	Biological level	**Medical devices to alleviate complications of the disability**	Case management to help individual carry out day-to-day tasks	Therapy to help family cope with the needs of the developmentally disabled child	Creation of or collaboration with organizations that provide services to people with disabilities	Programs and activities in community for individuals with developmental disabilities	Advocacy for national policies around issues of concern to those with developmental disabilities
Eating disorder	Individual level	Vitamins and supplements to compensate for lack of nutrients in normal diet	**Counseling to help individual with eating disorder**	Family counseling to help friends and family cope with the individual's disordered eating	Work with organizations, such as schools, to provide workshops on body image and eating issues	Community programs designed to raise awareness around eating disorders	Advocacy for policies to change the portrayal of body images in the media
Abusive family	Family-group level	Sedatives to reduce anger spells	Individual counseling on anger management	**Family counseling on issues such as anger, communication, and relationship building**	Development of organizations that focus on family support issues	Creation of community-wide hotlines to help provide support during stressful situations	Advocacy for policies aimed at reducing family stress and providing support to families
Worker burnout	Organizational level	Antidepressant medications to reduce depression related to burnout	Individual counseling around burnout and depression, employment counseling about finding a new job	Group counseling for employees about reducing burnout and/or finding new job skills	**Programs that provide new incentives for employees; work with organization to redesign atmosphere and create work-friendly policies**	Work with community to provide support programs for workers, create new job skill classes in community	Advocacy for policies that will allow workplaces to adopt family-friendly and worker-friendly policies (i.e., job sharing, day care, incentive programs)

| High levels of community unemployment | Community level | Physical therapy to help workers on disability to go back to work | Mentoring to help individuals determine career options and education needs | Case management for families to help them plan for future employment | Organizations that target individuals who are unemployed and help to move them back into workforce; organizations that provide ancillary supports to enable individuals to work | **Organization of a community-wide planning session on strategies to lure new business to the community** | Advocacy at national level for better vocational training and job training policies (e.g., JTPA, TANF work programs) |
| Juvenile smoking | Society level | Drugs to help alleviate cravings for nicotine | Provision to individuals of information about dangers of smoking; work with youth around issues of smoking and image | Work with families to address issues of juvenile smoking in the home, provision of information to families about signs of youth smoking | Work with local organizations to provide programs around youth smoking; programs by organizations to educate about dangers of smoking | Organization of a community-wide rally against tobacco use by minors | **Advocacy for laws that prevent minors from purchasing and consuming tobacco; creation of awareness campaigns on the dangers of tobacco** |

SOURCE: Based on J. E. Tropman (1976), "The Loci of Social Change." In J. E. Tropman et al. (Eds.), *Strategic Perspectives on Social Policy*. Elmsford, NY: Pergamon.

NOTE: Boldface items (where system cause and system target intersect) are *direct* interventions; those to the right of the boldface items are *contextual* interventions, those to the left are *compositional* interventions.

the family/group level, we might wish to deal with it at the organization, community, or societal level. Contextual interventions are also available. On the left of the boldface boxes are those systems that compose the system in question. Compositional intervention is an indirect intervention that involves changing the composing elements of a system as a way of dealing with a particular problem at a system level. Hence, if a problem occurs at an organizational level, we might wish to change work groups or even individuals within the organization rather than attack the problem directly.

Table 4.1 is one tool to help determine an appropriate intervention. In summary, we have suggested that there are four key elements to review before engaging in any social work intervention: the system and its functioning, the composition of the system, the system's context, and the relationships that exist in the system. Once these elements are understood, the social worker must choose the type of intervention to pursue—a direct intervention or an indirect intervention.

Direct Intervention

The most typical and well-understood kind of social work intervention is direct. We seek to intervene at the level where the problem exists. For the individual, this is traditionally thought of as casework or interpersonal practice, and a variety of modes, such as counseling, behavioral modification, and so on are used to help individuals deal with problems that are confronting them.

Group work technology seems most appropriate for problems that emerge at the group level. Family interventions involving all members of an affected family are another example. Gathering together various kinds of voluntary groups, such as adult children of alcoholics, parents of murdered children, and so on, are further examples.

At the level of the organization, improving administrative technology—personnel, budgeting, policy management—offers ways to approach organization-level problems. At the level of the community, difficulties have been most often approached with the use of community organization technology. More specifically, social planning, community or locality development, and social action have been useful strategies.

At the level of society, policy technologies have been the method of choice, including the proposing of laws and ordinances at all levels of government, the changing of executive regulations, and the use of judicial interventions. Each of these represents a different approach to policy change. In addition to proposing policy, the implementation, review, and refurbishment of policy have been appropriate methods.

Indirect Intervention: Contextual Strategies

Sometimes, it is not possible to intervene at the level at which a problem occurs, either because intervention is impossible, unwise, politically prohibited, or for other reasons. In that case, contextual interventions are an alternative. Thus, for a particular medical problem, one might seek to modify individual health attitudes and behaviors as opposed to giving someone a particular drug. Changes in medical care organization and medical care policy might also be useful.

Similarly, at the individual level, in lieu of (or in support of) counseling with an individual person, family treatment might be used. Intervention in the workplace, self-help groups, or policy shifts might be possible. A number of other examples are suggested by Table 4.1. We should add that it is not necessarily the case that contextual strategy be used in lieu of direct strategy. It may be used to supplement or to work on other aspects of the problem or to complete a treatment plan. For example, individual counseling with a particular person may be important, but without family treatment, the same problems may repeat themselves.

Indirect Intervention: Compositional Strategies

Compositional strategies are another possible indirect intervention and may be used for the same reasons as a contextual intervention. In this case, the systems that compose the particular level—or some of the systems—might be themselves targets of change. Consider the case of an individual suffering from substance abuse. Apart from casework technology and individual counseling, drugs might be needed to address the biological system, both to stabilize and to enhance the results of individual casework.

The Mix of Strategies

The system-levels approach offers the social worker a mix of strategies. One may choose a direct strategy, either of the indirect strategies (contextual and compositional), or all three simultaneously. It is important for social workers to keep this grid in mind. Two other observations are important. First, the social work profession takes the view that all direct strategies are valid. The problems of reduction or overcontextualization should be avoided. Individual problems cannot be argued away in terms of system responsibility or cause, nor can problems at the system level be reduced to and explained by the particular components. A full program of social welfare and social services addresses both context and composition, as well as the direct cause/target system involved.

But what are the bases on which we might choose a strategy for intervention? If all are valid, then what ideas might be available to help in the selection? Although we cannot prescribe completely, some bases are worth consideration.

1. *Agency mission.* Sometimes, a strategy is chosen because it is what the agency does.
2. *Worker skill.* Another reason for picking a particular approach is because it is what the worker does well. A particular social worker, for example, might be expert with family work. Hence, if you come to that worker (or agency, as in the previous example) you receive family work. The problem, of course, is that you should not get family work whether you need it or not, but only if it is appropriate for you.
3. *Client/customer preference.* The client/customer may have something to say about what kind of approach he or she wishes to take. This makes sense, of course, up to a point. Professional practice promotes "starting where the client is" but does not require that we stay there if the client is not making progress, or if the choice is a defense mechanism to avoid other painful elements in the presenting problem.
4. *Pragmatism.* What is easy and available might be the ticket; again, one might use the strategy of "small wins" that Weick (1993) discusses. A particular intervention may not deal with all

the problems, but it is a chance to make a successful start.

THE ORCHESTRATION OF SYSTEM-LEVEL INTERVENTION

It should be clear from the foregoing discussion that social work takes place on different system levels and around a particular client system. Hence, an individual may have a problem that requires work with that individual, particularly on precipitating causes and short-term solutions, but may also require community-oriented or policy-oriented work around longer-term solutions and predisposing causes. That different system levels are involved becomes at times a problem for some social workers. Not only does their time not always permit multilevel work, but there are differences in the characters of system levels that may make the competence required for one system level different from that required for another.

Hence, it is often appropriate to have different workers involved with respect to the same cases. This enhances the need for case management skills that, in effect, allow for intersystem as well as intrasystem coordination around a particular case. The issue of time is often an administrative one related to the needs and foci of particular agencies. Therefore, we will now examine the issue of differential character both between and within systems.

Familiarization With All Levels

The first point to be made, of course, is that workers must familiarize themselves with the overall structure and functioning of all system levels. This perspective strengthens the intellec-

tual rationale for generic training, at least in the beginning phase of social work practice. All workers should know something about the basic structures of the individual personality system, the biological system, groups, organizations, communities, and societies. Precipitating and predisposing elements of client system problems do not locate themselves neatly within the totality of one or another system level. Social workers should take it on themselves to maintain some ongoing responsibility for breadth as well as depth of knowledge.

Current and historical propensities on the part of the social work profession to divide into level-related methods such as case work, group work, community organization, and policy does make a certain sense. What does not make sense, however, is that individuals become so specialized in one level or another that they have no knowledge of adjacent system levels. Lipsky (1980) offers a useful discussion of the disconnection between social policy makers and the realities of frontline staff. Furthermore, it can be positively problematic when hostility among workers within different system levels erupts. Such hostility is most likely to occur in cases of reductionism or contextualism.

Juxtaposed Characteristics

A second important point lies in the observation that system levels appear to contain contradictory tendencies within themselves. Workers who have had experience with individual counseling know how much individuals vary. Great difference exist along dimensions of trust versus suspicion, open and revealing versus closed and unsharing, privately versus publicly oriented, ambitious versus lethargic, and so on.

Not only do individuals vary among each other, but individuals vary within themselves. Hence, univariate or stereotypic characterizations of individuals or categories of individuals invariably select and articulate some subset like color or gender while remaining silent on other aspects of the individual. The same point, of course, can be made for families, groups, organizations, communities (e.g., see Fellin, 1995), and societies. Each of these levels contains contradictory tendencies among and within its members.

Societies can be both open and welcoming to immigrants, as American society has generally been, or restrictive and hostile, as the experience of Japanese internment camps and Indian reservations also indicates (see Tropman, 1989, for further discussion on values). Social workers must be aware of the contradictory nature of systems and be prepared to bring such an understanding to their work. Reducing diagnoses to simplistic univariate statements does a disservice to the complexity, variety, and texture of system levels.

SUMMARY

From a social work perspective, the system-level concept is extremely important. First, it articulates "the client system" at a particular level. In making that articulation, it also locates the particular client system in its own structure and identifies contextual and compositional elements that may bear importantly on the potential problems and solutions of the particular client system. The concept of system levels not only lays out a course of study for social workers throughout our life course but also provides

a handy scheme for diagnosis and intervention—a set of checkpoints that we can go over as we are thinking about particular client systems and their contexts and conditions.

As we articulated, it is essential for social workers to have the skills and abilities to work within and across systems and levels. For example, school social workers should understand students' systems, but they should also understand the organizational system of the school; community workers should understand the community as a system but also the systems of the individuals and organizations that inhabit the community, and so forth. Furthermore, we have highlighted the importance of understanding the functioning of systems and the context and composition of systems to make appropriate interventions.

The breath and depth of knowledge needed by social workers today and in the future behooves us to critically examine our field, as questions remain. One deals with definition. How do we define and divide systems, and are we careful to do so in culturally sensitive ways? For example, can we make a determination of what defines a community in ways that are rich and inclusive?

A second involves analysis. Once we have defined systems, can we understand them? Do we have the skills and tools to determine system context and system functioning? Can we be sensitive to both manifest and latent aspects?

Third, there is a question of intersection. Systems equilibrate. When we intervene, we upset that balance. Sometimes, the intervention worsens the situation. For example, when should children be removed from their birth parents? Some situations are clear. But often, the question is open—and it is less clear. Would removing the children put them in more detrimental situations? Would using a systems analysis allow social workers to determine if the replacement systems are functioning better?

Answers to these questions and to many others lie in future analysis and social work research.

REFERENCES

Anderson, R. E., & Carter, I. (1990). *Human behavior in the social environment: A social systems approach* (4th ed.). Chicago: Aldine.

Buckley, W. (1967). *Sociology in modern systems theory.* Englewood Cliffs, NJ: Prentice Hall.

Fellin, P. A. (1995). *The community and the social worker* (2nd ed.). Itasca, IL: F. E. Peacock.

Friedlander, W. A., & Apte, R. Z. (1980). *Introduction to social welfare* (5th ed.). Englewood Cliffs, NJ: Prentice Hall.

Gerard, R. W. (1968). Units and concepts of biology. In W. Buckley (Ed). *Modern systems research for the behavioral scientist* (pp. 51-58). Chicago: Aldine.

Gilbert, N., Miller, H., & Specht, H. (1980). *An introduction to social work practice.* Englewood Cliffs, NJ: Prentice Hall.

Hearn, G. (Ed.). (1969). *The general systems approach: Contributions toward an holistic conception of social work.* New York: Council on Social Work Education.

Kretzmann, J., & McKnight, J. (1993). *Building communities from the inside out: A path toward finding and mobilizing a community's assets.* Evanston, IL: Northwestern University, Center for Urban Affairs and Policy Research.

Lipsky, M. (1980). *Street-level bureaucracy: Dilemmas of the individual in public services.* New York: Russell Sage Foundation.

Mehr, J. (1998). *Human services: Concepts and intervention strategies* (7th ed.). Boston: Allyn & Bacon.

Merton, R. (1958). *Social structure and process* (Rev. ed.). Glencoe, IL: Free Press.

Meyer, H. J., Litwak, E., Thomas, E., & Vinter, R. (1967). Social work and social welfare. In P. F. Lazarsfeld, W. H. Sewell, & H. L. Wilensky (Eds.), *The uses of sociology* (pp. 156-190). New York: Basic Books.

Miller, J. G. (1978). *Living systems.* New York: McGraw-Hill.

Olsen, M. (1968). *The process of social organization.* New York: Holt, Rinehart & Winston.

Rapoport, A. (1968a). Foreword. In W. Buckley (Ed.), *Modern systems research for the behavioral scientist* (pp. xi-xxii). Chicago: Aldine.

Rapoport, A. (1968b). General systems theory. In D. L. Sills (Ed.), *International encyclopedia of the social sciences* (pp. 452-485). New York: Macmillan.

Rothman, J., Erlich, J., & Tropman, J. (1995). *Strategies of community organization* (5th ed.). Itasca, IL: F. E. Peacock.

Ruark, J. (1999, February). Redefining the good life. *Chronicle of Higher Education,* p. A13.

Sayles L. R., & Chandler, M. K. (1971). *Managing large systems: Organizations for the future.* New York: Harper & Row.

Schein, E. (1992). *Organizational culture and leadership* (2nd ed.). San Francisco: Jossey-Bass.

Schelling, T. (1972). Egonomics, or the art of self-management. *Journal of the American Economic Association,* 68(2), 290-294.

Skidmore, R. A., & Thackeray, M. G. (1988). *Introduction to social work* (4th ed.). Englewood Cliffs, NJ: Prentice Hall.

Tropman, J. E. (1989). *American values and social welfare.* Englewood Cliffs, NJ: Prentice Hall.

Tropman, J. E., Erlich, J. L., & Cox, F. M. (1977). Introduction. In F. M. Cox, J. L. Erlich, J. Rothman, & J. E. Tropman (Eds.), *Tactics and techniques of community practice* (pp. 1-15). Itasca, IL: F. E. Peacock.

Tropman, J. E., & Johnson, H. (1979). Settings of community practice. In F. M. Cox, J. L. Erlich, J. Rothman, & J. E. Tropman (Eds.), *Strategies of community organization* (3rd ed., pp. 213-223). Itasca, IL: F. E. Peacock.

Weick, K. (1993, Winter). Small wins in organizational life. *Dividend,* pp. 21-23.

PART II

Frameworks for Practice

We have identified several frameworks related to the profession's quest for social justice that should govern how practitioners use specific theories and approaches. One such framework is that of prevention. A professional focus that is limited to such concepts as "therapy" or even "rehabilitation," although we accept the importance of these types of interventions, is not likely to confront the harm that large social systems can impose on the recipients of social work services. These more individually directed approaches, when used inappropriately, represent what has been called "blaming the victim." The placement of prevention as a major framework for practice, along with resto-ration, rehabilitation, and enhancement of the quality of life, emphasizes bringing about changes in conditions and environments that place people at risk of developing unhealthy or illegal ways of surviving. There are ways, also, of helping people to cope with environmental stresses so that they can function on their own behalf to ameliorate the effects of noxious systems.

In Chapter 5, Fraser, Randolph, and Bennett portray how practice knowledge regarding prevention has evolved in social work. They then strengthen our understanding of prevention by linking it to two important concepts: risk and resilience. As they state, risk factors increase the probability of future negative events. Resilience draws from studies of how individuals cope with adversity. By drawing on these types of understanding, these authors lead us into an analysis of promising prevention approaches and research that is related to these.

Another framework is that of empowerment. We believe that all social work practice should result in ways that empower people to effectively seek changes in the systems that oppress them. Unfortunately, the term empowerment has at times become another catchword that is used by social workers to describe all their actions. Thus, it has at times become synonymous with increasing self-care or personal responsibility. To be meaningful in describing emerging forms of practice, the term empowerment must be defined in a political sense as enhancing the skills, motivation, and knowledge that vulnerable people have relevant to changing oppressive systems; these skills are also used when people join with each other in groups to strengthen the effectiveness of the actions they take.

In Chapter 6, Cox and Parsons begin with a theoretical base for empowerment practice. In addition to raising philosophical issues, they discuss such social science theories as systems theory, conflict theory, and theories related to the idea of powerlessness. They relate these ideas to empowerment practice in a variety of contexts, such as group work, and to approaches, such as competency-based practice. Empowerment practice principles are identified, and practice models are presented in

detail. The importance of evaluating empowerment practice is stressed, and ways of doing this are described.

We also believe that it is unconscionable for practitioners to develop approaches that primarily or even exclusively meet the needs of the more privileged groups in society while adding to the oppression of other groups. An understanding of diversity in its cultural, historical, and structural richness—integrated with an awareness of the strengths that people bring to their tasks of living—must be acquired by all practitioners who desire to be relevant and effective.

In Chapter 7, Spencer, Lewis, and Gutiérrez appropriately link their ideas of multiculturalism to those of empowerment. Not only do they elaborate on their own ways of thinking about multicultural practice, but they provide a sound and much needed critique of the multiculturalism literature. This creates a new and interdisciplinary definition that is linked to issues such as social class and to other forms of oppression such as that experienced on the basis of sexual orientation.

Perhaps a more controversial assertion is that feminist thinking must pervade the practice of social work. At least one reason for this controversy is that there is not one "feminism" but many feminist writers, who often take issue with one another. Nevertheless, we are mindful that many of the pioneers of social work were women, who built on a legacy of caring for others a knowledge base, a set of values, a broad range of skills, and a political understanding that was undoubtedly related to their experiences of gender-based oppression. The word *feminist* may not have been used by Jane Addams or Grace Coyle or Mary Richmond or Edith Abbott, to name only a few of such early leaders, but modern feminists may still learn from them or certainly owe them an intellectual debt. Our inclusion of feminism goes deeper than this, however. It stems from our understanding that one of the most consistent forms of oppression in all societies and throughout history is that suffered by women. Thus, we declare that an understanding of this dynamic must be used in our judgment of the appropriateness of theories, interventions, and concepts. In addition, feminist ideas can teach many things that will benefit both men and women about the use and abuses of power, the linkages between gender oppression and other forms of social exploitation, and the means of becoming empowered.

Bricker-Jenkins's Chapter 8 on feminist practice differs from many other chapters in this book in its use of personal narrative as well as conceptual discussion. But this is highly consistent with what we expect from a leading feminist thinker. Bricker-Jenkins has played a major role in promoting a feminist perspective in social work, and a history of her experience illuminates better than any abstract exposition what fighting for human equality and against oppression is all about. On this base, Brinker-Jenkins erects an exciting structure of feminist practice principles and approaches.

CHAPTER FIVE

Prevention: A Risk and Resilience Perspective

MARK W. FRASER

KAREN A. RANDOLPH

M. DANIEL BENNETT

Prevention will require both selected specific programs directed
especially at known causes and general strengthening of our fundamental
community, social welfare, and educational programs.

—*John F. Kennedy, 1963*

In 1964, Gerald Caplan wrote an influential book called *Principles of Preventive Psychiatry*. Defying canons on the institutional treatment of mental disorders and building on President Kennedy's enthusiasm for the country's nascent community mental health programs, Caplan argued that mental disorders could be prevented. Many experts regard this book as marking the beginning of a new era in social welfare, an era in which prevention found a toehold in public policy.

To be sure, prevention was not a new idea. Throughout history and across the development of many disciplines in the social and health sciences, it emerges time and again. Elements of prevention can be found, for example, in the teachings of Greek gods. The mythical god of medicine, Asklepius, and her daughter, Hygeia, advocated early intervention and admonished city-state citizens to pursue healthy lifestyles (Buckner & Cain, 1998). Prevention has long been acknowledged in social work. In *Social Diagnosis,* Mary Richmond (1917) argued that "the promotion of preventive measures . . . made varied treatment possible" (p. 32). But, arguably, it was Caplan who made prevention seem feasible. Prior to his descriptions of primary, secondary, and tertiary interventions, prevention was widely regarded as impractical and potentially harmful. Prevention programs that focused on broad community problems and made services universally available were thought too costly. Conversely, prevention programs that focused on target populations were thought to err too often, labeling and stigmatizing healthy people as at risk.

Today, prevention looms large on the landscape of social intervention. In the years since Caplan's landmark text, the gap between discourse on the need for prevention and actual practice with a prevention focus has closed significantly. With support from the National Institute of Mental Health (NIMH) and the Institute for Medicine, researchers and practitioners have articulated a new field of prevention science. Residing at the intersection of social work, psychology, public health, education, psychiatry, nursing, sociology, criminology, and other disciplines, prevention science combines knowledge of the epidemiology and etiology of social and health problems with knowledge of the effectiveness of interventions.

The purpose of this chapter is to describe this emerging field and to discuss the concept of resilience in the context of prevention science.

First, we will define prevention science and describe principles that underpin the development of practice knowledge in the field of prevention. Second, we will define resilience and describe its relation to prevention science. Finally, we will discuss progress in the field of prevention, including a framework for classifying prevention interventions and examples of prevention programs that appear to be successful. At the end of the chapter, we will attempt to distill implications for social work practice from the increasingly rich research on prevention and resilience.

Prevention Science: Building Knowledge for Practice

To prevent something, one must stop it from occurring. In the words of Coie et al. (1993), the purpose of prevention science "is to prevent or moderate major human dysfunctions" (p. 1013). This implies that to prevent a mental disorder, efforts must be undertaken before the occurrence of major dysfunction, and if efforts are to be effective, they must eliminate or reduce those factors that cause the disorder. In this sense, prevention science seeks to identify the precursors of social and health problems and, then, to construct interventions that block or moderate these precursors—some of which may be causes.

From a prevention science perspective, the development of practice knowledge involves five phases or related activities. Shown in Figure 5.1, the first step entails developing an understanding of the epidemiology of a problem through systematic study. This includes being able to answer such questions as: Who has the problem? What are the demographic character-

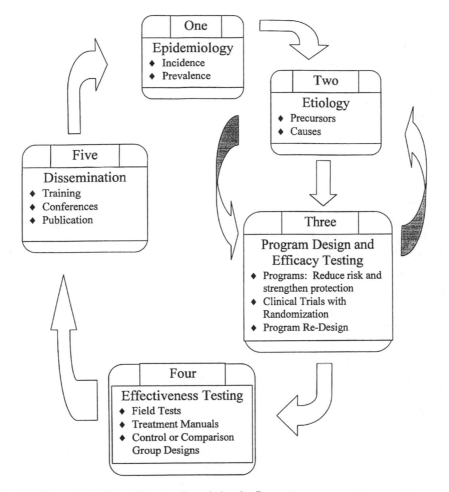

Figure 5.1. Five Phases in Building Practice Knowledge for Prevention

istics of people with the problem? Where do they live? How often does the problem occur? In the second phase, one seeks to identify the precursors of problems. Ideally, this requires developing an understanding of the causes of problems. But in practice, causes are rarely known. So we must rely on knowledge of the correlates and markers of problems, on factors that covary with problems and that may in the long run prove to be causes.

In the language of program design, this set of hypothesized causes is a conceptual framework. It consists of those risk and protective factors on which services may be targeted. The development of a conceptual framework must be informed by a deep understanding of the way environmental conditions contextualize risk and protective conditions (Trickett, 1996, 1997). Data from national surveys and studies are informed and enriched by an assessment of neighborhood, cultural, language, religious, and other factors that give a unique face to the development of problems across communities (Fraser & Galinsky, 1997). If services are to be successful, they should be tailored—or have the potential to be tailored—to local conditions.

Phase Three is characterized by a dynamic interplay between the conceptualization of causes and the design of prevention programs. In this phase, prevention programs are evaluated using research designs involving randomly assigned control groups, implementation of carefully monitored experimental services, and rigorous outcome assessment. Often, activities in this phase take place in a university setting, where researchers are deeply involved in an iterative refinement of the intervention, a highly supervised implementation of prevention services, and a multimeasures approach to observing outcomes. From this clinical trials approach, both refined prevention services and deeper understandings of the etiology of problems often emerge. Through a circular process involving experimental intervention, measurement of outcomes, and refinement of conceptual frameworks, the results of what is called efficacy testing provide feedback that informs a reconceptualization of problems and a revision of the program design. This often results in a new round of clinical trials. Some programs such as parenting training are based on decades of development, design, and efficacy testing.

Phase Four involves application. After a program has been positively evaluated in a con-trolled setting, the next phase of development—effectiveness testing—requires testing in the real world of practice in agencies, where workers are subject to conflicting public policies, high caseloads, media pressure, and so on. Using control and comparison group research designs, effectiveness testing seeks to answer the question: Can a prevention program that has produced positive outcomes in efficacy testing produce meaningful outcomes in the field? In providing agency-based services, staff are often trained by researchers and services are guided by the use of treatment manuals. However, the basic idea is to test the new service under routine agency conditions (for more information on efficacy and effectiveness studies, see Hoagwood, Hibbs, Brent, & Jensen, 1995). Large field experiments often uncover serious problems in bringing a promising program to scale and in faithfully implementing multicomponent interventions (see, e.g., Henggeler, Schoenwald, Borduin, Rowland, & Cunningham, 1998; Schuerman, Rzepnicki, & Littell, 1994). At this phase, one seeks to identify and resolve these implementation issues.

Finally, in Phase Five, a prevention program that has been found effective in field tests is disseminated. The difficulty in disseminating knowledge about promising programs is vastly underestimated. Dissemination involves publication in journals or books and training at professional conferences. Sometimes, too, public policies are altered to permit reimbursements for new and promising programs. If widely used, a new prevention program should affect the epidemiology of the problem. Few programs eradicate problems, but—as in the case of tobacco cessation programs—they can change public policies and attitudes, which may affect the distribution of the problem and initiate a new round of program development and design (Sussman, Dent, Burton, Stacy, & Flay, 1995).

Risk and Protective Factors

Experience in trying to identify the precursors of problems and in conducting prevention interventions has produced a set of new concepts and terms that many social workers are beginning to use (Fraser, 1997a). Suggested above, these terms include: risk factor, protective factor, and resilience. A *risk factor* increases the probability of a negative future event, such as the onset of an illness or digression to a more serious state of illness. A *protective factor* decreases this probability. Not the polar opposite of a risk factor, protective factors must be conceptually different from risk factors (for a discussion of this, see Jessor, Van Den Bos, Vanderryn, Costa, & Turbin, 1997). Although they are sometimes conceived as directly suppressing a problem (i.e., main effects), they are more frequently defined as interacting with and moderating the effect of risk factors (i.e., interaction effects) (Rutter, 1987). Protective factors act as buffers, ameliorating or building resistance to risk.

Risk and protective factors may be individual traits or characteristics of the environment, such as family or neighborhood conditions. For example, exposures to family dysfunction, marital violence, and child maltreatment are risk factors for delinquency. In contrast, high academic achievement is a protective factor for delinquency (Williams, Ayers, & Arthur, 1997). Research strongly suggests that delinquency is associated with risk and protective factors at the individual, family, or neighborhood level (Loeber, Farrington, Stouthamer-Loeber, & Van Kammen, 1998).

Latent in many risk factors are interactional processes that produce a higher probability for negative outcomes. These are sometimes called *risk chains*. Gerald Patterson and his colleagues at the Oregon Social Learning Center have described a family risk chain in which parents and children engage in mutually coercive relationships that inadvertently reward children for aggressive behavior and increase vulnerability for youth violence (Fraser, 1996; Patterson, 1995). Such risk chains are sequences of contingent events that elevate the odds for a social or health problem. Many trait- and event-related risk and protective factors probably represent complex chains involving individual and environmental factors.[1]

Common and problem-specific factors. We are still learning about risk and protective factors. Clearly, problems arise from the complicated interplay of multiple risk and protective factors, and the same factors may be associated with several problems (Jessor, 1993, 1998). In applying the principles of prevention science to children, Kirby and Fraser (1997) described both common and problem-specific risk and protective factors. Common factors elevate risks for a variety of childhood problems. They affect or play a causal role in more than one problem. Low academic achievement, hyperactivity, and poor parental supervision are common or shared risk factors that influence delinquency, substance abuse, depression, and other problems (Loeber et al., 1998). In contrast, specific risk factors affect one problem markedly more than other problems. Failure to use contraception may not affect delinquency but, among sexually active adolescents, it has a dramatic effect on the risk of contracting a sexually transmitted disease. It is a specific risk factor for sexually transmitted diseases, including HIV.

Differential effects of factors. The effect of risk and protective factors on the probability of experiencing a negative future event appears to vary, and in some cases, it may be multiplicative (Rutter, 1993). Some factors exert small effects, whereas others exert large effects. Moreover, the number of risk factors is not an additive predictor of their cumulative effect. For example, the effect of four risk factors—depending on the nature of the risk factors—might not be twice that of two risk factors. Rather, the effect could be more—possibly exponentially more (Rutter, 1997). The degree to which factors influence problems has led some scholars to identify "keystone" risk and protective factors. Keystone factors are thought to exert relatively more influence than other factors. The identification of keystone factors that can be changed through prevention intervention is a central aspect of developing a conceptual framework for program design.

Caution. In spite of the salience of a strengths perspective that emphasizes protective factors, it is not clear how much protective factors dampen risk. In a study of more than 78,000 children, Pollard, Hawkins, and Arthur (1999) recently found that risk, as compared to protective factors explained more than twice as much variability in substance abuse, delinquency, and other social problems. This suggests that a pure strengths orientation may be less efficacious than a perspective that focuses both on risk reduction and protection promotion.

Defining Resilience

Perhaps the most fascinating concept in prevention science is resilience. An age-old idea, resilience is used to describe individuals who prevail over adversity (Garmezy, 1974, 1991). It is evident in stories of Horatio Alger, Michael Jordan, Helen Keller, Abraham Lincoln, and others who have surmounted disadvantage. Children who grow up to be successful entrepreneurs, scholars, or leaders in spite of having a serious disabling condition or coming from a socially disadvantaged neighborhood or family are often described as resilient (Masten, Best, & Garmezy, 1990). People who are resilient do not merely adapt to their environments; rather, they are recognized as being highly successful. More than adaptation, unexpected success characterizes resilience (Rutter, 1997).

By definition, resilience requires exposure to risk; and although it connotes extraordinary strength or resources, it does not imply immunity to stress or suffering (Luthar, Doernberger, & Zigler, 1993). People who are resilient are not invulnerable, and they are not usually comprehensively successful. They experience pain, and some research suggests that their success varies across developmental domains. An adult who was abused as a child may experience painful flashbacks or have difficulty sustaining close friendships, but in spite of this, he or she may be quite successful at work (Luthar, 1993). Similarly, a child who prevails over adversity may be resilient in early adolescence but, when confronted with the challenges of *late* adolescence, may lack essential skills for success.

The factors that produce resilience are not clear. Scholars now think that protective factors may buffer individuals from risk, providing resistance to risk or directly suppressing problematic behavior. These protective factors include (but are not limited to) language competence, high intelligence, an easygoing temperament, high self-efficacy, high expectations for achievement, coping skill, racial or ethnic identity, high involvement in productive activities, closeness to one parent, attachment to someone outside the family, and access to high quality schools (Arroyo & Zigler, 1995; Bowman & Howard, 1985; Doll & Lyon, 1998; Miller & MacIntosh, in press). The processes that produce resilience are scarcely researched. It may be, for example, that having at least one loving adult as a child reduces rejection-sensitivity or builds self-regulatory skills that permit children to ignore disadvantage or partition the effects of stress so as to allow concentration on studies, sports, or other activities (Freitas & Downey, 1998). If we can begin to understand the processes that allow some individuals to prevail over adversity, we may find a rich source of knowledge for strengthening prevention interventions.

Resilience and Prevention

Resilience research and prevention share a common goal. Each is focused on understanding the factors that produce behavior. Resilience is focused on the precursors of adaptive behavior—the mix of risk and protective factors that reduces vulnerability and promotes successful adaptation. Because by their very nature prevention programs focus efforts on problems before they become fully developed, prevention requires an understanding of the precursors of behavior (Cowan, Cowan, & Schulz, 1996). Knowledge of risk and protective factors that are related to vulnerability holds the potential to inform the development of prevention programming. Of course, not all

risk and protective factors can be changed. But some are targetable in social and health programs. Coie et al. (1993) argued that it is the purpose of prevention to "counteract risk factors and reinforce protective factors in order to disrupt processes that contribute to human dysfunction" (p. 1013). Thus, the concepts of risk and protection lie at the heart of prevention science.

PREVENTION: A RISK AND RESILIENCE PERSPECTIVE

What Is the Status of Prevention Science?

Recent studies support a prevention science perspective. In a meta-analytic review of 177 rigorously evaluated primary prevention programs for children and adolescents, Durlak and Wells (1997) found mean intervention effects ranging from .24 to .93. On measures of behavioral and social problems, the performance of an average participant in a prevention program surpassed the performance of 59% to 82% of the children in control groups. Findings such as these contribute to the growing optimism about prevention science.

Contextual dependence and reciprocal causation. Successful prevention programs appear to share three common assumptions (see, e.g., Bloom, 1996; Caplan, 1964; Coie et al., 1993; Durlak, 1997; Leavell & Clark, 1953; Mrazek & Haggerty, 1994). First, problem conditions are conceptualized as the result of a dynamic, sometimes reciprocating process of influence between personal attributes and environmental events or circumstances. That is, social and health problems are seen to arise from the interaction between individuals and their environments over time. Problems are thought to be contextually dependent, and this dependence on person-environment interaction makes it difficult to sort out the causal order. Some relationships may, in fact, be reciprocal. In a survey of 1,655 adolescents, Agnew (1991) found a reciprocal relationship between delinquent behaviors and association with delinquent peers. The more a youth engaged in delinquent acts, the more he or she was likely to have delinquent peers, and vice versa. Conceptualizing prevention interventions is complicated by these twin notions of reciprocal causation and contextual dependence.

Time dependence. Second, the interactive, context-dependent processes that produce problems are thought to evolve or change over time. That is, the importance or strength of risk factors waxes and wanes developmentally. The effect of poor parental discipline (supervision and the use of physical punishment) increases as children move from early childhood into adolescence (Loeber et al., 1998, p. 235). Parents who fail to monitor their children after school and in the evening hours and who resort to physical punishment are likely find their children engaged in more and more problematic behavior. Although we are just beginning to learn about them, many of the factors that produce problems are thought to be time-dependent, influenced by a complex array of risk and protective conditions that range from biological predispositions to broad societal conditions.

Interrupting risk chains. Third, using the ideas of reciprocal causation, context dependence, and time dependence, effective preventive intervention attempts to interrupt problem-producing processes early in their course. This requires extraordinary specificity about the risk chains that produce problems. Moreover, it requires developing an understanding of *local* risk and protective factors, that is, the way local traditions, culture, and language may affect risk and protective mechanisms. This has led some experts to develop community mobilization processes that guide prevention practitioners in a step-by-step protocol for identifying local risk and protective factors, matching keystone factors with interventions, and allocating resources for comprehensive initiatives (Hawkins & Catalano, 1992). Not yet evaluated, these community involvement strategies appear to offer communities the means to restructure existing service plans by using a risk and resilience perspective.

Growth of Prevention Science: Interrupting Proximal Risk Processes

The focus of prevention science is to "systematically study the precursors of dysfunction and health and to address risk and protective factors associated with a variety of disorders" (Coie et al., 1993, p. 1013). As experts have recognized that treatment technologies per se do not always reduce the incidence of social and health problems, funding for prevention research has grown (Heller, 1996). For instance, the NIMH established the Center for Prevention Research (CPR) in 1982 as a way of promoting and coordinating preventive intervention research. Moreover, one school of social work, at the University of Washington in Seattle, recently received NIMH funding to establish a prevention research center in social work. One of the goals of these programs is to collect information on prevention at the theoretical, methodological, and applied levels (Spilton-Koretz, 1991). As a consequence of increased prevention research, the knowledge base about the developmental markers, correlates, and causes of social problems has evolved. These centers serve important roles in aggregating and testing new knowledge.

Currently, two widely held beliefs guide a conceptual framework for interrupting risk chains. First, *intervention must address keystone risk and protective factors at a variety of levels* (see, e.g., Hawkins et al., 1992). Werner and Smith (1982), in their longitudinal study of more than 600 children on the island of Kauai, found that protective influences included having a sense of humor and a bond of attachment with at least one adult within or outside of the family. Such studies suggest that individual risk factors (such as a sense of humor, problem-solving skills, or planfulness) are nested within family (such as parent-child communication) and other contextual risk factors (such as neighborhood safety). Providing clues for individual and family interventions, Loeber et al. (1998) recently found that many contextual factors are mediated by individual and family factors. The implication of these research findings for program design is that efforts to reduce risk and promote protection need to be focused on a variety of individual and family conditions. Moreover, extrafamilial factors should be addressed because they provide a context that conditions family functioning, work opportunities, and broader connectedness to others.

Second, *intervention must be dynamic.* Because the relationship of risk and protective factors to behaviors varies over the life course, interventions must be based on a developmental conceptualization of social and health problems. For children, this means that prevention

programs should be tailored to the cognitive, social, and other developmental characteristics of the risk or target population. Moreover, a continuum of prevention interventions should be laddered in such a way that the complexity and content changes with development across the life course.

Classifying Prevention Interventions

Prevention interventions can be classified on the basis of *target population* and major *domain* (see, e.g., Durlak, 1997; Gordon, 1983, 1987; Mrazek & Haggerty, 1994). The target group is the audience to whom change efforts are directed. The domain is the focus or venue of activity.

Using Gordon's (1983, 1987) typology, we identify two targeting strategies: universal and selected (see Table 5.1). Universal prevention interventions are directed toward entire populations. They attempt to provide a benefit for everyone in a target population. Thus, this strategy may affect incidence rates. However, the danger in providing services to all clients at a clinic, all schools in a school district, or all counties in a state is that some people who do not need services will receive them. Because this can waste resources, recent research has attempted to "sharpen the focus of prevention targeting" (Schinke, 1994, p. 47). In contrast to universal interventions, selected prevention interventions are directed toward groups of people who have characteristics known to increase vulnerability for social and health problems. Target populations (individuals, family, schools, and neighborhoods) are selected on the basis of high levels of risk.[2]

Shown also in Table 5.1, the second classification criterion is the domain. Based on the idea

TABLE 5.1   Typology of Prevention Programs: Representative Promising Programs

	Target Population	
Domain of Activity	Universal	Selected
Individual	• Immunization • PKU testing	• Breast cancer screening • Prostate examination Nurse Home Visitation Program
Family	• Family Medical Leave Act	• Multisystemic treatment Functional family therapy

School, neighborhood, societal levels	• Metal detectors
	• School resource officers
	  Car safety devices
		• Metropolitan Area Child Study
		• Seattle Social Development Project
		  Boston Gun Project

that problems are contextually dependent, the domain represents the level at which the intervention is directed. Interventions can focus on individual, family, school, neighborhood, and broad social conditions. At the individual level, practitioners work directly with individuals. At the family level, efforts may be focused on improved outcomes in family communication, problem solving, home habitability, and other risk factors. At higher orders of this ecological framework, practitioners work in schools, neighborhoods, and in political environments to effect change.

Our framework includes six types of prevention interventions defined by the six cells in Table 5.1. From the top left to right, Cell 1 represents interventions that are directed at the individual level and designed for all. Cell 2 includes individual level interventions for those at risk of developing certain problem conditions. Cells 3 and 4 consist of interventions focused on the family. Cell 3 includes family level interventions that are geared toward all families, whereas Cell 4 contains interventions for families at risk. The final pair of cells represents interventions directed at schools, neighborhoods,

or other higher order systems; for example, interventions planned for all schools or neighborhoods in a community are found in Cell 5. Finally, Cell 6 includes interventions for at-risk schools, neighborhoods, or larger systems, such as a state with a high incidence of HIV or a nation with a high incidence of tuberculosis.

Although this model includes six types of prevention interventions, in practice, the boundaries between cells tend to be permeable. In fact, many prevention interventions are—or should be—targeted toward multiple domains, attempting to produce positive effects at more than one level (Durlak, 1997). We use this framework both to classify the major domains of prevention activity and to show the need for multi-element prevention programs that address a variety of risk and protective factors. Using this framework, we highlight promising prevention programs in the next few pages.

Promising Prevention Programs

The knowledge base for effective interventions has expanded dramatically in recent years (Hawkins, Arthur, & Catalano, 1995; Mrazek

& Haggerty, 1994). As suggested above, prevention programs are generally designed to reduce or counterbalance risk factors that place an individual, family, neighborhood, or even a nation at risk. Sometimes, too, they are designed to promote protective factors. Current research suggests that timing plays a key role in prevention intervention because risk and protective factors must be developmentally targeted (Coie et al., 1993). So, whether early in the life course (e.g., home-visiting public health programs for mothers with newborn children), or at points later in life where risk is thought to increase (e.g., free breast and prostate cancer screenings for older people), early intervention increases the likelihood of preventing (or at least postponing) disorder, disease, or dysfunction.

In addition to preventing or delaying disorders, an oft-purported benefit of prevention is cost-effectiveness (see Lipsey, 1984). Generally, preventing a problem should be less expensive than treating it after it occurs; however, to be cost-effective, programs must accurately target (predict) who will experience a problem and then provide a universal or selected intervention to reduce risk. Although this is a challenging task, recent data suggest that it is not impossible. For example, a comparative analysis of California's "three strikes" law, which mandates life imprisonment for offenders convicted of three felonies, and early intervention revealed that early intervention efforts prevent just as much crime but at one fifth the financial cost of "three strikes" imprisonment (Greenwood, Model, Rydell, & Chiesa, 1996). Studies like this one demonstrate that prevention can be more cost-effective than programs designed to provide services after serious problems develop. But more research will surely be needed if prevention is to make further advances.

As Durlak and Wells (1997) suggest, prevention offers practitioners and policymakers an increasingly salient alternative to treatment. In the next section, we review exemplary programs that are generating excitement about the potential for prevention. This review is neither exhaustive nor systematic. We have attempted to highlight empirically supported programs that reduce risk while enhancing protective factors.

Individual Universal and Selected Prevention Interventions

A wide range of individual level factors are targetable—subject to change via intervention prevention programs. These factors include general health, gender-specific health, cognitive development, and socio-emotional development (Wasserman & Miller, 1998). Individually focused universal prevention interventions are designed to improve outcomes or reduce risk for general populations. On the other hand, individually focused selected prevention interventions are designed to improve outcomes for a specific population, a population that is characterized by set of risk factors.

The Childhood Immunization Initiative is an individually focused universal prevention intervention. Its goal is to develop and maintain a comprehensive vaccination delivery system. The initiative has two objectives: (a) to ensure that all 2-year-olds receive each of several critical vaccines and (b) to reduce to zero the incidence of diseases preventable by childhood vaccinations (Centers for Disease Control, 1997). Like immunization programs, Phenylketonuria (PKU) testing, whether by venipuncture or heel lancing, is a method of screening for inborn errors of metabolism in neonates (Larsson, 1998). Across the country, this test is administered to all newborns. Both the Childhood Immunization Initiative and PKU testing can be considered individually universal prevention interventions.

In contrast, the Prenatal and Early Childhood Nurse Home Visitation Program is an individually focused selected prevention intervention. The goal of this program is to help low-income, first-time parents improve their prenatal health and avoid pregnancy problems. In addition, the program seeks to improve the health of infants and toddlers and to assist women in planning future pregnancies, in making personal development plans, and in preparing to enter or re-enter the workforce. A series of randomized clinical trials developed to test the Prenatal and Early Childhood Nurse Home Visitation Program suggests that it improves maternal and child functioning (Olds, Hill, Mihalic, & O'Brien, 1998). Moreover, recent longitudinal data indicate that the program significantly reduces both the risk of child maltreatment and, in the long run, the risk of antisocial behavior in children (Olds, Hill, & Rumsey, 1998).

Widely used in Big Brothers and Big Sisters programs, mentoring is also an individually focused selected prevention intervention. Mentoring involves pairing a nonprofessional volunteer with an individual youth identified as being at risk. Generally, mentoring interventions use such a relationship to buffer children from factors such as alienation and association with delinquent peers (Catalano, Arthur, Hawkins, Berglund, & Olson, 1998). Moreover, they attempt to enhance protection by emphasizing academic assistance, structured recreation, and positive peer relationships. Although research

on the impact of mentoring interventions is not yet convincing, recent evidence suggests that these programs are successful in building attachments to prosocial adults, a protective factor thought to buffer youths from family and school risk factors (Galbraith & Cohen, 1995; Harvey & Rauch, 1997; Tierney, Grossman, & Resch, 1995).

Family-Based Universal and Selected Prevention Interventions

Across the life span, family is a critical concept. Whether universal or selected, family-based prevention interventions are designed to improve family functioning and family-related outcomes. The Family and Medical Leave Act (FMLA) of 1993 is widely regarded as a universal family-based prevention intervention. The FMLA requires businesses with 50 or more employees to provide 12 weeks a year of unpaid leave for birth, adoption, foster care, or personal or family illness (Scharlach & Grosswald, 1997). The FMLA may help to reduce risk by providing families with time to deal with stressful life transitions.

Although we use it here as representative of a universal program, the FMLA has been criticized for failing to extend benefits to all employees regardless of marital status (and other issues of difference). Intended to support families in a universal way, the controversy surrounding the FMLA points to the fact that universal programs rely on sometimes disputed definitions of terms such as family, school, and neighborhood (Zipper & Simeonsson, 1997).

No field of prevention has been more fertile than that of selected family-focused intervention. These interventions usually target the families of children who are at risk of serious social problems. Much of the work in this area has focused on children with conduct problems (see, e.g., Eron, Gentry, & Schlegel, 1996; Loeber & Farrington, 1998). Functional Family Therapy (FFT), for example, uses an array of behavioral and communications techniques to intervene with families where children are oppositional, hostile, or truant (Alexander et al., 1998; Alexander, Barton, Schiavo, & Parsons, 1976). In a series of rigorous studies, FFT has been shown to be effective in improving family communication and reducing conduct problems in children (Wasserman & Miller, 1998).

Broader in scope and design than FFT, home-based family preservation services assist families in dealing with problems of such magnitude that placing children in foster or group care is often under consideration. With origins in child welfare, these programs have been tested most rigorously in juvenile justice programs designed to reduce recidivism rates. Home-based services generally seek to improve family functioning by providing concrete services (e.g., assistance in paying rent or obtaining food or health care) plus supportive training in budget management, problem solving, anger management, parenting, and other skills. In doing this, these programs attempt to strengthen families and reduce the risk of out-of-home placement (for reviews, see Burns, Hoagwood, & Mrazek, in press; Fraser, Nelson, & Rivard, 1997).

Perhaps the best known family preservation intervention is multisystemic therapy (MST), which is based on family systems and social ecological theories. MST uses components of family therapy, parental management training, and problem-focused interventions in peer and school settings to provide a set of intensive services to children and families (Henggeler et al., 1998). MST has proved effective with serious juvenile offenders (Henggeler & Borduin, 1995; Wasserman & Miller, 1998). When compared with standard treatment offered by the South Carolina Division of Youth Services, MST was found to positively affect family cohesiveness, adaptability, and support in addition to reducing overall family conflict (Henggeler, Melton, & Smith, 1992). In addition, follow-up studies indicated that families and children who received MST had lower arrest rates than those who received standard treatment (Henggeler & Borduin, 1995).

School-Based Universal and Selected Prevention Interventions

School-based prevention interventions are generally aimed at improving behavioral and academic outcomes for children and adolescents (Catalano et al., 1998). Risk factors for children and adolescents within a school setting include a wide range of school and classroom characteristics (e.g., school size and classroom management practices). Moreover, they include factors that affect students in making transitions from school to school, in being academically successful (e.g., poor school readiness), and in participating fully in school programs (e.g., poor school attachment and association with delinquent peers) (for a review, see Miller, Brehm, & Whitehouse, 1998). Protective factors include a strong attachment to school, social and cognitive competence, and academic achievement. Universal school-based prevention interventions are designed to improve outcomes or reduce risk for all students. Selected school-based interventions, on the other hand, are designed to improve outcomes for a specific population based on an identified set of risk factors.

The Seattle Social Development Project (SSDP) is a universal school-based intervention. It consists of parent management training (PMT), social competence training (SCT), classroom contingency training (CCT), and positive reinforcement of academic achievement. PMT encourages the positive reinforcement of children's adaptive and prosocial behaviors while consistently ignoring or mildly punishing antisocial behavior. PMT strategies typically include reducing corporal punishment and developing clear standards and expectations for child behavior. SCT teaches children to develop and use prosocial behaviors and social-cognitive processes such as conversational skills, academic performance, and behavioral control. CCT builds on PMT with similar techniques adapted for classroom use. These techniques include developing clear expectations and routines for attendance, behavior, and classroom procedures. Teachers are trained in the use of positive reinforcement, contingent encouragement, and praise (Wasserman & Miller, 1998). Focused on aggressive behavior, the general aim of this intervention is to increase children's attachments to school and family (protective factors) while reducing involvement with antisocial peers (risk factors) (Hawkins et al., 1992).

Studies from the SSDP indicate that the intervention has a significant impact on school attachment, academic achievement, and school misconduct. In addition, although the SSDP focuses on elementary school-age children, it appears to have distal effects. Recent data suggest that children in experimental versus control conditions had significantly lower rates of problem behavior well into adolescence (Wasserman & Miller, 1998).

Unlike SSDP, the Metropolitan Area Child Study (MACS) is a selected school-based intervention directed at preventing serious antisocial behavior in children ages 7 to 13 who are at risk because they live in urban areas characterized by high levels of violence. With three graduated levels of intervention, the program involves 7,000 children across 16 schools in a large urban area. Each intervention condition represents an increasingly intensive and comprehensive level of intervention. Level A is a general enhancement, classroom-based, social-cognitive and peer relations training program. Level B uses the same methods as Level A in conjunction with a small-group social-cognitive and peer relations training program for high-risk children. Level C uses the same methods as Level B in conjunction with a family intervention (Huesmann et al., 1996).

The general aim of the MACS is to modify the social-cognitive processes and social environmental factors that place children at risk for antisocial behavior. In a comparative analysis of the three levels of the MACS intervention, significant main effects for participants across treatment conditions were not found. However, when participants' initial levels of aggression were taken into account, the MACS intervention was found to have the greatest impact on the most aggressive children (Guerra, 1998).

Far less complicated than multi-element programs that involve training and altering existing or introducing new practices, some prevention programs attempt to promote changes in schools by increasing deterrence. As examples of universal school-based prevention intervention, these programs may, for example, increase use of metal detectors, hire school-based police officers, or institute no-notice locker inspections. Although some question the ethics and legality of these prevention initiatives, they are widely adopted and represent growing public concern about violence on school grounds (Ginsberg & Loffredo, 1993). Although they are easier to implement than MACS, SSDP, afterschool programs, or school restructuring programs that require changes in school practices or policies, it is not clear that these universal school-based interventions are effective. For instance, the much-acclaimed positive outcomes of the New York City School District's violence prevention interventions may be related to the drop in the city's overall crime rate (Tyre, 1998). Notwithstanding, elements of the New York program have been brought to scale in school districts across the country. We mention these largely unevaluated programs because the urgency of need (e.g., the press to take action on youth violence after 12 high school students were murdered in 1999 at Columbine High School in Littleton, Colorado) sometimes exceeds the capacity of prevention science to generate knowledge for public policies.

Community-Based Universal and Selected Prevention Intervention

Because communities are composed of individuals, families, schools, and other institutions and agencies, effective prevention intervention at the community level must be comprehensive in nature. Community-based prevention strategies typically involve mobilizing community members to actively participate in planning and implementing prevention efforts. Building social cohesion and informal social control (the sum of which may be thought of as the collective efficacy of a community) is critical in successful community-based interventions. Experts argue that reducing social disorganization and promoting strong bonds of attachment and ownership of the community build the effectiveness of families, schools, and informal resident networks (Hawkins & Catalano, 1992). Neighborhood Watch programs are based on these premises. Through collective monitoring and supervision, community residents are thought to establish social connections that increase collective efficacy. However, evaluations of the effectiveness of Neighborhood Watch programs have not yet produced positive findings (Catalano et al., 1998; see also Lindsay & McGillis, 1986; Rosenbaum, Lewis, & Grant, 1986).

More comprehensive and systematic than watch programs, Communities That Care (CTC) is a universal prevention intervention based on a social development perspective (Hawkins & Catalano, 1992; Catalano & Hawkins, 1996). CTC seeks to reduce risk and enhance protection by promoting systemic, collective, community action to develop targeted prevention strategies. CTC has proven effective in some aspects of community mobilization (i.e., bringing community leaders together to develop a risk reduction and protective factor approach to prevention). The CTC model has been adopted by the U.S. Office of Juvenile Justice and Delinquency Prevention to assist community coalitions to plan for spending Title V delinquency-prevention block grants (Catalano et al., 1998). To date, however, the full effects of the CTC intervention strategy have yet to be evaluated (Loeber & Farrington, 1998).

The Midwestern Prevention Project is a universal community-based intervention designed to prevent substance abuse (Pentz, Brannon, et al., 1989). The intervention project was implemented across 42 middle and junior high schools in Kansas City, Missouri. It consisted of five components: (a) mass media programming, (b) school-based educational curricula, (c) parent education and organization, (d) community organization, and (e) health policy. Beginning with the mass media, school curricula, and parent interventions, these components were introduced sequentially during the middle and junior high school years over a 4-year period (Pentz, Dwyer, et al., 1989). One year of the intervention significantly lowered the prevalence of drug use in schools in the treatment condition, when compared to schools in a mass media-only control condition. A net *increase* in drug use prevalence among schools in the treatment condition was about half that of schools in the control condition (Pentz, Dwyer, et al., 1989). A 3-year follow-up revealed stable significant differences between schools in the treatment and control conditions. Such findings reinforce the notion that multicomponent prevention programs (ones that address many different risk factors at multiple domains) are more effective than single-component programs.

In a community-wide program, the city of Boston recently implemented an exemplary multicomponent prevention initiative. Targeted for communities with high rates of violence, the initiative consists of the Youth Violence Strike Force, Operation Nightlife, Operation Cease-Fire, and the Boston Gun Project. The Youth Violence Strike Force (YVSF) is composed of law enforcement officers from the city of Boston and outside agencies (e.g., state police, Bureau of Alcohol Tobacco and Firearms and the state

Department of Corrections). The YVSF uses various criminal statutes and civil forfeiture laws as a means to remove violent offenders from the streets. Operation Nightlife is a collaborative effort between the YVSF and the Massachusetts Department of Probation. To ensure compliance with the terms of probation, officers work in teams and make nightly visits to homes of youths who are under court supervision. In an effort to reduce truancy and increase academic performance, these teams also work to increase parental involvement and foster communication with schools. Like Operation Nightlife, Operation Cease-Fire can be characterized as a gang-suppression strategy. Using computer databases and geographic mapping, the program focuses on specific areas thought to be at increased risk for gang activity and violence. Mediation specialists also known as "street workers" are sent to these hot spots and work alongside Nightlife teams to help resolve conflicts and link youths with community services. Gang-mediation specialists and crisis-intervention teams are deployed into areas with known gang activities. In addition, heightened surveillance for shootings, assaults, and other incidents, as well as intensive monitoring in the event of violent retaliations between gangs in conflict, is used (Howell & Hawkins, 1998). Finally, the Boston Gun Project seeks to halt the use of gun violence by coerced use-reduction strategies, including limiting access to firearms (Kennedy, Piehl, & Braga, 1996). The program relies heavily on federal firearm laws to make the illicit gun market much less viable and to remove the most violent gang and drug offenders from the streets (Howell & Hawkins, 1998). Overall, Boston's community prevention intervention is believed to be a significant contributor to the near 80% reduction in juvenile homicide from 1990 to 1995 (U.S. Department of Justice, 1996).

Societal Universal and Selected Prevention Interventions

At the societal level, prevention interventions often take the form of policies or legislation. Legislation regulating product redesign has had a significant impact on injury prevention. For example, legislation requiring the manufacture of flame-retardant sleepwear for children and the Poison Prevention Packaging Act of 1970 requiring potentially hazardous products to be sold in specially designed child-proof packaging appears to have contributed to reductions in death and injury to children (Durlak, 1997).

Although legislation alone may have an impact on some social and health problems, legislative efforts often must be accompanied by additional measures designed to change behavior, reflecting the need for multidimensional prevention efforts. Such is the case with regard to car-safety devices (CSD) (Durlak, 1997). Legislation requiring the use of CSD in conjunction with behavioral community-based interventions has proven to be successful in increasing the use of seat belts and child safety seats. Roberts, Fanurik, and Wilson (1988) report that employing relatively inexpensive incentives to reward children who are in child safety seats or wearing seat belts has the ability to change safety behavior significantly. An intervention designed to improve car-safety behavior was implemented with 9,000 children across 25 elementary schools in Tuscaloosa, Alabama. Local businesses provided funding and in-kind donations for the program. Information about the program was disseminated at Parent-Teacher Association meetings. Local media popularized the use of car seats and seat belts by running public service announcements and news stories. To evaluate the program, children and adults were observed arriving at school each morning. Those who used car safety devices were given stickers, bumper stickers, or lottery tickets good for a drawing for a free family dinner at a local restaurant. The use of these incentives was discontinued after 3 weeks, but observation continued for an additional 2 weeks. The initial observation period (baseline) indicated that only 18% of people in vehicles were using CSD. During the intervention phase of the project, CSD use increased to 65% (Roberts et al., 1988). During the follow-up phase of the intervention (without incentives), CSD use dropped to 49%, still a significant overall increase. Thus, demonstrating the interplay between societal and individual preventive interventions, the use of relatively inexpensive incentives appears to have played a major role in augmenting CSD legislation (Roberts et al., 1988; see also Roberts, Layfield, & Fanurik, 1992).

CONCLUSION

Prevention programs cannot substitute for major social structural reforms that redistribute economic, health, and social resources equitably; however, in the absence of major social reforms, prevention programs are beginning to produce impressive behavioral outcomes across a variety of fields of practice. In this chapter, we reviewed the emergence of a new interdisciplinary field called prevention science. Prevention science grew out of and is rooted deeply in a risk and resilience perspective on social and health problems. In the context of a prevention science perspective on the development of knowledge for social work practice, we discussed risk and resilience, introduced a typology for prevention programs, and reviewed representative prevention programs.

Across promising prevention programs, several common features emerge. These shared features constitute principles for a still-developing risk and resilience orientation in prevention practice. Prevention programs engage in a process of:

1. Selecting target populations by examining local, state, and national epidemiological data
2. Developing an understanding of the risk and protective factors influencing the selected population
3. Tailoring interventions to the unique cultural, ethnic, gender, racial, religious, and other issues of difference in local communities
4. Interrupting risk chains and strengthening protective factors
5. Assessing outcomes by measuring changes in risk and protective factors

The findings from programs that employ this perspective are encouraging. In rigorous studies where research subjects were randomly assigned to control groups,[3] participants in experimental prevention services did better than 59% to 82% of participants in control conditions (Durlak & Wells, 1997). Described in part above, promising prevention programs often address chains of risk factors at the individual, family, and school levels. Moreover, many programs attempt to strengthen protective factors while concomitantly addressing risk factors. This is the basis for an emerging resilience orientation in social work practice and for a renewed sense of optimism about the effectiveness of prevention and early intervention services.

Amid this promise, however, new challenges are emerging. First, both the chains of risk factors that produce poor developmental outcomes and the relative impact of protective factors on these chains are not well understood. A few scholars are attempting to specify risk chains and identify points at which they might be disrupted. Patterson (1996, 1997) and his colleagues have developed an interactionist perspective on family and peer processes that appear to produce delinquent behavior. Similarly, Crick and Dodge (1994) have developed a theory of processing social information that appears to explain hostile, aggressive behavior in some children. Other similar works that attempt to develop causal linkages or risk sequences in the context of cultural, ethnic, gender, and racial differences are needed.

Second, the risk and resilience perspective is only beginning to inform intervention. Risk chains should be elucidated in such a way that practitioners can develop interventions that interrupt risk processes. In the past 15 years, over 29,000 children have participated in more than 100 longitudinal studies from which more than 60 risk factors have been identified (Burns et al., in press). However, less than 10% of these risk factors have been causally analyzed or used as the basis for intervention research. Because some risks are cross-cutting and appear to influence several problems (for a review, see Kirby & Fraser, 1997), prevention programs that interrupt risk mechanisms could potentially affect many social problems at one time. This is grounds for growing sanguinity. But before this can happen, a new generation of research is required to more fully identify causal mechanisms, the environmental contingencies that maintain them, and the protective factors or processes that suppress them. Moreover—and this may be an important role for social work research—this growing body of knowledge must be incorporated into the design and development of more effective social and health programs.

Third, resilience—a concept that has great salience for practitioners and public policy makers—is easily misunderstood and too broadly applied. At best, resilience is due only in part to individual traits such as perseverance, intelligence, planfulness, and motivation. Certainly, these are important individual attributes that serve protective functions. However, individual attributes are often related to environmental conditions. Resilience arises from the transaction of individual factors and environmental contingencies. It is a person-in-environment phenomenon.

Moreover, resilience is rare; it is the exception to the rule. Perhaps as few as 5% of the children exposed to high risk have high levels of protection (Pollard et al., 1999). The majority of children who are exposed to adversity do not enjoy high levels of protection and are not able to overcome disadvantage. That some children prevail over adversity must never become an excuse for failing to develop a basic web of environmental supports. The cost of failing to provide supportive programs for families, resources to make neighborhoods safe, and adequate funding for schools, health care agencies, and other institutions will trivialize knowledge about resilience.

Finally, to acknowledge resilience is to acknowledge an ecological perspective on the development of social and health programs. Research suggests that resilience emerges in the context of strong families and community supports that permit individual growth (Fraser, 1997b). Thus, although it is tempting to attribute the success of talented people to individual traits, it is the confluence of exceptionally—perhaps paradoxically—strong environmental supports that reduces high levels of risk and that permits talent to flourish.[4] In this sense, John F. Kennedy's comments seem equally applicable today. The promise of a risk and resilience perspective lies both in selective prevention initiatives and in "general strengthening of our fundamental community, social welfare, and educational programs."

NOTES

1. For example, being female is often described as a protective factor against aggressive behavior, and the death of a child's parents is described as a risk factor for depression. The former is usually thought of as a trait-related risk, and the latter is thought of as an event-related risk. The effects of both are likely related to a variety of socialization and adaptational processes that affect life-course outcomes. Many risk factors appear to mark these processes, the elaboration of which is an ongoing challenge both for researchers and for practitioners.

2. The degree of risk is cause for some experts to develop categories of selected prevention intervention. Selective prevention is sometimes thought to address populations at high risk for the development of disorder. The term *indicated prevention* is used to describe strategies addressing populations where signs or symptoms of disorders have become observable, implying the highest magnitude of risk. Finally the term *relapse prevention* is used to describe strategies addressing populations that have specific disorders that are in remission. The purpose of relapse prevention is to prevent the re-emergence of florid symptoms or the re-occurrence of declines in functioning associated with an active disorder and conditions co-morbid with disorders.

3. Or where some other method was used to ensure that comparison and experimental groups were equivalent on basic demographic characteristics and pretest risk factors.

4. See, for example, the story of Michael Jordan and his family (Jordan & Lewis, 1996).

REFERENCES

Agnew, R. (1991). A longitudinal test of social control theory and delinquency. *Journal of Research in Crime and Delinquency, 28*(2), 126-156.

Alexander, J. F., Barton, C., Gordon, D., Grotpeter, J., Hansson, K., Harrison, R., Mears, S., Mihalic, S., Parsons, B., Pugh, C., Schulman, S., Waldron, H., & Sexton, T. (1998). *Functional family therapy.* Boulder, CO: Center for the Study and Prevention of Violence.

Alexander, J. F., Barton, C., Schiavo, R. S., & Parsons, B. V. (1976). Systems-based intervention with families of delinquents: Therapist characteristics, family behavior, and outcome. *Journal of Consulting and Clinical Psychology, 44,* 656-664.

Arroyo, C. G., & Zigler, E. (1995). Racial identity, academic achievement, and the psychological well-being of economically disadvantaged adolescents. *Journal of Personality and Social Psychology, 69*(5), 903-914.

Bloom, M. (1996). *Primary prevention practices.* Thousand Oaks, CA: Sage.

Bowman, P. J., & Howard, C. (1985). Race-related socialization, motivation, and academic achievement: A study of black youths in three-generation families. *Journal of the Academy of Child Psychiatry, 24*(2), 134-141.

Buckner, J. C., & Cain, A. C. (1998). Prevention science research with children, adolescents, and families: Introduction. *American Journal of Orthopsychiatry, 68,* 508-511.

Burns, B. J., Hoagwood, K., & Mrazek, P. J. (in press). *Effective treatment for children and adolescents.* Report prepared for the Surgeon General's Report on Mental Health.

Caplan, G. (1964). *Principles of preventive psychiatry.* New York: Basic Books.

Catalano, R. F., Arthur, M. W., Hawkins, J. D., Berglund, L., & Olson, J. J. (1998). Comprehensive community and school-based interventions to prevent antisocial behavior. In R. Loeber & D. P. Farrington (Eds.), *Serious & violent juvenile offenders: Risk factors and successful interventions* (pp. 248-283). Thousand Oaks, CA: Sage.

Catalano, R. F., & Hawkins, J. D. (1996). The social development model: A theory of antisocial behavior. In J. D. Hawkins (Ed.), *Delinquency and crime: Current theories* (pp. 149-197). New York: Cambridge University Press.

Centers for Disease Control. (1997). *Facts about the Childhood Immunization Initiative* [On-line]. Available: http://www.cdc.gov/od/media/fact/cii.htm

Coie, J. D., Watt, N. F., West, S. G., Hawkins, J. D., Asarnow, J. R., Markman, H. J., Ramey, S. L., Shure, M. B., & Long, B. (1993). The science of prevention: A conceptual framework and some directions for a national research program. *American Psychologist, 48,* 1013-1022.

Commission on Chronic Illness. (1957). *Prevention of chronic illness* (Vol. 1). Cambridge, MA: Harvard University Press.

Cowan, P. A., Cowan, C. P., & Schulz, M. S. (1996). Thinking about risk and resilience in families. In E. M. Hetherington & E. A. Blechman (Eds.), *Stress, coping, and resiliency in children and families* (pp. 1-38). Mahwah, NJ: Lawrence Erlbaum.

Crick, N. R., & Dodge, K. A. (1994). A review and reformulation of social information-processing mechanisms in children's social adjustment. *Psychological Bulletin, 115*(1), 74-101.

Cullen, F. T., Wright, J. P., Brown, S., Moon, M. M., Blankenship, M. B., & Applegate, B. K. (1998). Public support for early intervention programs: Implications for a progressive policy agenda. *Crime & Delinquency, 44*(2), 187-204.

Doll, B., & Lyon, M. A. (1998). Risk and resilience: Implications for the delivery of educational and mental health services in schools. *School Psychology Review, 27,* 348-363.

Durlak, J. (1997). Basic concepts in prevention. In J. Durlak (Ed.), *Successful prevention programs for children and adolescents* (pp. 1-25). New York: Plenum.

Durlak, J., & Wells, A. (1997). Primary prevention mental health programs for children and adolescents: A meta-analytic review. *American Journal of Community Psychology, 25*(2), 115-152.

Eron, L., Gentry, J. H., & Schlegel, P. (1996). *Reason to hope: A psychosocial perspective on violence and youth.* Washington, DC: American Psychological Association.

Fraser, M. W. (1996). Aggressive behavior in childhood and early adolescence: An ecological-developmental perspective on youth violence. *Social Work, 41*(4), 347-361.

Fraser, M. W. (1997a). The ecology of childhood: A multisystem perspective. In M. Fraser (Ed.), *Risk and resilience in childhood: An ecological perspective* (pp. 1-9). Washington, DC: NASW Press.

Fraser, M. W. (Ed.). (1997b). *Risk and resilience in childhood: An ecological perspective.* Washington, DC: NASW Press.

Fraser, M. W., & Galinsky, M. (1997). Toward a resilience-based model of practice. In M. W. Fraser (Ed.), *Risk and resilience in childhood: An ecological perspective* (pp. 265-276). Washington, DC: NASW Press.

Fraser, M. W., Nelson, K. E., & Rivard, J. C. (1997). The effectiveness of family preservation services. *Social Work Research, 21,* 138-153.

Freitas, A. L., & Downey, G. (1998). Resilience: A dynamic perspective. *International Journal of Behavioral Development, 22*(2), 263-285.

Galbraith, M. W., & Cohen, N. H. (Eds.). (1995). *Mentoring: New strategies and challenges.* San Francisco: Jossey-Bass.

Garmezy, N. (1974). The study of competence in children at risk for severe psychopathology. In E. J. Anthony & C. Koupernik (Eds.), *The child in his family* (Vol. 3, pp. 77-97). New York: John Wiley.

Garmezy, N. (1991). Resilience in children's adaptation to negative life events and stressed environments. *Pediatric Annals, 20*(9), 459-466.

Ginsberg, C., & Loffredo, L. (1993). Violence-related attitudes and behaviors of high school students—New York 1992. *Journal of School Health, 63,* 438-439.

Goldston, S. (1976). An overview of primary prevention programming. In D. Klein & S. Golston (Eds.), *Primary prevention: An idea whose time has come* (pp. 3-32). Rockville, MD: National Institute of Mental Health.

Gordon, R. (1983). An operational definition of disease classification. *Public Health Reports, 98*(2), 107-109.

Gordon, R. (1987). An operational classification of disease prevention. In J. Steinberg & M. Silverman (Eds.), *Preventing mental disorders.* Rockville, MD: National Institute of Mental Health.

Greenwood, P. W., Model, K. E., Rydell, C. P., & Chiesa, J. (1996). *Diverting children from a life of crime: Measuring costs and benefits.* Santa Monica, CA: RAND.

Guerra, N. G. (1998). Serious and violent juvenile offenders: Gaps in knowledge and research priorities. In R. Loeber & D. P. Farrington (Eds.), *Serious & violent juvenile offenders: Risk factors and successful interventions* (pp. 389-404). Thousand Oaks, CA: Sage.

Harvey, A., & Rauch, J. (1997). A comprehensive Afrocentric rites of passage program for black male adolescents. *Health and Social Work, 22,* 30-36.

Hawkins, J. D., Arthur, M. W., & Catalano, R. (1995). Preventing substance abuse. In M. Tonry & D. P. Farrington (Eds.), *Building a safer society* (Vol. 19). Chicago: University of Chicago Press.

Hawkins, J. D., & Catalano, R. F., Jr. (1992). *Communities that care.* San Francisco, CA: Jossey-Bass.

Hawkins, J. D., Catalano, R. F., Morrison, D. M., O'Donnell, J., Abbott, R. D., & Day, L. E. (1992). The Seattle Social Development Project: Effects of the first four years on protective factors and problem behaviors. In J. McCord & R. E. Tremblay (Eds.), *Preventing antisocial behavior: Interventions from birth through adolescence* (pp. 139-161). New York: Guilford.

Heller, K. (1996). Coming of age of prevention science. *American Psychologist, 51*(11), 1123-1127.

Henggeler, S. W., & Borduin, C. M. (1995). Multisystemic treatment of serious juvenile offenders and their families. In I. M. Schwartz & P. AuClaire (Eds.), *Home-based services for troubled children* (pp. 113-130). Lincoln: University of Nebraska Press.

Henggeler, S. W., Melton, G. B., & Smith, L. A. (1992). Family preservation using multisystemic therapy: An effective alternative to incarcerating serious juvenile offenders. *Journal of Consulting and Clinical Psychology, 60*(6), 953-961.

Henggeler, S. W., Schoenwald, S. K., Borduin, C. M., Rowland, M. D., & Cunningham, P. B. (1998). *Multisystemic treatment of antisocial behavior in children and adolescents.* New York: Guilford.

Hoagwood, K., Hibbs, E., Brent, D., & Jensen, P. (1995). Introduction to the special section: Efficacy and effectiveness in studies of child and adolescent psychotherapy. *Journal of Consulting and Clinical Psychology, 63,* 683-687.

Howell, J. C. (1998). Promising programs for youth gang violence prevention and intervention. In R. Loeber & D. P. Farrington (Eds.), *Serious and violent juvenile offenders: Risk factors and successful interventions* (pp. 284-312). Thousand Oaks, CA: Sage.

Howell, J. C., & Hawkins, J. D. (1998). Prevention of youth violence. In M. Tonry & M. H. Moore (Eds.), *Youth violence* (Vol. 24, pp. 263-316). Chicago: University of Chicago Press.

Huesmann, L. R., Maxwell, C. D., Eron, L., Dahlberg, L., Guerra, N. G., Tolan, P., VanAcker, R., & Henry, D. (1996). Evaluating a cognitive/ecological program for the prevention of aggression among urban children. *American Journal of Preventive Medicine, 12*(5), 120-128.

Jessor, R. (1993). Successful adolescent development among youth in high-risk settings. *American Psychologist, 48*(2), 117-126.

Jessor, R. (1998). *New perspectives on adolescent risk behavior.* New York: Cambridge University Press.

Jessor, R., Van Den Bos, J., Vanderryn, J., Costa, F. M., & Turbin, M. S. (1997). Protective factors in adolescent problem behavior: Moderator effects and developmental change. In G. A. Marlatt & G. R. Van Den Bos (Eds.), *Addictive behaviors: Readings on etiology, prevention, and treatment* (pp. 239-264). Washington, DC: American Psychological Association.

Jordan, D., & Lewis, G. A. (1996). *Family first: Winning the parenting game.* San Francisco, CA: Harper.

Kennedy, D. M., Piehl, A. M., & Braga, A. A. (1996). Youth violence in Boston: Gun markets, serious youth offenders, and a use reduction strategy. *Law and Contemporary Problems, 59*(1), 147-196.

Kennedy, J. F. (1963, February 5). *Message to the Congress of the United States from The President of the United States on Mental Illness and Mental Retardation.* Washington, DC: Committee on Interstate and Foreign Commerce.

Kirby, L. D., & Fraser, M. W. (1997). Risk and resilience in childhood. In M. W. Fraser (Ed.), *Risk and resilience in childhood: An ecological perspective* (pp. 10-33). Washington, DC: NASW Press.

Larsson, B. (1998). Venipuncture is more effective and less painful than heel lancing for blood tests in neonates. *Journal of the American Medical Association, 280*(2), 112.

Leavell, H. R., & Clark, E. G. (Eds.). (1953). *Textbook of preventive medicine.* New York: McGraw-Hill.

Lindsay, B., & McGillis, D. (1986). Citywide community crime prevention: An assessment of the Seattle program. In D. P. Rosenbaum (Ed.), *Community crime prevention: Does it work?* (pp. 46-67). Beverly Hills, CA: Sage.

Lipsey, M. W. (1984). Is delinquency prevention a cost-effective strategy? A California perspective. *Journal of Research in Crime and Delinquency, 21*(4), 279-302.

Loeber, R., & Farrington, D. P. (Eds.). (1998). *Serious and violent offenders: Risk factors and successful interventions.* Thousand Oaks, CA: Sage.

Loeber, R., Farrington, D. P., Stouthamer-Loeber, M., & Van Kammen, W. B. (1998). *Antisocial behavior and mental health problems: Explanatory factors in childhood and adolescence.* Mahwah, NJ: Lawrence Erlbaum.

Luthar, S. S. (1993). Methodological and conceptual issues in research on childhood resilience. *Journal of Child Psychology and Psychiatry, 34,* 441-453.

Luthar, S. S., Doernberger, C. H., & Zigler, E. (1993). Resilience is not a unidimensional construct: Insights form a prospective study of inner-city adolescents. *Development and Psychopathology, 5,* 703-717.

Masten, A. S., Best, K. M., & Garmezy, N. (1990). Resilience and development: Contributions from the study of children who overcome adversity. *Development and Psychopathology, 2,* 425-444.

Miller, D., & MacIntosh, R. (in press). Promoting resiliency in urban African American adolescents: Racial socialization and identity as protective factors. *Social Work Research.*

Miller, G. E., Brehm, K., & Whitehouse, S. (1998). Reconceptualizing school-based prevention for antisocial behavior within a resiliency framework. *School Psychology Review, 27*(3), 364-379.

Mrazek, P., & Haggerty, R. (1994). *Reducing risks for mental disorders.* Washington, DC: National Academy Press.

Olds, D. L., Hill, P. L., Mihalic, S. F., & O'Brien, R. A. (1998). *Prenatal and infancy home visitation by nurses.* Boulder, CO: Institute of Behavioral Science, Center for the Study and Prevention of Violence.

Olds, D., Hill, P., & Rumsey, E. (1998). *Prenatal and early childhood nurse home visitation.* Washington, DC: Office of Juvenile Justice and Delinquency Prevention.

Patterson, G. R. (1995). Coercion as a basis for early age onset for arrest. In J. McCord (Ed.), *Coercion and punishment in long-term perspective* (pp. 81-105). New York: Cambridge University Press.

Patterson, G. R. (1996). Some characteristics of a developmental theory for early-onset. In M. Lenzenweger & J. J. Haugaard (Eds.), *Frontiers of developmental psychopathology* (pp. 81-124). New York: Oxford University Press.

Patterson, G. R. (1997). Performance models for parenting: A social interactional perspective. In J. E. Grusec & L. Kuczynski (Eds.), *Parenting and children's internalization of values: A handbook of contemporary theory* (pp. 193-226). New York: John Wiley.

Pentz, M. A., Brannon, B. R., Charlin, V. L., Barrett, E. J., MacKinnon, D. P., & Flay, B. R. (1989). The power of policy: The relationship of smoking policy to adolescent smoking. *American Journal of Public Health, 79,* 857-862.

Pentz, M. A., MacKinnon, D. P., Flay, B. R., Hansen, W. B., Wang, E. Y., Johnson, C. A., & Dwyer, J. H. (1989). Primary prevention of chronic diseases in adolescence: Effects of the Midwestern Prevention Project on tobacco use. *American Journal of Epidemiology, 130,* 713-724.

Pollard, J. A., Hawkins, J. D., & Arthur, M. W. (1999). Risk and protection: Are both necessary to understand diverse behavioral outcomes in adolescence? *Social Work Research, 23*(3), 145-158.

Richmond, M. E. (1917). *Social diagnosis.* New York: Russell Sage Foundation.

Roberts, M. C., Fanurik, D., & Wilson, D. R. (1988). A community program to reward children's use of seat belts. *American Journal of Community Psychology, 16,* 395-407.

Roberts, M. C., Layfield, D. A., & Fanurik, D. (1992). Motivating children's use of car safety devices. *Advances in Developmental and Behavioral Pediatrics, 10,* 61-88.

Rosenbaum, D. P., Lewis, D. A., & Grant, J. A. (1986). Neighborhood-based crime prevention: Assessing the efficacy of community organization in Chicago. In D. P. Rosenbaum (Ed.), *Community crime prevention: Does it work?* Beverly Hills, CA: Sage.

Rothman, J., & Thomas, E. J. (1994). *Intervention research: Design and development for human service.* New York: Haworth.

Rutter, M. (1987). Psychosocial resilience and protective mechanisms. *American Journal of Orthopsychiatry, 57,* 316-331.

Rutter, M. (1993). Resilience: Some conceptual considerations. *Journal of Adolescent Health, 14,* 626-631.

Rutter, M. (1997). *Risk and resilience.* Paper presented at Risk and Resilience in Youth Violence, School of Social Work, Jordan Institute for Families, Chapel Hill, NC.

Scharlach, A., & Grosswald, B. (1997). The Family and Medical Leave Act of 1993. *Social Service Review, 71*(3), 335-360.

Schinke, S. P. (1994). Prevention science and practice: An agenda for action. *The Journal of Primary Prevention, 15*(1), 45-57.

Schuerman, J. R., Rzepnicki, T. L., & Littell, J. H. (1994). *Putting families first: An experiment in family preservation.* New York: Aldine de Gruyter.

Spilton-Koretz, D. (1991). Prevention-centered science in mental health. *American Journal of Community Psychology, 19*(4), 453-459.

Sussman, S., Dent, C. W., Burton, D., Stacy, A. W., & Flay, B. R. (1995). *Developing school-based tobacco use prevention and cessation programs.* Thousand Oaks, CA: Sage.

Tierney, J. P., Grossman, J. B., & Resch, N. L. (1995). *Making a difference: An impact study of big brothers/big sisters.* Philadelphia: Public/Private Ventures.

Trickett, E. J. (1996). A future for community psychology: The contexts of diversity and the diversity of contexts. *American Journal of Community Psychology, 24,* 209-234.

Trickett, E. J. (1997). Ecology and primary prevention: Reflections on a meta-analysis. *American Journal of Community Psychology, 25*(2), 197-205.

Tyre, P. (1998, May 22). *How schools got safer.* [On-line]. Available: http://cnn.com/US/9805/22/school.reduced.violence/index.html

U.S. Department of Justice. (1996). *Youth violence: A community-based response* [Pamphlet]. Washington, DC: Author.

Wasserman, G. A., & Miller, L. S. (1998). The prevention of serious and violent juvenile offending. In R. Loeber & D. P. Farrington (Eds.), *Serious & violent juvenile offenders: Risk factors and successful interventions* (pp. 197-247). Thousand Oaks, CA: Sage.

Werner, E., & Smith, R. (1982). *Vulnerable but invincible: A study of resilient children.* New York: McGraw-Hill.

Williams, J. H., Ayers, C. D., & Arthur, M. (1997). Risk and protective factors in the development of delinquency and conduct disorder. In M. W. Fraser (Ed.), *Risk and resilience in childhood* (pp. 140-170). Washington, DC: NASW Press.

Zipper, I. N., & Simeonsson, R. (1997). Promoting the development of young children with disabilities. In M. W. Fraser (Ed.), *Risk and resilience in childhood: An ecological perspective* (pp. 244-264). Washington, DC.: NASW Press.

CHAPTER SIX

Empowerment-Oriented Practice: From Practice Value to Practice Model

ENID O. COX

RUTH J. PARSONS

This chapter will describe the basic characteristics of empowerment-oriented practice, selected theoretical perspectives that support this form of practice, and the challenges and potential of empowerment practice for coming decades. The 1980s and 1990s have witnessed an explosion of the use of the term *empowerment*. This term has become a central theme for popular psychology and self-help publications and seminars, as well as a mantra for political conservatives to use as justification for cutting social services and other human resources. However, the variety of popular definitions is no less wide or complex than the historical evolution of the meaning of empowerment as it has evolved in social work practice.

Barbara Simon (1994) has provided a comprehensive history of empowerment in social work. She identifies practice efforts that include both social action and client change strategies, efforts that emphasize client strengths and abilities, and efforts that reflect the social justice-oriented intellectual, religious, and political movements of particular eras, as examples of empowerment in social work practice. Activities of the Settlement House Movement (Axinn & Levin, 1997; Day, 1997), efforts of social workers who were members of the Rank-and-

File Movement of the 1930s (Fisher, 1980), and the critical and radical practice movements of the 1960s and early 1970s (Galper, 1980; Pivin & Cloward, 1975) provide rich examples of ongoing professional efforts to integrate these characteristics into practice. Many components of empowerment practice have been incorporated into systems-based social work models, which have defined mainstream social work practice since the 1960s. However, most earlier social work methods and/or models of practice did not explicitly use the term empowerment in defining a specific practice model and/or describing models of practice that incorporate the multiple dimensions of empowerment practice into a single framework.

The definition of empowerment as it relates to today's social work practice has evolved from earlier definitions, which often referred to social action activities, self-help activities, or advocacy for individual clients; it supports the multilevel, multistrategy activities that reflect the current models of empowerment practice that we will discuss in this chapter. Empowerment for purposes of this discussion will be defined as a process in which (a) social workers and clients engage in activities "that aim to reduce the powerlessness that has been created by negative valuations based on membership in a stigmatized group" (Solomon, 1976, p. 19) and (b) clients become strong enough to participate within, share in the control of, and influence events and institutions that affect their lives. Participation in empowerment processes may require that people gain particular skills, knowledge, and sufficient power to influence their lives and the lives of those they care about (Torre, 1985). Definitions with these components underlie the recently developed empowerment-oriented social work practice models.

Prior to discussion of the basic characteristics of these models, a brief discussion of important related social science theory will be presented.

THEORETICAL BASE OF EMPOWERMENT PRACTICE

Empowerment-oriented practice has developed its current nature through an interactive combination of philosophy and values, insights gained from social and psychological science and practice experience.

Philosophy and values. The philosophical orientation, especially commitment to social justice and practice activity of the social work profession from its beginning to the present, has offered empowerment practice a rich legacy of inspiration and illustration. The Civil Rights Movements of the 1960s and early 1970s, based in Gandhi's philosophy, provided many illustrations of the powerful potential for change that participation in a empowerment process could provide for individuals and for communities. The emergence of leaders from oppressed communities, the successful life status changes made by many individual clients, and the significant policy gains that resulted from collective action increased the many social workers' awareness of the potential for empowerment-oriented change for individuals as well as the larger environment. The social programs generated by the era also offered opportunities for community practice that allowed attention to both the personal and political dimensions of social issues and problems.

In addition to encouragement from practice experience, professional social work's commitment to diversity and social justice issues through its code of ethics (National Association of Social Workers, 1998) and regulation of training content (Council on Social Work Education, 1997) provide a strong sanction base for empowerment practice. For example, social work values include providing services in a manner that respects diversity, promotes self-determination, and promotes client-worker partnership as the basis for professional relationships. Professional values also promote focus on issues of poverty, discrimination, and other aspects of social justice. Curriculum content in schools of social work is also required to represent these values.

The Social/Psychological Science Theory Contributions

Empowerment practice models have found support from a variety of economic, social, and psychological theories. Many of these theories both provided insight into and gained insight from the nature of social change inspired by the events of the 1960s and 1970s. Because empowerment practice encompasses concern with personal, interpersonal, and political aspects of life and related multiple practice approaches within one framework, it is not surprising that empowerment practice models are informed by many knowledge areas.

Macro theories that have provided guidance for empowerment-oriented social workers include general systems theory and conflict theory. Systems theory challenged social work as a whole to increase its awareness of the importance of the larger environment to problem assessment and intervention (Payne, 1997). Conflict theory, including Marxian and neo-Marxian theory, focused attention on the social and structural inequities that form the con-

tent of existing social systems (Rojek, 1986; Sherman, 1987). Conflict theorists have also been useful to our understanding of ways in which problems and issues are internalized, often with the assistance of powerful socialization processes (Marcuse, 1964).

Postmodern critiques of macro theory and of its basic assumptions about society further elucidate the process of social construction of the self that begins in Marxist critiques of social problems and issues. In sum, these theories have enhanced understanding of powerlessness/oppression within the larger political arena and set the context for many areas of middle-level theory development. Theory development has been predominately focused on the nature of powerlessness, the impact of powerlessness on individuals seen through a psychological lens, and, more recently, theory that systematically addresses empowerment as a three-dimensional construct as it relates to empowerment-oriented practice.

Theory development that illuminates the nature of powerlessness includes older psychosocial theories related to powerlessness (Seeman, 1959, 1967) and learned helplessness (Maier & Seligman, 1976), as well as more recent efforts in this area (Seligman, 1995). Freire's (1970) development of the "culture of silence" concept applied the sense of powerlessness to the poor (in particular suggesting that a state of powerlessness exists as individuals and groups are alienated from the process of constructing social reality). In addition, many feminist scholars have explored the processes involved in oppression. Their exposure of the role of social structure in both internalized and external perceptions of women's roles (status) and capabilities has further documented the need for empowerment practice models

(Chodorow, 1989; East, 1998; Hanisch, 1971; McIntosh, 1996). The works of observers who have captured the experience of oppression from the perceptions of members of ethnic minority populations have also provided insight to the phenomena of powerlessness (Feagin, 1989; Solomon, 1976, 1985).

Theoretical developments that suggest the impact of powerlessness on individuals include theory related to the concept of self-efficacy (Bandura, 1995; Maddux, 1995) and the role of social support in efficacy (Antonucci & Hiroko, 1997; Carstensen & Frieder, 1997). This work also provides strong support for the development of empowerment-oriented practice.

The health professions have also demonstrated an increasing interest in empowerment-related efforts. Concerns related to patient compliance, self-care behaviors, and issues of autonomy have fueled debate, study, and innovation in medical fields during the past two decades. The recognition of the critical role that patient attitude and behavior play in health-related outcomes has led to increasing emphasis on the importance of self-care (Carroll, 1995; Ory & DeFriese, 1998; Segall & Goldstein, 1989; Spitzer, Yoram, & Ziv, 1996). For example, in their study of 142 primary care patients, Punamaki and Aschan (1994) identified the most frequent causes of feelings of helplessness as "disease symptoms, discrepancies between demands and capabilities, and negative psychological and emotional states" (p. 740). They conclude that self-care interventions are the most promising approach. Health researchers have also explored the critical role that self-efficacy plays in self-care behaviors and recovery (Maddux, Brawley, & Boykin, 1995; Schwarzer & Fuchs, 1995). A final area of work that has affected interventions in health care

settings is findings of studies related to social support and health outcomes (Antonucci & Akiyama, 1994). This emphasis on patient role has led to increasing interest in interventions that develop patient knowledge and skills to better address health challenges.

Practice-Based Theory Development

Simultaneous with the development of theoretical insights, and as part of that development, social work practice and psychology-based practice added many important insights to the current models of empowerment practice. In the 1960s, social work practice began to include more work that emphasized citizen participation, advocacy, and community organization. This emphasis led to a movement away from strong boundaries that had developed between casework, group work, community work, and social action (Brinker-Jenkins & Joseph, 1980; Galper, 1980; Moreau, 1979). The emphasis on "consciousness raising" as an integral part of social change and social action— fostered by the work of Freire (1970, 1973) and various feminists perspectives (Brinker-Jenkins, 1991), critical and radical social work practice perspectives (Galper, 1980; Piven & Cloward, 1975), the black power movement, and other social movements of the period—called attention to this process as a powerful tool for empowerment-oriented social work practice.

Social group work has been identified as the method of choice among most proponents of empowerment-oriented practice due to the powerful impact of collectivity as a factor in the empowerment process (Cox & Parsons, 1994; Gutiérrez, 1990; Lee, 1994). In addition, social group work advocates began to reconstruct models to incorporate more of the political aspects of collective action as an essential part of social group work practice (Breton, 1994; Cox, 1988).

Competency-based practice approaches have incorporated an empowerment-oriented strategy of education and skills development as a central part of social work practice (Maluccio, 1981). Work on a strengths-based approach to practice emphasized the key role that client strengths play in empowerment and an increased sense of self-efficacy (Saleeby, 1992). In addition to these social work practice efforts, an anti-psychiatry movement flourished in the late 1960s and 1970s. This movement called attention to the important role of the political/economic environment in personal problems and the need to focus on these issues in treatment (Brown, 1974; Hanisch, 1971; Ingleby, 1980; Rappaport, 1981; Steiner, 1971).

A final area of practice development, of perhaps great value to the goal of moving empowerment-oriented practice approaches from the margins of social work interest to central attention, is the integration of empowerment principles and practice strategies into some generalist models of practice. These models are taught in schools of social work, both at the bachelor's and master's level. One such practice approach is the generalist practice model of Miley, O'Melia, and DuBois (1998), built on ecosystems, cultural competence, strengths, and empowerment. Called an empowering approach to generalist practice, the model uses roles across the micro and macro levels. These roles include consultant, enabler, facilitator, planner, colleague and monitor, broker and advocate, convenor and mediator, activist, catalyst, teacher, trainer, and outreach. The authors deliberately avoided a problem-solving framework and instead proposed a phased process that

consists of the Dialogue Phase, the Discovery phase, and the Development Phase. The model describes how generalist practice, using an empowerment-based approach, can meet the purposes of social work to enhance human functioning and promote social justice. In addition, the book describes the practice processes related to constructing and maintaining client-system-worker relationships, communicating effectively with diverse clients about their situation, and defining a purpose for the work. In this book, empowerment provides a theoretical base for generalist practice.

Parsons, Jorgensen, and Hernandez (1994), in *The Integration of Social Work Practice,* provide a framework for developing and organizing advanced generalist curricula for social work practice education. In this book, social work practice is conceived as intervention across multilevel client systems, from micro to macro, and through six roles of social workers—conferee, enabler, broker, advocate, mediator, and guardian—applied to multilevel client systems. The theoretical foundation includes empowerment as the overriding principle in generalist practice.

Mondros and Wilson (1994), in their book, *Organizing for Power and Empowerment,* use the concept of empowerment as an undergirding principle for looking at social action organizations. They propose that social action groups are a viable means of empowerment for citizens of all social classes and agendas.

In sum, many separate practice efforts in social work practice and psychology/psychiatry have incorporated key elements of empowerment-oriented practice such as attention to personal, interpersonal, and political aspects of client problems and renewal of our philosophical commitments to respect for clients as partners in intervention efforts. More elaborate efforts to design and evaluate empowerment-oriented practice models are described below.

Research and the Multidimensional Approach

Research on empowerment that addresses empowerment as a practice model was initiated in the 1980s and 1990s by individuals who had practice intervention experience (Cox, 1988; Gutiérrez, 1990; Torre, 1985) as well as other social science researchers (Kieffer, 1981; Zimmerman, 1990, 1995). Empowerment has been conceptualized as a three-dimensional construct (Gutiérrez, 1990; Kieffer, 1984; Segal, Silverman, & Temkin, 1993; Torre, 1985; Zimmerman, 1990, 1995), and relationships among these dimensions have been explored. Research supports the thesis that these three dimensions—personal, interpersonal, and political—interact and influence one another and are subconcepts of a larger construct that has to do with power, both perceived and objective.

Practice-related research that describes the ways in which the personal, interpersonal, and social participation dimensions interact and influence each other has also been initiated. Kieffer (1984), using biographic interviewing with a sample of 15 individuals, found a substantial relationship between attitudes about self-efficacy and self-worth and both individual and group actions taken to resolve the problems or issues that were facing these individuals. A study by Parsons and Cox found a positive correlation between self-efficacy attitudes and higher voting rates in isolated elders (reported in Kimboko & Parsons, 1987). Zimmerman and Rappaport (1988) compared the results on 11 indices of perceived self-efficacy and auton-

omy with attitudes and actual participation in community activities and organizations.

In each of these studies, individuals reporting a greater amount of participation scored higher on indices indicating levels of perceived autonomy and self-efficacy. Later, Zimmerman (1990) found a positive correlation between perceived self-efficacy and community participation and a negative relationship between both and attitudes of alienation. He concluded that "learned hopefulness" (contrasting it with helplessness) is possible through community participation and positive attitudes toward self-efficacy.

In a path analysis, Dunst, Trivette, and Deal (1988) found the variable action-taking to be a predictor of perceptions of self-efficacy. Similarly, Zimmerman, Israel, Schult, and Checkoway (1992) found a positive correlation between high levels of participation and high levels of intrapersonal empowerment. (Zimmerman uses the term *intrapersonal* to refer to what is called *personal* in this chapter.) As they pointed out, however, their findings do not necessarily confirm that the increased attitudes of self-efficacy resulted from being more active and participatory. Segal et al. (1993) found "personal empowerment" in consumers of mental health services to be related to quality of life and independent functioning. "Organizational and extra-organizational empowerment" were related to involvement in work, both paid and volunteer. Self-efficacy was the bridging concept between these two dimensions of empowerment.

Although this research is limited, it has been most useful in our efforts to both explain and test empowerment practice. Specific evaluation efforts are described below as part of the practice model.

SOCIAL WORK EMPOWERMENT-ORIENTED PRACTICE MODELS

During the 1990s, the ongoing dialogue between practice and research has led to a comprehensive articulation of empowerment-based practice models. Three such models will be summarized as examples: the models suggested by Cox and Parsons (1994) and Gutiérrez, Parsons, and Cox (1998), by Lee (1994), and by Sadan (1997). From these examples, common principles and strategies will be identified.

The practice model offered by Cox and Parsons (1994) and Gutiérrez et al. (1998) addresses blockages and barriers at three levels (Solomon, 1976). These levels are: personal (feelings, attitudes, perceptions, and beliefs regarding the ability to influence and manage one's social problem situation), interpersonal (experiences with others that facilitate or hinder problem management or resolution), and sociopolitical participation (behavior in relation to societal institutions/organizations that facilitate or hinder individual and group efforts toward meeting needs and social change). Practice strategies are focused on all three levels to facilitate client empowerment. The relationship between worker and client is based on shared power, or "power with" and is participant driven, with the professional becoming a facilitator, partner, or a resource rather than an authority. The relationship is built around consciousness-raising on the part of both worker and client. Roles and responsibilities become mutual and shared. Recognizing that there are many barriers to such a relationship, the authors suggest a dialogue regarding values, roles, each other's strengths, respect for diversity, and exploration of common interests.

Empowerment is a process that involves:

1. A critical review of attitudes and belief about one's self and one's sociopolitical environment
2. The validation of one's experience
3. An increased knowledge and skills for self care, critical thinking, and action
4. Action taking for personal and political change

The practice model is organized around a multidimensional framework with intervention in four dimensions. Dimension 1 consists mainly of interventions with individuals involving assessing needs and resources, both personal and environmental; finding needed resources; and broadening the scope and understanding of the problem into its sociopolitical context. Dimension 2 consists of interventions geared toward acquiring knowledge and skills necessary to address identified problems. The methods here include education in the form of conferences, workshops, small-group formats, mutual aid efforts, newspapers, and other written materials. Ongoing small groups allow the formation of support networks in which individuals can discover the strength of common interests and find validation of their perceptions and experiences. The definition and scope of the problem and its power dynamics continue in this phase, with a key factor being reflection regarding situations that are shared with others. Self-help and mutual aid are key strategies. Dimension 3 consists of interventions focused on change or mediation of the environment. Learning how to access social service, health care, and other resources; how policy-making boards function, and where resource decisions are made are examples of activities that might occur in addressing this dimension. Dimension 4 consists of interventions that involve clients in the broader political aspects of their problems. These include social action and other collective efforts to affect environmental forces that contribute to individual and community problems. The dimensions are nonlinear and are not mutually exclusive. Instead, they are often simultaneous and cyclic. The social worker serves as a catalyst through this process by raising questions about the relationship between various private troubles and related public issues, resource access, and rights and by providing information and resources that assist client groups to act on their own behalf.

Outcomes are expected in three system levels of power: personal, interpersonal, and sociopolitical participation. At the personal level, an increase is expected in self-awareness, self-efficacy, self-esteem, an awareness of having rights, and critical thinking. At the interpersonal level, an increase is expected in knowledge and skills, assertiveness, learning to ask for help, problem solving, and resource access. In sociopolitical participation, expected change is in giving back to others, making a contribution, and taking action on one's behalf and on behalf of others, joining action groups, voting, writing letters, and engaging in other forms of political action.

Lee's (1994) model is quite similar and focuses on the goal of elevating oppression at the personal, interpersonal, and societal levels. Five perspectives, or "a fifocal vision" contribute to her practice framework:

a) historical view of oppression, including the history of social policy related to oppressed groups; b) an ecological view, encompassing knowledge of individual adaptive potentialities and ways people cope and/or power structures and their inequities; c) an ethclass perspective focusing on realities of class structure, racism, ethnocentrism, and classism as well as heterosexism; d) a feminist perspective focusing on the oppression of women, the different voice, the personal as political (and nature of power—e.g., power may be infinite); and e) a critical perspective, the critique and conscious awareness of the above four perspectives. (p. 22)

Lee (1994, p. 8) also suggests eight principles of empowerment-oriented practice:

1. All oppression is destructive of life and should be challenged by social workers.
2. Social workers should maintain holistic vision in situations of oppression (the fifocal vision).
3. People empower themselves: Social workers should assist.
4. People who share common ground need each other to attain power.
5. Social workers should establish an "I and I" relationship with clients.
6. Social workers should encourage the client to say her own words.
7. The worker should maintain a focus on the person as victor and not victim.
8. Social workers should maintain a social change focus.

The method rests on empowerment values and purposes, as well as these principles, and it is used in one-to-one, group, or community relations systems. A collaborative relationship that encompasses mutuality, reciprocity, shared power and shared human struggle is a critical component of empowerment intervention, as is the use of empowerment groups to identify and work on direct and indirect power blocks toward the ends of personal, interpersonal, and political power, as well as collective activity that reflects a raised consciousness regarding oppression.

A Comprehensive Model by Sadan (1997) uses the problem-solving framework to facilitate the empowerment process to create both individual and community empowerment outcomes. The empowerment facilitation process contains developing relationship, focusing on a target group, creating a participatory infrastructure that fits the group, defining practitioners' roles and creating valuable roles for target group participants, developing a strategy of achievement for the identified solution, and evaluating both the outcome and the empowering qualities of the intervention.

Outcomes are sought at both the community and individual level. At the community level, expected outcomes include the discovery of common critical characteristics as a source of support and networking, the creation of togetherness (finding commonality) and self-definition (redefining the personal/social situation), acquisition of new skills for self-advocacy and self-management, resistance to the existing state of solution, creation of an independent or alternative solution, and evaluation of the empowerment process.

Outcomes at the individual level include sharing feelings with others, feeling a part of a group, being committed to the group, developing self-awareness and conscientization or contextual understanding of social and political reality, acquiring new coping skills (gaining self-confidence, exercising influence), mastering sociopolitical skills, performing activist and leadership roles in organizations and communities, and learning self-evaluation and impact assessment.

Common Principles and Components of Empowerment-Oriented Practice

Although empowerment-oriented models have developed from different philosophical and practice perspectives, most share key principles. As suggested by discussion of the three models presented above, basic principles include:

1. A commitment to focus practice on the issues of the most oppressed populations is made.
2. Models foster a belief that personal and group issues must be addressed with understanding of personal and political aspects of their nature. This requires emphasis on a critical review of attitudes and beliefs, which often results in an increased belief in personal and collective rights (Gutiérrez et al., 1998) and renaming and reconstruction of realities (Lee, 1994).
3. Emphasis on a multisystem approach (strategies that target multiple levels, including individual, family, small group, community, organizational, and social/economic/political levels) is integrated into daily practice efforts.
4. Worker-client relationships must be egalitarian in nature, stressing development of a partnership between clients and workers; hence, our emphasis on mutual respect and respect for diversity and strengths. Empowerment implies an integration of methods and strategies from the various social work client system levels.

Several authors have provided intervention examples that demonstrate the way these principles are applied, especially through small-group interventions. Empowerment practice relies heavily on the group work method as a means for validation and strength building, for mutual aid and mutual education, and for action taking. The "collective we" is a central concept in releasing hopelessness to gain a great sense of hopefulness. Critical thinking about the relationship between social problems and the social structure is a major part of the empowerment process, and consciousness-raising is essential to the reconstruction of internalized powerlessness.

As reported elsewhere (Breton, 1994; Cox, 1988), clients who participate in small groups are able to share their common struggles and ways of coping. As they reflect together on problems and challenges, they often begin to engage in a critical analysis of the ways in which their problems (e.g., poverty) are generated by the larger environment.

Women who have experienced poverty often become more aware of the personal and political aspects of their poverty and are able to engage in individual and collective efforts both to resist the internalization of negative self-valuations they have held and to find ways to affect some of the environmental aspects of the problem. The group is the medium for both consciousness-raising and planning and implementing social action.

As emphasized above, empowerment relies on a different kind of relationship between clients and workers than the traditional expertise and authority-based relationship. Through the group medium, the worker is a participant in consciousness-raising processes (learning together) and a participant in social action (struggling with issues of common concern) as well as a group facilitator of initial stages of the group process.

Regardless of the strength generated from commonality among developing models of empowerment practice, further development must meet the challenge of demonstrating the effectiveness of these interventions and their applicability to diverse populations in diverse situations and facilitating opportunities to expand empowerment practice. The following section reviews key issues that have been identified in measurement of empowerment-oriented practice and briefly describes current efforts.

Evaluating Empowerment and "Empowering" Evaluation

The assessment of empowerment process and state(s) is extremely complex. The evaluation of empowerment practice must meet the demands of both potential funders and other decision makers who control resources related to the expansion of empowerment-oriented practice. In keeping with the principles of empowerment, assessment of empowerment must support rather than undermine the empowerment of the participants. An assessment should amplify the expertise of clients and benefit their own problem situation in its context; it should be collaborative and focus on strengths, not deficits (Rapp, Shera, & Kisthardt, 1993; Rappaport, 1990; Whitmore, 1991).

Participatory evaluation research literature provides a conceptual basis for empowerment in practice evaluation. (See Sohng, 1998.) A major goal of participatory evaluation research is to provide participatory roles to those with whom research is conducted (Hall, 1992; Whitmore, 1991). Participation is a key process in facilitating empowerment (Kieffer, 1984), and the key to this process is the extent to which participants are able to exercise power in decision making (Whitmore, 1991, p. 2). Using these important guides to research can enhance the validity of empowerment evaluation and facilitate empowerment in client and consumer groups.

A feminist action research perspective was used in an evaluation of a project targeting low-income women. Observation, fieldnotes, interviews, and taped group meetings were used to create their story. The story was taken back to them for validation. They discussed the story and its relevance for their lives and made modifications where necessary. Finally, they helped tell the story at a national conference. Parsons, East, and Boesen (1994) identified three ways this approach furthers the empowerment process:

1. The research process is not only about the discovery or verification of theoretical concepts; it is also about the development of people. Use of strategies such as oral history and examination of experience lead to components of empowerment such as validation of experience and the development of critical thinking.

2. Participatory Action Research (PAR) uses the experience of the participants to validate and expand their own expertise. This growing knowledge, which comes from within and not from an external authority, leads to information, which leads to power.

3. Because of reciprocity between researchers and participants, the research creates social spaces in which members can make meaningful contributions to their own well-being.

These characteristics have been incorporated into various assessments of empowerment practice principles and expected outcomes. An accumulation of empirical evidence suggests that an empowerment approach to the personal and social dysfunction of people who are mentally ill is promising in terms of such client outcomes as social functioning and quality of life (Hall & Nelson, 1996; Kimboko & Parsons, 1987; Manning, 1994; Paulson, 1991; Rappaport, Reishl, & Zimmerman, 1992; Segal et al., 1993). Qualitative research studies of empowerment-based services to adults with severe and persistent mental illness have identified the experiences of consumers, practice elements that characterize empowerment, outcomes, and

specific structures and processes necessary in an agency setting (Manning & Suire, 1996; Manning, Zibalese-Crawford, & Downey, 1994; Parsons, 1998). Manning (1998) evaluated a program for consumers and family members that was meant to increase empowerment by use of consumer and family-run support groups and centers. Key elements of empowerment in consumer-driven programs were identified as maintaining an environment that provides (a) acceptance regardless of level of functioning, (b) an individualized system of care, (c) activities based on need, not structure or rules, (d) a safe and stigma-free setting for discussion, and (e) responsiveness and respect. Consumers said these characteristics facilitated their empowerment by providing the opportunity to grow, make mistakes, and learn from the mistakes; and a place to help them transition to the larger community.

Parsons (1998) used group interviews and individual qualitative interviews to identify program processes, client change processes, and client outcomes in five programs. These qualitative interviews gave clients and staff an opportunity to voice their understandings of empowerment, their interactive experiences in these programs, descriptions of how change occurs in clients who are involved in these experiences, and perceived outcomes for clients. Data from clients and staff were combined to form a profile of practice principles in the programs and change outcomes in clients. The categorical themes were used to conceptualize outcome surveys for both practice principles and client outcomes. After extensive piloting of these instruments, along with validation through focus group data of their use for mental health consumers, an empowerment outcome assessment survey and an empowerment practice principles survey with 95 consumers of mental health services was tested. The principles survey was intended to assess whether helping strategies carried out by social workers contain empowerment principles, as identified by clients of social work services. The scale was built on four subscales derived from the themes and categories of the qualitative research cited above. These subscales included a cohesive collective for work, collaborative relationships between professionals and clients, strength-based assessment, and an educational focus. The correlation relationships among the four subscales of the survey were strong but not so strong that each measured the same domain, and they provided strong support for the validity of the scale as a whole.

The empowerment outcome assessment contained three dimensions (subscales) reported earlier—personal, interpersonal, and sociopolitical— that are found in other similar research (Bolton & Brookings, 1996; Chamberlin, 1997; Cox & Parsons, 1994; Zimmerman, 1995). Items for this survey instrument were selected from Torre's (1985) personal empowerment scale; Paulson's (1991) client empowerment scale, which he developed with consumers of mental health; and Segal's (Segal et al., 1993) organizational empowerment scale and extra-organizational empowerment scale. These three subscales were combined into a 40-item, single survey instrument and assigned a common Likert-type response set. The correlation between the subscales was tested by the use of a Pearson r and ranged from .21 (personal and political) to .54 (sociopolitical and interpersonal). The strengths of the correlations among the three subscales suggest that these three domains of empowerment are different from one another but are correlated sufficiently to be considered a single construct.

In sum, empowerment-oriented social workers are finding forms of program evaluation that are responsive to the values of empowerment practice, including participation, partnership in client-worker relationship, responsiveness to diversity, and, at the same time, responsiveness to potential funding sources, private and public. The above examples of work indicate the powerful potential of research as a tool for empowerment as well as for program development guidance. (For more examples, see Fleming & Ward, 1997; Sohng, 1998.)

Future Potential of Empowerment Oriented-Models

Empowerment-oriented practice has much to offer as an approach to addressing problems of individuals and communities. Increasing gaps in resources between the wealthy and the poor, internationalization of the economy, increased diversity in population, and other factors causing rapid environmental change set a context in which oppressed populations face obvious need to struggle for policies that force social justice and strengthen communities (Davey, 1995; Karger & Stoesz, 1998). Five characteristics of empowerment practice that are especially suited to these issues are (a) the strong orientation toward social justice issues that provides the base for empowerment practice, (b) commitment to oppressed populations, (c) strong support of multiculturalism as part of a strengths perspective, (d) emphasis on the use of collectivity and community development, and (e) the potential of empowerment-practice activities to support new social movements that share similar values. Success of the overall goal of empowerment to engage individuals and groups in an empowerment process that builds on strengths, increases knowledge and skills, and promotes social action continues to be a critical need of oppressed communities.

Empowerment-oriented practice also has strong potential to affect client needs in the areas of aging, mental health, and physical disability. As noted in the section on program evaluation, current research efforts are in progress to establish a strong linkage between empowerment practice and improved mental health. Linkages to physical health and increased sense of self-efficacy and knowledge and skills that enable self-care are also being affirmed (Ewart, 1995; Prohaska, 1998; Rakowski, 1998). The last area of potential that comes from the basic characteristics of empowerment practice is for increased integration and or collaboration in three arenas: (a) multidisciplinary collaboration, (b) partnership between professional social work practice and client constituencies, and (c) integration of social work practice methods.

Multidisciplinary connections are strongly reinforced by the shared theoretical approaches noted above in areas of self-sufficiency, self-care, self-efficacy, and empowerment. Not only psychology, medicine and other health sciences, and social work but education, applied sociology, gerontology, and many related fields share these constructs and related approaches.

Empowerment-oriented practice models require that social workers simultaneously address individual counseling, crisis management, resource development, and other issues while engaging with clients in social action and self-help activities. Consequently, the barriers between direct and indirect practice interventions must be overcome. Practitioners must have skills in all areas or strong partnerships with other practitioners with different skills.

Perhaps the most important potential for empowerment practice is its potential to forge stronger partnerships between the social work profession and client constituencies. When partnership relationships are achieved, clients identify common interests with professional social workers, especially in social justice-related areas such as health care and more equitable income distribution. Empowerment practice models encourage working together for solutions to these common problems.

Challenges in the Coming Decades

Empowerment practice advocates are faced with the dual task of (a) developing and refining practice strategies, including measurement and (b) expanding the use of empowerment practice by social workers with diverse populations and in many settings. Resources for both development and implementation of empowerment-oriented practice are scarce. In the late 1990s, traditional social service agencies and programs were experiencing tremendous upheaval due to large governmental cuts in funding, increased for-profit competition, increasing caseloads, increased demands for outcome measurement, lack of resources for staff training, and related cost-cutting efforts. These changes are situated in a conservative political environment that fosters blaming those in need for their circumstances and promoting interventions that are individualized and isolating in nature (Cox & Joseph, 1998; Fabricant & Burghardt, 1992; Riffe & Kondrat, 1997).

Specific challenges to expansion of empowerment practice have been identified by several observers (Cox & Joseph, 1998; Gutiérrez,

Glenmaye, & DeLois, 1994; Shera, 1995). Gutiérrez et al. identified the following barriers from the perspective of agencies that were attempting to incorporate empowerment practice into their programs:

- Funding issues, particularly the resistance of funding sources who are concerned about the longer times required to document results in empowerment-oriented approaches
- A social environment that involves political and philosophical differences with other agencies and agency competitors
- Interpersonal issues related to client-worker relationships and characteristics of clients or workers that seem to interfere with empowerment practice
- Conflict between empowerment goals and methods with other modes of practice that dominate social work practice and are reflected in various state licensure laws that severely limit the nature of client worker relationships, for example prohibit providing transportation to clients, informal meetings, and so on
- Conflict between empowerment-oriented practice approaches and generally accepted practice approaches that dominate school of social work curricula, for example, the informal nature of client-worker relationships and the strong relationship of empowerment practice activity to sociopolitical movements

Overcoming these obstacles will require strong political advocacy, including ongoing work at several levels. Empowerment practice by its very nature will lead to power struggles with oppressed populations for increased resources and other forms of social justice. Positive outcomes from the programs' perspective may be met with strong political resistance. Other outcomes, such as increased capacity for self-care among people with disabilities, may,

on the other hand, be well-received in the current political milieu. Varying definitions of professionalism may lead to challenges of the perceptions of practitioners who believe that models of intervention must be based on hierarchical client/worker relationships and who do not subscribe to the idea that personal and political aspects of problems are interrelated and approachable simultaneously. Advocates of empowerment practice will be required to lobby both schools of social work and service delivery networks, such as the aging network, mental health networks, and public welfare and private voluntary agencies to provide training for social workers in empowerment practice. The clients of empowerment practice will need to be engaged in the support of these interventions if we are to more fully broaden the base of practice. In sum, empowerment-oriented practice has much to offer society if its advocates are able to mobilize the necessary resources during the years to come.

REFERENCES

Antonucci, T. C., & Hiroko, A. (1997). Social support and the maintenance of competence. In S. L. Willis, K. Schaie, & M. Hayward (Eds.), *Societal mechanisms for maintaining competence in old age.* New York: Springer.

Axinn, J., & Levin H. (1997). *Social welfare: A history of the American response to need.* White Plains, NY: Longman.

Bandura, A. (Ed.). (1995). *Self-efficacy in changing societies.* New York: Cambridge University Press.

Bolton, B., & Brookings, J. (1996). Development of a multifaceted definition of empowerment. *Rehabilitation Counseling Bulletin, 39*(4), 256-264.

Breton, M. (1994). On the meaning of empowerment and empowerment-oriented social work practice. *Social Work with Groups, 17*(3), 23-37.

Brinker-Jenkins, M. (1991). The propositions and assumptions of feminist social work practice. In M. B. Brinker-Jenkins, N. R. Hooyman, & N. Gottlieb (Eds.), *Feminist social work practice in clinical settings* (pp. 271-304). Newbury Park, CA: Sage.

Brinker-Jenkins, M., & Joseph, B. (1980, September). *Social control and social change: Toward a feminist model of social work practice*. Paper presented at the National Association of Social Workers Conference on Social Work Practice in a Sexist Society, Washington, DC.

Brown, P. (1974). *Toward a Marxist psychology*. New York: Harper & Row.

Carroll, D. (1995, January/February). The importance of self-efficacy expectations in elderly patients recovering form coronary artery bypass surgery. *Heart and Lung, 24,* 50-59.

Carstensen, L., & Frieder, R. (1997). Commentary: Social relationships in context and as context: Social support and the maintenance of competence in old age. In S. L. Willis, K. Schaie, & M. Hayward (Eds.), *Societal mechanisms for maintaining competence in old age*. New York: Springer.

Chamberlin, J. (1997). A working definition of empowerment. *Psychiatric Rehabilitation Journal, 20*(4), 43-46.

Chodorow, N. (1989). *Feminism and psychoanalytical theory*. New Haven, CT: Yale University Press.

Council on Social Work Education. (1997). *Handbook of accreditation standards and procedures* (Curriculum policy statement for master's degree programs in social work education). Alexandria, VA: Author.

Cox, E. (1988). Empowerment of low-income elderly through group work. *Social Work with Groups, 39*(3), 262-268.

Cox, E., & Joseph, B. (1998). In L. Gutiérrez, R. Parsons, & E. Cox (Eds.), *Empowerment in social work practice: A sourcebook*. Pacific Grove, CA: Brooks/Cole.

Cox, E., & Parsons, R. J. (1994). *Empowerment-oriented social work practice with the elderly*. Pacific Grove, CA: Brooks/Cole.

Davey, J. D. (1995). *The new social contract*. Westport, CT: Praeger.

Day, P. J. (1997). *A new history of social welfare* (2nd ed.). Boston: Allyn & Bacon.

Dunst, C. J., Trivette, C., & Deal, A. (1988). *Enabling and empowering families*. Cambridge, MA: Brookline Books.

East, J. (1998). In-dependence: A feminist postmodern deconstruction. *Affilia, 16*(3), 273-288.

Ewart, C. K. (1995). Self-efficacy and recovery from heart attack: Implications for a social cognitive analysis of exercise and emotion. In J. E. Maddux (Ed.), *Self efficacy, adaptation, and adjustment: Theory, research, and application* (pp. 203-226). New York: Plenum.

Fabricant, M. B., & Burghardt, S. (1992). *The welfare state crisis and the transformation of social service work*. Armonk, NY: M. E. Sharpe.

Feagin, J. R. (1989). *Racial and ethnic relations* (3rd ed.). Englewood Cliffs, NJ: Prentice Hall.

Fisher, J. (1980). *The response of social work to the Depression*. Cambridge, MA: Schenkman.

Fleming, J., & Ward, D. (1997, September 25-26). *Research as empowerment: The social action approach*. Paper presented to Conference on Empowerment Practice in Social Work, Faculty of Social Work, University of Toronto.

Freire, P. (1970). *Pedagogy of the oppressed*. New York: Seabury.

Freire, P. (1973). *Education for critical consciousness*. New York: Seabury.

Galper, J. (1980). *Social work practice: A radical perspective*. Englewood Cliffs, NJ: Prentice Hall.

Gutiérrez, L. M. (1990). Working with women of color: An empowerment perspective. *Social Work, 35*(2), 149-153.

Gutiérrez, L. M., DeLois, K. A., & GlenMaye, L. (1994). Understanding empowerment based practice: Building on practitioner based knowledge. *Families in Society, 76*(9), 534-542.

Gutiérrez, L. M., Glenmaye, W., & DeLois, K. (1995). The organizational context of empowerment practice: Implications for social work administration. *Social Work, 40,* 249-258.

Gutiérrez, L. M., Parsons, R. J., & Cox, E. O. (1998). *Empowerment in social work practice: A sourcebook*. Pacific Grove, CA: Brooks/Cole.

Hall, B. L. (1992, Winter). From margins to center? The development and purpose of participatory research. *The American Sociologist, 23*(4), 15-28.

Hall, B. L., & Nelson, G. (1996). Social networks, social support, personal empowerment, and the adaptation of psychiatric consumers/survivors: Path analytic models. *Social Science and Medicine, 43*(12), 1743-1754.

Hanisch, C. (1971). The personal as political. In J. Agel (Ed.), *The radical therapist*. New York: Ballantine.

Ingleby, D. (Ed.). (1980). *Critical psychiatry*. New York: Pantheon.

Karger, H. J., & Stoesz, D. (1998). *American social welfare policy: A pluralist approach* (3rd ed.). New York: Longman.

Kieffer, C. (1981). *The emergence of empowerment: The development of participatory competence among individuals and organizations*. Unpublished doctoral dissertation, University of Michigan.

Kieffer, C. (1984, Winter/Spring). Citizen participation: A developmental perspective. *Prevention in Human Services, 3,* 9-36.

Kimboko P., & Parsons R. J. (1987). *Elder empowerment project final report.* Denver: Colorado Division of Mental Health.

Lee, J. (1994). *The empowerment approach to social work practice.* New York: Columbia University Press.

Longres, J. F., & McCloud, E. (1980). Consciousness raising and social work practice. *Social Casework, 61*(5), 267-276.

Maddux, J. E. (Ed.). (1995). *Self-efficacy, adaptation, and adjustment: Theory, research, and application.* New York: Plenum.

Maddux, J. E., Brawley, L., & Boykin, A. (1995). Self-efficacy and healthy behavior: Prevention, promotion, and detection. In J. E. Maddux (Ed.), *Self-efficacy, adaption, and adjustment: Theory, research, and application* (pp. 173-202). New York: Plenum.

Maier, S. F., & Seligman, M. E. (1976). Learned helplessness: Theory and evidence. *Journal of Experimental Psychology, 105*(1), 3-46.

Maluccio, A. N. (Ed.). (1981). *Promoting competence in clients: A new/old approach to social work practice.* New York: Free Press.

Manning, S. S. (1994). *Colorado mental health consumer and family development project: Program evaluation report.* Denver: Colorado Division of Mental Health.

Manning, S. S. (1998). Empowerment in mental health programs: Listening to the voices, In L. M. Gutiérrez, R. J. Parsons, & E. O. Cox (Eds.), *Empowerment in social work practice: A sourcebook.* Pacific Grove, CA: Brooks/Cole.

Manning, S. S., & Suire, B. (1996). Bridges and road blocks: Consumers as employees in mental health. *Psychiatric Services, 47*(9), 939-943.

Manning, S. S., Zibalese-Crawford, M., & Downey, E. (1994). *Colorado mental health consumer and family development project, program evaluation report.* Denver, CO: University of Denver.

Marcuse, H. (1964). *One dimensional man.* New York: Vintage.

McIntosh M. (1996). Feminism and social policy. In D. Taylor (Ed.), *Critical social policy: A reader* (pp. 13-26). London: Sage.

Miley, K., O'Melia, M., & DuBois, B. (1998). *Generalist social work practice: An empowering approach* (2nd ed.). Boston: Allyn & Bacon.

Mondros, J. B., & Wilson, S. M. (1994). *Organizing for power and empowerment.* New York: Columbia University Press.

Moreau, M. (1979). A structural approach to social work practice. *Canadian Journal of Social Work Education, 5*(1), 78-94.

National Association of Social Workers. (1998, April 4). *NASW code of ethics: Ethical standards* [On-line]. Available: *http://www.naswdc.org/Code/CDSTAN1.HTM*

Ory, M., & DeFriese, G. H. (Eds.). (1998). *Self-care in later life: Research, program, and policy issues.* New York: Springer.

Parsons, R. J. (1998). Evaluation of empowerment practice. In L. M. Gutiérrez, R. J. Parsons, & E. O. Cox (Eds.), *Empowerment in social work practice: A sourcebook.* Pacific Grove, CA: Brooks/Cole.

Parsons, R. J., East, J. F., & Boesen, M. B. (1994). Empowerment: A case study with AFDC women. In L. M. Gutiérrez & P. Nurius (Eds.), *Education and research for empowerment practice.* Seattle: University of Washington, Center for Policy and Practice Research.

Parsons, R. J., Jorgensen, J. D., & Hernandez, S. H. (1994). *The integration of social work practice.* Pacific Grove, CA: Brooks/Cole.

Paulson, R. (1991). Professional training for consumers and family members: One's road to empowerment. *Psychosocial Rehabilitation Journal, 14*(3), 69-80.

Payne, M. (1997). *Modern social work theory* (2nd ed.). Chicago: Lyceum.

Piven, F. F., & Cloward, R. A. (1975). Notes toward a radical social work. In R. Bailey & M. Brake (Eds.), *Radical social work.* New York: Pantheon.

Prohaska, T. (1998). The research basis for the design and implementation of self-care programs. In R. S. Schweiker (Ed.), *Self-care in later life* (pp. 62-84). New York: Springer.

Punamaki, R., & Aschan, H. (1994). Self-care and mastery among primary health care patients. *Social Science Medical, 39*(5), 733-741.

Rakowski, W. (1998). Evaluating psychosocial interventions for promoting self-care behaviors among older adults. In M. Ory & G. H. DeFriese (Eds.), *Self-care in later life: Research, program, and policy issues.* New York: Springer.

Rapp, C. A., Shera, W., & Kisthardt, W. (1993). Research strategies for consumer empowerment of people with severe mental illness. *Social Work, 38*(6), 727-735.

Rappaport, J. (1981). In praise of paradox: A social policy of empowerment over prevention. *American Journal of Community Psychology, 9*(1), 1-25.

Rappaport, J. (1990). Research methods and the empowerment social agenda. In P. Tolan, C. Keys, F. Chertok, & L. Jason (Eds.), *Researching community psychology.* Washington, DC: American Psychological Association.

Rappaport, J., Reishl, T. M., & Zimmerman, M. A. (1992). Mutual help mechanisms in the empowerment of former mental patients. In D. Saleeby (Ed.), *The strengths perspective in social work practice* (pp. 87-97). New York: Longman.

Riffe, H. A., & Kondrat, M. E. (1997). Social worker alienation and disempowerment in a managed care setting. *Journal of Progressive Human Services, 8*(1), 41-55.

Rogers, E. S., Chamberlin, J., Ellison, M. L., & Crean, T. (1997). A consumer-constructed scale to measure empowerment among users of mental health services. *Psychiatric Services, 48*(8), 1042-1047.

Rojek, C. (1986). The "Subject" in social work. *British Journal of Social Work, 16*(1), 65-77.

Sadan, I. (1997, September 24-26). *Empowerment in social work: A comprehensive model*. Paper presented at Challenges of Conducting Research on Empowerment Practice, Faculty of Social Work, University of Toronto.

Saleeby, D. (Ed.). (1992). *The strengths perspective in social work practice*. New York: Longman.

Sands, R., & Nuccio, K. (1992). Postmodern feminist theory and social work. *Social Work, 37*(2), 489-494.

Schwarzer, R., & Fuchs, R. (1995). Changing risk behaviors and adopting health behaviors: The role of self-efficacy beliefs. In A. Bandura (Ed.), *Self-efficacy in a changing society* (pp. 259-288). New York: Cambridge University Press.

Seeman, M. (1959). On the meaning of alienation. *American Sociological Review, 24*(1), 783-791.

Seeman, M. (1967). Powerlessness and knowledge: A comparative study of alienation and learning. *Sociometry, 30*(2), 105-123.

Segal, S. P., Silverman, C., & Temkin, T. (1993). Empowerment and self-help agency practice for people with mental disabilities. *Social Work, 38*(6), 705-712.

Segall, A., & Goldstein, J. (1989). Exploring the correlates of self-provided health care behavior. *Social Science and Medicine, 29*(2), 153-161.

Seligman, M. (1995). *Helplessness*. Thousand Oaks, CA: Sage.

Shera, W. (1995). Empowerment for organizations. *Administration in Social Work, 19*(4), 1-15.

Sherman, H. J. (1987). *Foundations of radical political economy*. London: M. E. Sharpe.

Simon, B. (1994). *The empowerment tradition in American social work*. New York: Columbia University Press.

Sohng, L. (1998). Research as an empowerment strategy. In L. M. Gutiérrez, R. J. Parsons, & E. O. Cox (Eds.), *Empowerment in social work practice: A sourcebook*. Pacific Grove, CA: Brooks/Cole.

Solomon, B. B. (1976). *Black empowerment: Social work in oppressed communities*. New York: Columbia University Press.

Solomon, B. B. (1985). Community social work practice in oppressed minority communities. In S. H. Taylor & R. W. Roberts (Eds.), *Theory and practice of community social work* (pp. 217-257). New York: Columbia University Press.

Spitzer, A., Yoram, B., & Ziv, L. (1996). The moderating effect of age of self-care. *Western Journal of Nursing Research, 8*(2), 137-148.

Steiner, C. M. (1971). Radical psychiatry: Principles. In J. Agel (Ed.), *The radical therapist*. New York: Ballantine.

Torre, D. (1985). *Empowerment: Structured conceptualization and instrument development*. Unpublished doctoral dissertation, Cornell University, New York.

Whitmore, E. (1991). Evaluation and empowerment: It's the process that counts. *Networking Bulletin, 2*(2), 1-7.

Zimmerman, M. (1995). Psychological empowerment: Issues and illustrations. *American Journal of Community Psychology, 23*(5), 581-599.

Zimmerman, M. A.(1990). Toward a theory of learned hopefulness: A structural model analysis of participation and empowerment. *Journal of Research in Personality, 24*, 71-86.

Zimmerman, M. A., Israel, B. A., Schult, A., & Checkoway, B. (1992). Further explorations in empowerment theory: An empirical analysis of psychological empowerment. *American Journal of Community Psychology, 20*(6), 707-727.

Zimmerman, M. A., & Rappaport, J. (1988). Citizen participation, perceived control, and psychological empowerment. *American Journal of Community Psychology, 16*(5), 725-750.

CHAPTER SEVEN

Multicultural Perspectives on Direct Practice in Social Work

MICHAEL SPENCER

EDITH LEWIS

LORRAINE GUTIÉRREZ

Within the past 30 years a paradigm shift has occurred in most models of direct practice in social work. This shift has moved from a view that encourages practice that is culture-free and universal to one that seriously considers the role that gender, culture, sexual orientation, race, and other social identities play in the experiences, problems, and solutions of the communities with which we work. These changes and developments in practice reflect conflicts that have occurred within our field regarding the kind of work we do and the increasing visibility of people of color, gays and lesbians, and people with disabilities as leaders in our profession. Although a paradigm shift has occurred, there is no consistent view of how social workers should integrate a multicultural view into their practice.

In this chapter, we address the waves of interest in the topic of multiculturalism in social work and its current iterations and operational definitions for social work practice. We use historical, social, and political lenses to examine the development of multiple definitions of multiculturalism, the social science research using the term, and the implications for social work practice. We also propose a definition of multiculturalism that we think is useful in the development of our knowledge base on this construct.

DEVELOPING A MULTICULTURAL PERSPECTIVE ON PRACTICE

The term *multicultural* has been used as a noun, adjective, and verb for over 30 years in social science discourses. During those decades, it has been clear that the operational definitions and their resultant methodologies and outcomes have been inconsistent. How do we deconstruct multiculturalism so that it has utility for social work practice education in this new millennium? What is the status of multiculturalism in social science research? Can evidence-based criteria for multiculturalism be developed and consistently used in social work so that the body of knowledge on this construct can grow? What are social work practitioners and faculty to do with the literature on multiculturalism in the interim?

Multiculturalism as meta-theory. When one looks back at well-developed bodies of knowledge in the social sciences, one can trace the literature on the meta-theories and subtheories to a time when these bodies of knowledge were simply untested conceptualizations. One example is life-span or developmental theories of the family. The constructs related to the life-span were first conceptualized primarily through descriptive methods, tied together by the early theorists, then taught to students at institutions of higher education, and eventually, they became part of the practice knowledge of "family therapy" practitioners. Other scholars began to empirically test the theories using qualitative and quantitative studies. By the early 1980s, one of the benchmarks of a fine family theory was whether or not it had one or many corresponding scales measuring its major constructs. The validity and reliability of these scales were

determined through statistical tests. Later, single-scale validation alone was insufficient—theories were supported through meta-analyses of empirical studies, often more likely to be quantitative than qualitative, to support or refute the conceptual frameworks.

Studies advanced developmental/life-span theory by creating subtheories or linking the basic constructs of the developmental method with other established or recognized conceptual frameworks. Other process-stage approaches, such as those of Erickson and Piaget, were identified as apparent support for the concept that certain developmental processes are required during particular life stages for the overall well-being of individuals or families.

While larger studies of these theories and subtheories were being conducted, many students whose professional work focused on providing service were still using the earlier and not necessarily empirically supported conceptual frameworks in their practice. Ideas stemming from the life-span or developmental framework were included in programmatic and policy recommendations made to social welfare institutions at the state and federal levels. For example, this area of research has influenced discussions about the work requirement in the Personal Responsibility Act. In this example, practice strategies implementing the conceptual frameworks occur simultaneously with their debate, testing, and reconceptualization.

We posit that the conceptual framework(s) of multiculturalism has followed the same path as that of developmental theory, but the consequences have not been the same. As was the case with life-span theory, much of the early multicultural work has been descriptive in nature. Only during the last 20 years has any consistent codification taken place, and then, only on subtheories within the meta-theory of multiculturalism, not on its entirety. However, it would appear that multicultural theory is more susceptible to critique and dismissal than life-span developmental theory was at this same point.

Van Soest (1995) posits that the multicultural discussion has been so polarized in education and in the general society that only debate between neo-conservatives and liberals has been possible. This debate has, more important, been completely stifled in social work, due in part to the Council on Social Work Education (CSWE) Curriculum Policy Statement, which requires all social work programs to give primacy to multicultural issues, and to a passivity on the part of dissenters (and even proponents) in the field. In some respects, this non-debate has prevented the full articulation of multicultural perspectives in social work.

Another issue influencing the integration of multiculturalism in empirical study is the different uses of the term in different disciplines. Unlike many discipline-specific conceptual frameworks, multiculturalism as a construct, theory, or meta-theory has been included in the humanities and physical sciences as well as the social sciences. The operational definitions of the term have not been consistent, making comparisons even of empirical findings difficult.

An example of how multiculturalism is ill defined is in the conceptualization of multicultural education in schools. The goals of multicultural education are to foster a sense of understanding and respect for differences, to overcome prejudice and discrimination, to provide an understanding of the dynamics of racism, to replace historical and cultural misnomers with accurate information, and to ensure that all students receive equitable benefits from the education system (Drum & Howard, 1989). In prac-

tice, the term *multiculturalism* is used to describe a wide variety of school practices, policies, and programs designed to increase cultural awareness. For example, in a study of the use of multicultural education in schools, it was found that teachers included lessons on cultures such as the Greeks and Vikings as part of their multicultural efforts (Morelli & Spencer, in press; Spencer, 1998). Banks (1984) provides an explanation for the incongruence between the goals of multicultural education and its practice. He states that when educational innovations arise, disparate programs and practices often emerge and claim the new title. Perhaps, multicultural social work practice has fallen victim to a similar fate, as programs and providers strive to meet new pressures and mandates that require greater sensitivity to diverse populations.

The development of multicultural theory in social work. In previous work, we have identified one model for understanding the development of multicultural social work practice (Gutiérrez & Lewis, 1999). That model looked historically at large trends in practice that moved from a more individually focused perspective that was ethnocentric to a more contextualized practice leading to the development of culturally competent practice (Green, 1995; Gutiérrez & Nagda, 1996; Iglehart & Becerra, 1995; Lum, 2000). This movement and change has been due to dialogue, debate, and difference within our profession, between our profession and allied fields, and between our profession and the communities it services. The more contextualized view of the development of multicultural theories, which we discuss here, recognizes that different constructs were added to the theory base between the

1960s and 1990s as a result of the waves of deconstruction, debate, and empirical analysis. These waves correspond to movements within professional social work organizations as well.

Before the waves of change. How has our profession traditionally dealt with racial and ethnic diversity? (See Table 7.1.) The roots of social work practice reflect a monocultural or ethnocentric perspective that considers, either explicitly or implicitly, the norms, values, and needs of the majority culture to be the most desirable (Chau, 1991; Gallegos, 1982; Morales, 1981). This perspective places little or no value on the unique experiences of people of color and may approach their cultures as the source of many of the problems they face.

The ethnocentric perspective has been the dominant orientation of social services. It was reflected in the development of the social services by predominantly upper-class men and women, who created programs that often reflected classist, racist, and nativist social mores (Iglehart & Becerra, 1995; Wenocur & Reisch, 1989). In response, immigrant, Native American, and African American communities developed their own systems of self-help and mutual aid (Iglehart & Becerra, 1995; Mankiller, 1993; Wenocur & Reisch, 1989)

Ethnocentrism has manifested itself in social service organizations as the provision of segregated services (Stehno, 1982), in the deportation of "aliens" (Guerin-Gonzales, 1994), or in "Americanization" programs that resulted in the loss of culture and community (Carpenter, 1980). The presence of some ethnic groups, such has Asian Americans, has been ignored by service planners and providers (Lee, 1986). Some ethnic groups and their needs have been overlooked based on the notion that they "take

care of their own" or may not respond well to the treatments offered at agencies (Land, Nishimoto, & Chau, 1988; Lee, 1986; Starret, Mindel, & Wright, 1983). In its more subtle form, ethnocentrism has led to stereotyping of clients tracking or differential treatment within the human services (Gutiérrez, 1992). Rather than looking at ways in which existing agency procedures, structures, or treatments can be altered to better respond to the needs of ethnic minorities, the ethnocentric approach assumes that the "problem" in accessing and using services exists in the client group and that it is their responsibility to change.

First wave—race and ethnicity. The first wave, ending in the early 1970s, focused on issues of race and ethnicity as the primary constructs in understanding multiculturalism. Anthropologists, social workers, and psychologists studied the impact of constructs such as assimilation and acculturation on the lives and well-being of "minorities" in the United States (Anderson & Hill-Collins, 1992; Keanau, Green, & Valencia-Weber, 1982). Debate on the benefits and consequences of using "colonizer" and/or umbrella terms such as *minorities, Chicanos,* or *Native Americans* to describe populations of color in the United States appeared in much of the early social work scholarship during this period (Asamoaoh, Garcia, Hendricks, & Walker, 1991). Two other events also characterized the period. First, the CSWE, after several years of discussion, began to require that all accredited social work programs include information about minorities in their curriculum. Second, when conference delegates and other social workers could not come to some resolution of conflict about the issue of transracial adoption and the ability of African American communi-

TABLE 7.1 Waves of Addressing Multiculturalism in Social Work Practice

Wave/Date (Approximate)	Topics Included	Major Constructs Addressed	Practice Models	Implications for the Social Work Profession	Implications for Social Work Education and Research
Pre Waves: Pre 1965	Ethnocentrism	None	Established practice models	No attention to social group memberships; only people of color have race or ethnicity	Research methods are "color blind"
Wave 1: 1965-1974	Race, ethnicity	Assimilation, acculturation, emphasis on race and ethnic justice, identity	Ethnic sensitive practice	Emergence of the National Association of Black Social Workers; dichotomous "black/white" perspectives; only people of color should work with other people of color	Use of back-translation methods; curricular attention to populations of color mandated via standards of the Council on Social Work Education (CSWE)
Wave 2: 1975-1984	Race, ethnicity, gender	Social justice, social change, race/class confounded	Emergence of feminist practice methods	Trabajadores de la Raza, organization; recognition of changing demographics	Curricular attention to women mandated via CSWE standards; Commissions on Women, People of Color established
Wave 3: 1985-1995	Race, ethnicity, gender, sexual orientation	Multiple social group memberships; each addressed independently, target/agent groups, praxis	Culturally competent practice	Expansion of workshops, literature on social work practice with specific target populations	CSWE Commission on Gay, Lesbian, Bisexual, Transgender Issues established; culturally competent practice literature expands
Wave 4: 1995-??	Race, gender, ethnicity, sexual orientation, physical/mental ability, class	Intersectionality, pluralism, allocation of resources, power	Ethnoconscious practice	Focus on larger system interventions with individuals, families, and groups; community-and social systems-oriented practice; empowerment methods	See Table 7.2 for Multicultural Practice Principles

ties to determine the best interests of their children, a group of African American social workers walked out of a National Association of Social Workers conference and established what is now known internationally as the National Association of Black Social Workers.

Organizing within communities of color led to the development of ethnic sensitive and culturally competent approaches to social service organizations and programs (Chau, 1991; Devore & Schlesinger, 1987; Gallegos, 1982; Scott & Delgado, 1979). The goal of the ethnic sensitive or ethnic competent approach is to create or re-create programs and organizations that will be more responsive and responsible to the cultures of people of color. Training for cultural competence and the delivery of ethnic sensitive services requires understanding one's own personal attributes and values, gaining knowledge about the culture of different groups, and developing skills for cross-cultural work (Chau, 1991; Gallegos, 1982). It is based on the notion that the nature of our society is multicultural and that positive gains can result from learning about different cultural groups and incorporating culture into agency procedures, structures, and services (Comas-Díaz & Griffith, 1988; Devore & Schlesinger, 1987; Gallegos, 1982).

One of the limitations of early work during this first wave was that it mirrored the dichotomous perspective of the United States. Moving with the U.S. Census categories from "White and Non-White" to "White and Black" or "White and Minority," an emphasis was often placed on interactions between those of European and African descent, with an absence of focus on individuals and families whose origins were in other parts of the world (Jackson, Tucker, & Bowman, 1982; Orlandi, 1992).

Remnants of this dichotomy remain in current research, making it difficult to distinguish the parameters of the sample under study and its generalizability to the realities of U.S. demographics (Marger, 1997).

Second wave—race, ethnicity, and gender. The second wave spanned the period between the mid-late 1970s and the mid 1980s. In addition to race and ethnicity, gender emerged as a social group membership for examination and intervention (Bricker-Jenkins & Hooyman, 1986). CSWE commissions were established on issues related to race/ethnicity and gender. Distinctions between race and ethnicity became more common during this period, but much of the research of the period confounded race and class, leading to several debates in the literature about the homogeneity of racial groups in the United States (Jackson et al., 1982). Other ethnic groups of color founded social work practitioner interest groups, such as Trajabadores de la Raza, during this period as well. Given the projections about the changing demographics of the country, interest heightened about ethnicity. Work during the period also began to highlight the ethnicity of European descendants, and everyone was recognized as having an ethnic background (McGoldrick, Giordano, & Pierce, 1996). Women's movements in the United States also focused attention on issues of gender. A body of conceptual literature on feminism began to find publishers, and methods for feminist practice were included in this category (Bricker-Jenkins, Hooyman, & Gottlieb, 1991; Figuiera-McDonough, Netting, & Nichols-Casebolt, 1998).

Third wave—race, ethnicity, gender, and sexual orientation. During the years between the mid-1980s and mid 1990s, a third wave of multiculturalism emerged in the social work profession and in social work education and research circles. A further expansion of CSWE commissions occurred, which included attention to sexual orientation. Differences developed between those who believed that sexual orientation was restricted to content and those who believed the issue of sexual orientation was a policy issue in practice, research, and education (Greene, 1993; Lorde, 1984). The reactance to the inclusion of sexual orientation as part of the list of mandated curricular areas in social work continues today.

Another shift in practice models occurred during this period, from ethnic sensitive practice to culturally competent practice (Castex, 1993; Chau, 1990; Lum, 1996). Partially to accommodate the recognition of multiple group statuses that went beyond race, ethnicity, and gender, the conceptual construct of multiple social group membership began to emerge in the field. Recognition of "target-agent" statuses instead of majority/minority statuses allowed for the discussion of the separate impact of exclusion, oppression, and discrimination (Iglehart & Becerra, 1995; Tatum, 1997). Although multiple social group memberships were recognized, their interactions were not measured or addressed in most of the research (Orlandi, 1992). One interesting outcome of this omission was that women of color felt excluded in two categories rather than one (Baines, 1997; Boyd-Franklin, 1987; Figuiera-McDonough et al., 1998; Gutiérrez & Lewis, 1994). Their experiences were different from the white women developing feminist practice and theory; the issues raised about women usually meant about white women. Their experiences also differed from the experiences of men of color. A need for a more integrative set of methods was evident (Baca Zinn, 1994; Pyant & Carlson, 1991).

Although the development of the ethnic sensitive approach to social services has led to changes in the training and thinking of individual service providers and the creation of new programs, this was not an adequate response to challenges related to the low status and power of people of color. These methods were limited by their focus on individual change and cultural factors. They ignored the role of power in the social order and social work practice (McMahon & Allen-Meares, 1992), were more concerned with individual change at the expense of maintaining an institutional status quo (McMahon & Allen-Meares, 1992), equated ethnicity and culture with the danger of stereotyping and typifying clients (Green, 1995; Jayasuriya, 1992; Longres, 1991), were more suited for working with refugees than with ethnic minorities who have been in the United States for more generations (Longres, 1991), and lacked a social development agenda (Midgley, 1991). The question arose as to how the profession could respond to societal changes in more comprehensive and effective ways.

This question was partially addressed by the movement to culturally competent practice, rather than culturally sensitive practice. Competence in working with people from different social group memberships was determined to be good practice in social work. It was thought that being sensitive to the different life circumstances of others was good but did not require anything other than acknowledgment. In response to this limitation, social workers began to be trained about their role as change agents rather than simply facilitators (Cohen, 1990; Green, 1995). Social workers also began to be charged with integrating a praxis perspective in their work, moving from self-reflection through action. This perspective on social worker self-reflection as a critical part of the intervention endeavor was borrowed from the work of Paulo Freire (1972).

Fourth wave—race, gender, ethnicity, sexual orientation, physical and mental ability, class. Most would argue that this period, stemming from the mid 1990s, is not the final wave of attention to multiculturalism in social work practice, education, and research (Van Soest, 1995). This period has been marked by the introduction of the construct of intersectionality, or the acknowledgment that (a) we all have multiple group memberships and identities, (b) the impact of these on our daily lives is not simply additive, and (c) each social group membership cannot be completely extracted from all others (Hill-Collins, 1997; Johnsrud & Sadao, 1998; Schiele, 1995). Returning to an earlier example, the differences in being a woman of color are much more complex in their interaction than those simply of being a man of color or a woman (Comas-Díaz & Greene, 1994; Gutiérrez & Lewis, 1999).

Recognizing intersectionality and the importance of including the uniqueness of individual's families and groups in the intervention process, the types of social group memberships social work educators and researchers have been concerned about have expanded to include categories such as age, physical or mental ability, and economic class (Gutiérrez & Lewis, 1998; Lum, 2000). These categories have now joined race, ethnicity, gender, and sexual orientation as parts of the larger construct termed multiculturalism in some of the social work literature. How these are combined and affect the allocation of resources and power for individuals, families, and groups has become the research

challenge for the fourth wave (Drisko, 1997; Watts-Jones, 1990).

The fourth wave has also moved social work to make connections between multiculturalism and other constructs such as social justice (Garvin & Reed, 1995). Social justice and social change issues require that more attention be paid to pluralism and/or assimilation, allocation of resources, and power. An additional outcome of the fourth wave has been the shift in the focus of the intervention from the target individual, family, or group to the wider society or global interactions, with the target group influencing change (Cohen, 1990). The larger context is viewed as playing a complex role in shaping the experience of the target population.

Research suggests that if ethnic sensitive services do not lead to structural changes in organizations and a greater participation of people of color in the governance of the agency, efforts toward change are be mostly symbolic and marginal (Gutiérrez, 1992; Mizio, 1981; Morales, 1981; Solomon, 1976; Washington, 1982). The ethnoconscious approach, which combines an ethnic sensitive orientation and an empowerment perspective on practice, holds promise for creating empowering services, programs, and organizations.

The ethnoconscious approach is based on an appreciation and celebration of the strengths existing in communities of color (Gutiérrez, 1992, Pinderhughes, 1989; Solomon, 1976). At its center is a concern with power, confronting social inequality through work with individuals, families, groups, organizations, and communities. The process of helping is that of partnership, participation, and advocacy. In all work, people of color are active agents in individual and social transformation.

At the center of the ethnoconscious approach is empowerment: the process of gaining personal, interpersonal, and political power (Gutiérrez, DeLois, & GlenMaye, 1995; Gutiérrez & Lewis, 1999; Pinderhughes, 1989; Simon, 1994; Solomon, 1976). The empowerment perspective on practice is not new but reflects a tradition that challenges the conceptualization of social workers as benefactors or liberators of the less fortunate (Simon, 1994) The first two traditions, with their paternalistic assumptions, have most often been tools for social control. The empowerment tradition is identified as one that can most effectively work for both social and individual change through active engagement of community members in change efforts at all levels (Simon, 1994).

We have chosen to operationalize multicultural practice in a manner that incorporates an ethnoconscious perspective and includes fourth wave criteria. Multicultural practice, by our definition, refers to methods that work toward the development of disenfranchised groups while creating mechanisms for greater intergroup interaction and change. It is work that attempts to address the central challenge of living in a diverse society—how do we respect diversity and reduce inequality while working toward a common good? It is built on a pluralistic foundation, while going beyond pluralism to recognize and work to eliminate social injustices and oppression based on group membership through practice with individuals, groups, families, communities, and organizations.

RESEARCH ON MULTICULTURAL SOCIAL WORK

The social work literature on multicultural practice is growing. However, much of this literature is primarily descriptive and theoretical. Our journals and books provide many interest-ing examples of how this practice can be conducted in the field. However, very few articles use quantitative or qualitative methods to assess the effectiveness of these methods. Therefore, one of the specific obstacles facing us in this chapter is the dearth of empirical research on the constructs of multiculturalism in social work practice. This leads to the following questions: What constructs have been addressed empirically? What are their importance for practice, policy, and research? What constructs require further codification? What types of analysis would be more fruitful in helping us to understand the utility of the concept in our practice literature? Can these studies be conducted by community members or practitioner/researchers, or is the work restricted to trained researchers external to the community environment?

Most of the empirical multicultural work, and much of the empirical testing of other practice theories, has been done by a small number of researchers with advanced degrees (Schiele, 1995). Schiele posits,

> Without diversification, the profession's knowledge base can become restricted and influenced by a small cadre of knowledge producers. This can lead to a form of oppression wherein the majority of social work faculty, as well as social workers in general, are subject to the ideas and perspectives of a few. (p. 53)

If there are so few researchers actually responsible, and these are addressing all aspects of social work research, it should come as no great wonder that multiculturalism gets little attention in the social work research. Researchers also work on topics of interest to them, and the information on multiculturalism increased significantly with the increased numbers of faculty of color. At the same time, calls for more ethnic sensitive or culturally competent practice increased with the number of practitioners of color. As described by Van Soest (1995) "as a result of [CPS] standards, as well as faculty and student recruitment strategies, social work is the only profession in which African Americans have ever attained parity of access and equity in graduation rates" (p. 57).

Given the limited empirical evidence on the effectiveness of multicultural practice in social work, why do we continue to espouse its tenets and promote its value? What is it about the concept of multicultural practice that is so appealing to us? Does multicultural practice simply strike a chord with our intuition and emotions? Is there no place for intuition in empirical social work to establish the validity of multicultural practice? The determination of validity in research begins with the establishment with face validity. The intuitions and emotions of the many scholars who support multicultural social work practice certainly should not be discounted. These intuitions and emotions are developed over years of personal and practice experiences. Related to face validity is the concept of content validity, which is based on experts' decisions about the adequacy of the concept and its appeal to reason. Indeed, the intuition of the growing number of scholars' knowledge of multiculturalism will have a greater influence on the "panel of experts" who establish content validity. Certainly, there were many health professionals whose intuition told them that smoking was bad for one's health long before the Framingham studies of the 1960s and 1970s identified it as a major risk factor for cardiovascular disease. But the current multicultural movement is based on more than just intuition and emotion—it makes sense.

Then, perhaps, the empirical research on multicultural social work practice is merely forthcoming and highlights a need in our current research efforts. Shifting demographics within American society point to the need to consider the worldviews of others. Evidence of the problematic nature of mainstream models for people of color and other target identities suggest the need for new models. Thus, at least, the need for models of practice that take culture into consideration is more than mere intuition and emotion.

Too often, when the effectiveness of multicultural social work practice is questioned by empiricists, advocates question why they are being required to "prove" the merit of practice, when mainstream models have gone unchallenged for years. Although well intended, this argument is not entirely accurate. Social work practice's effectiveness, as a whole, has been repeatedly challenged. Fischer's (1973) call to the profession to incorporate empiricism in practice models came at a time when demonstrating effectiveness was only beginning to be an issue. The development of single-subject research and experimental designs to test interventions grew out of this movement. Total quality management and the importance of consumer satisfaction in the 1980s and 1990s added to the need for accountability to our client/consumer base. Today, social workers are subject to pressure from third-party managed care organizations to prove the effectiveness of social work practice under conditions of diminishing resources. Asking proponents of multicultural practice to show their effectiveness is no longer merely a strategy of attack from nonbelievers but a necessary reality. Social work has evolved to a point at which our professional values and education and training standards encourage multiculturalism, but this does not mean that threats to these values do not exist. Rather, it means that we must remain focused in our efforts to show the effectiveness of current methods and continue to develop new models that incorporate strong evaluative standards. We must adopt a proactive stance toward evidence-based multicultural practice.

AN AGENDA FOR EMPIRICALLY BASED MULTICULTURAL SOCIAL WORK PRACTICE: WHAT SHOULD WE DO?

Developing a foundation for empirical multicultural social work practice will require research on the importance of both service providers' characteristics and the processes geared toward specific communities. To date, research on the effectiveness of service providers with diverse populations has focused on the demographic characteristics of the providers, such as ethnicity and gender. Existing studies focus on whether the matching of service providers and clients on the basis of social group membership makes a difference in service use, length of treatment, and outcome of treatment. Sue, Fujino, Hu, and Takeuchi (1991) found that therapist-client ethnic matching was associated with length of treatment for Asian American, African American, and Mexican American clients. Language matching was related to treatment outcomes for Mexican Americans. Takeuchi, Uehara, and Maramba (1999) summarized a host of empirical studies that demonstrate the association between ethnic and language match and decreases in dropout rates and increases in use of services by ethnic minorities. Evidence also suggests that the use of ethnic-specific mental health service centers for children is related to less dropout from services after the first session, more use of services, and

higher functioning scores at discharge, compared to children who received services from mainstream centers (Yeh, Takeuchi, & Sue, 1994).

Although these studies provide a useful framework for exploring how service providers' demographic and organizational characteristics can influence services to target populations, they do not take into consideration the attitudinal characteristics of service providers. We must also consider the worldview of social workers working in diverse communities, regardless of target or agent group status. Mahalik, Worthington, and Crump (1999) found that therapists shared similar worldviews, regardless of group membership. This was described as a "therapist culture," and differences between therapists based on racial/ethnic membership were minimal. Ethnic matching alone does not assure effective multicultural practice.

Rather, understanding the attitudes of service providers toward target group members, that is, bias, prejudice, and stereotypes, is critical. Equally important is the service providers' awareness of their own multiple identities, both as targets and agent group members, and their willingness to self-reflect on these identities and its impact on the provider-client relationship. Research is needed that explores the effectiveness of willingness to self-reflect on these identities and their impact on the provider-client relationship. Research that explores the effectiveness of social workers who are aware of privileged status and its contribution to the cycle of oppression is also necessary. The correlation between critical consciousness and effective multicultural social work practice would be a major step toward understanding the usefulness of training and education efforts in this area. Although we have come a long way in training students for culturally competent practice, we must continue to work toward the further infusion of curricula that promote self-awareness and proficiency in critically analyzing and revising existing "laws of universal behavior."

The development of critical consciousness among service providers, in turn, influences the way we work with specific communities, including our conceptualization of the problems and strengths of the community, as well as the design of our preventive interventions programs. Without this knowledge of critical consciousness, social workers may fall victim to the maintenance of procedural norms, those conventional canons that tell us what the problem is, how it should be dealt with, and what practices and orientations are acceptable and not so (Rogler, 1999). Cultural insensitivities arise as a consequence of unconscious assumptions that remain unrecognized. These unconscious assumptions are present in all phases of practice, from the assessment of individuals to the selected form of treatment. For example, Rogler (1999) describes how the unconscious assumption involved in maintaining the original language in standardized assessment forms can be problematic for Latino populations. In an attempt to overcome language differences, Spanish versions of these assessments are sometimes developed. Unfortunately, these instruments often contain syntax or grammar errors and colloquial expressions that, when translated, literally make no sense, all in the name of attaining standardization and equivalence with the original version (Velez-Diaz & Gonzalez-Reigosa, 1987). The solution suggested: Treat the original language version as open to revi-

sion. Make conscious the assumptions of our rigid worldview and the procedural norms we carry with us.

The responsibility of critical consciousness does not fall only on practitioners but also requires great sensitivity and creativity on the part of researchers who work in this area. Continuous self-reflection, community collaboration, and empowerment are potentially important elements of culturally competent research. Self-reflection must be prevalent in all aspects of the research process from the conceptualization of research questions to the interpretation of the data. Research models that solicit the input of the community in the definition of the problem and their collaboration in the design of studies are at the forefront of multicultural social work research (Uehara et al., 1996). These models of research are congruent with the value base of social work and hold promise for further empiricism in multicultural practice.

Based on this brief discussion, it is clear that the area of multicultural practice in social work should be a research priority. Many of the complex ideas that characterize the fourth wave of multicultural practice have emerged from the humanities, ethnic and gender studies, or qualitative research. Concepts such as oppression may be considered in practice research without connection to change or social justice. Similarly, very few studies have looked specifically at intersectionality. This has led us to a discussion of the hierarchies of "isms" rather than a consideration of how interlocking identities can be a source of risk or resilience. Future research on practice with diverse populations must be more deeply grounded in our current thinking regarding multiculturalism.

TABLE 7.2   Principles for Multicultural Direct Practice

- Multicultural practice will need to be flexible in addressing the dynamic changes and processes of the future.
- Multicultural practice requires self-reflection and action by practitioners at the interpersonal through societal levels.
- Multicultural practice benefits from the inclusion of the community's perspective in assessing problems and resources.
- Multicultural practitioners employing multicultural methods in practice must be aware of the "wave" of practice from which they have drawn the concepts and methods they use.
- Multicultural practice is enhanced by expanding the use of research by social work practitioners in the practice setting.
- Multicultural practice recognizes the importance of language used in instruments for assessment and intervention.
- Multicultural practice requires the consistent use and operationalization of constructs to further the knowledge base.
- Multicultural practice at all levels is enhanced by the involvement of community-based service centers.

PRINCIPLES AND METHODS FOR MULTICULTURAL PRACTICE

The development of multicultural social work practice is dynamic, and it will certainly continue to evolve as it is further critically analyzed. Rather than suppress the discussion and debate around these issues, we must engage in the discourse about its usefulness and efficacy. The future of multicultural social work practice will rely heavily on the articulation of new principles and methods that may in fact lead to a new wave of practice that builds on the momentum of the previous wave.

Given the dynamic nature of multicultural practice, we recognize that models of practice must be flexible and malleable to remain useful over time. The principles and methods for practice presented below are both a combination of what we have learned from previous waves and points of departure for future directions (see also Table 7.2). The purpose of these principles

and methods is to provide a framework for practice and a lens through which practitioners and researchers can examine and evaluate their current practice and methods.

Multicultural practice will need to be flexible in addressing the dynamic changes and processes of the future. These will include geographic differences, changes in family forms and backgrounds, and policy changes (which generally lag behind the realities of families in the United States). From an ecological perspective, we understand that the world is a complex interaction of individuals and their environments. These environments are ever changing, and our understanding of their influence on individual behavior is developing. Shifting demographics, the urbanization and suburbanization of our communities, and acculturation of second- and third-generation immigrants will influence our conceptualization of multiculturalism and its practice. Not only must we be cognizant of the contemporary context, but we must also be mindful of the historical context that has led to the current situation. We also must be prepared to defend programs and policies that influence multicultural communities and remain proactive in the development and implementation of new policies that reflect the changing face of these communities.

Multicultural practice requires self-reflection and action by practitioners at the interpersonal through societal levels. Our success in achieving flexible practice is contingent on our ability to reflect on our own assumptions about multicultural communities and to address the core issues that disadvantage and oppress these communities. Self-awareness is perhaps the most important skill that we must strive for to do effective multicultural social work practice. Coming to grips with our own privilege and the ways in which our practice supports a system of oppression is key. Making our unconscious biases and assumptions about multicultural communities' conscious is critical. Recognition that the process is lifelong and requires continual self-reflection in all phases of our lives, both professional and personal, sustains our effort and our flexibility. If we can understand that our awareness as multicultural social workers is dynamic and developing, we are in a better position to address the issues that arise within the communities where we work. Multicultural practice also embodies praxis, a process of reflection and action. Recognition alone is not sufficient. We must be committed to action that promotes social change and social justice. We must become allies and take a greater role in the education of multiculturalism and promote self-reflection in our entire sphere of influence, including our personal, professional, and community life.

Multicultural practice benefits from the inclusion of the community's perspective in assessing problems and resources. Although an important theme in the education of social workers has been "starting where the client is," its practice within multicultural communities has not been consistent. Problems and resources within these communities are often identified using our knowledge of theory and research developed with mainstream society in mind. What may be apparent to the practitioner or researcher may not be of immediate concern to multicultural communities. Interventions designed with practitioner-identified problems and resources may not be relevant to the needs of the community or cater to the existing strengths of the community. Rather, multicultural practice should appreciate and value strengths, resources, needs, and cultural backgrounds as defined by specific community members. Collaboration in all phases of practice, from problem definition and assessment to implementation and evaluation, is invaluable to meet the needs of multicultural communities and effective practice. This can be accomplished by collaborating with community and social service organizations and by recruiting individuals who may be less likely to be a part of such organizations due to their disenfranchised status.

Multicultural practitioners employing multicultural methods in practice must be aware of the "wave" of practice from which they have drawn the concepts and methods they use. As successive generations enter the field of multicultural social work practice, new levels of awareness and techniques are sure to emerge. Although it is important to continually examine the state of multicultural practice, it may or may not be necessary to discard previous conceptualizations and methods. Rather, a more productive approach might include a recognition of these previous waves of knowledge development, a greater understanding of the historical context in which they were developed, and an assessment of their utility in our contemporary and future practice. Although current models of practice call for an examination of the intersectionality of social identities, it may be useful to isolate one or two identities to tease out the complex interactions. Once we have gained some clarity about these specific identities, we can begin the process of re-layering the other contextual factors that influence the client perspective.

Multicultural practice is enhanced by expanding the use of research by social work practitioners in the practice setting. Multicultural practice must be proactive in its development of an accessible empirical knowledge base. Despite a groundswell of courses and an infusion of content on multiculturalism in direct practice education, many still question of the utility, if not the possibility, of infusing such content into research courses. The need for social work students to have adequate knowledge of traditional research designs and methods and to become intelligent consumers of the research literature is important to social work education. Equally important is expanding the proficiency of students in methods of research that not only develops our knowledge base but is also congruent with the values of multiculturalism. Such methods include models of community-based and participatory action research. Qualitative analysis can also be an important tool for analyzing interviews, process recordings, and other forms of narrative we encounter in practice. In fact, these qualitative recordings are underused

as sources of data that could help to evaluate our practice.

Multicultural practice recognizes the importance of language used in instruments of assessment and intervention. It also recognizes the need to revise the original language text when using tools with another target group. When an instrument is determined to be reliable and valid—that is, it has been analyzed for its psychometric properties and has been used repeatedly in the literature—its status as a standard tool for measuring a specific construct is enhanced. Over time, these standards may become an accepted part of our practice, being used with individuals and communities with which the instrument's validity was never tested. The tool's application is thought to be universal, when it may be culturally bound. Normally, the term *culturally bound* is reserved for conditions that are found almost exclusively within another culture, and thus, it is not immediately applicable to the dominant culture. The notion that conditions might be culturally bound to the dominant culture and not applicable to minority cultures must be considered. The language we use to measure specific constructs and conditions may be culturally bound, as well. For example, the use of the word *blue* to identify symptoms of depression does not translate well and make little sense outside the dominant culture.

Multicultural practice requires the consistent use and operationalization of constructs to further the knowledge base. As work on multicultural direct practice has grown, we have not always been consistent in our use of specific terms or concepts. Many ideas, concepts, and theories have been undefined or used with little specification. If we are going to advance our knowledge and skills for multicultural work, we need to work toward the consistent use and definition of concepts such as critical consciousness, empowerment, and cultural competence. A large body of practice literature is available to use in developing these definitions. This work is difficult but necessary if we are going to conduct practice and research that incorporate multicultural perspectives.

Multicultural practice at all levels is enhanced by the involvement of community-based service centers. As societal understandings of multicultural practice become fluent, more agencies will be equipped to work effectively with multicultural communities. In the current state of multicultural practice, community-based agencies have been shown to be highly effective in meeting the needs of these communities. Agencies that specialize in certain populations may be better able to do outreach and find members of target groups to provide services, may be more likely speak the language of the community, and may have a greater understanding of the needs and strengths of the community due to experience (Delgado, 1999). Often, these organizations originated in the community, among its members, through social activism or grassroots organization. However, regardless of an agency's specialization, it should be proficient in the principles outlined above to provide efficacious multicultural services.

CONCLUSION

In this chapter, we have identified ways in which direct practice in social work is developing models to work more effectively in an increasingly diverse society. These models have evolved from those that have ignored or disparaged the role of culture and social identity in individual lives to those that attempt to bring an individual's standpoint into practice. In this fourth wave of multicultural practice, our focus is increasingly on the intersection of identities and how those identities shape experience, opportunities, and resources. However, this interest in social identity and cultural experience should not prevent us from developing this work toward social justice more completely. Ethnoconscious practice requires that we pay closer attention to issues of social justice and to methods that will build on the strengths, capacities, and values of the individuals, families, and communities with which we work. This form of practice will require us to develop methods to work more effectively in partnership with others and to view ourselves as learners in the helping process (Reed, Newman, Suarez, & Lewis, 1997).

The most recent *NASW Code of Ethics* (1996) explicitly supports the use of social work methods focused on cultural competence, social justice, empowerment, and collaborative practice. However, existing trends regarding managed care, welfare "reform," and efforts to eliminate affirmative action and further restrict immigration may create further barriers to this work. Taking the path toward multicultural practice will require taking risks, speaking out, and challenging current trends. It requires applying empowerment methods for ourselves in our workplaces and daily lives so we can act on our convictions and professional responsibilities. To engage in this critical work, we will require support and resources from each other, our professional organizations, and the institutions in which we work. By recognizing the challenges we face, and the means to meet those challenges, we can be effective agents for improving the social conditions in which we all live.

REFERENCES

Anderson, M. L., & Hill-Collins, P. (Eds). (1992). *Race class and gender: An anthology*. Belmont, CA: Wadsworth.

Asamoah, Y., Garcia, A. O., Hendricks, C. O., & Walker, J. (1991). What we call ourselves: Implications for resources, policy, and practice. *Journal of Multicultural Social Work, 1*(1), 7-22.

Baca Zinn, M. (1994). Feminist rethinking from racial-ethnic families. In M. Baca Zinn & B. Dill (Eds.), *Women of color in U.S. society* (pp. 303-314). Philadelphia: Temple University Press.

Baines, D. (1997). Feminist social work in the inner city: The challenges of race, class, and gender. *Affilia, 12*(3), 297-317.

Banks, J. A. (1984). *Multicultural education in western societies*. New York: Praeger.

Boyd-Franklin, N. (1987, July). Group therapy for black women: A therapeutic support model. *American Journal of Orthopsychiatry, 57*(3), 394-401.

Bricker-Jenkins, M., & Hooyman, N. (1986). *Not for women only: Social work practice for a feminist future*. Silver Spring, MD: National Association of Social Workers.

Bricker-Jenkins, M., Hooyman, N., & Gottlieb, N. (Eds.). (1991). *Feminist social work practice*. Newbury Park, CA: Sage.

Carpenter, E. (1980). Social services, policies, and issues. *Social Casework, 61,* 455-461.

Castex, G. M. (1993). Frames of reference: The effects of ethnocentric map projections on professional practice. *Social Work, 38*(6), 713-726.

Chau, K. L. (1990, Spring-Summer). Social work practice: Towards a cross-cultural practice model. *Journal of Applied Social Sciences, 14*(2), 249-275.

Chau, K. L. (1991). Social work with ethnic minorities: Practice issues and potentials. *Journal of Multicultural Social Work, 1*(1), 23-39.

Cohen, H. (1990). My client, myself. *Family Therapy Networker, 14*(3), 19-23.

Comas-Días, L., & Greene, B. (Eds.). (1995). *Women of color: Integrating ethnic and gender identities in psychotherapy*. New York: Guilford.

Comas-Días, L., & Griffith. E. E. H. (Eds.). (1988). *Clinical guidelines in cross-cultural mental health*. New York: John Wiley.

Delgado, M. (1999). *Social work in non-traditional urban settings*. New York: Oxford University Press.

Devore, W., & Schlesinger, E. (1987). *Ethnic-sensitive social work practice*. St. Louis, MO: C. V. Mosby.

Drisko, J. W. (1997). Strengthening qualitative studies and reports: Standards to promote academic integrity. *Journal of Social Work Education, 33*(1), 185-197.

Drum, J., & Howard, G. (1989, January). *Multicultural and global education: Seeking common ground (Summary)*. Paper presented at a conference cosponsored by Las Palomas de Taos, REACH Center for Multicultural and Global Education, and the Stanley Foundation, Taos, NM.

Figueira-McDonough, J., Netting, F. E., & Nichols-Casebolt, A. (Eds.). (1998). *The role of gender in practice knowledge: Claiming half the human experience*. New York: Garland.

Fischer, J. (1973). Is casework effective? A review. *Social Work, 18,* 5-20.

Freire, P. (1972). *The pedagogy of the oppressed*. New York: Seabury.

Gallegos, J. (1982). The ethnic competence model for social work education. In B. White (Ed.), *Color in a white society* (pp. 1-9). Silver Spring, MD: NASW Press.

Garvin, C., & Reed, B.(1995). Sources and visions for feminist social work: Reflective processes, social justice, diversity, and connection. In N. van Den Bergh (Ed.), *Feminist practice in the 21st century* (pp. 41-69). Washington, DC: NASW Press.

Green, J. (1995). *Cultural awareness in the human services* (2nd ed.). Needham Heights, MA: Allyn & Bacon.

Greene, B. (1993). Human diversity in clinical psychology: Lesbian and gay sexual orientations. *The Clinical Psychologist, 46*(2), 74-82.

Guerin-Gonzales, C. (1994). *Mexican workers and American dreams*. New Brunswick, NJ: Rutgers University Press.

Gutiérrez, L. (1992). Empowering clients in the twenty-first century: The role of human service organizations. In Y. Hasenfeld (Ed.), *Human service organizations as complex organizations* (pp. 320-338). Newbury Park, CA: Sage.

Gutiérrez, L., DeLois, K., & GlenMaye, L. (1995). Understanding empowerment practice: Building on practitioner based knowledge. *Families in Society, 76*(9), 534-542.

Gutiérrez, L., & Lewis, E. (1994). Community organizing with women of color: A feminist perspective. *Advances in Community Organization and Social Administration, 1*(2), 23-44.

Gutiérrez, L., & Lewis, E. (1998). A feminist perspective on organizing women of color. In J. Erlich & F. Rivera (Eds.), *Community organizing in a diverse society* (pp. 97-116). Boston: Allyn & Bacon.

Gutiérrez, L., & Lewis, E. (1999). *Empowering women of color.* New York: Columbia University Press.

Gutiérrez, L., & Nagda, B. (1996). The multicultural imperative in human services organizations: Issues for the 21st century. In P. Raffoul & A. McNeece (Eds.), *Future issues for social work practice.* Boston: Allyn & Bacon.

Hill-Collins, P. (1997, November). *Women in families: Race, gender, and class.* Keynote speech presented at the annual meeting of the National Council on Family Relations, Chicago.

Iglehart, A., & Becerra, R. (1995). *Social services and the ethnic community.* Boston: Allyn & Bacon.

Jackson, J. S., Tucker, M. B., & Bowman, P. J. (1982). Conceptual and methodological problems in survey research on black Americans. In W. T. Lui (Ed.), *Methodological problems in minority research* (pp. 11-39). Chicago: Pacific/Asian American Mental Health Research Center.

Jayasuriya, L. (1992). The problematic of culture and identity in social functioning. *Journal of Multicultural Social Work, 2*(4), 37-58.

Johnsrud, L. K., & Sadao, K. C. (1998). The common experience of "otherness": Ethnic and racial minority faculty. *The Review of Higher Education, 21*(4), 315-342.

Keanau, E. J., Green, V., & Valencia-Weber, G. (1982, March). Acculturation and the Hispanic woman: Attitudes toward women, sex-role attribution, sex-role behavior, and demographics. *Hispanic Journal of Behavioral Studies, 4*(1), 21-40.

Land, H., Nishimoto, R., & Chau, K. (1988). Interventive and preventive services for Vietnamese Chinese refugees. *Social Service Review, 62,* 568-584.

Lee, J. (1986). Asian-American elderly: A neglected minority group. *Journal of Gerontological Social Work, 9*(4), 103-116.

Longres, J. (1991). Toward a status model of ethnic sensitive practice. *Journal of Multicultural Social Work, 1*(1), 41-56.

Lorde, A. (1984). *Sister outsider.* Freedom, CA: The Crossing Press.

Lum, D. (2000). *Social work practice and people of color* (4rd Ed.). Pacific Grove, CA: Brooks/Cole.

Mahalik, J. R., Worthington, R. L., & Crump, S. (1999). Influence of racial/ethnic membership and "therapist culture" on therapists' worldview. *Journal of Multicultural Counseling and Development, 27,* 2-17.

Mankiller, W. (1993). *Mankiller: A chief and her people.* New York: St. Martin's.

Marger, M. N. (1997). *Race and ethnic relations: American and global perspectives* (4th ed.). Belmont, CA: Wadsworth.

McGoldrick, M., Giordano, J., & Pearce, J. (Eds.). (1996). *Ethnicity and family therapy* (2nd ed.). New York: Guilford.

McMahon, A., & Allen-Meares, P. (1992). Is social work racist? A content analysis of the recent literature. *Social Work, 37*(6), 533-539.

Midgley, J. (1991). Social development and multicultural social work. *Journal of Multicultural Social Work, 1*(1), 85-100.

Mizio, E. (1981). Training for work with minority groups. In E. Mizio & A. Delaney (Eds.), *Training for service delivery to minority clients* (pp. 7-20). New York: Family Service Association of America.

Morales, A. (1981). Social work with third world people. *Social Work, 26,* 48-51.

Morelli, P. T., & Spencer, M. S. (in press). The use and support of multicultural and antibigotry education: Research-informed interdisciplinary social work practice. *Social Work.*

National Association of Social Workers.(1996). *NASW code of ethics.* Washington, DC: Author.

Orlandi, M. A. (Ed.). (1992). *Cultural competence for evaluators.* Rockville, MD: U.S. Department of Health and Human Services.

Pinderhughes, E. (1989). *Understanding race, ethnicity, & power: The key to efficacy in clinical practice.* New York: Free Press.

Pyant, C. T., & Carlson, B. T. (1991). Relationship of racial identity and gender-role attitudes to black women's psychological well-being. *Journal of Counseling Psychology, 38*(3), 315-322.

Reed, B., Newman, P., Suarez, Z., & Lewis, E. (1997). Interpersonal practice beyond diversity and toward social justice: The importance of critical consciousness. In C. Garvin & B. Seabury (Eds.), *Interpersonal practice in social work* (pp. 44-77). New York: Garland.

Rogler, L. (1999). Methodological sources of cultural insensitivity in mental health research. *American Psychologist 54*(6), 424-433.

Schiele, J. H. (1995). Submission rates among African-American faculty: The forgotten side of publication productivity. *Journal of Social Work Educaion, 31*(1), 46-54.

Scott, J., & Delgado, M. (1979). Planning mental health programs for Hispanic communities. *Social Casework, 60,* 451-456.

Simon, B. L. (1994). *The empowerment tradition in American social work.* New York: Columbia University Press.

Solomon, B. (1976). *Black empowerment*. New York: Columbia University Press.

Spencer, M. S. (1998). Reducing racism in schools: Moving beyond rhetoric. *Journal of Social Work in Education, 20,* 25-36.

Starret, R., Mindel, C., & Wright, R. (1983). Influence of support systems on the use of social services by the Hispanic elderly. *Social Work Research and Abstracts, 19,* 35-40.

Stehno, S. (1982). Differential treatment of minority children in service systems. *Social Work, 27,* 39-45.

Sue, S., Fujino, D. C., Hu, L., & Takeuchi, D. T. (1991). Community mental health services for ethnic minority groups: A test of the cultural responsiveness hypothesis. *Journal of Consulting and Clinical Psychology, 59,* 533-540.

Takeuchi, D. T., Uehara, E., & Maramba, G. (1999). Cultural diversity and mental health treatment. In A. V. Horwitz & T. L. Scheid (Eds.), *A handbook for the study of mental health: Social contexts, theories, and systems.* New York: Cambridge University Press.

Tatum, B. (1997). *"Why are all the black kids sitting together in the cafeteria?": And other conversations about race.* New York: Basic Books.

Uehara, E., Sohng, S. L., Bending, R. L., Seyfried, S., Richey, C. A., Keenan, L., Spencer, M., Morelli, P., Ortega, D., & Kanuha, V. (1996). Towards a values-based approach to multicultural social work research. *Social Work, 41,* 613-623.

Van Soest, D. (1995). Multiculturalism and social work education: The non-debate about competing perspectives. *Journal of Social Work Education, 31,* 143-150.

Velez-Diaz, A., & Gonzalez-Reigosa, F. (1987). The Spanish version of the Clinical Analysis Questionnaire: A precautionary note. *Journal of Personality Assessment, 51,* 414-416.

Washington, R. (1982). Social development: A focus for practice and education. *Social Work, 27,* 104-109.

Watts-Jones, D. (1990). Toward a stress scale for African-American women. *Psychology of Women Quarterly, 14,* 271-275.

Wenocur, S., & Reisch, M. (1989). *From charity to enterprise: The development of American social work in a market economy.* Chicago: University of Illinois Press.

Yeh, M., Takeuchi, D. T., & Sue, S. (1994). Asian-American children treated in the mental health system: A comparison of parallel and mainstream outpatient service centers. *Journal of Clinical Child Psychology, 23,* 5-12.

CHAPTER EIGHT

Feminist Social Work Practice: Womanly Warrior or Damsel in Distress?

MARY BRICKER-JENKINS

This chapter seeks to contribute to an assessment of the state of the art in feminist social work practice against the vision it fashioned some 20 years ago. It is based in part on a survey of feminist practitioners that replicated one done at the height of feminist activism in social work. It is also a plea for us to claim our victories but to redouble our efforts to fashion theory and practice for the compelling conditions of interpersonal and institutionalized exploitation and marginalization that women—and growing numbers of men—face today.

A HISTORICAL OVERVIEW: THREE DECADES OF TRIUMPHS ON THE *TITANIC*

Since the current wave of the women's movement rose on the political and cultural shores of North America in the late 1960s, we have indeed created a new feminist culture and consciousness. Safe spaces for battered women—although mainstreamed into "domestic violence services"—are available in nearly every community, but so are growing numbers of

AUTHOR'S NOTE: Special thanks to Professor Barbara Kasper of the Underground Railroad, SUNY-Brockport Depot, who rescued this chapter.

shelters for homeless families (read "women and their children"). Rape and sexual abuse services are now listed in telephone directories, but there is little evidence that misogynist assaults themselves have decreased. Moreover, the degree to which we attend to the injuries of women is often contingent on our willingness to reframe them to secure the billable hour—from wounds inflicted by an assailant to a pathology women must claim to access help. After decades of legal and cultural work, it is easier today for women to divorce and/or choose single parenthood, but it is harder for us to survive economically in these "liberated" families. Indeed, after years of struggling for the right to work outside the home, we now find that, under welfare reform, the work of women (and men) who are raising children at home is no longer worthy of public support. Having walked or been pushed to the right politically, many social workers are now running to the trough for "welfare to work" contracts and the subsidized labor of (unpaid or underpaid) welfare moms placed for "work experience" under a system that looks much like indentured servitude.

True, for those women fortunate enough to be able to consider a career, just about everything is available: We can be cops or bankers, builders or farmers, engineers, astronauts, entrepreneurs, construction workers. Our influence in these and nearly every other occupation is undeniable, but we search in vain for the evidence that we have managed to transform these fields in the ways we had hoped. In the end, the degree to which we believe in and trust the triumphs of the women's liberation movement is likely to rise and fall with our location in the economic structure. For too many women to-

day, it seems that some of their sisters have claimed the lifeboats while they are left to ride the *Titanic* to the bottom.

THE PLACE OF SOCIAL WORK: ACTIVISM AND AMBIGUITY

Where does social work fit into this picture? Like feminist activism, social work places itself at the nexus of individual biography and social processes, at the intersection of the personal and the political. Of all the helping professions, social work is the only one that claims to reside there. Even before this current wave of feminism, social workers embraced and sometimes invented theories and practices that potentiated a feminist perspective. From the settlement house to the halfway house, social workers have insisted on attending to the ways that people shape social, political, cultural, and economic dynamics—and could confound each other through them. Activism to challenge oppression and promote peace and justice has long been a prominent theme in the social work community, if not the literature. Early efforts to define the common theoretical base of social work practice held promise for helping social workers move seamlessly from the personal to the political (Bartlett, 1970; Germain, 1973; Pincus & Minahan, 1973; Towle, 1945/1965).

Given this heritage, it seems odd that it took so long for feminism to take hold among social workers. While in 1980 our sisters in psychology were celebrating "the first decade of feminist influence on psychotherapy" with a major publication (Brodsky, 1980), social workers were just convening our first national conference on Women in a Sexist Society. This was a spirited gathering that focused more on "women's issues" than on feminism (Weick & Vandiver, 1982), but many of us who had embraced feminism in our quest for a liberatory social work seized the opportunity to organize a campaign to promote the feminist presence in our profession.

Defining Feminist Social Work Practice Principles: The NASW/NCOWI's FPP

As part of that campaign, Nancy Hooyman and I asked the National Association of Social Workers' National Committee on Women's Issues (NCOWI) to sponsor a research effort to define the feminist social work practice we knew was being invented in the field. Although NCOWI was supportive, the NASW program committee was not. They told us we had to provide a working definition of *feminist practice* before we could ask for funds to define it. We argued that feminist research alternatives to positivist research designs were necessary and appropriate, but our arguments were to no avail. Undaunted, Nancy and I used bootlegged resources and a rather unusual distribution system to implement the Feminist Practice Project (FPP) Pilot Study in 1983.[1] Modeling the practice we wished to promote, we joined with others to establish the Association for Women in Social Work (AWSW), thereby changing the political environment in which our request for funds would be evaluated. The next year, our application for funds was approved by NASW's Program Advancement Fund, and we launched the FPP.

That project used the pilot study results to guide an in-depth inquiry into the work of a diverse group of practitioners who defined their work as feminist. A set of overarching propositions of and assumptions about feminist practice was gleaned from that study. Although the participants in the study differed dramatically in every way, these principles were reflected in their work, albeit in different configurations and with different emphases (Bricker-Jenkins, 1991). Participants also showed a preference for certain methods and techniques and a dedicated creativity in "feminizing" some conventional ones (Bricker-Jenkins & Lockett, 1995). Other empirical studies have since confirmed that a nascent feminist social work practice theory exists and is distinguishable from that of nonfeminists (Katz-Porterfield, 1998; Sandell, 1993).

The Problem With Principles

However, two trends in the development of feminist social work theory/practice are problematic. First, the overarching practice principles are often too abstract to guide the concrete work of daily practice, particularly of social workers who are isolated from an activist feminist community. Thus, while a "gendered" sociopolitical focus has continued to inform assessments, the *locus* of work has generally been restricted to such "accessible environments" as interpersonal relations and intrapersonal processes. Women are helped to renegotiate power relations at home and sometimes at work; they depathologize, deconstruct, and "re-story" their lives; they claim their healing time. But, it seems that less and less time goes into changing the structures that drive women into treatment in the first place or—most urgently—the racist, classist, and misogynist beliefs that have permitted the dismantling of the welfare state

(Abramovitz, 1988, 1996; Hill, 1998; Land, 1998; Miller, 1990).

Second, and perhaps more harmful for practice/theory development, broad principles tend to erase the sharp differences among social workers who claim a feminist identity. Feminist practice can no longer be discussed monolithically (if ever it should have been). The community has diversified—some say splintered or even shattered—and it is increasingly difficult to map its terrain and boundaries. In search of concrete application and theoretical refinement, the community's primary efforts in the last decade have been to apply feminist perspectives to various fields of practice and modalities (especially in clinical work) and to incorporate concepts from the transdisciplinary field of Women's Studies into social work. However, we tend to incorporate these concepts uncritically and sometimes inappropriately. We have romanced shamelessly the deconstructionists and some postmodernists, for example, apparently unaware of the debates about their "conservatizing" influence and reactionary turns (see, e.g., Collins, 1998; Kenney & Kinsella, 1997; Murray, 1997). Although they help us refine clinical technique, the uncritical use of some of these concepts may unwittingly be neutralizing and devitalizing the original liberatory and transformative agendas of feminist practice.

Back to the Future

To find the ways that feminists continue to address those agendas (if we do), it is necessary to re-explore the terrain between the global precepts of feminist practice and their concrete applications—to re-ground the definitions of feminist social work practices (now clearly plu-

ral). To that end, I turned to my colleagues in the Association for Women in Social Work and asked for assistance as I prepared to write this chapter. We decided to return to the root system of feminist practice, to conduct a reprise of the 1983 Pilot Study for the FPP.[2] In the remainder of this chapter, I present some of the initial findings from this 1998 FPP Pilot Reprise (FP98 Reprise) as well as my (admittedly idiosyncratic) interpretations of them as I compare them to the 1983 findings against the backdrop of contemporary events.[3]

In so doing, I hope to affirm the gains we have made in the past 15 years and, as we open another decade and century, to reopen some blocked pathways for further exploration. Thus, this chapter presumes some knowledge of feminist social work practice and literature about it.[4] Obviously, the findings and my reflections on them must be regarded as suggestive only, clues to some likely treasures and troubles of feminist social work practice today and a possible framework for future work.

THE 1998 FEMINIST PRACTICE PILOT STUDY: A 15-YEAR REPRISE

The FP 1998 Reprise, like the 1983 original, used a limited and opportunistic network sample of people who identified themselves as feminist social workers. In the fall of 1998, we mailed questionnaires to 268 AWSW members; the six-page survey, consisting primarily of open-ended questions, was nearly identical to the FPP study instrument used in 1983. As in 1983, we did not propose an a priori definition of feminism or feminist practice, allowing people to "self-select" and bring their own definitions to the study. We ensured an appropriate population by distributing the survey questionnaire through the AWSW membership.[5] Given the time-consuming nature of the survey, we were not surprised that only 23 were returned; because we did not have the resources for a second mailing, we had to be satisfied with this small sample.

The purpose of both pilot studies was not so much to answer questions as to formulate questions and identify possible trends; given this limited purpose, the small sample can serve. However, the study approach itself has clear limitations that must be kept in mind throughout this presentation. It is as if we were examining static, two-dimensional snapshots of a rapidly growing and unfolding tree—one with many buds and branches that can only be inferred or intuited from the data. The following sections present, with all appropriate caveats and cautions, those questions and trends that arise from one comparison of the snapshots.

The Practitioners and Their Work

The FP98 Reprise participants roughly matched the original 1983 group in credentials and type of practice: There were 22 women who held Master's of Social Work degrees, of whom 10 also held doctorates, and one licensed professional clinical counselor. Eleven were agency-based practitioners, three were in private practice, and six were academics with a nonacademic practice; three identified academic work as their only practice. There were no Bachelor of Social Work respondents in either pilot group. Like the original pilot participants, the 1998 practitioners were involved in every major practice arena and issue, including health, mental health, drugs and alcohol; families, aging, child, and adolescent welfare; poverty, homelessness, welfare, employment, prisons; violence against women, people of color, lesbians; peace, politics, communities, and administration.

The first notable difference to emerge in this 15-year reprise was in the ordering of the respondents' identified issues/areas of concentration. Whereas the 1983 group focused primarily on mental health, violence against women, and education (in that order), the 1998 group named poverty or welfare reform with greatest frequency, followed by mental health and violence. Again, caution is in order, but it is quite possible that the urgency, pervasiveness, and depth of poverty in the midst of an "economic boom"—along with the constrictions in services resulting from privatization, managed care, and welfare cuts—have demanded increased attention of feminist practitioners.

Also worth exploring is the marked increase in the proportion of practitioners who named *lesbians/homophobia* as a primary focus of their work (30% in 1998 versus only 8% in 1983). Because the study populations were roughly comparable, it is quite possible that the years of feminist and lesbian activism in the profession and in the world have altered the climate and consciousness, legitimating lesbianism and homophobia as appropriate practice concerns. Of course, it is also possible that there has been a comparable rise in the attention to lesbianism on the part of antagonists (including some professionals) and that this trend has demanded the attention and protection of feminist social workers.

Whatever the explanations, these shifts in attention of feminist practitioners over the 15-year period underscore the need to explore the ways that practice systems shape and are shaped by political environments. These data suggest that some feminist practitioners may be taking on some obdurate realities that most endanger women today, particularly poverty. Although poverty clearly cuts across all race/ethnic populations, it has disproportionately affected communities of color. Inattention to poverty and welfare issues by large sectors of feminist communities has sometimes been cited as evidence that feminism is for white women only.[6] There is a suggestion in this data that change may be taking place, both in the focus of our concerns and, as we shall see, in our efforts to use theories that inform practice where racism, sexism, classism, and other oppressions intersect with the objective economic forces that produce poverty.

The Goals of Feminist Social Work Practice

We asked participants about their goals with reference to their primary issues/areas of concentration. Despite today's obdurate realities, there was considerable reaffirmation of participants' belief in the transformational potential[7] of feminist practice (Bricker-Jenkins & Hooyman, 1986).[8] For some, there was retreat: "I've given up believing in revolution," said one, "and work on problem solving at the individual, family, and community levels." What appeared to change between 1983 and 1998 was the degree to which differences in types of goals were articulated. Some goals were described as explicitly transformative:

A humane, just, peaceful, cooperative society based on equality

Overthrowing the current system

Social and economic justice

Some goals were implicitly transformative—that is, they attempted to reveal the connections between the personal and the political in ways that would stimulate collective action toward fundamental structural changes:

Planting seeds of activism against oppression

Understanding of points of individual and collective interventions and change to be made in their worlds by them

Another category of goals was potentially transformative in one of two ways: (a) attempts to reveal personal-political connections but with no reference made to collective action for change in sociopolitical environments ($N = 3$), or (b) attempts to make radical (but not necessarily transformative) changes in social work theories, practices, or services ($N = 9$):

Broaden the theoretical perspective [in a practice arena] from behavioral/cognitive behavioral to a systems perspective

Work with others to . . . integrate spiritual and physical wellness [into mental health practice]

Provide a safe environment in which women can begin to explore themselves, . . . learn to problem-solve and take action for themselves

Of all the stated goals, only six might be classified as primarily personal growth—reduction in self-blame, increased self-esteem, improved relationships, and the like—and these were often accompanied by transformative goal statements. Finally, a new goal category appeared in the FP98 Reprise: Self-nurturance was mentioned by four participants as integral to the achievement of their practice goals for and with others. In conclusion, it is clear that at least this group of respondents is holding fast to the hope and expectation that feminist social work practice can change the world. But how?

Can We Get There From Here?
Issues in Defining Feminist Social Work Practice

At least to some degree, the methods we use to achieve our goals are predicated on the ways we define our practice. One of the participants in the FP98 Reprise referred to feminist practice as "who I am, what I do, what I hope for." This suggests three ways to approach the task of defining feminist practice: as *identity*—a way of seeing and being in the world; as *metatheory*—a constellation of beliefs, values, and visions that motivate and guide choices; and as *method* (or methods) that build toward a model. Participants in the study approached defining feminist practice in all of these ways, often simultaneously. Because a lack of clarity about definitional issues can hamper development of a practice model, I will present and offer some reflections on problems and potentials of each approach.

Feminist Practice as Identity:
"Who I am . . ."

The inherent logic in this approach is "I am feminist; therefore, everything I do in my practice is feminist practice." The problems posed by this approach are obvious. Not only are definitions of feminism contested, but the approach is "essentially essentialist"—that is, it presumes that certain identity categories are ontologically fixed, not primarily or predominately shaped by sociopolitical processes. Feminist scholarship that assumes that women's experiences, values, and visions are *essentially* different than men's shares the same problem.[9] This approach

can lead to the kind of "women's issues first and foremost" position that obscures perceptions of the ways that multiple identities/oppressions/agendas interact in people's real lives; thus, it can inhibit efforts to join with others who are attempting to create a liberatory practice.

On the other hand, there is certainly something "out there" in the phenomenological world that women identify with as women. Similarly, there is something called feminism that draws some people—people who are often very different from one another—to connect with it and each other. Each of the study participants described some life event or influence that precipitated her identifying as a feminist, however much they differed in the ways they experienced that identity.

Studies of feminist practice are themselves predicated on this approach to definition; some (like this one) attempt to glean definitions from the data, whereas others start with definitions and focus on ways people implement the a priori definitions.[10] Each method has merit, but each must grapple with the problem of essentialism. The major benefits of the identity approach to definition are that (a) it is potentially most inclusive and (b) it provides an opportunity to ask people who view the world primarily through the lens of this identity how they see the world and how this angle of vision shapes every detail of their practice.[11]

Feminist Practice as Metatheory:
"What I do . . ."

Metatheory, as used here, refers to a philosophy or approach to practice that has less specificity than a model or method but comprises a set of propositions and assumptions that guide practice.[12] In the case of feminist practice, it is unabashedly a normative approach. As such, it is both an espoused theory—a vision of practice, including its hoped-for outcomes—and a dynamic "theory-in-use" (Schön, 1983) devolving from practitioners' attempts to create alternatives to patriarchal, particularly Eurocentric, theories and practices.

The concepts and principles of feminist practice metatheory were derived from the experience and literature of the women's liberation movement of the 1970s. Feminist practitioners translated ideological themes of the movement into propositions, assumptions, and characteristics of practice. The NASW-sponsored FPP was an attempt to articulate these as they were being reflected in actual practice; other studies and essays state them in similar and compatible terms (Collins, 1986; Gould, 1987; Morell, 1987; Norman & Mancuso, 1980; Valentich, 1986; Wetzel & The Feminist World View Educators, 1986). The FP98 Reprise data suggest that feminist practitioners continue to embrace them to some degree and in some configuration.

Social workers in virtually every kind of setting have reinvented practice by using feminist precepts or "guiding principles" pertaining to the nature and purposes of practice, the sociopolitical dynamics on which practice should focus, the relationships through which work should be done, and—to some degree—the methods and techniques that should be used. Particularly notable are the applications in social work with families (Laird, 1995; McGoldrick, 1998; Walters, Carter, Papp, & Silverstein, 1988) and with survivors of violence against women (Stout & McPhail, 1998), as well as in the fields of addictions (Babcock & McKay, 1995; Collins, 1993; Ebben, 1995;

Favorini, 1995; Haaken, 1993; Simmons, Sack, & Miller, 1996) and mental health (Austrian, 1995; Land, 1998; Worell & Remer, 1992). Metatheoretical precepts have been used as lenses to help us identify and understand some experiences that affect women quite differently or in greater frequency than they affect men; homelessness, battering, incest and sexual assault, mental health labeling, imprisonment, and poverty are examples. Used as a scaffolding for practice, these precepts have helped us decide what might be incorporated from other disciplines and practice models; examples include narrative and various "postmodern" approaches to clinical practice.

As noted earlier, the metatheory of feminist practice does have some empirical grounding and, being both abstract and distinguishable from mainstream metatheories, it has stimulated inspiration and innovation by a wide variety of practitioners. In this strength lies its disadvantage, of course: Its precepts are open to such a wide variety of interpretations that their utility is limited. Moreover, practitioners pick and choose among them—they are not a closed ideological system—and this has resulted in contradictions and conflicts among practices labeled feminist. Indeed, many clinical practitioners appear to have abandoned sociopolitical activism altogether, even while acknowledging that the need to change sociopolitical structures is the raison d'être of feminist practice (Hill & Ballou, 1998; Land, 1998). Similarly, the use of metatheory as scaffolding has been problematic. Into a somewhat disjointed structure, we have imported more dislocation and contradiction in postmodernism, which is not a single system of thought but a collection of hotly contested positions on everything to do with reality including reality itself.

Little wonder that a recent study of feminist therapists' efforts to render their espoused precepts in daily practice found considerable surface but little deep integration of them—that is, practitioners had become more gender aware but had not fundamentally transformed their practices (Hill & Ballou, 1998, pp. 4-5). The FP98 Reprise data are similar in this regard: Most respondents describe "feminizing" or "gendering" traditional practice methods and techniques rather than inventing new ones. Correlatively, Katz-Porterfield (1998) found that many *non*feminist practitioners had recently changed their practices, making them more gender-sensitive and even consonant with some feminist precepts but remaining significantly different overall from those who identified as feminists.

Katz-Porterfield's finding suggests a particular advantage of the "feminist practice as metatheory" approach to definition: It is more likely than the identity approach to help us build bridges to and alliances with others who share some of its precepts and values. Moreover, the traffic flows both ways across the bridge: Feminist practitioners have opportunities to test and refine our approaches as we collaborate with others having similar interests and agendas. Thus, it seems wise at this stage of model development to resist the temptation to make the precepts of feminist practice prescriptive in any way.

Feminist Practice as Method: "What I hope for . . ."

On the other hand, as we saw in our review of the stated goals of the FP98 Reprise participants, feminism is still experienced by many, perhaps most, as a theory and practice of integrated personal/sociopolitical transformation.[13] One who works with battered women said she seeks "support and assistance to individuals *and* social reform/change. I don't see one happening without the other." Feminism seeks change across the continuum from personal to political, individual to institutional. If the liberatory and transformative agendas of feminism are to be met in this process, it is not enough to ameliorate a condition; both the contexts and the consciousness that are related to the condition must change. Feminist practice as method would provide concrete guidelines, specific courses of action, and the necessary techniques to accomplish this multidimensional purpose in a variety of settings. It would move a general metatheoretical approach to a specific integrated practice system.

From the beginning, some feminist practitioners have been at work on this project, incorporating such methods as consciousness-raising, collective decision making, community development, and selected group work approaches, often working with natural allies from the empowerment practice and strengths-based practice movements (see, e.g., Gutiérrez, 1990; Guitérrez, Parsons, & Cox, 1998; Saleebey, 1992, 1996; Simon, 1994; Weick, 1986). Feminist practice as method is definitely a work-in-progress, although there is a suggestion in the FP98 Reprise data that some of the techniques mentioned above are being used less.

In part, this may be due to the way services are organized and sanctioned today, with emphases on billable hours and structured, outcome-driven methods pervading all arenas of practice. But if the project of developing an integrated practice of personal/political transformation has stalled, it is also due to the nature of the task itself. It is much easier, for example, to theorize and practice about the gendered political economy of particular families in our practice than to change the political economy that shapes those families and constrains their options. It is easier to help a woman on welfare learn to think differently about herself and her options than to create real options and, ultimately, end poverty. Nonetheless, the stated purpose of feminism is to end patriarchy, not to renegotiate the terms on which it will operate; similarly, most feminist practitioners appear to be holding fast to the aim of meeting human needs through systems of social and economic justice, not to create islands of safety for a few. Clearly, there is much work to be done. The next section is intended to reflect and support some of the theoretical work being done to define feminist practice as method.

A (REVISED) DEFINITION OF FEMINIST PRACTICE: DISCOVERING METHOD; BUILDING A MODEL

You can put your foot in the stream, but the water has moved on.

—Zen proverb[14]

Any overarching definition of feminist practice as method will surely omit some key information and obscure important detail, but attempts must be made. With all due caveats and cautions, we derived one from the 1983 data (Bricker-Jenkins & Hooyman, 1986, pp. 26-27), and now, we will attempt to reflect the changes we see in the 1998 data. In the following material, new and revised concepts are italicized, and each component is illustrated by quotations from the FP98 Reprise surveys.

Feminist social work practice as method is both the water and the stream. No two practitioners are likely to emphasize the same elements of the definition or apply them in the same way, but the data suggest that, in general, those who strive to create feminist practice as method do the following:

Approach all issues *and opportunities* presented by social living and social relationships with a view to identifying *the power dynamics operating in them and* their implications for *diverse groups of* women

> I am always prompted to act when particular conditions affect women and children—whether social policy, cultural abuse (advertising, for example), and the personal enactment of these [as in] domestic violence and institutional violence.

> [I teach people] my understanding of power dynamics (how to assess who has power, how to get and use power) . . . to identify oppressive conditions and points of change.

Are concerned with the ways in which institutionalized sexism (and, usually, other oppressive ideologies and behaviors) create problems for all persons and for women in particular

> I include more cultural and political influences [than my nonfeminist colleagues] . . . i.e., connections between race, class, and drug use; sexism and oppression reflected in people with trauma histories.

> In the oppression of women one finds a description of and prescription for what needs to be changed for everybody. Ineluctably, with women of color, you have all of this, the whole thing.

Are committed to the development *and use* of specific actions and techniques[15] to *create op-*

portunities for and remove barriers, both material and ideological, to the fullest possible development of the abilities of individuals and groups

> I look for teaching/learning moments when analysis and the need to *act* can come together.

> Ideological, cultural, social behaviors practiced personally and collectively. I do [these] when and where I can and as much as possible.

> I'm working for individual emancipation *and* social change in whatever context.

Identify and build on the strengths and opportunities of individuals, groups, communities, and cultures

> Strengths-oriented/belief in fostering hope and resiliences

> Assist the families . . . to acknowledge their expertise regarding their own lives.

> [In my work on] rape, woman abuse, women in prison . . . I'm using a feminist strengths approach.

> Valuing diversity, acceptance, and consensus decision-making are a major component of domestic violence shelter work.

Are committed to collaborative relationships with people with whom they are working as clients while recognizing and negotiating the differential power inherent in all relationships, including professional relationships

> I try not to ever exert my power and I explore the power differential in sessions. I explicitly encourage exploration of political issues as they emerge—racism, classism, sexism, welfare reform, poverty—and connections to "illness."

> [My feminism is] in listening to a child's story in his/her own words, in working with a problem of the child's own choosing, in selecting interventions collaboratively.

Tend to view social work practice as a "political," *liberatory, and transformative* practice, that is, as a normatively based and directed effort to enable people to control the conditions of their lives by *redefining and* moving *individual and institutional* power in a more egalitarian direction

> Placing events in a context of who benefits and who does not . . . realizing that if one person is helped to "escape," they will be replaced by someone else. It is the system that requires a certain number of unemployed, a group to do unpaid labor, a certain level of consumption, etc.

> Having a worldview that includes social influences in personally experienced problems, and transmitting that view to clients in terms that they will understand. When possible . . . being involved in community change efforts . . . Political should be an *action* adjective.

While working to create options for and with people, respect and support their natural healing and helping processes and the choices they make in relation to their conditions of concern

> I hope to provide a safe environment where women can begin to explore themselves. I hope to empower women to learn to problem-solve and take action for themselves.

> I used to hope to join with others in spreading the feminist vision. Now I hope to alleviate a bit of the pain momentarily. . . . On a "macro level" [I] try to turn the tide with whatever allies I can find.

> I treat the people [with whom] I work with dignity and respect. . . . This treatment includes respecting their choices even if I disagree. . . . [I do]

encourage women to look at societal pressures and expectations which influence their choices and perhaps try to help them make choices that are less influenced by outside influences.

I take the time necessary for feminist process in decision making.

In sum, a good many feminist social workers continue to attempt a practice method that can accomplish the goal of personal/political transformation espoused by most feminists. Elements of the approach may have been refined over the past 15 years; the most notable differences between the 1983 and 1998 data appear to be in practitioners' thinking about diversity/the differential effect of sexism on various groups of women; an increased emphasis on the need to include effects on men in our analyses; refinements in notions of power and the pervasiveness of power; a distinction between practice that is liberatory/transformational and that which is more narrowly political; a more explicit strengths orientation; and emphasis on the centrality of relationships and respect in feminist practice, including the imperative to engage people's expertise and support their choices.

VARIATIONS OF FEMINIST PRACTICE REVISITED

Changes in feminist theory and practice will continue to emerge from conversations among members of a very diverse and increasingly differentiated community. The FP98 Reprise data suggest that the nature of the variations (and/or our understanding of them) is also changing. About variations in feminist practices, the report on the 1983 pilot survey concluded "If feminist theory provides the lens through which

the world is viewed, political and demographic characteristics influence the specific qualities of the lens and in some cases may compel the development of an entirely new one" (Bricker-Jenkins & Hooyman, 1986, p. 31).[16] Today's assessment is different:

- Espoused political orientation does *not* appear to have a direct influence on most practitioner's actual practice behaviors; however, their implicit beliefs about ontology, epistemology, and change (which are related to but distinguishable from political orientation) might be very influential in shaping practice and its variations.
- Demographic categories and identities (race/ethnicity, sexual orientation, geography, and so on) also appear to be less directly determinant of practice than they appeared (or were assumed) to be in the past, not because they are less important in people's lives, but because attention to identity-related issues may be more complex and infused into all feminist practice.
- Similarly, attention to spirituality and the commitment to a "wholistic" practice appear to be more fully established throughout the feminist practice communities.

The more consequential variations in feminist practice today may be in these dimensions:

- Field of practice (addictions, families, mental health, poverty and welfare reform, etc.) and/or modality specialization;
- *Within* each of these, whether the practitioner's orientation is primarily woman-centered, gendered, or feminist transformational; and
- The practitioner's implicit operant beliefs about reality, truth, and change.

In the remainder of this chapter, I will reflect on what I believe to be the significance of the changes I see in the terrain of feminist practice and some of the challenges they pose. It seems to me that the choices we have to make as we encounter these challenges are clearer and more urgent than they were 15 years ago.

SOME DIFFERENCES OF THE PAST

Political orientation has provided a convenient way to categorize definitions and variations of feminist practice (see, e.g., Bricker-Jenkins & Hooyman, 1986; Nes & Iladicola, 1986; Saulnier, 1996). However, studies that attempt to derive principles from actual practice (rather than examining applications of principles in practice) have found that these categories have a tenuous relationship to practice behaviors (Bricker-Jenkins, 1989; Katz-Porterfield, 1998; Sandell, 1993). In the FP98 Reprise, for example, democratic socialism was most frequently named among the top three political theories influencing practice (receiving 15 votes from the 23 respondents), whereas reformism/liberalism—the political theory that appeared to be most reflected in the respondent's descriptions of their practice—was named only eight times.[17]

This is not to say that such categories are useless; the raging debates between and among their adherents have sharpened our thinking, often by illuminating and "naming" collective experiences, thus laying a foundation for the creation of community and the potential for political power. However, using these categories can also produce a form of brand loyalty that can actually inhibit analysis, render it irrelevant, or cause us to abandon our goals as unrealistic. At this juncture, setting aside a priori political categories might lead to more useful approaches to understanding and developing feminist social work practices today.

Similarly, the role of demographic variables and the discourse on identities in shaping practice may have changed during the past 15 years. The 1983 pilot and much of the feminist social work literature of the last two decades bear witness to the fact that at least some definitions of feminist practice have always incorporated such concepts as diversity, oppression, privilege, and multiple positionalities (e.g., examining the intersecting dynamics of racism, classism, and heterosexism as well as sexism); at least some have always seen the ending of all forms of domination and subordination, exploitation, and supremacy as integral to the feminist practice agenda.

The FP98 Reprise data suggest that these concepts are quite fully integrated into the language of feminist practice if not the practice itself. For example, a "liberal white feminist" is likely to be aware that her positionality shapes her consciousness and privileges, although racist thinking and behaviors have hardly been eliminated from feminist (or any other) practice. Similarly, identity as a woman of color, or a lesbian, or a rural woman, or a Christian or Muslim or Jewish feminist, or even a man does not lead one inexorably to attach an identity modifier to one's practice. We do see in this data a continuation of perspectives based in or influenced by identity, but one's identity cannot be assumed to preclude or bind one to a group loyalty, much less to an ideological position. For example, a "black feminist perspective" will not be the same as a "womanist" perspective; it may have relatively few black adherents but many white ones; it may or may not be *radical* as that term is differentially understood in feminist and African American communities; its position on lesbianism (whatever position it takes) will be a lightning rod; someone is sure to critique its implicit class position; and other women of color will (justifiably) say "This does not speak for me!" When it comes to making assumptions about the ways that people will experience and negotiate their many interlocking identities, all bets are off.[18]

In this study, some practitioners illustrated another dimension of identity-based politics: They felt angry, betrayed, and dismayed when feminists (or fill in other identity categories) did not act the way they "should," implying both an assumption that identity is important and a clarity that it is not important in the same way for everybody. Perhaps, as many academic feminists argue, the days of essentialism, universalism, and identity politics are numbered (or should be). On the other hand, until we eliminate the conditions that give rise to whatever it is that people experience as collective alienation and systematic exploitation, at least some of these practitioners are going to be looking for concepts and forms of practice that name and address these experiences. The roles of identity as well as ideology are both less clear and more complex today than they were a decade and a half ago. In their very fluidity and complexity, we might find hope for a more powerful practice or a hopeless tangle of failed theory, but a closer look is surely warranted.

The place of spirituality and wholistic perspectives (for lack of a better term) in feminist practice is also difficult to discern and perhaps in flux. In 1983, it seemed that some feminist practitioners were developing a distinguishable approach to practice based on their commitment to address the unity—not just the interactions—of the intellect, emotions, spirit, body, and their sociopolitical contexts. Although this work may continue to be a primary preoccupation for some, the more interesting possibility is

that the perspective has greater currency in all branches of feminist practice (and perhaps in social work at large). This possibility is reflected not only in comments about what people do or attempt to do in practice but in the theories that people identified as informing their practice. Many respondents chose *both* democratic socialism or socialism/marxism *and* cultural or radical feminisms. At least until recently, these were thought to be discordant if not irreconcilable approaches to viewing and being in the world. It is possible, of course, that respondents were imprecise or confused in their replies, and we do not always seem to understand that some differences among schools of thought are quite irreconcilable; however, there is some evidence that the particular alchemy of feminist practice involves combining elements that appear to be incongruent (Bricker-Jenkins, 1991; Diamond, 1994; Finley, 1991; Hobgood, 1991). We turn now to an examination of some of the elements—incongruent and not—with which feminist practitioners are working.

SOME DIFFERENCES FOR THE FUTURE

The greatest area of development in the 15 years between the two pilot studies appears to have been in applying feminist concepts to various fields of practice—addictions, family practice, mental health, violence against women, and the like—and in such practice modalities as clinical practice, group work, community organization, policy analysis, and administration.[19] As noted earlier, much of this work has used the metatheory approach, using feminist precepts as a lens through which to view the world differently, modifying practice in accordance with what can be seen through this lens. In recent years, it appears that most feminist practitioners have used a convex lens to view at close quarters the operations of gender bias in microsystems more often than the concave lens through which earlier feminists examined the connections between the personal and the political, the biographical and the sociostructural. Thus, most of the developments have been in discreet areas of practice and particularly in what is called clinical practice.

For the most part, the considerable gains in fields of practice and modalities have involved modifications of existing methods—creating woman-centered or gendered approaches—rather than development of the integrated feminist transformation method espoused by many. Our sister field of feminist therapy appears to be gaining and stalling in the same places: In their study of the enactment of feminist principles in therapy, Hill and Ballou (1998) found a good deal of surface integration—modification of conventional techniques and attention to power dynamics in relationships—but little of the deep integration that would incorporate action to foster social change into the therapeutic process itself.

Some of the reasons for this are not hard to discern: Not only is social work increasingly organized by fields of practice and method, but increased regulation and reduced resources have constricted opportunities and energy for innovation. The related demand to "show results" in concrete terms has also deflected attention from achievements that are difficult to document and—more to the point—not of much interest to funding sources. Efforts to develop an "empowerment scale," for example, have focused primarily on the psychological and relational dimensions of empowerment, although changes in the structural contexts of people's

lives have been regarded from the beginning as integral to empowerment practice, at least in the social work milieu (Parsons, Gutiérrez, & Cox, 1998; Simon, 1994; Solomon, 1976). In other words, we may be seeing increased and more sophisticated attention to power in feminist practice (and in social work at large), but the cost of that attention may be the abandonment of our transformational agenda. If the core feminist concept of power is stripped of its structural dimension, what is left? The economic and political contexts in which feminist practice is attempting to survive and thrive may very well be precipitating a transmutation of the conceptual "gene pool" of that practice, leaving us bereft of the material we need to develop theories and practices that challenge those structures, leaving us only the rhetoric and dream of transformation.

If the FP98 Reprise participants are at all representative of feminist social work practitioners today, we are not ready to abandon the dream. Let us examine more closely, then, the space in which much of the work must take place: the gap between espoused theory and theory-in-use (Schön, 1983). The disjunction between them is not surprising; an imperfect fit is characteristic of most practice. Bringing them together into a unified theory/practice system (or praxis), however, requires more than a commitment to reflective practice or the now-fashionable documentation of practice process and outcomes. It requires action rooted in analysis of power.

The actual power and opportunities that people have to translate their consciousness into the historical/material world are generally limited by their social locations. As feminist practitioners (who are still mostly women) and as social *workers* (with little control over the resources needed to accomplish our stated objectives), we live with a dual consciousness as a matter of survival—using it as a form of resistance and, when the opportunities are there, for rebellion. Perhaps, we encode our dreams and desires in the theories we espouse as we look for opportunities for insurrection and, sometimes, for sustained campaigns to change the conditions of practice.

In the current context of practice, there is a growing tendency to become self-limiting in our perceptions of the potential of our practice, to abandon our analyses and aspirations as too quixotic or intellectually spent. But is it possible to find among the dreamers today examples of feminist practitioners' resistance, rebellion, and insurrection that form the bridges between our aspirations and our day-to-day practices? Can these be combined so that they become elements of a liberatory *and* transformative practice model and method? These questions are certainly raised by this study, and they are no less compelling today than they were 15 years ago. Indeed, the current level of danger to women and our allies is such that they are more urgent than ever. Before we abandon the goal, we can be clear about the very real material impediments to achieving it and the enormous creativity we have shown thus far.

If we are to continue developing along these lines—a healthy diversity of theories and practices and something akin to a transformational agenda—feminist social workers will need to take back and examine closely the elements of practice theory over which we *do* have control. These include some elements that underpin all practices that we usually do not think about much: ontology, epistemology, and theory of change. Implicit beliefs we hold about the nature of reality and ways we can "know" it appear to influence practice behaviors much more powerfully and directly than espoused political theories.[20] For example, those who espouse the primacy of subjectivity and discourse may be more likely to emphasize goals and techniques that are intended to help people think differently about themselves and their worlds than those who work in a materialist tradition. Although associated with several different political traditions, such techniques as cognitive reframing, restructuring family narratives, self-esteem/self-reliance work, feminist psychoanalysis, and even hypnotherapy are consistent with the notions that "reality is what we make of it" and that oppressed people do not have to buy into the definitions and discourses imposed on them by others. On the other hand, those who believe there is "something out there" that is at least partially independent of subjective experience will continue to demand attention to the material and structural contexts of people's lives as a locus of influence and action. For them, practice is incomplete without structural change in the material world; thus, their practice is more likely to include advocacy, organizing, group work, cultural work, and other forms of activism—again, packaged differently according to political orientation and agenda—intended to produce sociopolitical and cultural changes.

This discussion assumes that feminist social workers can and should attempt changes in the sociopolitical realm; as we have seen, there are those who believe we cannot or should not—and some who are not sure there *is* such a realm, at least in a material sense.[21] Our core of assumptions about the nature of change itself is another critical area for study and choice. The theory of change that appears to be pre-eminent in social work today is an accretion theory: "Feminist therapists create revolution insidiously, one person at a time" (Hill, 1998, p. xv). Some of us think that the world is a much too dangerous place, especially for women, to rely on this theory alone. When it comes to personal/political transformation, not all theories are created equal. So whatever our theory-in-use—be it microstructural or cultural, magic or movement-based—we need to be clearer than we have been about stating it, interrogating it, connecting the dots. We need also to continue to distinguish between what is political practice—pertaining to distributions of power—and what is transformative practice—pertaining to changes in the nature and bases of power as well as distributions of it. And we need to be clear about when a system *can* meet a need and *won't* (requiring a reform strategy) and when it cannot meet needs because it was not intended to (requiring another strategy).[22]

On the surface, at least, these sets of assumptions appear to be opposing and contradictory, but the history of feminist social work practice tells us it is better to think of them as contrapuntal themes that could go off in different directions but could resolve creatively into new themes. In some measure, what happens to them will depend on how we decide to play them. The FP98 Reprise study shows that we have been making some choices and perhaps need to make some more consciously. It also suggests some new questions about change that we might consider if we choose to travel the path of personal/political transformation:

- What do I/we believe are the "realities" that must change here?

- Who says? (Whose "truth" is being privileged in this situation?)
- What do I/we believe about the relationships and interactions among between the personal and political, individual and institutional, biographical and structural dimensions of change? In other words, what beliefs about the nature and possibility of social change are being chosen?
- Can the need/condition of concern be addressed within the current context, or are changes needed in the contexts and consciousness that create or sustain the need?
- If the latter, what methods are available or imaginable to make those changes?
- What path do I choose for feminist social work practice and its hope for personal/political transformation in the midst of the realities of my daily practice?

NOTES

1. The findings formed the basis for a Practice Institute we did at the next NASW national conference and for our first book, *Not for Women Only: Social Work Practice for a Feminist Future* (Bricker-Jenkins & Hooyman, 1986).

2. The original pilot study results were reported in Bricker-Jenkins and Hooyman (1986), pp. 25-33.

3. Currently, the entire reprise pilot study data set is being examined in depth by a study group of AWSW members including Doris Correa-Capello, Marcie Lazzari, Bernice Liddie, Nancy Hooyman, and me. Hoping to stimulate further empirical research on feminist social work practice, we expect to report on the full pilot study findings in another format.

4. For some introductory sources, see overview in Bricker-Jenkins and Lockett (1995).

5. In 1983, we engaged a less formal but comparable network of social workers who self-identified as feminists—the network that, in fact, constituted the core of the founding members of AWSW in 1984.

6. The FPP interviews, conducted from 1984 to 1986, revealed that feminism was of much greater interest to some people of color in social work than was generally

assumed. In fact, the majority of participants (12 of 23) were people of color (Bricker-Jenkins, 1989).

7. In this context, *transformational* refers to changes not only in the conditions we experience but also in the consciousness and sociopolitical contexts that sustain those conditions.

8. One participant sent along a bumper sticker to express her indignation at the position of some feminists: that we should abandon the theory and practice of revolutionary transformation. It reads, "I'll be post-feminist in the post-patriarchy!"

9. The definition of *feminist* currently in use by social work's feminist journal, *Affilia,* falls into this category. The journal seeks scholarship that "places women at the center of analysis."

10. Saulnier (1996) provides an excellent recent example of the latter method. She reviews nine branches or schools of contemporary feminist theory/ies with implications for social work.

11. Through applying this approach in the FPP, we came to understand the similarities between feminist approaches and others that emerge from experiences of oppression and liberatory practice (such as some Afrocentric approaches).

12. This is similar to the notion of the *ideological base* of feminist practice, but the use of the term *ideology* has been problematic, as it is often presumed to mean (and lead to) doctrinaire imposition of "politically correct" behaviors.

13. Thus, many authors have underscored the consonance of the goals of feminist social work and those articulated by the profession as a whole. See especially Collins (1986), Morell (1987), Stout and McPhail (1998), and Valentich (1986).

14. Feminists and others who find Jungian archetypes useful note that a similar notion is attributed to the Heraclitis of Ephesus (c. 540-480 BC): "You could not step twice into the same river, for other waters are ever flowing on to you."

15. For examples of preferred techniques, see Bricker-Jenkins and Lockett (1995).

16. The "new one" referred to what we labeled "the psychic-healer perspective" in the report of that study.

17. Others most frequently cited were cultural and radical feminisms (11 and 9 respectively). Marxism/socialism got only three mentions, but others emerging from or related to Marxist and socialist feminist literatures received several more (standpoint, social structural, and oppression theories and others).

18. Beyond the scope of this chapter but certainly important is the fact that feminists of various stripes and dis-

ciplines are contesting the very notions of oppression, identity, and other concepts on which the practice of social work today is based.

19. These developments have been assisted greatly by the 1986 introduction of *Affilia—The Journal of Social Work with Women,* which has provided an outlet for research and conceptual discussion among feminist social workers.

20. Each of the political theories makes core assumptions about ontology and epistemology, of course; I am suggesting that these components can and should be looked at separately from the totality of the theory.

21. Figueira-McDonough (1998) provides an excellent overview of the epistemological issues as applied to social work knowledge.

22. With thanks to Willie Baptist, Education Director of the Kensington Welfare Rights Union, for this formulation.

REFERENCES

Abramovitz, M. (1988). *Regulating the lives of women: Social welfare policy from colonial times to the present.* Boston: South End Press.

Abramovitz, M. (1996). *Under attack, fighting back: Women and welfare in the United States.* New York: Monthly Review Press.

Austrian, S. (1995). *Mental disorders, medication, and clinical social work.* New York: Columbia University Press.

Babcock, M., & McKay, C. (Eds.). (1995). *Challenging codependency: Feminist critiques.* Toronto: University of Toronto Press.

Bartlett, H. M. (1970). *The common base of social work practice.* New York: National Association of Social Workers.

Bricker-Jenkins, M. (1989). *Foundations of feminist social work practice: The changer and the changed are one* (Publication No. 9015943). Ann Arbor, MI: University Microfilms International. (UMI Dissertation Abstract # 5104 A)

Bricker-Jenkins, M. (1991). The propositions and assumptions of feminist social work practice. In M. Bricker-Jenkins, N. Hooyman, & N. Gottlieb (Eds.), *Feminist social work practice in clinical settings* (pp. 271-303). Newbury Park, CA: Sage.

Bricker-Jenkins, M., & Hooyman, N. (Eds.). (1986). *Not for women only: Social work practice for a feminist future.* Silver Spring, MD: National Association of Social Workers.

Bricker-Jenkins, M., & Lockett, P. W. (1995). Women: Direct practice. In *Encyclopedia of social work* (pp. 2529-2538). Silver Spring, MD: NASW Press.

Brodsky, A. (1980). A decade of feminist influence on psychotherapy. *Psychology of Women Quarterly, 4,* 331-344.

Bounds, E. M., Brubaker, P., & Hobgood, M. E. (Eds.). (1999). *Welfare policy: Feminist critiques.* Cleveland, OH: Pilgrim Press.

Collins, B. (1993). Reconstructing codependency using self-in-relation theory: A feminist perspective. *Social Work, 38,* 470-476.

Collins, B. G. (1986). Defining feminist social work. *Social Work, 31,* 214-219.

Collins, P. H. (1998). *Fighting words: Black women and the search for justice.* Minneapolis: University of Minnesota Press.

Diamond, S. (1994). Religion and the rise of feminism. *Women's Review of Books, 11,* 174.

Ebben, M. (1995). Off the shelf salvation: A feminist critique of self-help. *Women's Studies in Communication, 18,* 111-122.

Favorini, A. (1995). Concept of codependency: Blaming the victim or pathway to recovery? *Social Work, 40,* 827-830.

Figueira-McDonough, J. (1998). Toward a gender-integrated knowledge in social work. In J. Figueira-McDonough, F. E. Netting, & A. Nichols-Casebolt (Eds.), *The role of gender in practice knowledge: Claiming half the human experience* (pp. 227-256). New York: Brunner/Mazel.

Finley, N. J. (1991). Political activism and feminist spirituality. *Sociological Analysis, 52,* 349-362.

Germain, C. (1973). An ecological perspective in casework practice. *Social Casework, 54,* 323-330.

Gould, K. (1987). Feminist principles and minority concerns: Contributions, problems, and solutions. *Affilia, 3,* 6-19.

Gutiérrez, L. M. (1990). Working with women of color: An empowerment perspective. *Social Work, 35,* 97-192.

Gutiérrez, L. M. (1991). Empowering women of color: A feminist model. In M. Bricker-Jenkins, N. Hooyman, & N. Gottlieb (Eds.), *Feminist social work practice in clinical settings* (pp. 199-214). Newbury Park, CA: Sage.

Gutiérrez, L., Parsons, R. J., & Cox, E. O. (Eds.). (1998). *Empowerment in social work practice: A sourcebook.* Pacific Grove, CA: Brooks/Cole.

Haaken, J. (1993). From AL-ANON to ACOA: Codependence and the reconstruction of caregiving. *Signs, 18,* 321-348.

Hill, M. (Ed.). (1998). *Feminist therapy as a political act.* New York: Harrington Park Press.

Hill, M., & Ballou, M. (1998). *Making therapy feminist: A practice survey.* In M. Hill (Ed.), *Feminist therapy as a political act.* New York: Harrington Park Press.

Hobgood, M. E. (1991). *Catholic social teaching and economic theory: Paradigms in conflict.* Philadelphia: Temple University Press.

Katz-Porterfield, S. L. (1998). *Feminist social work: An analysis of practice.* Unpublished doctoral dissertation, Barry University, Miami.

Kenney, S. J., & Kinsella, H. (Eds.). (1997). *Politics and feminist standpoint theories.* New York: Haworth.

Laird, J. (1995). Family-centered practice: Feminist, constructionist, and cultural perspectives. In N. Van Den Bergh (Ed.), *Feminist practice in the twenty-first century* (pp. 20-40). Washington, DC: NASW Press.

Land, H. (1998). The feminist approach to clinical social work. In R. Dorfman (Ed.), *Paradigms of clinical social work* (pp. 227-256). New York: Brunner/Mazel.

Lee, J. A. B. (1994). *The empowerment approach to social work practice.* New York: Columbia University Press.

McGoldrick, M. (Ed.). (1998). *Re-visioning family therapy: Race, culture, and gender in clinical practice.* New York: Guilford.

Miller, D. C. (1990). *Women and social welfare: A feminist analysis.* New York: Praeger.

Morell, C. (1987). Cause is function: Toward a feminist model of integration for social work. *Social Service Review, 61,* 144-155.

Murray, G. (1997). Agonize, don't organize: A critique of postfeminism. *Current Sociology, 45,* 37-47.

Nes, J., & Iadicola, P. (1989). Toward a definition of feminist social work: A comparison of liberal, radical, and socialist models. *Social Work, 34,* 12-21.

Norman, E., & Mancuso, A. (Eds.). (1980). *Women's issues and social work practice.* Itasca, IL: F. E. Peacock.

Parsons, R., Gutiérrez, L., & Cox, E. (1998). A model for empowerment practice. In L. Gutiérrez, R. J. Parsons, & E. O. Cox (Eds.), *Empowerment in social work practice: A sourcebook* (pp. 1-23). Pacific Grove, CA: Brooks/Cole.

Pincus, A., & Minahan, A. (1973). *Social work practice: Model and method.* Itasca, IL: F. E. Peacock.

Saleebey, D. (Ed.). (1992). *The strengths perspective in social work practice.* White Plains, NY: Longman.

Saleebey, D. (1996). The strengths perspective in social work practice: Extensions and cautions. *Social Work, 41,* 296-305.

Sandell, K. S. (1993). *Different voices: Articulating feminist social work.* Unpublished doctoral dissertation, Mandel

School of Applied Social Sciences, Case Western Reserve University, Cleveland, OH.

Saulnier, C. F. (1996). *Feminist theories and social work: Approaches and applications.* New York: Haworth.

Schön, D. (1983). *The reflective practitioner: How professionals think in action.* New York: Basic Books.

Simmons, K. P., Sack, T., & Miller, G. (1996). Sexual abuse and chemical dependency: Implications for women in recovery. *Women & Therapy, 19,* 17-30.

Simon, B. L. (1994). *The empowerment tradition in American social work: A history.* New York: Columbia.

Stout, K. D., & McPhail, B. (1998). *Confronting sexism and violence against women: A challenge for social work.* New York: Longman.

Towle, C. (1965). *Common human needs* (Rev. ed.). New York: National Association of Social Workers. (Original work published 1945)

Valentich, M. (1986). Feminism and social work practice. In F. Turner (Ed.), *Social work treatment: Interlocking theoretical frameworks* (3rd ed., pp. 564-589.). New York: Free Press.

Walters, M., Carter, B., Papp, P., & Silverstein, O. (1988). *The invisible web: Gender patterns in family relationships.* New York, Guilford.

Weick, A. (1986). The philosophical context of a health model of social work. *Social Casework, 67,* 551-559.

Weick, A., & Vandiver, S. T. (Eds.). (1982). *Women, power, and change.* Silver Spring, MD: NASW Press.

Wetzel, J. W., & The Feminist World View Educators. (1986). A feminist world view conceptual framework. *Social Casework, 67,* 166-173.

Worell, J., & Remer, P. (1992). *Feminist perspectives in therapy: An empowerment model for women.* New York: John Wiley.

P A R T   I I I

Approaches to Change

When serving individuals, families, and groups, practitioners relate practice principles to many theories. Some of those most often noted are ego psychology, behaviorism, and cognitive psychology, as well as a range of social psychological propositions about group dynamics, family systems, human ecology, and organizational functioning. Some practitioners operate in a broadly eclectic manner, whereas others restrict their thinking to a small set of theories. This is not to deny that many propositions about intervention come from so-called "practice wisdom," which represents the accumulated wisdom of the profession about "what works."

In this book, we have decided not to organize chapters around one or another theory, as we have concluded that effective practice must not make the assumption that there is only one truth. Practice should draw on the knowledge base that leads to effective intervention in the specific situation. We decided, instead, to provide the frameworks that have implications for the application of appropriate theories. In this and the next section of the book, we shall illustrate this principle further as we focus on types of practice targets and practice fields.

As we indicated in the introduction to Part II, we decided that it was most representative of contemporary practice ideas to organize our discussion of theories and procedures around types of client behavior or types of client systems rather than around discrete theories. Each of these behavioral or client system targets requires unique ways of using theory or integrating several theories.

With respect to types of behavior, we adopted a frequently used typology (Garfield, 1980; Kanfer & Goldstein, 1991; Kanfer & Schefft, 1988) of categorizing behavior. All behavior, according to this schema, has cognitive, affective, and instrumental components. It is rare to have a practice situation that involves only one of these; however, this typology leads to useful ways of conceptualizing, planning, and executing professional interventions. Thus, Chapter 9 presents current ideas on how to understand and work with the client's cognitive processes. In Chapter 9, Berlin and Barden elaborate on the basic premise that "our human species has evolved a way of adapting to the world by generating mental models of what is going on" (p. 175). This leads to the practice premise that we can try to help our clients change the meanings of their lives. This occurs by altering available information and patterns for formulating meanings. The bulk of the chapter expands on these principles as well as the empirical basis for a cognitively oriented practice.

Chapter 10 does the same thing with respect to instrumental behaviors, such as client actions and activities. Thyer and Myers believe that behavioral theory, and practices derived from it, is the most desirable way of approaching this issue, and they explicate this assertion. This leads them to a detailed discussion of such processes as those of reinforcement, punishment, and various forms of conditioning and how these are employed in a variety of practice situations.

Chapter 11 deals with clients' affective responses, such as depression and anxiety. These were chosen by Himle because of the frequency with which these responses are troublesome in practice situations. Himle provides a broad array of procedures that empirical work has demonstrated to be effective with these types of problems.

With respect to types of client systems, we have adopted a traditional typology based on working with individuals, families, and groups. When we came to consider work with individuals, however, we encountered significantly different contexts when the focus is on an adult compared to when it is on a child. We, therefore, commissioned separate chapters for these age categories.

In Chapter 12, Reid and Misener undertake the portrayal of individual work with adults. They precede their discussion of practice procedures with a review of research and theories related to adult change. They consider such procedures as motivators for change. Such motivators, in turn, represent either the "push of discomfort" or the "pull of hope." These authors indicate a broad array of social work practices derived from these simple ideas and indicate the types of situations appropriate for various practices.

In Chapter 13, Faller organizes her presentation of work with children in a way that takes into consideration the ways children are brought into a social work practice context. The legal status of children and their relative powerlessness are important issues. Children also can rarely be a focus in the absence of their families. These are important considerations for Faller as she portrays such important social concerns as child abuse and neglect and the plight of children from socially oppressed groups.

We believe that it is essential that workers be able to work with multiperson situations, typically families and groups of unrelated individuals. In Chapter 14, on social work practice with groups, Pollio, Brower, and Galinsky consider such environmental impacts as managed care requirements as well as resources in the form of new technologies for interpersonal communication. It is exciting to consider how group practice on a face-to-face basis will be supplemented, and even at times replaced, by telephone and computer-based group interactions. In Chapter 15, on families, Walsh and Crosser take a stance that is highly compatible with the other chapters in the book. This is a stance that understands the social contexts of family life, the strengths that families bring to their struggles with such contexts, and the need

for environmental changes to strengthen families.

Specific practice principles are drawn on with clients who are in a state of crisis compared to those who seek service because of longer-standing problems. In Chapter 16, Roberts and Corcoran offer a useful review of the crisis literature as well as the history of crisis intervention and then discuss such practice issues as how diversity affects what social workers should do in crises. The authors draw on a rich research literature on crisis intervention in support of the practice models they explore.

Also, we recognized that the increasing emphasis on prevention requires still another set of theories and approaches, and this led to our selection of an author for a chapter on coping and stress. In Chapter 17, Nurius draws our attention to the rapidly expanding literature on this topic; this is a literature that has not yet been sufficiently plumbed for its practice implications. This chapter is particularly useful as it organizes the findings under such headings as "Building a Reserve of Coping-Related Resources," "Recognition of Potential Stressors," "Preliminary Coping," and "Elicitation and Use of Feedback."

Finally, we are deeply committed to the idea that direct service practitioners must be able to work, often collaboratively with their clients and others, for changes in the social environment. We do not see a sharp delineation between the skills of these workers and community organizers or even administrators. We consequently asked an outstanding scholar of macro practice to write a chapter on this topic. Thus, in Chapter 18, Weil presents an extensive set of ways that practitioners can and should act with clients, or on behalf of clients, in seeking change in systems in the environment.

REFERENCES

Garfield, S. (1980). *Psychotherapy: An eclectic approach.* New York: John Wiley.

Kanfer, F. H., & Goldstein, A. P. (Eds.). (1991). *Helping people change* (4th ed.). New York: Pergamon.

Kanfer, F. H., & Schefft, B. K. (1988). *Guiding the process of therapeutic change.* Champaign, IL: Research Press.

CHAPTER NINE

Thinking Differently:
The Cognitive-Integrative
Approach to Changing a Mind

SHARON B. BERLIN

JANE E. BARDEN

The cognitive part of this practice approach encompasses the notion that our human species has evolved a way of adapting to the world by generating mental models of what is going on. In other words, we adapt according to our sense of what things mean. In our daily lives, we are constantly attempting to make sense of the events that are going on around us and within us in order to adapt—to do whatever seems to be in the best interest of our goals and enhances our feelings of security and predictability. We anticipate, arrange, and add to informational cues that are generated by interpersonal and other environmental sources and by our own feelings, thoughts, actions, and physiological states.

This search for meaning is not just a matter of passively picking up the sensations that originate in the external world; rather, what we know is a result of our active attempts to respond to environmental challenges. By anticipating and giving organization to the cues that we encounter, we not only respond to the environment but also participate in shaping the situations to which we respond. Nonetheless, the information that is available to us is not completely neutral, to the extent that we can make events and things mean whatever our whims might dictate and still maintain an adaptive balance. Our personal awareness and understanding is influenced by our encounters with the concrete realities of the physical world and, perhaps more important, by the pre-formed meanings that are conveyed to us through the beliefs, practices, and symbols of our culture; the families, communities, and opportunity structures that we are born into and grow up in; and the ongoing interpersonal messages we receive throughout our lives. All of these orient us toward certain modes of understanding and locate us on such basic dimensions as safety, power, worth, and affiliative connections. Similarly, informational cues that we might see as stemming from primarily personal sources (e.g., cues regarding our level of behavioral skills, the feel of our own bodies, the action implications of our emotions) do not afford an unlimited range of interpretations.

Even though it is not possible to make a distinct differentiation between internal and external sources of meaning, for heuristic purposes, we can conclude that all of the important meanings of our lives—who we are, how we stand in relation to others, what kinds of prospects and options we have—are a function of (a) the nature of the information that we encounter and (b) our own patterns or systems for organizing informational cues—in other words, our schemas.

These assumptions about sources of meaning also apply to problematic meanings. We tend to experience problems under two main conditions. The first is when the informational cues from social or personal sources that are available and that we pay attention to are essentially negative—difficult life conditions, conflictual relationships, lack of skills, emotional numbness or a state of constant emotional arousal, or bombardment with negative self-assessments. Sometimes, this negative information is chronically available, and sometimes, it occurs suddenly and intensely to shatter what we had always believed and held on to as anchors of stability in our lives (as in the case of traumatic life events). Second, we construct problematic meanings when our memory models (schemas) for organizing information are overly restrictive, so that we keep anticipating and acting on the basis of old, inflexible, narrow perspectives such as, "I can't trust anyone," "I never get what I deserve," "I'll never measure up." Not surprisingly, in many instances, problems result from an interplay between realistically difficult life circumstances and schemas that restrict one's ability to see a way out.

All of this suggests that when we try to help our clients change the meanings of their lives, we can differentially focus our attempts on altering (a) the kinds of information that is available to them and (b) their patterns for formulating meanings. Attempts to alter the flow of information from the environment can include working to change problematic relationships or to meet basic needs for food, shelter, and safety. In the realm of personal sources of information, we can work to alter available cues by helping clients to acquire new skills, gain more comfort with their emotions, or engage in less punitive self-appraisals. When the focus is on changing overly narrow or inflexible schematic patterns of organizing meanings, we work in a similar way to ensure the availability of new information and, in addition, we attempt to reorient the individual to attend to new cues, organize new meanings, and repeatedly bring these new meanings to awareness and use them to guide understanding and action.

✗ To provide direction about how to intervene with such a broad spectrum of potential targets, the cognitive-integrative perspective draws from a number of intervention approaches including behavioral, psychodynamic, family systems, experiential, cognitive, and environmental interventions, each of which is designed to focus in on a particular information domain. This is the integrative part of the C-I perspective. (See Table 9.1 for a summary of the basic assumptions.)

Everything included in the C-I approach directly links to a number of other theories and therapeutic approaches, but it can be distinguished from other cognitive therapies on the basis of (a) its emphasis on social sources of meaning, (b) its reliance on a wide range of therapeutic approaches (including social work approaches) for changing the character of available information, and (c) its reliance on memory models for understanding how our minds work.

Applicability to Direct Practice in Social Work

With its emphasis on the ways in which external circumstances influence personal meanings and, in turn, how these meanings anticipate and create external circumstances, the C-I perspective fits within and adds detail to social work's commitment to a person-environment approach. Specifically, it explains the ways in which environmental conditions and interpersonal interactions shape, reinforce, and interact with a person's cognitive-emotional processes.

TABLE 9.1   Central Assumptions

We constantly work to make sense of things.
We do that by responding to various internal and external sources of information.
The sense we make is influenced by the nature of the information we encounter and by our own schematic organizing systems.
These schemas themselves carry the mark of culture and family and experiences of daily life.

And from the person side of the interaction, it describes how individuals can marshal their own intentions, motivations, attention, talents, and social resources to create, add to, ignore, or make salient additional options for understanding, living in, and contributing to the social world.

The C-I perspective will not always be the most informative framework for understanding or intervening in the case situation at hand, nor the only theoretical perspective that practitioners should understand and use. Nonetheless, its value is in providing a broad framework for thinking about and intervening with the range and mix of person-environment problems that people experience and organizing interventions that can address these problem configurations at whatever level of simplicity or complexity they require. As suggested above, depending on where the delimiting information is coming from, social workers might variously work to alter living conditions, service organizations, interpersonal relationships, or personal skills, feelings, and ways of understanding. Whether the mix of internal and external factors suggests that the focus of change should primarily be directed inward to cognitive patterns or outward to social circumstances or back and forth in both directions, in all cases, the C-I approach requires that we work in the service of the wants, goals, and real world concerns of our clients.

MEANING AND THE MIND

To understand the personal side of person-environment interactions, we need to understand the workings of the mind. Our concern here is the extent to which the individual's memory patterns of perceiving and understanding will hold her to a narrow spectrum of responses or allow her to expand her personal realities to create, exploit, and/or incorporate positive differences. In other words, we are interested in how the mind works to both preserve the stability of meaning and allow meaningful change.

Theorists approach the study of the mind at varying levels of abstraction, but at the most concrete and specific level, we need to understand that the mind is the work of a biological brain that has evolved over millions of years through processes of natural selection. In his analysis of motivation and its fundamental role in human life, Klinger (1996) reminds us that our species evolved because of the built-in motivation of our ancestors to survive. He explains that the primary survival strategy for the earliest moving organisms was to seek out the vital substances and conditions necessary for survival. As a consequence, we have inherited a refined sensitivity—a hair-trigger emotional reactivity—to occurrences that bear on our primary survival goals and on the range of learned goals that are derivatives of them.

The Mind as the Brain

It has been estimated that our brains contain something on the order of 1 trillion neurons that are interconnected in functional networks by roughly 70 trillion synaptic connections (Hall, 1998). Edelman (1992) reminds us of the impressiveness of the organic arrangements that make up the mind:

> When this exquisite arrangement of cells (their microanatomy, or morphology) is taken together with the number of cells in an object the size of your brain, and when one considers the chemical reactions going on inside, one is talking about the most complicated material object in the known universe! (p. 17)

Some of these neural networks pick up input from the world from specialized neurons known as transducers that make up the sense organs. Others provide output through neurons that are connected to the muscles and glands. Despite these connections with the outside world, most of the brain only receives signals from and sends signals to other parts of the brain, without prompting from the outside world. In other words, the brain mostly communicates with itself (Edelman, 1992, pp. 18-19).

These internal-internal and external-internal communications occur as "massive numbers of neurons act in parallel in amazing numbers of combinations" (Edelman, 1992, p. 22). The remarkable thing is that adjustments in rates of firing across participating neurons create a pattern—a weighted circuit—that means something (Hall, 1998). When this same pattern is re-created, we access the same meaning.

Evolution has also equipped our species with what might be called an ecological brain in the sense that it is specifically designed to develop in response to environmental experiences. In fact, "three quarters of connections in the human brain develop outside the womb in direct relationship with an external environment" (B.

Shore, 1997, p. 3). Most scientists agree that the brain of the infant and young child develops through a pruning process in which certain preformed connections fall into disuse and essentially die, whereas others are strengthened. The disagreement is over the extent to which these processes are governed by genetic mapping of a delicate infrastructure, which may then be fine-tuned by experience, versus the extent to which the brain is a more pliable and flexible organ, which builds complex interconnections that tend to reflect experiences (Blakeslee, 1997). Rima Shore (1997) summarizes a large body of neuroscience and early childhood intervention research to argue for an interactionist position, in which the influence of genes on brain development and subsequent behavior is often dependent on specific input from the environment (also see Ramey & Ramey, 1998). Shore contends that available evidence should resolve the nature or nurture debate once and for all.

> All of this evidence . . . leads to a single conclusion: how humans develop and learn depends critically and continually on the interplay between nature (an individual's genetic endowment) and nurture (the nutrition, surroundings, care, stimulation, and teaching that are provided or withheld). The roles of nature and nurture in determining intelligence and emotional resilience should not be weighted quantitatively; genetic and environmental factors have a more dynamic, qualitative interplay that cannot be reduced to a simple equation. Both factors are crucial. (R. Shore, 1997, pp. 26-27)

No contemporary cognitive scientist would argue that the brain (and the rest of the body) is irrelevant to understanding the mind, but most would claim that there is utility in zeroing in on the patterns of transmitting and organizing information at a mid-level of analysis. Although

these analyses should at least be neurally plausible, there are differences of opinion among experts on the issue of how much one needs to understand the actual anatomy and chemistry of brain structures as opposed to leaving these tasks to others in favor of focusing on the mind functions of the brain. Nonetheless, over the last decade, there has been a shift away from the computer and toward the brain as the ruling metaphor for the mind. Because this shift is occurring at an uneven rate among theorists, we are currently faced with a somewhat confusing array of theories that rely on different concepts, language, and frameworks to capture similar mind/brain phenomena.

The Mind as an Information-Processing Computer

Ever since Alan Turing developed his theoretically possible computing machine in 1936, scientists have been fascinated with the prospect that the computer and the brain share some similar functions. The basic idea has been that, despite differences in their physical makeup, if the two systems generate the same conclusions, they must be carrying out similar functions. Over the years, numerous computational models of the mind have been developed, tested, merged, discarded, and revised to explain how we are able to apprehend and sort through the overwhelming complexities in our worlds and to respond to them with such an amazing degree of correspondence or accuracy (Gardner, 1985; Pinker, 1997).

For the past several decades (and until the more recent interest in the operations of the biological brain), notions of computation and representation have served as the central dogma of cognitive science. Within this orientation, the mind has been viewed as an organic computational or information-processing system: selecting, encoding, storing, transforming, and retrieving information (Tataryn, Nadel, & Jacobs, 1989, p. 86). Although computational perspectives have evolved and proliferated, for the most part, the mind has been portrayed as a serial processor in which thoughts or feelings are the result of serial or sequential mental activity. Like the old digital computer, the serial processing mind operates as a relatively passive responder to sensory inputs. In other words, the meanings that people "crank out" are a function of stimulus inputs and the overlap of inputs with previously stored memory representations. Input symbols (or representations) are transformed into output symbols through rule-governed computational processes.

Particularly during the 1970s and 1980s, as cognitive therapies imported information-processing concepts from the fields of cognitive psychology and social cognition and applied them to clinical concerns, they primarily borrowed (loosely) from explanations of serial information processing that were being developed at the time. The result was an emphasis on therapeutic interventions to correct client errors in the information-processing stages of attending, encoding, storing, and retrieving (Beck, Rush, Shaw, & Emery, 1979). In particular, clinical attention was given to cognitive schemas (networks of related beliefs and emotions) as the basic unit of cognitive architecture. The interest here was in undermining the accessibility and stability of clients' maladaptive schemas.

In recent years, serial processing explanations have been criticized by cognitive scientists for being too inflexible and slow to account for the complexities of human thought and emotion (Stinson & Palmer, 1991). To some extent,

they have been replaced by emerging models of the mind as a parallel processor that is capable of organizing multiple, simultaneous, distributed, and subsymbolic memory elements in the service of perception, learning, and memory. A handful of clinical theorists have begun considering the implications of parallel distributed processing for practice (e.g., Horowitz, 1991; Stein & Young, 1992; Teasdale & Barnard, 1993).

One of the more promising aspects of these massively distributed, parallel models (known as parallel distributed processing or connectionist models) is the extent to which they correspond with neurobiological accounts of the way the in which "massive numbers of neurons act in parallel in amazing numbers of combinations" to keep us breathing, moving, thinking, and acting (Edelman, 1992, p. 22).

The Mind Constructs Reality

The discovery that the components of the mind are constantly interacting among themselves and generating some of their own input is in some ways also compatible with the notion that we construct our own experiences, a notion that has been flourishing in the humanities and social sciences during recent decades. In Mahoney's (1998) words, "connectionism may . . . represent a conceptual bridge . . . to the recent rise of constructivist and evolutionary theories of learning" (p. 7).

Various forms of this idea of constructivism have made a distinctive mark on cognitive therapies by emphasizing the constructive and subjective nature of reality. As a theory about the nature of knowledge, constructivism has long historical roots, dating back to the philosophical writings of Vico (1668-1744), Kant (1724-

1804), and Vaihinger (1852-1933). Beginning with the work of Hayek (1952), the re-emergence of constructivist perspectives in the mid-20th century raised powerful challenges to prevailing assumptions of objective realism and rationalism.

As Mahoney (1998) elaborates,

> Constructivism is a family of theories and therapies that emphasizes at least three interrelated principles of human experience: (a) that humans are proactive (and not passively reactive) participants in their own experience—that is, in all perception, memory, and knowing; (b) that the vast majority of the ordering processes organizing human lives operate at tacit (un- or superconscious) levels of awareness; and (c) that human experience and personal psychological development reflect the ongoing operation of individualized, self-organizing processes that tend to favor the maintenance (over the modification) of experiential patterns. Although uniquely individual, these organizing processes always reflect and influence social systems. (p. 7)

With this latter statement, Mahoney recognizes the relationship between constructivism and theories of social constructionism, which posit that personal and social meanings are the result of social processes of defining meanings, norms, boundaries, and power relationships.

Although early versions of cognitive therapy tended to at least implicitly adhere to notions of objective reality and the superiority of rational thought (e.g., Beck, 1970, 1976; Ellis, 1962), more recent clinical models have explicitly emphasized the constructive nature of human knowing (e.g., Greenberg, Rice, & Elliott, 1993; Guidano & Liotti, 1983; Mahoney, 1991; Safran & Segal, 1990) and the active and generative properties of the mind. Rather than viewing the mind as the passive processor of sensa-

tions and receptacle for memories, this line of thinking focuses on the mind as an active agent of adaptation in charge of preparing us for adaptive responses by anticipating how events are likely to unfold and generating actions on the basis of these expectations. In this way, individuals not only register sensations but also generate them. As Mahoney (1995) suggests, we "feed forward" our own realities.

Most contemporary cognitive therapies have been influenced by a modified version of constructivism known as critical constructivism. In contrast to more radical positions that argue against an objective reality beyond one's experience, critical constructivism asserts that there is something "out there"; there is an external world that places limits on the viability of our constructions. Among constructive models of cognitive therapy, the concern is not so much with the absolute validity or rationality of personal knowledge but rather with its viability—the extent to which it allows the person to adapt and develop (Franklin, 1998).

In sum, the C-I perspective owes some large part of its theoretical heritage to the cognitive tradition and its approach to the study of the mind. At the same time, the assumptions and practical guidelines that make up the C-I perspective are also drawn from a broader, intersecting set of biological, cognitive, and constructivist/constructionist notions that variously suggest that meanings are the product of (a) an active, self-communicating brain (biological); (b) schematic patterns emerging from the simultaneous activity of distributed memory elements (cognitive); and (c) people's constant involvement in constructing meanings to make sense of the world and themselves and the preformed social meanings that are available to us (constructivist/constructionist). The values that frame this perspective and set its purpose are a product of the social work tradition and our commitment to extending the opportunities available to people—especially those who are the least advantaged—to maximize their "ability to act and give shape to their own destiny" (Witkin & Gottschalk, 1988, p. 221).

SCHEMAS TO LIVE BY

Among the concepts that cognitive therapies have borrowed from cognitive psychology, the idea of schemas has proven to be a particularly useful way to think about how the mind organizes meanings. Schemas can be understood as memory patterns—learned ways of anticipating and organizing information in a particular domain—that are developed out of repeated encounters with similar experiences. Beyond simply registering and classifying incoming stimuli, our memory processes organize sensory and semantic cues (what we see, hear, smell, taste, feel, do, and think) into meaningful themes or patterns of experience. Some of our memory patterns are innate and, over the course of development, through repetitions of experiences, we learn many more. For example, "You are driving me nuts! Can't you be quiet? Go play in the street or something! You're always underfoot! Don't you have some place to go? Look, I've had a hard day, just give me some peace and quiet, OK? Can't you see, we're talking? Butt out!"

As a result of repeated similar experiences, we learn what to expect, what to do, how to relate to others, what to hope for, and how to understand our own worth, capacities, feelings, needs, and resources. These recurring commonalities or patterns are maintained in our memories. As we continue to draw on them to understand new events, they become increasingly accessible and increasingly stable. This stability gives us a feeling of security, allows us some predictability so that we can orient ourselves to what is likely to happen, and provides us with a sense of continuity. And yet, we do learn new patterns; we do sometimes change our minds. In fact, we are able to maintain an adaptive balance by relying on our dual capacities for stability and plasticity—for assimilation and accommodation.

Self-Schemas

Although self-schemas are like other highly developed schemas in the way that they are organized, they are unique in their affective and motivational qualities and their close connection to personal history (Strauman & Higgins, 1993, p. 23). As Kihlstrom (1990) suggests, self-schemas include memory links that connect schematic patterns of sensation and conception to designations of oneself (me, I, my) as the experiencer or agent. In his analysis, Greenberg (1995) further suggests that it is our "bodily felt sense" that activates this designation or symbolization. In other words, the sensations we feel in our bodies as we act and experience and conceptualize activate the link that Kihlstrom describes and give us the knowledge of a self— ourself—at the center of the experience or action. Greenberg (1995) elaborates,

> Construction of conscious personal meaning involves three important moments. First, the synthesis of a feeling or "felt sense;" second, a moment of consciously symbolizing the tacit felt sense to form a subjective reality. Third, a moment of generating explanations of the symbolized experience to produce a coherent narrative

and/or identity. It is the combination of these three processes of synthesizing feeling, symbolizing, and explaining that leads to the construction of new views of self and reality. (p. 325)

From this and related explanations, it becomes clear that even though self-schemas are often described as self-concepts in semantic terms, our memory patterns about ourselves are more than propositional symbolizations. They also contain knowledge that is procedural, evaluative, relational, and emotional (Strauman & Higgins, 1993).

At any one time, only a subset of our memories of self is active in working memory (the part of the memory system that gains conscious attention in any one instant). Whatever array of self-relevant sensations, definitions, images, feelings, and actions is on-line at the moment makes up what is variously referred to as the "working self concept" (Markus & Nurius, 1987) or the "working model" of interpersonal relations (Bowlby, 1969; Horowitz, 1991).

Multiple Selves

In the course of our lifetimes, if we have logged in a variety of experiences of ourselves in different roles and relationships, then, we are likely to have access to a variety of self-defining and self-guiding schemas (Linville, 1985; Markus & Nurius, 1987). In contrast to the view that mental health is achieved through a highly integrated and cohesive concept of self, increasing evidence suggests that a larger repertoire of self-schemas offers a range of options to select from in responding adaptively to life's circumstances (Nurius & Berlin, 1993; Stein & Markus, 1994). These multiple self-structures are sources of personal flexibility. They allow us

to differentially access the facets of ourselves (the traits, roles, abilities, and possibilities) that fit best with the opportunities and demands of the moment (Stein & Markus, 1994). Moreover, to the extent that these multiple patterns for understanding ourselves are not inextricably interconnected, we are able to experience stress or an assault to self-esteem in one area of our lives without feeling as if our entire identity is compromised. A level of independence among self-schemas allows us to compartmentalize our vulnerabilities and respond to them from our areas of strength. For example, Rich is a police officer, a husband, a sports enthusiast, a Little League coach, a deacon in his church, and an involved uncle to a small group of nieces and nephews. If these "selves" are not tightly linked, when Rich runs into trouble on his job and experiences a blow to his police officer identity, he may still feel a general sense of demoralization, but at the same time, he is more likely to be successful in limiting the problem to the domain where it occurs and coping with the difficulty as "a problem" rather than a deficient self.

Possible selves. As one subset of our repertoire of selves, self-schemas of possibility represent our fears and desires for the future: in other words, our motivations. The more that these possible selves are elaborated with detailed plans, compelling emotions, and relevant skills, the more likely it is that they will actually serve as guides for our current functioning. In this vein, we work with our clients to locate and hold onto what they want and then to develop and fill out these possibilities. We engage with them in an iterative and interactive process of imagining, feeling, planning, practicing, and generating social support for these emerging self-aspects.

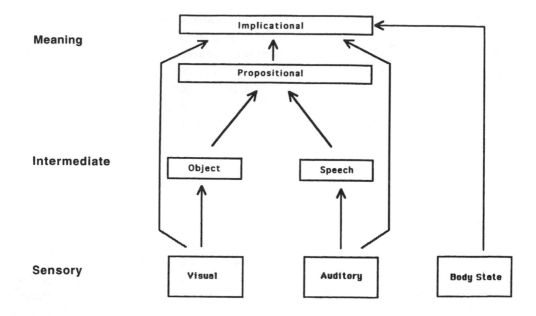

Figure 9.1. Interacting Cognitive Subsystems

SOURCE: This figure is adapted from Teasdale and Barnard (1993, Figure 5.1).

Schemas as a Function of Interacting Cognitive Subsystems

In recent years, British theorists John Teasdale and Philip Barnard developed an explanatory model of memory that organizes a set of observations emerging from clinical, neurological, and cognitive accounts of the mind (Teasdale, 1996; Teasdale & Barnard, 1993). Assuming a general parallel distributed-processing architecture, their model of Interacting Cognitive Subsystems (ICS) gives us a comprehensive rendition of how the mind works to organize memory elements that are active in various subsystems of the mind into larger schematic patterns of meaning.

ICS operates on the basis of several qualitatively different kinds of information represented by different kinds of memory codes. At the sensory level of information organization, one group of codes represents raw sensory experiences "such as patterns of light, shading, and color; the pitch, timbre, and temporal patterns of sounds"; and the proprioceptive sensations that are generated by the body (Teasdale, 1996, p. 28). At the intermediate level, object and speech codes represent larger patterns of regularities that have been extracted from visual and auditory data at the sensory level. Finally, co-occurring patterns in speech and object codes are transformed into codes that convey meaning. There are two meaning subsystems. In the first, propositional codes represent specific meanings in terms of discrete concepts and the relationships between them; and in the second, implicational codes capture co-occurring regularities at the sensory, intermediate, and concept levels to represent the most abstract, holistic, contextual, felt-in-the-body level of meaning. In Teasdale and Barnard's model, this activated pattern of meaning constitutes a schematic model of experience (see Figure 9.1).

When the implicational pattern is of personal significance, it automatically generates body state output—what emotion theorists call physiological action tendencies. These autonomic and expressive motor sensations are integrated back into the implicational pattern to yield an emotional sense of things. Because meanings that are organized at the implicational level go beyond semantic concepts, they are hard to describe in words. Although it is usually possible to come up with the words to convey the gist or basic themes of implicational meanings such as *something wrong, confident, hopeless,* and *ecstatic,* these words cannot fully encompass the overall, multifaceted experience (Bohart, 1993).

Each code in ICS has its own separate memory store and specialized information processing activities. Altogether these structures, codes, and processes constitute a cognitive subsystem. Information processing depends on information flowing from one subsystem to another. There are two basic processes that occur: (a) a transforming operation that transposes information from one code to another and (b) a copying operation in which information that is received as input is copied into the subsystem memory store.

Input into the system comes from both externally instigated patterns of sensory information and internally derived patterns of codes that are active in the system, "arising from previous processing or from access to memory" (Teasdale, 1996, p. 29). This means that whatever we attend to in our external experience meets up with whatever else is going on in the system and whatever else is accessible in memory because of recency or frequency of activation. Altogether these bits of information are organized to create meaning. On the basis of previous experience (procedural knowledge of "what goes with what"), when the Implicational Subsystem recognizes that the sensory and semantic codes flowing through the system belong with one another, they are automatically bound together to give us a holistic experience of how things are and how we are.

One of the implications of ICS for our therapeutic work comes from the explanation that distressing emotional states can be prolonged as a result of "heavy traffic" between the Implicational and Propositional Subsystems and between the Implicational and Body State Subsystems. For example, as propositional codes symbolize the more abstract, holistic experiences (e.g., I am worthless, I always have bad luck), these word-based descriptions may be incorporated back into an overall pattern to extend, affirm, or otherwise reactivate it. Similarly, the body response to a generic meaning (the slump, the grimace, the state of high arousal) provides further signals that are reintegrated into an overall sense of things. As Teasdale (1996) suggests, "Given [such] reciprocal relationships, there is an inherent possibility that the exchange of information . . . can 'settle' into a pattern in which only a narrow range of thematically related cognitive contents are processed" (p. 34). Because each subsystem can only recognize one coherent stream of information at a time, these recycling streams take up processing capacity and keep other information out. From this perspective, we can understand how we (our clients and ourselves) sometimes get caught up in states of experiencing and acting, even when we have vowed to handle situations differently. Here is a common scenario: Jenny wants to be more patient and good-humored with her children and to find the stamina, efficiency, and concentration to also do well in her studies at the community college. But when she comes home tired after a day of struggling through her classes to kids who are whining, teasing, and demanding, these cues make up enough of the "You can't do anything right . . . you'll never make anything of yourself" pattern to activate the entire schema. Jenny feels defeated, lashes out at her kids, and spends the evening trying to block out her worries through TV.

Given a lifetime of repeated experiences with a total pattern, on those occasions when only some of the elements are present, they may still be sufficient to instantiate an entire integrated set of feelings, thoughts, and action tendencies. Similarly, when discrepant elements are present along with those that make up the pattern, the discrepancies may not be processed. The elements that make up the pattern will be integrated and the parts that do not fit may simply be ignored. So, you may say to yourself "No big deal, this is just one glitch . . . it is not a crisis," but chances are you are still feeling CRISIS! This one new piece of discrepant propositional information ("no big deal") will not have much of an impact in preventing a re-synthesis of the "Life's too hard and I'm too weak" pattern if a wider array of crisis-related information (from memory and from current sounds, sights, and body feel) is also present (Teasdale, 1996).

Knowing that overlearned patterns tend to operate automatically, sometimes in a regenerating fashion and sometimes on the basis of only partial sets of memory elements or without regard to discrepant information that is also present, we can better understand why it is so difficult to get beyond entrenched habits of understanding. Nonetheless, people do change. We revise and adjust and deviate and generally are able to maintain an adaptive balance that allows us to maintain stability and incorporate difference (Wachtel, 1993).

Mechanisms of Schematic Change

Within the ICS model, the two essential requirements for effecting changes in implicational patterns of meaning are discrepancy and selection (Teasdale & Barnard, 1993). At the most basic level, change requires discrepancy or difference. This means that externally and/or internally generated inputs into the system have to represent different sensations and body feelings and propositional assessments (either as new occurrences or activated memories). The more discrepancies there are, and the greater their personal importance, the greater the likelihood of schematic change. Thus, the first requirement of change is to alter the nature of the information that is available to the system. When we apply this notion to our clinical work, we say that to effect change, our clients need to have information options in their lives and in their memory systems. As practitioners, we engage in a wide range of environment-changing, relationship-changing, and behavior-changing interventions to get to this point.

Second, these differences have to be selected into the system and given processing priority. As noted above, limits on processing capacity mean that each transforming process can only recognize one coherent stream of input information at a time. Selection between data streams usually occurs on the basis of procedural knowledge about which data stream has paid off in the past (i.e., which is the most personally salient or related to automatic goals), but selection can also be guided by intentions. We can intentionally focus on one stream of information over another (or activate one set of memories instead of another) and consciously direct our attentional resources to it (Bargh, 1996). In regulating our attention in this kind of purposeful way, we are moving from the realm of automatic processing to the realm of effortful, controlled processing in which we give ourselves instructions about what outcome we are trying to create and what we have to do to get there (Bargh, 1996; Gollwitzer & Moskowitz, 1996).

At the first levels of change, we may be able to at least temporarily block a pattern by changing some of the peripheral elements (shifting attentional focus to different sights and sounds, altering body-state feelings and actions, providing different conceptualizations, activating different emotional memories) that are part of the unwanted pattern to achieve immediate and short-term change. Under the best scenario, these changes in the informational elements not only block an old pattern, they are also are sufficient to activate and strengthen an already existing, but perhaps relatively weak, alternative schematic model.

For example, if we have stored up memory records of coping and if these memories are accessible—if they are stored in some of the more recent sections of implicational memory—then we only have to remember to intentionally access these memories during tough times to activate an alternative schematic model and by extension an alternative emotional state (Teasdale, 1996, p. 39). By consciously searching for this alternative pattern, using it, extending it, and feeling good about it, we develop it. For example, Jenny, from the previous example, might remember that she knows how to manage irascible kids and shift right into her "Mommy's home and let's spend a little time together catching up and organizing ourselves mode" and get the feedback (sensory, specific meaning, body state) that maintains and elaborates an "I can do this" implicational schematic model. Because all of this new information will be saved in memory stores, this elaborated implicational pattern should be easier to activate the next time.

From the discussion above, we know that multiple self schemas are the sources of personal flexibility. Although any one well-established pattern can be hard to change, when we have multiple patterns, we have memory-based options that we can consciously prime to get us into the coping mode or the stand your ground mode or the admit you're wrong and face up mode.

In the absence of these alternative models, we have to be concerned with how to develop them. The most arduous way is simply a longer version of the blocking and building strategy just mentioned. It involves heavy reliance on controlled processing to disrupt or terminate the old pattern and consciously bring in and attend to the elements that make up a new pattern repeatedly—over and over again. We get several tips from the self-regulation literature about how to "hang in there" with this task. For example, desirable and feasible goals, incremental versus all-or-none achievement expectations, detailed plans, practice, a focus on achievements and not setbacks, and social supports are all components of self-regulation strategies that can help us steer our experiences in directions that we choose, and that social constraints and opportunities will allow (Gollwitzer & Moskowitz, 1996; Mischel, Cantor, & Feldman, 1996). We also know that another real incentive for "hanging in" is the presence or at least the feasible possibility of social opportunities. This is why real options (such as companionship, employment, education, care) stand as the first necessity of change.

Teasdale and Barnard (1993) suggest that there may also be a more efficient way to effect schema change by altering some critical elements within the overall patterns but still retaining certain core configurations. In this way, we exploit the availability and the accessibility of the old pattern but graft new elements onto it, so that its overall meaning is changed. This strategy circumvents some (but not all) of the effortful controlled processing that is required to build accessible alternative patterns "from scratch." For example, reframing that is made possible by metaphors, stories, and paradoxes seems to work in this way by nesting a familiar set of particulars within a different frame (Rosenbaum, 1996). And sometimes changing a subset of particulars makes the critical difference: "Life is too hard, barely keeping my head above water, *and* all this is temporary . . . I will have a better time again." In the example that Teasdale and Barnard give, "While I may not be very good at things and often fail, this time I did actually succeed," they note that the appraisal, "I may not be very good . . . and often fail" serves as a discriminating marker, a component that is so key to the overall pattern that it will activate memory records of the pattern despite discrepancies. When the pattern is activated along with key discrepancies, in this case the sensations, words, and feelings that go along with "I actually succeeded," the discrepancies

are likely to be incorporated into the pattern and change its meaning. When we adopt and adapt this latter strategy in our clinical work, it puts us in the position of validating the client's reality and respecting his or her inclination for stability overall, but it still allows us to look for the personal strengths and social opportunities that can contribute to critical differences in what things mean.

This review of ICS suggests that, depending on the clients situation, there may be utility in focusing some of our attention on understanding and creating change within the cognitive subsystem level of the client's functioning. Even so, the ICS picture is not the whole picture. We need to move back and forth from a focus on the mechanisms of client information processing to a much broader focus on the client's life—his or her life in a culture, in a family, in a socioeconomic niche, as a parent, a student, a person with hopes and goals and worries and frailties. We think about the internal information-processing context, but we also have to think about the broader external social context from which meanings were derived in the first place and which continually provides cues that contribute to current meanings.

SOCIAL SOURCES OF MEANING

The ways we code information and interpret reality reflect the cultural meanings that have been provided to us. Culture provides "individuals in a community with a stock of common orientational models for constructing experience" (B. Shore, 1997, p. 16). Because these cultural meanings are so fundamental and intertwined with natural phenomena, we often fail to recognize their cultural roots and treat them instead as part of the natural world. Thus, we believe that it is "human nature" to do whatever the culture prescribes, whether it be striving for individual recognition or expressing our innermost feelings or taking multiple wives (D'Andrade, 1984).

Cultural Influences

We know that culture is not monolithic; within a general cultural system, there are many streams of social meaning that we have differential access to—depending on our income, race, gender, age, ethnicity, sexual orientation, education, or geographic region. In fact, each of us is influenced by a number of subsidiary contexts, none of which produces exactly uniform effects. As Hannerz (1992) reminds us, culture can be seen as "the organization of diversity" (as cited in Markus, Kitayama, & Heiman, 1996, p. 867).

In some ways, the discrepancies between our personal views and broader social views create a tension or dissonance that can be the impetus for change, for considering alternative meanings at the personal or cultural level (D'Andrade, 1984). But under a variety of circumstances, discrepancies can also result in a chronic sense of marginalization (e.g., when promises for opportunities are held out, but the pathways to achieving them are repeatedly blocked). Although we are all defined by and participate in various streams of cultural meanings, we are not all a part of the mainstream. Sociocultural context and status positions differ in their "authority, legitimacy and power to define realities for individuals and society as a whole" (Oyserman & Markus, 1993, p. 193).

In our social work role, our concern is to extend such authority, legitimacy, and power. In our attempts to be the agents of individuals who live in a variety of cultural contexts, we enter their worlds, not as fixers or experts or representatives of the "normal" dominant world, but as learners and perhaps contributors. We should recognize at the outset that the terms and metaphors of C-I therapy are likely to be alien to many of our clients. There is no need to—and every reason not to—foist this perspective onto them. Rather, our interest is in meeting our clients on their terms. We need to listen carefully to the details of their wants, difficulties, satisfactions, and ways of making change and then see if our background knowledge of C-I conceptions allows us to generate shared meanings with our clients and jointly create possibilities that hold significance for them.

Social Structures

As a part of culture, social structures such as political and economic forces, labor markets, and social institutions mold our self-definitions by positioning us within the larger society and constraining the range of opportunities and roles that are available to us (Kemp, Whittaker, & Tracy, 1997; Markus & Cross, 1990). These external conditions are sometimes referred to as life chances because they are largely outside of the realm of personal choice.

We know from numerous sources (Kleinman, 1988; McCloyd, 1989; Mirowsky & Ross, 1989; Sherraden, 1991) that people who have the worst life chances (because of poverty, victimization, joblessness) are at the highest risk for psychological distress. In reviewing a number of studies addressing the psychological correlates of social stress, Mirowsky and Ross (1989) suggest that the losses and failures that are prompted by these conditions influence

(a) feelings of alienation and powerlessness, (b) the development of narrow and rigid cognitive perspectives and coping capacities, and (c) an overall sense of unfairness and mistrust.

In our work with clients, we reach into their social worlds to open up opportunities that will energize their sense of hope and hopeful actions. In the greater scheme of things, the social changes that we and our client are able to effect are likely to be relatively small—linking up an estranged kid to an especially warm and gifted teacher; helping the daughter who has schizophrenia apply for SSI as a way of expanding the economic base of the family; working with the leaders of a tenant association at the housing project to organize their campaign for improvements in living conditions—but they are sometimes of major personal significance. We know that behind the difficulties that we have attempted to ameliorate, there remain larger social structural difficulties that we have not altered in any fundamental way—except to the extent that one by one, our clients have gained an enlarged sense of worth, possibility, and personal or social power.

Family Life

Finally, we are born into and develop within the interpersonal context of families. These people who are our mothers and fathers and siblings and aunts and grandmothers and grandfathers are our most direct source of input about what things mean and who we are. As noted earlier in the chapter, we are all born into the world with a similar genetic plan for the basic interconnections or synapses in our brains. Beyond these inherited patterns, early experiences will forge and strengthen links among trillions more neurons. If these are repeatedly activated as a function of day-to-day interactions, they are strengthened and will "become a part of the brain's permanent circuitry. If they are not used repeatedly, or often enough, they are eliminated" (R. Shore, 1997, p. 17). So all of the repeated early caregiver-child interactions—rocking, soothing, cooing, mirroring, babbling, limiting, yelling, spanking, ignoring—are likely to add up to something, to strengthen pathways that form rudimentary patterns. Where interactions are missing, so are the mental pathways and patterns that make up the self.

Stern (1985) describes the interpersonal nature of self-development in terms of an inborn, primary motivation to establish and maintain relationships. This affiliation motivation operates in both the parent and the child, and under optimal conditions, it results in a "finely tuned interdependency that characterizes the caregiver-child relationship from its beginning" (Markus & Cross, 1990, p. 582). Over the course of repetitions of this internal and external reciprocity, the infant begins to form memory representations of consistent aspects of these experiences—episodes of co-occurring "sensations, perceptions, actions, thoughts, affects, and goals" (Stern, 1985, p. 95). These representations of interactions that have been generalized (or RIGS) are the preverbal core of memories about the self. These are the same memory structures that neuroscientists might label as rudimentary patterns of reinforced synapses, that Piaget (1926) refers to as the sensorimotor self, and that Guidano and Liotti (1983) describe as the nucleus of self-knowledge. They are ultimately elaborated into more complex patterns, which Bowlby (1969) terms "working models of the self" and which we refer to as self-schemas.

Guidano and Liotti (1983) explain that early relationships with caregivers that are particularly contradictory and conflictual are likely to interfere with subsequent development because they will require children to concentrate all of their cognitive-emotional resources on obtaining some kind of adaptive equilibrium. Under these circumstances, children develop a strong motivation to detect and respond to cues of threat. This focus on a narrow band of survival-relevant information is likely to result in rigid early patterns and the constriction of cognitive growth (Guidano & Liotti, 1983, p. 106).

At the same time, ongoing interactions with family members and an array of others in the wider society continue to contribute to one's overall sense of self well beyond infancy and childhood (Markus & Cross, 1990). The foundation of memories that we organize early in life develops and moderates in response to these ongoing experiences. What happens to us in our earlier years may create particular areas of strength or vulnerability, but it does not seal our fate. Whatever else we experience along the way can serve to strengthen, buffer, weaken, or provide alternatives to early formed patterns. Two girls grow up under the influence of the same neglectful parents. Both are now adults; Melanie seems withdrawn, meek, and tentative while Karisa is much more confident and outgoing. What makes the difference? We can speculate that, at least in part, it's grandma. When Karisa was about 4, grandma moved in next door and played a pivotal role in affirming, teaching, and soothing both of the little girls. Melanie was already 11 when grandma came, not too old to profit from her warm attention; but Karisa, who had also been carefully looked after by Melanie, formed a strong bond with grandma and had a greater opportunity to learn about herself and life through these interactions.

Because early caregivers are the first source of information about self and other and because the information they convey necessarily forms the foundation for subsequent knowledge development, there are powerful reasons for focusing prevention and intervention efforts on this early parenting process. But every time we zero in on a parent who is struggling with this caregiving task, we see more (or should see more) than an individual who is too rigid or too withdrawn or too inconsistent. Caregivers who are unable to give their children the kinds of early and ongoing experiences that reflect a secure and capable self are likely to be held back by some combination of overly narrow, rigidly held memory models of their own difficult experiences; limits in their general knowledge about how things work; and ongoing interpersonal and environmental constraints that interfere with new learning.

COGNITIVE-INTEGRATIVE SOCIAL WORK PRACTICE

The overall C-I strategy for helping the individual is to look hard for and/or create differences in their environmental, interpersonal, and personal circumstances and make positive meaning out of them. To capsulize this change process, we turn to Kegan's (1982) notion that in therapy and in the course of development, schematic change results from the cumulative press of "repeated and varied encounters in natural experience" that affirm and reaffirm that the old system of operating is too limiting and that alternatives exist (p. 41).

Intervention Strategies

As suggested above, the necessity for repeated and varied encounters means that the external situation has to provide or allow the possibility for options or opportunities. As social workers, our job is to search out options in areas that matter for a particular client. This may include helping him or her gain the basic necessities of life, negotiate more supportive and secure social and family relationships, tap into cultural and spiritual sources of sustenance, and reclaim ties that provide a sense of belonging (see Aponte, 1994). It may include showing, doing, caring, or calming in such a respectful, honest, and steady way that clients gradually begin to understand that this relationship with their social worker is different and that it means something good about them and their prospects. It could also mean going to bat for clients in our own agency or other agencies by organizing efforts to change policies and practices that obstruct good services.

For opportunities to really matter, however, clients have to notice them and see them as potentially valuable openings. Clients must use this emerging awareness to formulate or strengthen goals or possible selves. Some clients come in with goals that provide the direction for our work together. These goals should also work to provide clients with an active intention and readiness to focus on goal-related opportunities and achievements. For other clients, generating a meaningful goal is the product of much work. But in all cases, goals are important. To the extent that clients generate goals—and fill them out with words, images, feelings, and actions—they have other sensory and body and propositional elements to select and a reason for doing so. There are a variety of strategies that we can

use to help the client do this work of finding options and using them. They span a large range of intervention models, from relational and interpersonal, to strategies of advocacy, community action, and organizational change as well as many others in between that cannot be adequately represented here.

Intervention Process

How the intervention process actually unfolds depends on a number of factors, including the nature of the difficulty, the intrinsic pull of the client's goals, the availability of options, and the strength of competing patterns. Like most intervention models, the C-I version begins with a relationship-building and assessment phase that merges into a working-through phase and finally an ending phase. In engaging in initial assessment explorations, we try to figure out the various personal and social components that make up the problem or support it, to clarify targets for change. Our C-I model provides us with some pre-formed notions of what constitutes problems (Schön, 1987). Essentially, we look for the sources of information and/or patterns of organizing information that seem to be constraining adaptive meanings. For example, if our search tells us that the client's difficulties are primarily a function of inadequate environmental opportunities, then logic tells us to scan the environmental situation for undeveloped resources that might be exploited. If it suggests that the client lacks the basic information and skills necessary for using and expanding opportunities, then we are alerted to consider how to assist the client in learning the relevant concepts and skills. If our review suggests that the client's current pattern of organizing information is the main source of problematic meanings, then our attention will primarily be drawn to figuring out how to assist the client in "disattending" to old patterns and creating and strengthening new ones.

Although problems are the targets of our interventions, change comes from strength (Miller, 1986). As a consequence, we look for the skills, the conceptions of possibility, the supportive relationships, the underused schemas, and we build on them. We rely on the emotional pull of goals—the adaptive action tendencies of goal-related emotions such as stay safe, protect loved ones, find comfort and connection—to energize change efforts. In eliciting this kind of information and exploring it with clients, we will need to go back and forth between soliciting their descriptions and perspectives and asking for concrete details about specific factors or sources of information that may contribute to the problem, while simultaneously keeping our own antennae out for recurring cognitive themes that may suggest underlying cognitive schemas.

The understanding that we and our clients develop through this initial exploration is dynamic and evolving. It is refined, revised, and elaborated over the course of the therapeutic encounter. As work proceeds, our initial understanding is deepened by considering the nature of problematic meanings in the context of our efforts to change them. For example, from this vantage point, we are better able to understand the tensions between pulls to realize new goals and to stay the same, and to grasp the social dynamics and memory mechanisms underlying them.

Once we have a beginning idea of what the client wants, what gets in the way of securing those wants, and the strengths that the client might draw on, we look for an "obvious place" (where a small amount of effort is likely to make a significant difference) to start changing information or revising overall meanings. Under optimal circumstances, all of these factors (the clients' desires, their resources and strengths, the scope of the problems) should bear on the scope—the depth, breadth, and length—of the intervention effort. Although cognitive therapies are typically short term, in cases in which individuals are working to revise very entrenched and chronically accessible maladaptive schemas (e.g., personality patterns), short-term work can only provide a start to a longer effort that is likely to require ongoing conscious regulation of their motivations, emotions, actions, and thoughts to create and make accessible new patterns of anticipation and action (Mischel et al., 1996).

The C-I approach follows a relatively structured format in which sessions are used to analyze problems, plot strategies, work through difficulties, and plan for between-session tasks. A great deal of work should occur between sessions, for example, as clients practice using broadened ways of taking in and responding to particular circumstances and the workers track down various opportunities. Sessions are flexibly organized around a format in which time is allocated for setting an agenda, reviewing the relevant events since the last meeting, reviewing homework, attending to the main agenda items, generating new homework, and reviewing the central features of the session. This structure is intended to help the worker and clients maintain a focus so that the session does not wander. On the other hand, it is critically important to tailor the arrangement to take into account the changes in the clients' circumstances and their overall comfort with a more organized versus free-flowing or selfdirected working environment (Beutler, Paulo, Machado, & Mohr, 1993).

As noted above, we use early assessment information to help us find a place to start, but having started, we watch, listen, and feel closely to get a sense of how clients are responding so that we can be more precisely helpful in what we do next. To aid in this process, we need some system for keeping track of how clients are doing and what seems to be helping. Are clients developing new behavioral skills? Is the interpersonal conflict being reduced? Were we able to open up new possibilities in terms of child care or housing? And, to what extent are clients able to use these new "facts" in understanding themselves differently and operating differently down the line? Where are they in their struggle to remember and reformulate and feel and act the difference? We can rely on standardized or individualized measures to give us a quick read of shifts in problem levels, but to gauge the clients' sense of themselves in relation to problematic meanings, it is also helpful to systematically record qualitative shifts in the basic themes of meaning that are at issue (Berlin & Marsh, 1993).

Under optimal circumstances, we end our work with clients when they have achieved their goals. In real life, endings are also a function of competing demands on the clients' attention, flagging motivation in the face of little progress or distrust, time limits that are imposed by third-party payers, and so on. Under all of these circumstances, however, it is important to leave clients with a useable, individualized framework for continuing to move around or burrow through the issues that are troublesome, and to expand the aspects of themselves and their lives that give pleasure, freedom, and a sense of personal control. According to the C-I perspective, this framework includes guides for focusing on the areas of potential and possibility in one's life circumstances and then making them real in one's consciousness and day-to-day existence.

REFERENCES

Aponte, H. (1994). *Bread and spirit: Therapy with the new poor.* New York: Norton.

Bargh, J. A. (1996). Automaticity in social psychology. In E. T. Higgins & A. W. Kruglanski (Eds.), *Social psychology: Handbook of basic principles* (pp. 169-183). New York: Guilford.

Beck, A. T. (1970). Cognitive therapy: Nature and relation to behavior therapy. *Behavior Therapy, 1,* 184-200.

Beck, A. T. (1976). *Cognitive therapy and the emotional disorders.* New York: International Universities Press.

Beck, A. T., Rush, A. J., Shaw, B. F., & Emery, G. (1979). *Cognitive therapy for depression.* New York: Guilford.

Berlin, S. B., & Marsh, J. C. (1993). *Informing practice decisions.* New York: Macmillan.

Beutler, L. E., Paulo, P. P., Machado, D. E., & Mohr, D. (1993). Differential patient-treatment maintenance among cognitive, experiential, and self-directed psychotherapies. *Journal of Psychotherapy Integration, 3,* 15-33.

Blakeslee, S. (1997, November 4). Recipe for a brain: Cup of genes and dash of experience? *The New York Times,* p. B12.

Bohart, A. C. (1993). Experiencing: The basis of psychotherapy. *Journal of Psychotherapy Integration, 3*(1), 51-67.

Bowlby, J. (1969). *Attachment and loss: Vol. 1. Attachment.* New York: Basic Books.

D'Andrade, R. G. (1984). Cultural meaning systems. In R. A. Shweder & R. A. LeVine (Eds.), *Culture theory: Essays on mind, self, and emotion* (pp. 88-119). Cambridge, UK: Cambridge University Press.

Edelman, G. M. (1992). *Bright air, brilliant fire: On the matter of the mind.* New York: Basic Books.

Ellis, A. (1962). *Reason and emotion in psychotherapy.* Englewood Cliffs, NJ: Prentice Hall.

Franklin, C. (1998). Distinctions between social constructionism and cognitive constructivism: Practice applications. In C. Franklin & P. S. Nurius (Eds.), *Constructivism in practice* (pp. 57-96). Milwaukee, WI: Families International.

Gardner, H. (1985). *The mind's new science* (2nd ed.). New York: Basic Books.

Gollwitzer, P. M. (1990). Action phases and mind sets. In E. T. Higgins & E. M. Sorrentino (Eds.), *Handbook of motivation and cognition* (Vol. 2, pp. 53-92). New York: Guilford.

Gollwitzer, P. M., & Moskowitz, G. B. (1996). Goal effects on action and cognition. In A. W. Kruglanski (Ed.), *Social psychology: Handbook of basic principles* (pp. 361-399). New York: Guilford.

Greenberg, L. S. (1995). The self is flexibly various and requires an integrative approach. *Journal of Psychotherapy Integration, 5*(4), 323-330.

Greenberg, L. S., Rice, L. N., & Elliott, R. (1993). *Facilitating emotional change: The moment-by-moment process.* New York: Guilford.

Guidano, V. F., & Liotti, G. (1983). *Cognitive processes and emotional disorders.* New York: Guilford.

Hall, S. S. (1998, February 15). Our memories, our selves. *The New York Times Magazine,* pp. 26-33.

Hannerz, U. (1992). *Cultural complexity: Studies in the social organization of meaning.* New York: Columbia University Press.

Hayek, F. A. (1952). *The sensory order.* Chicago: University of Chicago Press.

Horowtiz, M. J. (Ed.). (1991). *Person schemas and maladaptive interpersonal patterns.* Chicago: University of Chicago Press.

Kegan, R. (1982). *The evolving self.* Cambridge, MA: Harvard University Press.

Kemp, S. P., Whittaker, J. K., & Tracy, E. M. (1997). *Person-environment practice: The social ecology of interpersonal helping.* New York: Aldine de Gruyter.

Kihlstrom, J. F. (1990). The psychological unconscious. In L. A. Pervin (Ed.), *Handbook of personality: Theory and research* (pp. 445-464). New York: Guilford.

Kleinman, A. (1988). *Rethinking psychiatry: From cultural category to personal experience.* New York: Free Press.

Klinger, E. (1996). Emotional influences on cognitive processing, with implications for theories of both. In P. M. Gollwitzer & J. A. Bargh (Eds.), *The psychology of action: Linking cognition and motivation to behavior* (pp. 168-192). New York: Guilford.

Linville, P. W. (1985). Self-complexity and affective extremity: Don't put all of your eggs in one cognitive basket. *Social Cognition, 3,* 94-120.

Mahoney, M. J. (1991). *Human change processes.* New York: Basic Books.

Mahoney, M. J. (1995). Cognitive psychology and contemporary psychotherapy: The self as an organizing theme. *Journal of Psychotherapy Integration, 4,* 417-424.

Mahoney, M. J. (1998). Continuing evolution of the cognitive sciences and psychotherapies. In C. Franklin & P. S.

Nurius (Eds.), *Constructivism in practice* (pp. 3-27). Milwaukee, WI: Families International.

Markus, H., & Cross, S. (1990). The interpersonal self. In L. A. Pervin (Ed.), *Handbook of personality: Theory and research* (pp. 63-78). New York: Guilford.

Markus, H. R., Kitayama, S., & Heiman, R. J. (1996). Culture and basic psychological principles. In E. T. Higgens & A. W. Kruglanski (Eds.), *Social psychology: Handbook of basic principles* (pp. 857-914). New York: Guilford.

Markus, H. R., & Nurius, P. S. (1987). Possible selves: The interface between motivation and the self-concept. In K. Yardley & T. Honess (Eds.), *Self and identity: Psychosocial perspectives* (pp. 157-172). Chichester, UK: John Wiley.

McCloyd, V. C. (1989). Socialization and development in a changing economy. *American Psychologist, 44,* 293-302.

Miller, J. B. (1986). *What do we mean by relationships.* (Work in progress). Stone Center: Wellesley, MA.

Mirowsky, J., & Ross, C. E. (1989). *Social causes of psychological distress.* New York: Aldine de Gruyter.

Mischel, W., Cantor, N., & Feldman, S. (1996). Principles of self-regulation: The nature of willpower and self-control. In E. T. Higgins & A. W. Kruglanski (Eds.), *Social psychology: Handbook of basic principles* (pp. 329-360). New York: Guilford.

Nurius, P. S., & Berlin, S. B. (1993). Treatment of negative self-concept and depression. In D. K. Granvold (Ed.), *Cognitive and behavioral treatment: Methods and applications* (pp. 249-271). Pacific Grove, CA: Brooks/Cole.

Oyserman, D., & Markus, H. R. (1993). The sociocultural self. In J. Suls (Ed.), *Psychological perspectives on the self* (Vol. 4, pp. 187-220). Hillsdale, NJ: Lawrence Erlbaum.

Piaget, J. P. (1926). *The language and thought of the child.* New York: Harcourt Brace.

Pinker, S. (1997). *How the mind works.* New York: Norton.

Ramey, C. T., & Ramey, S. L. (1998). Early intervention and early experience. *American Psychologist, 53,* 109-120.

Rosenbaum, R. (1996). Form, formlessness, and formulation. *Journal of Psychotherapy Integration, 6*(2), 107-117.

Safran, J. D., & Segal, Z. V. (1990). *Interpersonal processes in cognitive therapy.* New York: Basic Books.

Schön, D. (1987). *Educating the reflective practitioner.* San Francisco: Jossey-Bass.

Sherraden, M. W. (1991). *Assets and the poor: A new American welfare policy.* Armonk, NY: M. E. Sharpe.

Shore, B. (1997). *Culture in mind: Cognition, culture, and the problem of meaning.* New York: Oxford University Press.

Shore, R. (1997). *Rethinking the brain.* New York: Work and Families Institute.

Stein, D. (1992). Clinical cognitive science: Possibilities and limitations. In D. Stein & J. E. Young (Eds.), *Cognitive science and clinical disorders* (pp. 3-19). San Diego: Academic Press.

Stein, D. J., & Young, J. E. (Eds.). (1992). *Cognitive science and clinical disorders.* New York: Academic Press.

Stein, K. F., & Markus, H. R. (1994). The organization of the self: An alternative focus for psychopathology and behavior change. *Journal of Psychotherapy Integration, 4*(4), 317-353.

Stern, D. N. (1985). *The interpersonal world of the infant: A view from psychoanalysis and developmental psychology.* New York: Basic.

Stinson, C. H., & Palmer, S. E. (1991). Parallel distributed processing models of person schemas and psychopathologies. In M. J. Horowitz (Ed.), *Person schemas and maladaptive interpersonal patterns* (pp. 339-378). Chicago: University of Chicago Press.

Strauman, T. J., & Higgins, E. T. (1993). The self-construct in social cognition: Past, present, and future. In Z. V. Segal & S. J. Blatt (Eds.), *The self in emotional distress: Cognitive and psychodynamic perspectives* (pp. 3-40). New York: Guilford.

Tataryn, D., Nadel, L., & Jacobs, W. J. (1989). Cognitive therapy and cognitive science. In A. Freeman, K. S. Simon, H. Arkowitz, & L. Beutler (Eds.), *A handbook of cognitive therapy.* Cambridge: MIT Press.

Teasdale, J. D. (1996). Clinically relevant theory: Integrating clinical insight with cognitive science. In P. Salkovskis (Ed.), *Frontiers of cognitive therapy* (pp. 26-47). New York: Guilford.

Teasdale, J. D., & Barnard, P. J. (1993). *Affect, cognition, and change: Re-modeling depressive thought.* East Sussex, UK: Erlbaum.

Wachtel, P. L. (1993). *Therapeutic communications.* New York: Guilford.

Witkin, S. L., & Gottschalk, S. (1988). Alternative criteria for theory evaluation. *Social Service Review, 62*(2), 211-224.

CHAPTER TEN

Approaches to Behavioral Change

BRUCE A. THYER

LAURA L. MYERS

Preparing a chapter dealing with approaches to behavioral change within social work is a daunting task, because in a very meaningful sense, *all* of social work practice is focused on changing behavior, be it of individuals, small groups, communities, or society at large. Although the editors have made it clear that this chapter is to deal with how to change overt, publicly observable behavior, it is important to note at the onset that the very term *behavior* implies much more than this. For example, the *Social Work Dictionary* defines behavior as "any action or response by an individual, including observable activity, measurable physiological changes, cognitive images, fantasies, and emotions" (Barker, 1999, p. 42).

Although in the first part of this century, the American psychologist John Watson attempted to limit psychology to conducting research on observable behavior, this definition was never widely adopted. The inherent attractions of studying mental life and affective states were simply too reinforcing. In the late 1930s, B. F. Skinner contended that within the radical behavioral framework he was developing, behavior essentially means anything the body does, and that this of course subsumes all so-called mental and affective phenomena in exactly the same sense that the physical movement of the body is behavior. As he later put it, "What is felt or introspectively observed is not some nonphysical world of consciousness, mind, or mental life, but the observer's own body" (Skinner, 1974, p. 17).

Skinner always contended that a genuine science of behavior was certainly possible, including the study of cognition and feelings, as well as overt comportment. Where radical behaviorism differed from most alternative social science theories (and subsequently in the development of derivative schools of intervention in the human services, including social work) was not in its focus on dependent variables (actions, thoughts, and feelings) but in it emphasis on independent variables, accounting for the causes of these phenomena. Simply put, behavior analysis and therapy has always attempted to help alleviate dysfunctional affective states (e.g., depression or anxiety) or cognitive states (e.g., self-statements promoting unassertiveness). However, change efforts consist of training in various social and self-control skills (i.e., behaviors), environmental modification, and manipulation of the antecedents to and consequences of selected behavior. A frequent misconception in our social work literature is that "behaviorists" are only interested in overt behavior. This is decidedly not true now and has not been accurate for over 60 years (see Myers & Thyer, 1994; Thyer, 1991).

In turning more directly to the subject matter, how to change behavior, the following definition can serve as our initial position:

> Behavioral social work is the informed use by professional social workers of interventive techniques based upon empirically derived learning theories, including but not limited to, operant conditioning, respondent conditioning, and observational learning. Behavioral social workers may or may not subscribe to the philosophy of behaviorism. (Thyer & Hudson, 1987, p. 1)

The balance of this chapter will address the above definition in reverse order, philosophical assumptions first, followed by a review of the theoretical concepts, empirical evidence, diversity considerations, and directions for the future.

Philosophical Foundations

The philosophical foundations of behaviorism have recently been reviewed in Thyer and Wodarski (1998), although more primary sources are certainly recommended (e.g., Chiesa, 1994; Skinner, 1974). A selection of these principles is summarized in Table 10.1. Each of these points of view has experienced central controversies within philosophy for hundreds of years, and in some cases, millennia. In offering them as characteristic of the behavioral position, we make no pretense that any one of them can be considered irrefutably justified, either by logic or by empirical data. Like Euclid's axioms, consider them as undemonstrated propositions (although behaviorists would likely contend that they are self-evident) that serve as intellectual pivot points around which the behavioral perspective revolves.

Like contemporary biology, behaviorism has abandoned the concept of purpose as a causal factor in explaining phenomena. Just as evolution by natural selection is not said to have the purpose of creating human beings, we do not say that human beings exist for the purpose of evolving to another (presumably higher) stage of existence. According to the behavior analytic position, people's actions are not seen as purposive. One does not *do* certain things to *get* certain consequences (e.g., rewards). Rather, one does certain things now because they have been reinforced in the past. The mechanism of agency is seen in the past, not in the future. Philosophically, it is difficult to attribute causal influence to the future, which by definition is something that has never existed and therefore cannot be considered to be the cause of something occurring in the present (according to the doctrine of post hoc, ergo prompter hoc). This

TABLE 10.1   Selected Philosophical Foundations of Behaviorism

	Definition
Acceptance of:	

Acceptance of:

   Realism   The point of view that the world has an independent or objective existence apart from the perceptions of the observer

   Monism   The point of view that there exists only one kind of reality (e.g., physical matter)

   Determinism   The assumption that all phenomena have physical causes (which are potentially amenable to scientific investigation)

   Positivism   The belief that valid knowledge about the objective world can be arrived at through scientific research

   Rationalism   The belief that reason and logic are useful tools for scientific inquiry, and that ultimately, truthful explanations of human behavior will be rational

   Empiricism   A preference to rely on evidence gathered systematically through observation or experiment and capable of being replicated (i.e., verified) by others, using satisfactory standards of evidence

   Operationism   The assertion that it is important to develop measures of phenomena (and of social work interventions) that can be reliably replicated by others

   Parsimony   A preference for the simpler of the available adequate explanations for a behavioral phenomena

   Environmentalism   The assertion that most (but *not* all) causal factors responsible for an individual's behavior reside in the past and present transactions with his/her physical environment

   Pragmatism   The view that the meaning or truth of anything resides in its consequences in action

   Scientific skepticism   The point of view that all claims should be considered of doubtful validity until substantiated by credible scientific data

Rejection of:

   Nihilism   A doctrine that all values are baseless and that nothing is knowable or can be communicated

   Teleology   The assumption that behavior is purposive or goal directed

   Vitalism   The doctrine that life processes possess a unique character radically different from physiochemical phenomena

   Dualism   The view that the world consists of the two fundamental entities of mind and matter.

   Reification   Treating an abstract concept as if it has a physical reality (e.g., the Freudian ego)

   Circular reasoning   An explanation for human behavior in which cause and effect cannot be distinguished from one another

   Mentalism/Cognitivism   The view that one's mind(cognition) causes oneself to behave in certain ways

is an important distinction to make, given the frequency with which it is erroneously asserted that the behaviorist position is that people behave in certain ways to get rewards.

Theoretical Foundations

Like contemporary social work, behavior analysis focuses on the history of transactions that occurred between individuals and their environment to account for the present behavioral repertoire. Here are some representative quotes illustrating the behaviorist person-in-environment (PIE) position:

Men act upon the world and change it, and are changed in turn by the consequences of their action. Certain processes . . . alter behavior so that it achieves a safer and more useful interchange with a particular environment. . . . If by chance the environment changes, old forms of behavior disappear, while new consequences build new forms. (Skinner, 1957, p. 1)

We no longer look at behavior and environment as separate things or events but at the interrelation among them. (Skinner, 1969, p. 10)

Thus, the stimulating conditions that constitute the environment produce changes in behavior; these behavior changes alter the environment; . . . the altered environment produces further behaviors that again modify the environment, etc., resulting in the construction of unique cultures (modified environments), on one hand, and unique individual psychological developments on the other. (Bijou & Baer, 1978, p. 12)

The modern behaviorist believes that in every interaction with the environment, the child contributes her own responses and internal stimuli, which have been determined by her genetic structure and personal history. Furthermore, as the child develops, she responds increasingly to stimuli and environmental factors she herself has produced, so that she is engaging in active self-management. (Thomas, 1992, p. 221)

Compare and contrast the behavioral position with the point of view promulgated by systems and ecological models within social work:

[A goal is] building more supportive, helpful, and nurturing environments for clients through environmental helping, and increasing their competence in dealing with the environment through teaching basic life skills. (Whittaker & Garbarino, 1983, p. 34)

A basic assumption . . . is that human behavior is the product of the transactions between the individual and his environment. (Northen, 1982, p. 63)

The ecological metaphor of mutual adaptation suggests that the connectedness referred to is reciprocal—that is, a certain adaptiveness takes place between the person and others in the environment they share. (Meyer, 1988, p. 276)

The human being and the environment reciprocally *shape* [italics added] each other. People mold their environments in many ways, and in turn, they must then adapt to the changes they created. (Germain, 1992, p. 407)

The parallels are striking. However, unlike the metaphorical systems and ecological models, which lack substantive empirical evidence of the validity of their propositions and which fail to provide guidance to practitioners in terms of prescriptive assessment and intervention strategies (Gallant & Thyer, in press; Wakefield, 1996), contemporary social learning theory fleshes out the language of PIE with solid principles relating to the acquisition and change of behavior among individuals, couples, families, groups, organizations, and communities. In turn, these principles have led to the development and validation of a large number of psychosocial interventions (see O'Donohue, 1998) firmly grounded in the social work PIE perspective, which can be prescriptively applied to selected client problems.

A selected number of the basic assumptions of social learning theory are listed in Table 10.2. Although a comprehensive review of the principles of respondent, operant, and observational learning are beyond the scope of the present chapter, more extensive descriptions can be found in some of the authors' prior work (e.g., Thyer, 1987, 1988, 1992; Thyer & Myers, 1997a, 1997b). No doubt readers are familiar with the general concepts of respondent conditioning, for example, how a neutral stimulus, although paired with an unconditioned stimulus, becomes a conditioned stimulus; the general ideas behind operant conditioning, such as

TABLE 10.2 Selected Basic Assumptions of Social Learning Theory

- Human behavior consists of everything that a person *does*. This includes observable behavior and private events such as thoughts and feelings, as well as all those phenomena called *cognitive* and *affective*.
- Human behavior is, to a very large (but undetermined) extent, *learned*.
- There are three major biological processes by which people learn: respondent conditioning (i.e., Pavlovian), learning from past consequences that have followed behavior (i.e., operant conditioning), and learning by imitating others (modeling). These three processes are the mechanisms of social learning theory.
- The underlying biological processes by which people acquire behavior are similar across racial, cultural, and ethnic groups, by gender, social class, and all other methods of categorizing human beings.
- Similar learning processes taking place in different environments, within an individual's life span, and across this history of the human race (via genetic mediation) have given rise to the diversity of expressions we call the human experience.
- Assessment of clients involves an analysis of past and present learning experiences that may be responsible for giving rise to problematic situations. This is called a functional assessment. By definition, social learning theory takes into account the person-in-environment.
- Behavioral intervention involves providing a client with remedial/corrective learning experiences and/or restructuring the client's psychosocial environment so that adaptive behavior is reinforced and maladaptive behavior is weakened. There is an explicit preference, guided by data, to use reinforcing contingencies rather than punitive ones.
- Behavioral practice is embedded in traditional social work values of respect for individuals, maximizing client autonomy, and working toward the elimination of racism, discrimination, and social injustice.

SOURCE: Based on Thyer (1994, p. 136).

reinforcement, punishment, extinction, and shaping; and so forth. But what may not be appreciated is the incredible degree of depth and complexity into which these deceptively simple concepts develop. Contemporary social workers could well profit from beginning with some fairly elementary sources (e.g., Fischer & Gochros, 1975; Pryor, 1984; Skinner, 1953), then delving into mid-level abstractions and applications (e.g., Chance, 1998; Malott, Whaley, & Malott, 1993), and perhaps, for the truly intellectually daring (or the doctoral student preparing for comprehensive examinations!), looking at advanced content (e.g., Catania & Harnad, 1988; Hayes, 1989; Skinner, 1957). In Table 10.3, we have provided some simple definitions of the major practice principles, derived from the assumptions found in Table 10.2.

Practice Procedures

The development of specific intervention procedures derived from social learning theory, sometimes used alone but most often in combination, has been very rapid. Fifteen years ago, Bellack and Hersen (1985) edited the *Dictionary of Behavior Therapy Techniques,* which contained entries for almost 200 interventions. No doubt this list would be greatly expanded if it were brought up to date. This makes it difficult to list, much less describe in detail, a selection of important behavioral methods and the empirical research supporting their use. Any partial selection could be seen as an arbitrary listing and critiqued on the grounds of selectiveness or of not properly representing the field. Therefore, we have opted to organize the balance of this chapter, not on practice procedures, but rather along the lines of principles of learning theory as these undergird the rationale and development of all methods of behavior analysis and therapy. Understanding these theoretical principles may be seen as a prerequisite for the informed and professional use of prac-

TABLE 10.3   Major Principles Governing Overt
              Behavioral Change

Principle	Definition
Positive reinforcement	The presentation of a stimulus contingent on the occurrence of a behavior so as to strengthen that behavior (p. 202)
Negative reinforcement	The removal of an aversive stimulus contingent on the occurrence of a behavior so as to increase that behavior (p. 204)
Positive punishment	The reduction of the probability that a behavior will occur by presenting an aversive stimulus contingent on its occurrence (p. 209)
Negative punishment	The removal of a positive reinforcer contingent on the occurrence of an undesired behavior (p. 210)
Operant extinction	The discontinuance of the presentation of any and all reinforcement for a specific behavior contingent on the occurrence of that behavior such that its probability or occurrence is reduced (p. 212)
Shaping	The development of a desired behavior—either completely missing from the client's repertoire or in rudimentary form—through the sequential reinforcement of successively closer approximations to that behavior (p. 203)
Modeling	A change in behavior as a result of the observation of another's behavior (p. 96)

SOURCE: Page numbers are from Fischer and Gochros (1975).

tice techniques. We will review some techniques derived from respondent conditioning first, then those based on the operant model.

RESPONDENT LEARNING

Respondent Extinction

Respondent extinction is a practice method used to decrease dysfunctional behavioral responses to conditioned stimuli. Essentially, the approach involves exposing a client to a conditioned stimulus that has come (largely through each person's unique learning history) to elicit a conditioned response. Ideally, this exposure should be of long duration, not brief, and clinically, it is usually more acceptable to titrate the exposure, beginning with low intensity/duration stimulation and gradually increasing to that of higher intensity/duration. In Chapter 11 of this volume, Joseph Himle presents an extensive discussion of how this principle is used to treat clients suffering from various clinical anxiety disorders, such as agoraphobia, specific and social phobias, and obsessive compulsive disorder, but the approach can be applied to many disorders other than anxiety, for example, morbid grief (see Artelt & Thyer, 1998) or extreme jealousy.

Respondent extinction is also a component of treating sex offenders with the procedure known as masturbatory reconditioning. In this approach, male sex offenders (e.g., pedophiles) privately masturbate to orgasm while viewing pictures/videotapes of appropriate adult sexual content. Immediately after orgasm, clients continue to masturbate while observing pedophiliac stimuli. Masturbation for 10 to 15 minutes postorgasm does not serve as the same type of unconditioned stimulus (pleasant physical stimulation) as does the same stimulation when aroused and erect, prior to orgasm. By pairing pedophiliac stimuli with nonarousal, it is hoped that the respondent linkages between masturbation to orgasm (an extremely powerful unconditioned response) and young children will be extinguished. Etiologically, in the case of paraphilias, it is hypothesized that sexual arousal to deviant stimuli has been adventitiously respondently conditioned during the lifetime. Once such a link has been established (perhaps only one or two pairings are necessary), an individual's subsequent use of deviant stimuli (e.g., children, fetish objects, inflicting pain) in real-life sexual activities or masturbatory fantasies leading to orgasm serves to respondently strengthen these associations. *Delinking* a conditioned stimulus (e.g., a young child, female underwear) with orgasm using masturbatory reconditioning represents a direct application of respondent extinction conditioning principles to direct practice. Now, of course, respondent extinction used in this manner is only one of a number of concurrently applied interventions that can be used in the treatment of sexual paraphilias, but the approach is widely used by practitioners who specialize in the treatment of such individuals, and it seems to work well in routine clinical practice (see Crolley, Roys, Thyer, & Bordnick, 1998; Kelly, 1982).

Similar respondent extinction principles are employed in one form of treatment of substance abuse, known as cue exposure. The substance abuser's learning history has led to the establishment of profound conditioned responses. Use of certain substances (which are themselves unconditioned stimuli) certainly produces naturally occurring pleasant reactions (unconditioned responses). The "high" of alcohol intoxication, the "rush" of amphetamine or cocaine, the mellowness of opiates—these are all unlearned reactions of the body to unconditioned stimuli (the abused substances themselves). But a history of substance abuse has resulted in previously neutral stimuli coming to elicit conditioned responses, for example, craving and associated frantic efforts to obtain the drug. This is important, given the salient role of craving as a determinant of relapse among treated substance abusers. The originally neutral sights, sounds, and smells associated with using crack (for example) can themselves come to elicit craving reactions. Here is how one group of experts describes this phenomenon:

> When detoxified former cocaine users are confronted with stimuli previously associated with cocaine use, they report cocaine craving despite their expressed and apparently genuine intention to refrain from returning to drug use. Some report intense urges to use cocaine along with arousal and palpitations when they encounter stimuli as diverse as seeing a friend with whom they had used cocaine or seeing any powdery substance such as sugar or talcum powder . . . patients also experience similar responses when they encounter drug-buying locations, a pharmaceutical odor, or almost anything that has been repeatedly associated with getting and using cocaine. . . . After years of using cocaine, there are usually numerous stimuli within the patient's normal environment that have strong links to cocaine. (O'Brien, Childress, McLellan, & Ehrman, 1992, pp. 81-82)

Treatment of substance abusers, using respondent extinction via cue exposure to reduce craving and drug acquisition behaviors, involves the intentional exposure of the client to stimuli that elicit craving. Artificial powdered cocaine and crack rocks are laid out on a table with all the paraphernalia the user's history (not the user's cognitions) has associated with using drugs. He mixes it up, lights it, or taps the syringe, does everything except ingest it. Music, movies, and magazines previously associated with drug abuse are arranged around the client. Craving is measured in various ways (usually via quantitative self-report by the client). As you might imagine, craving and agitation are initially quite high. But an amazing phenomenon occurs. With the passage of time (anywhere from a few minutes to a few hours), craving begins to decrease without ingesting the drug. Such sessions are repeated, perhaps several times a day. Gradually, the conditioned behavioral reactions become less intense via the mechanism of respondent extinction. Each session tends to elicit less severe craving, and it diminishes more rapidly within sessions. With success in the contrived setting of the hospital in-patient unit or outpatient clinic, some specialized treatment centers then take their clients on field trips to the street, wherein less controlled exposure to those cues that elicit craving (the street corner where one purchased drugs, crack vials and empty cocaine packets on the sidewalks, drug-using acquaintances, etc.) are encountered. This is a grueling approach to treatment, and respondent extinction is usually combined with a multifaceted intervention package as opposed to being used as a singular technique. See McLellan, Childress, Ehrman, and O'Brien (1986), O'Brien, Childress, McLellan, and Ehrman (1990), and Acierno, Donohue, and Kogan (1994) for more complete descriptions of cue exposure as a treatment and for a summary of the research evidence on its effectiveness.

Respondent Conditioning

In the treatment of pedophiles described above, the intentional pairing of appropriate sexual stimuli (watching an age-appropriate videotape and verbalizing aloud appropriate sexual fantasies) while masturbating to orgasm represents an example of deliberately using respondent conditioning principles to establish associations between neutral stimuli (pornographic videotapes of adult sexual activity) and unconditioned responses (self-stimulation and orgasm), in an effort to generate a conditioned response (age-appropriate stimuli produce sexual arousal).

Social workers Young and Morgan (1972) have conducted a number of outcome studies on the bell-and-pad conditioning treatment for childhood enuresis. Most readers will be familiar with this effective technique. A child with nocturnal enuresis sleeps atop a pad that, when dampened, sounds an alarm. This wakes the child, who then (perhaps with parent assistance) completes voiding in the toilet. The respondent conditioning model is as follows: The alarm is an unconditioned stimulus that produces the unconditioned response of waking up. A full bladder is linked with the alarm that causes awakening. With a number of pairings, the full bladder assumes the properties of a conditioned stimulus and elicits awakening (a conditioned response) on its own, in the absence of the alarm.

OPERANT CONDITIONING

Positive Reinforcement

Sedentary living is encouraged by institutional environments that house people with chronic mental illness. Thyer, Irvine, and Santa (1984) describe one attempt to partially remedy this. A group home caring for five to six individuals with chronic mental illness was located in rural Michigan. The home's activity therapist was singularly unsuccessful in getting her heavily medicated clients to participate with her in any form of exercise program. The author's attempt to resolve this situation involved the home's acquisition of an exercise bicycle with an odometer that kept track of mileage ridden. The residents were encouraged to ride the bike, which had been placed in the living room in view of the television. Careful data were taken on clients' bike-riding behavior. This was easy, because none did it. After a 1-week baseline, staff were instructed to provide the clients with small reinforcers (consumables) contingent on riding the bike a prescribed distance (1/10th of a mile, 2/10ths, etc., up to 5/10ths of the mile, where the standard remained). Bike riding escalated to several miles per day. This was continued for 1 week, and then the reinforcement program was deliberately halted. Bike riding declined to baseline levels. After another week had passed, the positive reinforcement program was reinstituted, and riding surged back to several miles a day. The demonstrable success of the program, as evidenced by the compelling nature of the data gathered through the use of an A-B-A-B design, was so strong that the positive reinforcement system remained in place as a permanent part of the home's activity therapy program.

Clearly, small-scale programs such as this are not cures for serious mental illness, but they do provide promising leads to small-scale solutions for the everyday types of problems encountered by human services staff charged with caring for such individuals. And, we believe, there is real value in such small-scale efforts. A more impressive study is described next, again making extensive use of positive reinforcement in caring for people with chronic mental illness.

Paul and Lentz (1977) conducted a controlled study of three different inpatient treatment programs at one large state mental hospital. Patients were randomly assigned to either a specially structured social learning (SL) theory-based inpatient unit, a specially structured milieu therapy inpatient unit, or a "treatment as usual" program at the same hospital. Hospital staff were trained in the three different modalities and rotated every 3 weeks across the units (this controlled for possible disparities in the staff's characteristics between the units).

A major treatment modality on the SL unit was the use of staff-distributed tokens contingent on prosocial, nonpsychotic, normal behavior, tokens serving as positive reinforcers that could be redeemed for desired goods and activities. All clients had noncontingent access to the normal goods and services essential to proper inpatient psychiatric care, but access to augmented, highly desired services, goods, and activities was earned via the acquisition of tokens. All client rights were protected; the study was conducted in an ethical manner and carefully monitored.

This project involved the most severely impaired patient population ever studied. Highly detailed and reliable measures were continuously taken of dysfunctional and functional patient behavior across all three programs. Striking results were obtained favoring the SL program, with more than 97% of the SL patients being discharged for more than 90 days (vs. 71% for milieu, and 45% standard care). "The social learning program produced significant sustained improvement in all classes of functioning . . . about 25% improved to levels that were indistinguishable from the 'normal' population" (Paul & Menditto, 1992, p. 52). Space does not permit detailed delineation of the positive results—the declines in aggression, lethargy, psychotic behavior, and use of time-outs and restraints obtained on the SL unit, along with a dramatic reduction in the use of antipsychotic medications. Paul and Lentz (1977) is a landmark study in the care of the chronically mentally ill and should be required reading for any social worker serving this client population.

Readers will recognize the ubiquitousness of positive reinforcement processes in everyday social work practice. Almost all approaches to practice now recognize the importance of having social workers make conscious use of positive reinforcement to strengthen client functional behaviors. Some evidence suggests that even in those practice approaches that theoretically strive for a neutral (e.g., psychoanalytic) stance or for the use of noncontingent reinforcement, the selective use of therapist empathy, warmth, and directiveness occurs. Truax (1966), for example, carefully analyzed tape recordings of a long-term therapy case conducted by Carl Rogers and found that the founder of so-called nondirective therapy himself was inadvertently selective in his responses to the client and that this tended to strengthen certain types of client verbal behaviors within therapy. This suggests that because reinforcement is such a fundamental mechanism of behavior change, social workers should be well schooled in the underlying theory and application of the procedure in practice.

Negative Reinforcement

Noncompliance in taking antipsychotic medications is a serious problem for some individuals, so Azrin and Powell (1969) developed an automated pill dispenser for use in the outpatient medication treatment of mentally ill patients. Simply put, the dispenser was loaded with prescribed medications, and the timer was set to go off when it was time to take them. When the alarm went off, the device had to be manually reset, and when this occurred, the medications were automatically dispensed into the client's hand. The desired behavior of getting the medications was negatively reinforced by the cessation of the aversive alarm. A conceptually similar arrangement was contrived by Greene and Hoats (1969) to help maintain the vocational behavior of a mildly retarded man in a correctional institution, whereby a television playing in the work area displayed a mildly distorted picture, unless the client was properly engaged in his work task. While he worked, the picture was clear and undisturbed, but when he engaged in off-task behaviors the screen began to flicker and roll. An A-B-A-B design clearly demonstrated the effectiveness of removing picture distortion as a negative reinforcer for work. The work requirement was a modest one, and working sessions lasted only 1 hour each day, so the client was in no danger of being abused or exploited for his labors.

Sometimes, it is difficult for dentists to manage the behavior of noncooperative children requiring dental care. One approach to getting children to cooperate involved the use of negative reinforcement. Allen, Loiben, Allen, and Stanley (1992) arranged a system whereby if otherwise noncooperative children remained quietly in the dental chair for brief periods of time and permitted the dentist to work, this would be followed by the children being allowed to get out of the chair (this could be called "relief" or "escape" and is very negatively reinforcing for both children and adults!). Initially, the dentist only asked for a few seconds of cooperation before allowing the child out of the chair for 10 to 20 seconds. Gradually, the amount of cooperative time required to get out of the chair was increased. This approach, evaluated using a multiple baseline across clients design, was found to be highly effective in gaining the cooperation of heretofore non-compliant children and did not result in any increase in the amount of time required to complete treatments.

Positive Punishment

Generally, within the behavioral model, interventions focusing on reinforcement are preferred over those initially involving punishment, but in selected circumstances, treatment regimens involving aspects of punishment may be warranted. Social workers Fischer and Nehs (1978) provide a simple illustration of using positive punishment. An 11-year-old boy, Mark, living in a group home, swore profusely, and staff instructions and coaxing had no evident effect on his use of profanity. A 5-day baseline was taken by staff of Mark's swearing; this was followed by a 10-day intervention phase. Simply put, the staff began requiring Mark to wash windows (this was normally done by staff) for 10 minutes each time he swore. Failure to perform window-washing would result in the curtailment of privileges. During the baseline, Mark swore 8 to 14 times a day (totaling 56 times in 5 days). This rapidly decreased following the implementation of the positive punishment program, with swearing ranging from 9 to 0 times and totaling 13 times in 10 days (on 6 of the 10 days, no cursing at all occurred). The punishment program was then discontinued for 5 days and cursing increased (23 times in 5 days). When the punishment program was reinstituted, swearing immediately dropped to 0 times a day and remained there all 5 days. The program was then discontinued, and cursing remained very low, well below baseline levels (four times during 6 probe days) during the following 15 days. Fischer and Nehs (1978) were able to format their data in an A-B-A-B design, and the clarity of the data permitted concluding that the punitive intervention caused Mark's swearing to decrease, as opposed to some rival variables.

Social worker Stephen Wong (Wong, Larrow, & Fuqua, 1983) provides another illustration of positive punishment (for brevity's sake, much clinical detail is omitted from these descriptions). A 36-year-old mother of five was seriously troubled by three discrete, disturbing somatic sensations, breathing difficulty, throat discomfort, and difficulty swallowing. Extensive medical work-ups failed to disclose an organic basis for these problems, and various other treatments had been tried and not found to be successful. Wong had the client create a baseline for each problem separately, recording the number of times a day it occurred. After a 1-week baseline for breathing difficulty, the client agreed to write out a positive statement of at least five words, 50 times (e.g., "I can overcome this problem.") immediately following the occurrence of the difficulty. Today, advocates of holistic healing would call this an *affirmation,* but the astute reader will recognize it for what it really is, positive punishment: presenting the clients with a boring, repetitive task contingent on the occurrence of an undesired behavior. After 1 week of baseline, the punishment program was begun, and it took about 2 weeks for the breathing difficulty to disappear completely.

Meanwhile, baselines continued to be taken of throat discomfort and swallowing difficulties. Following a 3-week baseline of throat discomfort, the same intervention (contingent writing) was implemented. The problem disappeared in less than a week. Swallowing difficulties proved less amenable to remediation using this approach, and their resolution will be described below in the section labeled "Operant Shaping." Nevertheless, Wong's (Wong et al., 1983) report, formatted as a multiple baseline design across three problems, provides a nice example of using positive punishment. It should be stressed that the client's problems were of long duration; they had resisted prior treatment approaches, both medical and psychosocial; and the treatment program was entered into completely voluntarily on her part.

Negative Punishment

Early (1995) used negative punishment to reduce the self-stimulatory and self-injurious behavior exhibited by a 20-year-old man, Matthew, who met the criteria for autistic disorder. Self-stimulation and self-injury can be dysfunctional behaviors that not only interfere with a person's ability to learn, or to be integrated into mainstream settings (self-stimulation), but also cause permanent disfigurement or harm (retinal detachment, scarring, loss of hearing, infections) (see Underwood & Thyer, 1990). Working in a classroom setting, the school social worker provided Matthew with 25 popsicle sticks at the beginning of a tutoring session. At the end of each session, the sticks could be exchanged for consumables (peanuts). Each time Matthew engaged in self-stimulation or self-injury, the social worker removed one of the sticks (thereby reducing the peanuts earned that session). This simple approach resulted in a rapid reduction in dysfunctional behaviors.

Social worker Barbara Hudson used the principle of negative punishment in her work with "Mrs. Evans," a woman with many complex problems. Here is how Hudson described this element of intervention:

I told Mrs. Evans that from now on I would want to hear a piece of good news each time I visited. We planned a series of tasks, starting with what seemed easiest and progressing to the more difficult. Examples from our list are hoovering (vacuuming) a room, doing some mending, later sorting out bills, re-organizing the kitchen, and later still, looking for a part-time job and attending an evening class. If the agreed upon task was done, my pleasure was lavishly expressed; if it was not done, I expressed disappointment and *left early* [italics added] but first tried to ensure that the failure was not because the task was too much of a contrast in difficulty . . . . Later I took to telephoning and if the task was not done, I would *postpone my visit until it was* [italics added]. (Hudson, 1975, p. 507)

Assuming that Hudson's visits were reinforcing events, the tactic of leaving early or of postponing an appointment until a task was accomplished represents the use of negative punishment (the removal of a positive reinforcer contingent on the occurrence of an undesired event, e.g., failing to accomplish a task).

The general concept of fines can be used as a shorthand term for the procedure of negative punishment—something pleasant (e.g., money) is taken away contingent on engaging in an undesired (by society as a whole, anyway) behavior (speeding while driving). Another term used synonymously with negative punishment is *response cost*. Armstrong and Drabman (1998) describe the treatment of public masturbation on the part of a 9-year-old girl. The third grader was observed by her teacher to be masturbating apparently nearly constantly in class. The intervention consisted of having her mother prepare 10 drawings for her daughter, which she was given at the beginning of the school day and took to class. Each time the teacher observed the student to be touching her genitals, a drawing was taken away. New drawings were made by the student and her mother each night. Masturbation at school was eliminated almost immediately. A similar contingency involving response cost was employed by Reynolds and Kelley (1997) to decrease aggression in preschoolers. Bullying preschool boys were given a small supply of "smiley faces" at the beginning of class. Each time they were observed to be aggressive against a classmate, they lost a smiley face. If they retained at least one smiley face at the end of a given class segment, they could choose from a choice of small rewards. This approach was highly effective in reducing bullying in four preschoolers, as assessed using a multiple baseline across-subjects design.

Operant Extinction

In Figueroa, Thyer, and Thyer (1992), the authors helped treat a boy with severe mental retardation who seemed to fear the close proximity of others and who reacted by physically aggressing against them. His aggression was so severe as to warrant his being placed in a long-term residential care facility, as his parents were unable to care properly for him at home (he had attacked other children in the neighborhood). The authors hypothesized that the aggression was inadvertently negatively reinforced. The child found the close proximity of others to be aversive, and when he acted aggressively, others responded by moving away and leaving him alone, thus strengthening aggression. In a very real sense, the child's aggression was quite functional for him, in the short run, although quite dysfunctional in the long run, as it precluded him from being placed in a less restrictive, community-based living environment.

A tentative treatment plan was formed, based on this hypothesis. Several pilot sessions were arranged wherein one of the authors (BAT), wearing heavy clothes and leather gloves, entered a small treatment room with the child and sat next to him. This prompted the boy to aggress—hit with his fists, scratch, spit, bite, pinch, kick, and so on. Rather than move away, the clinician simply engaged in moderate self-protection but otherwise allowed the child to aggress. Other staff videotaped the session and took reliable data on the occurrence of aggression. At the end of the 45-minute session, aggression was much lower in both quantity and quality. These pilot sessions were repeated with the same therapist on two more occasions, and aggression eventually diminished and became virtually absent. The positive results of this pilot work with one clinician led the practitioner-researchers to continue the extinction program, eventually involving many different staff (which attempted to promote generalization of treatment effects). Similarly positive results were obtained.

Operant Shaping

Earlier, the report by Wong et al. (1983) was outlined, and it was noted that the client's swallowing difficulties did not respond to the contingent writing intervention. A careful analysis of her swallowing problems revealed that they tended to occur in the later stages of a meal. The instructed intervention was for the client to limit herself to 10 bites for a meal. After she had experienced two successive meals with no swallowing problems, she could increase her intake to 11 bites. Once she had two more meals without difficulties, she could increase to 12, and so forth. After 43 days she was up to 28 bites (a complete meal) without problems. Hunger, of course, was the therapist's ally, as were the naturally occurring, positively reinforcing effects of enjoying good food and the negatively reinforcing effects of alleviating hunger through eating.

Sluckin and Jehu (1969) describe an early use of shaping in the treatment of a 5-year-old girl, Tesse, with elective mutism. Tesse spoke normally in the presence of her family but not when others were around. The social worker laid out a simple program, whereby Tesse was asked to read aloud to her mother and would receive candy for doing so. Initially, the social worker stationed herself a good distance from the child and mother, with her back to them. When Tesse whispered a word, the goodies were proffered. Three or four times a week, these sessions were held for about 20 to 30 minutes. Gradually, Tesse was required to whisper not simply one word, but a whole line of the story, then a paragraph, and so on. Meanwhile, the social worker moved gradually closer and closer to mother and child, and Tesse was required to speak more and more audibly. Over a few months, the girl began reading directly to the social worker in an audible voice and soon began to speak to others, even though no specific training was provided in this area.

Modeling

Pediatric social worker Jill Koepke (Koepke & Thyer, 1985) described her intervention with a young mother who had a 2-year-old child hospitalized due to failure-to-thrive. Observations within the hospital demonstrated that the mother possessed very poor feeding skills and that she inadvertently reinforced her child's maladaptive behavior during eating. For example, social reinforcement tended to be given for screaming, regurgitation, and refusing to eat, as opposed to ingesting food. A major component of the intervention was having the social worker model functional feeding skills: reinforce the child for allowing food to be placed in her mouth, reinforce swallowing food, discontinue social reinforcement of non-eating behaviors, read to the child (a favored activity) for 30 minutes following a successful meal, and so on. Gradually, the mother replaced the social worker in conducting the meal times, with judicious use of praise and correction. The child was discharged after 17 days of hospital treatment. Weight gain only occurred after the behavioral program began on Day 11. At 7-month follow-up, her weight had continued to improve, and self-induced vomiting was absent.

Generally, modeling is an effective method to help clients acquire new skills, particularly those that may be a bit complex. And often, modeling conducted using small groups is an efficient way to serve clients, as well as to take advantage of the naturally occurring opportunities for mutual modeling and reinforcement processes. Social worker Sheldon Rose has had a productive career making use of small groups as a vehicle for inducing behavior change with clients and of employing modeling, reinforcement, and other behavioral methods as a major intervention. For example, Rose (1974a, 1974b) describes some of his early work with parents receiving welfare and with the parents of children with mental retardation, using modeling as a means to teach parenting skills. The parents helped each other in the development of monitoring and intervention plans, and

the parents themselves served as models for other parents for the purposes of demonstrating various behavior modification techniques. Behavioral rehearsal involved the parents practicing these techniques in the presence of other parents before using them at home. Modeling and behavioral rehearsal were particularly useful in training parents in the expression of appropriate affect in the application of reinforcement and time out. (Rose, 1974b, p. 137)

The development of assertiveness skills, dating skills, and social skills in general often relies heavily on modeling as a means of transmitting new abilities. Moote, Smyth, and Wodarski (1999) found over 25 intervention research studies on social skills training with youth in school settings, and almost all made use of modeling as a treatment component. Twenty-three of the 25 studies obtained positive results.

Exactly why modeling works remains unclear. It is known that other animals learn from observing each other and that imitation by human babies of adults (e.g., facial expressions) occurs very shortly after birth, so it would seem than evolutionary selection has favored the capacity of learn via modeling. Clearly, operant processes are at work as well—if the client is reinforced after imitating a model, both the specific imitated act and modeling in general are strengthened.

CONTEMPORARY STATUS

Assessing the role played by any theoretical perspective within contemporary social work practice is a difficult undertaking. One approach to do this is by surveying direct practitioners themselves, and there are at least two such studies bearing on the topic. Jayaratne (1980-1981) surveyed clinical social workers and found that about 30% reported making use of the behavioral theoretical orientation in their practice. More recently, Strom (1994) randomly surveyed licensed clinical social workers in private

practice from across the United States and asked them, among other issues, about the theoretical orientations they used in practice. About 62% claimed to use a cognitive-behavioral orientation and 37% a behavioral one (respondents could list multiple orientations).

Another approach is to examine the course offerings at schools of social work. A survey is one way to conduct this review, but a more direct way is to examine school bulletins and review course descriptions. This latter approach was the one selected by Thyer and Maddox (1988), who wrote to all programs accredited by the Council on Social Work Education, requesting their bulletin. Sixty-seven responded, and the course offerings were evaluated in terms of the presence of content in behavior therapy. These authors found that 28% of the 67 responding schools offered an entire course in behavior therapy, and 39% offered this content as a part of another class (e.g., practice methods).

Thus, the admittedly somewhat dated information cited above suggests that the behavioral perspective has been a viable one within the practice and educational social work communities for several decades. It is by no means a dominant influence, however. The picture is somewhat different when one examines the practice-research literature describing social work outcome studies, described below in the section headed "Empirical Foundations." The authors' informal observations suggest that most contemporary practice textbooks give at least a respectful tip of the hat, and sometimes a great deal more, to the behavioral perspective.

Diversity Issues

From a pragmatic perspective, the most important consideration in evaluating the appropriateness of a particular model of practice, with respect to diversity issues, is the empirical evidence that the approach in question can be effective in helping clients from diverse backgrounds, including racial, ethnic, and gender factors. One of the authors has addressed this point as follows:

> One operational definition of a social worker's skills in culturally diverse practice is his or her ability to effectively help clients from varying cultural backgrounds. The behavioral social worker does not see a practitioner's choice of theory, purported cultural sensitivity, knowledge of unique family systems, and so on as being as important the query: What evidence is there that your client's situation improved? Social workers capable of providing such evidence have, ipso facto, demonstrated their capacity to effectively work with culturally diverse clients. On the other hand, the "culturally sensitive" social worker could nevertheless provide services that are not helpful to minority or oppressed clients. (Thyer, 1994, p. 141)

From its inception, behavior analysis and therapy has been concerned about, and provided services to, clients from exceedingly diverse backgrounds. Where the behavioral perspective stands out is in the impressive number of empirical outcome studies documenting the practice effectiveness of this approach with racial and ethnic minorities living in North America and in practice contexts found in other countries around the world (see Thyer, 1994, for a review).

Empirical Foundations

The literature reporting outcome studies conducted in social work practice can be divided into two crude areas, those with negative outcomes and those with generally positive ones. Comprehensive reviews conducted in the early 1970s of studies conducted in the 1960s and earlier, produced the dismaying result that when selected social work interventions were tested in terms of their effectiveness in helping clients, clients generally did not benefit, or even got worse (as prime examples of such reviews, see Fischer, 1976; Segal, 1972). This provoked what has been called a crisis in social casework, resulting in two divergent responses. One was to generally disparage scientific methodology as an insufficiently subtle research tool to reliably detect the otherwise undoubtedly beneficial results of our efforts. The other was to focus evaluation efforts in the direction of better proceduralized interventions on more specific problems, using progressively more sophisticated research designs. Both types of responses have continued to the present.

Beginning in the 1980s, however, the case for social work's effectiveness has been much more promising, and for two decades, the behavioral perspective has prominently figured in bringing about this change. For example, in Reid and Hanrahan's (1982) comprehensive review of controlled experimental studies on direct social work practice, published between 1973 and 1979, 18 of the 29 included studies were behavioral in nature, leading the authors to conclude, "The influence of the behavior modification movement is apparent and pervasive. The majority of the experiments involve evaluation of skills training or contingency contracting within the frame of reference of learning theory" (Reid & Hanrahan, 1982, p. 329). A similar review of more current studies found much the same thing: "Most of the studies with unequivocally positive outcomes tested forms of practice that relied heavily on problem-solving and task-centered methods, usually in conjunction with behavioral methods" (Rubin, 1985, p. 474).

A decade later, this dominance was maintained. MacDonald, Sheldon, and Gillespie (1992) reviewed 95 published social work outcome studies that appeared between 1979 and 1991, found very positive outcomes for most of these, and noted that "The majority of positive results within research of an experimental and quasi-experimental nature are accounted for by behavioral and cognitive-behavioral approaches" (p. 635). Fully 31 of the 95 studies were behavioral in nature, almost one third, more than any other perspective.

More recently, Kevin Gorey and his colleagues published a meta-analysis of 45 social work outcome studies published from 1990 to 1994. Almost 49% ($n = 22$) of these even more current examples of evaluation research were behavioral in theoretical orientation, a far greater proportion than any other single orientation, and they were found to have very strong effect sizes. Among the conclusions was the following: "The empirical social work practice knowledge base is much greater for cognitive-behavioral models" (Gorey, Thyer, & Pawluck, 1998, p. 274). Thus, to the extent that the profession is committed to following the lead of empirical research, our field should clearly enhance its commitment to the provision of such cognitive-behavioral methods of behavior change.

FUTURE DIRECTIONS

What are the likely future developments in behavioral social work? Speculation is always risky but here are a few of our best guesses.

In terms of theory we predict that in time, the current distinctions among respondent, operant, and observational learning will be subsumed under a singular, more comprehensive conceptual framework. This is not meant to imply that respondent, operant, or observational learning theory principles will necessarily be shown to be incorrect in themselves, but rather, eventually, the underlying biological mechanisms of each will be elucidated better and make possible conceptualizing these three forms of learning as one process. Already, conceptual and empirical research is afoot in melding respondent and operant learning as one, not two, mechanisms of learning (see Pear & Eldridge, 1984), and it is possible that observational learning will eventually be seen as a special form of operant conditioning (see Baer & Deguchi, 1985).

We will also see empirically based learning principles further extrapolated to better account for behavioral phenomena beyond that of the individual, to the level of small groups, families, organizations, and communities. This process would be the social and behavioral sciences' counterpart to work in physics to arrive at a so-called grand-unified theory, a truly exciting prospect.

In terms of social work research, we shall see parallel increases in the use of randomized controlled clinical trial methodology to evaluate the outcomes of social services, pre-experimental and quasi-experimental group research designs for the same purpose, and single-system designs permitting individual practitioners to gather credible data regarding behavioral change with individual clients. Still in its embryonic stages, qualitative research methods may have a greater role in program evaluation as well, embedded in the context of studies possessing an overall quantitative, positivist character.

Generally, more attention shall be given to outcome studies in social work practice. An exceedingly small proportion of social work research investigations have heretofore involved outcome studies. According to Proctor's (1998) analysis, only about 3% of the articles published in social work journals consist of research evaluating replicable interventions. It is little wonder that direct practitioners seem to rarely consult the professional literature.

This greater emphasis on the evaluation of social work practice will be stimulated by the demands of managed care firms, the general sense within the field that it is a good thing to empirically document practice outcomes using scientifically credible research designs, and preliminary evidence that empirically evaluating practice may result in improved practice outcomes (see Faul, McMurtry, & Hudson, in press; Slonim-Nevo & Anson, 1998).

The changes described above, if they occur at all, are likely to take place slowly, and there will likely always be a market for practitioners to provide non-empirically-based treatments. However, the greater integration of social and behavioral science within the practice of social work, a goal present from the very inception of our field, is proceeding apace. A good word to describe this process is *progress*.

REFERENCES

Acierno, R., Donohue, B., & Kogan, E. (1994). Psychological interventions for drug abuse: A critique and summation of controlled studies. *Clinical Psychology Review, 14,* 417-442.

Allen K. D., Loiben, T., Allen, S., & Stanley, R. T. (1992). Dentist-implemented contingent escape for management of distruptive child behavior. *Journal of Applied Behavior Analysis, 25,* 629-636.

Armstrong, K. J., & Drabman, R. S. (1998). Treatment of a nine-year-old girl's public masturbatory behavior. *Child & Family Behavior Therapy, 20,* 55-62.

Artelt, T., & Thyer, B. A. (1998). Treating chronic grief. In B. A. Thyer & J. S. Wodarski (Eds.), *Handbook of empirical social work practice* (Vol. 2, pp. 341-356). New York: John Wiley.

Azrin, N. H., & Powell, J. (1969). Behavioral engineering: The use of response priming to improve prescribed self-medication. *Journal of Applied Behavior Analysis, 2,* 39-42.

Baer, D. M., & Deguchi, H. (1985). Generalized imitation from a radical-behavioral viewpoint. In S. Reiss & R. R. Bootzin (Eds.), *Theoretical issues in behavior therapy* (pp. 179-217). New York: Academic Press.

Barker, R. (Ed.). (1999). *The social work dictionary* (4th ed.). Washington, DC: NASW Press.

Bellack, A. S., & Hersen, M. (Eds.). (1985). *Dictionary of behavior therapy techniques.* New York: Pergamon.

Bijou, S., & Baer, D. M. (1978). *Behavior analysis of child development.* Englewood Cliffs, NJ: Prentice Hall.

Catania, A. C., & Harnad, S. (1988). *The selection of behavior.* New York: Cambridge University Press.

Chance, P. (1998). *First course in applied behavior analysis.* Pacific Grove, CA: Brooks/Cole.

Chiesa, M. (1994). *Radical behaviorism: The philosophy and the science.* Boston, MA: Authors Cooperative.

Crolley, J., Roys, D., Thyer, B. A., & Bordnick, P. S. (1998). Evaluating outpatient behavior therapy of sex offenders: A pretest-posttest study. *Behavior Modification, 22,* 485-501.

Early, B. P. (1995). Decelerating self-stimulating and self-injurious behaviors of the student with autism: Behavioral intervention in the classroom. *Social Work in Education, 17,* 244-255.

Faul, A. C., McMurtry, S. L., & Hudson, W. W. (in press). Can empirical clinical practice techniques improve social work outcomes? *Research on Social Work Practice.*

Figueroa, R., Thyer, B. A., & Thyer, K. B. (1992). Extinction and DRO in the treatment of aggression in a boy with severe mental retardation. *Journal of Behavior Therapy and Experimental Psychiatry, 23,* 133-140.

Fischer, J. (1976). *The effectiveness of social casework.* Springfield, IL: Charles C. Thomas.

Fischer, J., & Gochros, H. (1975). *Planned behavior change: Behavior modification in social work.* New York: Free Press.

Fischer, J., & Nehs, R. (1978). Use of a commonly available chore to reduce a boy's rate of swearing. *Journal of Behavior Therapy and Experimental Psychiatry, 9,* 81-83.

Gallant, J. P., & Thyer, B. A. (in press). A critique of general systems theory in social work practice. In R. R. Greene & P. Ephross (Eds.), *Human behavior theory and social work practice* (2nd ed.). New York: Aldine de Gruyter.

Germain, C. B. (1992). A conversation with Carel Germain on human development in the ecological context. In M. Bloom (Ed.), *Changing lives: Studies in human development and professional helping* (pp. 406-409). Columbia: University of South Carolina Press.

Gorey, K., Thyer, B. A., & Pawluck, A. (1998). Differential effectiveness of prevalent social work practice models: A meta-analysis. *Social Work, 43,* 269-278.

Greene, R. J., & Hoats, D. L. (1969). Reinforcing capabilities of television distortion. *Journal of Applied Behavior Analysis, 2,* 139-141.

Hayes, S. (Ed.). (1989). *Rule-governed behavior: Cognition, contingencies, and instructional control.* New York: Plenum.

Hudson, B. (1975). An inadequate personality. *Social Work Today, 6,* 506-508.

Jayaratne, S. (1980-1981). Characteristics and theoretical orientations of clinical social workers: A national survey. *Journal of Social Service Research, 4*(2), 17-30.

Kelly, R. J. (1982). Behavioral reorientation of pedophiliacs: Can it be done? *Clinical Psychology Review, 2,* 387-408.

Koepke, J. M., & Thyer, B. A. (1985). Behavioral treatment of failure-to-thrive in a two-year-old infant. *Child Welfare, 64,* 511-516.

MacDonald, G., Sheldon, B., & Gillespie, J. (1992). Contemporary studies of the effectiveness of social work. *British Journal of Social Work, 22,* 615-643.

Malott, R., Whaley, D., & Malott, M. (1993). *Elementary principles of behavior* (2nd ed.). Englewood Cliffs, NJ: Prentice Hall.

McLellan, A., Childress, A., Ehrman, R., & O'Brien, C. (1986). Extinguishing conditioned responses during treatment for opiate dependence: Turning laboratory findings into clinical procedures. *Journal of Substance Abuse Treatment, 3,* 33-40.

Meyer, C. H. (1988). The ecosystems perspective. In R. Dorfman (Ed.), *Paradigms of clinical social work* (pp. 275-294). New York: Brunner-Mazel.

Moote, G. T., Smyth, N. J., & Wodarski, J. S. (1999). Social skills training with youth in school settings: A review. *Research on Social Work Practice, 9,* 427-465.

Myers, L. L., & Thyer, B. A. (1994). Behavioural therapy: Popular misconceptions. *Scandinavian Journal of Behaviour Therapy, 23,* 97-107.

Northen, H. (1982). *Clinical social work.* New York: Columbia University Press.

O'Brien, C., Childress, A., McLellan, T., & Ehrman, R. (1990). Integrating systematic cue exposure with standard treatment in recovering drug dependent patients. *Addictive Behaviors, 15,* 355-365.

O'Brien, C., Childress, A., McLellan, T., & Ehrman, R. (1992). Developing treatments that address classical conditioning. In F. Tims & C. Leukefeld (Eds.), *Cocaine treatment: Research and clinical perspectives* (pp. 71-91). Rockville, MD: National Institute on Drug Abuse.

O'Donohue, W. (Ed.). (1998). *Learning and behavior therapy.* Boston, MA: Longwood.

Paul, G. L., & Lentz, R. J. (1977). *Psychosocial treatment of chronic mental patients: Milieu versus social learning programs.* Cambridge, MA: Harvard University Press.

Paul, G. L., & Menditto, A. A. (1992). Effectiveness of inpatient treatment programs for mentally ill adults in public psychiatric facilities. *Applied and Preventive Psychology, 1,* 41-63.

Pear, J. J., & Eldridge, G. D. (1984). The operant-respondent distinction: Future directions. *Journal of the Experimental Analysis of Behavior, 42,* 453-467.

Proctor, E. (1998). Social work research and the quest for effective practice. In *Proceedings on the Tenth National Conference on Doctoral Research in Social Work* (pp. 1-27). Columbus: Ohio State University, School of Social Work.

Pryor, K. (1984). *Don't shoot the dog!* New York: Bantam.

Reid, W., & Hanrahan, P. (1982). Recent evaluations of social work: Grounds for optimism. *Social Work, 27,* 328-340.

Reynolds, L. K., & Kelley, M. L. (1997). The efficacy of a response cost-based treatment package for managing aggressive behavior in preschoolers. *Behavior Modification, 21,* 216-230.

Rose, S. D. (1974a). Group training of parents as behavior modifiers. *Social Work, 19,* 156-162.

Rose, S. D. (1974b). Training parents in groups as behavior modifiers of their mentally retarded children. *Journal of Behavior Therapy and Experimental Psychiatry, 5,* 135-140.

Rubin, A. (1985). Practice effectiveness: More grounds for optimism. *Social Work, 30,* 469-476.

Segal, S. P. (1972). Research on the outcome of social work therapeutic interventions: A review of the literature. *Journal of Health and Social Behavior, 13,* 3-17.

Skinner, B. F. (1953). *Science and human behavior.* New York: Macmillan.

Skinner, B. F. (1957). *Verbal behavior.* Englewood Cliffs, NJ: Prentice Hall.

Skinner, B. F. (1969). *Contingencies of reinforcement: A theoretical analysis.* Englewood Cliffs, NJ: Prentice Hall.

Skinner, B. F. (1974). *About behaviorism*. New York: Knopf.

Slonim-Nevo, V., & Anson, Y. (1998). Evaluating practice: Does it improve treatment outcome. *Social Work Research, 22*, 66-74.

Sluckin, A., & Jehu, D. (1969). A behavioural approach in the treatment of elective mutism. *British Journal of Social Work, 10*, 70-73.

Strom, K. (1994). Social workers in private practice: An update. *Clinical Social Work Journal, 22*, 73-89.

Thomas, R. M. (1992). *Comparing theories of child development*. Belmont, CA: Wadsworth.

Thyer, B. A. (1987). Contingency analysis: Toward a unified theory for social work practice. *Social Work, 32*, 150-157.

Thyer, B. A. (1988). Radical behaviorism and clinical social work. In R. Dorfman (Ed.), *Paradigms of clinical social work* (pp. 123-148). New York: Guilford.

Thyer, B. A. (1991). Behavioral social work: It is not what you think. *Arete, 16*(2), 1-9.

Thyer, B. A. (1992). A behavioral perspective on human development. In M. Bloom (Ed.), *Changing lives: Studies in human development and professional helping* (pp. 410-418). Columbia: University of South Carolina Press.

Thyer, B. A. (1994). Social learning theory: Empirical applications to culturally diverse practice. In R. R. Greene (Ed.), *Human behavior theory: A diversity framework* (pp. 133-146). New York: Aldine de Gruyter.

Thyer, B. A., & Hudson, W. W. (1987). Progress in behavioral social work: An introduction. *Journal of Social Service Research, 10*(2/3/4), 1-6.

Thyer, B. A., Irvine, S., & Santa, C. (1984). Contingency management of exercise by chronic schizophrenics. *Perceptual and Motor Skills, 58*, 419-425.

Thyer, B. A., & Maddox, K. (1988). Behavioral social work: Results of a national survey on graduate curricula. *Psychological Reports, 63*, 239-242.

Thyer, B. A., & Myers, L. L. (1997a). Behavioral and cognitive theories. In J. R. Brandell (Ed.), *Theory and practice in clinical social work* (pp. 18-37). New York: Free Press.

Thyer, B. A., & Myers, L. L. (1997b). Social learning theory: An empirically based approach to understanding human behavior in the social environment. *Journal of Human Behavior in the Social Environment, 1*, 33-52.

Thyer, B. A., Thyer, K. B., & Massa, S. (1991). Behavior analysis and therapy in the field of gerontology. In P. Kim (Ed.), *Serving the elderly* (pp. 117-135). New York: Aldine de Gruyter.

Thyer, B. A., & Wodarski, J. S. (1998). First principles of empirical social work practice. In B. A. Thyer & J. S. Wodarski (Eds.), *Handbook of empirical social work practice: Vol. 1. Mental disorders* (pp. 1-21). New York: John Wiley.

Truax, C. B. (1966). Reinforcement and nonreinforcement in Rogerian psychotherapy. *Journal of Abnormal Psychology, 71*, 1-9.

Underwood, L., & Thyer, B. A. (1990). Social work practice with the mentally retarded: Reducing self-injurious behaviors using non-aversive methods. *Arete, 15*(1), 14-23.

Wakefield, J. (1996). Does social work need the eco-systems perspective? Part 2. Does the perspective save social work from incoherence? *Social Service Review, 70*, 183-213.

Whittaker, J., & Garbarino, J. (1983). *Social support networks: Informal helping in the human services*. New York: Aldine.

Wong, S. W., Larrow, L. D., & Fuqua, W. (1983). Self-administered behavioral treatment of disturbing somatic sensations. *Behavioral Engineering, 8*, 130-135.

Young, G. C., & Morgan, R. T. (1972). Overlearning in the conditional treatment of enuresis: A long-term follow-up study. *Behaviour Research and Therapy, 10*, 419-420.

CHAPTER ELEVEN

Affective Change: Depression and Anxiety Disorders

JOSEPH A. HIMLE

The concept of affect potentially involves just about any emotion from sadness, anger, grief, regret, guilt, fear, and anxiety to pleasure, joy, and happiness. Although certain affective states are vigorously pursued, others become a target for change. The affective states most often targeted by clinical social workers for change are various forms of anxiety, depression, and excessive anger. Clearly, most every well-functioning adult experiences some measure of anxiety, anger, and sadness, affective states that apparently can be helpful and adaptive (Nesse & Williams, 1994). Social workers usually get involved when their clients judge these affective states to be a source of interference in their lives. Our clients ultimately judge how much anxiety, anger, and depression is too much. The purpose of this chapter is to review the "state of the art" with respect to the identification and treatment of anxiety disorders and depression, and a brief review of anger management techniques.

Anxiety disorders and depression are of particular relevance to the field of social work, given that these disorders are collectively the most prevalent psychiatric conditions in the United States. Kessler and colleagues (1994) report that 25% of the population meet criteria for at least one anxiety disorder over their lifetime. Kessler et al. further report that 17% of individuals in the United States meet diagnostic criteria for major depression, and over 6% meet criteria for dysthymia at some time in their lives. The prevalence of anger-control problems is not known, but excessive anger is a common complaint in counseling centers. Beyond issues related to prevalence, these conditions are especially relevant to social work because mental health agencies are the among the most common settings in which social workers are employed (Chess & Norlin, 1991). Given the historical focus of social work on the person-in-the-environment, anxiety disorders, anger-management problems, and depression are also of relevance to social work, given the many environmental factors that can be associated with the development of these symptoms. Problems such as low income (Kessler et al., 1994), traumatic experiences (Coyne & Downey, 1991), and other adverse living situations can increase the risk of developing anxiety and depressive disorders. In addition, the connection between difficult environmental circumstances and excessive anger is obvious.

Interventions that have been demonstrated as effective in controlled studies are included in this chapter. Emphasis will be given to those techniques where empirical support has been replicated across research centers. Promising new interventions with limited empirical support will also be included where appropriate. This chapter is meant to be a review that captures state-of-the-art thinking in social work practice related to affective disorders. Many of the interventions included in this chapter have a direct focus on the social environment, including cognitive-behavioral and interpersonal psychotherapies.

The interventions described in this chapter are in keeping with a significant trend toward prescriptive treatment in mental health care over the past decade (Ammerman, Hersen, & Last, 1999). Prescriptive treatments refer to specifically designed intervention programs to match particular presenting problems. This trend has led to uniquely designed interven-

tions for depression, anger-control problems, obsessive-compulsive disorder, posttraumatic stress disorder, panic disorder, and phobic disorders. These prescriptive treatments are often well defined and thus easily transferable from one setting to another, allowing for efficient transfer of knowledge for clinical and research purposes. Although the trend toward prescriptive treatments has been generally positive, one drawback of this approach can be the heavy emphasis on psychiatric diagnoses. Prescriptive treatments based on particular diagnoses can lead practitioners to adhere to treatment protocols when adjustment in interventions related to cultural differences or environmental issues is warranted. Readers should take these issues into account when noting that the chapter is organized according to psychiatric diagnoses obtained from *The Diagnostic and Statistical Manual of Mental Disorders,* Fourth Edition *(DSM-IV)* (American Psychiatric Association, 1994). This assessment system has been criticized for its emphasis on psychiatric symptoms without appropriate attention given to the environmental context in which the affected individual functions (Karls & Wandrei, 1992). The social work literature has responded to this difficulty by creating the person-in-the-environment (PIE) classification system, which incorporates a method of coding role functioning in people's work and social environment (Karls & Wandrei, 1992).

Although women are well represented in the treatment studies reviewed in this chapter, unfortunately, most studies do not include many individuals from minority groups. Several reasons for the underrepresentation of minority group members in research studies in mental health have been suggested. A distrust of motives for research and fear that minority groups will be portrayed negatively may discourage individuals from participating in research (Neal & Turner, 1991). Second, nearly all of the treatment research reviewed in this chapter has been conducted at academic medical centers or universities. Minority group members may be more likely to seek help for anxiety or depression from clergy, general physicians, or hospital emergency rooms (Neighbors, 1988). If mental health professionals are sought out, private psychotherapists or community mental health agencies appear to be preferred over academic medical centers (Neighbors, 1988). In addition, it is likely that many researchers do not seek out minority research subjects vigorously because cultural issues are not an integral part of the research plan. However, the National Institute of Mental Health (NIMH, 1997) has attempted to address this issue by requiring funded studies to include minority group members.

The following portion of this chapter presents two main sections. The initial section describes the primary anxiety and depressive disorders described in the *DSM-IV,* (American Psychiatric Association, 1994). The second section describes treatments, with empirical support for these conditions, in addition to a description of empirically based anger-management techniques.

ANXIETY DISORDERS

Specific and Social Phobia

Specific phobia is a single name for a complex of heterogeneous fears of various objects or situations (Himle, McPhee, Cameron, & Curtis, 1989). Specific phobias include four subtypes: an animal and insect group, which includes fears of cats, dogs, spiders, snakes, and various other creatures; a situational phobia group, which includes fear of enclosures, flying, and driving; a third group, commonly referred to as specific phobias of the natural environment, which includes fears of storms, heights, and water; and, finally, a fourth group referred to as blood, injury, and injection phobias, which includes fear and avoidance of various medical stimuli. The lifetime prevalence rate of specific phobia is just over 11% (Kessler et al., 1994). Specific phobias are substantially more common among females, and there is some evidence of greater prevalence among minority groups (Eaton, Dryman, & Weissman, 1991). Neal and Turner (1991) suggest that this elevated prevalence may be due to higher levels of chronic stress and negative life events, which may make African Americans more vulnerable to developing fears. In addition, they speculate that cultural differences in the way fears are expressed may account for differing rates of phobia.

The *DSM-IV* characterizes social phobia as an unreasonable fear of situations in which the individual is exposed to the scrutiny of others. Social phobic individuals fear that they will act in a humiliating or embarrassing way or that they will experience anxiety that is observable to others. Social phobia includes two subtypes, specific and generalized. Specific social phobia includes performance fears, such as speaking in public or playing an instrument, as well as fears of eating, writing, or using public restrooms. Other social fears, such as problems dating or talking to people in authority, are considered specific social phobias. Social phobias are referred to as generalized if an individual fears most social situations. The prevalence of social phobia has been inconsistent in epidemiologic studies, ranging from about 2.7% (data from the Epidemiologic Catchment Area Survey/ECA)

(Eaton et al., 1991) to just over 13% in the National Comorbidity Study (NCS) (Kessler et al., 1994). Women who are single, less educated, and of lower socioeconomic status appear to be most vulnerable to social phobia (Magee, Eaton, Wittchen, McGonagle, & Kessler, 1996; Schneier, Johnson, Horning, Liebowitz, & Weissman, 1992). Brown, Eaton, and Sussman (1990), using the data from the ECA study, found an elevated rate of social phobia among African Americans after controlling for education, occupation, age, and marital status. However, the NCS study did not find increased rates of phobia among African Americans (Kessler et al., 1994), making conclusions about the prevalence of social phobia across culture difficult to determine.

Panic Disorder and Agoraphobia

Panic Disorder is a condition that comprises panic attacks and enduring complications that result from them. The *DSM-IV* (APA, 1994) defines a panic attack as a discrete period of intense fear or discomfort, in which at least 4 of a list of 13 symptoms develop abruptly and reach a peak within 10 minutes. Panic attack symptoms include: palpitations, pounding, or racing heart; sweating; trembling or shaking; shortness of breath or smothering; feeling of choking; chest pain or discomfort; feeling dizzy, unsteady, lightheaded, or faint; derealization or depersonalization; fear of losing control or going crazy; fear of dying; numbness or tingling sensations; and chills or hot flushes. The *DSM-IV* describes panic disorder as recurrent, unexpected panic attacks where at least one attack is followed by 1 month (or more) of at least one of the following: persistent concern about having

additional attacks, worry about the implications of the attack or its consequences, and/or a significant change in behavior related to the attacks. There are two subtypes of panic disorder, panic disorder without agoraphobia and panic disorder with agoraphobia.

Agoraphobia is defined in the *DSM-IV* as anxiety about being in places or situations from which escape might be difficult (or embarrassing) or in which help may not be available, in the event of a panic attack or experiencing panic-like symptoms. Agoraphobic fears include anxiety about leaving the home; being in a crowded area; traveling in a bus, train, or automobile; visiting a mall or grocery store; going to the theater; eating in a restaurant; or entering other places where panic attacks have occurred previously. Agoraphobia can occur with or without panic attacks (see description of panic disorder).

In the United States, panic disorder without agoraphobia and panic disorder with agoraphobia are present in about 2% and 1.5% of the population, receptively (all rates are lifetime prevalence) (Eaton, Kessler, Wittchen, & Magee, 1994). Agoraphobia without panic disorder is present in about 5.2% of the U.S. population (Eaton et al., 1994). As with most psychiatric disorders, a range of impairment is noted among people meeting criteria for agoraphobia and panic disorder. However, when panic disorder and agoraphobia are both present, impairment is often significant (Magee et al., 1996).

Obsessive-Compulsive Disorder

According to *DSM-IV* (APA, 1994), obsessive-compulsive disorder (OCD) involves two components, obsessions and compulsions. Obsessions are repetitive ideas, thoughts, or impulses that are not under an individual's voluntary control. Obsessions are often very anxiety-provoking. Individuals with OCD recognize obsessive thoughts as the product of their own mind, which is important in differentiating OCD from psychotic disorders. Obsessions often involve worries about contamination or dirt, concerns about having made a mistake that could lead to large consequences (e.g., starting a fire by not being careful enough when turning off the stove), concern regarding symmetry or orderliness, obsessions about losing things, obsessions about harm coming to others or harming others directly, or blasphemous thoughts of a religious nature. Compulsions involve repetitive behaviors, or mental acts, which are often performed according to certain rules or in a stereotyped fashion. Usually, these compulsive behaviors are performed to reduce obsessive thoughts and accompanying anxiety. Compulsive behaviors include repetitive washing or cleaning, checking (e.g., stove, door locks), straightening or ordering, hoarding or collecting, touching, tapping or rubbing, or compulsive prayer. Most clients with OCD suffer from both obsessions and compulsions. However, some individuals experience obsessions without compulsions or more rarely, compulsions without obsessions (Fischer, Himle, & Hanna, 1997).

The lifetime prevalence of OCD in the general population is thought to be about 2.6%. Women appear to outnumber men in meeting criteria for OCD but after controlling for marital status, vocation, age, and ethnicity, the gender difference no longer holds (Karno & Golding, 1991). There are no significant differences in lifetime prevalence of OCD with respect to race (Karno & Golding, 1991). OCD

often has a significant impact on a person's day-to-day functioning and quality of life. Many clients with OCD experience marked interference with social or occupational functioning due to their condition (Karno & Golding, 1991).

Posttraumatic Stress Disorder

The *DSM-IV* (APA, 1994) criteria for posttraumatic stress disorder (PTSD) begins with an individual experiencing or witnessing an event that includes actual or threatened serious injury or threat to physical integrity of the self or others. The response to this experience is intense fear, hopelessness, or horror. The traumatic event is re-experienced in one or more ways, including distressing recollections of the event that are recurrent and intrusive, recurrent dreams related to the traumatic event, a sense that the traumatic event is reoccurring (e.g., flashback episodes), and/or intense physical distress when confronting situations or sensations that are reminiscent of those experienced during the trauma. In addition to re-experiencing the event in one of the ways mentioned above, people with posttraumatic stress disorder also experience significant avoidance of stimuli related to the trauma, such as avoidance of thoughts and feelings associated with the traumatic event and avoidance of places or individuals that trigger recollection of the trauma. People with PTSD also can experience a numbing of general responsiveness including difficulty recalling important aspects of the trauma, diminished interest in activities, feeling of estrangement from others, difficulty feeling a full range of emotions, and a sense of a foreshortened future. In addition to these problems, people with PTSD experience symptoms of increased arousal, including difficulty staying or falling asleep, anger outbursts or irritability, difficulty concentrating, hypervigilance, and an overly active startle response. There are three subtypes of PTSD, acute (less that 3 months, duration), chronic (over 3 months), and delayed onset, where at least 6 months elapses between the trauma and the occurrence of PTSD symptoms. The prevalence of PTSD in the general population is about 8% (Kessler, Sonnega, Bromet, & Nelson, 1995). Nonwhites appear to be at greater risk for PTSD, but this difference does not remain after controlling for other sociodemographic factors (Breslau et al., 1998).

Generalized Anxiety Disorder

The primary symptoms of generalized anxiety disorder (GAD) are multiple repetitive worries that are difficult to control (APA, 1994). These worries relate to problems in many areas, such as finances, family life, work, and social relations. Although most people have concerns in these areas, worries in GAD are excessive and unreasonable; they are present most of the time for 6 months or more. In addition to repetitive worry, individuals with GAD also experience irritability, muscle tension, difficulty sleeping, problems concentrating, fatigue, and feelings of restlessness and being keyed-up. The lifetime prevalence of generalized anxiety disorder is about 5% in the general population (Kessler et al., 1994). GAD (only when present without comorbid panic attacks and depression) is apparently more prevalent among women, African Americans, and people under 30 (Blazer, Hughes, George, Swartz, & Boyer, 1991).

DEPRESSIVE DISORDERS

Major Depression and Dysthymia

Major depressive disorder and dysthymia are the two primary disorders of depressed mood in the *DSM-IV* (APA, 1994). Major depressive disorder includes at least one of two primary symptoms, persistent depressed (sad or empty) mood and/or markedly diminished interest or pleasure in all or almost all activities. In major depression, at least one of these problems is present most of the day, nearly every day, for a period of at least 2 weeks. Other symptoms of major depression include significant weight loss or gain or a decrease or increase in appetite, insomnia or hypersomnia, psychomotor agitation or retardation that is observable by others, fatigue or loss of energy, feelings of worthlessness or excessive guilt, difficulty concentrating, and recurrent thoughts of death, thoughts of suicide, specific plan for committing suicide, or a suicide attempt. To meet criteria for major depressive disorder, an individual must experience at least four of the above symptoms (including at least one of the two primary symptoms described above).

Dysthymic disorder also includes depressed mood most of the day, but the duration criteria extends for a period of at least 2 years. In addition to depressed mood, two or more of the following are present while depressed: poor appetite or overeating, insomnia or hypersomnia, low energy or fatigue, low self-esteem, poor concentration or difficulty making decisions, and feelings of hopelessness. Major depression and dysthymia are common disorders, with 17% and 6% meeting criteria (lifetime) for these conditions, respectively (Kessler et al., 1994). Both disorders are substantially more common among women. Several explanations for high rates of female depression have been proposed, ranging from biological differences (Brown, 1996) to cognitive schema that lead women to defer self-interest to attend to the needs of others (Jack, 1987). African Americans are significantly less likely to meet criteria for depressive disorders compared to Caucasian Americans. Hispanic Americans exceed Caucasian Americans in rates of depressive disorders (Kessler et al., 1994).

EMPIRICAL TREATMENT OF AFFECTIVE DISORDERS

The following portion of this chapter reviews treatments with empirical support for anxiety and depressive disorders, with a brief section summarizing the empirical treatment of anger-management problems. Graded exposure therapy, systematic desensitization, and relaxation therapy apply mainly to the anxiety disorders. Cognitive therapy is relevant to both anxiety and depressive disorders, whereas interpersonal psychotherapy is primarily used to treat depression. In addition to a general discussion of each therapeutic technique, specific applications to particular disorders are included where relevant. Anger-management techniques usually involve multiple interventions, and a special section describing these techniques follows the discussion of treatments for anxiety and depressive disorders.

Graded Exposure Therapy

The central feature of graded exposure therapy involves real life (in vivo), prolonged confrontation with anxiety-evoking stimuli. Occasionally, imaginal exposure is conducted, especially in the treatment of PTSD, but for most anxiety conditions, live exposure to the actual anxiety-evoking stimulus is preferred. Exposure therapy typically begins with the social worker and client collaborating to generate a hierarchy of progressively more challenging encounters with a phobic object or situation. For instance, individuals with a fear of snakes may be asked to give an estimate of how much anxiety they might experience upon encountering a snake under various conditions, ranging from looking at a picture of a snake, to handling a rubber snake, to viewing an enclosed snake at a substantial distance, ending finally with handling a live snake. As an aid in constructing the hierarchy, the social worker and client often assign a 0 to 100 rating (0 representing calm and 100 representing extreme terror) to each potential encounter with a phobic stimulus. Close collaboration with the client is necessary during this phase of treatment, and the construction of the hierarchy is usually facilitated by using a brainstorming technique where phobic situations are reviewed without initially attempting to place them in a hierarchical order. Once the list of encounters is complete, hierarchical ordering can be conducted, and the social worker and client can negotiate an item of mild to moderate difficulty as an initial phobic stimulus to encounter.

After completion of the hierarchy and reaching agreement regarding where to begin, exposure sessions are initiated. These sessions are conducted according to a set of practice standards that include: graded exposure to progressively more challenging stimuli, prolonged sessions of 1 to 2 hours in duration, frequent sessions occurring one time weekly or more, focus of attention during exposure trials rather than engaging in distraction, and ending each session with improved anxiety (Marks, 1987). Another important principle of exposure therapy is for clients to ultimately be responsible for guiding the pace of treatment. The social worker serves the role of a coach, encouraging clients to attempt challenging exercises without forcing them to confront stimuli against their will. Throughout the exposure sessions, the social worker asks clients to give ratings of their anxiety level, often using the 0 to 100 scale as described above. These ratings are used to guide the pace of treatment. One important issue relates to when the social worker suggests to the client that it is time to move from one encounter on the exposure hierarchy to the next. The most logical process would be to move from one encounter to the next after the anxiety associated with the present exercise has been eliminated. However, clinical experience suggest that clients often have difficulty eliminating anxiety completely, because some portion of their anxiety relates to the task at hand and some to anxious anticipation of the next exercise to come. Often, the social worker is wise to encourage the client to move from one encounter to the next in an exposure hierarchy after the client's anxiety has declined by about one half. Ratings of anxiety near 0 are often reserved for the last items in the hierarchy.

The number of sessions required to complete exposure treatment varies greatly according to severity and phobic disorder. Specific phobias can be successfully treated in as little as 1 session (Ost, 1989) but are typically completed within 5 to 10 sessions. Specific social phobias, such as public speaking or fears of eating in public, are also often treated within 10 sessions, but exposure treatment for severe generalized social phobias may extend for many months. Clinical experience also suggests that exposure therapy for agoraphobia, especially among those who are house-bound, can sometimes extend beyond 1 year.

As exposure therapy progresses, homework assignments are given to enhance generalization to the natural environment and to extend improvement beyond what can be accomplished in session. Clients are usually asked to set aside 1 to 2 hours each day for self-conducted exposure practice. These sessions are usually spent practicing exercises of moderate difficulty and are often similar to those conducted with the social worker. A discussion of the use of homework assignments in the treatment of phobic disorders serves as an opportunity to discuss whether the social worker's presence during sessions is a necessary component in the exposure therapy. Clearly, self-conducted exposure has been shown to be effective (Ghosh & Marks, 1987). Self-conducted exposure programs are especially relevant for agoraphobia, generalized social phobia, and certain situational specific phobias where phobic stimuli are easily found and controlled. Self-conducted exposure can be difficult when attempting to address small animal phobias because it is often difficult to obtain and manage the phobic stimulus.

A final general issue related to graded exposure therapy is the question of whether to include techniques to reduce the anxiety experienced during encounters with the phobic stimulus. Relaxation techniques and distraction are not recommended as adjuncts to behavioral exposure therapy (Barlow, 1988). Exposure therapy is thought to function through a learning process known as habituation (Marks, 1987), which apparently operates most effectively when anxiety is allowed to elevate and decline naturally.

Moving beyond the technical guidelines related to exposure therapy described above, exposure therapy presents the social worker with important cultural issues to address. Neal-Barnett and Smith (1997) point out the importance of interacting with African Americans in the therapeutic setting in a manner that communicates respect for them. Issues such as using appropriate titles (Dr., Mr., Mrs., Ms.) and taking time to learn to pronounce names properly are a few of the recommendations they make. In the exposure treatment of phobic disorders, one may be especially vulnerable to displaying behaviors that are interpreted as disrespectful. Prolonged periods of time spent together in worker-assisted exposure sessions often leads to a casual manner of interaction between client and the social worker, which could be viewed as offensive by a minority client. A second issue related to exposure therapy and culture is the directive nature of the treatment. Minority group members may resent being told what to do by their social worker, especially a social worker from a majority group. Fostering a collaborative spirit where the client and the social worker jointly create exposure assignments may be especially important with minority clients.

Graded Exposure Therapy— Issues Related to Specific Disorders

Specific Phobia

Graded exposure for specific phobias has been shown to be effective in reducing anxiety and phobic avoidance (Ost, 1989). Improvements achieved with graded exposure therapy for specific phobia are often quite durable, with improvements usually maintained after conclusion of successful exposure therapy (Hellstroem & Ost, 1996). Most specific phobias are relatively straightforward, from an exposure therapy perspective, as long as a cooperative pet store, a small enclosure, a tall building, and an expressway are nearby. However, certain specific phobias require special consideration when designing an exposure hierarchy. Phobias of flying and thunderstorms present a substantial challenge in creating a graded exposure hierarchy. Obviously, commercial airline companies are not able to accommodate repetitive attempts at gradually leaving the ground, so the social worker is required to improvise. If funds permit, a small private aircraft can be chartered for graded exposure purposes, which would allow the client to begin with looking at the plane and progress to sitting in the plane, taxiing, and finally lifting off. If funds are not available, a less desirable alternative would be imaginal exposure to challenging phobic imagery. Unfortunately, imaginal exposure, although somewhat helpful, is generally considered less effective than real life exposure for specific phobias (Dyckman & Cowan, 1978). Storm phobias also present a similar challenge, given that one is not able to conjure up a suitable storm at the time of the therapy appointment. This difficulty requires the social worker and the client to be flexible in scheduling their exposure sessions. When the weather looks promising, exposure sessions need to be quickly scheduled. Imagery and other attempts to create challenging stimuli for storm phobics, such as watching intense storm videotapes, are sometimes helpful as well. A final consideration relates to blood, injury, and injection phobias. These phobias are the only anxiety disorders in which fainting commonly occurs (Curtis & Thyer, 1983).

Asking the client to lie down during exposure, and instructing the client to vigorously tense major muscle groups during exposure (Ost, Fellenius, & Sterner, 1991), can be helpful in preventing fainting.

Social Phobia

Several controlled studied have demonstrated that exposure therapy for social phobia is an effective treatment (Feske & Chambless, 1995). Group sessions with other socially phobic individuals can be especially helpful in facilitating exposure through interacting with and performing in front of other group members (Hope, Heimberg, & Bruch, 1995). Depending on the nature of the social phobic complaint, arranging exposure exercises can be relatively simple or quite cumbersome. Difficulties such as writing in front of others or eating in public are easily encountered through visits to public places where others are present. However, fears of public speaking, dating, or speaking to people in authority can present a challenge when attempting to arrange repetitive, prolonged, and gradually more difficult encounters. The main difficulty with these exercises is arranging for prolonged exposure. People with public speaking fears have usually avoided situations where they would be asked to give speeches, so therefore, they rarely have opportunities for extended speaking engagements. Short speeches, such as those available by taking a speech class or joining a community public speaking group (e.g., Toastmasters), can require a considerable amount of repetition before improvement is observed. The same duration difficulty can take place when conducting exposure to other social phobic situations. Authority figures often do not allow time for long conversations, a person met at a party may soon drift off to the punch bowl, and classmates may need to get to their next class in a hurry. Substantial trial and error, considerable knowledge of community resources, and significant clinical creativity are sometimes required to design an exposure therapy program for social phobia that is both prolonged and gradually more challenging.

Agoraphobia

For agoraphobia, real life exposure to phobic situations is also a well-established method of treatment with an extensive amount of empirical support (Barlow, 1988; Marks, 1987). Exposure treatments for agoraphobia usually involve encouraging clients to confront feared situations such as leaving the home, visiting a large department store, or using public transportation. However, a few special issues related to exposure therapy for agoraphobia would be helpful to address. Agoraphobic clients often find it difficult to consistently follow the exposure guideline of ending each session only after anxiety has improved. Most clients who seek professional help for agoraphobia experience panic attacks in addition to their fears. When panic attacks occur, many agoraphobics flee the situation, leaving when they are feeling most anxious. Social workers are wise to anticipate this possibility and to encourage clients to remain in the situation until the panic attack dissipates. A second issue relates to the use of protective behaviors during exposure therapy. Many agoraphobic clients bring along trusted companions, bottles of water, cellular telephones, food, tranquilizing medication, paper bags to breathe in, and so on to protect themselves from extreme anxiety. Over time, these protective behaviors should be withdrawn to enhance the outcome of exposure therapy.

Panic Disorder

Exposure-based treatment aimed directly at panic attacks is usually referred to as interoceptive exposure or exposure to internal panic cues (Barlow & Cerny, 1988). According to this method, certain internal states (e.g., dizziness, increased heart rate, shortness of breath), once associated with a panic attacks, can serve as conditioned triggers of panic attacks. Internal cue exposure involves exposing clients to internal sensations present during panic attacks (Barlow & Cerny, 1988). Exercises such as running in place, whirling about, and hyperventilating are used to confront challenging bodily sensations. Clients performing internal cue exposures are thought to habituate in a similar manner as they would during therapeutic exposure to external panic cues such as grocery stores, shopping centers, and driving.

Internal cue exposures are often initiated in the social worker's office and are then given to the client as homework assignments. Initially, clients often experience panic attacks when conducting internal cue exposure exercises. However, over time, the panic responses dissipate as clients practice the exercises. Internal cue exercises differ from exposure to external panic triggers with respect to the duration of the practice sessions. Clients cannot often hyperventilate, jog in place, spin around, and so on for prolonged periods of time as is typical for exposure exercises at the mall or on the highway. Instead, exposure is often shorter in duration and involves intermittent rest periods. Empirical support for internal cue exposure is limited by the fact that it has only been tested in combination with other cognitive and behavioral methods. However, preliminary research suggests that it may enhance outcome when included with other treatments for panic disorder (Margraf, Barlow, Clark, & Telch, 1993).

Posttraumatic Stress Disorder

The unique feature of exposure therapy for PTSD is the extensive use of imaginal exposure techniques. Because it would be impossible, dangerous, and unethical to expose clients to repetitive trauma, behavioral exposure therapy for PTSD involves repetitive exposure to detailed descriptions of the traumatic event. If multiple traumatic events have been experienced, an especially difficult situation would typically be selected as the target of exposure. Behavioral exposure for PTSD is begun with the client describing the traumatic event, using the present tense and including as much detail as possible (Foa et al., 1996). Prolonged exposure sessions are then conducted where the client recites an account of the traumatic event. Sessions are usually audiotaped for daily review as exposure homework. In addition to exposure to recollections of the event, other stimuli related to the event can be included in the exposure program. These stimuli may include clothing related to the trauma, smells related to the trauma, and exposure to the actual site of the trauma, if the client's safety can be assured. It is important to note that clients often experience substantial anxiety and sadness associated with exposure therapy for PTSD. It is important for clinicians to prepare clients for these challenging emotions and to encourage them to continue to participate even if the sessions are difficult. To date, several studies (Foa et al., 1996; Hickling & Blanchard, 1997; Marks, Lovell, Noshirvani, Livanou, & Thrasher, 1998) have found exposure therapy to be helpful in reducing symptoms of PTSD.

An exposure-related treatment with empirical support for PTSD is eye-movement desensitization and reprocessing (EMDR). EMDR is similar to exposure therapy for PTSD in that it involves imaginal exposure to images related to the traumatic event. However, two additional procedures are included with exposure to the traumatic images, rapid saccadic eye movements and coping self-statements. The rapid eye movements are usually produced by asking the client to track the social worker's finger as it is moved from side to side (Shapiro, 1991). How much the eye movements add, beyond exposure, to the efficacy of EMDR is uncertain and has been a source of controversy in the field (VanEtten & Taylor, 1998). The usual number of sessions involved in EMDR for PTSD is between one and four (Shapiro, 1991). The number of sessions required for successful outcome in EMDR may be less than the amount required for exposure alone, but this is uncertain given the lack of controlled studies comparing the two treatments for PTSD. However, a recent meta-analytic study, including several controlled studies, found EMDR to be helpful in treating symptoms of PTSD (VanEtten & Taylor, 1998).

Obsessive-Compulsive Disorder

Exposure therapy for OCD actually involves two components, exposure to stimuli that elicit anxiety and obsessive thinking, coupled with prevention of rituals (exposure and response prevention—ERP). For example, people with contamination obsessions would be encouraged to deliberately handle contaminated surfaces while attempting to delay washing afterward. Someone with straightening obsessions may be encouraged to deliberately put items in disarray (exposure) while refraining from the temptation to straighten them (response prevention). Likewise, an individual who compulsively checks the stove would be advised to repetitively use the stove throughout the day while attempting to prevent checking afterward. Unfortunately, performing these exercises is often difficult, time-consuming, and anxiety-provoking. The anxiety-provoking nature of the exercises can be reduced somewhat by gradually introducing progressively more difficult exercises. For example, an individual with fears of contamination may begin with handling a seldom-handled portion of a door or wall, progressing to a door handle, a well-traveled floor, and finally to a public restroom surface. The difficulty of ERP therapy for OCD can also be reduced by using a friend, family member, social worker, or inpatient setting for help with response prevention, as resisting ritualistic behavior is often challenging.

ERP, in addition to being an effective individual treatment (Foa, Steketee, Grayson, Turner, & Latimer, 1984; Steketee, 1993), is also effective when delivered in a group format (Fals-Stewart, Marks, & Shafer, 1993; Krone, Himle, & Nesse, 1991). There is also evidence of enhanced outcome by involving family members in the treatment program (Van Noppen, Steketee, McCorkle, & Pato, 1997).

SYSTEMATIC DESENSITIZATION

A second treatment with empirical support for phobic disorders is systematic desensitization

(Wolpe, 1958). This technique involves two central components, imaginal exposure to imagery related to the feared object or situation and deep muscle relaxation (see below for a complete description of muscle relaxation training). Sessions begin with the client practicing deep muscle relaxation. Once a state of relaxation has been achieved, the social worker introduces a scene that involves an encounter with the phobic stimulus. When the imagery begins to elicit anxiety, the client signals the social worker and the scene is withdrawn until a state of relaxation is again achieved. This method is repeated until the client can imagine the scene without experiencing anxiety. After the client is able to imagine very challenging scenes involving the anxiety-evoking stimulus without anxiety, he or she is encourage to confront real life stimuli. The efficacy of systematic desensitization in the treatment of phobias is well established (Paul, 1969). However, real life exposure to phobic stimuli is likely superior to primarily imaginal methods, such as those used in systematic desensitization (Dyckman & Cowan, 1978).

RELAXATION THERAPIES

One of the best known relaxation procedures with empirical support is progressive muscle relaxation (Bernstein & Borkovec, 1973). This technique is often used in the treatment of generalized anxiety disorder (Borkovec, Mathews, Chambers, & Ebrahimi, 1987). In progressive muscle relaxation, the anxious client is asked to apply tension to one of several muscle groups for approximately 5 seconds followed by a 20-second period of rest. The client progresses from one muscle group to the next following this tension and relaxation procedure. The typi-

cal sequence of muscle groups begins with applying tension to the hands and arms, continuing through the head, shoulders, chest, abdomen, buttocks, legs, and feet. During the progressive muscle relaxation exercises, clients are asked to focus their attention on the difference between sensations of tension experienced during the muscle tension phase and the state of relaxation achieved through releasing the muscle groups. The initial phase of progressive muscle relaxation usually lasts about 20 to 30 minutes. After a few weeks, the treatment shifts to a release only phase where tensing muscles is abandoned and clients relax muscles in sequence without prior tension. In addition, slow-paced breathing techniques can be added especially for clients who experience panic attacks or overbreathing (Butler, Fennell, Robson, & Gelder, 1991).

A second relaxation training is a method referred to as applied relaxation (Ost, 1987). Applied relaxation has primarily been evaluated as a treatment for panic disorder (Ost, Westling, & Hellstrom, 1993) and, to a lesser extent, phobic disorders (Ost et al., 1991; Ost, Johansson, & Jerremalm, 1982). This technique begins with a 2-week course of daily progressive muscle relaxation exercises similar to that described above. The full tension and release phase is then followed by several methods designed to reduce the length of time to achieve a relaxed state. These techniques include a release-only phase, where clients release tension from various muscle groups, and a cue-controlled relaxation phase, where clients with panic disorder learn to relax quickly by pairing the word *relax* with a slow-paced breathing technique. The final stages of applied relaxation involve application training, where clients use cue-controlled relaxation exercises initially in nonstressful situations and finally in stressful situations. The effectiveness of applied relaxation is somewhat in question, with certain investigators finding it equal to cognitive therapy for panic disorder (Ost et al., 1993) and others finding it inferior (Clark, Salkovskis, Hackmann, Middleton, Anastasiades, & Gelder, 1994).

A final relaxation technique, also mainly used in the treatment of panic disorder, is breathing retraining (Barlow & Cerny, 1988). Breathing retraining involves teaching clients to slow down their breathing while using a meditational counting technique. The meditational technique begins with the client counting each inhalation followed by exhaling while thinking the word *relax*. Clients are asked to time each breath so that they inhale for about 3 seconds, then slowly release air, again for about 3 seconds. Empirical support for breathing retraining is limited due by the fact that it has not been tested as a stand-alone treatment for panic disorder. However, breathing retraining is often included as a component in cognitive-behavioral interventions with an established record of efficacy in the treatment of panic disorder (Craske, Brown, & Barlow, 1991).

COGNITIVE RESTRUCTURING

The essential feature of cognitive restructuring therapy involves collaboration between the social worker and the client in which the pair seeks to identify and modify habitual errors in thinking that are associated with maladaptive affective states. The general theoretical model of the cognitive approach is that correcting errors in thinking and altering erroneous beliefs will result in improved affect. The therapeutic process used to correct these thoughts and beliefs is often referred to as *collaborative empiricism* (Beck, Rush, Shaw, & Emery, 1979). Beck and associates (1979) have identified several common errors in thinking, often referred to as negative automatic thoughts or cognitive distortions. A sampling of these automatic thoughts include: magnification (exaggerating one's shortcomings or negative personal attributes), discounting the positive (dismissing one's accomplishments or positive personal attributes), fortune telling (predicting failure or rejection without supporting evidence), overgeneralization (viewing negative events or mistakes as evidence of enduring patterns), and selective abstraction (attending to a single negative aspect of an event until the entire event is viewed as substandard) (adapted from Beck, 1995; see Beck, 1995, for a complete list of negative automatic thoughts).

The initial portion of cognitive restructuring therapy involves identifying distorted thoughts that are commonly present when the client is experiencing the affect that has been targeted for change (e.g., sadness, fear, anger, etc.). Several strategies can be used to identify habitual errors in thinking including: simply asking clients to report their thinking when depressed or anxious; inquiring about thinking when mood changes within the session are observed; roleplaying interpersonal situations that were associated with problematic affect; or using a self-help book about cognitive therapy (Burns, 1980) or other material, where clients can identify examples of distorted thinking that are relevant to their situation.

Once a sampling of distorted thoughts has been elicited, the process of cognitive restructuring begins. Therapy often begins by focusing on a thought that is often present, commonly associated with the targeted affect, and judged by the social worker as a likely candidate for modification. After the client and the social worker select an initial thought, the worker uses questions, rather than argument, to find information that is counter to the distorted thought. Although the manner in which these interchanges are conducted varies from social worker to social worker, some common elements are usually present. The questioning process usually begins with the social worker inviting the client to begin the process of examining a particular thought, (e.g., Can we work together to see if the thought, "I am alone in the world" is accurate?). After the invitation to begin is complete, the social worker typically uses information from several sources including the client's present living situation, past history, and possibilities in the future to find evidence counter to the targeted distorted thought. When contradictory evidence is found, the social worker typically follows with comments that are designed to highlight differences between the distorted thought and the actual situation (e.g., How does that fact that we have discovered three people who consider you a friend fit with the thought that you are alone in the world?). The next step in the process usually involves a recommendation to use this new evidence to counter the distorted thought when it surfaces again in the future (e.g., Do you think that the next time the thought "I am alone in the world" occurs, you could counter it with the information we have gathered today?). Finally, in support of this within-session technique, homework assignments are given for the client to record distorted thoughts as they occur, and in-

structions are given to respond to these thoughts using a written homework log.

Moving beyond the conversational method described above, cognitive therapy often includes a behavioral activation component, where clients are asked to engage in certain behaviors to gain further information contrary to their distorted thinking. For instance, depressed clients who believe they cannot enjoy anything may be asked to engage in several potentially enjoyable activities as method of testing out whether the thought is accurate. Similarly, clients with social anxiety, who believe that everyone will reject them, may be asked to seek out contact with several people to determine whether their thoughts are distorted. Finally, clients who are certain they cannot accomplish anything and cannot imagine that they could solve any of their problems may be given small assignments aimed at completing certain tasks or solving problems. Behavioral activation exercises such as these can also be helpful in improving mood by increased involvement in enjoyable activities and encouragement of clients to initiate problem-solving strategies.

The final phase of cognitive therapy often involves attention to altering personal rules or standards, known as schema. Examples of schema include: My work is equal to my worth; I must be thin to be worthwhile; I must do everything perfectly; I must be universally liked by others; People can only have a good life if they have a romantic partner. Schema, when threatened or violated, are thought to give rise to distorted thoughts and affective problems. Maladaptive schema can be addressed using several strategies. One valuable strategy is known as the cost-benefit analysis (Beck, 1995). This technique involves working with the client to exhaustively review both the negative and positive effects of strongly adhering to the maladaptive personal standard. A second helpful strategy for modifying schema involves reviewing how following these standards might interfere with achieving important life goals. The purpose of these and other methods is to assist clients in moderating their personal schema to a more balanced view. This strategy is thought to reduce distorted thinking and improve affective symptoms.

COGNITIVE THERAPY— ISSUES RELATED TO SPECIFIC DISORDERS

Specific and Social Phobia

Although the use of cognitive methods in the treatment of specific phobias is not common, cognitive restructuring is often used in the treatment of social phobia (Feske & Chambless, 1995). Social phobic individuals often exaggerate the consequence of social failure (e.g., It would be terrible if I ran out of things to say), predict that social encounters will lead to failure (e.g., No sense in going to that party, I will just make a fool of myself), and assume that others are reacting negatively to them without evidence to support this belief (e.g., She looked away, she must think I am a loser). Cognitive therapy for social phobia involves the general cognitive strategies described above in addition to specialized techniques designed specifically for social phobia. One important technique involves the challenging beliefs related to social failure. Many social phobic clients believe that it would be horrible to make a social mistake, which often leads to excessive anticipatory anxiety and avoidance behavior. One strategy that

can be helpful for this concern is encourage the client to make purposeful social blunders to observe that they do not generally lead to the predicted catastrophic consequences. Overall, cognitive therapy for social phobia has been shown to be effective for treating both generalized and specific social phobics (Feske & Chambless, 1995). In addition to individual sessions, group therapy for cognitive restructuring has also been shown to be helpful (Hope et al., 1995).

Panic Disorder

Cognitive therapy is also commonly used in the treatment of panic disorder. Clark (1986) proposes a cognitive model of panic disorder, which suggests that inaccurate and catastrophic thinking contributes to the development of panic attacks. During panic attacks, people suffering from panic disorder often experience thoughts that they are about to die, suffocate, go crazy, lose control, or have a heart attack (Ottaviani & Beck, 1987). These cognitions are thought to contribute to a positive feedback loop where thoughts of catastrophe lead to an increase in physical symptoms, only to be followed by further distorted thoughts and even more intense physical sensations. After describing this model of panic disorder to the client, the cognitive social worker begins to work with the client to replace inaccurate thinking with more truthful self-statements.

The cognitive social worker will use information from several sources to find evidence against faulty thinking. The first source of information that a cognitive social worker can use to assess the accuracy of a client's thinking during a panic attack is the client's past history. Usually, by the time panic-disordered clients present for treatment, they have experienced several attacks. Often, these attacks have been associated with dire predictions of catastrophe (e.g., I am going to die, I am going crazy). Thankfully, these catastrophes do not take place during panic attacks. Using questioning, the social worker can help clients recognize that their concerns have not materialized, and the social worker can encourage clients to use this information to counter distorted thoughts.

A second source of information that the social worker can use is what is known about other clients with panic disorder. The social worker can inform the client about erroneous predictions that others have made and how these concerns have not come to pass. If the social worker has not worked with many panic-disordered clients, informing clients about cases of panic disorder found in the literature can serve as a good substitute.

A third source of information is often referred to as a behavioral test. It is often difficult to understand why clients hold on to beliefs that panic attacks are dangerous when they, almost by definition, have not experienced any dangerous consequences. It appears that many clients with panic disorder do not get a chance to learn that panic attacks are not dangerous because they engage in self-protective behavior designed to prevent disastrous consequences. Distracting themselves, fleeing, quickly taking a medication, drinking water, seeking out a trusted companion just in time, and so on all have one thing in common: They support the belief that the panic attack might have been dangerous if they did not intervene. Behavioral tests involve the client allowing panic attacks to run their natural course without interference from these safety behaviors. The technique leads the client to discover that the panic attacks only seem dangerous and are not truly danger-

ous. Behavioral tests can be supplemented by aggravating panic attacks (e.g., running in place during a panic attack), thus allowing the client to develop even more confidence that panic attacks are not likely to lead to catastrophe. The four sources of information described above can be brought together to form a truly convincing argument that panic attacks are not dangerous. The client can then practice replacing distorted thinking with more accurate self-statements.

There is substantial empirical support for the cognitive therapy of panic disorder (Barlow, Craske, Cerny, & Klosko, 1989; Clark et al., 1994; Craske, Maidenberg, & Bystrintsky, 1995). Cognitive techniques are also useful when delivered to small groups of panic-disordered clients (Penava, Otto, Maki, & Pollack, 1998). In addition, involving the family in treatment may enhance outcomes, especially if there is pre-existing marital strain (Barlow, O'Brien, & Last, 1984).

Generalized Anxiety Disorder

Cognitive restructuring for generalized anxiety disorder usually focuses on replacing inaccurate thoughts (e.g., It would be awful if I made a mistake; I just know things are going to turn out badly, they always do; This worry is dangerous, and it will hurt me). Wells (1997) believes this concept of worry about worry, or as it is sometimes referred to, *meta worry,* is particularly important in the treatment of GAD. Special attention to gathering information contrary to the thought that worry is harmful can be especially helpful in reducing the core symptom of GAD, worry that is difficult to control. Later in treatment, attention to schema such as "I must do everything perfectly" or "I must have everything under control at all times" can also often be fruitful.

Significant empirical support exists for cognitive-behavioral methods in the treatment of GAD (Borkovec & Costello, 1993; Butler et al., 1991). The efficacy of group therapy for GAD and the benefits of including family members in the treatment of GAD are not known.

Major Depression and Dysthymia

As with anxiety disorders, cognitive therapy of depression begins with the client and the social worker attempting to identify inaccurate thinking associated with emotional distress. Depressed clients often experience distorted thoughts about themselves (e.g., I am stupid), their environment (e.g., My life is terrible), and their future (e.g., No sense in going forward, nothing will work out for me). These negative thoughts are sometimes referred to as the Cognitive Triad of Depression (Beck et al., 1979). These thoughts are typically addressed using the process of collaborative empiricism described in the above general section on cognitive therapy. One issue in cognitive therapy related to depression is the central role of behavioral activation strategies. Engaging in enjoyable activities can enhance mood by increasing reinforcement and testing whether the thought, "I can't enjoy anything," common in depression, is accurate. Similarly, encouraging clients to take small steps aimed at solving their problems can help counter the thought "I can't accomplish anything" in addition to improving mood by gradually intervening to solve problems. Cognitive-behavioral therapy has been established in several controlled studies as an effective treatment for depression (Beck, Hollon, Young, Bedrosian, & Budenz, 1985; Elkin et al.,

1989; Murphy, Simons, Wetzel, & Lustman, 1984).

INTERPERSONAL PSYCHOTHERAPY

Interpersonal psychotherapy (IPT) has mainly been developed and tested in the treatment of depression. IPT is focused on the relationship between interpersonal problems and depressed mood. Little attention is given to past interpersonal relationships; instead, the focus of IPT is on current problems in relationships. The therapy begins with an interpersonal inventory, which is an overview of the client's social relationships. An attempt is made to focus attention on relationship changes that may have occurred near the onset of the client's depressed mood. Markowitz (1998) organized interpersonal problems into four types: grief, interpersonal role disputes, role transitions, and interpersonal deficits. Particular strategies are used to respond to each problem area (Klerman, Weissman, Rounsaville, & Chevron, 1984). For grief, the social worker attempts to help the client establish new relationships and a set of new activities. Interpersonal role disputes relate to conflicts in close relationships: with a spouse, close friend, family member, or work colleague. These conflicts are explored, and strategies are enacted in an attempt to resolve problems. If conflicts cannot be resolved, plans are made to circumvent the problem or end the relationship. Role transitions refers to interpersonal problems related to life events, such as starting or terminating a relationship, obtaining a promotion, retiring, graduating, or moving. Clients are helped to explore both the positive and negative aspects of adopting the new role and terminating the old role. Finally, interpersonal deficits in social skills are assessed, and strategies are put in place to improve verbal and non-verbal communication patterns. Interpersonal psychotherapy is usually a short-term treatment, with weekly sessions lasting about four months (Markowitz, 1998). IPT was found to be equal to cognitive-behavioral therapy and medication in the treatment of major depression in a large multicenter, randomized, controlled study of major depressive disorder (Elkin et al., 1989). In this study, IPT was particularly effective for clients with moderate to severe depression.

SOCIAL SKILLS TRAINING

Social skills training's main use in affective disorders is to assist a portion of social phobics with social skill deficits (Wlazlo, Schroeder-Hartwig, Hand, & Kaiser, 1990). Social skills training can also play a role in the treatment of depression, in that clients may be deficient in social skills required to extend their social network, obtain a new job, or solve a difficult interpersonal problem (Becker, Heimberg, & Bellack, 1987). Social skills training involves both verbal and nonverbal social skills. Nonverbal skills—appropriate eye contact, body positioning and movement, voice tone and volume, grooming, and personal hygiene—are among the typical nonverbal skills that are assessed and altered, if appropriate. Verbal social skills such as asking open-ended questions, following up questions by inviting further discussion, using appropriate topics for initiating conversations, and deflecting disagreement are often part of a social skills training program. Social skills training sessions can be enhanced by the use of videotaping equipment for practice and review of

progress. Cultural issues play a central role in social skills training. Social standards of eye contact, body positioning, topic selection, and voice tone and volume vary greatly across culture, particularly among Asian Americans (Iwamasa, 1997). A cultural match between the social worker and the client can be especially helpful when conducting social skills training. If a cultural match is not possible, sensitive collaboration with the client or the client's family is imperative in understanding what social behaviors are in need of modification. The efficacy of social skills training in social phobia has not been extensively studied. However, Wlazlo and associates (Wlazlo et al., 1990) found social skills training to be comparable in outcome to exposure in the treatment of social phobia.

ANGER MANAGEMENT STRATEGIES

Cognitive and behavioral strategies, most often used in combination, are generally considered the empirically based treatment of choice for anger-management problems (Beck & Fernandez, 1998). A recent meta-analysis of 50 studies of cognitive-behavioral therapy for anger problems found it to be moderately effective when compared to various control conditions (Beck & Fernandez, 1998). The main cognitive-behavioral intervention strategy employed for anger-management difficulties is a variation of Meichenbaum's (1975) stress-inoculation therapy adapted for anger problems mainly by Novaco (1975). This technique involves three main phases: preparing cognitively for anger-inducing situations, learning new skills for anger management, and applying the strategies learned. Training in adaptive cognitive self-statements is the primary technique in stress-inoculation therapy for anger problems. When preparing for the potential anger-inducing situation, statements such as "This is going to upset me, but I know how to deal with it," or "Easy does it, remember to keep your sense of humor" are used. Self-statements for use during the confrontation might include "You don't need to prove yourself" or "As long as I keep my cool, I'm in control." When arousal increases, statements such as "Time to take a deep breath" or "My muscles are starting to feel tight, time to relax and slow things down" are recommended. Finally, self-statements after the anger-provoking situation such as, "I handled this one pretty well . . . it worked!" are used. In addition to practicing self-statements, Novaco's program includes relaxation training, modeling, and role-play of anger-inducing situations.

FUTURE DIRECTIONS IN SOCIAL WORK PRACTICE WITH AFFECTIVE DISORDERS

One of the future directions in empirical practice with affective disorders relates to the multiple components involved in many intervention programs. Although already under way, much work remains in identifying active components within a multimodal intervention. For instance, what are the relative effects of cognitive restructuring, internal cue exposure, external cue exposure, and breathing retraining in the treatment of panic disorder? A limited amount of research has been completed addressing this issue, but much work remains.

Prevention of affective disorders is another important area for future research. Given the substantial cost of depression and anxiety to society in terms of work productivity (Kessler &

Frank, 1997) and family problems (Kessler et al., 1997; Kessler, Walters, & Forthofer, 1998), further development of prevention programs is vital. As an example of the value of preventative interventions, Swinson and colleagues (Swinson, Soulios, Cox, & Kuch, 1992) found that a brief 1-hour intervention for panic attacks substantially reduced future panic attacks and agoraphobic avoidance among of group of people seeking help for a panic attack in a hospital emergency room.

Another important area for future research relates to issues of diversity. Few interventions have been evaluated for their differential effects according to gender, race, culture, socioeconomic status, or sexual orientation. A first step in this research is to include more diversity in the subject pools used in treatment research. Second, it is important for researchers to report the differential effect of interventions as a standard practice in their intervention research reports. Finally, interventions designed from the ground up to fit specialized needs of the economically disadvantaged, minority groups, men, and women are needed.

A fourth important area for future research relates to the method of delivering interventions. Individual or group therapies, involvement of family members, optimal timing of sessions, and the optimal duration of therapy are all issues to be investigated. Research in this area can be very valuable in terms of health care financing and enhancing outcomes. For instance, in a recent treatment study of OCD, a 7-week group behavioral therapy program was found to be superior in outcome and satisfaction when compared to a 12-week format (Himle, Rassi, Nesse, & Abelson, 1999). Further research of this type can be helpful in refining current treatments.

Finally, although the interventions reviewed in this chapter are known to be helpful, a portion of clients with anxiety and depressive disorders do not improve with treatment. Treatment failures are observed even when treatment is provided by experts under optimal conditions. Clearly, the field is in need of new and refined procedures to reach those who attempt treatment and fail. It is also clear that most people with anxiety and depressive disorders never receive treatment (Kessler et al., 1994). Assuring availability of service throughout the United States is a critical issue. In addition, the further development of methods to encourage people to enter treatment is needed. Clearly, effective treatments for depression and anxiety disorders exist, but substantial work is needed to get treatment to those who need it.

REFERENCES

American Psychiatric Association. (1994). *The diagnostic and statistical manual of mental disorders* (4th ed.). Washington, DC: Author.

Ammerman, R. T., Hersen, M., & Last, C. G. (1999). A prescriptive approach to treatment of children and adolescents. In R. T. Ammerman, M. Hersen, & C. G. Last (Eds.), *Handbook of prescriptive treatments for children and adolescents* (2nd ed.). Needham Heights, MA: Allyn & Bacon.

Barlow, D. H. (1988). *Anxiety and its disorders.* New York: Guilford.

Barlow, D. H., & Cerny, J. A. (1988). *Psychological treatment of panic.* New York: Guilford.

Barlow, D. H., Craske, M. G., Cerny, J. A., & Klosko, J. S. (1989). Behavioral treatment of panic disorder. *Behavior Therapy, 20,* 261-282.

Barlow, D. H., O'Brien, G. T., & Last, C. G. (1984). Couples treatment of agoraphobia. *Behavior Therapy, 15,* 41-58.

Beck A. T., Hollon, S. D., Young, J. E., Bedrosian, R. C., & Budenz, D. (1985). Treatment of depression with cognitive therapy and amitriptyline. *Archives of General Psychiatry, 42,* 142-148.

Beck, A. T., Rush, A. J., Shaw, B. F., & Emery, G. (1979). *Cognitive therapy of depression.* New York: Guilford.

Beck, J. S. (1995). *Cognitive therapy: Basics and beyond.* New York: Guilford.

Beck, R., & Fernandez, E. (1998). Cognitive-behavioral therapy in the treatment of anger: A meta-analysis. *Cognitive Therapy and Research, 22,* 63-74.

Becker, R. E., Heimberg, R. G., & Bellack, A. S. (1987). *Social skills training treatment for depression.* New York: Pergamon.

Bernstein, A. D., & Borkovec, T. D. (1973). *Progressive relaxation training.* Champaign, IL: Research Press.

Blazer, D. G., Hughes, D., George, L. K., Swartz, M., & Boyer, R. (1991). Generalized anxiety disorder. In L. N. Robins & D. A. Regier (Eds.), *Psychiatric disorders in America: The epidemiologic catchment area study.* New York: Free Press.

Borkovec, T. D., & Costello, E. (1993). Efficacy of applied relaxation and cognitive-behavioral therapy in the treatment of generalized anxiety disorder. *Journal of Consulting & Clinical Psychology, 61,* 611-619.

Borkovec, T. D., Mathews, A. M., Chambers, A., & Ebrahimi, S. (1987). The effects of relaxation training with cognitive and nondirective therapy and the role of relaxation-induced anxiety in the treatment of generalized anxiety. *Journal of Consulting and Clinical Psychology, 55,* 883-888.

Breslau, N., Kessler, R. C., Chilcoat, H. D., Schultz, L. R., Davis, G. C., & Andreski, P. (1998). Trauma and posttraumatic stress disorder in the community. *Archives of General Psychiatry, 55,* 626-632.

Brown, D. R., Eaton, W. W., & Sussman, L. (1990). Racial differences in prevalence of phobic disorders. *Journal of Nervous & Mental Disease, 178,* 434-441.

Brown, G. W. (1996). Psychosocial factors and depression and anxiety disorders—Some possible implications for biological research. *Journal of Psychopharmacology, 10,* 23-30.

Burns, D. D. (1980). *Feeling good: The new mood therapy.* New York: Morrow.

Butler, G., Fennell, M., Robson, P., & Gelder, M. (1991). Comparison of behavior therapy and cognitive behavior therapy is the treatment of generalized anxiety disorder. *Journal of Consulting and Clinical Psychology, 59,* 167-175.

Chambless, D., & Gillis, M. M. (1993). Cognitive therapy of anxiety disorders. *Journal of Consulting and Clinical Psychology, 61,* 248-260.

Chess, W. A., & Norlin, J. M. (1991). *Human behavior in the social environment: A social systems method* (2nd ed.). Boston: Allyn & Bacon.

Clark, D. M. (1986). A cognitive approach to panic. *Behavior Research and Therapy, 24,* 461-470.

Clark, D. M., Salkovskis, P. M., Hackmann, A., Middleton, H., Anastasiades, P., & Gelder, M. (1994). A comparison of cognitive therapy, applied relaxation, and imipramine in the treatment of panic disorder. *British Journal of Psychiatry, 164,* 759-769.

Coyne, J. C., & Downey, G. (1991). Social factors and psychopathology: Stress, social support, and coping processes. *Annual Review of Psychology, 42,* 401-425.

Craine, M. H., Hanks, R., & Stevens, H. (1992). Mapping family stress: The application of family adaptation theory to Post-Traumatic Stress Disorder. *American Journal of Family Therapy, 20,* 195-203.

Craske, M. G., Brown, T. A., & Barlow, D. H. (1991). Behavioral treatment of panic disorder: A two year follow-up. *Behavior Therapy, 22,* 298-304.

Craske, M. G., Maidenberg, E., & Bystrintsky, A. (1995). Brief cognitive behavioral versus non-directive therapy for panic disorder. *The Journal of Behavior Therapy and Experimental Psychiatry, 26,* 113-120.

Curtis, G. C., & Thyer, B. A. (1983). Fainting on exposure to phobic stimuli. *American Journal of Psychiatry, 140,* 771-774.

Dyckman, J. M., & Cowan, P. A. (1978). Imagining vividness and the outcome of *in vivo* and imagined scene desensitization. *Journal of Consulting and Clinical Psychology, 48,* 1155-1156.

Eaton, W. W., Dryman, A., & Weissman, M. M. (1991). Panic and phobia. In L. N. Robins & D. A. Regier (Eds.), *Psychiatric disorders in America: The epidemiologic catchment area study.* New York: Free Press.

Eaton, W. W., Kessler, R. C., Wittchen, H. U., & Magee, W. J. (1994). Panic and panic disorder in the United States. *American Journal of Psychiatry, 151,* 413-420.

Elkin, I., Shea, M. T., Watkins, J. T., Imber, S. D., Sotsky, S. M., Collins, J. F., Glass, D. R., Pilkonis, P. A., Leber, W. R., Docherty, J. P., Fiester, S. J., & Parloff, M. B. (1989). National Institute of Mental Health treatment of depression collaborative research program. *Archives of General Psychiatry, 46,* 971-982.

Fals-Stewart, W., Marks, A.P., & Shafer, J. (1993). A comparison of behavioral group therapy and individual therapy in treating obsessive-compulsive disorder. *Journal of Nervous and Mental Disease, 181,* 189-193.

Feske, U., & Chambless, D. L. (1995). Cognitive behavioral versus exposure-only treatment for social phobia: A meta-analysis. *Behavior Therapy, 26,* 695-720.

Fischer, D. J., Himle, J. A., & Hanna, G. L. (1997). Age and gender effects on obsessive-compulsive symptoms in children and adults. *Depression and Anxiety, 4,* 237-239.

Foa, E. B., Freund, B. F., Hembree, E., Dancu, C. V., Franklin, M. E., Perry, K. J., Riggs, D. S., & Molnar, C. (1996). *Efficacy of short-term behavioral treatments of PTSD in sexual and nonsexual assault victims.* Unpublished manuscript, Medical College of Pennsylvania at Eastern Pennsylvania Psychiatric Institute, Philadelphia.

Foa, E. B., Steketee, G. S., Grayson, J. B., Turner, R. M., & Latimer, P. R (1984). Deliberate exposure and blocking of obsessive-compulsive rituals: Immediate and long-term effects. *Behavior Therapy, 15,* 450-472.

Gath, D., & Mynors-Wallis, L. (1997). Problem-solving treatment in primary care. In D. M. Clark & C. G. Fairburn (Eds.), *Science and practice of cognitive behaviour therapy.* Oxford, UK: Oxford University Press.

Ghosh, A., & Marks, I. M. (1987). Self-directed exposure for agoraphobia: A controlled trial. *Behavior Therapy, 18,* 3-16.

Hellstroem, K., & Ost, L. G. (1996). Prediction of outcome in the treatment of specific phobia: A cross validation study. *Behaviour Research and Therapy, 34,* 403-411.

Hickling, E. J., & Blanchard, E. B. (1997). The private psychologist and manual-based treatments: Post-traumatic stress disorder secondary to motor vehicle accidents. *Behaviour Research and Therapy, 35,* 191-203.

Himle, J. A., McPhee, K., Cameron, O. G., & Curtis, G. C. (1989). Simple phobia: Evidence for heterogeneity. *Psychiatry Research, 28,* 25-30.

Himle, J. A., Rassi, S., Nesse, R. M., & Abelson, J. A. (1999). *Seven- versus twelve-week group therapy for obsessive compulsive disorder.* Unpublished manuscript, University of Michigan, Department of Psychiatry, Ann Arbor.

Hope, D. A., Heimberg, R. G., & Bruch, M. A. (1995). Dismantling cognitive-behavioral group therapy for social phobia. *Behaviour Research and Therapy, 33,* 637-650.

Iwamasa, G. Y. (1997). Asian Americans. In S. Friedman (Ed.), *Cultural issues in the treatment of anxiety.* New York: Guilford.

Jack, D. (1987). Silencing the self: The power of social imperatives in female depression. In R. Formanek & A. Gurian (Eds.), *Women and depression.* New York: Springer.

Karls, J. M., & Wandrei, K. E. (1992). PIE: A new language for social work. *Social Work, 37,* 80-85.

Karno, M., & Golding, J. M. (1991). Obsessive compulsive disorder. In L. N. Robins & D. A. Regier (Eds.), *Psychiatric disorders in America: The epidemiologic catchment area study.* New York: Free Press.

Kessler, R. C., Berglund, P. A., Foster, C. L., Saunder, W. B., Stang, P. E., & Walters, E. E. (1997). Social consequences of psychiatric disorders: II. Teenage parenting. *American Journal of Psychiatry, 154,* 1405-1411.

Kessler, R. C., & Frank, R. G. (1997). The impact of psychiatric disorders on work loss days. *Psychological Medicine, 27,* 861-873.

Kessler, R. C., McGonagle, K. A., Zhao, S., Nelson, C. B., Hughes, M., Eshleman, S., Wittchen, H., & Kendler, K. (1994). Lifetime and 12-month prevalence rates of *DSM-III-R* psychiatric disorders in the United States. *The Archives of General Psychiatry, 51,* 8-19.

Kessler, R. C., Sonnega, A., Bromet, E., & Nelson, C. B. (1995). Posttraumatic stress disorder in the National Comorbidity Study. *Archives of General Psychiatry, 52,* 1048-1060.

Kessler, R. C., Walters, E. E., & Forthofer, M. S. (1998). The social consequences of psychiatric disorders: Probability of marital stability. *American Journal of Psychiatry, 155,* 1092-1096.

Klerman, G. L., Weissman, M. M., Rounsaville, B. J., & Chevron, E. S. (1984). *Interpersonal psychotherapy of depression.* New York: Basic Books.

Krone, K., Himle, J. A., & Nesse, R. N. (1991). A standardized behavioral group treatment for obsessive-compulsive disorder: Preliminary outcomes. *Behaviour Research and Therapy, 29,* 627-631.

Magee, W. J., Eaton, W. W., Wittchen, H. U., McGonagle, K. A., & Kessler, R. C. (1996). Agoraphobia, simple phobia, and social phobia in the National Comorbidity Survey. *Archives of General Psychiatry, 53,* 159-168.

Margraf, J., Barlow, D. H., Clark, D. M., & Telch, M. J. (1993). Psychological treatment of panic: Work in progress on outcome, active ingredients, and follow-up. *Behaviour Research and Therapy, 31,* 1-8.

Markowitz, J. C. (1998). *Interpersonal psychotherapy.* Washington DC: American Psychiatric Press.

Marks, I. M. (1987). *Fears, phobias, and rituals.* New York: Oxford University Press.

Marks, I. M., Lovell, K., Noshirvani, H. Livanou, M., & Thrasher, S. (1998). Treatment of posttraumatic stress disorder by exposure and/or cognitive restructuring: A controlled study. *Archives of General Psychiatry, 55,* 317-325.

Meichenbaum, D. H. (1975). *Stress inoculation training.* New York: Pergamon.

Murphy, G. E., Simons, A. D., Wetzel, R. D., & Lustman, P. J. (1984). Cognitive therapy and pharmacotherapy: Singly and together in the treatment of depression. *Archives of General Psychiatry, 41,* 33-41.

National Institute of Mental Health. (1997). Collaborative R-O1s for clinical studies of mental disorders. In *NIH Guide, Vol. 26.* Washington, DC: Author.

Neal, A. M., & Turner, S. M. (1991). Anxiety disorders research with African Americans: Current status. *Psychological Bulletin, 109,* 400-410.

Neal-Barnett, A. M., & Smith, J. (1997). African Americans. In S. Friedman (Ed.), *Cultural issues in the treatment of anxiety.* New York: Guilford.

Neighbors, H. W. (1988). The help-seeking behavior of black Americans. *Journal of the National Medical Association, 80,* 1009-1012.

Nesse, R. M., & Williams, G. C. (1994). *Why we get sick: The new science of Darwinian medicine.* New York: Times Books.

Novaco, R. W. (1975). *Anger control: The development and evaluation of an experimental treatment.* Lexington, MA: D. C. Heath.

Ost, L. (1989). One session treatment for spider phobias. *Behaviour Research and Therapy, 27,* 1-8.

Ost, L. G. (1987). Applied relaxation: Description of a coping technique and review of controlled studies. *Behaviour Research and Therapy, 25,* 397-410.

Ost, L. G., Fellenius, J., & Sterner, U. (1991). Applied tension, exposure *in vivo,* and tension-only in the treatment of blood phobia. *Behaviour Research and Therapy, 29,* 561-574.

Ost, L. G., Johansson, J., & Jerremalm, A. (1982). Individual response patterns and the effects of different behavioral methods in the treatment of claustrophobia. *Behaviour Research and Therapy, 20,* 445-460.

Ost, L. G., Westling, B. E., & Hellstrom, K. (1993) Applied relaxation, exposure *in vivo,* and cognitive methods in the treatment of panic disorder with agoraphobia. *Behaviour Research and Therapy, 31,* 383-394.

Ottaviani, R., & Beck, A. T. (1987). Cognitive aspects of panic disorders. *Journal of Anxiety Disorders, 1,* 15-28.

Paul, G. L. (1969). Outcome of systematic desensitization II: Controlled investigations of individual treatment, technique variations, and current status. In C. M. Franks (Ed.), *Behavior therapy: Appraisal and status.* New York: McGraw-Hill.

Penava, S. J., Otto, M. W., Maki, K. M., & Pollack, M. H. (1998). Rate of improvement during cognitive-behavioral group treatment for panic disorder. *Behaviour Research and Therapy, 36,* 665-673.

Perl, J., Westin, A. B., & Peterson, L. G. (1985). The female rape survivor: Time-limited group therapy with female-male co-therapists. *Journal of Psychosomatic Obstetrics and Gynecology, 4,* 197-205.

Schneier, F. R., Johnson, J., Horning, C. D., Liebowitz, M. R., & Weissman, M. M. (1992). Social phobia: Comorbidity and morbidity in an epidemiological sample. *Archives of General Psychiatry, 49,* 282-288.

Shapiro, F. (1991). Eye movement desensitization: A new treatment for post-traumatic stress disorder. *Journal of Behavior Therapy and Experimental Psychiatry, 20,* 211-217.

Sipprelle, R. C. (1992). A vet center experience: Multievent trauma, delayed treatment type. In D. W. Foy (Ed.), *Treating PTSD: Cognitive and behavioral strategies.* New York: Guilford.

Steketee, G. (1993). Social support and treatment outcomes of obsessive compulsive disorder at 9-month follow-up. *Behavioral Psychotherapy, 21,* 81-95.

Swinson, R. P., Soulios, C., Cox, B. J., & Kuch, K. (1992). Brief treatment of emergency room patients with panic attacks. *American Journal of Psychiatry, 148,* 944-946.

Thyer, B. A. (1987). *Treating anxiety disorders.* Newbury Park, CA: Sage.

VanEtten, M. L., & Taylor, S. (1998). Comparative efficacy of treatments for post-traumatic stress disorder: A meta analysis. *Clinical Psychology and Psychotherapy, 5,* 126-144.

Van Noppen, B., Steketee, G., McCorkle, B. H., & Pato, M. (1997). Group and multi-family behavioral treatment for OCD: A pilot study. *Journal of Anxiety Disorders, 11,* 431-446.

Wells, A. (1997). *Cognitive therapy of anxiety disorders: A practice manual and conceptual guide.* New York: John Wiley.

Williams, K. E., & Chambless, D. L. (1994). Behavioral therapies. In B. B. Wolman & G. Stricker (Eds.), *Anxiety and related disorders: A handbook.* New York: John Wiley.

Wilson, S. A., Becker, L. A., & Tinker, R. H. (1997). 15-month follow-up of EMDR treatment for psychological trauma. *Journal of Consulting and Clinical Psychology, 65,* 1047-1056.

Wlazlo, Z., Schroeder-Hartwig, K., Hand, I., & Kaiser, G. (1990). Exposure *in vivo* vs social skills training for social phobia: Long-term outcome and differential effects. *Behaviour Research and Therapy, 28,* 181-193.

Wolpe, J. (1958). *Psychotherapy by reciprocal inhibition.* Stanford, CA: Stanford University Press.

CHAPTER TWELVE

Adult Change

WILLIAM J. REID
ELIZABETH MISENER

This chapter is concerned with the kind of change that social workers usually seek in their work with adult clients who are seen for problems in their functioning, for example, problems of addiction, emotional distress, and interpersonal conflict. Change goals generally involve significant modifications of feelings, cognitions, and behavior, which may be needed to achieve alleviation of the person's problem. Moreover, change is intentional (Prochaska, DiClemente, Velicer, & Rossi, 1992). That is, the person is deliberately engaging in activities to effect change. This conception includes involuntary clients. Clients who do change usually do so intentionally, even though their change efforts may be brought about by social pressures, fear of sanctions, and so on. Thus, an abusing father, mandated to see a social worker,

may stop drinking as a requirement for having his children returned from foster care. The change, although done under pressure, is nevertheless intentional.

This kind of change can be contrasted with change brought about through biological mechanisms (e.g., medication) or change that may occur without intent or even awareness, as a function of such factors as aging or role transitions (Watson & Sher, 1998). The chapter will then focus on intentional, self-generated change. Within this focus, we will attempt to identify motivators for change, origins and dynamics of change processes, and stages of change. Implications for social work practice will be drawn.

Our hope is to contribute to a research-based theory of change that can be used to inform clinical work. Social work interventions are based on explicit or implicit theories of client change. Thus, practitioner interpretations made to enhance the client's insight into his or her behavior are predicated on assumptions of how the interpretations will cause the client to experience cognitive-emotional change and ultimately change in his or her actions. Usually, such theories lack both adequate explication and a sound research base.

VALUE CONSIDERATIONS

However change is examined and measured, it must be seen within a value context. Although our focus is on constructive change, what is considered to be constructive or how constructive it is seen to be are always value determinations and open to debate. Mrs. Roy might place a high degree of value on relief of her symptoms following an initial session, regard her problem as resolved, and not return for a second. The clinician might dismiss this change as superficial and temporary and label her termination as a "flight into health." Getting a divorce, having an abortion, giving up a child for adoption, and placing an elder in a nursing home are a few among many examples of change that might be valued differently from different perspectives. Lack of consensus on intervention outcome obtained from different sources of data has been a consistent finding in research on professional helping (Lambert & Hill, 1994). A factor that appears to contribute to this divergence is "the differing value orientations of the individuals supplying the data" (Lambert & Hill, 1994, p. 81). Solutions for this dilemma have included having outcome or change rated from multiple perspectives (Strupp & Hadley, 1977).

Although value considerations may affect how change is appraised, they need not necessarily influence formulations about how change occurs. Observers may disagree about whether achieving controlled use of a substance is desirable, but they may agree on the processes of change that enable an addict to achieve control. However, no theory is completely value-free. Thus, in the formulations to follow, we emphasize the individual as a generator of change—a bias that reflects the American ethos of individual responsibility. Theorists from other cultures might place greater emphasis on other sources—social units, for example.

RESEARCH AND THEORIES RELATING TO ADULT CHANGE

At first glance, there appears to be a plethora of research relating to adult change. Potentially relevant are thousands of studies from the helping professions that have assessed the effects of different modes of intervention designed to bring about changes in adults. Although such research may document how much change, if any, has taken place as a result of a certain type of intervention, it may not provide much information about change processes. Moreover, most interventions draw on complex theories of change, and it may not be clear from the results which of different theoretical components caused change to occur and by what means. Finally, it is difficult to disentangle factors common to most interventions, such as practitioner empathy and client suggestibility, from the effects of the specific theory in question. Despite these limitations, this body of research can yield inferences as well as supporting evidence concerning change phenomena.

Although there is certainly no shortage of theorizing, both within and outside the intervention literature, on why and how adults change, the amount of empirical research devoted to the topic is surprisingly limited. Two research strategies have been used for the most part.

One approach has been to study change processes primarily within intervention contexts. Perhaps the leading example of this kind of approach has been the work of Prochaska and his colleagues (Grimley, Prochaska, Velicer, Blais, & DiClemente, 1994; Prochaska & DiClemente, 1986; Prochaska, DiClemente, & Norcross, 1992). Their program of research and theory development, which has extended over the past two decades, has constructed a research-based, transtheoretical model of change. Another body of research has consisted of microscopic studies of intervention to determine the change processes that clients are experiencing (Berlin, Mann, & Grossman, 1991; Greenberg & Pinsof, 1986; Jones, Ghannam, Nigg, & Dyer, 1993; Reid, 1990).

A second approach has been to focus study on change processes under natural (i.e., nontherapeutic) conditions in respect to particular issues, such as alcoholism and addiction (Klingemann, 1991, 1992; Stall & Biernacki, 1986; Watson & Sher, 1998) or self-esteem (Baumeister, 1994), or in response to life events or crises (Heatherton & Nichols, 1994; Schaefer & Moos, 1992). Such studies focus on the kind of change processes that are especially useful in intervention theory. They typically examine motivation to achieve particular change goals and the mechanisms people use to attain them.

Neither research strategy has produced an empirically based, social work-oriented theory of change. The closest approximation, the transtheoretical model of Prochaska and colleagues, originated in the field of psychology and was grounded in smoking cessation and other addiction programs. It bears the stamp of that discipline and those programs. Work on building a theory of change for social work is clearly needed.

In our view, such a theory needs to fit basic characteristics of clinical social work practice: involvement of multiple client systems and use of a broad spectrum of interventions. Because a large proportion, if not the majority, of social work clients do not take the initiative in seeking help or are ambivalent about receiving it, motivation needs to be emphasized. Finally, a theory needs to be based to the extent possible in research on change processes, both outside and within service contexts.

THEORETICAL FRAMEWORK

The theoretical direction we propose views adult change as occurring through the interaction of multiple systems. In this conception, the individual and his or her social environment are seen as an ecology of systems. The individual is composed of a variety of systems—the neurological system, circulatory system, the cognitive-emotional system, and so on. The individual as a system interacts with numerous other systems, such as the family, formal organizations, and the community. Often, these systems can be organized hierarchically, that is, the cognitive-emotional system is part of the individual, who may be part of a family, which in turn is part of a community (Tomm, 1982). In this formulation, the social environment becomes specified in terms of the systems with which the person interacts or of which he or she is a part. Guided by this conception, we will examine two essential aspects of adult change: motivators (what prompts the person to want to change) and change activities (actions necessary to bring change about).

Motivators

For people to engage in intentional change efforts, they must be motivated to do so. Accordingly, it makes sense to focus on motivation as a personal phenomenon, although motivators may have their source in higher level systems. For example, a person's motivation to become "more responsible" may have been prompted by events at the family or organizational levels. Still, the events do not become motivators until they have been processed by that person.

For our purposes, we will assume that the motivational process becomes activated in the cognitive-emotional system of the individual. Significant change is initiated by challenges to the stability of this system. Such challenges have been described by French (1952) as the "push of discomfort" and the "pull of hope" (p. 50). This conception of motivation has been expressed in less elegant form as the "carrot and stick." Whatever terms one uses, motivators either prod us to change our course or attract us toward desirable goals. Our focus will be on those motivators most relevant to the kind of changes of concern to clinical social workers. We shall begin with some prods.

Crystallization of discontent. This apt phrase is used by Baumeister (1994) to describe the "forming of associative links among a multitude of unpleasant, unsatisfactory, and otherwise

negative features of one's current situation" (p. 282). Other expressions capture similar meanings: I was completely fed up! I couldn't take it any more! Something had to give! I hit bottom! A person comes to realize, often abruptly, that his or her situation has become intolerable. Past events that may have caused problems are reappraised, not as isolated incidents but as a dominating theme. This realization may be triggered by a specific incident (the last straw) which may not be important in itself but serves to catalyze the reappraisal. The reappraisal is usually accompanied by negative emotional reactions, such as disgust, self-hatred, or despair. The crystallization is then a cognitive-emotional event, a reappraisal accompanied by negative affect.

The dominance of this kind of motivator has been seen in studies of self-changing (naturally recovering) alcoholics and addicts (Klingemann, 1991, 1992; Ludwig 1985; Tuchfeld 1981; Watson & Sher, 1998). In their research, Heatherton and Nichols (1994) compared narratives of successful and unsuccessful efforts to make major and sudden changes (of any type). Successful changers were more likely than the unsuccessful to experience strong negative emotions prior to the change and to attach importance to focal events. Almost 60% of the successful self-changers had experienced a "crystallization of discontent" as opposed to only 13% of the unsuccessful. Miller and C'deBaca (1994) found that the majority of "quantum changers," people reporting profound and abrupt changes in their lives, reported being "emotionally distressed or upset" prior to the change.

Social pressure. Negative appraisals leading to crystallization of discontent may include rejection and disapproval expressed by others. However, social pressure as a change motivator involves a different set of dynamics. Here, the instigation for change is not inwardly driven by a revulsion over one's behavior or situation but is rather related more to a need to conform to social norms, to secure or retain the approval of important others, or to maintain important relationships.

Social pressures for change are likely to arise when a person's behavior deviates from the norms of those with whom he or she interacts. Often, the source of pressure is a system, such as the family, peer group, or organization of which the individual is a part. The pressures will become motivators, however, only if the person is responsive to the norms of others or of higher level systems. Thus, in family relationships, the person under pressure to change must have a sufficient degree of investment in the relationships so that a threat to their stability becomes a motivator to behave differently. The motivational effects of social pressures are consistently found in studies of self-changers (Heatherton & Nichols, 1994; Klingemann, 1991, 1992). Certain practice approaches have made successful use of social pressures to persuade individuals to enter treatment programs for substance abuse. One example is the Johnson Intervention, in which members of a person's social network (family members, employer, etc.) confront the person (in a caring manner) about his or her abuse problem (Loneck, Garrett, & Banks, 1996). Another is unilateral family therapy, in which spouses are trained to use social pressures to promote sobriety in their partners (Thomas, Santa, Bronson, & Oyserman, 1987).

Negative consequences. The perception that negative consequences may be imposed if one fails to do something about a problem is a frequently reported motivator in studies of self-changers (Stall & Biernacki, 1986). For some individuals, the threat of sanctions may bring about changes in behavior. For example, some abusing or neglectful parents may alter how they treat their children if faced with the threat that their children will be removed if they do not. Public assistance recipients may seek work in the face of a loss or reduction of their grant. Licensing sanctions and imposed counseling have been found effective with people convicted of driving while intoxicated (Wells-Parker, Bangert-Drowns, McMillen, & Williams, 1995).

Not all individuals react to sanctions with expected behavior change, however. As Rooney (1988, 1992) has suggested, the person's response to sanctions can be fruitfully understood through reactance theory—an empirically based social psychological theory that is concerned with people's responses to the loss of valued freedoms (Brehm & Brehm, 1981). In terms of this theory, the threat of a loss of freedom that sanctions usually convey may cause reactance; that is, people may "dig in" and resist expected changes, even though they may "go through the motions" to give the appearance of compliance. Such situations often occur, of course, in work with nonvoluntary clients. Reactance theory and related research suggest ways of engendering motivation to change where clients might be inclined to react negatively to possible sanctions. For example, practitioners should emphasize the client's right of choice, even if the choice is either to accept service or to face a dire consequence, such as going to jail (Rooney, 1988, 1992).

Crises. Life crises have long been seen as instigators of positive change (Ell, 1995). The motivators discussed above arise out of problem behavior and seek to change that behavior. Although crises can also originate in such behavior, they often do not, as illustrated by such crisis-producing events as physical illness, the death of a loved one, and rape. Whatever their origins, crises produce change by creating severe emotional dislocations that overwhelm the individual's usual mode of response. In responding to a crisis, an individual may be pushed to learn new modes of adaptation and coping. As Schaefer and Moos (1992) point out, "Personal growth can be fostered by the disruption that crises generate and the subsequent reorganization that occurs in their wake" (p. 150). Positive effects of crises have been found in a variety of investigations, including survivors of divorce (Wallerstein, 1986), rape (Frazier & Burnett, 1994), combat (Yarom, 1983), heart attacks (Affleck, Pfeiffer, Tennen, & Fifield, 1988; Dhooper, 1983), and the death of a loved one (Lehman et al., 1993). Constructive changes that have been reported include formation of new support networks, enhancement of self-reliance and self-efficacy, positive shifts in values and priorities, increased spirituality, and the development of coping skills (McMillen & Fisher, 1998; Schaefer & Moos, 1992).

Incentives. We turn now to those motivators that pull rather than push. Incentives to change may come in many forms. Of particular importance is the hope that desired goals are possible, accompanied by the conviction that they are attainable. Bandura (1989) has referred to this configuration as a *self-efficacy belief.* As Bandura (1989) has noted, "People's self-efficacy beliefs determine their level of motivation, as reflected in how much effort they will exert

in an endeavor and how long they will persevere in the face of obstacles" (p. 1176). Research has suggested that the stronger the belief in one's capabilities, the stronger will be the effort to reach the goal (Bandura, 1988). In their hallmark study of family agency clients, Ripple, Alexander, and Polemis (1964) found that a favorable discomfort-hope balance (similar to a self-efficacy belief) was highly related to measures of outcome and more influential than measures of the client's capacity to change.

Goal setting is particularly important in enhancing self-efficacy. There is a good deal of evidence that setting and attaining subgoals can increase motivation by providing immediate gratification as well as increased confidence that more demanding goals can be achieved (Strecher et al., 1995). For these reasons, perhaps, expressions such as "one day at a time" and "start small" have become watchwords of so many change efforts.

New horizons. Motivation can be instigated and strengthened by learning that one has a problem or by learning about the problem. Human beings have the capacity to view almost any difficulty they endure as natural or inevitable ("That's life," or "Just born that way."). Such an attitude precludes the possibility that a remedial problem exists, and hence there is no motivation to change it. Education, psycho-education, conscious-raising, client self-monitoring, feedback from tests, and interpretive or confrontational methods are among the awareness-enhancing tools that can help a person become aware of a problem.

For example, standardized self-report measures can be used to help clients become aware of problems of depression or anxiety. Such measures, as well as physical tests (e.g., of liver enzyme function), can be used to promote aware-ness of problems with alcohol and addiction. In one alcohol program (Drinker's Check-up), this approach led to immediate reductions in drinking (Miller & Sovreign, 1989).

Change Activities

Motivators alone are not sufficient to pro-duce meaningful change. They must be accom-panied by activities that bring change about. We start with activities that are initiated and carried out by the person. Our focus of attention then shifts to activities initiated by other social sys-tems of which the person is a part. Although motivators alone are not enough to bring about change, their continued presence is essential to maintain change activities.

Cognitive-emotional. Modifications in the cognitive-emotional system are seen as essential change activities in most clinical practice theo-ries, although theories vary in terms of the kinds of changes deemed essential and how these may be brought about. Alternative views of cognitive-emotional change processes in two major theories will be briefly examined. In psychodynamic theories, such changes, referred to as insight, are thought to emerge from the uncovering of repressed thoughts and feelings. The uncovering experience must involve a "re-living" of past experience and must be emotion-ally laden for change to be effective. Once change has been solidified or "worked through," changes in behavior will be a natural concomitant. In cognitive and cognitive-behav-ioral theories, it is assumed that cognitions—for example, beliefs and underlying assumptions about self and the world—control feelings and actions. Problems arise from distorted or dys-

functional cognitions, which become the target of change activities. Most of these cognitions can be identified through questioning and, once identified, can be examined critically and modi-fied. It is not assumed that modification needs to be accompanied by reliving of experience or intense affect.

However, there has been surprisingly little direct testing of either of these theories. Most of the evidence that each works in the way de-scribed comes from studies of the effectiveness of therapies based on the theories. Although ev-idence supporting both psychodynamic and cognitive therapies can be found, this kind of evidence, as noted earlier, is not the best, be-cause it may reflect factors other than the change theory. Adequate testing for specific ef-fects of these theories has just begun to emerge. For example, Whisman, Miller, Norman, and Keitner (1991) compared patients receiving standard pharmacological treatment and cogni-tive therapy. Although the two groups did not differ at post-test in respect to symptoms of de-pression, the group receiving cognitive therapy showed fewer dysfunctional cognitions, sug-gesting that cognitive change did in fact have an impact on depression. In studying psycho-dynamic theories of change, use has been made of naturalistic single-subject designs to deter-mine the relationship between client change and use of techniques such as interpretation (Jones et al., 1993; O'Connor, Edelstein, Berry, & Weiss, 1994).

Studies of the kind just discussed can help de-termine which change processes can be empiri-cally validated. Processes with adequate empiri-cal credentials can become a part of a theory of change, even though they may originate from different schools of thought. It would be up to the change theorist to develop constructs that could resolve differences in perspective and vocabulary.

Cognitive-emotional change may not always take place in the incremental way suggested by the theories discussed above. In certain instances, major change may occur quite suddenly, as in some religious conversions. In their study of quantum changers, individuals who experienced dramatic and sudden transformations, Miller and C'deBaca (1994) found that the overwhelming majority (almost 90%) reported revelations "of an important truth." Although the changes appeared to be cognitive-emotional, it was not clear why they occurred. Sudden shifts in perception—seeing things in a new way as might happen in figure-ground exercises—seemed to play a part. Such changes, the authors suggest, may be related to the sudden cognitive shifts that supposedly occur from time to time in response to a practitioner's use of paradoxical injunction.

Although the processes by which cognitive-emotional change occurs may not be well understood, we would argue that such processes are central to meaningful adult change. Regardless of their nature or their points of origin, change processes must affect the cognitive-emotional realm if they are to matter, as we try to show below.

Overt action and its consequences. Most types of change require some new form of overt action—forsaking alcohol or drugs, venturing into feared situations, behaving differently with others, and so on. Action may also lead to further change, depending on its outcome and how this is evaluated by the cognitive-emotional system. If the outcome is positively evaluated, that is, if it is seen as providing gratification, furthering goals, contributing to mastery

and heightened self-efficacy, and the like, the action is likely to be repeated. From a cognitive-behavioral perspective, the action has been reinforced.

In systematic change efforts, reinforcements may be planned. In token economies for adults, often those with mental illnesses or disabilities, reinforcers may take the form of tokens or points that can be "cashed in" for rewards of value to the individual. Token economies have been demonstrably effective in bringing about behavioral changes, such as improved self-care and diminished interpersonal aggression (Corrigan, 1995). Such changes may be useful to facilitate clients' adaptation to their current situation even if the changes may not generalize to other settings. A broader application of planned reinforcement occurs within the context of self-change or self-regulatory programs, which are widely used for emotional and health-related problems of adults. The principal components of these programs comprise self-evaluation or self-monitoring (in which the person keeps track of a particular behavior), self-evaluation (in which the behavior is viewed in relation to a goal), and self-reinforcement (in which the individual provides himself or herself with a reinforcer). Self-monitoring and self-evaluation also have reinforcement potential if they reveal that positive change has occurred. In their meta-analysis of 22 studies evaluating the effectiveness of self-change programs, Febbraro and Clum (1998) found that the use of these components yielded small to medium effect sizes, with the strongest effects obtained when either self-evaluation or self-reinforcement was added to self-monitoring. The amounts of change suggested by the effect sizes approach those achieved in forms of treatment in which practitioners play a much larger role.

Reinforcement may be seen as a component of any overt action designed to bring about change. If the action appears successful to the person, it is likely to be repeated. It is apparent also that the cognitive-emotional system is an integral part of reinforcement. The person must evaluate the outcome of the action, a cognitive process. The evaluation further provides information about how the action might be altered to achieve an even better result. Reinforcement then describes a feedback loop that guides a person's action strategies.

Using such guidance, clients can employ a variety of action strategies to effect change relating to their problems or functioning. A fundamental strategy is coping, which Lazarus and Folkman (1984) define as "constantly changing cognitive and behavioral efforts to manage specific external and/or internal demands that are appraised as taxing or exceeding the resources of the person" (p. 141). These authors further distinguish two types of coping. In problem-focused coping, people attempt to deal with external situations through such means as problem-solving (defining the problem, generating alternative solutions, selecting and implementing one), learning new skills, or finding alternative sources of gratification. Emotion-focused coping is concerned with "regulating emotional response to the problem" (p. 151) and may include such devices as avoidance, selective attention, minimization (There are more important things to worry about), positive comparisons (Others have it worse), and emphasis on the positive side of the problem (This will teach me a lesson). The change resulting from coping may be temporary but still vital, like the balancing movements of a high-wire acrobat. When accustomed modes of coping are severely disrupted, as in crises, or when coping with similar situations becomes prolonged, new coping patterns can emerge and become a part of a person's functioning.

Almost any action strategy used in coping can be systematically learned and applied (Reid, in press) Problem-solving and skill acquisition are two examples mentioned above. Training in problem-solving has been found to be an effective means of helping people deal with a range of taxing situations, such as disciplining children (Whiteman, Fanshel, & Grundy, 1987) and depression (Nezu, Nezu, & Perri, 1989). The acquisition of skills in social interaction is a lifetime learning venture for most people and probably has been since the beginnings of civilization. Through observation of others (modeling), taking advice, reading, using trial-and-error, and so on, we try to improve our social lives and interpersonal competencies. Over the past several decades, methods have been developed to train people in such skills as assertiveness, conversation, job interviewing, parenting, and anger management. Extensive research has demonstrated that such methods can be effective agents of change (Corrigan, 1991; Penn & Mueser, 1996). Skills training is most often used for people with gross deficits, such as the mentally ill, people with disabilities, or abusing parents, but as Wachtel (1997) has observed, it is also quite useful as a method of individual treatment for people with less obvious deficits whose emotional problems have limited the development of their social competencies.

Hal Jones, a recovering alcoholic, is visiting friends. One of them asks, "Would anyone like a drink?" Hal knows that if he stays in a situation in which others are drinking, he will be likely to drink himself. As his anxiety mounts, he decides to leave and politely does so. This kind of coping response has traditionally been known as "avoiding temptation." To shift to a more modern and technical term, we can say that Hal has dealt successfully with *stimulus control.* In stimulus control situations, certain stimuli or cues can elicit a response—the aroma of good food gives us an appetite. When the response may be undesirable, an action strategy is to avoid the situation. Self-changing alcoholics and addicts consistently report use of stimulus-control strategies (Klingemann, 1991, 1992), and they are generally a component of substance abuse programs. To be maximally effective, such strategies need to include a plan for finding desirable alternatives to stimulus-control situations. Thus, an addict must not only find ways of breaking away from a drug culture but must also develop new social relationships that can take its place.

Conquering fear by doing what one is afraid of is an age-old coping strategy. This strategy has been refined into forms of *exposure* interventions for a variety of anxiety conditions, including phobias and obsessive-compulsive disorders. In exposure, a person learns to approach feared objects or situations incrementally. Mrs. Green is afraid of driving on the expressway. Her first step may be to drive onto the expressway and exit immediately. She continues to do this until she feels comfortable. She may then drive to the next exit, a short distance away, and then leave the highway. This step is also repeated until she feels comfortable. The process continues until she is able to drive on the expressway for as long as necessary without anxiety. For people too afraid to take even the first step (or if a first step is not practical, as in fear of flying), exposure may be imagined. Exposure therapy has received considerable empirical support (DeRubeis & Crits-Christoph, 1998; Mattick, Andrews, Hadzi-Pavlovic, & Chris-

tensen, 1990) and is generally regarded as the most effective intervention available for agoraphobia. Although the reasons for its effectiveness are not completely clear, it is likely that experiencing fear for a brief period (at the beginning of an exposure progression) without anticipated catastrophes fosters the belief that perhaps "there is nothing to fear except fear itself." Self-efficacy beliefs that the fear can be mastered are heightened. These cognitive events encourage the person to attempt a longer or more difficult exposure.

As can be seen, action strategies involve behavior that is integrated with cognitive processes. Action results from cognitive appraisals and is cognitively guided and evaluated. The evaluation helps determine if the action is worth repeating and how it might be made more effective in helping the person reach his or her goals.

One-on-one interaction: The two-person system. A person's interaction over time with another has long been viewed as an important source of change in adults. Included here would be relationships with mentors, friends and confidants, and, of course, social work practitioners and other professional helpers. In terms of our framework, the source of change shifts from the individual to a two-person system.

The dynamics of change are multifaceted. Confiding painful feelings or distressing experiences to a trusted and accepting other may provide emotional relief and restore self-esteem—the well-known values of catharsis or the "corrective emotional experience." The other's empathic responses may stimulate the person to be more self-revealing and hence to achieve great self-understanding. The other may reinforce actions by demonstrations of approval and encouragement. In addition, a person may imitate desired characteristics of the other, who serves as a model for new attitudes and behavior. Such attributes have been referred to as "common characteristics" of helping relationships and are assumed to account for some degree of change, apart from change resulting from specific interventions on the part of the helper.

Almost all of the research on these characteristics has been conducted within the context of professional helping relationships. Studies have consistently shown positive associations between the degree to which these characteristics are present and measures of client change (Orlinsky, Grawe, & Parks, 1994). In recent years, increased attention has been given to the "therapeutic alliance" between client and helper, a notion that focuses on relational aspects, including not only good helper characteristics but also the client's attachment to and identification with the helper and the client and helper's agreement about the goals/tasks of intervention. It has been posited that the alliance can contribute to change directly as well as indirectly by increasing the effectiveness of the practitioner's interventions. Measures of the alliance taken early in the relationship have been generally found to be predictive of client change later in the relationship or at termination (Henry, Strupp, Schacht, & Gaston, 1994). Although the concept of the alliance originated in the psychodynamic practice tradition, it was been applied to a wide range of modalities. For example, in perhaps the largest-scale application to date, Connors, Carroll, DiClemente, Longabaugh, and Donovan (1997) obtained early measures of the alliance in 1,726 cases of alcoholism treatment reflecting multiple sites and a range of therapeutic orientations. The alliance was consistently predictive of treatment participation and positive drinking outcomes for outpatient alcoholics but only sporadically predictive for alcoholics in aftercare programs.

Studies of common characteristics and the therapeutic alliance have provided evidence that one-to-one relationships can generate and facilitate change. As the Connors et al. (1997) study illustrates, more research is needed to identify sources of variation in the effects of the alliance. Moreover, more work is needed to disentangle the effects of the alliance per se from confounding factors such as tendencies for clients already on the road to change to form better relationships with practitioners.

Groups. Treatment, self-help, skills training, and other such groups introduce change dynamics not available to self-changers proceeding on their own or to individuals being helped in one-on-one relationships (Garvin & Seabury, 1997; Kurtz, 1990; Ramsey, 1992; Toseland & Rivas, 1998; Toseland & Siporin, 1986). Groups can provide input from peers—suggestions, feedback, encouragement, sharing of experiences, and the like. A person may be particularly responsive to peer input because peers may have had similar experiences, may speak the same language, and do not represent possibly mistrusted or resented authority figures. The acceptance and support of peers (plus a leader, if one is present) may be more influential than acceptance and support received from a single other. Being part of a group can help develop identity—for example, being a member of Alcoholics Anonymous reinforces an individual's identity as a "recovering person." A member can learn vicariously from others in the group and gain hope from their progress. Moreover, through peer interactions, clients can learn and practice interpersonal behaviors.

Finally, helping others in the group can be a form of self-help, because the helper's own self-efficacy and learning may be enhanced (Kurtz, 1990; Ramsey, 1992). The special dynamics of the group experience may enhance changes, such as skill acquisition, that may be achieved on an individual basis or in one-on-one relationships.

Although there is abundant evidence to suggest that groups are an effective agent of adult change (Bednar & Kaul, 1994; Kurtz, 1990; Ramsey, 1992; Toseland & Siporin, 1986), it is not clear what types of problems or people may benefit more from group experiences than from one-on-one relationships or self-change efforts (Garvin & Seabury, 1997). Also, research evidence is lacking on how change dynamics in groups might affect different types of individuals.

The family. Most adults, including those with problems, live with families—their parents or their spouses and children. Like the formed groups discussed above, families can provide acceptance, support, feedback, and encouragement. The effects of such family responses may be accentuated by family members' intimate knowledge of one another and the powerful emotional bonds they share. When the family maintains or aggravates the problems of its adult members, change in the family may be the key to change in the member.

Studies of intervention with families provide evidence of the role of families in effecting such changes. For example, in their meta-analysis of 15 controlled, comparative studies, Stanton and Shadish (1997) found that family and couples treatment for drug abuse had better outcomes than individual counseling, peer group therapy, or psychoeducational approaches. These find-

ings have been supported by other reviews (see, e.g., Diamond, Serrano, Dickey, & Sonis, 1996). Among the reasons appears to be that altering the family environment—the reduction of family stress or "enabling" behaviors and the strengthening of family support for nonuse of drugs—has positive consequences for the addicted member. Modifications of the family environment of people with schizophrenia, which include maintaining a low-key emotional climate in the home, improving family communication and problem-solving, and helping family members expand their social networks, have been found to be important in relapse prevention (Baucom, Shoham, Mueser, & Daiuto, 1998; Hogarty, 1993). Involving spouses and family members in treatment of such problems as anxiety and depression has either matched or surpassed results of individual treatment, with the added benefit, in some studies, of improved family relationships (Baucom et al., 1998).

Social networks. In addition to being connected to families, most adults are a part of social networks consisting of relatives, friends, neighbors, coworkers, service providers, and the like. Social networks can provide many of the supports and inputs that are obtained from groups and families. When networks function in a positive way, for example, to decrease social isolation, buffer stress, and provide constructive feedback, they are viewed as supportive or as support systems. Studies have suggested that people with inadequate support systems are more likely to maltreat their children (Berry & Cash, 1998) or become re-addicted (Havassy, Hall, Sharon, & Wasserman, 1991). Systematic involvement of social networks has been found to be effective in the treatment of alcoholism (Sisson & Azrin, 1993). Not all social networks provide constructive support, however. A person's network may consist of substance abusers, hostile relatives, and friends in need of money. As Berry and Cash (1998) point out, "the inclusion of kin and extended family and friends cannot be assumed to be a naturally beneficial component of a service plan" (p. 19). Practitioners may need to help clients discern who in their social networks may be able to provide the support they most need.

Macro systems. Larger systems involved in individual change include formal organizations, such as employers, insurers, and health and welfare agencies; neighborhoods; communities; and state and federal levels of government. Through policies as well as specific transactions with individuals, macro systems have a multifaceted and complex role in fostering the kind of adult change on which we are focusing. First, macro systems constitute or provide support for most intervention and remedial systems that aim to help people change. Second, they may pursue policies that can have a profound effect on what services are given and how this is done or, more broadly, on social behavior. Managed care, welfare reform, drug laws, deinstitutionalization, Medicare/Medicaid programs, and mandatory sentencing are just some of the examples that come to mind. Of course, it is not always clear what changes such policies may bring about or whether they resemble the kind that social workers strive for or that social workers deplore. Often, such changes appear to produce a mixture of both kinds. For example, there is little doubt that the welfare reform policies of recent years have improved the lives of some poor people by helping them become independent of the welfare system. At the same time, there is little doubt that such policies have adversely affected many others. We lack definitive research on which policies produce optimal changes, not only in respect to welfare reform but in respect to most social policies.

Finally, macro systems may provide milieus that may lead to changes in individuals who are a part of them. The revitalization of a neighborhood can infuse its residents with new hope and motivation for individual change. Formal organizations, such as residential settings, can be structured as therapeutic milieus in which all contacts with residents on the part of all staff, from janitors to administrators, are designed to be therapeutic (Jones, 1953; Murray & Baier, 1993). For example, in one study of institutional milieus, residents in a home for seniors that emphasized self-help appeared to experience higher levels of self-esteem and social involvement than residents of a conventional home (Berkowitz, Waxman, & Jaffe, 1988).

INTERACTIONS BETWEEN CHANGE ACTIVITIES

Collectivities, such as the group, family, and social networks, and macro systems have been described as initiating or facilitating change. But the principle that change results from multiple systems in interaction continues to apply. Thus, if a person acts in a socially skilled manner to elicit support from a group, he or she is more likely to receive it. Two-person systems may serve to mediate between the individual and a collectivity. For example, Mallinckrodt (1996) found that the extent of the therapeutic alliance was positively associated with social network changes, which in turn were related to lessening of symptoms. Changes in the therapeutic alliance in itself were not sufficient to bring symptom relief.

STAGES OF CHANGE

An important contribution of Prochaska and his associates, and perhaps the one most widely used, has been their formulation of stages of change (Grimley et al., 1994; Prochaska, DiClemente, & Norcross, 1992). They posit the following five stages:

Precontemplation (no awareness of a problem or, if aware, no change is planned)

Contemplation (an awareness of the problem, considering change but possibly ambivalent; no commitment to change)

Preparation (intent to change in the near future—within a month—often with beginning attempts to change)

Action (active engagement in eliminating the problem)

Maintenance (active efforts to prevent relapse)

To put these stages in a social work context, we might say that nonvoluntary clients tend to be precontemplators; this is also true of many voluntary clients who see problems, not in themselves, but in others, such as family members. Our guess would be that the modal group of voluntary clients is probably in the contemplation stage, considering change but not yet committed to action. Only a minority, as least at the beginning of service, would be in preparation or action stages.

Perhaps the most interesting and stable findings that have emerged from the extensive research program carried out by Prochaska and colleagues have concerned the relationship between the stages and processes of change

(Prochaska, 1995). For example, individuals in the contemplation stage may be more open to consciousness-raising processes, such as observations, interpretations, and confrontations, than to actions, such as use of stimulus control (Prochaska, DiClemente, & Norcross, 1992).

Another useful set of findings from this program concerns the maintenance stage. In maintenance, clients make use of action strategies that have proven successful in problem reduction to prevent problem recurrence. Often, these strategies fail, and relapses occur. Individuals who relapse, however, seldom go back to square one and stay there. The more likely tendency is to progress forward again through the stages of change. Thus, a cyclical model of progression, in which a person may repeat stages of change before maintenance is achieved, emerged as the dominant model in their studies (Grimley et al., 1994). Although their research has dealt largely with smoking cessation and other fairly specific behavioral problems, the cyclical model of change appears to have relevance to a large range of issues facing social workers.

Finally, the notion of stages of change can be related to research on the duration of active change efforts. There is reason to suppose that this duration is relatively brief, well under 6 months for most psychosocial problems, with most of the change occurring during the early part of this period. This generalization is in keeping with studies of the efficacy of planned brief treatment (Koss & Butcher, 1994; Steenbarger, 1994), as well as studies of change curves during the course of longer term treatment (Koptka, Krause, & Orlinsky, 1986). For some problems, however, such as those exhibiting chronic distress symptoms, active change efforts may be sustained for longer periods (Koptka, Howard, Lowry, & Beutler, 1994).

IMPLICATIONS FOR CLINICAL SOCIAL WORK PRACTICE

In this chapter, we have attempted to contribute to the development of theory relating to adult change. In so doing, we have tried to accommodate to, as well as advance some trends in social work practice. Such practice is becoming increasingly eclectic, leading to the emergence of integrative frameworks; it is also becoming more empirically based (Reid, 1998). We have presented an integrative, research-grounded framework that would permit the incorporation of perspectives from different practice schools.

What practice principles might be suggested from the theoretical work we have presented? A first principle would be to pay considerable attention to change motivators. We cannot impose change on clients. They must do their own changing. Without strong and active motivators to stimulate and sustain their efforts, they are not likely to change. The theory should sensitize practitioners to a range of potential motivators. Those that are relevant in a given case should be clarified and, in collaboration with the client, strengthened through motivational interviewing (Miller & Rollnick, 1991) or other techniques. This principle applies especially to nonmotivated involuntary clients. Determining and building on whatever motivators may work for the client and the use of reactance theory to clarify and maximize client choices should be key components of the practitioner's approach.

A second principle would be to carry out interventions in tune with the client's readiness for change. Interventions should be "stage-matched" to use Prochaska's (1995) expression. Perhaps the most important application of this principle is in the initial phase of service. It would suggest that the clients' motivation for change should be clearly established and clients should have moved into the preparation or action stage before social workers attempt to engage them in change activities. For example, Bob Morris agreed to see a social worker when his wife threatened to leave him because of his violent, abusive behavior. He remarked initially that "he would do anything to have her stay." It might be tempting to start working with him immediately on anger control. However, it would be better first to help Bob see his behavior as a problem and make sure he is ready to do something about it before having him take steps to curb his anger. Another application of the principle would be to fit the length of treatment to the duration of the client's active change efforts. In most cases, this would mean use of planned, short-term modalities, but with the awareness that some clients may need to—and are able to—continue change efforts beyond the usual norms to resolve their difficulties.

A final application would concern maintenance. Keeping in mind that relapse is a likely event for many problems, ways of coping with relapse (a relapse plan) should be developed with the client prior to termination. The plan should include specification of what the client can do to avoid a recurrence of the problem, information about the warning signs of a recurrence and actions to be taken at that point, and description of what the client can do, including return to treatment, should a relapse occur. For problems or clients where relapse may be a strong possibility, follow-up contacts with the option of short-term "booster" treatment should be considered.

A third principle suggests that practitioners draw on interventions related to a multisystemic range of change activities, integrating them to fit the client, problem, and stage of change. Toni Harris is seeking help for depression. She may need first to develop insight into interpersonal stressors contributing to her problem and correct distortions of beliefs about herself (DeRubeis & Crits-Christoph, 1998; Jensen, 1994). She might then improve her interpersonal competence by learning new social skills (Corrigan, 1991). Additional change activities aimed at relieving her depression might include participating in a group (Peterson & Halstead, 1998) and enlarging her social network (Mallinickrodt, 1996).

Where available, empirical evidence should be used to determine which activity is most likely to work, as in the example given above. When such evidence cannot provide clear guidance, the social worker can discuss alternative approaches with the client and develop a plan based on the client's informed wishes (Garvin & Seabury, 1997).

A final principle relates to the effect of macro systems on adult change. The social worker's awareness of macro level influences on change can be important in two ways. First, it may provide a direction for intervention in a particular case. Denise, a recent Haitian immigrant, applied to a work-training program 2 months earlier but has heard nothing. Her social worker knew that the agency to which she applied had an informal policy of discouraging Haitian immigrants, which was contrary to its own admissions criteria. Armed with this knowledge, the practitioner confronted the agency. Denise was soon accepted. Second, through their professional organizations and their workplaces, or as individuals, social workers can advocate for policies that seem the most likely to facilitate the kind of changes that they are attempting to help individual clients achieve.

REFERENCES

Affleck, G., Pfeiffer, C., Tennen, J., & Fifield, J. (1988). Social support and psychosocial adjustment to rheumatoid arthritis: Quantitative and qualitative findings. *Arthritis Care and Research, 1,* 71-7.

Bandura, A. (1988). Self-regulation of motivation and action through goal systems. In V. Hamilton, G. H. Bower, & N. H. Frijda (Eds.), *Cognitive perspectives on emotion and motivation* (pp. 37-61). Dordrecht, Netherlands: Kluwer.

Bandura, A. (1989). Human agency in social cognitive theory. *American Psychologist, 44*(9), 1175-1184.

Baucom, D. H., Shoham, V., Mueser, K. T., & Daiuto, A. D. (1998). Empirically supported couple and family interventions for marital distress and adult mental health problems. *Journal of Consulting and Clinical Psychology, 66*(1), 53-88.

Baumeister, R. F. (1994). The crystallization of discontent in the process of major life change. In T. Heatherton & J. L. Weinberger (Eds.), *Can personality change?* Washington, DC: American Psychological Association.

Bednar, R. L., & Kaul, T. K. (1994). Experimental group research: Can the cannon fire? In A. E. Bergin & S. L. Garfield (Eds.), *Handbook of psychotherapy and behavior change.* New York: John Wiley.

Berkowitz, M. W., Waxman, R., & Jaffe, L. (1988). The effects of a resident self-help model on control, social involvement, and self-esteem among the elderly. *The Gerontologist, 28*(5), 620-624.

Berlin, S. B., Mann, K. B., & Grossman, S. F. (1991). Task analysis of cognitive therapy for depression. *Social Work Research and Abstracts, 27,* 3-11.

Berry, M., & Cash, S. (1998). Creating community through psychoeducational groups in family preservation work. *Families in Society: The Journal of Contemporary Human Services, 79*(1), 15-24.

Brehm, S., & Brehm, J. W. (1981). *Psychological reactance: A theory of freedom and control.* New York: Academic Press.

Connors, G.-J., Carroll, K. M., DiClemente, C., Longabaugh, R., & Donovan, D. M. (1997). The therapeutic alliance and its relationship to alcoholism treatment participation and outcome. *Journal Consulting & Clinical Psychology, 65,* 588-598.

Corrigan, P. (1991). Social skills training in adult psychiatric populations: A meta-analysis. *Journal of Behavior Therapy and Experimental Psychiatry, 22*(3), 203-210.

Corrigan, P. (1995). Use of a token economy with seriously mentally ill patients: Criticisms and misconceptions. *Psychiatric Services, 46,* 1258-1263.

Davis, R., Olmsted, M., & Rockert, W. (1990). Brief group psychoeducation for bulimia nervosa: Assessing the clinical significance of change. *Journal of Consulting and Clinical Psychology, 58*(6), 882-885.

DeRubeis, R. J., & Crits-Christoph, P. (1998). Empirically supported individual and group psychological treatments for adult mental disorders. *Journal of Consulting and Clinical Psychology, 66*(1), 37-52.

Dhooper, S. S. (1983). Family coping with the crisis of heart attack. *Social Work in Health Care, 9,* 15-31.

Diamond, G. S., Serrano, A. C., Dickey, M., & Sonis, W. A. (1996). Current status of family-based outcome and process research. *Journal of American Child Adolescence Psychiatry, 35,* 6-16.

Ell, K. (1995). Crisis intervention: Research needs. In *Encyclopedia of social work* (19th ed.). Washington, DC: National Association of Social Work Press.

Febbraro, A. R., & Clum, G. A. (1998). Meta-analytic investigation of the effectiveness of self-regulatory components in the treatment of adult problem behaviors. *Clinical Psychology Review, 18*(2), 143-161.

Frazier, P. A., & Burnett, J. W. (1994). Immediate coping strategies among rape victims. *Journal of Counseling and Development, 72,* 633-639.

French, T. M. (1952). *The integration of behavior: Basic postulates.* Chicago: University of Chicago Press.

Garvin, C. D., & Seabury, B. A. (1997). *Interpersonal practice in social work* (2nd ed.). Needham Heights, MA: Allyn & Bacon.

Greenberg, L. S., & Newman, F. L. (1996). An approach to psychotherapy change process research: Introduction to the special section. *Journal of Consulting and Clinical Psychology, 64*(3), 435-438.

Greenberg, L. S., & Pinsof, W. M. (Eds.). (1986). *The psychotherapeutic process: A research handbook.* New York: Guilford.

Grimley, D., Prochaska, J. O., Velicer, W. F., Blais, L. M., & DiClemente, C. C. (1994). The transtheoretical model of change. In T. M. Brinthaupt & R. P. Lipka (Eds.), *Changing the self: Philosophies, techniques, and experiences* (pp. 201-227). Albany: State University of New York Press.

Hamm, F. B. (1992). Organizational change. *Journal of Substance Abuse Treatment, 9*(3), 257-260.

Havassy, B. E., Hall, E., Sharon, M., & Wasserman, D. A. (1991). Social support and relapse: Commonalities among alcoholics, opiate users, and cigarette smokers. *Addictive Behaviors, 16*(5), 235-246.

Heatherton, T., & Nichols, P. (1994). Personal accounts of successful versus failed attempts at life change. *Personality and Social Psychology Bulletin, 20*(6), 664-675.

Henry, W. P., Strupp, H. H., Schacht, T. E., & Gaston, L. (1994). Psychodynamic approaches. In A. E. Bergen & S. L. Garfield (Eds.), *Handbook of psychotherapy and behavior change* (4th ed., pp. 278-376). New York: John Wiley.

Hogarty, G. E. (1993). Prevention of relapse in chronic schizophrenic patients. *Clinical Psychiatry, 54,* 3.

Jensen, C. (1994). Psychosocial treatment of depression in women: Nine single-subject evaluations. *Research on Social Work Practice, 4*(3), 267-282.

Jones, E. E., Ghannam, J., Nigg, J. T., & Dyer, J. F. P. (1993). A paradigm for single-case research: The time series study of a long-term psychotherapy for depression. *Journal of Consulting and Clinical Psychology, 61*(3), 381-394.

Jones, M. (1953). *The therapeutic community: A new treatment method in psychiatry.* New York: Basic Books.

Klingemann, H. K. (1991). The motivation for change from problem alcohol and heroin use. *British Journal of Addiction, 86,* 727-744.

Klingemann, H. K. (1992). Coping and maintenance strategies of spontaneous remitters from problem use of alcohol and heroin in Switzerland. *The International Journal of the Addictions, 27,* 1359-1388.

Koptka, S. M., Howard, K. I., Lowry, J. L., & Beutler, L. E. (1994). Patterns of symptomatic recovery in psychotherapy. *Journal of Consulting and Clinical Psychology, 62*(5), l009-l016.

Koptka, S. M., Krause, M. E., & Orlinsky, D. E. (1986). The dose-effect relationship in psychotherapy. *American Psychologist, 41,* 159-164.

Koss, M. P., & Butcher, J. N. (1994). Research on brief psychotherapy. In A. Bergin & S. Garfield (Eds.), *Handbook of psychotherapy and behavior change* (4th ed., pp. 627-670). New York: John Wiley.

Kurtz, L. F. (1990). The self-help movement: Review of the past decade of research. *Social Work with Groups, 13*(3), 101-115.

Lambert, M. J., & Hill, C. E. (1994). Assessing psychotherapy outcomes and processes. In A. E. Bergin & S. L. Garfield (Eds.), *Handbook of psychotherapy and behavior change* (4th ed., pp. 72-113). New York: John Wiley.

Lazarus, R. S., & Folkman, S. (1984). *Stress, appraisal, and coping.* New York: Springer.

Lehman, D., Davis, C., DeLongis, A., Wortman, C., Bluck, S., Mandel, D., & Ellard, J. (1993). Positive and negative life changes following bereavement and their relations to adjustment. *Journal of Social and Clinical Psychology, 12,* 90-112.

Loneck, B., Garrett, J. A., & Banks, S. M. (1996). The Johnson intervention and relapse during outpatient treatment. *American Journal of Drug Alcohol Abuse, 22*(3), 363-375.

Ludwig, A. M. (1985). Cognitive processes associated with "spontaneous" recovery from alcoholism, *Quarterly Journal of Studies on Alcohol, 46,* 53-57.

Mallinckrodt, B. (1996). Change in working alliance, social support, and psychological symptoms in brief therapy. *Journal of Counseling Psychology, 43*(4), 448-455.

Mattick, R. P., Andrews, G., Hadzi-Pavlovic, D., & Christensen, H. (1990). Treatment of panic and agoraphobia: An integrative review. *Journal of Nervous and Mental Disease, 179*(9), 567-576.

McLeavey, B. C., Daly, R. J., Ludgate, J. W., & Murray, C. M. (1994). Interpersonal problem-solving skills training in the treatment of self-poisoning patients. *Suicide and Life Threatening Behavior, 24*(4), 382-394.

McMillen, J. C., & Fisher, R. H. (1998). The perceived benefit scales: Measuring perceived positive life changes after negative events. *Social Work Research, 22*(3), 129-192.

Miller, W. R., & C'deBaca, J. (1994). Does thought content change as individuals age? Can personality change? In T. F. Heatherton & J. L. Weinberg (Eds.), *Quantum change: Toward a psychology of transformation* (pp. 253-280). Washington, DC: American Psychological Association.

Miller, W. R., & Rollnick, S. (1991). *Motivational interviewing.* New York: Guilford.

Miller, W. R., & Sovreign, R. G. (1989). The check-up: A model for early intervention in addictive behaviors. In T. Loberg, W. R. Miller, P. E. Nathan, & G. A. Marlatt (Eds.), *Addictive behaviors: Prevention and early intervention* (pp. 219-231). Amsterdam: Swets & Zeitlinger.

Murray, R. B., & Baier, M. (1993). Use of therapeutic milieu in a community setting. *Journal of Psychosocial Nursing 31*(10), 11-16.

Nezu, A. M., Nezu, C. M., & Perri, M. G. (1989). *Problem-solving therapy for depression: Theory, research, and clinical guidelines.* New York: John Wiley.

O'Connor, L., Edelstein, S., Berry, J. W., Jr., & Weiss, J., Jr. (1994). The pattern of insight in brief psychotherapy: A series of pilot studies. *Psychotherapy, 31*(3), 533-544.

Orlinsky, D. E., Grawe, K., & Parks, B. K. (1994). Process and outcome in psychotherapy: Noch einmal. In A. E. Bergin & S. L. Garfield (Eds.), *Handbook of psychotherapy & behavior change* (pp. 270-376). New York: John Wiley.

Penn, D. L., & Mueser, K. T. (1996). Research update on the psychosocial treatment of schizophrenia. *American Journal of Psychiatry, 153,* 607-617.

Peterson, A. J., & Halstead, T. S. (1998). Group cognitive behavior therapy for depression in a community setting: A clinical replication series. *Behavior Therapy, 29,* 3-18.

Prochaska, J. O. (1995). Common problems: Common solutions. *Clinical Psychology Science & Practice, 2,* 101-105.

Prochaska, J. O., & DiClemente, C. (1986). The transtheoretical approach. In J. C. Norcross (Ed.), *Handbook of eclectic psychotherapy* (pp. 163-200). New York: Brunner/Mazel.

Prochaska, J. O., DiClemente, C. C., & Norcross, J. C. (1992). Applications to addictive behaviors: In search of how people change. *American Psychologist, 42,* 1102-1114.

Prochaska, J. O., DiClemente, C. C., Velicer, W. F., & Rossi, J. S. (1992). Comments on Davidson, Prochaska, and DiClemente's model of change: A case study? *British Journal of Addiction, 87,* 1102-1114.

Ramsey, P. W. (1992). Characteristics, processes, and effectiveness of community support groups: A review of the literature, *Family Community Health, 15*(3) 38-48.

Reid, W. J. (1990). Change process research: A new paradigm? In L. Videka-Sherman & W. J. Reid (Eds.), *Advances in clinical social work research* (pp. 130-148) Silver Spring, MD: NASW Press.

Reid, W. J. (1998). The paradigms and long-term trends in clinical social work. In R. Dorfman (Ed.), *Paradigms of clinical social work* (pp. 231-242). New York: Brunner/Mazel.

Reid, W. (in press). *The task planner.* New York: Columbia University Press.

Ripple, L., Alexander, E., & Polemis, B. W. (1964). *Motivation, capacity, and opportunity.* Chicago: University of Chicago Press.

Rooney, R. (1992). *Strategies for work with involuntary clients.* New York: Columbia University Press.

Rooney, R. (1988). Socialization strategies for involuntary clients. *Social Casework: The Journal of Contemporary Social Work, 69*(3), 131-140.

Schaefer, J., & Moos, R. (1992). Life crises and personal growth. In B. N. Carpenter (Ed.), *Personal coping: Theory, research, and application* (pp. 149-170). Westport, CT: Praeger.

Sisson, R. W., & Azrin, N. H. (1993). Community reinforcement training for families: A method to get alcoholics into treatment. In T. J. O'Farrell (Ed.), *Treating alcohol problems: Marital and family interventions* (pp. 242-258). New York: Guilford.

Stall, R., & Biernacki, P. (1986). Spontaneous remission from the problematic use of substances: An inductive model derived from a comparative analysis of the alcohol, opiate, tobacco, and food/obesity literatures. *The International Journal of the Addictions, 21*(1) 1-23.

Stanton, M., & Shadish, W. (1997). Outcome, attrition, and family-couples treatment for drug abuse: A meta-analysis and review of the controlled, comparative studies. *Psychological Bulletin, 122*(2), 170-191.

Steenbarger, B. N. (1994). Duration and outcome in psychotherapy: An integrative review. *Professional Psychology: Research and Practice, 25*(2), 111-119.

Strecher, V., Seijts, G., Kok, G., Latham, G., Glasgow, R., DeVillis, B., Meertens, R., & Bulger, D. (1995). Goal setting as a strategy for health behavior change. *Health Education Quarterly, 22*(2), 190-200.

Strupp, H. H., & Hadley, S. W. (1977). A tripartite model of mental health and therapeutic outcomes: With special reference to negative effects in psychotherapy. *American Psychologist, 32*, 187-196.

Thomas, E. J., Santa, C., Bronson, D., & Oyserman, D. (1987). Unilateral family therapy with the spouses of alcoholics. *Journal of Social Service Research, 10*, 145-162.

Tomm, K. (1982). Towards a cybernetic systems approach to family therapy. In F. W. Kaslow (Ed.), *The international book of family therapy* (pp. 70-90). New York: Brunner/Mazel.

Toseland, R. W. (1995). *Group work with the elderly and family caregivers.* New York: Springer.

Toseland, R. W., & Rivas, R. E. (1998). *An introduction to group work practice.* Needham Heights, MA: Allyn & Bacon.

Toseland, R. W., & Siporin, M. (1986). When to recommend group treatment: A review of the clinical and research literature. *International Journal of Group Psychotherapy, 36*(2), 171-201.

Tuchfeld, B. S. (1981). Spontaneous remission in alcoholics—empirical observations and theoretical implications, *Journal of Studies on Alcohol, 42*, 626-641.

Wachtel, P. L. (1997). *Psychoanalysis, behavior therapy, and the rational world.* Washington, DC: American Psychological Association.

Wallerstein, J. S. (1986). Women after divorce: Preliminary report from a ten-year follow-up. *American Journal of Orthopsychiatry, 56*, 65-77.

Watson, A. L., & Sher, K. J. (1998). Resolution of alcohol problems without treatment: Methodological issues and future directions of natural recovery research. *Clinical Psychology: Science and Practice, 5*, 1-18.

Wells-Parker, E., Bangert-Drowns, R., McMillen, R., & Williams, M. (1995). Research report: Final results from a meta-analysis of remedial interventions with drink/drive offenders. *Addiction, 90*, 907-926.

Whisman, M. A., Miller, I. W., Norman, W. H., & Keitner, G. I. (1991). Cognitive therapy with depressed inpatients: Specific effects on dysfunctional cognitions. *Journal of Consulting and Clinical Psychology, 59*(2), 282-288.

Whiteman, M., Fanshel, D., & Grundy, J. F. (1987). Cognitive-behavioral interventions aimed at anger of parents at risk of child abuse. *Social Work, 32*, 469-474.

Yarom, N. (1983). Facing death in war: An existential crisis. In S. Brezmotz (Ed.), *Stress in Israel* (pp. 3-38). New York: Van Nostrand Reinhold.

CHAPTER THIRTEEN

Individual Change in Children and Direct Social Work Practice

KATHLEEN COULBORN FALLER

Social workers endeavoring to effect individual change using direct practice with children are to be found in a wide range of settings: public child welfare agencies, public mental health agencies, public delinquency programs, preschool and school settings, medical care facilities, voluntary social services agencies, and group and private practices. Moreover, these social workers may take on a spectrum of roles: These include case manager, evaluator, therapist or counselor, educator, and advocate. In their practice, social workers may employ a range of conceptual frameworks for effecting change, for example attachment, developmental, psychodynamic, behavioral, and problem-solving. Finally, social workers practicing with children rely on underlying philosophical and value assumptions.

Of necessity, this chapter is selective. In it, I will discuss the four topics above in the following order: value and philosophical issues related to work with children, typical social work roles in direct practice with children, contexts in which this practice takes place, and theoretical frameworks for practice with children. Special emphasis will be placed on the first topic and its implication for direct practice with children.

Topics and issues covered in this chapter will be illustrated by drawing on a case example. The case is typical of situations in which children require direct social work services. What will be described are children in a family with complex problems but real strengths as well as vulnerabilities. As will be evident, the children's problems and social workers' difficulties resolving them derive in considerable part from the broader ecology, which includes deficits in the service delivery system. In addition, the case example was selected because it illustrates the kind of children I think social workers *should* be helping.

Case example. The names in the Abbott case have been changed to protect confidentiality. Names were changed, and only first names are used for the professionals because social workers who work with children and those in non-traditional settings often prefer that clients refer to them by their first names. As this case will illustrate, the Abbott children and their mother encounter social workers in a number of settings, performing a variety of functions, and with different levels of training and expertise. Some facts in the Abbott case have been altered slightly to demonstrate more fully the roles and responsibilities of social workers engaging in direct practice with children. In addition, the Abbott case will be used to highlight how the situation for the children in this family could have been improved.

Abbott Family Members	Professionals
Maude, maternal grandmother, age 45	Jane, shelter social worker
Betina, mother, age 29	Evan, James's therapist
James son, age 9	Dana, social work evaluator
Jason, son, age 8	Lucy, social work evaluator
Jackson, son, age 6	Welfare worker
Jackie, daughter, age 4	Sally, day care social worker
Jacine, daughter, age 2	Child Protective Services (CPS) worker

Betina is a single, African American mother of five children, who relocated from an inner-city community to a nearby small town because she and her children were being harassed by a relative, Uncle Steve. Uncle Steve had sexually abused her oldest son, James, and James was to testify against Uncle Steve in a criminal trial.

Betina arrived with her five children in the small town shortly before Christmas, with no place to live. Betina, at age 29, has a high school equivalency diploma, possesses little work experience, is about 50 pounds overweight, and suffers from high blood pressure. Betina and her children were sheltered by a program for homeless families, where Jane, the shelter social worker, assisted Betina and the children in getting Temporary Assistance for Needy Families (TANF). To receive her welfare benefits, Betina had to work at least 20 hours a week. Betina's TANF worker enrolled her in a nurse's aide program that guaranteed her employment after she completed it. Jane placed Betina and her children in transitional housing and helped her enroll her children in school and in a day care center with an afterschool program. Betina needed an afterschool program because the nurse's aide training required her to attend from 2 p.m. to 9 p.m. most days. A condition of the training program was that Betina had to attend every session, including those on Christmas Eve and Christmas Day, a total of 80 hours, or start the program over.

Jane also arranged for James to see a social worker at a university-based clinic to address his experience of sexual abuse. Fortunately, there was a program that would treat James free of charge, and Evan, James's social worker therapist, could see James in his afterschool program rather than requiring him to come to the office. James was doing well academically in school, but his mother reported he was easily angered at home and at school. James agreed to work with Evan on his anger. The first complication in the therapy for James was the discovery that, in addition to having been sexually abused himself, he had also sexually acted out with an 8-year-old boy. Because this incident had already been reported to CPS, Evan did not have to jeopardize his developing therapeutic relationship with James by making a report. Nevertheless, Evan had to develop a relationship with James before he could address James's sexual acting out. He sought to assure there were safe-guards to prevent further sexual acting out in the meantime.

However, after a few weeks, other problems began to emerge. Jason, the second son, was expelled from the afterschool program for sexual activity with younger children. Sally, the day care social worker, reported this to CPS. The CPS worker did not investigate because the sexual acting out occurred out of the home; the case was referred to the police. Jane from the shelter program remained concerned about risks in the family because Jason also reportedly had acted out sexually with Jackie, his 4-year-old sister. With Betina's agreement, Jane referred all of the children for evaluation at the university-based program where Jason was being treated. A team of three social workers, Dana, Lucy, and Evan (James's therapist), worked with the family.

Maude, the children's maternal grandmother, relocated to the small town where the family had moved to assist Betina. She was a considerable support to Betina and the children, but she also revealed facts about James and the family that Betina had not mentioned. Maude reported to Evan that both she and her daughter had been sexually abused as children but had never received any treatment. Maude also reported that James had tried to set the family's house on fire after he was sexually abused. He was found sitting in his mother's room while she slept and the fire burned. Evan wondered whether Betina failed to tell him of the severity of James's problems because she did not trust him, as a white person, or because she was overwhelmed by her situation. Betina had recently learned that James was to be charged as a sex offender for his sexual interaction with the 8-year-old boy.

Three days before the university clinic evaluations, Sally made another report to CPS because Jacine's vaginal area was red when the day care worker changed her diaper. After interviewing Betina, the CPS worker did not pursue the investigation further and denied the case because the physician who examined Jacine said he could not confirm that the redness came from sexual abuse.

Dana conducted a psychosocial evaluation of Jason, the second son. Jason reported that he also had been sexually abused by his Uncle Steve. In addition, Jason said that his mother beats him and the other

children with a belt when they misbehave. Jason was also described as a very active, observant, and bright child. When the findings, including Jason's activity level, were discussed with Betina, she said that he had been on Ritalin, but she took him off because she did not want him to be dependent on medication the rest of his life.

Dana also did a psychosocial evaluation of Jackson. Jackson was described as a bright, engaging, anxious 6-year-old, who reported being sexually accosted by his two older brothers. He also said James had engaged in sexual activity with Jackie and had paid him a dollar to engage in sexual activity with Jacine. He used anatomical dolls to show this was intercourse.

Lucy evaluated Jackie. At 4, Jackie was developmentally delayed by about a year and had a marked speech anomaly. These problems had not been attended to in her preschool program. She appeared to be deprived emotionally. She hugged and clung to Lucy, whom she had just met. She cried when reprimanded by her mother. Jackie also communicated that she had experienced sexual abuse from her older brother, Jason, by pointing to places on her own body where he had touched her.

Jacine was too young to be interviewed but was engaged by Lucy in play. Her play appeared to be normal, but, like her sister, she was quite clingy with Lucy. She fell and hurt herself but did not cry. Lucy was concerned about Jacine's preference, at least in the evaluation context, for Lucy over her mother and Jacine's pain agnosia, sometimes a signal of maltreatment or deprivation.

The social work evaluators, Dana, Lucy, and Evan, found Betina to have both strengths and weaknesses as a parent. She appeared physically exhausted by the requirements of her nurses aide training, as well as emotionally drained. When interviewed, her first comments were about how tired and sore she was. However, she was also evidently proud of herself for being able to stick with the training. Her strengths were demonstrated in several other ways. She had brought all of her children to be evaluated, even though she was not required to do so, and she verbalized wanting to find out what was going on with them. She was preparing to go to court on her day off to support James, when he testified against Uncle

Steve. Even though she was exhausted during the evaluation, she read a book to the children in the waiting room. She spoke of her plans to have her mother take the children to the movies Christmas Day while she worked, and, after enduring the stress of her children's lengthy evaluation, she took them all with her to buy food for Christmas dinner.

At the same time, she minimized her children's sexual activity as experimentation and defended her use of the belt to punish them. In addition, although it was clear that Betina loved all of her children, at times, she was harsh and threatening with them when they were noncompliant.

Lucy, Dana, and Evan were quite concerned about the level of sexual activity among Betina's children, including coercive activity. They were worried that this activity would continue and escalate, resulting in further trauma to the children and likely CPS intervention and removal of all the children from Betina's care. In addition, they thought hitting the children with a belt, although not a good method of discipline, did not constitute reportable abuse in the family's cultural context. They decided to do three things. First, they urged Betina to use other forms of discipline, rather than the belt. Second, with Betina's knowledge, they filed a report with CPS about the sexual activity among her children, but with a specific request for supportive services and treatment for the children (their program could not accommodate four more children). Third, with Betina's permission, Lucy did an immediate intervention. She and Evan met with the entire family, including Betina. Lucy spoke to the children about the sexual activity that was going on in their family, telling them all that it had to stop, that no one was to touch or do anything to anyone else's private parts. She asked them what could happen if they kept doing this, and Jackson said they could get in trouble. The children were asked whom they could tell if any touching happened in the future, and the older children said their mother. Lucy and Evan supported both of these responses.

This is not the end of social work involvement in the Abbott case, but it represents an appropriate end point for issues to be discussed in this chapter.

VALUE AND PHILOSOPHICAL ISSUES

The issues discussed in this section are the need for direct practitioners to be aware of the ecology of children's lives, implications of knowledge about children's ecology for direct practice, and the involuntary nature of most relationships children have with social workers.

Direct practitioners should be aware of children's ecology. Social workers engaged in direct practice with children must be ever mindful of the ecology or larger contexts in which children live. These contexts can be characterized as political, economic, environmental, cultural, and family.

In *political* terms, children are disenfranchised. They do not vote, and they have no political power and virtually no voice in the political arena. Numerous individuals, groups, and constituencies speak on behalf of children. However, these individuals and groups may not be in a position to discern children's best interest, or they may not always make children's best interest the primary issue. Moreover, in the last analysis, politicians do not have to worry about children rebelling and voting or throwing them out of office.

In *economic* terms, children do not earn their living. Throughout most of their childhood, they are dependent on adults for food, shelter, clothing, and medical care. When families cannot meet children's economic needs and the state steps in, what the state provides is hardly a living but, rather, a standard of care at about two thirds of the poverty level (Lewitt, Terman, & Behrman, 1997; Long, Clark, Ratcliffe, & Olson, 1998). Because two thirds of welfare recipients are children, more children will be affected than adults as the inadequate safety net of the Aid to Families With Dependent Children (AFDC) program is dismantled and replaced by TANF, with use-specific (2 years) and lifetime limits (5 years) on benefits (Plotnick, 1997).

Illustrative of children's political and economic disadvantage is their poverty rate. Although the poverty rate in the general population is unconscionably high for the world's richest country, 11.3%, the rate for children is more than twice as high, about 25% (Children's Defense Fund, 1997; Lewitt et al., 1997), and the poverty rate for children has been steadily increasing since 1970 (Albelda, Folbre, & the Center for Population Economics, 1996). Moreover, when the United States is compared to other industrialized countries, 15 other countries have lower poverty rates (Lewitt et al., 1997). Thus, direct practitioners should be aware that, as a society, we could do and should do better by our children.

The political and economic disadvantage of the Abbott children speaks for itself. These children are not regarded by society as deserving a mother to parent them. Rather, society, as represented by the TANF provisions, deems it more appropriate for Betina to toil long hours, at best for a minimum wage. Her children spend their time in school, day care, and afterschool care. They rarely see Betina unless it is when she must accompany them to court or to an appointment where her presence is required. When they do see her, she is exhausted and has little energy for them.

Children's *environmental* context includes school, neighborhood, and a larger urban, suburban, or rural community. It also encompasses social agencies and community resources available to children. Environmental contexts can offer advantage or entail disadvantage. Additional environmental characteristics have an impact on child well-being. The quality of the school is an important predictor of how well children perform academically. Neighborhoods may be war zones or safe havens. Communities may be racist or enlightened, poor or rich.

Illustrative of the importance of environment are recent findings from LONGSCAN (Hunter & Knight, 1998), an ongoing, multisite study of children at risk. LONGSCAN researchers are engaged in an action research endeavor to identify factors they describe as social capital; presently, these include church affiliation, family social support, and support within the neighborhood. The presence of social capital was strongly associated with child well-being; the presence of one factor increased children's odds of doing well by 29% and of two factors by 66% (Hunter & Knight, 1998).

When working with disadvantaged children, whether programs such as Head Start, Family Support, Well Child Clinics, and adequate housing exist will make a great deal of difference in how successful direct practice will be (Garbarino & Eckenrode, 1997).

The Abbott children left a community with gangs, high unemployment, and substandard schools. It was also a community where Steve, their abusive uncle, was free to stalk James, and he and his family to threaten Betina. The Abbotts were more fortunate in their new community. They encountered a very supportive social worker in the homeless shelter, Jane, who obtained services for them, including temporary housing, TANF, therapy for James, evaluations of all of the children, and child care. Betina moved from a community that, in many respects, was a war zone, to a community that was relatively resource-rich for families who comply with social welfare agency rules.

Children are raised in a *cultural* context, often a strong source of identity. For the majority of children with whom social workers practice, the child's culture will be different from the social worker's. Most social workers achieve middle-class status, but most clients of social workers are disadvantaged, usually poor. Moreover, a substantial and increasing proportion of the children social workers try to help are children of color. To practice effectively with children, social workers must learn about their cultures and honor cultural differences. This means appreciating that differences are not deficits and in fact may be strengths. A child's culture must be taken into account in both assessment and intervention.

In addition, direct practitioners should not lose sight of the fact that racism is the underlying cause for disproportionate numbers of children of color requiring their services. As a consequence, disenfranchisement and disadvantage, which affect children in general, disproportionately affect children of color. Whereas about 25% of all children are poor, half of children of color are poor (Children's Defense Fund, 1997). Children of color are not only more likely to be poor, they are likely to be poor for longer periods of time than white children (Lewitt et al., 1997). Similarly, children of color are more likely to live in dangerous and resource-disadvantaged communities, to attend substandard schools, and to receive second-rate or no health care (Weissbourd, 1996; Wilson, 1987). Although minorities are no more likely than whites to maltreat their children (Sedlak & Broadhurst, 1996), they are disproportionately reported to CPS (Lewitt et al., 1997).

Betina's reticence about the severity of James's problems likely reflects the distrust many people of color have for social agencies, which are also agents of social control.

Perhaps more important than any of these previously described larger contexts in which children exist and function is the *family*. All children have parents, and most children live in families. Increasingly, these families vary in structure. Thus, the "traditional family," a two-parent family in which the mother stays at home and cares for the children and the father works outside the home, is a minority family form. More than 15% of children live in single-parent families, most of them headed by mothers (Long et al., 1998), and more than half of children spend some of their childhood in single-parent families (Furstenberg & Cherlin, 1991). Mother-headed households are especially likely to be poor and African American. These structural changes influence direct practice with children in a variety of ways. It is simply insensitive and unrealistic to expect single parents, especially those who also work outside the home, to do what was previously expected of two parents. Other formal and informal resources must be accessed. In addition, divorce and living in a single-parent family are often issues direct practitioners need to address as they work with children.

Moreover, although most children live with their families, a substantial minority spend some of their childhood in substitute care; presently, about half a million children are not living with their families (Courtney, 1998). These children are disproportionately children of color.

The Abbott children are among the increasing numbers of children who are growing up in single-parent, poor households. Although they have some supportive relatives on whom they can rely in times of stress—for example, Betina's mother—they also have extended family members, specifically Uncle Steve, who are predatory. Moreover, Uncle Steve's relatives have joined forces with him to make the situation for James, who is scheduled to testify against Steve in a criminal trial, so frightening that Betina decided to move herself and her children out of the community.

Furthermore, Betina probably feared, and with good reason, placement of one or more of her children, should the extent of the children's sexual problems become known. Thus, she minimized the problems as sexual experimentation.

Implications of understanding children's ecology. What are the implications of this ecological perspective for direct social work practice with children?

First, if social workers are to work effectively with children, they cannot do so in a vacuum. They cannot ignore children's families, schools, and communities. They should beware the temptation to try to rescue children, to be a better parent than the child's caretaker, or to be a better teacher than the child's classroom teacher. The goal of the social worker is to work *with* these individuals, not in competition with them. In addition, social workers cannot be oblivious to children's need for food, shelter, clothing, and medical care and merely address their needs for therapy. Such an approach is both insensitive and likely to be counterproductive. Case advocacy is an honorable role for social workers practicing with and on behalf of children.

Jane, the shelter worker, exemplifies commitment to work collaboratively and advocate for her clients. Her strategy is to mobilize resources for the family, thereby empowering Betina.

Second, trying to effect individual change in children, in some cases against overwhelming odds—for example, poverty, neighborhood gangs, inadequate housing, and a substandard school system—can be very discouraging and frustrating. Social workers involved in direct practice with children are at risk of burning out. Particularly when working with children whose lives are fraught with adverse circumstances, direct practitioners may feel totally impotent. However, theory and research from widely divergent arenas document the importance of primary relationships (e.g., Anthony & Cohler, 1988; Bowlby, 1973; Mahler, Pine, & Bergman, 1975), including relationships with children who are disadvantaged (e.g., Kotlowitz, 1991; Weissbourd, 1996). As a consequence, children may learn from relationships with social workers and other adults in their lives—people who are caring, dependable, and invested—that their lives can change and that there is a different way to live than in dangerous, abusive, or deprived circumstances. Children can carry that experience with them, and it can form a basis for future relationships and more positive expectations. Maintaining a perspective that the alliance the social worker forms with the child is the most crucial element in change can overcome disillusionment and burnout.

For Evan, who was new to direct practice with children, feeling overwhelmed was an issue. He was appalled by the insensitivity of the welfare system, the obstacles faced by James and his family, and the emergence of new family problems and crises virtually every week. He was helped to appreciate the potential positive impact of his work with James and how to address the other problems Betina and her children encountered by his supervisor and by working with a team of social workers.

Who is the client? Another important value and philosophical issue for direct practitioners with children is that, as a rule, children do not identify themselves as having a problem requiring social work and other intervention. Usually, an adult or an institution governed by adults defines the child as needing services. As a consequence, most child clients are involuntary or only quasivoluntary. If they do see themselves as having a problem, it may be different from that defined by the referring person. It follows that practitioners providing direct services must be clear about who their client is. If their role is to serve the child, the child is the client. The older the child, the more autonomy the child should be given. Even so, in the majority of cases, the social worker must negotiate his or her role and intervention goals with the child. The agreement with the child client may place the social worker in conflict with the referring party, with other adult stakeholders, and with invested institutions. Although it is important not to be foolhardy and ignore the potential impact of institutions (e.g., the Juvenile Court) and individual adults on the fate of children, it is also important to remember the child is the client.

> In the Abbott case, Jane has a very different perspective on Betina and what sort of intervention is appropriate than Sally, who in fact only met Betina briefly. Jane essentially sees Betina as her client and advocates and tries to support her. Sally sees the children as her clients and twice made reports to CPS when she thought the children were at risk.
>
> Because Jane was the one who thought James needed therapy—not James—Evan was challenged in negotiating a treatment contract with James. James was happy enough to spend time with Evan and enjoyed board games with him. He initially denied any concerns about his experience of sexual abuse. However, he agreed to work on his anger, and

> Evan's anger-management interventions with James were effective. Nevertheless, as the case history indicates, anger was not the only manifestation of James's problems.

ROLES OF DIRECT PRACTITIONERS WITH CHILDREN

As with other populations, social workers serving children have a variety of roles. Mentioned in the introduction, these include *case manager, evaluator, therapist or counselor, educator, and advocate.*

Because of the way in which children are embedded in larger contexts, such as schools, day care, communities, and families, the case manager and advocate roles are especially important in direct practice with children. These and other roles social workers play in work with children rely on the availability of resources, such as tutors, big brothers, medical care, and transportation. Especially when social workers are acting as case managers and advocates, they employ a resource-linkage model to guide their intervention. That is, the social worker cannot do it all but can select appropriate resources and persuade the child of their efficacy and utility. A frequent frustration is the absence of or paucity of needed resources.

> As noted above, Jane's interventions illustrate the importance of case management and advocacy roles. However, even she was challenged when she needed to find free therapy for five children, rather than one child.

Moreover, even when a social worker is functioning as an *evaluator* or a *therapist*, these interventions rarely involve seeing the child in isolation. A school social worker who is assessing a child to develop an Individual Educational Plan, works with a multidisciplinary team. A social worker treating a child for behavior problems associated with trauma usually involves the child's caretaker(s) because they must support and, in some instances, carry out the intervention.

> In the Abbott case, the need for input from other disciplines begins to emerge. A medical consultation will be needed to assess Jason's need for medication. A legal consultation will be sought to help the family respond to the delinquency charge against James for his sexual activity with the 8-year-old.

In fact, often the intervention of choice is not individual treatment for the child but family or group treatment. Although children's individual treatment needs should not be overlooked, often it is the child's caretakers who need to change more than the child. The caretakers bring the child to the social worker to be "fixed," when in fact the child is not the one, or the only one, needing fixing. In addition, children who have been stigmatized or traumatized often benefit from treatment in a group context with other children with comparable problems. Merely exposing the child to others with similar difficulties can overcome a sense of isolation and stigmatization.

> In the Abbott case, Lucy, Dana, and Evan determined that a family intervention was needed to prevent further sexual activity among the children (known as the "cut that out" intervention). They decided that Betina could not, by herself, perform that protective function, and each child's separate awareness of the inappropriateness of the sexual activity was not enough protection.

Direct practitioners often do not see themselves as *educators*. However, both in direct work with children and with their parents, a psychoeducational approach is often the intervention of choice. A *psychoeducational* approach may involve providing information about the characteristics and likely effects of trauma, common issues at different developmental stages, resources available to the child or family, or choices the child or family may make. Often, the goal is to empower the client by providing information rather than to impose change.

> Illustrative of a psychoeducational approach in the Abbott case was imparting to Betina that what her children were doing was not just sexual exploration. Because of the age differences and use of bribery, the behavior was exploitive.

SETTINGS FOR DIRECT PRACTICE WITH CHILDREN

As noted at the beginning of the chapter, direct practice with children can take place in a variety of settings. Social workers can be found working with children in *public child welfare agencies, public mental health agencies, public delinquency programs, preschool and school settings, medical care facilities, voluntary social services agencies* such as family and children services or sectarian agencies, and *group and private practices.* Moreover, an individual child or the child's family often needs social work services from several sources. Some of these settings (e.g., mental health, health care) will be discussed in other chapters; settings to be discussed in this chapter are child welfare, school, and delinquency settings. The voluntary social services sector will not be discussed separately, but in many states, public sector agencies, such as child welfare or mental health, contract with the voluntary sector for services for their clients, especially for therapy.

Public child welfare. The current array of public child welfare services consists of preventive services, protective services, placement services, and adoption.

Preventive services target at-risk families and attempt voluntary intervention to avoid more serious situations, such as child maltreatment or placement of children. Preventive Service workers usually function as case managers and counselors. Such services may take the form of family support (Adoption Assistance and Family Support Act, 1994), teen parenting programs, outreach counseling, or intensive in-home intervention (e.g., Barthel, 1991; Forsythe, 1992; Rossi, 1992). The central issue for most workers providing preventive services is maintaining family continuity for children. A framework that includes the importance of attachment and bonding for the child's psychological well-being and later functioning underlies concern about family continuity. As a consequence, prevention workers focus primarily on the caretakers, supporting, empowering, and confronting them, rather than on direct work with children. Largely dependent on federal funds, resources for all child welfare services are insufficient, but especially for preventive services (Courtney, 1998).

Protective services workers investigate reports of suspected child maltreatment and make decisions about appropriate intervention. The major roles performed by protective services workers are evaluator and case manager. Thus, protective services workers interview children and their suspected abusers and gather other information to decide whether or not the child has been maltreated. If it is determined

that the child was maltreated, the worker, in consultation with a supervisor, then decides whether or not to ask the court to remove the child to a safe place. In their case manager role, protective services workers determine what concrete and supportive interventions are needed to restore the family to minimum sufficient level of child care and link the family to these services. To a lesser extent, they are involved in advocacy, and they rarely function as therapists or counselors.

These workers must balance competing issues, including child safety, child well-being, family continuity, and family preservation. The assessment and decision-making skills these workers need are not taught in most schools of social work. Moreover, research documents that predicting violence is at best very imprecise (e.g., Wang & Daro, 1998). Finally, more than other child welfare workers, protective services workers find their errors subject to scrutiny by the public and the press. As a consequence, their practice is probably governed more by the environment in which they work than by social work knowledge or skills.

If the child is determined to be at risk in his/her own home, *placement services* or *foster care* becomes involved. In most public child welfare systems, the placement worker is a different person from the protective services worker. Placement may be in a shelter, perhaps just temporarily, or with relatives, in a foster home, in a group home, or in a residential setting. According to statute (Adoption Assistance and Child Welfare Act, 1980), the placement is supposed to be the least restrictive that can manage the child and to be located close to the child's family. This determination is made by the placement worker, usually in consultation with a supervisor, but it is greatly influenced by the availability of placements. After placement, a worker, usually someone different from the worker who made the placement decision, is responsible for the case.

This worker serves as an evaluator, case manager, and sometimes as a counselor and an advocate. The presumptive goal of the placement worker is family reunification, which is pursued by helping the parents, the child, and sometimes the child's current caretakers. Thus, in the evaluator role, the worker determines what services are needed to facilitate family reunification and later evaluates the effectiveness of the services. In the worker's case manager role, he or she links parents with concrete resources, such as transportation and emergency funds; with supportive services, such as parenting classes and parent aides;[1] and with treatment, which may be individual, family, or group therapy. Therapy may also be provided for the child. Some placement workers provide counseling to children, their parents, or substitute caretakers, but this counseling is usually limited to issues related to the child's placement and to making use of and cooperating with the services and resources to which the worker has referred them.

Having a presumptive goal of family reunification means that the importance of family continuity to child well-being and the child's attachment to his or her family are likely to receive greater weight than child safety. Nevertheless, if family reunification efforts are unsuccessful, or deemed inappropriate, the parents' rights are terminated in the Juvenile Court, and an alternative permanent placement for the child is sought. In most cases, optimally this placement is in an adoptive home.

At this point, *adoption services* becomes involved. The adoption services worker functions as an evaluator. In that capacity, the worker recruits potential adoptive parents, studies prospective adoptive parents, studies children available for adoption, and makes matches between adoptive parents and children. The adoption worker also functions as a case manager, an educator, a counselor, and sometimes an advocate, by providing supervision, support, and resources to adoptive parents and children. These resources are often financial, in the form of medical and mental health adoption subsidies (Adoption Assistance and Child Welfare Act, 1980).

Important issues for adoption workers are helping children develop attachments to their new adoptive family and helping the adoptive family and professionals handle any problems in functioning children may have. In addition, the children's psychobiological connection to their birth family is a salient issue for adoption workers.

As already suggested, there is an ongoing tension in the public child welfare system between protecting children and preserving families. Child welfare policy has varied over time as to whether the mission of child safety or family preservation has received priority. Recently, the balance has shifted toward greater emphasis on protecting children (Adoption Assistance and Safe Families Act, 1997).

At the same time, relationships children develop with foster parents and other substitute caretakers are deemed therapeutic because they substitute for the less than optimal attachments with parents. It is, therefore, somewhat ironic that the child welfare system is structured in a way that precludes the formation of primary relationships between the child and the child welfare worker. Workers usually have segmented, instrumental role relationships with the children they serve, rather than ongoing relationships that could form the basis for individual change.

In describing the various worker roles in the public child welfare system, the term *worker* was used advisedly. Unfortunately, beginning in the 1970s, public child welfare systems declassified positions, so master's or even bachelor's degrees in social work were no longer required. When trained social workers are found in the public child welfare system, they tend to be in supervisory and administrative roles, rather than on the front line (e.g., State of Michigan, 1995). Moreover, trained social workers have also abandoned public child welfare agencies, citing bureaucratic red tape, high caseloads, inadequate resources, and dangerous working conditions as reasons. Both the structure of public child welfare and the current paucity of trained social workers in the system mean that crucial decisions, which may involve life or death or affect the long-term well-being of children and families, are being made by people with minimal and on-the-job training (Faller, 1981, 1985).

The Abbott family is on the verge of child welfare system involvement. The CPS worker denied the first two reports, not because there was no abuse, but because he took a narrow view of his responsibility. When Lucy, Dana, and Evan feel they must make a third report, they attempt to orchestrate the intervention so that it is helpful to the family and not overly intrusive.

The Abbott case illustrates the short-sightedness of TANF. It unrealistically expects Betina to work for her benefits when society would be better served if she put all her resources into caring for her five children. Even if she were allowed to stay home and care for them, she would need additional resources to parent effectively. A potential danger is that, because of

her absence, her children's problems will get worse; the children will then be removed; and her efforts at self-sufficiency will result in failure as a parent. Of course, without her children, she will not qualify for TANF, and welfare will no longer be responsible for her and her children. The child welfare system will.

Schools. Social workers are found in elementary and secondary schools and in preschool programs. School social workers function principally as case managers, educators, and advocates. They see themselves as providing linkages between children and teachers, between children in school and their families, and between the school and the community. For example, a teacher may consult with the school social worker about a student's classroom behavior problem, and the social worker may work with the teacher and student to effect a behavior-management program. A school social worker may communicate with parents about child problems or behaviors noted at school. School social workers often facilitate referrals of children to mental health and other services in the community. In some school systems, school social workers also have the role of therapist or counselor, providing individual treatment and group intervention for children in school.

School social workers focus on children's abilities to function academically, behaviorally, and socially in school. They rely on knowledge related to academic and social development, behavioral dysfunction, and behavior management. Children's ability to function adequately in school has implications for children's success in the outside world and for their future well-being.

To a degree, the roles of school social workers overlap with those of school counselors and educators, and in some instances, the social work roles have been taken over by these other professions. However, in 1975 federal legislation, the Individuals with Disabilities Education Act (IDEA; PL 94-142), which requires assessment of children with special needs, secured the place of school social workers, because they are designated members of multidisciplinary teams who conduct these assessments. In fact, in many school settings, the primary role of school social workers is as part of the team, and they have little contact with children without disabilities.

Nevertheless, there is a fairly new and potentially exciting role open to school social workers in programs that provide school-linked services. Education is the one universal social welfare benefit in the United States and, therefore, is a potential gateway for intervention with all children. The principle of school-linked services is that other services, such as health and mental health care, welfare benefits, parenting classes, and even employment assistance, should be provided on site at schools. The assumptions are that schools are in the best position to know children's service needs and that having all services at a single site will assure better service coordination and more complete service provision ("School-Linked Services," 1998). Because school social workers have traditionally linked students to community resources, it is logical they should play a key role in school-linked service programs.

Presently, scores of schools are experimenting with school-linked services. The actual services that are provided vary depending on the availability of programs and resources, community needs, and community decisions. These programs have already demonstrated the capacities of communities to collaborate, but evaluations of most of these programs are still

in progress. The few that have results show modest or mixed results ("School-Linked Services," 1998). However, it is unrealistic to expect such programs to be a panacea for poverty stricken, disadvantaged children and families.

The Abbott family would have benefited from more effective school and day care-based intervention. Even though Jackie's developmental delay was marked, and her speech practically unintelligible, her day care program had not sought services for her. Jason's hyperactivity was not addressed at school. In defense of the day care program and the school, the children had only been enrolled 2 months.

Similarly, the immediate response of the after-school program to Jason's sexual acting out was to exclude him from the program, rather than trying to address his problem. In fact, the service the Abbott children received from the social worker in their school settings was two referrals to CPS.

If the Abbott children had attended a school with school-linked services, their situation might have been greatly improved. For example, if welfare benefits were administered at the school site, likely Betina would not have been required to work at the expense of her children's welfare, and perhaps the school and day care would have been more sensitive to the family's needs.

Delinquency programs. Direct intervention is provided for children, who are usually but not always adolescents, in delinquency programs. These programs are connected to juvenile courts and departments of social services. As in the case of child welfare, some services are delivered through contracts with voluntary agencies and even group and private practices. Children become involved in the juvenile justice or delinquency system when they commit crimes against property (e.g., theft, vandalism) and against people (e.g., assault) and when they commit status offenses, that is, acts that are offenses because children are minors (e.g., home and school truancy, incorrigibility). Children involved in the child welfare system may also be involved in the juvenile justice system, and maltreated children are at risk of becoming delinquent as they become older (Widom, 1992).

Workers perform case manager, advocate, evaluator, counselor, and educator roles in the delinquency system. However, as in public child welfare, the social work profession has abdicated its responsibility for serving delinquents, a population in dire need of skilled intervention. Many of the workers in delinquency have bachelor's level training in criminal justice rather than master's level training in social work. Criminal justice training may increase the probability their response to youth will be punitive. Research on youth involvement in the delinquency system indicates that recidivism rates are lower when responses are less punitive, even when types of delinquency are controlled for (Greenwood, 1996).

Regardless of the training of the professionals, the knowledge base that delinquency workers draw on relates to their ability to understand deviant behavior and interventions that result in more appropriate behavior. These behaviors include antisocial, noncompliant, and nonconforming behaviors, as well as performance in school and in the workplace.

> The relationship between abuse and delinquency is evident in the Abbott case. Because of James's sexual abuse by Steve, he was vulnerable to sexual activity with an 8-year-old. Indeed, the juvenile justice system is looming large in James's life. Although he states the 8-year-old was the initiator, reportedly, James is being charged because he was older, the younger boy being viewed as James's victim. Jason is also at risk for involvement in the delinquency system because of

his sexual acting out in the afterschool program. His case has been referred to the police.

CONCEPTUAL FRAMEWORKS FOR CHANGE

Direct practice with children builds on a variety of conceptual frameworks, although these are often not well articulated. In addition, as the discussion of settings indicated, conceptual frameworks vary somewhat by the settings in which social workers practice. The frameworks are not necessarily discrete but rather overlapping. In fact, an accomplished social worker will approach a case and/or a problem using more than one framework to pursue change. The frameworks to be discussed here are *attachment, developmental, psychodynamic, behavioral,* and *problem solving.*

An attachment framework. Theories of attachment underlie much of policy and practice in child welfare settings, but related theories about mentoring and role models are frameworks for intervention in school and delinquency settings. These theories posit the importance of primary relationships in psychological well-being (Ainsworth, 1973; Bowlby, 1973; Freud, 1943, 1944; Greenspan, 1981), in adherence to societal norms (e.g., Kotch et al., 1997; Kotlowitz, 1991), and in bringing about change (Faller, 1988).

In child welfare, professionals believe that lack of parental attachment plays an important role in child maltreatment and in the failure of maltreating parents to change as a requirement for keeping their children or having custody returned (Steele, 1976; Thompson, 1981). Furthermore, concerns about breaking parent-child bonds and family attachments are factors that underlie reluctance to place children (Fahlberg, 1979, 1981) and a preference for kinship care.

In child welfare, school, and delinquency programs, numerous interventions are built on assumptions about the importance of primary relationships that may be substitutes for inadequate relationships provided by the child's family. These include foster care, mentoring programs, some recreational programs, and Big Brothers and Big Sisters. Moreover, school social workers, delinquency workers, probation officers, and children's therapists can all be viewed and may function as substitute attachment figures. In one approach to treatment for traumatized and attachment-disordered children, the relationship with the therapist is regarded as fundamental to the child's healing (James, 1989; Karp & Bulter, 1996).

A developmental framework. All social workers must be cognizant of their clients' ages; however, age is especially important with children. Their capacities and their tasks vary markedly depending on developmental stage. Moreover, the younger the child, the more central the child's caretaker is to the intervention. For example, helping infants and preschoolers almost always means helping their parents. In contrast, when working directly with adolescents, social workers may not involve their caretakers and often seek the youth's permission before communicating with caretakers.

Developmental issues are reflected in many ways in work with children. One way is through the use of play, media, or activities when working with children. Whereas for most adults, communication in words is the preferred and most accomplished medium, this is not neces-

sarily so for children. Moreover, as noted above, because children are usually reluctant clients, they may not be disposed to talk about their problems. Media used in direct practice with children may include the dollhouse, dolls, the sand tray, stuffed animals, illustrations, picture drawing, puppets, books, writing, games, and computers. The choice of media will vary depending on the child's developmental stage, the child's interests and talents, and issues the social worker wants to address with the child. These media may be used for direct communication or communication in metaphor. Play or activities have other uses aside from communication in social work with children. For example, they can be used to mediate the impact of discussion of stressful material or to enhance the attractiveness of therapy and the therapist.

Whereas traditional play therapy assumes children, when allowed to play in the presence of a supportive therapist, will work through their problems (Axline, 1947), contemporary play therapists take a more directive approach. They may structure the play by choice of media, by interpreting the child's play or drawing analogies based on it, and by direct involvement in the play (Cattanach, 1992; Gil, 1991; Schaefer, 1994).

Despite the extensive use of play or activities with children, play as a framework for communication and change has not been the subject of extensive study (e.g., Finkelhor & Berliner, 1995). However, research with preschool and school-age children demonstrates the efficacy of communication using anatomical dolls (Everson & Boat, 1997), the utility of computers with young children (Faller & DeVoe, 1995; Steward et al., 1996), and their superiority to verbal and written communication with adolescents (e.g., Bagley & Genuis, 1991).

In the Abbott case, media were used by social workers in their evaluation and treatment with the children. To enhance the attractiveness of therapy for James, Evan played board games with him. Dana used anatomical dolls to gather information about sexual activity among the children when she interviewed Jackson. Lucy observed Jacine's play to assess her developmental level and overall functioning.

A psychodynamic framework. Although the use of play or media can be conceptualized from a developmental perspective, it also can be viewed from a psychodynamic perspective. Axline (1947) saw free play with children as the rough equivalent of free association for adults in psychoanalysis.

More globally, in terms of a psychodynamic approach, the underlying assumptions are that expressing or talking about problems and associated feelings, receiving interpretations from the therapist (e.g., reframing), and obtaining support or affirmation are therapeutic (e.g., Mishne, 1983; Pearce & Pezzot-Pearce, 1997). Once the problem is articulated and feelings expressed, the child can move on to other issues in development and functioning. Much of child treatment that addresses trauma is built on this framework (Conte, Forgarty, & Collins, 1991).

Although there have been efforts to assess client satisfaction with interventions based on a psychodynamic approach, few studies have been controlled (Bonner, Walker, & Berliner, 1994; Finkelhor & Berliner, 1995). However, one of the findings from controlled studies of sexually abused children is that they improve over time whether or not they receive therapy (Berliner & Saunders, 1996).

In the Abbott case, Evan unsuccessfully attempted to get James to talk about his sexual abuse and associated feelings, assuming it would enhance his ability to cope with this experience. It is likely that the reason James engaged in sexual activity with his younger siblings was because he was unable to talk about his feelings about what Steve did to him.

Behavioral and cognitive behavioral frameworks. A lot of direct practice with children is based on behavioral frameworks (e.g., Bloomquist, 1996; Breen & Altepeter, 1990; Mash & Barkley, 1998; Schaefer & Millman, 1981). These include both operant and respondent paradigms and cognitive behavioral models. When behavioral approaches are employed in schools to effect behavior control, attendance, or assignment completion, an operant paradigm usually underlies the intervention. That is, the child is rewarded for appropriate activities and sanctioned for inappropriate activities.

Treatment of child behavior problems in other contexts, such as mental health settings, delinquency programs, and residential treatment facilities, is also based on behavioral or cognitive behavioral frameworks. In addition, with some delinquent populations, for example, adolescent sex offenders, respondent conditioning components are used. Covert sensitization and thought-stopping may be employed as techniques to terminate inappropriate sexual arousal (e.g., Becker & Hunter, 1997).

In the treatment of trauma, cognitive behavioral interventions are often employed (Cohen & Mannarino, 1998; Deblinger & Heflin, 1996; Deblinger, Lippmann, & Steer, 1996; Kolko, 1996), and some respondent techniques are used, for example, stress inoculation and systematic desensitization (Berliner & Saunders, 1996).

With most child populations, behavioral interventions have shown the capacity to effect short-term change (e.g., Friedrich, 1990; Schaeffer & Millman, 1981). The efficacy of behavioral approaches has been demonstrated in a variety of contexts (e.g., the classroom, delinquency programs, mental health settings) and with a range of problems (e.g., aggressive behavior, avoidant behavior, bed-wetting). The challenges are identifying an appropriate adult caretaker to assist in the intervention and sustaining change after formal intervention ceases. A series of controlled studies is now under way to test cognitive behavioral interventions with abused children and their families (Cohen & Mannarino, 1998; Deblinger & Heflin, 1996; Deblinger, Lippmann, & Steer, 1996; Kolko, 1996). Preliminary findings suggest that cognitive behavioral interventions are more effective than nondirective, supportive therapy (Cohen & Mannarino, 1997, 1998).

> In the Abbott case, if James had been able to talk about his abuse and its relationship to his sexual acting out with the 8-year-old, then Evan could have helped James develop some behavioral strategies to prevent subsequent sexual acting out. Because Betina has so many other responsibilities, making her the linchpin in a behavioral intervention with James or her younger children would not likely be successful.

A problem-solving framework. A problem-solving framework undergirds much of social work practice, including that of social workers involved in direct practice with children. It is a process of defining the problem, generating possible solutions, selecting and implementing a solution, and monitoring the results. The involuntariness of child clients is taken into account in this framework, in that both problem definition and solution can be negotiated. Most other frameworks can be recast as problem-solving approaches, including psychodynamic

and behavioral interventions. In addition, a problem-solving framework is compatible with all social work roles and is not primarily limited to roles of evaluator and therapist, a limitation of other frameworks described in this chapter.

> Examples from the Abbott case of the use of a problem-solving framework include the case management interventions employed by Jane and the approach that Evan took to treatment of James. Evan had to negotiate with James the problem he would work on first, his anger.
>
> A problem-solving framework might be used in the future to help Betina with her children's sexual activity. One solution might be using a family session to generate rules that would reinforce boundaries. These could include: (a) only one person in the bathroom at a time, (b) children always wear clothing, (c) each child sleeps in his/her own bed, and (d) older children don't baby-sit for younger ones, at least for now.

CONCLUSION

In this chapter, I have attempted to show that direct practice with children should to take into account the broader context in which children live and that social workers must be flexible if they are to respond appropriately to children's needs. Direct practitioners need to function beyond the dyadic relationship between themselves and the child. This broader concept of practice is widely espoused and is taught in many schools of social work, but it may be undermined in agencies where social workers ultimately practice. One reason for resistance to a broader perspective is that it is antithetical to the way services are generally delivered and to value and philosophical positions held by those responsible for design and delivery of social work and social welfare services.

Future social work practice must take into account the changing face of children in the United States. The population projections suggest that the children of the future will be predominantly children of color. This demographic fact presents opportunities but also poses challenges for direct practice with children. Strategically placed social workers can play pivotal roles in helping children of color celebrate their culture, overcome adversity, and maximize their potential. At the same time, this population likely will be in greater need of a safety net of adequate food, clothing, shelter, and medical care and of education that will assure them a decent start in life, than the current generation of children. Some might argue that direct practitioners should abandon their efforts at individual change and seek more global change on behalf of children. This might be a good strategy if it were likely to be successful, but history suggests it will not be. In the meantime, there are millions of children who cannot be abandoned and require individual attention. Direct practitioners will continue to have a vital mission.

Nevertheless, if direct practice is to be successful with the future population of children, who will be substantially children of color, social workers of color must represent a substantial cohort of practitioners providing this service. Schools of social work must take the lead in recruiting, supporting, and training professionals who can inspire and assist diverse client populations.

Finally, social workers should work in the settings that serve the children most in need. They need to "take back" public child welfare, public mental health, preschool and school settings in disadvantaged communities, and delinquency programs.

NOTE

1. Parent aides act as support persons, friends, and sometimes surrogate parents to maltreating parents. They are usually volunteers who commit to work with one family for a year or more.

REFERENCES

Adoption Assistance and Child Welfare Act (P.L. 96-272). (1980). Washington, DC: Government Printing Office, Child Abuse and Neglect Clearinghouse.

Adoption Assistance and Family Support Act (P.L. 103-). (1994). Washington, DC: Government Printing Office, Child Abuse and Neglect Clearinghouse.

Adoption and Safe Families Act (P.L. 105-89). (1997). Washington, DC: Government Printing Office, Child Abuse and Neglect Clearinghouse.

Ainsworth, M. (1973). The development of infant-mother attachment. In B. Caldwell & R. Biscuitti, (Eds.), *Review of child developmental research* (Vol. 3, pp. 1-94). Chicago: University of Chicago Press.

Albelda, R., Folbre, N., & the Center for Population Economics. (1996). *The war on the poor.* New York: The New Press.

Anthony, J., & Cohler, B. (1988). *The invulnerable child.* New York: Guilford.

Axline, V. (1947). *Play therapy.* New York: Ballentine.

Bagley, C., & Genuis, M. (1991). Psychology of computer use: Sexual abuse recalled: Evaluation of computerized questionnaire in a population of young adult males. *Perceptual and Motor Skills, 72*(1), 287-288.

Barthel, J. (1991). *For children's sake: The promise of family preservation.* New York: Edna McConnell Clark Foundation.

Becker, J., & Hunter, J. (1997). Understanding and treating child and adolescent sex offenders. In T. Oliendick & R. J. Prinz (Eds.) *Advances in clinical child psychology* (Vol. 19, pp. 177-197). New York: Plenum.

Berliner, L., & Saunders, B. (1996). Treating fear and anxiety in sexually abused children: Results of a controlled 2 year follow-up study. *Child Maltreatment, 1*(4), 294-309.

Bloomquist, M. (1996). *Skills training for children with behavior disorders.* New York: Guilford.

Bonner, B., Walker, C. E., & Berliner, L. (1994). *Children with sexual behavior problems* (Grant funded by the National Center on Child Abuse and Neglect, No.

90CA1469). Unpublished manuscript, Oklahoma Health Sciences Center, University of Oklahoma.

Bowlby, J. (1973). *Attachment and loss* (Vols. 1 and 2). New York: Basic Books.

Breen, M., & Altepeter, T. (1990). *Disruptive behavior disorders in children: Treatment-focused assessment.* New York: Guilford.

Cattanach, A. (1992). *Play therapy with abused children.* London: Jessica Kingsley.

Children's Defense Fund. (1997). *Children's Defense Fund budget.* Washington, DC: Author.

Cohen, J., & Mannarino, A. (1997). A treatment study of sexually abused pre-school children: Outcome during one year follow-up. *Journal of the American Academy of Child and Adolescent Psychiatry, 39*(6), 1228-1235.

Cohen, J., & Mannarino, A. (1998). Interventions for sexually abused children: Initial treatment outcome findings. *Child Maltreatment, 3*(1), 17-26.

Conte, J., Forgarty, L., & Collins, M. E. (1991). National survey of professional practice in child sexual abuse. *Journal of Family Violence, 6*(2), 149-166.

Courtney, M. (1998). The costs of child protection in the context of welfare reform. In *The Future of Children: Protecting Children from Abuse and Neglect, 8*(1), 88-103.

Deblinger, E., & Heflin, A. (1996). *Treating sexually abused children and their non-offending parents: A cognitive behavioral approach.* Newbury Park, CA: Sage.

Deblinger, E., Steer, R., & Lippmann, J. (1999). Maternal factors associated with sexually abused children's psychosocial adjustment. *Child Maltreatment, 4*(1), 13-20.

Everson, M., & Boat, B. (1997). Anatomical dolls in child sexual abuse assessments: A call for forensically relevant research. *Applied Cognitive Psychology, 11,* S55-S74.

Fahlberg, V. (1979). *Attachment and separation.* Lansing: Michigan Department of Social Services.

Fahlberg, V. (1981). *Children in placement: Common behavior problems.* Lansing: Michigan Department of Social Services.

Faller, K. C. (1981). *Social work with abused and neglected children.* New York: Free Press.

Faller, K. C. (1985). Unanticipated problems with the United States child protection system. *Child Abuse and Neglect: The International Journal, 9,* 63-69.

Faller, K. C. (1988). *Child sexual abuse: An interdisciplinary manual for diagnosis, case management, and treatment.* New York: Columbia University Press.

Faller, K. C., & DeVoe, E. (1995). *Final report: Computer-assisted interviewing with children who may have been sexually abused.* Available from K. C. Faller, University of Michigan School of Social Work, 1080 S. University, Ann Arbor, MI 48109-1066.

Finkelhor, D., & Berliner, L. (1995). Research on the treatment of sexually abused children: A review and recommendations. *Journal of the American Academy of Child and Adolescent Psychiatry, 34,* 1408-1423.

Forsythe, P. (1992). Homebuilders and family preservation. *Child and Youth Services Review, 14,* 37-47.

Freud, A. (1943). *War and children.* New York: International Universities Press.

Freud, A. (1944). *Infants without families.* New York: International Universities Press.

Friedrich, W. (1990). *Psychotherapy with sexually abused children and their families.* New York: Norton.

Furstenberg, F., & Cherlin, A. (Eds.). (1991). *Divided families: What happens to children when parents part?* Cambridge, MA: Harvard University Press.

Garbarino, J., & Eckenrode, J. (1997). *Understanding abusive families: An ecological approach to theory and practice.* San Francisco: Jossey-Bass.

Gil, E. (1991). *The healing power of play.* New York: Guilford.

Greenspan, S. (1981). *Psychopathology and adaptation in infancy and early childhood.* New York: International Universities Press.

Greenwood, P. (1996). Responding to juvenile crime: Lessons learned. *The Future of Children: The Juvenile Court, 6*(3), 75-85.

Hunter, W., & Knight, E. (1998). *LONGSCAN Research briefs, 1.* Available: http://www.calib.com/nccancn/pubs/Resbrief

James, B. (1989). *Treating traumatized children.* Lexington, MA: Lexington Books.

Karp, C., & Bulter, T. (1996). *Treatment strategies for abused children.* Thousand Oaks, CA: Sage.

Kolko, D. (1998). Treatment efficacy and program evaluation with juvenile sexual abusers. *Child Maltreatment, 3*(4), 362-373.

Kotch, J. B., Browne, D., Ringwalt, C., Dufort, V., Ruina, E., Stewart, P., & Jung, J. W. (1997). Stress, social support, and substantiated maltreatment in the second and third years of life. *Child Abuse & Neglect, 21*(11), 1025-1037.

Kotlowitz, A. (1991). *There are no children here.* New York: Anchor.

Lewitt, E., Terman, D., & Behrman, R. (1997). Children and poverty: Analysis & recommendations. *The Future of Children, 7*(2), 4-24.

Long, S., Clark, S., Ratcliffe, C., & Olson, K. (1998). *Assessing the new federalism* [On-line]. Available: http://newfederalism.urban.org.html

Mahler, M., Pine, F., & Bergman, A. (1975). *The psychological birth of the human infant*. New York: Basic Books.

Mash, E., & Barkley, R. (Eds.). (1998). *Treatment of childhood disorders*. New York: Guilford.

Mishne, J. (1983). *Clinical work with children*. New York: Free Press.

Pearce, J., & Pezzot-Pearce, T. (1997). *Psychotherapy of abused and neglected children*. New York: Guilford.

Plotnick, R. (1997). Childhood poverty can be reduced. *The Future of Children, 7* (2).

Rossi, P. (1992). Assessing family preservation programs. *Child and Youth Services Review, 14*, 77-97.

Schaefer, C. (1994). *Handbook of play therapy*. New York: John Wiley.

Schaefer, C., & Millman, H. (1981). *Therapies for children*. San Francisco: Jossey-Bass.

School-linked services: Research and practice. (1998). Available: http://eric-web.tc.columbia.edu/families/School_Linked/pract. html

Sedlak, A., & Broadhurst, D. (1996). *National incidence study of child abuse and neglect* (NIS-3). Washington, DC: National Clearinghouse on Child Abuse and Neglect.

State of Michigan. (1995). *Children's services employees: Education and years of experience*. Unpublished document available from the Michigan Family Independence Agency.

Steele, B. (1976). *Working with abusive parents from a psychiatric point of view*. Washington, DC: National Clearinghouse on Child Abuse and Neglect.

Steward, M. S., Steward, D. S., Farquhar, L., Myers, J., Welker, J., Joye, N., Driskill, J., & Morgan, J. (1996). *Interviewing young children about body touch and handling* (Monograph series of the Society for Research on Child Development). Chicago: University of Chicago Press.

Thompson, A. (1981). Normal child development. In K. C. Faller (Ed.), *Social work with abused and neglected children* (pp. 219-237). New York: Free Press.

U.S. Department of Health and Human Services. (1998). *Fiscal year 2000* [On-line]. Available: http://www.calib.com/nncanch/pubs/fatality.htm

Wang, C.-T., & Daro, D. (1998). *Current trends in child abuse reporting and fatalities*. Chicago: National Committee to Prevent Child Abuse.

Weissbourd, R. (1996). *The vulnerable child*. New York: Addison-Wesley.

Widom, C. S. (1992). *The cycle of violence*. Washington, DC: National Institute of Justice.

Wilson, W. J. (1987). *The truly disadvantaged: The inner city, the underclass, and public policy*. Chicago: University of Chicago Press.

CHAPTER FOURTEEN

Change in Groups

DAVID E. POLLIO

AARON M. BROWER

MAEDA J. GALINSKY

Group work practice is a mature field, with a long and illustrious history dating back to the beginnings of the profession. It has an extensive and well-developed literature (Garvin, 1997; Schopler & Galinsky, 1995). Analyses of current trends in practice suggest that group work will continue to be a core method of service delivery to most of the populations traditionally served by social workers. Furthermore, various factors, including market forces (e.g., managed care), the push toward treatment-effectiveness and cost-effectiveness in practice, technological innovations that allow increased access to services, and the desire to reach and serve greater numbers of clients all support the conclusion that knowledge of group work practice will become even more important in our future.

This chapter serves two purposes. First, given the increasing prominence of group work as a practice modality in social work, it is critical that all social workers acquire group skills—making it essential for all social workers to be exposed to the current state of group work knowledge and practice modalities. Thus, this chapter will discuss such group work knowledge as the impact of group purposes on group conditions and variations in group practices. This review is intended not to provide readers with in-depth knowledge but rather to expose social work practitioners to the breadth of available groups, key issues relevant to creating successful groups, and issues of group development. (For greater detail on these issues, see Garvin, 1997; Schopler & Galinsky, 1995; Toseland & Rivas, 1998.)

The second purpose of the chapter is to examine current trends and issues in group work practice, research, and theory. This will serve as the springboard from which we can identify issues in group work as we move into the 21st century. Three factors that we believe will have considerable impact on future group work practice are managed care, technological innovations, and empirically validated curriculum-based groups. The last section of this chapter will focus on issues arising from these trends that can present challenges to group workers, such as group confidentiality and worker privilege, the impact of diversity on practice models, and directions in evaluation of group work practice.

GROUP WORK KNOWLEDGE AND CONSTRUCTS

Groups serve as ideal settings for sharing experiences with, giving help to, and taking help from others with similar needs, interests, and goals. Social change actions gather momentum when they are initiated by a group whose members share common experiences and purpose. Group norms, rules, and goals facilitate personal change and growth by providing a supportive and safely challenging atmosphere.

Groups also provide ideal opportunities for creative problem-solving because members can share common experiences and goals while responding to these experiences differently based on their different life situations. Groups also serve as a fertile ground in which to try out solutions and receive feedback from other members. Groups represent a microcosm of society: They provide a safe environment in which individuals can re-create or re-experience aspects of the outside world. Group support can also enhance social action. Furthermore, given the number of individuals requiring services, the economy of being able to work with a number of individuals at once stands as a cogent argument for groups.

Group work practice has a strong foundation that is based on group dynamics and systems theory (Schopler & Galinsky, 1995). Group work practitioners use common methods for intervening at the individual, group, and environmental levels. In addition, all group workers share an appreciation for the mutual aid that develops as members form reciprocal relationships with and responsibilities to each other (Gitterman, 1989). Group work also requires awareness that the group is both the means for service and the setting in which the service takes place (Vinter, 1985). For example, even in an interaction between the group facilitator and a single individual, all other group members observe the interaction (Kurland & Salmon, 1993) and are likely to be influenced by it.

Group Purposes

Group work has been developed for such purposes as treatment, support, education, self-help, recreation, social action, community organization, work, task performance, team meetings, and management. Sometimes, group purpose focuses on facilitating individual change (e.g., treatment, support, education, and self-help) and at other times, on organizational or social change (e.g., social action, community organization, teamwork). Group leadership roles (e.g., facilitator or adviser) and membership issues (e.g., composition for expertise or for similarity of problems) vary based on group purpose.

Groups workers employ different theoretical perspectives, including cognitive behavioral (Rose, 1989, 1998; Rose, Duby, Olenick, & Weston, 1996), psychosocial (Northen, 1988), task (Garvin, 1992), interactionist (Shulman, 1999), humanist (Glassman & Kates, 1990), mutual aid (Steinberg, 1997), and feminist (Butler & Wintram, 1991; Lewis, 1992). The social work literature also reports many examples of groups to address specific issues, including domestic violence (Evans & Shaw, 1993; Tutty & Wagar, 1994), coping with adolescence (Malekoff, 1994, 1997), drug treatment (Jones, 1996), and coping with aging (Brennan, Downes, & Nadler, 1996; McCallion & Toseland, 1995; Ryan & Doubleday, 1995; Toseland, 1990). Recently, the group work literature has seen an increase in groups developed in response to needs of specific populations, including African American men (Fagan & Stevenson, 1995; Franklin, 1999), African American and other adolescents of color (Bilides, 1990, 1992; Lopez, 1990; Salmon-Davis & Davis, 1999; Tannenbaum, 1990), women of color (Lewis & Ford, 1991; Suarez, Lewis, & Clark, 1995), and gays and lesbians (Gambe & Getzel, 1989; Getzel, 1998; Mallon, 1998; Peters, 1997).

One recent trend, noted in the early 1990s (Schopler & Galinsky, 1995), has been an emergence of groups with a focus on both empowerment and individual change. This trend is reflected in both self-empowerment in group work (Berman-Rossi, 1992; Breton, 1995; Gutiérrez & Ortega, 1991) and a recommitment to social action by group workers (Garvin, 1991; Lewis, 1991; Ramey, 1992; Shapiro, 1991; Wood & Middleman, 1991). One increasingly common feature of these groups is that they are designed to incorporate unique strengths of specific populations. For example, in reporting on groups for homeless populations, a number of authors have described how common activities (such as preparing and eating communal meals or playing basketball) can be used to facilitate individual growth and community empowerment at the same time (Berman-Rossi & Cohen, 1988; Breton, 1988, 1994; Cohen, 1994; Cohen & Wagner, 1992; Glasser & Suroviak, 1988; Johnson & Lee, 1994; Martin & Nayowirth, 1988; Pollio, 1995; Pollio, McDonald, & North, 1996; Sachs, 1991). These models focus more on using individual and collective skills for coping with homelessness and less on pathologies of individuals.

This proliferation of groups based on theoretical models and aimed at specific populations and issues increases the richness and appropriateness of group work and thus represents a strength for our field. Furthermore, the focus on empowering populations through group work remains an ongoing significant trend in the literature. As we will discuss later in this chapter, however, the proliferation of theoretical models, especially with specific populations, will require a complementary proliferation of assessment methods that can measure the impact of these models on these populations.

Group Structure

In addition to varying by purpose, groups also vary according to structure. Most groups fall into one of four categories: (a) brief/time-limited with closed membership (e.g., problem-solving groups), (b) brief/time-limited with open membership (e.g., social action committees), (c) long-term with closed membership (e.g., personal growth), and (d) long-term with open membership (e.g., self-help or recreational groups). We shall highlight three issues related to these categories, namely composition, size, and leadership.

Group composition can significantly enhance or decrease a group's chance to reach its goals. One compositional principle is that group members should share some similarity with respect to descriptive characteristics (e.g., color, gender, age) and some heterogeneity with respect to behavioral attributes (e.g., assertiveness, passivity, verbal skills) (Bertcher & Maple, 1985). Although there is some debate in the literature currently about the influence of race and gender on composition (Davis, Cheng, & Strube, 1996), there is a general consensus that we should not create groups in which individuals may feel isolated because of descriptive characteristics (Proctor & Davis, 1994). Additional discussion of diversity will be presented later in this chapter.

Despite some general agreements about desirable sizes for groups, there is no clear guideline for precisely the right size. For groups focusing on individual change, for example, consensus places optimal group size between five and eight individuals (Brown, 1991; Garvin, 1997). For neighborhood or social change groups, however, recommendations on group size vary considerably. Community meetings consisting of large groups of individuals (literally hundreds of participants) can achieve social change goals when these large-group formats are combined with smaller task-specific groupings.

A third dimension along which groups vary is type of leadership. The influence of individual and group needs, cultural considerations, organizational and community contexts, and the leader's preferred style are all considerations for leadership choices. When creating a group, one key decision is whether to have one or more facilitators, with further deliberations on the role that each will assume. Co-leaders present both advantages and challenges to group functioning. Regardless of the number of leaders, decisions must be made in each session concerning when to intervene, how much to intervene, and how much direction to provide.

Groups not led by professionals have proliferated. These include Alcoholics Anonymous-type Twelve Step groups (Powell, 1987) and multifamily psychoeducation groups for family members of individuals who suffer from severe mental illness (Burland, Mayeux, & Gill, 1992). The relationship between social workers and leaderless groups can include referring members to these groups as adjuncts to treatment, consulting with groups about problematic situations, and evaluating group effectiveness. The role of social workers with these groups represents an important issue for the future of group practice (Ephross & Vassil, 1988).

Group Development

Development of positive group interactions, with clear communication patterns and roles, helps to create cohesive units while facilitating positive change in members. Conversely, the development of negative group interactions can lead to antisocial norms and suppression of opinion that can retard goal achievement. Issues for practitioners to consider for the development of their groups include creating shared meanings and norms, developing group cohesion, clarifying member power, sharing leadership, enhancing communication and resolution of conflict, and defining member roles. Readers can supplement the information presented here with more detailed descriptions of these concepts in Sundel, Glasser, Sarri, and Vinter (1985) and Cartwright and Zander (1968).

Charting the stages of group development has generated much interest and study. The classic view is that groups go through a sequence of stages of development and that worker and group tasks and themes vary based on the stage of development. Garland, Jones, and Kolodny (1976) and Sarri and Galinsky (1985) provide two classic conceptualizations of group development. These models include stages of pre-affiliation, formation, power and control, intimacy and differentiation, and separation. Tuckman (1965; Tuckman & Jensen, 1977) focuses on task and interpersonal features, identifying their developmental stages as forming, storming, norming, performing, and adjourning.

Although these models suggest that group development is a sequential process, research finds many variations, with a number of factors influencing the variety of ways in which groups develop. For example, in open-ended groups where there is a slow infusion of new members, groups go through a cyclical set of stages (Moreland & Levine, 1982). Galinsky and Schopler (1989a) describe variations in group development and possible worker interventions based on the amount and frequency of change in open-ended groups. Furthermore, empirical evidence has found that some groups, rather than going through a linear development process, go through several cycles repeated throughout the life of the group (Garvin, 1998; Worchel, 1994). Brower (1986) found that

groups will progress through their stages at different rates and in different sequences based on the content of their discussions (see also Wheelan & Kaeser, 1997). Schiller (1997) has argued that groups composed entirely of women may have different stages of development than groups of men. The ongoing increase in sophistication of understanding group development has significant impact on interventions across the life of the group. Glassman and Kates (1993), for example, write about how the appropriateness of interventions will differ according to stages of group development.

We wish to highlight one final area of research related to group development that draws from a literature variously labeled constructivism, social constructionism, and social cognition. This body of research describes and explains how we attend to cues from situations, how we put these cues together to form an understanding of the situation, and how we respond to what we see and understand ("meaning making"). Constructivism has been characterized as being the flip side to the old saying, "seeing is believing"—that is, from a constructivist point of view, "believing is seeing" (see Brower & Nurius, 1993, and Franklin & Nurius, 1998, for summaries of this research applied to social work).

Nowhere is the phenomenon of meaning-making more clearly seen, and more essential to understand, than in groups—where the group modality forces members to develop a shared understanding of the group setting (Llewelyn & Dunnett, 1987; Nye & Brower, 1996). Many small-group dynamics processes, particularly those of cohesion, development, norm setting, and boundary setting, can be understood using constructivist language and concepts. One aspect of group cohesion, for example, results from group members creating a shared understanding of events in their group. In addition, these reinterpretations of classic small-group dynamics can be directly and effectively communicated to group members to help them make sense of their own behaviors and the behaviors of others in their group (Brower, 1996).

Intervention Processes

Group workers use the following set of intervention processes: composition, assessment, goal setting and contracting, programming, evaluation, and termination (Schopler & Galinsky, 1995). The guidelines for using these processes are derived from social work values, group work practice theory, group work research, practice wisdom, concepts and findings from the social sciences, and group approaches developed in such other professional areas as group psychotherapy and counseling.

Composition of groups draws on knowledge of the kinds of skills and attributes a group requires to carry out its purposes, the ways subgroups form, and the dangers that come from having too few members who share crucial attributes. Current realities of group work practice lead to the possibility that the group worker may have too few members to draw on to create the "best" group; therefore, workers must employ interventions to compensate for compositional problems.

Assessment requires attention to how the group is developing, members' problems and strengths, how well members are attaining their goals, and how the environment affects the group. The group worker can use assessment instruments that have been developed for practice with individuals but must also devise ways to assess *group* conditions, such as the ways

members communicate, experience attraction or rejection, create norms, and resolve conflicts.

Group workers help members formulate goals and contracts that facilitate what will be worked on and how their work will take place. Group workers strive to be creative in this process with individuals who find this task difficult because of their age, psychological status, or previous experience. Members in involuntary or social control groups may be particularly resistant to forming goals because of legal or social pressure to be there (Garvin, 1997).

Group workers have been in the forefront of developing program tools for and with group members. These have included the use of music, dance, drama, role-playing, food preparation, and trips away from the agency. These program tools are used to help build cohesiveness, new means of communication, deeper ways to understand member concerns, and creative problem solving.

The way the group worker assists the group, when some or all members are ready to leave, is crucial to the ultimate success of the group. Members are helped at this time to again evaluate the group experience, cope with feelings of loss, reinforce gains, and plan for how they will use resources in the future.

CURRENT TRENDS IN GROUP WORK PRACTICE

Three trends that are receiving increasing emphasis are the move to managed care, the development of technology, and the pressure to develop effective practice models. These trends represent challenges and opportunities to group workers, particularly those working in treatment and community settings. Understanding the tensions that group workers experience as they respond to these trends gives us more insight into these critical issues.

Managed Care and Time-Limited Models

Market-driven service delivery may represent the single greatest challenge to social work. Increasingly, social workers of all types are being asked to make do with less. At the same time, although group workers report being discouraged by having to cope with these changes (Zimet, 1997), there is growing recognition that groups can play an increased role in the managed care environment (Budman, 1996; Crosby & Sabin, 1995; Steenbarger & Budman, 1996). We shall also discuss brief and time-limited models—a trend in group work that is fueled at least partially by managed care market forces.

Programmatic opportunities. Programmatic strategies have been created by group workers to respond to pressures from the managed care market (Winegar, Bistline, & Sheridan, 1992). For example, Crosby and Sabin (1995, 1996) highlight the ways group services can be provided in a health maintenance organization (HMO): having a clinical group coordinator, screening for appropriate groups at intake, developing clear group referral criteria, and developing an array of group treatment models.

However, although the potential for increasing group services on a programmatic level can be an opportunity, the market force of managed care creates clear challenges. One challenge is that managed care administrators ration treatment—deciding who gets services, what services are provided, and how much or how many units of service are given. (Many managed care administrators themselves are nonprofessionals whose performance is evaluated on how effectively they limit service access.) This is a particular challenge for group workers, as group work is often viewed as a supplement to individual treatment (Rosenberg & Zimet, 1995). Group workers are faced with the need to reframe groups as a core service.

When groups are the primary service options, as is the case in some managed care programs, pressures exist to compose groups based on client availability rather than optimal characteristics. Furthermore, most managed care situations require individuals to begin groups within a short period of time, further pressuring workers to compose groups from available clients or to enroll individuals in existing groups without regard to goodness of fit.

Another challenge for managed care-based group work lies in the fact that reimbursement (particularly insurance) drives service development. Many of social work's traditional populations (e.g., individuals and families in extreme poverty, children in school systems) have little or no access to insurance-driven services, and many group types (e.g., recreational, prevention, or community action groups) have limited potential for reimbursement. Therefore, opportunities for involvement in these groups may decrease. As social workers, we have a duty to resist these limitations of managed care services by advocating for the insuring of marginalized populations and the inclusion of prevention and other group types as part of covered treatments.

Short-term and brief models. Hand in hand with the impact of managed care on group practice is the increasing importance of short-term and brief group models. Brief group models have been reported in the social work literature for a variety of populations, such as sexual abuse (de Jong & Gorey, 1996), sexual high-risk behavior (Flowers, Miller, Smith, & Booraem, 1994), divorce (Charping, Bell, & Strecker, 1992), mental illness (Mailick, 1984; Turnbull, Galinsky, Wilner, & Meglin, 1994; Wolozin & Dalton, 1990), physical illness (Ebenstein, 1998), pain management (Rose & Subramanian, 1986), and employee stress (Gladstone & Reynolds, 1997). Both multimethod (Rose, 1989, 1998) and task-centered group approaches (Garvin, 1985, 1992; Garvin, Reid, & Epstein, 1978) provide empirical support for the effectiveness of interventions that are time-limited and problem-specific.

One current issue concerns the precise definition of *brief* or *time-limited* treatment. Brief can range from single-session models (Ebenstein, 1998; Flowers et al., 1994; Gladstone & Reynolds, 1997; Turnbull et al., 1994) to those lasting 18 months (Budman, Cooley, et al., 1996; Budman, Demby, Soldz, & Merry, 1996). A general review of current models suggests that most last between 8 and 16 sessions. MacKenzie (1994), in summarizing treatment effectiveness of psychotherapy in general (including group treatment), posits the existence of an asymptote of effective gains at about the 8-session mark. He further notes that at this point about 80% of all individuals have dropped out of treatment. These results can provide guidance when determining the length of group treatment: 8 sessions might be the most useful unit for brief treatment.

Another issue in brief group treatment is the seeming paradox of providing rationed services to individuals suffering from chronic condi-tions. Although brief treatment for populations with chronic illness seems paradoxical, group treatments focusing on limited issues and acute exacerbations (e.g., periods of inpatient treatment) have suggested that true brief models for these populations represent an appropriate treatment option (Ebenstein, 1998). In addition, Hardy and Lewis (1992) present an intriguing model for combining short-term and long-term groups. They construct their intervention around a segmented approach—providing a series of 12-week, time-limited groups that members may rejoin after an appropriate hiatus. Group workers can also play a role in facilitating referrals to groups outside of a managed care system. For example, they may refer clients to no-cost, long-term, self-help groups. Finding creative ways to provide focused, brief groups for those with chronic conditions represents a way for practitioners to provide continuing services in the managed care framework.

The issue of integrating brief group models into longer-term work has repercussions for service provision in general. For example, issues of further limiting services to populations with little access (a traditional population for social work) become an even greater challenge facing social workers in general. Although market forces are currently driving the emergence of short-term or brief group models, these models will remain even if managed care no longer provides an impetus for these groups. Increased emphasis on accountability and the easy dissemination of these types of models across agencies and environments, along with evidence of their effectiveness, argue for the increasing prominence of short-term and brief models within group work as it moves into the 21st century.

Technology and Group Work

In recent years, social workers and other human service professionals have used technology-based group work services for education, support, treatment, and enhancement of organizational functioning. Group work practice is likely to rely more on technology in the future. As advances in technology occur, it will increasingly become possible for groups of people to be connected across time and space. We will describe how technology-based groups have been used in practice, their advantages and disadvantages, and the development of theory for technology-based groups.

Technology-based groups in practice. Since the late 1970s, groups employing telephone conferencing have been used for a variety of purposes (Schopler, Abell, & Galinsky, 1998). Populations that have been served in this manner include the blind elderly (Evans & Jauregy, 1982; Thomas & Urbano, 1993), people with physical disabilities (Evans, Smith, Werkhoven, Fox, & Pritzl, 1986; Kennard & Shilman, 1979), people affected by HIV disease (Meier, Galinsky, & Rounds, 1995; Rittner & Hammons, 1992; Roffman et al., 1997; Rounds, Galinsky, & Despard, 1995; Wiener, 1998; Wiener, Spencer, Davidson, & Fair, 1993), cancer patients (Colon, 1996), and patients with multiple sclerosis (Stein, Rothman, & Nakanishi, 1993). Computer groups have been used with caregivers of people with dementia (Brennan, Moore, & Smyth, 1992; Smyth & Harris, 1993), breast cancer patients (Weinberg, Schmale, Uken, & Wessel, 1996), seriously ill hospitalized children (Holden, Bearison, Rode, Rosenberg, & Fishman, 1999), social workers

experiencing stress (Meier, 1997), and adults in group psychotherapy (Colon, 1998). Computer self-help groups have also been used with survivors of sexual abuse as an adjunct to their individual treatment (Finn & Lavitt, 1994).

The advantages of using technologically based groups are their accessibility, convenience, and anonymity (Galinsky, Schopler, & Abell, 1997; Schopler, Galinsky, & Abell, 1997). These features enable those who live in rural areas, those who fear stigma, and those who are homebound to obtain help and support. People often share information more easily and form relationships more quickly due to the anonymity these groups offer. There are also possibilities for creative programming through the use of computer games and interactive educational sessions.

Technology-based groups also have limitations, such as fewer interpersonal cues, difficulties with the use of technology, and problems with group process (Galinsky et al., 1997; Schopler et al., 1997). For example, participants must have access to telephones and computers. Lack of confidentiality of computer records may be a problem, and organizations may need additional resources to manage the technology. Members have a greater opportunity to deceive each other or not join in when they cannot see and/or hear each other.

Theory development for technology-based groups. Group work theory designed for use with face-to-face groups forms a foundation for practice with technology-based groups; however, group work theorists have begun to examine the unique features of technology-based groups and to design models of group work practice that will be appropriate for technology-based groups (Schopler et al., 1998). Although we have combined the examination of telephones and computers here, there are important distinctions between them, such as the types of social cues available to participants, and practice theory must take such distinctions into account. More fine-grained variations within each medium need to be examined as well; for example, there are differences in computer groups among listservs, discussion forums, and chat rooms.

Social psychologists are increasing their study of technology-based groups. Especially relevant to the development of practice theory are the concepts of social presence and social impact (e.g., Latane & Todd, 1996; Walther & Burgoon, 1992) and those of deindividuation and social loafing (e.g., Connolly, Jessup, & Valacich, 1990; Kiesler & Sproull, 1992; Siegel, Dubrovsky, Kiesler, & McGuire, 1986). Other aspects of computer groups are receiving greater attention, such as aspects of group development (Bordia, DiFonzo, & Chang, 1999), social support (Mickelson, 1997), feedback (McKenna & Bargh, 1998), communications (Walther, 1996), and social networks (Wellman, 1997). As group work practice theory is extended to technology-based groups, it will increasingly rely on the findings of this social science literature to build a theoretical base and establish practice theory. Using knowledge of traditional group work theory and practice, distinctive features of technology-based groups, and the social science literature, Schopler et al. (1998) have begun to formulate principles of practice specifically tailored to technology-based groups.

This review has concentrated on groups designed to meet the needs of individual clients. However, technology-based groups can also be employed within organizations and to connect organizations and communities with one another (e.g., Boiney, 1998; Calhoun, 1986; Schoech, Cavalier, & Hoover, 1993). Task completion, team decision making, and problem-solving are examples of this application of technology (Graetz, Boyle, Kimble, Thompson, & Garloch, 1998; Hedlund, Ilgen, & Hollenbeck, 1998; Hollingshead & McGrath, 1995; Hollingshead, McGrath, & O'Connor, 1993).

Additional technological formats. Although we have highlighted the use of computers and telephones, other forms of technology link people together—for example, voice mail groups for people with severe and persistent mental illness have been described by Craig (1997). As technology is further advanced and becomes less expensive to use, visual images of participants may be used in conjunction with the telephone and the computer, audio effects may be linked to computers, and other technological formats will undoubtedly be developed for group work practice.

Empirically Validated and Curriculum-Based Groups

Determining what works in clinical practice, a trend that occurs concurrently with the push toward managed care but is in many ways independent of it, has become a multidisciplinary imperative. Two primary trends in the literature appear to reflect group work's response to this: using curriculum-based models and determining treatment integrity and generalizability.

Curriculum-based models. The literature increasingly contains descriptions of curriculum-based group models, such as those for families with an adult member with severe mental illness (Hogarty et al., 1986; North et al., 1998; Pollio, North, & Foster, 1998; Solomon, Draine, Mannion, & Meisel, 1997), families with children with disorders (McKay, Gonzalez, Stone, Ryland, & Kohner, 1995; McKay, Nudelman, McCadam, & Gonzalez, 1996; Rhodes, 1995; Stone, McKay, & Stoops, 1996), elderly populations and their caretakers (Ryan & Doubleday, 1995; Walker, Pomeroy, McNeil, & Franklin, 1994), families of color (Bentelspacher, DeSilva, Goh, & LaRowe, 1996; Jordan, Lewellen, & Vandiver, 1995), children (Fraser, Nash, Galinsky, & Darwin, in press; Rose, 1998), and populations with HIV/AIDS (Pomeroy, Kiam, & Abel, 1999; Pomeroy, Rubin, Van Laningham, & Walker, 1997; Roffman et al., 1997; Subramanian, Hernandez, & Martinez, 1995). Many of these curricula carry an educational or psychoeducational label (Brown, 1998). Their distinguishing features are incorporation of educational content (usually in every session); focus on problem solving, skill development, and prevention; and inclusion of elements encouraging the development of mutual support.

Treatment integrity and generalizability. In using these curricula, treatment integrity may vary significantly. In addition, models may have limited generalizability or may be less effective when transferred to other populations not intended by the developers. When generalizing PACT (Program of Assertive Community Treatment, a team treatment of people with mental illness), for example, researchers found that implementation in different environments led to model changes, many of which were associated with decreased effectiveness (McGrew, Bond, Dietzen, & Salyers, 1994).

The issue of treatment integrity is particularly problematic for group workers. Traditionally, group work has incorporated respect for practitioner acumen as well as client wishes. Although many of the aforementioned models allow for periods of interpersonal processing, group workers understand that groups often come to take on a life of their own. This creates a treatment integrity dilemma for the replication of group work models. How and when should groups diverge from established models? Incorporating the opportunity for some degree of flexibility into the curriculum is one means of addressing this dilemma.

CRITICAL ISSUES

A number of issues have emerged from the discussion to this point that will have a crucial impact on the future development of group work. Increasing third-party reimbursements, concurrent increase in likelihood of legal involvement about treatment decisions and payment, and privacy in cyberspace require a serious consideration of confidentiality and privilege. Changes in population demography highlight the need to deepen our understanding of issues related to diversity in group work practice. Finally, the move toward accountability and the need to develop empirically valid models lead to emphasis on evaluation and empirical methods in group work.

Confidentiality and Privilege

Confidentiality and privilege represent linked issues that have received scant attention by group work practitioners (Northen, 1998). Although social workers have an ethical duty to present and discuss issues of confidentiality, limitations of member confidentiality and rules for privileged communication at a group level represent an important challenge for social workers (VanWinkle, 1998).

Group workers rarely inform members about the limits of confidentiality (Roback, Ochoa, Block, & Purdon, 1992), often out of a concern that doing so will discourage new members from participating (Applebaum & Greer, 1993; Roback, Moore, Block, & Shelton, 1996). Complexities of confidentiality for groups within settings in which participants have interactions across a variety of settings (e.g., support groups in community centers) must be carefully considered. When subgroups are likely to have the opportunity to congregate outside the group, assuring that what's said in the group stays within the group is particularly difficult.

Group workers have an ethical duty to discuss confidentiality and privileged communication early in the group and to emphasize their relevance for the group worker, members, and the agency as a whole (Congress & Lynn, 1997; Dolgoff & Skolnick, 1992). Congress and Lynn (1997) delineate three useful guidelines for group confidentiality: (a) discuss confidentiality and related issues early, (b) develop an explicit group norm for confidentiality, and (c) continue to revisit and refine confidentiality over the life span of the group. Furthermore, it is necessary to include worker privilege and its limitations in this ongoing discussion.

The legal issue of worker-client privilege is difficult to define, primarily because levels of protection vary from state to state. Group workers often mistakenly presume that group members are protected in much the same manner as individual clients (Parker, Clevenger, & Sherman, 1997). Although the vast majority of states have laws on legal protection in therapeutic dyads (*Jaffe v. Redmond,* 1996; Klein, 1995), these statutes and case law are generally silent on privilege in group situations. In a few states, privilege has been extended for both therapists and group members to group therapy situations (Parker et al., 1997). Although case law on privilege varies, a number of recent decisions appear to support the inclusion of group therapy under counselor-client statutes. The current situation is in sufficient flux that group workers should closely monitor regulatory statutes and legal case law at state and federal levels.

In delineating future directions for discussions of worker confidentiality and privilege, it is necessary to consider how these issues intersect with technology-based groups. The point often made in the media is that it is impossible to assure electronic confidentiality. Technology makes information available to people not at all involved in the group (e.g., hackers entering private cyberspace). Furthermore, privilege has much less meaning when on-line discussions are available to outside parties. Some researchers have given attention to this issue. Roffman et al. (1997), for example, protects his users by having them choose pseudonyms when participating in telephone groups.

Diversity

Changes in population demography suggest that issues of incorporating diversity into group work are becoming even more central—workers can now anticipate that addressing issues of multicultural membership in groups will be necessary in all settings. Issues of race, gender, and sexual orientation (Schopler & Galinsky,

1995) are increasingly addressed in the group work literature.

McLeod, Lobel, and Cox (1996) found that ideas generated by ethnically diverse groups were judged to be of higher quality than those of homogeneous European American groups. They concluded that heterogeneity in composition along dimensions of ethnicity improves production of ideas relevant to ethnicity. Recent research suggests that groups composed along single dimensions of diversity (e.g., only African American men versus men and women) may limit group process and options. Davis and colleagues (1996), for example, found that racial group composition had a unique impact on members' perceptions about the group but that there were significant differences in findings between male-only and female-only groups. Incorporating unique strengths and capabilities of members into groups with homogeneous membership represents an important future challenge to group workers. To further inform group practitioners, however, future research should delineate the advantages as well as the consequences of homogeneous group composition.

Social workers also need to be educated in culturally competent practice and to develop conceptual models of racially and ethnically sensitive group work. One recent construct that synthesizes the various issues facing diverse groups is the Recognize, Anticipate, Problem-solve (RAP) model (Davis, Galinsky, & Schopler, 1995; Schopler, Galinsky, Davis, & Despard, 1996). The RAP model represents a significant step forward in working with issues of race in multicultural group settings in that it presents a framework for addressing issues of race in group practice situations. Further development and testing of the RAP model and development of similar models (e.g., Chau, 1992)

focusing on other types of diversity (as well as multiple categories of diversity at the same time) are important directions for future research.

Although the need for diversity is clear and the importance of incorporating this issue into practice has been stated repeatedly, the sum of knowledge about issues of diversity remains limited. This is true of social work in general, and it is especially true in group work. Generally speaking, only a few major works on diversity are discussed in current group work texts (e.g., Davis, 1984; Davis & Proctor, 1989; Proctor & Davis, 1994), and only a few basic issues are presented. It is critical in our multicultural society to continue to increase the sophistication of our conceptual and practice models for groups and to pay increasing attention to diversity in small-group research.

Current Directions in Evaluation

We have argued throughout this chapter that research and knowledge development play an increasingly important role in group work. Previous researchers have noted a gradual increase in the number and sophistication of methods for small-group evaluations (Brower & Garvin, 1989; Magen, 1995; Rose & Tolman, 1994; Tolman & Molidar, 1994). Recent group work research, however, no longer reflects Tolman and Molidar's (1994) conclusion that empirical group work is largely cognitive behavioral group work, as there is a trend toward evaluating group practice derived from a variety of theoretical orientations. Nevertheless, the majority of reports do not include rigorous evaluations.

Evaluation of group work practice effectiveness cannot focus exclusively on outcomes. As we have noted repeatedly, groups are uniquely influenced by within-group dynamics. Group work evaluation, therefore, should incorporate attention to group processes. A recent review has argued that researchers are indeed increasingly focusing their attention on the role played by group processes in outcomes (Magen, 1995), although this attention is still sporadic and generally poorly operationalized.

Group work evaluation needs to include attention to appropriate research designs (Brower & Garvin, 1989), using outcome measures with established reliability and validity, providing clear descriptions of interventions, and attending to group-level and process measurements (e.g., Kacen & Rozovski, 1998; Macgowan, 1997, in press). Although we believe in the importance of incorporating rigorous evaluation methods, we also recognize the real challenges in doing so—challenges that may discourage even motivated and evaluation-minded group workers. Given increasing pressures for accountability, we recommend that group workers incorporate some form of systematic collection of data into their work. This information can be gathered through case studies or pilot studies and can use qualitative interviews, standardized evaluation instruments, or data already available in records.

TOWARD THE 21ST CENTURY

We have delineated a number of issues that will continue to require attention and resolution as we move into the 21st century. We have highlighted a number of trends and critical issues facing group work and have noted the increasing number of group models available to practitioners. We have described the challenges and opportunities inherent in managed care and ar-

gued that the trend toward brief treatment is likely to continue—even without the impetus of rationed services. We have illustrated the increasing importance of technology to group practice. In addition, we have advocated for the incorporation of empirical methods of knowledge development and practice evaluation.

Critical to the continued success of group work will be practitioners who not only respond to current trends in the field of social work but also have strong voices in determining its direction. We need to build on our traditions while we create new pathways into the future.

REFERENCES

Applebaum, P. S., & Greer, A. (1993). Confidentiality in group therapy. *Law and Psychiatry, 44*(4), 311-312.

Bentelspacher C. E., DeSilva E., Goh, T. L. C., & LaRowe, K. D. (1996). A process evaluation of the cultural compatibility of psychoeducational family group treatment with ethnic Asian clients. *Social Work with Groups, 19*(3/4), 41-59.

Berman-Rossi, T. (1992). Empowering groups through understanding stages of group development. *Social Work with Groups, 15*(2/3), 239-255.

Berman-Rossi T., & Cohen M. B. (1988). Group development and shared decision making: Working with homeless mentally ill women. *Social Work with Groups, 11*(4), 63-78.

Bertcher H. J., & Maple F. (1985). Elements and issues in group composition. In M. Sundel, P. Glasser, R. Sarri, & R. Vinter (Eds.), *Individual change through small groups* (pp. 180-202). New York: Free Press.

Bilides, D. G. (1990). Race, color, ethnicity, and class: Issues of biculturalism in school-based adolescent counseling groups. *Social Work with Groups, 13*(4), 43-58.

Bilides, D. G. (1992). Reaching inner-city children: A group work program model for a public middle school. *Social Work with Groups, 15*(2/3), 129-144.

Boiney, L. G. (1998). Reaping the benefits of information technology in organizations: A framework for guiding appropriation of group support systems. *Journal of Applied Behavioral Science, 34*(3), 327-346.

Bordia, P., DiFonzo, N., & Chang, A. (1999). Rumor as group problem-solving: Development patterns in informal computer-mediated groups. *Small Group Research,* *30*(1), 8-28.

Brennan F., Downes, D., & Nadler, S. (1996). A support group for spouses of nursing home residents. *Social Work with Groups, 19*(3/4), 71-82.

Brennan, P. F., Moore, S. M., & Smyth, K. A. (1992). Alzheimer's disease caregivers' uses of a computer network. *Western Journal of Nursing Research, 14*(5), 662-673.

Breton, M. (1988). The need for mutual aid groups in a drop-in center for homeless women: The Sistering case. *Social Work with Groups, 11*(4), 47-61.

Breton, M. (1994). On the meaning of empowerment and empowerment-oriented social work practice. *Social Work with Groups, 17*(3), 23-37.

Breton, M. (1995). The potential for social action in groups. *Social Work with Groups, 18*(2/3), 5-14.

Brower, A. M. (1986). Behavior changes in psychotherapy groups: A study using an empirically based statistical model. *Small Group Behavior, 17*(2), 164-185.

Brower, A. M. (1996). Group development as constructed social reality revisited: The constructivism of small groups. *Families in Society, 77*(6), 336-344.

Brower, A. M., & Garvin, C. D. (1989). Design issues in social work group research. *Social Work with Groups, 12*(3), 91-102.

Brower, A. M., & Nurius, P. S. (1993). *Social cognition and individual change.* Newbury Park, CA: Sage.

Brown, L. N. (1991). *Groups for growth and change.* New York: Longman.

Brown, N. W. (1998). *Psychoeducational groups.* Bristol PA: Accelerated Development.

Budman, S. H. (1996). Introduction to special section on group therapy and managed care. *International Journal of Group Psychotherapy, 46*(3), 293-295.

Budman, S. H., Cooley, S., Demby, A., Koppenaal, G., Koslof, J., & Powers, T. (1996). A model of time-effective group psychotherapy for patients with personality disorders: The clinical model. *International Journal of Group Psychotherapy, 6*(3), 329-354.

Budman, S. H., Demby, A., Soldz, S., & Merry, J. (1996). Time-limited group psychotherapy for patients with personality disorders: Outcomes and drop-outs. *International Journal of Group Psychotherapy, 46*(3), 357-376.

Burland, J. C., Mayeux, D. M., & Gill, D. (1992). *Journey of hope family education and support.* Baton Rouge, LA: Alliance for the Mentally Ill.

Butler, S., & Wintram, C. (1991). *Feminist groupwork.* London: Sage.

Calhoun, C. (1986). Computer technology, large-scale social integration, and the local community. *Urban Affairs Quarterly, 22,* 329-349.

Cartwright, D., & Zander, A. (1968). *Group dynamics: Research and theory* (3rd ed.). Evanston, IL: Row, Peterson.

Charping, J. W., Bell, W. J., & Strecker, J. B. (1992). Issues related to the use of short-term groups for adjustment to divorce: A comparison of programs. *Social Work with Groups, 15*(4), 15-41.

Chau, K. L. (1992). Needs assessment for group work with people of color: A conceptual formulation. *Social Work with Groups, 15*(2/3), 53-66.

Cohen, M. B. (1994). Who wants to chair the meeting? Group development and leadership patterns in a community action group of homeless people. *Social Work with Groups, 17*(1/2), 71-88.

Cohen, M. B., & Wagner, D. (1992). Acting on their own behalf: Affiliation and political mobilization among homeless people. *Journal of Sociology and Social Welfare, 19*(4), 21-39.

Colon, Y. (1996). Telephone support groups: A nontraditional approach to reaching under-served cancer patients. *Cancer Practice, 4*(3), 156-159.

Colon, Y. (1998). Chatt(er)ing through the fingertips: Doing groups online. In J. Fink (Ed.), *How to use computers and cyberspace in the clinical practice of psychotherapy* (pp. 61-68). Northvale, NJ: Jason Aronson.

Congress, E. P., & Lynn, M. (1997). Group work practice in the community: Navigating the slippery slope of ethical dilemmas. *Social Work with Groups, 20*(3), 61-74.

Connolly, T., Jessup, L. M., & Valacich, J. S. (1990). Effects of anonymity and evaluative tone on idea generation in computer-mediated groups. *Management Science, 36,* 689-703.

Craig, J. (1997). Convening groups on "voice-mail" systems. *Social Work with Groups Newsletter, 12*(3), 13.

Crosby, G., & Sabin, J. E. (1995). Developing and marketing time-limited groups. *Psychiatric Services, 46*(1), 7-8.

Crosby, G., & Sabin, J. E. (1996). A planning check-list for establishing time-limited psychotherapy groups. *Psychiatric Services, 47*(1), 25-26.

Davis, L. E. (1984). The essential components of group work with black Americans. *Social Work with Groups, 7*(3), 95-109.

Davis, L. E., Cheng, L. C., & Strube, M. J. (1996). Differential effects of racial composition on male and female groups: Implications for group work practice. *Social Work Research, 20*(3), 157-166.

Davis, L. E., Galinsky, M. J., & Schopler, J. H. (1995). RAP: A framework for leading multiracial groups. *Social Work, 40*(2), 155-165.

Davis, L. E., & Proctor, E. K. (1989). *Race, gender, and class: Guidelines for practice with individuals, families, and groups.* Englewood Cliffs NJ: Prentice Hall.

de Jong, T. L., & Gorey, K. M. (1996). Short-term versus long-term group work with female survivors of childhood sexual abuse: A brief meta-analytic review. *Social Work with Groups, 19*(1), 19-27.

Dolgoff, R., & Skolnick, L. (1992). Ethical decision making, the NASW code of ethics, and group work practice: Beginning explorations. *Social Work with Groups, 15*(4), 99-112.

Ebenstein, H. (1998). Single-session groups: Issues for social workers. *Social Work with Groups, 21*(1/2), 49-60.

Ephross, P. H., & Vassil, T. V. (1988). *Groups that work: Structure and process.* New York: Columbia University Press.

Evans, D., & Shaw, W. (1993). A social group work model for latency aged children from violent homes. *Social Work with Groups, 16*(1/2), 97-116.

Evans, R. L., & Jaureguy, B. M. (1982). Group therapy by phone: A cognitive behavioral program for visually impaired elderly. *Social Work in Health Care, 7*(2), 79-89.

Evans, R. L., Smith, K. M. S., Werkhoven, W. S., Fox, H. R., & Pritzl, D. O. (1986). Cognitive telephone group therapy with physically disabled elderly persons. *Gerontologist, 26*, 8-10.

Fagan, J., & Stevenson, H. (1995). Men as teachers: A self-help program on parenting for African American men. *Social Work with Groups, 17*(4), 29-42.

Finn, J., & Lavitt, M. (1994). Computer-based self-help for survivors of sexual abuse. *Social Work with Groups, 17*(1/2), 21-47.

Flowers, J. V., Miller, T. E., Smith, N., & Booraem, C. D. (1994). The repeatability of a single-session group to promote safe sex behavior in a male at-risk population. *Research on Social Work Practice, 4*(2), 240-247.

Franklin, A. J. (1999). Therapeutic support groups for African American men. In L. E. Davis (Ed.), *Working with African American males: A guide to practice* (pp. 5-14). Thousand Oaks, CA: Sage.

Franklin, C., & Nurius, P. S. (1998). *Constructivism in practice: Methods and challenges.* Milwaukee, WI: Families International.

Fraser, M. W., Nash, J. K., Galinsky, M. J., & Darwin, K. M. (in press). *Making choices: Social problem-solving skills for children.* Washington, DC: NASW Press.

Galinsky, M. J., & Schopler, J. H. (1989a). Developmental patterns in open-ended groups. *Social Work with Groups, 12*(2), 99-114.

Galinsky, M. J., & Schopler, J. H. (1989b). The social work group. In J. B. P. Schaffer & M. J. Galinsky (Eds.),

Models of group therapy (pp. 18-40). Englewood Cliffs, NJ: Prentice Hall.

Galinsky, M. J., Schopler, J. H., & Abell, M. D. (1997). Connecting members through technology: Telephone and computer groups. *Health and Social Work, 22*(3), 181-188.

Gambe, R., & Getzel, G. S. (1989). Group work with gay men with AIDS. *Social Casework, 70*(3), 172-179.

Garland, J. A., Jones, H. E., & Kolodny, R. L. (1976). A model for stages of group development. In S. Bernstein (Ed.), *Explorations in group practice* (pp. 17-71). Boston: Charles River Books.

Garvin, C. D. (1985). Task-centered groups. In A. Fortune (Ed.), *Task-centered practice with families and groups.* New York: Springer.

Garvin, C. D. (1991). Barriers to effective social action by groups. *Social Work with Groups, 14*(3/4), 65-76.

Garvin, C. D. (1992). A task-centered group approach to work with the chronically mentally ill. *Social Work with Groups, 15*(2/3), 67-80.

Garvin, C. D. (1997). *Contemporary group work* (3rd ed.). Englewood Cliffs, NJ: Prentice Hall.

Garvin, C. D. (1998). *Potential impact of small group research on social group work practice.* Unpublished manuscript.

Garvin, C. D., Reid, W., & Epstein, L. (1978). A task-centered approach. In R. W. Roberts & H. Northen (Eds.), *Theories of social work with groups.* New York: Free Press.

Getzel, G. S. (1998). Group work practice with gay men and lesbians. In G. P. Mallon (Ed.), *Foundations of social work practice with lesbian and gay persons.* New York: Haworth.

Gitterman, A. (1989). Building mutual support in groups. *Social Work with Groups, 12*(2), 5-21.

Gladstone, J., & Reynolds, T. (1997). Single-session group work intervention in response to employee stress during work force transformation. *Social Work with Groups, 20*(1), 33-49.

Glasser, I., & Suroviak, J. (1988). Social group work in a soup kitchen: Mobilizing the strength of the guests. *Social Work with Groups, 11*(4), 95-109.

Glassman, U., & Kates, L. (1990). *Group work: A humanistic approach.* Newbury Park, CA: Sage.

Glassman, U., & Kates, L. (1993). Feedback, role rehearsal, and programming enactments: Cycles in the group's middle phase. *Social Work with Groups, 16*(1/2), 117-136.

Graetz, K. A., Boyle, E. S., Kimble, C. E., Thompson, P., & Garloch, J. L. (1998). Information sharing in face-to-face, teleconferencing, and electronic chat groups. *Small Group Research, 29*(6), 714-743.

Gutiérrez, L. M., & Ortega, R. (1991). Developing methods to empower Latinos: The importance of groups. *Social Work with Groups, 14*(20), 23-43.

Hardy, J., & Lewis, C. (1992). Bridging the gap between long- and short-term group psychotherapy: A viable treatment model. *Group, 16*(1), 5-17.

Hedlund, J., Ilgen, D. R., & Hollenbeck, J. R. (1998). Decision accuracy in computer-mediated versus face-to-face decision-making teams. *Organizational Behavior and Human Decision Processes, 76*(1), 30-47.

Helfmann, B. (1994). Here is now. *International Journal of Group Psychotherapy, 44*(4), 429-435.

Hogarty, G. E., Anderson, C. M., & Reiss, D. J. (1987). Family psychoeducation, social skills training, and maintenance chemotherapy in schizophrenia: The long and short of it. *Psychopharmacological Bulletin, 23*, 12-13.

Hogarty, G. E., Anderson, C. M., Reiss, D. J., Kornblith, S. J., Greenwald, D. P., Javna, C. D., & Madonia, M. J. (1986). Family psychoeducation, social skills training, and maintenance chemotherapy in the aftercare of schizophrenia. *Archive of General Psychiatry, 43*, 633-642.

Holden, G., Bearison, D. J., Rode, D. C., Rosenberg, G., & Fishman, M. (1999). Evaluating the effects of a virtual environment (STARBRIGHT World) with hospitalized children. *Research on Social Work Practice, 9*(3), 365-382.

Hollingshead, A. B., & McGrath, J. E. (1995). Computer-assisted groups: A critical review of the empirical research. In R. A. Guzzo, E. Salas, & Associates (Eds.), *Team effectiveness and decision making in organizations* (pp. 46-78). San Francisco: Jossey-Bass.

Hollingshead, A. B., McGrath, J. E., & O'Connor, K. M. (1993). Group task performance and communication technology: A longitudinal study of computer-mediated versus face-to-face work groups. *Small Group Research, 24*(3), 307-333.

Jaffee v. Redmond, 518 U.S. 1, 116 S. Ct. 1923 (1996).

Johnson, A. K., & Lee, J. A. B. (1994). Empowerment work with homeless women. In M. A. Mirkin (Ed.), *Women in context: Toward a feminist reconstruction of psychotherapy* (pp. 408-432). New York: Guilford.

Jones, D. M. (1996). Termination from drug treatment: Dangers and opportunities for clients of the graduation ceremony. *Social Work with Groups, 19*(3/4), 105-116.

Jordan, C., Lewellen, A., & Vandiver, V. (1995). Psychoeducation in minority families: A social work perspective. *International Journal of Mental Health, 14*, 27-43.

Kacen, L., & Rozovski, U. (1998). Assessing group processes: A comparison among group participants', direct observers', and indirect observers' assessment. *Small Group Research, 29*(2), 179-197.

Kennard, W. W., & Shilman, R. P. (1979). Group services with the homebound. *Social Work, 24*, 330-332.

Kiesler, S., & Sproull, L. (1992). Group decision making and communication technology. *Organizational Behavior and Human Decision Processes, 52*, 96-123.

Klein, J. G. (1995). I'm your therapist, you can tell me anything: The supreme court confirms the psychotherapist-patient privilege in Jaffee v. Redmond. *DePaul Law Review, 79*.

Kurland, R., & Salmon, R. (1993). Not just one of the gang: Group workers and their role as an authority. *Social Work with Groups, 16*(1/2).

Latane, B., & Todd, L. H. (1996). Spatial clustering in the conformity game: Dynamic social impact in electronic groups. *Journal of Personality and Social Psychology, 37*, 822-832.

Lewis, E. (1991). Social change and citizen action: A philosophical exploration for modern group work. *Social Work with Groups, 14*(3/4), 23-34.

Lewis, E. (1992). Regaining promise: Feminist perspectives for social group work practice. *Social Work with Groups, 15*(2/3), 271-284.

Lewis, E., & Ford, B. (1991). The Network Utilization Project: Incorporating traditional strengths of African-American families into group work practice. *Social Work with Groups, 14*(1), 7-22.

Llewelyn, S., & Dunnett, G. (1987). The use of personal construct theory in groups. In R. A. Neimeyer & G. J. Neimeyer (Eds.), *Personal construct therapy casebook* (pp. 245-258). New York: Springer.

Lopez, J. (1990). Groupwork as a protective factor for immigrant youth. *Social Work with Groups, 13*, 29-42.

Macgowan, M. J. (1997). A measure of engagement for social group work: The Group Engagement Measure (GEM). *Journal of Social Service Research, 23*(2), 17-37.

Macgowan. M. J. (in press). Evaluation of a measure of engagement for group work. *Research on Social Work Practice.*

MacKenzie, K. R. (1994). Where is here and when is now? The adaptational challenge of mental health reform for group psychotherapy. *International Journal of Group Psychotherapy, 44*(4), 407-428.

Magen, R. H. (1995, March). *Ten years of group work: Lessons learned and lessons to learn.* Paper presented at Council on Social Work Education, 41st Annual Program Meeting.

Mailick, M. D. (1984). The short-term treatment of depression of physically ill hospital adults. *Social Work in Health Care, 9,* 51-61.

Malekoff, A. (1994). A guideline for group work with adolescents. *Social Work with Groups, 17*(1/2), 5-20.

Malekoff, A. (1997). *Group work with adolescents: Principles and practice.* New York: Guilford.

Mallon, G. P. (1998). *Foundations of social work practice with lesbian and gay persons.* New York: Haworth.

Martin, M. A., & Nayowirth, S. (1988). Creating community: Group work to develop social networks with homeless mentally ill. *Social Work with Groups, 11*(4), 79-93.

McCallion, P., & Toseland. R. W. (1995). Supportive group interventions with caregivers of frail older adults. *Social Work with Groups, 18*(1), 11-25.

McCleod, P. L., Lobel, S. A., & Cox, T. H. (1996). Ethnic Diversity and creativity in small groups. *Small Group Research, 27*(2), 248-264.

McGrew, J. H., Bond, G. R., Dietzen, L., & Salyers, M. (1994). Measuring the fidelity of implementation of a mental health model. *Journal of Clinical and Consulting Psychology, 62*(4), 670-678.

McKay, M. M., Gonzalez, J. J., Stone, S., Ryland, D., & Kohner, K. (1995). *Social Work with Groups, 18*(4), 41-56.

McKay, M. M., Nudelman, R., McCadam, K., & Gonzalez, J. (1996). Evaluating a social work engagement approach to involving inner-city children and their families in mental health care. *Research on Social Work Practice, 6*(4), 462-472.

McKenna, K. Y. A., & Bargh, J. A. (1998). Coming out in the age of the Internet: Identity "demarginalization" through virtual group participation. *Journal of Personality and Social Psychology, 75*(3), 681-694.

Meier, A. (1997). Inventing new models of social support groups: A feasibility study of an online stress management support group for social workers. *Social Work with Groups, 20*(4), 35-53.

Meier, A., Galinsky, M. J., & Rounds, K. A. (1995). Telephone support groups for caregivers of persons with AIDS. In M. J. Galinsky & J. H. Schopler (Eds.), *Support groups: Current perspectives on theory and practice* (pp. 99-108). Binghamton, NY: Haworth.

Mickelson, K. D. (1997). Seeking social support: Parents in electronic groups. In S. Kiesler (Ed.), *Culture of the Internet* (pp. 157-178). Mahwah, NJ: Lawrence Erlbaum.

Moreland, R. L., & Levine J. M. (1982). Socialization in small groups: Temporal changes in individual-group relations. In L. Berkowitz (Ed.), *Advances in experimental social psychology* (15th ed., pp. 137-192). New York: Academic Press.

North, C. S., Pollio, D. E., Sacher, B., Hong, B., Isenberg, K., & Bufe, G. (1998). The family as caregiver: A group psychoeducation model for schizophrenia. *American Journal of Orthopsychiatry, 68*(1), 39-46.

Northen, H. (1988). *Social work with groups* (2nd ed.). New York: Columbia University Press.

Northen, H. (1998). Ethical dilemmas in social work with groups. *Social Work with Groups, 21*(1/2), 5-18.

Nye, J., & Brower, A. M. (Eds.). (1996). *What's social about social cognition: Social cognition in small groups.* Newbury Park, CA: Sage.

Parker, J., Clevenger, J. E., & Sherman, J. (1997). The psychotherapist-patient privilege in group therapy. *Journal of Group Therapy, Psychodrama, and Sociometry, 49*(4), 157-161.

Peters, A. J. (1997). Themes in group work with lesbian and gay adolescents. *Social Work with Groups, 20*(2), 51-69.

Pollio, D. E. (1995). Hoops group: Group work with young "street" men. *Social Work with Groups, 18*(2/3), 107-122.

Pollio, D. E., McDonald, S. M., & North, C. S. (1996). Combining a strengths-based approach and feminist theory in groupwork with persons "on the streets." *Social Work with Groups, 18*(2/3), 107-122.

Pollio, D. E., North, C. S., & Foster, D. A. (1998). Content and curriculum in multifamily psychoeducation. *Psychiatric Services, 49*(6), 816-822.

Pomeroy, E. C., Kiam, R., & Abel, E. M. (1999). The effectiveness of a psychoeducational group for HIV-infected/affected incarcerated women. *Research on Social Work Practice, 9*(2), 148-171.

Pomeroy, E. C., Rubin, A., Van Laningham, L., & Walker, R. J. (1997). The effectiveness of psychoeducational group intervention for heterosexuals with HIV/AIDS. *Research on Social Work Practice, 7*(2), 149-164.

Powell T. J. (1987). *Self-help organizations and professional practice.* Silver Spring, MD: National Association of Social Workers.

Proctor, E. K., & Davis, L. E. (1994). The challenge of racial difference: Skills for clinical practice. *Social Work, 39*(3), 314-323.

Ramey, J. H. (1992). Group work practice in neighborhood centers today. *Social Work with Groups, 15*(2/3), 193-206.

Rhodes, R. (1995). A group intervention for young children in addictive families. *Social Work With Groups, 18*(2-3), 123-134.

Rittner, B., & Hammons, K. (1992). Telephone group work with people with end-stage AIDS. *Social Work with Groups, 15*(4), 59-72.

Roback, H. B., Moore, R. F., Block, F. S., & Shelton, M. (1996). Confidentiality in group psychotherapy: Empirical findings and the law. *International Journal of Group Psychotherapy, 45*(1), 117-134.

Roback, H. B., Ochoa, E., Block, F., & Purdon, S. (1992). Guarding confidentiality in clinical groups: The therapist's dilemma. *International Journal of Group Psychotherapy, 42*(1), 81-101.

Roffman, R. A., Picciano, J. F., Ryan, R., Beadnell, B., Fisher, D., Downey, L., & Kalichman, S. C. (1997). HIV-prevention group counseling delivered by telephone: An efficacy trial with gay and bisexual men. *AIDS and Behavior, 1*(2), 137-154.

Rose, S. D. (1989). *Working with adults in groups.* San Francisco: Jossey-Bass.

Rose, S. D. (1998). *Group therapy with troubled youth: A cognitive-behavioral interactive approach.* Thousand Oaks CA: Sage.

Rose, S. D., Duby, P., Olenick, C., & Weston, T. (1996). Integrating family, group, and residential treatment: A cognitive-behavioral approach. *Social Work with Groups, 19*(2), 35-48.

Rose, S. D., & Subramanian, K. (1986). *A group leader's guide to pain management training.* Madison WI: Interpersonal Skill Training and Research Project.

Rose, S. D., & Tolman, R. M. (1994). Social work group research: Challenges for the 1990s. *Research on Social Work Practice, 4*(2), 139-140.

Rosenberg, S. A., & Zimet, C. N. (1995). Brief group treatment and managed mental health care. *International Journal of Group Psychotherapy, 45*(3), 367-378.

Rounds, K. A., Galinsky, M. J., & Despard, M. R. (1995). Evaluation of telephone support groups for persons with HIV disease. *Research on Social Work Practice, 5,* 442-459.

Ryan, D., & Doubleday, E. (1995). Group work: A lifeline for isolated elderly. *Social Work with Groups, 18*(2/3), 65-78.

Sachs, J. (1991). Action and reflection in work with a group of homeless people. In *Social action on group work* (pp. 187-202). Binghamton NY: Haworth.

Salmon-Davis, S., & Davis, L. E. (1999). Group work with sexually abused African American boys. In L. E. Davis (Ed.), *Working with African American males: A guide to practice* (pp. 15-28). Thousand Oaks, CA: Sage.

Sarri, R., & Galinsky, M. J. (1985). A conceptual framework for group development. In M. Sundel, P. Glasser, R. Sarri, & R. Vinter (Eds.), *Individual change through small groups* (pp. 70-86). New York: Free Press.

Schiller, L. Y. (1997). Rethinking stages of development in women's groups: Implications for practice. *Social Work with Groups, 20*(3), 3-19.

Schoech, D., Cavalier, A. R., & Hoover, B. (1993). Using technology to change the human services delivery system. *Administration in Social Work, 17*(2), 31-52.

Schopler, J. H., Abell, M. D., & Galinsky, M. J. (1998). Technology-based groups: A review and conceptual framework for practice. *Social Work, 43*(3), 254-268.

Schopler, J. H., & Galinsky, M. J. (1995). Group practice overview. In *Encyclopedia of social work* (pp. 1129-1142). Washington, DC: NASW Press.

Schopler, J. H., Galinsky, M. J., & Abell, M. D. (1997). Creating community through telephone and computer groups: Theoretical and practice perspectives. *Social Work with Groups, 20*(4), 19-34.

Schopler, J. H., Galinsky, M. J., Davis, L. E., & Despard, M. (1996). The RAP model: Assessing a framework for leading multiracial groups. *Social Work with Groups, 19*(3/4), 21-39.

Shapiro, B. Z. (1991). Social action, the group, and society. *Social Work with Groups, 14*(3/4), 7-21.

Shulman, L. (1999). *The skills of helping individuals, families, groups, and communities* (4th ed.). Itasca, IL: Peacock.

Siegel, J., Dubrovsky, V., Kiesler, S., & McGuire, T. W. (1986). Group processes in computer-mediated communication. *Organizational Behavior and Human Decision Processes, 37,* 157-187.

Smyth, K. A., & Harris, P. B. (1993). Using telecomputing to provide information and support to caregivers of persons with dementia. *Gerontologist, 33,* 123-127.

Solomon, P., Draine, J., Mannion, E., & Meisel, M. (1997). Effectiveness of two models of brief family education: Retention of gains by family members of adults with severe mental illness. *American Journal of Orthopsychiatry, 67*(2), 177-187.

Steenbarger, B. N., & Budman, S. H. (1996). Group psychotherapy and managed behavioral health care: Current trends and future challenges. *International Journal of Group Psychotherapy, 46*(3), 297-309.

Stein, L., Rothman, B., & Nakanishi, M. (1993). The telephone group: Accessing group service to the homebound. *Social Work with Groups, 16*(1/2), 203-215.

Steinberg, D. M. (1997). *The mutual aid approach to working with groups: Helping people help each other.* Northvale NJ: Jason Aronson.

Stone, S., McKay, M. M., & Stoops, C. (1996). Evaluating multiple family groups to address the behavioral difficulties of urban children. *Small Group Research, 27*(3), 398-415.

Suarez, Z. E., Lewis, E., & Clark, J. (1995). Women of color and culturally competent feminist social work practice. In N. Van Den Bergh (Ed.), *Feminist practice in the 21st century* (pp. 195-209). Washington DC: NASW Press.

Subramanian, K., Hernandez, S., & Martinez, A. (1995). Psychoeducational group work for low-income Latina mothers with HIV infection. *Social Work with Groups, 18*(2/3), 53-64.

Sundel, M., Glasser, P., Sarri, R., & Vinter, R. (Eds.). (1985). *Individual change through small groups.* New York: Free Press.

Swenson, L. (1993). *Psychology and the law for helping professionals.* Belmont, CA: Books Core.

Tannenbaum, J. (1990). An English conversation group model for Vietnamese adolescent females. *Social Work with Groups, 13*(2), 57-68.

Thomas, T., & Urbano, J. (1993). A telephone support group program for the visually impaired elderly. *Clinical Gerontologist, 13*(2), 61-71.

Tolman, R. M., & Molidar, C. E. (1994). A decade of social group work research: Trends in methodology, theory, and program development. *Research on Social Work Practice, 4*(2), 142-159.

Toseland, R. W. (1990). *Group work with older adults.* New York: New York University Press.

Toseland, R. W., & Rivas, R. F. (1998). *An introduction to group work practice* (3rd ed.). Boston: Allyn & Bacon.

Tuckman, B. W. (1965). Developmental sequence in small groups. *Psychological Bulletin, 63,* 384-399.

Tuckman, B. W., & Jensen, M. A. C. (1977). Stages of small group development revisited. *Group and organization studies, 2,* 419-427.

Turnbull, J. E., Galinsky, M. J., Wilner, M. E., & Meglin, D. E. (1994). Designing research to meet service needs: Single-session groups for families of psychiatric inpatients. *Research on Social Work Practice, 4*(2), 192-207.

Tutty, L. M., & Wagar, J. (1994). The evolution of a group for young children who have witnessed family violence. *Social Work With Groups, 17*(1-2), 89-104.

VanWinkle, J. (1998). *A guide for social group workers on current legal aspects of privileged communication.* Unpublished manuscript.

Vinter, R. D. (1985). Essential components of social group work practice. In M. Sundel, P. Glasser, R. Sarri, & R. Vinter (Eds.). (1985). *Individual change through small groups* (pp. 11-34). New York: Free Press..

Walker, R. J., Pomeroy, E. C., McNeil, J. S., & Franklin, C. (1994). A psychoeducational model for caregivers of patients with Alzheimer's disease. *Journal of Gerontological Social Work, 22*(1/2), 75-91.

Walther, J. B. (1996). Computer-mediated communication: Impersonal, interpersonal, and hyperpersonal interaction. *Communication Research, 23*(1), 3-43.

Walther, J. B., & Burgoon, J. K. (1992). Relational communication in computer-mediated interaction. *Human Communication Research, 19*(1), 50-88.

Weinberg, N., Schmale, J., Uken, J., & Wessel, K. (1996). On-line help: Cancer patients participate in a computer-mediated support group. *Health and Social Work, 21*(1), 24-29.

Wellman, B. (1997). An electronic group is virtually a social network. In S. Kiesler (Ed.), *Culture of the Internet* (pp. 179-208). Mahwah, NJ: Lawrence Erlbaum.

Wheelan, S., & Kaeser, R. (1997). The influence of task type and designated leaders on developmental patterns in groups. *Small Group Research, 28*(1), 94-121.

Wiener, L. S. (1998, May). Telephone support groups for HIV-positive mothers whose children have died of AIDS. *Social Work, 43*(3), 279-285.

Wiener, L. S., Spencer, E. D., Davidson, R., & Fair, C. (1993). National telephone support groups: A new avenue toward psychosocial support for HIV-infected children and their families. *Social Work with Groups, 16*(3), 55-71.

Winegar, N., Bistline, J. L., & Sheridan, S. (1992). Implementing a group therapy program in a managed care setting: Combining cost effectiveness and quality care. *Families in Society: The Journal of Contemporary Human Services, 73*(1), 56-58.

Wolozin, D., & Dalton, E. (1990). Short-term group therapy with the "father-absent father" in a maximum security psychiatric hospital. *Social Work with Groups, 13*(1), 103-111.

Wood, G. C., & Middleman, R. R. (1991). Advocacy and social action: Key elements in the structural approach to direct practice in social work. *Social Work with Groups, 14*(3/4), 53-63.

Worchel, S. (1994). You can go home again: Returning group research to the group context with an eye on developmental issues. *Small Group Research, 25*(2), 205-223.

Zimet, C. N. (1997). Coping with the new world of health care. *International Journal of Group Psychotherapy, 47*(1), 17-21.

CHAPTER FIFTEEN

Advances in Family Therapy: Theory and Practice

FROMA WALSH

CARMEN CROSSER

Family therapy has emerged as a major approach to clinical practice. This chapter first examines the growing diversity and unprecedented challenges of families and offers a framework for assessment of family functioning. Next, a brief overview of major models of family therapy is presented, highlighting the recent development of strength-based approaches and application of a biopsychosocial orientation, addressing the family impact of biologically based illnesses and powerful sociocultural influences concerning race, ethnicity, religion, class, gender, and sexual orientation. Challenges and opportunities for the continuing development of family systems research and practice are identified. This overview reveals the growth and vitality of the field of family therapy in its efforts to be responsive to the challenges facing families in our rapidly changing world.

EVOLUTION OF THE FIELD

The family and larger social forces have been recognized as major influences in individual development from the early focus in social work on the concept of person-in-environment. With the ascendency of the psychoanalytic model in the mental health field, attention narrowed to the mother-child dyadic relationship in early childhood, with linear-causal attributions of maternal deficiencies blamed for any child disturbance. A paradigm shift occurred in the late 1950s with the development of general system theory, communications theory, and cybernetics (Ruesch & Bateson, 1951; Watzlawick, Beavin, & Jackson, 1967). Direct observation of whole families in studies of schizophrenia shifted attention from etiological questions to ongoing transactional processes that reinforced disturbed behavior or symptoms. It was a natural step to design therapeutic interventions to alter dysfunctional processes in sessions with whole families.

The 1960s was a period of rapid expansion of theory and innovative family approaches to treat a wide range of problems. The emergence of distinct models in the 1970s brought a refinement of strategies and techniques based on particular views of problem formation and the process of change. Over the past two decades, that foundation has been reformulated and expanded with a broader biopsychosocial perspective. Most important has been the redirection from family deficits to family resources in a range of collaborative approaches aiming to strengthen and support families. Although family therapy approaches vary, they do share a common conceptual base in systems theory.

FAMILY SYSTEMS ORIENTATION

The practice of family therapy is grounded in a set of basic assumptions about the interplay of individual, family, and social processes that operate according to certain principles that apply to all human systems (Bateson, 1979; Bertalanffy, 1968). Ecological and developmental perspectives are interwoven in viewing the family as an open system that functions in relation to its broader sociocultural context and evolves over the life cycle and across the generations.

Systemic Lens: Patterns That Connect

Family therapy is not simply a therapeutic modality in which all members are seen conjointly. A family systems approach is distinguished less by who is in the room and more by how the clinician attends to the relationship system in problem formulation and intervention planning. Therapy may focus on a couple relationship or combine individual and conjoint sessions with the whole family, parents, siblings, or key extended family members. Systems-based approaches offer the principles and methods for direct interventions to foster both individual and relational well-being. Individual counseling that attends only to a symptomatic member may leave other family members—and the family unit—at risk. For instance, the death of a child poses a heightened risk for marital estrangement and divorce unless partners can support each other through their devastating loss.

Interactional view: Process and context. Family therapy puts into practice social work's core principle of person-in-environment: Problems cannot be adequately understood or resolved apart from their psychosocial context (Nichols & Schwartz, 1997). The family as a whole is greater than the sum of its parts and cannot be described simply by summing up characteristics of individual members. The devilish behavior of a child and the angelic behavior of a sibling may both contribute in a complementary way to the overall family balance. Problems presented as within a person are viewed interactionally. A label of *hysteric* might be redefined as a wife's futile attempt to get attention from her unresponsive husband. In a vicious cycle, the more she complains, the more he withdraws; the more he distances, the more upset she becomes.

Circular causality and accountability. Family members are interrelated such that each individual affects all others and the group as a whole, in turn, affecting the first member in a circular chain of influence. Every action in a sequence is also a reaction: A single parent's upset, provoked by a child's tantrum, may exacerbate the child's out-of-control behavior. In tracking the sequence of interactions around a presenting problem, repetitive patterns often involve other family members, such as a grandparent's criticism. Regardless of how a sequence began, family members can be helped to pull together to handle problems more effectively. Although processes may be circular, not all participants have equal influence over others. Feminist critique of early family therapy brought recognition of the culturally based gendered power differential in families and the imperative of holding an individual accountable for abuse of others (McGoldrick, Anderson, & Walsh, 1989).

Biopsychosocial Orientation

Family therapy has increasingly broadened from focus on the family as the source of symptoms to a biopsychosocial view. Assessment and intervention attend to the family impact of biologically based conditions and larger cultural influences, including race, class, gender, ethnicity, religion, and sexual orientation. The family is most often the focal point for assessment of

this multiplicity of forces. Yet, therapists are cautioned not to equate family distress with family pathology nor to type a family by the disturbance of a member. With multiple influences, there is no one-to-one correlation between an individual's problems and a pattern of family dysfunction. Labels such as "schizophrenogenic mother" carry faulty attributions of parental blame (Walsh & Anderson, 1988). Problems may be primarily biologically based, as in schizophrenia, and/or largely fueled by social or economic conditions. Family distress may result from unsuccessful attempts to cope with an overwhelming situation. Therefore, the interaction of individual, family, and larger social influences must always be carefully evaluated. A systemic assessment may lead to a variety of approaches, depending on the relevance of various system levels to problem resolution and individual/family well-being. Putting an ecological view into practice, interventions increasingly involve community-based collaboration and change in workplace, school, and health care systems (Imber-Black, 1988).

Family Developmental View

Family systems approaches attend to processes over time, from ongoing transactions to family life-cycle passage and multigenerational influences. In a systemic model of human development, individual development is seen to coevolve with the family and culture over time (Carter & McGoldrick, 1998). It would be an error to presume that a particular origin or event determines an outcome (Watzlawick et al., 1967). The same outcome may result from different origins and multiple influences over time. The same origin may lead to different outcomes. For instance, although most perpetrators of abuse have been abused themselves, as children, most individuals who have been abused as children do not go on to abuse others (Kaufman & Ziegler, 1987). The impact of initial conditions or events, such as early life trauma, may be outweighed by mediating influences, especially strong relationships that foster recovery and resilience (Walsh, 1996).

Family Coping, Adaptation, and Resilience

Symptoms of family distress are often triggered by a disruptive life transition or crisis, such as traumatic loss (Walsh & McGoldrick, 1991), or they may be associated with persistent adversity, such as living in a blighted neighborhood (Garmezy, 1991). How a family handles stressful challenges is crucial for coping, adaptation, and resilience of all members and for the family unit (McCubbin & Patterson, 1983; Walsh, 1996). One family may be disabled while another rallies in response to similar conditions. Resilience is the ability to rebound from crises strengthened and more resourceful through an active process of self-righting and growth out of adversity (Walsh, 1998b).

Even with family breakup, the presumption that divorce inevitably damages children fails to take into account the many variables that can make a difference over time, from the predivorce climate, to postdivorce parental cooperation, conflict, or cutoff; financial security; and how a remarriage is handled (Hetherington, Law, & O'Connor, 1993). In fact, most children do better after divorce than counterparts in high-conflict families that stay together. Research identifying family processes that distinguish those who recover well from those who fare poorly can inform prevention and in-

tervention efforts for optimal postdivorce child and family adaptation. Therapy and mediation approaches can draw on such research findings to facilitate amicable divorce processes and workable arrangements for ongoing care and support of children (Walsh, 1991; Walsh, Jacob, & Simons, 1995). Similarly, studies of successful stepfamily formation can inform approaches to decrease the high risk of divorce and foster integration of biological and step-relations (Visher & Visher, 1996).

ASSESSMENT OF FAMILY FUNCTIONING

What Is a Normal Family?

Perspectives from social constructionism (Hoffman, 1990) have heightened awareness that clinical views of normality, health, and pathology are socially constructed. Clinicians coconstruct the patterns they "discover" in families, just as family and therapist beliefs about healthy functioning influence therapeutic objectives. We need to be aware of our own assumptions, values, and biases embedded in cultural norms, professional orientations, and personal experience. Most research has assessed family health based on studies of white, middle-class, intact families who are not under stress, viewing differences from norms as deficits. Clinical theory, practice, and nomenclature have been so pathology based that a normal family might be defined, only half-jokingly, as one that has not yet been clinically assessed (Walsh, 1993a).

The very concept of the family has been undergoing redefinition, with major social and economic transformations in recent decades.

The idealized 1950s norm of the intact nuclear family, headed by a breadwinner-father and supported by a homemaker-mother, now accounts for less than 7% of households (Skolnick, 1991). Nearly 70% of mothers of school-age children are in the workforce, most out of financial necessity, as dual-earner families have become the norm and single-parent households have increased (undersupported by noncustodial parents). Despite a high divorce rate, now leveled off at just under 50%, most individuals continue to seek loving, lasting relationships. After divorce, three fourths of men and two thirds of women go on to remarry, making stepfamilies increasingly common. Commitment vows and parenting by lesbians and gay men are on the rise. Over the life cycle, children and their parents are likely to move in and out of varied and increasingly complex family constellations, each transition posing new adaptational challenges.

To be responsive to the growing diversity of families, a broad and open definition of family normality is required. The myth that one family form is essential for the healthy development of children has continued to stigmatize those who do not fit the standard. In reifying one particular model, unique to the affluent post-World War II era, it is forgotten that family diversity has always been common historically and cross-culturally (Walsh, 1993a). A growing body of research finds that healthy children can be found in a variety of family structures (Coontz, 1997). What matters more than family form are family processes, the quality of caring, committed relationships.

Research and conceptualization of normal family processes over the past two decades have important clinical utility, providing empirical grounding for assessment to identify compo-nents of healthy family functioning that can be fostered in intervention with distressed families (Walsh, 1987, 1993a). It should be kept in mind that any assessment must consider functioning in context: relative to each family's structure, values, and life challenges. We can, nonetheless, identify key processes that tend to distinguish well-functioning families in three domains of family functioning: family belief systems, organization patterns, and communication processes (Walsh, 1998b).

Family Belief Systems

Family members develop and share meaning systems through their transactions. Relationship rules, both explicit and unspoken, serve as norms, providing a set of expectations about roles, actions, and consequences that guide family life. Reiss (1981) found that members construct a family paradigm, an enduring structure of shared beliefs, convictions, and assumptions about the social world shaped by pivotal family experiences. In turn, these beliefs influence the family's perception of events, meanings ascribed, problem-solving styles, and expectations about consequences—from hopeful, to benign, to catastrophic.

Family members' beliefs about their ability to master life challenges are keys to family resilience (Walsh, 1998b). Family history and relationship patterns are transmitted down the generations, influencing future expectations, hopes, and dreams, as well as catastrophic fears. Multigenerational legacies reinforce family myths, secrets, and taboos. They become encoded into family scripts that provide conscious or covert blueprints guiding behavior when facing a dilemma or crisis (Byng-Hall, 1995). Culture, class, race, ethnicity, and religion contribute greatly to family beliefs and practices (Falicov, 1995; McGoldrick, Giordano, & Pearce, 1996; Walsh, 1999). For instance, all couples form an implicit bargain—a relational quid pro quo—defining themselves and their expectations of each other and the relationship. A gender-based power differential reinforces assumptions that a wife must subordinate her needs in deference to those of her husband (Walsh, 1989).

Well-functioning families tend to be bolstered by a transcendent moral or spiritual value orientation and cultural heritage (Beavers & Hampson, 1993; Walsh, 1998b). Racism and other forms of social and institutionalized discrimination disempower marginalized groups, generating stigma and shame. Aponte (1994) contends that families in poor minority communities suffer from an impoverishment of spirit as well as bread, or financial needs, requiring investment in family and community programs that restore hope for the future.

Family identity and beliefs are conveyed through family rituals, including celebrations of holidays, rites of passage (e.g., bar/bat mitzvah), family traditions (e.g., annual gatherings), and routine interactions (e.g., family dinner). Rituals foster community and continuity over time and facilitate transitions, as by the inclusion of children in a remarriage ceremony. Family therapists (Imber-Black, Roberts, & Whiting, 1988) often use rituals in therapeutic intervention to foster change or healing, as in cases such as stillbirth where a loss has not been adequately marked.

Clinicians should routinely inquire about family, ethnic, and spiritual beliefs, exploring differences between partners, with families of origin, or in the dominant culture. For instance, traditional faith-healing beliefs and practices, common in many immigrant families, may not be mentioned unless a therapist inquires respectfully about them (Falicov, 1998; Walsh, 1999).

Family Organizational Patterns

Families require effective organization to maintain integration, foster healthy development of members, and master life challenges. Varying family structures have varied configurations, resources, and constraints. For instance, a stepfamily must coordinate parenting and support across households to involve biological and step-networks. Likewise, dual-earner families must organize their roles and work/family lives differently than a traditional breadwinner/homemaker family. All families have to develop their own ways to achieve adaptability and connectedness.

Adaptability fosters effective family functioning and resilience (Beavers & Hampson, 1993; Olson, 1993). Stability (homeostasis) and flexibility (morphogenesis) are counterbalancing tendencies in family systems. To function well, families need clear leadership with predictable, consistent rules, roles, and patterns of interaction. They also need to adapt to changing conditions or developmental priorities. Lacking this flexible structure, families at dysfunctional extremes are either overly rigid and autocratic or chaotically disorganized and leaderless. Crisis events, such as significant losses, may require major adaptational shifts to ensure the continuity of family life. For instance, a husband's disability may require a traditional couple to alter gender-based roles as his wife becomes the primary breadwinner and he assumes most homemaking responsibilities.

Connectedness, or cohesion, is vital for family functioning and resilience. Well-functioning families balance needs for closeness and mutual support with respect for separateness and individual differences. Extremes of enmeshment or disengagement tend to be dysfunctional. An enmeshed pattern sacrifices individual differences, privacy, and separation for unity and family survival. Differentiation is blocked, with distorted, rigid role assignments. In a disengaged pattern, the family unit is fragmented and lacks mutual support, leaving members isolated to fend for themselves. The functional balance of connectedness shifts as families move through the life cycle. Cultural norms and personal preferences also vary. Thus, clinicians must be cautious not to reflexively label highly cohesive relationships as enmeshed or presume they are dysfunctional. One study, for instance, found that although lesbian couples scored at the high extreme on cohesion, the relationships were not fused but were mutually satisfying and functioned to fortify the relationship in a homophobic social environment (Zacks, Green, & Marrow, 1988).

Structural boundaries need to be clear and firm, yet permeable. Interpersonal boundaries define and separate individual members, fostering their differentiation and autonomous functioning. Generational boundaries uphold grandparent, parent, and child roles, rights, and obligations, maintaining hierarchical organization in families. Established by the parents, in turn, they reinforce their leadership, authority, and privacy. The complexity of divorced and stepfamily configurations poses challenges to sustain workable parenting coalitions across households and to knit together biological and step-relations, including step-siblings and extended families (Walsh, 1991). It may be functional, and necessary, for older children to assist parents with responsibilities, especially in single-parent or large families, or in cases of parental disability, as long as a child is not overburdened. Generational boundaries are breached when a parent abdicates leadership, assuming a childlike position, or most destructively when a child is sexually abused (Trepper & Barrett, 1989). Family-community boundaries in well-functioning families maintain a clear sense of the family unit while connecting members with the community. Social networks are vital for support and resilience, especially in crisis. In a closed system, family isolation contributes to dysfunction and blocks socialization and emancipation of growing children.

The concept of the triangle and the dysfunctional process of triangulation (Bowen, 1978; Haley, 1976) refers to the tendency of two members to draw in a third person when tension develops between the two. A couple may avoid conflict by joining in mutual concern about a symptomatic child. A triangulated child may serve as a go-between for parents or may be drawn by one parent into a coalition against the other. A grandparent-child coalition may be formed against a single parent. In more troubled families, such patterns are more rigid and likely to be replicated in multiple interlocking triangles throughout the family system.

Gender, power, and privilege. Gender, like generation, is a basic structural axis in families (Goldner, 1988). Feminist family therapists have challenged constraining gender-based rules and roles in marriage and family life (e.g., Hare-Mustin, 1987; McGoldrick et al., 1989; Walters, Carter, Papp, & Silverstein, 1988). Studies find that an equitable sharing of authority, responsibility, and privilege between partners fosters couple intimacy and optimal family functioning (Beavers & Hampson, 1993;

Walsh, 1998b). Yet, such balance is difficult to achieve with the reinforcement of traditional role relations in the larger culture and the interplay of racism and power for people of color (Pinderhughes, 1989).

Communication Processes

Communication processes facilitate family functioning and resilience. Every communication has two functions: a content (report) aspect, conveying information, opinions, or feelings; and a relationship (command) aspect, defining the nature of the relationship (Ruesch & Bateson, 1951). The statement "Eat your vegetables" conveys an order with expectation of compliance and implies a hierarchical status or authority in the relationship, as between parent and child. All verbal and nonverbal behavior, including silence (or spitting out the vegetables), conveys interpersonal messages, (e.g., I won't obey you!).

In family evaluation, clinicians assess members' ability to communicate openly about both instrumental and emotional issues. Clarity and congruence in verbal and nonverbal messages are important (Epstein, Bishop, Ryan, Miller, & Keitnor, 1993), although cultural norms vary considerably in directness and expressivity (McGoldrick, Giordano & Pearce, 1996). Still, well-functioning families establish a climate of mutual trust that encourages open expression of a range of feelings and empathic responses, with respect for differences. Troubled families, in contrast, perpetuate a climate of mistrust, marked by blaming and scapegoating. Highly reactive emotional expression can fuel destructive cycles of conflict, escalating in violence. Cascading effects of criticism, stonewalling, contempt, and mutual withdrawal contribute to

despair and divorce (Gottman, 1993). It is important to note areas of conflict as well as toxic or sensitive issues where communication is blocked. Also, clinicians should be aware of the personal and relational constraints of gender-based socialization, as in expectations that men (and boys) should be tough and invulnerable.

Problem-solving is crucial for family functioning and is central in all family therapy approaches. Every family has problems; resilience requires joint problem-solving and conflict resolution. Families need to master instrumental problems, such as juggling job, child care, and elder care demands, and to handle socioemotional needs of members. Families can falter at various steps in a problem-solving process (Epstein et al., 1993): identifying the problem, communicating with appropriate people about it, brainstorming possible solutions, deciding on an approach, taking initiative, following through, and evaluating its effectiveness. Family resilience builds on small successes, with mistakes viewed as learning experiences. A systemic assessment attends to the collaborative process: How decisions are made can be as crucial as the decision itself. Negotiation and compromise are important and can be blocked by rivalry or power struggles. Mutual accommodation, respect for each member's needs and contributions, and reciprocity over time foster long-term relational balance and harmony (Walsh, 1989).

Key processes in family resilience are summarized in Table 15.1. Family belief systems support resilience when they help members make meaning of a crisis, encourage a positive outlook, and foster transcendence and spirituality. Family organization bolsters resilience by flexibility, connectedness with strong leadership and teamwork, and kin/community/financial resources. Communication facilitates

TABLE 15.1   Key Processes In Family Resilience

Belief Systems

Making meaning of adversity
- Affiliative value: Resilience as relationally based
- Family life-cycle orientation: Normalize, contextualize adversity and distress
- Sense of coherence: Crisis as meaningful, comprehensible, manageable challenge
- Appraisal of crisis, distress, and recovery: Facilitative versus constraining beliefs

Positive outlook
- Active initiative and perseverance
- Courage and en-*courage*-ment;
- Sustain hope, optimistic view, confidence in overcoming odds
- Focus on strengths and potential
- Master the possible; accept what can't be changed

Transcendence and spirituality
- Larger values, purpose
- Spirituality: Faith, communion, rituals
- Inspiration: Envision new possibilities; creativity
- Transformation: Learning and growth from adversity

Organizational Patterns

Flexibility
- Capacity to change: Rebound, reorganize, adapt to meet challenges over time
- Counterbalanced by stability: Continuity, dependability through disruption

Connectedness
- Mutual support, collaboration, and commitment
- Respect individual needs, differences, and boundaries

- Strong leadership: Nurture, protect, guide children and vulnerable family members
- Varied family forms: Cooperative parenting/ caregiving teams
- Couple/Co-parental relationship: Equal partners
- Seek reconnection, reconciliation of troubled relationships

Social and economic resources
- Mobilize extended kin and social support; models and mentors
- Build community networks
- Build financial security; balance work/family strains

Communication Processes

Clarity
- Clear, consistent messages (words and actions)
- Clarify ambiguous information: Truth seeking/truth speaking

Open emotional expression
- Share range of feelings (joy and pain; hopes and fears)
- Mutual empathy; tolerance for differences
- Responsibility for own feelings, behavior; avoid blaming
- Pleasurable interactions; humor

Collaborative problem solving
- Creative brainstorming; resourcefulness
- Shared decision making: Negotiation, fairness, reciprocity
- Conflict resolution
- Focus on goals; take concrete steps; build on success; learn from failure
- Proactive stance: Prevent problems; avert crises; prepare for future challenges

resilience through clarity, open emotional expression, and collaborative problem solving (see Walsh, 1998b).

Multigenerational Family Cycle

Family functioning is assessed in the context of the multigenerational system moving forward over time (Carter & McGoldrick, 1998). A *genogram* and *family time line* (McGoldrick, Gerson, & Shellenbeger, 1999) schematize relationship information and track system patterns to guide intervention planning. A drawing of the family field includes all members of the household, the extended family (including noncustodial parents and relatives after separation or divorce), and other relationships that have been significant and/or could become potential resources. It is crucial to note linkages between the timing of symptoms and stress events, such as a father's recent cancer recurrence or the anniversary of a teenage son's death in a car crash (Walsh, 1998b).

Current stresses impinge on a family as it moves forward through time, coping with stressful events and transitions. These include both the predictable, normative stresses and unpredictable, disruptive circumstances, such as untimely death. Family members may lose perspective on time when a problem arises, becoming overwhelmed by a crisis or catastrophic fears. They may confound immediate situations with past events, become stuck in the past, or cut themselves off emotionally from painful memories and contacts. Healthy families are better able to balance intergenerational continuity and change and to maintain links between their past, present, and future direction.

Relationships evolve over the course of the family life cycle. Boundaries and roles are redefined. Family life-cycle models identify stages of family development, each presenting salient developmental tasks. Divorce, single parenting, and remarriage pose additional life-cycle challenges (Carter & McGoldrick, 1998). With the increasing diversity of families and their timing of nodal events, no single model or life trajectory should be deemed essential for proper development (Walsh, 1993a).

Frequently symptoms coincide with stressful events or transitions. A family's coping ability depends on the convergence of developmental and multigenerational strains. Although all change is stressful, strain increases exponentially when current stressors intersect with sensitive multigenerational issues. Nodal events are likely to reactivate past unresolved conflicts and losses, particularly when similar developmental challenges are confronted. For instance, a man whose mother died in childbirth may avoid intimacy when his wife desires to become pregnant. One partner's vulnerability can be eased by a spouse's support in a trusting couple relationship.

Many families function well until they reach a critical point in the life cycle at which complications arose a generation earlier. A mother may become upset that her daughter is sexually active at 16 years of age—the same age that the mother became pregnant. Therapy helps parents draw lessons from their past to best support their children's healthy development.

MAJOR APPROACHES TO FAMILY THERAPY

Over the past three decades, a number of approaches to family therapy have been developed. This overview will focus on the major foundational models and those most influential in the evolving practice field. The models can be usefully categorized as intergenerational approaches, which tend to be more exploratory, growth oriented, and historically focused, and problem-solving approaches, which are typically brief, pragmatic interventions focused on resolving immediate problem situations. Discussion will highlight distinctions in views of family functioning and dysfunction, therapeutic objectives, and strategies and techniques (as summarized in Table 15.2).

INTERGENERATIONAL GROWTH-ORIENTED APPROACHES

Psychodynamically Oriented Approaches

Early in the field of family therapy, growth-oriented intergenerational approaches sought to bridge psychodynamic, object relations, and family systems theories. Attention shifted from maternal influences in early childhood to ongoing dynamic processes in the multigenerational family system. Family interaction is conceptualized in terms of object relations, internalizations, and introjection and projection processes. The capacity to function as a spouse or parent is viewed as largely influenced by each individual's experiences in the family of origin. Couple relationships are successful to the extent that they are organized in terms of a well-differentiated sense of self, uncontaminated by pathogenic introjects (Scharff & Scharff, 1987).

The interlocking of projection and introjection processes forms a shared projection process based on need complementarity, influencing mate choice as well as couple and parent-child relationships. Reciprocal bargains involve implicit agreements among family members to relate on the basis of unfulfilled needs. Current life situations are interpreted in light of parents' inner object world and role models. Unresolved conflict or loss interferes with realistic appraisal and response to other family members. Symptoms or scapegoating may result from unconscious attempts to re-enact, externalize, or master intrapsychic conflicts from the past through current relationships (Ackerman, 1958; Framo, 1970) or an irrational role assignment ritualized into the family's structural pattern (Byng-Hall, 1995). With the loss of a significant family member, emotional shockwaves ripple through the family system, affecting all (Bowen, 1978; Paul & Paul, 1975).

Assessment and treatment explore the complex multigenerational family patterns and their connection to disturbances in current functioning and relationships. The therapeutic aim is for family members to deal directly with one another, either in or between sessions, to work through unresolved conflicts and losses.

Negative introjects from the past are tested out and altered or updated through contacts with the family of origin, rather than by analysis of transference patterns. The therapist acts as a catalyst, encouraging members' awareness of intense conflictual emotions and shared defenses, interpreting their sources and consequences. The contextual approach of Boszormenyi-Nagy (1987) examines multigenerational legacies of parental accountability and filial loyalty toward the resolution of grievances. Families are thought to be strengthened by moves toward trustworthiness and relational equitability, considering all members' welfare. The therapist takes charge in preparing, guiding, and processing such highly charged work. Covert family processes are made overt and accessible to resolution through insight and action. The conjoint process builds empathy and mutuality, strengthening couple and family bonds.

Bowen Model

Bowen (1978) developed a theory of the family emotional system and a method of therapy based on the view that functioning is impaired by poorly differentiated relationships with high anxiety and emotional reactivity. Stresses on the family system, especially by death, can decrease differentiation, heighten reactivity, and fuel triangulation or cutoffs of highly charged relationships. The therapeutic goal is to assist individuals to repair troubled relationships with their families of origin, resolving issues that block their growth. Through a coaching process, clients refocus from futile attempts to change others to efforts to change themselves in relationships through information gathering and contacts between sessions. Both partners/parents are encouraged to work on their own extended family issues that are in-

TABLE 15.2 Major Approaches to Family Therapy

Intergenerational/
Growth-Oriented Approaches

Family Therapy Model	View of Problems	Therapeutic Goals	Process of Change
Psychodynamic Ackerman Boszormenyi-Nagy Framo Paul and Paul	• Symptoms due to shared family projection process stemming from unresolved past conflicts or losses in family of origin	• Resolution of family-of-origin conflict and losses • ↓ Family projection processes • Individual and family growth	• Insight-oriented, linking past and present dynamics • Assist in resolution of conflicts, losses • Facilitate healthier modes of relating

Bowen approach
Bowen
Carter
McGoldrick
	• Functioning impaired by relationships with family of origin
	  • Poor differentiation
	  • Anxiety (reactivity)
	  • Triangulation
	  • Cutoffs
		• Differentiation
		• ↑ Cognitive functioning
		• ↓ Emotional reactivity
		• Modify relationships in family system:
		  • Detriangulation
		  • Repair cutoffs
			• Survey multigenerational field (use of genogram)
			• Plan focused interventions to change self directly with family
			• Therapist coaches action outside session

Experiential
Satir
Whitaker and Keith
	• Symptoms are nonverbal messages expressing current communication dysfunction in system	• Direct, clear communication
		• Individual and family growth
			• Change here-and-now interaction
			• Share feelings about relationships
			  • Self-disclosure
			  • Direct communication
			  • Experiential techniques
			• Therapist uses experience with family to catalyze process

Approach	View of Problem	Goals	Therapist Role/Techniques
Structural Minuchin Philadelphia Child Guidance Clinic	Symptoms result from current family structural imbalance • Malfunctioning hierarchy and boundaries • Maladaptive reaction to developmental, environmental changes	Reorganize family structure: • Parental leadership, authority • Clear, flexible subsystems and boundaries • Promote more adaptive coping	Therapist shifts interaction patterns • Joining family • Enactment of problem • Map structure, plan stages of restructuring • Tasks and directives
Strategic/systemic Palo Alto group Haley and Madanes Milan approach	Symptoms maintained by family's unsuccessful problem-solving attempts	Solve presenting problem; specific behaviorally defined objectives	Pragmatic, focused, action-oriented: • Change symptom-maintaining sequence to new outcome • Interrupt feedback cycles • Relabeling, reframing • Circular questions
Postmodern Solution-focused Berg and deShazer Narrative White and Epston Conversational Anderson and Goolishian	• Normality is socially constructed • Problem-saturated narratives	• Envision new possibilities • Re-author life stories	• Externalize problems • Future oriented potential • Search for exceptions and unique outcomes • Collaborative
Cognitive-behavioral Patterson et al. Alexander et al. Jacobson	Maladaptive, symptomatic behavior reinforced by family attention and reward	Concrete, behavioral goals Improved communication and problem-solving	• Therapist models, educates • Change interpersonal consequences of behavior • Guide family to reward desired behavior • Teach negotiation and problem-solving skills
Psychoeducational Anderson Goldstein Falloon et al.	• Biologically-based disorders; stress/diathesis • Normative and non-normative adaptational challenges; e.g., remarriage; chronic illness	• Family management of stressful conditions • Reduction of stress and stigma • Mastery of family adaptational challenges	• Information • Management guidelines • Social support • Respectful collaboration

truding into relationships. The therapist serves as a coach, preparing and guiding change efforts and toning down reactivity to toxic family issues and contact.

A family evaluation surveys the entire family field. A genogram (McGoldrick et al., 1999) is sketched to diagram the network of relationships, important facts, events, and information (e.g., conflicts, triangles, cutoffs, alcoholism, abuse, secrets, and unresolved losses). A time line is constructed to note patterns in the timing of symptoms and stress events, such as a significant grandparent's death. Client are encouraged to contact family members to clarify obscured or missing information, gaining new perspectives on parents, key relationships, and family history.

In the process of change, clients redevelop more differentiated personal relationships with family members, repairing cutoffs and changing their own part in emotionally charged cycles. The therapist encourages clients to take an I-position, clearly asserting their own thoughts and feelings without attacking, defending, or withdrawal. Techniques of detriangling and reversals (acknowledging the other side of an issue) are two of many means employed to open up rigid patterns. Sessions may start at weekly or biweekly intervals and be spaced out as work proceeds. Follow-through is essential, given the anxiety generated and the need to handle others' self-correcting reactions that can undermine change. Developments by Betty Carter, Monica McGoldrick, and colleagues (e.g., McGoldrick, 1998) have expanded this work to explore and modify the impact of the larger cultural forces of racism, classism, sexism, heterosexism, and other forms of discrimination, such as the effects of slavery across the generations.

Experiential Approaches

Experiential approaches to family therapy were developed by two leading pioneers, Virginia Satir (1964, 1988), who blended a communication approach with a humanistic orientation, and Carl Whitaker (Whitaker & Keith, 1981), who practiced an idiosyncratic style of intervention. Experiential approaches are highly intuitive and relatively atheoretical. Current behavior and feelings are seen as the natural consequence of life experience. Regardless of intent, old pains can be aroused by current interaction. The aim of these growth-oriented approaches is fuller awareness and appreciation of self in relation to others, achieved through an intense, affective experience with open communication of feelings and differences.

In a phenomenological approach to assessment and intervention focused on the immediate experience, the therapist elicits important information in current transactions, emphasizing the holistic nature of human relational systems. The approach encourages exploration, experimentation, and spontaneity of members' responses to one another. Experiential exercises, such as family sculpting and role-play, are used to catalyze this process. The therapist is facilitative, following and reflecting family processes and stimulating genuine relating. Marital enrichment approaches (Guerney, 1991) draw on these ideas and methods.

Problem-Solving Approaches

Structural Model

Structural family therapy, developed by Salvador Minuchin (1974) and colleagues at the

Philadelphia Child Guidance Center (Minuchin, Montalvo, Guerney, Rosman, & Schumer, 1967), has emphasized the importance of family organization for the functioning of the family unit and the well-being of members. The model focuses on the patterning of transactions in which symptoms are embedded. Problems are viewed as an indication of imbalance in family organization, particularly, a malfunctioning hierarchical arrangement with unclear parent and child subsystem boundaries. Commonly, symptoms are a sign of a maladaptive reaction to environmental or developmental changes, such as a life-cycle transition. Child-focused problems often detour conflict between parents or between a single parent and grandparent.

Therapy is short term and directed to strengthen the structural foundation for family functioning. It aims to modify dysfunctional patterns so that the family can better function and cope with life stresses. It is expected that presenting problems, a symptom of family distress, will be resolved as this reorganization is accomplished. Therapy involves three processes: joining, enactment, and restructuring. First, the therapist joins the family system in a position of leadership to form the therapeutic system, connecting with family members, especially parents, to bring about change. Second, the therapist assesses the family experientially as members enact presenting problems in the interview. Third, based on an interactional diagnosis and structural mapping of the immediate family field, tasks and directives are used to restructure the family around its handling of problems. Therapy is action oriented, based on the conviction that behavior change occurs independently of members' insight. The therapist is active in sessions, shifting triangular patterns, blocking dysfunctional coalitions, and promoting healthier alliances. Efforts are made to strengthen the parental subsystem and reinforce appropriate generational boundaries. Live observation of sessions facilitates training and implementation of therapeutic intervention.

The structural model was developed to work effectively with poor, inner-city, multiproblem families and was later applied successfully to problems ranging from psychosomatic disorders to anorexia nervosa, most often with child-focused cases (Minuchin & Fishman, 1981). Recent efforts are directed to change traditional foster care and child welfare systems, criticized for "dismembering families" in fragmented approaches, toward practices that strengthen families and knit together biological and foster relationships (Minuchin, Colapinto, & Minuchin, 1998).

Strategic/Systemic Approaches

Among the most innovative early approaches were the strategic and systemic models of the MRI (Mental Research Institute) group in Palo Alto (Weakland, Fisch, Watzlawick, & Bodin, 1974), the problem-solving approach of Jay Haley (1976) and Cloe Madanes (1981), and the Milan team approach (Selvini Palazzoli, Boscolo, Cecchin, & Prata, 1980). These models focus on clients' immediate social situation. Assuming multiple origins of problems, they view a presenting problem as both a symptom and a response to current stresses, a communicative act that is part of a repetitive sequence of interactions. They focus on how a family has attempted to resolve its problems, because a misguided attempt may make matters worse. The models contend that most families do what they do because they believe it is the best way to approach a problem or it is the only way they know. The Milan approach stresses the importance of learning a family's language and beliefs, seeing the problem through various members' eyes, and taking into account the values and expectations that guide their approach to handling problems and inability to change.

The goal of these brief therapies is limited to solving the particular presenting problem. The therapist's responsibility is only to initiate change that gets a family "unstuck" from unworkable interactional patterns maintaining symptoms. Therapy focuses on problem resolution by altering the feedback loop that maintains symptomatic behavior. Early strategic approaches assumed that change depends more on indirect means of influence than on insight or improved communication. The therapist's stance was highly intellectual and remote from personal involvement, yet active and pragmatic, planning and carrying out a strategy to achieve specific objectives.

Several techniques were developed to this end. Relabeling, reframing, and positive connotation involve strategic redefinition of a problem situation to cast it in a new light. They are commonly used to redefine what has been viewed negatively as a well-intentioned attempt to adapt or protect other family members. The techniques can be useful in shifting a family's rigid view or stereotypic response, altering an unproductive blaming process, or overcoming barriers to change. In reformulation of a problem or set, new solutions become apparent. Circular questioning (Selvini Palazzoli et al., 1980) elicits and enlarges perspectives of various family members about relationship patterns. Directives, widely used by family therapists, are care-

fully designed behavioral tasks assigned for families to carry out between sessions. They are useful in gathering direct information about the ways family members interact and how they respond to change efforts. When well-formulated and well-timed, they can be a highly effective way to bring about structural as well as behavioral change. Indirect techniques are seemingly in opposition to objectives but actually serve to move the family toward them. In paradoxical instructions, no longer widely used, a therapist might prescribe the symptom, or direct clients to do the opposite of their intended goal. Neutrality was advised in the therapist's avoidance of judgment, criticism, or moral alignment with any part of the system. With recognition that therapists cannot be neutral, emphasis has shifted to a therapeutic stance of respectful curiosity (Boscolo, Cecchin, Hoffman, & Penn, 1987; Cecchin, 1987).

Cognitive-Behavioral Approaches

Behavioral approaches to family therapy developed from behavior modification and social learning traditions, increasingly incorporating a cognitive component. Families are viewed as critical learning contexts, created and responded to by members. Therapy attends to transactional rules, behaviors, and conditions under which social behavior is learned, influenced, and changed. Following social exchange principles, family interactions offer many opportunities for rewarding exchanges likely to enhance relationships. In well-functioning families, positive behavior is reinforced far more than troublesome behavior through attention and approval. Poor communication and reliance on coercive control also exacerbate maladaptive behavior and relationship distress.

Intervention objectives are specified in concrete, observable behavior. The therapist guides family members in a straightforward way to learn more effective modes of dealing with one another by changing the interpersonal consequences of behavior (contingencies of reinforcement). Individuals learn to give each other approval and to acknowledge desired behavior instead of reinforcing maladaptive behavior by attention or punishment. The therapist builds communication skills in negotiation and problem solving and fosters adaptability in using varied reponses in different situations. Reciprocity and equitability are encouraged. The therapist, within a positive alliance, serves as a social reinforcer in a role as educator, model, and facilitator. Numerous empirical studies have documented the effectiveness of these approaches with marital conflict (Baucom, Epstein, & Rankin, 1995; Christensen, Jacobson, & Babcock, 1995) and with families of conduct-disordered adolescents (Alexander, Pugh, & Parsons, 1998; Patterson, Reid, Jones, & Conger, 1975).

Recent Developments in Strength-Based Approaches

The field of family therapy has shifted increasingly from a deficit to a resource perspective and from a hierarchical stance of the therapist as expert to a respectful collaboration with family members. Assessment and intervention are redirected from problems and how they are maintained to solutions and how they can be attained. Therapeutic efforts aim to identify and amplify existing and potential competencies and resources. Therapist and client work in partnership to see new possibilities in a problem-saturated situation and to overcome impasses to change and growth. This positive, future-focused orientation shifts the emphasis of therapy from what went wrong to what can be done for enhanced functioning and well-being.

A family resilience-based approach (Walsh, 1998b) builds on these developments to strengthen each family's ability to deal with recent, ongoing, or threatened stress events to reduce vulnerability and master family challenges. This approach draws together studies of individual resilience (e.g., Anthony, 1987; Luther & Ziegler, 1991; Rutter, 1987; Werner, 1993), along with systems-based research on normal family processes (see Walsh, 1993b) and models of family coping and adaptation (McCubbin & Patterson, 1983). A basic premise guiding this approach is that serious life crises and persistent adversity have an impact on the whole family and that, in turn, key family processes influence the recovery and resilience of the family unit and all of its members. How a family manages a disruptive or threatening experience, buffers stress, effectively reorganizes, and reinvests in life pursuits will influence adaptation for all members. Fostering the family's ability to master its immediate crisis situation also increases its capacity to meet future challenges. In strengthening the family as problems are resolved, each intervention is also a preventive measure.

Postmodern Approaches

Growing out of strategic-systemic models, more recent solution-focused and narrative approaches are based in constructivist and social constructionist views of reality (Foucault, 1980; Geertz, 1986; Gergen, 1985; Hoffman, 1990; Laird, 1998; Maturana & Varela, 1980). These approaches refocus attention from problems and the patterns that maintain them to solutions and the processes that enable them. Less concern is given to the nature of problems or how they have developed, and more is directed to future possibilities (Penn, 1985). Therapists search for exceptions: solutions that have worked in other situations and might work now and in the future. As in the MRI Model, people are thought to be constrained by their narrow, pessimistic views of problems, which limits the range of alternatives for resolution. However, these newer approaches do not assume that symptoms necessarily serve ulterior functions for the family and do assume that clients really want to change. The therapeutic relationship eschews the hierarchical power-based position of earlier structural-strategic approaches. Instead, it is built on trust and respect of clients and oriented toward recognizing and amplifying the positive strengths and resources that clients bring and the potentials they may have lost sight of.

Solution-focused approaches avoid complex formulations when simple assumptions will lead more quickly to change (deShazer, 1988; O'Hanlon & Weiner-Davis, 1989). It is believed that complicated problems do not necessarily require complicated solutions. Berg (1997) offers a useful brief approach for social services settings. A risk lies in too narrow a focus that fails to address the broader web of influences in the social context of a problem situation.

Narrative and conversational approaches emphasize the therapeutic conversation and process of "restory-ing" a problematic experience. At the core of therapy is the postmodern conceptualization that reality is subjective and is socially constructed through language. These approaches are underpinned by a philosophy of language suggesting that meaning arises in particular contexts. Therapists do not consider themselves experts in interpreting their client's lives; rather, their skills are in listening well to the narrative, being curious about their story, and "wondering" about alternative possibilities (Anderson, 1997). The client's story is questioned, looked at, and expanded through the collaborative efforts of therapist and client. The goal is to develop new narratives that are more empowering and satisfying. Although critics worry that any story is deemed to be good if useful, therapy attends to the ways language reflects our cultural heritage and larger social context, opening space for voices that have not been heard or views marginalized by dominant stories in the culture. Narrative therapy is finding broad use with a range of difficulties, such as child fears and behavioral problems, couple distress, eating disorders, sexual abuse, and depression (Freedman & Combs, 1996).

The technique of externalization (White & Epston, 1990) serves as a means, through language, to reframe problem situations toward more enabling and empowering constructions for problem resolution. Essentially, it shifts conversation to talk about problems as problems, rather than people as the problem. By separating people from their problems, clients are able to release themselves from overidentification with the problem and lessen pressures of guilt and defensiveness. This allows therapists to acknowledge the power of labels without reinforcing people's attachment to them or letting them escape responsibility for their behavior. An external force may be defined as wreaking havoc on the lives of clients. The therapist then aligns with a symptomatic child (or with a couple or family) as a therapeutic team who, together, will gain control over and defeat this negative force, which is often given a name. Clients are viewed as accountable for the choices that they make in relation to the problem. The goal is to leave clients feeling successful and victorious, shifting a vicious cycle to a virtuous cycle.

Psychoeducational Approaches

The psychoeducational model was developed for family intervention with schizophrenia and other persistent mental and physical illnesses. This multifamily group approach is also finding application with a range of stressful life challenges such as stepfamily formation and adaptation of refugee families (Walsh, 1998b). It provides family education and support for coping and adjustment, with concrete guidelines for crisis management, problem solving, and stress reduction. The rationale for family intervention is explicitly based on the importance of support, practical information, and problem-solving assistance through the predictably stressful periods that can be anticipated in the course of a chronic illness or life transition.

With major mental illness, families are engaged as valued and essential collaborators in the treatment process, with respect for their challenges. This approach does much to correct the blame-laden causal attributions experienced by many families of the mentally ill (Hatfield & Lefley, 1990). The approach is based on a stress-diathesis model, with the assumption that environmental stresses interact negatively with a core biological vulnerability to produce disturbed cognitions and behaviors. Assisted by

concrete support and information, families are viewed as caregiving resources for the long-term management of the condition. Goldstein (1981) first demonstrated the combined effectiveness of brief family therapy and drug maintenance in helping schizophrenic patients maintain functioning in the community in the high-risk months following hospitalization. Falloon (Falloon, Boyd, & McGill, 1984) developed a cost-effective home-based family intervention, emphasizing behavioral problem-solving techniques. The psychoeducational model developed by Anderson and her colleagues (Anderson, Reiss, & Hogarty, 1986) demonstrated effectiveness in the treatment of chronic schizophrenia and reduction of family distress. Family intervention, combined with drug maintenance and social skills training, produced the best results, dramatically reducing relapse rates and improving functioning. A highly structured family-oriented program was designed to avoid treatment dropout, to sustain functioning in the community, and to decrease family stress. As families increase their knowledge about the illness and their confidence about their ability to manage it, reciprocal pressures between the patient and family are reduced. All psychoeducational approaches focus on solving daily problems one at a time, measuring success in small increments, and maintaining family morale.

Psychoeducational family interventions have been adapted to a number of formats including periodic family consultations, workshops, and time-limited or ongoing multifamily groups (McFarlane, 1991). Brief psychoeducational modules, timed for critical phases of an illness or life challenge (Rolland, 1994), support families in digesting manageable portions of a long-term coping process and in handling periodic flareups. Such cost-effective approaches are especially valuable with families at high risk of maladaptation or relapse of a serious condition.

PROGRESS AND CHALLENGES FOR FAMILY SYSTEMS-BASED RESEARCH AND PRACTICE

Table 15.2 provides a summary of the major approaches to family therapy, noting for each the view of problems, therapeutic goals, and process of change. Currently, most clinicians with a family systems orientation combine elements from the various approaches and incorporate multidimensional views of family functioning (Breunlin, Schwartz, & Karrer, 1992). Family therapy training programs value group supervision with live observation of sessions through a one-way mirror to gain a meta-perspective of the therapeutic system and direct feedback to benefit the therapist and family, as in the reflecting team approach (Andersen, 1987).

The field of family therapy, with its rich diversity, continues to flourish and find broad application. Family systems approaches are being used effectively with problems ranging from child or adolescent behavior disorders and couple/family relationship problems to illness, disability, and loss (Campbell & Patterson, 1995; McDaniel, Hepworth, & Doherty, 1992; Rolland, 1994; Walsh & McGoldrick, 1991). It is combined with other therapeutic approaches for substance abuse (Stanton & Todd, 1982; Steinglass, 1987). Multisystemic approaches have been developed to work effectively with eating disorders, trauma survivors, domestic violence, and sexual abuse (Schwartz, 1995; Trepper & Barrett, 1989). (For reviews of appli-

cation and effectiveness, see Almeida & Durkin, 1999; Bograd, 1999; Bograd & Mederos, 1999; Goldner, 1999; Lebow & Gurman, 1995, Pinsof & Wynne, 1995).

Pioneering family systems research has developed multidimensional empirically based models for assessment of family functioning. Notably, the Beavers Family Systems Model, Olson's Circumplex Model, and the McMaster Model (see Walsh, 1993b) have found wide application. The self-report inventory PREPARE (Fowers & Olson, 1986) is being used with premarital couples to predict marital success and identify problem areas. Recently advanced family resilience models (McCubbin, McCubbin, McCubbin, & Futrell, 1998; McCubbin, McCubbin, Thompson, & Fromer, 1998; Walsh, 1998b) also offer potential for intervention planning and outcome research, enabling clinicians to assess a family's current functioning on key system dimensions and target focal priorities for strengthening families. Several challenges and opportunities ahead are important to note.

Strength-oriented family approaches. We need to shift focus from how families fail to how families can succeed. Family research, policy, and funding priorities must be rebalanced from psychopathology to health and prevention if we are to move beyond the rhetoric of family strengths to clearer understanding of key variables and needed intervention and prevention programs for healthy family functioning. Concerted efforts between family therapy and family support movements hold untapped potential, particularly in strengthening the most vulnerable families (Kagan & Weissbourd, 1994; Kaplan & Girard, 1994; Walsh, 1998b).

Multidisciplinary collaboration. The bridges between the social sciences, the clinical field, and social policy need to be strengthened for greater mutual exchange of perspectives and concerted approaches to understanding and supporting family well-being. Greater dialogue between clinicians and researchers and across mental health disciplines will be mutually beneficial.

Quantitative and qualitative methods. Our knowledge and practice will be enriched through the contributions of both quantitative and qualitative research methodologies. Quantitative family-process research has focused on organizational and communication patterns that can be measured through observation, rating scales, and self-report measures. Qualitative methods hold potential for exploring beliefs, the meaning of experiences, and other subjectivities in family life. Ethnographic methods and narrative life accounts can be particularly valuable for understanding family development over time. Postpositivist research, now coming to the fore, does not reject empirical research, but rather emphasizes the contextual and self-referential nature of the research process, findings, and interpretation of data (Doherty, Boss, LaRossa, Schumm, & Steinmetz, 1993).

Challenges of family diversity. Family process research, clinical training, and public policy need to keep pace with the dramatic changes and growing diversity of families. A fundamental problem concerns the relevance of categories and scales based on samples representing a narrow band on the wide spectrum of today's families. Recent studies have expanded the database to many cohorts, yet they still tend to compare families to one standard, as if one size fits all (Walsh, 1996).

Falicov (1995) offers a useful multidimensional framework, viewing each family as occupying a complex ecological niche, sharing borders and common ground with other families, as well as differing positions (e.g., gender, economic status, and life stage). A holistic assessment includes the varied contexts a family inhabits, aiming to understand constraints and resources. A family resilience framework shares this perspective, striking a balance that allows us to identify common threads of family functioning while also taking each family's unique challenges into account.

Future research and intervention must be better attuned to emerging family challenges and opportunities. Attention should be expanded beyond the household to mobilize extended and informal kin networks, which have fortified African American and immigrant families (Boyd-Franklin, 1989; Falicov, 1998) and "families of choice" in gay communities (Laird, 1993; Laird & Green, 1996). Also, with the aging of societies, more attention is required to families in later life and in particular to chronic illness, disability, and end-of-life issues (Walsh, 1998a), refocusing from a primary caregiver (usually female) to support a family caregiving team. Finally, the clinical field is now just beginning to recognize—and research is documenting—the importance of spirituality as a vital dimension of human experience. We need to incorporate it into clinical practice, as we do other aspects of culture, to understand spiritual sources of distress and to help clients tap faith and congregational support for healing and growth (Walsh, 1999).

CONCLUSION

As a basic worldview, a systems perspective is distinguished by attention to problems in context; interactions between individuals, families, and larger systems; circular versus linear processes; and patterns that connect over time. For any presenting problem, the context can be punctuated in a more broadly inclusive or focused way. A systemic assessment includes inquiry about the family and social context of a problem, interactional processes surrounding it, timing in the family life cycle, and relevant multigenerational and cultural influences. The inclusion of many family members yields more information and potential resources. Family functioning and resilience involve the interweaving of belief systems, organizational patterns, and communication processes.

A clinician's ethical stance must be carefully considered in all situations. We need to be careful not to impose our values on clients and yet, we cannot remain silent when harmful abuses are taking place. We must remain mindful of societal influences that maintain gender bias, racism, heterosexism, and violence. Family therapists have become attentive to issues of social justice in our theory and practice, and we increasingly view our responsibility as extending beyond the therapy room to address larger system patterns that affect the well-being of children and families.

An integrative strength-promoting approach to family therapy involves a crucial shift in emphasis from family damage to family challenge. A family resilience model for research and practice (Walsh, 1996, 1998b) seeks to understand how families can survive and rebound through stressful crisis or persistent adversity and fosters key processes for resilience with clients in distress. As family therapy has evolved from a focus on family deficits to family strengths and resources, the therapeutic relationship has become more collaborative and empowering of our clients' potentials. We have come to recognize that successful interventions rest as much on tapping into family resources as on a therapist's change techniques (Karpel, 1986). The need to strengthen families has never been more urgent. Family therapists may differ in approach, yet, all share a deep conviction in the potential for healing, resilience, and growth in all families.

REFERENCES

Ackerman, N. (1958). *The psychodynamics of family life.* New York: Basic Books.

Ahrons, C. (1994). *The good divorce: Keeping your family together when your marriage comes apart.* New York: HarperCollins.

Alexander, J. F., Pugh, C., & Parsons, B. (1998). *Blueprints for violence prevention: Functional family therapy.* Golden, CO: Venture.

Almedia, R., & Durkin, T. (1999). The cultural context model: Therapy for couples with domestic violence. *Journal of Marital and Family Therapy, 25*(3), 313-324.

Andersen, T. (1987). The reflecting team: Dialogue and meta-dialogue in clinical work. *Family Process, 26,* 415-428.

Anderson, C. M., Reiss, D., & Hogarty, G. (1986). *Schizophrenia and the family.* New York: Guilford.

Anderson, H. (1997). *Conversation, language, and possibilities: A postmodern approach to therapy.* New York: Basic Books.

Anderson, H., & Goolishian, H. (1988). Human systems as linguistic systems: Preliminary and evolving ideas about the implications for clinical theory. *Family Process, 27,* 371-393.

Anthony, E. J. (1987). Risk, vulnerability, and resilience: An overview. In E. J. Anthony & B. Cohler (Eds.), *The invulnerable child.* New York: Guilford.

Aponte, H. (1994). *Bread and spirit: Therapy with the new poor.* New York: Norton.

Bateson, G. (1979). *Mind and nature: A necessary unity.* New York: Dutton.

Baucom, D., Epstein, N., & Rankin, L. (1995). Cognitive aspects of cognitive-behavioral marital therapy. In N. Jacobson & A. Gurman (Eds.), *Clinical handbook of couple therapy* (pp. 65-90). New York: Guilford.

Beavers, W. R., & Hampson, R. (1993). Measuring family competence: The Beavers Systems Model. In F. Walsh (Ed.), *Normal family processes* (2nd ed., pp. 73-103). New York: Guilford.

Berg, I. (1997). *Family-based services: A solution-focused approach.* New York: Norton.

Bertalanffy, L. (1968). *General system theory and psychiatry: Foundation, developments, applications.* New York: Braziller.

Bograd, M. (1999). Strengthening domestic violence theories: Intersections of race, class, sexual orientation, and gender. *Journal of Marital and Family Therapy, 25*(3), 275-289.

Bograd, M., & Mederos, F. (1999). Battering and couples therapy: Universal screening and selection of treatment modality. *Journal of Marital and Family Therapy, 25*(3), 291-312.

Boscolo, L., Cecchin, G., Hoffman, L., & Penn, P. (1987). *Milan systemic family therapy: Conversations in theory and practice.* New York: Basic.

Boszormenyi-Nagy, I. (1987). *Foundations of contextual family therapy.* New York: Brunner/Mazel.

Bowen, M. (1978). *Family therapy in clinical practice.* New York: Jason Aronson.

Boyd-Franklin, N. (1989). *Black families in therapy: A multi-systems approach.* New York: Guilford.

Breunlin, D., Schwartz, R., & Karrer, B. (1992). *Metaframeworks: Transcending the models of family therapy.* San Francisco: Jossey-Bass.

Byng-Hall, J. (1995). *Writing family scripts: Improvisation and systems change.* New York: Guilford.

Campbell, T., & Patterson, J. (1995). The effectiveness of family interventions in the treatment of physical illness. *Journal of Marital & Family Therapy, 21, 545-583.*

Carter, B., & McGoldrick, M. (1998). *The expanded family life cycle: Individual, family, and social perspectives* (3rd ed.). Needham Hill, MA: Allyn & Bacon.

Cecchin, G. (1987). Hypothesizing, circularity, and neutrality revisited: An invitation to curiosity. *Family Process, 26, 405-414.*

Christensen, A., Jacobson, N., & Babcock, J. (1995). Integrative behavioral couple therapy. In N. Jacobson & A. Gurman (Eds.), *Clinical handbook of couple therapy* (pp. 31-64). New York: Guilford.

Coontz, S. (1997). *The way we really are: Coming to terms with America's changing families.* New York: Basic Books.

de Shazer, S. (1988). *Clues: Investigating solutions in brief therapy.* New York: Norton.

Doherty, W., Boss, P., LaRossa, R., Schumm, W., & Steinmetz, S. (1993). Family theory and methods: A contextual approach. In P. Boss, W. Doherty, W. LaRossa, W. Schumm, & S. Steinmetz (Eds.), *Sourcebook of family theories and methods* (pp. 3-30). New York: Plenum.

Epstein, N., Bishop, D., Ryan, C., Miller, I., & Keitnor, G. (1993). The McMaster model: View of healthy family functioning. In F. Walsh (Ed.) *Normal family processes* (2nd ed., pp. 138-160). New York: Guilford.

Falicov, C. (1995). Training to think culturally: A multidimensional comparative framework. *Family Process, 34,* 3733-388.

Falicov, C. (1998). *Latino families in therapy.* New York: Guilford.

Falloon, I., Boyd, J., & McGill, C. (1984). *Family care of schizophrenia: A problem-solving approach to the treatment of mental illness.* New York: Guilford.

Foucault, M. (1980). *Power/knowledge: Selected interviews and other writings, 1972-1977.* New York: Pantheon.

Fowers, B., & Olson, D. (1986). Predicting marital success with PREPARE. *Journal of Marital & Family Therapy, 12,* 403-413.

Framo, J. (1970). Symptoms from a family transactional viewpoint. In N. Ackerman (Ed.), *Family therapy in transition.* Boston: Little, Brown.

Framo, J. (1976). Family of origin as a therapeutic resource for adults in marital and family therapy: You can and should go home again. *Family Process, 15,* 193-210.

Freedman, J., & Combs, G. (1996). *Narrative therapy: The social construction of preferred realities.* New York: Norton.

Garmezy, N. (1991). Resiliency and vulnerability to adverse developmental outcomes associated with poverty. *American Behavioral Scientist, 34,* 416-430.

Geertz, C. (1986). Making experiences, authoring selves. In V. Turner & E. Bruner (Eds.), *The anthropology of experience.* Chicago: University of Chicago Press.

Gergen, K. J. (1985). The social constructionist movement in modern psychology. *American Psychologist, 40,* 31-329.

Goldner, V. (1988). Generation and gender: Normative and covert hierarchies. *Family Process, 27,* 17-21.

Goldner, V. (1999). Morality and multiplicity: Perspectives on the treatment of violence in intimate life. *Journal of Marital and Family Therapy, 25*(3), 325-336.

Goldstein, M. (1981). *New developments in interventions with families of schizophrenics.* San Francisco: Jossey-Bass.

Gottman, J. (1993). A theory of marital dissolution and stability. *Journal of Family Psychology, 7,* 57-75.

Guerney, B. (1991). Marital and family enrichment research: A decade review and look ahead. In A. Booth (Ed.), *Contemporary families*. Minneapolis: National Council on Family Relations.

Haley, J. (1976). *Problem-solving therapy*. San Francisco: Jossey-Bass.

Hare-Mustin, R. (1987). The problem of gender in family therapy theory. *Family Process, 26,* 15-33.

Hatfield, A., & Lefley, H. (1990). *Families of the mentally ill: Coping and adaptation*. New York: Guilford.

Hetherington, M., Law, T., & O'Connor, T. (1993). Divorce: Challenges, changes, and new chances. In F. Walsh (Ed.), *Normal family processes* (2nd ed.) New York: Guilford.

Hoffman, L. (1990). Constructing realities: An art of lenses. *Family Process, 29,* 1-13.

Imber-Black, E. (1988). *Families and larger systems*. New York: Guilford.

Imber-Black, E., Roberts, J., Whiting, R. (Eds.). (1988). *Rituals in families and family therapy*. New York: Norton.

Kagan, S., & Weissbourd, B. (1994). *Putting families first*. San Francisco: Jossey-Bass.

Kaplan, L., & Girard, J. (1994). *Strengthening high-risk families*. New York: Lexington.

Karpel, M. (1986). *Family resources*. New York: Guilford.

Kaufman, J., & Ziegler, E. (1987). Do abused children become abusive parents? *American Journal of Orthopsychiatry, 57,* 186-192.

Laird, J. (1993). Lesbian and gay families. In F. Walsh (Ed.), *Normal family processes* (2nd ed.). New York: Guilford.

Laird, J. (1998). Family-centered practice in the postmodern era. In C. Franklin & P. Nurius (Eds.), *Constructivism in practice* (pp. 217-233). Families International.

Laird, J., & Green, R.-J. (1996). *Lesbian and gays in families and family therapy*. San Francisco: Jossey-Bass.

Lebow, J., & Gurman, A. (1995). Research assessing couple and family therapy. *Annual Review of Psychology, 46,* 27-57.

Luther, S. S., & Ziegler, E. (1991). Vulnerability and competence: A review of research on resilience in childhood. *American Journal of Orthopsychiatry, 61,* 6-22.

Madanes, C. (1981). *Strategic family therapy*. San Francisco: Jossey-Bass.

Maturana, H., & Varela, F. (1980). *Autopoiesis and cognition: The realization of living*. Boston: D. Reidel.

McCubbin, H., McCubbin, M., McCubbin, A., & Futrell, J. (Eds.). (1998). *Resiliency in ethnic minority families: Vol. 2. African-American families*. Thousand Oaks, CA: Sage.

McCubbin, H., McCubbin, M., Thompson, E., & Fromer, J. (Eds.). (1998). *Resiliency in ethnic minority families:*

Vol. 1. Native and immigrant families. Thousand Oaks, CA: Sage.

McCubbin, H., & Patterson, J. (1983). The family stress process: The double ABCX Model of adjustment and adaptation. In H. McCubbin, M. Sussman, & J. M. Patterson (Eds.), *Social stress and the family: Advances in family stress theory and research*. New York: Haworth.

McDaniel, S., Hepworth, J., & Doherty, H. (1992). *Medical family therapy: Psychosocial treatment of families with health problems*. New York: Basic Books.

McFarlane, W. (1991). Family psychoeducational treatment. In A. Gurman & D. Kniskern (Eds.), *Handbook of family therapy* (Vol. 2). New York: Brunner/Mazel.

McGoldrick, M. (1998). *Revisioning family therapy*. New York: Guilford.

McGoldrick, M., Anderson, C., & Walsh, F. (1989). *Women in families: Framework for family therapy*. New York: Norton.

McGoldrick, M., Gerson, R., & Shellenberger, S. (1999). *Genograms: Assessment and intervention* (2nd. ed.) New York, Norton.

McGoldrick, M., Giordano, J., & Pearce, J. (Eds.). (1996). *Ethnicity and family therapy* (2nd ed.). New York: Guilford.

Minuchin, P., Colapinto, J., & Minuchin, S. (1998). *Working with families of the poor*. New York: Guilford.

Minuchin, S. (1974). *Families and family therapy*. Cambridge, MA: Harvard University Press.

Minuchin, S., & Fishman, C. (1981). *Family therapy techniques*. Cambridge, MA: Harvard University Press.

Minuchin, S., Montalvo, B., Guerney, B., Rosman, B., & Schumer, F. (1967). *Families of the slums*. New York: Basic Books.

Nichols, M., & Schwartz, R. (1997). *Family therapy: concepts and methods*. Needham Heights, MA: Allyn & Bacon.

O'Hanlon, W., & Weiner-Davis, M. (1989). *In search of solutions in brief therapy*. New York: Norton.

Olson, D. (1993). Circumplex model of marital and family systems: Assessing family functioning. In F. Walsh (Ed.), *Normal family processes* (2nd ed., pp. 104-137). New York: Guilford.

Patterson, G. R., Reid, J. B., Jones, R. R., & Conger R. (1975). *A social learning approach to family intervention*. Eugene, OR: Castalia.

Paul, N., & Paul, B. (1975). *A marital puzzle: Transgenerational analysis in marriage*. New York: Norton.

Penn, P. (1985). Feed forward: Future questions, future maps. *Family Process, 24,* 299-310.

Pinderhughes, E. (1989). *Understanding race, ethnicity, and power: The key to efficacy in clinical practice.* New York: Free Press.

Pinsof, W., & Wynne, L. (Eds.). (1995). The effectiveness of marital and family therapy [Special issue]. *Journal of Marital & Family Therapy, 21*(4).

Reiss, D. (1981). *The family's construction of reality.* Cambridge, MA: Harvard University Press.

Rolland, J. S. (1994). *Families, illness, and disability: An integrative treatment model.* New York: Basic Books.

Ruesch, J., & Bateson, G. (1951). *Communication: The social matrix of psychiatry.* New York: Norton.

Rutter, M. (1987). Psychosocial resilience and protective mechanisms. *American Journal of Orthopsychiatry, 57,* 316-331.

Satir, V. (1964). *Conjoint family therapy.* Palo Alto, CA: Science and Behavior Books.

Satir, V. (1988). *The new peoplemaking.* Palo Alto, CA: Science and Behavior Books.

Scharff, D., & Scharff, J. (1987). *Object relations family therapy.* New York: Jason Aronson.

Schwartz, R. (1995). *Internal family systems therapy.* New York: Guilford.

Selvini Palazzoli, M., Boscolo, L., Cecchin, G., & Prata, J. (1980). Hypothesizing—circularity—neutrality: Three guidelines for the conductor of the session. *Family Process, 19,* 3-12.

Skolnick, A. (1991). *Embattled paradise: The American family in an age of uncertainty.* New York: Basic Books.

Stanton, M., & Todd, T. (1982). *The family therapy of drug abuse and addiction.* New York: Guilford.

Steinglass, P. (1987). *The alcoholic family.* New York: Basic Books.

Trepper, T., & Barrett, M. J. (1989). *Systemic treatment of incest: A therapeutic handbook.* New York: Brunner/Mazel.

Visher, E., & Visher, J. S. (1996). *Therapy with stepfamilies.* New York: Brunner/Mazel.

Walsh, F. (1987). The clinical utility of normal family research. *Psychotherapy, 24,* 496-503.

Walsh, F. (1989). Reconsidering gender in the marital "quid pro quo." In M. McGoldrick, C. Anderson, & F. Walsh (Eds.), *Women in families: Framework for family therapy.* New York: Norton.

Walsh, F. (1991). Promoting healthy functioning in divorced and remarried families. In A. Gurman & D.

Kniskern (Eds.), *Handbook of family therapy* (2nd ed.). New York: Brunner/Mazel.

Walsh, F. (1993a). Conceptualization of normal family processes. In F. Walsh (Ed.), *Normal family processes* (2nd ed., pp. 3-69). New York: Guilford.

Walsh, F. (1993b). *Normal family processes* (2nd ed.). New York: Guilford.

Walsh, F. (1996). The concept of family resilience: Crisis and challenge. *Family Process, 35,* 261-281.

Walsh, F. (1998a). Families in later life: Challenge and opportunities. In B. Carter & M. McGoldrick (Eds.), *The expanded family life cycle.* Needham Heights, MA: Allyn & Bacon.

Walsh, F. (1998b). *Strengthening family resilience.* New York: Guilford.

Walsh, F. (Ed.). (1999). *Spiritual resources in family therapy.* New York: Guilford.

Walsh, F., & Anderson, C. (Eds.). (1988). *Chronic disorders and the family.* New York: Haworth.

Walsh, F., Jacob, L., & Simons, J. (1995). Facilitating healthy divorce processes: Therapy and mediation approaches. In N. Jacobson & A. Gurman (Eds.), *Clinical handbook of couple therapy.* New York: Guilford.

Walsh, F., & McGoldrick, M. (Eds.). (1991). *Living beyond loss: Death in the family.* New York: Norton.

Walters, M., Carter, B., Papp, P., & Silverstein, O. (1988). *The invisible web: Gender patterns in family relationships.* New York: Guilford.

Watzlawick, P., Beavin, J., & Jackson, D. (1967). *Pragmatics of human communication.* New York: Norton.

Weakland, J., Fisch, R., Watzlawick, P., & Bodin, A. (1974). Brief therapy: Focused problem resolution. *Family Process, 13,* 141-168.

Werner, E. E. (1993). Risk, resilience, and recovery: Perspectives from the Kauai longitudinal study. *Development and Psychopathology, 5,* 503-515.

Whitaker, C., & Keith, D. (1981). Symbolic-experiential family therapy. In A. Gurman & D. Kniskern (Eds.), *Handbook of family therapy.* New York: Brunner/Mazel.

White, M., & Epston, D. (1990). *Narrative means to therapeutic ends.* New York: Norton.

Zacks, E., Green, R. J., & Marrow, J. (1988). Comparing lesbian and heterosexual couples on the Circumplex Model: An initial investigation. *Family Process, 27,* 471-484.

CHAPTER SIXTEEN

Crisis Intervention Practices in Social Work Settings

ALBERT R. ROBERTS

JACQUI CORCORAN

Crisis intervention is operationally defined as the point in time when a clinical social worker enters into the life situation of an individual, group, or family to alleviate the impact of an acute crisis episode and to help mobilize the coping skills and resources of those differentially affected. This clinical assistance may be given over the telephone or in person (Roberts, 1990; Roberts & Dziegielewski, 1995).

An accurate definition of the term *crisis* must be based on subjective reality because what precipitates a crisis episode in one individual might not generate such a response in another person. A crisis state occurs when an individual perceives an event as a threat to need fulfillment, safety, or social functioning. The term crisis re-

fers to a person's perception of feelings of fear, shock, and distress about the disruption, not to the disruption or event itself (Roberts, 1990; Roberts & Dziegielewski, 1995). Roberts (2000) aptly stated,

> A person in a crisis state has experienced a highly threatening, hazardous, or traumatic event, is in a vulnerable state, has failed to cope and lessen the stress or trauma through customary coping strategies, and thus enters into a state of disequilibrium—an active or acute crisis state.

Several integrative crisis intervention approaches offer much promise for the future in terms of optimizing crisis resolution, behavioral change, and cognitive mastery. Clinical practice theories and models that have been integrated with crisis intervention are a strengths perspective, based on solution-focused therapy; a cognitive restructuring strategy, based on time-limited cognitive therapy; and a systems perspective. Roberts's (1995, 1996) seven-stage crisis intervention model is the first step-by-step clinical model that builds on clients' strengths, integrating cognitive therapy and solution-focused therapy techniques with crisis intervention. This chapter will include a full description of Roberts's crisis intervention model, with detailed information on Stage 1, lethality assessment, and the best ways to determine which clients are in imminent danger to self and/or others.

Solution-based therapy puts emphasis on working with client strengths. The client is viewed as being resourceful and having untapped resources or latent inner coping skills on which to draw. This approach uses specifically explicated clinical techniques (e.g., the miracle question, the scaling technique) appropriate for crisis intervention practice. Solution-based therapy and the strengths perspective view the client as being resilient. The resilient client generally has the high self-esteem, social support network, and problem-solving skills to cope with, bounce back, and thrive in the aftermath of a series of stressful life events or traumatic events.

CRISIS INTERVENTION PROGRAMS AND 24-HOUR CRISIS HOTLINES

During the last quarter of the 20th century, thousands of crisis intervention programs have been established throughout the United States and Canada. There are currently over 1,400 grassroots crisis intervention units and community crisis centers affiliated with the American Association of Suicidology or a local community mental health center. There are also over 9,000 victim assistance, rape crisis, and child sexual abuse intervention programs; police-based crisis intervention programs; and battered women's shelters and hotlines. In addition, crisis services are provided at thousands of local hospital emergency rooms, hospital-based trauma centers and emergency psychiatric services, suicide prevention centers, and pastoral counseling services (Roberts, in press).

24-Hour Hotlines

In American society, traumatic events and acute crisis episodes have become pervasive. Each year, millions of people are confronted with traumatic crisis-producing events that they are unable to resolve on their own, and they turn for help to a 24-hour telephone crisis line, crisis units of community mental health centers, and outpatient hospital-based programs (for an example of a call to a 24-hour hotline, see Box 16.1).

Crisis intervention units and hotlines provide information, crisis assessments, intervention, and referrals for callers with such problems as depression, suicide ideation, psychiatric emergencies, chemical dependency, AIDS, sexual dysfunction, woman battering, and crime victimization. Because of their 24-hour availability, hotlines can provide immediate, although temporary, intervention. Some crisis victims do not have a caring friend or relative to whom they can turn; they often benefit from an empathetic, active listener. Even when significant others are available to aid the person in crisis, hotlines provide a valuable service by

---

BOX 16.1

Case Example 1: Suicidal Crisis

Sylvia Jenkins, a white female of 23, called the 24-hour suicide crisis intervention hotline. She told the telephone counselor that her boyfriend of 3 years had broken up with her the week before. She said it hurt so much she felt like there was no choice but to die, and that without him, she didn't have anyone. When asked about friends, she said she had mainly hung around his friends and hadn't really developed any friendships on her own. As far as family support, Sylvia related she was estranged from her family, who lived in another state. She reported she had been sexually abused by her father when she was growing up. She had sought counseling for depression while she was at college and talked a lot about the sexual abuse. When she confronted her father, he denied its occurrence, and her mother sided with Sylvia's father. As a result, Sylvia cut off contact with her family.

Sylvia reported she had graduated from college the year before and had moved in with her boyfriend because he got a job as an engineer. Sylvia said she was unable to find a professional job with her liberal arts degree, and she was working as a secretary. She said she hated her job and described it as "boring" and "unfulfilling." Sylvia said that she didn't feel like she had anything left to live for.

---

linking the caller to appropriate community resources.

The large number of documented calls for help to crisis hotlines—an estimated 4.3 million calls annually—provides a major indicator of the importance of these hotlines (Roberts, 1995). The first national organizational survey of crisis units and centers yielded a response from 107 programs (Roberts, 1995). The researcher's summary findings indicated that a total of 578,793 crisis callers were handled by the crisis centers and programs in the 1-year period directly prior to receipt of the mailed questionnaire, or an annual average of 5,409 callers per crisis line/crisis program. In 1990, there were 796 crisis intervention units and programs (affiliated with a community mental health center) operating throughout the United States, and the annual average number of callers received by each program was 5,409. As a result of multiplying the average number of callers by the

number of crisis programs, Roberts (1995) estimated the annual number of callers to be 4.3 million or 4,305,787. If we broaden our estimate to all national and local 24-hour crisis lines, including crime victims, battered women, sexual assault victims, troubled employees, adolescent runaways, child abuse victims, and the crisis intervention units at the mental health centers, the total estimate would be about 35 million to 45 million crisis callers per year (Roberts, 2000).

The primary objective of a crisis intervention program is to intervene on behalf of the person in crisis at the earliest possible stage. Thus, given the immediacy and rapid response rate of telephone crisis counseling and referrals, 24-hour crisis lines generally meet their objective (Waters & Finn, 1995). With the development of crisis centers nationwide, there has been a considerable increase in the use of the telephone as a method of rapid crisis assessment and management. The 24-hour telephone crisis service maximizes the immediacy and availability of crisis intervention. It also provides anonymity to the caller while assessing the risk of suicide and imminent danger. The telephone crisis intervener is trained to establish rapport with the caller, conduct a brief assessment, provide a sympathetic ear, help develop a crisis management plan, and/or refer the caller to an appropriate treatment program or service. In most cases, effective crisis resolution can be facilitated by suicide prevention hotlines as long as they provide referral and follow-up services.

Professor Waters and Finn (1995) have reviewed and discussed the primary objectives and functions of different types of crisis hotlines for vulnerable and high-risk populations:

- Career-oriented and job information hotlines
- Employee assistance hotlines
- Information and referral hotline for dementia caregivers
- Kidline
- Media call-ins
- Police emergency calls, 911
- Substance abuse crisis lines
- Suicide prevention hotlines
- Teenlines
- Telephone reassurance programs for the elderly
- Telephone crisis treatment for agoraphobia
- University-based counseling hotlines
- 24-hour availability for telephone therapy with one of the 300 licensed family therapists, psychologists, or social workers on call

Suicide Prevention and Crisis Centers

Suicide prevention services began in England in 1906, when the Salvation Army opened an antisuicide bureau focused on helping people who attempted suicide. Also in 1906, the Rev. Harry M. Warren, Jr. (a minister and pastoral counselor), opened the National Save-a-Life League in New York City. Over the many decades of its existence, the league's 24-hour hotline has been answered by full-time staff, trained volunteers, and in a few instances, consulting psychiatrists who have served on the agency's board of directors.

By the 1960s and early 1970s, federal funding was made available as a result of the Community Mental Health Center Act of 1963 and by the National Institute of Mental Health (NIMH). Between 1968 and 1972, almost 200 suicide prevention centers were established (Roberts, 1979, p. 398). In the United States and Canada, that number now has increased more than sevenfold. These suicide prevention and crisis intervention programs help depressed children, youth, and adults; people with suicide ideation and prior suicide attempts; people experiencing marital conflict; people with adjustment disorders; and people in psychiatric emergencies.

National Domestic Violence Hotline

A toll-free, 24-hour national domestic violence hotline was established in February 1996. Operated by the Texas Council on Family Violence in Austin, the crisis phone line provides immediate crisis assessment and intervention, as well as referrals to emergency services and shelters throughout the United States. Initially, the national hotline received a $1 million grant from the U.S. Department of Health and Human Services, and its annual budget is $1.2 million per year.

In January 1997, the Center for Social Work Research at The School of Social Work of the

University of Texas at Austin completed the first evaluation study of the National Domestic Violence Hotline (Lewis, Danis, & McRoy, 1997).

The high frequency of incoming calls to the National Domestic Violence Hotline—61,677 calls—during its first 6 months of operation is an important initial indicator of success. The high volume of calls exceeded expectations (Roberts, 2000).

CRISIS INTERVENTION PRACTICES

Crisis clinicians should adopt an active and directive role without taking problem ownership away from the individual in crisis too quickly. The skilled crisis intervener should display acceptance and hopefulness to communicate to people in crisis that their intense emotional turmoil and threatening situations are not hopeless and that, in fact, they (like others in similar situations before them) will survive the crisis successfully and become better prepared to deal with potentially hazardous life events in their future.

To become an effective crisis clinician, it is important to gauge the stages and completeness of the intervention. Keep in mind that the following paradigm and seven-stage model should be viewed as a guide, not as a rigid process, because with some clients, the stages may overlap.

Roberts's (1991, 2000) seven-stage model of crisis intervention has been used for helping people in acute psychological crisis, acute situational crises, and acute stress disorders. The seven stages are as follows:

1. Plan and conduct a thorough assessment (including lethality, dangerousness to self or others, and immediate psychosocial needs)

2. Make psychological contact, establish rapport, and rapidly establish the relationship (conveying genuine respect for the client, acceptance, reassurance, and a nonjudgmental attitude)
3. Examine the dimensions of the problem to define it (including the last straw or precipitating event)
4. Encourage an exploration of feelings and emotions
5. Generate, explore, and assess past coping attempts
6. Restore cognitive functioning through implementation of an action plan
7. Follow up, leaving the door open for booster sessions 3 and/or 6 months later

1. Plan and conduct a thorough psychosocial and lethality assessment. In many cases, Stages 1 and 2 occur at the same time. However, first and foremost, basic information needs to be obtained to determine whether the caller is in imminent danger. Crisis clinicians are trained to perform an ongoing and rapid risk assessment with all clients in crisis. Crisis counselors, psychologists, and social workers encounter a full range of self-destructive individuals in crisis, including potentially lethal drug overdoses, depressed and lonely callers who have attempted suicide, and impulsive acting-out adolescents threatening to injure someone. In cases of imminent danger, emergency medical or police intervention is often necessary. All suicide prevention and other 24-hour crisis hotlines have access to paramedics and emergency medical technicians, poison control centers, the police, and the emergency rescue squad. It is critically important for the crisis intervener to be in close contact with the crisis caller before, during, and after medical stabilization and discharge.

In many other crisis situations, there is some potential for danger and harm. Because of potential danger from crisis callers with a history of reckless driving, binge drinking, chemical dependency, manic-depression, explosive anger, and/or pre-occupation with suicidal thoughts or fantasies, it is imperative that the crisis intervener use Stages 1 through 7 of Roberts's model as a framework and guide to crisis intervention.

Assessments of imminent danger and potential lethality should determine

- Whether or not the crisis caller needs medical attention (e.g., drug overdose, suicide attempt, or domestic violence)
- If the crisis caller is thinking about killing herself or himself (Are these general thoughts, or does the caller have a specific suicide plan or pact with the location, time, and method specified?)
- If the caller is a victim of domestic violence, sexual assault, and/or other violent crime. If the caller is a victim, ask whether the batterer is nearby or likely to return soon.
- Whether or not the children are in danger
- If the victim needs emergency transportation to the hospital or shelter
- If the crisis caller is under the influence of alcohol or drugs
- If the caller is about to injure herself or himself (e.g., self-injurious behaviors or self-mutilations)
- Whether or not any violent individuals are living in the residence (i.e., assaultive boarders, elder abusers, sibling abusers, etc.)

If time permits, the risk assessment should include the following (recognize that a client who is in imminent danger needs to immediately go to a safe place):

- In domestic violence situations, determine the nature of the woman's previous efforts to protect herself or her children to determine her ability to protect herself.
- In domestic violence cases, to fully assess the perpetrator's threat, inquire into the batterer's history of criminal activity, physical abuse, substance abuse, destruction of property, impulsive acts, mental disorders, psychiatric diagnosis, suicide threats or gestures, stalking behavior, and erratic employment or long periods of unemployment.
- If the caller is a victim of a violent crime, is there a history of prior visits to the hospital emergency room for physical abuse, drug overdose, or suicide attempts?
- Are there any guns or rifles in the home?
- Has anyone recently used a weapon against the crisis caller?
- Has the caller received any terrorist threats, including death threats?
- Determine whether the caller is suffering from major depression, intense anxiety, phobic reactions, agitation, paranoid delusions, acute stress disorder, adjustment disorder, and/or sleep disturbances. (Roberts, in press; Roberts & Burman, 1998)

2. *Make psychological contact and rapidly establish the relationship.* This second stage involves the initial contact between the crisis intervener and the potential client. The major task for the clinician at this point is to establish rapport by conveying genuine respect for and acceptance of the client. Clients also often need reassurance and reinforcement that they can be helped and that this is the appropriate place to receive such help. For example, sufferers of obsessive-compulsive disorders (OCD) and phobias, such as agoraphobia, often have strong feelings that they will never get better. This is often the case when they have been misdiag-

nosed with a psychosis or personality disorder by a crisis clinician who has never seen patients with OCD or agoraphobia. If the crisis clinician has helped many other clients suffering from agoraphobia, he or she might provide the client with some reassuring examples: for example, a patient from a few years ago could not even leave his room for a 4-month period and now is married and successfully working 5 days a week outside of his home.

3. *Examine the dimensions of the problem to define it.* It is useful to try to identify the following: (a) the "last straw" or precipitating event that led the client to seek help, (b) previous coping methods, and (c) dangerousness or lethality. Crisis counselors should explore these dimensions of the problem through specific open-ended questions. The focus must be on *now and how* rather than *then and why*. For example, key questions would be

What situation or event led you to seek help?
When did this event take place?

4. *Encourage an exploration of feelings and emotions.* Step 4 is closely related to examining and defining the dimensions of the problem, particularly the precipitating event. It is presented here as a separate step because some therapists overlook it in their attempt to make rapid assessment and find the precipitating event. It is extremely therapeutic for a client to ventilate and express feelings and emotions in an accepting, supportive, private, and nonjudgmental setting.

The primary technique for identifying a client's feelings and emotions is through active listening. This means that the crisis intervener listens in an empathic and supportive way to both the client's reflection of what happened and how the client feels about the crisis event.

5. *Explore and assess past coping attempts.* Most youths and adults have developed several coping mechanisms, some adaptive, some less adaptive, and some inadequate as responses to the crisis event. Basically, an emotionally hazardous event becomes an emotional crisis when the "usual homeostatic, direct problem-solving mechanisms do not work" (Caplan, 1964, p. 39). Thus, attempts to cope fail. One of the major focuses of crisis intervention involves identifying and modifying the client's coping behaviors at both the preconscious and conscious levels. It is important for the crisis intervener to attempt to bring to the conscious level the client's coping responses, which now operate just below the surface at the preconscious level, and then to educate the client in modifying maladaptive coping behaviors. Specifically, it is useful to ask the client how certain situations are handled, such as feelings of intense anger, loss of a loved one (a child or spouse), disappointment, or failure.

Integrating a strengths- and solution-focused approach involves jogging the clients' memory so they recall the last time everything seemed to be going well and they were in a good mood rather than depressed (Roberts, 2000). Here are some suggestions to use with clients:

How would you have coped with the divorce or death of your parents when you were in a good mood?
Write a letter to your parents, letting them know that you are setting a specific goal for yourself

to make them proud of the values and ambition they instilled within you.

If your deceased parents are in heaven looking down on you, what could you do to make them proud?

It is important to help the client generate and explore alternatives and previously untried coping methods and partial solutions. If possible, this involves the collaborative effort of the client and crisis intervener to generate alternatives. It is also important at this stage to explore the consequences of and feelings about each alternative. Most clients have some notion of what should be done to cope with the crisis situation, but they may well need assistance from the crisis clinician to define and conceptualize more adaptive coping responses. In cases where the client has little or no introspection or personal insights, the clinician needs to take the initiative and suggest more adaptive coping methods. Defining and conceptualizing more adaptive coping behaviors for the client can be a highly productive component in helping the client resolve the crisis situation (Roberts, 2000).

6. *Restore cognitive functioning through implementation of an action plan.* The basic premise underlying a cognitive approach to crisis resolution is that the ways in which external events and a person's cognitions of the events turn into personal crisis are based on cognitive factors. Using a cognitive approach, the crisis clinician helps the client focus on why a specific event leads to a crisis state (e.g., it violates a person's expectancies) and, simultaneously, what the client can do to effectively master the experience and be able to cope with similar events, should they occur in the future. Cognitive mastery in-

volves three phases. First, the client needs to obtain a realistic understanding of what happened and what led to the crisis. To move through and past the crisis and get on with life, it is important that the client have an understanding of what happened, why it happened, who was involved, and the final outcome (e.g., being locked out of one's house, a suicide attempt, death of an adolescent, a divorce, a child being battered).

Second, it is useful for clients to understand the specific meaning the event has for them, how it conflicts with their expectations, life goals, and belief system. Thoughts and belief statements usually flow freely when a client in crisis talks. The crisis intervener should listen carefully and note any cognitive errors or distortions (overgeneralizing, catastrophizing) or irrational beliefs. The clinician should avoid prematurely stating rational beliefs or reality-based cognitions for the client. Instead, the clinician should help the client discover distortions and irrational beliefs. This can be facilitated through carefully worded questions, such as

Do you still want to move out of state now that you know that the person who raped you and brutally killed his previous two victims will be electrocuted today in the electric chair?

Have you ever asked your doctor whether he thinks you will die from a heart attack at a young age?

The third and final part of cognitive mastery involves restructuring, rebuilding, or replacing irrational beliefs and erroneous cognitions with rational beliefs and new cognitions. This may involve providing new information through cognitive restructuring, homework assignments, or referral to others who have lived through and mastered a similar crisis (e.g., a support group for widows, rape victims, or students who have been confronted with school violence).

7. *Follow-up.* At the final session, clients should be told that if at any time in the future they need to come back for another session, the door is open, and the clinician is available. Sometimes, clients cancel their second, third, or fourth appointment prior to resolving the crisis. For example, the client who was raped at knifepoint is up half the night prior to her appointment with her clinician. She mistakenly thinks her nightmares and insomnia are caused by the clinician. In actuality, she has not come to grips with her vulnerabilities and fears that the rapist will return. The clinician, knowing that victims of violent crimes often go into crisis at the anniversary of the crime—exactly 1 month or 1 year after the victimization—informs the client that she would like to see her again and that as soon as she calls, she will be given an emergency appointment the same day.

Greene, Lee, and Rheinchild (2000) have demonstrated through case illustrations how to tap into and bolster clients' strengths in crisis intervention. They have demonstrated how to integrate Roberts's seven-stage crisis intervention model with solution-focused treatment in a stepwise manner. Using this integrated strengths approach, the clinician serves as a catalyst and facilitator for clients discovering their own resources and coping skills. Greene et al. systematically bolster their clients by emphasizing the person's resilience, inner strengths, and ability both to bounce back and to continue to grow emotionally. This chapter aptly applies the strengths-based approach to crisis intervention to a diverse range of previous clients in crisis situations, including suicidal, domestic violence, and alcoholic clients.

EMPIRICAL SUPPORT FOR CRISIS INTERVENTION

An extensive search of the empirical literature was conducted using key words *crisis theory* and *crisis intervention* with *outcome, outcome studies, outcome research, research,* and *evaluation* in the following databases: *Psychinfo, Social Work Abstracts, Socioabs, Criminal Justice Abstracts, Nursing and Allied Health Database,* and *Medline.* Because few studies were uncovered using this method, certain problem areas in which crisis intervention is commonly applied, such as *crime victimization, domestic violence, family violence, sexual assault, rape, suicide, cancer, stroke, heart attack, head injury, brain injury, HIV,* and *AIDS* were then searched on the above databases. When this avenue also failed to generate many studies, the articles and abstracts of two relevant journals for crisis intervention were reviewed. The articles of all issues of *Crisis Intervention and Time-Limited Treatment* and the abstracts for issues of *Suicide and Life Threatening Behavior* from 1985 were scanned for their relevance. Despite these extensive efforts, few empirical outcome studies on crisis intervention were found. Apparently, the state of research has not advanced much beyond its condition a decade or so ago when writers decried the lack of research in this area (Barth, 1988; Young, 1990).

To organize the literature that was found, studies will be discussed in terms of the following problem areas: crime victimization, suicide prevention, psychiatric emergencies, and child abuse.

Although most victim assistance programs have as their basis crisis intervention (Young, 1990), there is a lack of evaluation in this area. Furthermore, the evaluations that have been conducted on crime victimization are not always identified as crisis intervention (e.g., Skogan & Wycoff, 1987). One victim assistance program specifically testing the effects of crisis intervention randomly assigned 249 victims of crime to the following groups: (a) crisis intervention with supportive counseling, (b) crisis intervention with cognitive restructuring, (c) material assistance only, and (d) no-service control (Davis, 1987). Three-month follow-up indicated that crime-related problems decreased almost 50%, with most measures showing significant improvement; however, there were no differences between any of the experimental groups or the control group. Of note is that the vast majority of victims assigned to the counseling conditions opted for only one session (91% of those in the crisis counseling condition and 82% of those in cognitive restructuring treatment). Despite the low attendance at sessions, when queried, almost 90% of victims stated that they benefited from crisis intervention, particularly those who had been assigned to cognitive restructuring. The author attributed the low use of services and the weak effects of crisis intervention to the fact that time is a crucial healing factor for most crime victims' coping and readjustment.

Another prospective study on crime victims found that mental health services were only associated with improved adjustment when they were sought soon after the initial crime and when they continued over several months' duration (Norris, Kaniasty, & Scheer, 1990). The authors suggest that although service provision should probably be enacted as close to the crime as possible, crisis intervention, if defined as "one-shot" counseling efforts, is probably not effective. Therefore, the main role of crisis intervention may be to provide victims with a link to longer term support services in the community.

In this vein, Corcoran (1995) describes a police department-based victim assistance program using a crisis intervention model with child sexual abuse victims and their families. One of the objectives was to provide parents with referrals to the community for ongoing counseling and to assist them in completing Victims' Compensation applications for reimbursement of counseling expenses. An evaluation of services was conducted using a mailed follow-up survey to all those families who had contacted the child abuse victim assistance unit for a police investigation. Although it is difficult to generalize findings given the extremely small response rate (91 out of 1,200 surveys sent), 50% of the parents reported they had been in counseling and said that 65% of their children had attended sessions. In a majority of cases (70%), respondents reported either a positive or somewhat positive change in their children and/or their families as a result of attending counseling. Respondents also professed their satisfaction with services at the victim assistance unit, with 92% finding services were either helpful or somewhat helpful.

Suicide Crisis Intervention

Crisis intervention efforts involving suicide concern both those who survive the suicide of a family member and those who are considering suicide. Most of the studies in these areas describe services offered rather than discussing efficacy of programs. For example, Rubey and McIntosh (1996) surveyed suicide survivor groups listed with the American Association of Suicidology. Aspects of programs, such as treatment duration (average of eight sessions), program affiliation (the most significant proportion were associated with mental health centers), and leadership (most often professionals) were described, although it is unknown how soon after the death friends or relatives began attending such groups and how effective they were.

Lester (1997) reviewed 14 studies, published from the 1950s to the 1990s, on the effects on suicide rates of suicide prevention centers. Part of the review included a meta-analysis in which an overall program effect of −.16 was reported. This effect, although representing a positive association between the presence of programs and decreased suicide rates in communities, is very small (Cohen, 1977).

In Lester's (1997) review, when populations were broken down according to gender and age groups, certain populations seemed to have more significant benefits from the presence of suicide prevention centers. Females seemed to benefit more overall, as did individuals between the ages of 15 and 24 and those between the ages of 55 and 64.

Psychiatric Emergencies

Another area in which crisis intervention has been applied is in response to psychiatric emergencies. The few empirical studies in this area are marked by a number of limitations, most notably that comparison groups of individuals who did not undergo crisis intervention are lacking. In an attempt to make comparisons, authors of studies have compared groups of individuals on certain characteristics. For example, Andreoli et al. (1993) studied the effects of a psychiatric crisis intervention program on depressed individuals who either did or did not also have a personality disorder. Anthony

(1992) examined the impact of a crisis intervention program on those who required a transfer to a long-term care unit. Cluse-Tolar (1997) compared the responses of males and females to a crisis intervention program.

Crisis intervention programs also appear to vary by different psychiatric settings, although one limitation is that such programs are often not described (e.g., Anthony, 1992; Cluse-Tolar, 1997). An exception is Andreoli et al. (1993), who describe a program at a psychiatric center in Switzerland. The average length of the crisis intervention program was 6 weeks (Andreoli et al., 1992): a week of inpatient treatment followed by outpatient treatment, involving medication if needed and two to three sessions per week of time-limited psychotherapy. The 35 subjects were also tracked at 1- and 2-year follow-up. Depressed individuals without personality disorders tended to have positive outcomes in terms of briefer episodes of depression and fewer relapses than those with personality disorders. Treatment variables appeared to play a greater role for those who were also diagnosed with personality disorders. Factors associated with poor outcome in this group involved a poor therapeutic relationship and/or having had less long-term treatment at 2-year follow-up. Apparently, crisis intervention was often insufficient for individuals who had personality disorders and suffered from depression.

Child Abuse

Another area in which a crisis intervention model has been applied is in family preservation programs for child abuse victims and their families (for an example, see Box 16.2). These programs are designed with the main goal of keep-

---

BOX 16.2
Case Example 2: Risk of Imminent Placement of Child

Joanne Parker, an African American mother of three children (2-year old Rodney, 4-year old Deanna, and 6-year old Daryl) has been assigned to a crisis intervention family preservation program. As a single parent dependent on welfare, Joanne was already struggling to meet her family's needs. She was thrown into a crisis when she and her boyfriend of 3 years, Stephan, the father of her youngest child, got into an argument one night. She said that Stephan threatened to leave and take their child with him. Joanne said when she held her son so her boyfriend couldn't take him, Stephan started pushing her around and pulling her hair. He had also tried to pry her hands from the child, hurting Rodney's arm in the process. Her oldest son, Daryl, had awakened, hearing her screams and his younger brother's crying, and he called the police. When Joanne's boyfriend heard the police were coming, he left. After the police arrived and questioned Joanne and her family, paramedics were called to examine the youngest child's injury, and a child protective services worker was summoned to investigate.

Through the investigation, information on the family was gathered. Apparently, the children had witnessed many incidents in which Joanne's boyfriend had hit and pushed her during arguments. Joanne said she hadn't called the police before because if Stephan went to jail, he would lose his job, and then "who would help me pay my bills?" Plus, she said, he could be "real sweet except for when he got mad" and that he was a lot better than the men the rest of the women in her family were involved with.

---

ing children in their own home with caretakers to whom they are attached when risk of placement has occurred. Placement risk usually involves child abuse and/or neglect, although such programs have also been employed with juvenile offenders and children with emotional disorders and their families. The program based on crisis intervention is called Homebuilders and was developed in 1974 (Kinney & Dittmar, 1995; Kinney, Haapala, & Booth, 1991); now, about half of all states (53%) report modeling their family preservation program after Homebuilders, according to a 1996 Child Welfare League survey (Petit & Curtis, 1997).

Consistent with the assumption that there is a critical short-term period for restabilization to a former, more adaptable level of functioning,

Homebuilders provides immediate services (within a day of referral) in the home with 24-hour availability of workers (Kinney & Dittmar, 1995; Kinney et al., 1991). For this level of service intensity, workers carry a low caseload (a maximum of three families), and clients are usually seen for a brief period (between 4 and 6 weeks); after that, the crisis is assumed to be stabilized. Besides offering counseling, Homebuilders either supply or link families to a variety of concrete resources that may include helping families meet basic needs for food, clothing, housing, and medical care (Nelson, Landsman, & Deutelbaum, 1990; Pecora, Fraser, & Haapala, 1992).

The majority of studies of crisis intervention family preservation programs rely on pretest, posttest-only designs. These studies report favorable results, with placement prevention rates ranging from an average of 77% (Scannapieco, 1994) to nearly 99% (Bath, Richey, & Haapala, 1992) at case termination and from 65% (Fraser, Pecora, & Haapala, 1991) to 83% (Bath et al., 1992; Yuan & Struckman-Johnson, 1991) at follow-up.

To address the question of whether children involved with family preservation programs are truly at risk of placement, there has been some movement toward quasi-experimental designs with random assignment to family preservation or casework-as-usual services (Feldman, 1991; Walton, 1996; Walton, Fraser, Lewis, Pecora, & Walton, 1993) or the use of overflow comparison groups (Wood, Barton, & Schroeder, 1988). High percentages of successful outcomes were found in these studies in terms of maintaining and/or returning children to their homes, although prevention rates began to dissipate over time.

Although placement prevention has been the main criterion for program outcome, when standardized self-report measures were used rather than caseworker ratings of program effects, no significant differences were found between family preservation and casework-as-usual services (Feldman, 1991; Walton, 1996). Therefore, although family preservation programs appear to be able to keep children in the home, improved functioning of families and adjustment of children may not also follow. In addition, logistical concerns preclude the provision of intervention during the crucial crisis period (Tracy, 1991). When a child abuse referral is made, the case usually is not investigated immediately unless severe risk of harm to the child is present. After the caseworker completes his or her investigation, then the case must be staffed and an administrative decision is made about the case. Depending on the extent of involvement of child protective services, a court hearing may have to be held to mandate services. The time involved in this process means that the crisis that resulted in child abuse occurring or the family coming to the attention of the child protective services system may have already passed on its own accord. More discussion of the use of crisis intervention services with child abuse populations is presented in the next section on System Level Interventions.

SYSTEM-LEVEL INTERVENTION

A number of societal factors may influence clients' vulnerability to a crisis and their response to a crisis. Because there are such a multiplicity of factors, only those that have some basis in the empirical literature will be explored. These studies suggest the system levels to target for intervention. In addition, the focus of this section will be on populations at particular risk for certain crises and will therefore involve diversity issues. There is recognition, however, given the breadth of areas in which crisis intervention is employed, that this section will only address a few of the salient issues, and these are in the areas of gender and socioeconomic status. At the immediate social environment, the amount of support available from friends, family, and the school system, and at the individual system level, depression and cognitive coping, may be salient factors for determining those who are vulnerable to certain crises occurring or for impaired adjustment and coping after a crisis, and these factors will each be explored.

Larger Social Factors/Diversity

Socioeconomic Status

A particular person's socioeconomic status determines the amount of resources, supports, and opportunities available, with the chronic stress of poverty compromising individual and family functioning more than acute events associated with crises (Barth, 1988). Crisis intervention was originally formulated for individuals who were functioning at an acceptable level before being confronted with untenable circumstances. These circumstances were seen as overwhelming the individual's capacity for functioning, with the goal of intervention being to return the individual to prior adjustment (Parad & Caplan, 1960). Crisis intervention, therefore, is viewed as involving precipitating events rather than predisposing environmental factors, such as long-standing poverty. Lindsey (1994) argues that neither family preservation or any other residual program attempting to address problems that have already occurred can be effective when inadequate residence, food, and medical care undermines a family's ability to function. Poverty is a serious risk factor not only for abuse and neglect but also for a host of other problems and crises that may develop, such as teenage pregnancy, marital conflict, and family violence (Lindsey, 1994). Without addressing poverty and the lack of resources, individual efforts might be limited.

Gender

Because of the multiplicity of factors in systems and their interactive nature (Garvin & Tropman, 1998), it is sometimes difficult to as-

certain at what level factors are operating. For gender, the system under consideration could include biological aspects and therefore would be considered at the individual system level. Alternatively, the socialization process and societal expectations for males and females could be assessed as a societal level influence for differences in vulnerabilities for certain crises.

Women may be at risk for the occurrence of certain crises, such as domestic violence (U.S. Bureau of Justice Statistics, 1995), sexual assault (Kilpatrick, Saunders, Veronen, Best, & Von, 1987), and events related to the maternal role, such as medical crises with their children (e.g., Affleck, McGrade, Allen, & McQueeney, 1985; Graham, Thompson, Estrada, & Yonekura, 1987) and deaths of children. For example, in a study of family members' reactions to the suicide of an adolescent member, mothers still showed elevated rates of depression at 3-year follow-up, whereas siblings and fathers did not (Brent, Moritz, Bridge, Perper, & Canobbio, 1996). Women are also more at risk for suicide attempts beginning in adolescence, whereas males are more at risk to complete suicide (e.g., Canetto & Sakinofsky, 1998; Carnetto, 1997). It is further recognized that females are more likely to both exhibit depression and seek help for depression and other mental health problems (see section on depression below and Congress, 1995, who also addresses clinical issues with women using brief treatment).

At the same time, women may also find more benefits from seeking such help. For example, Cluse-Tolar (1997) evaluated a crisis intervention for individuals presenting to an emergency room for help with a psychiatric problem. The majority were female and, when measured over 6 weeks on psychological functioning, females tended to improve while the men did not.

Cluse-Tolar (1997) discusses findings in terms of the lack of responsiveness of services to men and the prohibitions against help-seeking that are present in this society. Such prohibitions may be in place by adolescence, suggests another study, finding that boys at highest risk for suicide would not use services offered in school such as crisis lines and education programs (Evans, Smith, Hill, Albers, & Neufeld, 1996). The following section will explore some of the supports available at the level of the immediate social environment so that vulnerabilities in both males and females will be ameliorated.

Immediate Social Environment

In a systemic conceptualization of individual behavior, an individual's behavior is affected not only by factors unique to individual functioning (Garvin & Tropman, 1998). The social environment also plays a large role in human behavior. Immediate social environments in which individuals regularly interface include their networks of family and friends and the support they receive from these networks; for children and youth, these include the school.

Social Support

The key role of social support in mitigating against the occurrence of crises and poor reactions to crisis has been discussed. For example, lack of family support has been tied to suicidal behavior in adolescents (e.g., King et al., 1995; Rohde, Seeley, & Mace, 1997; Wagner, Cole, & Schwartzman, 1995). Furthermore, interpersonal difficulties were found to be implicated in a substantial proportion of calls made to suicide crisis intervention hotlines in a western state (97,000 telephone contacts over a 6-year period) (Albers & Foster, 1995). Only 8% to 12% of the calls actually involved suicide, whereas 40% of callers reported interpersonal difficulties, such as grief, loneliness, and conflict.

Additional evidence is provided by data from the National Institute of Mental Health's Epidemiologic Catchment Area Study 1980-1985 (Nisbet, 1996). The presence of informal support networks (friends and family) is a protective factor against suicide for all race and gender categories. Support gained from professional sources, however, is correlated with an increased risk of suicide attempts. It may be that people seek professional help only when their emotional and mental condition has deteriorated to a severe state (Nisbet, 1996).

Social support may protect against the event of a suicidal crisis, and it may also improve the effectiveness of crisis intervention programs. Anthony (1992) examined hospital records of psychiatric inpatients who underwent a crisis intervention program and found that both treatment compliance and family support were significant factors associated with successful discharge to the community versus continued inpatient. In another psychiatric crisis intervention program, quality of relationships was also a crucial factor for positive outcome (Dazord et al., 1991).

Given the importance of social support, the crisis worker's interventions should be directed at those who have social influence on individuals who are undergoing crises to affect them more successfully (Norris et al., 1990). For instance, Kaniasty and Norris (1992) evaluated the effects of both perceived and received support and, within each of these types, different kinds of support on a representative state sample of crime victims. In terms of perceived support, appraisal support (consisting of emotional and informational support) had a positive effect on well-being, whatever the crime, and had a protective influence against anxiety and fear of crime. Tangible support, the availability of material assistance, produced positive effects by protecting victims of violent crime from anxiety and by buffering victims of both nonviolent and violent crime against depression. An implication at the practice level is that the crisis intervention worker can help members appropriately support those who are experiencing a crisis, offering both emotional and more practical kinds of support when required. The worker can also help victims of crises cultivate the types of support they most need from those close to them.

School

Given the risk of adolescent depression and suicide, suicide prevention programs have been developed in schools, as teens are not likely to depend on community suicide prevention hotlines. School interventions have typically been formulated as suicide awareness programs or suicide debriefings after another student has committed suicide. The available evidence suggests that such programs have not typically been effective and may even increase the risk of suicide by normalizing suicide as a coping response (Coie et al., 1993; Garland & Zigler, 1993). In addition, those at high risk for suicide, particularly high-risk males, may not seek out school-related suicide or crisis services (Evans et al., 1996). The argument has instead been made that school programs should emphasize the development of broad-based life skills (Coie et al., 1993; Garland & Zigler, 1993). Skills would therefore be built in the following areas:

feelings management, coping, decision making, social support, and conflict resolution. Such a program targeting suicide prevention, drug abuse prevention, and school attendance led to reduced suicidal risk (in both one-semester and two-semester programs) and increased protective factors against suicide (in two-semester programs) (Eggert, Thompson, Herting, & Nicholas, 1995). In this way, teens at risk for the development of problems such as suicide, depression, drug use, and anger management would gain individual coping skills, which would render them less vulnerable to crises of various kinds.

Individual System Level

This section on the individual system level will address depression and its role in crises and the development of cognitive coping strategies as a protective factor against risk. Because the individual is the system typically targeted by the crisis worker, implications for intervention will be explored.

Depression/Adjustment Problems

At the individual level, depression and other adjustment difficulties have been implicated in various types of crises. First, the existence of depression may place individuals at risk for certain types of crises, namely suicidal crises. Depression has been implicated as a strong risk factor for suicidal ideation, attempts, and behavior in adolescent (e.g., King et al., 1995; Rohde et al., 1997; Wagner, Cole & Schwartzman, 1996), adult (e.g., Lipschitz, 1995) and elderly samples (Ademek & Kaplan, 1996; McIntosh, 1995). Severe depressive episodes also may trigger a psychiatric crisis, and, as discussed, crisis intervention programs have been designed to address such psychiatric emergencies (Andreoli et al., 1993; Anthony, 1992; Cluse-Tolar, 1997).

In addition to creating greater vulnerability for certain types of crises, depression may also exacerbate crisis reactions. For example, in their prospective study, Norris and Kaniasty (1994) found that prior poor adjustment often made adjustment after crime victimization more difficult. Depression was also one of the factors motivating crime victims to seek mental health services (Norris et al., 1990).

The role that prior adjustment may play in increased vulnerability to crisis and impaired reactions calls into question the goal of crisis intervention, which is to return individuals to their prior level of functioning (e.g., Parad & Caplan, 1960). In many cases, this prior level of functioning may be less than optimal; therefore, efforts of the crisis intervention worker may have to include building skills and helping the individual achieve a higher level of adjustment. Therefore, it is important that crisis workers familiarize themselves with empirically validated treatment methods for depression. Many of these are brief in nature (12 sessions or so), such as interpersonal therapy (Klerman, Weissman, Rounsaville, & Chevron, 1984) or cognitive-behavioral therapy (Young, Beck, & Weinberger, 1993). (See Elkin, 1994, for review of National Institute of Mental Health studies on depression.)

Interpersonal therapy may be particularly helpful for individuals in crisis, as grief or loss is usually involved, whether an actual loss has occurred, such as theft of property or death of a loved one, or more symbolic losses, such as the loss of the view of the world as a benign place (Janoff-Bulman, 1992). The first phase of interpersonal therapy involves helping individuals resolve grief through two goals: facilitating the mourning process and helping individuals reestablish interests and relationships to replace the loss (Klerman et al., 1984).

The next major goal of interpersonal therapy is to work on current interpersonal relationships that are problematic and to address interpersonal deficits. These social arenas may be particularly salient for people who have experienced crises, given the significant role that social support plays in mitigating maladjustment in crisis situations (see earlier section).

The third phase of interpersonal therapy is also relevant for crisis because it involves coping with role transitions. A crisis may often stimulate a loss of a certain role or a change in that role. For example, a woman whose child has died may have lost her maternal role; a sudden onset of illness in adults may cause them to lose their role as employees.

Cognitive-behavioral therapy is another relatively brief, empirically validated treatment for depression (Young et al., 1993). According to this theory, depressed people have a negative view of self (as worthless, inadequate, unlovable, and deficient), the environment (overwhelming, involving unsurmountable obstacles, resulting in failure or loss), and the future (hopeless, efforts directed toward change will be insufficient and ineffective) (Young et al., 1993). These negative views are similar to the "shattered assumptions" involved in crime victimization (Janoff-Bulman, 1985, 1989, 1992; Janoff-Bulman & Frieze, 1983): the loss of the view of self as worthy and as being able to control what happens and of the world as a benign and meaningful place. Cognitive-behavioral therapy then works on challenging the distorted interpretations of events that maintain individuals' negative views.

COPING RESPONSES

A main premise of crisis intervention is that coping strategies need to be developed and bolstered, as they have been taxed by the demands of a crisis (Cluse-Tolar, 1997). Although literature has accumulated on cognitive coping (e.g., Folkman & Lazarus, 1985; Lazarus & Folkman, 1984),[1] it has not often been integrated into crisis intervention efforts. In this section, the relevant literature on coping will be briefly reviewed and then some suggestions for crisis intervention will be offered.

Coping has been defined as cognitive and behavioral strategies to overcome, reduce, or at least withstand the internal and external pressures that are stimulated by stress or a crisis (Folkman, 1984). These efforts have been classified into two main types: problem-focused and emotion-focused (Folkman, 1984). Problem-focused strategies focus on the use of problem-solving and action plans, whereas emotion-focused strategies involve the control of negative or distressing emotions. Which types of strategies are associated with the most beneficial short- and long-term adjustment is still unknown. Although some studies support the use of problem-focused coping over emotion-focused coping (Aldwin & Revenson, 1987; Vitaliano et al., 1987; Vitaliano, Russo, Carr, Maiuro, & Becker, 1985; Wells, Hobfoll, & Lavin, 1997), others indicate the use of both problem- and emotion-focused strategies (Folkman & Lazarus, 1985, 1988; Folkman, Lazarus, Gruen, & DeLongis, 1986).

One hypothesis is that the use of emotion-focused versus problem-focused strategies should be dictated by the extent to which individuals believe an event is under their control (Folkman, 1984). For example, if individuals appraise an event as under their control, problem-focused strategies may be more effective. However, for situations perceived as unchangeable, emotion-focused strategies, such as venting emotions, may be more helpful. If the person's perception of control is accurate, then using strategies that correspond to each appraisal would lead to better adjustment.

Another theoretical discussion in the coping literature involves the extent to which either internal or external attributions contribute better to coping. People with internal attributions feel they are responsible for playing a major role in bringing about the situations and events that occur. Janoff-Bulman (1992) further makes a distinction between characterological and behavioral self-blame. Characterological self-blame has to do with stable personality attributes whereas behavioral self-blame involves modifiable aspects of behavior. The argument for behavioral self-blame is that people gain a greater sense of control when they know certain actions can be taken to avoid the occurrence of a similar crisis in the future.

Despite the lack of positive effects for external attribution, other crisis situations may be better served by other-blame. Some evidence suggests that in cases of domestic violence, which may present substantial risk and harm, self- versus other-blame may be detrimental. In an English study examining factors that discriminated between staying in and leaving an abusive relationship, self-blame was associated with being in the relationship (Andrews & Brewin, 1995). Furthermore, when self-blame was broken down into behavioral and characterological self-blame, more women blamed their behavior (68%) rather than their character. Although characterological self-blame seemed particularly problematic, given its association with early childhood abuse and low social support, even women who used behavioral self-blame were still more likely to be in a violent relationship. Therefore, the adaptive functioning of behavioral self-blame (e.g., Janoff-Bulman, 1992) is questionable, at least perhaps for women coping with the crisis of domestic violence.

Other more systematic links need to be established between the coping literature and crisis intervention. For example, an understanding of both the short-term and long-term cognitive-emotional responses associated with different crises is required. Koss and Burkhart (1989) suggest that long-term impact has to be examined prospectively because certain effects may only be evident after more immediate cognitive responses to the trauma and the response of the social support systems have occurred. Furthermore, retrospective analyses of individuals who have a different adjustment in terms of type and severity of symptoms, coping strategies, and cognitive appraisals need to be examined to discover how trauma is resolved in various types of crises (Koss & Burkhart, 1989). Moreover, the link between type of coping strategy and the extent of perceived controllability of an event should be established so that crisis clinicians can encourage appropriate emotional and problem-solving responses in their clients (Roberts & Burman, 1998).

CONCLUSIONS

As should be evident as a result of our theoretical synthesis of crisis theory and review of the eclectic crisis intervention model and outcome studies, identifying the most important research areas for the future is complex. In addition, when we examined all of the methodological flaws in previous research, as well as the ethical dilemmas in obtaining baseline data and pretest measures, we found that making realistic suggestions becomes even more difficult. Nevertheless, future research and research questions regarding the efficacy of crisis intervention should include the following:

What will stronger research designs and between-group studies comparing different components of crisis intervention tell us about the effectiveness of crisis intervention?

What is the long-term impact of undergoing certain types of crises, and how is impact affected by the type of crisis intervention services provided, other types of social support available, and other coping strategies?

What are the optimal methods of crisis intervention? Are these associated with certain theories, such as solution-focused, cognitive behavioral, or Rogerian approaches?

How will future crisis intervention programs best involve naturally occurring support systems, such as the family and neighborhood? How will the research on social support be integrated into a knowledge base for crisis intervention?

How will crisis intervention services differ when individuals have already suffered much pre-crisis distress and their adjustment is already poor, and how does this challenge the assumption of crisis intervention that individuals should be returned to their prior level of functioning?

More systematic links need to be established between the coping literature and crisis intervention regarding the type of coping strategy, either problem-focused or emotion-focused, that more optimally contributes to improved adjustment at both the short and long term. We also need a better understanding of how attributions about a crisis event and the perceived controllability of an event interact with coping strategy and how this affects adjustment.

NOTE

1. Grateful acknowledgment to Jenny Mize, University of Texas at Austin, School of Social Work, graduate student, for review of cognitive coping literature.

REFERENCES

Ademek, M. E., & Kaplan, M. (1996). Managing elder suicide: A profile of American and Canadian crisis prevention centers. *Suicide & Life-Threatening Behavior, 26,* 122-131.

Affleck, G., McGrade, B., Allen, D., & McQueeny, M. (1985). Mothers' beliefs about behavioral causes for their developmentally disabled infants condition: What do they signify? *Journal of Pediatric Psychology, 10,* 293-303.

Albers, E., & Foster, S. (1995). A profile of 97,100 crisis intervention contacts over a six-year period. *Crisis Intervention, 2,* 23-29.

Aldwin, C. M., & Revenson, T. A. (1987). Does coping help? A reexamination of the relation between coping and mental health. *Journal of Personality and Social Psychology, 53,* 337-348.

Andreoli, A., Frances, A., Gex-Farby, M., Aapro, N., Gerin, P., & Dazford, A. (1993). Crisis intervention in depressed patients with and without *DSM-III-R* personality disorders. *Journal of Nervous and Mental Disease, 181,* 732-737.

Andreoli, A., Muehlebach, A., Gognalons, M., Abensur, J., Grimm, S., & Frances, A. (1992). Crisis intervention response and long-term outcome: A pilot study. *Comprehensive Psychiatry, 33,* 388-396.

Andrews, B., & Brewin, C. R. (1995). Attributions of blame for marital violence: A study of antecedents and consequences. In S. M. Stith & M. A. Straus (Eds.), *Understanding partner violence: Prevalence, causes, consequences, and solutions.* Minneapolis, MN: National Council of Family Relations.

Anthony, D. (1992). A retrospective evaluation of factors influencing successful outcomes on an inpatient psychiatric crisis unit. *Research on Social Work Practice, 2,* 56-64.

Barth, R. (1988). Theories guiding home-based intensive family preservation services. In J. Wittaker, J. Kinney, E. Tracey, & C. Booth (Eds.), *Improving practice technology for work with high-risk families: Lessons from the "Homebuilders" social work education project* (pp. 91-113). Seattle, WA: Center for Social Welfare Research.

Bath, H., Richey, C. A., & Haapala, D. A. (1992). Child age and outcome correlates in intensive family preservation services. *Children & Youth Services Review, 14,* 389-406.

Brent, D., Moritz, G., Bridge, J., Perper, J., & Canobbio, R. (1996). The impact of adolescent suicide on siblings and parents: A longitudinal follow-up. *Suicide & Life Threatening Behavior, 26,* 253-259.

Canetto, S. S., & Sakinofsky, I. (1998). The gender paradox in suicide. *Suicide & Life-Threatening Behavior, 28*(1), 1-23.

Caplan, G. (1964). *Principles of preventive psychiatry.* New York: Basic Books.

Carnetto, S. (1997). Meanings of gender and suicidal behavior during adolescence. *Suicide & Life Threatening Behavior, 27,* 339-351.

Cluse-Tolar, T. (1997). Gender differences in crisis theory recovery: Rethinking crisis theory. *Crisis Intervention, 3,* 189-198.

Cohen, J. (1977). *Statistical power analysis for the behavioral sciences.* New York: Academic Press.

Coie, J., Watt, N., West, S., Hawkins, J., Asarnow, J., Markman, H., Ramey, S., Shure, M., & Long, B. (1993). The science of prevention: A conceptual framework and some directions for a national research program. *American Psychologist, 48,* 1013-1022.

Congress, E. P. (1995). Clinical issues in time-limited treatment with women. In A. Roberts (Ed.), *Crisis intervention and time-limited cognitive treatment.* Thousand Oaks, CA: Sage.

Corcoran, J. (1995). Child abuse victim services: An exploratory study of the Austin, Texas, Police Department. *Family Violence and Sexual Assault Bulletin, 11,* 19-23.

Davis, R. (1987). Studying the effects of services for victims in crisis. *Crime & Delinquency, 33,* 520-531.

Dazord, A., Gerin, P., Iahns, J., Andreoli, A., Reith, B., & Abensur, J. (1991). Pretreatment and process measures in crisis intervention as predictors of outcome. *Psychotherapy Research, 1,* 135-147.

Eggert, L., Thompson, E., Herting, J., & Nicholas, L. (1995). Reducing suicide potential among high-risk youth: Tests of a school based prevention program. *Suicide & Life Threatening Behavior, 25,* 276-296.

Elkin, I. (1994). The NIMH treatment of depression collaborative research program: Where we began and where we are. In A. Bergin, & S. Garfield (Eds.), *Handbook of psychotherapy and behavior change* (5th ed., pp. 114-139). New York: John Wiley.

Evans, W., Smith, M., Hill, G., Albers, E., & Neufield, J. (1996). Rural adolescent views of risk and protective factors associated with suicide. *Crisis Intervention, 3,* 1-12.

Feldman, L. H. (1991). Evaluating the impact of intensive family preservation services in New Jersey. In K. Wells & D. E. Biegel (Eds.), *Family preservation services: Research and evaluation.* Newbury Park, CA: Sage.

Folkman, S. (1984). Personal control and stress and coping processes: A theoretical analysis. *Journal of Personality and Social Psychology, 46,* 839-852.

Folkman, S., & Lazarus, R. S. (1985). If it changes it must be a process: Study of emotion and coping during three stages of college examination. *Journal of Personality and Social Psychology, 48,* 150-170.

Folkman, S., & Lazarus, R. S. (1988). *Ways of coping questionnaire permissions set: Manual, test booklet, scoring key.* Redwood City, CA: Mind Garden.

Folkman, S., Lazarus, R. S., Gruen, R. J., & DeLongis, A. (1986). Appraisal, coping, health status, and psychological symptoms. *Journal of Personality and Social Psychology, 50,* 571-579.

Fraser, M. W., Pecora, P. J., & Haapala, D. A. (1991). *Families in crisis: The impact of intensive family preservation services.* Hawthorne, NY: Aldine de Gruyter.

Garland, A. F., & Zigler, E. (1993). Adolescent suicide prevention. *American Psychologist, 18*(2), 169-182.

Garvin, C. D., & Tropman, J. E. (1998). *Social work in contemporary society* (2nd ed.). Boston: Allyn & Bacon.

Graham, M., Thompson, S., Estrada, M., & Yonekura, M. (1987). Factors affecting psychological adjustment to a fetal death. *American Journal of Obstetrics and Gynecology, 157,* 254-257.

Greene, G., Lee, M., & Rheinchild, J. (2000). How to work with clients' strengths in crisis intervention: A solution-focused approach. In A. R. Roberts (Ed.), *Crisis intervention handbook: Assessment, treatment, and research.* New York: Oxford University Press.

Janoff-Bulman, R. (1985). Criminal vs. non-criminal victimization: Victim's reactions. *Victimology: An International Journal, 10*(1-4), 498-511.

Janoff-Bulman, R. (1989). Assumptive worlds and the stress of traumatic events: Applications of the schema construct. *Social Cognition, 7,* 113-136.

Janoff-Bulman, R. (1992). *Shattered assumptions.* New York: Free Press.

Janoff-Bulman, R., & Frieze, I. (1983). A theoretical perspective for understanding reactions to victimization. *Journal of Social Issues, 39,* 1-17.

Kaniasty, K., & Norris, F. (1992). Social support and victims of crime: Matching event, support, and outcome. *American Journal of Community Psychology, 20,* 211-241.

Kilpatrick, D., Saunders, B., Veronen, L., Best, C., & Von, J. (1987). Criminal victimization: Lifetime prevalence, reporting to police, and psychological impact. *Crime & Delinquency, 33,* 479-489.

Kinney, J., & Dittmar, K. (1995). *Homebuilders: Helping families help themselves.* Lincoln: University of Nebraska Press.

Kinney, J., Haapala, D. A., & Booth, C. (1991). *Keeping families together: The Homebuilders model.* New York: Aldine de Gruyter.

King, C., Segal, H., Kaminiski, K., & Naylor, M. et al. (1995). A prospective study of adolescent suicidal behavior following hospitalization. *Suicide & Life Threatening Behavior, 25,* 327-338.

Klerman, G., Weissman, M., Rounsaville, B., & Chevron, E. (1984). *Interpersonal psychotherapy in depression.* New York: Basic Books.

Koss, M., & Burkhart, B. (1989). A conceptual analysis of rape victimization. *Psychology of Women Quarterly, 13,* 27-40.

Lazarus, R. S., & Folkman, S. (1984). *Stress, appraisal, and coping.* New York: Springer.

Lester, D. (1997). The effectiveness of suicide prevention centers: A review. *Suicide & Life Threatening Behavior, 27,* 304-310.

Lewis, C. M., Danis, F., & McRoy, R. (1997). *Evaluation of the National Violence Hotline.* Austin: The University of Texas at Austin, Center for Social Work Research.

Lindsey, D. (1994). Family preservation and child protection: Striking a balance. *Children and Youth Services Review, 16,* 279-294.

Lipschitz, A. (1995). Suicide prevention in young adults. *Suicide & Life-Threatening Behavior, 25*(1), 155-170.

McIntosh, J. (1995). Suicide prevention in the elderly. *Suicide & Life Threatening Behavior, 25,* 180-192.

Nelson, K. E., Landsman, M. J., & Deutelbaum, W. (1990). Three models of family centered placement prevention service. *Child Welfare, 69,* 3-19.

Nisbet, P. (1996). Protective factors for suicidal black females. *Suicide & Life Threatening Behavior, 26,* 325-341.

Norris, F. H., & Kaniasty, K. (1994). Psychological distress following criminal victimization in the general population: Cross-sectional, longitudinal, and prospective analyses. *Journal of Consulting and Clinical Psychology, 62,* 111-123.

Norris, F. H., Kaniasty, K., & Scheer, D. A. (1990). Use of mental health services among victims of crime: Frequency, correlates, and subsequent recovery. *Journal of Consulting & Clinical Psychology, 58*(5), 538-547.

Parad, H. J., & Caplan, G. (1960). A framework for studying families in crisis. *Social Work,* 3-15.

Pecora, P. J., Fraser, M. W., & Haapala, D. A. (1992). Intensive home-based family preservation services: An update from the FIT preject. *Child Welfare, 69,* 177-188.

Petit, M. R., & Curtis, P. A. (1997). *Child abuse and neglect: A look at the states: 1997 CWLA stat book.* Washington, DC: CWLA Press.

Rohde, P., Seeley, J., & Mace, D. (1997). Correlates of suicidal behavior in a juvenile detention population. *Suicide & Life Threatening Behavior, 27,* 164-175.

Roberts, A. R. (1979). Organization of suicide prevention agencies. In L. Hankoff & B. Einsidler (Eds.), *Suicide: Theory and clinical aspects* (pp. 391-399). Littleton, MA: PSG Publishing.

Roberts, A. R. (Ed.). (1990). *Helping crime victims.* Newbury Park, CA Sage.

Roberts, A. R. (1991). Conceptualizing crisis theory and the crisis intervention model. In A. R. Roberts (Ed.), *Contemporary perspectives on crisis intervention and prevention* (pp. 3-17). Englewood Cliffs, NJ: Prentice Hall.

Roberts, A. R. (1995). *Crisis intervention and time-limited cognitive treatment.* Thousand Oaks, CA: Sage.

Roberts, A. R. (1996). The epidemiology of acute crisis episodes in American society. In A. Roberts (Ed.), *Crisis management and brief treatment.* Chicago: Nelson-Hall.

Roberts, A. R. (2000). An overview of crisis theory and crisis intervention. In A. R. Roberts (Ed.), *Crisis intervention handbook: Assessment, treatment, and research* (pp. 3-29). New York: Oxford University Press.

Roberts, A. R., & Burman, S. (1998). Crisis intervention and cognitive problem-solving therapy with battered women. In A. R. Roberts (Ed.), *Battered women and their families: Intervention strategies and treatment programs* (2nd ed., pp. 3-28). New York: Springer.

Roberts, A. R., & Dziegielewski, S. (1995). Foundation skills and applications of crisis intervention and cognitive therapy. In A. R. Roberts (Ed.), *Crisis intervention and time-limited cognitive treatment* (pp. 3-27). Thousand Oaks, CA: Sage.

Rubey, C., & McIntosh, J. (1996). Suicide survivors groups: Results of a survey. *Suicide & Life Threatening Behavior, 26,* 351-358.

Scannapieco, M. (1994). Home-based services program: Effectiveness with at risk families. *Children and Youth Services Review, 16,* 363-377.

Skogan, W., & Wycoff, M. (1987). Some unexpected effects of a police service for victims. *Crime & Delinquency, 33,* 490-501.

Tracy, E. M. (1991). Defining the target population for family preservation services. In K. Wells & D. E. Biegel (Eds.), *Family preservation services: Research and evaluation* (pp. 138-158). Newbury Park, CA: Sage.

U.S. Bureau of Justice Statistics. (1995). *Women usually victimized by offenders they know.* Washington, DC: U.S. Department of Justice.

Vitaliano, P. P., Katon, W., Russo, J., Maiuro, R. D., Anderson, K., & Jones, M. (1987). Coping as an index of illness behavior in panic disorder. *Journal of Nervous and Mental Disease, 175,* 78-84.

Vitaliano, P. P., Russo, J., Carr, J. E., Maiuro, R. D., & Becker, J. (1985). The ways of coping checklist: Revision and psychometric properties. *Multivariate Behavioral Research, 20,* 3-26.

Wagner, B., Cole, R., & Schwartzman, P. (1995). Psychosocial correlates of suicide attempts among junior and senior high school youth. *Suicide & Life-Threatening Behavior, 25,* 358-372.

Wagner, B., Cole, R., & Schwartzman, P. (1996). Comorbidity of symptoms among junior and senior high school suicide attempters. *Suicide & Life Threatening Behavior, 26,* 300-307.

Walton, E. (1996). Family functioning as a measure of success in intensive family preservation services. *Journal of Family Social Work, 1,* 67-82.

Walton, E., Fraser, M. W., Lewis, R. E., Pecora, P. J., & Walton, W. K. (1993). In-home, family-focused reunification services: An experimental study. *Child Welfare, 72,* 473-487.

Waters, J., & Finn, E. (1995). Handling client crises effectively on the telephone. In A. R. Roberts (Ed.), *Crisis intervention and time-limited cognitive treatment* (pp. 251-189). Thousand Oaks, CA: Sage.

Wells, J. D., Hobfoll, S. E., & Lavin, J. (1997). Resource loss, resource gain, and communal coping during pregnancy among women with multiple roles. *Psychology of Women Quarterly, 21,* 645-662.

Wood, S., Barton, K., & Schroeder, C. (1988). In-home treatment of abusive families: Cost and placement at one year. *Psychotherapy, 25,* 409-414.

Young, J., Beck, A., & Weinberger, A. (1993). Depression. In D. Barlow (Ed.), *Clinical handbook of psychological disorders: A step-by-step treatment manual* (2nd ed., pp. 240-277). New York: Guilford.

Young, M. (1990). Victim assistance in the United States: The end of the beginning. *International Review of Victimology, 1,* 181-199.

Yuan, Y. Y., & Struckman-Johnson, D. L. (1991). Placement outcomes for neglected children with prior placements in family preservation programs. In K. Wells & D. E. Biegel (Eds.), *Family preservation services: Research and evaluation.* Newbury Park, CA: Sage.

CHAPTER SEVENTEEN

Coping

PAULA S. NURIUS

The lay and professional literatures on coping have blossomed in recent years, spanning many different specific problem areas in addition to cross-cutting models. This growth has brought great strides yet has also resulted in a large umbrella being shared by an assortment of processes, responses, situations, styles, dispositions, strategies, moderators, and mediators. This chapter builds on current work, but it is not intended to review the sprawling coping literature, per se. Some very useful book-length resources for this are available (e.g., see Carpenter, 1992; Eckenrode, 1991; Goldberger & Breznitz, 1993; Gottlieb, 1997; Kaplan, 1996; Lazarus & Folkman, 1984; Zeidner & Endler, 1996).

Because of the importance of social context and person-environment interaction for social work practice, I focus on coping models that explicitly take these into account, and I summarize what happens "behind the scenes." Drawing from interdisciplinary literature, this chapter identifies some of the whats and hows of normative person-environment interaction as it relates to the components and process of coping: for example, factors that can help or hinder risk acknowledgment, threat perception, cognitive coping appraisal, emotional responding, and coping adaptability. I conclude with attention to recent developments that hold promise for proactive and preventive applications of coping research and practice.

WHAT IS COPING?

As awareness of the stress and coping concepts has grown, people have incorporated them into everyday life and language. When people talk of "being stressed out," "being in over their heads," "staying afloat," and "dancing as fast as they can" we feel we understand what they mean . . . but do we? Is every challenge or difficulty a threat or stressor? Is everything we do in responding to difficulties coping? Are stress or significant personal threats inherently negative? What differentiates adaptive coping from maladaptive coping? In practice efforts to help others improve or strengthen their coping, what underlying processes are we assuming carry these new effects?

To ask and answer questions about meaningful assessment and intervention effectiveness, the practitioner and researcher must have clear operational definitions and understand the mechanisms that are believed to be functioning in problem development and resolution. Concretely, coping includes responses whose purpose it is to (a) modify or avoid conditions producing stress or threat, (b) manage the meaning of the circumstances in a way that minimizes potency for harm, and (c) enhance the control and relief of distress associated with the threat or stressor[1] (Houston, 1987; Pearlin & Aneshensel, 1986). I limit my emphasis here primarily to coping with relatively discrete acute and short-term stressors. The longer term a threat or stressor, the more coping overlaps other practice constructs, such as rehabilitation and adjustment—topics addressed by other chapters—and the more that problem-specific factors become prominent in findings of what is most effective (for discussion of coping with chronic stressors see Compas, Connor, Osowiecki, & Welch, 1997; Lepore, 1997; O'Brien & DeLongis, 1997; for coping distinctions pertaining to children see Boekaerts, 1996; Zeidner & Hammer, 1990). The lines are by no means sharply drawn. Coping with a relatively discrete stressor such as injury, loss, or victim-

ization often takes place within a background of chronic stressors (e.g., work-related difficulties, chaotic life circumstances, environmental hazards or deficiencies, exposure to others with disordered functioning). After an event is over (e.g., an assault), coping in terms of the aftermath continues, including reinterpretation and redefinition of the stressful event as well as adjustment to the shattering loss of one's fundamental self and worldviews and rebuilding of new beliefs and expectations (Frieze & Bookwala, 1996; Janoff-Bulman, 1992).

Rather than being a special or separate class of reactions, coping is largely seen today as fueled by common human needs and motivations such as (a) a need for understanding, which motivates a search for meaning in the experience; (b) an inclination to interpret ambiguous events in a manner consistent with preexisting beliefs and expectancies, (c) an experience of stress stemming from loss of control and/or threat to well-being, which motivates efforts to maintain or regain a sense of mastery and emotional equilibrium; (d) a challenge to one's identity, worldviews, and related fundamental assumptions, which motivates efforts to reestablish essential perceptions and conditions; and (e) the need to maintain ties to valued others, particularly those who may be helpful in resolving the crisis (Janoff-Bulman, 1992; Moos & Schaefer, 1986; Taylor, 1983). As in so many areas of practice and research, early inquiries about coping were anchored in a problem/pathology orientation focusing on stressor-illness outcomes. Over the years, conceptualizations have evolved dramatically, with deepening attention to adaptive resources, coping strategies, and individual differences in understanding the process of coping and its outcomes (Goldberger & Breznitz, 1993). Although there is a long list of variations in ways that coping has been "de-chunked" and packaged, one fundamental distinction has been that of contextual (situation-person transactions) versus dispositional (relatively stable personality factors) focus regarding the predominant factors that shape an individual's choice or use of coping responses.

Stressors or threats can affect an individual who is unaware of them. Although they may not be noticed or interpreted (appraised) by the individual or generally defined in coping terms, such stressors can have clinically significant repercussions. Indeed, the massive evidence of the toll of stressors is part of what motivates the pursuit of stress management and coping interventions, through which these costs can be reduced if not altogether avoided. What can make a great deal of difference is whether, when, and how stressors are appraised—if the individual is to be effective in managing stresses in his or her life, this is an essential step—and the factors that impede or facilitate appraisal and response processes.

WHAT GOES ON BETWEEN STRESSOR AND ACTION?

The prevailing contextual view of coping sees it as a function of appraisal, or the meaning ascribed to a perceived stressor.[2] Whereas coping refers to what a person thinks or does to manage a taxing situation, appraisal refers to the interpretations or evaluations of what might be thought or done in that encounter (Lazarus, 1991). Specifically, appraisals are the interpretive processes through which the individual evaluates a given person-environment event or condition with respect to (a) its potential for harm, loss, challenge or benefit—primary ap-

praisal; and (b) the resources and options for affecting the event, condition, or outcome—secondary appraisal (Lazarus & Folkman, 1984). For example,

What is the nature of this threat?

Who is at fault or accountable?

What is my ability to act directly to affect the situation in the direction I desire?

What is my ability to manage my emotions or appraisals consistent with the direction I desire?

What other resources are available, and how well or likely can I draw on these?

What is the likelihood the situation will change to make it less threatening? (Smith, Haynes, Lazarus, & Pope, 1993; Smith & Lazarus, 1990, 1993)

The stipulation of appraised stress or threat has oriented recent practice and research to approach coping predominantly as a conscious process, although a mutable one that interacts with other factors, such as personal characteristics, prior stress-related experience, and environmental attributes.[3] When a threat is imminent, simple, and unambiguous (a speeding car coming toward us, a stranger leaping from the dark), appraisals and emotions can be relatively straightforward and similar across people. But, many of life's stressors are not so simple or unambiguous. Stressors often emerge subtly or incrementally within ordinary life circumstances or are multifaceted in the positive and negative potential they carry. Appraisals must often be undertaken under unclear or confounded circumstances. And people enter a coping sequence replete with histories, goals, and dispositions that will shape what they perceive and, thus, what they do. Because coping generally occurs within the fabric of everyday life, we must understand the ongoing social and psychological processes that surround it.

Confirmatory Bias in Information Processing

The individual's current mode of information processing significantly affects threat and coping appraisals. In familiar situations, information processing functions in a relatively automatic fashion with great reliance on knowledge and assumptions based on past experience and comparatively limited attention to situational detail (Bargh, 1989; Langer, 1989; Wyer & Bargh, 1997). For example, once we become familiar with what typically occurs in a classroom, office meeting, church/temple, conversation with neighbors, particular social event, and so forth, we "go on autopilot" to a much greater extent than when that situation was new or if something atypical is present. Deliberate or "mindful" attention to details in the environment and intensive processing of cues requires a state of vigilance and mindfulness. This is difficult to sustain for long and tends to be activated on an as-needed basis: for example, when meeting novel situations in which prior experience or constructs may not apply, when actively engaged in a choice or decision, or when a noticeable feature or event triggers alertness.

People are inherently biased to perceive information consistent with a presumed context or preferred conclusion (Ditto, Jemmott, & Darley, 1988; Holton & Pyszczynski, 1989; Kunda, 1987, 1990). When not in a deliberative mode, people's mind-sets are characterized by expectations and motivations relevant to whatever plans or activities are prominent at the time. Their information processing is markedly biased in service of these, thus limiting atten-

tiveness to environmental information (Gollwitzer, 1990, 1991; Taylor & Gollwitzer, 1995). Thus, familiarity, assumptions, and focus on a goal can cause one to overlook or misinterpret subtle threat information and thus delay active coping.

Attention, Activation, and Working Knowledge

Another element influencing coping involves how information gets processed and the limits of "working knowledge." Although people may amass a large repertoire of information—of any sort, but in this case about types of threat and coping responses—only a very limited amount of one's total cognitive repertoire can be retrieved from memory and held in active working awareness at any given moment (J. R. Anderson, 1983, 1995; Nurius, 1993). Which specific cognitive structures become active is partly a function of habit (much of our lives are sufficiently routine or comparable to prior experience that we develop assumptions, expectancies, and patterned sets of information we commonly draw on; see discussion on social niches in Brower & Nurius, 1993, 1997) and partly a function of what has been situationally cued.

If a situation does not provide enough threat information to trigger the person's attention, a person may have skills and knowledge relevant to coping with the stressor at hand, but these will not be active and working to the individual's benefit. Matthews and Wells (1996) amplify the relation of attentional processes and coping. Thus, education about stressors/threats and coping skills training are important practice components, but they are insufficient if specific types of coping information and strategies are not activated into working knowledge at the time and place needed. Because effective application of coping resources and strategies is highly contingent on situation-specific factors, it is essential to take information-processing features into account in practice (see Folkman et al., 1991).

The Power of Emotions

Because much of the work behind the scenes involves cognitive operations, it is all too easy to overlook the tremendous impact of emotion. Stress is by its very nature emotional. Emotions come into play at every juncture of coping. For example, activated cognitive constructs tend to be mood congruent, making it far easier to access constructs consistent with one's prevailing mood and difficult to access those at odds with one's emotional state (Brown & Taylor, 1986; Mayer, Gaschke, Braverman, & Evans, 1992; Nurius & Markus, 1990). People's prevailing moods can substantially color evaluative judgments, particularly under conditions such as time pressures or competing task demands (Forgas, 1994, 1995; Siemer & Reisenzein, 1998). Although emotions can play a galvanizing role in coping (e.g., discomfort or alarm triggering deliberate attention to environmental events), they can also hinder threat appraisal and impede access to knowledge or abilities relevant to coping (e.g., positive emotions are not consistent with threat; anxiety feelings can make it difficult to tap competence constructs).

Emotions can and do distract and overwhelm. Thus, managing emotions is critical to effective coping, whatever the type of stressor or specific coping strategy undertaken. The specific nature of an individual's emotional response to a stressor depends on his or her meaning analysis of the situation. Thus, if two people experiencing the same stressor cognitively appraise its meaning differently, they will have different emotions. This includes the extent to which a set of circumstances is congruent or incongruent with personal goals and beliefs and the specific nature of secondary appraisals. For example, anger has been associated with blaming someone for an unwanted situation, guilt with blaming oneself, fear with thinking that one is endangered, and hurt or sadness with perceived betrayal or loss (Folkman & Lazarus, 1988; Lazarus, 1991; Lazarus & Smith, 1988; Smith et al., 1993).

Emotions are also significantly tied to behavioral responses. People's emotions following appraisal of a situation reflect their interpretation of the implications of the situation for their well-being (however accurate/inaccurate, rational or not this may appear to others) and provide valuable predictors of what they will likely do, or at least have the strongest impulse to do (Smith & Lazarus, 1993). Different emotions predispose individuals to certain forms of action readiness or unreadiness (Frijda, 1987; Frijda, Kuipers, & ter Schure, 1989; Frijda, Markam, Sato, & Wiers, 1995). Different clusters of emotions are associated with action impulses such as moving toward, away from, or against an environmental interaction (e.g., joy, fear, and rage, respectively); others evoke states such as helplessness or an urge to disappear from view. Thus, if one feels shame in a situation, but really needs the types of behavioral strategie more closely related to feeling angry, effective coping will be difficult.[4]

In sum, if coping were merely a matter of being armed with a repertoire of strategies and/or skills, practice would be far easier. But coping is often most needed in situations when life is most messy, confused, and stressful. Coping is, by definition, far from neutral or formulaic. Goals, values, and commitments are part of what bring "heat" to cognition and coping. Confrontation, rejection, loss, failure, injury, illness—stressors threaten what we care about, and we must often juggle more than one at a time. We often experience a jumble of emotions and concerns: for example, in situations with conflicting outcomes, such as safeguarding security versus being ridiculed or rejected by valued others. Next, we will consider some aspects of human psychology in the social environment that can make a real difference in the efficacy of coping skills training.

SOME CONUNDRUMS IN COPING

Why didn't they just: say no, leave, get themselves to the doctor, stand up for themselves, see it coming (whatever seems the obvious "right" thing to do)? Looking at coping from the outside or with 20-20 hindsight misses much of the complexity involved. I have noted a few information processes that can work against threat and coping appraisal. I discuss here additional double-edged aspects of psychological functioning that practitioners must carefully consider in their practice efforts. Again, it is crucial to bear in mind that these factors normatively affect us all; they serve useful and reasonable functions along with their problematic aspects.

Positivity Bias

Positivity is used here to refer to a number of observed phenomena such as assumptions of control, perceived invulnerability, unrealistic optimism, positive illusions, and positive assumptive worlds. This is not a blanket positivity—people do understand and see that bad things happen. Rather, this refers to an egocentric bias that one's own likelihood of experiencing negative events is low, certainly lower than others' likelihood of experiencing the same problems, and one's good fortune and ability to handle situations is greater than that of others (McKenna,1993; Perloff & Fetzer, 1986; Taylor, 1989; Weinstein, 1980, 1984; Weinstein & Klein, 1995).[5] This perceptual bias presents a dilemma. On the one hand, strongly positive self-perceptions, assumptions of mastery or control, and positive expectations about others and the future are generally very important assets to mental health and have been found significantly associated with well-being factors such as higher motivation, greater contentment and confidence, more positive self-esteem, greater use of effective coping strategies, and better adjustment following adversity (Carver et al., 1993; Friedland, Keinan, & Regev, 1992; Taylor & Aspinwall, 1996; Taylor & Brown, 1988). On the other hand, perceptions of vulnerability are an important prelude to anticipating potential harm and appraising ambiguous threat information as self-relevant. Similarly, recognizing limits of personal control or barriers to self-protection is needed to motivate efforts to seek assistance or to adopt precautionary protective action.

Thus, although positivity bias is fundamentally valuable for coping engagement, persistence, and recovery, it can also work against coping by inclining one to overlook, disregard, or misinterpret threat information and overestimate one's efficacy in avoiding, deflecting, or controlling the threat (Nurius, 1999; van derPlight, 1996). Practice interventions must take this balance into account. Efforts to counter positivity bias run the risk of creating new problems, such as fostering anxiety, paranoia, loss of confidence, hypervigilance, difficulty trusting or taking reasonable risks, or denial. Thus, practice interventions designed to increase perceptions of vulnerability to certain threats and to enhance risk reduction and/or preparation for coping that is realistic to contextual constraints should be purposefully coupled with selective reinforcement of positivity such as having expectations of success, mobilizing active coping efforts, focusing on immediate effective consequences of specific behaviors, redefining the situation or struggle in a relatively positive way, persisting at goal attainment under adversity, feeling in control (over one's daily life and emotional reactions even if not over the stressor or outcome), and making active efforts to renormalize one's life (see Carver & Scheier, 1995; Richard, van der Plight, & de Vries, 1995; Thompson, Sobolew-Shubin, Galbraith, Schwankovsky, & Cruzen, 1993).

Threat Ambiguity and Context Confounds

From a practice perspective, detecting a potential threat as early as possible generally allows a more thorough appraisal of threat and coping options and may allow for a greater range of coping responses and resources than coping at later stages of threat development (e.g., when a threat is more imminent, severe, or less likely to respond to coping efforts). But, what makes an event or sign a "trigger" for coping? Because coping requires detection of a threat, there must be signs that differentiate the

presence and absence of danger and these signs must be "readable."

For some threats, it is just not possible to see them coming, and the practice emphasis is better placed on adaptive coping (e.g., productive secondary appraisals such as low self-blame and high coping potential, practice with emotion management, active coping strategies appropriate to the context) and expanding coping resources. In cases when risk is logically related to an event, action, or environmental feature and/or when the odds of a bad outcome are not slight, training to pair threat appraisal with the presence of risk markers strengthens the chance that these risk markers will get noticed and the coping process will be triggered. This is commonly a component of relapse prevention treatment, refusal and resistance training (e.g., peer pressure for illicit substance use, various health and public safety campaigns).

When risk is ambiguous or confounded in its initial encounter—arising in subtle or incremental form, from counterintuitive sources, or in circumstances that obscure threat appraisal—efforts to support self-protective coping are more complicated.[6] This dilemma may be particularly marked when the threat involves deception or duplicity by others, in that there is active effort to maintain ambiguity or erroneous situation interpretations. In the case of acquaintance sexual aggression, for example, risk is often embedded in normative situations, and efforts by the assailant to isolate or exert control over the woman are not patently evident (Norris, Nurius, & Graham, 1999; Nurius & Gaylord, 1998). Although not yet extensively explored, research related to deception—both what enables successful deception and what enables lie detection (e.g., fleeting emotion in facial expression)—may guide practice innovations to strengthen one's facility for threat appraisal (Ekman & O'Sullivan, 1991; Frank & Ekman, 1997; Vrij & Semin, 1996; Vrij, Semin, & Bull, 1996). In addition, recent findings suggest that sensitivity to situational characteristics—the ability to flexibly adapt one's vigilance level to different situations, called discriminative facility—is modifiable, and this may point to a skill set for threat appraisal that has not yet been well explored (Chiu, Hong, Mischel, & Shoda, 1995; Roussi, Miller, & Shoda, in press; Shoda et al., 1998).

Translating Global Information to Be Self-Referent

It is one thing to gain general information about potential threats and self-protective actions (e.g., related to vehicular accidents, health conditions, activity-related injuries). It is another thing to make that information truly self-relevant. Evidence indicates that general knowledge is not automatically translated into self-knowledge—for example, education about AIDS will not inherently be stored as self-referential—nor does general knowledge automatically generalize to or get activated in specific situations (Thompson, Anderson, Freedman, & Swan, 1996). An interesting set of findings in my own research illustrates this translation gap from general to self. Specifically, women have reported situational and behavioral information they associate with risk of acquaintance sexual aggression. They have reported vigilance on behalf of friends exposed to risk, and activities undertaken or mentally rehearsed to extricate friends from what they believe to be risky situations (Norris, Nurius, & Dimeff, 1996). The same women were much less specific about

how they would have or had applied this information in their own behalf. In spite of problems such as context conflict and ambiguous threat cues, people appear more able to undertake protective coping appraisals and actions on behalf of others than on their own behalf (see also Nurius, Furrey, & Berliner, 1992).

Thus, one practice goal is the translation of abstract knowledge about risk and protection into personally applicable appraisals, emotions, and responses (Cue, George, & Norris, 1996; Nurius, 1999; Sparks & Guthrie, 1998). Because repeated behaviors can influence a person's self-concept (Charng, Piliavin, & Callero, 1988), one strategy is to practice selected coping activities (e.g., precautionary behaviors, situation analysis related to the specific stressor or threat in question). These findings suggest that orienting this kind of coping preparation toward the protection of others similarly affected by the threat in question may circumvent impediments to acknowledging and preparing for one's own vulnerability (e.g., use of natural networks in which new patterns of coping appraisal and action are practiced in teams or small groups).

Aspinwall and Taylor (1997) note naturally occurring ways in which social networks can be important aids in the detection of warning signs and the determination of the extent of danger a potential stressor poses. For example, feedback from others can help individuals to see and sort out potential stressors in their financial affairs, workplace, residence, or interpersonal relationships. And, activities undertaken as coping assistance can themselves help build cognitive schemas about "psychologically active" features of situations relative to threat and protective coping skills, which may then be easier to translate into use for oneself (Nurius & Shoda, 1999).

Multitrack Coping

Not only can there be more than one stressor in any given set of circumstances, but any given stressor can represent multiple forms of threat or loss. Weighing multiple types of harm or loss against one another constitutes a kind of multivariate cost analysis of potentially conflicting goals and concerns. For example, fear of physical harm, social ridicule, and relationship rejection may all come into play in a situation where a social partner may have a sexually transmittable disease, may be capable of sexual aggression, or attempts to drive when intoxicated. What may appear a perplexing coping strategy relative to one kind of threat (e.g., physical safety) can be more easily understood if the threat that is most prominent for the individual in the moment is something else (Nurius, Norris, Young, Graham, & Gaylord, in press).

Relationships are one arena particularly vulnerable to multitrack coping and conflicting goals. The interplay between individual coping and one's social network is both crucially important and delicately complex. The need for belonging, to form and maintain meaningful bonds with others, is a fundamental human motivation that influences both cognition and affect (Baumeister & Leary, 1995). When individuals cope in ways that threaten their closeness with valued others and/or when the source of stress is among this pool, as in relationship-based threat, coping becomes double-edged (Nurius, Macy, Norris, & Haung, 2000). Icard and Nurius (1996), for example, provide an example of multilayered issues for gays and lesbi-

ans of color in coming out, and Laux and Weber (1991) illustrate the need to disentangle the purposes behind coping strategies, differentiating, for example, those directed toward preserving relationship (e.g.,, suppression of anger, reframing) or toward repairing a wound to self-esteem.

This list of conundrums is by no means exhaustive. Rather, these examples illustrate the complex social, cognitive, and emotional system within which coping is embedded and the importance of understanding this system for assessment and intervention planning. Otherwise, it is all too easy to pathologize what is actually normative and to insufficiently prepare clients to anticipate and grapple with factors such as these.

DIFFERENCES CAN MAKE A DIFFERENCE

Variations in situations and among people clearly make a difference in risk susceptibility, what is experienced as stressful, how people interpret and feel about the stress, what coping strategies they use, and how the whole process feeds into future stress and coping. Two aspects of situational variability broadly pertinent to practice are (a) the intensity of the stressor and (b) coping resources. Although intensity can be gauged in many ways (see Freedy, Saladin, Kilpatrick, Resnick, & Saunders, 1994; Hobfoll, Freedy, Green, & Solomon, 1996, for discussions related to extreme stressors, such as devastating natural disasters; and Katz, Ritvo, Irvine, & Jackson, 1996; Maes, Leventhal, & de Ridder, 1996, for issues related to chronic stressors), perhaps most common to practice are issues related to coping with multiple stressors.

Multiple Stressors

If personal threats came in single doses, coping would be far simpler. In reality, people often cope with multiple stressors simultaneously. Multiple stressors can be part of distinct circumstances, such as cataclysmic events or major life events, as well as repeated aspects of a person's life—daily stressors, ambient stressors, and role stressors. Some of these will be focal events; some will be secondary offshoots from the focal stressor (such as increase in daily stressors created by adisaster or major life event). Some people have different exposures to multiple stressors due to underlying causes such as economic or social conditions (e.g., poverty, crowding, noise, physical strain, pollutants, lack of safety or control).

Although considerable research has implicitly assumed that multiple stressors will have an additive effect on adjustment—a linear relationship wherein more stressors leads to greater negative impact—Lepore and Evans (1996) review compelling evidence that this is often not the case. There is a need for more careful assessment. For example, to what extent are multiple stressors relatively independent versus having an interactive or multiplicative relationship? If interactive, is the effect *potentiation* of stress (the combined effects are more negative than adding up the unique effects of each stressor) or *attenuation* of stress (the combined effects are less negative than the sum of all stressors)? And why? Do the interactive effects stem from the nature of the stressors in relation to one another (e.g., how specific factors related to illness, substance use, work-setting stress, and so forth

function) or from the coping used to date? Dimensions of coping that can potentiate stress include (a) stereotypic coping (indiscriminate use of a coping strategy or resource across diverse stressors; mismatch of coping response to demands of stressor), (b) behavioral constraints (coping strategies for one stressor are literally incompatible with strategies needed for another), and (c) residual arousal and fatigue. Although coping may reduce stress, it typically involves considerable effort, which, particularly with chronic or concurrent multiple stressors, can reduce the capacity to respond to other stressors and can require a longer period of time to recover.

Outcomes from coping with a stressor can foster expectations of control that can in turn affect how a person appraises and responds to subsequent stressors. When coping has resulted in perceived *lack* of control, subsequent coping is likely to be more palliative than instrumental and to reflect beliefs of helplessness and external control. When coping has resulted in mastery experiences, individuals are more likely to reflect a sense of self-efficacy in their secondary appraisals of stressors (regarding their coping potential, expectations about positive or negative outcome, accountability) and their choice of coping strategies. Multiple stressors would also be expected to affect people's primary appraisals; increasing sensitivity to subsequent stressors, for example, heightening the felt threat value to a greater extent than if one of those stressors were experienced alone.

Coping Resources

Coping resources is a broadly used term, including assets such as time, energy, cognitive load or busyness, environmental and personality characteristics, and material goods, in addition to the well-known resources of social supports and coping skills (Aspinwall & Taylor, 1997; Fiske & Taylor, 1991; Hobfoll, 1989). Not surprisingly, individuals with higher social status tend to have higher perceptions of personal control and levels of coping resources (Lefcourt, 1981; Pearlin & Schooler, 1978), and greater coping resources tend to be associated with more effective coping and lower distress (Booth & Amanto, 1991). However, having resources can cut both ways with respect to stress and coping. Hobfoll et al. (1996) describe the effects of loss spirals in that, following stressful experiences, people tend to have a depleted resource pool, which in itself can create vulnerabilities or difficulties in coping with subsequent stressors—of particular concern to those experiencing extreme, multiple, or chronic stress.

One of the most important and extensively studied resources is that of social support.[7] Research has generally indicated that the availability of social support as well as its receipt can affect coping at multiple points—appraisal of threat and degree of experienced stress, appraisal of coping, manner of coping, likelihood of stress effects, outcomes of coping effort, and recovery (for more detail on social support in coping, see Pierce, Sarason, & Sarason, 1996; Taylor, 1995). There are many forms of social support (e.g., perceived support, supportive relationships, supportive networks, moderation of stress via direct and stress-buffering effects), as well as distinctions within these forms. For example, social relationships involve demands as well as supports, supports are not always well matched to needs, support sources that are overused or misused can become part of negative spirals, and negative social interactions can

have as many or more adverse effects on coping and well-being as positive interactions have helpful effects (Gottlieb & Wagner, 1991; Taylor, 1995). Thus, it is crucial that social support not be oversimplified in "more-is-better" terms.

Through social support, one can see coping more concretely as a dynamic, transactional process between a person who has a set of resources, values, and commitments and an environment with its own resources, demands, and constraints (Lazarus & Launier, 1978; Thoits, 1986). Thus, rather than a one-shot set of appraisals and action, coping is a set of reciprocal exchanges through which—for better or worse—the person and environment influence one another.

Social Structural Factors

Another crucially important aspect of the social context is how broader social structures (e.g., socioeconomic status) engender differences in exposure to stressors, development and use of coping resources, and the shaping of coping appraisals and strategies; and how social structures can contribute to larger patterns in which institutional structures become involved in individuals' coping. Laumann, Michael, and Gagnon (1994) argue that gender, socioeconomic level, race/ethnicity, religion, marital status, and age are important variables because they act as "master statuses," exerting a strong influence on how one perceives and is perceived by one's social world in addition to more tangible factors such as differential life circumstances and access to and control over resources. These status characteristics have been found to be associated with identity, as well as patterns of social relationships and the meaning one ascribes to experiences. Wheaton (1982), for example, illustrates ways that fatalistic beliefs often associated with living in poverty can inhibit active, problem-focused coping, and Gore and Colten (1991) emphasize gender-linked socially structured differences in the nature of stressors and the role of social relationships in shaping coping. Uncertainty, cascading events, lack of direct control over stressors, and psychological distress generally increase linearly with a decrease of income level (Pearlin, 1993; Pearlin & Radabaugh, 1976), and those with fewest resources and least ability to control their lives, such as the elderly, ethnic minorities, and women, tend to hold different fundamental assumptions about themselves, the way the world works, and the future (Janoff-Bulman, 1992; Normoyle & Lavrakas, 1984).

To date, the bulk of work that has examined differences among societal subpopulations has focused on stress and vulnerability, with comparatively little on coping differences per se. However, recent research is stimulating promising new directions. Some of this work has focused on communication and public education goals and the need to attend to audience characteristics and historic schisms in designing effective intervention programs—for example, use of family- and community-based approaches to infuse health promotion information to communities of color (N. B. Anderson, 1995; Icard, Zamora-Hernandez, Spencer, & Catalano, 1996; U.S. Department of Health and Human Services, 1987). Other research has provided promising guides with respect to gender differences that can help or hamper women's risk perception and self-protective coping (Miller & Kirsch, 1987; Weidner & Collins, 1993)—for example, attention to issues of trust and relationship maintenance in developing HIV/AIDS

prevention programs targeting women (Kline & Strickler, 1993; Mantell, Schinke, & Akabas, 1988). Particularly important is increasing attention to the pathways through which environmental influences (socioeconomic status, residential factors, education, cultural and sociocultural variables, institutional and political forces, family and media influences) can affect health and well-being and, thus, ways that interventions designed to reduce exposure to stressors and to strengthen coping and related stress management may be informed by these findings (Anderson & Armstead, 1995; Johnson et al., 1995).

Much more research and carefully documented practice is needed to guide theory development and testing across diverse populations. Although this need is not unique to the topic of coping, it highlights the importance of a high-quality empirical base to the general applicability of models and findings. In this regard, it is encouraging that social cognition models have been found associated with health behavior across a wide variety of societies—applying successfully, for example, with individuals from individualist and collectivist cultures (Abraham & Sheeran, 1997; Earley, 1993). Knowing that individual or group differences exist is not enough. Research and practice findings must go beyond this basic descriptive level to explain why differences exist and how their effects are carried and sustained.

PROACTIVE COPING: REVERSING THE DIRECTION OF STRESS AND COPING

The general shift in coping research to look beyond strategies defined by threats and negative events encourages more proactive and preventive practice innovations as well as exploration of aspects of coping that can lead to mastery, growth, and flexibility (e.g., Holahan, Moos, & Schaefer, 1996; Parker & Endler, 1996). Work related to proactive coping is consistent with this general shift. There has been considerable attention over the years to various forms of anticipatory coping, which involves preparation for stress associated with specific events or phenomena that are certain or likely to occur (Breznitz, 1983; Folkman & Lazarus, 1985). Basic techniques of relaxation training and stress inoculation and management, for example, can be thought of as part of anticipatory coping and have been applied across a wide range of stressors (e.g., workplace, performance, or examination anxiety; substance misuse; various health and other chronic stressors).

Proactive coping is broader based (not directed toward any specific stressor but rather to prepare in general), involves somewhat different activities and skills than coping with extant stressors, and is fundamentally more prevention oriented. Because of its recency and positive promise, I will describe some of the key practice components and issues involved. Proactive coping has been differentiated into five sets of tasks (Aspinwall & Taylor, 1997):

1. *Building a reserve of coping-related resources* (e.g., time, energy, money, support network, organizational and planning abilities, personal environment that permits sufficient relief from overload). As Hobfoll (1989) has pointed out, such resources are important to many aspects of functioning. Insufficiency or erosion of such resources will hamper efforts to lead self-determined lives in many respects, including but not limited to coping. This is not to say that one cannot be proactive unless one is resource wealthy. Rather, it is to recognize the importance of securing and safeguarding resources as part of any realistic effort to help people avoid or head off stressors to the extent possible, in addition to actively coping and persevering with threats and life stress that are unavoidable. Aiding others in obtaining and sustaining needed resources has long been a core dimension of social work practice. A good match between type of resources sought and those most valuable for an individual's proactive coping is important (e.g., whereas emotional supports are often priorities for reactive coping, the ability of a support network to provide informational guidance germane to potential or ambiguous stressors is likely to be particularly valuable for proactive coping).

2. *Recognition of potential stressors.* The importance of early threat detection, which has become so evident in reactive coping, is similarly crucial to proactivity (e.g., Is this something I should keep an eye on? What is this likely to develop into?). Aspinwall and Taylor (1997) present stimulating findings about two facets often overlooked: (a) the usefulness of fostering a future temporal orientation to better enable individuals to think about and plan for desired futures such as cultivating preventive health behaviors, developing good parenting, sustaining safe-sex practices, and decreasing tobacco and alcohol use (Nurius, Lovell, & Edgar, 1988; Rothspan & Read, 1996; Strathman, Gleicher, Boninger, & Edwards, 1994) and (b) the need to explicitly engage a social network to assist in detection of potential stressors (as discussed under conundrums).

As noted earlier, a host of trade-offs must be considered regarding concepts such as vigilance and monitoring versus repression and blunting—referring to tendencies to either seek out potentially threatening information or to avoid and ignore threatening information (Miller, Shoda, & Hurley, 1996; Taylor & Clark, 1986; provide reviews). Whereas chronic repressors or avoiders will be seriously hampered in their ability to act in advance relative to potential stressors, there are liabilities associated with continually scanning one's environment for potential danger, such as hypervigilance, perseveration, and emotional and mental fatigue. More research findings about how people learn to regulate their attention to some but not all environmental information and to be flexible in responding is needed (Derryberry & Reed, 1994).

3. *Initial appraisal of emerging stressors.* For proactive coping, in addition to identifying potential threats, one must understand how they are likely to change: that is, how a stressor in an incipient or nebulous stage is likely to develop. One mechanism is purposefully engaging one's social network—talking to or observing others in similar circumstances, asking others to provide "perception checks," or exchanging information and appraisals. Although others' perceptions are by no means likely to be wholly accurate, establishing an exchange mechanism provides an ongoing conduit for information and mutual alert. Use of mental simulations is another mechanism. In addition to engaging one's natural social network, group work interventions are well suited to goals.

Another mechanism is the use of mental simulations, or systematically developing imaginative images and rehearsals of hypothetical or real events (Aspinwall & Taylor, 1997; Taylor

& Pham, 1996; Taylor & Schneider, 1989). In some cases, this may mean undertaking education about specific kinds of stressors to learn how a nebulous danger may evolve, such as early warning signs of aggression potential or substance misuse in a relationship. It also refers to a more general skill development, in which people acquire the habit of running through logical extensions of what a nebulous situation may develop into and what options for proactive and reactive coping appear most available. Planning and cognitive rehearsal are, of course, staple interventions for most any practitioner. In this case, these habits and skills are directed toward a problem-solving appraisal style that helps develop confidence and preparedness for averting or dampening potential stressors (see Skinner, in press, for a review controllability appraisals and their relation to range of action opportunities one).

4 and 5. *Preliminary coping and elicitation and use of feedback.* As with reactive coping, this is fundamentally about the question of "what can I do?" Aspinwall and Taylor (1997) suggest that successful proactive coping at this stage is inherently active rather than avoidant (e.g., planning, seeking input from others, taking behavioral action). The specific nature of the action would depend, of course, on the initial appraisals. Although some stressors are realistically not directly controllable, this determination may not be clearly discernible at an early stage, and an initial problem-solving effort will likely be needed to inform such an evaluation. This leads to a pivotal point with respect to proactive coping—that by its nature it typically begins with small steps (to match the as-yet-not-fully-developed threat) and is iterative. That is, the very emergent potential nature of

future threats often requires a give-and-take process wherein the individual seeks information or tries out an action and then watches to assess its impact on the stressor.

Although elicitation and use of feedback as a dynamic loop is implicit in the coping literature, its importance is made clearer and more salient in proactive coping. Questions such as "Has the event developed further and in what direction?," "Did my initial efforts have an effect?," and "What am I learning about this potential stressor and its relationship to my efforts and resources?" are key to fueling and directing effective proactive coping. The very nature of these questions suggests a proactivity—ongoing information seeking, targeted prevention or containment efforts, and readiness to continue experimentation with ways to exert control. On the face of it, all this may seem completely obvious. But, as considerable literature attests (Aspinwall & Taylor, 1997; Carver & Scheier, 1994; Scheier, Weintraub, & Carver, 1986; Taylor, 1989; Wiebe & Williams, 1992), these efforts are not so easily foreseen and undertaken prior to an encounter with an unambiguously threatening event, and many people are hampered at the start by aspects of their learning histories, dispositions, or coping resources.

Venturing into proactive coping is a bigger step than it may appear on the surface. "The problem" is not a clear, clean target. There is not yet a specific critical incident or a chronic or acute stressor to center an intervention around. Practice in targeting proactive coping is inherently prevention and strengths oriented, but it is not suited to everyone or to all situations. It involves building skills and resources that constitute a repertoire or capacity more than a one-

on-one problem-response readiness. Working toward proactive coping also requires an understanding of the normative social psychological processes that people engage in before they encounter problems that disable or overwhelm them. The directives of proactive coping are based on established theory and findings, but there is not yet an accumulated empirical base for the model as a whole, nor has the model been tested across diverse populations or problem types. Its articulation is emblematic of future directions of coping research and practice—to learn more about what works preventively, at least by way of fostering an alert, resilient base from which to cope.

In summary, most coping research to date has been literally defined by extant stressors and a context of reactivity versus proactivity. Our knowledge base includes limited information about people who may have encountered the stressor in question but whose actions or other characteristics offset the course of the development of the stressor. Thus, we lack indepth knowledge about how to best equip people to be proactive in heading off potential threats. Although many stressors are preventable or controllable, many are not (e.g., bereavement, certain chronic conditions, some forms of victimization and disaster). For life stressors that are not preventable, elements of proactive coping may hold promise for lessening suffering and supporting adaptive coping. For example, investing in one's support network and other coping resources, fostering future-oriented planning and problem-solving skills, and learning to manage negative emotions have very robust and broadly applicable empirical support. For stressors that are preventable or can be lessened, the coping process must necessarily be understood in terms of individual-in-environment variations.

WHAT DO WE KNOW AND WHERE DO WE GO FROM HERE?

Rather than providing a definitive set of do's and don'ts regarding coping effectiveness, the corpus of research has made it clear that intervention questions are most honestly met with "it depends." This is not to say that there are no robust findings. For example, aggregate data suggest a cluster of comparatively more adaptive strategies (active coping, planning, suppression of competing activities, restraint, positive reinforcement, seeking social support) and a cluster of strategies more likely to be maladaptive in managing stress (denial, behavioral disengagement, focus on negative emotions, misuse of alcohol and drugs; see Carver, Scheier, & Weintraub, 1989). Problem-focused coping has generally been found to be more effective than emotion-focused coping or avoidance in reducing stress, providing a sense of mastery, producing problem resolutions, and fostering well-being. However, some studies report opposite effects for active coping, whereas others reveal the utility of emotion-focused coping and avoidance responses in some circumstances (see Carver & Scheier, 1994; Thoits, 1991; Zeidner & Saklofske, 1996; for findings illustrating differences in coping effects at different points in the coping process).

Research findings overall reinforce a view of coping as sensitive to situational variables and greater consistency within stressor domains (e.g., depression, physical illness, substance misuse, work settings, criminal victimization). The following summary list of adaptive coping findings illustrates this point (for elaboration see Lazarus, 1993; Zeidner & Saklofske, 1996).

- No one coping response is uniformly adaptive.
- Coping strategies should fit the context and the individual.
- Coping strategies vary between and within individuals.
- Adaptive coping involves a flexible repertoire and combined use of coping strategies.
- Coping behaviors may influence some but not other outcomes.
- What is adaptive can be different for chronic versus acute stressors.
- Coping adaptiveness may vary across phases of a stressful encounter.
- Those with favorable external coping resources tend to have better outcomes.

Where do we go from here? Some of the cutting edge questions posed by coping researchers suggest some of the likely future directions for research and practice inquiry (see, for elaboration, Carver, 1996; Costa, Somerfield, & McCrae, 1996; Holahan et al., 1996; Lazarus, 1993):

- What is the ordinary balance of helpful coping to harmful coping? What should we use as a referent for healthy, realistic goals regarding balance?
- Are there generalizations we can make about the match of coping responses to type of situation in which responses are helpful? In which they are harmful?
- What outcome measure (or measures) are most appropriate to assess coping as being successful or unsuccessful? To assess other dimensions such as distress, task performance while under stress, flexibility versus rigidity?
- How long a time lag should there be between assessment of coping and assessment of the

consequences of coping? Are there critical periods within which coping is most important and after which it matters less?

- Is coping that is undertaken in advance of encounter with a stressor the same phenomenon as coping in direct reaction to a stressor? Is there more involved than time sequence?

- Do we adequately assess the personal meaning aspects of stress? Are we overly inclined to focus on evident environmental pressures and neglect more individualized threat meanings?

- Do people's reports about the ways they coped tell us how they really coped, or only how they think they coped?

- Does it make sense to use the word *cope* when people are responding to challenges (opportunities), as opposed to threats (situations with potential for harm)?

- Do we tend to overrationalize coping? Do we have an adequate understanding of the roles of emotions and motivations?

- Have we adequately examined the reciprocal and longitudinal relationships of stress and coping factors with one another—for example, ways that ongoing stressors and a lack of social resources may predict new stressful conditions, which, in turn, augment the stress load and erode social resources?

- What answers can personality psychology make to applied coping? What implications does this hold for revising ways we think about personality?

- Are responses like blunting threat information, self-blame, avoidance, and denial inherently bad things? What do we need to ask and examine to fairly answer this question?

Although many of the phenomena that define coping are individual in nature (e.g., appraisals, emotions, responses), there is increasing recognition that people, and thus coping, are always embedded within larger networks, systems, and dynamics that impinge on and are affected by individual coping. Pearlin (1991;

see this reference for further examples and elaboration) eloquently illustrates several aspects of this interconnectedness that are relevant for social work practice:

- Although coping education and skills training are crucial practice tools, factors such as the social and economic characteristics of people's lives are powerful forces affecting what will be attractive, realistic, or effective for people coping in different problem conditions.

- The problems that created the stress in the first place often go unchanged even when coping with the problem is significantly improved. Although this is not unique to coping, it points to the ongoing need to target sources of problem development as well as strengthening resistance and problem management.

- Particularly for collectivities sharing difficult life circumstances, both indigenous, naturally arising coping "interventions" and planned, formal interventions can make a unique contribution to the relief from or prevention of the problematic circumstances. We need to better understand such relationships and ways that each form may help to optimize the usefulness of the other.

- Whether it is stress in the workplace, education, or treatment setting, or the bureaucratized social welfare structures themselves, it is often beyond the power of the individual to alter the stress-producing situation. Because personal problems are often embedded in formal organizations or extensions of social problems, public policy and other meso or macro-interventions provide important complements to individual interventions.

- Public policy holds particular potential to remove or reduce threats and onerous conditions and to enhance coping, yet, this has been neglected as a player to date. Rather than segregating social work's efforts along traditional micro to macro roles or pitting levels against one another as ideologically superior, the future requires us to look for synergistic combinations of coping, social support, community programs, and public policy thatcontribute to greater effectiveness than any one level can provide.

In conclusion, evaluation of the successfulness or adaptiveness of coping efforts must take into account diverse levels of analysis (e.g., what outcome indicators do we deem most important and why), the specific circumstance or type of stressor, the short-term versus long-term consequences of the strategy in question, and the purposes and perspective of those involved—both the client and the practitioner or researcher (Beehr & McGrath, 1996; Monat & Lazarus, 1991; Schwarzer & Schwarzer, 1996). To be effective in promoting positive outcomes such as stress resistance, new coping skills, enhanced bolstering resources, crisis growth, and proactivity, we must have a strong and constantly upgrading empirical base about what to assess, what to change, and how. This requires ongoing informational commerce between theory-driven practice and theory-driven research. Both must be accountable to evidence bases and open to scrutiny and debate such that, ideally, the profession benefits from the inductive/deductive exchange among theory, research, and application. Moreover, because the need for coping is inherently defined by changing and challenging relationships between people and their environments, what we need to understand and foster effective coping will continually change and evolve as well.

NOTES

1. There are also literatures focused at the biological and physiological levels, and attention within sociology is paid to coping by societies and large groups. These literatures tend to require familiarity with specialized information (e.g., about biochemical processes, drug effects and interactions), are not broadly applicable, and, thus, are not directly germane to the issues reviewed here. Interested readers may want to see review chapters on topics such as chronic illness and substance misuse for examples of physiological factors (Maes, Leventhal, & de Ridder, 1996; Wills & Hirky, 1996).

2. Although appraisal models are the most widely empirically examined and currently used, there are challenges to the notion of appraised stress and calls to better differentiate the impact of stress from positive and negative events (see Hobfoll et al., 1996). In addition, stress and coping have often been defined and studied separately. Thus, appraisal coping researchers do not maintain, for example, that there are no stress effects even when stress is not perceived, just that one cannot invoke the concept of coping unless and until stress does become detected and assessed in some form. The interested reader is referred to Parker and Endler (1996) for a review of how the coping definition has evolved over the decades, including the ebb and flow of attention to situation and person variables.

3. This stipulation does not mean that appraisal is necessarily neither accurate nor within conscious awareness—although they can be, particularly when effort is taken by the person or a helper to review prior responses or to monitor and regulate future stress responses. In a similar vein, the contemplation and decision-making processes involved in"selecting" coping strategies are not necessarily fully within awareness nor, in some situations, as deliberative as they could be. Increasing self-awareness and use of methods to consciously revise one's coping methods is indeed part of how coping intervention can be helpful. Appraisal coping research and practice is generally distinguished from the tradition of defense mechanism research. However, psychodynamic and cognitive science approaches are no longer as distinct as they once were. Dissatisfaction with the limited viability and empirical defensibility of classical psychoanalytic definitions of defense for applicability to coping, for example, motivated more precision in defining operational terms; for example, what specifically is meant by various mechanisms. Horowitz, Znoj, and Stinson (1996) provides a useful summary of several points of linkage with cognitive approaches reviewed in this chapter and the important contributions by researchers such as Haan, Valiant, Horowitz, and others.

4. Although the roles of emotion are crucially important in coping, it is also important not to overinterpret or lose precision in systematic ways in which emotion, cognition, and behavior interrelate. For example, not all emotion necessarily goes through these appraisal components.

After all, people do more than cope. Emotions have additional roots important to broader aspects of functioning and self-regulation; the interested reader is referred to Carver and Scheier (1990), Frijda (1986), Neisser (1988), Parkinson and Manstead (1992), Scherer (1984), and Zajonc (1980).

5. There are additional dimensions of this positivity such as self-aggrandizing self-perceptions and a general tendency to seek and maintain positive mood as well as findings regarding the flip side of negative affectivity, pessimistic explanatory style, and lack of perceived control and self-efficacy. Although these other dimensions are related and important regarding broader practice aims of inoculation and preparing people to be "hardy," they are not central to current discussion. The interested reader is referred to Carver and Scheier (1998), Taylor (1995), and Taylor, Aspinwall, and Giuliano (1994).

6. Here, I am not referring to personal perception factors such as denial, minimizing, or repression, which have been found to impede processing of threat-related information but rather to the nature of contextual factors that can render situational information difficult to "read;" recall prior discussion related to information processing.

7. The literature on social support is, in fact, so massive that a review of it is well beyond scope of this chapter and is interwoven with many of the handbook's chapters. The interested reader may find the following useful: Pierce, Sarason, and Sarason (1990, 1996), Richey (1994), Sarason, Sarason, and Pierce (1990), and Stroebe and Stroebe (1995).

REFERENCES

Abraham, C., & Sheeran, P. (1997). Cognitive representations and preventive health behavior: A review. In K. J. Petrie & J. A. Weinman (Eds.), *Perceptions of health and illness: Current research and applications* (pp. 213-240). Australia: Harwood.

Anderson, J. R. (1983). *The architecture of cognition.* Cambridge, MA: Harvard University Press.

Anderson, J. R. (1995). *Rules of the mind.* Hillsdale, NJ: Lawrence Erlbaum.

Anderson, N. B. (1995). Appealing to diverse audiences: Reaching the African-American community. *Journal of the National Medical Association, 87,* 647-649.

Anderson, N. B., & Armstead, C. A. (1995). Toward understanding the association of socioeconomic status and health: A new challenge for the biopsychosocial approach. *Psychosomatic Medicine, 57,* 213-225.

Aspinwall, L. G., & Taylor, S. E. (1997). A stitch in time: Self-regulation and proactive coping. *Psychological Bulletin, 121,* 417-436.

Bargh, J. A. (1989). Conditional automaticity: Varieties of automatic influence in social perception and cognition. In J. S. Uleman & J. A. Bargh (Eds.), *Unintended thought.* New York: Guilford.

Baumeister, R. F., & Leary, M. R. (1995). The need to belong: Desire for interpersonal attachments as a fundamental human motivation. *Psychological Bulletin, 117,* 497-529.

Beehr, T. A., & McGrath, J. E. (1996). The methodology of research on coping: Conceptual, strategic, and operational-level issues. In M. Zeidner & N. S. Endler (Eds.), *Handbook of coping: Theory, research, applications* (pp. 65-82). New York: John Wiley.

Boekaerts, M. (1996). Coping with stress in childhood and adolescence. In M. Zeidner & N. S. Endler (Eds.), *Handbook of coping: Theory, research, applications* (pp. 452-484). New York: Wiley.

Booth, A., & Amanto, P. (1991). Divorce and psychological stress. *Journal of Health and Social Behavior, 32,* 396-407.

Breznitz, S. (1983). Anticipatory stress and denial. In S. Breznitz (Ed.), *The denial of stress* (pp. 225-255). New York: International Universities Press.

Brower, A., & Nurius, P. S. (1993). *Social cognition and individual change: Current theory and counseling guidelines.* Newbury Park, CA: Sage.

Brower, A. M., & Nurius, P. S. (1997). Schemas, nodes, and niches: Social cognition resources for contemporary social work practice. In D. J. Tucker, C. Garvin, & R. Sarri (Eds.), *The integration of social work and social science.* Westport, CT: Greenwood.

Brown, J. D., & Taylor, S. E. (1986). Affect and the processing of personal information: Evidence for mood-activated self-schemata. *Journal of Experimental Social Psychology, 22,* 436-452.

Carpenter, B. (Ed.). (1992). *Personal coping: Theory, research, and practice.* New York: Praeger.

Carver, C. S. (1996). Foreword. In M. Zeidner & N. S. Endler (Eds.), *Handbook of coping: Theory, research, applications.* New York: John Wiley.

Carver, C. S., Pozo, C., Harris, S. D., Noriega, V., Scheier, M. F., Robinson, D. S., & Ketcham, A. S. (1993). How coping mediates the effects of optimism on distress: A study of women with early stage breast cancer. *Journal of Personality and Social Psychology, 65,* 375-390.

Carver, C. S., & Scheier, M. F. (1990). Origins and functions of positive and negative affect: A control-process view. *Psychological Review, 97,* 19-35.

Carver, C. S., & Scheier, M. F. (1994). Situational coping and coping dispositions in a stressful transaction. *Journal of Personality and Social Psychology, 66,* 184-195.

Carver, C. S., & Scheier, M. F. (1995). The role of optimism versus pessimism in the experience of the self. In A. Oosterwegel & R. A. Wicklund (Eds.), *The self in European and North American culture: Development and processes* (pp. 193-204). Netherlands: Kluwer.

Carver, C. S., & Scheier, M. R. (1998). *On the self-regulation of behavior.* New York: Cambridge University Press.

Carver, C. S., Scheier, M. F., & Weintraub, J. K. (1989). Assessing coping strategies: A theoretically based approach. *Journal of Personality and Social Psychology, 56,* 267-283.

Charng, H.-W., Piliavin, J. A., & Callero, P. L. (1988). Role identity and reasoned action in the prediction of repeatedbehavior. *Social Psychology Quarterly, 51,* 303-317.

Chiu, C., Hong, Y., Mischel, W., & Shoda, Y. (1995). Discriminative facility in social competence: Conditional versus dispositional encoding and monitoring-blunting of information. *Social Cognition, 13,* 49-70.

Compas, B. E., Connor, J., Osowiecki, D., & Welch, A. (1997). Effortful and involuntary responses to stress: Implications for coping with chronic stress. In B. H. Gottlieb (Ed.), *Coping with chronic stress* (pp. 105-130). New York: Plenum.

Costa, P. T., Somerfield, M. R., & McCrae, R. R. (1996). Personality and coping: A reconceptualization. In M. Zeidner & N.S. Endler (Eds.), *Handbook of coping: Theory, research, applications* (pp. 44-61). New York: John Wiley.

Cue, K. L., George, W. H., & Norris, J. (1996). Women's appraisals of sexual-assault risk in dating situations. *Psychology of Women Quarterly, 20,* 487-504.

Derryberry, D., & Reed, M. A. (1994). Temperament and attention: Orienting toward and away from positive and negative signals. *Journal of Personality and Social Psychology, 66,* 1128-1139.

Ditto, P. H., Jemmott, J. B., III, & Darley, J. M. (1988). Appraising the threat of illness: A mental representational approach. *Health Psychology, 7,* 183-200.

Earley, P. C. (1993). East meets west meets midwest: Further explorations of collectivistic and individualistic work groups. *Academy of Management Journal, 36,* 319-348.

Eckenrode, J. (Ed.). (1991). *The social context of coping.* New York: Plenum.

Ekman, P., & O'Sullivan, M. (1991). Who can catch a liar? *American Psychologist, 46,* 913-920.

Fiske, S. T., & Taylor, S. E. (1991). *Social cognition* (2nd ed.). New York: McGraw-Hill.

Folkman, S., Chesney, M., McKusick, L., Ironson, G., Johnson, D. S., & Coates, T. J. (1991). Translating coping theory into an intervention. In J. Eckenrode (Ed.), *The social context of coping* (pp. 239-260). New York: Plenum.

Folkman, S., & Lazarus, R. S. (1985). If it changes, it must be a process: Study of emotion and coping during three stages of a college examination. *Journal of Personality and Social Psychology, 48,* 150-170.

Folkman, S., & Lazarus, R. S. (1988). Coping as mediator of emotion. *Journal of Personality and Social Psychology, 54,* 466-475.

Forgas, J. P. (1994). The role of emotion in social judgments: An introductory review and an Affect Infusion Model (AIM). *European Journal of Social Psychology, 24,* 1-24.

Forgas, J. P. (1995). Mood and judgment: The Affect Infusion Model (AIM). *Psychological Bulletin, 117,* 39-66.

Frank, M. G., & Ekman, P. (1997). The ability to detect deceit generalizes across different types of high-stake lies. *Journal of Personality and Social Psychology, 72,* 1429-1439.

Freedy, J. R., Saladin, M. E., Kilpatrick, D. G., Resnick, H. S., & Saunders, B. E. (1994). Understanding acute psychological distress following natural disaster. *Journal of Traumatic Stress, 7,* 257-273.

Frijda, N. H. (1986). *The emotions.* Cambridge, UK: Cambridge University Press.

Frijda, N. H. (1987). Emotion, cognitive structure, and action tendency. *Cognition and Emotion, 1,* 115-143.

Frijda, N. H., Kuipers, P., & ter Schure, E. (1989). Relations among emotion, appraisal, and emotional action readiness. *Journal of Personality and Social Psychology, 57,* 212-228.

Frijda, N. H., Markam, S., Sato, K., & Wiers, R. (1995). Emotions and emotion words. In J. A. Russell, J.-M. Fernandez-Dols, A. S. R. Manstead, & J. Wellenkamp (Eds.), *Everyday conception of emotion* (pp. 121-144). Dordrecht: Kluwer.

Friedland, N., Keinan, G., & Regev, Y. (1992). Controlling the uncontrollable: Effects of stress on illusory perceptions of controllability. *Journal of Personality and Social Psychology, 63,* 923-931.

Frieze, I. H., & Bookwala, J. (1996). Coping with unusual stressors: Criminal victimization. In M. Zeidner & N. S. Endler (Eds.), *Handbook of coping: Theory, research, applications* (pp. 303-321). New York: John Wiley.

Goldberger, L., & Breznitz, S. (Eds.). (1993). *Handbook of stress: Theoretical and clinical aspects* (2nd ed.). New York: Free Press.

Gollwitzer, P. M. (1990). Action phases and mind-sets. In E. T. Higgins & R. M. Sorrentino (Eds.), *Handbook of motivation and cognition: Foundations of social behavior* (Vol. 2, pp. 53-92). New York: Guilford.

Gollwitzer, P. M. (1991). *Abwagen and Planen* [Deliberation and planning]. Goettingen, Germany: Hogrefe.

Gore, S., & Colten, M. E. (1991). Gender, stress, and distress: Social-relational influences. In J. Eckenrode (Ed.), *The social context of coping* (pp. 139-163). New York: Plenum.

Gottlieb, B. H. (Ed.). (1997). *Coping with chronic stress.* New York: Plenum.

Gottlieb, B. H., & Wagner F. (1991). Stress and support processes in close relationships. In J. Eckenrode (Ed.), *The social context of coping* (pp. 165-188). New York: Plenum.

Hobfoll, S. E. (1989). Conservation of resources: A new attempt at conceptualizing stress. *American Psychologist, 44,* 513-524.

Hobfoll, S. E., Freedy, J. R., Green, B. L., & Solomon, S. (1996). Coping in reaction to extreme stress: The roles of resource loss and resource availability. In M. Zeidner & N. S. Endler (Eds.), *Handbook of coping: Theory, research, applications* (pp. 322-349). New York: John Wiley.

Holahan, C. J., Moos, R. H., & Schaefer, J. A. (1996). Coping, stress resistance, and growth: Conceptualizing adaptive functioning. In M. Zeidner & N. S. Endler (Eds.), *Handbook of coping: Theory, research, applications* (pp. 24-43). New York: John Wiley.

Holton, B., & Pyszczynski, T. (1989). Biased information search in the interpersonal domain. *Personality and Social Psychology Bulletin, 15,* 42-51.

Horowitz, M. J., Znoj, H. J., & Stinson, C. H. (1996). Defensive control processes: Use of theory in research, formulation, and therapy of stress response syndromes. In M. Zeidner & N. S. Endler (Eds.), *Handbook of coping: Theory, research, applications* (pp. 532-553). New York: John Wiley.

Houston, B. K. (1987). Stress and coping. In C. R. Snyder & C. E. Ford (Eds.), *Coping with negative life events* (pp. 373-399). New York: Plenum.

Icard, L., & Nurius, P. S. (1996). The loss of self incoming out: Special risks for African American gays and lesbians. *Journal of Personal and Interpersonal Loss, 1,* 29-47.

Icard, L. D., Zamora-Hernandez, C. E., Spencer, M. S., & Catalano, R. (1996). Designing and evaluating strategies to recruit African Americans for AIDS/HIV interventions: Targeting the African-American family. *Ethnicity & Disease, 6,* 301-310.

Janoff-Bulman, R. (1992). *Shattered assumptions.* New York: Free Press.

Johnson, K. W., Anderson, N. B., Bastida, E., Kramer, B. J., Williams, D., & Wong, M. (1995). Panel II: Macrosocial and environmental influences on minority health. *Health Psychology, 14,* 601-612.

Kaplan, H. B. (Ed.). (1996). *Psychosocial stress: Perspectives on structure, theory, life-course, and methods.* New York: Academic Press.

Katz, J., Ritvo, P., Irvine, M. J., & Jackson, M. (1996). Coping with chronic pain. In M. Zeidner & N. S. Endler (Eds.), *Handbook of coping: Theory, research, applications* (pp. 252-278). New York: John Wiley.

Kline, A., & Strickler, J. (1993). Perceptions of risk for AIDS among women in drug treatment. *Health Psychology, 12,* 313-323.

Kunda, Z. (1987). Motivation and inference: Self-serving generation and evaluation of evidence. *Journal of Personality and Social Psychology, 53,* 636-647.

Kunda, Z. (1990). The case for motivated reasoning. *Psychological Bulletin, 108,* 480-498.

Langer, E. J. (1989). *Mindfulness.* Reading, MA: Addison-Wesley.

Laumann, E. O., Michael, R. T., & Gagnon, J. H. (1994). *The social organization of sexuality: Sexual practices in the United States.* Chicago: University of Chicago Press.

Laux, L., & Weber, H. (1991). Presentation of self in coping with anger and hostility: An intentional approach. *Anxiety Research, 3,* 233-255.

Lazarus, R. S. (1991). *Emotion and adaptation.* New York: Oxford University Press.

Lazarus, R. S. (1993). Coping theory and research: Past, present, and future. *Psychosomatic Medicine, 55,* 234-247.

Lazarus, R. S., & Folkman, S. (1984). *Stress, appraisal, and coping.* New York: Springer.

Lazarus, R. S., & Launier, R. (1978). Stress-related transactions between person and environment. In L. A. Pervin & M. Lewis (Eds.), *Perspectives in interactional psychology* (pp. 287-327). New York: Plenum.

Lazarus, R. S., & Smith, C. A. (1988). Knowledge and appraisal in the cognition-emotional relationship. *Cognition and Emotion, 2,* 281-300.

Lefcourt, II. M. (1981). Locus of control and stressful life events. In B. S. Dohrenwend & B. P. Dohrenwend (Eds.), *Stressful life events and their contexts* (pp. 157-166). New York: Prodist.

Lepore, S. J. (1997). Social-environmental context of coping with chronic stress. In B. H. Gottlieb (Ed.), *Coping with chronic stress* (pp. 133-160). New York: Plenum.

Lepore, S. J., & Evans, G. W. (1996). Coping with multiple stressors in the environment. In M. Zeidner & N. S.

Endler (Eds.), *Handbook of coping: Theory, research, applications* (pp. 350-377). New York: John Wiley.

Maes, S., Leventhal, H., & de Ridder, D. T. D. (1996). Coping with chronic diseases. In M. Zeidner & N. S. Endler (Eds.), *Handbook of coping: Theory, research, applications* (pp. 221-251). New York: John Wiley.

Mantell, J. E., Schinke, S. P., & Akabas, S. H. (1988). Women and AIDS prevention. *Journal of Primary Prevention, 9*, 18-40.

Matthews, G., & Wells, A. (1996). Attentional processes, dysfunctional coping, and clinical intervention. In M. Zeidner & N. S. Endler (Eds.), *Handbook of coping: Theory, research, applications* (pp. 573-601). New York: John Wiley.

Mayer, J. D., Gaschke, Y. N., Braverman, D. L., & Evans, T. W. (1992). Mood-congruent judgments is a general effect. *Journal of Personality and Social Psychology, 63*, 119-132.

McKenna, F. P. (1993). It won't happen to me: Unrealistic optimism or illusion of control? *British Journal of Psychology, 84*, 39-50.

Miller, S. M., & Kirsch, N. (1987). Sex differences in cognitive coping with stress. In R. C. Barnett, L. Biener, & G. K. Baruch (Eds.), *Gender and stress* (pp. 278-307). New York: Free Press.

Miller, S. M., Shoda, Y., & Hurley, K. (1996). Applying cognitive-social theory to health-protective behavior: Breast self-examination in cancer screening. *Psychological Bulletin, 119*, 70-94.

Monat, A., & Lazarus, R. S. (1991). Introduction to stress and coping—Some current issues and controversies. In A. Monat & R. S. Lazarus (Eds.), *Stress and coping: An anthology* (pp. 1-15). New York: Columbia University Press.

Moos, R. H., & Schaeffer, J. A. (1986). Life transition and crises: A conceptual overview. In R. H. Moos (Ed.), *Coping with life crisis* (pp. 3-28). New York: Plenum.

Neisser, U. (1988). Five kinds of self-knowledge. *Philosophical Psychology, 1*, 35-59.

Normoyle, J., & Lavrakas, P. J. (1984). Fear of crime in elderly women: Perceptions of control, predictability, and territoriality. *Personality and Social Psychology Bulletin, 10*, 191-202.

Norris, J., Nurius, P. S., & Dimeff, L. (1996). Through her eyes: Factors affecting women's perception of and resistance to acquaintance sexual aggression. *Psychology of Women Quarterly, 20*, 123-145.

Norris, J., Nurius, P. S., & Graham, T. L. (1999). When a date changes from fun to dangerous. *Violence Against Women, 5*, 230-250.

Nurius, P. S. (1993). Human memory: A basis for better understanding the elusive self-concept. *Social Service Review, 67*, 261-278.

Nurius, P. S. (1999). Women's perception of risk for acquaintance sexual assault: A social cognitive assessment. *Aggression and Violent Behavior: A Review Journal, 5*, 63-78.

Nurius, P. S., Furrey, J., & Berliner, L. (1992). Coping capacity among women and abusive partners. *Violence and Victims, 7*, 229-243.

Nurius, P. S., & Gaylord, J. (1998). Coping with threat from intimate sources: How self-protection relates to loss for women. In J. H. Harvey (Ed.), *Perspectives on personal and interpersonal loss: A sourcebook* (pp. 281-291). Philadelphia: Brunner/Mazel.

Nurius, P. S., Lovell, M., & Edgar, M. (1988). Self-appraisals of abusive parents: A contextual approach to study and treatment. *Journal of Interpersonal Violence, 3*, 458-467.

Nurius, P. S., & Markus, H. (1990). Situational variability in the self-concept: Appraisals, expectancies, and asymmetries. *Journal of Social & Clinical Psychology, 9*, 316-333.

Nurius, P. S., Macy, R., Norris, J., & Haung, B. (2000, January). *Contextualizing coping with sexual violence: Implications for preventive interventions.* Paper presented at the Society for Social Work and Research Annual Conference, Charleston, SC.

Nurius, P. S., Norris, J., Young, D., Graham, T. L., & Gaylord, J. (in press). Interpreting and defensively responding to threat: Examining appraisals and coping with acquaintance sexual threat. *Violence Victims.*

Nurius, P. S., & Shoda, Y. (1999). *Coping and the psychologically active environment.* University of Washington, manuscript in preparation.

O'Brien, T. B., & DeLongis, A. (1997). Coping with chronic stress: An interpersonal perspective. In B. H. Gottlieb (Ed.), *Coping with chronic stress* (pp. 161-190). New York: Plenum.

Parker, J. D., & Endler, N. S. (1996). Coping and defense: A historical overview. In M. Zeidner & N. S. Endler (Eds.), *Handbook of coping: Theory, research, applications* (pp. 3-23). New York: John Wiley.

Parkinson, B., & Manstead, A. S. R. (1992). Appraisal as a cause of emotion. In M. S. Clark (Ed.), *Review of personality and social psychology* (Vol. 13, pp. 122-149). Newbury Park, CA: Sage.

Pearlin, L. I. (1991). The study of coping: An overview of problems and directions. In J. Eckenrode (Ed.), *The social context of coping* (pp. 261-276). New York: Plenum.

Pearlin, L. I. (1993). The social contexts of stress. In L. Goldberger & S. Breznitz (Eds.), *Handbook of stress: Theoretical and clinical aspects* (pp. 303-315). New York: Free Press.

Pearlin, L. I., & Aneshensel, C. (1986). Coping and social supports: Their functions and applications. In L. H. Aiken & D. Mechanic (Eds.), *Applications of social science to clinical medicine and health* (pp. 53-74). New Brunswick: NJ: Rutgers University Press.

Pearlin, L. I., & Radabaugh, C. (1976). Economic strains and the coping functions of alcohol. *American Journal of Sociology, 82,* 652-663.

Pearlin, L. I., & Schooler, C. (1978). The structure of coping. *Journal of Health and Social Behavior, 19,* 2-21.

Perloff, L. S., & Fetzer, B. K. (1986). Self-other judgments and perceived vulnerability to victimization. *Journal of Personality and Social Psychology, 50,* 502-511.

Pierce, G. R., Sarason, B. R., & Sarason, I. G. (1990). Integrating social support perspectives: Working models, personal relationships, and social support. In S. Duck with R. C. Silver (Eds.), *Personal relationships and social support* (pp. 173-189). London: Sage.

Pierce, G. R., Sarason, I. G., & Sarason, B. R. (1996). Coping and social support. In M. Zeidner & N. S. Endler (Eds.), *Handbook of coping: Theory, research, applications* (pp. 434-451). New York: John Wiley.

Richard, R., van der Plight, J., & de Vries, N. K. (1995). The impact of anticipated affect on (risky) sexual behavior. *British Journal of Social Psychology, 34,* 9-21.

Richey, C. A. (1994). Social support skill training. In D. Granvold (Ed.), *Cognitive and behavioral treatment: Methods and applications* (pp. 299-338). Pacific Grove, CA: Brooks/Cole.

Rothspan, S., & Read, S. J. (1996). Present versus future time perspective and HIV risk among heterosexual college students. *Health Psychology, 15,* 131-134.

Roussi, P., Miller, S. M., & Shoda, Y. (in press). Discriminative facility in the face of threat and its relationship to psychological distress. *Psychology and Health.*

Sarason, B. R., Sarason, I. G., & Pierce, G. R. (Eds.). (1990). *Social support: An interactional view.* New York: John Wiley.

Scheier, M. F., Weintraub, J. K., & Carver, C. S. (1986). Coping with stress: Divergent strategies of optimists and pessimists. *Journal of Personality and Social Psychology, 51,* 1257-1264.

Scherer, K. R. (1984). Emotion as a multicomponent process: A model and some cross-cultural data. In P. Shaver (Ed.), *Review of personality and social psychology* (Vol. 5, pp. 37-63). Beverly Hills, CA: Sage.

Schwarzer, R., & Schwarzer, C. (1996). A critical survey of coping instruments. In M. Zeidner & N. S. Endler (Eds.), *Handbook of coping: Theory, research, applications* (pp. 107-132). New York: John Wiley.

Shoda, Y., Mischel, W., Miller, S. M., Diefenback, M., Daly, M. B., & Engstrom, P. F. (1998). Psychological interventions and genetic testing: Facilitating informed decisions about BRCA1/2 cancer susceptibility. *Journal of Clinical Psychology in Medical Settings, 5,* 3-17.

Siemer, M., & Reisenzein, R. (1998). Effects of mood on evaluative judgments: Influence of reduced processing capacity and mood salience. *Cognition and Emotion, 12,* 783-805.

Skinner, E. A. (in press). Planning and perceived control. In S. Friedman & E. Scholnick (Eds.), *Why, how, and when do we plan? The developmental psychology of planning.* Hillsdale, NJ: Lawrence Erlbaum.

Smith, C. A., Haynes, K. N., Lazarus, R. S., & Pope, L. K. (1993). In search of the "hot" cognitions: Attributions, appraisals, and their relation to emotion. *Journal of Personality and Social Psychology, 65,* 916-929.

Smith, C. A., & Lazarus, R. S. (1990). Emotion and adaptation: In L. A. Pervin (Ed.), *Handbook of personality: Theory and research.* New York: Guilford.

Smith, C. A., & Lazarus, R. S. (1993). Appraisal components, core relational themes, and the emotions. *Cognition and Emotion, 7,* 233-269.

Sparks, P., & Guthrie, C. A. (1998). Self-identity and the theory of planned behavior: A useful addition or an unhelpful artifice? *Journal of Applied Social Psychology, 28,* 1393-1410.

Strathman, A., Gleicher, F., Boninger, D. S., & Edwards, C. S. (1994). The consideration of future consequences: Weighing immediate and distant outcomes of behavior. *Journal of Personality and Social Psychology, 66,* 742-752.

Stroebe, W., & Stroebe, M. S. (1995). *Social psychology and health.* Pacific Grove, CA: Brooks/Cole.

Taylor, S. E. (1983). Adjustment to threatening events: A theory of cognitive adaptation. *American Psychologist, 38,* 1161-1173.

Taylor, S. E. (1989). *Positive illusions: Creative self-deception and the healthy mind.* New York: Basic Books.

Taylor, S. E. (1995). *Health psychology* (3rd ed.). New York: McGraw-Hill.

Taylor, S. E., & Aspinwall, L. G. (1996). Mediating and moderating processes in psychosocial stress: Appraisal, coping, resistance, and vulnerability. In H. B. Kaplan (Ed.), *Psychosocial stress: Perspectives on structure, theory, life-course, and methods* (pp. 71-110). New York: Academic Press.

Taylor, S. E., Aspinwall, L. G., & Giuliano, T. A. (1994). Emotions as psychological achievements. In S. H. van Goozen, N. E. van de Poll, & J. A. Sergeant (Eds.), *Emotions: Essays on emotion theory* (pp. 219-239). Hillsdale, NJ: Lawrence Erlbaum.

Taylor, S. E., & Brown, J. D. (1988). Illusion and well-being: A social psychological perspective on mental health. *Psychological Bulletin, 103,* 193-210.

Taylor, S. E., & Clark, L. F. (1986). Does information improve adjustment to noxious events? In J. J. Saks & L. Saxe (Eds.), *Advances in applied social psychology* (Vol. 3, pp. 1-28). Hillsdale, NJ: Lawrence Erlbaum.

Taylor, S. E., & Gollwitzer, P. M. (1995). Attitudes and social cognition. *Journal of Personality and Social Psychology, 69,* 213-226.

Taylor, S. E., & Pham, L. B. (1996). Mental simulation, motivation, and action. In P. M. Gollwitzer & J. A. Bargh (Eds.), *The psychology of action: Linking cognition and motivation to behavior* (pp. 219-235). New York: Guilford.

Taylor, S. E., & Schneider, S. K. (1989). Coping and the simulation of events. *Social Cognition, 7,* 176-196.

Thoits, P. A. (1986). Social support as coping assistance. *Journal of Consulting and Clinical Psychology, 54,* 416-423.

Thoits, P. A. (1991). Gender differences in coping with emotional distress. In J. Eckenrode (Ed.), *The social context of coping* (pp. 107-138). New York: Plenum.

Thompson, S. C., Anderson, K., Freedman, D., & Swan, J. (1996). Illusions of safety in a risky world: A study of college students' condom use. *Journal of Applied Social Psychology, 26*(3), 189-210.

Thompson, S. C., Sobolew-Shubin, A., Galbraith, M. E., Schwankovsky, L., & Cruzen, D. (1993). Maintaining perceptions ofcontrol: Finding perceived control in low-control circumstances. *Journal of Personality and Social Psycholgy, 64,* 293-304.

U.S. Department of Health and Human Services. (1987). *Strategies for diffusing health information to minority populations.* Washington, DC: Government Printing Office.

Van der Plight, J. (1996). Risk perception and self-protective behavior. *European Psychologist, 1,* 34-43.

Vrij, A., & Semin, G. R. (1996). Lie experts' beliefs about nonverbal indicators of deception. *Journal of Nonverbal Behavior, 20,* 65-80.

Vrij, A., Semin, G. R., & Bull, R. (1996). Insight into behavior displayed during deception. *Human Communication Research, 22,* 544-562.

Weidner, G., & Collins, R. L. (1993). Gender, coping, and health. In H. W. Krohne (Ed.), *Attention and avoidance: Strategies for coping with aversiveness* (pp. 241-265). Seattle, WA: Hogrefe & Huber.

Weinstein, N. D. (1980). Unrealistic optimism about future life events. *Journal of Personality and Social Psychology, 38,* 806-820.

Weinstein, N. D. (1984). Why it won't happen to me: Perceptions of risk factors and susceptibility. *Health Psychology, 3,* 431-457.

Weinstein, N. D., & Klein, W. M. (1995). Resistance of personal risk perceptions to debiasing interventions. *Health Psychology, 14,* 132-140.

Wheaton, B. (1982). The sociogenesis of psychological disorder: An attributional theory. *Journal of Health and Social Behavior, 24,* 2-15.

Wiebe, D. J., & Williams, P. G. (1992). Hardiness and health: A social psychophysiological perspective on stress and adaptation. *Journal of Social and Clinical Psychology, 11,* 238-262.

Wills, T. A., & Hirky, A. E. (1996). Coping with substance abuse: A theoretical model and review of the literature. In M. Zeidner & N. S. Endler (Eds.), *Handbook of coping: Theory, research, applications* (pp. 279-302). New York: John Wiley.

Wyer, R. S., Jr., & Bargh, J. A. (1997). The automaticity of everyday life. In *Advances in social cognition* (Vol. 10). Mahwah, NJ: Lawrence Erlbaum.

Zajonc, R. B. (1980). Feeling and thinking: Preferences need no inferences. *American Psychologist, 35,* 151-175.

Zeidner, M., & Endler, N. S. (Eds.). (1996). *Handbook of coping: Theory, research, applications.* New York: John Wiley.

Zeidner, M., & Hammer, A. L. (1990). Life events and coping resources as predictors of stress symptoms in adolescents. *Personality and Individual Differences, 11,* 693-703.

Zeidner, M., & Saklofske, D. (1996). Adaptive and maladaptive coping. In M. Zeidner & N. S. Endler (Eds.), *Handbook of coping: Theory, research, applications* (pp. 505-531). New York: John Wiley.

CHAPTER EIGHTEEN

Social Work in the Social Environment: Integrated Practice— An Empowerment/ Structural Approach

MARIE WEIL

An empowerment/structural approach engages social workers in social change with clients and in their social environments. Social change-oriented direct practice focuses on structural interventions designed to encourage transformative change for individuals and families—as well as change in their social networks, the communities in which they live, and the organizations and institutions that provide services and distribute social goods. This approach integrates work with client systems and natural helping systems, along with macro-oriented interventions to reform agencies and service systems and improve the quality of life in vulnerable communities. Positive social change is change that improves the quality of life for the most disadvantaged and increases individual liberty and community-based interdependence.

The empowerment/structural approach can be applied with people whose lives reflect major social problems, such as poverty and homelessness; it can also be applied in helping people with debilitating health and mental health problems, behavior and social relations problems, families where violence abuse and neglect occur, and other individual and family problems that diminish quality of life and ability to access needed resources. This approach can also be used with groups and in organizational and community practice to improve service systems and community conditions or in preventive and protective policy practice. Macro social change strategies may focus on direct practice organizing in geographic or functional communities, on building of coalitions with and for an at-risk group such as the homeless or children in poverty (Weil & Gamble, 1995), on community social and economic development, or on social planning or political and social action (Kramer & Specht, 1983; Rothman, 1996; Weil & Gamble, 1995). Direct practice workers are involved in change at all these levels.

For practitioners to be able to effectively integrate practice interventions based on what clients need (rather then on what workers or their agencies do!), a structural approach that fully integrates perspectives, knowledge, and skills for both social service provision and social change activities is needed for practice in the 21st century (Lee, 1994; Withorn, 1984; Wood & Middleman, 1989). A structural approach requires an understanding of societal as well as interpersonal issues and the knowledge and skills to articulate the connections between individual or family troubles and social problems. Macro practice strategies geared toward structural change in the social environment make these connections and involve social workers in

direct work with groups and community-based organizations and, as called for, in social and economic development, partnership-oriented program and community development, social planning, political and social action, and social movements (Rubin & Rubin, 1992; Weil & Gamble, 1995).

If social workers take the empowerment tradition seriously, the focus of the profession will be on helping vulnerable and at-risk populations gain power and change the conditions of their lives and on systemic work for positive social change (Gamble & Weil, 1995; Lee, 1994; Simon, 1994; Solomon, 1976; Wagner, 1989; Wrong, 1979). For many practitioners, this implies strengthening skills for intervention in the social environment. A considerable literature is available on systems theory, ecosystems theory, and person-in-environment approaches (Martin & O'Connor, 1989). However as previous analysis has indicated, it can become too easy for social workers to emphasize the personal/interpersonal issues in practice and consequently to give insufficient attention to work in the social environment. Work with social networks, larger systems, and macro strategies are needed to develop client-level support and to engage in more general social change focused on preventing problems, assisting groups of people with similar problems, and working to ameliorate serious social problems (Longres, 1995; Martin & O'Connor, 1989; see also Fisher & Karger, Chapter 1, this volume). Given the potential to pay closest attention to client issues that seem immediate and very much "up front," it is important to critically analyze the reasons for "private troubles" and consider needed structural change and supports that could make a difference. Asking such questions will help in applying social change and structural theory and approaches directly in practice. From early in the profession's history, leaders have emphasized that it is important for social workers to oppose injustice and oppression and to work toward social justice and nonexploitive relations, particularly for those who are oppressed or in economically or socially disadvantaged positions (Addams, 1910; Lee, 1929; Reynolds, 1964; Lurie in Schriver, 1987; Wagner, 1989). Given the growing disparity in income between the rich, the working class, and the poor, this practice will be critically important in coming decades.

Gil (1998) defines *oppression* as "a mode of human relations involving domination and exploitation—economic, social, and psychologic" (p. 10) that can occur interpersonally, or between groups, classes and societies (even on a global level). He defines *injustice* as "coercively established and maintained inequalities" (p. 10) that would include social problems such as unemployment, poverty, inadequate health care and education, and lack of opportunity structure. *Social justice* then includes the concepts of liberty, freedom, civic participation, and equality. Gil notes that oppression is a complex phenomenon and that, in many societies, the same individuals may be oppressed in some relationships and oppressors in others. In *A Theory of Justice,* John Rawls (1971) explains and expands the concept of distributive justice in ways quite useful for social work. The primary subject of justice, he holds is "the basic structure of society, . . . [particularly] the way in which the major social institutions distribute fundamental rights and duties and determine the division of advantages from social cooperation" (p. 7). Rawls presents two essential principles to promote social justice that provide a useful backdrop for the empowerment tradition in social work:

1. Each person is to have an equal right to the most extensive basic liberty compatible with a similar liberty for others. (p. 60)
2. Social and economic inequalities are to be arranged so that they are both handled: (a) to the greatest benefit of the least advantaged and (b) so that democratic equality guides individual and group access to opportunity and institutional operations. (pp. 65, 302)

In a structural approach, social workers can enact aspects of distributive justice in work to increase opportunities and access for clients and to reform social services and other institutions to make them more responsive to vulnerable populations and democratic principles.

Gil (1998) analyzes six value dimensions for workers to use when planning strategies to overcome injustice and oppression. His dichotomous list makes clear that if workers do not choose the first options in practice, they are by default choosing the second options, which diminish opportunities in human life (p. 46):

- Equality versus inequality
- Liberty versus domination and exploitation
- Individuality versus selfishness and individualism
- Life affirmation versus disregard for life
- Collectivity orientation versus disregard for community
- Cooperation versus competition

Rawls's principles and Gil's value dimensions, added to the basic social work values promoting rights of the individual and mutual interdependence (Dromi & Weil, 1984), provide a means of reviewing practice plans and strategies to see that (a) interventions are focused on empowerment and (b) that direct practice interventions engage with the social environment to remedy system inequalities. Practice grounded in these precepts will be structurally oriented social change practice (Simon, 1994; Solomon, 1976; Withorn, 1984; Wood & Middleman, 1989). This approach to practice recognizes social inequity and power issues in systems and is committed to transformative change for individuals, families, groups, communities, organizations, and societies (Bombyk, 1995; Fabricant & Burghardt, 1992; Galper, 1980; Garvin, 1985; Hardcastle, Wenocur & Powers, 1997; Kretzmann & McKnight, 1996; Lee, 1994; Wood & Middleman, 1989; Wrong, 1979).

THE EMPOWERMENT/ STRUCTURAL MODEL

The empowerment/structural model for direct work with clients and work in the social environment builds on the work of several practice theorists. It integrates the following views of practice: structural approaches (Withorn, 1984; Wood & Middleman, 1989), empowerment approaches to working with families (Dunst, Trivette, & Deal, 1988), empowerment group work and work with social networks (Garvin, 1985, 1987; Lee, 1994; Middleman & Goldberg, 1977; Whittaker & Garbarino, 1983), organizational and interorganizational work on behalf of clients (Alter, 1990, 1997; Alter & Hage, 1993; Netting, Ketner, & McMurtry, 1993), direct community work practice (Hardcastle et al., 1997; Homan, 1994), and community practice and other macro interventions on behalf of classes of clients and to deal with social problems (Kramer & Specht, 1983; Rothman, 1995; Rubin & Rubin, 1992; Weil & Gamble, 1995).

To consider the building blocks of the empowerment/structural model, let us first examine the approach taken by Wood and Middleman (1989) in their book, *The Structural Approach to Direct Practice in Social Work.* They present a structural model for direct service practice that integrates practice methods and incorporates the above principles. They state in their approach that

> social change is not separated from social work, not relegated to specialists within the social work profession. Rather, it is pursued at every level of assignment, every working day by all social workers, and especially by those who must face the clients directly. (p. 16)

In their structural perspective on direct practice, they stress activities and actions that develop mutual partnership with clients, promote mutual problem solving, and involve clients, client support systems, and workers in activities that can change the problematic and/or oppressive conditions of their lives. Their frame of reference for a structural approach involves direct practice workers in intervening in four major ways that can occur in any order:

> (a) working with clients in their own behalf; (b) working with clients on behalf of themselves and others like them; (c) working with others, i.e., nonsufferers in behalf of a category of sufferers; and (d) working with others, i.e., nonsufferers in behalf of clients. (Wood & Middleman, 1989, pp. 20-23)

The model presented in this chapter expands this framework and incorporates empowerment/structural strategies from each major social work practice arena.

Within the empowerment/structural frame of reference, it seems logical that workers would employ dialogue and methods to build critical consciousness in themselves and with clients to help people with serious problems understand the structural elements of their situation, whether they are affected by limitations managed care is placing on needed treatments or by employment and opportunity issues relating to changes in the local and the global economy—that is, Where have the jobs gone, and how many others are in situations like mine? (Freire, 1973a, 1973b, 1990; Gil, 1998). To be fully human, people need community and they need to work toward strengthening their communities. Social workers also need a sense of community and the skills to help clients connect to communities that can support them. Earlier social work leaders often wrote about common human needs and our common humanity (Bartlett, 1970/1958; Towle, 1953). Jane Addams (1910) frequently talked and wrote about these issues:

> Nothing so deadens the sympathies and shrivels the power of enjoyment as the persistent keeping away from the great opportunities for helpfulness and a continual ignoring of the starvation struggle which makes up the life of at least half the [human] race. To shut one's self away from that half of the race's life is to shut one's self away from the most vital part of it; it is to live out but half the humanity to which we have been born heir and to use but half our faculties. (pp. 116-117)

> The best speculative philosophy sets forth the solidarity of the human race; that the highest moralists have taught that without the advancement and improvement of the whole, no man can hope for any lasting improvement in his own moral or material living condition. (p. 127)

To this end, we all—clients and workers alike—need to understand the social, economic, and political realities that affect our lives and our access to opportunities. Development of critical consciousness then should be a basic aspect of working with people in each arena of practice—with individuals or families, with groups of people with similar problems, with natural networks, with human service systems, and in macropractice and policy arenas.

Integrated Practice and the Empowerment/Structural Model

Integrated practice, as noted, draws on the methods of practice needed by clients. Where workers do not already have the skills for a particular intervention in a particular arena of practice, they can learn them, refer clients to a relevant program that engages in those interventions, or join with other agencies and/or citizens' groups in collaboration to see that service and community needs are met. Workers who begin at the macro level also will refer groups and organizations and clients to more direct services and will provide leadership in social change strategies to positively change communities, reform service systems, engage in political and social action, and develop more just social policy. Complex social conditions in people's lives will need to be addressed by multiple action systems to promote positive outcomes and longer term social change. More and more, workers need the skills to engage multiple actors and strategies in an integrated approach.

For many direct practice workers, entry into integrated practice will occur in neighborhood-based or functional community-focused services (Fraser, 1997; Hardcastle et al., 1997; Weil & Gamble, 1995). For example, a neighborhood-based child abuse prevention program

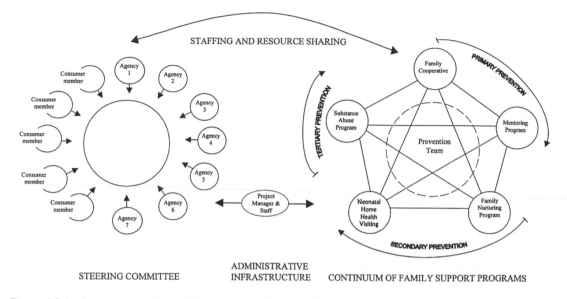

Figure 18.1. Interorganizational Collaboration to Prevent Child Abuse: A Neighborhood Network (Mulroy & Shay, 1998).

SOURCE: Reprinted with permission from the National Association of Social Workers. All printed material is copyrighted.

uses multifocused interventions that have been documented empirically to be "the most appropriate way to ameliorate child maltreatment in situations of urban poverty and social decay" (Mulroy & Shay, 1998, p. 98). The CARES project seeks to enhance factors that are protective of children and to reduce factors that place children at risk of maltreatment and placement (Fraser, 1997; Mulroy & Shay, 1998); it uses empowerment strategies with clients and has developed means to "work with low-income residents as partners rather than as clients" (Solomon, 1976). Building on a community asset approach in work with residents (Delgado, 1996; Kretzman & McKnight, 1996; Shiffman & Motley, 1990), the staff use a "multipronged" strategy of intervention employing collaboration, resource development, educa-

tion, services, and advocacy (Mulroy & Shay, 1998, pp. 98-100).

To decrease risk and increase resiliency in children, Fraser and Galinsky (1997) also argue for a multisystemic assessment and intervention. Clients, citizens, and practitioners are major sources of information about a community, its assets, and its conditions (Fraser & Galinsky, 1997; Kretzman & McKnight, 1996). Resilience-based practice is seen as community-wide, builds on strengths and empowerment perspectives, and uses empowerment work to combat discrimination (Fraser & Galinsky, 1997; Gutiérrez, 1990; Solomon, 1976). Mulroy and Shay (1998) describe an integrated model of practice that builds social networks and supports through informal groups and community-based programs engaging in pri-

Figure 18.2. Conceptual Framework of Neighborhood-based Child Abuse Prevention (Shay, 1995).

SOURCE: Reprinted with permission from the National Association of Social Workers. All printed material is copyrighted.

mary (Family Cooperatives and Mentoring programs), secondary (Family Nurturing and Neonatal Home Health Visiting programs), and tertiary prevention (a substance abuse program and connections to other agencies). Project management and staff relate to this continuum of family support programs and to the CARES steering committee, which is composed of seven agency representatives and five consumer representatives (Mulroy & Shay, 1998, pp. 100-102).

Figure 18.2 illustrates the CARES ecological model, which focuses on families and communities simultaneously (Co ulton, 1996; Shay, 1995). Building on ecological theory, the family is seen at the center of practice and is assisted with access to levels of informal support, interagency prevention services, and community systems (Bronfenbrenner, 1979; Shay, 1995). The

community ecology of families, informal supports, and social service programs is one way to view empowerment-oriented practice that focuses on both family and community assets and stresses service system collaboration around community needs. This approach is an exemplar of future-oriented practice. In the macro practice discussion of the integrated model, a broader ecological/social change perspective will be presented.

Another approach to seeing the connections of integrated practice is presented by Lee (1994), who stresses the relations between people, their environments, and collective action engaged through mediating structures. Figure 18.3 presents Lee's perspective on the transactional relationships between political and personal change. The figure encapsulates her

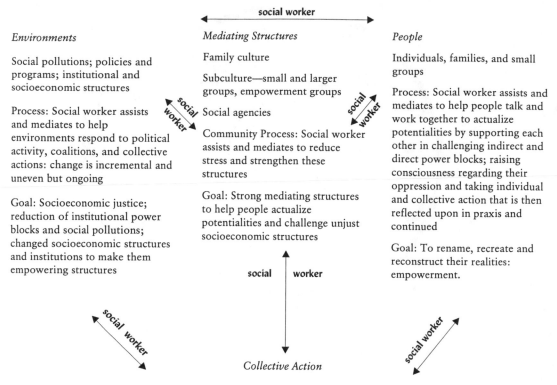

Environments

Social pollutions; policies and programs; institutional and socioeconomic structures

Process: Social worker assists and mediates to help environments respond to political activity, coalitions, and collective actions: change is incremental and uneven but ongoing

Goal: Socioeconomic justice; reduction of institutional power blocks and social pollutions; changed socioeconomic structures and institutions to make them empowering structures

Mediating Structures

Family culture

Subculture—small and larger groups, empowerment groups

Social agencies

Community Process: Social worker assists and mediates to reduce stress and strengthen these structures

Goal: Strong mediating structures to help people actualize potentialities and challenge unjust socioeconomic structures

People

Individuals, families, and small groups

Process: Social worker assists and mediates to help people talk and work together to actualize potentialities by supporting each other in challenging indirect and direct power blocks; raising consciousness regarding their oppression and taking individual and collective action that is then reflected upon in praxis and continued

Goal: To rename, recreate and reconstruct their realities: empowerment.

Collective Action

Social and political action

Process: Social worker assists and mediates to help people reconstruct reality and participate in the collective change process, create building blocks for developing effective political actions and movements

Goal: Changes in oppressive, unjust structures that remove direct blocks to empowerment and allow all people access to resources, opportunities, and options; to make an optimum fit between all people and environments through political empowerment

Figure 18.3. A Transactional View of Political and Personal Change—The Unity of Professional Purpose in the Empowerment Approach
SOURCE: Lee (1994).

empowerment approach to work with individuals, families, special populations, groups, and communities, highlighting the roles of social workers among people, their environment, me- diating structures, and collective action for so- cial change (Lee, 1994).

A special population that should always be a primary focus of social work is families and individuals living in poverty, who not only lack basic resources but are overrepresented in both health and mental health service populations because of life stressors and lack of resources. From a global perspective, Friedmann (1996) argues for a political model to understand the disempowerment of poverty. Building on the assumption that poor households often "lack the social power to improve the condition of their member's lives," he analyzes social power and considers the ability of families to gain access to eight types of social power: social networks, needed information, surplus time, instruments of work and livelihood, social organization, knowledge and skills, defensible life space (including neighborhood factors), and financial resources. If a family lacks the ability to participate in and negotiate access to these power bases, they are poor. Relative access to these power bases determines the degree of poverty and disempowerment that families face (Friedmann, 1996, pp. 66-71). Structural work is therefore needed to increase access to bases of social and economic power.

The empowerment/structural model presented in this chapter is guided by the strengths and empowerment perspectives and is directed toward transformative individual, family, and group change and structural change in communities, organizations, institutions, society, and the political structures that distribute resources. According to Gutiérrez (1990), the empowerment approach involves

> combining a sense of personal control with the ability to affect the behavior of others, a focus on enhancing existing strengths in individuals or communities, a goal of establishing equity in the distribution of resources, an ecological (rather than individual) form of analysis for understanding individual and community phenomena, and a belief that power is not a scarce commodity but rather one that can be generated. (p. 150)

As noted earlier, structural approaches to practice emphasize social change to increase social justice—this can happen in families (eliminating violence), in communities (creating access to services and opportunities), and in societies (legislating equal civil rights or increasing the operations of distributive justice). Increasingly, we can expect social work practice to be community-based with connections to families, groups, and neighborhoods, with horizontal connections to the service system, and with vertical connections from communities to national policies, institutions, and political systems. Intervention research to discover and document what works, along with practitioner and planner commitment to find ways to grow progressive models in multiple localities, fuels these efforts (Rothman & Thomas, 1994; Schorr, 1997). The growing focus on outcomes-oriented practice, as well as the historic value base and expanding knowledge base of the profession, add momentum to the model. This empowerment/structural model is integrated in its perspective and multipronged in intervention strategies. Combining these two major trends in practice and practice theory results in an integrated model of practice that can work on individual empowerment and distribution of resources, group empowerment and policy change, family problems and community building, organizing and development, and community interventions and legislative change.

Figure 18.4 presents these possibilities in an integrated empowerment/structural model of social work with clients and their social environments that will involve multiple interven-

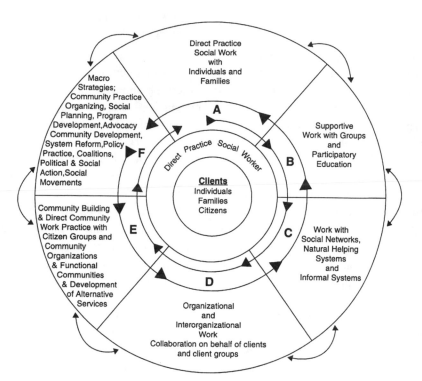

Figure 18.4. Integrated Practice: An Empowerment/Structural Model for Social Work Practice With Clients and in the Social Environment

tions to make immediate and longer term change in the lives of families and communities.

Moving among these practice arenas may be done by a worker and client system connecting to other natural networks and agency systems. Viewing the model, integrated practice could move in a clockwise fashion (from A to F or in between) or counterclockwise from (F to A or in between) or in any order, depending on where a need is recognized. Each arena connects quite naturally to the ones on either side; however, the modes of intervention may "hop or skip" depending on the nature of issues and community resources. The boundaries of prac-

tice arenas are permeable, and workers and clients can pull together the needed sets of practice strategies to maximize achievement of desired goals.

Implicit in the model's success are excellent face-to-face direct practice skills; connective and supportive skills in work with informal systems; collaboration, boundary-spanning skills, and managing skills in organizational and interorganizational work; and facilitating, organizing, planning, development, advocacy, policy practice, and social change skills in community and macro practice. The next section of this chapter briefly lists possible direct client-level interventions. These illustrate some practice examples to be expanded on in the remainder of this chapter, tracing the extension from the face-to-face work with clients to work with people with similar concerns, to mobilizing efforts with informal and formal systems and related macro-level interventions.

Direct Practice With Individuals and Families

In direct practice, social workers engage with many people who are coping with a wide variety of types of problems. For many families and groups, their individual problems are embedded in major social problems. America has the highest percentage of children living in poverty of any western democracy (Blank, 1997; Institute for Wisconsin's Future, 1999). Many individuals with severe and persistent mental illnesses and many poor families make up major segments of the homeless population. While the shift from Aid to Families With Dependent Children (AFDC) to Temporary Assistance for Needy Families (TANF) promotes the work ethic and has moved considerable numbers of people into the workforce, the effectiveness of this strategy for longer term employment remains unproved. Indeed, studies in several states already indicate that although TANF gets people "off the welfare rolls," it does not seem to move substantial numbers of people out of poverty (Burtless, 1997; Rooney, 1998). Unemployment and underemployment take on new ramifications as increasing numbers of jobs move offshore and into the global economy. Many other families and groups of people suffer with long-term or serious acute physical or mental illnesses, more younger children exhibit

behavior problems (or at least problems dealing with expectations of school systems), and problems of delinquency and alcohol and drug use are prevalent with both homeless youth and youth of more financially stable backgrounds. Adults deal with normal life crises as well as acute life-changing conditions or situations.

Direct Practice Exmaples

The following situations are examples of direct work with clients that will be used in this chapter to illustrate the structural approach:

1. Children in a family are suspected of being victims of physical and sexual abuse.
2. An infant born to young parents is diagnosed with physical problems and suspected developmental delays.
3. A youth is diagnosed with behavior disorders, attention deficit-hyperactivity disorder (ADHD), and aggressive behavior.
4. A young adult experiences the first onset of schizophrenia.
5. A young adult contracts HIV.
6. Members of a homeless family are beaten and robbed, and the mother is brutally raped.
7. A woman in her 40s leaves a physically and emotionally abusive partner for the third time and seeks shelter.
8. A woman in her 30s is diagnosed with breast cancer; her brother with prostate cancer.
9. A very old couple experiences the increasing physical disability of one partner and the decreasing mental capacity of the other, who had intended to continue as primary caretaker for the physically disabled partner.

These typical practice situations, based on real cases, require social workers to change the social environment to improve the quality of life of the individual client or family with whom they are working. The following sections of this chapter describe work in the social environment in the ever-widening circles of the ecological system.

SUPPORTIVE/EMPOWERMENT WORK WITH GROUPS

Wood and Middleman (1989) describe this aspect of structural social work as activities in which workers directly engage several people in similar situations for the benefit of themselves and others like them—that is, working with clients in groups. A worker may form a group to address their common issues and situation or connect clients to existing support groups. With the worker, the group might engage in personal problem-solving or expand further to develop a new support or mutual aid group. Supportive and connective work is needed in all fields of current practice and is an early level of "putting the social in social work." Becoming connected to a group whose members share a similar problem or concern may be the first time an individual deeply feels "I am not alone in this." Paulo Freire's influential works, *Pedagogy of the Oppressed* (1973b) and *Education for Critical Consciousness* (1973a), underscore the importance of workers and clients engaging in critical consciousness-raising about problematic situations and the importance of social and power analysis, whatever the situations of clients may be. Connections to others like ourselves can place us in dialogue about our situation and our direction. Freire sees this process as an essential part of our efforts to become fully human, to liberate ourselves and others, and to create social settings and transform societies to foster equality, freedom, and social development. Participatory education, a model of work with groups elaborated from Freire's work in Latin America, is focused on critical consciousness and problem-solving. This approach to groups can be applied in work with the dispossessed and by staff working with oppressed/disadvantaged groups (Castelloe, 1999). This approach is clearly a structural/empowerment model focused on social change.

Judy Lee (1994) discusses the empowering properties of groups, noting that they may promote development, growth, collective problem solving, and social change and that they have a major impact on identity and self-concept (Garvin, 1987; Hartford, 1971; McRoy & Shorkey, 1985). Groups can help us develop flexibility to change, learn new roles, take on new tasks, and enhance role performance (Garvin, 1987; Lee, 1994; Toseland & Rivas, 1998). If workers have skills in supporting and facilitating personal and group processes from an empowerment framework, then groups can be "the optimum medium for empowerment" (Lee, 1994, p. 209). This potential can develop however, only if the worker has skills in "defining empowerment as group purpose, challenging obstacles to the work, and enhancing the group processes that develop the group's power as a group" (Lee, 1994, p. 209). Lee presents potent examples of empowerment group work with women in homeless shelters. In these examples, the women discuss not only personal issues but the connection of their situation to the wider political level.

Empowerment may have a different thrust in groups, depending on population and purpose. At the very least, groups should support achieving interpersonal empowerment, developing self-efficacy (Pecukonis & Wenocur, 1994), learning new skills or roles, and becoming more active and engaged members of the community. Members of groups also should learn how to advocate for themselves and others like themselves. Frequently, group participants who have attained this level of self-advocacy move on to involvement in formal advocacy groups related to their concerns.

As direct practice social workers have embraced the empowerment approach to social work, many have broadened their skills in outreach and in work with groups. Many have also adopted new roles as coaches or consultants to groups on particular issues or systems issues. If workers really understand empowerment, they will also be engaged in critical consciousness-raising so that mutual learning and mutual empowerment can occur. It is not unusual for a group that begins in support and mutual aid to engage in system change or advocacy. For example, a group of people with HIV/AIDS in a rural community might lobby the system for a broader array of services for people like themselves (Griffith, 1999).

Supportive, connective work with clients and others like them takes place in many fields of practice and at different levels of empowerment focus. A group worker for example, might engage groups of parents of preschool children in learning aspects of early childhood development, discussing appropriate discipline, and learning how to promote positive learning and social development for their children. Programs such as Parents As Teachers or Family Support Programs promote mutual support among parents (trading off baby-sitting or planning for group outings to parks) and help new parents learn more about their roles and community and educational supports available to them. In one empowerment-oriented new Family Support Program, participants and staff per-

suaded a rural county council to provide an unused school for their center. The program and its board (with 40% membership being family program participants) then developed a wide range of supportive social and recreational programs and provided office space for a pediatric dentist and a medical practice, as well as afterschool educational programs for both children and adults (Trivette & Dunst, 1997; Weil & Hodges, 1996). Work with groups of parents and groups of families is developing as a hallmark of family support programs and family resource centers, as is inclusion of a substantial percentage of family members on governing boards and program monitoring committees (Goetz & Peck, 1994; Weil et al., 1997; Kagan, Powell, Weissbourd, & Zigler, 1987).

Supportive work with groups has a long history in social work in health and mental health, in school social work, and in senior centers, and it continues in settlements and neighborhood centers (Allen-Meares, Washington, & Welsh, 1996; Gottlieb, 1981; Lieberman, Borman, & Associates, 1979; Singer et al., 1988). More recently, explicitly empowerment-oriented work has increased with disadvantaged and oppressed groups (Garvin, 1985; Lee, 1994). The following brief practice examples illustrate how workers may move from direct work with clients to empowerment/structural supportive work with groups of clients.

Supportive/Empowerment Group Work Examples

Supportive/empowerment work with groups can take the form of participatory education with members of oppressed or disadvantaged groups and/or may focus on building support among clients dealing with serious mental health or health problems, or groups of children or adults engaged in life development tasks in hostile environments. It includes consciousness-raising and a civil rights orientation.

1. *A youth is diagnosed with behavior disorders, ADHD, and aggressive behavior.* The middle school social worker and mental health case manager work together with an afterschool enrichment program from the child's cultural group. While issues of medication and treatment are being considered, the program engages the child in a community-based children's theater and dance group program that reflects his home culture. The school arranges for the child to stay with his class "pod" for part of the day and to work with volunteer mentors from the Communities in Schools Program on small-group learning activities with other students with ADHD. The mentor and school social worker help the child's grandparents connect to a support group that also discusses how to cope with aggressive behavior in the home and provides information on community resources. The youth's minister and Sunday school teacher are also available to support the family, encouraging the grandparents to have the youth participate in a camping, outdoor skill, and physical development program co-sponsored by a group of churches and a small nonprofit organization. Here also, the intervention builds on group work and work in the youth's social network. The close connection to community resources and the family's social network is an example of the need to embed troubled youth in a supportive community.

2. *A young adult experiences the first onset of schizophrenia.* Initially, she is placed in a hos-

pital shortly after diagnosis. The staff engages her siblings in planning for her later placement in a small group home. The residents have regular house meetings and a resident manager who helps them connect to needed services. He also coaches residents on advocating for services and supports that can lead to employment. Members of the Alliance of the Mentally Ill come to the group home every other month to offer information and means to connect to community resources.

3. *A woman in her 30s is diagnosed with breast cancer, her brother with prostate cancer.* Connecting with the same hospital social worker, both are able to join a support group of recently diagnosed cancer patients and to connect individually with cancer-survivor support volunteers. The parents and other siblings are able to participate in cancer information meetings offered by the American Cancer Society.

4. *A very old couple experiences the increasing physical disability of one partner and the decreasing mental capacity of the other, who had intended to be the physically disabled partner's lifelong caretaker.* The couple is connected to outreach programs at a senior center. Their children in distant cities are able to visit and to engage a family case manager to help the couple remain at home initially and to participate in some senior center activities. The senior center worker arranges for some home care and provides transportation so that both partners can come to programs at the center several times a week. The case manager provides information to the siblings about their parents' conditions and progress and helps two of them connect with "sandwich generation" support groups at their respective local Jewish community centers.

These examples of structural/empowerment-oriented practice provide support for people in crisis, helping them to deal with long-term changes in their life situation and to improve or maintain their quality of life. Group interventions with people sharing similar problems or situations can be very powerful. They can strengthen identity, promote critical consciousness-raising and engage members in work on organizational and system change. The examples illustrate workers engaging in mutual problem-solving with client groups and their support systems. They also illustrate how workers collaborate to connect individuals, families, and groups with the services they need and initiate their connections with mutual aid groups and community-based services. Connections to larger social networks are also initiated. The next structural level takes practice further into the community and broader levels of the social environment, engaging workers and the people they serve more deeply in social networks and natural helping systems.

SOCIAL NETWORKS AND NATURAL HELPING SYSTEMS

Throughout human history, mutual support has frequently been the primary instrument for survival, whether in prehistorical hunter-gatherer groups, on the American frontier, or in current efforts to rebuild natural networks in communities. Barn raisings and extended family help in times of health crises are typical examples of natural systems at work. In an early sociologically oriented study of America, Alexis de Tocqueville (1835/1956) commented that a traveler could hardly spend time in a commu-

nity without finding a small group of Americans involved together in some joint project.

As social work developed as a profession, one of its tasks was to learn to work with and strengthen natural support systems through group-focused work and community work. More recently, direct practice workers have put an emphasis on engaging with natural helping systems to help effect longer term positive change for individuals and families dealing with social and health issues. Collins and Pancost (1976) had a major influence on the increased professional focus on intervention with and support of informal systems with their book, *Natural Helping Networks.* This work and subsequent literature mapped out the ways such networks could improve the immediate social environment for individuals and families (Collins, 1980; Collins & Pancost, 1976; Leutz, 1976; Unger & Powell, 1980).

Two streams of literature have been primary forces in shaping this professional/natural system interaction to provide safety, support, and mutual help for individuals and families. The community mental health movement, with its focus on least restrictive environment and community-based care, has emphasized work with natural support systems for people with severe and persistent mental illnesses. Indeed, it has developed mutual support groups where none existed (Gottlieb, 1981, 1988; Lieberman et al., 1979).

Multipronged strategies to develop family-centered/community-based services have fostered a movement that is grounded in principles of family-focused practice, with an emphasis on professional involvement in natural helping networks to strengthen families and their environments (Hartman & Laird, 1983; Pecora, Whittaker, & Maluccio, 1992; Weissman,

1978; Whittaker & Garbarino, 1983). These efforts range from the family support movement (Goetz & Peck, 1994; Kagan et al., 1987) to the enlarged emphasis on services for families whose children have developmental disabilities or delays, to the development of intensive and less intensive family preservation services (Pecora, Fraser, Nelson, McCroskey, & Meezan, 1995; Whittaker, Kinney, Tracy, & Booth, 1990). One of the earliest efforts in this arena was the development of the Lower East Side Family Union in New York, founded by five Settlement Houses to integrate services for troubled families and to build mutual support (Weissman, 1978). Another early effort was the St. Paul Multiproblem Family Project, which also sought to assist families and develop informal support (Overton, Tinker, & Associates, 1957).

In 1982, Brown, Finch, Northen, Taylor, and Weil called for the development of a comprehensive model for neighborhood-based services and family-centered child welfare practice. Specialized work to enable and empower families with children with disabilities or developmental delays was championed by Dunst et al. (1988), and a strong literature related to early childhood development and disabilities has since developed, with a major focus on building natural supports (Zipper, Rounds, & Weil, 1993).

The particular needs of children of color have prompted studies of both the child welfare system and natural support systems in the African American and Latino communities (Billingsley & Giovannoni, 1972; Cross, Bazron, Dennis, & Isaacs, 1989; Hernandez & Isaacs, 1998; McAdoo, 1988; Solomon, 1976; Sotomayor, 1991; Stack, 1974). Culturally responsive practice is a major tenet of the family-centered/community-based services movement.

Recent efforts to introduce Family Group Conferencing in the United States are also grounded in working with natural support systems to promote good outcomes for children and their families (Pennell & Burford, in press). In most of the literature on family-centered work, intervention in mutual support or natural helping networks is at least a subtext recognized as a requisite to enable long-term support when professionals move out of the picture.

Social network intervention is, in a number of ways, the cardinal example of social work intervention to improve the "fit" between person and environment, not in ways that adjust someone to an unjust system, but rather in ways that strengthen the ties, connections, and mutual concerns that can enable people to help each other over the long term. As Gottlieb (1981, 1988) has pointed out, when people need help, most first seek out relatives, friends, neighbors or coworkers—people in their primary association networks. Next, they are most likely to seek out clergy, physicians, or teachers—members of the professional community with whom they have established relationships. Indeed, some of the early research in the community mental health movement revealed that people were more likely to seek advice from "community gatekeepers" such as bartenders or beauticians than to seek out specialized professionals (Gottlieb, 1981). Representatives of the formal human service system rank relatively low on the list of "Who you gonna call?" There is a large body of literature on social networks in both sociology and anthropology (Whittaker & Garbarino, 1983). People's support networks grow out of the interactions that they have on a regular basis. As Whittaker and Garbarino (1983) define it,

A social support network is a set of interconnected relationships among a group of people
that provides enduring patterns of nurturance (in
any or all forms) and provides contingent reinforcement for efforts to cope with life on a day-to-
day basis. (p. 5)

Most individuals and families have some
form of support or natural helping network
that social workers can connect with to help
solve problems. Sometimes, natural support
systems work well to assist problem-solving
processes and provide social and tangible resources—and sometimes they fail. If an individual or a family lacks or has "used up" the natural
support network, social workers can connect
with and help to revitalize or develop a network. Social workers' involvement in social
support networks is intended to help build mutual support for longer term resilience and increase the ability of clients to deal with obstacles and issues in their lives and social
environment. This may be a humbling experience for professionals, but it illustrates the
power of mutuality, trust, and love, underscor-
ing the reality that human services professionals
are not always present to assist clients and that
families' support networks are closer to home—
literally and figuratively. Natural helping networks may in fact be the best means for professionals to take seriously the old maxim of
"working ourselves out of a job."

Professionals can identify and put a client or
family in closer touch with their support systems—re-engage estranged members and build
new connections. A number of forms of service
seek to build social networks—such as the "circle of friends" for children with disabilities, the
self-help group for women surviving breast cancer, or high school-age gay and lesbian student

support groups. An important and too often ignored professional responsibility is not only to
identify social support networks, but to actively
collaborate with them to promote healthy functioning and development of individuals and
families. Work with such mutual helping systems extends the work of professionals into the
community and can become a form of community education and development of community
as well as family resiliency (Fraser, 1997).
Whittaker and Garbarino (1983) make a convincing argument for the connection of social
treatment and social support and have provided
evidence of informal helping in a range of systems: mental health; health care and health promotion; services to the elderly, children, and
their families; programs for families with disabled members and those involved in day care,
schools, and youth and substance abuse programs. A number of intervention models are
grounded in work with extended families and
informal support systems, including Family
Group Conferencing, Family Preservation, and
Family Resource Centers.

Family Group Conferencing, for example,
intervenes with families when children are at
risk of out-of home placement in the child welfare or juvenile justice system. A social worker
works with a family that wants to become engaged in conferencing and helps them decide
who should be invited to a family group conference. Careful planning is done to secure everyone's safety and to assure that all who should be
heard are invited. Indeed, some programs are
able to fly in distant relatives to participate. At
the conference, all family members and support
people hear a presentation of the facts of the
case, and the involved professionals are present
to answer questions. After the presentation, all

professionals leave, and the family is charged with developing a plan to provide safety for the child and any family members at risk. The family can call in workers if members have concerns or questions. When their plan is formulated, the social services (or juvenile services) representative is called back to review it. If the plan is acceptable in terms of policy and good practice, it is put into effect, and monitoring is done by family members as well as professionals. In studies in Newfoundland and Labrador, this intervention has been shown to (a) reduce recurrence of abuse, (b) increase extended family and community supports, and (c) improve cooperation between family members and local authorities (Burford & Pennell, 1998). It is now being tested in several parts of the United States.

Alternative services form an interesting category, frequently founded in informal systems that evolve into macro strategies of community practice and service development with specific populations. Alternative services are developed by concerned individuals and groups when it is clear that particular groups have serious unmet needs or that they are excluded from available mainstream services. The most obvious recent examples are the development of the alternative services network for women (Gottlieb, 1980; Van den Berg & Cooper, 1986) and the development of a range of services for the gay and lesbian community. These social networks evolved into social movements that focused strongly on organizing and service development. Therefore, they will be discussed in the macro section of this chapter.

The basic practice principles guiding work with natural helping systems include professionals learning mutual approaches to problem-solving and promoting healthy development with families, their networks, and their communities—both geographic and functional. Implicit in work with natural systems is the confidence that people and their close supporters have knowledge and skills to remedy problems and that professionals can help to make connections to larger systems of service or support as needed. Power-sharing is crucial, as are explicit empowerment strategies. For intervention with natural support systems to be effective, approaches should include collaborative planning and implementation of strategies, along with mutual monitoring of outcomes. Figures 18.1 and 18.2 provide pictorial illustration of some of these processes. Some of these principles are illustrated in the following examples.

Examples of Social Networks and Natural Helping Systems

1. Children in a family are suspected of being victims of physical and sexual abuse. Following a family group conference, if the family's plan is accepted by the local authority, efforts are made to further strengthen the natural network and to connect each family member with services and supports needed. Parents might join Twelve Step programs or a parent support group. They might initiate further planning meetings with their network. The model builds partnerships within the family and natural network and between the family and participating agencies.

2. A child born to young parents has physical problems and suspected developmental problems. Over time, the parents become leaders in the early education advocacy group and volunteer workers. Their own social network is expanded through development of a Circle of Friends drawn together out of concern for the child and family to support them in different aspects of their lives and their child's development.

3. A young adult experiences the first onset of schizophrenia. The young woman is able to participate in group home activities and to become a cofacilitator in a young adults group at the community clubhouse's mental health program. These activities widen her social network and improve her quality of life.

As social workers help their clients use social networks and natural helping systems, they should seriously consider doing a power analysis as proposed by Friedmann (1996). This will ascertain which aspects of disempowerment affect clients and client groups and their social networks. Much of what social workers do relates to the domains of social organizations (including both formal and informal organizations) and social networks (based on reciprocity). The range of a family's social network typically expands when members are engaged in social organizations. Friedmann (1996) holds,

> Households with extensive horizontal networks among family, friends, and neighbors have a larger space of maneuver than households without them. Vertical networks, up through the social hierarchy, give households a chance to access other forms of power but may lead to dependent patron-client relationships. (pp. 68-69)

This analysis provides useful cautions to social workers:

1. We need to give far more attention to helping families and individuals develop their horizontal, reciprocal social networks.

2. We need to help families develop and use a broader array of vertical linkages to assist them in accessing needed resources.

3. We need to consciously employ an empowerment model of practice to prevent a "patron-client" relationship, to build a mutual worker-client relationship, and to help clients gain skills in interactions and self-advocacy that will assist them in longer term social development.

Specht and Courtney (1994) provide a strong rational for social workers' engagement with natural helping networks:

> The objective of social work is to help people make use of social resources—family members, friends, neighbors, community organizations, and social service agencies and so forth—to solve their problems. . . . They (i.e., social workers) deal with social problems, which concern the community, rather than personality problems of individuals. Helping people to make use of their social resources is one of the major functions of social work practice. And just as important is the social worker's function of developing and strengthening these resources by bringing people together in groups and organizations, by community education, and by organizational development. (p. 24)

ORGANIZATIONAL AND INTERORGANIZATIONAL WORK: COLLABORATION ON BEHALF OF CLIENTS AND CLIENT GROUPS

The next structural level of intervention illustrates workers moving into organizational development and interorganizational work on behalf of clients and groups of clients. Organizational development incorporates all the strategies to help make human service organizations more effective in terms of outcome and more efficient in use of resources. An important focus of current organizational development is illustrated in all the newer forms of organizations that seriously seek to engage clients and their representatives in the planning, operation, and evaluation of services. The growing literature on learning organizations is one illustration of how organizations need to be responsive to their environments and, from a social work perspective, to structure services to empower clients and client groups (Bennis & Nanus, 1985; Fabricant & Burghardt, 1992; Garvin, 1998; Withorn, 1984). Indeed, social service organizations should strive to mirror in their organizational activities the value base that guides quality service.

Organizations and organizational networks are part of the larger ecosystem, and a major function of direct practice social workers is to help clients and client groups connect effectively to useful organizations. Human service organizations are complex (Drucker, 1990; Hasenfeld, 1992); they are often viewed as open systems that have their own culture and life cycle, which may or may not be responsive to clients (Holland, 1995; Schein, 1992; Scott, 1998). A particular tension for many human service organizations is that there may be considerable divergence between the perspectives of clients and potential service consumers and those of the nonprofit boards or governmental bodies to which public agencies report.

Organizational development and organizational change may be sparked by shifts in policy, political changes, increased or decreased resources, and new knowledge and new models of practice (Brager & Holloway, 1978; Kimberly, Miles, & Associates, 1980; Lee, 1994; Romanelli, 1991; Weissman, 1978; Withorn, 1984). When policy perspectives positively

converge with new knowledge and practice models, the organizational environment is ripe for change. Such convergence can be moved forward when direct practice workers promote change from within (Homan, 1994; Netting et al., 1993; Resnick & Patti, 1980). Organizational change, like community change, can come from the bottom up as well as from the top down (Austin, 1988; Netting et al., 1993). To create responsive organizations and integrate service systems so that vulnerable populations are served more effectively requires leadership development at all organizational levels. Program supervisors and direct service staff must take on administrative and planning tasks, and staff must become increasingly engagegd in boundary spanning, interagency planning, and collaborative roles (Edwards, Yankey, & Altpeter, 1998; Williams, Weil, Zipper, & Hays, 1995). These trends move direct service staff into the forefront in organizational change and organizational-community linkages.

The recent developments in family-centered and community-based strategies of intervention challenge organizations to have parallel processes in their internal operations: processes that empower workers as they seek to empower clients (Homebuilders, 1994). For example, the Methodist Home for Children in Raleigh, North Carolina (formerly the Methodist Orphanage), has reorganized services significantly to meet changing needs and to respond to the growing knowledge base. First, the Methodist Home changed from being a large institutional orphanage operation to providing small group homes for foster care of children (*The News & Observer,* June 18th, 1999). With the family-centered practice movement, and in the face of much criticism from other group facilities, the Methodist Home led the charge among voluntary agencies to develop family preservation services and to advocate for policies for family preservation and family support services throughout North Carolina. Benefiting from visionary leadership at multiple levels, within a short span of years, this long-established organization was able to bring on new staff and new models of practice to focus on in-home services and intensive family preservation, when assessments predicted that children could be safe at home with such services. The Methodist Home has since become partners with the state to develop less intensive services and family resource centers. This is one example of thousands throughout the nation, as agencies develop and implement services that are family centered and responsive to changing conditions. In such organizational change—particularly in the case of in-home services focused on treatment, network intervention, and development of collaborative services—direct service staff carry increased leadership responsibility not only in work with individuals and families but also in dealing with other organizations and interorganizational networks. This shift in roles marks a major direction in practice and should be fundamental to a new MSW's work expectations.

With the stronger development of community-based services has come an increased emphasis on service collaboration, coordination, and integration—again growing from the community mental health movement, the family-centered practice movement, and corollary movements in education and early intervention. Collaboration involves a specific set of skills, requiring staff to understand their own and other organizations' missions and methods of work; staff members must be able to work toward the common good for clients, even when the missions of their organizations are somewhat different (Weil, 1977). Vulnerable families and vulnerable groups most often need multiple services. Recognizing this means staff must learn to pull together needed services and to work effectively with a variety of agencies and organizations (Melaville & Blank, 1993; Stroul, 1993; Weil, 1986). Because collaboration is so important in today's service environment, skills involved in working with other professionals and organizations on behalf of clients are just as important as skills needed for social treatment methods (Zipper & Weil, 1995).

Efforts at collaboration for specific populations in several fields of practice have grown into ongoing interorganizational work, both to coordinate services for children and their families and to build a service network. In both services for families and children and for adult mental health, these efforts have further encouraged local and state advocacy. Interorganizational work and collaboration are challenging aspects of practice and now involve staff at every organizational level. Efforts to implement a comprehensive system of care for children with mental, emotional, or behavioral disorders have required strong administrative and managerial leadership; much more boundary spanning and system networking are asked of direct service staff (Friesen & Poertner, 1995; Hernandez & Isaacs, 1998; Stroul, 1993).

In western North Carolina, for example, several counties joined to have a conference on interagency work to create a smoothly working system of care. The large conference was called after some other efforts failed to identify all agencies and organizations involved in the system and to hammer out procedures and protocols to promote positive interagency collaboration. Principles were developed at this conference, and a standing committee was formed to continue work on difficult issues related to differing agency missions, responsibilities, and standards of confidentiality (Zipper & Weil, 1995).

Similar efforts to develop better functioning systems of care for vulnerable groups have occurred throughout the nation; in many of these efforts, gaining advanced cultural competence has been a major thread of service development and community interaction (Hernandez & Isaacs, 1998). These efforts depend on the competency and skills of direct service workers to make services culturally responsive, family centered, and community based. The Wilder Foundation (1992) has published research-based work to guide service collaboration; and the federal Departments of Education and of Health and Human Services sponsored the *Together We Can* monograph and website to promote learning communities and strategic development of pro-family service systems (Melaville & Blank, 1993). Interorganizational work has long been a part of social work practice and is now an indispensable aspect of direct practice. Figure 18.1 illustrates aspects of organizational/interorganizational systems. Social workers need to be alert advocates for clients and client groups, given the various pressures of organizational and interorganizational work; a social justice perspective needs to be worked on in each setting each day (Lee, 1994; Long & Holle, 1997; Wood & Middleman, 1989). Where populations are underserved, coalitions can be developed to advocate for policies and

to develop services (Mizrahi & Rosenthal, 1993). The following examples illustrate organizational and interorganizational efforts to strengthen services for vulnerable populations.

Organizational and Interorganizational Work Examples

1. AIDS/HIV survivors need long-term services. A rural hospice program receives increasing referrals for AIDS/HIV patients who, because of new treatments, have much longer life expectancies. With intense efforts in the local service network, specialized services for AIDS/HIV survivors are developed.

2. A homeless family is beaten and robbed, and the mother is brutally raped. The Battered Women's Shelter helps the formerly homeless family to reconnect with estranged family members in a rural community in a neighboring state. They are able to relocate, and the mother is able to find work through a connection to the local rural women's center. Over time, and with the shelter worker's assistance, the mother is able to participate in the shelter's collaborative program with the local vocational rehabilitation agency's job training program, join a peer lending group, and develop a microenterprise that can adequately support her family.

3. Refugee service needs. With the rapid growth of the Southeast Asian refugee community in Los Angeles, the Asian American Community Mental Health Training Center recognizes the need for specialized services, as well as bridges from the refugee community to the service community. Its representatives work with new groups to train lay leaders and to develop the supports and connecting services needed by new arrivals—children, youth, and adults—

who have suffered severe mental and physical trauma in their homelands (Weil, 1981).

DIRECT COMMUNITY PRACTICE AND COMMUNITY BUILDING

Community practice can be a direct form of practice in which a worker engages face-to-face with groups and citizens' organizations to help them achieve their own goals for community development, community organization, and improvement of quality of life (Gamble & Weil, 1995; Homan, 1994; Rothman, 1996; Rubin, 1997; Rubin & Rubin, 1992; Weil & Gamble, 1995). It also encompasses more macro-focused processes of organizing, coalition development, social planning, and policy practice (Checkoway, 1997; Rothman, 1996; Weil & Gamble, 1995). Quite frequently, these two areas feed into each other. For example, social worker/planners at World Vision (an internationally focused NGO) might design and fund a variety of community development efforts to be carried out "on the ground" in multiple countries. Both the international and local work are processes of community development. However, one focuses on direct work with local citizens in planning and implementation of social and economic development strategies, whereas the other focuses on global planning and resource development to enable local work. Both involve development, organizing, planning, and social change (Weil, 1996). The difference is not so much in the processes but in the scale of operation, specific activities, and the differing amounts of time spent working directly with citizens on their own issues as compared to working with other organizations for larger scale change. Because direct practice social workers are very likely to engage in direct community practice activities and community-building efforts, those activities are highlighted in this section.

Direct community practice grows out of the Settlement Movement, which focused on learning what was needed from neighborhood residents, engaging them in assessments and planning, providing programs to meet local needs, and engaging in advocacy and social planning to strengthen communities in their social structure and their physical environment (Addams, 1895/1930). It also has roots in the rural development movement, the labor movement, projects and programs related to religious institutions such as the Catholic Worker movement, and the struggles for equality by African Americans, Native Americans, women, and other oppressed groups (Betten & Austin, 1990; Garvin & Cox, 1995).

To engage effectively in community change, social workers need to understand not only community practice models and intervention strategies but the ways in which people interpret community as well as basic community structures and functions: production, distribution, consumption (access to resources for day to day life), socialization, social control, social and civic participation, and mutual support (Gamble & Weil, 1995; Hardcastle et al., 1997; Netting et al., 1993; Warren, 1978). Human ecological theory, community systems theory, and participation theory are major knowledge bases to draw on in these areas (Fellin, 1995; Gamble & Weil, 1995). A community strengths perspective is requisite (Castelloe, 1999; Homan, 1994; Kretzman & McKnight, 1996; Netting et al., 1993; Saleebey, 1997) as is an empowerment approach directed toward actually increasing the power and control disadvantaged groups have over the circumstances of their lives. Power is variously described as (a) the "capacity to move people in a desired direction to accomplish some end" (Homan, 1994, p. 110), (b) "the ability to accomplish one's will with or without opposition" (Rubin & Rubin, 1992, p. 13), and (c) the ability to influence or "the capacity to produce a change" (Miller, 1983, p. 4). Many feminists define power as a capacity that enlarges with power sharing (Gutiérrez & Lewis, 1994; Gutiérez, Alvarez, Nemon, & Lewis, 1996; Van den Berg & Cooper, 1986).

These definitions help practitioners understand people's diverse interactions in community settings and gain a perspective on vested interests and divergent values that shape behavior. In communities, power is visible in personal, interpersonal, social, and political aspects. With this understanding, workers can help groups and organizations deal realistically with issues of power (internally and externally) and develop strategies for making change and for surmounting obstacles to change (Kahn, 1991; Netting et al., 1993).

Social workers may be involved in direct work with people who want to form an action group about a social issue, or they may work with already organized citizen groups or coalitions. This is face-to-face work with people to improve the conditions and quality of their lives. Although processes for direct intervention with citizens in communities are similar in some ways to processes of more clinically focused practice, they are also distinct—especially in the types of techniques and tools used for information gathering and in the strategies for larger system change (Locke, Garrison, & Winship, 1998; Long & Holle, 1997). To ac-

complish goals, Hardcastle et al. (1997) recommend a problem-solving strategy including

> (1) recognition of a problem and establishment of the need for change; (2) information gathering; (3) assessment and the development of a case theory and plan for change; (4) intervention and the change effort; and (5) evaluation and termination of the change effort. (pp. 14-16)

In all of these processes, it is important to analyze community situations and interventions using both gender and multicultural lenses and to check approaches and worker actions in relation to the community culture and context (Gutiérrez & Alvarez, 1998). Judith Lee extends this concern, reminding workers that it is important not to use a limited "bifocal" lens, but to broaden into a "fifocal" examination— one that considers an historical view of the community; an ecological view; an ethnicity/social class perspective (Gordon, 1978) that includes adaptive behaviors (Lum, 1999); a feminist perspective—which highlights the particular oppression of women, seeks unity of concepts, and envisions power itself in limitless terms (Van den Berg & Cooper, 1986; Weil, Gamble, & Williams, 1998); and a critical perspective to critique all forms of oppression and to develop strategies that link individual and social change (Freire, 1973a, 1973b; Longres, 1995).

Community practice in both direct and macro aspects involves working with both citizens and service providers and engaging in system change and social reform. The objectives of direct community practice are

> to develop the organizing skills and abilities of citizen groups, to make social planning more accessible and inclusive in a community, to connect so-

cial and economic investments to grassroots groups, to advocate for broad coalitions in solving community problems, and to infuse the social planning process with a concern for social justice. (Weil & Gamble, 1995, p. 580)

Eight current models of community practice (Weil & Gamble, 1995, p. 581) are

Neighborhood and Community Organizing—developing the capacity of members to change conditions in their neighborhoods and deal with political and economic forces

Organizing Functional Communities—engaging in action for social justice focused on advocacy and changing public attitudes—groups may also provide services

Community Development (Social & Economic)—initiates development plans from a grassroots perspective and prepares citizens to make use of social and economic investments

Social Planning—creation of larger-scale plans for developing a service system or system of care; also citywide or regional proposals developed in the governmental sector or human service planning councils

Program Development and Community Liaison—expansion or redirection of an agency program to improve community service effectiveness; organizing a new service.

Political and Social Action—action for social justice focused on changing policy or policy makers

Coalitions—building a multiorganizational power base large enough to influence program direction and/or draw down resources

Social Movements—action for social justice that provides a new paradigm for a particular population, group, or issue

Engagement in each of these practice models requires high levels of interpersonal, process, task, and technical skills. Much of direct community practice involves mutual learning and teaching. Group members and workers learn from each other and hone their own leadership styles. For example, meetings are a basic means of work and communication in community practice; workers need to be able to facilitate a meeting themselves and to to teach others—citizens in a new group or board members of an agency—how to do so, using process skills to complete the group's tasks. To engage in community practice, social workers need to be committed to positive social change, to analyze large systems and social problems, to invest time and expand their role repertoire, and to speak truth to power.

Work with groups often involves helping them to learn to work together effectively to plan and carry out strategies. Facilitating a group involves seeing not only that a meeting goes well but also that people are prepared for the meeting and ready to take action. Internally, people may need coaching in collaboration, planning, and conflict management. Work to effect change in larger systems often requires the use of a range of tactics, from education to marketing, to collaboration, to pressure to gain the attention of public bodies or protest unjust conditions (Brager, Specht, & Torczyner, 1987; Homan, 1994; Rubin & Rubin, 1992). Particular models of practice call for other specific skills. For example, in organizing either geographic or functional communities, workers need to know how to organize people and tasks and how to carry a plan forward to completion. They also coach others in learning these coordination skills. In internal work with groups, skills are needed in mediation; and in externally focused work, groups will need skills in advocacy and public and media communication.

Community building is an approach to community practice that is increasingly discussed because of widespread concern about the decline of "community" in America, evidenced in increasing housing segregation by income as well as race, increasing income disparity, structural unemployment, and growth of the global economy (Bellah, Madsen, Sullivan, Swidler, & Tipton, 1990; Blank, 1997; Fisher & Karger, Chapter 1, this volume; Fisher & Karger, 1997; Flacks, 1995). These negative trends also result from the critical lack of resources in inner-city and rural communities, as well as alienation and separation of people even in affluent suburban neighborhoods (Bellah, Madsen, Sullivan, Swidler, & Tipton, 1992; Ewalt, Freeman, & Poole, 1998; Fitchen, 1998; Weil, 1997; Wilson, 1987). Community building is conceived of in a variety of ways, but it usually includes social development (or development of human capital) and economic development (strategies of reinvestment in underresourced areas) (Ewalt, 1998; Kretzman & McKnight, 1996; Rubin, 1997).

Community building can take place through projects such as Habitat for Humanity; youth and community development strategies, such as Communities in Schools; combined economic and social development projects, such as Bethel New Life in Chicago; and strategies for developing civil society and local infrastructure (Bailey & Koney, 1995, 1996; Barry, 1989; Morrison et al., 1998; Richman & Bowen, 1997; Weil, 1997). Major approaches to community building include comprehensive community initiatives, economic revitalization to build community self-sufficiency, development of local collaboratives, functional community organizing based on affiliations, housing initiatives, school-based community development, and community health partnerships (Dupper &

Poertner, 1998; Ewalt et al., 1998; Morrison et al., 1998; Naparstek & Dooley, 1998; Poole & Van Hook, 1998; Schorr, 1997).

There are opportunities for social workers to engage in organizing, planning, and development in mental health and health fields, in services for families and children, and in programs for the aging. There are also growing opportunities in major efforts to assist rural and urban low-income neighborhoods through development of affordable housing, social and economic development strategies including microenterprises, and development of collaborative networks of social services and community-based organizations (Bailey & Koney, 1995; Banerjee, 1998; Locke, Garrison, & Winship, 1998; Gutiérrez, 1990; Rubin, 1997; Schorr, 1997). Comprehensive community initiatives include the above activities and seek a synergy among them to revitalize communities (Kubisch et al., 1995). A number of major foundations have and continue to invest in such initiatives to strengthen families, communities, and service systems (Ewalt et al., 1998).

Direct community practice engages both citizens and social workers in the larger and more public arena of their social environment and offers challenges for development of citizen advocacy, organization to remedy injustices or develop new programs, and community improvement—in both relationships and infrastructure. For citizens, it is health-promoting to engage in active citizen advocacy, planning, and assessment activities. This engagement enlarges our lives, our sphere of influence, and our sense of self as actors in the world (Gamble & Weil, 1995).

For social workers, it is important to engage in community practice because it offers the means to follow the guidance of an old Hassidic teaching. As the story goes, the bodies of slain Jews were found floating in the river. Three courses of action followed. Some lifted the bodies out of the river and dug graves; some ran to the village to seek help; but one rabbi set out on foot up the river to see who was committing mass murder and determine what could be done to stop the slaughter. Community practice moves us from efforts to heal the immediate physical and emotional injuries of individuals who have suffered disadvantage and oppression and into efforts to develop immediate and long-term strategies and means to change organizations, institutions, and society so that vulnerable groups not only receive quality services but, more crucially, that they gain power, equality of citizenship, and opportunities.

When groups have dealt with discrimination, oppression, or exclusion from mainstream services and opportunities, their members have often organized to advocate for their cause and to develop alternative services (Garvin & Cox, 1995; Weil & Gamble, 1995). Macro-practice social workers often are engaged with such groups in the development and implementation of new and alternative services. Alternative services emerge when mainstream service systems are unresponsive the the needs of particular groups; that is, people organize these services themselves, because no one else sees the need as clearly and is as willing to do the complex organizing work. The development of the alternative services system for women is perhaps the most broadly recognized among recent efforts. As the Women's Movement developed, and more and more women sought help in areas that had primarily been relegated to the "private troubles" ledger—that is, as women openly sought help for health and mental health concerns, including treatment of sexual assault or domestic violence, and for job discrimination— a web of services was developed by women for women to respond to these serious social problems (Gottlieb, 1980; Gutiérrez, 1999; Hyde, 1996; Masi, 1981; Mauney, Williams, & Weil, 1993). Specialized literature and intervention strategies have been developed to assist women in particular service sectors and with specific problems, such as single parenthood or inability to access credit (Burden & Gottlieb, 1987; Figueira-McDonough, Netting, & Nichols-Casebolt, 1998; Sherraden & Ninacs, 1998; Van den Berg & Cooper, 1986).

The gay and lesbian community has engaged in a decades-long project to develop health care and other services for adults and youth. The AIDS/HIV crisis and development of related specialized services have received the most public attention. However, a wide variety of services have been developed including support groups for youth, peer support for career advancement, support from allies, and specialized services such as health centers. Over time, such alternative services may become incorporated in mainstream service networks.

Another example of alternative services arises from the Grameen Bank/low-income credit movement. Developed in Bangladesh by Mohammed Yunus, the Grameen Bank provides loans to women living in poverty to help develop a stronger household economy (Jansen & Pippard, 1998). Some lending programs in the United States have adopted and adapted this peer-support credit model (Varma, 1999). Alternative services represent a major way that social workers become engaged in social reform.

All forms of direct community practice should be empowerment based and focus on mutuality in relationships. In work with individuals and groups, many of the skills in direct practice are immediately transferable. There are, however, additional roles that are needed to work effectively with larger groups, organizations, and service networks. Direct practitioners moving into community practice will find themselves taking on roles as advocates, organizers, coaches, facilitators, mediators, negotiators, and planners (Weil & Gamble, 1995). They will be engaged in processes of social and economic development (Estes, 1993; Midgley, 1995; Rubin, 1997; Rubin & Rubin, 1992; Sherraden & Ninacs, 1998), organizing (Kahn, 1991; Mondros & Wilson, 1994; Rubin & Rubin, 1992; Taffe & Fisher, 1997), planning (Checkoway, 1997; Friedmann, 1996; Noponen, 1996), and social change with citizens and organizations committed to strengthening communities (Fabricant & Burghardt, 1992; Fisher & Karger, Chapter 1, this volume; Fraser & Leavitt, 1990; Lee, 1994; Withorn, 1984). The following examples provide vignettes of direct community practice and community building.

Direct Community Practice and Community Building Examples

1. *Responses to the problems of youth with behavior disorders.* A local school becomes involved with the Communities in Schools program, which not only offers supportive services to children and their families, but also works on neighborhood conditions to encourage community development and build safer more nurturing environments for children in risky environments (program development, community liaison; neighborhood organizing). Local communities including health professionals, citizens, cultural groups, and religious groups organize to fight labeling of minority children, to develop community programs emphasizing child development within their cultural context, and to obtain increased funding for recreation and school programs for at-risk youth (neighborhood organizing, program development, coalition building, local advocacy for policy and system change)

2. *Responses to HIV/AIDS and issues in the gay and lesbian community.* Alternative service systems are developed to meet the health, social, and developmental needs of people living with AIDS (alternative service system and program development). The Gay Community Service Center does outreach with local homeless youth, forms support groups, and works with the gay and lesbian community to provide employment training and job placement for homeless youth, as well as to offer community education about safe sex and HIV prevention (functional community organizing, program development, economic development, health education). Locally and nationally, the gay and lesbian community, their families, and their supporters organize to press for equal civil rights for gays and lesbians (functional community organizing, social action; social witness; political and social action).

3. *Responses to need for services for the very old.* Staff and board members of a senior center conduct an outreach program to identify seniors with increasing health or physical problems. The results of the assessment are used to secure funding for an adult day program that can assist with the physical, emotional, and social needs of a variety of older people. The new program is located in the same building as an early childhood day care program; each program has its own "side," with program rooms and eating facilities in the middle. The adult day program adopts environmental enrichment

policies, bringing in plants and pets, and provides structured activities for young children and seniors together (functional community organizing, program development, social planning).

COMMUNITY PRACTICE MACRO INTERVENTIONS: ON BEHALF OF GROUPS, COMMUNITIES, AND CLASSES OF CLIENTS

In macro-focused community practice, social workers are involved in larger-scale efforts of community and service organization, including functional community organization, social and economic development, and social planning (Checkoway, 1997; Rothman, 1996; Rubin, 1997; Rubin & Rubin, 1992). They are also involved in macro processes of program and system development, coalitions to strengthen services or advocate for the needs of underserved or oppressed populations, political and social action with citizens and organizations, and social movements to develop a more just society and world (Weil & Gamble, 1995). These efforts move social workers more sharply into public arenas: system integration, advocacy and negotiation on community issues, and research to document community and population strengths and needs. Social workers in macro-community work engage in leadership facilitation with community representatives and sharpen their own leadership skills in organizing, planning, research, advocacy and public speaking, and documentation of social change.

At first glance, these forms of social work practice might seem far removed from the basics of direct practice work with individuals,

groups, and families; however, macro strategies for changing organizations, systems, and society grow directly out of the unmet needs of clients, potential clients, citizens, and communities. Macro work embodies the social reform mission of social work (Hardcastle et al., 1997). Earlier social work theorists argued strongly for the connection between and movement from case work—private troubles of individuals and families—to cause work—transforming those private troubles into public issues and developing strategies to redress injustice, exclusion, and oppression (Lee, 1929; Reynolds, 1964). To be true to its historical mission, the profession and individual social workers need to embrace macro strategies of reform, social action, and social change, as well as social treatment of individuals, families, and groups (Hardcastle et al., 1997; Lee, 1994; Wood & Middleman, 1989). Despite several historical efforts to define the profession narrowly in more clinical terms, social work has and does emphasize: intervention with individuals and families to improve quality of life, intervention in the social environment to develop resources and reform organizations and systems, and macro interventions and social, political, and policy action to transform organizations, communities, and society in the direction of social justice (Hardcastle et al., 1997; Pumphrey, 1980; Weil & Gamble, 1995).

In Figure 18.4, macro strategies are pictured adjacent to direct practice interventions to illustrate this relationship. Social needs are discovered and documented not only in census and research data but, critically, in social workers' daily encounters with the families and individuals we serve. Information from even one case can spark a class action suit: for example, the *State of North Carolina vs. Willie M,* which established the right to treatment for aggressive/

violent children with mental and emotional disorders. The creative problem-solving of direct practice workers often produces new models of practice, which macro strategies then adapt and transfer to additional locations or other populations (Fraser & Leavitt, 1990; McCroskey & Meezan, 1998; Schorr, 1997). Macro strategies for policy reform often depend on the "telling examples" from experiences of particular families and individuals. Conversely, the clients of direct practice workers benefit from positive policy and social change and from efforts to reform organizations and build collaborative service systems.

With the devolution of decision making to states and localities in recent policy changes, and with the growing focus on comprehensive community initiatives and system reform, it is less and less likely that social workers will have their roles narrowly circumscribed by an exclusive focus on treatment (Ewalt et al., 1998; Hernandez & Isaacs, 1998; Wood & Middleman, 1989). Recent changes in the larger social environment, in policies and practices, make it much more likely that social workers will need to operate from an empowerment/structural model that integrates all arenas of practice. Direct practice workers now typically engage in case management, and more and more often, they are engaged in boundary spanning, outreach to populations and citizens' organizations, system development, advocacy, and other community practice processes (Rose & Moore, 1995; Weil & Karls, 1985; Zipper, Rounds, & Weil, 1992). The balance of micro and macro responsibilities will be different with each worker but may well involve representing their organization, strengthening empowerment approaches, building public support for programs, presenting issues to community forums and po-

litical bodies, and advocating for the needs of special populations. Social workers who view themselves as having primary skills in direct practice need to connect to macro strategies for the good of the people they serve; and conversely, those with macro practice portfolios need to learn about local conditions and issues from direct service workers and the individuals and families they serve. Netting et al. (1993) argue,

> Being a social worker requires seeing the client as part of multiple, overlapping systems that comprise the person's social and physical environment. The profession of social work is committed to seeking social justice in concert with vulnerable and underserved populations, and macropractice skills are necessary in confronting these inequalities. If the social worker is not willing to engage in some macropractice activities relating to these environments, then he or she is not doing social work. (p. 10)

Macro practice responsibilities typically require competencies in communication, facilitation, organizing, advocacy, planning, social and economic development, proposal writing, program management, research, public speaking, mediation, negotiation, and policy analysis (Castelloe, 1999; Edwards et al., 1998; Hyde, 1996; Jansson, 1997; Kahn, 1991; Perlmutter, 1994; Rubin, 1997; Weil & Gamble, 1995). As macro practice carries forward the social reform mission of social work, it needs workers who can envision new strategies, new programs, and new solutions for social problems and who can engage in mutual problem solving, education, collaboration, and campaign and contest strategies as needed to deal with social issues (Brager et al., 1987; Mellaville & Blank, 1993; Schorr, 1997). Practice needs to be seen holistically, recognizing that the interventions offered should depend not on the particular specialty of individuals but on the client's or community's strengths and needs. There is a vast literature on macropractice. This section provides only the briefest of introductions. The following examples illustrate some aspects of macro practice and indicate the specific models used in each.

Community Practice Macro Intervention Examples

1. Macro responses to child abuse and neglect. Locally, social workers design and implement a Family Group Conferencing program (program planning). Family Preservation and Family Support programs are extended across a state, using funds allocated from the federal Family Support Act to assist the child welfare system to become more family- and community-oriented and to protect children with the least possible disruption in their lives (social planning). System reform is undertaken to make the welfare of children a central community issue, to make the child welfare system more accountable to communities, and to make practice family-centered—as in the Kellogg Foundation's multistate Families for Kids initiative (system reform and public/private partnership). Globally, many developing nations strive to make their nascent child welfare and social programs develop in accord with the United Nations Declaration on the Rights of the Child (global human rights movement).

2. Macro responses to homelessness and woman abuse. A local coalition for the homeless is formed, which builds new interagency and interfaith community partnerships and includes numerous homeless and formerly home-

less representatives (functional community organizing; partnership building; coalition development). A national housing coalition connects to nonprofit housing development corporations in a campaign to emphasize housing construction for homeless families over a 10-year period (coalition building, economic development). Interagency groups mobilize to provide educational, social development, and employment development training for adults who have been homeless (partnership building, system reform, development of alternative services for a stigmatized population).

3. Macro responses to domestic violence. A state-level coalition against domestic violence engages in research and program development to help battered women move beyond crisis and into economic self-sufficiency. Micro enterprise peer-loan and business-development groups are organized, Co-housing is developed for formerly battered women and their children. Local shelters lead in developing interagency work groups to foster intensive employment training for formerly battered women (coalition action, social and economic development, local system reform, and partnership building). The coalition is successful in having state grant programs for domestic violence refocus on moving women beyond the crisis of domestic violence (state system reform and legislative advocacy).

4. Macro response to poverty. In response to increasing pressures of poverty and homelessness, a "Poor People's Summit" drawing 300 people was held in Philadelphia in October 1998 to build solidarity and plan for a "Poor People's March of the Americas" from Washington, D.C., to the United Nations in October 1999. These social action plans grow out of a North/South Dialogue held at the Highlander Center in Tennessee in October 1997. The

Summit and the March were envisioned as a way to advance the movement to end poverty in the Americas. "Speaking from the crucible of their own experiences, . . . participants in the Highlander gathering began to challenge assumptions underpinning current public policy and to insist upon new analyses and actions based on their truths. . . . Signaling their commitment to the work of ending poverty, they chose the theme, 'First Things First: Let's Get Organized!' " A bus tour, "The New Freedom Bus," helped to organize for the coming events with local rallies, demonstrations, speak-outs, and teach-ins. Contradictions between current welfare policies and the provisions of the U.N. Declaration of Human Rights were sharply drawn in tour events. The summit provided a means to organize for the 1999 March. Leadership in the movement is primarily from the poor and formerly homeless, though many social workers are "allies" in the struggle. As one participant noted at the conclusion of the Summit: "As long as people are willing to take a stand for change; I know there is a chance!" (Baptist & Bricker-Jenkins, 1999) (social action, social movements, global human rights movement, and social change).

Community practice strategies are about increasing those chances, enlarging opportunities, changing policies, and moving toward social justice.

REFERENCES

Addams, J. (1910). *Twenty years at Hull-House*. New York: Macmillan.

Addams, J. (1930). *Hull House maps and papers, by residents of Hull House, a social settlement, a presentation of nationalities and wages in a congested district of Chicago, together with comments and essays on problems growing out of the social conditions*. New York: Crowell. (Original work published 1895)

Allen-Meares, P., Washington, R. O., & Welsh, B. L. (1996). *Social work services in schools* (2nd ed.). Boston: Allyn & Bacon.

Alter, C. (1990). An exploratory study of conflict and coordination in interorganizational service delivery systems. *Academy of Management Journal, 33,* 478-501.

Alter, C. (1997). Family support as an intervention with female long-term AFDC recipients. In P. L. Ewalt, E. M. Freeman, S. A. Kirk, & D. L. Poole (Eds.), *Social policy: Reform, research, and practice* (pp. 217-237). Washington, DC: NASW Press.

Alter, C., & Hage, J. (1993). *Organizations working together*. Newbury Park, CA: Sage.

Austin, M. J. (1988). Managing up: Relationship building between middle management and top management. *Administration in Social Work, 12,*(4), 29-46.

Bailey, D., & Koney, K. (1995). Community-based consortia: One model for creation and development. *Journal of Community Practice, 2,* 21-41.

Bailey, D., & Koney, K. (1996, February). *From community collaboratives to public policy: Lessons from two stories in progress*. Paper presented at the Association for Community Organization and Social Administration Symposium, Council on Social Work Education, Washington, DC.

Banerjee, M. (1998). Micro-enterprise development: A response to poverty. In M. S. Sherraden & W. A. Ninacs (Eds.), *Community economic development and social work*. New York: Haworth.

Baptist, W., & Bricker-Jenkins, M. B. (1999). *"Gonna take back what he stole from me. . .": A report on the Poor People's Summit*. Philadelphia: Temple University, School of Social Administration.

Barry, P. (1989). *Rebuilding the walls: A nuts and bolts guide to the community development methods of Bethel New Life, Inc. in Chicago*. Chicago: Bethel New Life.

Bartlett, H. M. (1958, April). Toward clarification and improvement of socal work practice. *Social Work, 3,* 5-9.

Bellah, R. N., Madsen, R., Sullivan, W. M., Swidler, A., & Tipton, S. M. (1990). *Habits of the heart*. New York: Vintage.

Bellah, R. N., Madsen, R., Sullivan, W. M., Swidler, A., & Tipton, S. M. (1992). *The good society*. New York: Vintage.

Bennis, W., & Nanus, B. (1985). *Leaders: The strategies for taking charge*. New York: Harper & Row.

Betten, N., & Austin, M. J. (Eds.). (1990). *The roots of community organizing, 1917-1939*. Philadelphia: Temple University Press.

Billingsley, A., & Giovannoni, J., (1972). *Children of the storm: Black children and American child welfare.* New York: Harcourt Brace Jovanovich.

Blank, R. M. (1997). *It takes a nation: A new agenda for fighting poverty.* Princeton, NJ: Princeton University Press/Russell Sage Foundation.

Bombyck, M. (1995). Progressive social work. In R. L. Edwards (Ed.), *Encyclopedia of social work* (19th ed., pp. 1933-1942). Washington, DC: NASW Press.

Brager, G., & Holloway, S. (1978). *Changing human service organizations: Politics and practice.* New York: Free Press.

Brager, G., Specht, H., & Torczyner, J. (1987). *Community organizing* (2nd ed.). New York: Columbia University Press.

Bronfenbrenner, U. (1979). *The ecology of human development.* Cambridge, MA: Harvard University Press.

Brown, J., Finch, W. A., Northen, H., Taylor, S. H., & Weil, M. (1982). *Child, family, neighborhood: A master plan for social service delivery.* New York: Child Welfare League of America.

Burden, D., & Gottlieb, N. (Eds.). (1987). *The woman client: Social curriculum for practice with women.* London: Tavistock.

Burford, G., & Pennell, J. (1998). *Family group decision-making project: Outcome report* (Vol. 1). St. John, Newfoundland: Memorial University.

Burtless, G. (1997). Welfare recipients' job skills and employment prospects. *The Future of Children, 7*(1), 39-51.

Castelloe, P. E. (1999) *Community change and community practice: A qualitative inquiry into an organic model of community practice.* Unpublished dissertation, University of North Carolina, Chapel Hill.

Checkoway, B. (1997). Core concepts for community change. *Journal of Community Practice, 4*(1), 11-29.

Collins, A. (1980). Helping neighbors intervene in cases of maltreatment. In J. Garbarino, S. H. Stocking, & Associates (Eds.), *Protecting children from abuse and neglect.* San Francisco: Jossey-Bass.

Collins, A. H., & Pancost, D. L. (1976). *Natural helping networks.* Washington, DC: NASW Press.

Coulton, C. (1996). Effects of neighborhood on families and children: Implications for services. In A. Kahn & S. Kamerman (Eds.), *Children and their families in big cities* (pp. 87-110). New York: Columbia University, Cross-National Studies Research Program.

Cross, T. L., Bazron, B. M., Dennis, K. W., & Isaacs, M. R. (1989). *Toward a culturally competent system of care: Vol. 2. Programs which utilize culturally competent principles.* Washington, DC: Georgetown University, Child Development Center.

Delgado, M. (1996). Community asset assessments by Latino youths. In P. A. Ewalt, E. M. Freeman, & D. L. Poole (Eds.), *Community building: Renewal, well-being, and shared responsibility* (pp. 202-212). Washington, DC: NASW Press.

Dromi, P., & Weil, M. (1984, November). *Social work values: Their role in a technological age.* Paper presented at the sixth annual symposium for the Advancement of Social Work with Groups, Chicago.

Drucker, P. F. (1990). *Managing the nonprofit organization.* New York: Harper Business.

Dunst, C., Trivette, C., & Deal, A. (1988). *Enabling and empowering families: Principles and guidelines for practice.* Cambridge, MA: Brookline Books.

Dupper, D. R., & Poertner, J. (1998). Public schools and the revitalization of improverished communities: School-linked family resource centers. In P. A. Ewalt, E. M. Freeman, & D. L. Poole (Eds.), *Community building: Renewal, well-being, and shared responsibility* (pp. 306-315). Washington, DC: NASW Press.

Edwards, R. L., Yankey, J. A., & Altpeter, M. A. (Eds.). (1998). *Skills for effective management of nonprofit organizations.* Washington, DC: NASW Press.

Estes, R. J. (1993). Toward sustainable development: From theory to praxis. *Social Development Issues, 15*(3), 1-29.

Ewalt, P. L. (1998). The revitalization of impoverished communities. In P. A. Ewalt, E. M. Freeman, & D. L. Poole (Eds.), *Community building: Renewal, well-being, and shared responsibility* (pp. 3-5). Washington, DC: NASW Press.

Ewalt, P. L., Freeman, E. M., & Poole, D. L. (Eds.). (1998). *Community building: Renewal, well-being, and shared responsibility.* Washington, DC: NASW Press.

Fabricant, M., & Burghardt, S. (1992). *The welfare state crisis and the transformation of social service work.* Armonk, NY: M. E. Sharpe.

Fellin, P. (1995). Understanding American communities. In J. Rothman, J. L. Erlich, J. E. Tropman, & F. Cox (Eds.), *Strategies of community intervention macro practice* (pp. 114-128). Itasca, IL: F. E. Peacock.

Figueira-McDonough, J., Netting, F. E., and Nichols-Casebolt, A. (Eds.). (1998). *The role of gender in practice knowledge: Claiming half the human experience.* New York: Garland.

Fisher, R., & Karger, H. (1997). *Social work and community in a private world: Getting out in public.* New York: Longman.

Fitchen, J. M. (1998). Rural poverty and rural social work. In L. H. Ginsberg (Ed.), *Social work in rural communities* (3rd ed.). Alexandria, VA: Council on Social Work Education.

Flacks, D. (1995). The revolution of citizenship. In J. Rothman, J. L. Erlich, J. E. Tropman, & F. Cox (Eds.), *Strategies of community intervention macro practice* (5th ed., pp. 368-380). Itasca, IL: F. E. Peacock.

Fraser, M., & Leavitt, S. (1990). Creating social change: "Mission"-oriented research and entrepreneurship. In J. K. Whittaker, J. Kinney, E. M. Tracy, & C. Booth (Eds.), *Reaching high risk families: Intensive family preservation in human services* (pp. 165-178). New York: Aldine de Gruyter.

Fraser, M. W. (Ed.). (1997). *Risk and resilience in childhood: An ecological perspective.* Washington, DC: NASW Press.

Fraser, M. W., & Galinsky, M. J. (1997). Toward a resilience-based model of practice. In M. W. Fraser (Ed.), *Risk and resilience in childhood: An ecological perspective.* Washington, DC: NASW Press.

Freire, P. (1973a). *Education for critical consciousness.* New York: Continuum.

Freire, P. (1973b). *Pedagogy of the oppressed.* New York: Seabury.

Freire, P. (1990). A critical understanding of social work. *Journal of Progressive Human Services, 1*(1), 3-9.

Friedmann, J. (1996). *Empowerment: The politics of alternative development.* Cambridge, MA: Blackwell.

Friesen, B., & Poertner, J. (1995). *From case management to service coordination for children with emotional, behavioral, or mental disorders.* Baltimore, MD: P. H. Brookes.

Galper, J. (1980). *Social work practice: A radical perspective.* Englewood Cliffs, NJ: Prentice Hall.

Gamble, D., & Weil, M. (1995). Citizen participation. In R. L. Edwards (Ed.), *Encyclopedia of social work* (19th ed., pp. 483-494). Washington, DC: NASW Press.

Garvin, C. (1985). Work with disadvantaged and oppressed groups. In M. Sundel, P. Glasser, R. Sarri, & R. Vinter (Eds.), *Individual change through small groups* (2nd ed., pp. 461-472). New York: Free Press.

Garvin, C. (1987). *Contemporary group work* (2nd ed.). Englewood Cliffs, NJ: Prentice Hall.

Garvin, C. D., & Cox, F. M. (1995). A history of community organizing since the Civil War with special reference to oppressed communities. In J. Rothman, J. L. Erlich, & J. E. Tropman (Eds.), *Strategies of community intervention* (5th ed., pp. 64-99). Itasca, IL: F. E. Peacock.

Garvin, D. A. (1998). Building a learning organization. In *Harvard Business Review on knowledge management*

(pp. 47-80). Boston, MA: Harvard Business School Press.

Gil, D. G. (1998). *Confronting injustice and oppression: Concepts and strategies for social workers.* New York: Columbia University Press.

Goetz, K., & Peck, S. (Eds.). (1994). *The basics of family support.* Chicago: Family Resource Coalition.

Gordon, M. M. (1978). *Human nature, class, and ethicity.* New York: Oxford University Press.

Gottlieb, B. H. (Ed.). (1981). *Social networks and social support.* Beverly Hills, CA: Sage.

Gottlieb, B. H., (Ed.). (1988). *Marshaling social support: Formats, processes, and effects.* Newbury Park, CA: Sage.

Gottlieb, N. (1980). *Alternative social services for women.* New York: Columbia University Press.

Griffith, D. (1999). *The networking for humanity initiative.* Unpublished paper, University of North Carolina School of Social Work, Community Practice Course.

Gutiérrez, L. M. (1990). Working with women of color:An empowerment perspective. *Social Work, 35*(2), 149-153.

Gutiérrez, L. M., & Alvarez, A. R. (1998, March). *Educating and training students for multicultural and community practice.* Paper presented at the annual program meeting of the Council on Social Work Education, Association for Community Organization and Social Administartion Symposium, Orlando, FL.

Gutiérrez, L., Alvarez, A. R., Nemon, H., & Lewis, E. (1996). Multicultural community organizing: A strategy for change. *Social Work, 41*(5), 501-508.

Gutiérrez, L. M. & Lewis, E. A. (1994.) Community organizing with women of color: A feminist approach. *Journal of Community Practice 1*(2), 23-44.

Hardcastle, D. A., Wenocur, S., & Powers, P. R. (1997). *Community practice: Theories and skills for social workers.* New York: Oxford University Press.

Hartford, M. (1971). *Groups in social work: Applications of small group theory and research to social work practice.* New York: Columbia University Press.

Hartman, A., & Laird, J. (1983). *Family-centered social work practice.* New York: Free Press.

Hasenfeld, Y. (Ed.). (1992). *Human services as complex organizations.* Thousand Oaks, CA: Sage.

Hernandez, M., & Isaacs, M. R. (Eds.). (1998). *Promoting cultural competence in children's mental health services.* Baltimore: Paul H. Brookes.

Holland, T. P. (1995). Organizations: Context for social services delivery. In R. L. Edwards (Ed.), *Encyclopedia of* social work (19th ed., pp. 1787-1794). Washington, DC: NASW Press.

Homan, M. S. (1994). *Promoting community change: Making it happen in the real world.* Pacific Grove, CA: Brooks/Cole.

Homebuilders, Intensive Family Preservation Training. (1994, September). Held at Methodist Home for Children, Raleigh, NC.

Hyde, C. (1996). A feminist response to Rothman's "The interweaving of community intervention approaches." *Journal of Community Practice, 3*(3/4), 127-145.

Institute for Wisconsin's Future. (1999, Spring). W-2 problems reach across Wisconsin, frustration in communities is growing, *W-2 Connection, 2*(2).

Jansen, G. G., & Pippard, J. L. (1998). The Grameen Bank in Bangladesh: Helping poor women with credit for self-employment. In M. S. Sherraden & W. A. Ninacs (Eds.), *Community economic development and social work* (pp. 103-124). New York: Haworth.

Jansson, B. S. (1997). *The reluctant welfare state* (3rd ed.). Pacific Grove, CA: Brooks/Cole.

Kagan, S. L., Powell, D. R., Weissbourd, B., & Zigler, E. F. (Eds.). (1987). *America's family support programs.* New Haven, CT: Yale University Press.

Kahn, S. (1991). *Organizing: A guide for grassroots leaders.* Washington, DC: NASW Press.

Kimberly, J. R., Miles, R. H., & Associates. (1980). *The organizational life cycle.* San Francisco: Jossey-Bass.

Kramer, R., & Specht, H. (1983). *Readings in community organization practice* (3rd ed.). Englewood Cliffs, NJ: Prentice Hall.

Kretzmann, J., & McKnight, J. (1996). *Building communities from the inside out: A path toward finding and mobilizing a community's assets.* Chicago: ACTA.

Kubisch, A. C., Brown, P., Chaskin, R., Hirota, J., Joseph, M., Riochman, H., & Roberts, M. (1995). *Voices from the field: Learning from comprehensive community initiatives.* Washington, DC: Aspen Institute.

Lee, J. A. B. (1994). *The empowerment approach to social work practice.* New York: Columbia University Press.

Lee, P. (1929). Presidential address to the National Conference on Social Welfare.

Leutz, W. N. (1976). The informal community caregiver: A link between the health care system and local residents. *American Journal of Orthopsychiatry, 46,* 678-688.

Lieberman, M. A., Borman, L. D., & Associates. (1979). *Self-help groups for coping with crisis.* San Francisco: Jossey-Bass.

Locke, B., Garrison, R., & Winship, J. (1998). *Generalist social work practice: Context, story, and partnerships.* Pacific Grove, CA: Brooks/Cole.

Long, D. D., & Holle, M. C. (1997). *Macro systems in the social environment.* Itasca, IL: F. E. Peacock.

Longres, J. (1995). *Human behavior and the social environment.* Itasca, IL: F. E. Peacock.

Lum, D. (1999). *Culturally competent practice: A framework for growth and action.* Pacific Grove, CA: Brooks/Cole.

Martin, P., & O'Connor, J. (1989). *The social environment: Open systems applications.* New York: Longman.

Masi, D. A. (1981). *Organizing for women: Issues, strategies, and services.* Lexington, MA: Lexington Books/D. C. Heath.

Mauney, R., Williams, E., & Weil, M. (1993). *Beyond crisis: Developing comprehensive services for battered women in North Carolina.* Winston-Salem, NC: Z. Smith Reynolds Foundation.

McAdoo, H. P. (1988). *Black families* (2nd ed.). Newbury Park, CA: Sage.

McCroskey, J., & Meezan, W. (1998). Family-centered services: Approaches and effectiveness. *The Future of Children, 8*(1), 54-71.

McRoy, R. G., & Shorkey, C. T. (1985). Alcohol use and abuse among blacks. In E. M. Freeman (Ed.), *Social work practice with clients who have alcohol problems* (pp. 202-213). Springfield, IL: Charles C Thomas.

Melaville, A. I., & Blank, M. J. (1993). *Together we can: A guide for crafting a profamily system of education and human services.* Washington, DC: Government Printing Office.

Middleman, R. R., & Goldberg, G. (1977). *Social service delivery: A structural approach to social work practice.* New York: Columbia University Press.

Midgley, J. (1995). *Social development: The development perspective in social welfare.* Thousand Oaks, CA: Sage.

Miller, J. B. (1983). Women and power. *Social Policy, 13*(4), 3-6.

Mizrahi, T., & Rosenthal, B. R. (1993). Managing dynamic tensions in social change coalitions. In T. Mizrahi & J. D. Morrison (Eds.), *Community organization and social administration.* New York: Haworth.

Mondros, J. B., & Wilson, S. M. (1994). *Organizing for power and empowerment.* New York: Columbia University Press.

Morrison, J. D., Howard, J., Johnson, C., Navarro, F. J., Plachetka, B., & Bell, T. (1998). Strengthening neighborhoods by developing community networks. In P. A.

Ewalt, E. M. Freeman, & D. L. Poole (Eds.), *Community building: Renewal, well-being, and shared responsibility* (pp. 107-116). Washington, DC: NASW Press.

Mulroy, E. A., & Shay, S. (1998). Nonprofit organizations and innovation: A model of neighborhood-based collaboration to prevent child maltreatment. In P. A. Ewalt, E. M. Freeman, & D. L. Poole (Eds.), *Community building: Renewal, well-being, and shared responsibility* (pp. 95-106). Washington, DC: NASW Press.

Naparstek, A. J., & Dooley, D. (1998). Countering urban disinvestment through community building initiatives. In P. A. Ewalt, E. M. Freeman, & D. L. Poole (Eds.), *Community building: Renewal, well-being, and shared responsibility* (pp. 6-16). Washington, DC: NASW Press.

Netting, F. E., Ketner, P. M., & McMurtry, S. L. (1993). *Social work macro practice* (2nd ed.). New York: Longman.

The News & Observer [Raleigh, NC]. (Friday, June 18, 1999). The Methodist Home for Children: A Timeline. Available: http://www.News-Observer.com/daily/1999/06/18/Faith00_side1.html

The News & Observer [Raleigh, NC]. (Friday, June 18, 1999). The Methodist Home for Children: 100 years of Giving. Available: http://www.News-Observer.com/daily/1999/06/18Faith/00.html

Noponen, H. (1996, May 16). *A gender analysis framework for understanding women's roles in sustainable development*. Paper presented at an International Forum, Women, Community, and Sustainable Development: Collaborative Approaches to Skills, Theory, and Practice, University of North Carolina at Chapel Hill.

Overton, A., Tinker, K., & Associates. (1957). *The casework notebook*. St. Paul, MN: Community Chest and Councils, Inc.

Pecora, P., Fraser, M. W., Nelson, K.,E., McCroskey, J., & Meezan, W. (1995). *Evaluating family-based services*. New York: Aldine de Gruyter.

Pecora, P., Whittaker, J. K., & Maluccio, A. N. (1992). *The child welfare challenge: Policy, practice, and research*. New York: Aldine de Gruyter.

Pennell, J., & Burford, G. (in press). Family group decision making: Protecting children and women. *Child Welfare*.

Perlmutter, F. D. (Ed.). (1988). *Alternative social agencies: Administrative strategies*. New York: Haworth.

Perlmutter, F. D. (Ed.). (1994). *Women and social change*. Washington, DC: NASW Press.

Poole, D. L., & Van Hook, M. (1998). Retooling for community health partnerships in primary care and prevention. In P. A. Ewalt, E. M. Freeman, & D. L. Poole (Eds.), *Community building: Renewal, well-being, and shared responsibility* (pp. 407-410). Washington, DC: NASW Press.

Pumphrey, R. E. (1980). Compassion and protection: Dual motivations of social welfare. In F. R. Breul & S. J. Diner (Eds.), *Compassion and responsibility: Readings in the history of social welfare policy in the United States* (pp. 5-13). Chicago: University of Chicago Press.

Rawls, J. (1971). *A theory of justice*. Cambridge, MA: Harvard University Press.

Region A Child and Youth Planning Council. (1993). *Our children today and tomorrow: A call to action for the children of Western North Carolina*. Bryson City: Southwestern North Carolina Planning and Economic Development Commission.

Resnick, H., & Patti, R. (1980). *Change from within: Humanizing social welfare organizations*. Philadelphia: Temple University Press.

Reynolds, B. C. (1964). *An uncharted journey*. Hebron, CT: Practitioners Press.

Richman, J. M., & Bowen, G. L. (1997). School failure: An ecological-interactional-developmental perspective. In M. W. Fraser (Ed.), *Risk and resilience in childhood: An ecological perspective*. Washington, DC: NASW Press.

Romanelli, E. (1991). The evolution of new organizational forms. *Annual Review of Sociology, 17*, 79-103.

Rooney, B. J. (1998). *Reconceptualizing poverty as quality of life: Implications for theory, measurement, and intervention*. Unpublished manuscript, University of North Carolina, Chapel Hill.

Rose, S. M., & Moore, V. L. (1995). Case management. In R. L. Edwards (Ed.), *Encyclopedia of social work* (19th ed.). Washington, DC: NASW Press.

Rothman, J. (1995). Approaches to community intervention. In J. Rothman, J. L. Erlich, & J. E. Tropman (Eds.), *Strategies of community intervention* (5th ed., pp. 26-63). Itasca, IL: F. E. Peacock.

Rothman, J. (1996). The interweaving of community intervention approaches with personal preface by the author. *Journal of Community Practice, 3*(3/4), 69-99.

Rothman, J., & Thomas, E. J. (Eds.). (1994). *Intervention research: Design and development for human service*. New York: Haworth.

Rubin, H. J. (1997). Being a conscience and a carpenter: Interpretations of the community-based development model. *Journal of Community Practice, 4*(1), 57-90.

Rubin, H. J., & Rubin, I. S. (1992). *Community organizing and development* (2nd ed.). New York: Macmillan.

Saleebey, D. (Ed.). (1997). *The strengths perspective in social work practice* (2nd ed.). New York: Longman.

Schein, E. H. (1992). *Organizational culture and leadership* (2nd ed.). San Francisco: Jossey-Bass.

Schorr, L. B. (1997). *Common purpose: Strengthening families and neighborhoods to rebuild America.* New York: Anchor Books/Doubleday.

Schriver, J. M. (1987). Harry Lurie's critique: Person and environment in early casework practice. *Social Service Review, 61*(3), 523-529.

Scott, W. R. (1998). *Organizations* (4th ed.). Saddle River, NJ: Prentice Hall.

Shay, S. (1995). *Building the twenty-first century ark: The CARES model for comprehensive family support* (Final report to the National Center on Child Abuse and Neglect, Grant No. 90-CA1417). Washington, DC: Government Printing Office.

Sherraden, M. S., & Ninacs, W. A. (1998). Introduction: Community economic development and social work. In M. S. Sherraden & W. A. Ninacs (Eds.), *Community economic development and social work.* New York: Haworth.

Shiffman, R., & Motley, S. (1990). *Comprehensive and integrative planning for community development.* New York: Community Development Research Center, New School for Social Research.

Simon, B. L. (1994). *The empowerment tradition in American social work: A history.* New York: Columbia University Press.

Solomon, B. B. (1976). Community social work practice in oppressed minority communities. In S. H. Taylor & R. W. Roberts (Eds.), *Theory and practice of community social work* (pp. 217-257). New York: Columbia University Press.

Sotomayor, M. (Ed.). (1991). *Empowering Hispanic families: A critical issue for the '90's.* Milwaukee, WI: Family Service America.

Specht, H., & Courtney, M. (1994). *Unfaithful angels: How social work abandoned its mission.* New York: Free Press.

Stack, C. (1974). *All our kin: Strategies for survival in a black community.* New York: Harper & Row.

Stroul, B. (1993). *Systems of care for children and adolescents with severe emotional disturbances: What are the results?* Washington, DC: Georgetown University, Child Development Center.

Taffe, L., & Fisher, R. (1997). Public life in Gulfton: Multiple publics and models of community organization. In M. Weil (Ed.), *Community practice: Models in action* (pp. 31-56). New York: Haworth.

Tocqueville, A. de. (1956). *Democracy in America* (R. D. Heffner, Ed.). New York: Mentor. (Original work published 1835)

Toseland, R. W., & Rivas, R. F. (1998). *An introduction to group work practice* (3rd ed.). Boston: Allyn & Bacon.

Towle, C. (1953). *Common human needs.* Washington, DC: Federal Security Agency, Social Security Board.

Trivette, C., & Dunst, C. (1997). *North Carolina family resource centers evaluation: First year of implementation—What we have learned.* Raleigh: North Carolina Department of Human Resources, Division of Family Development.

Unger, D. G., & Powell, D. R. (1980). Supporting families under stress: The role of social networks. *Family Relations, 29*(4), 566-575.

Van den Berg, N., & Cooper, L. (Eds.). (1986). *Feminist visions in social work practice.* Washington, DC: NASW Press.

Varma, S. (1999). *Microenterprise programs in the United States: A literature review.* Doctoral qualifying paper, University of North Carolina at Chapel Hill, School of Social Work.

Wagner, D. (1989). Radical movements in the social services: A theoretical framework. *Social Service Review, 63*(2).

Warren, R. L. (1978). *The community in America.* Chicago: Rand McNally.

Weil, M. (1977). *Practicum in law and social work: An educational program in interprofessional collaboration.* New York: City University of New York, Graduate Center.

Weil, M. (1981). Southeast Asians and service delivery: Issues in service provision and institutional racism. In *Bridging cultures: Social work with southeast Asian refugees.* Los Angeles: Asian American Mental Health Training Center.

Weil, M. (1986). Women, community, and organizing. In N. Van Den Berg & L. Cooper (Eds.), *Feminist visions in social work practice.* Washington, DC: NASW Press.

Weil, M. (1996). Model development in community practice: An historical perspective. In *Community practice: Conceptual models* (pp. 5-67). New York: Haworth.

Weil, M., & Gamble, D. (1995). Community practice models. In R. L. Edwards (Ed.), *Encyclopedia of social work* (19th ed., pp. 577-594). Washington, DC: NASW Press.

Weil, M., Gamble, D. N., & Williams, E. S. (1998). Women, communities, and development. In J. Figueira-McDonough, F. E. Netting, & A. Nichols-Casebolt (Eds.), *The role of gender in practice knowledge: Claiming half the human experience* (pp. 241-286). New York: Garland.

Weil, M., & Hodges, V. G. (1996, February). *Planning and evaluation for family preservation and family support.* Washington, DC: ACOSA Symposium, Council on Social Work Education.

Weil, M., Hodges, V., vander Straeten, S., & Castelloe, P. (1997, October). *North Carolina's Family Preservation and Family Support Services Programs: Final evaluation report.* Chapel Hill: University of North Carolina School of Social Work

Weil, M., & Karls, J. (1985). *Case management in human service practice: A systematic approach to mobilizing resources for clients.* San Francisco: Jossey-Bass.

Weissman, H. H. (1978). *Integrating services for troubled families.* San Francisco: Jossey-Bass.

Whittaker, J. K., & Garbarino, J. (Eds.). (1983). *Social support networks: Informal helping in the human services.* New York: Aldine De Gruyter.

Whittaker, J. K., Kinney, J., Tracy, E. M., & Booth, C. (1990). *Reaching high-risk families: Intensive family preservation in human services.* New York: Aldine De Gruyter.

Wilder Research Center, Amherst H. Wilder Foundation. (1992). *Collaboration: What makes it work—a review of research literature on factors influencing successful collaboration.* St. Paul, MN: Author.

Williams, E. S., Weil, M. O., Zipper, I. N., & Hays, C. (1995). Module XIV: Supervision and cross-system management. In I. N. Zipper & M. O. Weil (Eds.), *Case management for children's mental health: A curriculum for child serving agencies.* Raleigh: North Carolina Division of Mental Health, Developmental Disabilities and Substance Abuse Services.

Wilson, W. J. (1987). *The truly disadvantaged: The inner city, the underclass, and public policy.* Chicago: University of Chicago Press.

Withorn, A. (1984). *Serving the people: Social services and social change.* New York: Columbia University Press.

Wood, G. G., & Middleman, R. R. (1989). *The structural approach to direct practice in social work.* New York: Columbia University Press.

Wrong, D. H. (1979). *Power: Its forms, bases, and uses.* New York: Harper Colophon Books.

Zipper, I. N., Rounds, K. A., & Weil, M. O. (1993). *Service coordination for early intervention programs: Parents and professionals.* Cambridge MA: Brookline Books.

Zipper, I. N., & Weil, M. O. (1995). *Case management for children's mental health: A curriculum for child serving agencies.* Raleigh: North Carolina Division of Mental Health, Developmental Disabilities and Substance Abuse Services.

PART IV

Fields of Practice

The previous section attested to the divergence in theories, methods, and models of practice with reference to different kinds of behavior and different sizes of client systems. Some types of practice objectives also require such variance, and we singled out crisis situations and prevention.

In this section, we stress practice variations that are required for practice in different fields. We see *fields* as created by the social welfare system with reference to different types of social problems. Social problems are created by a lack of fit between human needs and the environmental resources to meet these needs. The social, structural, and historical conditions that create such problems vary, and consequently,

the solutions are likely to vary. We have, therefore, commissioned chapters that correspond to our typology of such conditions and related problems and that prescribe practice models for their amelioration. The specified problems are as follows:

1. Problems in the fit between the ways people accomplish developmental tasks and the resources required for this accomplishment

In Chapter 19, Freeman discusses this topic in terms of promoting healthy development across the life span, in such settings as schools, family service agencies, and health care settings. For example, the school is the strategic institution in the lives of children—it is located at the intersection of home and community. Freeman also makes a strong case for the use of developmentally sensitive practice approaches. This life-span perspective holds special relevance for other client populations, for example, children, families, and the elderly. The coordination of services across systems for the purpose of mutual planning is fundamental to a life-span perspective and essential in our efforts to increase effectiveness. The coordination of in-school services, with services provided by health, mental health, and other service systems is essential in addressing, for example, the child's total needs. Negotiating complicated organizational boundaries will become even more significant in the future in the provision of services to the elderly. It will also affect some families as they develop and grow dynamically over time. A strengths and ecological perspective, and such theories as empowerment, family network, and organizational and community development theories, are explored in this chapter, all within a multicultural context.

2. Problems in the fit between the needs of people to function in mentally or physically healthy ways and the resources required for this healthy functioning

According to Snowden in Chapter 20, a new world of practice will evolve in the next century—one that integrates physical health with mental health and that takes into consideration demographic shifts and the managed care environment. Evidence for this prediction becomes pronounced if one merely examines what has occurred in these areas in the last two decades of the 20th century. Such terms as *co-morbidity, cultural competence,* and *capitation* have crept into our vocabulary. There is increasing violence in our society across socioeconomic class, ethnicity/race, and age groups. Downsizing of health and mental health systems is occurring. Social workers are the largest providers of mental health services in the United States. The questions that arise include: Are social workers prepared in terms of knowledge and skills to function in this new environment? Do they have the ability to coordinate tasks/activities/functions across complicated arrangements of "human services?" Do they have sufficient knowledge of co-occurring disorders? How will social workers advocate for their clients in a managed care environment that is more concerned with the reduction of cost, in some instances, than with the client's self-determination or need for assistance beyond a time-limited intervention? What new knowledge will be needed as the United States continues to diversify? New immigrant groups will challenge yesterday's notion of what is a culturally competent practitioner. What practice/program evaluation designs will be needed to demonstrate social workers' contributions to this area of practice?

3. Problems in the fit between the needs of people to act in prosocial ways and the resources required for prosocial (as compared to deviant) adaptation

Criminal behavior, and in particular, violent behavior, is on the rise in the United States. As Sarri points out in Chapter 21, arrest rates vary among people of color, social classes, and gender. In other words, this system is not blind to race, gender, and social class. During the past two decades, our society has been more concerned with building prisons than its human infrastructure. To prevent the isolation of criminal behaviors among our youth and adults, we will be called on to invest more time and dollars in the provision of preventive and rehabilitative services and in those critical institutions that support healthy development, for example, the family, community, and schools. Overreliance on laws and punitive approaches/programs/policies must be replaced with attention to poverty, racism, sexism, ageism, unemployment, the availability of guns, and social alienation and isolation. As Sarri suggests, social workers have important roles to play to influence the current state of affairs; in the past, their involvement has been too limited. It is indeed timely for us to marshal our professional knowledge and apply it to the field of criminal justice.

4. Problems in the fit between the way people seek to meet their needs for intimacy and the supportive responses of the environment to alternative ways of meeting these needs

In Chapter 22, Longres and Fredriksen consider this topic as they examine social work practice with lesbians and gay men.

They call our attention to the fact that during the 20th century, these groups were viewed as a deviant subculture in America, and in the next century, they will be viewed as a mainstream group in a multicultural society. The pathological perspective that dominated our view of these groups and the related professional literature that depicted them as deviants will be replaced by a focus on normalcy. The authors trace the origin of sexual orientation and coming out by examining biological, psychological, and sociological factors, research, and theories. They discuss practice implications across a life-span perspective (e.g., from adolescent to elderly gay men and lesbians). They conclude the chapter with a litany of concerns and issues that holds importance for the development of a greater understanding of same-sex attraction, that calls our attention to the need for empirically validated theory, and that recommends a more proactive stance on the part of the social work profession.

5. Problems in the fit between the ways people seek to earn a livelihood and the environmental opportunities and supports for such employment

In Chapter 23, Akabas describes the challenges and opportunities social workers will face in the world of work. She takes the view that social work must adopt a fresh look at its practice and actions if it is to have a meaningful role in the next century in the field of practice. In her chapter, she accentuates the fact that ethnic, racial, and gender discrimination will continue to exist in the next century and that it is the profession's responsibility to promote employment opportunity and economic justice for all. We must challenge the dominant economic system that has left so many behind in the 20th century. She takes the position that a combination of economic development and community organizing will be required to empower the most vulnerable members of our society.

6. Problems in the fit between the needs of people for sufficient income to survive and to maintain their quality of life and the adequacy of programs to provide sufficient resources

From the early beginning of the profession, social workers have been involved in working with the poor. As the economic structure of the country continues to change in drastic ways, fueled by a growing global economy and technological advancements, there will be increasing demand for a highly skilled and knowledgeable labor force. Groups that were vulnerable—for example, the less educated, those who suffer from chronic illness and health problems, those who are welfare dependent, single-parent households, some ethnic and racial minorities, and the aged—will find themselves even more at-risk in terms of their economic status. During the last half of the 20th century, much was written about the feminization of poverty and the long-term consequences on children born into poverty, the growing number of homeless indi-

viduals in America, and the fact that a disproportionate number of ethnic and racial minorities lived in poverty. In Chapter 24, Segal and Stromwall address the issue of poverty in America, current and futuristic practice strategies, and broad-based interventions that social workers should embrace, given current and future trends. Illustrative examples include employment training for vulnerable groups, the adoption of a strengths perspective, advocacy strategies that challenge discriminatory practices, and investment asset-based approaches. The editors of this book believe that macro practice and the economic empowerment of communities and vulnerable groups will take on more significance in the decades to come. The question is: Are schools of social work prepared to offer cutting-edge curriculum to promote this macro agenda?

Although the traditional fields of practice will continue to endure, with perhaps some modifications as a consequence of service integration and reorganization, new areas and populations will evolve, offering opportunities to expand the profession. This section of the book explores fields of practice, such as mental health, social work services in schools, health, social work in the workplace and correctional settings, gay and lesbian clients, and poverty and homelessness. A cross-cutting theme is the adoption of a life-span perspective. There are numerous other fields of service and client populations the authors could have examined—far too many to discuss within this book.

CHAPTER NINETEEN

Direct Practice in Fields Related to Developmental Tasks: A Life-Span Perspective

EDITH M. FREEMAN

Although social workers and other helping professionals in all practice fields should consider the impact of life-span issues on clients' situations (Berger, McBreen, & Rifkin, 1996), certain practice fields and settings *require* the use of developmentally sensitive practice approaches. These approaches are defined as client-involved, accessible services that include a normative focus on clients' developmental strengths and needs across the life span (Franklin & Allen-Meares, 1997; Freeman, 1987). School social work, family service agencies, and health care settings are areas in which such services should be provided to individuals at particular points in the life span: to children and youths, families, and the elderly (Beaver & Miller, 1992; Freeman, 1995; Hartman, 1995).

To increase effectiveness, workers in these settings often collaborate with those in other organizations in a mutual planning and coordination process for improving delivery of their developmentally sensitive services. Coordination is obviously beneficial to clients, but it adds complexity to an already complicated service delivery process. For example, effective life-span services for the elderly involve coordination among hospitals, home health care agencies, age-specific supported housing, adult day care organizations, health promotion or wellness programs, community service programs that use the expertise of the elderly (as mentors or consultants), adult protective services, long-term care agencies, and Elderhostel and other educational, leisure time, and recreation programs for the elderly (Bellos & Ruffolo, 1995; Bumagin & Hirn, 1990; Cox & Parsons, 1994; Steinberg & Carter, 1983). To add to this complexity, there is a current movement away from simple informal coordination of such services toward more integrated service models. For children and youths, these models formally link mental health, child welfare, education, and health care services (Franklin & Allen-Meares, 1997).

This chapter presents an overview of the life-span perspective, using certain practice fields as exemplars for illustrating the perspective's value and theoretical underpinnings. That discussion clarifies the importance of linking direct practice and policy issues when using such a perspective to address social justice issues. Practice roles and practice principles related to integrated service models are emphasized, along with methods for engaging in empirically based practice from a life-span perspective. Future trends and issues that are emerging in practice fields directly related to developmental tasks are identified.

VALUE AND THEORETICAL ISSUES IN THE LIFE-SPAN PERSPECTIVE: IMPLICATIONS FOR FIELDS OF PRACTICE

Overview and Definition of This Perspective

The life-span perspective is defined as a framework for understanding life changes and processes. It assumes that life is a series of transitions, events, and processes that occur at any point in human existence. This series of changes does not follow a predictable sequence because unexpected disruptions and disorders are common occurrences throughout the life course, as are examples of people's resiliency and strength (Berger et al., 1996). The life-span perspective incorporates but goes beyond life-cycle models and stage theories, such as developmental theory. Germain (1994) emphasizes that such theories and models "contain underlying assumptions about what constitutes normative behavior and do not take into account cultural and historic contexts, variations in sexual orientations, and the influence of poverty and oppression" (p. 259).

Human life, from a life-span perspective, is seen as a moving spiral with infinite twists and turns, rather than a straight linear path from birth, to old age, to death (Germain, 1994). An underlying assumption of this perspective is that all open systems share a common characteristic, that they exhibit unique aspects of growth and change throughout the life span while, nevertheless, continuously interacting and mutually influencing one another. Berger et al. (1996) point out that these interdependent yet unique patterns are observable across the life course at various levels, from individuals, families, small groups, organizations, and communities to large systems. In addition to its compatibility with this multisystems focus, the life-span perspective is consistent with a range of human behavior theories and social work values.

Value and Philosophical Issues

Social work values are implicit in the life-span perspective across the various practice fields in which it is applied. Although a number of values are involved, this discussion is limited to examples of values that address cutting edge issues in direct practice. The following values are discussed: being inclusive, viewing clients as experts, normalizing behavior, supporting strengths and resiliency, and providing client-centered accessible services.

The value of inclusion. This value is extremely important in practice with groups, such as children and youths, who typically have little power and for whom services may be mandated. Life-span, integrated services models involve a restructuring of services to eliminate fragmentation and to increase the client- and family-centeredness of those services. Therefore, for school-linked integrated services, Aguirre (1995) recommends that children and youths, family members, and community residents be included in policy decisions and in the daily implementation of those service. They might serve liaison functions, become advisory board members, or assume roles on governance or evaluation committees. Inclusion within these models covers a broad range, from simple location of services in the same place and informal input from constituents to jointly developed and fully collaborative services in which children and youths, families, and community members are included as formal partners (Briar-Lawson, Lawson, Collier, & Joseph, 1997). The value of inclusion also encourages partial to full integration of special education students into regular classes and social programs as much as possible (Freeman, 1998).

Clients as experts in the school social work field. In integrated services models involving formal partnerships with constituents, clients are viewed as experts. Formal mechanisms should draw on the specialized knowledge that youths in public schools possess, for example, about their needs, peer support networks, assets mapping, their process of "getting better" related to problem resolution, and barriers and supports in those settings (Carley, 1997; Delgado, 1996). Carley's process of videotaping at-risk youths' stories about getting better documented the importance of feedback to school staff who had not previously understood their facilitative roles in this process or acknowledged students' progress. Freeman and Pennekamp (1988) have identified some complementary roles for school social workers and other school and community staff that support the value of clients as experts. These roles include facilitating youths' skill development in leadership, communication, conflict mediation, time management, problem solving, and academic areas.

Normalizing behavior in the field of family services. Philosophically, a life-span perspective is not consistent with current social program reforms, such as welfare-to-work and managed care in child welfare, mental health, and health care. These reforms tend to blame and pathologize individuals in certain life circumstances (e.g., those who are living in poverty) or people at particular points in their life spans (e.g., families with young children) (Freeman, 1996). In contrast, staff of family service agencies can use the life-span perspective to provide a normative framework for their practice. This framework can help social workers understand the universal but seemingly conflicting needs that develop among family members over the life course.

For instance, it is not uncommon for teenagers to seek decision-making power by breaking their curfew and other family rules that they may not have challenged previously. The normalization value helps social workers maintain appropriate objectivity by pointing out how family members often have parallel but different realities. The parents need to understand how their teenagers' response is a normal reaction to the developmental task of separation from the family at this point in the life span. Helping them understand that most parents struggle when they are confronted with the need to renegotiate various rules with their teenagers normalizes this somewhat typical parental response.

Similarly, teenagers need to understand that their desire for more freedom and power in some areas is normal at this point in their life course. It is useful to clarify how a parental tendency to become inflexible rather than more flexible about the rules often comes from a desire to be an effective parent. Youths also need help in developing more appropriate ways of initiating and maintaining change within the family. This internal conflict-resolution process reflects a parallel application of the normalization value across generational boundaries.

Supporting client resiliency in the aging and health practice fields. The life-span perspective encourages practitioners and policymakers to explore how people's unique resiliency and strength allow them to successfully address their needs and overcome problems. Thus, social workers in health care and related agencies that serve the elderly and other clients with chronic illnesses use the life-review process as a strengths-based intervention. This process implicitly supports the value of the uniqueness of the individual by helping clients to discover resiliency that has helped them to cope with cer-

tain adverse transitions such as aging or a diagnosis of AIDS (Borden, 1989, 1992).

For instance, a recently widowed client provided a home health care social worker an opportunity to build on the client's resiliency. This elderly widow was struggling with how to cope with her husband's death and told a story that she interpreted as evidence of a lifelong dependency problem. In listening to her story, the social worker was able to validate the woman's current pain and struggles. But the worker also raised the question of how the client had managed to care for her bedridden spouse and run a household successfully across many life transitions. This coping question (Freedman & Combs, 1996) highlighted the client's resiliency and helped the client reinterpret the narrative's meaning from a problem-saturated to a solution-focused context.

Making client-centered services accessible in the aging field. Finally, the value of increasing service accessibility builds on and is related to the other three values that have been discussed. Providing nutrition, recreation, medical care, legal, and social services, such as life-review groups, in supported housing sites for the elderly is an example of increasing service accessibility. However, the simple location of services at housing sites is not sufficient. Service accessibility implies the following additional value assumptions related to the life-span perspective. It is important to provide developmentally sensitive services (a) at key points in the life span; (b) in an organized, comprehensive, and integrated service delivery model; (c) in sites that are physically and psychologically accessible to the target group; and (d) in sites that are nonstigmatizing to consumers. In the field of aging, this last value assumption could result in pre-retirement as well as health promotion services being provided in work settings. As another application of this value, HIV/AIDS prevention could be provided as part of in-home health care services for older adults, or it could be integrated into Twelve-Step groups for elderly recovering people.

Life-Span Theories

Values discussed in the previous section are often an explicit aspect of life-span theories. Berger et al. (1996) believe practitioners should be knowledgeable about how such theories explain human behavior from a life-span perspective. Those authors include four theories of human behavior: biological, psychological, social-structural, and cultural. Biological theories, which will not be discussed here, focus on genetics and the impact of that area on mental and behavioral disorders, basic human characteristics, human development, gender, sexual orientation, racial characteristics, and intelligence (Jones, 1993). Psychological theories of personality, also not addressed in this discussion, focus on people's perceptions, cognition, and emotional growth and development (Berger et al., 1996). Social-structural theories focus on social structure and organization, whereas cultural theories explore people's acquired knowledge, traditions, and negotiated meanings (Brunner, 1986; Spradley, 1994). Because the latter two groups of theories are often omitted from discussions on life-span issues, they are summarized in this section.

Social-Structural Theories

Life-span development and narrative theories. Social-structural theories include life-span development, narrative, empowerment, family network, organizational, and community development theories, as well as the strengths and ecological perspectives. Life-span development theory implies that each individual is born with a unique genetic makeup that is expressed in his or her behavior. Genetic-based behavior is shaped and influenced, in turn, by social-cultural factors in the immediate environment or family and in the larger environment (Berger et al., 1996). Moreover, the interplay of historical factors, such as family relocations and deaths, with these social-cultural factors is called the *life course.* Certain life events occur across the life course in predictable ways, although the timing, meaning, and patterns of coping with those events are often unique to the individual.

Narrative theory suggests that the meaning of those events is interwoven into life narratives that people tell themselves about pivotal periods in their life span (Borden, 1992; Carley, 1997). Saleebey (1994) indicates that such stories may center around people's narrative adversities (e.g., environmental injustices and barriers) or narrative resources (e.g., successes in overcoming adverse situations). It is understood that narratives about previous points and transitions across the life course may influence current narratives, along with people's ongoing life narratives. Targeting services for meaningful points in people's life spans, such as movement from middle to high school or movement from independent living to a long-term care facility, provides opportunities for social workers to help clients to heal themselves and re-narrate or revise their life narratives. Clients can be helped to anticipate future life-course transitions and to speculate about how those transitions might influence their coping and life narratives about those events (Borden, 1992).

The strengths and ecological perspectives. The strengths perspective highlights people's individual strengths and environmental resources as well as problems and barriers that confront them in those multilevel environments. It is assumed that the dynamic balance between those ecological factors shifts at particular points over the life span (Beckett & Coley, 1987; Freeman & O'Dell, 1997; Saleebey, 1996). Strengths-based case-management approaches focus on the person-in-environment. Hence, these approaches help clients to change environmental resource deficits or barriers to their effective coping with life transitions. Teenage pregnancy, parental divorce, and chronic illness are examples of unexpected developmental crises/transitions that shift the balance between individuals' resources and needs. Workers can use case-management approaches to provide the necessary coaching and social support interventions for improving the match between new or changing needs and resources, both in the individual and in the environment (Germain & Gitterman, 1996).

Empowerment theory. Empowerment theory is relevant to a life-span perspective because it links knowledge with power. Knowledge about the institutional roots of people's problems and about their common struggles to overcome those problems is assumed to be a positive source of power (Freire, 1989; Gutiérrez & Ortega, 1991). At the same time, skill development related to changing large systems and policy or engaging in political action to negotiate additional power is an implicit principle of this theory (Gutiérrez, 1990; Solomon, 1987). Life-span psychoeducational approaches teach people why such power transfers are critical during life transitions. They also clarify the negative effects of disempowerment experiences during those events. These approaches help clients to educate themselves about how environmental factors can support oppression, while hindering their efforts to address certain developmental tasks necessary for their continued growth (Cox & Parsons, 1994; Freeman, 1993).

Family network theory. This theory focuses on network traditions and rituals that help members to bond and provide social supports to one another, particularly during life-span and cultural transitions (Beckett & Johnson, 1995; Hartman, 1995). During those transitions, prevention and problem resolution are assumed to occur through the members' natural process of mobilizing themselves and marshaling or pooling their resources. Although nuclear and extended family members typically make up the network, this theory highlights the importance of internal definitions of the family network, which may include nonrelated individuals and social units.

In the child welfare field, a family decision-making model helps members use their family network to address family crises that could typically lead to out-of-home placements. By drawing on a broader set of problem-solving and placement resources beyond the immediate family, the child welfare system attempts to build on families' resources and strengths. Another goal is to prevent institutionalization of children and further family disruption. This model has been especially important in addressing the needs of families of color, single-parent families, and poor families. Those families are overrepresented in traditional out-of-home placements, which tend to disrupt the family network, its natural helping traditions, and its resilience (Everett, 1995; Tatara, 1993).

Organizational and community development theories. Organizational theories assume that organizations may embody the same norms and rules about power and status that are reflected in larger society. They also involve social structures and processes that are unique to each organization's culture. Although organizational goals may emphasize meeting the needs of certain populations at particular points in the life span, goal displacement can often occur. Goal displacement may lead to a de-emphasis on clients' life-span needs and strengths. In the school social work field, for instance, practitioners are often faced with demands from school personnel to help students become more compliant in ways that may limit their growth and individual learning styles. Therefore, during the transition from home to elementary school, the goal of meeting children where they are and creating a supportive learning environment may be displaced by the system's need for early uniformity and compliance.

Community development theory focuses on ways residents can address environmental barriers to their community's growth and autonomy, as well as ways they can build or enhance their collective capacities. The theory and methods are "designed to create social environments that support social justice through influencing policies, developing programs, or governing locally" (Gutiérrez, Alvarez, Nemon, & Lewis, 1996, p. 502). Social justice is achieved by encouraging the members to acknowledge environmental influences on their problems and to change relevant systems through economic, political, and social development strategies (Harrison, 1995).

A community's successful use of these strategies can be affected by differences in the members' priorities. Priorities can vary across the life span and according to other circumstances, reflecting the range of conflicting needs and issues that often coexist within communities. In one example, a family resource center in a multicultural community used assets mapping to document the needs of community members who were at different points of the life span. Many of the community's families with young children and adolescents were concerned about recreation, education, and substance abuse issues, whereas aging community members cited issues such as transportation and safety related to grocery shopping and church attendance. These generational differences also influenced their ideas about current personal-collective power for resolving the identified issues and the amount of individual versus environmental blame they attributed to the community's lack of growth.

Cultural Theories

Theories of cultural pluralism or multiculturalism. Cultural theories are the means by which practitioners enter and view the cultural worlds of their clients. Theories of social construction and postmodernism assume that there are multiple realities rather than the single reality projected by the dominant discourse (Berger & Kelly, 1995; White & Epston, 1990). These theories explain how the dominant discourse ignores and marginalizes the voices and expert local knowledge of oppressed groups. Theories of cultural pluralism provide the means for practitioners to understand clients' cultural interpretations of their reality and beliefs. Those meanings and beliefs are assumed to be reflected in clients' narratives about important life-span events such as a family's loss of a young child or its forced immigration to a new country and culture. Saleebey (1994) notes that clients' cultural stories may contain important clues about their solutions and their strengths. Such stories may instruct them on how to survive, accept, or overcome difficult life events, while remaining centered culturally.

Theories of oppression and cultural maintenance. Other cultural theories illustrate how people's stories may reveal the culturally biased environmental barriers to their growth that are frequently embedded in large institutions. Theories of oppression and institutionalized racism explain the impact of external factors on cultural groups' growth opportunities and on their coping patterns. Scholars have applied this concept of oppressed cultural groups to people of color, as well as more broadly to include groups that are different in terms of age, religion, gender, sexual orientation, disabling conditions, and location (Beaver & Miller, 1992; Berger & Kelly, 1995; Delgado, 1996; Freeman & McRoy, 1986; Gutiérrez, 1990; Hunter & Schaecher, 1987). In contrast, theories of biculturality and cultural maintenance help to identify cultural resources and other strengths in people's narratives about important life events (Freeman, 1991). Such narratives and other accounts may reflect cultural norms and traditions that strengthen their ability to manage conflicting expectations in dominant society versus their cultural group. Managing such conflicting expectations makes it possible for them to maintain their cultural traditions and values (Freeman, 1991).

Social workers can solicit narratives about previous life transitions that clarify the sources of people's current cultural patterns and resiliency. A family service practitioner may have difficulty helping a Native American family to grieve the loss of a child without understanding the family's cultural rituals about loss. The practitioner should understand the impact of culturally insensitive health care staff and policies on the family's coping with this life transition. Examples of insensitive policies include ignoring cultural norms about what medical information should be shared with families and how it should be shared and about restricting the number of relatives allowed in intensive care to two individuals at a time. To influence the latter policy, the social worker should be aware of the family's cultural pattern of having a large number of tribal members present in those circumstances and at other rituals. However, awareness of within-group cultural differences that can affect the situation is equally important. Such differences may be related to family, generational, tribal, or geographic cultural norms about loss and other life-span issues.

Summary of Life-Span Theories and Values Related to Diversity

This discussion of values, along with cultural and social-structural theories, indicates that simply addressing life-course issues at the individual or family level is insufficient in terms of environmental and social justice issues. To do so fails to address what Gutiérrez (1990) indicates are often the institutional roots of culturally diverse individuals' and families' problems. The life-span framework requires, therefore, that practitioners and policy makers examine social-structural factors that may delimit oppressed clients' individual and social identities, values, goals, and behaviors and help resolve those barriers at various points in clients' life spans. The oppression may stem from differences in race or ethnicity, religion, sexual orientation, gender, disabling conditions, age, socioeconomic status, and/or location.

Hence, the framework encourages linkage between direct practice, policy development, and reforms by social workers in practice fields related to developmental and life-span issues. For effective practice, health care practitioners should, for example, help aging clients manage chronic illnesses by increasing their coping skills. However, they also should help address institutional barriers such as Medicaid regulations and family leave policy related to caretakers that may be affecting their clients' situations.

PRACTICE ROLES AND PRACTICE PRINCIPLES

An Organizational Study: Hilton High School

Institutional barriers such as those in the health care example above are the focus of the organizational study discussed in this section. This organizational study demonstrates how practitioners can operationalize the life-span perspective and its underlying theories and values. The study clarifies, for instance, appropriate practice roles and principles for helping clients to identify and address social justice issues that are affecting their problem situations and strengths. Struggles to address those issues often occur in practice settings and other organizations in which cultural diversity may not be valued and organizational policies and other barriers to consumers' growth are not acknowledged by decision makers.

This organizational study begins with a practitioner's observations of 16-year-old Allan in a public school setting. However, the practitioner's focus gradually expands to include the system itself. Allan is a white student who lives with his 17-year-old sister, 20-year-old brother, and their parents. The family is from a working-class background. Allan often compares their lifestyle and resources unfavorably with those of other, more affluent families in his community and school. Allan attends Hilton, a suburban high school where Ed Weisner, the school social worker, observed him informally for several weeks while Allan was experiencing a number of difficulties.

The first situation involved a verbal conflict between Allan and other students when he tried to place an announcement about an organizational meeting for gay and lesbian students on a student bulletin board. Ed prevented a fight from developing after one student said Allan could not place a notice about a "fag" meeting on the board. Allan was later told by the school principal that he could not start a new organization without obtaining a faculty sponsor. A second incident involved a meeting with student leaders who were reviewing nominations for student elections. Allan's petition to nominate himself for one of the positions was thrown out. Although the petition had the minimum number of signatures, it did not meet other school requirements. In both situations, Ed encouraged Allan to stop by his office to discuss his concerns. In a third situation, Ed and the school counselor presented a session on HIV/AIDS education in several Family Life Education classes. During the sessions in Allan's class, Ed noticed that Allan participated actively in the discussion but raised questions about whether the school was sincerely interested in the topic.

A few days later, Allan asked to talk with Ed. During this session, Allan indicated that gay and lesbian students were being discriminated against in the school. When Allan asked for permission to start a gay/lesbian newsletter, the principal told him he should use the existing student newspaper, like other students. When Allan tried to secure a faculty sponsor for the gay/lesbian organization he wanted to start, none of the faculty he asked would agree to sponsor the organization. Allan wanted to develop a support system for those students because he had been unable to get nominated for a student office to represent their interests. He believed that most of the school officers were from more affluent families and that students from poor families were subtly discouraged from running for office.

Allan thought that, unlike him, other gay and lesbian students were uncomfortable about exploring and addressing their sexual orientation within the school. Therefore, Allan wanted to become a more effective activist, but he acknowledged he had been working alone in his efforts. He agreed to meet with Ed for three to four sessions focused on the following goals and interventions:

1. Identify potential individuals and groups with which Allan could align himself to enhance his support within his family and the school-community, including resources within Hilton's new Integrated Services Project (intervention: mutually developed ecomaps of those systems)

2. Identify school barriers to validate his frustrations in trying to increase his involvement and find ways to overcome those barriers (interventions: analysis of the ecomaps, power analyses of relationships between key actors in the school, clarification of relevant formal/informal school policies, and changing adverse policies and other barriers)

3. Advocate for a peer-support group for gay and lesbian students (intervention: psychoeducation

about the political action process, sexual identity development, the effects of oppression, and related skills)

4. Identify and recruit a faculty sponsor and other supporters for this group and for a newsletter for gay/lesbian students (intervention: psychoeducation on communication skills, involving coaching and role-playing exercises, and on training to increase tolerance of diversity and collaboration at multisystems levels)

Organizational Analysis: Practice Roles and Other Issues

Practice roles. A number of the practice roles illustrated in the above organizational study are shown in Table 19.1, although this list is not exhaustive. For example, Ed, the social worker, helped Allan to educate himself about sexual orientation issues/development, oppression related to this area, and systems impact skills. In a parallel fashion, Ed provided Allan with opportunities to educate him about the school's informal policies on the inclusion and exclusion of students, while coaching him through "real life" situations in which Allan applied his new systems impact (political action) skills. For example, Allan and a coalition of students were able to get the policy on nominations for student offices revised so that it was easier for students who did not represent a formal institutionalized group to get nominated.

Ed also facilitated Allan's analysis of power differentials between students and school staff and between heterosexual and gay/lesbian students by constructing and analyzing an ecomap. This mutual mapping process, which was designed to identify organizational supports and other resources in Allan's school/community environment, required Ed to assume a broker/linker role in connecting Allan to resources

TABLE 19.1   Practice Roles: Life-Span Development Perspective

Example of role	Focus of roles
Educator/learner	Mutual psychoeducation: (knowledge and application)
	Life-span development issues, transitions, and tasks
	Skill development and capacity building (e.g., communication)
	Policy analysis (regarding inclusion, leadership development, mutual help)
	Sources of power and leadership
Coach	Articulation of clients' strengths and areas of expertise
	Use of real life experience
	Opportunities to apply skills
Facilitator/mediator	Mutual mapping and identification of resources
	Power analysis
	Negotiation of group process: peer networks, family units, large systems
Broker/linker	Development of and access to social support and other resources (informal and formal)
	Coalition building/partnering
Advocate	Negotiation of power-sharing opportunities
	Engagement in political/social action
	Work to affect and reform policies
	Dissemination of developmental data
Consultant	Provision of technical assistance
	Documentation of systems changes (consumer involvement, cultural sensitivity of the system, feedback loop)

such as other gay and lesbian students. That role was useful also in helping Allan to connect with and use other services provided through Hilton's newly developing, integrated school-linked services project. For instance, that project included a mentoring program that paired Allan with a journalist role model from the local newspaper.

Ed served as an advocate for Allan and other gay/lesbian students during their collaborative efforts to establish a special interest newsletter and identify a faculty sponsor for their peer-support group. The counselor who presented the HIV/AIDS Education sessions with Ed was enlisted to become the support group's faculty sponsor. Although their efforts to start a newsletter were not successful, those efforts allowed Allan and the other students to apply their systems change skills and to analyze what they had learned from this process. Finally, Ed was the support group's consultant on an as-needed basis when the brief individual work with Allan ended.

As shown in Table 19.1, this organizational study illustrates the dynamic interplay between the various life-span roles for practitioners and how each role can reinforce the others. Ed assumed all of the roles included in Table 19.1. However, he could have expanded some of those roles even more. For instance, Ed could have used psychoeducation, as needed, to help Allan's family learn about the sexual orientation issues with which he was struggling. This role could have improved family members' support of Allan and addressed other individual and unit issues that confronted them. Ed might have used brokering to help Allan identify and use community resources, such as a support group for gay and lesbian youths. These non-school based groups often have more flexibility and tolerance for helping to decrease the risk of problems such as suicide and substance abuse among youths. Such groups support positive coping and self-esteem, as well as political action for changing environmental barriers (Hunter & Schaecher, 1987)

Although Ed helped the students successfully negotiate with school officials to initiate a student-staff cultural diversity training program, additional efforts were needed to institutionalize the program. Ed should have used advocacy and consultation roles with Hilton's Integrated Services Coordinating Committee to point out this gap in the project's services and administration. None of the existing services were focused on identifying and serving at-risk, sexually different students or on establishing a system wide cultural diversity psychoeducation process. Moreover, students had not been included on the project's advisory board and coordinating committee or in other aspects of its administrative-operational structure. These gaps limited the client-centered nature of the services, as well as opportunities for student capacity-building and empowerment and systems change possibilities.

Life-span, value, and theoretical issues. In addition to these systems change mistakes and successes, Ed used social supports to help Allan address life-span issues such as identity development and friendship. Adolescent identity issues such as Allan's are related to all youths' ethnicity, self-image, and gender, as well as their sexual orientation (Freeman & McRoy, 1986). Allan attempted to develop a positive self-image and attitude about his sexual orientation, while also trying to make his school environment more inclusive for him and other gay and lesbian students. However, school policies hindered Allan's positive identity-development process and made it difficult for him to address the friendship task in terms of creating a positive peer network. Organizational policies that exclude gay and lesbian youths like Allan, even unintentionally, make those students invisible and essentially marginalize them and their special life-span needs (Hunter & Schaecher, 1987).

Several of the values discussed in the section on life-span values and theories are implicit in the collaborative work that Ed engaged in with Allan. Ed operationalized the value of clients as experts in a number of important ways. He encouraged Allan to identify issues of concern to him, then validated those concerns and Allan's previous efforts to address them. Ed acknowledged Allen's expertise about supports and barriers for his goals within the school, and most important, he agreed, although somewhat reluctantly, with Allan's decision that the support group should be facilitated by peers rather than by Ed. This work reflected the value of inclusion, encouraging Allan to influence policies that limited his participation and that of other gay and lesbian youths in the life of the school. The work also supported Allan's strengths and resilience, another important value, as he per-

TABLE 19.2   Guiding Principles Relevant to a Life-Span Perspective and Empirically Based Practice

1. Mutual exploration of clients' current developmental transitions and tasks within a culturally meaningful context (at the individual, family, group, organization, community, or large system level)

2. Emphasis on clients' strengths and past successes in addressing developmental transitions and tasks

3. Collaborative analysis of environmental supports and barriers, including sources of empowerment and disempowerment

4. Normalization of clients' situations by helping them to understand the uniqueness and universality of their concerns, needs, and problems

5. Externalization and deconstruction of clients' problems to generate alternative solutions for individual, interpersonal, and systems changes

6. Elicitation of narratives and stories about clients' developmental transitions and tasks to reflect the cultural meanings of those transitions to clients

7. Power sharing and knowledge building through the use of mutual assessment and mapping tools

8. Use of social support networks as rich sources of natural helping, coalition building, and role modeling for the management of life-span transitions

9. Provision of health promotion and wellness services that can lead to clients' continuous growth and development

10. Documentation of client and environmental changes in a manner that promotes their self-knowledge, ownership, and self-efficacy

sisted in challenging the school to develop a more culturally sensitive environment.

In terms of life-span theories, Ed drew on the strengths and ecological perspectives. Ed used mapping to encourage Allan to explore his ecological environment by identifying individual and environmental supports and barriers during this critical life transition. Normalizing Allan's identity-development struggles by using life-span developmental theory helped to shift the focus from Allan as the problem to organizational issues, which drew on organizational theory. Thus, Ed helped Allan reinterpret the school's policies as inadequate organizational responses to student diversity and as examples of institutionalized oppression, using cultural oppression theory.

Essentially, this combination of life-span theories helped Allan to externalize the problem and stop blaming himself. The theoretical framework maintained a focus on the cultural context, on Allan's identity development and efforts to gain power, and on contextual factors such as negative school policies. In contrast, following a fixed developmental stage theory, Ed would have focused solely on Allan's needs as evidence of individual pathology, perhaps without moving to assess and intervene in the oppressive organizational environment.

Organizational Analysis: Practice Principles

The practice principles shown in Table 19.2 are also based on the combination of theories in the previous section, consistent with the life-span perspective. The first principle in Table 19.2 forms the basis for all life-span work, across different practice fields and population groups. This principle encourages practitioners to clarify the developmental issues/tasks each client is attempting to accomplish and to explore his or her perceptions about how those tasks are relevant culturally. The cultural aspects may be related to age, ethnicity or race, religion, gender, sexual orientation, disabling conditions, socioeconomic status, or location.

Applying this principle in the situations of Allan and other youths leads to a focus on the life-span tasks of friendship and identity development, involving locating and using a peer network. A network was essential to support Allan's struggles to develop a positive self-image and sexual orientation as a young gay male. Developmental tasks also included participating meaningfully in the life of the school, a socially and culturally appropriate way for typically disempowered youths to gain power. In contrast, in work with families, this first principle should lead practitioners to help families address, as needed, individuation and socialization of their children, along with other developmental tasks (McGoldrick, 1989). For elderly clients, work on life-span tasks often includes exploring generativity and the meaning and value of life events and decisions (Borden, 1992).

Principle 4, stressing normalization, is useful for spreading the problem to other potential clients, which is helpful for destigmatizing the identified client's situation. Normalization also helps to spread the problem to systems or environmental factors. Identifying the environmental roots of problems, as in Allan's situation, frees clients to externalize the problem in an adaptive way (Principle 5). Helping Allan to normalize and externalize the problem decreased the guilt and shame he was experiencing. It also allowed him to focus more clearly on feasible ways to develop coalitions and resolve the problem rather than continuing his role as "The Lone Ranger."

This metaphor of Allan's was useful in helping Ed to understand the meaning Allan was attributing to his unsuccessful attempts to become involved in the school. It underscored the societal myth about the strong, independent,

self-sufficient male who does not need others, which was reinforcing Allan's sense of inadequacy and failure. Ed asked Allan whether, in terms of this life-span narrative and metaphor, it was better to be an unsuccessful Lone Ranger or an effective catalyst of collective (peer group) action (Principle 6). This question helped Allan to reframe the cultural meaning of his current life-transition struggles, along with the narrative he had developed about those struggles. Allan's increased self-awareness and knowledge about the school environment was facilitated by the mutual mapping process (Principle 7) and by coalition building among other students and school staff (Principle 8).

IMPLICATIONS FOR EMPIRICALLY BASED PRACTICE

The practice principles and strategies discussed in the previous section reinforce the importance of empirically based practice for social workers who use the life-span perspective. This perspective's emphasis on clients as experts and on supporting their resiliency shifts the focus from practitioner-driven evaluations of the work to client-centered process and outcome evaluations. The following organizational study and analysis of empirical practice guidelines reflect this client-centered process.

An Organizational Study: St. Joseph Hospital

Initial contacts. Ms. Moses was a 90-year-old African American patient at St. Joseph Hospital. She was brought into the hospital emergency room after the police found her unconscious near a small gas heater in an abandoned warehouse. The warehouse was located in the industrial district of a small city. A physical examination revealed that she had been overcome by carbon monoxide fumes from the heater and that she was diabetic and had a heart condition. When Ms. Moses told the medical staff she had been living for a week in the abandoned warehouse when she was found, they referred her for social services.

Traci Richardson, the social worker assigned to the referral, learned, after their initial contacts, that Ms. Moses was supposed to be living with her two grandsons, 35-year-old Ben and 30-year-old Delbert. The men had moved into her house 2 years earlier to take care of her after she suffered a heart attack. Ms. Moses gradually revealed to Traci that she had left her home the week before she had been found in the warehouse because her grandsons' parties with their friends disrupted her sleep at night. Traci's efforts to interview the grandsons were unsuccessful because they visited their grandmother only at night when Traci was off duty. Consequently, Traci called the Adult Protective Services hotline and referred the case for investigation. She felt it was unsafe for Ms. Moses to return to her home as long as the grandsons lived with her, even though Ms. Moses thought she could convince "the boys" to stop partying.

Goal setting. Traci began exploring the possibility of a nursing home placement for Ms. Moses. She learned that Ms. Moses' husband, son, and daughter were dead. The client had two other grandchildren who lived out of town and with whom she was not in regular contact. She had a neighbor with whom she attended church and often had coffee. Traci felt that because the neighbor was elderly, too, she was probably not a resource for the client. There-

fore, Traci began to educate Ms. Moses about the potential benefits of nursing home placements. Although it was clear that Ms. Moses' goal was to return to the home where she lived with her grandsons, Traci continued to work toward the goal of placement.

In the meantime, Ms. Moses and another patient in the same room, 72-year-old Ms. Edwards, began to "swap stories" about their life situations. Ms. Edwards convinced Ms. Moses to contact her out-of-town relatives after learning that Ben and Delbert were addicted to crack cocaine. They were using Ms. Moses' retirement check to pay for their drugs, and she often did not have enough money for food. Ms. Edwards had her daughter call Ms. Moses' relatives and explain the situation to them. One of the granddaughters, Alice Taylor, and her husband arrived in town the next day and visited Ms. Moses at the hospital. When Traci met with them, they disagreed with her plans for a nursing home placement, indicating that they planned to take Ms. Moses to live with them when she was discharged. Ms. Taylor believed Ms. Moses was depressed because of the death of her daughter in an automobile accident 2 years earlier. She thought having her grandmother live with her in a safe and more comfortable environment would help Ms. Moses to mourn her loss. Traci agreed that living with her granddaughter was a better plan for Ms. Moses than a nursing home placement.

Summarizing the process and outcomes of the ongoing work. Traci used the few remaining days of Ms. Moses' hospitalization to prepare the family to care for Ms. Moses' health needs and to help her make the transition to her new living arrangements. The hospital's on-site home health care unit provided psychoeducation services to the client and her grand-daughter, providing information about coping with her nutrition needs related to the diabetes and her heart condition. They also helped the family understand how to administer Ms. Moses' diabetic medication. When Ms. Moses remained ambivalent about the move, Traci met with Ms. Moses and Ms. Taylor and the latter's husband as a family network intervention. Encouraging the client to review the reasons she had moved to the warehouse helped to convince her that living with her grandsons was not good for her health. Also, listening to Mr. and Ms. Taylor's ideas about how much more comfortable her life would be with them convinced Ms. Moses that the move would be beneficial.

After hearing about Ms. Moses' incomplete mourning for the loss of Ben and Delbert's mother, Traci recommended that Ms. Moses also receive mental health counseling before the granddaughter moved her out of the city. One of the city's mental health centers had a specialized unit providing mental health services for the elderly. Traci was certain the small town in which the granddaughter lived did not provide such services. Ms. Taylor agreed with Traci's recommendation, although reluctantly, because she felt that more natural resources such as counseling with her minister would be more meaningful to her grandmother. However, the hospital was currently embroiled in billing and service coordination conflicts with the mental health center, and for the present, it was refusing to discharge patients to that facility. When Traci told Ms. Taylor that the family would have to refer Ms. Moses to the mental health center themselves after her hospital discharge, the family decided to use the resources in their hometown.

Traci completed an informal evaluation of her work in this case, using her direct observations and SOAP notes (written analysis of the Situation, Options, Analysis, and Plan for each contact) (Freeman & Pennekamp, 1988). She believed her goals of protecting Ms. Moses from an unsafe environment and finding an alternative placement had been achieved successfully. Although she had concerns about failing to obtain mental health services for Ms. Moses, she believed the family's ambivalence might have prevented Ms. Moses from benefiting from such services. Traci wrote a memo to her supervisor about the effects of the hospital's continuing dispute about interagency collaboration with the mental health center. She pointed out how Ms. Moses' situation indicated the need for a more integrated service arrangement among organizations that provide aging and health care services.

Analysis of Empirical Practice Guidelines

Initial contacts for identifying strengths and baselining problems. Table 19.2, which includes a set of life-span practice principles, also provides important guidelines for empirically based practice. These guidelines are applicable across a range of practice settings in which, typically, clients are helped to address their life-span development issues. For example, Principles 1, 2, and 3 focus on initial contacts between clients and practitioners for exploring such issues, along with clients' strengths and problems, regardless of the presenting problem. In this way, the presenting problem can be explored within its culturally meaningful context, a beginning step in empirically based practice.

In the case of Ms. Moses, Traci explored the presenting problem isolated from its cultural context. She should have explored Ms. Moses' life-span tasks related to cultural issues such as age, gender, and ethnicity. In terms of age, Ms. Moses might have been concerned about the meaning and value of her earlier life, juxtaposed against her struggles to find continuity and meaning in her current situation (Borden, 1992). Moreover, elderly African Americans often have a need to mentor the young for reasons of cultural maintenance and generativity (Freeman, 1991). If the presenting problem had been explored with Ms. Moses within this context, the process could have clarified the meaning she attributed to having her grandsons live with her. It would have been a way for Traci to tune into Ms. Moses' reality and strengths, as well as her problems, and therefore to better appreciate her client's goals.

Goal setting as the foundation of empirical practice. Principle 7 in Table 19.2, the use of mutual assessment and mapping tools, aids in the goal-setting process. Tools such as the ecomap and life-history grid provide baseline data on both problems and resources, identifying the strengths in a client's ecological environment (Anderson & Brown, 1980; Hartman, 1995). These maps should be constructed in collaboration with clients; hence, they facilitate inclusion and ownership of the process by clients. As seen in Principle 8, these tools also reveal clients' individual and environmental resources and how those resources can be used in the assessment and work phases, related to clients' motivations and goals for change. Because the criteria for evaluating the process and outcomes of the work are the goals that have been mutually determined, goal setting is an impor-

tant second component of empirically based practice (Rose, 1995). This component is not sequential, however; it is a continuous dynamic process that should be revised throughout the intervention-evaluation continuum.

Traci's SOAP notes served as documentation of her work with Ms. Moses. Those progress notes reveal the lack of involvement that Ms. Moses had in the goal-setting process. Although the goals of having a meaningful relationship with her grandsons and influencing their development in positive ways, such as helping to eliminate their drug use, could be inferred, there is no clear statement of Ms. Moses' goals in those notes. Instead, Ms. Moses no doubt felt that the goals of protecting her and finding an alternative placement had been imposed on her, because her goals were not explored, listened to, or validated by Traci. Moreover, because resources in her environment had been ignored— including her neighbor, minister, and other church members, her granddaughter, and her hospital roommate—no goals were set to help her access those natural resources. When the granddaughter arrived from out of town, Traci responded effectively to Ms. Taylor's desire to change the goals in the situation. However, Traci involved Ms. Moses more actively in the process only after it became apparent that she was ambivalent about the move.

Monitoring the process and outcomes of the ongoing work. Methods for monitoring the work can help to reveal the extent of clients' involvement in the intervention and evaluation process, along with evidence of the work's effectiveness (Cheetham, 1992). Principles 9 and 10 (Table 19.2) provide guidelines for the ongoing monitoring process. The focus should be on clients' health promotion and growth from a capacity-building and prevention perspective. This growth process is facilitated by monitoring tools that provide clear feedback about clients' growth areas and developing skills, along with their ability to articulate the process of change (Carley, 1997). Freire (1989) emphasizes that articulation and ownership of change are prerequisites for clients to experience self-efficacy and empowerment. Thus, Freire's assumptions about the sources of empowerment imply that clients' involvement in the ongoing evaluation process is essential.

In the process of working with Ms. Moses, Traci missed an opportunity to involve her in the intervention process as well as in evaluation of the work. Traci should have discussed with Ms. Moses the progress and quality of the work in terms of what was helpful or not helpful, especially because of the strict time limits currently imposed on hospital social work. Such discussions could have revealed the importance of her hospital roommate's brokering and linking interventions as a natural helper. Those discussions would perhaps have revealed the resentment Ms. Moses may have felt when Traci did not acknowledge her desire to return home.

Potential losses from the move to her granddaughter's hometown could have been identified through this monitoring process, by using an ecomap and other reflective tools. Ms. Moses' potential losses included her grandsons, the home where she had lived with her husband and raised her children, the neighbor, and her church. If Traci had used the ecomap to identify those losses as part of the current work, or as part of the future work after the move, this step might have prevented later problems and enhanced Ms. Moses' growth. Finally, involving Ms. Moses in an exit evaluation of the work could have facilitated her life-span task of life

review. A second monitoring tool, such as a written or taped journal with only a few entries, is often effective. A journal could have expressed the cultural meaning of Ms. Moses' current changes and the effects of the interventions on her, placing those experiences within the context and continuity of her whole life.

CONCLUSION

A number of trends related to developmental issues have emerged and will continue to emerge in practice areas, such as the health care and aging fields. The organizational studies involving Ms. Moses and Allan illustrate three of these trends. One trend involves managed care policies and the privatization of services, which are developing in tandem. Because managed care policies are designed to facilitate cost-containment measures (Edinbergh & Cottler, 1995), they restrict the time allowed for addressing social problems. Such linear thinking underestimates the complexity of social problems and the multiple systems and stakeholders that are involved. Similar restrictions apply in managed care policies related to children's mental health, child welfare, and family support services.

Privatization of services imposes parallel time restrictions on service delivery and the quality of services (Chamberlain, 1995). In treatment planning and decision making, contractors often make decisions on the basis of the least costly and time-consuming alternatives, to break even or receive maximum profit. In Ms. Moses' situation, these constraints led to a superficial exploration of the problem and an arbitrary goal-setting process by the hospital social worker. The hospital had been purchased by a private health care corporation 2 years earlier.

A second important trend is the movement toward integrated services models for delivering services to clients at particular points in the life span. However, this trend has not been accompanied by the necessary integrated funding structure (Pennekamp, 1980). Thus, many of these newly developing service models can involve as many as 10 to 15 separate and often conflicting funding sources. These conflicts lessen opportunities to coordinate and improve direct services and discourage the type of client involvement and client-centered services that are consistent with a life-span perspective. Funding and service priority conflicts between the hospital and the mental health center impeded their collaboration in getting Ms. Moses referred to the mental health center to address her loss and grief issues. This vital service could have increased Ms. Moses' natural resiliency to cope effectively with her upcoming transition, her relocation away from familiar surroundings and relationships.

A third trend is the reduction in funding overall for social programs. As not-for-profit programs are forced to merge or compete for funds sought by privatized organizations, they tend to decrease their focus on prevention or serving at-risk youths such as Allan. Services tend to focus on the short-term needs of well-adjusted youths, without attention to the long-term developmental needs of these and other adolescents. Not-for-profit programs are also unable to find the time necessary for following up on referrals in situations like that of Ms. Moses. Weeks after this case was closed, a quality assurance review revealed that Traci had neither received nor pursued a follow-up contact on her referral to Adult Protective Services.

These service gaps are barriers to the development of integrated services approaches that can enhance interorganizational collaboration as well as the quality and accessibility of services.

REFERENCES

Aguirre, L. M. (1995). California's efforts toward school-linked, integrated, comprehensive services. *Social Work in Education, 7,* 217-225.

Anderson, B., & Brown, R. A. (1980). Life history grid for adolescents. *Social Work, 25,* 321-322.

Beaver, M. I., & Miller, D. A. (1992). *Clinical social work practice with the elderly: Primary, secondary, and tertiary intervention* (2nd ed.). Belmont, CA: Wadsworth.

Beckett, J., & Coley, S. (1987). Ecological intervention with the elderly: A case example. *Journal of Gerontological Social Work, 11*(1), 37-157.

Beckett, J., & Johnson, H. C. (1995). Human development. In R. L. Edwards (Ed.), *Encyclopedia of social work* (19th ed., Vol. 2, pp. 1385-1404). Washington, DC: NASW Press.

Bellos, N. S., & Ruffolo, M. C. (1995). Aging: Services. In R. L. Edwards (Ed.), *Encyclopedia of social work* (19th ed., Vol. 1, pp. 165-173). Washington, DC: NASW Press.

Berger, R. M., & Kelly, J. J. (1995). Gay men overview. In R. L. Edwards (Ed.), *Encyclopedia of social work* (19th ed., Vol. 2, pp. 1064-1075). Washington, DC: NASW Press.

Berger, R. L., McBreen, J. T., & Rifkin, M. J. (1996). *Human behavior: A perspective for the helping professions.* White Plains, NY: Longman.

Borden, W. (1989). Life review as a therapeutic frame in treatment of young adults with AIDS. *Health and Social Work, 14,* 253-259.

Borden, W. (1992). Narrative perspective in psychosocial intervention following adverse life events. *Social Work, 37,* 135-141.

Briar-Lawson, K., Lawson, H. A., Collier, C., & Joseph, A. (1997). School-linked comprehensive services: Promising beginnings, lessons learned, and future challenges. *Social Work in Education, 19,* 136-148.

Brunner, J. (1986). *Actual minds, possible worlds.* Cambridge, MA: Harvard University Press.

Bumagin, V. E., & Hirn, K. (1990). *Helping the aging family: A guide for professionals.* New York: Springer.

Carley, G. (1997). The getting better phenomena: Video-tape applications of previously at-risk high school student narratives. *Social Work in Education, 19,* 115-120.

Chamberlain, R. (1995). *Kansas mental health managed care: Enhancing client lives while controlling costs* (Executive summary). Lawrence: University of Kansas, Office of Social Policy Analysis.

Cheetham, J. (1992). Evaluating social work effectiveness. *Research on Social Work Practice, 2,* 265-287.

Cox, E. V., & Parsons, R. J. (1994). *Empowerment-oriented social work practice with the elderly.* Lexington, MA: Lexington Books.

Delgado, M. (1996). Community asset assessments by Latino youths. *Social Work in Education, 18,* 169-178.

Edinbergh, G. M., & Cottler, J. M. (1995). Managed care. In R. L. Edwards (Ed.), *Encyclopedia of social work* (19th ed., Vol. 2, pp. 1635-1641). Washington, DC: NASW Press.

Everett, J. E. (1995). Child foster care. In R. L. Edwards (Ed.), *Encyclopedia of social work* (19th ed., Vol. 1, pp. 375-389). Washington, DC: NASW Press.

Franklin, C., & Allen-Meares, P. (1997). School social workers are a critical part of the link. *Social Work in Education, 19,* 131-135.

Freedman, J., & Combs, G. (1996). *Narrative therapy.* New York: Norton.

Freeman, E. M. (1987). Interaction of pregnancy, loss, and developmental issues in adolescents. *Social Casework, 68,* 38-46.

Freeman, E. M. (1991). Social competence as a framework for addressing ethnicity and teenage alcohol problems. In A. R. Stiffman & L. E. Davis (Eds.), *Ethnic issues in adolescent mental health* (pp. 247-266). Newbury Park, CA: Sage.

Freeman, E. M. (1993). Empowerment opportunities for black adolescent fathers and their nonparenting peers. In J. Gordon (Ed.), *The African American male: His present status and future* (pp. 195-212). New York: Nelson-Hall.

Freeman, E. M. (1995). School social work overview. In R. L. Edwards (Ed.), *Encyclopedia of social work* (19th ed., Vol. 3, pp. 2087-3000). Washington, DC: NASW Press.

Freeman, E. M. (1996). Welfare reforms and services to children and families: Setting a new practice, research, and policy agenda. *Social Work, 41,* 521-532.

Freeman, E. M. (1998). School social work at its crossroad: Multiple challenges and possibilities [Editorial]. *Social Work in Education, 20,* 83-89.

Freeman, E. M., & McRoy, R. (1986). Group counseling program for unemployed black teenagers. *Social Work with Groups, 9,* 73-89.

Freeman, E. M., & O'Dell, K. (1997). Ethnographic research methods for multicultural needs assessments: A systems change perspective. In J. Gordon (Ed.), *A systems change perspective* (pp. 55-67). New York: Mellon.

Freeman, E. M., & Pennekamp, M. (1988). *Social work practice: Toward a child, family, school, community perspective.* Springfield, IL: Charles C Thomas.

Freire, P. (1989). *Pedagogy of the oppressed.* New York: Continuum.

Germain, C. (1994). Emerging conceptions of family development over the life course. *Families in Society: Journal of Contemporary Human Services, 75,* 259-267.

Germain, C., & Gitterman, A. (1996). *The life model of social work practice: Advances in theory and practice* (2nd ed.). New York: Columbia University Press.

Gutiérrez, L. (1990). Working with women of color: An empowerment perspective. *Social Work, 35,* 149-154.

Gutiérrez, L., Alvarez, A. R., Nemon, H., & Lewis, E. A. (1996). Multicultural community organizing: A strategy for change. *Social Work, 41,* 501-508.

Gutiérrez, L. M., & Ortega, R. (1991). Developing methods to empower Latinos: The importance of groups. *Social Work with Groups, 14,* 23-43.

Harrison, W. D. (1995). Community development. In R. L. Edwards (Ed.), *Encyclopedia of social work* (19th ed., Vol. 1, pp. 555-562). Washington, DC: NASW Press.

Hartman, A. (1995). Family therapy. In R. L. Edwards (Ed.), *Encyclopedia of social work* (19th ed., Vol. 2, pp. 983-991). Washington, DC: NASW.

Hunter, J., & Schaecher, T. (1987). Stresses on lesbian and gay adolescents in schools. *Social Work in Education, 9,* 180-189.

Jones, S. (1993). *The language of genes: Solving the mysteries of our genetic past, present, and future.* New York: Anchor Books.

McGoldrick, M. (1989). Women through the family life cycle. In M. McGoldrick (Ed.), *Women in families: A framework for family therapy* (pp. 200-226). New York: Norton.

Pennekamp, M. (1980). Merged funding alternatives: A base for integrated services delivery (Trends and Issues). *Social Work in Education, 1,* 66-73.

Rose, S. D. (1995). Goal setting and intervention planning. In R. L. Edwards (Ed.), *Encyclopedia of social work* (19th ed., Vol. 2, pp. 1124-1128). Washington, DC: NASW Press.

Saleebey, D. (1994). Culture, theory, and narrative: The intersection of meanings in practice. *Social Work, 39,* 351-359.

Saleebey, D. (1996). *The strengths perspective in social work practice* (2nd ed.). White Plains, NY: Longman.

Solomon, B. (1987). *Empowerment: Social work in oppressed communities.* New York: Columbia University Press.

Spradley, J. (1994). Ethnography and culture. In J. Spradley & D. McCurdy (Eds.), *Conformity and conflict: Readings in cultural anthropology* (8th ed., pp. 49-57). New York: HarperCollins.

Steinberg, R., & Carter, G. W. (1983). *Case management and the elderly.* Lexington, MA: Lexington Books.

Tatara, T. (1993). *Characteristics of children in substitute and adoptive care.* Washington, DC: Voluntary Cooperative Information System, American Public Welfare Association.

White, M., & Epston, D. (1990). *Narrative means to therapeutic ends.* New York: Norton.

CHAPTER TWENTY

The New World of Practice
in Physical and Mental Health:
Comorbidity, Cultural Competence,
and Managed Care

LONNIE R. SNOWDEN

The world of practice has changed over the past decade and will continue to change at a rapid pace. These changes are irreversible: There will be no return to more familiar and, in certain respects, more comfortable arrangements. No matter how heartfelt, expressions of indignation will produce only marginal adjustments to structures and procedures that have been altered in their fundamentals and constitute a new status quo.

Consider the public mental health system in Colorado as a case in point (Bloom et al., 1998). Before 1995, the system consisted of 17 community mental health centers (CMHCs), four specialty clinics, and two state hospitals. Concerned by rising costs in its Medicaid program and by system fragmentation, the Colorado legislature took action in 1992. Legislators enacted policies requiring the state mental health authority to create and evaluate, on a pilot ba-

AUTHOR'S NOTE: Preparation of this chapter was supported in part by Award R01 MH52908 from the National Institute of Mental Health.

sis, programs of services having a single point-of-entry in which treatment was financed on a prepaid, capitated basis.

Fourteen community mental health centers competed successfully and entered the demonstration after reorganizing themselves into seven new entities called Mental Health Assessment and Service Agencies (MHASAs). One multi-CMHC MHASA and three single-CMHC MHASAs continued to operate independently on a not-for-profit basis (Model 1). Two multi-CMHC MHASAs and one single-CMHC MHASA entered separately into joint venture with a for-profit managed behavioral health care corporation, which provided administrative and inpatient services (Model 2). Three remaining CMHCs were not part of the demonstration and continued to operate as they had previously (Bloom et al., 1998).

Under both models, MHASAs receive contracts and are required, either directly or by way of subcontract, to provide an array of specific services and to coordinate efforts with other human services agencies including child welfare, schools, and juvenile justice. Other children's services, such as respite care, family preservation, and interventions targeting infants and children, are recommended but not required.

MHASAs are paid according to a capitated rate based on historical patterns of use by Medicaid eligibility category and by the region in which they are located. The payment reflects the number of Medicaid-eligible clients in each group and is made prospectively each month with subsequent adjustments to correct to actual enrollment. Although they do not pay for selected services, MHASAs are at full risk for delivery of the services for which they have contracted. They pay for certain services and are re-sponsible for delivery of those services, but not for others (Bloom et al., 1998).

The state has become a purchaser rather than a provider of care. It buys services through contracts that include for-profit partners with not-for-profit agencies. These organizations must coordinate their activities with an array of other human service providers. Although they are autonomous and encouraged to create innovative approaches and services, they carry a burden of risk: If the rate of payment falls short of the amount required to provide necessary care, they may go bankrupt.

The transformation of mental health services systems is but a manifestation of a larger transformation of health care. Health Maintenance Organizations (HMOs) and other managed care arrangements have come to dominate the private sector. They have made substantial inroads in the public sector as well as Medicaid; other public payers for care have pursued cost containment. For longer than their counterparts in mental health, and perhaps to a greater extent, social work practitioners in health care settings find themselves subject to prior authorization, utilization review, and other forms of managed care oversight (Dziegielewski, 1998).

SOCIAL WORKERS IN DIRECT PRACTICE

Living through such transitions, social workers in health and mental health practice might find the experience unsettling—a transformation of their expectations about conditions and forms of practice. The challenge facing practitioners is to understand these developments and to cope effectively, continuing to deploy skills of direct practice in a manner that permits them to engage, and even thrive, under new organizational arrangements and financial systems. In facing this challenge, social workers must continue to affirm values—including, as will be discussed shortly, social justice, diversity, and commitment to successful adaptation in the social environment—at the core of social work.

However, if social work practitioners are successful, they can expect more than merely to survive. They might prosper, discovering that their orientation toward practice has been vindicated.

As we confront this new world of practice, it is timely again to consider the values and orientation to helping that anchor the profession. Core values commit practitioners to a sense of concern for the vulnerable, the oppressed, and the poor. Even among mental health private practitioners who have been accused of retreating from this commitment, there is evidence that social workers accommodate their practice styles more than other professionals to make room for the poor: They not only show a greater willingness to accept Medicaid-funded clients, they also continue at least part-time practice in a mental health or social service agency (Knesper, 1985; Peterson et al., 1996). Therefore, in their search for autonomy and income—factors that motivate entry into private practice—many social work private practitioners do not appear to entirely abandon core values of the profession.

The training of social work practitioners disposes them to seek ways of enhancing the well-being of their clients and to meet basic human needs with an eye toward promoting successful living in the day-to-day environment. As will be shown later, these values and this stance toward practice prepare social work practitioners for future professional challenges.

MANAGED CARE

The term *managed care* refers not to a specific organizational form or administrative technique but to a family of structures and policies potentially deployed individually or in combination under a variety of arrangements (Harden, 1994). Familiar examples of organizations constructed on managed care principles are HMOs and Preferred Provider Organizations (PPOs). In recent years, firms specializing in "carve out"—administering mental health or other benefits of special concern based on managed care principles and provided by insurance companies—have gained prominence. All managed care organizations must somehow strike a balance between provider and client autonomy, on the one hand, and centralized control and conformance to policy, on the other.

Despite the diversity of managed care, both in principle and practice, most observers would recognize a number of features as characteristic:

1. People enrolled in managed care plans are encouraged and often required to seek care from a designated group of providers. These providers either are employed by a managed care organization or agree to policies that limit their fees and constrain their styles of practice. The organization thereby retains control over client use of services and provider patterns of practice.

2. Access to care is limited to people who are enrolled in the managed care plan or otherwise meet eligibility criteria. For its part, the organization is obligated to offer or make available a package of services.

3. An active role is taken toward monitoring the status of clients and the provision of care. Mechanisms are established to screen clients for eligibility, evaluate their needs, and monitor their movement through a system.

4. The decision making of providers is overtly constrained. Policies such as limits on certain forms of care are established, and treatment plans and activities are reviewed, by people employed directly by the managed care organization or engaged by the organization under contract.

5. The following incentives may be introduced to reduce costs: paying providers a salary rather than a fee-for-service basis, creating bonus plans, and setting requirements for cost sharing. All are designed to encourage conservative styles of practice.

6. Emphasis is placed on using interventions of proven effectiveness, particularly those that are cost-effective.

Capitated financing goes hand in hand with managed care (Masland, Piccagli, Snowden, & Cuffel, 1996). Under capitation, providers are paid per client instead of per procedure: They receive a fixed amount and must, within limits, provide all necessary care. Providers stand to lose money if costs exceed the per-client rate at which they are being paid. For this reason, they are vulnerable and operate at financial risk.

Although managed care originated in the private sector and remains most widely practiced there, public sector managers have increasingly turned to managed care. They sometimes purchase the services of managed care specialty firms operating on either a for-profit or not-for-profit basis to provide services ranging in scope from technical assistance (e.g., management information system design) to complete operational control. For this reason and others, the boundary between public and private is less than hard and fast. Nevertheless, the public-private distinction continues to be important: The public system remains an accountable

agent of multiple and overlapping constituencies (Cuffel, Snowden, Masland, & Piccagli, 1996).

Managed care is controversial. Incentives are felt within the organization to solely enroll clients who are least needy and easiest to serve—to "cream" the population. Receiving widespread attention in the popular press is a related problem of "skimping" on care, or undertreating. Consumers also complain of restrictions on their freedom of choice: Under some arrangements, they are no longer able to select their preferred provider, which may include the provider with whom they have an ongoing and successful relationship.

The conditions of managed care may prove especially challenging for social work practitioners. Inclined by professional values and personal commitment to place the well-being of clients above all other considerations, they may find themselves unwilling—even ethically constrained—to adhere to protocol-imposed restrictions and limitations on care.

Styles of practice encouraged under managed care have several features. They focus on specific complaints and time-limited interventions. They reflect concern with improving the functional capacity of the client—with restoring his or her ability to successfully meet demands posed by day-to-day living—for example, in maintaining constructive family relationships and holding a job. These styles of practice sometimes demand advocacy: When practitioners believe that managed care protocols compromise the quality of care they are able to provide, they must speak out. There are appeals procedures under managed care arrangements, whereby additional treatment can be requested on grounds of medical necessity. These procedures are meaningful and can be influenced by informed argument and thoughtful, strategic action. For these reasons, the style of practice necessary for managed care is suited to the training and values of social work practitioners.

CULTURAL COMPETENCE AND ETHNIC MINORITY POPULATIONS

Part of the new landscape of practice is defined by the large and growing presence of ethnic minority populations in the United States (del Pinal & Singer, 1997; O'Hare, Pollard, Mann, & Kent, 1991). Social work practitioners are committed to serving a diverse clientele because of the values within their profession and the overrepresentation of minority group members among vulnerable populations such as the poor. In any event, well-established demographic trends make it increasingly difficult to avoid serving minority clients.

As professional helpers seek to practice effectively with a diverse clientele, they confront issues relating to culture. Scholars have identified dimensions along which cultures vary; among those, they have focused on several as especially pertinent (Triandis, 1996). Some cultures are active, stressing competition, action, and self-fulfillment; others are more passive, stressing reflection and deferral to others. Some cultures emphasize individualism—personal goals take precedence—whereas other cultures emphasize collectivism—group goals take precedence over personal goals. Some cultures are more hierarchical, promoting guidance from authority figures and authoritative texts; others are more egalitarian. Some cultures are oriented toward honor, with special concerns about giving and taking offense; others are more pragmatic. These differences and others complicate the task of developing successful, beneficial relationships and promoting positive client change.

Minority communities and individuals vary in their adherence to a traditional cultural outlook and their identification with community and cultural concerns. The oldest means by which to analyze such differences is through the concept of acculturation. Historically, acculturation referred to a dimension of social distance in which members of an ethnic group were separated from the wider society in beliefs, values, and primary group relations (e.g., work, social clubs, family, friends) (Gordon, 1964).

Along with acculturation, ethnic or cultural identity constitutes another basis on which differences must be considered. Ethnic or cultural identity seeks to specify a reference group—an identifiable social entity with whom a person identifies and to whom he or she looks for standards of behavior (Cooper & Denner, 1998).

Minority advocates have called for a culturally competent direct practice—a recognition and response to differences in outlook on personal problems and on traditions for intervention. From this point of view, professional practice must consider cultural differences and reflect an appropriate degree of sensitivity.

Within the development of performance indicators used to judge human service organizations, cultural competence has sometimes been included as a standard. The translation of cultural competence in this context has included a number of requirements, such as consulting with cross-cultural experts, training staff, providing services in languages other than English, and monitoring caseloads to ensure proportional racial and ethnic representation (Snowden, 1996).

Another response has been to develop guidelines for social workers to use in direct practice. After synthesizing a number of approaches, Lum (1999) devised a framework of several facets. Lum's framework encompasses cultural awareness (e.g., recognizing personal culturally related experience, societal racism, and discrimination), knowledge acquisition (e.g., knowing history, demographics, and values of cultural groups), skill development (e.g., overcoming resistance, identifying problems, and making appropriate use of self disclosure), and *inductive learning* or information gathering. Domains of cultural competence are ordered hierarchically, ranging from beginning (generalist) to advanced levels.

In the final analysis, cultural competence is practice that works—practice that successfully ameliorates whatever problems have led clients to seek professional help. Cultural competence implies that to work, practice must be adapted to take account of cultural influences. However, not all modifications made in the name of cultural competence produce improved results. In treating a Mexican American male, for example, to minimize chronic, severe abuse of alcohol from a belief in cultural sanction of such behavior would yield a worse result, not a better one. Whatever the intention, such a practice cannot be considered truly culturally competent. (Snowden, 1996).

Social work practitioners are committed by the values of their profession to consider the needs of culturally diverse and politically marginalized populations. Their tradition has emphasized such an orientation longer than other professions; accordingly, their training more often includes diversity-enhancing experiences. As

the effort to achieve cultural competence moves forward, social work practitioners may find themselves better situated than are other professionals to make an active contribution.

THE SEVERELY AND PERSISTENTLY MENTALLY ILL

Through the efforts of advocacy groups, most notably the National Alliance for the Mentally Ill, the field of mental health, focusing on people with severe and persistent forms of illness, is receiving considerable attention. Precisely what is severe and persistent mental illness? In 1993, the National Advisory Mental Health Council put forward an influential three-part definition (Kessler et al., 1996). One element is diagnosis, which referred to several specific disorders including schizophrenia, schizoaffective disorder, manic depressive disorder, autism, and severer forms of major depression, panic disorder, and obsessive compulsive disorder. A second element, disability, refers to impairment in capacity for day-to-day functioning in major life domains, including community and family relationships but especially vocational capacity and employment. The third element of the definition indicates that the problem is long-standing rather than transient.

According to estimates (Kessler et al., 1996), about 2.6% of the population suffers from severe and persistent mental illness: about 4.8 million people. The severely and persistently mentally ill are especially likely to be female, unmarried, and having less than a high school education (Kessler et al., 1996). They are high users of services: About 46.6% used medical or mental health services within a 1-month period.

The number and problems of people with severe and persistent mental illness grew considerably over recent decades (Mechanic, 1989), giving rise to great societal concern. One reason for this increase was deinstitutionalization, by which the census of mental hospitals was substantially reduced. Less well known but also of great importance are demographic trends. As the baby boom generation approached the age of risk for the onset of severe mental illness, a marked increase in the number of severely mentally ill accompanied the large number of baby boomers.

Treatment of the severely and persistently mentally ill requires a wide-ranging response to potential sources of emotional and functional disability. One model of care, the program of Assertive Community Treatment (Test, 1992), is well supported by research and actively promoted for dissemination by the federal Center for Mental Health Services, the National Alliance for the Mentally Ill. Other beneficial methods, including case management and family psychoeducation, also draw from social work traditions and contributions of social workers.

Originally developed in Madison, Wisconsin, Assertive Community Treatment calls for a multidisciplinary team that provides a spectrum of services (e.g., housing and vocational assistance, medication, substance abuse treatment, crisis care, etc.) to a small group of clients. The emphasis is on monitoring the status of clients and actively developing their living skills within the communities in which they live. Practitioners must not only work side by side with other specialists but also take a hands-on role in providing assistance.

This model embodies an active, environment-oriented style of intervention and serves a neglected and stigmatized sector of the population. For these reasons and others, Assertive Community Treatment embodies the values and professional orientation of social work.

THE MEDICALLY INDIGENT

Poor and disenfranchised members of society are plagued by acute and chronic medical conditions. For example, people with incomes less than $10,000 per year are more likely than others to suffer from all acute medical conditions, including infectious and parasitic conditions, respiratory conditions, digestive disorders, and injuries (U.S. Department of Health and Human Services, 1991). These and other illnesses compromise the quality of their lives and put them at risk of early death.

These problems are exacerbated by inadequacies in the U.S. health care system, especially in financing. About 17% of the population lack health insurance (Vistnes & Monheit, 1997). Most are poor and either unemployed or employed in low wage jobs that fail to provide health care and other fringe benefits. Others rely on Medicaid and other public sources with limited access to health care programs and providers.

The uninsured and publicly insured are less likely than others to seek routine and preventative care and more likely to visit the emergency room. For many, the emergency room becomes a primary health care resource: Compared to people with private coverage, the uninsured and publicly insured are more than five times as likely to report the emergency room as their usual source of health care (Weinick, Zuvekas, & Drilea, 1997).

Several facets of the social worker role and the customary social work practice are particularly well suited to the problems of the medically indigent. Their lives are characterized by high levels of stress resulting from the pressures of poverty and community discord. Their reliance on emergency care arises in part from stress-related illnesses and conflict-related injuries.

Social workers are especially oriented toward the larger environment in which illnesses and injuries arise; this perspective is well suited to effective work with the medically indigent. Crisis intervention (Dziegielewski, 1997), a characteristic mode of social work in health care settings (Dziegielewski, 1998), can help resolve frequently accompanying immediate turmoil.

Another responsibility of social workers, discharge planning, can potentially contribute to longer term resolution. The medically indigent are not only more likely to rely on emergency and hospital-based care, they are also more likely to be repeat users of the system (Snowden, 1999). They reappear under circumstances similar to those of their initial appearance, largely because underlying psychological and social conditions remain unchanged. Clients whose substance abuse or confrontational interpersonal style embroil them in chronic conflict, for example, will sustain repeated injury until necessary changes in lifestyle take place.

To interrupt these cycles, careful attention must be paid to personal and community sources that place the medically indigent at risk. Social work practitioners in health care settings are well situated to address this social adversity. They take a comprehensive approach and are attuned to social dynamics that underlie recurrent patterns of illness and injury (Dziegielewski, 1998). Their experience in discharge planning

holds out the best hope, among existing approaches, to interrupting patterns of crisis that undermine personal well-being and contribute to family and societal burden.

OVERLAPPING PROBLEMS AND FADING BOUNDARIES: HEALTH, SUBSTANCE ABUSE, AND MENTAL HEALTH

As long realized by many social workers and other kinds of practitioners, the problems of clients tend to occur in clusters, not in isolation. Circumstances in living that cause one problem tend to cause a concomitant problem; once established, these problems themselves tend to feed on each other. In such a manner, difficulties compound.

The comorbidity of mental health and substance abuse problems is referred to routinely as *dual diagnosis.* The two disorders occur jointly to a substantial extent. Among people with a lifetime diagnosis of any mental disorder, about 29% also suffer from a substance abuse disorder. The rate of alcohol abuse has been estimated as being about twice as high among such people as it is among the general population, and the rate of substance abuse is about four times as high (Regier et al., 1990).

The prevalence of mental illness among people suffering from a substance abuse problem has been shown to be even greater than the reverse prevalence discussed above. Among people with a lifetime alcohol disorder, about 37% indicated a co-occurring mental disorder; about 53% of those with another kind of drug abuse problem also reported a mental illness (Regier et al., 1990).

People suffering from mental illness are at risk not only for substance abuse problems but also for physical illness and premature death. Thus, people with schizophrenia demonstrate a two-fold increase in overall mortality compared with people from the population at large (Regier et al., 1990); people suffering from depression demonstrate about a 1.5-fold increase (Wells, Sturm, Sherbourne, & Meredith, 1996). The differential reflects both increased rates of health-related problems and suicide.

Similarly, people suffering from alcohol and other drug abuse problems also experience elevated rates of problems in health. Illness and death rates from alcohol- and drug-related causes, as well as emergency room use, are particularly high (U.S. Department of Health and Human Services, 1991).

The increasing awareness of the overlap among mental health, substance abuse, and general health problems is accompanied by an increasing interest in revising treatments and programs accordingly. The most comprehensive approach to date involves integrating elements of mental health and substance interventions into a single, unified program of treatment (e.g., Drake, Teague, & Warren, 1990). Reliance on model programs targeting clients with comorbid substance abuse and mental illness helps to overcome barriers to integrating existing programs from mental health and substance abuse treatment sectors—differences in treatment philosophy, staffing patterns, and administrative history and structure.

Concurrently, efforts have increased to more effectively recognize and treat problems in mental health and substance abuse as they appear in general medical care settings. Administrators and researchers have paid closest attention, perhaps, to depression (e.g., Attkisson & Zich, 1990). They have been motivated by the high prevalence of depression in primary care, which remains mostly undetected and, if detected, and untreated (Wells et al., 1996). In many places, the restructuring of health care delivery to better respond to mental health problems in primary care is already under way.

Whatever the sector and style of intervention for people with multiple problems in living, there is increasing concern with improving their functional status (cf. McGlynn, 1996). Improvement in the capacity to work and to participate successfully with family, friends, neighbors, and others has become accepted as a target for intervention in general medical, drug and alcohol, and mental health sectors of care alike.

Social work is the profession with the greatest understanding of these spheres of day-to-day activity and the longest-standing tradition of intervention. The real-world orientation of this profession affords social work practitioners with a distinctive advantage when addressing the functional status of multiproblem clients. They are better prepared to improve those dimensions of client functioning in which all professionals now have taken such an active interest.

RESEARCH

The relationship between research and practice also has been altered as part of the transformation of the world of practice. A frequently discussed and long-lamented gap between the two has shrunk, not through academic debate or development of new theoretical models but through increasing pressure from payers and other stakeholders for practitioners to be held accountable.

But what standards should be used to judge helping professionals? A number of organizations, including the National Committee on Quality Assurance, the Mental Health Statistics Improvement Program of Substance and Mental Health Services Administration, the American College of Mental Health Administration, and the National Association of State Mental Health Program Directors Research Institute, have developed performance indicators for evaluating mental health and substance abuse treatment systems (Mazade, 1998).

One objective has been to develop "report cards"—assessments of system performance followed by dissemination of results to consumers and other stakeholders. This assessment of performance indicators is carried out through rigorous empirical research. For example, a county mental health system might investigate as performance indicators its clinic waiting times, proportion of minority clients, and referral and emergency care rates, then report its findings to consumers and families. In turn, consumers and families might critique the findings, thereby providing the basis for a new study. This cycle of research and dissemination greatly reduces the research-practice gap.

Critical to performance assessment is the assessment of client outcomes. Improvement in client functioning, according to critics, constitutes the very rationale of services systems: "The ultimate criterion for judging the quality of health care is that it lead to positive health outcomes that are valued by the consumer, the payer, and society" (Steinwachs, Flynn, Norquist, & Skinner, 1996, p. 1).

Outcomes assessment in health care and mental health and substance abuse treatment encompasses several domains. The National Association of State Mental Health Program Directors Task Force identified several of these domains as symptom relief, employment, adequate residential arrangements and social functioning, and freedom from various adverse conditions (e.g., injury, victimization, criminal justice involvement) (Mazade, 1998).

In a performance assessment, outcomes are assessed to understand the *effectiveness* of care (provided under circumstances of everyday routine practice) rather than its *efficacy* (provided under ideal circumstances). The distinction reflects a recognition of the fact that what is true in an artificial world created for research need not be true in the real world of practice.

The performance assessment might apply to many treated disorders or focus on particular tracer conditions; it might also vary in intensity, scope, or measurement perspective (e.g., client, clinician, family member) (Smith, 1996). If monitoring and feedback are provided on an ongoing basis, outcomes assessment forms the basis for continuous quality improvement; it permits "real-time, real-place feedback to managers, clinicians, and consumers" (Burnam, 1996, p. 5). With such ongoing feedback from research to practice, the gap between research and practice vanishes.

Under continuous quality improvement, the influence between research and practice is reciprocal: Research affects practice, but practice also affects research. Practitioners are enlisted as partners in the design of instruments and otherwise in the development of research procedures.

Social work practitioners are well situated to make an active and important contribution. Their orientation toward understanding the systems in which services are provided and the environments in which clients live provides them with an important vantage point for comment and critique. Their involvement can help to ensure that subsequent research is realistic and relevant.

Consider, for example, a service system that has targeted levels of client social interaction as a goal for intervention, and in which a program of research on client outcomes is contemplated. In considering measures of social interaction, there would be a need for input from people knowledgeable about life in the community—about opportunities and constraints on interaction.

Because of their knowledge of community dynamics, social workers would become important participants. Their perspective would better permit development of a measure that is realistic in that it is grounded in possibilities available in the community and sensitive to nuances of day-to-day living.

The challenge does not call for new research tasks or methods. To select and adapt valid and reliable measures, to gather data such that internal and external validity are maximized, to bring appropriate statistical techniques to bear and powers of critical judgment—none of these strategies are new, but all acquire renewed importance when decisions about acceptable forms of practice and officially sanctioned levels of client well-being rest in the balance.

EDUCATION AND TRAINING

To prepare social workers to succeed in the new world of practice, educational programs must successfully meet several challenges. They must prepare students with knowledge that is contemporary, specific, and informative in meeting professional tasks as they are encountered in the real world of practice.

Thus, educational programs must prepare students with knowledge that is specific to the problem at hand, rather than broad. As accountable practitioners performing in a competitive environment, social workers must be equipped to understand problems and communicate to clients and to other professionals, not from a general orienting framework, which by its nature cannot be particular, but from a foundation of well-documented fact and cutting-edge theory (Wakefield, 1996).

This orientation runs counter to a growing emphasis on generalist education. It is becoming necessary, however: Public and private entities paying for care increasingly are favoring a task-centered rather than a profession-centered approach. In the new world of practice, what professionals can do is coming to count more than what credential they possess.

Much of the necessary knowledge has been contributed by social workers, but other important knowledge has not. Disciplinary boundaries do not clearly mark or effectively contain the welter of information necessary to solve the broad and interconnected problems we face; this will become ever more apparent within the new structures of practice. Knowledge must be sought out and applied whatever its source.

As medicine draws on chemistry, physiology, biology, and other fields of basic science, so social work must draw on the social sciences and allied professions. Thus, to best understand managed care, one must consult organizational theory and applied economics; to understand the medically indigent and the severely mentally ill, public health and health services; to understand ethnic minority populations, anthropology, sociology, and psychology. The drive to preserve a distinctive professional identity must not overwhelm a commitment to equip students with the most useful information available.

The need for a more interdisciplinary approach and more particular rather than general knowledge will become increasingly apparent as professions are pressed to justify themselves by advocates and by the public-at-large. The rise of problem-oriented advocacy groups is hastening this process. Thus, professional practitioners have increasingly felt the power of breast cancer survivors, people living with HIV/AIDS, former foster youth, and others who have raised their voices on behalf of their interests as they perceive them, not as mediated by professionally trained advocates.

These groups display skepticism toward professions and professional training, which they sometimes perceive as self-serving. They recognize and are convinced by knowledge perceived as useful, without regard to professional boundaries. They are likely to be less impressed with broad perspectives and unifying frameworks.

In its recently published consumer and family guide to treatment of schizophrenia, for example, the National Alliance for the Mentally Ill (NAMI) does not mention professions or disciplines by name. Instead, it recommends specific interventions—for example, vocational rehabilitation, Assertive Community Treament, the "right kind" of psychotherapy, and particular medicines. It is likely that NAMI will look with favor on mental health curricula address-

ing these modes of service, which are specific and up-to-date, and with disfavor on curricula that omit them.

CONCLUSION

After an adjustment period, a new era of practice into which we have entered need not disconcert social workers engaged in direct practice. Fundamental commitments of the profession—its core values, which, as previously noted, include social justice, diversity, and successful client functioning in day-to-day social surroundings—are highly compatible with new developments and trends.

Managed care has transformed the landscape, and social workers may find it difficult to conform to its restrictions and limitations. On the other hand, the orientation toward here-and-now interventions and willingness to advocate will serve social workers well. Their greater experience with culturally diverse populations, social service agencies, and day-to-day client environments position social workers to take the lead in serving the severely and persistently mentally ill, the medically indigent, and other people suffering from multiple problems. Their experience and advice will become integral in the design and interpretation of realistic, decision-oriented research. Ultimately, social workers might come to believe that certain long-standing concerns of their profession have at long last been vindicated.

REFERENCES

Attkisson, C., & Zich, J. M. (1990). *Depression in primary care: Screening and detection.* New York: Routledge.
Bloom, J. R., Hu, T. W., Wallace, N., Cuffel, B., Hauseman, J., & Scheffler, R. (1998). Mental health costs and ac-

cess under alternative capitation systems in Colorado: Early results. *Journal of Mental Health Policy and Economics, 1,* 1-11.

Burnam, A. (1996). Measuring outcomes of care for substance abuse and mental disorders. In D. M. Steinwachs, L. M. Flynn, G. S. Norquist, & E. A. Skinner (Eds.), *Using client outcomes to improve mental health and substance treatment.* San Francisco: Jossey-Bass.

Cooper, C. R., & Denner, J. (1998). Theories linking culture and psychopathology: Universal and community-specific processes. *Annual Review of Psychology, 49,* 559-584.

Cuffel, B. J., Snowden, L. R., Masland, M., & Piccagli, G. (1996). Managed care in the public mental health system. *Community Mental Health Journal, 32,* 109-124.

del Pinal, J., & Singer, A. (1997). Generations of diversity: Latinos in the United States. *Population Bulletin, 52,* 1-44.

Drake, R. E., Teague, G. B., & Warren, S. R. (1990). Dual diagnosis: The New Hampshire Program. *Addiction and Recovery, 10,* 35-39.

Dziegielewski, S. F. (1997). Time-limited brief therapy: The State of practice. *Crisis Intervention and Time Limited Treatment, 3,* 217-228.

Dziegielewski, S. F. (1998). *The changing face of health care social work.* New York: Springer.

Gordon, M. M. (1964). *Assimilation in American life.* New York: Oxford University Press.

Harden, S. L. (1994). *What legislators need to know about managed care.* Washington, DC: National Conference of State Legislatures.

Kessler, R. C., Berguland, P. A., Zhao, S., Leaf, P. J., Kouzis, A. C., Bruce, M. L., Friedman, R. M., et al. (1996). The 1-month prevalence and correlates of serious mental illness (SMI). In R. W. Manderscheid & M. A. Sonnenschein (Eds.), *Mental health, United States* (DHHS Publication No. SMA 96-3098). Washington, DC: Government Printing Office.

Knesper, D. (1985). Similarities and differences across mental health service providers and practice settings in the United States. *American Psychologist, 40,* 1352-1369.

Lum, D. (1999). *Culturally competent practice.* Pacific Grove, CA: Brooks/Cole.

Masland, M., Piccagli, G., Snowden, L. R., & Cuffel, B. (1996). Planning and implementation of capitated mental health services in the public sector. *Evaluation and Program Planning, 19,* 253-262.

Mazade, N. A. (1998, Summer). NRI and NASMHPD managed care perfomance indicator project. In *Outlook* (pp. 4-7). Cambridge, MA: The Evaluation Center.

McGlynn, E. A. (1996). Setting the context for measuring patient outcomes. In D. M. Steinwachs, L. M. Flynn, G.

S. Norquist, & E. A. Skinner (Eds.), *Using client outcomes to improve mental health and substance treatment.* San Francisco: Jossey-Bass.

Mechanic, D. (1989). The evolution of mental health services and mental health services research. In C. A. Taub, D. Mechanic, & A. Hohman (Eds.), *The future of mental health services research* (DHHS Publication No. ADM 91-1762). Washington, DC: Government Printing Office.

O'Hare, W. P., Pollard, K. M., Mann, T. L., & Kent, M. M. (1991). African Americans in the 1990s. *Population Bulletin, 46,* 1-40.

Peterson, B. D., West, J., Pincus, H., Kohout, J., Pion, G. M., Wicherski, M. M., et al. (1996). An update on human resources in mental health. In R. W. Manderscheid & M. A. Sonnenschein (Eds.), *Mental health, United States* (DHHS Publication No. SMA 96-3098). Washington, DC: Government Printing Office.

Regier, D. A., Farmer, M. E., Rae, D. S., Locke, B. Z., Keith, S. J., Judd, L. L., & Goodwin, F. K. (1990). Comorbidity of mental disorders and alcohol and other drug abuse: Results from the epidemiologic catchment area (ECA) study. *Journal of the American Medical Association, 264,* 2511-2518.

Smith, G. R. (1996). State of the science of mental health and substance abuse outcomes assessment. In D. M. Steinwachs, L. M. Flynn, G. S. Norquist, & E. A. Skinner (Eds.), *Using client outcomes to improve mental health and substance treatment.* San Francisco: Jossey-Bass.

Snowden, L. R. (1996). Ethnic minority populations and mental health outcomes. In D. M. Steinwachs, L. M. Flynn, G. S. Norquist, & E. A. Skinner (Eds.), *Using client outcomes to improve mental health and substance treatment.* San Francisco: Jossey-Bass.

Snowden, L. R. (1999). *Barriers to providing effective mental health services to African Americans.* Manuscript under review.

Steinwachs, D. M., Flynn, L. M., Norquist, G. S., & Skinner, E. A. (1996). Editors' notes. In D. M. Steinwachs, L. M. Flynn, G. S. Norquist, & E. A. Skinner (Eds.), *Using client outcomes to improve mental health and substance treatment.* San Francisco: Josscy-Bass.

Test, M. A. (1992). Training in community living. In P. Robert (Ed.), *Handbook of psychiatric rehabilitation* (pp. 153-170). Boston: Allyn & Bacon.

Triandis, H. C. (1996). The psychological measurement of cultural syndromes. *American Psychologist, 51,* 407-415.

U. S. Department of Health and Human Services. (1991). *Health status of minorities and low-income groups.* Washington, DC: Government Printing Office.

Vistnes, J. P., & Monheit, A. C. (1997). *Health insurance status of the civilian noninstitutionalized population* (Publication No. 97-0030). Rockville, MD: Agency for Health Care Policy and Research.

Wakefield, J. C. (1996). Does social work need the ecosystems perspective? Is the perspective clinically useful? *Social Service Review, 70,* 1-32.

Weinick, R. M., Zuvekas, S. H., & Drilea, S. K. (1997). *Access to health care: Sources and barriers* (Publication No. 98-0001). Rockville, MD: Agency for Health Care Policy and Research.

Wells, K. B., Sturm, R., Sherbourne, C. D., & Meredith, L. S. (1996). *Caring for depression.* Cambridge, MA: Harvard University Press.

CHAPTER TWENTY-ONE

The Juvenile Justice System in Crisis: Challenges and Opportunities for Social Workers

ROSEMARY C. SARRI

During the 1990s, the United States experienced a level of increase in incarceration that was unprecedented in our history. Regrettably, this places us in the unenviable position of having a higher rate than any other country in the world. Moreover, given recent legislative and judicial actions, there is little reason to be optimistic about declines in the future. The entire system is in crisis because of overcrowding, the elimination of almost all educational and rehabilitation programs inside prisons and jails, overrepresentation of minority populations, and increasingly long sentences for even minor crimes. Nowhere is that truer than in the juvenile justice system. Juvenile confinement has grown more rapidly than adult incarceration because juveniles have been in the forefront of much of the punitive legislation passed and implemented in the 1980s and 1990s (Snyder & Sickmund, 1999). In all states, minors can now be tried as adults with little or no input from the juvenile court or social agencies (Griffin, Torbet, & Szymanski, 1998). Following conviction, youth as young as 11 are placed in adult prisons. These changes are sharply at odds with the views of those who founded juvenile justice programs: Their explicit position was that an 11- or 12-year-old should not be judged by the same standards as an adult (Gittens, 1977). The year 2000 marks the 100th anniversary of the founding of the juvenile justice system, but unfortunately, there has been a serious retrogression in the handling of juveniles during the last quarter of the 20th century. The situation in 2000 is even more problematic than the conditions that led to the establishment of the juvenile justice system.

More than 2.8 million youth under the age of 18 were arrested in 1997, 19% of all arrests in the United States that year (Snyder, 1998). Of those who are adjudicated by the court, about 600,000 spent some time within that year in an out-of-home placement, detention, or a residential institution. In addition, an unknown number participated in some local justice program. Despite a popular myth that juvenile crime is worse than it has ever been, Bernard (1992) points out that in 1952, the youth population was larger than it was in 1992, and youth arrests then were 45% of all arrests, including 15.4% of all arrests for serious violent crime. Gun-related violence is higher today than it was in 1952, but it has declined since 1994 (Snyder, 1998).

Recent national concern about youth violence has provoked varied responses. It is true that violent crime by juveniles rose sharply in the early 1990s, but since 1996, there has been a decline in all crime, particularly in the most serious crimes, such as murder and rape. However, assaults and other violent crime are still higher than in the early 1980s. Attention to punishing offenders for several school-linked homicides has taken attention away from what is occurring inside the justice system following the passage of more and more punitive laws, under which thousands of youth are charged with minor crimes and institutionalized, often for very long periods of time.[1] Also incarcerated for long periods of time are youth charged with

status and sex offenses as well as drug offenses, both those who are charged with trafficking and those who may be diagnosed as mentally ill and substance abusers.

The criminal justice system is reactive rather than proactive or preventive, largely because it assumes that the system can do little to alleviate the complex cultural causes of crime, racism, poverty, urban disorganization, sexism, unstable employment, widespread availability of alcohol and other drugs, and ineffective K–12 or vocational education (Currie, 1998). Little emphasis has been given to prevention or advocacy strategies that would require a proactive approach.

Because of the size and complexity of the justice system, it is inadvisable to address critical contemporary issues that are relevant for social work practice in both the adult and juvenile systems. Therefore, I have chosen to focus on the juvenile justice system in this chapter, because it is where social workers are more likely to be employed today and where the opportunities for social work are greater. The adult system is primarily concerned with punishment, retribution, public safety, and deterrence. If we can be more successful in reducing subsequent crime by juveniles, then, the volume of people in the adult system will also decline. At present, many youth ultimately find themselves in adult criminal careers (Blumstein, Farrington, & Morris, 1985).

This chapter is written for social workers who are presently practicing in the juvenile justice system or who are considering opportunities to do so. There are numerous opportunities for social workers to function within juvenile justice as treatment personnel, family and community liaisons, advocates on behalf of youth, and policy analysts and administrators. As of

1993, Gibelman and Schervish reported that only 1.2% of social workers were working in the justice system, down from 12% in 1950. Thirty years ago, social workers were in leadership positions in juvenile justice in the majority of states. In the 1980s, a gradual decline began in agencies and in social work education for practice in juvenile justice. Some have suggested that the decline was at least partially due to professional resistance to working in coercive settings with involuntary clients. However, given the millions of people now caught up in the criminal justice system who are not receiving the social services they desperately need, it is a priority that social work return to a more central role in criminal justice. There is a great need for professionally trained practitioners in all areas of juvenile justice, including prevention and diversion, alternatives for incarceration, probation, alternative schools, group homes, residential treatment centers, training schools, and reintegration programs. We will address some of the key areas in which social workers can make important contributions because of urgent contemporary needs. These include practice principles, from the evaluation of a range of juvenile programs, diversity issues, risk and needs assessment and other approaches, to structured decision making, minority overrepresentation, community-based services, and gender-sensitive programming. Before examining specific issues it is important to consider the values and ideologies that have influenced the developments in juvenile justice.

VALUES AND PHILOSOPHICAL ISSUES

Although society has sanctioned juvenile misconduct for thousands of years, youth were typically processed with adults until the 20th century. The juvenile justice system was established as a separate system at the beginning of the 20th century by judges, social workers, and concerned citizens. Juveniles were to be processed and treated separately from adults with the primary goal being rehabilitation rather than punishment. Youth were viewed as malleable when provided with proper guidance and support. Court and service agency procedures were to be flexible, informal, child-centered, and based on scientific knowledge (Feld, 1995). The needs of youth were paramount rather than the offenses that they committed. Due process and other civil liberties protections were deemed unnecessary when what the child needed was treatment. Although implementation of these goals was less than ideal, this model operated in all of the states, until U.S. Supreme Court decisions of the late 1960s and 1970s asserted that juveniles were entitled to at least some due process protections. In the 1980s, state legislatures began to pass laws formalizing court procedures, de-emphasizing rehabilitation, and treating juveniles like adults in many instances. This movement accelerated throughout the 1990s in response to the increase in juvenile violent crime and greater punitiveness in the adult system. At the beginning of the 21st century, there is little difference in the processing of juveniles and adults in many states, with one major exception: Juveniles can still be adjudicated as delinquents for status offenses, behaviors that are not crimes for adults. For females, in particular, status offenses may lead to long periods of institutionalization as delinquents.

Many philosophies are manifested in the juvenile justice system, as Guarino-Ghezzi and Loughran (1998) point out. They identified as liberal those who believe that rehabilitation can and should be the primary goal; libertarians favor the least restrictive and nonintervention approaches by the state; conservatives argue that juveniles need to be punished and held accountable for their crime and damage to victims; and fundamentalists present religious values as moral precepts to be followed, denying the need for education and community and job development as critical to nondelinquent behavior. Abolitionists would remove all distinction between adults and juveniles as far as criminal law and processing is concerned. Each of these ideologies can be identified in aspects of the juvenile justice system, but none is clearly dominant except for a synthesis of the conservative and abolitionist philosophies.

Some general values in U.S. society have been relevant for the justice system. It is often said that youth are our most valuable asset, and such statements are used to justify various sanctions, programs, and appropriations. Unfortunately, it appears that we are really much closer to George Bernard Shaw's dictum, "Youth is such a wonderful thing—what a shame to waste it on children." Youth are undervalued and underused. Moreover, millions of young people are affected by poverty, poor health, unemployment, substance abuse or mental illness, and lack of education. Youth are more likely to die from homicide or suicide than anything else. They are growing up in neighborhoods that are permeated by crime and deviant behavior, with almost no opportunity for normal recreation and sports. Youth lack the protections that are afforded adults in most spheres of life. They have almost no political power and few acknowledged civil rights.

Americans prefer short-term and crisis-oriented solutions. Thus, little emphasis is placed on primary prevention. We respond with great generosity to "real" people in crises, but we do not respond to statistical realities such as poverty, illness, or injustice experienced by a group of people. Individualism and independence are two of our most prized values, and we tend to view even youth in trouble as largely responsible for their behavior.

These values of adult mainstream society influence developments in the justice system. Our failure to establish prevention programs to control juvenile crime results in high social and economic costs, as Lipsey (1984) points out. Prevention programs, to be effective, would need to be established outside the justice system by social agencies, schools, churches, and other community organizations. Unfortunately, few of these organizations are being funded today for such prevention services.

THEORETICAL FOUNDATIONS AND LITERATURE

Theories of delinquent behavior and related literature are extensive, so this chapter will highlight those that appear to be particularly relevant for practice with delinquent youth. Shoemaker (1996) provides an excellent summary including detailed discussion of the following:

1. Classical theories of Beccaria emphasized free will and rational choice by individuals to reach desired goals (Platt, 1977). Although not widely used today, elements of this approach are found in learning and differential association explanations of crime.

2. Biological and biosocial theories assume that behavior is caused by internal mechanisms that predispose an individual to crime (Booth & Osgood, 1993). A rich literature

on these theories goes back to Lombroso, but these ideas are also represented in contemporary theory about genetic factors in criminal behavior (Walters, 1989).

3. Psychological theories have abounded as explanations of delinquency, from the time of Freud to the present, as is evident in the recent instruments for structured decision making in juvenile justice (Wilson & Herrnstein, 1985). Despite recent emphasis on the importance of environmental interaction, the search for a unique set of personal, psychological antecedents of delinquency continues.

4. Social disorganization and anomie have been influential in the work of Durkheim (1951), Merton (1957), and Shaw and McKay (1964), but Spergel's (1995) studies of youth gangs also emphasize the crucial contribution of environmental conditions. Moreover, Spergel develops his community intervention principles using these theories.

5. Working-class and underclass theories are represented in the work of Cohen (1955) on goal displacement; of Cloward and Ohlin (1961) on opportunity theory; of Wolfgang, Figlio, and Sellin (1972) on subcultural values and norms; and of Miller (1958) on lower class culture. More recently, the work of Wilson (1987) on the underclass falls into this category.

6. Interpersonal and situational theories are represented in the work of Sutherland and Cressey (1978) on differential association and of Matza (1964) on delinquency and drift. These authors postulate that delinquency is behavior learned and reinforced in interpersonal interaction. These theories have been very influential in probation strategies about relationships between offenders.

7. Control theories cover a broad range, but all assume that a person must be held in check if delinquent tendencies are to be suppressed (Kempf, 1993). Closely linked is social bond theory as developed by Hirschi (1983),

which incorporates attachment, commitment, involvement, and beliefs. Contemporary juvenile justice policy is dominated by control theories.

8. Labeling theory as espoused by Lemert (1974) and Mahoney (1974) asserts that characteristics such as sex, race, residence, and class may increase the likelihood of being identified as delinquent but that individuals also define themselves as delinquent after repeated acts.

9. Radical theory has not been very influential with respect to intervention, but it does highlight the importance of economic factors in crime (Quinney, 1980).

10. Feminist theory has been developed in recent years because of the differences between males and females in delinquent behavior and in the conditions affecting their entry into the justice system. Power-control theories have been challenged by those who argue that differences in socialization are important, as is the need to examine behavior from a gender-context perspective (Belknap, 1996; Chesney-Lind, 1997).

DIVERSITY ISSUES

Unfortunately, a significant characteristic of criminal justice is minorities are more overrepresented here than in any other social institution. Youth of color are arrested and incarcerated at higher rates than white youth, and the gap continues to widen each year (Tonry, 1995). Those in the justice system are also more likely to be males and victims of violent crime than any other age or sex group (Bastian & Taylor, 1994; Fagan, Forst, & Vivona, 1987). According to 1992 national population data, minority youth compose about 32% of the youth population but 65% of youth held in detention centers and 66% of those in training schools (U.S. Office of Juvenile Justice and Delinquency Prevention, 1995). Although the majority of the nonwhite youth are African American, the numbers of Hispanic and Asian youth are increasing rapidly. Moreover, Hispanic and Native American youth are often counted as white and are not identified with their minority group.

Recently, Bonczar and Beck (1997) estimated that at birth today, 5.1% of all people in the United States can expect to be incarcerated in a prison, but 28.1% of all black males can expect to be incarcerated. That number is six times the rate of whites and eight times the rate for women. In fact, by age 25, 15.9% of black males and 6.3% of Hispanic males, compared to 1.7% of white males, can expect to have served time in a state or federal prison. Miller (1996) estimates that 75% of all 18-year-old African American males in Washington, D.C., can look forward to being arrested and jailed at least once before they reach age 35. The reality of these predictions is supported by the fact that in 1994, 11.7% of African American males in the age group 20 to 29 years were incarcerated (Mauer, 1997; Mauer & Huling, 1995). More than 10 years ago, Blumstein et al. (1985) pointed out that the disproportionate arrest of African American males over a lifetime occurs primarily in the juvenile years before 18, so it is particularly important to try to determine how and why this disproportion occurs. Moreover, they note that if you include misdemeanors as well as felonies, 90% of African American males can expect to be arrested at least once in their lifetime.

The disproportionate representation of minority youth in the juvenile justice system oc-

curs not just at apprehension or arrest; it may also increase at later stages of juvenile justice processing: adjudication, institutional commitment, and placement in public training schools rather than in private facilities (Bortner, Sunderland, & Winn, 1985). In some instances, as Kempf-Leonard and Sontheimer (1995) have noted, disproportionate representation of minority youth increases at successive stages of processing, but that is not a general pattern in all instances. This process is often referred to as the *amplification* effect (Tonry, 1995).

The differential processing of minority people by both the juvenile and adult criminal justice systems is a matter of increasing national concern, but despite the provisions and policy priorities of the Juvenile Justice and Delinquency Prevention Act (JJDPA), little concrete action has been taken to date to reverse this pattern of minority overrepresentation in the justice system; in arrests, jail or detention, court convictions, commitments to secure facilities, or probation or parole (Bishop & Frazier, 1990; Bishop, Henretta, & Frazier, 1992). In 1999, a serious effort was initiated to eliminate the policy priority of reducing minority overrepresentation in the juvenile justice system through Senate Bill 254.

Some refer to this disproportionate representation as a manifestation of serious institutionalized racism and relate it to prejudice, the lack of opportunity for minority people in education and legitimate employment, the quality of life in inner-city ghettos, and housing segregation (Aguirre & Baker, 1994; Axelrad, 1952; Currie, 1998; Kempf-Leonard, Pope, & Feyerherm, 1995; Kirk, 1996; Leiber, 1994; Mann, 1993; Sampson, 1997; Wu, 1997). Others interpret the situation as a reflection of greater involvement of minority people in criminal behavior (Blumstein, 1995), particularly the involvement of young males in violent and drug-related crime. This issue has been studied quite extensively for adults, but less attention has been given to examining the causes or correlates of the disproportionate processing of juveniles. The long-term consequence of this processing of youth may be even more problematic than it is for adults, because early in the 21st century, the majority of young people in this society will be from groups now classified as minority.

Wordes, Bynum, and Corley (1994) documented the disproportionate processing of juveniles in the early stages of the Michigan juvenile justice system—apprehension, arrest, and detention. They used a multimethod design, including both police and court case processing. The overrepresentation of minorities was most severe for youth taken to court and placed in secure detention, as well as in formal case processing. Bynum, Wordes, and Corley (1993) observed that the initial decision to detain was the critical one. Indirect affects were associated with social factors such as social class and family structure, but even when controlling for these factors, there was a residual effect associated with race. No differences were observed in age at apprehension, age at first offense, and number of prior offenses. Caucasian youth were more likely to be dropped or diverted than youth of color.

Nationally, data from the *Children in Custody* (U.S. Office of Juvenile Justice and Delinquency Prevention, 1995) report provides information about changes that have occurred in the past 15 years. There has been a marked increase in the institutional placements of both males and females in public and private facilities, with a larger increase for males (110%), but the rate of increase for females is greater. There has been an increase in the proportion of minority youth from 52% to 64% in public facilities and 37% to 43% in private facilities.

In a study of disproportionate minority representation in Michigan, we examined all male commitments to the state in a 3-year period (Sarri, Rollin, Wolfson, Farmer, & Ward, 1998). Of these, 32.6% were non-Hispanic white and 67.4% were minority youth. The largest group were African Americans, making up 61.5% of the total. The overall percentage of minority youth in public training schools slightly exceeded the national percentage of 66% reported by the Office of Juvenile Justice and Delinquency Prevention in 1994.

Commitment by county was selected as a critical variable for analysis, because it is the county juvenile court that makes the decision about commitment to the state. Fourteen counties were selected for more detailed analysis because only these counties had two or more minority youth commitments between 1991 and 1994. All of these were male youth committed to state public institutions for crimes they had committed in their respective counties. Females and youth sent to out-of-state institutions are not included in this analysis. Table 21.1 presents commitment information for the 14 counties, overall and separately for minority youth. The overall in-state commitment rate for Wayne County was 406 per 100,000 youth, far higher than in the next highest county, Kalamazoo, with 278.8, followed by Van Buren with 210.5 per 100,000 youth. At the low end was Calhoun County, with a rate of 37.6 youth committed per 100,000 youth population. However, in

TABLE 21.1 Juvenile Male Commitment Rate, by County and Race/Ethnicity (N = 1,746)

| | Number of Commitments | | | Youth Population and Total Commitments | | | | Commitment Rate per 100,000 | | |
County	Majority	Minority	Total	Total Youth Population	Minority Youth Population	Majority Youth Population	Total Commitments per 100,000 Youth	Majority Rate	Minority Rate	Ratio, Minority to Majority
Muskegon	13	9	22	18,880	3,889	14,991	116.5	86.7	231.4	2.7
Genesee	36	48	84	53,575	15,629	37,946	156.8	94.9	307.1	3.2
Ottawa	28	6	34	22,718	1,363	21,355	146.7	131.1	440.2	3.4
Calhoun	3	3	6	15,978	2,668	13,310	37.6	22.5	112.4	5.0
Oakland	60	48	108	114,746	1,5491	99,255	94.1	60.4	309.9	5.1
Wayne	161	836	997	245,592	123,532	122,060	405.8	131.9	676.7	5.1
Berrien	6	11	17	19,371	4,901	14,470	87.8	41.5	224.4	5.4
Macomb	34	9	43	74,658	3,359	71,299	57.6	47.6	267.9	5.6
Washtenaw	9	17	26	24,505	4,999	19,506	106.1	46.1	340.0	7.4
Ingham	10	23	33	27,797	6,199	21,598	118.7	46.3	371.0	8.0
Kalamazoo	22	41	63	22,596	3,887	18,709	278.8	117.6	1,054.8	9.0
Saginaw	4	19	23	26,854	8,190	18,664	85.6	21.4	232.0	10.9
Van Buren	7	2	19	9,026	1,155	7,871	210.5	88.9	1,039.0	11.7
Kent	25	65	90	56,080	8,748	47,332	160.5	52.8	743.0	14.0

NOTE: These data include all males committed to state residential juvenile correctional facilities between 1991 and 1994 in Michigan. See Sarri et al. (1998), for further description of these data.

TABLE 21.2 Total Commitments by Youth Arrest, Poverty, Minority Rates, School Dropout, and Unemployment[a]

	R2	B	T	Significance T
Youth arrest rate	.0042	−.005888	−.740	.4617
Youth poverty rate	.0120	11.7888	.099	.9213
Youth minority rate	.4525	1090.5409	8.037	.0000
School dropout rate	.0299	23.241529	1.579	.1181
Unemployment	.0059	−2.744909	−.695	.4893

a. Youth arrest rate is for Part I or serious crimes only. The rate was also calculated for total arrest rates, and nearly identical results were obtained. Data for the above analysis are presented in Table 21.1.

Calhoun County, the rate per 100,000 majority youth is 22.5, compared to 112.4 per 100,000 minority youth. Muskegon, a relatively poor, industrial county, had the lowest ratio of difference (2.7) but still a high rate of minority youth commitments (231.4 per 100,000 youth). Overall, Kalamazoo County had the highest rate of commitment of minority youth (1054.8), but Kent County had the largest ratio of difference. Minority youth in the latter county were 14 times more likely to be committed than were majority youth.

Offenses varied among these youth, but there were no clearly discernible patterns indicating that minority youth committed more serious crimes. They were more likely to be committed for drug-related offenses, although our data about the youth indicated that a higher proportion of majority youth were substance abusers. In one county, which used structured decision-making instruments, judges were far more likely to override the recommendation for community placement for a minority youth than a majority youth. Factors such as family characteristics were associated with commitment rather than the juvenile's offense pattern.

Table 21.2 presents the results of an analysis in which we tried to identify the variables that were correlated with county commitments of juveniles to determine if crime, poverty, unemployment, or education might explain some of this difference.[2]

Most of the variance in county commitments was explained by the percentage of the minority youth who were selected for commitment versus the percentage of majority youth who were selected. Poverty and unemployment rates explained less than would be expected; however, when one considers that all but one county in Michigan must pay the state half or more of the costs of commitment of their delinquent youth, the counties with fewer resources are less likely to commit youth and will keep them in the county on probation or in some similar program. Wayne County was the exception, in that it was not obliged to pay 50% of the cost; not surprisingly, this county committed many more youth to the state than the other counties. In addition, it was noteworthy that almost no community-based programs were developed for youth in Wayne County because it had no financial incentive to do so. Youth arrest rates explain almost none of the variance in commitments, although this would be expected to be an important predictor.[3] The findings from this study illustrate the complexity of decision making associated with minority overrepresentation. If we compare these results for males with similar data for females, the same patterns prevail except that the level of minority overrepresentation is even higher for females.

Almost no information is available about how the juvenile justice system has responded to diversity issues related to sexual orientation in the juvenile justice system. Only sexual offending really receives attention. Given the identity crisis typically experienced by adolescents, many could be expected to experience confusion regarding sexual orientation, but this issue has seldom been addressed. With respect to issues of age, the majority of juvenile offenders in the system are between the ages of 15 and 18 years. Many of the issues for this age group also reflect problems in adolescent development for which adult society has little or no tolerance (Welsh, Harris, & Jenkins, 1996). A public health approach could be applied successfully to address much of delinquency because it has long been recognized as a time-limited phenomenon. Age is becoming a human rights issue for the justice system, in that youth as young as 7 may now be processed and tried as adults. In many states, there are no lower age limits. International human rights groups such as Amnesty International have criticized the United States for its failure to adhere to the International Human Rights Standards that the world community has adopted pertaining to children and the justice system.

We will address the issues of diversity and gender later in the chapter. We will now examine some of the current practice issues in juvenile justice, first presenting practice principles that have been developed from evaluation of a variety of programs.

PRACTICE ISSUES

It is frequently asserted that effective treatment in juvenile corrections is no longer worth attempting because the results from systematic evaluation of many programs have produced pessimistic outcomes. Those who support this position argue that juveniles convicted of violating the law should be committed to programs whose goals are protection of society, deterrence, and retribution. At the same time, the number of programs and technologies for needs-based services to juvenile delinquents is growing. The conflict between these two contending parties remains unresolved, although there has clearly been a shift in resource allocation to control and custody rather than treatment and rehabilitation. A particularly large reduction has occurred in community-based nonresidential programs of all types.

It is not possible in a few pages to discuss the range of practice literature about work with juvenile delinquents or efforts directed toward the prevention of delinquency. We will focus on the literature that relates to social work in direct practice with youth in community or residential programs. To set the context for our review, a few quotes by adolescent juveniles in the justice system illustrate major challenges for social workers with clients in the juvenile justice system today (Sarri et al., 1998).

One youth (now in an adult prison) observed about the neighborhood in which he lived,

> I grew up in the southwest part of town, and it's not a good neighborhood. It's just full of kinds of drugs, violence, you know, all that. All packed in one of those neighborhoods. It's no place to grow up. You expect somebody to turn out right, you can't raise them in a neighborhood like that. . . .

We was all poor, you know, and we was trying to get money and we'd try to do everything and anything to make money . . . but they [my family] could pay the rent much, 'cause my SSI was paying for most of the helping out with the family and all that. And when I moved, they couldn't pay the rent and got behind in rent. So they had to move out, into my grandmother's house. (Sarri et al., 1998, pp. 129-130)

Another observed,

You know, the 'hood was crazed, man. There sure were a lot of people like me, man, people who never really came up with nothing, and when they got old, just decided that they was gonna go get it on their own. (Sarri et al., 1998, p. 140)

Exposure to trauma and violence characterized the early lives of many youth, as another explained:

I became a criminal when I was a little kid. When I was a little kid, I'd seen people get killed. I'd seen people steal stuff, fights, all types of stuff. I grew into it, and it became a part of my life. Basically, almost everybody had a gun. (Sarri et al., 1998, p. 130)

In commenting about reintegration services by social agencies, another said,

When I was a juvenile, they never once asked me what did I want or what was going on with me or nothing like that, you know. It was always, they'd set me down and tell me what kind of problems I got. They wouldn't listen to me to see what was really going on with me. (Sarri et al., 1998, p. 157)

What is known about empirically based practice principles for working with delinquent youth? There is a rich literature based on extensive careful evaluation of juvenile justice pro-grams that address various phases of intervention, from diversion programs to reintegration services. Some evaluative studies are of primary or secondary prevention, but the majority tend to be of tertiary intervention, involving work with more serious and chronic offenders. The following principles are illustrative of the syntheses that have been done by several authors to identify practice principles. These principles refer to intervention practice in interpersonal services with clients and their families and also to social work interventions in the community with other agencies and organizations.

Altschuler and Armstrong (1994 and 1996)

Based on extensive evaluation of programs throughout the United States, Altschuler and Armstrong (1996) identified several factors linked to recidivism by juvenile delinquents: frequency and severity of prior offenses, early entry into the juvenile justice system, number of prior commitments, family resources, peer-group and school experiences, and involvement with drugs and/or alcohol. Using an integration of strain, social learning, and social control theories of delinquency, the authors offer five principles for effective reintegration services, which have been empirically tested in several states:

1. Prepare youth for increasing responsibility and freedom in the community.
2. Help youth become involved in the community, and get the community to interact and support these youth.
3. Work with youth, their families, peers, schools, and employers to identify the qualities needed for legitimate success in that community.

4. Integrate surveillance and services based on risk factors. The community support system must be actively involved.

4. Develop new community resources and supports where needed.

5. Monitor and evaluate youth and the community on their abilities to interact effectively so that youth will not return to crime.

Altschuler (1994) also emphasizes that reintegration must be an integral part of the juvenile justice system: It must be able to cut across traditional bureaucratic domains and professional ideologies. Agencies and workers must collaborate closely in the design and provision of services. He further advocates that the youth have a single worker whose role is that of case manager, advocate, and confidant. Services must be coordinated, consistent, and mutually reinforcing. Some form of behavioral or contingency contracting is recommended, as is a relationship of trust and predictability. Procedures for identifying high-risk youth are necessary, as is assessment of the risk level of the community. Case planning, assessment, and management must be individualized. Ongoing monitoring and evaluation must also be a component, if agencies are to demonstrate whether or not their services are effective.

Greenwood, Deschenes, and Adams (1993)

In a study of reintegration services of chronic juvenile offenders, Greenwood, Deschenes, and Adams (1993) reported on their evaluation of the Skillman Intensive Aftercare Program. The program involved a 2-month early release from residential placement and intensive aftercare supervision in their home community for 6 months. Program components included prerelease contacts and planning between the af-

tercare worker, the youth, and his family; intensive supervision and counseling involving several contacts per day; efforts to resolve family problems affecting the youth; and efforts to mobilize community resources. The program was modeled on an aftercare program in Massachusetts. One hundred youth were randomly assigned to experimental and control conditions at each site. The control program included the usual agency services. Differences in the offense characteristics, timing of release, intensity of supervision, and use of sanctions varied between the experimental and control groups. It should be noted that only 22% of the youth in the experimental group were rearrested, and of those, only 28% were arrested for a felony index crime.

The findings revealed that differences in program content produced no measurable differences in final outcomes. The experimental program did not appear to have a significant effect on the behavior of participating youth. The authors suggest that the surveillance/casework approach was inappropriate or inadequate to meet the needs of these young men. They further recommend that more explicit educational and training efforts, using cognitive-behavioral techniques might be more effective.

When community-based programs were compared with institutional programs, the authors state that where there were no differences in recidivism; the community program should be chosen because of its cost advantage and also because there is less disruption in the youth's life. In a review of the literature on what works with juvenile offenders, Greenwood et al. (1993) points out that behavioral, skill-oriented, and multimodal methods produced the largest effects, and more positive effects occurred in the community than in institutional settings. He further noted that more effective programs used these methods to address anger management, conflict resolution skills, and substance abuse resistance training. In a later monograph, Greenwood, Model, Rydell, and Chiesa (1996) developed a model for effectively diverting youth from a life of crime. In that, they found that investment in education provided the biggest payoff in preventing subsequent recidivism.

Barton and Butts (1990)

A study completed by Barton and Butts (1990) drew similar conclusions to those of Greenwood and his colleagues. Barton and Butts compared three contrasting community programs that were alternatives to residential placement but had components similar to those in reintegration programs. Their findings indicated that 56% of the youth in these three programs offended again, but the program that provided intensive in-home care had only 46% recidivism, and there was a program suppression effect in that youth in the program were arrested for less serious crimes than they had committed earlier. Barton and Butts reported that community-based alternatives were as effective as institutional programs in terms of recidivism but were far more cost-effective. Particularly relevant here, for our purposes of attempting to identify the prerequisites for effective program components, they emphasize:

1. A stronger focus should be placed on youths' peer network, restricting contact with friends known to be delinquent and facilitating the selection of friends who are more pro-social in their orientation.
2. Job training, job creation, and placement all need to receive greater attention because of the high rates of chronic unemployment in urban communities and because of the relationship between unemployment and crime.
3. Programs should provide services (especially job-related services) to other members of the youths' families.
4. Youths not involved in criminal activity after 1 year should be appropriately terminated, with the opportunity for re-contact if the youth deems it necessary.
5. Small programs appear to be more effective because they can adapt to changing circumstances more readily and are not overly bureaucratized.
6. Programs need adequate resources and some assurance of continuance, provided they can demonstrate effectiveness. Delinquency aftercare/reintegration services will be needed for the foreseeable future; therefore, agencies need to have some stability if they are to select, train, and maintain excellent staff and if they are to have the necessary resources for programming.

Lerman and Pottick (1994)

Because several programs address the family as a critical element in reintegration, the research of Lerman and Pottick (1994) is relevant. They note that all too often, parents or family members are blamed for a youth's deviance, yet, parents may be dealt with superficially and in a highly bureaucratic manner. Moreover, they may be expected to be responsible for a youth's behavior when that may be nearly impossible by the time a youth is an older adolescent. Lerman and Pottick emphasize the importance of treating parents as subjects who actively participate in treatment, not as mere objects who are peripheral to the intervention. It is also important, they say, to consider how the parents see the problems of their youth, when and how they observed the problems, and how they function as third-party help seekers. In a study completed with a large sample of troubled adolescents in Newark, Lerman and Pottick recommended that workers should:

1. Improve the ability of parents to become better help seekers and providers
2. Be more responsive and helpful when families seek help in caring for their children
3. Avoid stereotypical handling (e.g., of single-mother families)
4. Offer services that promote alternative pro-social behavior in which the parents can be involved
5. Keep parents well-informed about any actions that are taken with respect to their children
6. Treat parents with respect

Blechman (1992)

Because some parents may not be available or interested in their youth, alternative programs need to be provided. Blechman (1992) recommends that mentoring programs can be successful with high-risk youth involved in delinquency. This approach appears to be particularly effective for reintegration from a residential setting to semi-independent or independent living in the community. She indicates that such service can be effectively provided by a paraprofessional or professional. Mentors can assist youth in conflict resolution, development of effective communication and other interpersonal skills, education, and job search. Mentors also serve as a viable role model.

Gendreau (1980 and 1998)

The research and reviews of Gendreau and his colleagues about effective programs for working with serious delinquents emphasize the cognitive behavioral approach that we have already noted as the more effective means for successful reintegration. His conclusions about effective programs emphasize the following:

1. Intensive services should occupy 40% to 70% of the youth's time each day and should last at least 3 months, although longer is often required.
2. Program contingencies should be enforced in a firm but fair manner to motivate changes in youth's behavior.
3. The responsivity principle should be followed. Wherever possible, individual differences of clients should be matched with characteristics of staff and with the style of the program delivery.
4. Workers should relate to offenders in interpersonally sensitive and constructive ways and should be trained and supervised appropriately.
5. The program's structure and activities should disrupt the criminal network.
6. Relapse prevention services should be provided in the community by planning and rehearsing alternative pro-social responses, monitoring and anticipating problem situations that might lead to relapse, practicing new pro-social behaviors in increasingly difficult situations, rewarding improved competencies to combat relapse, training significant others to provide reinforcement of pro-social behaviors, and offering "booster" sessions that return to the formal treatment phase.

Gendreau emphasizes the importance of pro-social modeling opportunities in pro-social environments, of being action oriented and flexible in using extent community resources, and of providing roles for advocacy and peer support.

Spergel (1995)

In his discussion of intervention with youth gangs, Spergel (1995) offers action strategies at five levels: suppression, social intervention, opportunities provision, organizational change and development, and community mobilization. He also identifies the setting in which activities for youth take place at each of these levels. These settings include streets and parks, homes, police stations, schools, prosecution, judges, probation, corrections, parole and reintegration, employment and training, community-based agency, grass-roots organization (especially churches), emerging gang situations, and chronic gang contexts. Very specific protocols are identified for each of these targets. The protocols include individual worker activity with clients, collaborative work in the family and community, organizational collaboration and development, and a large variety of activities in community mobilization.

Price, Cioci, and Penner (1993)

In their review of school and community programs, Price et al. (1993) emphasize active involvement of youth and family members in programs for adolescents, including programs that:

1. Provide supportive aid and material benefits
2. Encourage active youth participation in community projects, mobilizing the support of parents and other adults
3. Are sensitive to the goals of adolescents and provide opportunities to learn desired skills
4. Are responsive to the rapid changes that occur in early adolescent social and physical development

5. Exist where organizational support for programs is consistent and continuing

Price et al. also note the need for alternative approaches to program evaluation.

In addition to the issues and principles presented by the above authors, there are several current areas of concern in the United States, in which social workers can make a particular contribution because of their knowledge and skill in working with at-risk youth populations. These include community-level approaches to addressing youth violence, structured decision making regarding juvenile placements, prevention programs, and services to female juvenile offenders.

The Community and Youth Violence

Youth violence concerns the entire country and has provoked a variety of responses, not the least of which are those from the criminal justice system (Bilchik, 1996). However, the justice system may be the least effective way to address this problem. The criminal justice system is always reactive after the tragedy has occurred. Even in the case of gun violence, it has not had an effective prevention or pro-active strategy. The presence of guns as a critical instrument of violence is reflected in Blumstein's report (1998) that gun suicide rates by young people, especially young African Americans, escalated at the same time as homicide rates, when there were no comparable trends in nongun homicides or suicides. Thus, the argument of Prothrow-Stith (1991 and 1998) and many others is that a public health approach to violence prevention and reduction will be more effective than one focused on punishment and deterrence. This approach focuses on the community as the central target in any primary prevention approach (Center for Disease Control, 1997). Although this approach recognizes that violence is a multifaceted problem requiring solutions at various levels, the community must inevitably be the critical target. The community is where social workers in local agencies can play important roles in their own practice and in collaborative work with other agencies. We have an excellent model in the Boston Violence Prevention Project, which began in 1986 and resulted in zero homicides of youth in Boston in 1996 (U.S. Department of Justice, 1996). The 10-year community collaborative effort included churches, schools, police, business, voluntary social agencies, associations, marketing organizations, and a special violence prevention curriculum that was widely implemented in youth organizations. Thousands of people, lay and professional, as well as youth were trained to address violence prevention and reduction in their respective organizations. In addition, secondary and tertiary prevention programs were implemented with selected youth.

Another approach that is being tried in many communities, and one in which social workers can actively participate, is the development of conflict resolution mechanisms in which youth learn to resolve conflict in schools, in the neighborhood, and in the family. In some instances, social workers in local agencies have collaborated with police and the court in developing quasi-judicial mechanisms for dealing with status offenses and misdemeanors outside the justice system. Juvenile panels or family councils, as they have been termed, are used extensively in Australia, New Zealand, and Scotland, and they were previously used in New Jersey and Connecticut. Many communities are establishing mediation and conflict resolution mechanisms for addressing a variety of community problems. In some communities, youth have been trained to conduct conflict resolution training with peers in middle and secondary schools. Strategies to increase youth involvement in violence prevention and reduction may have other unanticipated results in the form of pro-social behavior and general interest in community betterment (Garbarino & Kostelny, 1996; Hawkins et al., 1992; Sarri, Mogane, & Rollin, 1992). The issue of reintegration of the juvenile offender can be directly addressed in restorative justice programs.

Restorative justice programs are being developed in many communities as a means through which juvenile offenders can aid or compensate people whom they have victimized. Offenders are helped to accept responsibility for their behavior and to repair the damage that was caused. Such programs also encourage offenders to mitigate the harm and bring about reconciliation through dialogue. In some instances, restorative justice may also include service projects that provide a level of offender accountability to the community. Klein (1991) and Lipsey (1984) have shown that restorative justice programs have positive effects on recidivism.

These various community approaches to addressing violence are likely to have other positive effects because they will increase contact between offenders and other community residents and thereby increase understanding (Singer, 1996). However, to be effective, they have to be carefully planned and executed by trained people.

Structured Decision Making

To rationalize decision making in the juvenile justice system regarding detention and subsequent postdisposition decision making, many states and local jurisdictions have implemented structured decision making (Baird, Storrs, & Connelly, 1984; Lovegrove, 1989; Maupin, 1993; Petersilia & Turner, 1985). A youth's sociodemographic characteristics as well as delinquent behavior can be analyzed within a framework of risk or needs analysis. Those "at risk" are usually identified by the fact that they have already engaged in illegal behavior. Components of a risk definition, as developed by Resnick, Burt, Newmark, and Reilly (1992), include risk antecedents, risk markers, problem behaviors, and outcomes. Antecedents are environmental conditions such as poverty, family attributes, or neighborhood conditions. Markers refer to behaviors associated with negative outcomes for youth, for example, school performance. Outcomes are serious negative behaviors such as crime, substance abuse, and so forth, which identify the group at risk of an outcome such as dropping out of school or being suspended.

A realistic and relevant framework for evaluating risk is not limited to either an individual or an environmental approach but rather in some measure considers the influence of both. Research has consistently revealed that "the same outcomes may arise from different combinations of risk factors; one cannot predict risk without considering both the individual and the environment with which the individual interacts" (Resnick et al., 1992, p. 16). Similar systems, as well as sentencing guidelines, are used by many states in decision making regarding the placement of juvenile and adult offenders in various types of programs (Champion, 1994). The variables and the scoring systems are based on empirical information about the characteristics of youth, their families, and their environments, so that decision making about placement will be more objective and les discretionary (Hawkins & Catalano, 1992). It is important, however, to examine the theory and philosophy that underlie risk assessment because this may be correlated with disproportionate representation of minorities in residential placements (Lovegrove, 1989).

Young people's development, individual attitudes, and behavior, pro-social or antisocial, are molded by their personality and experience, family, and significant people in their immediate environment and community. One useful approach to understanding the impact and interplay of factors influencing the development of youth is the community-school-family-youth model. This model is layered like an onion, with each layer creating pressures and exerting demands on the ones on either side. On the outside are neighborhood/community characteristics: resources, role models, supports, dangers, and opportunities. In the next layer are the characteristics of the caregiver: beliefs, physical and mental health, quality of social support, experience with other children, and perceptions of the neighborhood. In the next layer are family characteristics: child-rearing methods, aspirations for the child, and perceptions of the child's strengths and weaknesses. In the next layer are the characteristics of the child, keeping in mind that as children mature, they develop their own strategies for dealing with their neighborhood. At the center of the model is the child (Earls & Reiss, 1994, p. 30).

Risk scores are supposed to predict the probability of re-offending and also to aid in determining the security level that needs to be considered in placement of a youth. The actual decision regarding placement of a delinquent will be made by a law enforcement or judicial official, but social workers (as probation officers) play important roles in selection, administration, and interpretation of risk assessment instruments. Many judges have been reluctant to use structured decision making for two reasons: (a) They believe that disposition is their decision and that standardized instruments control their discretion, and (b) resources for alternative placements in the community are often unavailable so the judge is forced to a more restrictive placement.

There has been limited evaluation of the validity as well as reliability of structured decision making, but it is being applied widely in sectors other than juvenile justice, including mental health and children's protective services. Many of the instruments currently being used include primarily psychological level variables and unrelated characteristics of the family as risk factors. The occurrence of both false negative and false positive predictions has not been fully analyzed. An additional factor noted by several in the field is that interadministrator reliability is often not addressed when several different assessors are used, who themselves may have variable responses to criteria that require subjective judgement. Last, initial interest in structured decision making was based on findings from the assessment of needs of the youth but has declined sharply in recent years as the justice system has been more focused on information to assure legal accountability in the sanctions that are assigned to a youth. Thus, programs are more interested in risk and are likely to ignore need.

Prevention

The concept *delinquency prevention* is widely supported, but intervention efforts have produced mixed results for a variety of reasons: programs were too broad in their focus; programs were never fully implemented as planned; evaluation results indicated that the program was ineffective (Howell, 1998; Lipsey, 1984; Maxon & Klein, 1997). Although some prevention programs were designed to reach youth in general through the media, most have targeted specific populations who were at risk because of individual or community characteristics or because they lacked attributes that would protect them from delinquency. Most prevention programs exist outside the formal justice system agencies, as would be expected. When formal justice system agencies attempt prevention, they often fail, because they adopt a negative approach only—that of trying to keep the juvenile from engaging in deviant behavior. In interviews with young people in the justice system, they reported that their workers always spoke to them about their negative behavior and failed to provide positive guidance, nor did workers help youth gain access to positive opportunities for their pro-social development (Sarri et al., 1998). Positive approaches that emphasize opportunities for healthy physical, social, and mental development have a greater likelihood of success (Dryfoos, 1990).

Prevention services in social work are construed as programs, policies, and clinical efforts directed toward helping clients avoid future problems (Schinke, 1997). In addition, prevention also includes efforts that promote individual and societal well-being. Thus, for example, we may provide conflict resolution and mediation training to youth so that they can address future conflicts in ways that will not lead to violence. But prevention also includes efforts to see that neighborhoods will have sports and recreation facilities, effective schools, and safe streets, so that the healthy functioning of youth is actively promoted.

Hawkins and Catalano (1992; Hawkins et al., 1992) emphasize the community as the critical target in prevention effort. They state that successful prevention interventions must do the following:

1. Address the highest-priority risk and protective factors
2. Focus on populations exposed to multiple risks
3. Address risk and protective factors early and at the appropriate developmental age
4. Address multiple risk factors in multiple domains
5. Create a continuum of prevention services for children at different developmental stages
6. Reach and communicate effectively with the target populations
7. Involve a service delivery system with well-trained staff

Among the prevention programs that have been evaluated, the following have been shown to produce positive results:

1. Youth employment and vocational training with an intensive educational component
2. Structured school and playground activities
3. Conflict resolution and peer mediation
4. Afterschool academic enrichment, sports, and recreation

5. Gang prevention, crisis intervention, and mediation
6. Youth service programs
7. Control on the sale, transfer, purchase, and possession of guns
8. Family treatment that incorporates parent training

It is clear from what is known about prevention that social workers in a variety of public and private agencies could be engaged in meaningful and effective prevention efforts. Strong advocacy of such programs is needed at present, when so much effort and so many resources are going to punishment and incarceration.

Social Services for Females in the Juvenile Justice System

Much of what we have considered in terms of practice issues applies equally to males and females, but many issues apply only to females, so we need to consider programming for them separately. Females are treated quite differently in the justice system because their delinquent behavior substantially differs from that of males. About 25% of all juveniles who are arrested are female, but arrests of juvenile females are increasing at a more rapid rate than those of males. However, significant differences are observed: Females are much less likely to be charged with serious felonies or misdemeanors (Belknap, 1996; Chesney-Lind, 1997; Giordano & Cernovich, 1992). Following the implementation of the JJDPA legislation in 1974, there was a decline in the apprehension and institutional placement of female status offenders, but processing is again increasing. Particularly noteworthy is the increasingly disproportional representation of minority females in the juvenile justice system. African American females are often processed and institutionalized unfairly (Young, 1994). Females charged as incorrigible are being placed for extended periods in institutions. Moreover, parents may refer their daughters to the court for placement, whereas such an action would be extremely rare in the case of male youth.

Adolescent female offenders are likely to have been victims of abuse, to be status offenders, to live in unstable living arrangements, to have a history of family incarceration, to abuse drugs and alcohol, to have had early contact with police and courts, to be pregnant or parenting or at risk for such, to have been victimized by older males, and to lack knowledge or skill in developing or maintaining appropriate, healthy boundaries in relationships (Chesney-Lind, 1997; Greene & Peters, 1998). It is estimated that 70% of females in the juvenile justice system have been physically and/or sexually abused. As was noted earlier, minority overrepresentation is more prevalent among females in the justice system than among males. Increasingly, parenting and pregnant teens are being placed in institutions, and their children in foster care, for extended periods of time. *Incorrigibility* is the label applied to these young women when they are committed to residential institutions because they have been rejected by parents, are living on the street, or insist on being with their child when such a decision is not supported.

Concern has been expressed about the increase in violent crime by juvenile females, but when the context of those offenses is examined, most violent behavior by female teens falls within the home and needs to be classified as domestic violence involving multiple people (U.S. Department of Justice, 1999). Young

women are often the victims as well as perpetrators, but they are the ones likely to be arrested. Fighting among peers has also increased, but again, the level of seriousness is questionable, according to special analysis of FBI arrest data (U.S. Department of Justice, 1999). Because of the classification of the behavior at home and with peers, female teens are being identified as a serious problem requiring a strict law enforcement response. Nonetheless, the issue of violence is one requiring intervention, but intervention as we have previously outlined.

After lagging in the development of gender-specific programming to address the special needs of females, states are now developing plans to address the needs of female juvenile offenders within their systems (Community Research Associates, 1998). Several states have already developed special programs that are producing positive results. In some states, such as Minnesota and Illinois, programs for female offenders are being blended with other services for at-risk adolescent females, with the result that the label of being a delinquent is muted.

All of these characteristics indicate that social work practice with this population will be more effective when it responds to gender-specific needs and characteristics. Urgently needed are community-based programs for adolescent girls that address issues of women's roles, societal barriers to women's growth and development, appropriate development of relationships, and adequate knowledge of reproductive behavior. Treating females equally does not imply that they receive processing or services identical to those provided to males. Gender-specific programs encourage healthy attitudes, behavior, and lifestyles, promoting social competence in females. Young women need to be directly involved in programming so as to have a stake in goals that are set.

CONCLUSIONS: CHALLENGES FACING SOCIAL WORK

After a century of emphasizing why children and youth need to be treated differently in the justice system because of their vulnerability and potential for change, as well as their inability to exercise civil rights as adults, the juvenile justice system took a step backward in the 1980s and 1990s to emphasize punishment and retribution and juveniles' similarity to adults for criminal justice processing. The separate juvenile court with its distinctive policies and procedures has been abolished in many states. Juveniles are mingled with adults and given similar sentences for their crimes. There appears to be minimal recognition of the likelihood of negative long-term consequences, nor is their awareness of the denial of civil and human rights to children and youth.

In this chapter, we have reviewed an extensive literature from systematic empirical evaluation of intervention programs in a variety of different locations and contexts, programs that serve different types of delinquent youth. The authors generally agree on a number of practice principles:

1. Youth and their families must have the necessary material and social support so that they can survive legitimately before they can participate effectively in treatment.
2. Well-structured programs are necessary to train youth in useful and skills that are relevant to today's and tomorrow's economy. When most youth leave the juvenile justice system, they are 17 to 18 years of age and lack the knowledge and skill to succeed in today's economy. Frey (1999) emphasizes using a variety of interventions that assist these youth in successful transition into the adult global economy.
3. Collaboration among workers is essential for effective results, including staff engaged in social work, law enforcement, education, health, employment, churches, sports, and recreation.
4. Reintegration and relapse services need to be available for extended periods of time because delinquents often face a hostile environment and re-offend because they lack ongoing support. Particularly critical is ongoing assistance with employment and avoidance of substance abuse.
5. Advocacy on behalf of youth, individually and collectively, is a necessary role for social workers working with juvenile delinquents and the communities in which they reside.
6. Youth need to be actively involved in decision making regarding their treatment and program; they should also be engaged in community activities so that they gain acceptance and a sense of legitimate belonging there.
7. Parents should be informed, consulted, and actively involved when they and the youth agree on their involvement.
8. Interventions should be provided at multiple levels to increase the probability of positive outcomes. The evidence suggests that community-level intervention is critically important. (Corbett & Petersilia, 1994)

These principles are ones that social workers can apply in their work with children and youth at risk for delinquency. Their approach is urgently needed in the majority of communities where large numbers of children are being punitively processed into the justice system, particularly poor and minority children. The focus of this chapter has been on practice principles and issues that are relevant for social workers engaged in interpersonal practice with delinquents and their families.

We have discussed a variety of programs that have been deemed successful through careful evaluation, but no matter how knowledgeable and skilled a worker is, a clinical practice approach alone will not succeed. Social workers must equally emphasize advocacy and the importance of social justice and human rights in the way this society treats its young people (Davis, 1999). Likewise, collaborative work with other professionals in and out of the justice system is also crucial. In many states today, civil and human rights protections of youth are being jeopardized by legislators who rush to pass short-sighted and punitive legislation.

The character of the justice system is critically shaped by the attitudes and behaviors of local communities. Communities can escalate or alleviate the problems of youth and families. Community opportunities, resources, and services define basic life conditions and generate motives for normative or deviant behavior. Community toleration of crime directly affects the rates and volume of cases presented for formal handling. Thus, if there were more primary and secondary prevention programs, the negative consequences of formal handling could be alleviated. The majority of juvenile offenders in state training schools or other secure institutions could be served in the community, as was demonstrated in Massachusetts in the 1970s (Miller, 1991). The responsiveness of community institutions determines whether individuals in trouble will be isolated in the justice system or will be offered service and assistance to achieve a conventional life. The newly developing restorative justice and conflict resolution efforts will facilitate movement toward normative and conventional lives. As Guarino-Ghezzi and Loughran (1998) state, we need a balanced continuum of juvenile justice services, but to

achieve that, social work practice will need to include community mobilization, advocacy, and interorganizational collaboration in addition to interpersonal services to individual clients and their families.

Delinquency is really a property of the social system in which many people are enmeshed, rather than a characteristic of those people called delinquents by agents of social control. Today, we need to develop constructive, community-based social institutions in which families, friends, neighbors, businesses, churches, law enforcement, and schools are engaged cooperatively with youth in the development of policies and programs to enhance youth wellbeing. Social workers can be the catalysts for the development of such a system.

NOTES

1. The 1-day count of children and youth under the age of 18 in juvenile correctional and detention facilities was 108,700 in 1997, a 47% increase since 1980. The rate of institutionalization per 100,000 youth between the ages of 5 and 17 was 151.38 in 1983 versus 234.49 in 1997, a substantial increase despite a decline in the population in this age group of more than 2 million nationally (U.S. Office of Juvenile Justice and Delinquency Prevention, 1998).

2. We were limited in the choice of variables to those for which county-level data regarding juveniles were available.

3. The results obtained in this analysis closely parallel those obtained by Downs in 1976, when he analyzed information on deinstitutionalization correlates in the 50 states during the early 1970s.

REFERENCES

Aguirre, A., & Baker, D. (1994). *Perspectives on race and ethnicity in American criminal justice.* St. Paul, MN: West.

Altschuler, D. M. (1994). Tough and smart juvenile incarceration: Integrating punishment, deterrence, and rehabilation. *Saint Louis University Public Law Review,* 14(1), 217-237.

Altschuler, D. M., & Armstrong, T. L. (1996). *Intensive aftercare for high-risk juveniles: A community care model.* Washington, DC: U.S. Department of Justice.

Arnold, W. R. (1971). Race and ethnicity relative to other factors in juvenile court dispositions. *American Journal of Sociology, 77*(2), 211-227.

Axelrad, S. (1952). Negro and white institutionalized delinquents. *American Journal of Sociology, 57,* 569-574.

Baird, S. C., Storrs, G. M., & Connelly, H. (1984). *Classification of juveniles in corrections: A model systems approach.* Washington, DC: Arthur D. Little.

Barton, W., & Butts, J. (1990). Viable options: Intensive supervision programs for juvenile delinquents. *Crime and Delinquency, 36,* 238-255.

Bastian, L. D., & Taylor, B. M. (1994). *Young black male victims.* Washington, DC: U.S. Department of Justice.

Belknap, J. (1996). *The invisible woman: Gender, crime and justice.* Belmont, CA: Wadsworth.

Bernard, T. (1992). *The cycle of juvenile justice.* New York: Oxford University Press.

Bilchik, S. (1996). *Reducing youth gun violence: An overview of programs and initiatives.* Washington, DC: U.S. Department of Justice, Office of Juvenile Justice and Delinquency Prevention.

Bishop, D. M., & Frazier, C. E. (1990). Race effects in juvenile justice decision-making: Findings of a statewide analysis. *The Journal of Criminal Law and Criminology, 86*(2), 392-414.

Bishop, D., Henretta, J., & Frazier, C. (1992). The social context of race differentials in juvenile justice dispositions. *The Sociological Quarterly, 33,* 447-458.

Blechman, E. A. (1992). Mentors for high-risk minority youth: From effective communication to bicultural competence. *Journal of Clinical Child Psychology, 21*(2), 160-169.

Blumstein, A. (1995). Violence by young people: Why the deadly nexus? *National Institute of Justice Journal,* No. 229, 2-9.

Blumstein, A. (1998). The context of recent changes in crime rates. In *What can the federal government do to decrease crime and revitalize communities?* (pp. 15-21). Washington, DC: Goverment Printing Office.

Blumstein, A., Farrington, D., & Morris, S. (1985). Delinquency careers: Innocents, amateurs, and persisters. In N. Morris & M. H. Tonry (Eds.), *Crime and justice: An annual review of research* (Vol. 6). Chicago: University of Chicago Press.

Bonczar, R., & Beck, A. (1997). *Lifetime likelihood of going to state or federal prison.* Washington, DC: U.S. Department of Justice, Office of Justice Programs.

Booth, A., & Osgood, D. W. (1993). The influence of testosterone on deviance in adulthood: Assessing and explaining the relationship. *Criminology, 31,* 93-117.

Bortner, M. A., Sunderland, M. L., & Winn, R. (1985). Race and the impact of juvenile deinstitutionalization. *Crime and Delinquency, 31*(1), 35-46.

Bynum, T., Wordes, M., & Corley, C. (1993). *Disproportionate representation in juvenile justice in Michigan: Examining the influence of race and gender.* East Lansing: Michigan State University School of Criminal Justice.

Center for Disease Control and Prevention. (1997). *Youth violence in the United States.* Available at: http://www.cdc.gov/ncipc/dvp/yvfacts.htm)

Champion, D. (1994). *Measuring offender risk: A criminal justice sourcebook.* Westport, CT: Greenwood.

Chesney-Lind, M. (1997). *The female offender: Women, girls, and crime.* Thousand Oaks, CA: Sage.

Cloward, R., & Ohlin, L. (1960). *Delinquency and opportunity.* New York: Free Press.

Cohen, A. (1955). *Delinquent boys: The culture of the gang.* New York: Free Press.

Community Research Associates. (1998). *Female juvenile offenders: A status of the states report.* Washington, DC: U.S. Department of Justice, Office of Juvenile Justice and Delinquency Prevention.

Corbett, R., Jr., & Petersilia, J. (1994). What works with juvenile offenders: A synthesis of the literature and experience. *Federal Probation, 58* (No. 4).

Currie, E. (1998). *Crime and punishment in America.* New York: Holt.

Davis, N. (1999). *Youth crisis: Growing up in a high-risk society.* Westport, CT: Praeger.

Downs, G. (1976). *Bureaucracy, innovation, and public policy.* Lexington, MA: Lexington Books.

Durkheim, E. (1951). *Suicide* (J. Spaulding & G. Simpson, Trans.). New York: Free Press.

Earls, F. J., & Reiss, A. J., Jr. (1994). *Breaking the cycle.* Washington, DC: U.S. Department of Justice, National Institute of Justice Research.

Fagan, J., Forst, M., & Vivona, T. S. (1987). Racial determinants of the judicial transfer decision prosecuting violent youth in criminal court. *Crime and Delinquency, 33*(2), 259-286.

Feld, B. C. (1995). The social context of juvenile justice administration: Racial disparities in an urban juvenile court. In K. Kempf-Leonard, C. E. Pope, & W. H. Feyerherm (Eds.), *Minorities in juvenile justice* (pp. 66-98). Thousand Oaks, CA: Sage.

Frey, H. (1999). *Employment and training for court-involved youth* (Fact Sheet No. 102). Washington, DC: U.S. Department of Justice, Office of Justice Programs.

Garbarino, J., & Kostelny, K. (1996). What do we need to know to understand children in war and community violence? In R. Apfel & B. Simon (Eds.), *Minefields in their hearts: The mental health of children in war and communal violence.* New Haven, CT: Yale University Press.

Gendreau, P. (1980). *Effective correctional treatment.* Toronto: Butterworth.

Gendreau, P. (1998). *Community corrections: Probation, parole, and intermediate sanctions.* New York: Oxford University Press.

Gibelman, M., & Schervish, P. (1993). *Who we are: The social work labor force as reflected in NASW membership.* Washington, DC: National Association of Social Workers Press.

Giordano, P. C., & Cernovich, S. A. (1992). School bonding, race, and delinquency. *Criminology, 301,* 261-291.

Gittens, J. (1977). *For usefulness and heaven: The juvenile reform movement in anti-bellum period.* Ann Arbor: University of Michigan.

Greene, L., & Peters, S. (1998). *Gender-specific programming for girls.* Nashville, TN: Greene & Peters Associates.

Greenwood, P., Deschenes, E., & Adams, J. (1993). *Chronic juvenile offenders: Final results from the Skillman Aftercare Experiment.* Santa Monica, CA: Rand.

Greenwood, P., Model, K., Rydell, C. P., & Chiesa, J. (1996). *Diverting children from a life of crime: Measuring costs and benefits.* Santa Monica, CA: RAND.

Griffin, P., Torbet, P., & Szymanski, L. (1998). *Trying juveniles as adults in criminal court: An analysis of state transfer provisions.* Washington, DC: U.S. Department of Justice.

Guarino-Ghezzi, S., & Loughran, E. J. (1998). *Balancing juvenile justice.* New Brunswick, NJ: Transaction Press.

Hawkins, D., & Catalano, R. (1992). Risk and protective factors for alcohol and other drug problems in adolescence. *Psychological Bulletin, 112,* 64-105.

Hawkins, J. D., Catalano, R. F., Morrison, D. M., O'Donnell, J., Abbott, R. D., & Day, L. E. (1992). The Seattle Social Development Project: Effects of the first four years on protective factors and problem behaviors. In J. McCord & R. Tremblay (Eds.), *The prevention of antisocial behavior in children* (pp. 139-161). New York: Guilford.

Hirschi, T. (1983). Causes of delinquency: A partial replication and extension. *Social Problems, 20*(3), 471-487.

Howell, J. (Ed.). (1998). *Guide for implementing the comprehensive strategy for serious, violent and chronic juvenile offenders.* Washington, DC: U.S. Department of Justice, Office of Juvenile Justice and Delinquency Prevention.

Kempf, K. (1993). The empirical status of Hirschi's social control theory. In F. Adler & W. Laufer (Eds.), *New directions in criminological theory.* New Brunswick, NJ: Transaction Press.

Kempf, K. L., Decker, S. H., & Bing, R. L. (1990). *An analysis of apparent disparities in the handling of black youth within Missouri's juvenile justice system.* St. Louis: University of Missouri, Department of Juvenile Justice.

Kempf-Leonard, K. Pope, C. E., & Feyerherm, W. H. (Eds.). (1995). *Minorities in juvenile justice.* Thousand Oaks, CA: Sage.

Kempf-Leonard, K., & Sontheimer, H. (1995). The role of race in juvenile justice in Pennsylvania. In K. Kempf-Leonard, C. E. Pope, & W. H. Feyerherm (Eds.), *Minorities in juvenile justice* (pp. 98-128). Thousand Oaks, CA: Sage.

Kirk, B. (1996). *A simple matter of black and white and examination of "race" and the juvenile justice system.* Brookfield, VT: Avebury.

Klein, A. R. (1991). Restitution and community work service: Promising core ingredients for effective intensive supervision programming. In T. L. Armstrong (Ed.), *Intensive interventions with high risk youth.* Monsey, NY: Willow Tree Press.

Leiber, M. J. (1994). A comparison of juvenile court outcomes for Native Americans, African Americans, and whites. *Justice Quarterly, 11*(2), 257-277.

Lemert, E. (1974). *Social pathology.* New York: McGraw-Hill.

Lerman, P., & Pottick, K. J. (1994). *The parent's perspective.* Switzerland: Harwood.

Lipsey, M. (1984). Is delinquency prevention a cost-effective strategy? A California perspective. *Journal of Research in Crime and Delinquency, 21*(4), 279-302.

Lovegrove, A. (1989). *Judicial decision making and sentencing policy.* New York: Springer-Verlag.

Mahoney, A. (1974). The effect of labeling upon youth in the juvenile justice system. *Law and Society Review, 8,* 583-614.

Mann, C. R. (1993). *Unequal justice: A question of color.* Bloomington: Indiana University Press.

Matza, D. (1964). *Delinquency and drift.* New York: John Wiley.

Mauer, M. (1997). *Intended and unintended consequences of state racial disparities in imprisonment.* Washington, DC: The Sentencing Project.

Mauer, M., & Huling, T. (1995). *Young black Americans and the criminal justice system: Five years later.* Washington, DC: The Sentencing Project.

Merton, R. (1957). *Social theory and social structure.* New York: Free Press of Glencoe.

Miller, J. (1991). *Last one over the wall: The Massachusetts experiment in closing reform schools.* Columbus: Ohio State University Press.

Miller, J. (1996). *Search and destroy: African American males in the criminal justice system.* New York: Cambridge University Press.

Miller, W. (1958). Lower-class culture as a generating milieu of gang delinquency. *Journal of Social Issues, 14*(1), 5-19.

Petersilia, J., & Turner, S. (1985). *Guideline-based justice: The implication for racial minorities.* Santa Monica, CA: RAND.

Platt, A. (1977). *The child savers.* Chicago: University of Chicago Press.

Price, R., Cioci, M., & Penner, W. (1993). Web of influence and community programs that enhance adolescent health and education. *Teachers College Record, 94,* 487-521.

Prothrow-Stith, D. (1991). *Deadly consequences.* New York: Harper Perennial.

Prothrow-Stith, D. (1998). Revitalizing communities: Public health strategies for violence prevention. In *What can the federal government do to decrease crime and revitalize communities?* (pp. 59-65). Washington, DC: Government Printing Office.

Quinney, R. (1980). *Class status and crime.* New York: Longman.

Resnick, G., Burt, M., Newmark, L., & Reilly, L. (1992). *Youth at risk: Definitions, prevalence, and approaches to service delivery.* Washington, DC: Urban Institute.

Sampson, R. (1997). Racial and ethnic disparities in crime and criminal justice in the United States. In M. Tonry (Ed.), *Ethnicity, crime, and immigration: Comparative and cross-national perspectives.* Chicago: University of Chicago Press.

Sarri, R., Mogane, M., & Rollin, J. (1992). *Community education for substance abuse prevention: Evaluation of the Wolverine Human Services Program.* Ann Arbor: University of Michigan, Institute for Social Research.

Sarri, R., Rollin, J., Wolfson, C., Farmer, F., & Ward, G. (1998). *Minority overrepresentation and outcomes in juvenile justice in Michigan.* Ann Arbor: University of Michigan, Institute for Social Research.

Schinke, S. (1997). Prospects for prevention. In M. Reisch & E. Gambrill (Eds.), *Social work in the 21st century.* Thousand Oaks, CA: Pine Forge Press.

Shaw, C., & McKay, H. (1964). *Juvenile delinquency and urban areas.* Chicago: University of Chicago Press.

Shoemaker, D. (1996). *Theories of delinquency: An examination of explanations of delinquent behavior.* New York: Oxford University Press.

Singer, S. (1996). *Decriminalizing delinquency: Violent juvenile crime and juvenile justice reform.* New York: Cambridge University Press.

Snyder, H. (1998). *Juvenile arrests, 1997.* Washington, DC: U.S. Department of Justice, Office of Justice Programs.

Snyder, H. N., & Sickmund, M. (1999). *Juvenile offenders and victims: 1999 national report.* Washington, DC: U.S. Dept. of Justice.

Spergel, I. (1995). *The youth gang problem: A community approach.* New York: Oxford University Press.

Sutherland, E., & Cressey, D. (1978). *Criminology.* New York: Lippincott.

Thornberry, T. (1979). Sentencing disparities in the juvenile justice system. *Journal of Criminal Law and Criminology, 70,* 164-171.

Tonry, M. (1995). *Malign neglect: Race crime and the law.* New York: Oxford University Press.

U.S. Department of Justice. (1996). *Youth violence, a community-based response: One city's success story.* Washington, DC: Author.

U.S. Department of Justice. (1999). Juvenile female crime: A special study. In *Uniform crime report* (pp. 288-295). Washington, DC: Author.

U.S Office of Juvenile Justice and Delinquency Prevention. (1995). *Children in custody, 1994.* Washington, DC: U.S. Department of Justice.

U.S. Office of Juvenile Justice and Delinquency Prevention. (1998). *Children in custody, 1997.* Washington, DC: U.S. Department of Justice.

Walters, G.W. T. (1989). Heredity and crime: Bad genes or bad research. *Criminology, 27*(4), 455-485.

Welsh, W. N., Harris, P. W., & Jenkins, P. H. (1996). Reducing overrepresentation of minorities in juvenile justice. *Crime and Delinquency, 42,* 76-98.

Wilson, J. Q., & Herrnstein, R. J. (1985). *Crime & human nature.* New York: Simon & Schuster.

Wilson, W. J. (1987). *The truly disadvantaged.* Chicago: University of Chicago Press.

Wolfgang, M., Figlio, R., & Sellin, T. (1972). *Delinquency in a birth cohort.* Chicago: University of Chicago Press.

Wordes, M., Bynum, T. S., & Corley, C. J. (1994). Locking up youth: The impact of race on detention decisions. *Journal of Research in Crime and Delinquency, 31*(2), 149-165.

Wu, B. (1997). The effect of juvenile justice processing. *Juvenile and Family Court Judges, 17*(1), 43-51.

Young, V. D. (1994). Race and gender in the establishment of juvenile institutions: The case of the South. *Prison Journal, 73*(2), 244-265.

CHAPTER TWENTY-TWO

Social Work Practice With Lesbians and Gay Men

JOHN F. LONGRES

KAREN I. FREDRIKSEN

Social work practice with lesbians and gay men has come a long way. Pivotal events that provided new directions for practice in the third quarter of the 20th century included the publication of the Kinsey studies, the emergence of a gay rights movement, psychological studies showing no significant differences in the psychological profiles of heterosexuals and homosexuals, the Stonewall riots, and the decision by the American Psychiatric Association to eliminate homosexuality from its list of mental disorders. American social attitudes have also changed significantly. In 1993, 80% of Americans favored equal job opportunities for lesbians and gay men, compared to 74% and 56% in 1992 and 1982, respectively. By 1994, eight states and almost 90 cities or counties had en-

acted protections against sexual orientation discrimination in private employment (Klawitter & Flatt, 1994).

In spite of the AIDS pandemic, organizing on behalf of lesbians and gays has continued strong in the last quarter of the century. Clinical social work practice perspective has shifted significantly, from curing the pathology of homosexuality to affirming the normalcy of same-sex relations. Some helping professionals, including social workers, have been of enormous help in the movement, providing supportive policies and a cadre of leaders who have developed services to fill the spiritual, material, interpersonal, and health needs of lesbians and gays. As we enter the 21st century, many lesbians and gays have emerged from the shadows of a deviant, urban subculture and have begun to enter the mainstream of a multicultural society.

These successes have not come easily, and there is no assurance that progress will prevail. Social work practice with lesbians and gay men continues to take place within a context of cultural conflict. Conservative interests still consider same-sex erotic attraction pathological and promote social policies to suppress it and social services to cure it. Progressive social service administrators and workers often remain unaware of the sexual identities of their clients, thereby relegating this crucial element of self to the margins of their service closets. When confronted with presenting problems of a sexual nature, these same service providers are likely to confuse the orientation of their clients with the causes of the difficulties they experience.

In this chapter, we clarify the meaning of sexual orientation, discuss cultural variations, and examine theories of sexual orientation and coming out. We take a life-span approach to identify common practice issues and concerns.

SEXUAL ORIENTATION

The concept of sexual orientation is a product of contemporary Western thought. Although some define it more broadly, sexual orientation refers here to the phenotypic sex of a person's "sustained erotic attraction" (Murphy, 1997, pp. 15-24). Three sexual orientations are commonly recognized, that is, people may be attracted to members of the opposite sex, the same sex, or both sexes. In colloquial terms, these three are called *heterosexual, homosexual,* and *bisexual.* To have a sexual orientation implies that individuals believe their sexual

needs are singularly important to their essential being. In the context of contemporary society, however, sexual orientation has moved beyond mere sexual conduct and erotic attachment. It has become synonymous with an identity—a master identity or civil status akin to social class, race, ethnicity, gender, or age. Furthermore, sexual orientation has become a statement about community life. It can no longer be assumed that society is one single heterosexual community. The concept of sexual orientation brings with it the notion of distinguishable communities, norms, reference points, and lifestyles to which their members are attached.

Like heterosexual conduct, homosexual conduct is never given free reign in communal life. Heterosexual society defines a range of acceptable behaviors by which it expects its members to abide. For instance, adult-child sexual relations are forbidden, as are nonconsensual heterosexual relations between adults. In a similar way, the rise of the lesbian and gay community has led to a reshaping of the boundaries of acceptable homosexual behavior and development. Although there is still considerable debate, behaviors that might have been acceptable during a time of severe oppression are being rethought. Presently, social norms surrounding the selection of sexual partners, dating, coupling, setting up households, interfacing with careers, and joining churches and other voluntary associations are creating a kind of gay and lesbian person who increasingly aspires to be an integral part of America's multicultural mosaic. This is very different from homosexuals in other periods of Western history, who lived as a deviant subculture with little hope of being accepted by the larger society.

Lesbian and gay communities are heterogeneous, and the individuals composing them come in many political stripes. Generation, class, and ethnic differences are also clearly evident. Nevertheless, the quest for human rights has led many to emulate American middle-class norms and values. The quest for the American Dream, with all its implications for acceptance and respectability, is becoming as much a reality for some gays and lesbians as it is for some ethnic and racial minorities.

It is not just that many lesbians and gays aspire to join the American mainstream and thus conduct themselves accordingly. Lesbians and gays are also fundamentally altering mainstream society. In part, the consumer society has altered the nature of family, such that the institutional supports once relied on by heterosexuals no longer function to give stability to their intimate relationships. Heterosexual relations are becoming more like homosexual relations, in that couples must now find internal sources of support for building and sustaining households (Giddens, 1992). The American mainstream is also changing as a result of the strength of the lesbian and gay movement. In particular, lesbians and gays are influencing the way that children are reared and treated in a heterosexually dominant society. Lesbians and gays have influenced parent, school, and church attitudes about gender nonconformity in childhood and about the treatment of adolescent sexual development. They have carved a niche for themselves among society's increasingly diverse family, friendship, and neighborhood networks. They are normalizing the place of lesbians and gays in the delivery of needed services across the life span.

Sexual orientation is a concept that has been made a public issue through the emergence of a lesbian, gay, and bisexual social movement. Heterosexuals often take their orientation as a given and fail to see anything but a natural order in their behavior. For these same reasons, white Americans often fail to recognize that they have a racial or ethnic identity or even a unique set of cultural norms by which they live and by which they judge others. The term *heterosexism* has been coined to describe the way that heterosexual norms have been woven into the fabric of society such that only other forms of intimacy require explanation and, more often than not, defense.

Diversity and Sexual Orientation

Because of its Western origins, the concept of sexual orientation may have limitations in practice. It might not be transferable to practice in international settings, especially when these are in non-European nations. And it may not be completely useful in working with immigrants and historically marginalized racial and ethnic individuals, who hold different ideas about sexuality and its place in civil society.

A number of cross-cultural issues are important to contemporary practice. These are offered as generalizations that may help practitioners better understand their clients. Social workers should not assume, however, that they apply to each and every person. There is as much variation within groups as between groups; social class, age, generation, and level of assimilation must always be taken into account.

First, for a good number of people, homosexuality is a sexual behavior with little implication for an all-encompassing, primary identity. Although traditional values are strongly antihomosexual, there appears to be less contradiction between homosexuality and heterosexuality among African, Asian, Latino, and

Native Americans. A man or woman may accept the primacy of heterosexual marriage with procreative and child-rearing responsibilities but separate this from the realm of sexual desire and attraction, which is reserved for a same-sex person. When homosexuality does become an identity, it may be less a function of same-sex attraction than of the role one assumes in society and, often enough, in the sexual act. To the extent, for instance, that a Latino or African American man is married with children, or sees himself in an active, masculine, or impersonal role in sexual encounters, he is not likely to think of himself as homosexual (Icard, 1996; Zamora-Hernandez & Patterson, 1996). Similar thinking is found among homosexually active Filipino men (Rodriguez, 1996).

Given the generally antihomosexual values of their communities, these men are often aware that they are crossing the boundary of acceptable conduct, participate discretely in same-sex relations, and live under fear of exposure. Yet, the label homosexual accrues more easily to unmarried men who display gender nonconformity in mannerisms and clothing and who may be more willing to assume a passive, feminine, or more interested role in same-sex relations. Often, these men, or their female-gender nonconforming counterparts, are severely stigmatized within their communities.

Two-spirited Native American people may be an exception in terms of stigmatization. The term *two-spirited* was recently coined as a way of distinguishing same-sex behavior and attraction among Native Americans. It is an attempt to understand sensuality, not just in erotic terms but in spiritual terms as well, in keeping with the history of same-sex relations among Native people (Herdt, 1997). Native Americans are unusual, in that many tribes did not repress same-sex conduct. Supported by spiritual beliefs, homosexuals were seen as a third sex and often considered sacred. These women and men often passed through coming out rituals, wore articles of clothing associated with members of their opposite sex, and served useful and specialized functions in family life, religion, and war (Williams, 1986). Historically, the term two-spirited would have only applied to people occupying these special roles. When they partnered, they did not partner with other two-spirited people, nor did they form a community of two-spirited people within Native American societies. Their partners were what we might call heterosexual men and women because they carried out the social roles and expectations associated with men and women. In the contemporary context, however, two-spirited includes "Native American gays and lesbians as well as people who have been referred to as 'berdache' by anthropologists and other scholars." In addition, two-spirited now includes a full range of sexual orientations including transvestites, transsexuals, and transgendered people, as well as "drag queens and butches" (Jacobs, Thomas, & Lang, 1997).

Although the concept of sexual orientation has its limitations, social workers should also be aware of the appeal of the lesbian and gay rights movement and the effects it is having on the identities of immigrants as well as subordinated racial and ethnic groups in the United States. Processes of biculturation—including the role of cultural translators, mediators, and models—are creating shifts in attitudes such that sexual orientation may merge with ethnic identity (Lukes & Land, 1990). For some, ethnic and racial identity may remain primary (Icard, 1986) whereas for others, a lesbian and gay identity may become primary (Chan, 1989).

Origin of Sexual Orientation and Coming Out

We will use the concept of coming out to describe both the origins of sexual orientation and the process by which people come to understand and accept their sexual orientation. The expression "coming out" is usually reserved for gay men, lesbians, and bisexuals but is no less relevant for heterosexuals. The process by which people take on a sexual identity is important regardless of type of orientation or cultural variation.

There are no theories that satisfactorily explain the origins of sexual orientation. It is not a product of simple biological determinism, nor is it easily understood in terms of social learning processes. Contemporary research suggests that complex biological, psychological, and sociocultural factors work in transaction to produce sexual inclinations. In this section, we describe current psychological, biological, and cultural thinking on sexual orientation.

Psychodynamic Theories

Theories of heterosexual development usually privilege it, that is, make it a problematic but normal outcome of human development, while relegating other orientations to the status of problematic and abnormal. Psychodynamic theories of development are a good example. Freud proposed that humans are born polymorphous perverse, that is, able to experience a wide range of psychosexual gratification. He believed people take on an exclusive heterosexual orientation only as a result of identification processes in early childhood. In the phallic stage, boys come to identify with the gender of their father, shut down erotic feelings for their

mothers, and transfer their sexual yearnings to people of the same gender as their mother. Girls, on the other hand, come to identify with their mothers while shifting erotic feeling from the mother and her gender to people of the father's gender. The process of coming out heterosexual is solidified during puberty, when childhood sexual urges are reawakened and reworked, and in young adulthood, when heterosexual intimacies lead to marital or long-term commitment.

Freud's theory raises a number of vexing questions that are beyond the scope of this chapter. Suffice it to say that Freud was never able to adequately account for the convoluted shifts required for exclusive heterosexuality. It is not surprising, therefore, that his writings on homosexuality are contradictory. On the one hand, his theory does suggest that homosexuality represents stunted development, that is, a failure to make the expected identification adjustments. On the other hand, Freud wrote that homosexuality was not a pathology and that the role of psychoanalysis was to support homosexuals in achieving their needs and living fuller lives (Mitchell, 1975).

Contemporary psychoanalysts generally support Freud's progressive inclinations on sexual orientation. Nicolosi and Freeman (1993) are exceptions to this rule. Focusing only on adult males, they argue that homosexuality is the result of psychic injury suffered by children at the hands of their fathers during the second year of life. Nicolosi and Freeman's work has been discredited because it is based on case studies of men who sought reparative therapy. They do not provide clear conceptual and operational definitions that would enable other researchers to verify their findings (Murphy, 1997).

Richard Friedman (1988) is more representative of contemporary psychoanalytic thinking. He believes that the origin of sexual orientation is a complex function of prenatal neuroendocrine factors in transaction with childhood psychological processes and family interaction patterns. Friedman recognizes that gender nonconformity in childhood is a major predictor of adult homosexuality and acknowledges that alienation from the father may be a contributing factor. He concludes, however, that there are no readily discernable family patterns associated with sexual orientation and that greater monitoring of parental behavior will not assure a heterosexual orientation. Furthermore, homosexual, bisexual, and heterosexual men are not distinguishable in terms of personality subtype (e.g., hysteric, obsessive, narcissistic), psychostructural levels (e.g., neurotic, borderline, or psychotic), or position on the schizophrenic-manic/depressive continuum (pp. 85-95).

Psychodynamic thinkers have given less attention to the formation of a lesbian identity. To be sure, feminist psychodynamicists have tended to understand lesbian identity formation within the broader context of a female sexual identity process. As such, a lesbian identity is seen as one of several normative possibilities emerging from a core mother-daughter infant relationship. Empathy and the capacity for mutuality in relationships, rather than the object of the relationship, is the essence of a positive developmental outcome. On the other hand, psychodynamic feminists have been criticized for their failure to account for the different passionate interests of women and the implications of that for attachment and relationships (Brown, 1995).

Biology and Sexual Orientation

Recent biological research has received considerable media attention. Biological researchers do not aspire to demonstrate that a single, linear, biological determinism is at the root of sexual orientation. They aim merely to establish a link between biology and sexual inclination. Biological researchers consistently affirm that a complete understanding of the origins of sexual orientation must include biological, psychological, and sociocultural factors.

Earlier research suggested that prenatal levels of androgen might be implicated in the development of a lesbian or gay male orientation. For instance, Money, Schwartz, and Lewis (1984) found a high incidence of lesbian attraction and behavior among women born with adrenogenital syndrome. Although phenotypically female, such women secrete masculinizing androgens instead of cortisol during fetal life and continuously thereafter.

Recent research has moved away from the study of neuroendocrine processes to the study of possible brain and genetic differences. LeVay (1991, 1993), for instance, found correlational evidence linking sexual orientation with the size of the interstitial nuclei of the anterior hypothalamus (INAH), a part of the brain involved in sexual behavior. Studying a sample of deceased men and women, he found that, on average, the nuclei of homosexual men were smaller than those of heterosexual men, although larger than those of women (of unidentified sexual orientation). Michael Bailey and his colleagues (Bailey, Neale, & Agyei, 1993; Bailey & Pillard, 1991) reported that the identical twin of lesbians and gays was more likely to be gay or lesbian than a fraternal twin or an unrelated sibling. He found a male identical twin concordance of 52% and a female identical twin concordance of 48%. The concordance for fraternal or dizygotic twins and for adopted siblings was considerably lower. Using genetic pedigrees, Dean Hamer and his colleagues (Hamer & Copeland, 1994) found that male homosexuals were significantly more likely than male heterosexuals to report having brothers, maternal uncles, and male cousins (related through maternal aunts) who were gay. Using blood samples, they concluded that homosexuality may be inherited through the mother and may involve a shared region (q28) of the X chromosome.

The results of biological studies can only be taken as suggestive because of conceptual and methodological flaws. LeVay's small sample of corpses included only homosexual men who died of AIDS. It also turns out that the second-largest INAH was that of a gay male, and the third smallest was that of a heterosexual male. Bailey's and Hamer's findings also rely on small convenience samples. Although a 50% average identical twin concordance rate is high, one might expect an even higher level of concordance if genetics alone were operating. In an attempt at replication, Pattatucci and Hamer (1995) found no evidence of an Xq28 link among lesbians.

Sexual orientation may indeed have its roots in biology. Many gay men and lesbians feel strongly that they had no choice in their sexual orientation, that it was present at birth. Many gays and lesbians believe that if researchers could show that sexual orientation had roots in biology, this would dispel the idea that homosexuality is a pathological childhood adjustment. Nevertheless, lesbians and gays have re-

ceived the results of biological studies with mixed feelings. On the one hand, biological explanations do support the contention that sexual orientation is not an idle choice. On the other, they do not dispel the idea of pathology so much as shift it from the psychological to the biological. Even if sexual orientation were rooted in biology or genetics, might not this be seen as evidence of dysfunction and a reason to terminate pregnancy or perform reparative surgery?

Culture and Sexual Orientation

The cultural origins of homosexuality have also been studied. Social constructionists and queer theorists, for instance, argue that all forms of sexual orientation are learned in the context of ever-changing historical and cultural forces (Seidman, 1996). As Herdt (1997, pp. 50-61) emphasizes, it is clear that a gay, lesbian or bisexual orientation, as described in this chapter, is not a universal phenomenon. It has emerged from a number of economic, political, and social forces operating in Western industrial societies. On the other hand, if the question is shifted to whether same-sex intimate relationships are present across history and across all cultures, we may reach the conclusion that, in fact, it is a universal phenomenon.

Some scholars assert that culture itself gives rise to same-sex relationships. In this formulation, cultures may be divided between those where same-sex relationships have been found and those where they have not. Margaret Mead (1935) hypothesized, for instance, that societies—like Western societies—that distinguished sharply between male and female gender role expectations gave rise to homosexuality, whereas those that fostered more diffuse gender roles did not. Greenberg (1988) casts doubt on this proposition, however, after reviewing archival data on pre-industrial societies. He concludes that anthropologists often did not inquire about same-sex relations or if they did, confused condemnation of it with its absence. A good example of this confusion is seen in the study of homosexuality among African tribal societies. Anthropologists have long asserted that homosexuality was absent from most African tribal societies, largely because their informants condemned it. Murray and Roscoe (1998), however, have recently attacked this myth by editing a volume on the diverse forms homosexuality takes in black Africa.

Seidman (1996) suggests that social constructionists, in spite of statements to the contrary, have always assumed that homosexuals were "a stable, unified, and identifiable human type" (p. 11). We propose, therefore, that culture is not a cause of same-sex conduct or even attraction. Rather, culture shapes the expression of sexual conduct, including whether it will become an orientation, an identity, or a community of like-minded people. With this in mind, social constructionists have made a singular contribution to the study of the coming out process.

Coming Out

Coming out describes the process by which people achieve a sexual identity. Sexual orientation is generally taken as a given in most descriptions of coming out. Whatever processes incline people toward heterosexuality, bisexuality, or homosexuality, coming out has to do with becoming aware of the sexual self, working through possible role confusions, and taking on a positive achieved identity. As might be expected, most descriptions of coming out begin with the re-awakening of sexual desires in adolescence and trace development through early adulthood. However, Morris (1997) suggests that with regard to women, the process of coming out actually begins in early childhood with the development of gender identity. Likewise, coming out is not necessarily an adolescent or even a young adult phenomenon, as people may become aware of different sexual inclinations at different times during the life span.

Heterosexual coming-of-age stories are commonly celebrated in fiction, film, and art. The rituals and ceremonies associated with coming of age in different cultures, including our own, also attest to the rewarding ways that children and adolescents are systematically socialized into a heterosexual gender role. Coming of age generally takes place during a relatively protracted period when a young man or woman's sexual yearnings are first awakened and fulfilled. This period is generally marked by a series of institutionalized religious (e.g., confirmation, bar mitzvah) and social events (proms, debutante balls, engagement parties, bridal showers, stag parties, and the like) aimed at integrating young people into the heterosexual community. Coming of age presumably ends with positive feelings of having joined the society of adult heterosexuals.

Coming out lesbian, gay, or bisexual, on the other hand, is usually described as an extended process that can be divided into a series of more or less discrete phases (Cass, 1979; Coleman, 1981; Mallon, 1997; Morris, 1997; Troiden, 1993). The stages and processes may be somewhat different for women and men, although the tasks are generally similar. Morris (1997) suggests, for example, that sexual expression and behavior may come after sexual identification for women, whereas for men, sexual expression and behavior may come first.

The context for coming out is the personal struggle against heterosexist social institutions; there are no rituals, no celebrations and parties, and no general social support for this process. Each step in the coming out process—whether it be experiencing the first sensations of difference and the confusion that stems from these sensations, grappling to assume the identity, or committing to it—requires coming to terms with the stigma associated with being lesbian and gay. Coming out lesbian, gay, or bisexual represents a show of strength and resilience in the face of repressive social forces.

Research suggests that the acquisition of a gay identity begins in childhood with the sense of difference from one's peers. Many gay men and lesbians report sensing something different about themselves, often as young as 4 to 5 years of age, long before an awareness of their sexual orientation (Newman & Muzzonigro, 1993). Most researchers agree that the majority do not self-identify as gay or lesbian until the teen years. The average age that lesbians "come out" is between 16 and 19, whereas gay males tend to come out at a younger age, generally between the ages of 14 and 16 (GLSEN, 1996). There is also some evidence that lesbians and gays are coming out at an earlier age today than they did in the past (Herdt & Boxer, 1993).

Although empirical evidence does not confirm the existence of fixed and invariant coming out stages (Cass, 1984; Gonsiorek & Rudolph, 1991), the tasks described are common to the lives of many lesbians and gays. Early in life, lesbians and gays come to feel that they are at-

tracted to members of their same sex. Because of fears of social stigma, these feelings are usually met with confusion and denial. Some will immediately acknowledge their desires and struggle directly against family, peer, and school repression. For others, however, identity confusion may go on for a long time, during which they may date, have sexual relations, or marry members of the opposite sex. In this period, some live in the hope that their erotic feelings for same-sex partners will eventually disappear.

At some point, lesbians and gays act on their same-sex attractions. As suggested above, this may be earlier for young men than for young women (Morris, 1997). At first, their experiences may be furtive or in circumstances associated with drinking and other substance use, to more easily deny the implications of their behaviors. Denial may become less possible if a lesbian or gay male connects with someone for whom he or she feels a strong attachment. This first affair can lead to the acceptance of a gay or lesbian identity, or, if it is an aversive affair that ends badly, it may lead to further denial and identity confusion.

Once an identity is assumed, lesbians and gays are faced with social consequences both in the heterosexual community and in their newfound gay and lesbian community. They are likely to make friends with other lesbians and gays and thereby become influenced by the norms and mores of that community. Over the past 25 years, lesbian and gay communities have grown dramatically in terms of resources for friendship and social support. Taverns and bars are no longer the only places to meet friends and potential partners. Especially in large urban areas, voluntary associations, representing many different social, political, religious, and creative interests, are now available to help lesbians and gays find a network of compatible friends.

As lesbians and gay men strive to locate a comfortable niche in the community, they are also likely to experience its contradictions and tensions. Among these contradictions may be the competing allegiances arising from racial and ethnic group affiliations (Gonsiorek, 1995; Icard, 1985/86), class background, occupational involvement, gender, religious and spiritual preferences, and ability status friendships (Luczak, 1993). In addition, many secondary attributes of sexual orientation begin to take shape. These may range from the relatively simple, such as clothing, hair style, and argot, to the more complex, such as sexual image and political alliances.

As individuals become more deeply identified with their sexual orientation, they aspire to intimate commitments, building household units, and learning to sustain them. Deeper identification with a lesbian or gay lifestyle also provokes the need to redefine past and present relationships with heterosexuals. Lesbians and gays must determine in whom—among family members and heterosexual friends and acquaintances—they can confide. Research suggests that most gay men and lesbians first come out to a friend, rather than a family member (D'Augelli & Hershberger, 1993). However, most lesbians and gays are strongly attached to their families of origin, and these attachments have to be renegotiated in the context of their newly accepted identity. A number of crises may have to be confronted, and it is important to understand that the adaptations involved in coming out are mutual. Parents and other family members are often concerned about social stigma, the causes of sexual orientation (self-blame), and fears of loss and isolation in rela-

tion to having a lesbian or gay male family member (Bernstein, 1990). Families holding orthodox religious and social values tend to be less accepting of homosexuality than families with more progressive values (Newman & Muzzonigro, 1993).

On the other hand, given changing mores, many lesbians and gays may find unanticipated support from heterosexual loved ones. Although it may be a difficult process, parents often become accepting of a child's gay or lesbian identity (Anderson, 1998). For practitioners and others assisting gay men and lesbians, support from biological family members is an important and often overlooked resource. Support groups, educational materials, and discussions with other gay men and lesbians and their family members have all helped heterosexual family members explore their fears and prejudices about homosexuality. In a recent survey, gay and lesbian respondents reported experiencing a fairly high degree of support from biological family members (Fredriksen, 1999), a finding that runs counter to the stereotype that gay men and lesbians are isolated from their families of origin.

Coming Out Bisexual

Sexual orientation is often treated as a dichotomy; one is either homosexual or heterosexual. As a result, bisexuals are sometimes described as immature people who cannot make up their minds. They are thought to be in denial, or at least in a transitional stage toward exclusive homosexuality. Not surprisingly, bisexual people often feel marginal to both the heterosexual and homosexual communities. Increasingly, however, bisexuality is being defined as a separate orientation, neither heterosexual nor homosexual (Fox, 1995).

Very little is known about the origin of bisexuality. As indicated earlier, Freudian theory suggests that humans are born polymorphous perverse and therefore have a bisexual propensity. Gender nonconformity in childhood, a condition that often distinguishes homosexuals from heterosexuals, apparently does not distinguish bisexuals (Bell & Weinberg, 1978; Bell, Weinberg, & Hammersmith, 1981). As noted, some cultures are less likely to draw a sharp line between heterosexual and homosexual, thus allowing for a kind of bisexuality. Some tribal societies, like the Sambia of New Guinea, mark the life span in terms of succeeding periods of homosexuality, bisexuality, and heterosexuality (Herdt, 1997).

Coming out bisexual has been described as adding on to a basic heterosexual identity. Twinning (cited in Fox, 1995) describes four tasks associated with this process among women. Bisexual women must come to accept themselves, resolve internalized homophobia, develop a support network, and make decisions about to whom and under what circumstances to disclose their orientation. While acknowledging the relevance of these coming out tasks, Fox (1995) argues that bisexuality may as easily evolve from homosexuality. Klein (1993) describes bisexuality in terms of four possible types: (a) transitional, where bisexuality is a phase in becoming either heterosexual or homosexual; (b) historical, where someone might have spent a good amount of time in exclusively heterosexual relations but at a later point in life, became exclusively homosexual; (c) sequential, or going back and forth between monogamous heterosexual and homosexual relations; or (d) concurrent, being involved in heterosexual and homosexual relationships simultaneously. Each of these suggests that coming out bisexual will not involve the inherent linearity apparent in many models of homosexual coming out. Achieving a bisexual identity may be a lifelong process where people feel differently about themselves at different times.

Coming Out and Mental Health

As a hidden minority, gay men and lesbians must continually decide whether or not to disclose their sexual identity. The vast majority of those surveyed now openly identify as lesbian or gay in at least some settings. Bradford and Ryan (1988), for example, report that the vast majority of lesbians were "out" to friends, and 27% were out to all of their family members. In the workplace, 17% were out to all of their coworkers. On the other hand, 19% were not out to any family members, and 29% were not out to any coworkers. Research suggests that psychological health is related to openness about one's sexual orientation (Franke & Leary, 1991; Jordan & Deluty, 1998).

By not being out, some may be trying to protect their privacy and themselves from potential discrimination, harassment, and violence. These are reasonable decisions because lesbians and gay men are among the most frequent victims of hate crimes. Several national studies have documented the severity of anti-gay violence, the anguish it causes in survivors, and the pall it casts over the larger gay and lesbian community (Berrill, 1990; Herek, 1990). Among gays and lesbians, it has been found that more than 90% have experienced some type of victimization, with more than 40% threatened with physical violence and about 20% physically assaulted.

Herek and Berrill (1992), in an analysis of 26 surveys, found that about 70% of gays and lesbians had been verbally harassed, and 20% had been physically assaulted in response to their sexual orientation.

PRACTICE ISSUES ACROSS THE LIFE SPAN

The service needs of gays and lesbians can be considered across the life span. A life course, developmental approach illustrates the changing landscape of people's lives—a restructuring through time that incorporates both contemporary and historical influences. A developmental approach should not be taken to mean that there are clear periods of the gay and lesbian life span, each with a unique set of tasks and issues. Many developmental issues (e.g., grief and loss, relationship building) recur throughout life. Similarly, there are a great many differences in the timing of developmental tasks such that individuals may address them at very different points in their lives. Besides being a function of individual personality and life circumstances, these differences are often rooted in ethnic, racial, or religious group affiliations. In this section, we will highlight issues having to do with adolescence, adulthood, and old age.

Adolescence

The following illustrates the role of the social work educator in helping students become sensitive to lesbian and gay issues. Heterosexism is such a pervasive force that social workers often need to be reminded of diversity around sexual orientation.

Students in a class on school social work chose to participate in a project on adolescent sexuality. They developed and tested a questionnaire to better understand the sexual needs and knowledge of the teenagers they worked with in their practicum. When the students presented their results to the class, they provided data on such topics as dating, sexual knowledge, experiencing pressure to have sex, sexual harassment, and actual sexual experiences. Many of their survey questions included language something to the effect of "with a member of the opposite sex." When the professor commented about the exclusionary language, the students were horrified by their insensitivity to lesbian and gay teens. An excellent discussion ensued over the importance of creating a school and social service environment that would respect gay and lesbian teens.

Adolescence is a period of tremendous biological, cognitive, psychological, and social development. Negotiating the many challenges associated with puberty, adolescents move toward a more autonomous and independent sense of self. For most gay and lesbian youth, adolescence is a period of growing up as well as coming out. As gay youth respond to the unique features of their own development, they are adjusting to a potentially socially stigmatized role.

The majority of research on gay and lesbian youth highlights the experiences of the most vulnerable individuals and consequently focuses on risk factors and difficulties. A strengths perspective, however, illustrates the resiliency among gay youth as they cope with the stresses of adolescence and being gay. Gay male youth, for example, develop both internal and external resources that are protective in nature and that assist them in coping with the adversities they encounter (Anderson, 1998). They report higher levels of self-esteem and higher levels of internal locus of control than adolescents in general. Interestingly, gay youth of color report higher levels of self-esteem than white gay youth, likely due to earlier experiences confronting racism and oppression. Factors associated with higher levels of self-esteem and an internal locus of control include being older; having a strong social support network of family members as well as gay, lesbian, and bisexual friends; and a pre-adolescent awareness of being different.

Although the majority of lesbian and gay youth are able to negotiate adolescence and the process of coming out in a healthy way, some clearly experience distress. Positive familial and cultural role models may not be available to many gay and lesbian youth, resulting in feelings of isolation. Not being able to confide in parents in particular may heighten the sense of alienation (Savin-Williams, 1989, 1995). Although children born into subordinated groups are often socialized to deal with discrimination and prejudice on a broader scale, most gay and lesbian children do not share a collective experience with other family members who can teach them how to live successfully with their sexual orientation. At least initially, most young people fear the reaction of family members to a disclosure of their homosexuality. Many parents do not know how to affirm and support the struggles of their gay and lesbian children. In one study of gay and lesbian youth, 50% reported that their parents rejected them for being gay, and 80% of these reported feelings of extreme isolation (GLSEN, 1996). Other studies suggest that the problems may be more acute among gay and lesbian youth of color, those from families with more traditional religious values, and those from lower socioeconomic backgrounds (Anderson, 1998; Newman & Muzzonigro, 1993).

Because of isolation and desperation, there is a relatively high incidence of suicide and suicidal ideation among lesbian and gay adolescents. Suicide is the leading cause of death among lesbian, gay, bisexual, and transsexual youth (U.S. Department of Health and Human Services, 1989). Gay and lesbian youth account for almost one third of all youth suicides and are two to three times more likely to attempt suicide than are other youth. Lesbian and gay youth are at risk for other serious problems as well, including drug use, sexual abuse, and homelessness. Gay and lesbian youth are estimated to account for about 25% of the youth living on the streets in the United States (U.S. Department of Health and Human Services, 1989).

As adolescents negotiate the many changes in their lives, it is important that they receive accurate information about homosexuality, rather than rely on the inaccurate stereotypes presented by those trying to suppress their orientation. There is a need within the school system to provide comprehensive education on sexuality, including sexual orientation, to all students. Traditionally, schools have been reluctant to provide accurate information on homosexuality and to protect gay and lesbian students from harassment. Recently, this has been changing, as legal damages have been awarded to gay students who were not adequately protected in their schools from physical abuse or verbal harassment. Such court rulings have forced administrators and teachers to become more sensitive to the need for respect and protection of all their students.

A number of large urban areas have established programs for gay and lesbian youth to enable access to peer and adult role models. For example, a gay and lesbian community service center in Long Beach, California, provides a drop-in center for gay youth and has developed a group to provide opportunities for social skill development among these adolescents (O'Donnell, Ferreira, & Malin, 1997). Gay and lesbian youth also participate in the planning and implementation of the program, fostering leadership development among the youth.

Adulthood and Family

As U.S. society becomes more diverse, family practice social workers are increasingly serving nontraditional families. The following case illustrates the important role that social workers can have in effectively serving lesbian and gay parents and their children.

> Two lesbian mothers were raising their 6-year-old son in a large urban area. Shortly after the boy entered elementary school, one of the older kids teased him and called his mother a "queer." The teacher on the playground, who witnessed the teasing, disciplined the boy and brought the matter to the attention of the school social worker. The social worker suggested that she also meet with the boy and his mothers. She helped the mothers discuss the issue with their son. They discussed what it is like to be different; that some people understand and others may not. By the end of the discussion, they all agreed that "love makes a family" and that a school program was needed to promote respect for all types of families.

Adulthood is a time for setting up households and families, and this is as true for gays and lesbians as it is for heterosexuals. Yet research on family relationships has focused on traditional families and has only recently given attention to the family lives of lesbians and gay men. In fact, theoretical approaches informing the study of family life are generally based on the presumption of heterosexuality and do not

adequately address the experiences and needs of gay and lesbian families.

Nevertheless, extensive familial relationships and responsibilities are evident among lesbians and gay men. Family, when defined as people related by blood, legal ties, commitment, or close emotional bonds, incorporates a liberal range of households created by gay men, lesbians, and bisexuals. Intrafamilial and interfamilial diversity can be seen in terms of household and nonhousehold family members, arrangements between couples, and relationships with biological, extended, and step-family members. Furthermore, there is considerable diversity in terms of cultural, ethnic and racial, and other social differences among gay and lesbian families.

Gay and Lesbian Couples

Despite increasing support for basic civil rights, support for family development and maintenance among gays and lesbians remains under attack. The Defense of Marriage Act (DOMA), for example, was recently enacted to prohibit the recognition of interstate same-sex marriages. In spite of the lack of legal and social recognition, there is ample evidence that lesbians and gays form stable and caring intimate relationships. Gay and lesbian couples generally report fairly high levels of satisfaction and commitment (Blumstein & Schwartz, 1983; Mendola, 1980).

Studies that compare lesbian, gay male, and heterosexual couples have found both similarities and differences. In a comprehensive study of American couples, Blumstein and Schwartz (1983) reported basic similarities in values, problems encountered, and problem-solving strategies. Differences noted include higher levels of egalitarianism (Kurdek, 1995) and higher levels of cohesion and flexibility (Greene, Bettinger, & Zacks, 1996) among gay and lesbian compared to heterosexual couples. There are also differences between gay and lesbian couples. Lesbians report the highest levels of couple satisfaction, whereas gay males and heterosexual couples report fairly comparable levels of satisfaction (Greene et al., 1996). Gender, perhaps, is more likely than sexual orientation to influence some of these differences. For example, women, regardless of their sexual orientation, are more likely to value monogamy than are men (Blumstein & Schwartz, 1983).

Some gay and lesbian couples, like their heterosexual counterparts, experience dysfunction, with potentially serious consequences. For example, research suggests that personality characteristics and sociocultural factors, rather than sexual orientation, are most likely to predict domestic violence among intimate partners (Coleman, 1994). Domestic violence within same-sex relationships seems to follow the same cycle of abuse found in heterosexual relationships. When comparing lesbian, gay male, and heterosexual couples, Gardner (1989, as cited in Coleman, 1994) found no significant differences in the prevalence of abuse, although others have found differences by type of abuse (Lockhart, White, Causby, & Isaac, 1994) and the conceptualization of abuse (Letellier, 1994).

Gay and Lesbian Parents

Parenthood is a role that some gays and lesbians embrace during adulthood. There are a variety of means by which gays and lesbians become parents, including having children while in heterosexual relationships, adopting as a single parent, adopting as a gay or lesbian couple, using donor insemination, or becoming the nonbiological parent of a child conceived by a partner.

Although studies have repeatedly shown that sexual orientation is not related to the ability to parent or to child-related outcomes, such as emotional health, interpersonal relationships, social adjustment, gender identity, or sexual orientation (Patterson, 1992; Tasker & Golombok, 1995; Victor & Fish, 1995), lesbians and gay men are often denied custody and visitation with their biological children as well as the opportunity to adopt or become foster parents. A number of legislative initiatives and judicial rulings have negated the significance of relationships within gay and lesbian families. Existing research, however, suggests that ways need to be found to strengthen gay and lesbian primary relationships to promote mental health within their families. For example, among families with gay fathers, family satisfaction was higher when the father's partner participated and was included in the family (Crosbie-Burnett & Helmbrecht, 1993). Huggins (1989) found that daughters of lesbian mothers had higher self-esteem when the mother's partner lived with the family.

The number of gay men and lesbians who have dependent children and who have experienced problems with legal custody highlights the need to educate judges and health and human service professionals regarding the diversity of American families. In addition, only a few states currently grant second-parent adoptions to lesbians or gay men; in most cases, there is no legally recognized relationship between a child and the nonbiological gay or lesbian parent. Thus, it is essential that service providers be aware of the need for advocacy and professional legal planning to ensure the protection of all family members.

Illness and Bereavement

AIDS and HIV are serious health issues that have significantly affected the gay and lesbian community. AIDS is unique in a variety of ways. In addition to a high prevalence of the disease among stigmatized groups, there is a high degree of multiple loss experienced by people with AIDS and the family members who care for them (Nord, 1997). Providing care can be physically and emotionally taxing and cause disruptions in a caregiver's employment, living arrangements, and personal relationships.

With respect to other diseases, lesbians may be at higher risk for certain types of cancer, such as breast cancer, because they are less likely than heterosexual women to bear children (Peterson & Bricker-Jenkins, 1996). As with AIDS, an informal network of friends and family is most likely to provide the majority of care to ill and disabled lesbians and to suffer a great deal of stress in the process.

Lesbian and gay male family members may potentially encounter limited access to seriously ill or disabled partners, friends, or other family members. Because gay and lesbian relationships are not legally recognized, the magnitude of the loss associated with the death of a partner or extended family member is also often not recognized (Kochman, 1997). Only recently has the gay and lesbian community itself developed an increased awareness and language for loss and bereavement, acknowledging the experience and meaning of widowhood (Shernoff, 1997).

Although the numbers are increasing, only a relatively small number of employers provide gay and lesbian access to family leave, bereavement leave, or health care benefits for ill or disabled partners. Prohibitive costs and lack of support have often been cited as reasons for not implementing such coverage. Research suggests, however, that allowing domestic partner registration and health care coverage is substantially less costly than anticipated and does not require a significant increase in outlay for benefits (Fox, 1996).

Older Gay Men and Lesbians

Social work and related records may contain information on sexual orientation that can be used against clients. The following case illustrates the importance of confidentiality in the face of possible discrimination.

A 55-year-old gay man had always kept his sexual orientation to himself, especially in professional relationships with physicians and others in the medical field. On joining a Health Maintenance Organization, however, his primary care physician brought him out, stating that such information was necessary in the fight against AIDS. It was a nerve-wracking experience but a good one, especially since his partner of many years was seriously ill with AIDS, the physician was supportive, and the referral to the clinic social worker proved very helpful. Two years later the man applied for long-term care insurance. Because of a cancer earlier in life, the long-term care provider insisted on reviewing his entire medical history. The man was unsure what his physician had included in his records and feared he would be denied coverage not for the cancer, which had been long cured, but for his sexual orientation and the fact that his partner had died of AIDS (although he himself was negative). He called the clinic social worker and asked her to look over his records and let him know what had to be sent to the insurance provider. The social worker arranged an appointment for the man and the physician to meet to discuss the report to the insurance company. They expunged all information on sexual orientation and the death of the partner from his medical records.

Older gays and lesbians must be understood within the historical and cultural context of their lives. Each generation has had a different set of experiences; elderly gay men and lesbians were raised during a period of extreme intolerance, when homosexuality was considered a pathology and homosexuals a security risk.

Because of past and present discrimination, older gay men and lesbians are hardly visible in society. Moreover, age discrimination is also internal to the gay and lesbian community, reflecting the larger community. Most older gays and lesbians do not openly identify as gay or lesbian, with the resulting invisibility often becoming part of the fabric of their lives.

Beginning with Berger (1980), contemporary researchers have dispelled the myth that older gay men and lesbians lead isolated, lonely, and unhappy lives. The vast majority of older gay men and women are satisfied with their lives and have a strong sense of self (Quam & Whitford, 1992). Older gay men and lesbians report strong support systems, mostly composed of partners and close friends. It is possible that gays and lesbians, having already faced the major shift in identity and acquired the flexibility to come to terms with their sexual orientation, may find it easier to adjust to aging.

But like older adults in general, many elderly gay men and lesbians fear loneliness, declining health, and limited income (Quam & Whitford, 1992). They express concerns about potential discrimination particularly in relation to health care, employment, housing, and long-term care. They fear the potential ramifications of identifying as gay to service providers, the lack of control over their lives in the event of serious illness or disability, and the potential lack of legal protection of life partnerships (Kochman, 1997). Advocacy and legal planning are necessary to assist lesbian and gay elders in ensuring their self-determination and maintaining the integrity of their significant relationships.

A few urban communities have developed programs to exclusively serve gay and lesbian elders. One such program, Senior Action in a Gay Environment (SAGE), was founded in New York City in 1977 and now has chapters in several states and regions. SAGE is a multiservice organization that provides home care, social support, recreation, education, professional training, and advocacy for lesbian and gay elders (Kochman, 1997).

Even with the establishment of specialized services, most lesbian and gay seniors will still need to rely on mainstream services for support. To ensure accessibility, administrators of mainstream service agencies need to implement staff development and training to address attitudes and values in relation to homophobia and heterosexism and to develop skills for effectively serving gay and lesbian elders.

FUTURE ISSUES AND PRACTICE IMPLICATIONS

The past 20 years have witnessed some very positive changes for lesbians and gay men, not the least of which has been the shift toward an affirming social work practice. If gay men and lesbians are to become fully integrated into American society, however, a number of tasks remain to be accomplished. These can be articulated at the level of research, policy, and practice.

Researchers have documented the absence of a homosexual personality and have demonstrated that gay men and lesbians do not differ from heterosexual men and women with respect to their psychological health. Researchers have yet to fully demonstrate, however, how normal human development—from embryo to old age—encompasses same-sex attraction. Similarly, they have not fully demonstrated that the psychological problems of lesbians and gay men—like those of their heterosexual counterparts—are not caused by sexual orientation. This is a key issue. Without an empirically supported theory of normal human development, we will constantly be fighting those who would promote the need for social marginalization and reparative therapy.

At the policy level, the social service system must begin to lead rather than follow national patterns. Gay-affirming practice can only take place under the protection of supportive social and public policies. Presently, intimate same-sex conduct remains a criminal offense in several states, and lesbians and gay men are not allowed to join the military in defense of their country. Official definitions of the family exclude, and federal law impedes, marriage between same-sex couples. Although domestic partner legislation exists in some state and local jurisdictions, as well as in many large corporations, the great majority of lesbians and gays are not affected by it. These sources of institutional discrimination are reflected in the policies of many mainstream social agencies, departments, and programs. They result in lackluster services that often ignore the community and family of choice support systems so central to the well-being of lesbians and gay men. Inclusive definitions of family should be promoted throughout the social services, and taking note of sexual orientation should be as natural as taking note of gender, race, ethnicity, and religion. All administrators should ensure that direct service workers are trained to be gay and lesbian affirming.

Throughout this chapter we have called attention to issues of importance in working with lesbians and gay men. We close by listing some principles that emerge from our discussion and that collectively describe a gay and lesbian affirming practice.

1. Working with lesbians and gay men means participating in a movement for human rights. In spite of many advances, gays and lesbians continue to be a subordinated class and are at risk for suffering the effects of institutionalized discrimination. Gay and lesbian affirming social workers need to join the struggle against homophobia and heterosexism.

2. Social workers must examine their own sexuality as well as their beliefs and values about sexual orientation. In particular, social workers need to acknowledge the psychological normalcy of same-sex expression.

3. Social work theory has long held that primary family and household relationships were central to assessment and intervention planning. To effectively meet the needs of lesbian and gay clients, social workers must make room for self-disclosure and recognize people that are significant in the lives of their clients. It is essential to ask questions in a nonthreatening and inclusive manner, without assuming the sexual orientation, gender, or marital status of clients.

4. Sexual orientation should not be seen as the identified problem, the cause of an identified problem, or the target for change. This is perhaps the most distinguishing feature of a lesbian and gay affirming practice, and is in keeping with the *Diagnostic and Statistical Manual*

of *Mental Disorders* (*DSM IV*; American Psychiatric Association, 1994). In the past, the focus of practice with lesbians and gays was to determine how their orientation came about, because the orientation was believed to be related to the difficulties they were experiencing in their adult lives. Gay-affirming direct service practice acknowledges the need to understand the origin of sexual orientation, as such knowledge is central to establishing the normalcy of same-sex attractions and, therefore, promoting the general well-being of the lesbian and gay communities. However, the origin of sexual orientation has limited application when working with clients. Although we are still unable to explain how sexual orientation emerges, we can reassure people who are coming out and parents of gender-nonconforming children and adolescents that a lesbian or gay orientation does not preclude healthy psychological development. In most direct practice with lesbians and gay men, however, sexual orientation—like gender, ethnicity, or class—forms the context from which to understand individual, family, and communal needs, tensions, and resources.

The concept of sexual orientation, with all that it implies, is a very recent invention of Western industrialized societies. Social workers must be careful not to impose a Western cultural identity on immigrant and historically marginalized ethnic minority clients, who may have different understandings about same-sex intimacy and its place in their lives. We must respect the right of each individual to maintain his or her own cultural understanding, so long as it does not cause injury to self or others.

Working with gay men and lesbians means acknowledging their strengths. Although their subordinated status puts them at risk, most lesbians and gays can call on personal, familial, and communal resources as they negotiate the many challenges they face. Across the life course, most tend to embody resiliency in the face of adversity.

A life-span model may be quite useful in helping social workers understand presenting problems. Social workers should support the struggles of lesbians and gay men as they come out, take on an identity, choose families and friends, work to maintain these sources of social support, age, or die.

Coming out to families and friends is a major dilemma for most young lesbians and gay men. It represents a potential conflict with society: their attempt to define themselves as good within a world that deprecates them. Assisting in the coming out process involves problem solving around the common tasks of confusion, acceptance, and pride in self. It also involves helping lesbians and gays reach out to friends and families of origin and locate their niche in lesbian and gay circles.

Working with adult lesbians and gays often involves problem solving around couple, household, and family of choice issues, including violence and the care of sick members. It may also include counseling with respect to parenting and child care arrangements.

Working with lesbian and gay seniors requires sustaining social support and providing needed health services, including long-term care. Social workers should not minimize lesbian or gay widowhood.

Direct service providers must also accept their role as social change agents. The organizational and policy context of social work practice needs to be examined. Policies on the definition of family and family members are deserving of special scrutiny. In-service training on gay and lesbian issues should include information on promoting a welcoming and supportive environment, ensuring nondiscrimination and equal opportunity, and participating in gay pride celebrations. In concert with providing a welcoming environment, agency staff have the opportunity to validate gay men and lesbians by honoring the significant relationships in their lives. When clients are in need of referral, social workers should seek out agencies that respect lesbians and gay men. If these do not exist, social workers need to advocate for new or better services on behalf of all people, regardless of sexual orientation.

REFERENCES

American Psychiatric Association. (1994). *Diagnostic and statistical manual of mental disorders* (4th ed.). Washington, DC: Author.

Anderson, A. L. (1998). Strengths of gay male youth: An untold story. *Child and Adolescent Social Work Journal, 15*(1), 55-71.

Bailey, M. J., Neale, M. C., & Agyei, Y. (1993). Heritable factors influence sexual orientation in women. *Archives of General Psychiatry, 50,* 217-233.

Bailey, M. J., & Pillard, R. C. (1991). A genetic study of male sexual orientation. *Archives of General Psychiatry, 48,* 1089-1096.

Bell, A. P., & Weinberg, M. S. (1978). *Homosexualities: A study of diversity among men and women.* New York: Simon & Schuster.

Bell, A. P., Weinberg, M. S., & Hammersmith, S. K. (1981). *Sexual preference: Its development in men and women.* Bloomington: Indiana University Press.

Berger, R. M. (1980). Psychological adaptation of the older homosexual male. *Journal of Homosexuality, 5*(3), 161-175.

Bernstein, B. E. (1990). Attitudes and issues of parents as gay men and lesbians and implications for therapy. *Journal of Gay and Lesbian Psychotherapy, 1*(3), 37-53.

Berrill, K. T. (1990). Anti-gay violence and victimization in the United States. *Journal of Interpersonal Violence, 5*(3), 274-294.

Blumstein, P., & Schwartz, P. (1983). *American couples: Money, work, sex.* New York: William Morrow.

Bradford, J. B., & Ryan, C. (1988). *The National Lesbian Health Care Survey: Final report.* Washington, DC: National Lesbian and Gay Health Foundation.

Brown, L. (1995). Lesbian identities: Concepts and issues. In A. R. D'Augelli & C. J. Patterson (Eds.), *Lesbian, gay, and bisexual identities over the life span: Psychological perspectives* (pp. 1-23). New York: Oxford University Press.

Cass, V. C. (1979). Homosexual identity formation: A theoretical model. *Journal of Homosexuality, 4,* 219-235.

Cass, V. C. (1984). Homosexual identity formation: Testing a theoretical model. *Journal of Sex Research, 20*(2), 143-167.

Chan, C. S. (1989). Issues of identity development among Asian-American lesbians and gay men. *Journal of Counseling & Development, 68,* 16-20.

Coleman, E. (1981). Developmental strategies of the coming out process. *Journal of Homosexuality, 7*(2/3), 31-43.

Coleman, V. E. (1994). Lesbian battering: The relationship between personality and the perpetration of violence. *Violence and Victims, 9*(2), 139-152.

Crosbie-Burnett, M., & Helmbrecht, L. (1993). A descriptive empirical study of gay male stepfamilies. *Family relations, 42*(3), 256-262.

D'Augelli, A. R., & Hershberger, S. L. (1993). Lesbian, gay, and bisexual youth in community settings: Personal challenges and mental health problems. *American Journal of Community Psychology, 21*(4), 421-448.

Fox, R. C. (1995). Bisexual identities. In A. R. D'Augelli & C. J. Patterson (Eds.), *Lesbian, gay, and bisexual identities over the life span: Psychological perspectives* (pp. 48-86). New York: Oxford University Press.

Fox, S. W. (1996, January 31). *Testimony before the House Committee on HB2262 relating to same gender marriage.* Olympia, Washington.

Franke, R., & Leary, M. R. (1991). Disclosure of sexual orientation by lesbians and gay men: A comparison of private and public processes. *Journal of Social and Clinical Psychology, 10,* 262-269.

Fredriksen, K. I. (1999). Family caregiving responsibilities among lesbians and gay men. *Social Work, 44*(2), 142-155.

Friedman, R. C. (1988). *Male homosexuality: A contemporary psychoanalytic perspective.* New Haven, CT: Yale University Press.

Gardner, R. (1989). Method of conflict resolution and characteristics of abuse and victimization in heterosexual, lesbian, and gay male couples (Doctoral dissertation, University of Georgia, 1988). *Dissertation Abstracts International, 50,* 746B.

Giddens, A. (1992). *The transformation of intimacy: Sexuality, love, and eroticism in modern societies.* Stanford, CA: Stanford University Press.

GLSEN (The Gay, Lesbian, and Straight Education Network). (1996). *Making schools safe.* Seattle, WA: Author.

Gonsiorek, J. (1995). Gay male identities: Concepts and issues. In A. R. D'Augelli & C. J. Patterson (Eds.), *Lesbian and gay identities over the lifespan: Psychological perspectives* (pp. 24-47). New York: Oxford University Press.

Gonsiorek, J., & Rudolph, J. (1991). Homosexual identity: Coming out and other developmental events. In J. Gonsiorek & J. Weinrich (Eds.), *Homosexuality: Research implications for public policy* (pp. 161-176). Newbury Park, CA: Sage.

Greenberg, D. F. (1988). *The construction of homosexuality.* Chicago: University of Chicago Press.

Greene, R. J., Bettinger, M., & Zacks, E. (1996). Are lesbian couples fused and gay male couples disengaged? Questioning gender straitjackets. In J. Laird & R. J. Greene (Eds.), *Lesbians and gays in couples and families: A handbook for therapists* (pp. 185-227). San Francisco: Jossey-Bass.

Hamer, D., & Copeland, P. (1994). *The science of desire: The search for the gay gene and the biology of behavior.* New York: Simon & Schuster.

Herdt, G. (1997). *Same sex, different cultures: Exploring gay and lesbian lives.* Boulder, CO: Westview.

Herdt, G., & Boxer, A. (1993). *Children of horizons: How gay and lesbian teens are leading a new way out of the closet.* Boston: Beacon.

Herek, G. M. (1990). The context of anti-gay violence: Notes on cultural and psychological heterosexism. *Journal of Interpersonal Violence, 5*(3), 316-333.

Herek, G. M., & Berrill, K. (1992). *Hate crimes: Confronting violence against lesbians and gay men.* Newbury Park, CA: Sage.

Huggins, S. L. (1989). A comparative study of self-esteem of adolescent children of divorced lesbian mothers and divorced heterosexual mothers. In F. W. Bozet (Ed.), *Homosexuality and the family* (pp. 123-135). New York: Harrington Park Press.

Icard, L. (1985-1986). Black gay men and conflicting social identities: Sexual orientation versus racial identity. *Journal of Social Work and Human Sexuality, 4*(1-2), 83-93.

Icard, L. (1986). Black men and conflicting social identities. In J. Gripton & M. Valentich (Eds.), *Social work practice in sexual problems* (pp. 25-49). New York: Haworth.

Icard, L. (1996). Assessing the psychosocial well-being of African American gays: A multidimensional perspective. *Journal of Gay and Lesbian Social Services, 5*(2/3), 23-50.

Jacobs, S. E., Thomas, W., & Lang, S. (Eds.). (1997). *Two spirited people.* Chicago/Urbana: University of Illinois Press.

Jordan, K. M., & Deluty, R. H. (1998). Coming out for lesbian women: Its relation to anxiety, positive affectivity, self-esteem, and social support. *Journal of Homosexuality, 35*(2), 41-63.

Klawitter, M. M., & Flatt, V. (1994, October). *Antidiscrimination policies and earnings for same-sex couples.* Paper presented at the annual meeting of the Association of Public Policy and Management, Chicago.

Klein, F. (1993). *The bisexual option* (2nd ed.). New York: Harrington Park Press.

Kochman, A. (1997). Gay and lesbian elderly: Historical overview and implications for social work practice. *Journal of Gay and Lesbian Social Services, 6*(1), 1-10.

Kurdek, L. A. (1995). Lesbian and gay couples. In A. R. D'Augelli & C. J. Patterson (Eds.), *Lesbian and gay identities over the lifespan: Psychological perspectives* (pp. 243-261). New York: Oxford University Press.

Letellier, P. (1994). Gay and bisexual male domestic violence victimization: Challenges to feminist theory and response to violence. *Violence and Victims, 9*(2), 95-106.

LeVay, S. (1991). A difference in hypothalamic structure between heterosexual and homosexual men. *Science, 253,* 1034-1037.

LeVay, S. (1993). *The sexual brain.* Cambridge: MIT Press.

Lockhart, L., White, B. W., Causby, V. & Isaac, A. (1994). Letting out the secret: Violence in lesbian relationships. *Journal of Interpersonal Violence, 9*(4), 469-492.

Luczak, R. (Ed.). (1993). *Eyes of desire: A deaf gay & lesbian reader.* Boston: Alyson.

Lukes, A. C., & Land, H. (1990). Biculturality and homosexuality. *Social Work, 35*(2), 155-161.

Mallon, G. (1997). Toward a competent child welfare service delivery system for gay and lesbian adolescents and their families. *Journal of Multicultural Social Work, 5*(3/4), 177-194.

Mead, M. (1935). *Sex and temperament.* New York: Morrow.

Mendola, M. (1980). *The Mendola report: A new look at gay couples in America.* New York: Crown.

Mitchell, J. (1975). *Psychoanalysis and feminism.* New York: Vintage.

Money, J., Schwartz, M., & Lewis, V. G. (1984). Adult erotosexual status and fetal hormonal masculinization and demasculinization: 46, XX congenital virilizing adrenal hyperplasia and 46, XY androgen-insensitivity syndrome compared. *Psychoneuroendocrinology, 9,* 405-414.

Morris, J. F. (1997). Lesbian coming out as a multidimensional process. *Journal of Homosexuality, 33*(2), 1-22.

Murphy, T. F. (1997). *Gay science: The ethics of sexual orientation research.* New York: Columbia University Press.

Murray, S. O., & Roscoe, W. (1998). *Boy-wives and female husbands: Studies of African homosexualties.* New York: St. Martin's.

Newman, B. S., & Muzzonigro, P. G. (1993). Effects of traditional family values in the coming out process of gay male adolescents. *Adolescence, 28,* 213-226.

Nicolosi, J., & Freeman, L. (1993). *Healing homosexuality: Case stories of reparative therapy.* Northvale, NJ: J. Aronson.

Nord, D. (1997). *Multiple AIDS-related loss: A handbook for understanding and surviving a perpetual fall.* Washington, DC: Taylor & Francis.

O'Donnell, J., Ferreira, J., & Malin, M. (1997). Collaboration between youth and adults in a support group for gay and lesbian youth. *Journal of Gay and Lesbian Social Services, 6*(3), 77-81.

Pattatucci, A. M. L., & Hamer, D. H. (1995). Development and familiarity of sexual orientation in females. *Behavioral Genetics, 25,* 407-420.

Patterson, C. J. (1992). Children of gay and lesbian parents. *Child Development, 63,* 1025-1042.

Peterson, K. J., & Bricker-Jenkins, M. (1996). Lesbians and the health care system. *Journal of Gay and Lesbian Social Services, 5*(1), 33-47.

Quam, J. K., & Whitford, G. S. (1992). Adaptation and age-related expectations of older gay and lesbian adults. *The Gerontologist, 12*(3), 367-374

Rodriguez, F. I. (1996). Understanding Filipino male homosexuality: Implications for social services. *Journal of Gay & Lesbian Social Services, 5*(2/3), 93-114.

Savin-Williams, R. C. (1989). Parental influences on the self-esteem of gay and lesbian youths: A reflective appraisals model. In G. Herdt (Ed.), *Gay and lesbian youth* (pp. 93-110). New York: Harrington Park Press.

Savin-Williams, R. C. (1995). Lesbian, gay male, and bisexual adolescents. In A. R. D'Augelli & C. J. Patterson (Eds.), *Lesbian and gay identities over the lifespan: Psychological perspectives* (pp. 165-189). New York: Oxford University Press.

Seidman, S. (Ed.). (1996). *Queer theory/sociology.* Malden, MA: Blackwell.

Shernoff, M. (Ed.). (1997). *Gay widowers: Life after the death of a partner.* New York: Haworth.

Tasker, F., & Golombok, S. (1995). Adults raised as children in lesbian families. *American Journal of Orthopsychiatry, 65*(2), 203-215.

Troiden, R. R. (1993). The formation of homosexual identities. In L. D. Garnets & D. G. Kimmel (Eds.), *Psychological perspectives on lesbian and gay male experiences* (pp. 119-217). New York: Columbia University Press.

U.S. Department of Health and Human Services. (1989). *Report of the Secretary's Task Force on Youth Suicide.* Washington, DC: Government Printing Office.

Victor, S. B., & Fish, M. C. (1995). Lesbian mothers and the children: A review for school psychologists. *School Psychology Review, 24*(3), 456-479.

Williams, W. (1986). *The spirit and the flesh: Sexual diversity in American Indian culture.* Boston: Beacon.

Zamora-Hernandez, C. E., & Patterson, D. (1996). Homosexually active Latino men: Issues for social work practice. *Journal of Gay & Lesbian Social Services, 5*(2/3), 69-92.

CHAPTER TWENTY-THREE

Practice in the World of Work: Promise Unrealized

SHEILA H. AKABAS

What would you like to be when you grow up? What do you do? What did you do before you retired? These are probably some of the most frequently asked questions, and not surprisingly, they all have to do with work. That is because work is probably the most universal phenomenon in American society. Our fantasies are about accomplishments at work, and our sorrows are about the pain at work. When we are young, we prepare for it; when we are in middle years, we depend on it, hoping it will bring fulfillment economically, socially, and psychologically; and when we are older, we reminisce about it, finding our memories of it happier, often, than those about other aspects of our lives. Freud recognized its importance when he declared that the two hallmarks of adult functioning are the ability to love and to work

(Freud, 1930), and few have quarreled with that particular observation of his ever since. The very roots of our country are in the search for a life of work. Even when people hit the lottery, their most frequent future plan is to continue working (Akabas, 1990b). *Working* by Studs Terkel (1974) achieved the position of 54 on the list of the 100 best nonfiction books written in English in the 20th century, selected by an illustrious panel of the Modern Library. Although Terkel is a great raconteur, it is surely the importance of the subject that helped place the book on the prestigious list. It has been said that most immigrants come to America because they believe the streets are paved with gold. Once here, they learn that they have come to pave them. And pave them they do, for to become a true American, work must be on your mind and in your heart.

All is not well in the world of work nor in the outcomes that result from participating in that world. This chapter will identify the importance of work in people's lives and will provide contextual background for looking at the present state of work in relation to available data, legislative action, and theoretical concepts. The conclusion will be apparent—that problems are countless and wide ranging. Three will be the focus of this chapter, namely, the difficulties in

- Securing a viable balance between work demands and family needs
- Achieving an inclusive workplace where all participants experience comfort and support
- Assisting disadvantaged and oppressed groups to attain economic self-sufficiency

The relevance of these problems to social work is based on our understanding that the workplace is the opportunity system where much of the power and many of the rewards of American society are distributed. It is there that social work gains access to a population in need and to powerful sponsors—labor and management. The specific issues are chosen because they meet several conditions. First, each has ethical implications for social work, with its dual mission of meeting individual needs and promoting social justice (Kurzman, 1988). Each provides an ideal path for the profession to contribute to the general good. Second, their solution cannot occur without a significant contribution from labor and management. The world of work may not be a sufficient ally, but it is a necessary one (Marx, 1996). Third, social work can provide leadership in attacking these problems through its practice roles in the world of work. Fourth, and finally, working toward solution of these problems fulfills both the essence

of democracy and the human rights mission of the profession, related to Watkins's (1998) directive,

> Social work's concern for meeting basic human needs, its respect for differences, and its social change orientation position is at the forefront of human rights struggles. However, we need to do a better job of using human rights to inform our practice, scholarship, and teaching. (p. 198)

Work is not acknowledged in mainstream social work literature as the underpinning of American society. Yet, it is the contention here that work is ignored at a risk to our profession and our clients. Ozawa (1982) has attempted to explain how work became so dominant in our culture:

> One of the main foundation stones on which this nation has been built has been the common understanding that work by everyone is valued and will be fairly rewarded. True, work by all was not the *only* idea on which the nation was built. Some people came to this land to escape political or religious persecution, and their chief objective was to build a nation in which people enjoyed political and religious freedom. From the seventeenth century on, many also came to get away from rigid class barriers, and they have endeavored to break down these barriers and strive for more equality. But the majority who have come or who have been born in this country, in the early years or later, have embraced the idea that all who are able to work should do so, and that there should be opportunities for employment for all who want to work (albeit not equal access to all jobs). (p. 35)

As the recent movement championing welfare-to-work programs attests, the work goal remains the defining model for American society. A careful reading of Ozawa, however, suggests that the importance of work is paralleled by a commitment to fair rewards and employment opportunities for all. In these latter criteria, we have not fared as well. Our society is plagued by the greatest income inequity ever (Mishel, Bernstein, & Schmitt, 1997). Modern jobs require high levels of education at a time when our educational systems seem to falter in preparing students, particularly inner-city youths, for the demands of work. Although technology has brought amazing wonders to medical science, we depend largely on occupational benefits to cover health costs, leaving more than 43 million people, in 1997, without insurance to afford advanced care. Among poor workers, about half were uninsured. In fact, workers were less likely to be insured than nonworkers, among those with household incomes of less than $25,000 (U.S. Bureau of the Census, 1998). There is still a wide gap in the pay between men and women doing similar work, and people of color record an even greater gap in relation to white workers when performing like jobs. Although unemployment is at a three decade low, more than 6 million Americans are still actively looking for work (U.S. Bureau of Labor Statistics, 1999). The Equal Employment Opportunity Commission (EEOC) in 1998 received almost 80,000 complaints documenting discrimination based on race, gender, condition of disability, age, national origin, religion, and equal pay, in that order, and state human rights commissions record many more such claims (U.S. Equal Employment Opportunity Commission, 1999).

ISSUES IN THE WORKPLACE

Confirming the dominance of work in American society, it is noteworthy that, between the ages of 16 and 65, most of us spend the major portion of our waking hours working. In April 1999, the civilian labor force, comprising those who are employed and those who have actively sought work within the last month, accounted for a total of 139.1 million of the total of 272 million living Americans (U.S. Bureau of Labor Statistics, 1999). At no time in our history has the proportion of those in the relevant age group who are labor force participants been higher, standing at 67.1% overall (U.S. Bureau of Labor Statistics, 1999). There is variation by gender, age, and race in this participation rate, which suggests that it is harder for African American men to gain entry and for all men to maintain participation and that women's employment rates drop off during child-bearing years. The rate of participation for females, nonetheless, has risen steadily over the past several decades.

In most dimensions, significant variation occurs. In 1996, when the poverty guideline for a family of four was $16,036 income annually, 5.5% of workers earned less than that, particularly those with low educational levels. This meant that 4.1 million families lived below the poverty level despite having at least one member in the labor market. The poverty rate for families with just one member in the labor force was over seven times higher than that of families with two or more members in the workforce, at 14.6% versus 1.9% (U.S. Bureau of Labor Statistics, 1997). For a significant portion of families, the only means of staying above the poverty line is having two earners in the family. This has pulled mothers of young children into the workplace in record numbers (Akabas, 1990a). Yet, the top 5% of families, according to 1996 figures, earned a disproportionate 21.4% of the total aggregate income, and the top 20% reported earnings that accounted for 49% of the total aggregate (U.S. Bureau of the Census, 1997). It is possible to offer a far longer list of statistical data to confirm the inequities of the economy in relation to opportunities and reward distribution from the world of work, but this data set suffices to establish the obvious.

As the most significant institutional force in American society, the workplace might serve as the great equalizer by providing opportunity for all, but it does not appear to do so (Marlow, 1990; Potocky, 1996). Instead, it contributes to each of the three arenas of difficulty we discuss here. It causes workers to have to focus on the demands of work rather than on the needs of their families; it contributes to the discomfort and lack of inclusion that whole groups of employees experience; and it tends to bar the way to self-sufficiency for the most disadvantaged—those with modest education, those with physical and mental health disabilities, the aging, and people of color.

It is important to place this record in perspective. If one compares our economic circumstances with the rest of the world, the United States looks relatively benign. Aside from Japan and a few countries in western Europe, the United States guarantees its citizens greater security and a more comfortable lifestyle than other places in the world, and this is so for the vast majority of our inhabitants. But if one compares our status with our value system concerning fairness and our beliefs in the effectiveness of employment and democracy as efficient engines of distributive justice, one is left disappointed. The land of opportunity is a land of opportunity for some but not all, the rewards from work may have more to do with predetermined factors such as skin color and gender—and certainly neighborhood where one lives

and the work chosen by one's parents—than the common wisdom suggests.

The disparate impact of many of our economic and social policies and practices has brought us to this situation (Halter, 1996; Waldfogel, 1997). For example, if employers require a college degree for jobs that do not need that level of education, the disparate impact of the educational requirement may reduce the number of aging or African American applicants (both of which tend to have lower education than other population groups) who can meet the hiring criterion for the job. The message that those not hired take away is one of exclusion. If strength requirements are established that exceed the demands of certain manual work, the disparate impact on women and people with disabilities may eliminate them from qualifying for work that they could do. In both of these instances, the result of this disparate impact is that the supply of labor for these jobs is unnecessarily reduced, eliminating competition in securing these jobs. Automatically, the wage rate for those positions rises, increasing the competition for other work and thereby lowering the earnings and the possibility of economic self-sufficiency from alternative opportunities. Systemic inequity has gained a foothold through the operation of the world of work (Googins & Burden, 1987; Jones, 1992).

The major parties in the work system are employers and trade unions. There are about 6 million employers in the United States, including profit-making corporations, not-for-profit institutions, and government agencies. They vary in size and many other dimensions of their operation. Each has the potential to affect the lives of those in its employ. Almost universally, the first priority of each organization is to accomplish its production task. Although a large body of research links productivity to attention paid to the workforce (Chitwood, 1978; Ouchi, 1981; Peters & Waterman, 1984; Thomas, 1991), few employers have established policies and practices that evidence their acceptance of that link. Lambert (1993) has argued, in fact, that even when employers develop programs that look like they are responsive to the needs of individuals and families, their actual goal is to remove family responsibility so that the employee can pay priority attention to the demands of the workplace. The short-term thinking of most of American industry leaves little time for attention to the longer run payoffs stemming from providing a caring environment for employees. Unfortunately, this lack of attention is reinforced by a societal culture that values different people differently. Not only do people of color view the police differently than white Americans do, but in the workplace, people of color, and especially African American working women (who are doubly differentiated by race and gender), experience the workplace as a place of exclusion and discomfort (Hopkins, 1997). The ease with which organizations downsize, for example, not only results in lack of loyalty to an employer but in high levels of stress among employees (Schore & Atkin, 1993) and, ultimately, loss of economic well-being. Families, too, have suffered, and researchers even suggest that the level of violence among teenagers can be attributed, in part, to the lack of time and energy parents have left to invest in their children following their efforts to fulfill workplace demands. Ultimately, actions in the workplace affect employees, and through them, families and communities.

In the meantime, trade unions, which historically offered a relatively strong voice on behalf of social goals and economic justice, have be-

come increasingly impotent. The forces contributing to this change include the rise of global competition, decline of the manufacturing sector, expansion of part-time and contract work, and the development of a hostile legal and legislative environment. In the 1950s, unions represented 35% of the labor force; by 1998, only 13.9% of all wage and salary workers were union members (AFL-CIO, 1999). Furthermore, the unions have maintained their model of male domination in an era when almost half the labor force is female. This has limited both their ability to understand the needs of that half of the workforce and their general appeal to potential members. As Albee (1986) has suggested,

> The forces that are barriers to a just world are some of the same forces that block significant efforts at reducing psychopathology in our society: exploitation, imperialism, excessive concentration of economic power, nationalism, institutions that perpetuate powerlessness, hopelessness, poverty, discrimination, sexism, racism, ageism. (p. 894)

POLICY AND PRACTICE RESPONSES

This reality has not gone unnoticed in our national political debates. Legislative efforts have been made to remedy policies and practices that have unequal impact on various labor force participants. The National Labor Relations Act of 1935, which guaranteed the right of workers to organize and bargain collectively concerning their wages, hours, and working conditions, might be considered the birth of the legislative response to economic inequity. Although somewhat eroded over the years, the NLRA established the power of workers and their trade unions as a countervailing force to the power of employers. Since 1935, a Congressional agenda, more prevalent under Democratic than Republican administrations, has been directed at equalizing power and promoting the equality of rights among participants in the economy. A set of laws that deal with discrimination, as it manifests itself in the acceptance that different groups experience in the labor market, covers one dimension of this initiative. Title VII of the Civil Rights Act of 1964, which forbids discrimination in all aspects of employment based on race, sex, gender and national origin, is the showpiece of this trend. Regulations, issued to define the basis for compliance with this act, have been effective in establishing that sexual harassment in the workplace is unacceptable and in explicating the conditions under which affirmative action is required to reduce the residue of prior discrimination (Wilk, 1988). Further protection for women is provided by both the Equal Pay Act of 1963, which sets a standard of equal pay for equal work in a not entirely successful effort to close the wage gap between men and women with equal education and experience, and the Pregnancy Discrimination Act of 1978, which requires that pregnancy be dealt with like any other disability occurring among active workers.

The Age Discrimination in Employment Act of 1967 covers unfair labor market responses to those over 45, while the Immigration Control and Reform Act of 1986 protects from discrimination eligible workers born outside the United States. Those with disabilities finally earned similar protection under the Americans with Disabilities Act (ADA) of 1990. Title 1 of the ADA outlaws discrimination in employment toward qualified people with disabilities who can perform the essential functions of the job with reasonable accommodation, provided that such accommodation does not cause undue hardship (usually tested by its cost relative to the resources of the employer). Taken together, these laws have attacked some of the barriers to entry, advancement, and sustained participation in the labor market (Ledvinka & Scarpello, 1991; West, 1991; Wilk, 1988). Acceptance and support, however, cannot be legislated, and this remains an open field for social work intervention.

Other issues have also received attention. The Family Medical Leave Act of 1993 tried to assist family members in balancing their work/family responsibilities. This is important for all family members, but most particularly for women, who despite their massive entry into the labor market, continue to carry major responsibilities for care of children, the ill, and the aged, according to all research reports (Akabas, 1988). In recognition of the fact that the only safety net in American society is having a job, income loss resulting from loss of work caused by layoff, onset of disability, and aging are each a basis for benefit payments under provisions of the Social Security Act. Income maintenance is assured, as well, for those unable to work because of injury or illness precipitated by work through the Workers Compensation Act in each state. In addition, economic self-sufficiency was also the subject of the Fair Labor Standards Act of 1938, which established a minimum wage. At the time of passage, the required minimum payment per hour allowed full-time workers to earn more than a poverty-level income. Like other legislative mandates, however, the minimum wage law no longer offers protection from poverty. Efforts to raise the minimum to a level that would assure above-poverty earnings have been opposed by believers in the free market, who claim, without supportive evidence, that an increase in the minimum wage will reduce employment overall, and most particularly for the most disadvantaged (Chilman, 1995). Social work professionals have not raised their advocacy voice on these issues.

Finally, a set of laws seeks to improve the quality of the resources that unemployed individuals bring with them to the workplace. The Joint Training and Partnership Act and related legislation offer enhancement training to youths, the unemployed, people with disabilities, aging workers, and those displaced by the workings of the global economy. The programs established to carry out this initiative are usually devoted to a quick fix despite considerable evidence that enhancing human resources is a long, expensive, and labor-intensive process (Halter, 1996). Once again, social work voices have been scarce in discussions of these issues. Hagen (1992) argues for attention by the profession, noting that the variety of roles social workers could play in these programs include direct practice, management, staff development and training, policy analysis, advocacy, and research, concluding, "What social work brings to this challenge is an awareness that it is the client who is to be served, not the bureaucracy" (p. 12).

Although many other laws bear on conditions in the workplace, this list is sufficient to establish that it is a matter of accepted national social policy to recognize that our romance with the free market has not been an unmitigated blessing in relation to other values that we as a nation hold dear. The passage of legislation, as an expression of social policy, may be a necessary condition for correction, but it is in the enforcement of these laws that the determination

of a society is ratified. Judged not just by the lack of interest in amendments that could keep the laws synchronized to changing economic conditions, as in the case of the minimum wage, but by the allocation of funds for enforcement, our will as a nation has not been sufficient to protect the goals of protective legislation. If we claim to be against discrimination in the marketplace and then underfund, as we do, the EEOC, which has enforcement responsibility in relation to discrimination in the workplace, we cannot assure the goal of fair treatment. If we protect the jobs of those taking leave for family health issues, but unlike all of western Europe, we offer no income support during the period of leave, it is not clear that we really mean to help workers balance work demands and family needs. If we offer training through the JTPA, but do not parallel it with adequate day care arrangements, it is hard to believe that we really want young workers to enhance their skills and improve their competitive position in the labor market to achieve self-sufficiency.

These contradictions demonstrate our national ambivalence in accepting legislative initiatives that represent a change in underlying social assumptions. For example, because of past practices and their disparate impact, the Civil Rights Law of 1964 promotes a national policy of affirmative action. But affirmative action contradicts our long-standing assumption that equal treatment should be available to everyone. For our society, however, where groups such as women or minority populations are placed at a competitive disadvantage through no fault of their own, equality does not provide equity. Forces on the right, nonetheless, have rejected efforts to change that assumption, and they have weakened the national commitment to affirmative action as a means of reversing the results of disparate impact. Supporting the intent of the Family and Medical Leave Act, research documents that well-being of workers leads to productivity (Bond, Galinsky, & Swanberg, 1997). But payment for such leave would challenge the long-held assumption that family is not a business matter. The new assumption would be that anything that interferes with productivity *is* a business concern. Accepting that, a related view that family and children's needs are a women's issue would be replaced by an understanding that balancing work and family is an issue of interest to all workers (Bond et al., 1997). Then, instead of assuming that care for children and the elderly should be ignored because it holds the potential for liability claims, employers could develop a business commitment to support (and use) community services as an opportunity to provide evidence of their concern for the quality of life for all (Marx, 1996; Smith, 1994; Zippay, 1992). Thus, a change of assumptions establishes a new course of action, one that could resolve the national ambivalence with regard to our social agenda. These issues stand waiting for social work attention. This is not meant to suggest that we can change the situation alone or immediately, but surely, our professional voice should be heard loudly and clearly promoting and even demanding policies that further community support and personal independence.

The gap between policy enactment and its fulfillment is matched by a gulf between our practice potential and its achievement. Social workers have become the profession of choice in delivering services to workers. Both Employee Assistance Programs (EAPs) and their union counterparts, Membership Assistance Programs (MAPs), whether in-house or contracted off-site services, have become integrated into the workplaces of America. The workplace is seen as an appropriate site for identifying and treating a host of individual problems. It is well known that although employers may recruit workers, they get human beings. Not unexpectedly, these human beings are accompanied by all the marital, family, health, disability, and substance abuse problems one might expect to find among the adult working population. Occupational social work services, therefore, have included counseling for the gamut of problems faced by individuals. But too often, social workers in the workplace have settled for a narrow definition of their role. They have attended to individual problems rather than integrating their practice into organizational or community needs. Yet, a vast population is uncomfortable with their position in, or seeking entry into, the world of work. For them, and the millions of working poor for whom economic self-sufficiency is difficult to achieve, social workers, and especially occupational social workers, have missed the opportunity to provide leadership or assistance (Akabas & Kurzman, 1982; Mor-Barak & Tynan, 1993; Mudrick, 1991). The remainder of this chapter will examine the theoretical base for a systems approach to workplace-related practice intervention and then describe the nature of the practice that can affect the desired changes.

THEORETICAL CONSIDERATIONS

As indicated, social workers in the workplace are called on often to help with a myriad of personal problems ranging, to name just a few, from child care to elder care, from marital issues to domestic violence, from substance abuse to deteriorating physical health, from career planning to retirement issues, and including problems faced by workers trying to balance family and work demands and facing perceptions of discrimination in the workplace. Too, social workers are aware of the problems of those who experience economic dependence because they cannot gain access to jobs that pay enough to support families. Practice that allows intervention at the individual, organizational, and community level can inform the process of moving from case (private troubles) to cause (public issues) (Schwartz, 1969) to deal with these issues. In the armory of knowledge and skills available to social workers, there reside many potential responses to the problems in or of the workplace.

Underlying all practice in the world of work is the strengths perspective, which assesses personal and social resources and the capacity of individuals to respond constructively despite the problems in their lives (Saleeby, 1997). This focus, although valid for all practice, is particularly relevant to anyone who has managed home and work life, or who has persevered in an organization despite feeling discriminated against and undervalued, or who, regardless of lack of skill or the existence of serious mental, physical, or social problems, focuses on gaining entry into the world of work and seeking self-sufficiency. These behaviors speak to strengths within the individuals involved, strengths that can be the basis for individual problem solving (El-Bassel, 1996). The task of the effective social worker is valuing and building on these strengths or, as Weick and Chamberlain (1997) suggest, "meeting people where they are and joining with them in discovering and reaffirming the talents, abilities, and aspirations that will form a path away from the problem" (p. 42).

But even the strong cannot go it alone. At the individual level, workers need to feel support. There is much evidence to indicate that support serves as a buffer for stress in one's life. House's (1981) views on the importance of social support in achieving effectiveness in the workplace are instructive. He notes that, for most employees, stress at work interferes with performance. He identifies four types of support—(a) informational, (b) instrumental, (c) emotional, and (d) feedback or appraisal—that help alleviate stress and, therefore, are fundamental to productive performance. Assuming that an individual's well-being at work hinges on being able to feel satisfied with his or her performance, (LaRocco, House, & French, 1980), the challenge facing the social worker is how to establish an environment in which these various types of support are available.

Over the long run, the change required is not only, or even primarily, individual in nature. Organizational culture and societal definitions must change if solutions to problems are to be sustained. Lewin (1951) sheds light on how we can begin to understand the potential for change and establish a game plan for its accomplishment. An analysis using Kurt Lewin's force field theory can provide guidelines for such an endeavor. Too often, the culture of a workplace is wed to work processes rather than the underlying conditions that make work possible. Managers do not appreciate the possibilities of redesign that can improve the employees' sense of themselves and their potential. Suppose that we are interested in changing the culture of the workplace so that it offers the support that would enhance work performance. Lewin views an organization as in a state of equilibrium. If one seeks to achieve change, it is necessary to carry out an analysis that looks at the existing equilibrium (culture) and identifies its underpinnings. This allows the change agent (social worker) to identify how either to increase the forces that might promote change, reduce the forces that might restrain change, or bring about some combination thereof. What are the forces restraining and promoting the present equilibrium and what would it take to accomplish a change in culture, in this case, the creation of a supportive environment? Achieving this change is particularly important if diverse populations are to experience and feel the necessary level of support to be comfortable and, therefore, committed and productive at work.

Conceptually, the idea of accommodation, borrowed from the ADA, is relevant to the change process needed to help employees balance work and family demands or to influence work cultures to accept and reward diversity. Some might question whether the world of work can provide accommodation to the needs of the many and still fulfill its prime mission of productivity and profit. The author would argue that it already does so in countless informal and probably discriminatory ways. When a valued secretary has a child in a kindergarten play, she is allowed to take half a day to attend the performance. When the best salesman has a sick parent, no one questions his or her time away from the field to attend to the family member's needs. When the manager's daughter starts college, he or she is not charged with vacation time for the two days needed to drive her there and get her settled. When the young administrator, already identified as a fast-track possibility for top management, requests a leave to undertake a master's of business administration, he or she is reassured that his or her job will be protected and his or her return welcomed. The workplace accommodates every day, by informal means, to the interests and the needs of those deemed to be stars. Questions arise when the needs expressed are unexpected, or the requestor is merely an ordinary player in the bigger system. Time off needed by a cashier with a disability for a regular medical appointment may be an accommodation required by law, but it is one likely to be regarded with suspicion. The single-parent machine operator who asks for flextime because he or she cannot leave her children at nursery school early enough to arrive at the beginning of the shift is likely to be considered unreliable. Like the dilemmas surrounding assumptions, those surrounding actual behavior are challenging.

Kets De Vries and Balazs (1999) provide an insight that helps explain why change is so difficult to achieve and how we might organize to be more successful in its attainment. They argue that organizations have a tendency to continue even dysfunctional patterns, because people basically are inhibited from change for reasons ranging from fear to inability. They reason that when we try to institute an organizational change, we have not given sufficient attention to the forces that resist change within the individuals involved. They conclude that, in moving all individuals toward a new vision, it is the leadership of people at the top—how much they make it a public issue by staging a "focal event" and, by public announcement, making their support clear, and how safe they make those who have to change feel in the changed circumstances—that is the primary influence on the outcome.

The importance of the need to feel safe under conditions of change, discussed by Kets De Vries and Balazs (1999), is reinforced by research reported by Kim and Mauborgne

(1997). They have found that to achieve maximum outcome in a change process, it must be understood and regarded as fair by the constituents. Their research indicates that fairness releases creativity whereas change by fiat results in people doing what they are told to do but withholding their commitment. Fair process is based on (a) involving individuals in decisions that affect them by asking for their input, (b) explaining the basis for the final decision, and (c) making expectations based on that decision clear. Fair process, the authors point out, does not require consensus in the final decision. They conclude, "Individuals are most likely to trust and cooperate freely with systems—whether they themselves win or lose—when fair process is observed" (p. 69).

In short, a model of change emerges that is based on vision and understanding of individual and organizational issues. To enlist the commitment and productivity of the constituents in the world of work, leaders (Kets De Vries & Balazs, 1999) must assess the field of forces and their interests in the issue (Lewin, 1951), build on the strength of their constituents (Saleeby, 1997), offer maximum support (House, 1981), and assure a process that is fair and widely understood (Kim & Mauborgne, 1997).

PRACTICE POSSIBILITIES

Let us consider the application of these concepts to the issues social workers meet in helping the world of work contribute more positively to the solution of the individual, organizational, and community problems involved in balancing work and family demands, in helping diverse populations feel safe and cared for within the organization, and in having the world of work participate in improving access to and equity in economic well-being.

Balancing family needs and work demands. Faced with a situation in which an employee, trying to balance family and work, is having difficulty managing time, the traditional intervention might be individual counseling, building on the individual's already established strength in coping. EAPs try to help employees plan to manage better their multiple family and work demands by offering information (on child care programs, for example) and emotional support (House, 1981). Sometimes, looking at their caseloads as a needs assessment, social workers may move from case to class; that is, EAP social workers will recognize that balancing time is an issue for many employees (Lechner, 1993). They may even advocate successfully for accommodations in organizational policy that allow flextime, job sharing, telecommuting, or other means of providing an individual employee with more control over time at work (Schwartz, 1969). Without an organizational culture change, however, most employees will not take advantage of such new benefits, believing, according to all research findings, that time at the workplace is observed and counted and that "face time" is correlated with advancement. Then, the social worker must look for ways to influence the organization (Brager & Holloway, 1978; Hagen & Davis, 1992).

A Lewinian force field analysis might find a restraining force in the attitude of many supervisors, who believe that work is work and that workers should leave their "family business" at home. The advocacy of the EAP social worker would not be a sufficient promoting force to overcome the negative attitudes of the supervisors (Lewin, 1951). But if the social worker can give the issue sufficient visibility so that it captures the interest of corporate leadership, a different outcome can result (Googins & Davidson, 1993). A clear message from the leadership in a well-heralded public forum can shift the balance sufficiently to secure a change in organizational culture that would make the time-related accommodations usable benefits rather than paper privileges (Kets De Vries & Balazs, 1999). Training supervisors to apply the newly supported accommodations would reinforce the response. Were the leadership to reaffirm its interest in helping workers achieve a balance between family needs and work demands by financially contributing to community child care resources, for example, the private troubles of a few workers would have been parlayed into improved community well-being. In sum, starting with an advocacy effort that makes a business case for the cost of not responding (turnover will be high, workers will not be committed and loyal, supervisors will not be trusted, productivity will be impaired), the social worker can mainstream the problem and its solution (Mor-Barak, 1988; Warren & Johnson, 1995) by involving top management in a strategic decision that changes the essence of the organization and has repercussions for the community as well. The important lesson is that no one solution is mandated, and a desirable response can be a continuous dynamic process. Ultimately, the change in culture through commitment and action ripples through the society (Marx, 1996; Smith, 1994).

Creating a workplace culture where diversity is valued. Another issue for which this type of analysis and practice intervention can produce meaningful change surrounds diversity within organizations. Affirmative action, once it be-

came the law of the land, helped open doors to organizations for women and minorities (Bronner, 1998). Although they were inside, they never secured positions of power, acceptance, and decision making within the organization. This is the stage of diversity that Gummer (1998) refers to as a condition under which newcomers are allowed entry but are expected to act like others and conform to the existing culture rather than assert their individuality. Their entry does not make a difference in the organization. White men continue to rule, leaving most other organizational members with a sense that processes are neither fair nor safe for them (Hopkins, 1997; Kim & Maugborne, 1997). As Fong and Gibbs (1995) note,

> In terms of the individual multicultural worker in a dominant culture setting, this means . . . other staff members are likely to be preserving their commonality, keeping the worker outside. . . . Thus, new staff are usually organizationally powerless. (pp. 7-8)

EAP social workers are privy to many reports of dehumanizing experiences that continue to marginalize workers who gained entry through affirmative action (Wilk, 1988). In fact, it has been suggested that being an affirmative action hire is, itself, marginalizing. To gain the most productive performance from employees, however, employers benefit from building the workers' sense of identity with the organization. What is needed is to go beyond Gummer's (1998) first stage of diversity acceptance; through the stage in which people are allowed to be different, but organizations ignore their difference; to the true diversity situation, where the differences of the diverse are celebrated by the employer, and they are enlisted to contribute to the organization's accomplishments.

A social worker can orchestrate an intervention that improves communication and understanding between people and allows their full creativity to enhance the organization's work. An adaption of a technique first described by Tracy and Whittaker (1990) is appropriate here. They developed a social network mapping process to identify sources of social support that could be enlisted to preserve families at risk of out-of-home placement of children. Recognizing that similar support makes it possible for those in the workplace to fulfill their productivity potential, the author and colleagues (Gates, Akabas, & Oran-Sabia, 1998) used the circle map and grid developed by Tracy and Whittaker to record information about the network available to workers with mental health conditions who needed support from coworkers and supervisors to sustain employment. The map and its grid are completed jointly by the social worker and the worker who feels isolated, excluded, or undervalued, resulting in a picture of that individual's perception of his or her work group and its support levels. This technique, as reported elsewhere (Gates, Akabas, Oran-Sabia, 1998), identifies the work group members and uses House's (1981) categories of support to record work group size, criticalness, closeness, reciprocity, directionality of help, stability, and frequency of contact between the person needing support and others in the work group. Although applied to workers with mental health problems, this model of data collection seems applicable more broadly to workers who experience themselves as different from the members of their work groups.

Based on the collection of data just described, recording the individual's perception, it is possible for a social worker to facilitate a meeting of the work group during which a discussion can take place on the meaning of social support, the reasons different people need different kinds and degrees of social support, and how the work group has or has not fulfilled mutual needs for social support with the individual who is being treated as the outsider. The resulting communication and understanding can release the energy and commitment not only of the outsider but of the entire membership of the work group, to improve the work environment and offer support for all. This creates a culture aimed at promoting long-term assistance rather than crisis stabilization. As with the intervention concerned with improving the environment for work/family balance, the individual intervention works best when accompanied by a leadership initiative that truly supports and integrates people of all races, genders, and other differences into positions at all levels in the hierarchy and decision process. A culture of comfort will result because constituents will experience the process as fair, and the community in which this population lives will experience a reduced level of stress and a higher degree of citizen participation (Schore & Atkin, 1993).

Increasing access to self-sufficiency and economic independence. Finally, the issue of the world of work's contribution to self-sufficiency and economic independence is amenable to action by social workers who are knowledgeable about the workplace, through interventions that include public policy advocacy. The profession's involvement with all aspects of the human condition has helped us understand what public laws and policies are needed to create a more equitable society. There is extensive evidence to establish that legislative and program initiatives designed to reduce dependency and increase economic self-sufficiency have been inadequately conceived and poorly implemented, given the complexity of the problem for many of those seeking entry into the labor force (Hagen & Davis, 1995; Halter, 1996; Jones, 1992). Research evidence indicates that the problem with the poor is not their motivation or attitude but sometimes their lack of education and more often the lack of jobs that provide income adequate to support a family, the absence of support services such as day care and transportation to make jobs accessible, and the disadvantaged nature of the economies in the communities in which they live (Chilman, 1995; Coulton, 1996; Hagen & Davis, 1995; Halter, 1996). The practice implications seem clear. Individual counseling with poor people who are interested in gaining access to employment, but who lack fundamental skills for contemporary employment or are homeless, in poor physical health, or lacking knowledge of the job search process can help, and it is in keeping with the theory that views unemployment as due to a gap in human capital embodied by the unemployed person. Even here, however, providing individual services must be combined with attention to assure sufficient resources to allow intensity of service because, in welfare-to-work and youth employment initiatives, "the most successful work programs shared one critical component: intensive, long-term, individualized, multilevel services" (Iversen, 1998, p. 554).

But if, as most analyses and research suggest, individual service is a minor part of the answer, social work is participating in the problem rather than its solution if its efforts are all victim-focused individual interventions. There is a need to challenge the dominant economic system and its basic assumption of the effectiveness of the free market, which has left so many be-

hind. At one time, the profession was a voice for the disenfranchised. For too long, however, social work, in its search for its own professional status, has worked less and less with the poor. We need, once again, to legitimate the validity of their voices and language (Watkins, 1998). What is needed is a well-developed political advocacy effort based on professional expertise. The profession's voice and organizing ability can be a powerful catalyst to spark a more appropriate public response to those looking into the world of work, but unable to gain effective entry there. We would argue that occupational social workers are the ideal candidates to provide leadership for such an action. Occupational social workers' expertise concerning the "work" involved in serving the population allows them to claim jurisdiction for this wider context of practice. Only a modest reformulation of our practice is required to take our understanding of the meaning of work in people's lives and of the interests of labor and mangement, knowledge of advocacy, benefit counseling, experience in linking with resources, ability to provide education concerning workplace culture, and awareness of outplacement and other career concerns, using all of these to handle the full spectrum of work situations from pre-entry through postretirement (Akabas & Gates, 1995). Using our experience and knowledge, it is possible to establish our "place" as the appropriate professional group to handle this issue. Vourlekis, Edinburg, and Knee (1998) suggest that "strengthening a profession takes place by creating turf, not just defending it" (p. 567). Other professionals which face similar opportunities are also urged to accept an activist role. For example, Jenkins and Strauser (1999) admonish rehabilitation counselors to broaden their perspective to include services to employers or "remain niche players and eventually be replaced by professionals who are able to offer more comprehensive services" (p. 4).

Coulton (1996) argues that because social disadvantage is so linked to the nature of the neighborhood and the community, there also is a need to understand the factors that affect both the preconditions that do or do not encourage work as an outlook and the opportunities for work in local circumstances. She recommends that, to empower the poor to pursue economic independence, professionals should pursue a combination of economic development and community organizing based on an understanding of the importance of helping residents learn how to link to community economic resources and to develop a locally initiated network of social service support. Success in achieving these goals seems to require a connection with the world of work and an understanding of the language and practice in that world, again the province of the occupational social worker.

In short, what is suggested here is that the occupational social worker engage in the kind of integrated practice recommended by Parsons, Hernandez, and Jorgensen (1988). Such practice operates on the micro, meso, and macro levels and is directed at the social problem rather than its victim. They note,

> Rather than assuming that the problem is within an individual, the problem also may be defined as located in the interaction between the individual and the environment or within the environment. Moreover, the question of where to intervene is open. The location of the problem and the focus of the intervention need not always be the same. (p. 147)

Although this practice may look a little different from what social workers traditionally see themselves as trained to do, and able to influence, the author believes that what is suggested is merely a systems approach to the usual generalist practice applied to the occupational related arena. What seems apparent is that although we face a world in considerable flux, there does not appear to be any likelihood that the significance of work in American society will lessen. As a profession, therefore, we need a presence that will make the world of work more benign for all, and most particularly for the vulnerable populations that are the prime target of much of social work's attention and service initiatives.

In the early 1960s, when affirmative action became law, the author was called in by a major telephone company subsidiary to help them understand why they were experiencing such lack of success in the retention of black telephone operators. The company managers felt they were doing everything right. Their recruitment previously had been only at the local parochial high schools, where they filled their need for operators right out of the graduating class with an expectation, confirmed by experience, that these young women would remain with them until marriage (and until retirement if they did not marry). Now they had added a work training program for minority mothers to their recruitment source. Although this latter program referred well-trained operators, the young women worked for several weeks and almost inevitably quit. The telephone company was ready to say that black women did not want to be telephone operators, but given affirmative action legislation, managers were anxious to have their finding confirmed before making such a public statement.

An analysis of the situation identified that the problem was not with the women but with the structure used by the telephone company. Their policy was to use new operators on a split shift to handle high volume periods of demand. For the first year or so of employment, operators were expected to work from 10 a.m. to 2 p.m. and from 6 p.m. to 10 p.m. Thereafter, they were moved to continuous 8-hour shifts as openings developed. Although this schedule was fine for young single women, and the intervening hours were easy to fill with pleasant activity and plenty of colleague companionship, it proved deadly for young mothers, who could not access adequate child care coverage and missed the most important part of their child's day. The law (public policy) had made the company take a look at the issue, but it was generalist practice, using research, analysis, prior understanding, and negotiation skill, that solved the problem. Restructuring the system so that split shifts became voluntary, and all new employees were assigned continuous hours, eliminated the retention issue and opened well-paid, secure jobs that would allow any of the occupants to support a family, both socially and economically. Ultimately, everyone was better off.

CONCLUSION

As important as it is for the profession to be involved with labor and management and the world of work settings, we cannot escape from some of the baggage that accrues with that affiliation. As a profession concerned with the poor and disadvantaged, we cannot ignore the contribution of the world of work to the growth of a society of haves and have nots. The faster technology moves ahead to create the booming profits and job openings of the current era, the

further and further behind those without advantages can fall. Social workers can give voice to this concern. As we contribute to the world of work, we can gain credibility in that world. We can use that status to give visibility to the needs of those who are in danger of becoming even more marginal than they already are to that world. It is the job of social workers to clarify the mutual interest of labor and management with the least advantaged in our society. As customers, employees, and parents of future workers, the disadvantaged must contribute to the greater whole if we are to maximize our potential as a society. General well-being is increased by better schools, universal medical care, and equity in economic opportunity. Social workers in the workplace can give voice as a countervailing force to the short-term and ill-conceived rush for immediate return on investment that appears to drive the powers of the workplace today.

It is worthwhile at this juncture to ask, What role should the profession have, and how should it approach the future of, and in, the world of work?" With work as a core issue, there is a need for social work to pay increasing and knowledgeable attention to the ways in which the economy can become more inclusive, helping to realize the profession's goal of social equity. We need to use our knowledge of the world of work and the language it speaks and combine it with our role of advocacy. We need to see the inclusion of management and labor as vital to achieving the profession's agenda. We need to believe that the world of work can provide accommodation to these many needs and still fulfill its prime mission of productivity and profit, that actually meeting these needs will have a positive impact on its primary goals. We need to help spread information and foster improved communication not only among our clients but among the population in general. Raising awareness can have an impact on the social atmosphere and lead to restructured policies and cultures. That is our work and assures our place in the grand scheme of social outcomes.

Adaptation is a lengthy process. This discussion is not meant to make the process appear simple or swift. It is meant, however, to empower social work professionals to become activists in the interest of solving the problems encountered by constituents in the world of work.

REFERENCES

AFL-CIO. (1999). *The union advantage: Union membership trends* [On-line]. Available: http://www.aflcio.org/uniondifference1.1htm

Akabas, S. (1988). Women, work, and mental health: Room for improvement. *Journal of Primary Prevention, 9*(1&2), 130-39.

Akabas, S. (1990a, June). Reconciling the demands of work with the needs of families. *Families in Society: The Journal of Contemporary Human Services,* pp. 366-371.

Akabas, S. (1990b). The work ethic is alive and well: Its impact on persons with disabilities. In S. Scheer (Ed.), *Multidisciplinary perspectives in vocational assessment of impaired workers* (pp. xvii-xxii). Rockville, MD: Aspen.

Akabas, S., & Gates, L. (1995). *Planning for disability management: An approach to controlling costs while caring for employees.* Scottsdale, AZ: American Compensation Association.

Akabas, S., & Kurzman, P. (1982). The industrial social welfare specialist: What's so special. In S. Akabas & P. Kurzman (Eds.), *Work, workers, and work organizations: A view from social work* (pp. 197-235). Englewood Cliffs, NJ: Prentice Hall.

Albee, G. (1986). Toward a just society: Lessons on observations on the primary prevention of psychopathology. *American Psychologist, 41,* 891-898.

Bond, J., Galinsky, E., & Swanberg, J. (1997). *National study of the changing workforce.* New York: Families and Work Institute.

Brager, G., & Holloway, S. (1978). *Changing human service organizations: Politics and practice.* New York: Free Press.

Bronner, E. (1998, September 9). Study strongly supports affirmative action in admissions to elite colleges. *New York Times,* Section A, 1.

Chilman, C. (1995). Programs and policies for working poor families: Major trends and some research issues. *Social Service Review, 69*(3), 515-524.

Chitwood, S. (1978). Social equity and service productivity. In S. Slavin (Ed.), *Social administration* (pp. 326-336). New York: Harworth.

Coulton, C. (1996). Poverty, work, and community: A research agenda for an era of diminishing federal responsibility. *Social Work, 41*(5), 509-519.

El-Bassel, N. (1996). Correlates of return to work after an onset of short-term disability among female union members. *Employee Assistance Quarterly, 12*(1), 47-72.

Fong, L., & Gibbs, J. (1995). Facilitating services to multicultural communities in a dominant culture setting: An organizational perspective. *Administration in Social Work, 19*(2), 1-24.

Freud, S. (1930). *Civilization and its discontents.* New York: J. Cape & H. Smith.

Gates, L., Akabas, S., & Oran-Sabia, V. (1998). Relationship accommodations involving the work group: Improving work prognosis for persons with mental health conditions. *Psychiatric Rehabilitation Journal, 21*(3), 264-272.

Googins, B., & Burden, D. (1987). Vulnerability of working parents: Balancing work and home roles. *Social Work, 32*(4), 295-299.

Googins, B., & Davidson, B. (1993). The organization as client: Broadening the concept of employee assistance programs. *Social Work, 39*(4), 477-484.

Gummer, B. (1998). Current perspectives on diversity in the workforce: How diverse is diverse? *Administration in Social Work, 22*(1), 83-111.

Hagen, J. (1992). Women, work, and welfare: Is there a role for social work? *Social Work, 37*(1), 12.

Hagen, J., & Davis, L. (1992). Working with women: Building a policy and practice agenda. *Social Work, 37*(6), 495-502.

Hagen, J., & Davis, L. (1995). The participants' perspective on the job opportunities and basic skills training program. *Social Service Review, 69*(4), 656-678.

Halter, A. (1996). State welfare reform for employable general assistance recipients: The facts behind the assumptions. *Social Work, 41*(1), 106-110.

Hopkins, K. (1997). Supervisor intervention with troubled workers: A social identity perspective. *Human Relations, 50*(10), 1215-1238.

House, J. (1981). *Work stress and social support.* Reading, MA: Addison-Wesley.

Iversen, R. (1998). Occupational social work for the 21st century. *Social Work, 43*(6), 551-566.

Jenkins, W., & Strauser, D. (1999). Horizontal expansion of the role of the rehabilitation counselor. *Journal of Rehabilitation, 1,* 4-9.

Jones, L. (1992). The full employment myth: Alternative solutions to unemployment. *Social Work, 37*(4), 359-364.

Kets De Vries, M., & Balazs, K. (1999). Transforming the mind-set of the organization: A clinical perspective. *Administration & Society, 30*(6), 640-675.

Kim, W., & Mauborgne, R. (1997, July-August). Fair process: Managing in the knowledge economy. *Harvard Business Review,* pp. 65-75.

Kurzman, P. (1988). The ethical base for social work in the workplace. In G. Gould & M. Smith (Eds.), *Social work in the workplace* (pp. 16-27). New York: Springer.

Lambert, S. (1993, June). Workplace policies as social policy. *Social Service Review, 67,* 237-260.

LaRocco, J., House, J., & French, J. (1980). Social support, occupational stress, and health. *Journal of Health and Social Behavior, 21,* 202-218.

Lechner, V. (1993). Support systems and stress reduction among workers caring for dependent parents. *Social Work, 38*(4), 461-469.

Ledvinka, J., & Scarpello, V. (1991). *Federal regulation of personnel and human resource management* (2nd ed.). Belmont, CA: Wadsworth.

Lewin, K. (1951). *Field theory in social sciences: Selected theoretical papers.* New York: Harper.

Marlow, C. (1990). Management of family and employment responsibilities by Mexican American and Anglo American women. *Social Work, 35*(3), 259-265.

Marx, J. (1996). Strategic philanthropy: An opportunity for partnership between corporations and health/human service agencies. *Administration in Social Work, 20*(3), 57-73.

Mishel, L., Bernstein, J., & Schmitt, J. (1997). *The state of working America: 1996-1997.* Armonk, NY: M. E. Sharpe.

Mor-Barak, M. (1988). Social support and coping with stress: Implications for the workplace. *Occupational Medicine, 3*(4), 663-676.

Mor-Barak, M., & Tynan, M. (1993). Older workers and the workplace: A new challenge for occupational social work. *Social Work, 38*(1), 45-55.

Mudrick, N. (1991). An underdeveloped role for occupational social work: Facilitating the employment of people with disabilities. *Social Work, 36*(6), 490-495.

Ouchi, W. (1981). *Theory Z: How American business can meet the Japanese challenge.* Reading, MA: Addison-Wesley.

Ozawa, M. (1982). Work and social policy. In S. Akabas & P. Kurzman (Eds.), *Work, workers, and work organizations: A view from social work* (pp. 32-60). Englewood Cliffs, NJ: Prentice Hall.

Parsons, R., Hernandez, S., & Jorgensen, J. (1988). Integrated practice: A framework for problem solving. *Social Work, 33*(6), 417-421.

Peters, T., & Waterman, R. (1984). *In search of excellence.* New York: Warner.

Potocky, M. (1996). Refugee children: How are they faring economically as adults? *Social Work, 41*(4), 364-373.

Saleeby, D. (Ed.). (1997). *The strengths perspective in social work practice.* New York: Longman.

Schwartz, W. (1969). Private troubles and public issues: One social work job or two? In *Social welfare forum* (pp. 22-43). New York: Columbia University Press.

Schore, L., & Atkin, J. (1993). Stress in the workplace: A response from union member assistance programs. In P. Kurzman & S. Akabas (Eds.), *Work and well-being: The occupational social work advantage* (pp. 316-331). Washington, DC: NASW Press.

Smith, C. (1994, May-June). The new corporate philanthropy. *Harvard Business Review,* pp. 105-115.

Terkel, S. (1974). *Working.* New York: Pantheon.

Thomas, R. (1991). *Beyond race and gender: Unleashing the power of your total work force by managing diversity.* New York: AMACOM.

Tracy, E., & Whittaker, J. (1990, October). The social network map: Assessing social support in clinical practice. *Families in Society: The Journal of Contemporary Human Services,* pp. 461-470.

U.S. Bureau of the Census. (1997). *Money income in the United States: 1996 (with separate data on valuation of noncash benefits)* (Current Population Reports, P60-197). Washington, DC: Government Printing Office. Available: www.census.gov/prod/3/97pubs/p60-197.PDF, B-6

U.S. Bureau of the Census. (1998, September 28). *Health insurance coverage: 1997.* Available: http://www/census.gov/Press-Release/cb98-172.hmtl

U.S. Bureau of Labor Statistics. (1997, December). *A profile of the working poor, 1996.* Available: http://www.bls.gov/cpswp96.html

U.S. Bureau of Labor Statistics. (1999, May 7). *The employment situation news release.* Available: www:http://stats.bl.gov/newsrels.html

U.S. Equal Employment Opportunity Commission. (1999). *Charge statistics FY 1992 through FY 1998.* Available: http://www.eeoc.gov/stats/charges.html

Vourlekis, B., Edinburg, G., & Knee, R. (1998). The rise of social work in public mental health through aftercare of people with serious mental illness. *Social Work, 43*(6), 567-575.

Waldfogel, J. (1997). Understanding the "family gap" in pay for women with children. *Journal of Economic Perspectives, 12*(1), 137-156.

Warren, J., & Johnson, P. (1995). The impact of workplace support on work-family role strain. *Family Relations, 44,* 163-169.

Watkins, S. (1998). Editorial: Human rights and social work. *Social Work, 43*(3), 197-201.

Weick, A., & Chamberlain, R. (1997). Putting problems in their place: Further explorations in the strengths perspective. In D. Saleeby (Ed.), *Strengths perspective in social work practice* (pp. 29-48). New York: Longman.

West, J. (Ed.). (1991). The Americans with disability act: From policy to practice. *The Milbank Quarterly, 69,* Supplements 1/2.

Wilk, R. (1988). Assisting in affirmative action and equal employment opportunity. In G. Gould & M. Smith (Eds.), *Social work in the workplace* (pp. 213-228). New York: Springer.

Zippay, A. (1992). Corporate funding of human service agencies. *Social Work, 37*(3), 210-214.

CHAPTER TWENTY-FOUR

Social Work Practice Issues Related to Poverty and Homelessness

ELIZABETH A. SEGAL

LAYNE K. STROMWALL

*P*overty, the condition of lacking essential resources, is not a new social condition. Poor people and the societal challenge to care for them have existed throughout history. Even dating back to biblical times, societies have faced the question of how best to care for the poor. However, considering today's progress and this country's resources, how does˙this problem continue in the United States, which boasts the greatest national wealth and progress of any nation in the world? The seeming contradiction of poverty amid wealth is a challenge for American social work practitioners.

This chapter opens with an exploration of the characteristics and dimensions of poverty in the United States. The chapter continues with an identification of the ethical mandate for social work practice in relation to poverty. The pressing practice concerns faced when working with people who are poor are presented, followed by how we might intervene to alleviate this social problem.

HOW DO WE DEFINE POVERTY?

Defining the general condition of poverty is easier than actually defining who is and is not poor. A dictionary definition of poverty is "the state or condition of having little or no money, goods, or means of support; deficiency; insufficiency" (*Webster's College Dictionary*, 1991,

p. 1058). Although most of us might agree on what is a complete lack of resources, how many people have absolutely nothing? Most adults in the United States have some possessions, have some access to resources, and often have a history of working and earning wages. For example, "Earnings from work are the primary source of income for a majority of poor families. Even among families that get welfare assistance in a given year, half of such families have a parent who worked at least part of the year" (Lazere, 1997, p. 1). Given that most people have some resources, how do we define little, deficient, or insufficient resources?

The official definition of poverty is based on the poverty threshold (also referred to as the poverty index or line), which was developed in 1963. In an effort to be more precise in identifying who was poor, the Social Security Administration (SSA), which at that time was charged with overseeing government programs designed to address the problem of poverty, turned to existing research to inform the development of a poverty line. Based on the economic conditions of the time, families typically spent one third of their income on food. Therefore, if a minimum food allowance could be determined and then multiplied by three, a minimum economic standard could be designated.

The U.S. Department of Agriculture had already established the cost of an emergency food plan, the minimum amounts of food that would sustain a person in the case of a national emergency. Thus, taking the Department of Agriculture's food costs and multiplying by three provided the SSA with the first official poverty threshold or line. In 1963, that amount was $3,100 for a family of four, and it has only been adjusted to account for inflation and size of household since that time (Institute for Re-

search on Poverty, 1998). In 1997, the amount for a family of four was $16,333 (U.S. Bureau of the Census, 1998b). Any households below that set amount are officially counted as living in poverty, and households above that amount are not.

How valid is that measure? The official poverty line, although supposedly determined scientifically, is not at all based on solid research. In fact, the director of the SSA, who was responsible for creation of the poverty line in 1963, writes that "the standard itself is admittedly arbitrary, but not unreasonable. It is based essentially on the amount of income remaining after allowance for an adequate diet at minimum cost" (Orshansky, 1965, p. 4). However, many conditions have changed since 1963.

Of primary concern is that the relative cost of food has changed over the past 30 years. Today, food costs are nearer one fifth of a household's expenses (Haveman, 1992-1993) rather than one third. The result is that once the minimum cost of food is determined, it should be multiplied by five rather than three. This change alone would officially count millions more households as being in poverty.

There is also disagreement over the cost of a minimum diet. Such a diet was designed for emergency use, not at a level of consumption for a child growing up over an extended period of time. The cost of an adequate minimum diet, coupled with the change in distribution of income for households today, raises serious doubts about the validity of the poverty line.

WHO IS POOR?

Despite significant debate about the validity of the poverty line, it has consistently been used

TABLE 24.1   1997 Poverty Statistics

	Number	Percentage
People below poverty line	35.6 million	13.3
Children below poverty line	14.1 million	19.9
Families below poverty line	7.3 million	10.3
Female-headed households below poverty line	4.0 million	31.6
Married-couple families below poverty line	2.8 million	5.2
Elderly people below poverty line	3.4 million	10.5

over the past 30 years to determine how many people are poor. Table 24.1 lists the number of people in poverty and some of the key demographic characteristics of that population in 1997. The poverty population in this country tends to be households with young children, particularly single-parent, female-headed households. Whereas 13% of the overall population are living below the poverty line, the percentage of children (19.9%) is almost twice as high as that of all adults over the age of 18 (10.9%) (Dalaker & Naifeh, 1998).

The tendency for poverty to affect children and women has been identified and documented as the dual trends of the feminization of poverty (Pearce, 1978; Sidel, 1986) and the juvenilization of poverty (Segal, 1991; Wilson, 1985). These trends reveal the higher likelihood that women and children will be poor. Examination of the data reveals that one out of every five children, especially children being raised by a female single parent, live in a household with income below the poverty line. Although children make up about one fourth of our overall population, they account for 40% of the poor population (Dalakar & Naifeh, 1998).

Although poverty of the elderly was a historical concern, over the past few decades, the economic condition of the elderly has improved. Currently, the poverty rate of 10.8% for people over 65 years of age is almost half that of children (Rawlings, 1998). This compares with a poverty rate for the elderly of 28.5% in 1966 and 15% in 1976, both rates higher than the rates for children in those same years (Lamison-White, 1997). Thus, in addition to the negative trends of feminization and juvenilization of poverty, there has been a positive trend: significant progress in improving the economic conditions of elderly people. The improvement in the rate of poverty among the elderly coincides with the full implementation of the Social Security Benefits Program and the creation of Medicare, the program that provides medical coverage to the elderly.

Other factors are related to poverty. Race is a critical correlate of poverty. In 1997, the median household income for whites was $38,972, whereas for black households it was $26,628 (U.S. Bureau of the Census, 1998b). Although the absolute numbers of majority population living in poverty are greater than those of minority populations, the percentages of minorities are disproportionate. In 1997, when the poverty rate for whites was 11%, it was almost 27% for blacks and 27% for Hispanics (Dalaker & Naifeh, 1998). Thus, the overall tendency in this country is that poverty disproportionately affects children, woman-headed households, and people of color. For social work practice, these concentrations of people in poverty represent a critical challenge for effective intervention.

POVERTY AND HOMELESSNESS

Living without a permanent place to call home is certainly a deficiency in our society. Some theorists argue that homelessness is not poverty but rather a choice or the consequence of personal deficiency (Baum & Burnes, 1993). Those deficiencies include mental illness or alcohol and drug abuse. However, other research identifies homelessness as an extreme condition of poverty resulting from a lack of affordable housing and adequate employment. For urban leaders, the decrease in affordable housing was one of the most pressing issues of the 1980s (U.S. Conference of Mayors, 1988). Urban development resulted in a major decrease in the number of inexpensive housing units, leaving poor families and individuals struggling to find affordable places to live (U.S. General Accounting Office, 1992).

These two perspectives on the cause of homelessness alternately argue that homelessness is individual or that it is structural. The individual perspective denies that homelessness is a social problem, whereas the structural view ignores any contributions of the personal characteristics of homeless individuals. Recent research

places these two perspectives in balance. Wright, Rubin, and Devine (1998) argue that based on a decade of research, homelessness is part of the social problem of poverty and that although personal deficiencies are part of the problem, they are not causal. They argue,

> Poverty and housing trends have created a situation where some people are destined to be homeless; personal factors such as mental illness or substance abuse are useful in predicting who those people will turn out to be. In brief, social structural developments put people at risk of homelessness; personal failings actualize that risk for specific individuals. (p. xiv)

The distinction between structural causes of poverty and the vulnerability of people to poverty because of personal circumstances raises issues when providing services to people who are homeless. Do we work to create jobs and affordable housing, which are structural interventions, or do we treat a person's mental illness or substance abuse problem as an individual intervention, or do we work on both? This question will be discussed later in this chapter as we address the role of social work intervention in relation to poverty and homelessness.

ETHICAL MANDATE FOR SOCIAL WORK PRACTICE WITH POOR POPULATIONS

The answer to the question of how much is deficient or insufficient resources requires an examination of values and ideology. Social work values stress the need to address poverty as a professional concern. The *National Association of Social Workers' Code of Ethics* (1997), which governs all professional social workers, mandates that we must "strive to end discrimination, oppression, poverty, and other forms of social injustice" (p. 1). The *Code of Ethics* goes on to include, as part of the ethical principles that make up social work's core values, the belief that "social workers challenge social justice" and do so by pursuing social change efforts to alleviate poverty.

The Council on Social Work Education (1997) also identifies the professional mandate to address poverty. The promotion of social and economic justice is part of the professional foundation of social work education. Social work programs of education "must provide students with the skills to promote social change and to implement a wide range of interventions that further the achievement of individual and collective social and economic justice."

Thus, the two major bodies representing professional social work today identify as an ethical principle the understanding and alleviation of poverty. This principle is not new to social work. The profession has a long history of involvement in the amelioration of poverty.

HISTORICAL PRECEDENCE

Social workers have historically been involved in working with people who are poor. Two major periods in history witnessed the involvement of social workers in organized efforts to provide services to ameliorate poverty and the effects of poverty: the Progressive Era at the turn of the century and the New Deal of the 1930s.

The foundations of professional social work can be traced to the Progressive Era of the late 1800s and early 1900s, through the Charity Organization Societies (COS) and the Settlement Movement. These two social service systems took very different approaches to addressing poverty. The COS created methods to identify the individual causes of poverty and work with the person to remove those causes (Erickson, 1987), whereas the Settlement Movement directed its efforts to ameliorate poverty through social reform to lessen structural economic disparity (Davis, 1984). These two perspectives on intervention—change the individual or change the environment—evolved out of the social work efforts of the COS and the settlements. The COS philosophy was embodied in the work of Mary Richmond, as outlined in her book *Social Diagnosis,* which stressed intervention with the individual. The settlement philosophy was embodied by the efforts of Jane Addams and her social action and political advocacy to change the economic structure of society. These different approaches continue to be evident in poverty-related services today.

The period of the 1930s and the New Deal gave rise to the first permanent government efforts to ameliorate the effects of poverty and also change structural economic inequality. These efforts included the enactment of the Social Security Act in 1935, which included the original cash assistance program of Aid to Dependent Children (ADC), Aid to the Blind, and Old Age Assistance. Social workers such as Harry Hopkins and Frances Perkins, close aides to President Roosevelt, played key roles in developing these New Deal programs.

By the 1960s, the public assistance components of the Social Security Act were firmly entrenched in the American social welfare system. Poverty reemerged as a major social concern as evidenced by the work of Michael Harrington in his 1961 book *The Other America,* which is credited with fueling the new War on Poverty.

The existing programs of ADC, Aid to the Blind, and Old Age Assistance were expanded, and additional programs were established. In 1962, ADC was changed to Aid to Families with Dependent Children (AFDC) to reflect the expanded support of not only poor children but those adults who were single parents (Abramovitz, 1996). In 1965, medical care for poor people was created through enactment of Title XIX of the Social Security Act, the Medicaid program. Also during the 1960s, housing programs, education, and food supplement efforts expanded.

The growth in these anti-poverty programs and other initiatives to address poverty resulted in the expansion of social services and increased employment roles for social work practitioners. Social workers became involved in anti-poverty efforts through newly created positions in community action programs and the Comprehensive Employment Training Act program, as welfare rights organizers, and as case managers for expanded public assistance efforts.

The historical roots of social work practice centered around work with people who were poor. As poverty is still a pressing social problem, the need for social work intervention to address poverty and its correlates continues today.

INTERVENTION

Social workers play major roles in programs designed to improve the circumstances of people in poverty. In this section, we discuss contemporary and emerging social work interventions and practice concerns related to work with people in poverty. We begin by discussing social work practice skills that cut across poverty programs. We also discuss how competing personal and structural theories of poverty drive social work practice within contemporary U.S. poverty programs.

Generalist Practice Skills and Methods

People experiencing poverty are beset by a range of stresses. Poor people live in more crowded households, in older buildings, and have less access to needed heating and cooling (Ambert, 1998). Other sources of stress stem from uncertainty and lack of control experienced when a person does not have sufficient funds to meet basic human needs each day. For example, poor people may worry about whether they will be able to eat that day, whether they will find shelter for the night, or whether they will be able to pay the next month's rent. Parents who are poor may blame themselves for their inability to provide basic needs for their children as well as themselves. Stress may also take the form of fear; for example, fear because of living in an unsafe neighborhood and being unable to afford to move to another location. Stress may also result from a lack of control over one's circumstances, because one's best efforts have not improved economic circumstances. Whatever the specific source, mental health researchers have demonstrated that the stresses of living in poverty have negative health (Anderson & Armstead, 1995; Link & Phelan, 1995) and mental health consequences, including increased depression, particularly among single mothers (McLoyd & Wilson, 1990).

Strengths-based generalist practice interventions are used by social workers practicing across the range of poverty programs. These interventions are directed at such client change as enhancing self-esteem, promoting empowerment, generating a sense of hope for the future, and developing a sense of self-competence. The following intervention methods, posed from a generalist perspective, are particularly helpful for work with people in poverty.

1. Application of the strengths perspective (Saleebey, 1998) helps to identify and reinforce individual, family, and community strengths. Social workers who practice from a strengths perspective assume that poor people are doing the best they can in a difficult situation and identify the strengths people possess that allow them to do so. For example, homeless people often display superior organizational skills to navigate a public welfare system that requires them to produce the written documentation that domiciled people keep at home.

2. Mutual aid (self-help) groups provide a vehicle for the kind of dialogue identified by Freire (1970) as leading to critical consciousness and empowerment. Group dialogue can help clients to publicly articulate their experience and share solidarity with others who have similar experiences. This method relies on Mills's (1961) invocation of the "sociological imagination" to assist clients in moving from a "private troubles" definition of poverty to a group-generated understanding of systemic forces that affect social issues like poverty (Stromwall & Stucker, 1997).

3. Social network interventions (Kemp, Whittaker, & Tracy, 1997) are directed at the structure of a social network and the way it functions. Social network interventions may activate natural helpers, facilitate the functioning of a support system, or teach clients skills for ac-

tivating and maintaining a supportive social network.

4. Solution-focused methods (DeJong & Berg, 1998), although in no way denying the realities of poverty, structure discussion around times when the presenting issue is less burdensome or "not a problem." This directly counters the prevalent medical model of practice, which diagnoses problems and prescribes a remedy. Emphasizing solutions instead of dissecting problems promotes self-determination and empowerment by acknowledging clients' real efforts toward improving their circumstances. Solution-focused methods provide a mechanism for operationalizing the strengths perspective by building on clients' existing capacities and problem-solving abilities. Clients are assisted in identifying strategies they have already found useful in dealing with life challenges; in suspending disbelief that change can occur; and in identifying workable strategies, grounded in clients' own experience, that have not yet been tried.

Solution-focused methods should be combined with environmental interventions that connect people with the resources they need. For example, a single mother on public assistance who has already pursued job applications without success could be connected with a professional clothing bank and affordable, flexible child care to improve her success in job interviews.

5. Narrative methods, theoretically rooted in social constructionism, identify stories or narratives as the way human beings organize their lives. Changing, or "re-authoring" the story allows actual life change to occur. An important aspect to narrative methods with people in poverty is the practitioner's action of listening to the client's personal story. This action validates and gives voice to an individual devalued by society.

6. *Social work practitioners working in poverty programs must also understand how oppression has limited the economic choices of many poor people.* Oppression on the basis of race, national origin, gender, disability, appearance, or sexual orientation can have concrete, economic results: lower salaries or failure to obtain employment, specific housing, or even mentoring. Children growing up in poor school districts have less access to excellent instruction and school programs. Practitioners who are cognizant of these systemic impacts will actively seek social justice and an end to oppression as an effective intervention to end poverty.

Practice Strategies and Interventions Related to Theory

U.S. poverty programs derive from a theoretically fragmented policy that holds both economic structures and individual deficits as causes of poverty (Wright, Rubin, & Devine, 1998). In programs based on a structural understanding of poverty, social work practice contributes to economic development. Economic development interventions typically focus on modification of the rules of pure capitalism. Structural programs and services are designed to improve conditions for individuals less able to compete in the marketplace. Recently, theorists have advocated investment- and asset-based approaches (Kretzmann & McKnight, 1993; Ozawa, 1995; Sherraden, 1991), which focus on recognition of existing strengths and devel-

opment of functional capacity for economic security within families and communities.

In programs based on individual theories of poverty, social workers direct their efforts toward improving the individual's ability to compete within the capitalist economic system. Although the desired outcome—ending poverty—is the same in both, intervention methods aimed at ameliorating individual deficits are distinct from those aimed at intervening within a larger economic system. Table 24.2 provides an overview of social work practice interventions by theory and specific social work strategies.

Practice Based on Individual Deficit Theories of Poverty

Social workers who practice within programs primarily based on an individual deficit understanding of poverty direct their efforts at ameliorating personal deficits to improve the individual's ability to compete in the marketplace. Consequently, many programs seek the outcome of increasing the job market competitiveness of individuals, including both currently un- or under-employed workers and other adults deemed able to work.

Educational interventions. Most programs use an educational model to improve a person's abilities and access to employment. Educational programs typically assess clients' current competitive abilities and aptitudes, teach new educational and job skills, and place clients in internships or directly into paid employment. Basic educational skills may be related to obtaining a high school diploma or learning to read. Job skills may include skills specific to a career, such as computer programming. Other

TABLE 24.2 Practice Strategies and Interventions Based on Theory

Theory	Strategy	Intervention
Individual deficit	Interventions aimed at children to develop capacity for future self-sufficiency	Nutrition (brain research)—WIC programs Education and training—Head Start
	Increase economic survival skills	Money management Neighborhood barter
	Ameliorate correlates of poverty	Treat depression Locate housing/message center to indicate sense of stability to employer Treat alcohol/drug addiction
Structural deficits	Economic development	Create more jobs Create more higher-wage jobs
	Modify "rules" of capitalism	Raise minimum wage Provide direct subsidies to those deemed poor—TANF, SSI Provide subsidies for specific purposes to those deemed poor: • children's health insurance • public housing or Section 8 subsidies • child care • food stamps Provide social insurance to eligible: • Medicare • Social Security Protect workers discriminated against in marketplace: • affirmative action • Americans With Disabilities Act • family leave policies Intervene in crisis that results in downward slide: • social insurance • disaster relief • absent-parent financial responsibility for child support
	Community development	Assist people to start own businesses

employment-related skills needed for success in a variety of jobs include verbal and written communication skills, regular attendance, and promptness. These skills require potential workers to internalize the culture and structure common to U.S. work settings.

Social workers practice in these programs by referring clients and helping connect them with the environmental resources needed to overcome barriers to success in new employment. Barriers to employment are both external and internal to the client. Finding quality child care, obtaining clothing for job interviews, and securing transportation to and from job sites are some of the external barriers social workers can help clients overcome. Internal barriers may be categorized as health or mental health issues such as depression or physical health problems. Social workers address internal barriers through appropriate referrals to health or mental health professionals, including clinical social workers. Other internal barriers, such as demoralization, or lack of sense of hope for the future, can be addressed by social workers through the generalist interventions discussed earlier in this chapter.

Prevention of future poverty. Other programs seek to take a proactive approach to reducing poverty. Many efforts to prevent poverty include increasing the competitiveness of future workers. In these programs, social workers use knowledge of human development, including that from the emerging field of early brain research, to promote children's optimal development. Early interventions include a range of pre- and postnatal nutrition programs, early education such as Head Start, and childhood immunization and regular health care to prevent

health deficits. Social workers have a strong role in early parent education, through promoting knowledge of the requirements of health development, teaching about the contributions parents can make at home to their children's education, and assisting parents in healthy parenting strategies.

Later life interventions that center around formal education are key to future economic success. Table 24.3 shows how mean salary increases for women and men with eighth grade educations, high school diplomas, and college diplomas. Social workers play important roles in public schools, directed at increasing student attendance, promoting home-school cooperation, assisting teachers in dealing with classroom behavioral issues, and counseling students about issues that affect their educational achievement.

Other interventions are aimed at reducing the effects of poverty by increasing economic survival skills. If people experiencing poverty can get better value for their money, it is theorized that they will experience better quality of life. Examples of economic survival skills include money management, low-cost nutritional grocery shopping, and consumer product review. Another way of increasing economic survival skills is through the use of reciprocal barter systems, sometimes called time-dollar systems (Cahn, 1997), which rely on neighborhood and social support systems to provide needed goods and services without the use of currency. Examples might be a baby-sitting cooperative or a highly structured barter system that trades work for centralized credits that can be spent elsewhere. Social workers skilled in community development can help to develop these resources.

TABLE 24.3 Median Income, 1997, by Level of Education

	Median Income	
Education Completed	*Males*	*Females*
Less than 9th grade	$12,157	$ 7,505
9th to 12th grade (no diploma)	$16,818	$ 8,861
High school graduate (and equivalency)	$25,453	$13,407
Bachelor's degree or more	$47,126	$29,781

SOURCE: U.S. Bureau of the Census (1998b), pp. C-11–C-13.

Practice Based in a Structural Understanding of Poverty

Social work practice within a structural understanding of poverty requires macro level practice skills of community development, policy formulation, and legislative advocacy, as well as direct practice skills. Community economic development strategies include interventions aimed at the creation of more and higher-wage jobs and support for clients' own small businesses or cooperatives. A promising idea is the micro-credit approach (Briar-Lawson, 1998) in which community vouching substitutes for financial collateral. The micro-lending approach acknowledges that most poor people can never save sufficient collateral to be eligible for traditional business loans. By replacing that requirement with community support, many poor people, especially women, have been able to start businesses in developing countries (Jansen & Pippard, 1998) and neighborhoods worldwide.

Other strategies use policy-level interventions to modify pure capitalism to protect individuals judged less able to compete in the current economic system. Historic strategies to raise the minimum wage have been accomplished within the political arena, with the goal of raising the least-well paid workers out of poverty.

Social workers also practice in programs that provide direct cash assistance to people deemed poor who meet specific eligibility requirements. Examples include Supplemental Security Income (SSI), a program for people who are elderly or disabled and poor, and Temporary Aid to Needy Families (TANF), the primary income subsidy program for families with children. Other assistance is provided in the form of specific subsidies. Examples are Medicaid and other health insurance plans for people in poverty, food stamps, public housing and Section 8 housing vouchers, and child care assistance.

Social workers in macro practice roles develop policy, administer subsidy programs, and advocate for the development and modification of policies and programs. Direct practice roles may include referring clients to subsidy programs, assisting clients in completing complicated paperwork, obtaining needed documentation for qualification, determining eligibility (although this has become a primarily clerical role), and advocating for clients who have been denied eligibility. Generalist practice skills of clear communication, assessment, negotiation, understanding group dynamics and understanding human motivation are critical in these roles.

Programs that protect workers who have experienced historic discrimination in the marketplace also seek to reduce poverty. Programs of affirmative action for people of color and women; the Americans with Disabilities Act (ADA), which protects the rights of people with disabilities; and family leave policies, which protect parents and other caregivers, are examples. Other programs provide intervention in crises that have historically resulted in a downward slide into poverty for many people. These crises may include injury or death of a breadwinner (worker's compensation), weather-related damage (disaster relief), and desertion of a family by one parent (absent parent financial responsibility for child support).

FUTURE ROLES AND CHALLENGES FOR SOCIAL WORK PRACTITIONERS

The social problem of poverty has a very long history in this country. The disproportionate distribution of resources is not only long-standing, it is complicated by numerous other variables including race, age, gender, education, geographic location, and personal characteristics. The wide range of critical components of poverty make it a social and personal problem: Skill and training are required to intervene effectively, as well as a more complete understanding of theories of poverty. We have outlined these approaches to intervention with people and systems that are impoverished. However, we predict that social work practitio-

ners will continue to be faced with the problem of poverty and its correlates.

The U.S. economy is completing the sixth year of economic growth and prosperity, yet millions are still living in poverty. Through this period of economic expansion, we have witnessed significant changes in the national approach to poverty. "Welfare reform" raged through the mid-1990s, and with the Personal Responsibility Act of 1996, we have witnessed a major shift in the national approach to helping those who are poor. The former program of AFDC was revamped to become TANF. This new legislation has radically changed the approach to cash assistance for the poor, which dated back 61 years. The new legislation shifted the program from the previous guarantee of continuous cash assistance to people who are poor to time-limited help. Before, a poor family would be guaranteed AFDC for as long as the family was officially categorized as poor. Now, through TANF, that coverage is limited to a lifetime total of 5 years. That is a significant shift in how we approach poverty through social programs.

This change has come about within a period of economic growth, allowing welfare recipients to move off of public assistance and into employment while jobs are relatively plentiful. Welfare reform has its theoretical roots in capitalism—a cyclic economic system. What will happen when the next economic downturn occurs? Future direct social work practitioners must provide leadership. The general public needs to understand how the changing economy affects the numbers of people who are poor. People quickly move into poverty when they lose their jobs and cannot find another, a situation more likely to occur when economic times are bad. Advocacy will be strongly needed to ensure that poor people are not blamed for structural issues and that programs are responsive to needs.

Social workers are already faced with finding ways to enhance people's personal and social resources. In light of recent policy changes such as welfare reform, we social workers can continue to expect to practice in an environment where poverty and its most severe manifestation, homelessness, will continue. With the next economic downturn, we can expect a worsening of this social problem. We hope the tools for intervention outlined in this chapter will provide direction for future social work practice.

REFERENCES

Abramovitz, M. (1996). *Regulating the lives of women* (Rev. ed.). Boston: South End Press.

Ambert, A.-M. (1998). *The web of poverty: Psychosocial perspectives*. Binghamton, NY: Haworth.

Anderson, N. B., & Armstead, C. A. (1995). Toward understanding the association of socioeconomic status and health: A new challenge for the biopsychosocial approach. *Psychosomatic Medicine, 57*, 213-225.

Baum, A. S., & Burnes, D. W. (1993). *A nation in denial: The truth about homelessness*. Boulder, CO: Westview.

Briar-Lawson, K. (1998). Capacity-building for integrated family-centered practice. *Social Work, 43*, 539-550.

Cahn, E. S. (1997). The co-production imperative. *Social Policy, 27*(3), 62-67.

Council on Social Work Education. (1997). *Curriculum policy statement*. Arlington, VA: Author.

Dalaker, J., & Naifeh, M. (1998). *Poverty in the United States: 1997* (Current Population Reports, P60-201). Washington, DC: U.S. Bureau of the Census.

Davis, A. F. (1984). *Spearheads for reform*. New Brunswick, NJ: Rutgers University Press.

DeJong, P., & Berg, I. K.(1998). *Interviewing for solutions*. Pacific Grove, CA: Brooks/Cole.

Erickson, A. G. (1987). Family services. In *Encyclopedia of social work* (Vol. 1, pp. 589-593). Silver Spring, MD: NASW Press.

Freire, P. (1970). *Pedagogy of the oppressed*. New York: Continuum.

Harrington, M. (1962). *The other America: Poverty in the United States*. Baltimore, MD: Penguin.

Haveman, R. (1992-1993). Changing the poverty measure: Pitfalls and potential gains. *Focus, 14,*(3), 24-49.

Institute for Research on Poverty. (1998). Revising the poverty measure. *Focus, 19*(2).

Jansen, G. G., & Pippard, J. L. (1998). The Grameen Bank in Bangladesh: Helping poor women with credit for self-employment. *Journal of Community Practice, 5*, 103-123.

Kemp, S. P., Whittaker, J. K., & Tracy, E. M. (1997). *Person-environment practice: The social ecology of interpersonal helping*. New York: Aldine de Gruyter.

Kretzmann, J. P., & McKnight, J. L. (1993). *Building communities from the inside out: A path toward mobilizing a community's assets*. Evanston, IL: Northwestern University, Center for Urban Affairs and Poverty Research.

Lamison-White, L. (1997). *Poverty in the United States: 1996*. Washington, DC: U.S. Bureau of the Census.

Lazere, E. (1997). *The poverty despite work handbook*. Washington, DC: Center on Budget and Policy Priorities.

Link, B. G., & Phelan, J. (1995). Social conditions as fundamental causes of disease. *Journal of Health and Social Behavior* (Extra Issue), 80-94.

McLoyd, V. C., & Wilson, L. (1990). Maternal behavior, social support, and economic conditions as a predictor of distress in children. In V. C. McLoyd & C. A. Flanagan (Eds.), *Economic stress: Effects on family life and child development* (pp. 49-70). San Francisco: Jossey-Bass.

Mills, C. W. (1961). *The sociological imagination*. New York: Grove.

National Association of Social Workers. (1997). *Code of ethics*. Washington, DC: Author.

Orshansky, M. (1965). Counting the poor: Another look at the poverty profile. *Social Security Bulletin, 28*(1), 3-29.

Ozawa, M. N. (1995). Income security overview. In R. L. Edwards (Ed.-in-Chief), *Encyclopedia of social work* (19th ed., Vol. 2, pp. 1447-1464). Washington, DC: NASW Press.

Pearce, D. (1978). The feminization of poverty: Women, work, and welfare. *Urban and Social Change Review, 11*(1-2), 28-36.

Rawlings, L. (1998). *Poverty and income trends: 1996*. Washington, DC: Center on Budget and Policy Priorities.

Richmond, M. (1917). *Social diagnosis*. New York: Russell Sage Foundation.

Saleebey, D. (Ed.). (1998). *The strengths perspective in social work practice* (2nd ed.). New York: Longman.

Segal, E. A. (1991). The juvenilization of poverty in the 1980s. *Social Work, 36*(5), 454-457.

Sherraden, M. (1991). *Assets and the poor: A new American welfare policy.* Armonk, NY: M. E. Sharpe.

Sidel, R. (1986). *Women and children last.* New York: Viking Penguin.

Stromwall, L. K., & Stucker, J. R. (1997). A model for teaching the strengths perspective for work with low income persons: Methods and outcomes. *Arete, 21*(2), 61-66.

U.S. Bureau of the Census. (1998a). *Measuring 50 years of economic change.* Washington, DC: Author.

U.S. Bureau of the Census. (1998b). *Money income in the United States: 1997* (Current Population Reports. P60-200). Washington, DC: Author.

U.S. Conference of Mayors. (1988). *A status report on children in America's cities.* Washington, DC: Author.

U.S. General Accounting Office. (1992). *Homelessness: Single-room-occupancy program achieves goal, but HUD can increase impact* (GAO/RCED-92-215). Washington, DC: Author.

Webster's College Dictionary. (1991). New York: Random House.

Wilson, G. (1985). The juvenilization of poverty. *Public Administration Review, 45,* 880-884.

Wright, J. D., Rubin, B. A., & Devine, J. A. (1998). Beside the golden door: Policy, politics, and the homeless. New York: Aldine de Gruyter.

PART V

Research and Empirical Issues

As we indicated in our introduction to this volume, we strongly support the principle that social work practice should be grounded in evidence of effectiveness. This requires the profession of social work to maintain a vigorous research program in which data are collected to determine whether practice procedures are effective. Research activity also should be conducted to develop and test new approaches that produce better outcomes than those currently employed. This is in addition to the requirement that all practitioners should systematically determine whether their ways of practicing are effective.

Abell and Hudson, the authors of Chapter 25, consider the various ways that research procedures contribute to direct practice. Two types of designs are discussed, namely group and single-case designs. The chapter also puts research issues in a context of environmental factors; this is particularly important for research issues related to vulnerable, diverse, and disadvantaged populations, especially those oppressed by virtue of color, ethnicity, or gender. The authors are concerned that many practitioners do not use single-case designs, and they prescribe a solution to this problem.

Blythe and Reithoffer consider the important topic of assessment and measurement from both a research and practice point of view. They discuss how assessment affects client-worker relationships as well as the process of goal setting. A variety of types of measures are reviewed as well as criteria for their selection. The authors discuss how to introduce assessment tools to clients and how to analyze such data and use it to provide feedback to clients.

Finally, Flynn introduces the complex and rapidly growing field of information technology. Its use, as well as ethical issues arising from this use, are stressed. The discussion also argues that social workers are "low adopters" of technology. The reasons for this are suggested, along with ways to overcome sources of resistance that impede the development of the profession.

CHAPTER TWENTY-FIVE

Pragmatic Applications of Single-Case and Group Designs in Social Work Practice Evaluation and Research

NEIL ABELL

WALTER W. HUDSON

Social work academics seem almost continuously engaged in spirited, sometimes vitriolic debates over the role and function of practice evaluation research. Most recently, an invited book forum in *Social Work Research* (Kirk, 1996) stimulated a renewed outpouring of positions on the usefulness of the empirical perspective in social work. Thyer (1996) observed that, although such exchanges have certainly evolved over the history of the profession, they are far from new.

Contemporary concerns are numerous. Some debate the tacit acceptance of underlying assumptions extended from logical positivism, namely, that it is useful for practitioners to focus on measurable, operationalized outcomes in the context of single-subject designs employing systematic data collection (Bloom, 1997; Witkin, 1996). Others argue that empirical clinical practice as currently applied leaves out critical aspects of worker/client interactions, deemphasizing the social environment and artificially reducing the complexity of human problems to a level unpalatable to most practitioners and potentially disorienting to clients (L. Epstein, 1996; Meyer, 1996; Witkin, 1996). Wakefield and Kirk (1996) catalog the shortcomings of single-subject designs, concluding that advocates of empirical clinical practice have taken on the indefensible qualities of the unscientific zealots they intended to replace. Critiquing the absence of data-based arguments supporting the superiority of the "accountable professional," they write that "researchers who promote the scientist-practitioner model . . . appear to have created an empirically unsupported practice dogma of their own" (p. 93).

The new wrinkle in an old debate seems to be the advent (and rapid ascendency) of managed care, which I. Epstein (1996) observed "is likely to have a more profound effect on practice and research than decades of social work education, paradigmatic squabbling, or academic dreaming" (p. 99). Acknowledging the view that social workers should be more than passive respondents to dominant trends in the sociopolitical arena (Meyer, 1996; Witkin, 1996), we nevertheless share Bloom's (1997) view that "social work must demonstrate, clearly and in language understood in the professional and lay worlds, that what it does and how it is done is successful within increasingly defined and delimited time lines" (p. 191). Protesting, ostrich-like, that the current paradigm for service delivery is inequitable, ill-founded, or unfair is unlikely to advance our professional causes or enhance the lives of our clients. Indeed, the decades-old refusal of social workers to empirically demonstrate their effectiveness in medical settings is now resulting in the abandonment of social ser-

vices and the movement of those services into nursing. The question, we believe, is not whether social workers must engage in practice evaluation but how, with what expectations, and toward what ends.

In the sections that follow, we will address some of the challenges in determining the effectiveness of social work practice, emphasizing an understanding of the varying purposes of single-subject designs as compared to classical experimental and quasi-experimental designs. Consideration will be given to the complex (and sometimes contradictory) roles assumed by those charged with determining practice effectiveness and to the contexts (practice, academic, economic, social, and political) in which such work is undertaken.

METHODOLOGICAL DEBATES: INTEGRATING IDEALISM AND PRACTICALITY IN PRACTICE RESEARCH

Much of the debate over whether, where, and how to undertake practice research and/or evaluation revolves around the conflict between knowledge-building ideals and more pragmatic approaches to increasing one's understanding of practice effectiveness. The primary roles one occupies understandably shape the perspectives taken on these issues and are therefore critical to explore.

As Hudson, Nugent, and Sieppert (1999) have observed, practitioners are strongly obligated to pursuing the goals of practice—*not* the goals of science. Specifically, they must provide service, care, and treatment to clients. Concerns center on accurately assessing the client's problems; identifying the best interventions; delivering them in a timely, efficient, and sensitive manner; and (we hope) determining that the desired ends were reached *at least in part* as a result of the effort expended. In the typically demanding context of practice, the rules of evidence used to demonstrate achievement of these goals may be regarded as adequate and convincing for the practitioner, and even practice colleagues, but completely unpersuasive to the managed care administrator or the scientist. "Practice wisdom" (cf. Klein & Bloom, 1995), accrued from years of experience, trial, and error, carries little weight with those trained in the scientific method and is no longer adequate for practitioners and managers when practice wisdom is merely a euphemism for "unsubstantiated expertise" (Reid & Smith, 1989).

On the other hand, when one is in the role of researcher, one is obligated to pursue the goals of science. In this context, convincing one's peers (and oneself) requires adherence to demanding standards. Researchers must carefully control for a host of extraneous influences while isolating the factors most likely responsible for observed effects. Although reasonable researchers acknowledge that the "perfect" study does not exist, an atmosphere of careful critique prevails, as it should. In the best of circumstances, however, successful scientific studies are typically expensive and time-consuming to conduct, intrusive in the natural environment of client/practitioner exchange, and require a degree of technical expertise well beyond the skills of the practicing social worker (Thomas, 1978).

Recurrent tensions have been generated within the field by efforts to integrate these two roles into a "one size fits all" solution to the search for evidence-based practice knowledge. Before returning to a consideration of the scientist-practitioner concept, we turn our attention to the major modes of conducting practice evaluation and research, examining their current adaptations to empirical clinical practice concerns.

To understand and make best use of the tools of science, it is important to first distinguish between the broad methods that often are referred to as idiographic and nomothetic research. *Idiographic research* is based on a philosophy of science that says the best way to understand the relationships among variables is to study them intensively using one subject at a time. Idiographic research is largely seen in the use of single-case experimental and quasi-experimental designs and a variety of time-series studies. *Nomothetic research* is based on a philosophy of science that says the best way to understand the relationships among variables is to study them using large numbers of subjects. Nomothetic research is largely represented by three basic types of research we know as surveys, comparative studies, and planned group experiments. What is often very difficult to grasp is the fact that nomothetic research is used to develop a science of groups or populations, but idiographic research is used to develop a science of one person. Practitioners, for example, often care very little about the average depression score for the general population. However, they are vitally concerned about the score for a specific client and how that may change over time. On the other hand, a program manager might care very little about the score of that same client while expressing considerable interest in the mean score for the entire agency and how that might change over time.

SINGLE-SYSTEMS DESIGNS: ADAPTING THE GOALS OF KNOWLEDGE BUILDING TO THE REALITIES OF PRACTICE

Advocates of single-subject designs as a primary tool for practitioners face a litany of criticisms, often beginning with the well-documented observation that not many students trained in these models adopt them routinely in their practices after graduation. Arguments forwarded to explain the apparent phenomenon range from concerns that practitioners might too quickly become discouraged when charting unsupportive or ambiguous data (Rubin, 1996) to hesitations based on potential gender and ethnic biases (i.e., regarding who will be selected for or agree to participate in evaluation processes), excessive time requirements, and intrusiveness (Staudt, 1997). Wakefield and Kirk's (1996) critique argues that practitioners have largely shunned the use of single-subject designs not out of laziness but because they are "wisely reluctant to jump on one more therapeutic bandwagon" (p. 85) that has been oversold and underdocumented. Unfortunately, virtually all of these critics have also failed to support their claims with evidence of any kind—they, too, use little more than argument. For example, the wise reluctance to jump on the evaluation bandwagon is either a hypothesis capable of being tested or an unsupported opinion that completely fails to account for quite a long history of eagerly adopting sexier fads (e.g., the schizophrenogenic mother, codependency, penis envy, repressed memory syndrome, and past life therapy, to name but a few). Finally, it should be noted that virtually none of these critics have offered a viable alternative beyond a return to unsupported testimonial and heavy doses of anecdotal storytelling.

Whereas evidence in support of the use of single-subject designs has been late in coming and is only now beginning to emerge (cf. Faul, McMurtry, & Hudson, in press), others cite the accumulation of increasing levels of empirically supported intervention knowledge as an incentive to continue the drive toward refinement and application of single-subject methodology (Mattaini, 1996; Thyer, 1996; Thyer & Wodarski, 1998). In a recent survey of programs accredited by the Council on Social Work Education throughout the United States and Canada, educators indicated that single-subject designs currently received "moderate to considerable" attention in their programs ($M = 3.6$, $SD = 1.2$, where $1 = none$ and $5 = extensive$) and responded that they personally felt them to be *important* ($M = 4.0$, $SD = 1.2$, where $1 = very unimportant$ and $5 = very important$) to students' overall training (Abell & Hudson, 1999).

One argument that persists in critiquing single-subject designs is their failure to "live up" to their promises and claims regarding capturing causal relationships. Such critics appear to be wholly ignorant of a rather enormous experimental literature (e.g., *Journal of Applied Behavioral Analysis, Journal of Experimental Analysis of Behavior, Journal of Behavior Therapy and Experimental Psychiatry,* and *Research on Social Work Practice*) wherein causal knowledge is substantially advanced through the use of single-system designs. Although she was not addressing single-subject designs exclusively, Gambrill (1994) has usefully observed that "knowing 'more' is a long way from knowing what we want to know, but it is more than knowing nothing" (p. 362). Our intention in the following section is to offer suggestions for continued improvement in usefully adapting single-subject designs to clinical practice.

Chief among the methodological criticisms of single-subject designs is their inability to achieve sufficient control to truly isolate causal influences. The most commonly used design (i.e., the simple AB) provides opportunities, when data are collected using valid and reliable rapid assessment instruments (RAIs), to monitor client progress over time, capture change in identified target problems, and assess the correlation between timing of the intervention and onset of measured change (if any). By themselves, these could be considered substantial gains in self-critical practice, insofar as they encourage practitioners to closely scrutinize their case progress and to adapt intervention plans accordingly. Numerous threats to internal validity abound, however, and methodological purists will rightfully argue that the holes in such models are so numerous that the whole enterprise resembles a sieve far more than a knowledge-containing vessel.

Having noted these quite huge issues and problems, it is also essential to note that virtually all of these are directed toward the use of single-case designs in the conduct of science—*not* in the conduct of practice. That is, the major concerns have to do with the scientific enterprise, not the practice of service delivery. No doubt, some of these same purists will argue that any retreat from a standard of control associated with classical experiments (with sufficient samples, random assignment, clearly distinguished treatment and control conditions, etc.) amounts to a "white flag" of admission that single-subject designs are hopelessly damaged compromises not worthy of use in practice evaluation. Our view, however, is more optimistic and depends on recalling the essential purpose of such designs. They serve not as "stand-alone" determinants of practice knowledge but as pilot efforts designed to be informative, not definitive or universally generalizable in and of themselves.

A second, broadly held purist complaint is that single-subject designs are simply too mechanically intrusive and time-consuming to be applied in each and every practice interaction. We differ with the critics in refusing to accept this as yet another fatal blow to the use of single-subject designs in practice. If such designs are too cumbersome to be used formally in all cases (i.e., integrating measurement, controlled experimental designs, charting, and quantitative data analysis), we propose that substantial gains may still be realized by training students to informally apply the principles of empirical practice. Such applications involve constant, self-critical assessment of the operational nature of their clients' problems, attention to when and how they are specifically implementing intentional interventions, and monitoring client progress in relation to expended efforts on an ongoing basis.

The pragmatic issues then become: When should practitioners make use of single-subject designs, how should they apply them to minimize intrusiveness and maximize information gain, and how (if at all) should the new information be linked to broader, more formalized knowledge-building efforts?

Regarding when, our view is that all practitioners should be educated in the key principles of practice evaluation. Fluency in the basics of applied measurement theory, experimental control, implementation of practice evaluation methods (including single-subject designs), and analysis of case data should remain a central feature of social work education. At the heart of such training should be repeated emphasis on the value of critical thinking and the ethical mandate to ensure, to the greatest degree possible, that intervention methods are empirically grounded. Recent efforts by Thyer and Wodarski (1998) illustrate the emerging wealth of information from which practitioners may draw.

Students should be educated to appreciate both the potentials and the pitfalls of the current "state of the art" regarding practice evaluation. Understanding that scientific methods are themselves evolutionary should not excuse abandoning their clinical application simply because they are imperfect. Once so informed, practitioners should be encouraged to use formal evaluation techniques in at least three instances. First, when they are genuinely "in the dark" with respect to their interaction with a client and the severity of the client's problem. Such circumstances could arise because they are on new ground with an intervention as yet untried, or because, as novices for any other reason, they simply want reassurance that their efforts are (or are not) associated with desired gains for the client. Criticisms regarding the potential that any single analysis can be misleading (creating either false confidence that an intervention is working or premature discouragement that it is not) should be a part of prior training in evaluation techniques and will be addressed further below.

Second, practitioners should use formal single-subject designs when some external agent (funders, administrators, or supervisors, for instance) requires initial evidence that their intervention is yielding positive results. In this context (as in all others), such evaluation evidence should be represented as preliminary, not conclusive. Still, we argue that when low-budget, low-tech evidence of case progress is required, practitioners currently have no better recourse than the well-developed methods detailed in, for instance, Bloom, Fischer, and Orme (1999) and Hudson et al. (1999). Presented in the proper context (that is, with due attention to the cautions associated with interpretation), such data can encourage the continuation (or discontinuation) of funding for pilot intervention projects, provide material for case staffing, and, when aggregated across similar cases handled by practitioners employing similar techniques, provide supportive or corrective information for agency policy. Understanding the relations between idiographic and nomothetic research in these instances will help guide practitioners in deciding when more formal research is advisable and help prepare them for active participation in such projects.

Third, practitioners should make use of single-subject designs when the nature of their interventions and/or the problems or inclinations of their clients suggest it. One of the seldom emphasized strengths of single-subject methodologies is their capacity to provide feedback to clients and to practitioners in direct and immediate ways. Careful charting of case progress provides a visual record of change familiar to every parent who has ever instituted a token economy with a child, every trainer working to encourage independent living skills among vocational rehabilitation clients, or every caseworker seeking to motivate a discouraged client with evidence of gradual, positive change. Although the role of the scientist-practitioner may have been ambitiously defined when the term was first coined, embedded within it was the prospect of a practice method that would not only generate knowledge but also provide beneficial service. Arguments that such designs are primarily useful in behavioral and educational applications should not be used to undermine one their greatest demonstrated strengths in facilitating both worker and client goals.

If we pull all of the foregoing concerns together, we should state as clearly and as forcefully as we can that the overwhelming majority of all practitioners in all forms of service delivery settings should forever abandon any consideration of using the fully developed scientist-practitioner model. It is not efficient, and the purpose of "doing practice" is not the same as the purpose of "doing science"—the methods of doing each are radically different. The conduct of science is best reserved for those special environments that were created for that purpose or that have the generation of new knowledge as a major goal. Moreover, when conducting practice, it must be recognized that the essential purpose is to help one client solve or alleviate one or more problems; it is not to scientifically prove that one's intervention was the cause of any observed positive change or to help a population of clients.

Although we urge abandonment of the scientist-practitioner model, we also believe that self-evaluative practitioners (Bronson, 1994) always carry an enormous obligation to examine whether their clients are making reasonable progress. When this progress is not evident, the practitioner must develop a clear plan to change the treatment, refer the client to someone who is better able to help solve the problem, or provide supportive maintenance. We do not see any other ethically viable options. If a client is not making any progress, that fact alone suggests an

ethical obligation to (a) change the nature of the intervention so as to produce positive change, (b) transfer the case to someone who is better equipped to help the client make positive changes, or (c) defend the position that the client cannot improve and retention of the case is justified solely by the need to provide support and stability to forestall further deterioration or to meet minimum humanitarian requirements.

The question remains, of course, as to how one will determine whether positive change has occurred so that these basic case-planning decisions can be made. The solution to this problem is rooted in an axiomatic assertion concerning the nature of positive change or what is most often referred to as "effective service." That is, there is and can be no such thing as "effectiveness" unless or until there is change (Hudson et al., 1999; Nurius & Hudson, 1993). Stated differently, if there is no change, there is and can be no such thing as effectiveness. How then can we measure change so that we can demonstrate that a client's problem is improving, deteriorating, or not changing in either direction? The answer is simple enough—measure the client's problem repeatedly over time and graph the results. It is no more complicated than that, nor does it need to be.

If we do nothing but measure the client's problem repeatedly over time and graph the results, it is obvious that we are recommending the use of the simple B Design or what is also known as a simple monitoring design. Figure 25.1 provides an example of a simple monitoring design that shows a client to have improved quite remarkably over the period of a few weeks.

We have no doubt that methodological purists will shriek with great pain and despair at this point as they quickly and vigorously tell us

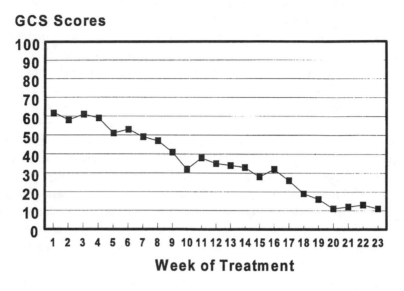

Figure 25.1. Evelyn S. Case 4219

that the so-called B-Design or monitoring de-sign is utterly worthless as a tool for demon-strating that the practitioner's intervention was responsible for the observed positive change that is reflected in Figure 25.1. Of course. We agree entirely. If one is pursuing the goals of sci-ence (demonstrating that it was the interven-tion that caused the positive change), then the B-Design and the data shown in Figure 25.1 are completely and utterly worthless. But we are not doing science—we are doing practice, and the simple B-Design is completely adequate to determine whether the client's problem is im-proving, deteriorating, or not changing during the period when we are working to help the cli-ent achieve positive results.

Once one is successfully engaged in practice evaluation using the most primitive single-sys-tem design, it is not a large step to move in the direction of practice research (i.e., toward

greater potential for drawing causal inferences) through adoption of more sophisticated de-signs. Adding an assessment or baseline (A) phase prior to treatment affords the self-evaluative practitioner a means for comparing a client's status before and during intervention.

Many difficulties arise in establishing such baselines, most related to ethical concerns re-garding the delay of intervention (a) at all or (b) for a period of time long enough to ensure that a stable picture of the target problem has been drawn. Acknowledging that there are legitimate instances when a concurrent baseline (one es-tablished from the initial intake and moving only forward in time) is unethical or unfeasible (i.e., in crisis contexts), retrospective baselines present a viable alternative. Working with cli-ents to establish a picture of what life was like during a relevant window prior to intake can serve as a reasonable basis for comparing the subsequent experience during intervention. The resulting AB design, which mimics the most common sequence of interactions in direct practice whether or not one is formally evaluating, increases practitioners' potential for critically analyzing the results of their work with clients.

Causal deficiencies notwithstanding, there remains a principle applied to single-systems designs that can benefit self-evaluative practitioners and ultimately contribute toward knowledge building and clarity. Replication (i.e., through multiple baselines across people, problems, or settings) assists one in ruling out (even to a degree) the likelihood that observations made in any single case might be entirely spurious or due to chance.

Again, purists will argue that the human condition is so varied and unique that the concept of replication is itself a reductionist fantasy. No client, they might say, exactly matches the characteristics or symptoms of another. Even when assessments reveal strong enough similarities across clients to warrant use of the same diagnostic labels, variations in symptom presentations, environmental circumstances, therapeutic styles, and intervention integrity all work against the hope that any meaningful accumulation of knowledge could ever accrue.

We respond by returning to the tension between the pragmatic and the ideal. Of course, no two circumstances are exactly the same. Taken to the extreme, however, this observation would leave us no choice but to "start from scratch" in each and every practice interaction. Setting aside the obviously unacceptable prospect of "pigeon-holing" clients and rushing to diagnostic judgements, the increasing emergence of treatment manuals geared toward specific client problems (anxiety, stress, depression) suggests that functional understandings of common problems do exist and can usefully guide interventions. Self-evaluative practitioners—trained in the principles of measurement, charting, and controlled observation—can, we believe, use the principle of replication to gradually accumulate impressions of effectiveness over time. Not in every case; not with all clients, but faithfully in those circumstances where repeated observations of treatments and outcomes are desired. Used in these ways, single-systems designs, even very simple ones, can gradually provide corrective feedback to clients and practitioners and, as pilot work, suggest directions for more elaborate practice research.

SINGLE-SYSTEM DESIGN APPLICATIONS FOR FAMILY TREATMENT

Concerns with control of potential alternative explanations, concurrent or retrospective baselines, and replication or aggregation of case data are also factors in applying single-system designs to evaluations of family therapy. As Reid (1993) observed, classically controlled single-system designs have limited usefulness in studies of family treatment, in part because of the systemic complexities of family intervention theories. Problems are often defined in terms of interactions or relationships, in addition to more traditional concerns with individual functioning.

Identifying target problems that capture systemic variables requires a broadened scope of measurement in a field where such progress has been slow in coming. Consequently, evaluative practitioners and researchers are often challenged to capture systemic problems with individual self-report scales that may be difficult to meaningfully aggregate across multiple family members or to attempt observational measures focused on systemic variables and interactions. In either case, measurement of theoretically valid target problems needs continued refinement.

Despite these limitations, the clinically intimate context of single-system designs (i.e., where practitioners may focus on one family at a time) provides opportunities for qualitative change process analyses, which can shed light on potential causal mechanisms or explore "informative events" (single incidents revealing information with value possibly extending beyond the immediate case, such as reactions to specific components of complex interventions) (Reid, 1993, p. 94). Taken together, quantitative and qualitative information gathered from single-system designs in these ways can provide the foundation for intervention research agendas (discussed further below).

Based on a multiple-baseline single-system design examining the effectiveness of narrative therapy with six families, Besa (1994, p. 324) identified the following strengths of the idiographic approach:

- People can participate in problem definition, data collection, and, potentially, data analysis.
- Each intervention can be tailored to the unique aspects of the family.
- The experimental design itself can be modified during the procedure if necessary.

GROUP DESIGNS: EMPHASIZING RESEARCH GOALS FOR ENHANCED EVIDENCE OF PRACTICE EFFECTIVENESS

Where more formal evidence of effectiveness is desired, traditional nomothetic research is often required. Group designs, employing sufficiently large samples and exercising more stringent experimental controls, provide greater opportunities for isolating causal influences and supporting claims of treatment effectiveness for groups of clients as compared to a single client. Compared to their idiographic counterparts, group designs offer more control over numerous threats to internal validity (cf. Cook & Campbell, 1979), aiding practice researchers in ruling out alternative explanations for observed outcomes. When studies are conducted on ideal (i.e., probability) samples of sufficient size, researchers can further claim that their findings generalize to larger, clinically relevant populations.

Such designs, as applied to clinical or direct-practice research, typically fall into one of three categories: true (or classical) experiments, quasi-experiments, and passive-observational or naturalistic studies (surveys and comparative studies) (Kazdin, 1994). The latter, historically referred to as correlational studies, have been renamed "to disentangle the design (nonmanipulation of independent variables and arrangement of selected conditions or groups) from the methods of data analyses (e.g., correlational)" (Kazdin, 1994, p. 24).

True experiments, which emphasize random assignment of subjects to conditions, control of condition variability (i.e., treatment/no treatment), and manipulation of various other sources of potential bias (i.e., therapist or setting characteristics), provide the strongest opportunities for drawing causal inferences. Viewed as the methodological "gold standard" for outcome studies, they may be contrasted with quasi-experiments, which approximate the elements of a true experiment and are conducted when the practice researcher lacks control over one or more classical design elements (i.e., cannot control for random assignment of subjects to groups). Ethical constraints often lead to concerns about the structure of "waiting list" or "no treatment" groups, for instance, impairing the practice researcher's ability to model ideal methodological conditions.

Experimental and quasi-experimental studies take numerous forms, each intended to maximize isolation of (and consequently, attention to the influence of) specified variable(s) (Kazdin, 1994; Wodarski, 1997). The pretest-posttest control group design (with random assignment), for instance, isolates the effect of the independent variable (treatment) on outcome. The Solomon four-group design calls attention to the potential interaction of assessment (or pretest) and intervention, and factorial designs allow examination of multiple treatments (i.e., cognitive-behavioral, psychoeducational) and/or group characteristics (i.e., HIV+, HIV−) in a single study.

Rosen, Proctor, and Staudt (1999) conducted a recent review of social work research literature on intervention effectiveness and employed a classification of studies grouped as descriptive, explanatory, or control. In their schema, descriptive studies were those that focused on central tendencies or sampling characteristics of single variables or (as in qualitative studies) were designed to conceptualize relevant variables. Explanatory studies reported on relationships among two or more variables (causal or correlational), including hypothesis-driven research on observed differences between groups.

Of special interest in their review were control studies focused on the effectiveness or efficacy of interventions. Critical to this latter category was the definition of interventions in clear, empirically measurable, and replicable terms

and the linking of intervention statements to specific outcome targets in such a way that rigorous examinations of their effectiveness could be conducted. Examining articles published in leading social work journals between January 1993 and July 1997, the authors found that 47% could be classified as research-focused. Of these, only 15% could be classified as control-oriented. Most disturbingly, "only 3 percent of all published articles (53 of 1,849) could inform a practitioner of how to implement reliably the intervention that was studied" (Rosen et al., 1999, p. 12). Clearly, studies lacking such detail are severely limited in their potential usefulness to evaluative practitioners and researchers alike.

The strengths of rigorous, experimental research, and the preference for such designs in competition for prestigious (and often substantial) federal funding, contribute to the favor they receive in education and training recommendations. The advantages they provide, however, are to some degree offset by the challenges faced in initiating, funding, and conducting them.

Successful conception and implementation of group designs require a degree of training not uniformly achieved in graduate social work education (Fraser, Jenson, & Lewis, 1993). Early optimistic conceptualizations of the scientist-practitioner notwithstanding, more realistic contemporary opinions and policy statements (cf. National Association of Deans and Directors, 1997) argue for the active promotion of practice researchers. In his *Report on Progress in the Development of Research Resources in Social Work,* Austin (1998) acknowledged substantial gains in practice research, among them: evidence of recurrent interest in traditional social work problems and populations (including child welfare, poverty, substance abuse, and chronic illness), the emergence of seven Social Work Research Development Centers supported by the National Institute of Mental Health (NIMH), and increases in academic research infrastructures nationwide. Continued progress may depend on substantial mentoring, sustained supports (i.e., academic resources of time, training, and funding), and active encouragement of interdisciplinary collaboration, beginning in doctoral education and continuing throughout an academic career.

Unlike single-system designs, group experiments are typically expensive to mount, require the formal consent (and, often, active involvement) of multilayered administrative and bureaucratic systems, and depend on favorable circumstances prevailing so that studies, once initiated, can be carried to completion as originally planned. Control groups, when they can be ethically justified and logistically mounted, become difficult to maintain when subjects refuse treatment or drop out prior to completion (sometimes in non-random fashion and for subsequently undetermined reasons) (Polansky, 1994). Limitations in interpretation of group data, including the loss of individual client responses in the group-averaging process and the related inability to learn the effects of treatments on individual subjects, severely limit the applicability of results to specific clients (Nugent, 1996). Together, these shortcomings arguably reduce the enthusiasm of agency staff for research involvement and, in part, led Polansky (1994) to caution that "if one is not absolutely convinced from clinical experience that a treatment works, there is seldom any point in subjecting it to large-scale testing" (p. 394).

Once again, tension between the pragmatic and the ideal presents itself. Social workers have made progress in the last decade (partially

through the advent of the NIMH centers), but that progress continues to be hampered by difficulties in the field (a) initiating such efforts and (b) maintaining and renewing them once begun. Some of these difficulties may be attributed to the research establishment swinging from one extreme of the practice evaluation-practice research continuum to the other, coming dangerously close to valuing only formal projects operating on a major scale with full federal funding. Realistically scaling the research agenda to allow for the integration of practice and research expertise remains a major challenge. As Austin (1998) noted, "the most critical issue for the future is to develop collaboration between social work researchers and social work practitioners in developing . . . evidence-based treatment and services, and in communicating the results of such research to the professional practice community" (p. 6). Fortunately, we believe a template for such efforts already exists.

INTERVENTION RESEARCH: INTEGRATING THE PRAGMATIC AND THE IDEAL

Intervention research, developed by Rothman and Thomas (1994), includes among its goals the design and development of innovative interventions. It has been identified as the potential "elusive bridge between practice and research" (Schilling, 1997, p. 174). Empirical research on new treatment strategies is pursued through a series of overlapping phases including: problem analysis and project planning, information gathering and synthesis, intervention design, early development and pilot testing, evaluation and advanced development, and dissemination (Thomas & Rothman, 1994). Although ambitious and admittedly a long-term strategy, the model, through its several elements, offers numerous specifics for developing practice research agendas that are explicitly sensitive to client needs.

Intervention research emphasizes respectful interaction between researchers and practitioners and interactive linkages between agencies and universities. As a whole, the model offers much to those wanting to get out of the extremist boxes we continue to posture in when advocating for knowledge building, and it provides a clear plan for productively resolving some of the old, recurrent methodological tensions.

In its earliest phases, from problem analysis through information gathering and the beginnings of design, the model underscores the value of clear communications among participants (researchers, administrators, practitioners, and clients) (Paine, Suarez-Balcazar, Fawcett, & Jameson, 1994; Rothman, Teresa, & Erlich, 1994). Taken seriously, the recommendations offered (active recruitment of stakeholder involvement, effective listening) are promising tools for overcoming the tendencies toward miscommunication and perceptions of elitism or ignorance that so often undermine research collaborations. In these phases, the model provides opportunities for qualitative data gathering and analysis (Schilling, 1997) and encourages the use of focus groups to ensure that all parties are sufficiently invested in the success of the project.

The phase of early development and pilot testing offers an excellent opportunity for the formal use of single-system designs (Thomas, 1994). Whether the work began in the less structured environment of practice evaluation or was instituted intentionally as a component of practice research, the value of early feedback on treatment effectiveness is viewed as critical in deciding whether and how to proceed to evaluation and advanced development. Because of the collaborative foundation laid in earlier phases of design and development, intervention researchers may experience fewer problems with ideal group designs that flounder due to unrealistic expectations for agency or client involvement. Similarly, where funding is required to execute the full evaluation, many of the steps described are directly responsive to recommendations for writing successful proposals (cf. Wodarski, 1997).

Emerging strategies for data analysis, in particular the use of hierarchical linear models (HLM), offer considerable promise for resolving long-standing dilemmas in integrating information from single-systems and group designs (Nugent, 1996). As use of such techniques becomes more widespread in social work research, reciprocal arguments against the use of either single-systems or group strategies may be further weakened. In the past, critics have argued that data from single cases could not be generalized to larger groups and that data from larger groups provided no useful feedback on the progress of individuals within a particular study. Both concerns underscored serious limitations and, for those looking for reasons to "opt out," justification for refusing participation or minimizing the implications of evaluation and research. For practitioners of intervention research methods, these analytic limitations contributed to difficulties along the whole spectrum, from project planning to dissemination.

As Nugent (1996) has demonstrated, increased sophistication in the use of HLM facilitates integration of single-system and group methodologies. Traditional analyses of group data were substantially limited to comparisons of pretest/posttest differences, with individual responses lost in examination of group means. Aggregation of single-system data for analysis via HLM provides, in addition, individual subject response profiles. These data can reveal individual paths between pre- and posttest scores, illuminating important aspects of intervention response, and leading to closer scrutiny of "active ingredients" (personal, social, or contextual) in treatment effectiveness. As with all innovations, cautions are in order. As Nugent (1996) notes, "HLM procedures are based on rather strong assumptions that may not be met in all circumstances, and we currently know little about the effects of violations of these assumptions" (p. 225).

SUMMARY AND INTEGRATION

In concluding this chapter, we would like to emphasize that single-system and group designs can actually be combined as a means of taking maximal advantage of each. Historically, evaluation research has largely been imposed on line workers from the top down, and those line workers have had little to say about the matter. Worse yet, those designs have traditionally been based on some variant of the planned group experiment, also known as the classical Fisherian pretest, posttest, control versus experimental group design and, as such, are virtually worthless to practitioners who are trying to help individual clients solve quite serious personal and social problems. The struggles for primacy in the practice evaluation/research continuum, with practitioners claiming the supremacy of intuitive wisdom and researchers arguing the same for empirical methods, have been prolonged and, to a degree, counterproductive.

It does not have to be this way. In the past decade, significant progress has been made in integrating qualitative and quantitative methods, arguably to the advantage of both. New degrees of rigor have been developed and articulated, and more attention has been paid to the fit between intention and method than to the seemingly endless arguments over the superiority of free-standing designs.

Similarly, although not as completely, academics seem to have reached some preliminary agreement over differentiating roles and expectations for varying levels of evaluation/research participation and are reconsidering educational goals (i.e., for bachelor's, master's, and doctoral degrees in social work) accordingly. Our discussion of the scientist-practitioner, the self-evaluative practitioner, and the practice researcher in this chapter was intended to clarify these distinctions and to further the view that the latter two roles, although distinct, can be useful in crafting pragmatic, appropriately targeted knowledge-building goals.

Bearing these distinctions in mind, we would make, for the sake of the self-evaluative practitioner, a radical recommendation that the simple B Design be championed for direct social work practice. Retaining the elements of objectively measuring clearly operationalized problems repeatedly over time, these designs, in themselves, would further the awareness of whether client change was happening and when. For practitioners and clients, evidence of change would, in most cases, be sufficient. But where would that leave the program evaluator and the administrator, who need evaluation data at the aggregate level, not at the single-case level?

As argued above, progress toward understanding why the desired change occurred would be left to those self-evaluative practitioners willing to advance to more elaborate designs (i.e., AB, ABA, ABAB, etc.) or, more appropriately, to practice researchers engaged in nomothetic science. Were we to do something as novel as is suggested here, it would not take long for a medium-size agency to find itself holding, for example, 400 to 1,000 cases of single-subject data that were collected over a very brief period of time. It would be quite a simple matter to classify those cases according to a number of criteria (type of problem, type of service, gender, ethnicity, etc.) and to then aggregate those single-case data. In short, it would be a relatively simple matter to capture the fullest advantage of using single-subject designs, which could be combined into one or more group comparison designs so that all professionals within the organization would have a decent chance of having their informational needs met. Nurius and Hudson (1993) discussed this possibility at length (cf. Chapter 11), and Nugent (1996) provides a complete statistical solution by imposing a design on both the responses and the sample.

In all cases, the observations of Rosen et al. (1999) must be borne in mind. If social work practice research is to advance and serve the purpose of informing practice knowledge for both practitioners and researchers, the field simply must increase its attention to clearly defined, replicable interventions focused on specific target problems. The desired goals, in this case, seem less challenging than finding the collective professional will to bring them into reality.

The advent of intervention research and the analytic advances illustrated through new uses of HLM both represent promising strategies for integrating single-subject and group designs for social work practice evaluation. Much work remains to be done before this pragmatic integration is itself ideal. Our hope is that clear delineation of goals, roles, and methods will advance the field and minimize our profession's proven tendencies toward arguing the micro issues at the expense of general progress in knowledge building, research, and service to our clients over time.

REFERENCES

Abell, N., & Hudson, W. W. (1999). *Research training in social work education: Translating professional priorities into policy and practice.* Unpublished manuscript.

Austin, D. M. (1998). *A report on progress in the development of research resources in social work.* New York: Ford Foundation.

Besa, D. (1994). Evaluating narrative family therapy using single-system designs. *Research on Social Work Practice, 4*(3), 309-325.

Bloom, M. (1997). The scientist-practitioner concept, revisited. *Social Work Research, 21*(3), 190-208.

Bloom, M., Fischer, J., & Orme, J. G. (1999). *Evaluating practice: Guidelines for the accountable professional.* Needham Heights, MA: Allyn & Bacon.

Bronson, D. E. (1994). Is a scientist-practitioner model appropriate for direct social work practice? In W. W. Hudson & P. S. Nurius (Eds.), *Controversial issues in social work research* (pp. 81-86). Needham Heights, MA: Allyn & Bacon.

Cook, T., & Campbell, D. (1979). *Quasi-experimentation: Design & analysis issues for field settings.* Boston: Houghton Mifflin.

Epstein, I. (1996). In quest of a research-based model for clinical practice: Or, why can't a social worker be more like a researcher? *Social Work Research, 20*(2), 97-100.

Epstein, L. (1996). The trouble with the researcher-practitioner idea. *Social Work Research, 20*(2), 113-117.

Faul, A. C., McMurtry, S. L., & Hudson, W. W. (in press). Can empirical clinical practice techniques improve social work outcomes? *Research on Social Work Practice.*

Fraser, M. W., Jenson, J. M., & Lewis, R. E. (1993). Research training in social work: The continuum is not a continuum. *Journal of Social Work Education, 29*(1), 46-62.

Gambrill, E. (1994). Social work research: Priorities and obstacles. *Research on Social Work Practice, 4*(3), 359-388.

Hudson, W. W., Nugent, W. R., & Sieppert, J. (1999). *Practice evaluation in the 21st century.* Unpublished manuscript.

Kazdin, A. E. (1994). Methodology, design, and evaluation in psychotherapy research. In A. E. Bergin & S. L. Garfield (Eds.), *Handbook of psychotherapy and behavior change* (pp. 19- 71). New York: John Wiley.

Kirk, S. A. (1996). Practice as science, science as practice. *Social Work Research, 20*(2), 67.

Klein, W., & Bloom, M. (1995). Practice wisdom. *Social Work, 40,* 799-807.

Mattaini, M. A. (1996). The abuse and neglect of single-case designs. *Research on Social Work Practice, 6*(1), 83-90.

Meyer, C. H. (1996). My son the scientist. *Social Work Research, 20*(2), 101-111.

National Association of Deans and Directors of Schools of Social Work, Task Force on Administrative Research Infrastructures Within Social Work Education Programs. (1997, April). *Challenges and opportunities for promoting federally funded research in social work programs.* Author.

Nugent, W. R. (1996). Integrating single-case and group-comparison designs for evaluation research. *Journal of Applied Behavioral Science, 32*(2), 209-226.

Nurius, P. S., & Hudson, W. W. (1993). *Human services practice, evaluation, and computers: A practical guide for today and beyond.* Pacific Grove, CA: Brooks/Cole.

Paine, A. L., Suarez-Balcazar, Y., Fawcett, S. B., & Jameson, L. B. (1994). Leading effective meetings: Encouraging members to listen actively and provide support. In J. Rothman & E. J. Thomas (Eds.), *Intervention research: Design and development for human service* (pp. 449-461). New York: Haworth.

Polansky, N. A. (1994). A historical perspective on evaluation research. *Research on Social Work Practice, 4*(3), 389-398.

Reid, W. J. (1993). Fitting the single-system design to family treatment. *Journal of Social Service Research, 18*(1-2), 83-99.

Reid, W. J., & Smith, A. D. (1989). *Research in social work* (2nd ed.). New York: Columbia University Press.

Rosen, A., Proctor, E. K., & Staudt, M. M. (1999). Social work research and the quest for effective practice. *Social Work Research, 23*(1), 4-14.

Rothman, J., Teresa, J. G., & Erlich, J. L. (1994). Fostering participation and promoting innovation: Handbook for human service professionals. In J. Rothman & E. J. Thomas (Eds.), *Intervention research: Design and development for human service* (pp. 377-426). New York: Haworth.

Rothman, J., & Thomas, E. J. (Eds.). (1994). *Intervention research: Design and development for human service.* New York: Haworth.

Rubin, A. (1996). The inflaming and defaming of the shrewd. *Research on Social Work Practice, 6*(1), 91-99.

Schilling, R. F. (1997). Developing intervention research programs in social work. *Social Work Research, 21*(3), 173-180.

Staudt, M. (1997). Pseudoissues in practice evaluation: Impediments to responsible practice. *Social Work, 42*(1), 99-106.

Thomas, E. J. (1978). Research and service in single-case experimentation: Conflicts and choices. *Social Work Research & Abstracts, 14,* 20-31.

Thomas, E. J. (1994). Evaluation, advanced development, and the unilateral family therapy experiment. In J. Rothman & E. J. Thomas (Eds.), *Intervention research: Design and development for human service* (pp. 267-296). New York: Haworth.

Thomas, E. J., & Rothman, J. (1994). An integrative perspective on intervention research. In J. Rothman & E. J. Thomas (Eds.), *Intervention research: Design and development for human service* (pp. 3-24). New York: Haworth.

Thyer, B. A. (1996). Forty years of progress toward empirical clinical practice? *Social Work Research, 20*(2), 77-81.

Thyer, B. A., & Wodarski, J. S. (1998). *Handbook of empirical social work practice.* New York: John Wiley.

Wakefield, J. C., & Kirk, S. A. (1996). Unscientific thinking about scientific practice: Evaluating the scientist-practitioner model. *Social Work Research, 20*(2), 83-95.

Witkin, S. L. (1996). If empirical practice is the answer, then what is the question? *Social Work Research, 20*(2), 69-75.

Wodarski, J. S. (1997). *Research methods for clinical social workers.* New York: Springer.

CHAPTER TWENTY-SIX

Assessment and Measurement Issues in Direct Practice in Social Work

BETTY BLYTHE

ANITA REITHOFFER

Assessment is a cornerstone of effective practice. It involves identifying the nature and extent of client needs and concerns, as well as critical information about client resources and supports and other environmental factors. The results of assessment activities form the basis for developing, implementing, and modifying a treatment plan. Measurement is the operationalization of assessment activities. In its broadest sense, measurement refers to "any endeavor attempting to assign numerals or symbols to properties of objects according to specified rules" (Bostwick & Kyte, 1985, p. 151). In everyday usage, measurement often suggests a wide range of tools that are available to carry out assessment tasks.

This chapter delineates the purposes of assessment and discusses the connection between assessment and the worker-client relationship. Goals, which are an important ingredient in practice, should be based on a thorough initial assessment. Subsequent monitoring of goal attainment further informs treatment planning and decision making. These connections between goals and assessment also are explored here. The major categories of the various measurement tools are reviewed, and factors involved in selecting measures are discussed. Because introducing and implementing measurement tools requires care and sensitivity, strategies for successfully incorporating measures in practice are examined.

PURPOSES OF ASSESSMENT

Several authors have described phases of practice, most of which are quite similar (Blythe & Tripodi, 1989; Compton & Galaway, 1989; Garvin & Seabury, 1984; Whittaker & Tracy, 1989). The phase model we will refer to here suggests that practice can be organized into four phases: assessment, planning interventions, implementing interventions, and termination and follow-up (Ivanoff, Blythe, & Tripodi, 1994). Assessment is most often associated with the initial phase of treatment. In this phase, assessment involves identifying client problems and issues and screening for certain risk or safety factors. But, assessment also is an ongoing part of practice that has implications for other phases. Assessing client problems and issues leads to a treatment plan that is developed in the second phase, planning interventions. Assessment plays a critical role in the implementing intervention phase, during which the practitioner can monitor client progress with regard to specific goals of treatment. Finally, assessment should inform decisions to terminate treatment and shape the follow-up efforts that ideally occur after termination. Thus, assessment serves a purpose during each phase of practice.

Assessment for Treatment Planning and Screening

Most practitioners agree that assessment must be carried out to determine the extent and nature of the client's problems and issues. Typically, the goal of assessment activities at this stage is to identify all potential client problems and issues. Depending on the nature of the client referral and the agency setting, the client, the practitioner, the referral source, significant others, and other members of the client's environment may contribute to the development of this inventory. Assessment involves not only identifying this inventory of problems but also collecting information about the nature and extent of these problems. Data about the nature and extent of each problem will help the client and the practitioner determine which problem(s) need to be addressed and the order in which they should be addressed. Of equal importance is information about the clients' strengths and resources or supports that should be gathered during the assessment phase. Data on the client's strengths and resources as well as other environmental and personal challenges help the practitioner develop a treatment plan that is tailored to the client's unique situation and allows the client to take as much responsibility as possible in resolving the situation.

Each client presents with a specific set of personal, developmental, and environmental attributes, which, in turn, suggest certain screening issues. It is critical to screen for these issues during the initial assessment phase. For example, an adolescent girl may suggest the need to screen for issues such as birth control and safe sex, substance use or abuse, suicide risk, eating problems, aggression, or educational difficulties, to name a few. Depending on the circumstances, this screening may involve directly questioning the adolescent, observing her behavior, or talking to parents, teachers, or other people in her network. Certain problems may be difficult for the client to divulge early in the relationship with the worker. As will be described later, certain screening issues may develop into goals if they cannot be resolved during the initial assessment phase.

Ongoing Assessment

Ongoing assessment involves both monitoring client progress and identifying any new issues or problems that may occur. Once treatment goals are developed and the intervention is implemented, the practitioner needs to routinely assess the client's progress toward goal attainment. This monitoring takes into account the time frame during which progress is reasonably expected to occur. Note that goals may be prevention or maintenance goals, in addition to change goals. Obviously, progress has a different connotation with prevention and maintenance goals than it has with change goals. Monitoring client improvement (or goal attainment in the context of prevention and maintenance goals) can use the same measures that were applied during the initial assessment phase, in which case the initial data provide a baseline. Alternatively, new or additional measures can be applied to allow a more refined examination of client progress.

Ongoing assessment serves many functions. The most obvious is that it allows the client and the worker to determine if the intervention is having the desired impact. If it is not, the practitioner must decide if the intervention should be revised, if another intervention technique should be added, or if an entirely new treatment plan needs to be developed for the targeted goal. Obviously, these decisions are not reached easily or quickly. The worker may need to collect additional assessment information to determine the possible factors contributing to the lack of sufficient progress. Ongoing assessment also can bolster the client's motivation and can encourage both the practitioner and the worker to continue their efforts.

Ongoing assessment also may identify new problems or issues. As in the assessment phase, the practitioner always must screen for other difficulties. If additional problems are uncovered, the worker and the client must decide how to proceed. As in working with the initial problem inventory, several factors must be weighed to decide how to handle these newly uncovered problems. These factors include the severity of the problem, the possibility that the problem is a factor in maintaining or resolving other issues, and the client's motivation, just to name a few. The worker and the client may decide to address this new problem at some point during their work together, or they may determine that it does not need to be addressed during this treatment period. Say, for example, that during ongoing assessment, the client realizes the extent of her estrangement from her sister. If this issue does not have serious consequences for the client's daily life at this point and appears unrelated to the goals of treatment, then, client and practitioner can simply note the problem and move on. On the other hand, the worker and the client may decide that the client needs to deal with this issue with her sister, but it is a lower priority and can be handled at a later time. In this case, the worker might make a referral or otherwise develop a plan with the client to address this problem in the future during the process of termination.

Special Assessment Issues

Assessment during any phase of practice may need to address special issues. If possible, these issues will be identified and dealt with during the initial assessment phase. This is not always possible, due to such factors as the nature of the issue or the amount of available information about the issue. For the most part, we are referring here to issues that are first identified by the worker, someone close to the client, or a collateral contact such as the referring worker. For example, during the initial assessment phase a practitioner may be concerned that an adult client, a single mother, is abusing drugs, based on the client's alertness during certain early morning sessions and comments made by the referral source, a child protective services worker. These issues must be dealt with as systematically as possible. On direct questioning, the client denies substance abuse, but several factors can explain this denial—insufficient trust in the worker, fear of losing her children, and so on. In such cases, we suggest that the worker develop an assessment goal, to be certain that the issue is not inadvertently overlooked. With a goal of assessing for possible substance abuse, the practitioner will need to develop an intervention plan. This plan might include making unannounced home visits, placing telephone calls in the morning, asking the client to record or report her daily activities, or continuing to share with the client the worker's concerns about possible substance

abuse. The critical points here are to pay attention to miscellaneous assessment information, particularly if it involves safety issues or high-risk behaviors, and to systematically monitor the accuracy of this information.

ISSUES RELATED TO ASSESSMENT AND CLIENT-WORKER RELATIONSHIPS

We have already suggested that timing and the state of the client-worker relationship have an important effect on the assessment process. The client-worker relationship always is a significant ingredient in direct practice in social work. In certain instances, however, it may be more difficult to develop a relationship with a given client or to maintain a relationship. Assessment tools can be used to monitor relationship development in such cases. Some clients are reluctant to participate in treatment for a variety of reasons. We believe that the practitioner needs to realize that such behavior is normal and understandable rather than labeling it resistant. Moreover, the practitioner needs to take active steps to engage such clients in treatment.

Suppose that a practitioner is working with the family of an adolescent charged with shoplifting and destroying public property. The father, who works full-time, may be reluctant to participate in family sessions despite the practitioner's efforts to schedule family sessions to meet his schedule. The worker can use simple assessment tools, such as a 5-point, self-anchored scale described later in this chapter, to systematically monitor the extent to which the father seems to be engaging in treatment. The practitioner may also be attempting simple interventions, such as exploring the father's other concerns or stressors or developing a short-term contract with the father regarding his participation, while assessing his engagement in treatment.

THE RELATIONSHIP BETWEEN GOALS AND ASSESSMENT

The relationship between goals and assessment is simple and straightforward. The results of assessment activities at any time during work with a client are some decisions about what issues need to be addressed and when. The issues that need to be addressed during the current period of work with a client are developed into goals. In effect, these goals are dependent variables to be measured by the assessment and monitoring tools selected by the practitioner, possibly with input from the client.

Why should measurement tools be employed to monitor goal attainment? Ethical social work practice requires that practitioners provide the best possible treatment to their clients. Part of determining if the treatment being provided is the best possible practice involves using all available methods of assessing the client's situation, including measurement tools. Another component of providing the best possible treatment is routinely monitoring the effects of one's interventions to determine if they are having the desired effect.

SELECTING MEASUREMENT TOOLS

Now that we have discussed why we need to assess and monitor our work with clients, it is important to explore the types of tools or measurement instruments that facilitate this process. There are a variety of types of measurement tools, ranging from the simple to the complex. As a practitioner, it is important to be familiar with the different ways to assess and monitor work with clients. This knowledge enables us to choose appropriate measures fitting the situation of our clients. Practitioners should not be limited to using one or two known measures repeatedly with their clients. The following is a discussion of the different types of measures most commonly used for clinical assessment and monitoring.

Quantitative Measures

Measurement tools can be quantitative and qualitative. Quantitative tools can measure concrete and specific aspects of the client, his or her situation, and the intervention. In assessment, quantitative measurements operationalize client behaviors, thoughts, and feelings, in an effort to obtain an objective estimate of client functioning (Jordan & Franklin, 1995). Guided by assessment, client progress can be monitored based on previously operationalized aspects of the problem or situation. For example, after completing a Beck Depression Inventory (Beck, 1967) in her first session, a client's score falls in the range of severely depressed. Suppose that this test is re-administered 2 months later, and the client's score indicates that she is moderately depressed. This information, taken together with other clinical data, can help the worker decide whether to continue, revise, or terminate the intervention plan. Five types of measurement tools are described here: standardized measures, self-anchored scales, self-monitoring measures, observational measures, and archival data.

Standardized measures, such as the Beck Depression Inventory, are a collection of questions with known psychometric properties organized

Fat Cow	/		/	OK	/		/	Thin Jeans
1		2		3	4	5	6	7

Figure 26.1 Fat Feelings

to measure the existence of a predetermined problem, like depression (Witkin, 1996). The client completes the measure, a score is tabulated, and then this is compared with a predetermined range of functioning from normal to poor. Or, the client's score is compared to his or her earlier score(s) on the same measure. The number and types of standardized measures are growing continuously, and access to them is improving. For more examples of clinical measures, refer to Corcoran and Fischer's (1999) *Measures for Clinical Practice*. Standardized measures have reported levels of reliability and validity, unlike other types of less complex measures discussed here.

Self-anchored scales are created by the client and worker, for the purpose of measuring the client's specific feelings, behaviors, or thoughts. Self-anchored measures or scales are especially appropriate for measuring situations that are unique to the client, for which other measures cannot work as precisely. To illustrate how self-anchored scales are created and used, let's refer to the previous example of the depressed client who completed the Beck Depression Inventory. The client is a teenage girl who has been struggling with depression, including suicidal thoughts, persistent cutting behavior, and an overwhelming feeling of "being fat." During the first few sessions, the girl discusses how feeling fat rules her life and states that she wants to work on accepting herself and her weight. So,

together with her worker they created a self-anchored scale that she called Fat Feelings (see Figure 26.1).

Because the girl desired to work on her intrusive feelings of being fat, the worker asked her to choose phrases or words that best describe her feelings of being extremely fat or extremely thin. As shown in Figure 26.1, she labeled "Fat Cow" and "Thin Jeans" as two extreme points on a continuum of feelings associated with her perceived body weight.

It is the role of the practitioner to help the client identify and verbalize these labels, commonly referred to as the anchors of the self-anchored scale. Generally, it is recommended that the two extreme points on the scale be anchored, plus one or more points in between. Because the client determines the anchors in his or her own words, this measure is referred to as a self-anchored scale. As a guide, creating a scale with 7 points is recommended by many researchers (see Jordan, Franklin, & Corcoran, 1992). If a client cannot reliably distinguish between all 7 points, however, fewer points are appropriate. But, there should not be too few points, or the scale will not reflect small degrees of improvement. The client and the worker may become discouraged, and they may not be able to detect the gradual progress toward goal attainment. Once this scale is created, it can be completed as often as the practitioner and client decide is appropriate. In the above example, the

			Behavior		
Time/Day	Setting	Precipitating Event	Did I cut?	If not, how did I stop myself?	If so, how did I feel afterward?

Figure 26.2. Chart for Monitoring Cutting

teenage client completed the scale at the beginning of each session to track her feelings and monitor her progress toward reaching her treatment goal.

Rating scales are a form of self-anchored scales but are completed by someone other than the client to monitor specific behaviors of the client. Parents or teachers of a child in treatment often complete rating scales in conjunction with that treatment. Rating scales can provide another perspective, which is especially useful in situations in which a client may not be aware of his or her behaviors or actions (Jordan & Franklin, 1995). Workers sometimes use a rating scale to monitor their relationship with a particular client over time, as mentioned above in the case of the father who was reluctant to participate in treatment.

Self-monitoring measures, like self-anchored scales, record specific aspects of client functioning. Self-monitoring measures are completed by the client, usually outside of the worker's office. These measures provide a way to systematically record thoughts, feelings, or behaviors. Depending on the client and the situation, jour-

nals, logs, or specially devised forms can be completed by the client and reported back to the worker during their sessions. For example, let us refer back to our teenage client. Because one of her goals was to stop her cutting behavior, she and her worker developed a chart for monitoring this behavior (see Figure 26.2).

This chart records the cutting behavior of the client, her feelings, antecedents or precipitating events associated with her desire to cut, and the outcome of the situation. Self-monitoring measures can be developed to assess a client's situation during initial assessment and to monitor progress during treatment. They can provide the worker and client with information about the client that may not have been available or evidenced in their sessions. Moreover, client self-monitoring is a useful way of assessing the accuracy of what a client reports to the worker during their sessions (Reid, 1993).

Observational measures monitor the behavior of clients. The person collecting the observational data can be someone from the client's environment, such as a parent, a teacher's aide, or a partner or spouse. Observational data might record the frequency and duration of client behavior or a combination of the two. The practitioner usually creates a form to facilitate systematic recording of the behaviors being observed. Ideally, two or more observers are available to check the reliability of their recording, but this often is not possible in practice. Observational measures can be time-consuming and difficult to implement. If clients are aware that they are being observed, their behavior may change. Having access to a setting in which one can be an unobtrusive observer is somewhat unusual in social work practice. On the other hand, if a client is not aware of this observation, ethical questions inevitably arise. Inpatient or residential settings and schools sometimes offer opportunities for collecting observational data. In other instances, only very simple observational recording is possible. For example, as part of the treatment of the aforementioned teenage client, her mother checks the forearms of her daughter on a daily basis to see if she has recently engaged in cutting herself. During the assessment period, the practitioner and teenage girl agreed to incorporate the mother, to reinforce and support her daughter's goal of discontinuing her cutting. In this instance, the mother's observations provide a reliability check of the daughter's self-report. Another example of observational measurement might involve a practitioner noting certain verbal or nonverbal client behaviors to assess the client-worker relationship.

Finally, practitioners may collect archival information for assessment and monitoring. Case files, school records, police reports, medical reports, and agency records are all excellent sources of information. Depending on the access and availability of this information, a practitioner can use archival measures, with the client's permission, to shed more light on certain aspects of a client's life.

To illustrate an instance of archival data, school attendance and academic performance are often used as indicators of the level of functioning of children and adolescents. In the case of the teenage client previously mentioned, the practitioner has access to her grades and attendance through her school. Before entering treatment, the girl had been missing at least 2 days of school per week, and her grades had fallen significantly. During the first few sessions, the girl stated that she was concerned about her absences and their possible effect on her ability to go to college. As one of her treatment goals, she agreed to try to attend school every day, unless she was physically ill. Every month during the treatment process, the practitioner monitored the client's school attendance record and grades and discussed them with her during their sessions.

Qualitative Measures

Whereas quantitative measures operationalize client behaviors, thoughts, and feelings in an effort to obtain an objective estimate of client functioning, qualitative measures capture the subjective experiences of the client. Qualitative measures are individualized to the client's problem or situation and examine a client's unique interpretation of his or her problem or situation. Qualitative measures rely on words and narratives or pictures and diagrams offered by the client (Jordan & Franklin, 1995). More than quantitative measures, qualitative measures can add depth and detail to the worker's understanding of the client.

Qualitative measures include interviews, narratives, and direct unstructured observations. The initial assessment interview that is conducted by the practitioner with the client is a clear example of a semistructured, often open-ended interview. It collects the client's account of the problem in his or her own words. Within this interview, the client offers information about the personal meaning of significant relationships with others and how these relationships influence his or her social conduct (Allen-Meares & Lane, 1990). This interview is a critical component of the initial assessment of a client and provides information that guides the planning and implementation of intervention. In subsequent sessions with the client, the worker collects additional information through such interviews. Feedback from clients about their situation often guides the decisions practitioners make about continuing, revising, or terminating interventions. Furthermore, session notes can be seen as qualitative measures of the client's situation. As the worker summarizes, organizes, and analyzes critical assessment information, qualitative measurement techniques can be employed to guide the worker's thinking. To the extent that a case-recording format requires this kind of critical thinking about assessment information, qualitative analysis occurs.

Jordan and Franklin (1995) stress the importance of monitoring the practitioner's role in applying qualitative measures. Qualitative measures should examine the client's view of reality rather than the practitioner's view of the client's reality. In an effort to ensure the reliability and validity of qualitative measures, Jordan and Franklin (1995) suggest that workers consider the following questions. Does the information collected from the client make sense? Do critical details seem to be missing? Are there contradictions in the information provided by the cli-

ent? Did the worker collaborate with the client in making formulations and interpretations? Is the client's language used? Finally, does the provided information lead to the same conclusions, when compared to other data sources? Answers to these questions can provide critical qualitative information to facilitate critical thinking in case planning and decision making.

CRITERIA FOR SELECTING MEASURES

Because there are so many possible measures for assessment and monitoring, the next step is to determine which measures are the most appropriate for a particular client. First, it is important to decide, with input from the client, what aspects of the presenting problem or situation can and should be measured. To do this, there should be a clear understanding between the client and practitioner of the specific problem and related treatment goals. Client characteristics that can be measured include personal and demographic information; thoughts, feelings, attitudes, and values; observable behaviors; and client knowledge and abilities. In addition, these variables can be specified in terms of problem existence, magnitude, duration, and frequency (Blythe, Tripodi, & Briar, 1994). Regardless of which specific aspect of the treatment the practitioner decides to measure, how a chosen measure relates to treatment goals must be clear. Simply put, the data collected must be relevant to treatment goals.

Another important factor in selecting measures relates to the client's resources and constraints. In what type of setting and how often is the client seeing the practitioner? Do they meet daily, weekly, or monthly—at the practitioner's office or the client's home? In home-based interventions, for instance, third-party observation may be considered too intrusive and not an option for the client. In the case of a woman involved in domestic violence counseling, completing diaries or self-monitoring measures at home may put her safety at risk. When selecting measures, it also is important to consider the strengths and skills that a client possesses. For example, can the client read and write? If not, standardized measures and questionnaires may be inappropriate. Also, what is the age of a particular client? Younger children may need simple, brief quantitative measures like self-anchored scales, or the practitioner may have to rely largely on qualitative measures. On the other hand, adults may have the capacity to complete longer standardized measures or more complex observational measures.

When selecting measures, the practitioner should not be limited to a single quantitative or qualitative measure. Multiple measures are preferable. The problems and situations that clients face are complicated, and one measure cannot accurately represent their complexity or provide enough information to effectively guide treatment decisions (Allen-Meares & Lane, 1990; Reid, 1993). Multiple measures, as well as multiple sources of information, provide "an approximation of reality to a degree that would not have been possible with the use of any one method alone" (Kazi, 1996, p. 109). As with developing and specifying treatment goals, the client should be involved in selecting measures, planning when to use the selected measures, and deciding how to involve other people in this process. Any additional information that a practitioner and the client are able to gather can only enrich the quality of treatment.

AVOIDING AND ADDRESSING PROBLEMS WHEN COLLECTING ASSESSMENT AND MONITORING DATA

Often, clients have had previous experience with social workers and other helping professionals, but this experience may not have involved the use of quantitative or qualitative measurement tools such as those described here. Therefore, the manner in which such tools for assessing and monitoring practice are introduced is critical. We suggest, and most experts agree, that the practitioner address this in the first session when giving the client other information about what to expect in the course of their work together (Corcoran & Fischer, 1999; Kazdin, 1993; Nelsen, 1990). The practitioner should explain that some tools, especially selected for this client, will be used to gather information. This information will aid in developing priorities for their work together and will give the practitioner important feedback as to whether the interventions are helping the client. One of the most important factors to consider when asking the client to participate in measurement activities is the client-worker relationship. A working relationship is essential not only for assessment and measurement of goal attainment; it is the foundation needed for providing assistance in the first place. The development of this client-worker alliance "will go a long way to assuring compliance and participation" (Woody, 1990, p. 286). Similarly, it is essential that the worker tell the client who will have access to all assessment and monitoring information and under what conditions other individuals will be allowed to review the data.

A primary reason for monitoring client progress toward goal attainment is to improve the worker's ability to help the client. Monitoring data help the practitioner decide if the intervention needs to be adjusted, continued, or terminated. Thus, we suggest that the worker emphasize that the measurement tools will help to determine the extent to which the intervention plan is supporting the client's efforts to achieve his or her objectives. In this way, the focus of evaluation is on the worker and the intervention plan rather than on the client.

Practitioners should continually solicit feedback and comments from clients about their feelings and experiences regarding measurement tools, just as other aspects of treatment are discussed. Over time, it is important to re-emphasize with clients that measuring progress toward their goals is a beneficial and necessary part of their treatment. Clients will be able to track and report their own progress or lack of progress toward goal attainment, so that the worker can change or modify the existing intervention to provide the best possible treatment. It is also crucial that a worker be "up front" with clients about the issue of social desirability (Corcoran & Fischer, 1999). The practitioner should openly discuss with the client the fact that it may be easier or desirable to complete measures in a way that is more positive than reality, in an effort to please the practitioner. The worker should reiterate that there are no right or wrong answers. In general, the more honest and forthright a practitioner is with the client, the better the chances are that measures will be consistently and accurately completed.

Despite the best introduction to assessment and monitoring practices, problems may develop at any point. Clients or other collateral contacts may be reluctant to complete measures, may complete them inconsistently, or may simply stop providing data. If any of these situations arise, the practitioner should initiate a frank and open discussion with the client or other person responsible for data collection. The rationale for collecting assessment or monitoring information should be reviewed. The worker should explore the reasons why data collection is not progressing as intended. Some of the possible reasons are unclear directions, requests for too much data, and concerns about who will have access to the data. If the practitioner conveys an open and flexible approach to addressing these issues, data collection problems usually can be resolved.

ISSUES OF ETHNICITY AND GENDER

Relatively little has been written about issues of ethnicity and gender when implementing assessment and measurement tools in direct social work practice. Nonetheless, some of the same guidelines that are offered for planning and implementing interventions apply here.

Obviously, practitioners must be aware of their own biases around issues of gender, culture, and ethnicity. These biases can subtly influence such things as the choice of measures or the interpretation of assessment information. For instance, when identifying potential screening issues for a client, as discussed earlier in this chapter, the worker needs to ensure that his or her own biases do not affect decisions about how the client's personal, developmental, or environmental attributes might suggest the need to screen for particular potential problems.

One way to reduce the impact of one's own biases is to actively involve the client in selecting measures, developing goals, and interpreting the information from assessment and monitoring tools. In reality, each of us looks at any given situation through our own lens. If clients are treated as colleagues, as individuals with expertise in describing and interpreting their experiences, values, and social environments, they can help workers recognize their own biases and reduce the likelihood that these biases will affect critical assessment and measurement decisions. Just as one example of operationalizing this approach, we earlier noted the importance of using the client's own words in developing the anchors on a self-anchored scale.

It is particularly critical to approach minority clients as colleagues. All too often, they are blamed or criticized for certain behaviors that may be adaptive, or understandable, in the context of their environments. In such instances, clients can help workers conduct assessments that are sensitive to environmental issues and may even highlight the need for environmental, rather than individual, interventions.

Certain types of measures discussed in this chapter present particular concerns about issues of ethnicity and gender. Qualitative measures, for example, hold the possibility of reducing worker bias insofar as the worker is able to focus on the client's view of reality. At the same time, the degree to which practitioners must organize, summarize, and analyze qualitative data opens possibilities for practitioner bias. Any measures using observers, such as rating scales or observational measures, are subject to biases presented by the observers. Standardized measures may be normed on a white, middle-class population or on some other population that is markedly different from the client's background. A widely used measure of child behavior, for instance, has been criticized by African American mothers for suggesting that

"healthy" children will respond in ways that seem "sissy" in their culture.

FUTURE DIRECTIONS

Some of the concepts presented in this chapter have long been a part of direct practice in social work and have stood the test of time. Other concepts presented here are newer ideas but are making their way into everyday practice. As with all of social work practice, assessment and measurement technology is continually evolving. The following are a few thoughts about future directions for assessment and measurement in social work practice.

Recent years have seen increased attention to qualitative measurement in social work research and practice. As we recognize the potential contribution of qualitative measurement strategies, it is likely that the number and types of qualitative measures will be expanded and that practitioners will have many more such measures in their repertoire. Also, the literature on social work practice is likely to contain more discussion of the issues surrounding the use of qualitative measures. Fortunately, the profession seems to be getting beyond the old debate that pitted quantitative measures and qualitative measures against each other. We now realize that our understanding of our client's reality is enhanced by combining both. More work is needed, however, to help practitioners combine the results of quantitative and qualitative assessment. Future work must provide guidelines for using both rich sources of data.

Practitioners often turn to standardized measures, particularly if their practice focuses on a specific client problem. For example, workers who routinely see families with parenting problems are looking for simple, yet rigorous standardized measures for assessing parenting skills. All too often, the available measures (of any given client behavior, feeling, or cognition) have not been normed on women and/or people of color. Ideally, the research community will respond to this need in the future and adapt existing measures or develop new measures that have more widespread application.

As we all know, applications of computer technology are growing at an incredibly rapid rate, as is the availability of computers. There are numerous instances of computerized assessment tools. Perhaps the most fully developed program is the Computer Assisted Assessment Package (Hudson, 1996), which, among other things, allows clients to complete assessment scales at the computer and to view scores including a graph of these scores. Given the plethora of emerging computer tools, it is likely that there will be new applications of computer technology to assessment and measurement in social work.

For the most part, this chapter has provided examples of assessment and measurement with single clients. We have noted that, for many reasons, practitioners may find it helpful to gather quantitative or qualitative data from significant others or collateral contacts in the client's environment. Social workers often work with dyads, families, or small groups. Essentially, the same recommendations and guidelines apply. The assessment data will lead to the development of treatment goals, which, in turn, suggest measures to monitor goal attainment. The entire client system may have the same goal, or all or some individuals in the system may have unique goals. Just as intervention planning and delivery are tailored to treatment goals, so are the assessment and monitoring strategies. Prac-

titioners who are comfortable using assessment and monitoring tools should not find this process more cumbersome when working with a client system as opposed to an individual client, but rather beneficial. Perhaps the only issue is when two or more members of a client system are working on the same goal, complete the same measure, and produce different results. This, in fact, can be very helpful and should be discussed openly in treatment. Other chapters on families and groups in this volume discuss assessment issues with these populations.

SUMMARY

This chapter has described the purposes of initial and ongoing assessment. The connections between worker-client relationships and assessment, as well as between goal development and monitoring and assessment were discussed. Both quantitative and qualitative measures were reviewed. We have tried to emphasize the importance of enlisting the client's support of and involvement in all data collection efforts. The results of initial and ongoing assessment efforts lead to the development of treatment goals and other treatment-planning activities. The results of ongoing monitoring influence case decision making as these data are analyzed as described in the following chapter.

REFERENCES

Allen-Meares, P., & Lane, B. (1990). Social work practice: Integrating qualitative and quantitative data collection techniques. *Social Work, 35,* 452-458.

Beck, A. (1967). *The Beck Depression Inventory.* San Antonio, TX: The Psychological Corporation.

Blythe, B. J., & Tripodi, T. (1989). *Measurement in direct practice.* Newbury Park, CA: Sage.

Blythe, B. J., Tripodi, T., & Briar, S. (1994). *Direct practice research in human service agencies*. New York: Columbia University Press.

Bostwick, G. J., Jr., & Kyte, N. S. (1985). Measurement. In R. M. Grinnell, Jr. (Ed.), *Social work research and evaluation* (2nd ed., pp. 149-160). Itasca, IL: F. E. Peacock.

Compton, B. R., & Galaway, B. (1989). *Social work processes* (4th ed.). Belmont, CA: Wadsworth.

Corcoran, K., & Fischer, J. (1999). *Measures for clinical practice: A sourcebook* (3rd ed.). New York: Free Press.

Garvin, C. D., & Seabury, B. A. (1984). *Interpersonal practice in social work: Processes and procedures*. Englewood Cliffs, NJ: Prentice Hall.

Hudson, W. W. (1996). *Computer assisted assessment package*. Tallahassee, FL: WALMYR.

Ivanoff, A., Blythe, B., & Tripodi, T. (1994). *Involuntary clients in social work practice: A research-based approach*. Hawthorne, NY: Aldine de Gruyter.

Jordan, C., & Franklin, C. (1995). *Clinical assessment: Quantitative and qualitative methods*. Chicago: Lyceum.

Jordan, C., Franklin, C., & Corcoran, K. (1992). Standardized measures. In R. M. Grinnell, Jr. (Ed.). *Social work research and evaluation* (4th ed., pp. 198-219). Itasca, IL: F. E. Peacock.

Kazdin, A. (1993). Evaluation in clinical practice: Clinically sensitive and systematic methods of treatment delivery. *Behavior Therapy, 24*, 11-45.

Kazi, M. (1996). The Centre for Evaluation Studies at the University of Huddersfield: A profile. *Research on Social Work Practice, 6*, 104-116.

Nelsen, J. (1990). Single-case research and traditional practice: Issues and possibilities. In L. Videka-Sherman & W. Reid (Eds.), *Advances in clinical social work research* (pp. 37-47). Silver Spring, MD: National Association of Social Workers.

Reid, W. (1993). Fitting single-system design to family treatment. *Journal of Social Service Research, 18*, 83-99.

Whittaker, J. K., & Tracy, E. M. (1989). *Social treatment: An introduction to interpersonal helping in social work practice* (2nd ed.). Hawthorne, NY: Aldine de Gruyter.

Witkin, S. (1996). If empirical practice is the answer, then what is the question? *Social Work Research, 20*(2), 69-75.

Woody, J. (1990). Clinical strategies to promote compliance. *The American Journal of Family Therapy, 18*, 285-294.

CHAPTER TWENTY-SEVEN

Computer-Mediated Communications in Direct Social Work Practice

MARILYN FLYNN

The purpose of this chapter is to examine computer-mediated communication in direct social work practice with individuals, families, and groups. The concept of computer-mediated communication has been subject to conflicting interpretation, depending on the extent to which the human-machine dichotomy is emphasized and whether automated communications systems such as the Internet are treated as similar or psychologically distinct from information and data-sharing functions of computers (Ferris, 1997; Hiltz & Turoff, 1993; Murray, 1997).

For the purposes of this analysis, computer-mediated communications are defined as nearly all forms of computer activity, from task-related data manipulation, archiving, and report production to connectedness through e-mail messaging, Internet chat rooms, other multi-user domains, and multimedia linkages with radio and television. The assumption is that the form of technology used to manage voice, image, and/or data transmissions is not as critical as whether a social act of communication is intended. And the tendency of human beings to bring a social and interpersonal dimension to interaction with—and among—computers has been irrepressible (Rheingold, 1993). This perspective of computers as social technology is well related to the methods and belief systems of practitioners, who daily harness the dynamics of social relationships as the working material of change in a variety of settings.

SOCIAL TECHNOLOGY IN DIRECT PRACTICE

Technology is usually defined as *any* systematic, structured process that produces practical replicable outcomes. Although mechanical components may be involved, many of the most interesting examples of technology are actually "soft" and consist of ideas that engender regular, predictable results. Social technology such as the social security system is one illustration. Progressive desensitization techniques to reduce fear and anxiety, some versions of the family preservation program in child welfare, manualized clinical programs in mental health, and Job Clubs for the disadvantaged are other examples.

Direct practice in social work, therefore, already employs many technologies that are designed to promote equity in treatment of applicants and clients, to make outcomes in therapy replicable, and to create consistency in process over time. Some of these technologies are as sweeping in scope as the social security system; some, as small as beepers and answering services. The interesting question is not whether social workers in direct practice wish to use technology, because they already do so, but which technologies hold the greatest potential for advancing the objectives of the profession.

THEORETICAL ISSUES IN COMPUTER-MEDIATED COMMUNICATION

Computer-mediated communications in social work were limited initially to management of repetitive administrative tasks such as document production, with workplace efficiency as the chief motivating factor in adoption. Once communications, computers, and other media systems were finally linked on a household, commercial, and global level in the 1980s, the foundation was finally laid for transformational applications of electronic technology in the profession.

Tools extend human beings—their hands, muscles, eyes, minds, abilities to use language for communication, and in the case of some forms of computer-mediated communication, their psyches and identities (Mitchum, 1994). Human potential for mobility, productivity, and interpersonal connection is speeded up, magnified, and ultimately altered. Because technologies like computer-mediated communication do actually modify the conditions under which learning, change, and organized living take place, computers themselves become agents of social and psychological transformation.

Consequently, computer-mediated communication is causing a slow reinterpretation of basic concepts such as shared space, personal "presence," identity, attachment, and even self (Lauria, 1997; McLuhan & McLuhan, 1988; Sanders & Rosenfield, 1998; Turkle, 1984). In virtual reality, for example, the conscious self interacts with digitized stimuli to create individually unique subjective experiences. That people see these projections of themselves and others as "real" has been demonstrated in personal accounts, case reports, and research. Users experience a high sense of personal presence in a space that is socially constructed with a multi-plicity of cues. Feelings of jointness, synchronicity, and fluid expressiveness characteristic of face-to-face relationships also transpire (Binik, Canot, Ochs, & Meana, 1997; Kirby, 1996; North, North, & Coble, 1997; Rothbaum et al., 1995; Schuemie, 1999; Suler, 1999; Turkle, 1997).

Practitioners have resisted the use of computer-mediated interventions with clients on the grounds that the environment created by machines is remote and impersonal. When communication is conducted only through text on a screen, it is hypothesized that conditions for a therapeutic relationship cannot be met. This view emphasizes the human-machine dichotomy and has been called the "cues filtered-out approach" (Culnan & Markus, 1987; Murphy & Pardeck, 1986a, 1986b; Short, Williams, & Christie, 1976; Walther & Burgoon, 1992). Critics believe that too much social presence seems to be missing in machine-based transactions: facial expressions, gestures, speech variations associated with language and emotion, body language, class and occupational symbols in dress and physical appearance, age/gender/ethnic markers, odors, and even the physical-social environment with its furnishings, colors, temperature, light, nearby people, and neighborhood or other contextual influences.

Aside from the vacuum in interpersonal exchange when multiple social cues are missing, the argument is also made that normal social inhibitions are undermined when people are cloaked in electronic anonymity. Individuals reading text-based messages on their computer screen may inadvertently respond to others in inappropriate and even painful ways. Worse, they may more freely engage in socially offensive or abusive actions. One example is "flam-ing," or the text equivalent of shouting, which happens more often on sites where users are anonymous. More perturbing, some women claim to have experienced the psychological sensation of rape in virtual environments (Baron, 1984; Kiesler, Siegel, & McGuire, 1985; Reid, 1992; Rice, 1989; Turkle, 1997).

On the other hand, most treatment technologies deliberately reduce social cues. In psychoanalytic therapy, for example, the patient's ability to make interpretations based on visual or nonverbal cues is minimized as much as possible. Light and noise are controlled to reduce distractions. Symbols or pictures in the office that would provide clues to the personal life of the therapist are removed, except for professional certificates and diplomas. The patient is often protected from contact with other patients to a significant extent, usually through separate exit and entry doors. In short, every technique is exercised to make the patient's subjective realities and perceptions the central focus.

Evidence is rapidly accumulating that evaluates positively the potential for attachment and trust in computer-mediated communications, whether text-based, animated, or multimedia. Observers have documented the emergence of trust, feelings of affinity, commitment, and even love among individuals interacting in machine-managed environments (Binik et al., 1997; Roberts, Smith, & Pollack, 1996; Turkle, 1997). Although evidence is still very limited, it appears that the anonymity of computer-mediated communications may actually reduce inhibitions in a way that allows people to speak more freely and to seek help when they otherwise might have felt too stigmatized to do so (Binik et al., 1997). Conventions have emerged even in text-based environments to convey emotion and identity—for example, "smileys" and other symbolic uses of punctuation marks and message signatures. These symbolic systems can reduce the likelihood that text-based messages will be misinterpreted, a problem noted by King, Engi, and Poules (1998).

The reinvention of language, emotion, and social conventions would be predicted if computer communications are conceptualized as social acts. For three decades, development in computer-mediated communications has built implicitly or explicitly on only one dimension of human psychology: reactions to external stimuli. These responses—such as the ability to focus attention, discriminate, and modify behavior based on feedback—represent the "easy" problems, according to Chalmers (1996). More difficult and less well-understood are the subjective aspects of cognition that give depth, color, and emotion to conscious experience. This duality in human experience has not been adequately recognized in current information theory, nor have the micro-, meso-, and macro-level effects on human behavior been conceptualized in an integrative way.

If it is granted that computer-mediated communications are an active, not passive force in change and that information is inherently subjective and social in meaning, then the profession faces a new horizon. The basic task of linking social science theory and social work practice in the use of computer-mediated communications has not yet been accomplished. It will demand from social workers an intellectual expansion into the fields of communication theory, engineering, medicine, and perhaps philosophy as well as sociology, psychology, and the policy sciences. A review of research on applications in direct practice will help to illustrate this point.

PRACTICE APPLICATIONS OF COMPUTER-MEDIATED COMMUNICATIONS

From a social work direct practice perspective, it is perhaps easiest to think of computer-mediated communications in reference to typical client pathways through a social program, from outreach and education, intake, and assessment to treatment, follow-up, and evaluation.

Outreach and Education

Outreach. Computer-mediated communications have not as yet played an important role in outreach to most groups in the human services. Karger and Levine (1999) list over 400 human service-related Internet sites with a broad utility for direct service workers; community organizations; people affected by social, emotional, or medical problems; and individuals seeking affinity with others in marginalized or socially dispersed groups. However, there are no well-designed studies of the level of activity, impact on service demand, or client characteristics that result from this new form of public information. Because Internet access remains limited to less than half the population in the United States, no systematic methods or guidelines for computer-mediated outreach have been created. This area is perhaps one of the least tapped empirically.

One example of research in the health care sector may be noted, however. The Division of Adolescent Medicine at Los Angeles Children's Hospital developed a computer-assisted adolescent referral system on diskette and the Internet directing HIV-infected and at-risk teenagers to services in the Hollywood area (Schneir, Kipke, Melchior, & Huba, 1998).

Education. The use of interactive computer programs for life skills development of school dropouts, prison inmates, the physically disabled, and other at-risk groups in agency settings began more than 30 years ago. Evidence has accumulated that populations ranging from learning disabled children and dislocated workers to institutionalized elderly have responded positively to computer-based learning and have shown learning gains equivalent to other forms of instruction. When fully interactive, computer-based educational content is absorbed more quickly and remembered longer than the usual mainstays of educational programming, such as videotapes, lectures, and books or pamphlets (Flynn, 1989; Flynn & DiBello, 1982; McConatha, McConatha, & Dermigny, 1994; Meyer, Ory, & Hinkely, 1983; Saracho, 1982).

Recent studies continue to test the same questions of whether users will be comfortable learning in an automated environment. Health educators have been encouraged by changes in knowledge and attitudes among bulimic and anorexic patients (Andrewes, O'Connor, Mulder, & McLennan, 1997), HIV-positive patients (Gustafson et al., 1999), and diabetics (Krishna, Balas, Spencer, & Griffin, 1997). Expense, costs of programming, and unfamiliarity with technology may help to account for the continuing minimal implementation of computer-assisted learning systems in social work direct practice.

Seen as computer-mediated communication, automated educational programs can suffer from all the plagues that afflict any instructional medium: low motivational appeal to the learner, inadequate reinforcement of gain, poor content, low relevance to individual learning needs, and sheer tediousness. The characteristics of people in the learner's social environment—that is, technical assistants, friends, social workers, and teachers—may support or undermine the achievement of lesson objectives. The significance of design and context in computer-assisted learning has been generally overlooked in the social work literature.

Intake

Large-scale computer-prompted and computer-based intake systems were launched in the human services about two decades ago. Reduced paper flow, improved timeliness in service response, reduction in errors relating to eligibility determination, and better use of professional time were expected. Initial experience was disappointing due to an array of issues related to software, lack of experience with computers by employees, high turnover, low morale, lack of needed linkages to other organizational divisions, and failure to install e-mail communications for direct service workers.

During the past decade, several local automated central intake systems have been introduced across the country, particularly in the area of health care and substance abuse (e.g., Becnel et al., 1998; Slack, 1999). These case studies and research reports are not focused on implications for direct service other than efficiency gains.

With the advent of the Internet, an entirely new avenue has been opened that can allow applicants for services to download application forms or even complete requests for service on line. According to one study, applicants feel comfortable—regardless of education, gender, or age—in entering data about themselves directly onto a computer with a touch-screen format (Shakeshaft, Bowman, & Sanson-Fischer, 1998). Internet-based applications are apt to become even more prevalent, once software experts improve the viability of voice recognition systems.

It is not known at this time whether Internet-based applications for public and private services will stimulate application rates, but some of the first cybertherapists have received up to 30 hits a day on their web sites. (Binik et al., 1997). Research is needed to determine whether computer-mediated applications might reduce stigma or fear in the intake process, shorten waiting and travel periods, and successfully deter and refer ineligible applicants to alternative programs.

Assessment

Computer-mediated assessments were prevalent by the 1970s for vocational aptitude, career planning, and psychological evaluations. As the 21st century begins, almost every personality and vocational inventory is automated and, in many instances, with computer-generated interpretations. The obvious adaptability of most tests and measures for computer delivery has contributed to use with all age groups (Murrelle, Ainsworth, Bulger, & Holliman, 1992; Newman, Consoli, & Taylor, 1997) and among certain ethnic groups.

In general, clients appear to react more favorably to computer-based assessment protocols than to traditional paper-and-pencil tests, and several recent studies have found no significant difference in reliability of responses when both methods are compared. Computer-generated assessment results tend to be more comprehensive, less affected by subjective impressions of the practitioner, more efficient to produce, and reliable when based on validated indexes (Butcher et al., 1997).

Some studies have shown that clients actually prefer computer-administered assessments or at least find them helpful as preparation for treatment (Bloom, 1992; Sloan, Eldridge, & Evenson, 1992). This is particularly true in cases where clients prefer anonymity due to a history of stigmatized problems such as drug abuse, suicide attempts, or sexually problematic behavior (Erdman, Klein, & Greist, 1985; Ford & Vitelli, 1992).

For example, Peterson, Johannsson, and Carlsson (1996) reported that when 57 patients in a general hospital environment were randomly assigned to touch-screen computers or paper-and-pencil tests, mean test results were comparable. However, the Beck Depression Inventory tended to show higher scores for patients using the computer, because this group was less likely to answer "no problem" to questions touching on sensitive content. One inference that might be drawn from these and other similar findings is that practitioners are systematically underestimating the amount of problem behavior at the point of assessment.

Investigators have been intrigued by the question of whether computers can be programmed to capture the important elements conferred by experience and intuition in traditional therapeutic assessment. An interesting study by Ames et al. (1994) compared the level of agreement between psychiatrists using the *Diagnostic and Statistical Manual of Mental Disorders* (*DSM III-R*; American Psychiatric Association, 1987) and a computer assessment program, AGECAT, in screening for depression and organic disorders among geriatric and general hospital patients, ages 71 to 98. With an overall kappa for all diagnostic groups of .78, the authors concluded that AGECAT could be used reliably as an assessment tool (Ames et al.,

1994). Similarly, one recent British study found that an expert computer-based system's ratings of clients as suited for psychotherapy were highly correlated with ratings by experienced clinicians (Buckingham & Birtle, 1997).

Questions about computer-mediated assessments persist. Automating a test exercises a legitimizing effect; an invalidated measure may receive an undeserved aura of authenticity. More serious is the question of whether computer-generated test interpretations are acceptable in the absence of widely shared norms for validity. At least for the MMPI, there is high consistency between interpretations by expert practitioners and computer-generated results (Butcher, 1997). Nonetheless, this remains an area for close scrutiny by social work practitioners, who may depend on this form of screening as part of an overall evaluation.

Intervention and Treatment

A well-designed study by Bass, McClendon, McKee, Brennan, and McCarthy (1998) systematically used both the communications and information functions of computers in a 12-month project with family caregivers for people with Alzheimer's disease. A sample of 102 caregivers were randomly assigned to an experimental group with access to a networked computer communications system or to a control group with no system access. The experimental subjects participated at home in an electronic support group with a public bulletin board, private e-mail, and a nurse-facilitated question-and-answer component. In addition, the experimental group was given a computer-based, modularized encyclopedia on Alzheimer's disease that could be individually accessed for information about treatment, symptom manage-

ment, self-care for caregivers, and services for patients and caregivers.

A buffering model was used for analysis of findings, in which different levels of caregiver strain and relationship of caregiver to the Alzheimer's patient were hypothesized to affect the amount of benefit to be derived from computer access. Four measures of caregiver strain were established and confirmed as separate dimensions by factor analysis. Findings were mixed but confirmed the assumption that the efficaciousness of computer-mediated communications differed depending on other characteristics of caregivers, not simply the type of communication or the extent to which it was used. For example, results suggested that a computer-mediated communications network for adult children and other non-spouse caregivers was particularly efficacious in reducing strains for this group compared to spousal caregivers. On the other hand, spousal caregivers experienced more initial reduction in perceived relationship strain when compared with controls.

Like the many studies of computer-mediated support groups and computer-assisted or computer-based therapy, this study did not analyze the content of communications, nor were other important elements of the social network for each caregiver examined. The most impressive example of content analysis in a computer-mediated group was conducted by Zimmerman (1987). He used the Harvard Psychological Dictionary to study differences in communication by a group of 18 severely disturbed adolescents as they interacted in face-to-face, e-mail, and computer conferencing groups on topics of concern to teenagers. He found that the computer-mediated communications were less likely to contain narcissistic references and reflected greater sensitivity to others.

Computer networks as devices for support groups have attracted the interest of practitioners. Advantages seem to include broadened access to service, reduction in the stigma of help seeking, and lessening of barriers imposed by certain physical disabilities or psychological conditions (Giffords, 1998; Finn, 1994; Weinberg, Schmale, & Uken, 1995; Weinberg, Schmales, Uken, & Wessel, 1996). Recent analyses suggest that electronically mediated groups do feel less stigma in treatment as a result of relative anonymity and can enjoy convenient group participation in the face of otherwise prohibitive distances, inadequate transportation, and other demands on time (Schopler, Abell, & Galinsky, 1998). At the same time, a random sample of members of the Association for the Advancement of Social Work with Groups indicated that respondents had little experience as leaders of computer-mediated groups, low levels of knowledge about computer networks, and feelings of discomfort in this domain (Galinsky & Schopler, 1997).

Weinberg et al. (1996) examined the interactions over a 6-month period in a computer-mediated support group for six women with breast cancer. Computers were provided by the project, with an easy posting system and an initial lesson so that lack of user experience was not an obstacle. The members connected 158 times, about twice a week. All women saw the connections as helpful, principally through reading the messages of others in the group rather than through formulating their own statements. This result is similar to that obtained by Miller and Gergen (1998), who tracked messages posted to a suicide bulletin board over an 11-month period. Ninety-eight participants made a total of 232 entries that were relatively brief. Findings showed that members gave each other support from a "safe distance." The authors concluded that "a network communication possesses limited but significant therapeutic potential" (p. 198). Finn and Lavitt (1994) have also reported some positive findings in working with sexual abuse survivors in computer-mediated self-help groups.

Outside of group work, practitioners in many fields with a theoretical orientation to cognitive behavioral therapy and progressive desensitization techniques have moved rapidly during the past decade to test the value of computer-mediated communication. Applications have been most extensive with populations affected by obsessive-compulsive disorders, anxiety and panic disorders, phobias, eating disorders, and disorganized thought processes associated with schizophrenia (e.g., Ahmed, Bayog, & Boisvert, 1997; Baer & Greist, 1997; Newman, Consoli, et al., 1997; Newman, Kennardy, et al., 1997; Olbrich, 1996). The research questions of most consistent interest among these reports are whether patients respond favorably to computer-mediated interventions, whether computer-based interventions achieve results that compare favorably with treatment by experienced clinicians or clinical groups, whether computer-mediated communication is a useful adjunct to traditional treatment methods, which clinical conditions appear to be most responsive to computer-medicated communication, and whether length of exposure to computer-mediated interventions affected treatment outcome. The value of findings from these studies is enhanced by the slightly greater rigor of research designs and the willingness of investigators to report mixed or negative results.

With some exceptions, investigators have found that in the context of short-term, structured interventions for certain anxiety disorders, depression, and obsessive-compulsive disorders, patients achieve significant symptom reduction following computer-based behavior modification regimens. Most studies that have adopted computer-based intervention as an adjunct rather than a substitute for human therapists have reported that the addition is useful and positively evaluated by clients. Palmtops, desktops, networks, and stand-alone versions all seem to be helpful. However, sample sizes in most studies tend to be small, with no controls.

Perhaps the most challenging to conventional beliefs is the finding in one controlled study that equivalent benefits in anxiety reduction were obtained by two groups randomly assigned to experienced clinicians or computer-based therapy. Both methods were equally acceptable to patients (Dolezal-Wood, Belar, & Snibbe, 1998). Another study reported more mixed results in attempting to help couples with sexual relationships (Ochs & Binik, 1998). Seventy-seven couples were assigned to counseling with a certified sex therapist, a sex-educational video, an expert computer system called "Sexpert," or a no-information control. The clinician and Sexpert received equivalent ratings regarding their ability to engage clients, but clients interacting with Sexpert adopted fewer behavior changes despite some changes in their relationships.

Among the more psychologically evocative uses of computer-mediated communications, virtual reality techniques for treatment of phobias and possibly some other psychological problems present the richest array of current possibilities. In "immersive virtual reality," a helmet is placed over the patient's head, completely controlling both sound and visual experiences of the individual. For this reason, immersive virtual reality, or the attempt to bring an individual "inside" electronically created space, is of considerable interest to philosophers, communication specialists, and an emerging group of cybertherapists. Lauria (1997) describes the essence of virtual reality as

> the inclusive relationship between the participant and the virtual environment. These environments may directly implicate what we can say about our very ability to know, that is, about consciousness itself. In this sense, virtual reality brings the psychological "presence" of the knowing self, with configurable digital phenomena to define "there."

Although simulations have long been used for training pilots, air traffic controllers, police, architects, and other professions, immersive virtual reality as a tool in therapy has been little developed and studied. A multidisciplinary team of clinical psychologists and computer scientists at the University of Amsterdam has, for example, experimented with using a virtual environment to desensitize patients suffering from agoraphobia and claustrophobia (Schuemie, 1999). In this case, a helmet-mounted display presented audiovisual stimuli, but patients were generally given considerable latitude in moving or rotating their perspective of a frightening situation such as an elevator. Therapists are allowed full control over simulated effects, shifting patients among locations or changing other features of the environment at will.

The University of Amsterdam investigators claim to have been successful in their limited early pilot projects. They point out that virtual reality treatment of anxiety disorders combines the virtues of safety, reduced patient embarrassment, and lower cost when compared to placing phobic individuals in real world situations.

The impact of treatment appeared to be directly related to presence, or the extent to which the patient experienced himself or herself to be present in a real situation. It is still not clear which anxiety disorders are most amenable to virtual reality therapy, and no techniques have been developed to respond to such unfavorable effects as simulator sickness. Furthermore, the interaction between patient and therapist in virtual reality has not been explored, and it is likely that new guidelines for practice will be needed (Schuemie, 1999).

In summary, the question of whether computers can be used in interventions has been answered through the more than 200 research reports written before 1991 and the myriad of narratives, case studies, small-scale studies, and "think pieces" that continue to appear regularly in professional journals (Bloom, 1992; Finn, 1994; Kaplan, 1997; King et al., 1998; Schopler et al., 1998).

However, principles underlying computerized automated psychotherapy, computer-mediated psychotherapy, computer-created virtual realities, e-mail and computer conferencing groups, and telephone therapy are not well distinguished. Variables related to the technology itself would include—but not be limited to—the rate at which transmissions are sent and received, the extent to which group leaders intervene and are experienced as present, whether private on-line or off-line communications between pairs of individuals are permitted, the presence or absence of graphic enhancements, the rules or structures established to guide communication, auditory enhancements, the complexity of instructions for use of the technology, experience and training of the group leader, and client role definition. The impact of social milieu and patient-related factors other than diagnosis have often not been considered as a relevant dynamic. Better-designed, theoretically based empirical reports are needed that would lead cumulatively to progressively better understanding of the role technology might play in supporting efficacious and effective interventions.

Evaluation and Follow-Up

Beginning in 1962, pressures for accountability, efficiency, and cost savings in the health and human services set the stage for the age of automated information systems. Most systems were ill-suited to the work of practitioners due to problems in reporting format, timing of feedback, lack of integration with other organizational units, lack of relevance to outcomes of intervention valued by practitioners, and poor functioning or inadequate technology support. Although these difficulties persist in many places, the quality of computer-mediated communications for evaluation and follow-up in practice is now somewhat better.

Just as computerized intake and assessment have taken hold in the human services field, automated evaluation has been widely introduced (Buetow, Douglas, Harris, & McCulloch, 1996). In one case report of early experience in Australia, patients and physicians in a general practice health care setting pilot-tested a computer-administered evaluation that recorded information about perceptions of service and service outcomes. As with automated assessments, participants were pleased with the experience. No comparisons were made with paper-and-pencil or face-to-face methods of data collection, and limitations were noted by both service providers and patients in their ability to convey fully the nature of their experience as a caregiver or recipient of care.

One of the enduring questions for practitioners is understanding the processes of help giving in relation to outcomes of intervention. Expert decision systems that permit practitioners to examine the quality and consistency of their clinical decision making continue to appear on the market (e.g., Pigott, 1997), but they have not been adopted widely by social workers. Questions persist regarding the underlying biases and conceptualization of treatment goals for these systems, and students are usually not exposed to expert systems as part of their graduate or undergraduate preparation.

In a similar vein, evolving methods of computerized textual analysis can permit practitioners to review outstanding sessions and turning points in work with individual clients. Ultimately, this approach might contribute to better selection of intervention methods in relation to issues presented by clients; at a minimum, it is likely to aid clinicians and other workers in their grasp of patterns of change in the intervention process (Mergenthaler & Kachele, 1996). The usefulness of computer-generated reminders and feedback on examination results has been tested in a few recent studies. Although conducted in health settings, the relevance to other social work populations can be readily extrapolated. For example, computer-generated follow-up with public assistance clients—and to a lesser degree, in child welfare—is common. How do people respond? In one controlled study of high-risk, under-served Australian women ages 18 to 70 who completed a computerized health risk survey, only the experimental group received computerized reports on survey results. Older women, age 50 or over, were significantly more likely to sched-

ule an examination within 6 months of receiving feedback, but no effect was observed for younger age groups (Campbell, Peterkin, Abbott, & Rogers, 1997).

Burack and Gimotty (1997) found that the effect of computerized reminders was most powerful only for the second year of a 2-year experiment involving a health maintenance organization (HMO) and a public health department setting. The authors speculated that agency characteristics were responsible for the lack of difference between experimental subjects and controls during the first year (45% response for both groups).

One of the more promising enhancements that has slowly made its way into the social service sector is geographic information systems (GIS), a mapping application that can be used in case management for matching clients with community resources and evaluating the effects of community intervention (Robinson & Wier, 1998).

Summary

Computer-mediated communications are now embedded in every component of human service programs, with the greatest development in health, substance abuse, and disability. Computerization with empirical testing has advanced the most in psychological assessment and adjunctive, short-term behavioral modification therapies. Social workers appear to have low levels of comfort with the Internet and computer-based communications for outreach, intake or intervention. Research in general is attuned more to consumer satisfaction and comparisons of tools (e.g., paper, computers) than with investigation of computer communications in a social context. The social work literature is silent on the role of the social worker or clinician in a computer-mediated environment.

COMPUTER-MEDIATED COMMUNICATION, GENDER, AND SOCIAL INEQUALITY

One of the most frequently repeated concerns about the explosion in computer-mediated communications is the exclusion of low-income populations from participation in this revolution. By implication, racial and ethnic minorities will suffer even more disproportionately. Only 1.6% of the world's population presently enjoys access to the about 100 million interconnected computers around the globe. And whereas 80% of websites are written in English, fewer than 1% of world's people speak this language (Dertouzos, 1999; United Nations Development Programme, 1999).

Extent of Household Computer and Communications Connection in the United States

In the United States, the National Telecommunications and Information Administration (NTIA) began measuring rates of household connection to telephones, computers, and the Internet in 1994. Between 1994 and 1998, all demographic groups and geographic areas expanded their connectivity. About 94% of the nation's population now has telephone service at home; 42% of all households own a personal computer; and 26% are Internet subscribers at home. Widening penetration has occurred among all age groups, income categories, ethnicities, and educational levels, including inner cities and rural communities. In 1997-1998

alone, Internet access grew for all demographic groups everywhere in the country, a rate of increase exceeding 52.8% for white households, 52.0% among African Americans, and 48.3% for Latinos (National Telecommunications and Information Administration, 1997, 1999).

The Roles of Race, Income, and Family Structure in Inequality of Access

However, rates of penetration have not been equal, and the NTIA's most recent data confirm a deepening disparity in access to personal computers and the Internet among certain subgroups. As has been true of access to many other forms of social benefit, computer ownership and Internet participation are closely associated with higher income, higher education, urban residence, two-parent family structure, and racial identity as white.

For example, adults with an elementary school education are 16 times less likely to have home Internet access and 8 times less likely to own a computer at home. Holding income constant, children from a low-income white families are three times more likely to have Internet access than those in African American families and four times more like than children in Latino homes. White children in two-parent homes are nearly twice as likely to have Internet access as children in white single-parent homes, and the difference is even more pronounced for African Americans. Children in a two-parent African American families are almost four times as likely to have access as those in female-headed, single-parent black households. In addition to lower Internet access, single-parent families also have lower rates of telephone and computer ownership than the general population. Finally, at almost every income level, homes in rural areas are less likely to own computers than households in urban or even central city areas, with Internet access half as likely among rural residents.

Gender and Computer-Mediated Communications

An underlying factor in low-income and single-parent households is gender. Although not analyzed in the NTIA report, the level of discomfort women feel in relating to computer-mediated communications has been the subject of numerous anecdotal reports and small-scale studies. Interaction patterns in computer-mediated environments are, not surprisingly, little different than elsewhere. Studies examining forms of social interaction in text-based virtual reality environments have found that when participants were perceived as women, they sometimes were criticized as "too talkative," more friendly and willing to collaborate, or in need of technical assistance; some were harassed by unwelcome attention and sexual overtures. Gender swapping, in which men masquerade as women on the Internet, happens relatively often (Spender, 1995; Turkle, 1995).

As Shade and We (1993) observed, "The new electronic frontier is unfortunately still a very masculine dominated space, one in which many women may feel uncomfortable at the best of times. Ensuring equitable gender access . . . should be a prerogative of this information age" (p. 10).

Federal Policies to Equalize Access

New federal policies and structures for implementation are emerging to address the problem of equal access to computer-mediated communications. None of these initiatives involves organizations with which social workers have historically been engaged.

The Federal Communications Commission operates a University Service Fund, which, with a 1998 budget of $1.7 billion, subsidizes costs for extension of service to rural areas by telecommunications companies. A special $500,000 fund supports the Lifeline Assistance and Link-Up America program, which assists poor families and individuals with installation and monthly service charges for telephones. A new E-rate program capped at $2.25 billion has also been inaugurated; it offers discounted rates to schools and libraries in economically or geographically disadvantaged areas. Over 80,000 schools and libraries in under-served areas have as a consequence been able to teach children and adults how to use computer-mediated communications through these new access points. The NTIA and the U.S. Department of Education also support community access centers (NTIA, 1999.)

For the near future, economically disadvantaged families, single parents, and geographically isolated households will obtain access to computer-mediated communications most readily through churches, grassroots organizations, public schools, and other community institutions where the social work profession has widespread relationships. New forms of outreach, including a version of the Peace Corps for the virtual community, are needed, following the precedent of undergraduate students at the Massachusetts Institute for Technology, who formed a Virtual Compassion Corps (Dertouzos, 1999).

Computer-mediated communications offer a promising package of relationships, community affiliations, information, and personal development that needs to be seen as a critical resource for the disadvantaged. Marginalized groups such as the homeless, people with low mobility, the chronically mentally ill, individuals who are members of underrepresented racial or ethnic minorities, and others may have a new avenue for social connection and even influence. Social workers could play a key role in ensuring that socially disenfranchised children and adults are brought more fully into the networked world of the future. It will, however, require direct practitioners to advocate more strongly for Internet linkages open to clients in major public agencies, computer consortia among social agencies that go beyond "computer competency" classes, acquisition of mobile devices for outreach to clients in the streets, and work with library personnel to evaluate how dispossessed and different clients can be best served with available technology.

ETHICAL ISSUES

The literature supports the contention that computer-mediated communications can have a powerful effect on people, whether as an adjunct to therapy or used independently of a clinician. In his experiments with programming natural language, this effect was noticed by (Weizanbaum, 1976), who created an interactive program (ELIZA) that unintentionally mimicked Rogerian-style therapy. He was astonished at the attraction staff and students felt to the program and their resistance to being interrupted in sessions with the computer. He subsequently argued strongly (1976, 1977) that computer-based therapy was dehumanizing and at root immoral and manipulative because a machine lacks genuine compassion and empathy.

The damage that might be done to vulnerable individuals through indiscriminate and unsupervised exposure to computer-mediated interventions is exacerbated by the tendency of some users to ascribe omnipotent qualities to the computer. Binik et al. (1997) maintains that it is in fact possible for clients to create a therapeutic alliance in computer-mediated communication. This leads to many of the same ethical issues that arise in all client-worker relationships: protecting clients from exploitation and indignity and avoiding harm through toxic or inappropriate treatment strategies.

Even for the most technically sophisticated client, there is still inadequate protection against commercially distributed programs that have not been adequately peer reviewed and thoroughly tested with intended target audiences. Relatively few restrictions are placed on who may administer these programs, leaving open the question of whether computer-based assessment and therapy is in the hands of competent and knowledgeable practitioners (Ford, 1993).

Many of these concerns have been magnified with the rapid penetration of the Internet into homes in this country and abroad. Cybertherapy through such programs as Shrink-Link are emerging, with on-line communication between therapists and clients, either in synchronous or asynchronous modes. Serious questions have been raised about the adequacy of monitoring and intervention by therapists, the failure of therapists to recognize influences on problem etiology that may be location-related, and problems in assessing the validity of data obtained via computer (Bloom, 1998). There is no systematic regulation of who may offer these services. Professional standard-setting organizations in social work and other professions have only just begun to consider these issues, with the American Psychological Association so far the most advanced.

The problem of confidentiality applies both to Internet and other forms of computer-mediated communications (Bloom, 1998; Ford, 1993; Gelman, Pollack, & Weiner, 1999). Safeguards are needed—and often lacking—to protect client records and communications. Modifications must include all three areas: software, hardware, and communications protocols. Examples include encryption methods that take advantage of the latest advances in copy protection, procedures for shielding client data from viruses, back-up procedures, security measures to prevent theft of hard drives, password systems for file access, and guidelines regarding what may be stored in electronic files.

CONCLUSION

Within the next 30 years, it is estimated that more than one quarter of the transactions in the world's economy will take place over interconnected computers, with as much as a 300% gain in human productivity. Equally significant, the free exchange or social aspects of computer-mediated communication will become embedded in almost every aspect of daily life, including family messages, social support, community-building exercises, and other yet-unimagined forms of contact. New speech recognition systems will allow people to interact with computers just as they do with other human beings. New wireless "chameleon-like" handheld devices will permit users to move about, switching freely from telephone, Internet use, data transmission, radio, and video on the same instrument (Dertouzos, 1999; Guttag, 1999; Zue, 1999).

It is encouraging that recent forms of development in computer and communications systems have potentially much higher compatibility with traditional direct practice methods and will be somewhat freer of prohibitive cost constraints. For example, "fuzzy logic" software systems and wireless communication will allow for more adaptiveness in software interaction with users and less dependency on geographic locale as a precondition for use. Fuzzy logic programming does not require the strict hierarchical relationships that give most computer applications their rigid and narrow linear feel. Other advances in programming, processing, storage, and retrieval will introduce lifelike and responsive systems for widespread use.

Interconnections between television, cable systems, telephone companies, and computer companies are now being established in the United States and Great Britain. This transforming advance means that by early in the 21st century, most homes and apartments will be able to access computer networks such as the Internet using a simple remote control device and, optionally, a wireless keyboard. E-mail, computer conferencing, enrollment in support groups, advice seeking, cybertherapy, and a whole range of yet-undeveloped cyberservices will be available directly to potential clients in low-income as well as affluent neighborhoods.

Virtual reality environments will permit unprecedented opportunities for observation of individual reactions to information under conditions where reality is physically manipulated. The implications of this perspective for practice theory are evident.

As the Internet and its successors grow even more ubiquitous in the lives of individuals, virtual reality may become as much a mainstay of people's experience as physical reality. This is not science fiction. Decision making may be electronically mediated (as in purchase of cars, clothing, movies, and books); electronically-mediated conferences and chat groups may become as common as face-to-face encounters; and private video and text messages may be more frequent than paper-based communication. To ignore this environment, to fail to give it leadership, and to segregate theories of behavior from this vast mechanism for influencing psychological and social relations would seem a sad retrogression for the profession.

REFERENCES

Ahmed, M., Bayog, F., & Boisvert, C. M. (October, 1997). Computer-facilitated therapy for inpatients with schizophrenia. *Psychiatric Services, 48*(10), 1334-1335.

Ames, D., Flynn, E., Tuckwell, V., & Harrigan, S. (1994, August). Diagnosis of psychiatric disorder in elderly general and geriatric hospital patients: AGECAT and *DSM-III-R* compared. *International Journal of Geriatric Psychiatry, 9*(8), 627-633.

Andrewes, D., O'Connor, P., Mulder, C., & McLennan, J. (1996). Computerized psychoeducation for patients with eating disorders. *Australian and New Zealand Journal of Psychiatry, 30*(4), 492-497.

Baer, L., & Greist, J. H. (1997). An interactive computer-administered self-assessment and self-help program for behavior therapy. *Journal of Clinical Psychiatry, 5*(Suppl 12), 23-28.

Baron, N. S. (1984.) Computer-mediated communication as a force in language change. *Visible Language, 18*(2), 118-141.

Bass, D. M., McClendon, M. J., McKee, J., Brennan, P. F., McCarthy, C. (1998, February). The buffering effect of a computer support network on caregiver strain. *Journal of Aging and Health, 10*(1), 20-43.

Becnel, J., Ray, S., Wolf, T., Lotten, T., Williams, J., Detiege, J., & Gable, W. (1998). The New Orleans patient tracking system (PTS): Data management for a network of community-based alcohol and drug treatment providers. *Computers in Human Services, 14*(3-4), 73-98.

Binik, Y. M., Canot, J., Ochs, E., & Meana, M. (1997). From the couch to the keyboard: Psychotherapy in cyberspace. In S. Kiesler (Ed.), *Culture of the Internet.* Mahwah, NJ: Lawrence Erlbaum.

Bloom, B. L. (1992). Computer-assisted psychological intervention: A review and commentary. *Clinical Psychology Review, 12,* 169-198.

Bloom, B. W. (1998, February). The ethical practice of WebCounseling. *British Journal of Guidance and Counseling, 26*(1), 53-59.

Buckingham, C. D., & Birtle, J. (1997, March). Representing the assessment process for psychodynamic psychotherapy within a computerized model of human classification. *British Journal of Medical Psychology, 70*(1), 1-16.

Buetow, S. A., Douglas, R. M., Harris, P., & McCulloch, C. (1996). Computer-assisted personal interviews: Development and experience of an approach in Australian general practice. *Social Science Computer Review, 14*(2), 205-212.

Burack, R. C., & Gimotty, P. A. (1997, September). Promoting screening mammography in inner-city settings: The sustained effectiveness of computerized reminders in a randomized controlled trial. *Medical Care, 35*(9), 921-931.

Butcher, J. N. (1997). Using the MMPI-2 in treatment planning. In J. Butcher (Ed.), *Personality assessment in managed health care: Using the MMPI planning* (pp. 153-172). New York: Oxford University Press.

Campbell, E., Peterkin, D., Abbott, R., & Rogers, J. (1997, November-December). Encouraging underscreened women to have cervical cancer screening: The effectiveness of a computer strategy. *Preventive Medicine, 26*(6), 801-807.

Chalmers, D. J. (1996.) *The conscious mind: In search of a fundamental theory.* New York: Oxford University Press.

Culnan, M. J., & Markus, M. L. (1987). Information technologies. In F. M. Jablin, L. L. Putnam, Notes on defining of computer mediated communication, *CMCMagazine* [On-line]. Available: http://www.december.com/cmc/mag/1997/jan/deccom.html

Dertouzos, M. L. (1999, August) The future of computing. *Scientific American, 281*(2), 52-55.

Dolezal-Wood, S., Belar, C. D., & Snibbe, J. (1998, March). A comparison of computer-assisted psychotherapy and cognitive-behavioral therapy in groups. *Journal of Clinical Psychology in Medical Settings, 5*(1), 103-115.

Erdman, H. P., Klein, M. H., & Greist, J. H. (1985). Direct patient computer interviewing. *Journal of Consulting and Clinical Psychology, 53*(19), 760-773.

Ferris, P. (1997, January). What is CMC? An overview of scholarly definitions. *CMC Magazine* [On-line]. Available: http://www.december.com/cmc/mag/1997/jan/ferris/html

Finn, J. (1994). Computer-based self-help groups for sexual abuse survivors. *Social Work with Groups, 17*(2), 21-46.

Finn, J., & Lavitt, M. (1994). Computer based self-help groups for sexual abuse survivors. *Social Work with Groups, 17,* 21-46.

Flynn, M. L. (1989). The potential of older adults for response to computer-assisted instruction. *Journal of Educational Technology Systems, 17*(3), 233-243.

Flynn, M. L., & DiBello, L. W. (1982) *Evaluating an automated career information system: Research results and techniques for system assessment.* Paper presented at the annual meeting of the American Vocational Association, St. Louis, MO.

Ford, B. D. (1993, March). Ethical and professional issues in computer-assisted therapy. *Computers in Human Behavior, 9*(3), 387-400.

Ford, B. D., & Vitelli, R. (1992, February). Inmate attitudes towards computerized clinical interventions. *Computers in Human Behavior, 8*(2), 223-230.

Galinsky, M., & Schopler, J. (1997). Connecting group members through telephone and computer groups. *Health and Social Work, 22*(3) 181-188.

Gelman, S. R., Pollack, D., & Weiner, A. (1999). Confidentiality of social work records in the computer age. *Social Work, 44*(3), 243-252.

Giffords, E. D. (1998). Social work on the Internet: An introduction. *Social Work, 4*(3), 243-251.

Gustafson, D., Hawkins, R., Boberg, E., Pingree, S., Serlin, R., Graziano, F., & Chan, C. (1999). Impact of a patient centered, computer-based health information/support system. *American Journal of Preventive Medicine, 16*(1), 1-9.

Guttag, J. V. (1999, August). Communications chameleons. *Scientific American, 281*(2), 58-59.

Hiltz, S. R., & Turoff, M. (1993). *The network nation: Human communication via computers.* Cambridge: MIT Press.

Kaplan, E. (1997). Telepsychotherapy: Psychotherapy by telephone, videotelephone, and computer videoconferencing. *Journal of Psychotherapy Practice and Research, 6*(3), 227-237.

Karger, H. J., & Levine, J. (1999). *The Internet and technology.* New York: Longman.

Kiesler, S., Siegel, J., & McGuire, T. W. (1985). Social-psychological aspects of computer-mediated communication. *American Psychologist, 39*(10), 1123-1134.

King, S. A., Engi, S., & Poules, S. T. (1998). Using the Internet to assist family therapy. *British Journal of Guidance and Counseling, 26,* 43-52.

Kirby, K. C. (1996, February). Computer-assisted treatment of phobias. *Psychiatric Services, 47*(2), 139-140.

Krishna, S., Balas, A., Spencer, D., & Griffin, J. (1997). Clinical trials of interactive computerized patient education: Implications for family practice. *Journal of Family Practice, 45*(1), 25-33.

Lauria, R. (1997, September). Virtual reality: An empirical-metaphysical testbed. *Journal of Computer Mediated Communication, 3*(2) [On-line]. Available: http://www.ascusc.org/jcmc/vole/issue2

McConatha, D., McConatha, J. T., & Dermigny, R. (1994, August). The use of interactive computer services to enhance the quality of life for long-term care residents. *The Gerontologist, 34*(4), 553-556.

McLuhan, M., & McLuhan, E. (1988). *Laws of media: The new science.* Toronto: University of Toronto Press.

Mergenthaler, E., & Kaechele, H. (1996, Fall). Applying multiple computerized text-analytic measures to single psychotherapy cases. *Journal of Psychotherapy Practice & Research, 5*(4), 307-318.

Meyer, L. A., Ory, M. C., & Hinkely, R. C. (1983). *Evaluation research in basic skills with incarcerated adults.* Unpublished report, Computer-Based Educational Research Laboratory, University of Illinois at Urbana-Champaign, Urbana, IL.

Miller, J. K., & Gergen, K. J. (1998). Life on the line: The therapeutic potentials of computer-mediated conversation. *Journal of Marital & Family Therapy, 24*(2), 189-202.

Mitchum, C. (1994). *Thinking through technology: The path between engineering and philosophy.* Chicago: University of Chicago Press.

Murphy, J., & Pardeck, J. T. (1986a). Computer clinical practice: Promises and shortcomings. *Psychological Reports, 59*(3), 1099-1113.

Murphy, J., & Pardeck, J. T. (1986b). Technology-mediated therapy: A critique. *Social Casework, 67*(10), 605-612.

Murray, P. J. (1997, January). A rose by any other name. *CMC Magazine* [On-line]. Available: http://www.december.com/cmc/mag/1997/jan/murray/html

Murrelle, L., Ainsworth, B., Bulger, J., & Holliman, S. (1992). Computerized mental health risk appraisal for college students: User acceptability and correlation with standard pencil-and-paper questionnaires. *American Journal of Health Promotion, 7*(2), 90-92.

National Telecommunications and Information Administration. (1999). *Falling through the net* [On-line]. Available: http://www.ntia.doc.gov/ntiahome/digitaldivide

National Telecommunication and Information Administration. (1997). *Falling through the net II: New data on the digital divide* [On-line]. Available: http://www.ntia.doc.gov/ntiahome/

Newman, M. G., Consoli, A., & Taylor, C. B. (1997, Spring). Computers in assessment and cognitive behavioral treatment of clinical disorders: Anxiety as a case in point. *Behavior Therapy, 28*(2), 211-235.

Newman, M. G., Kenardy, J., Herman, S., & Taylor, C. B. (1997, February). Comparison of palmtop-computer-assisted brief cognitive-behavioral treatment to cognitive-behavioral treatment for panic disorder. *Journal of Consulting & Clinical Psychology, 65*(1), 178-183.

North, M. M., North, S. M., & Coble, J. R. (1997.) Virtual reality therapy: An effective treatment for psychological disorders. In G. Riva (Ed.), *Virtual reality in neuro-psycho-physiology: Cognitive, clinical, and methodological issues in assessment and rehabilitation*(pp. 59-70.) Amsterdam: IOS Press.

Ochs, E. P., & Binik, Y. M. (1998, February). A sex-expert computer system helps couples learn more about their sexual relationship. *Journal of Sex Education & Therapy, 23*(2), 145-155.

Olbrich, R. (1996). Computer-based psychiatric rehabilitation: Current activities in Germany. *European Psychiatry, 11*(Suppl 2), 60s-65s.

Paulsen, A. S., Crowe, R. R., Noyes, R., & Pfohl, B. (1988). Reliability of the telephone interview in diagnosing anxiety disorders. *Archives of General Psychiatry, 45*(1), 62-63.

Peterson, L., Johannsson, V., & Carlsson, S. G. (1996, Fall). Computerized testing in a hospital setting: Psychometric and psychological effects. *Computers in Human Behavior, 12*(3), 339-350.

Pigott, H. E. (1997). Computer decision-support as a clinician's tool. In R. K. Schreter & S. S. Sharfstein (Eds.), *Managing care, not dollars: The continuum of mental health services* (pp. 245-263). Washington, DC: American Psychiatric Press.

Reid, E. M. (1992). Electropolis: Communication and community on Internet relay chat. *Intertek, 3*(3), 7-15.

Rheingold, H. (1993). *The virtual community: Homesteading on the electronic frontier.* Reading, MA: Addison-Wesley.

Rice, R. E. (1989). Issues and concepts in research on computer-mediated communication systems. In J. A. Anderson (Ed.), *Communication yearbook* (Vol. 12, pp. 436-476). Newbury Park, CA: Sage.

Roberts, L. D., Smith, L. M., & Pollack, C. (1996, September). *A model of social interaction via computer-mediated communication in real-time text-based virtual environments.* Paper presented at the 31st Annual Conference of the Australian Psychological Society, Sydney, Australia.

Robinson, J. G., & Wier, K. R. (1998, August). Using geographical information systems to enhance community-based child welfare services. *Child Maltreatment, 3*(3), 224-234.

Rothbaum, B. O., Hodes, L. F., Kooper, R., Opdyke, D., et al. (1995, April). Effectiveness of computer-generated (virtual reality) graded exposure in the treatment of acrophobia. *American Journal of Psychiatry, 152*(4), 626-628.

Sanders, P., & Rosenfield, M. (1998). Counselling at a distance: Challenges and new initiatives. *British Journal of Guidance & Counselling, 26*(1), 5-10.

Saracho, O. N. (1982.) The effects of a computer-assisted instruction program on basic skills achievement and attitudes toward instruction of Spanish-speaking migrant children. *American Educational Research Journal, 19*(4), 201-219.

Schneir, A., Kipke, M., Melchior, L., & Huba, G. (1998). Childrens Hospital Los Angeles: A model of integrated care for HIV-positive and very high-risk youth. *Journal of Adolescent Health, 23*(2, suppl.), 59-70.

Schuemie, M. (1999). *Virtual reality exposure therapy: Human interaction angle* [On-line]. Available: http://is.twi.tudelft.nl/schuemie/vrhei.html.

Schopler, J., Abell, M. D., & Galinsky, M. J. (1998). Technology-based groups: A review and conceptual framework for practice. *Social Work, 43*(3), 254-267.

Shade, L. R., & We, G. (1993). The gender of cyberspace. *The Internet Business Journal.*

Shakeshaft, A. P., Bowman, J. A., & Sanson-Fischer, R. W. (1998, April). Computers in community-based drug and alcohol clinical settings: Are they acceptable to respondents? *Drug and Alcohol Dependence, 50*(2), 177-180.

Short, J., Williams, E., & Christie, B. (1976). *The psychology of telecommunication.* London: John Wiley.

Slack, W. (1999). The patient online. *American Journal of Preventive Medicine, 16*(1), 43-45.

Sloan, K. A., Eldridge, K., & Evenson, R. (1992). An automated screening schedule for mental health centers. *Computers in Human Services, 8*(3-4), 55-61.

Spender, D. (1995). *Nattering on the net: Women, power, and cyberspace.* North Melbourne: Sponifex.

Suler, J. (1999). *Cyberspace as psychological space* [On-line]. Available: http://www.rider.edu/users/suler/psycyber/psychspace.html

Turkle, S. (1984). *The second self: Computers and the human spirit.* New York: Simon & Schuster.

Turkle, S. (1995). *Life on the screen: Identity in the age of the Internet.* New York: Simon & Schuster.

Turkle, S. (1997). Constructions and reconstructions of self in virtual reality: Playing in the MUDS. In S. Kiesler (Ed.), *Culture of the Internet* (pp. 143-156). Mahwah, NJ: Lawrence Erlbaum.

United Nations Development Program. (1999, July) *1999 human development report* [On-line]. Available: http://www.undp.org/hdro/99.html

Walther, J. B., & Burgoon, J. K. (1992). Relation communication in computer-mediated interaction. *Human Communication Research, 19*(1), 50-88.

Weinberg, N., Schmale, J. D., & Uken, J. (1995). Computer-mediated support groups. *Social Work with Groups, 17*(4), 19-34.

Weinberg, H., Schmale, J., Uken, J., & Wessel, K. (1996). On-line help: Cancer patients participate in a computer-mediated support group. *Health and Social Work, 21*(1), 24-29.

Weizenbaum, J. (1976.) *Computer power and human reason: From judgement to calculation.* San Francisco: Freeman.

Zimmerman, P. (1987). A psychosocial comparison of computer-mediated and face-to-face language use among severely disturbed adolescents. *Adolescence, 22*(88), 827-840.

Zue, V. (1999, August). Talking with your computer. *Scientific American, 281*(3), 56-57.

PART VI

Professional Issues

In this section, we asked authors to discuss issues that link direct practice to a set of professional issues that are the concern of all social workers. These issues are professional ethics, professional growth through educational processes, the place of direct practice in relationship to global issues, and enhancing social work's resource base. Although the profession's value and ethical bases have continued to develop and to be examined given ever-changing contexts, it is only very recently that social work's values and ethics have become substantive areas of research and intellectual inquiry. As Reamer points out in Chapter 28, "Ethical Issues in Direct Practice," "Relevant literature on ethical issues in the profession, ethical decision making, ethical standards, and ethical misconduct has burgeoned, especially since the early 1980s, as has professional education on the subject" (p. 598).

The editors believe that new and very complicated ethical issues will confront the social work profession, fueled by developments such as psychotropic medication, euthanasia, organ transplants, genetic engineering, breach of confidentiality to protect third parties, and end-of-life decisions. The challenge before the profession is to constantly review its ethics and values in light of its core ideology and mission, present-day forces, and laws. Keeping social work practitioners informed and educated about such issues, developing ways to periodically re-examine our values and ethics, and having social work curriculum and continuing education programs articulate to social work students and practitioners these topics will be our future challenge.

A consistent theme throughout many of the chapters contained in this volume is societal and economic restructuring. In Chapter 29 by Munson, societal and economic restructuring are covered from the perspectives of government and information technology and the implication for supervision standards. Clearly, social service delivery systems have undergone major structural changes—merging, realigning themselves, and downsizing, for example. Cost containment, bottom-line thinking, loss of autonomy, computerization, and privatization are terms that come to mind when one describes the 1980s and 1990s. Munson contends that these changes have and will continue to have major implications for the supervision of social workers. Supervisors will need to be well-grounded in the traditional domains—assessment, intervention, and measurement—as well as in the promotion of prevention, risk management, cultural diversity, and the potential risks of information technology in terms of record keeping and confidentiality.

There is greater socioeconomic interdependence among nations than in the past. This interdependency accentuates our need to appreciate human differences and cultural diversity. No longer can the United States continue its "foreign aid" approach to international affairs or posture that it has all the answers in terms of social justice, human rights, and social problems. We have much to learn from other countries in terms of how we promote the social and economic development of community and children's rights. In Chapter 30, Elliott and Mayadas agree that there are challenges and barriers to be overcome in increasing our international perspective. They suggest that the profession adopt a social development systems model of social work practice to facilitate internationalism and that the integration of macro and micro is fundamental to its advancement. Furthermore, they take the position that the goals of social development are consistent with those of social work—to create planned systematic social, economic, and institutional change with the objective to advance the quality of life here and around the world. There appears to be too much focus on differences among nations and people and not enough attention paid to commonalties. Internationalism will shift the paradigm from individualism to a model that encourages international exchange and empowerment at the micro, macro, and mezzo levels.

In Chapter 31, Lauffer points out the need for social workers to become more knowledgeable of fund-raising and grant procurement. Social services will become more dependent on a variety of fiscal sources—contracts, grants, charitable gifts, fee-for-services, and investments—to carry on their routine activities and to innovate and experiment with different approaches to present-day challenges. Governmental cutbacks could reduce the funding base for some service delivery systems. Social workers will need to become more knowledgeable regarding changes in the funding environment, the mechanisms for raising money, the importance of donor/foundation cultivation, and skills for marketing their agenda in such a way that others will extend in-kind and monetary support. Lauffer identifies a number of Internet resources useful for fund-raising purposes.

CHAPTER TWENTY-EIGHT

Ethical Issues in Direct Practice

FREDERIC G. REAMER

The maturation of social work ethics since the profession's formal inauguration in the late 19th century is remarkable. What began as preoccupation with clients' morality has evolved into a wide range of complex, intellectually rich attempts to assess and confront ethical issues in practice. Contemporary social workers have access to an array of conceptual tools and practical resources that were unimaginable to the profession's earliest practitioners.

Social workers who serve individuals, families, couples, and small groups must be prepared to address three sets of ethical issues that arise in practice: (a) the nature of core values in the profession and ethical dilemmas involving conflicts among them, (b) ethical decision-making strategies, and (c) ethics risk management. After presenting a brief overview of the evolu-

tion of social work ethics, we will explore these topics in depth.

THE EVOLUTION OF SOCIAL WORK ETHICS

Social work's approach to ethics spans four major, sometimes overlapping, periods: the morality period, the values period, the ethical theory and decision-making period, and the ethical standards and risk-management period (Reamer, 1998b). When social work began formally in the late 19th century, practitioners were much more concerned about *clients'* morality than about the morality or ethics of the profession, its intervention methods, or its members (Leiby, 1978; Lubove, 1965; Reamer, 1987b, 1995c;

Reid & Popple, 1992). During this morality period, particularly during the Charity Organization Society era, many social workers focused on providing organized relief to "paupers" (Paine, 1880; Siporin, 1992). This priority often took the form of paternalistic efforts to habilitate the poor from "shiftlessness," "indolence," or "wayward" moral character to rectitude.

Social workers' emphasis on the morality of the poor ebbed during the early 20th century, when many social workers—especially those involved in the settlement house movement—turned their attention to environmental causes of the social problems of individuals and communities (such as poverty, substandard housing, unemployment, alcoholism, mental health, and health problems). During this phase, many social workers focused on the profession's ethical obligation to address social justice and social reform issues (Brieland, 1995; Lee, 1930).

Emphasis on clients' morality continued to wane during the next several decades, as social workers cultivated a wide range of intervention theories and strategies, training programs, and educational models. During this phase, many social workers were eager to develop theoretical models and intervention approaches that would be indigenous to social work, partly in an effort to distinguish social work from professions such as psychology and psychiatry.

By the 1950s, a critical mass of literature on social work values and ethics had begun to emerge, building on several efforts earlier in the 20th century to explore social work values and ethics (Frankel, 1959). For example, as early as 1919, there were attempts to draft professional codes of ethics (Elliott, 1931; Joseph, 1989). In addition, there is evidence that at least some schools of social work were teaching courses on values and ethics in the 1920s (Elliott, 1931; Johnson, 1955).

Nearly a half century after its formal start, social work began to develop and publicize ethical standards and guidelines. In 1947, the Delegate Conference of the American Association of Social Workers adopted a code of ethics. In addition, during the 1950s, several important books and journal articles on the subject were published (Hall, 1952; Johnson, 1955; Pumphrey, 1959).

During the 1960s and early 1970s, social workers were especially concerned about issues of social justice, social reform, and civil rights. The profession's values and ideological commitment to human rights, welfare rights, equality, and nondiscrimination attracted legions of new practitioners (Emmet, 1962; Keith-Lucas, 1963; Levy, 1972, 1973; Lewis, 1972; McDermott, 1975; Plant, 1970; Vigilante, 1974). In addition, the National Association of Social Workers adopted its first code of ethics during this period, in 1960 (Reamer, 1997b).

Commentary on social work values was especially prominent during this time, especially concerning the nature of core values in the profession (Arnold, 1970; Bartlett, 1970; Bernstein, 1960; Biestek, 1957; Biestek & Gehrig, 1978; Gordon, 1962, 1965; Hamilton, 1940, 1951; Keith-Lucas, 1977; Levy, 1973, 1976; Lubove, 1965; Perlman, 1965, 1976; Plant, 1970; Pumphrey, 1959; Reynolds, 1976; Stalley, 1975; Teicher, 1967; Timms, 1983; Towle, 1965; Vigilante, 1974; "Working Definition," 1958; Younghusband, 1967). There were various critiques of social work values (e.g., Keith-Lucas, 1963; McDermott, 1975; Whittington, 1975; Wilson, 1978) and reports of empirical research on values held or embraced by social workers (e.g., Costin, 1964; McCleod & Meyer, 1967;

Varley, 1968). Noteworthy discussions during this period focused on the need for social workers to examine and clarify their own personal values (e.g., Hardman, 1975; McCleod & Meyer, 1967; Varley, 1968), based on the belief that social workers' personal beliefs and values related to such issues as people living in poverty, race relations, abortion, homosexuality, civil disobedience, and drug use may have a profound effect on their approach to and relationships with clients.

A new phase in the evolution of social work ethics began in the early 1980s, influenced largely by the development in the 1970s of a new field known as applied and professional ethics (Airaksinen, 1998; Callahan & Bok, 1980; Winkler, 1998). This field began primarily with developments in medical ethics or what has become known as bioethics (for discussion of the factors that led to the creation of the applied and professional ethics field, see Reamer, 1995a, 1995c). This new field developed and promoted a variety of conceptual and practical tools to help professionals facing ethical issues and dilemmas, especially by applying principles, concepts, and theories of moral philosophy, or ethics, to real-life ethical challenges faced by practitioners (McGowan, 1995). During this time, a small group of scholars began to write about ethical issues and challenges while drawing on literature, concepts, theories, and principles from the traditional field of moral philosophy and the newer field of applied and professional ethics (Loewenberg & Dolgoff, 1982; Reamer, 1982; Rhodes, 1986). Using somewhat different approaches, each of these scholars acknowledged explicitly for the first time the relevance of moral philosophy and ethical theory, concepts, and principles in the analysis and resolution of ethical issues in social

work. A significant portion of the literature since the mid 1980s has focused on decision-making strategies social workers can engage in when faced with difficult ethical judgments (to be discussed more fully below).

Most recently, social work has developed new ethical standards to guide practice and strategies to prevent ethics complaints and lawsuits (ethics risk management). Significant during this period was the 1996 ratification of a new *NASW Code of Ethics,* which significantly expanded ethical guidelines and standards for social work practice (Reamer, 1998a).

ETHICAL DILEMMAS IN DIRECT PRACTICE

Social workers in direct practice periodically face ethical dilemmas. An ethical dilemma occurs when social workers encounter conflicting values or professional duties and obligations. Consider, for example, the following scenarios:

A family service agency social worker provided counseling to a couple experiencing marital difficulties. For one counseling session, the husband appeared alone, because the wife was ill. During the session, the husband disclosed that he was having an extramarital affair. The husband asked the social worker not to share this information with his wife. However, the social worker felt uncomfortable continuing to work with the couple in light of the husband's ongoing deception. The social worker was torn between her loyalty to the wife and her obligation to respect the husband's right to privacy.

A social worker in private practice provided counseling services to a young woman who earned her living making repairs for homeowners. The client's insurance benefits ran out, but she was eager to continue her counseling. Weeks earlier, before the insurance issue arose, the social worker and client had chatted

briefly and casually about some home repairs the social worker was planning to make. Recalling the earlier conversation, the client proposed that she and the
social worker barter their services, exchanging counseling for home repairs. The social worker found the
offer tempting but was unsure whether the arrangement was ethical.

A social worker at a community mental health center
worked closely with a social work colleague in a local
school that referred many students to the center. Over
time, the community mental health social worker became concerned about the quality of the colleague's
work. At one point, the school social worker disclosed
to the community mental health center social worker
that she was a cocaine addict who had been in recovery but recently relapsed. The community mental
health social worker was unsure about her ethical responsibility to bring her colleague's impairment to
the attention of authorities in the profession.

Social work ethical dilemmas occur in direct
practice and indirect practice (e.g., in social
work organizing, policy work, social advocacy,
administration, education, and research). Common ethical dilemmas in direct practice—the
focus of this chapter—pertain to confidentiality
and privacy; clients' right to self-determination;
boundary issues; conflicts of interest; conflicts
of values among clients, social workers, agencies, and society; social workers' obligations to
address the unethical conduct, incompetence,
or impairment of colleagues; and service delivery (Reamer, 1998d, 1999).

Confidentiality and privacy. Social workers
understand the critical importance of confidentiality in the clinical relationship. However, social workers also understand that confidentiality
has its limits and that circumstances sometimes
arise requiring disclosure to third parties (Dickson, 1998; Kopels & Kagle, 1993; Reamer,
1994; VandeCreek, Knapp, & Herzog, 1988).

Consider the following examples requiring social workers' decisions:

1. Disclosing confidential information without
   clients' permission to protect third parties who
   have been threatened by clients
2. Disclosing confidential information to law enforcement or child protective services officials
   without clients' permission
3. Informing parents of confidential details
   about their children, over the objections of the
   minor clients
4. Sharing confidential information among parties involved in family, couples, or group counseling
5. Sharing confidential information about clients
   with clients' insurance providers

Social workers who face these circumstances
often need guidance concerning the proper
handling of confidential information and the
limitations of clients' right to confidentiality.

Self-determination and paternalism. Among
the most revered values in the profession is social workers' deep-seated respect for clients'
right to self-determination. As the *NASW Code
of Ethics* states, "Social workers respect and
promote the right of clients to self-determination and assist clients in their efforts to identify
and clarify their goals" (Standard 1.02).

Seasoned social workers know, however,
that extraordinary instances can arise that
may require interfering with clients' right to self-
determination (Biestek, 1957; Buchanan, 1978;
Carter, 1977; McDermott, 1975; Perlman,
1965; Stalley, 1975). Examples include clients
who threaten to seriously harm a third party or
commit suicide. Especially since the well-known
California Supreme Court decision, *Tarasoff v.
Board of Regents of the University of California*

(1976), there has been considerable consensus among social workers about their duty to take steps to protect from harm third parties who have been seriously threatened by social workers' clients, even if this means interfering with clients' right to self-determination. Furthermore, there is widespread agreement that social workers have a comparable duty to take steps to protect suicidal clients. As the *NASW Code of Ethics* goes on to say in the standard concerning self-determination, "Social workers may limit clients' right to self-determination when, in the social workers' professional judgment, clients' actions or potential actions pose a serious, foreseeable, and imminent risk to themselves or others" (Standard 1.02).

What is less clear is the extent of social workers' duty to interfere with clients' right to self-determination when clients plan to engage in, or are engaged in, threatening or self-destructive behavior that is harmful but not life threatening or not likely to result in serious bodily injury to third parties. Examples include a client who has been subjected to unrelenting emotional abuse by her partner and, nonetheless, wants to return to him, or a client who does not want to stop using dangerous, illegal drugs. The overriding question, of course, is to what extent people have the right to engage in behavior that is injurious to themselves, or what philosophers call the question of paternalism.

Paternalism involves interfering with a client's wishes, intentions, or actions "for his or her own good." Paternalism can take the form of interfering with or restraining self-destructive clients for their own good, requiring them to receive services or assistance against their wishes, withholding information from clients, or providing clients with misinformation (a form of lying).

Social workers disagree about the conditions under which various forms of paternalism are justifiable. Some believe that competent, informed, and thoughtful clients have a right to engage in self-destructive actions or behaviors, including taking serious risks, whereas others are more inclined to take steps against clients' wishes to protect them from harming themselves (Abramson, 1985; Dworkin, 1971; McDermott, 1975; Reamer, 1983).

Boundary issues. Social workers have always understood the need to maintain clear boundaries in their relationships with clients. Boundary violations can be profoundly damaging to clients.

Boundary violations entail inappropriate dual or multiple relationships between social workers and clients. Dual or multiple relationships occur when social workers relate to clients in more than one way, whether sexual, social, professional, or business. Some dual and multiple relationships are not inappropriate or unethical. Examples include social workers who happen to belong to the same church or synagogue as their clients or whose children attend the same grade school. In such instances, social workers are usually able to manage encounters with clients outside of the clinical setting.

Unethical dual or multiple relationships, in contrast, involve some kind of exploitation, manipulation, or deception that is, or is likely to be, harmful to the client (Jayaratne, Croxton, & Mattison, 1997). Examples include social workers who become sexually involved with their clients, borrow money from clients, or invest in clients' business ventures. In these instances, social workers take advantage of their clients to further their own interests. As Kagle and Giebelhausen (1994) argue,

Dual relationships involve boundary violations. They cross the line between the therapeutic relationship and a second relationship, undermining the distinctive nature of the therapeutic relationship, blurring the roles of practitioner and client, and permitting the abuse of power. In a therapeutic relationship, the practitioner's influence on the client is constrained by professional ethics and other protocols of professional practice. When a professional relationship shifts to a dual relationship, the practitioner's power remains but is not checked by the rules of professional conduct or, in some cases, even acknowledged. The practitioner and the client pretend to define the second relationship around different roles and rules. Behavior that is incompatible with a therapeutic relationship is made to seem acceptable in the context of the second relationship. Attention shifts from the client to the practitioner, and power appears to be more equally shared. (p. 217)

Some dual or multiple relationships raise boundary issues that are unclear, falling in an ethical "gray area." This is illustrated by the following examples:

A clinical social worker's client accepted an office job at the social worker's church. The two had little contact in the church setting. At a later time, the social worker was nominated to be on the church's governing board, which had administrative oversight responsibilities. The social worker was unsure about whether to accept the nomination in light of her client's position in the church office.

A clinical social worker's client moved to the social worker's neighborhood, and their children attended the same junior high school. The social worker was eager to become involved in the school's parent teacher association. He attended one of the organization's meetings and discovered that his client was actively involved in the organization. The social worker was torn about whether to continue his involvement.

A social worker at a family service agency joined a local fitness center. She went to the center one evening to use the exercise equipment and discovered that one of her long-term clients was an active member. The social worker felt uneasy about the prospect of regularly encountering her client in this social setting.

Experienced social workers know that when boundary issues are unclear, they must be exceedingly prudent and obtain competent consultation and supervision. According to the *NASW Code of Ethics*,

Social workers should not engage in dual or multiple relationships with clients or former clients in which there is a risk of exploitation or harm to the client. In instances when dual or multiple relationships are unavoidable, social workers should take steps to protect clients and are responsible for setting clear, appropriate, and culturally sensitive boundaries. (Standard 1.06[c]).

Divided loyalties and conflicts of interest. Some boundary issues involve situations where social workers feel caught between their obligation to their clients and to some other party, such as social workers' employers, public agencies, or the courts. In these situations, social workers may be unsure about to whom they owe their primary duty. Ordinarily, social workers' primary commitment is to their clients, but circumstances sometimes arise that require social workers to choose between their clients' interests and those of some other party. As the *NASW Code of Ethics* states,

Social workers are cognizant of their dual responsibility to clients and to the broader society. They seek to resolve conflicts between clients' interests and the broader society's interests in a socially responsible manner consistent with the values, ethical principles, and ethical standards of the profession. (p. 6)

Divided loyalties can be especially challenging in certain settings. For example, social workers in prisons sometimes feel caught between their duty to respect the right of clients (that is, inmates) to confidentiality and their obligation to report to prison officials confidential information about threatened escapes, drug transactions, sexual misconduct, or other security risks. Social workers in military settings may feel caught between the rights of their clients (that is, soldiers) and their duty to disclose compelling information related to military security, safety, or misconduct to superior officers. Social workers retained by employee assistance programs may feel caught between their clients' interests and their duty to disclose, for example, a client's serious drug-related impairment, which poses a threat to other employees who are supervised by the client.

Professional and personal values. Some ethical dilemmas involve conflicts between social workers' personal and professional values. In these instances, social workers find that their own values clash with traditional social work values or the official positions of social work agencies or organizations (Levy, 1976). Examples include social workers who personally oppose abortion but work in settings that support clients' right to choose abortion, social workers who disagree with political endorsements made by social work organizations, and social workers who oppose political or public policy stands taken by social work organizations.

Social workers may also find that their personal values conflict with those of their clients (Hardman, 1975). This can occur when, for example, clients engage in extramarital affairs, cheat on their income taxes, use illegal drugs, or refuse life-saving medication or procedures on religious grounds. In these situations, social workers must carefully examine the nature of their own values and the potential impact of these values on the way they serve clients and help clients struggle with moral issues in their own lives (Goldstein, 1998).

Whistle-blowing. Social workers, like all professionals, occasionally encounter wrongdoing by colleagues. This may involve colleagues engaged in unethical or illegal conduct as, for example, colleagues who are sexually involved with clients, submit fraudulent clinical reports to insurance companies to enhance reimbursement, falsify credentials or qualifications, or use coercive or harmful treatment techniques.

Decisions about whether to report colleagues' misconduct—for example, to professional associations or licensing bodies—can be very difficult. On the one hand, professional colleagues often feel loyal to one another and are reluctant to "blow the whistle" in a way that might end a colleague's career. Such situations can quickly become messy and stressful for the whistle blower, jeopardizing his or her own career. On the other hand, social workers typically feel a strong sense of duty and obligation to the profession and public at large. It is difficult for social workers to stand quietly on the sidelines when they have reason to believe that a colleague's misconduct is causing harm to clients and other parties (Barry, 1986; Bullis, 1995; McCann & Cutler, 1979; Reamer & Siegel, 1992; Westin, 1981). Thus, the major challenge is for social workers to weigh their obligation to clients, the profession, and the public at large against their duty to colleagues who are or may be involved in some kind of wrongdoing.

Managed care. Recent advances in managed care—carefully administered health and human services designed to enhance fiscal responsibility and cost containment—have created a number of ethical issues for social workers. Administrative policies concerning capitation, case rates, utilization review, diagnosis-related groups, and prospective reimbursement have forced social workers to make difficult ethical as well as clinical decisions about clientele served, services provided, and termination of services. Social workers operating under managed care sometimes face ethical choices about serving clients whose insurance benefits have been exhausted; providing inadequate or insufficient services to clients whose problems require more intervention than managed care authorities are willing to authorize; conflicting loyalties to their employers (whose resources may be limited) and clients (whose needs may require substantial resources); limiting their services only to clients who can pay for services out of pocket; exposing clients to privacy and confidentiality risks as a result of sharing information with managed care officials; and exaggerating clients' clinical symptoms, diagnoses, and prognoses to increase the likelihood that managed care officials will authorize services (American Medical Association, 1995; Corcoran & Vandiver, 1996; Davidson & Davidson, 1996; Reamer, 1997c, 1998c; Ross & Croze, 1997; Schamess & Lightburn, 1998; Schreter, Sharfstein, & Schreter, 1994; Strom-Gottfried & Corcoran, 1998). In addition to ethical decisions about individual clients, clinical supervisors and administrators also face challenging ethical decisions about allocating agency and program resources.

When resources are limited under managed care, which programs will be eliminated or cut back? Which clients will be assigned priority? On what conceptual criteria will decisions be based (Caughey & Sabin, 1995; Schamess & Lightburn, 1998)?

ETHICAL DECISION MAKING

Beginning in the mid-1970s, social workers, along with many other groups of professionals, began to develop ambitious conceptual frameworks to help practitioners identify ethical dilemmas and make ethical decisions. These frameworks, which often take the form of decision-making steps or protocols, encourage social workers to draw on a number of resources and tools when faced with ethical dilemmas. Typically, these discussions identify a series of steps and considerations that social workers can follow as they attempt to resolve difficult ethical dilemmas. Their focus must include a daunting range of components: the nature of conflicting values, ethical duties, and obligations; the individuals, groups, and organizations that are likely to be affected; possible courses of action; relevant ethical theories, principles, and guidelines; legal principles and pertinent codes of ethics; social work practice theory and principles; personal, cultural, and ethnic values; the need to consult with colleagues and appropriate experts; and the need to monitor, evaluate, and document decisions (Joseph, 1985; Loewenberg & Dolgoff, 1996; Reamer, 1999).

One of the key features of these decision-making frameworks is the application of standard or classic ethical theory and moral philosophy. Beginning with Socrates, Plato, and Aristotle, moral philosophers have developed various ethical theories, principles, and guidelines concerning matters of right and wrong, moral duty and obligation, social justice, and other key ethical concepts (Hancock, 1974). Briefly, relevant ethical theories focus on what is known as *metaethics* (abstract discussions of the formulation, derivation, justification, and validity of moral theories) and *normative ethics* (the application of existing ethical theories, principles, and guidelines to actual ethical dilemmas). Understandably, practitioners tend to find normative ethics more relevant to their needs than metaethics.

Theories of normative ethics are typically divided into two main schools of thought: *deontological* and *teleological* (Frankena, 1973; Reamer, 1990). Deontological theories (from the Greek *deontos,* "of the obligatory") assert that certain actions are inherently right or wrong, or right or wrong as a matter of fundamental principle. This perspective is most commonly associated with the 18th-century German philosopher Immanuel Kant. From a strictly deontological perspective, for example, social workers should never violate a law, regulation, or agency policy, no matter what the circumstances might be; should always tell the truth, even if telling the truth might be harmful; and should always honor their promises, even if doing so might have detrimental consequences. According to deontology, then, it would be unethical for a social worker to violate a mandatory reporting law concerning child neglect even if the social worker believes that doing so would be in his or her client's best interest (for example, to preserve the therapeutic relationship). Similarly, from this point of view, it would be unethical to lie to a client about his prognosis even if telling the truth might lead the client to engage in self-destructive behavior.

In contrast, according to teleological (from the Greek *teleios,* "brought to its end or purpose") or *consequentialist* theories, ethical decisions should be based on social workers' assessment of which action will produce the most favorable outcome or consequences—an ethical cost/benefit analysis. According to the most prominent teleological school of thought, *utilitarianism,* ethical choices should be based on estimates of what will result in the greatest good for the greatest number (positive utilitarianism) or what will minimize harm (negative utilitarianism). From a utilitarian perspective, for example, it may be justifiable to violate a statute or regulation if one can demonstrate that doing so is likely to produce more good than harm. Similarly, from this point of view, it may be legitimate to deceive clients or withhold information from them if doing so would prevent serious self-harm on their part.

Although there is much debate and constructive disagreement about the merits and limitations of various theories of normative ethics (Gorovitz, 1971; Smart & Williams, 1973), examining ethical dilemmas through these contrasting lenses can help social workers identify, grapple with, and think through all dimensions of the ethical dilemmas they face. In the end, this critical analysis may enhance the quality of the ethical decisions practitioners make. This process is analogous to clinical social workers' assessment of clients' needs and development of treatment plans using different clinical theories and schools of thought (for example, psychodynamic, behavioral, cognitive), recognizing there may never be consensus about which perspective is the most compelling and valid in any given circumstances. Despite such diverging views, the process involved in critically examining clients' needs using different perspectives and ideologies may enhance social workers' interventions.

Contemporary social workers can also draw on the now-substantial literature on social work ethics and, more broadly, applied and professional ethics. Relevant literature on ethical issues in the profession, ethical decision making, ethical standards, and ethical misconduct has burgeoned, especially since the early 1980s, as has professional education on the subject.

In addition, social workers who face ethical choices can access professional ethics consultants or agency-based ethics committees and institutional review boards. Ethics consultation is commonly found in health care settings and is expanding to other settings. Formally educated ethicists in these settings (usually moral philosophers who have experience working with professionals, or professionals who have obtained formal ethics education) provide advice on ethics-related matters. These consultants can help social workers identify key ethical issues, analyze ethical dilemmas, and make difficult ethical choices. They can acquaint social workers with relevant ethics concepts, literature, and other resources (Conrad, 1989; Fletcher, 1986; Fletcher, Quist, & Jonsen, 1989; La Puma & Schiedermayer, 1991; Reamer, 1995b; Skeel & Self, 1989). Social workers may also draw on the ethics expertise of NASW committees on inquiry (the panels that review and adjudicate ethics complaints) and on state licensing boards. Several NASW chapters also provide consultation through an ethics hotline.

Ethics committees, which exist in many health care and human service settings, often include social workers as members. The concept of ethics committees (often called institutional ethics committees or IECs) emerged in 1976, when the New Jersey Supreme Court ruled that

Karen Ann Quinlan's family and physicians should consult an ethics committee in deciding whether to remove her from life-support technology (a number of hospitals have had something like an ethics committee since at least the 1920s). Ethics committees usually include representatives from various disciplines found in health care and human service settings, such as physicians, nurses, allied health professionals, mental health professionals, agency administrators, and clergy.

Most ethics committees spend much of their time providing case consultation and nonbinding advice. Committees are available to agency staff, clients, and perhaps family members for consultation about challenging ethical dilemmas. Relevant issues may include termination of life support, the use of aggressive treatment, informed consent procedures, or release of confidential information (Cohen, 1988; Cranford & Doudera, 1984; Reamer, 1987a; Summers, 1989; Teel, 1975).

Many ethics committees also sponsor in-service or continuing education on ethical issues (for example, training on confidentiality or boundary issues) and critique, revise, or draft ethics-related agency policy. Education may take the form of informal workshops, formal conferences, or what have become known as "ethics grand rounds."

Social workers employed in settings that sponsor research (typically, health care organizations and educational institutions) may be involved in institutional review boards (IRBs). IRBs (sometimes known as human subjects protection committees) became popular in the 1970s as a result of increasing national interest in ethical issues in research and evaluation (Levine, 1991). As a result of strict federal regulations, all organizations and agencies that receive federal funds for research are required to have an IRB review the ethical aspects of proposals for research involving human subjects.

One of the most important tools in ethical decision making is the 1996 *NASW Code of Ethics*. This is only the third code in NASW's history and reflects significant changes over time in social work's approach to ethical issues.

The first code, which went into effect in 1960, included 14 proclamations concerning social workers' ethical obligations (for example, every social worker's duty to give precedence to professional responsibility over personal interests, respect clients' privacy, give appropriate professional service in public emergencies, and contribute knowledge, skills, and support to human welfare programs). The second code, which went into effect in 1979, was far more ambitious. It included six sections of 82 briefly stated principles related to social workers' conduct and comportment and their ethical responsibilities to clients, colleagues, employers and employing organizations, the social work profession, and society. Over time, however, particularly in light of the revolutionary changes taking place in the applied and professional ethics field following the ratification of the 1979 code, NASW leaders recognized that a new code was needed.

The NASW Code of Ethics Revision Committee was appointed in 1994 and spent 2 years drafting a new code. This committee, which I chaired and which included a professional ethicist and social workers from a variety of practice and educational settings, drafted a code that includes four sections and is far more detailed and comprehensive than the prior two codes (Reamer, 1998a). The first section, "Preamble," summarizes social work's mission and core values. For the first time in NASW's history, the association has adopted and published in the code a formally sanctioned mission statement and an explicit summary of the profession's core values. This mission statement and these core values focus on social work's enduring commitment to enhancing human well-being and helping meet basic human needs, empowering clients, serving people who are vulnerable and oppressed, addressing individual well-being in a social context, promoting social justice and social change, and strengthening sensitivity to cultural and ethnic diversity.

The second section, "Purpose of the NASW Code of Ethics," provides an overview of its main functions, including identifying the profession's core values, summarizing broad ethical principles that reflect social work's core values and specific ethical standards for the profession, helping social workers identify ethical issues and dilemmas, providing the public with ethical standards it can use to hold the profession accountable, orienting practitioners new to the field, and articulating standards that the profession itself can use to enforce ethical standards among its members. This section also highlights resources social workers can use when they face ethical issues and decisions.

The third section, "Ethical Principles," presents six broad principles that inform social work practice, one for each of the six core values cited in the code's preamble (service, social justice, dignity and worth of the person, importance of human relationships, integrity, and competence). Brief annotation for each principle is included.

The final and most detailed section, "Ethical Standards," includes 155 specific ethical standards to guide social workers' conduct and provide a basis for adjudication of ethics complaints filed against social workers. The 1996 code addresses a large number of issues that were not mentioned in the 1960 and 1979 codes, including limitations of clients' right to self-determination (e.g., when clients threaten harm to themselves or others), confidentiality issues involving electronic media (such as computers, facsimile machines, cellular telephones), storage and disposal of client records, case recording and documentation, sexual contact with former clients, sexual relationships with clients' relatives and close personal acquaintances, counseling of former sexual partners, physical contact with clients, dual and multiple relationships with supervisees, sexual harassment, use of derogatory language, bartering arrangements with clients, cultural competence, labor-management disputes, and evaluation of practice. The standards are placed into six categories concerning social workers' ethical responsibilities to clients, to colleagues, in practice settings, as professionals, to the profession, and to the broader society.

In general, the code's standards concern three kinds of issues (Reamer, 1994). The first includes mistakes social workers might make that have ethical implications, such as disclosing confidential information in public settings (e.g., restaurants, elevators) or inadvertently omitting important information on an informed consent or release of information form. The second category focuses on circumstances involving difficult ethical decisions, for example, related to ambiguous professional-client boundaries, release of information without client consent to protect third parties, labor-management disputes, social worker impairment, protection of research participants, termination of services, or allocation of scarce resources. The final category concerns issues pertaining to social worker misconduct and unethical behav-

ior, such as sexual indiscretions, financial exploitation of clients, or fraudulent or deceptive business practices.

ETHICS RISK MANAGEMENT

One of the reasons social workers have become more interested in ethical issues is that ethics complaints and lawsuits filed against them for alleged ethical negligence or misconduct have increased (Berliner, 1989; Bernstein, 1981; Houston-Vega, Nuehring, & Daguio, 1997; Kurzman, 1995; Reamer, 1994, 1998a). Members of NASW may have ethics complaints filed against them with NASW for alleged violations of the association's code of ethics. Licensed social workers may have complaints filed against them with their state licensing or regulatory board for alleged ethical infractions. In addition, social workers may have malpractice and negligence lawsuits filed against them in civil court.

Complaints filed against social workers— whether in the form of ethics complaints or lawsuits—typically allege some significant departure from the profession's standards of care. This key legal concept refers to the way an ordinary, reasonable, and prudent professional with similar training would act under the same or similar circumstances (Austin, Moline, & Williams, 1990; Cohen & Mariano, 1982; Gifis, 1991; Hogan, 1979; Madden, 1998; Meyer, Landis, & Hays, 1988; Reamer, 1994; Schutz, 1982). Departures from social work's standards of care may result from a practitioner's active violation of a client's rights (in legal terms, acts of commission, misfeasance, or malfeasance) or a practitioner's failure to perform certain duties (acts of omission or nonfeasance).

Some ethics complaints and lawsuits result from social workers' mistakes and oversights. Examples include social workers who disclose confidential information inadvertently based on an expired release of information form or who "slip" during a marriage counseling session and disclose sensitive confidential information to one party, forgetting that the other did not provide consent for the disclosure; others stem from difficult, deliberate ethical decisions, as, for example, when social workers disclose confidential information without a client's consent to protect a third party from serious harm, or when social workers terminate services being provided to uncooperative or noncompliant clients. In addition, some complaints result from social workers' alleged misconduct or unethical behavior, such as sexual contact with clients or other serious boundary violations.

When legal complaints are brought against social workers, plaintiffs (the parties bringing the lawsuit) must produce evidence to support their charges, including the following:

1. At the time of the alleged negligence, the social worker owed a duty of care to the client (that is, the social worker was providing professional services to the client).
2. The practitioner breached the duty or was derelict in the duty (that is, the social worker failed to perform the duty based on prevailing standards of care).
3. The client suffered some harm or injury (examples include emotional anguish or injury to reputation).
4. The harm or injury was directly and proximately caused by the professional's breach or dereliction of duty (often known as *proximate cause* or *cause in fact*).

For example, if a complainant alleges that a social worker was negligent because he violated the client's boundaries by initiating a sexual relationship, the complainant would need to show that (a) the social worker owed a broad duty of care to the client by virtue of providing her with professional services, (b) the social worker breached that duty by engaging in a sexual relationship with the client, (c) the client was injured, and (d) the injury was the direct and proximate result of the sexual relationship (as opposed to earlier trauma, for instance).

In some cases, prevailing standards of care are relatively easy to establish, through citations of the profession's literature, relevant codes of ethics, or expert testimony. Examples include standards concerning sexual relationships with current clients, fraudulent billing, and clients' right to examine their clinical records. However, in other cases, there is disagreement or confusion about standards of care. Examples include the appropriateness of nonsexual relationships with clients following termination of the professional-client relationship, the limits of clients' right to self-determination and right to engage in self-destructive behavior, termination of services to noncompliant clients, and disclosure of confidential information without a client's consent to protect third parties who have not been verbally threatened by one's client.

Relatively few social workers have received comprehensive education related to ethics risk management, that is, strategies designed to protect clients and, in turn, prevent ethics complaints and lawsuits. In recent years, several authors (Barker & Branson, 1993; Besharov, 1985; Besharov & Besharov, 1987; Dickson, 1995, 1998; Houston-Vega, Nuehring, & Daguio, 1997; Madden, 1998; Reamer, 1994, 1998a) have highlighted key topics related to ethics risk management in social work, including the following:

1. *Confidentiality and privacy:* evaluating ethical risks related to (a) the disclosure of confidential information to protect third parties; (b) compliance with mandatory reporting statutes related to abuse and neglect of children, elderly, and people with disabilities; (c) alcohol and substance abuse treatment; (d) disclosure of confidential information to outside agencies and professionals, such as social service organizations and colleagues, news media, law enforcement officials, insurers, and collection agencies; (e) disclosure of confidential information within organizations; (f) practice with families, couples, and small groups; (g) consultation and supervision; (h) deceased clients and minors; and (i) inadvertent disclosures, for example, verbal disclosures in agency waiting rooms and hallways, elevators, restaurants, on cellular telephones, or answering machines, or visual disclosures resulting from a failure to protect information on social workers' desks, computer screens, and faxed communications

2. *High-risk interventions:* using interventions that are questionable ethically (for example, massage therapy or "body work" during a psychotherapy session, past-life regression techniques) or without adequate training or education

3. *Informed consent:* failing to comply with standard informed consent procedures (for example, failing to explain the content of informed consent forms to clients or to provide them with an opportunity to ask questions about the form, omitting an expiration date, having clients sign a consent form before the blank spaces are filled in, failing to obtain the services of an interpreter when a client does not speak or understand the primary language used in the social service setting)

4. *Defamation of character:* libeling or slandering clients based on untrue written or verbal statements made by a social worker that are injurious to clients

5. *Boundary violations:* violating clients' boundaries based on, for example, inappropriate sexual or social contact, gifts, sharing of meals, self-disclosure, business dealings, religious activities, or barter

6. *Supervision:* failing to provide proper supervision (based on the legal theory of *respondeat superior* or vicarious liability, according to which a supervisor can, in principle, be found liable for the actions or inactions of supervisees, particularly if there is evidence of flawed supervision)

7. *Documentation and recording:* maintaining careful case records to enhance client assessment, case coordination, treatment planning, service delivery, supervision, and accountability (for example, to insurers, utilization review staff, courts)

8. *Consultation:* consulting with qualified colleagues when necessary to meet clients' needs

9. *Referral:* referring clients to qualified colleagues when necessary to meet clients' needs (e.g., when clients are not making sufficient progress in treatment or colleagues' specialized expertise is needed to address clients' problems)

10. *Fraud:* producing accurate billing and documentation

11. *Termination of services:* recognizing ethical risks involved in terminating services to clients in need of assistance, especially in a managed care environment, or in prolonging services beyond what is clinically appropriate (for instance, to generate revenue)

A significant problem reflected in many ethics complaints and lawsuits is social worker impairment (Reamer, 1992a). Impairment occurs when social workers' personal problems, psychosocial distress, substance abuse, or mental health difficulties interfere with their practice effectiveness (Bissell, Fewell, & Jones, 1980; Lamb et al., 1987). For example, many cases where there is evidence of boundary violations involve social workers who are leading troubled lives, in the form of substance abuse, problem-filled marriages, employment problems, or financial pressures. In one published prevalence study that included social workers, Deutsch (1985) found that more than half her sample of social workers, psychologists, and master's-level counselors reported significant problems with depression. About 82% reported problems with relationships, 11% reported substance abuse problems, and 2% reported suicide attempts. Bissell and Haberman (1984) found that in a sample of 50 alcoholic social workers they surveyed, 24% reported overt suicide attempts, a rate higher than that reported by the dentists, attorneys, and physicians in their sample.

Several key studies highlight the significant problem of sexual exploitation of clients by clinicians. Pope (1988) reviewed a series of empirical studies on sexual contact between therapists and clients and concluded that the aggregate average of reported sexual contact is 8.3% by male therapists and 1.7% by female therapists. Pope reported that one study (Gechtman & Bouhoutsos, 1985) found that 3.8% of male social workers admitted to sexual contact with clients.

Social work's first national acknowledgment of the problem of impaired practitioners came in 1979, when the NASW released a public policy statement on alcoholism and alcohol-related problems (NASW Commission on Employment and Economic Support, 1987). A NASW (1987) report, *Impaired Social Worker Program Resource Book,* noted that by 1980, a small nationwide support group for chemically dependent practitioners, Social Workers Helping Social Workers, had formed, although this group struggled to generate significant membership. In 1982, NASW established the Occupational Social Work Task Force, which was charged with developing a strategy to address the problem of impairment, and in 1984, the NASW Delegate Assembly issued a resolution on impairment. The most recent significant profession-wide effort was in 1987, when NASW published the *Impaired Social Worker Program Resource Book,* prepared by the NASW Commission on Employment and Economic Support, to help practitioners design programs for impaired social workers.

Beyond these nascent efforts and attempts by several NASW chapters to address this issue, social workers have paid relatively little attention to the phenomenon of practitioner impairment. Even today, the profession's literature contains few publications on impairment, and the subject receives inconsistent attention in social work education (Jayaratne et al., 1997; Reamer, 1992a). Social workers know relatively little about the prevalence of impaired practitioners or effective strategies for dealing with the problem.

AN AGENDA FOR THE FUTURE

Clearly, ethical issues in direct practice have come of age. Although many ethical issues have been constants in social work since the profession's formal beginning in the late 19th century (for example, a number of issues related to clients' right to self-determination, confidentiality, and boundaries), today's clinical social workers face a variety of ethical dilemmas that were unknown to previous generations of practitioners (for instance, ethical choices involving confidentiality and HIV/AIDS, termination of high-technology life-support systems, and privacy of computer-based records and Internet communications). Moreover, contemporary social workers have produced an enormous fund of knowledge and resources to enhance their ability to identify ethical issues and make ethical decisions when dilemmas arise. Recent advances related to ethical theory, codes of ethics, ethics consultation, agency-based ethics committees and IRBs, and applied and professional ethics literature provide social workers with a remarkable array of conceptual and practical tools.

Although these developments bode well for social workers who encounter ethical issues and dilemmas, the majority of contemporary social workers have received little, if any, systematic education or training related to ethics. Most practicing social workers completed their formal education before the full emergence of the applied and professional ethics field in the 1980s. In addition, the bulk of social work's literature on ethics has been published since the early 1980s. Currently relatively few social work education programs offer in-depth, comprehensive instruction on professional ethics (Black, Hartley, Whelley, & Kirk-Sharp, 1989).

Several steps are needed to ensure that contemporary social workers are equipped to handle the ethical issues and dilemmas they encounter:

1. Both social work education programs and social work settings (such as community mental health centers, family service agencies, health care facilities, prisons, schools, substance abuse treatment programs, programs for senior citizens, and child welfare programs) must offer formal education and in-service training on the subject. In addition, professional associations and groups (such as NASW and its state chapters, the Council on Social Work Education, the American Association of State Social Work Boards, and special interest groups related to group treatment, children's or mental health services, disabilities, and eating disorders) should sponsor continuing education workshops, seminars, and conferences devoted to social work ethics (Reamer & Abramson, 1982).

The content of such education should be wide-ranging. Potential topics include overviews of ethical issues and dilemmas in the profession generally or in specialty areas within it, ethical decision-making frameworks, the relevance of ethical and moral theory to practice, the *NASW Code of Ethics* (and other relevant codes), changes in the profession's ethical standards over time, institutional ethics committees, IRBs, and ethics risk management (relevant malpractice and liability issues, common problems leading to ethics complaints).

2. Social workers need to identify steps they can take in their own work settings to refine their handling of ethical issues. This may include appointing a task force or ethics committee that would be charged with identifying ethical issues in the setting that warrant attention (e.g., critiquing and revising the agency's confidentiality or informed consent policies and procedures, developing procedures for addressing worker impairment) or developing protocols for case consultation when ethical dilemmas arise.

3. Social workers need to be vigilant in their efforts to anticipate new and emerging ethical issues and develop relevant ethical standards to guide practice. Many social workers currently employed in health care settings, for example, face enormously complex ethical issues concerning phenomena that did not exist when they completed their formal education. Developments in medicine, biochemistry, biotechnology, and neuroscience have produced challenging ethical issues related to allocating scarce organs for transplantation, the use of artificial organs, genetic engineering, cloning, the use of psychotropic medication that alters individuals' personalities, legal euthanasia and "mercy killing," and sustaining the lives of extremely low-birthweight babies. Similarly, before the early 1980s, no social worker could have imagined the complex ethical issues that have emerged related to HIV/AIDS (e.g., concerning breaching confidentiality to protect third parties, contact tracing, mandatory testing and screening, end-of-life decisions), the use of the Internet, facsimile machines, and cellular telephones (Allen-Meares & DeRoos, 1997). As these phenomena have appeared, however, social workers have had to wrestle with their ethical implications.

With these as precedents, social workers should be alert to noteworthy developments that may introduce novel ethical dilemmas—for example, new computer-based technology and medical breakthroughs that push the ethics envelope—and do their best to educate themselves and their colleagues about key ethical issues and practical steps they can take to deal with them. For example, increasingly complex issues are likely to arise related to preserving client privacy and confidentiality as enhanced computer and electronic technology facilitates the circulation and sharing of client-based information among human service agencies, individual practitioners, insurance providers, managed care companies, and government agencies. Social workers will need to take aggressive steps to minimize breaches of client privacy and confidentiality. Also, the rapid expansion of managed care as the modus operandi in the social service field will likely result in new ethical challenges concerning the allocation of limited resources (distributive justice), respect for clients' right to self-determination (i.e., their preferences for specific social services), and premature termination of services (client abandonment). Especially in health care settings, new technological developments will probably lead social workers down paths filled with ethical dilemmas concerning the use of novel, aggressive interventions to enhance and sustain life. At present, we can only imagine what unprecedented ethical choices await us.

In a similar vein, social workers need to respond skillfully and earnestly to emerging ethical issues already on the horizon. One prominent example concerns clinical social workers' efforts to determine the nature and extent of their ethical obligation to evaluate their practice empirically—using an impressive panoply of research tools developed in recent years—and base their practice on empirically derived evidence of effectiveness. In the late 1970s and early 1980s, social workers became increasingly interested in monitoring and assessing the implementation and effectiveness of policies, programs, and interventions. By now, there is substantial agreement among social work educators that clinical practitioners should use, whenever feasible, research tools to monitor and evaluate their interventions with individuals, families, couples, and groups (Grinnell,

1997; Reamer, 1998e; Rubin & Babbie, 1997). These include various single-case designs and easy-to-use clinical measures and assessment instruments, client logs, and computer software designed for use in clinical (as opposed to primarily research) settings. Although some social workers were educated at a time when such tools and techniques were not available or well-known and, as a result, may resist their application in practice, it is important for all social workers to recognize that contemporary ethical standards have evolved and now require the active evaluation of practice. As the *NASW Code of Ethics* (1996) states, "Social workers should monitor and evaluate policies, the implementation of programs, and practice interventions" (Standard 5.02[a]).

Furthermore, new ethical standards contained in the *NASW Code of Ethics* (1996) require social workers to base their interventions on documented evidence of effectiveness. When evaluation and research evidence is available, social workers are ethically obligated to use this knowledge to guide their practice (Curtis, 1996; Myers & Thyer, 1997). According to the *NASW Code of Ethics*, "Social workers should base practice on recognized knowledge, *including empirically based knowledge* [italics added], relevant to social work" (Standard 4.01[c]).

Finally, a significant overarching ethical issue for the profession concerns social workers' future choices about the clientele they serve. Especially in recent years, social workers have debated the extent to which practitioners have a moral obligation to serve low-income, disadvantaged, and economically vulnerable clients (Austin, 1997; Billups, 1992; Gil, 1994, 1998; Keith-Lucas, 1992; Popple, 1992; Reamer,

1992b, 1997a; Reid, 1992; Specht & Courtney, 1994). Constraints imposed by managed care and other funding shortages have led some social workers to focus their practice on relatively affluent clients who can afford to pay fees out of pocket, thus bypassing the restrictions of insurers and third-party payers. If practiced widely, this response would lead to the virtual abandonment of social work's historic mission and defining character. Although it is certainly true that social workers must pledge to serve *all* people, including those who are relatively affluent and privileged, they must simultaneously hold to their long-standing, unique commitment to the most vulnerable members of our society. Social workers must be mindful of the assertive and compelling language added to the *NASW Code of Ethics* in 1996:

> The primary mission of the social work profession is to enhance human well-being and help meet the basic human needs of all people, *with particular attention to the needs and empowerment of people who are vulnerable, oppressed, and living in poverty* [italics added]. (p. 1)

Social workers should be proud of the remarkable growth of their collective knowledge related to ethical issues in the profession. Much of this knowledge is recent and demonstrates how rapidly issues can emerge and develop in a profession. At the same time, the stunning expansion of our understanding of ethical issues is sobering. Who knows what complex, controversial, and daunting issues await us in the 21st century? Our principal challenge is to be constantly alert to ethical issues in our midst and keep our antennae extended for signs of novel ethical issues that are not yet within range.

REFERENCES

Abramson, M. (1985). The autonomy-paternalism dilemma in social work practice. *Social Casework, 66,* 387-393.

Airaksinen, T. (1998). Professional ethics. In R. Chadwick (Ed.-in-Chief), *Encyclopedia of applied ethics* (Vol. 3, pp. 671-682). San Diego, CA: Academic Press.

Allen-Meares, P., & DeRoos, Y. (1997). The future of the social work profession. In M. Reisch & E. Gambrill (Eds.), *Social work in the 21st century* (pp. 376-386). Thousand Oaks, CA: Pine Forge Press.

American Medical Association. (1995). Ethical issues in managed care. *Journal of the American Medical Association, 273,* 330-335.

Arnold, S. (1970). Confidential communication and the social worker. *Social Work, 15,* 61-67.

Austin, D. M. (1997). The profession of social work in the second century. In M. Reisch & E. Gambrill (Eds.), *Social work in the 21st century* (pp. 396-407). Thousand Oaks, CA: Pine Forge Press.

Austin, K. M., Moline, M. E., & Williams, G. T. (1990). *Confronting malpractice: Legal and ethical dilemmas in psychotherapy.* Newbury Park, CA: Sage.

Barker, R. L., & Branson, D. M. (1993). *Forensic social work.* New York: Haworth.

Barry, V. (1986). *Moral issues in business* (3rd ed.). Belmont, CA: Wadsworth.

Bartlett, H. M. (1970). *The common base of social work practice.* New York: Columbia University Press.

Berliner, A. K. (1989). Misconduct in social work practice. *Social Work, 34,* 69-72.

Bernstein, B. (1981). Malpractice: Future shock of the 1980s. *Social Casework, 62,* 175-181.

Bernstein, S. (1960). Self-determination: King or citizen in the realm of values. *Social Work, 5,* 3-8.

Besharov, D. S. (1985). *The vulnerable social worker.* Silver Spring, MD: National Association of Social Workers.

Besharov, D. S., & Besharov, S. H. (1987). Teaching about liability. *Social Work, 32,* 517-522.

Biestek, F. P. (1957). *The casework relationship.* Chicago: Loyola University Press.

Biestek, F. P., & Gehrig, C. C. (1978). *Client self-determination in social work: A fifty-year history.* Chicago: Loyola University Press.

Billups, J. O. (1992). The moral basis for a radical reconstruction of social work. In P. N. Reid & P. R. Popple (Eds.), *The moral purposes of social work* (pp. 100-119). Chicago: Nelson-Hall.

Bissell, L., Fewell, L., & Jones, R. (1980). The alcoholic social worker: A survey. *Social Work in Health Care, 5,* 421-432.

Bissell, L., & Haberman, P. W. (1984). *Alcoholism in the professions.* New York: Oxford University Press.

Black, P. N., Hartley, E. K., Whelley, J., & Kirk-Sharp, C. (1989). Ethics curricula: A national survey of graduate schools of social work. *Social Thought, 15,* 141-148.

Brieland, D. (1995). Social work practice: History and evolution. In R. L. Edwards (Ed.-in-Chief), *Encyclopedia of social work* (19th ed., Vol. 3, pp. 2247-2258). Washington, DC: NASW Press.

Buchanan, A. (1978). Medical paternalism. *Philosophy and Public Affairs, 7,* 370-390.

Bullis, R. K. (1995). *Clinical social worker misconduct.* Chicago: Nelson-Hall.

Callahan, D., & Bok, S. (Eds.). (1980). *Ethics teaching in higher education.* New York: Plenum.

Carter, R. (1977). Justifying paternalism. *Canadian Journal of Philosophy, 7,* 133-145.

Caughey, A., & Sabin, J. (1995). Managed care. In D. Calkins, R. J. Fernandopulle, & B. S. Marino (Eds.), *Health care policy* (pp. 88-101). Cambridge, MA: Blackwell Science.

Cohen, C. B. (1988). Ethics committees. *Hastings Center Report, 18,* 11.

Cohen, R. J., & Mariano, W. E. (1982). *Legal guidebook in mental health.* New York: Free Press.

Conrad, A. P. (1989). Developing an ethics review process in a social service agency. *Social Thought, 15,* 102-115.

Corcoran, K., & Vandiver, V. (1996). *Maneuvering the maze of managed care: Skills for mental health practitioners.* New York: Free Press.

Costin, L. B. (1964). Values in social work education: A study. *Social Service Review, 38,* 271-280.

Cranford, R. E., & Doudera, E. (Eds.). (1984). *Institutional ethics committees and health care decision making.* Ann Arbor, MI: Health Administration Press.

Curtis, G. C. (1996). The scientific evaluation of new claims. *Research on Social Work Practice, 6,* 117-121.

Davidson, J. R., & Davidson, T. (1996). Confidentiality and managed care: Ethical and legal concerns. *Health & Social Work, 21,* 208-215.

Deutsch, C. (1985). A survey of therapists' personal problems and treatment. *Professional Psychology: Research and Practice, 16,* 305-315.

Dickson, D. T. (1995). *Law in the health and human services.* New York: Free Press.

Dickson, D. T. (1998). *Confidentiality and privacy in social work.* New York: Free Press.

Dworkin, G. (1971). Paternalism. In R. Wasserstrom (Ed.), *Morality and the law* (pp. 107-126). Belmont, CA: Wadsworth.

Elliott, L. J. (1931). *Social work ethics.* New York: American Association of Social Workers.

Emmet, D. (1962). Ethics and the social worker. *British Journal of Psychiatric Social Work, 6,* 165-172.

Fletcher, J. (1986). The goals of ethics consultation. *Biolaw, 2,* 36-47.

Fletcher, J. C., Quist, N., & Jonsen, A. R. (1989). *Ethics consultation in health care.* Ann Arbor, MI: Health Administration Press.

Frankel, C. (1959). Social philosophy and the professional education of social workers. *Social Service Review, 33,* 345-359.

Frankena, W. K. (1973). *Ethics* (2nd ed.). Englewood Cliffs, NJ: Prentice Hall.

Gechtman, L., & Bouhoutsos, J. (1985). *Sexual intimacy between social workers and clients.* Paper presented at the meeting of the Society for Clinical Social Workers, University City, CA.

Gifis, S. H. (1991). *Law dictionary* (3rd ed.). Hauppauge, NY: Barron's.

Gil, D. G. (1994). Confronting social injustice and oppression. In F. G. Reamer (Ed.), *The foundations of social work knowledge* (pp. 231-263). New York: Columbia University Press.

Gil, D. G. (1998). *Confronting injustice and oppression: Concepts and strategies for social workers.* New York: Columbia University Press.

Goldstein, H. (1998). Education for ethical dilemmas in social work practice. *Families in Society, 79,* 241-253.

Gordon, W. E. (1962). A critique of the working definition. *Social Work, 7*(6), 3-13.

Gordon, W. E. (1965). Knowledge and value: Their distinction and relationship in clarifying social work practice. *Social Work, 10,* 32-39.

Gorovitz, S. (Ed.). (1971). *Mill: Utilitarianism.* Indianapolis, IN: Bobbs-Merrill.

Grinnell, R. M., Jr. (Ed.). (1997). *Social work research and evaluation* (5th ed.). Itasca, IL: F. E. Peacock.

Hall, L. K. (1952). Group workers and professional ethics. *The Group, 15,* 3-8.

Hamilton, G. (1940). *Theory and practice of social casework.* New York: Columbia University Press.

Hamilton, G. (1951). *Social casework* (2nd ed.). New York: Columbia University Press.

Hancock, R. N. (1974). *Twentieth-century ethics.* New York: Columbia University Press.

Hardman, D. G. (1975). Not with my daughter you don't! *Social Work, 20,* 278-285.

Hogan, D. B. (1979). *The regulation of psychotherapists: Vol. 1. A study in the philosophy and practice of professional regulation.* Cambridge, MA: Ballinger.

Houston-Vega, M. K., Nuehring, E. M., & Daguio, E. R. (1997). *Prudent practice: A guide for managing malpractice risk.* Washington, DC: NASW Press.

Jayaratne, S., Croxton, T., & Mattison, D. (1997). Social work professional standards: An exploratory study. *Social Work, 42,* 187-198.

Johnson, A. (1955). Educating professional social workers for ethical practice. *Social Service Review, 29,* 125-136.

Joseph, M. V. (1985). A model for ethical decision making in clinical practice. In C. B. Germain (Ed.), *Advances in clinical practice* (pp. 207-217). Silver Spring, MD: National Association of Social Workers.

Joseph, M. V. (1989). Social work ethics: Historical and contemporary perspectives. *Social Thought, 15,* 4-17.

Kagle, J. D., & Giebelhausen, P. N. (1994). Dual relationships and professional boundaries. *Social Work, 39,* 213-220.

Keith-Lucas, A. (1963). A critique of the principle of client self-determination. *Social Work, 8,* 66-71.

Keith-Lucas, A. (1977). Ethics in social work. In J. B. Turner (Ed.-in-Chief), *Encyclopedia of social work* (17th ed., Vol. 1, pp. 350-355). Silver Spring, MD: National Association of Social Workers.

Keith-Lucas, A. (1992). A socially sanctioned profession? In P. N. Reid & P. R. Popple (Eds.), *The moral purposes of social work* (pp. 51-70). Chicago: Nelson-Hall.

Kopels, S., & Kagle, J. D. (1993). Do social workers have a duty to warn? *Social Service Review, 67,* 101-126.

Kurzman, P. A. (1995). Professional liability and malpractice. In R. L. Edwards (Ed.-in-Chief), *Encyclopedia of social work* (19th ed., Vol. 3, pp. 1921-1927). Washington, DC: NASW Press.

Lamb, D. H., Presser, N. R., Pfost, K. S., Baum, M. C., Jackson, V. R., & Jarvis, P. A. (1987). Confronting professional impairment during the internship: Identification, due process, and remediation. *Professional Psychology: Research and Practice, 18,* 597-603.

La Puma, J., & Schiedermayer, D. L. (1991). Ethics consultation: Skills, roles, and training. *Annals of Internal Medicine, 114,* 155-160.

Lee, P. R. (1930). Cause and function. In *National Conference on Social Work proceedings: 1929* (pp. 3-20). Chicago: University of Chicago Press.

Leiby, J. (1978). *A history of social work and social welfare in the United States.* New York: Columbia University Press.

Levine, C. (1991). AIDS and the ethics of human subjects research. In F. G. Reamer (Ed.), *AIDS and ethics* (pp. 77-104). New York: Columbia University Press.

Levy, C. S. (1972). The context of social work ethics. *Social Work, 17,* 95-101.

Levy, C. S. (1973). The value base of social work. *Journal of Education for Social Work, 9,* 34-42.

Levy, C. S. (1976). *Social work ethics.* New York: Human Sciences Press.

Lewis, H. (1972). Morality and the politics of practice. *Social Casework, 53,* 404-417.

Loewenberg, F., & Dolgoff, R. (1982). *Ethical decisions for social work practice.* Itasca, IL: F. E. Peacock.

Loewenberg, F., & Dolgoff, R. (1996). *Ethical decisions for social work practice* (5th ed.). Itasca, IL: F. E. Peacock.

Lubove, R. (1965). *The professional altruist: The emergence of social work as a career.* Cambridge, MA: Harvard University Press.

Madden, R. G. (1998). *Legal issues in social work, counseling, and mental health.* Thousand Oaks, CA: Sage.

McCann, C. W., & Cutler, J. P. (1979). Ethics and the alleged unethical. *Social Work, 24,* 5-8.

McCleod, D., & Meyer, H. (1967). A study of values of social workers. In E. Thomas (Ed.), *Behavioral science for social workers* (pp. 401-416). New York: Free Press.

McDermott, F. E. (1975). Against the persuasive definition of "self-determination." In F. E. McDermott (Ed.), *Self-determination in social work* (pp. 118-137). London: Routledge & Kegan Paul.

McGowan, B. G. (1995). Values and ethics. In C. H. Meyer and M. A. Mattaini (Eds.), *The foundations of social work practice* (pp. 28-41). Washington, DC: NASW Press.

Meyer, R. G., Landis, E. R., & Hays, J. R. (1988). *Law for the psychotherapist.* New York: Norton.

Myers, L., & Thyer, B. A. (1997). Should social work clients have the right to effective treatment? *Social Work, 42,* 288-298.

National Association of Social Workers. (1960). *NASW code of ethics.* Washington, DC: Author.

National Association of Social Workers. (1979). *NASW code of ethics.* Silver Spring, MD: Author.

National Association of Social Workers. (1996). *NASW code of ethics.* Washington, DC: Author.

National Association of Social Workers, Commission on Employment and Economic Support. (1987). *Impaired social worker program resource book.* Silver Spring, MD: National Association of Social Workers.

Paine, R. T., Jr. (1880). The work of volunteer visitors of the associated charities among the poor. *Journal of Social Science, 12,* 113.

Perlman, H. H. (1965). Self-determination: Reality or illusion? *Social Service Review, 39,* 410-421.

Perlman, H. H. (1976). Believing and doing: Values in social work education. *Social Casework, 57,* 381-390.

Plant, R. (1970). *Social and moral theory in casework.* London: Routledge & Kegan Paul.

Pope, K. S. (1988). How clients are harmed by sexual contact with mental health professionals: The syndrome and its prevalence. *Journal of Counseling and Development, 67,* 222-226.

Popple, P. R. (1992). Social work: Social function and moral purpose. In P. N. Reid & P. R. Popple (Eds.), *The moral purposes of social work* (pp. 141-154). Chicago: Nelson-Hall.

Pumphrey, M. W. (1959). *The teaching of values and ethics in social work* (Vol. 13). New York: Council on Social Work Education.

Reamer, F. G. (1982). *Ethical dilemmas in social service.* New York: Columbia University Press.

Reamer, F. G. (1983). The concept of paternalism in social work. *Social Service Review, 57,* 254-271.

Reamer, F. G. (1987a). Informed consent in social work. *Social Work, 32,* 425-429.

Reamer, F. G. (1987b). Values and ethics. In A. Minahan (Ed.-in-Chief), *Encyclopedia of social work* (18th ed., Vol. 2, pp. 801-809). Silver Spring, MD: National Association of Social Workers.

Reamer, F. G. (1990). *Ethical dilemmas in social service* (2nd ed.). New York: Columbia University Press.

Reamer, F. G. (1992a). The impaired social worker. *Social Work, 37,* 165-170.

Reamer, F. G. (1992b). Social work and the public good: Calling or career? In P. N. Reid & P. R. Popple (Eds.), *The moral purposes of social work* (pp. 11-33). Chicago: Nelson-Hall.

Reamer, F. G. (1994). *Social work malpractice and liability: Strategies for prevention.* New York: Columbia University Press.

Reamer, F. G. (1995a). Ethics and values. In R. L. Edwards (Ed.-in-Chief), *Encyclopedia of social work* (19th ed., Vol. 1, pp. 893-902). Washington, DC: NASW Press.

Reamer, F. G. (1995b). Ethics consultation in social work. *Social Thought, 18,* 3-16.

Reamer, F. G. (1995c). *Social work values and ethics.* New York: Columbia University Press.

Reamer, F. G. (1997a). Ethical issues for social work practice. In M. Reisch & E. Gambrill (Eds.), *Social work in the 21st century* (pp. 340-349). Thousand Oaks, CA: Pine Forge Press.

Reamer, F. G. (1997b). Ethical standards in social work: The NASW Code of Ethics. In R. L. Edwards (Ed.-in-Chief), *Encylopedia of social work* (19th ed., Suppl., pp. 113-123). Washington, DC: NASW Press.

Reamer, F. G. (1997c). Managing ethics under managed care. *Families in Society, 78,* 96-101.

Reamer, F. G. (1998a). *Ethical standards in social work: A critical review of the NASW Code of Ethics.* Washington, DC: NASW Press.

Reamer, F. G. (1998b). The evolution of social work ethics. *Social Work, 43,* 488-500.

Reamer, F. G. (1998c). Managed care: Ethical considerations. In G. Schamess & A. Lightburn (Eds.), *Humane managed care?* Washington, DC: NASW Press.

Reamer, F. G. (1998d). Social work. In R. Chadwick (Ed.-in-Chief), *Encyclopedia of applied ethics* (Vol. 4, pp. 169-180). San Diego, CA: Academic Press.

Reamer, F. G. (1998e). *Social work research and evaluation skills: A case-based, user-friendly approach.* New York: Columbia University Press.

Reamer, F. G. (1999). *Social work values and ethics* (2nd ed.). New York: Columbia University Press.

Reamer, F. G., & Abramson, M. (1982). *The teaching of social work ethics.* Hastings-on-Hudson, NY: Hastings Center.

Reamer, F. G., & Siegel, D. H. (1992). Should social workers blow the whistle on incompetent colleagues? In E. Gambrill & R. Pruger (Eds.), *Controversial issues in social work* (pp. 66-78). Boston: Allyn & Bacon.

Reid, P. N. (1992). The social function and social morality of social work: A utilitarian perspective. In P. N. Reid & P. R. Popple (Eds.), *The moral purposes of social work* (pp. 34-50). Chicago: Nelson-Hall.

Reid, P. N., & Popple, P. (Eds.). (1992). *The moral purposes of social work.* Chicago: Nelson-Hall.

Reynolds, M. M. (1976). Threats to confidentiality. *Social Work, 21,* 108-113.

Rhodes, M. (1986). *Ethical dilemmas in social work practice.* London: Routledge & Kegan Paul.

Ross, E. C., & Croze, C. (1997). Mental health service delivery in the age of managed care. In T. R. Watkins & J. W. Callicutt (Eds.), *Mental health policy and practice today* (pp. 346-361). Thousand Oaks, CA: Sage.

Rubin, A., & Babbie, E. (Eds.). (1997). *Research methods for social work* (3rd ed.). Pacific Grove, CA: Brooks/Cole.

Schamess, G., & Lightburn, A. (Eds.). (1998). *Humane managed care?* Washington, DC: NASW Press.

Schreter, R. K., Sharfstein, S. S., & Schreter, C. A. (Eds.). (1994). *Allies and adversaries: The impact of managed care on mental health services.* Washington, DC: American Psychiatric Press.

Schutz, B. M. (1982). *Legal liability in psychotherapy.* San Francisco: Jossey-Bass.

Siporin, M. (1992). Strengthening the moral mission of social work. In P. N. Reid & P. R. Popple (Eds.), *The moral purposes of social work* (pp. 71-99). Chicago: Nelson-Hall.

Skeel, J. D., & Self, D. J. (1989). An analysis of ethics consultation in the clinical setting. *Theoretical Medicine, 10,* 289-299.

Smart, J. J. C., & Williams, B. (1973). *Utilitarianism: For and against.* Cambridge, UK: Cambridge University Press.

Specht, H., & Courtney, M. (1994). *Unfaithful angels: How social work has abandoned its mission.* New York: Free Press.

Stalley, R. F. (1975). Determinism and the principle of client self-determination. In F. E. McDermott (Ed.), *Self-determination in social work* (pp. 93-117). London: Routledge & Kegan Paul.

Strom-Gottfried, K., & Corcoran, K. (1998). Confronting ethical dilemmas in managed care: Guidelines for students and faculty. *Journal of Social Work Education, 34,* 109-119.

Summers, A. B. (1989). The meaning of informed consent in social work. *Social Thought, 15,* 128-140.

Tarasoff v. Board of Regents of the University of California, 33 Cal. 3d 275 (1973), 529 P. 2d 553 (1974), 17 Cal. 3d 425 (1976), 551 P.2d 334 (1976), 131 Cal. Rptr. 14 (1976).

Teel, K. (1975). The physician's dilemma: A doctor's view: What the law should be. *Baylor Law Review, 27,* 6-9.

Teicher, M. (1967). *Values in social work: A re-examination.* New York: National Association of Social Workers.

Timms, N. (1983). *Social work values: An enquiry.* London: Routledge & Kegan Paul.

Towle, C. (1965). *Common human needs.* Washington, DC: National Association of Social Workers.

VandeCreek, L., Knapp, S., & Herzog, C. (1988). Privileged communication for social workers. *Social Casework, 69,* 28-34.

Varley, B. K. (1968). Social work values: Changes in value commitments from admission to MSW graduation. *Journal of Education for Social Work, 4,* 67-85.

Vigilante, J. (1974). Between values and science. *Journal of Education for Social Work, 10,* 107-115.

Westin, A. (Ed.). (1981). *Whistle blowing? Loyalty and dissent in the corporation.* New York: McGraw-Hill.

Whittington, C. (1975). Self-determination re-examined. In F. E. McDermott (Ed.), *Self-determination in social work* (pp. 81-92). London: Routledge & Kegan Paul.

Wilson, S. J. (1978). *Confidentiality in social work.* New York: Free Press.

Winkler, E. R. (1998). Applied ethics: Overview. In R. Chadwick (Ed.-in-Chief), *Encyclopedia of applied ethics* (Vol. 1, pp. 191-196). San Diego, CA: Academic Press.

Working definition of social work practice. (1958). *Social Work, 3*(2), 5-8.

Younghusband, E. (1967). *Social work and social values.* London: Allen & Unwin.

CHAPTER TWENTY-NINE

Supervision Standards of Practice in an Era of Societal Restructuring

CARLTON E. MUNSON

Social work practice has experienced a major transformation in the last decade, with significant implications for supervision practice. This chapter covers a historical review, highlighting social work practice and supervision trends. The topics affecting social work supervision include national and international economic restructuring, governmental changes, technology, and social work's unique historical contributions. Supervision practice is reviewed by focusing on diagnosis and assessment, intervention, ethics, stress, risk management, and recommendations for supervisors and the profession. These topics are covered from the per-

spective of the supervisor's role in promoting effective practice.

SOCIAL WORK'S UNIQUE CONTRIBUTION

In the social work profession, the recent increased restructuring of practice, which exceeds natural evolutionary change, has been connected to the growth of managed cost organizations (MCOs).[1] Social workers should always be looking for more effective and efficient ways to intervene, but the managed cost-efficiency movement has produced a shift from process to procedure that is fragmented. Schools of social work are continuing to teach a process and relationship model of intervention, whereas the MCO approach sanctions only mechanistic, task-oriented, linear models. As a result, social work graduates are entering a practice world for which they have not been trained, and this requires supervisors to aid practitioners in integrating the two conceptions.

Social work has made many contributions historically within the constellation of the primary helping professions, but four contributions stand out: (a) social reform; (b) focus on client advocacy; (c) a short-term, cost-effective model of intervention; and (d) an effective model of supervision.

Social work's strong emphasis on social reform was short-lived and peaked in the 1920s (Lundblad, 1995; Reeser & Epstein, 1990). Such efforts have been declining since the 1920s, with a few brief periods of increased activity. Social reform is no longer a part of individual practice or professional organizational emphasis (Specht & Courtney, 1994). This decline has coincided with the loss of concern for client advocacy and paralleled the development of the managed cost model in social work (Munson, 1998a). As MCOs target vulnerable groups for exclusion from participation to cut costs, client advocacy on a large scale becomes more and more necessary. It remains to be determined whether the social work profession will play a significant role in the new advocacy movement.

Lerner (1986) argues that powerlessness corrupts people, and professionals are not exempt from such corruption. Professional powerlessness has been manifested through the belief that clients will become dissatisfied with the MCO

system and demand changes. This has not occurred. When surveyed about health care priorities, people rank mental health care eighth. People are more concerned about catastrophic health coverage, long-term care, disability, prescription drugs, routine medical treatment, eye care, and dental care ("Professional Notes," 1996), and they show no inclination to organize against the MCO movement. This professional belief is a significant indicator of the degree to which the social work profession has pulled back from its historic advocacy role.

Social work evolved the short-term intervention model that is the hallmark of MCOs (Munson, 1998b). This can be traced from the works of Richmond (1917) to Perlman's (1957) problem-solving approach, to Reid and Epstein's (1972) task-centered model. The MCOs have added to this process the use of economic incentives to shorten intervention. This is illustrated by MCO's use of *case rates* to decrease the length of intervention by paying standard rates for a predetermined course of intervention (Pollock, 1998). The MCOs have carved out from the process the integration of individual intervention, advocacy, and social reform that social work had neatly and effectively integrated through its harmonious process of intervention and supervision, which was the hallmark of the social work profession. Supervision was the glue that held together these three functions. Before Mary Richmond, advocacy and social reform were the primary functions of social workers (Munson, 1993a). Richmond epitomized the shift to individual casework. However, she believed that reform, advocacy, and micro intervention could be integrated if supervisors gathered data from supervisees, generating statistics that would be supplied to social reformers to influence philanthropists and legislators to meet social needs and promote prevention (Munson, 1993a). Ironically, this is the integrative model that MCOs emphasize, but they make little effort to implement it. If social work could develop a model of supervision based on Richmond's earlier conception, it could play a key role in forging a new model of intervention. The dismantling of the social work historic model by MCOs was accomplished without any vocal defense of the model from the profession.

RESTRUCTURING EFFECTS ON SUPERVISION

The role of supervision has changed as the restructuring of service delivery has evolved. Historically, supervision was an autonomy issue in the social work profession. The decreased emphasis on supervision of practice paralleled the social work profession's quest for professionalization through autonomous practice. Supervision was replaced by multiple-choice examinations as the means of establishing competence. The monitoring function of supervision has been downgraded. Supervision is not required, because the MCO model of accountability has no need for this function; MCO managers view it as not cost-effective. The face-to-face, individual, and group supervision provided by a seasoned social worker has been replaced with telephone and written contact with MCO case managers, who often have no social work background. In this environment, practitioners not only lose control of the intervention process, but they also lose control of access to the people who make decisions regarding access to care,

outcomes of intervention, and duration of intervention.

In the last three decades, there has been a dramatic increase of theory and knowledge about human functioning. An enormous amount has been learned about the origin and nature of all forms of illness. The diagnosis and treatment of mental disorders have been refined. The medications to alleviate mental distress have improved and increased. Mental health and public assistance services have expanded dramatically since the 1970s. Licensing and certification of workers in the helping professions have been refined and expanded. Administrative supports for practitioners have grown, especially in the area of computer technology (Munson, 1988). These significant changes have been accompanied and partially offset by the emergence of the industry commonly referred to as *managed care* or *behavioral health organizations*. These businesses have become the chief administrators of mental health services in the United States and are beginning to have an impact on the delivery of public and private social services.

A number of books (Ackley, 1997; Alperin & Phillips, 1997; Aronson, 1996; Browning & Browning, 1996; Feldman & Fitzpatrick, 1992; Goodman, Brown, & Deitz, 1992) have been published in the last decade to assist professionals in how to "adjust" to the mandates of MCOs, but there has been limited literature regarding the role of supervision in the transformed MCO practice environments.

We live in a world that constantly threatens our individual autonomy. In our personal lives, we are threatened by big government, which is resented and seems impervious to change. At the same time, a new business philosophy and strategy of increasing profits through downsizing, reorganizing, and merging dominates

MCOs and further limits autonomy. People are increasingly at the mercy of the media and computers, even though we are presented with the illusion of "more options."

Lasch (1979) has historically argued, and Sullivan (1995) currently illustrates, that loss of control is the result of a complex mix of modern economic conditions, shifting family interaction and structures, and individual cognitive responses. The changes and resulting loss of autonomy have been in progress for the last three decades, in part related to a long-term, slow decline in economic growth (Madrick, 1995). The changes are not due to the effects of short-term policies of political administrations, as individual professionals and professional organizations tend to believe. The professional focus on the short-term political aspects and not on the long-term economic aspects of this change has caused professional groups to ignore and not challenge the changes that are having significant impact on professionals and their relationships with clients.

The economic restructuring has produced a revolution in information technology and communication methods that has affected the private, employment, and social spheres of all power relationships and is redefining the rules of social life and the concepts of freedom and justice (Altheide, 1995). The advances in technology have accelerated change. Large-scale computers and small personal computers have made it possible to manage, control, manipulate, and predict in ways that present new challenges for the social work profession. Computers and other technologies have led large corporations to eliminate jobs and centralize functions, increasing profits at the expense of employee and consumer satisfaction. Technology has produced an acceleration and stream-

lining of activity that increases stress for employees and consumers. For example, studies have shown that increasingly, administrative monitoring units and those who pay for services have more sophisticated technology available to accomplish tasks than supervisors or practitioners, resulting in imbalances in information management systems that can be frustrating for and even harmful to supervisors, practitioners, and clients.

There is evidence that technology will give rise to future models of supervision and practice that will involve less human contact. Supervision will be conducted through video, telephone, and Internet connections. These changes will produce unique communication advantages and problems for supervision practice (Munson, 1997).

RESTRUCTURING AND SERVICES

The loss of individual control is taking place in professional life (Sullivan, 1995). As government and private industry restructure to cut costs, social work practitioners and their clients are faced with loss of autonomy. Health care and mental health care delivery systems have been the first segments of the social welfare delivery system to be affected by the large-scale societal loss of autonomy. The management, cost, and delivery of social welfare services have become chaotic, but people perceive themselves as being unable to promote more rational functioning of the system in spite of a general belief that the system is in crisis (Goodman et al., 1992).

The restructuring in the social service and social work sectors is taking the form of privatizing and/or contracting services to MCOs

(Feldman & Fitzpatrick, 1992). There is a high degree of professional dissatisfaction with the restructuring ("Managed Care Notes," 1995; "Special Report," 1995) because there are no reliable indications that privatization cuts costs, but there is compelling evidence that it results in inadequate services for clients and hardship for professionals who work in the privatized environment (Motenko et al., 1995; Munson, 1993b, 1996a).

Restructuring and technology are producing larger, consolidated organizations. Corporate mergers and agency consolidations are producing larger bureaucracies (Schamess, 1998) as the globalization of economies increases, and international alliances increase competition. All human service delivery systems are national systems and are not connected to global economic disasters, recoveries, or reforms that blur national boundaries and cause rapid fluctuations in national markets. Economic consolidation and globalization are relevant to human service delivery systems in the United States because the dominance of MCOs mandates the people participate in the labor market to be eligible for services. The mergers of hospitals, long-term care facilities, managed cost companies, and large group practices of psychotherapy are a result of globalization and increased economic competition. These large entities can purportedly result in cost-efficiency, but any concomitant efficiency of social functioning in these quasi-monopoly environments remains in question. Although large organizations try to assure the public of their "entrepreneurial compassion" in dealing with consumers, clients, employees, and contractors (including human service professionals), when financial strains occur, profit becomes the ultimate criterion for action and change. In this climate, social work clients, practitioners, and supervisors are not provided supportive resources.

GOVERNMENT ROLE

The role of government has changed from one of advocate, protector, and guardian of freedom, justice, and fairness to that of self-protective entity (Day, 1997). Since the 1930s, social workers in the United States increasingly have been employed by various levels of government as participants in the government mission to protect the general welfare. This trend is reversing, and government-based social work practice is being transferred to the private sector. Social work is practiced in large private practice groups based on contractual relationships (Gibelman, 1995). The majority of government-employed social workers have practiced at the state and local level (Donahue, 1989). Handy (1995, 1996) has predicted that professionals in the future will be a "portfolio class" of independent contractors who will work for multiple organizations. This is a return to the model of social work practice of 100 years ago (Munson, 1996b).

Governments avoid the citizenry through privatization of services. This highlights the need for a return to advocacy. Research has shown that privatization of government services does not increase effectiveness and efficiency, can be detrimental to clients and staff, increases costs, and does not improve functioning (Munson, 1993b; Nicholson, Young, Simon, Bateman, & Fisher, 1996; Warres, Soderstrom, Marcus, Berman, & Liebman, 1996).

The combined rise of technology and privatization has transformed many social work services from a humanitarian commitment to a private industry. Some argue that mental health services have always been an industry, but this has not been the situation historically, especially in social work. The heritage in social work has been that work in mental health, like other social work practice areas, has been based on a calling, not manufacturing of product units motivated by profit. Officials of MCOs refer to services they provide as "product lines" and refer to clients as "bodies or lives covered." Social work supervisors have to confront this market orientation to services, which challenges the social commitment aspect of our professionalism, and must assist practitioners in reconciling these divergent approaches in an ethical and principled manner.

ROLE OF TECHNOLOGY

Technology components that practitioners and supervisors must contend with are the machines used to support and supplement practice. Computers are being used to generate social assessments and diagnostic reports. Telephone answering machines, pagers, and word processors are used for accounting and record keeping. The use of audio and video machines to record sessions for subsequent use in treatment and supervision is becoming more common. In some settings, videotaping is considered a valuable intervention agent; however, the guidelines for the use of such machines are limited. Employed properly, videotaping can enhance intervention, but improper applications can produce desultory intrusions into treatment (Munson, 1993a).

All of these technologies have implications for "high-tech/high-touch" (Naisbitt, 1982) issues in which increasingly, the client is not able to engage directly with the practitioner. Face-to-face contact with the client in a trusting relationship has been the hallmark of social work practice. As alternative models of intervention emerge, social work supervisors and practitioners will be required to use unfamiliar methods of intervention that limit contact or are based on no contact. The use of Internet counseling is an example of no-direct-contact intervention. Internet counseling raises licensing and supervision issues because Internet activity has no geographic boundaries. No studies have been done regarding the effects of these devices on the functioning of practitioners. There is no information about voluntariness in using such technologies. There have been no studies as to whether these instruments actually increase response time or effectiveness of practitioners. Supervisors need to be more cognizant of the effects of working with such devices and how practitioners can apply them most effectively. Increased use of machines for communication will most likely lead to models of supervision and practice that do not include direct contact with the client or supervisor (Handy, 1995).

Advances in technology necessitate greater emphasis on ethics in supervisory practice. Increased reliance on machines brings practitioners into closer contact with machine operators, designers, and analysts who have the "machine mentality," and practitioners may see their own values compromised in such interactions. This is the case in large agencies and medical settings, where machines are being used on a grand scale. Technology has increased electronic transmission of sensitive client information over telephone lines and the long-term archiving of information in computer storage devices. This offers new challenges to the practitioner related to confidentiality and privileged information. Practitioners are losing control of information generated about clients, and practitioners often fail to adequately inform clients about the use of confidential information by agencies and MCOs. It is a primary responsibility to be alert to threats to client confidentiality and to call breaches to the attention of higher-level administrators in organizations.

SUPERVISION PRACTICE

Supervisors must work to promote in practitioners the qualities of effective and ethical professionalism. Sullivan (1995) has reaffirmed the time-honored necessary components for professional status as specialized training, based on codified knowledge used to live out a commitment to public service that is carried out with a certain degree of autonomy as perceived and accepted by the public. These principles should be the core of supervisory practice. The historical psychoanalytic models (Caligor, Bromberg, & Meltzer, 1984; Jacobs, David, & Meyer, 1995; Lane, 1990), psychodynamic models (Alonso, 1985; Rock, 1997), role theory models (Kadushin, 1992), task-centered models (Mead, 1990), developmental models (Stoltenberg, McNeil, & Delworth, 1998), and interactional theory models (Munson, 1993a; Shulman, 1993) of supervision are being replaced by specific intervention areas with specific standards for practice and standards for supervision. The areas of standards are (a) diagnosis and assessment, (b) intervention and measurement, (c) task and relationship, (d) professional language, (e) scientific orientation, (f) populations served and advocacy, (g) culturally sensitive practice, (h) prevention, (i) risk management,

(j) stress reactions, and (k) ethics. Each of these areas will be reviewed below.

Diagnosis and Assessment

Diagnosis and assessment are critical to the new standards of practice. Direct practice social workers will need to develop standardized assessment for the client groups that are served, and the intervention plans used must be directly connected to an extension of the diagnosis and the assessment.

Supervisors need to be highly qualified in diagnosis and assessment and prepared to assist practitioners in developing good diagnostic assessment skills. Supervisors need to be skilled in the use of the *Diagnostic and Statistical Manual of Mental Disorders* (DSM-IV) classification system of the American Psychiatric Association (1994) and the person-in-environment system developed by the National Association of Social Workers (Karls & Wandrei, 1994). Standardized assessment screening instruments will be necessary in all assessments, and standardized measures of mood, anxiety, and various other mental disorders will be necessary for diagnosis and justification of interventions. Strategies for rapid assessment and diagnosis are becoming the hallmark of effective and efficient evaluation. Models for rapid assessment are emerging (Olin & Keatinge, 1998), and standardized formats are being adopted. Social workers historically have not developed specific intake measures and client-screening procedures beyond global categories of assessment. Supervisors need to develop standardized measures for the initial database to replace the old "social history" categories. Many models for evaluation and assessment exist and can be easily adapted for social work settings. The intake and screening measures developed by MCOs are generic and unreliable for many settings that employ social workers. Supervisors need to develop screening instruments unique to specific practice settings. Screening instruments are easy to develop and do not have to be standardized on large populations when they are designed for specific settings.

Intervention and Measurement

The evolution and expansion of diagnostic knowledge, as well as the expectation that practitioners connect diagnosis and treatment planning, require social work supervisees to develop more sophisticated research literature, behavior-based practice skills, and documented practice wisdom. These are roles that the supervisor should carry. The repertoire of techniques of intervention needs to be expanded for every practice situation and repeatedly tested. Development of practice guidelines and diagnosis-based recommended treatment plans makes it difficult for MCOs to exclude social work interventions from care plans and reimbursable services and procedures.

Intervention needs to be measurable and outcome focused. The profession has not devoted much attention to outcome measures or what constitutes successful intervention. More attention to objective measures and quantifiable outcomes is being demanded by service payers and monitoring organizations. The supervisor carries a primary role in promoting successful intervention. Models of planning for and assessment of successful intervention strategies through supervision have not been developed. The following guidelines can be helpful in planning successful intervention: (a) an intervention can be identified by the practitioner

that can be understood by the client; (b) there is an identifiable connection between the problem and the intervention; (c) the practitioner and client can implement the intervention with reasonable effort; (d) the practitioner, supervisor, and client can identify possible outcomes of the intervention in advance of its implementation; (e) the client has an identifiable reason or motivation to comply with the intervention; (f) an alternate intervention can be identified by the practitioner; and (g) the possible outcomes (intended and unintended, positive and negative) of the intervention can be observed and measured.

Task and Relationship

The intrusion of administrative and funding considerations in practice has caused treatment to be increasingly dominated by behavioral and task orientations. Relationship is losing recognition as a powerful curative factor. The supervisor's challenge is to develop a model that integrates intervention task and relationship process. The traditional view has been that one had to be articulated at the expense of the other. This is not necessary, and to maximize treatment outcome, there needs to be a merging of the two perspectives.

Supervisors must aid practitioners in developing skilled use of more techniques that enhance traditional relationship models. More emphasis should be placed on effective use of self-management models, cognitive approaches, psychoeducation methods, self-help groups, and prevention models.

Social workers have not been oriented to business models of service delivery (Austad, 1996). Unlike psychiatry and psychology, social work for the last 70 years has been practiced within the public sector. To return to a private sector model or a mixed model, individual practitioners and supervisors will have to change their attitudes and knowledge about business-based service delivery. Social work practitioners and supervisors need to integrate the financial and practice aspects of decision making to survive in the new model. Methods need to be devised to develop a more rational connection between financial and intervention decisions. The MCO model shift from focus on relationship to task and outcome has ethical implications. Practice based on tasks related to outcomes negates ethics. Unfortunately, MCOs have little concern about how practitioners conduct tasks or how outcomes are achieved, because only tasks or outcomes have value. In the social work relationship model, ethics are central to the process, because people always have expectations of how one should behave toward the other, regardless of the expected outcome. This is a basic point that practitioners and supervisors who work for MCOs must remember. Supervisors need to mediate the task-versus-relationship tension in the practice relationship and continue to promote relationship-focused practice based on ethical standards. Supervisory ethical principles need to integrate technique-based ethical standards with a relationship-focused ethical model. Supervisors need to apply ethical standards to each technique that practitioners use in the practice situation. Increased emphasis on techniques and tasks requires supervisors to monitor the use of techniques to ensure that (a) techniques used are related to the diagnosis and assessment, (b) the practitioner is trained in the techniques that are being applied, and (c) the techniques are generally accepted and appropriate. These are primary functions of the supervisor in the emerging practice environment.

Techniques that have not been subjected to clinical trials, or are not subject to regular and consistent monitoring, should not be used.

Supervisors should assist supervisees in using reliable techniques to counsel clients effectively under adverse conditions, such as trauma and loss. Supervisors should provide practitioners with skill in how to terminate with clients based on service cuts, not only because the intervention is completed. Practitioners are not trained in how to terminate for reasons other than completion of treatment, but MCOs frequently require practitioners to terminate before many client problems are resolved. Such shifts will require major reorientation for most social workers and can be accomplished only with the guidance and direction of a supervisor.

Professional Language

The self-help books for adapting to MCOs advocate strategies that decrease professional control. For example, some clinicians (Corpt & Reison, 1994) advocate that practitioners "behaviorize" the language they use in record keeping to please MCOs. The MCO "prescribed language" for practitioners goes to the essence of our professional being because language is the most fundamental connection between the individual and social functioning, and it is the "ultimate social tool" (Allman, 1994). Supervisors must mediate the replacement of our professional language with business-based language. Our professional language is the common core that allows social workers to communicate and maintain a unique professional identity. There is an old adage in supervision that the role of the supervisor is to be symbolically present looking over the shoulder of the practitioner as the intervention occurs

(Munson, 1979, 1993a). Unlike supervisors, MCOs do not share with the practitioner the results of these evaluations, even though they are rating the practitioner's effectiveness. For the educative and evaluative functions of supervision to remain valid, the social work profession will need to maintain its language base.

Scientific Orientation

Increased knowledge of disorders based on research has enhanced intervention. Differential diagnosis and diagnosis-specific treatment plans are being used. The neurobiology of mental disorders and the development of effective and diverse medication require practitioners to have knowledge of research, neurobiology, and medications. Practice guidelines for social workers developed by supervisors should take into account diagnostic and intervention outcome studies. Such studies are currently done by psychiatrists and psychologists, and social work supervisors must develop practice guidelines unique to our own form of practice. Psychiatry has initiated practice guidelines (American Psychiatric Association, 1996) that can serve as models for the development of social work practice guidelines that take into account the unique psychosocial perspective of clinical social work. Social workers are being compelled to justify claims of effectiveness and appropriateness of interventions through practice guidelines based on outcome studies. Social work has been slow to produce studies that meet the projected requirements for scientific practice (Munson, 1996b). A more unified and effective initiative in response to demands by MCOs is for psychiatrists and social workers to

collaboratively develop interdisciplinary practice guidelines. This would result in powerful comprehensive intervention genuinely based on biological, psychological, and social factors (Munson, 1997).

Populations Served and Advocacy

Social workers have traditionally served the poor and middle classes. Practitioners have worked with all age ranges, and most clients have been female. Based on the work of Ozawa (1997), it can be projected that in the future, the clients served by social workers will more likely be the poor and the upper middle classes. In the short term, children and adolescents and middle-class clients in general will be less served, and service to geriatric populations by social workers will increase in the long term. This will require a major shift in the client orientation of social work practice and supervision. Social work education is focused on the poor and on younger clients. Less than 4% of social work students express interest in work with geriatric populations. The most significant need for mental health work in geriatrics is related to family support, resource development, referral, and advocacy for people who have difficulty receiving services through MCOs. This need has been created because the elderly account for the largest share of health care costs, and MCOs target this population for cost cutting.

Women will continue to be the largest portion of social work clients. The number of single-parent households will continue to increase. Women are vulnerable in relation to MCOs in the same manner as the elderly. Limits placed on hospitalization for childbirth and restrictions of length of hospital stay for mastectomy have resulted in legislative regulation in some states and are indicators of the future need for advocacy for women.

Social work has historically been an urban profession. Although there has been a slight redistribution, rural areas continue to be underserved by social workers. There are no scientific studies of the urban/rural differences based on MCO models of service delivery. As mental health care is privatized and care increasingly is connected to the labor market, it is likely that service to the rural mentally ill will decrease. This is an area that deserves study because research has shown that the type and extent of mental disorders vary in rural and urban areas (Kessler, McGonagle, & Zhao, 1994).

Culturally Sensitive Practice

The U.S. population is increasingly diverse and during the next 50 years, projections are that racial and ethnic minorities will become the majority of U.S. citizens. The U.S. population is expected to grow by 50% from a total of 263 million in 1995 to a 2050 population that will consist of 206 million whites, 88 million Hispanics, 56 million African Americans, 38 million Asians, and 3.7 million American Indians (Ozawa, 1997). At the same time, there are no trends that would indicate that members of minority groups are increasingly entering the social work profession. Although no long-term projections of professional school enrollments are available, the enrollment trends of the last 20 years show no significant increase in minority enrollment. Minority enrollment has remained essentially unchanged for the 20-year period with bachelor's degree graduates averaging 24.6%, master's degree graduates averag-

ing 17.1% and doctoral graduates averaging 18.6%. If demographic trends and professional school graduate composition continue at the current levels, professionals of the dominant culture will be serving clients with varying cultural backgrounds in the short run. It is not clear in the long run whether increased presence of minorities in the population will result in more diversity in the social work profession. The demographic trends and factors that influence professional education choice will have significant implications for social work practice and supervision in the short and long term. Chetkow-Yanoov (1999) argues that new concepts and paradigms are needed by professionals to work with clients from different cultures and to work with different cultural groups that are in conflict. Modern individual, group, and community intervention by social workers and their supervisors requires a different focus than in the past.

Supervisors will have to increasingly monitor practitioners' sensitivity to the beliefs, attitudes, behaviors, and needs of clients who are different from the practitioner. Schools of social work have increased content related to vulnerable populations (Gitterman, 1991), but practitioners entering supervision have limited practical preparation for working with culturally different and vulnerable populations (Jivanjee, 1999). There is more literature regarding how to define culturally sensitive intervention than there is in how to define the supervisory relationship from a culturally sensitive perspective (Batten, 1990; Bernard, 1994; Brown & Landrum-Brown, 1995; Cashwell, Looby, & Housley, 1997; Cook & Helms, 1988; Douglas & Rave, 1990; Fong & Lease, 1997; Gopaul-McNicol & Brice-Baker, 1998;

Hipp & Munson, 1995; Lago & Thompson, 1997; Pope-Davis & Coleman, 1997; Priest, 1994; Ryan & Hendricks, 1989; Williams & Halgin, 1995). Key factors supervisors need to monitor in culturally sensitive supervision are:

1. Recognize differing perceptions of the meaning of functions, expectations, explanations, and behavior of the client, practitioner, and supervisor whenever difference is part of the client/practitioner/supervisor complex.

2. Ensure that respect and acceptance are shown for religious, spiritual, political, age, gender, and lifestyle differences.

3. Understand that assessment of communication during intervention may differ. For example, practitioner access to client perceptions may be impeded by differing views of language, styles of communication, valuing of socioeconomic and other statuses, acceptance of direct questioning, use of storytelling, role of privacy, work and leisure roles, family structure, authority, and importance of age.

These are general guidelines. The key is that the supervisor must ensure that the practitioner recognizes that each situation is unique, and any generalizations made about clients have the potential to produce practitioner bias and client resistance. Whenever a client is from a different background or group, the practitioner and supervisor must work to understand and assist the client within their own culture, and the client must be viewed in contrast to the dominant culture with which he or she must function. This orientation is a balancing act and creates conflicts, but the orientation is essential if the professional is to aid the client. Only through such an orientation can people from different cultures be comprehensively understood. Supervisors should be alert to uniqueness, diversity, and difference in clients, practitioners, and themselves as supervisors. The range of uniqueness can include, but is not limited to, race, ethnicity, culture, subculture, age, preferences, gender, physical and psychological limitations, and geographic location. Combinations of these categories can give rise to complex individuals and families that limit or enhance the intervention process, depending on how the differences are understood, accepted, and used. Each case explored in supervision should be screened and reviewed for differences and special circumstances that could be a source of communication and acceptance failure in the professional relationship. Uniqueness not only should be assessed in the context of identifying the difference; once identified, it should be interpreted in the context of its contribution to current functioning. If there is a functional problem, it must be decided whether it can be worked with through the dominant and background culture. For example, acculturation and assimilation can produce stress in families that lead to specific functional problems. This is especially the case for mothers engaged in child rearing. In situations where there are combinations of difference factors, supervisors must be alert to the practitioner's focus on one factor at the expense of another factor. For example, an immigrant with a severe physical disability may have a practitioner who focuses on assimilation issues and neglects the disability difficulties, whereas another practitioner may emphasize assistance with the disability and fail to recognize the assimilation difficulties. Combinations of differences can produce complex interactions among individuals and families that can cause distance and limitations or can enhance the intervention process, depending on how the combinations are understood, accepted and used by the practitioner and supervisor.

Prevention

Prevention is viewed by many as the way to reduce social service delivery costs. In the mental health field, specific prevention models have not been devised or implemented as they have been in the general health care field (Public Health Service, 1994). The MCOs have no structures for promoting behavioral health prevention. Prevention can save money in the long term, but money must be provided in the short term for prevention efforts. The question remains: Who will pay for prevention? The MCOs are interested only in self-motivated prevention and have no interest in costly large-scale programmatic prevention. Prevention will most likely remain a slogan, rather than a service, unless supervisors compile data to support specific strategies for effective preventive services based on documented solutions. Social workers are not trained in prevention, but this may become an important practice area in the future if supervisors develop a supervision practice standard for collecting data to support prevention efforts.

Risk Management

Risk management refers to risks in practice due to threats from clients or associates of clients and risks resulting from error made by practitioners. There is growing violence in society, in general, and violence aimed at social workers is rising. The increase of violence against children and by children is alarming. Violence against vulnerable groups, such as the elderly, is also increasing. Social workers face violence directly through threats and attacks and indirectly through the experiences of violence that their clients present in treatment. Supervi-

sors may experience the violence indirectly through having to aid a supervisee in making a decision to advise a woman to leave an abusive relationship. The supervisor may develop concern about what type of potential threat the abuser may represent for both the worker and the supervisor for their intervening in the situation. Supervisors have responsibility to ensure that supervisees are aware of risks to safety and take action to protect themselves and clients as well.

There is no organization gathering data on violent acts against social workers. In a limited study of violence against social workers (Munson, 1995a), some patterns occurred that are significant. First, violence was not random. The person committing the violent act had some complaint against the agency, real or imagined, that provoked him or her. Second, the precipitating incident was fairly recent and not long-standing. Third, a minor incident often preceded the serious violent incident. For example, the person gets in an argument with someone at the agency or telephones and becomes argumentative. Fourth, the violence incident occurred when the agency did something outside the established practices of the agency. Consider the following scenario: In a hospital shooting, when a client enters the hospital and becomes belligerent, the social worker agrees to interview the client in the waiting room. This is not normally done. After the social worker is shot, the client holds other people who are in the waiting room hostage for several hours. If normal procedures had been followed, it is possible that the tragedy could have been avoided, or the number of people involved could have been much smaller.

Supervisors and administrators frequently minimize the potential for violence in clients and inadvertently put workers at risk. One violent incident can have significant impact on staff, even when no serious physical harm occurs. When staff are held hostage, they suffer psychological and emotional stress for quite some time. Some people never completely recover from witnessing or being a part of a violent incident.

The supervisor has a responsibility to prepare practitioners by orienting them to the signs of potential violence in a client. Signs of agitation, such as heavy breathing, trembling, raising of the voice, trembling in the voice, glaring at the worker, sudden use of profanity, pacing, and clenched fists are primary signs of possible impending violence (for more detail, see Munson, 1995a; Shea, 1998).

The supervisor has a responsibility to take precautions to protect the safety of supervisees. If the agency does not have a policy on safety, the supervisor should take the lead in organizing the staff to develop a policy. A basic safety policy should include consideration of office arrangement, development of a "buddy system" for warning others when danger is present, installation of warning devices, strategies to deal with expressions of anger, establishment and implementation of a client restraint policy, and home visit precautions (Munson, 1995a).

Risk management also includes limiting risks to supervisees because of practice errors they may make. This is an important activity of the supervisor in an era when litigation has increased significantly. The most common errors relate to duty-to-warn requirements and child abuse reporting laws.

Duty to warn, also referred to as failure to warn and the Tarasoff rule, is closely related to confidentiality issues, and the concept has caused much concern and controversy in the helping professions. The essence of duty to warn is that if a professional learns that a client intends to do harm to others or to destroy property, there is a duty to warn the people who have been threatened. The supervisor has a responsibility to ensure that practitioners understand the concept of duty to warn and to offer guidelines for supervisees to follow.

Practitioners are required to report any known or suspected instances of child physical abuse, sexual abuse, or neglect. The practitioner can be at risk of legal sanction if there is a failure to report. There are many assumptions made about reporting, and the supervisor has a responsibility to ensure that practitioners act appropriately in child abuse situations. The rules regarding reporting of child abuse and neglect vary by jurisdiction. Supervisors should be aware of relevant statutes.

Even when the agency establishes guidelines, the practitioner will confront many situations that are ambiguous and will react to threats in different ways, given the circumstances. For example, it is easier for therapists to make a decision to warn when threats are made by clients with whom they have had a difficult relationship than by clients with whom they have had a positive relationship. It will be more difficult to report about a client whom the practitioner has seen for a long time than a client being seen for the first time.

Stress

Stress in professional life is increasing. A study by Schorr (1991) shows that in the United States, people are working substantially more hours per year than in the 1960s. The average American worked 163 more hours per year in 1991 than in 1969. The increase in work was significantly higher for women than men. Women were working 305 additional hours per year, compared with an increase of 98 hours for men. Other studies have confirmed this increased workload. During the same period, average wages declined 19%. One percent of families, those with incomes over $350,000, received 72% of U.S. income, while the 60% of people in the lowest income category lost ground economically (Danaher, 1996). Professionals have been identified as having been significantly affected by this trend. In the late 1970s and early 1980s, a series of studies focused on stress levels in social work practitioners, but the studies of stress have declined in the last 10 years. There are continuing signs that stress levels are quite high in social work practitioners, but there is little empirical research available to support the popular press and anecdotal reports of significant stress in practitioners.

A stressed, distracted, overwhelmed professional cannot be helpful to clients. Research has shown that supervision is effective in combating stress in professionals (Munson, 1993a). Supervisors have a responsibility to monitor workers and assist them with work-related, stress-induced functioning. A study by Bissell (1980) showed that social work supervisors are not sensitive to the behavioral manifestations of stress in practitioners, even when these behaviors are in the extreme form of arrests, hospital admissions, suicide attempts, alcohol abuse, and substance abuse.

Practice standards for supervision need to include visual and testing measures of stress in practitioners. There are scales available to assess stress in practitioners, as well as specific guidelines for treating stress reaction through supervision (see Munson, 1993a), and such measures should be used in supervision practice. Supervisors should discuss with supervisees perceptions of stresses in and outside the work setting. Stresses associated with the work setting should be a focus in supervision, but reactions to stress in a supervisee's personal life should be referred outside the supervision for intervention. The basic rule to follow is supervise the *position,* not the *person* (Munson, 1993a).

Supervisors are also subject to stress reactions, and supervisors should take steps to reduce stress levels. This is difficult because professionals are not sensitive to their own distress. C. Northcote Parkinson (1957) said that the patient and the surgeon should never be the same person. This is true when it comes to addressing stress by practitioners or supervisors. Supervisors should form support groups to address the stresses they face and to share the reactions they have to stress. If a person is the only supervisor in the practice setting, then the supervisor should join a group outside the practice setting. There are a growing number of traumatic stress centers in the United States that supervisors can contact for referral to support groups.

Ethics

Modern complex society generates many ethical issues for practitioners that must be addressed in supervision. Supervisors need to be well-grounded in and knowledgeable about the *National Association of Social Workers (NASW) Code of Ethics* (1996) and other codes of ethics that may be relevant to the supervisee's activity. It is now common for social workers to function under the mandates of several codes of ethics through licensing and membership in several professional organizations. The increasing legal and other mandated sanctions of social work practice present ethical problems for the practitioner that the supervisor must be prepared to address. Court mandated duty-to-warn requirements, for example, present conflicts for workers and supervisors. A case example illustrates such a conflict.

> Ms. Jones was receiving counseling in a public mental health clinic. She told her social worker that her teenage daughter had been raped by a man in the parking lot of a shopping mall. The man was found not guilty by a jury because of a technicality. Ms. Jones told the social worker that she would "give this man his punishment if she ever met him on the street." The social worker asked Ms. Jones the meaning of the statement, and she reached into her pocketbook, pulled out a handgun, and said, "This will be his conviction on appeal."

The supervisor must help the worker reconcile the worker's identification with Ms. Jones and the duty-to-warn requirements after a specific threat has been made against an individual. This is an example of the complex practice conflicts that supervisors and practitioners must resolve within current practice standards.

The actions of MCOs produce direct ethical conflicts for social work practitioners that can become a focus of attention in supervision. It is not surprising that the increase in professional concern about risk management and legal liability has paralleled the rise of MCOs. The *NASW Code of Ethics* (National Association of Social Workers, 1990, 1996) has contradictory statements that complicate its use, but it is the primary professional guide that we have, and the code does state that social workers who subscribe to it are required to abide by it. The *NASW Code of Ethics* contains the following guiding principles, which can create conflict issues for clinicians involved with MCOs as employees and contract providers: (a) honor obligations to the social work profession, to clients, to employing organizations, and to the general public; (b) foster self-determination of clients, respect privacy of clients, and honor confidentiality; (c) retain responsibility for quality of service that is performed; (d) act to prevent practices that are inhumane or discriminatory; (e) provide clients with information regarding services; (f) inform clients of risks and rights associated with service; (g) withdraw services precipitously only under unusual circumstances; (h) improve the agency employing them, and report unethical conduct by members of the profession; and (i) advocate for policies and legislation to improve social conditions and promote social justice. These items can be in conflict with common practices of MCOs. The profession has not provided practice standards or guidelines related to these conflicts. For example, is a social worker who contracts to provide services for an MCO an employee of that company? In the traditional sense of employment, this is not the case, but under current practices, it could be construed that the social worker is an employee of the MCO and obliged to "work to improve employing agency's policies and procedures." Social workers do not have a relationship with MCOs that would allow them to advocate for policy changes, and if they did advocate for company changes, they would most likely be removed from the MCO provider list. Some state licensing boards are struggling with this issue as a supervisory and employee/employer issue, but the ethical requirements of the social worker and MCO relationship have not been clarified.

There are ethics conflicts related to confidentiality (Sabin, 1997), self-determination, and rights to informed consent that are unresolved. Supervision is an appropriate forum to resolve these differences because there are no structures for practitioners to communicate with MCOs regarding professional and practice issues. An adversarial relationship exists between MCOs and professionals that is filtering down to the relationships between practitioners and clients and can foster conflict and resentment in professional relationships. This is a major flaw in the relationship between MCOs and providers that must be resolved if the system is to work effectively. The difficult but traditional role of supervisors as mid-level managers who mediate the relationship between practitioners and administration may be needed to address the problems that confront the MCO/practitioner interface.

It has been argued that professional ethics codes are outdated and in conflict with managed cost policy and procedures to the degree that the codes should be altered (Phillips, 1995; Wolf, 1994). The *NASW Code of Ethics* has been revised, and the new document (National Association of Social Workers, 1996) has modifications that reflect aspects of the managed-cost view of ethics. Ethics codes, to be effective, must have clarity, consistency, and endurance (Munson, 1995b). Supervisors should work to identify the enduring aspects of ethics and strive to have them applied with clarity and consistency. These questions are complex and need to be resolved at the professional organization level. At the same time, the supervisor must have a major role in aiding the supervisee in resolving ethical issues arising in daily practice. As the profession establishes supervisory standards of practice and guidelines to deal with such conflicts, the daily practice of supervision will become an easier task.

Psychiatry has taken initial steps to identify what is considered ethical practice in relation to MCOs (Macbeth, Wheeler, Sither, & Onek, 1995), and many of the items they identify are relevant to social work. To practice ethically in connection with MCOs, the practitioner and supervisor should determine that the following conditions are met:

1. Clients make informed treatment decisions based on knowledge of (a) their options, (b) benefit limitations, (c) authorization process, (d) rights to appeal utilization decisions, (e) limits on choice and copay requirements, and (f) potential invasion of privacy by the review process.
2. No exaggerated claims of excellence or quality are made by the MCO.
3. Treatment is competent and meets client needs within benefit limits.
4. The utilization review process is not invasive of the therapeutic relationship.
5. Reviewers are not financially rewarded for denying treatment or claims.

RECOMMENDATIONS

Recommendations are made at two levels. First, recommendations for individual supervisors are provided to assist in implementing a model of supervision based on standards of supervision practice and guidelines for effective supervision. Second, recommendations are made for implementation at the professional level to aid in fostering a model of supervision based on standards and guidelines and to promote a revival of the effective role of supervision to ensure quality service delivery by practitioners.

Recommendations for Supervisors

The following recommendations are made for implementation by supervisors to ensure that the quality standards and guidelines for supervision identified in this chapter are applied. Using a standards of practice model to implement these guidelines, supervisors should

1. Supervise practitioners only for tasks and functions the supervisors have performed

2. Have documented professional training in the areas for which they provide supervision.

3. Have documented formal training in supervision before assuming a supervisory position. On-the-job training should not be counted as sufficient supervisory training.

4. Be thoroughly knowledgeable regarding the code or codes of ethics under which they function and ensure that their supervisees have read and understood the code or codes.

5. Ensure that the supervisee understands the role of advocacy and is able to identify when the need for client advocacy exists.

6. Be knowledgeable about and monitor stress reactions in supervisees.

7. Identify agency/organization policy and professional organizational ethical conflicts and call them to the attention of supervisees, employing organizations, and professional organizations.

8. Have written risk-management policies for supervisees.

9. Have written requirements for intake procedures, diagnostic formats, assessment and evaluations criteria, and informed consent policies for clients.

10. Be knowledgeable about screening measures and familiar with basic standardized tests and measures relevant to populations served.

11. Have clear criteria for written treatment plans and foster supervisee understanding that treatment plans are related to diagnosis and initial assessment.

12. Have clear policies regarding the use of techniques during intervention. Supervisees should be able to explain, justify, and document existing research for techniques that are used.

13. Have clear criteria for evaluation of intervention that are applied equally to all supervisees.

14. Have clear protocols for termination with clients under differing circumstances (i.e., successful completion of intervention, loss of funding, client failure to pay, client failure to keep appointments, departure of the social worker).

15. Require supervisees to be aware of practice standards of other disciplines that may be relevant to the supervisee's practice (i.e., American Psychiatric Association, American Psychological Association, and American Association of Marriage and Family Therapy).

16. Be aware of the role of culture, race, ethnicity, lifestyle, preferences, and vulnerability in relation to clients and practitioners and monitor intervention to ensure that all practitioners and clients are treated with fairness and equality.

Recommendations for the Profession

The following recommendations are made for implementation at the professional organizational leadership level in setting standards:

1. Develop a national association of supervisors. It is not clear why no national organization exists to represent the interests of social work supervisors. Such an organization could be a powerful force for leadership in addressing many of the issues raised in this chapter.

2. Establish within the NASW a strong direct practice section that sets practice standards and establishes guidelines for practice.

3. Establish a direct practice section within the Council on Social Work Education that would set standards for direct practice components of the curriculum policy statement and would work closely with the NASW direct practice section mentioned above.

4. Integrate licensing regulatory bodies with practice-oriented professional organizations mentioned above.

5. Formulate a task group that monitors and evaluates practice technologies.

6. Develop standards of practice and standards of care for specific areas of clinical social work based on research on specific populations.

7. Develop a policy statement that makes a clear distinction between bachelor of social work, master of social work, and doctor of social work degrees in relation to practice and supervision.

8. Increase and clarify supervision requirements for field instruction that are associated with education for social work practice and supervision.

9. Increase sponsorship of interdisciplinary research directly related to treatment populations and aimed at establishing guidelines for practice and supervision.

10. Establish formal standards of practice related to culture, race, ethnicity, lifestyle, preferences, and vulnerability for practitioners and supervisors that ensure fair and just treatment.

NOTE

1. The term *managed care* is a misnomer. These companies provide managed cost, not managed care, and in this chapter, these companies will be referred to as managed cost organizations (MCOs). The abbreviations MCO and MCOs also refer to the philosophy and practice of managed cost organizations and do not refer to specific companies. This generic use of the term has been applied because public and private organizations have adopted managed cost methods.

REFERENCES

Ackley, D. C. (1997). *Breaking free of managed care: A step by step guide to regaining control of your practice.* New York: Guilford.

Allman, W. F. (1994). *The stone age present: How evolution has shaped modern life—from sex, violence, and language to emotions, morals, and communities.* New York: Simon & Schuster.

Alonso, A. (1985). *The quiet profession: Supervisors of psychotherapy.* New York: Macmillan.

Alperin, R. M., & Phillips, D. G. (1997). *The impact of managed care on the practice of psychotherapy: Innovation, implementation, and controversy.* New York: Brunner/Mazel.

Altheide, D. L. (1995). *An ecology of communication: Cultural formats of control.* New York: Aldine de Gruyter.

American Psychiatric Association. (1994). *Diagnostic and statistical manual of mental disorders* (4th ed.). Washington, DC: Author.

American Psychiatric Association. (1996). *Practice guidelines.* Washington, DC: Author.

Aronson, J. (1996). *Inside managed care: Family therapy in a changing environment.* New York: Brunner/Mazel.

Austad, C. S. (1996). *Is long-term psychotherapy unethical? Toward a social ethic in an era of managed care.* San Francisco: Jossey-Bass.

Batten, C. (1990). Dilemmas of crosscultural psychotherapy supervision. *British Journal of Psychotherapy, 7,* 129-140.

Bernard, J. M. (1994). Multicultural supervision: A reaction to Leong and Wagner, Cook, Priest, and Fukuyama. *Counselor Education and Supervision, 34,* 159-171.

Bissell, L. (1980). The alcoholic social worker: A survey. *Social Work in Health Care, 5,* 421-432.

Brown, M. T., & Landrum-Brown, J. (1995). Counselor supervision: Cross-cultural perspectives. In J. G. Ponterotto & J. M. Casas (Eds.), *Handbook of multicultural counseling* (pp. 263-286). Thousand Oaks, CA: Sage.

Browning, C. H., & Browning, B. J. (1996). *How to partner with managed care.* New York: John Wiley.

Caligor, L., Bromberg, P. M., & Meltzer, J. D. (Eds.). (1984). *Clinical perspectives on the supervision of psychoanalysis and psychotherapy.* New York: Plenum.

Cashwell, C. S., Looby, E. J., & Housley, W. F. (1997). Appreciating cultural diversity through clinical supervision. *The Clinical Supervisor, 15,* 75-85.

Chetkow-Yanoov, B. (1999). *Celebrating diversity: Coexisting in a multicultural society.* New York: Haworth.

Cook, D. A., & Helms, J. E. (1988). Visible racial/ethnic group supervisees' satisfaction with cross-cultural supervision as predicted by relationship characteristics. *Journal of Counseling Psychology, 35,* 268-274.

Corpt, E. A., & Reison, M. (1994). Behaviorizing your clinical language. *Managed Care News,* pp. 1-5.

Danaher, K. (Ed.). (1996). *Corporations are gonna get your mama: Globalization and the downsizing of the American dream.* Monroe, ME: Common Courage Press.

Day, P. J. (1997). *A new history of social welfare.* Boston: Allyn & Bacon.

Donahue, J. D. (1989). *The privatization decision: Public ends, private means.* New York: Basic Books.

Douglas, M. A. D., & Rave, E. J. (1990). Ethics of feminist supervision of psychotherapy. In H. Lerman & N. Porter (Eds.), *Feminist ethics in psychotherapy* (pp. 137-146). New York: Springer.

Feldman, J. L., & Fitzpatrick, R. J. (Eds.). (1992). *Managed mental health care: Administrative and clinical issues.* Washington, DC: American Psychiatric Press.

Fong, M. L., & Lease, S. H. (1997). Cross-cultural supervision: Issues for the white supervisor. In D. B. Pope-Davis & H. L. K. Coleman (Eds.), *Multicultural counseling competencies: Assessment, education and training, and supervision* (pp. 387-405). Thousand Oaks, CA: Sage.

Gibelman, M. (1995). *What social workers do.* Washington, DC: NASW Press.

Gitterman, A. (Ed.). (1991). *Handbook of social work practice with vulnerable populations.* New York: Columbia University Press.

Goodman, M., Brown, J., & Deitz, P. (1992). *Managing managed care: A mental health practitioner's survival guide.* Washington, DC: American Psychiatric Press.

Gopaul-McNicol, S. A., & Brice-Baker, J. (1998). *Cross-cultural practice: Assessment, treatment, and training.* New York: John Wiley.

Handy, C. (1995, May/June). Trust and the virtual organization. *Harvard Business Review,* pp. 40-50.

Handy, C. (1996). *Beyond certainty: The changing world of organizations.* Boston, MA: Harvard University Business School Press.

Hipp, J. L., & Munson, C. E. (1995). The partnership model: A feminist supervision/consultation perspective. *The Clinical Supervisor, 13,* 23-38.

Jacobs, D., David, P., & Meyer, D. J. (1995). *The supervisory encounter: A guide for teachers of psychodynamic psychotherapy and psychoanalysis.* New Haven, CT: Yale University Press.

Jivanjee, P. R. (1999). Social work field education to serve vulnerable populations: A case study. *Journal of Teaching in Social Work, 18,* 185-207.

Kadushin, A. (1992). *Supervision in social work* (3rd ed.). New York: Columbia University Press.

Karls, J. M., & Wandrei, K. E. (1994). *Person-in-environment system: The PIE classification system for social functioning problems.* Washington, DC: NASW Press.

Kessler, R. C., McGonagle, K. A., & Zhao, S. (1994). Lifetime and 12-month prevalence of *DSM-III-R* psychiatric disorders in the United States. *Archives of General Psychiatry, 51,* 8-19.

Lago, C., & Thompson, J. (1997). The triangle with curved sides: Sensitivity to issues of race and culture in supervision. In G. Shipton (Ed.), *Supervision of psychotherapy and counseling: Making a place to think* (pp. 119-130). Buckingham, UK: The Open University.

Lane, R. C. (Ed.). (1990). *Psychoanalytic approaches to supervision.* New York: Brunner/Mazel.

Lasch, C. (1979). *The culture of narcissism: American life in an age of diminishing expectations.* New York: Norton.

Lerner, M. (1986). *Surplus powerlessness: The psychodynamics of everyday life and psychology of individual transformation.* Atlantic Highlands, NJ: Humanities Press International.

Lundblad, K. S. (1995). Jane Addams and social reform: A role model for the 1990s. *Social Work, 40,* 661-669.

Macbeth, J. E., Wheeler, A. M., Sither, J. W., & Onek, J. N. (1995). *Legal and risk management issues in the practice of psychiatry.* Washington, DC: Psychiatrists' Purchasing Group.

Madrick, J. (1995). *The end of affluence: The causes and consequences of America's economic dilemma.* New York: Random House.

Managed care notes. (1995). *Psychotherapy Finances, 21*(10), 5.

Mead, D. E. (1990). *Effective supervision: A task-oriented model for mental health professions.* New York: Brunner/Mazel.

Motenko, A. K., Allen, E. A., Angelos, P., Block, L., DeVito, J., Duffy, A., Holton, L., Lambert, K., Parker, C., Ryan, J., Schraft, D., & Swindell, J. (1995). Privatization and cutbacks: Social work and client impressions of service delivery in Massachusetts. *Social Work, 40,* 456-463.

Munson, C. E. (Ed.). (1979). *Social work supervision: Classic statements and critical issues.* New York: Free Press.

Munson, C. E. (1988). Computers in social work education. *Computers in Human Services, 3*(1/2), 143-157.

Munson, C. E. (1993a). *Clinical social work supervision* (2nd ed.). New York: Haworth.

Munson, C. E. (1993b). The "P" word and mental health services. *Clinical Supervisor, 11*(2), 1-5.

Munson, C. E. (1995a). *Clinical supervision curriculum guide: Vol. 1. Training curriculum for supervisors of social workers seeking licensure as licensed clinical social workers (LCSW's) by the Virginia Board of Social Work.* Richmond: Virginia Board of Social Work.

Munson, C. E. (1995b, August). *Foundation concepts for survival of ethical social work practice in the health care environment.* Paper presented at the meeting of the National Institutes of Health, Bethesda, MD.

Munson, C. E. (1996a). Autonomy and managed care in clinical social work practice. In G. Schamess (Ed.), *The corporate and human faces of managed health care: The interplay between mental health policy and practice* (pp. 241-260). Northampton, MA: Smith College Studies in Social Work.

Munson, C. E. (1996b). Technology, change, and the clinical social work practice curriculum. In E. T. Reck (Ed.), *Modes of professional education II: The electronic social work curriculum in the twenty-first century* (pp. 86-106). New Orleans, LA: Tulane University, School of Social Work.

Munson, C. E. (1997). The future of clinical social work and managed cost organizations. *Psychiatric Services: A Journal of the American Psychiatric Association, 48*(4), 479-482.

Munson, C. E. (1998a). Evolution and trends in the relationship between clinical social work practice and managed cost organizations. In G. Schamess & A. Lightburn (Eds.), *Humane managed care?* (pp. 308-324). Washington, DC: NASW Press.

Munson, C. E. (1998b). Societal change, managed cost organizations, and clinical social work practice. *The Clinical Supervisor, 17,* 1-41.

Naisbitt, J. (1982). *Megatrends: Ten new directions transforming our lives.* New York: Warner Books.

National Association of Social Workers. (1990). *NASW code of ethics.* Washington, DC: Author.

National Association of Social Workers. (1996). *NASW code of ethics,* Washington, DC: Author.

Nicholson, J., Young, S. D., Simon, L., Bateman, A., & Fisher, W. H. (1996). Impact of medicaid managed care on child and adolescent emergency mental health screening in Massachusetts. *Psychiatric Services, 47,* 1344-1350.

Olin, J. T., & Keatinge, C. (1998). *Rapid psychological assessment.* New York: John Wiley.

Ozawa, M. N. (1997). Demographic changes and their implications. In M. Reisch & E. Gambrill (Eds.), *Social work in the 21st century* (pp. 8-27). Thousand Oaks, CA: Pine Forge Press.

Parkinson, C. N. (1957). *Parkinson's law and other studies in administration.* Boston: Houghton Mifflin

Perlman, H. H. (1957). *Social casework: A problem-solving process.* Chicago: University of Chicago Press.

Phillips, D. (1995). Professional standards and managed care. *National Federation of Societies for Clinical Social Work Progress Report, 13*(1), 11.

Pollock, E. J. (1998, January 5). With "case rates" cures come fast or the doctor incurs a loss. *The Wall Street Journal,* p. A1.

Pope-Davis, D. B., & Coleman, H. L. K. (Eds.). (1997). *Multicultural counseling competencies: Assessment, education and training, and supervision.* Thousand Oaks, CA: Sage.

Priest, R. (1994). Minority supervisor and majority supervisee: Another perspective of clinical reality. *Counselor Education and Supervision, 34,* 152-158.

Professional notes: Mental health ranks low on people's list of health care priorities. (1996). *Psychotherapy Finances, 22*(7), 10.

Public Health Service. (1994). *Clinician's handbook of preventive services.* Washington, DC: U.S. Department of Health and Human Services.

Reeser, J. C., & Epstein, I. (1990). *Professionalization and activism in social work: The sixties, the eighties, and the future.* New York: Columbia University Press.

Reid, W. J., & Epstein, L. (1972). *Task-centered practice.* New York: Columbia University Press.

Richmond, M. (1917). *Social diagnosis.* New York: Russell Sage Foundation.

Rock, M. H. (Ed.). (1997). *Psychodynamic supervision: Perspectives of the supervisor and the supervisee.* Northvale, NJ: Jason Aronson.

Ryan, A. S., & Hendricks, C. O. (1989). Culture and communication: Supervising the Asian and Hispanic social worker. *The Clinical Supervisor 7,* 27-40.

Sabin, J. E. (1997). Managed care: What confidentiality standards should we advocate for in mental health care, and how should we do it? *Psychiatric Services, 48*(1), 35-41.

Schamess, G. (1998). Corporate values and managed mental health care: Who profits and who benefits? In G. Schamess & A. Lightburn (Eds.), *Humane managed care?* (pp. 23-35). Washington, DC: NASW Press.

Schorr, J. B. (1991). *The overworked American.* New York: Basic Books.

Shea, S. C. (1998). *Psychiatric interviewing. The art of understanding: A practical guide for psychiatrists, psychologists, counselors, social workers, nurses, and other mental health professionals.* Philadelphia: W. B. Saunders.

Shulman, L. (1993). *Interactional supervision.* Washington, DC: NASW Press.

Specht, H., & Courtney, M. (1994). *Unfaithful angels: How social work has abandoned its mission.* New York: Free Press.

Special report: What is your professional organization doing for your practice? (1995). *Psychotherapy Finances, 21*(7), 6.

Stoltenberg, C. D., McNeil, B., & Delworth, U. (1998). *IDM supervision: An integrated developmental model for supervising counselor therapists.* San Francisco: Jossey-Bass.

Sullivan, W. M. (1995). *Work and integrity: The crisis and promise of professionalism in America.* New York: Harper Business.

Warres, N. E., Soderstrom, P., Marcus, L. A., Berman, P. C., & Liebman, M. C. (1996). The impact of managed care and utilization review: A cross-sectional study in Maryland. *Psychiatric Services, 47*(12), 1319-1322.

Williams, S., & Halgin, R. P. (1995). Issues in psychotherapy supervision between the white supervisor and the black supervisee. *The Clinical Supervisor, 3,* 39-61.

Wolf, S. (1994). Health care reform and the future of physician ethics. *Hastings Center Report, 24*(2), 28-41.

CHAPTER THIRTY

International Perspectives on Social Work Practice

DOREEN ELLIOTT

NAZNEEN S. MAYADAS

In a world where international events have long-ranging implications for the quality of people's lives, it is imperative for a human services profession such as social work to practice from a global rather than a parochial perspective. This chapter proposes a global model of social work practice for the future, based on social development, empowerment, and social justice. It incorporates new approaches such as human investment and micro economics and offers a framework for practice incorporating the possibility of mutuality of technology transfer and learning from the Third World.

INTERNATIONALISM IN SOCIAL WORK

Internationalism and globalization: Defining the terms. Internationalism in social work may be defined by its values and the scope of its activities. An international perspective in social work implies a global orientation toward professional activities. Midgley (1997a) suggests that globalization has a broader connotation than internationalization and is a preferred term: it is "a process of global integration in which diverse peoples, economies, cultures,

and political processes are increasingly subjected to international influences and people
are made aware of these influences in their everyday lives" (p. 21). Globalization, therefore,
implies a process by which we become increasingly aware of global connections and influences on our professional practice. Once these
connections are understood (for example, the
fact that the global north has prospered from
natural resources, labor, trade, and money
lending to countries in the global south), then a
global perspective has a moral obligation to assume certain values and goals such as freeing
the developing world of debt payments to the
industrialized nations, fostering world peace,
promoting a concern for the environment on a
worldwide basis, working to eliminate world
poverty, aiming for a more equal distribution of
resources between the global north and the
global south, promoting universal human
rights, and using people-centered sustainable
development. Whereas globalization is more
frequently used to describe these values and
goals, international social work is the term used
to describe activities that transcend national
boundaries and in which social workers engage
while subscribing to these values. Healy (1995)
suggests that three areas are dominant in defining international social work: comparative social policy, cross-cultural understanding, and
global social problems.

*Learning from the developed and developing
world.* Comparative social policy should inform our practice, not in the sense of our
blindly adopting programs from overseas, but
in our using the experience of others to solve
problems. We have much to learn from other
countries, including the developing world

(Midgley, 1990, 1997a). One such example is
the work of the Grameen Bank, which originated micro enterprise loans in Bangladesh.
Later, it successfully established similar programs in Chicago (Counts, 1996). Another
might be to learn lessons from French national
child welfare policy, which provides preschool
day care. Comparative research studies may offer the benefit of a new perspective on social issues leading to changes in social policy or service delivery (Midgley, 1997a).

World peace. Cross-cultural understanding
through international experiences broadens the
vision and enhances multicultural understanding at home. Ultimately, it works toward the
larger vision of world peace. Addressing global
problems may be a social work intervention either at the international or the local level. International and local socioeconomic systems are
inextricably linked. The plight of the Kosovar
refugees becomes a local problem once they arrive in their city of resettlement and local social
work agencies are called on for help.

Global social issues and social work practice.
International adoptions are an example of international practice where the social worker
has to interact with social and legal systems of
two countries. Issues of human rights such as female genital mutilation may need to be addressed more globally, along with issues of children's rights such as child labor, child
prostitution, and child soldiers. The work of
the large international agencies in dealing with
problems such as these—for example, the
United Nations (UN) High Commissioner for
Refugees (UNHCR), the UN Children's International Education Fund (UNICEF), Interna-

tional Committees of the Red Cross and Red Crescent, the Peace Corps, Oxfam, and Save the Children, to mention but a few—is generally well known. Their work with refugee resettlement and welfare, children's health and education programs, response to natural and man-made disasters, economic and community development projects, and so on represent a broad range of global social work interventions. Social workers may become involved at an international level when dealing with international adoptions or when working with refugee programs in a resettlement country under the auspices of federal government agencies such as the Office of Refugee Resettlement, a department of the Administration for Children and Families; local offices of national organizations, such as Catholic Charities and Lutheran Social Services; and local community centers and agencies.

The work of professional organizations such as the International Association of Schools of Social Work (IASSW), the International Federation of Social Workers (IFSW), the Inter University Consortium for International Social Development (IUCISD), the International Council on Social Welfare (ICSW), the International Commission of the Council on Social Work Education (CSWE), and the International Committee of NASW, all work toward the exchange of international ideas for social work education and practice through exchange of personnel, conferences, and sponsorship of professional journals.

We may extend the definition of internationalism in social work to include those activities that involve intervention in socioeconomic systems beyond national boundaries or the exchange of ideas and information between people residing within different national boundaries. These activities may take place through international, national, or local agencies; through conferences, journals, the World Wide Web, and other means of disseminating knowledge. Regardless of the location, the interventions will usually be directed according to a global values perspective as outlined above.

FOUR PHASES OF INTERNATIONALISM

Internationalism has always played an influential role in the development of American social work. However, this role has undergone many changes. Elsewhere, the authors have proposed four distinct phases, each characterized by different values and directions (Mayadas & Elliott, 1997). These phases are, first, the early pioneers; second, the era of professional imperialism; third, the period of reconceptualization and indigenization; and fourth, what we envisage as the future phase, that of internationalism based on a socioeconomic development model of social work practice.

Phase 1 of internationalism in social work, covering the last part of the 19th and the early 20th centuries, the early pioneers period, was characterized by paternalism and ethnocentrism. Services were predominantly based on a charitable/philanthropic model designed to maintain social control of the poor (Mayadas & Elliott, 1997). The Charity Organization Society, the Settlement Movement, and the ideas of Sigmund Freud, all imported from Europe, epitomized these values and significantly influenced the early history of the profession (Reinders, 1982).

Phase 2, from about 1940 to 1970, has been summarized as professional imperialism (Midgley, 1981). From the 1940s to the 1970s, the direction of exchange was predominantly from America to the rest of the world. The American professional education model was adopted in Britain, Europe, Asia, Africa, the Middle East, and South America (Ankrah, 1992; Bose, 1992; Elliott & Walton, 1995; Guttmann & Cohen, 1995; Lee, 1992; Leung, 1995; Maeda, 1995; Mandal, 1995; Matsubara, 1992; Midgley, 1981; Midgley & Toors, 1992; Ntusi, 1997; Queiro-Tajalli, 1997; Ragab, 1995; Resnick, 1995). The international growth of American social work took place through the economic influence of overseas aid, faculty and student exchanges, translation of social work texts, and the work of the Economic and Social Council of the United Nations. The values remained ethnocentric and paternalistic, and indigenous cultures were often treated patronizingly and put down as "backward." The focus was on individual change, with token recognition of the environment. Self versus other provided a value conflict between imported therapeutic models and indigenous values. The economics of poverty, family planning, and access to primary health care were issues that often remained outside the practice of social work. During this period, the lack of fit between the exported social work model and the needs of indigenous cultures has been well documented (Hampson, 1995; Midgley, 1981; Resnick, 1995).

Phase 3, from the 1970s to the 1990s, is indigenization and reconceptualization, marking

a clear rejection of the Western psychodynamic and individual paradigm (Asamoah, 1997; Resnick, 1995; Siddiqui, 1997; Walton & Abo El Nasr, 1988). Much of the developing world undertook a paradigm shift to the developmental model, while American social work withdrew from its colonial activities.

Phase 4 visualizes a new approach to social work at the millennium and beyond (Mayadas & Elliott, 1997). A social development model of social work practice, which is elaborated later in this chapter, has predominant values of internationalism, multiculturalism, empowerment, the strengths perspective, democracy, and participation. This represents a shift from the current paradigm, which focuses on individual therapy at the expense of a structural perspective (Barber, 1995; Frumkin & O'Connor, 1985; Specht & Courtney, 1994; Wakefield, 1988a, 1988b).

WHY AN INTERNATIONAL PERSPECTIVE FOR SOCIAL WORK?

The question may legitimately be asked, How does incorporation of an international perspective benefit social work practice? Before proposing our model for practice, which takes account of a global perspective, we will review some of the arguments that have been put forward in the literature regarding the benefits of an international dimension to practice.

Global links. That the nations of the world are inextricably interdependent, politically, socially, and economically, that we live in a global village, has become a universal platitude. Is it true, and what does this mean for social work?

Estes (1994) marshals a good list of statements drawn from the development literature. These are summarized below, with examples added by the present authors.

1. Quality of life in all regions of the world may be dependent on social, political, and economic events occurring in a remote place. For example, the collapse of the Asian stock markets has repercussions on Wall Street and affects the retirement income of individuals, whose lifestyle may be changed as a result.

2. The reasons for social injustice and the appalling conditions in which people live and work may have international causes. Examples include the use of cheap labor, including that of children, to provide consumer goods such as carpets and garments, or the exploitation of immigrant labor, especially illegal immigrant labor, as agricultural and sweatshop workers. The tourist trade contributes to the continued prostitution and sexual abuse of children in Thailand and other Asian countries.

3. Not only are poverty and discrimination maintained, but the poverty gap is widened in every country of the world by present socioeconomic policies. For example, the present global economy has created two worlds across the world:

> One world of material comfort and developed capabilities, the other of exclusion and crushing impoverishment. One world reflects the new global "network society" that benefits from the opportunities created by globalization and information technology. The other is at the very margin of that society, unable to cope with the challenge of the global market or to absorb the information revolution. (UNDP/UNDDSMS, 1997, p. 4)

4. Interpersonal violence may often have international origins, causing racial and cultural conflict and discrimination. For example, the World Trade Center bombing in New York, the violence in Northern Ireland, the atrocities in the Balkan nations.

5. International peace can accelerate and promote social and human development across the world. For example, the "peace dividend" that comes from the reduction of military spending in national budgets may be used to create social programs and to alleviate poverty.

Comparative studies. If social work is to keep pace with economic globalization, it needs to assume a more central international perspective, both in practice and professional education. This would encourage more comparative studies and research. To date, comparative studies have become more established in social policy. Were social work education and practice to focus on this area, it would give the profession a better opportunity to do comparative research and to develop a broad appreciation of cultural diversity (Midgley, 1997a; Sarri, 1997). This would lead to genuine exchange of learning between the global north and south, rather than a unidirectional dissemination of information from the industrialized countries to the developing world.

Technology transfer. Mutual exchange can be facilitated by carefully studied and appropriate technology transfer that is adaptable to local needs, values, and economy and by well-formulated attempts at furthering world peace and global understanding (Billups & Juliá, 1996). Although on the surface, technology transfer seems like the long sought-after answer for internationalism, it is fraught with dangers. It has been pointed out that the unidirectional approach taken by the West in helping developing countries often results in building facilities for the rich. For example, according to Billups and Juliá, in a developing country, technology transfer resulted in modern medical facilities that the poor could never afford. This is an example of technology transfer being implemented without cultural sensitivity or awareness of the needs of ordinary people—a form of professional imperialism. Billups and Juliá maintain that a prerequisite of technology transfer is the knowledge that it is the best use of resources for optimum numbers of people and that it is consistent with the ethics, values, and beliefs of the community.

Furthering world peace and global understanding. Another factor in support of an international perspective, furthering world peace and understanding needs to take into account that interpersonal relationships among diverse groups and ethnic and racial violence in communities may be associated with international social forces: the bombing of the World Trade Center in New York is one example of this. Thus, racial, ethnic, and cultural intolerance is fanned by events frequently outside national boundaries, but these problems must be faced and worked on at home (Estes, 1994). Furthermore, to address these issues, a global restructuring of relationships between nations, communities, and peoples is necessary to attain social justice and relieve worldwide poverty and suffering. A stronger international perspective in social work would bring greater influence of the profession in international issues and contribute to this end (Estes, 1994).

Practice issues in international social work. What then are some practice implications of international issues in social work? Work with international organizations such as Oxfam, Save

the Children, and UNICEF, as well as work with military families and refugees, clearly requires an international perspective; these are well-established areas of international practice. More recent practice settings are work with international adoptions and with families of employees of multinational corporations.

An example of international cooperation in social work and other human services is seen in the development of programs and policies worldwide in response to the UN Convention on the Rights of the Child (CRC). Children in all nations that have ratified the convention have benefitted from new programs and policies. According to UNICEF (1998a), "The CRC has broken all records as the most widely ratified human rights treaty in history" (p. 1). Since 1990, all nations except 2 (the United States and Somalia) have ratified the treaty, 14 countries have incorporated the CRC into their constitutions, 35 countries have passed new laws or amended existing laws to conform with the CRC, and 25 countries have created bodies to monitor progress on the implementation of the CRC. Specific country examples show different approaches to implementation of the CRC: El Salvador established 12 municipal councils on child rights; in Jamaica and Sweden, national public education initiatives publicized the convention; in Vietnam, a national children's competition was held on knowledge of the CRC; and Austria, Columbia, Costa Rica, and Spain have all designated ombudsmen for children at provincial and national levels (UNICEF, 1998b.) However, there are many challenges to the full implementation of the principles of the CRC worldwide. These may be viewed from a systems perspective at the macro, mezzo, and micro levels. At the macro level, political systems may provide a challenge. In 1995, the

United States signed (but has not subsequently ratified) the CRC. Concerns focus around national sovereignty and parental rights: For example, the CRC "undermines parental rights," "usurps national and state sovereignty, . . . would allow children to have abortions . . . and sue parents" (UNICEF, 1998c). Other barriers at the macro level include the effect of armed conflict, sociocultural practices such as female genital mutilation, and male child preference demonstrated through selected gender abortions and female infanticide.

At the mezzo level, institutional barriers such as sexual exploitation of children and economic exploitation through child labor provide significant challenges to the full implementation of child rights throughout the world. At the micro level of the individual and family, child physical abuse and neglect remain a worldwide problem (Finkelhor & Korbin, 1988; Melton, 1991; Segal & Ashtekar, 1994). Because we are part of a global socioeconomic system, we cannot ignore these international issues. Refugees and immigrants may continue their cultural practices in the country of resettlement. Some refugee populations in the United States practice female genital mutilation. As social workers, we need to be sensitive to and knowledgeable about the sociocultural beliefs of the refugees, the issues this creates for families in the United States, and other issues, such as not being accepting of the medicalization of this procedure. A knowledge of international human rights and children's rights helps social workers gain perspective on challenging issues.

Human migration. Social workers everywhere are faced with the issue of human migration. An international perspective increases understanding and competence in working with immigrants and refugees in any country. Human migration is a natural phenomenon in response to changing sociopolitical, religious, and economic conditions around the world. Currently, there are 22.4 million people of concern to the Office of the UNHCR (1998). Human migration is at an all-time high. Factors associated with migration are political, religious, and ethnic persecution; natural disasters; civil war; economic reasons; postcolonial affiliation; and a spirit of adventure. The accelerated expansion of international trade and free trade agreements has further contributed to the heavy movement of immigrants and economic migrants across political borders. This inflow of refugees, migrants, and immigrants brings new social and economic problems that fall into the domain of social services. An example of how human migration affects social work practice in the United States is a group of depressed refugee women living in an urban metropolitan area. They are attending classes for English as a Second Language (ESL) and are participating in asset-based cooperative programs operated by a local mental health agency to achieve economic self-reliance. An intervention strategy used is to muster their indigenous cultural strengths and skills in setting up micro-enterprise initiatives. Social workers involved with this client group will be more effective if they have some knowledge of the society and culture from which the refugees have come and some understanding of the process and traumatic events these clients have experienced prior to arriving in their country of resettlement.

Certainly, there are challenges to be addressed and barriers to be overcome in increasing our international perspective. (Elliott & Mayadas, 1999; Harris 1997). To facilitate internationalism, social work may need to adopt an overarching model of practice, sufficiently sensitive to local conditions, that can analyze and explain all levels of practice from macro to micro, where not only technology transfer but technology exchange is possible. We suggest that the social development systems model of social work practice, presented in the following section of this chapter, offers a beginning attempt to integrate both macro and micro social work practice; that this model can be applicable in differing political, cultural, and socioeconomic systems; and that it will encourage an international perspective (Elliott, 1997). It demonstrates that technology transfer can be a successful exchange process, with the incorporation of strategies such as micro-credit and micro-enterprise techniques first pioneered in Bangladesh. Indeed, the adoption of social development itself is an example of technology transfer from the developing world (Elliott & Mayadas, 1999).

This social development model integrates current social work thinking such as the strengths perspective, empowerment, social justice, and social systems with economic approaches such as people-centered sustainable development and human capital investment. The emphasis is on linking social and economic systems.

SOCIAL DEVELOPMENT

Social development has long been used as a focus for UN policies in the developing world. In 1995, the United Nations held the World Summit for Social Development in Copenhagen. Over 180 countries endorsed the Copenhagen declaration, indicating international consensus for the policy priorities set in broad terms at the conference so as to be capable of adaptation to local needs in different countries, both in the industrialized and the developing world. Agreement was reached on the following priorities:

- Creating an enabling economic and social environment for people-centered development
- Empowering all people for self-reliance
- Promoting broad-based and equitable growth
- Enhancing household food security
- Improving access to basic infrastructure and social services
- Promoting job-creation and sustainable livelihoods
- Ensuring equitable access to credit and productive assets
- Expanding social protection for vulnerable people
- Promoting gender equity and the full participation of women in development
- Preserving, maintaining, and regenerating the natural resource base
- Preserving people's security in the context of rapid and sometimes disruptive globalization. (United Nations, 1997, p. 51)

In recent years, the United Nations has focused on people-centered sustainable development, and the policy priorities listed above reflect that goal. These policy priorities summarize well the focus of the social development perspective. They incorporate values of empowerment, planned change for prevention and development, social investment, proactive optimal programs to address social problems, and the enhancement of access to services and resources for all. These goals also reflect the needs of many industrialized countries in addressing poverty and discrimination, yet social policy in industrialized countries has not incorporated developmental goals until recently.

Midgley (1995, 1997a, 1997b) has articulated the social development perspective for social welfare policy applicable to both developed and developing nations through an emphasis on linking the social and the economic. He defines *social development* as "a process of planned social change designed to promote the well-being of the population as a whole in conjunction with a dynamic process of economic development" (Midgley, 1995, p. 25). Midgley emphasizes a social investment approach to social policy and planning through the development of social and human capital to avoid "distorted development" (Midgley, 1995, pp. 2-7).

The goals of social development are consistent with those of social work: to create planned social, economic, and institutional change with a view to improving the lives of individuals. The values of social development are also consistent with those of social work: participatory democracy (client self-determination), social justice, gender equity, cooperation, investment in human resources, empowerment, and the fulfillment of individual potential (Meinert, Kohn, & Strickler, 1984). A review and analysis by Billups (1994a) of the literature linking social work and social development provides an excellent summary of key issues and problems for practice. Despite the commonalities between social work and social development, much of the literature on social development has focused on a macro approach to social policy, planning, and administration. Estes (1994) and Cox (1995) review issues relating to social development, social work practice, and social work education. However, less attention has been focused on the potential offered by social development as an integrative model for direct social work practice. Meinert and Kohn (1987) suggest a process model; Elliott (1993) suggests

a model linking social development and systems theory as an integrative model of social work practice; Billups (1994b) suggests an integrative framework linking micro and macro practice; Mayadas and Elliott (1995) link social group work and social development; and Elliott and Mayadas (1996) link social development with clinical practice in social work, arguing that one of the reasons why social development has not been incorporated into social work practice in North America, unlike other countries, is the predominant influence of the medical or clinical model in American social work. They point out that this is a needless, inhibiting factor to the acceptance of social development ideas, and they demonstrate their position by linking empowerment practice, the role of economics in clinical practice, multicultural practice, and psychotherapy as liberation. Social development has the potential to shift the paradigm in American social work from one in which, as Seidman (1983) has said, it is "trapped within the premise of individualism" to a model that would facilitate a global approach; greater international exchange; sustainable development; empowerment of individuals, families, and communities; and social and economic integration. The paradigm shift would be akin to the reconceptualization and indigenization of social work that has taken place in countries across the world. Social development offers the possibility of a new social work perspective and dynamic for the 21st century.

A SOCIAL DEVELOPMENT SYSTEMS MODEL FOR SOCIAL WORK

Figure 30.1 proposes a social development model for social work that addresses four sys-

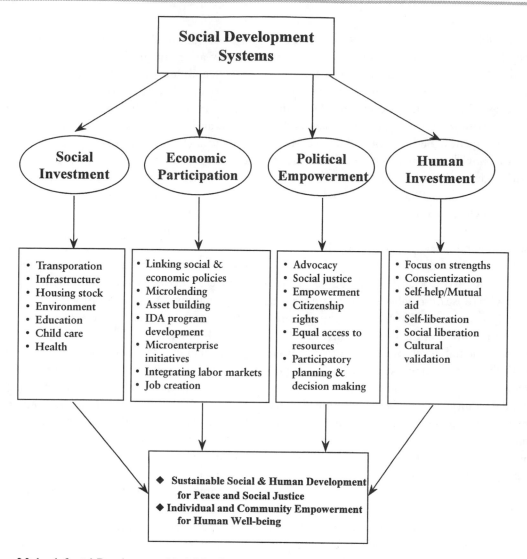

Figure 30.1. A Social Development Model for Social Work

tem levels: social investment, economic participation, political empowerment, and human investment. The social work intervention strategies that relate to each of these systems are set
out in the boxes corresponding to each sector.
The model extends the traditional approach to
social work by including sustainable developmental strategies for each system sector.

Social investment. Social work strategies related to this sector involve policy and planning,
with the goal of building a social infrastructure
designed not only to address social problems in
the remedial tradition but to preempt them in
the developmental mode. As an example of social investment, the provision of an adequate
stock of housing is important. In the United

States, the Census Bureau projects that the total number of households will increase from 101,683,469 in 1999 to 113,425,776 in 2010. In the same period, black households will increase by 3,032,970, and Hispanic households by 4,498,175 (U.S. Bureau of Census, 1996: Table 4n., text at www.census.gov). Given the disproportionate number of black and Hispanic people in poverty, a social investment program to ensure that adequate affordable housing is available for the projected increases in households would reduce the social costs incurred by homelessness or inadequate and substandard housing. In many developed nations, the provision of low-cost housing is also inadequate, and like public housing projects in the United States, often produces more social problems than it solves. Equal access to education for all children, whether inner-city, rural, or suburban residents, ethnic minority or ethnic majority, means the provision of equitable educational services and facilities as a function of social investment. In 1996, the Personal Responsibility and Work Opportunity Reconciliation Act replaced welfare with workfare. However, there was no national policy for child care. A social investment approach would take into account the fact that welfare recipients need child care arrangements if they are to enter the labor market and build a national child care policy accordingly, like the one that already exists in France. Similarly, adequate transportation and access to health care for all citizens foster equality of opportunity to participate in the labor market and achieve a reasonable standard of living for families. Recognition of changing economic conditions, such as the increasing number of women of child-bearing age who participate in the labor market, necessitates child welfare policies and employment legisla-

tion that incorporate provision of adequate day care facilities as part of the normal social order. Environmental issues are also a matter of social investment. Rogge and Darkwa (1996) attest that market globalization and economic expansion are destructive to the physical environment of the poor, especially in countries of the global south. For example, toxic waste and pesticide-related deaths in developing countries are directly linked to unrestricted marketing strategies of large multinational corporations, which are banned from similar operations in their own Western countries. This suggests that in the future, multidimensional interventions at the local, national, and international levels, based on social action, public participation, and legislation, should address environmental problems and maximize the person-in-environment perspective. To address environmental problems arguably represents the fullest extent of the person-in-environment perspective that is part of the mainstream tradition of American social work.

Economic participation. Midgley's (1995) definition of social development, quoted earlier in this chapter, stresses the link between the social and the economic. Although, traditionally, social work has had as its mission work with the poor, it has also been reactive in nature, addressing the consequences of poverty rather than influencing the causes. Social work has not been involved with economics until recently. The call for sustainable human development has led to the need for new policies, marking a departure from charity-based welfare, designed only to maintain individuals at the poverty line, to an investment approach that would empower them to achieve sustainable economic viability.

In the area of micro lending and micro finance, we have much to learn from the developing world. The Grameen Bank, which began its operations in Bangladesh and set a model for micro-loan and micro-enterprise programs worldwide, bases its operation on group liability in loans to people in poverty who have no collateral (Counts, 1996; Elliott & Mayadas, 1999; Livermore, 1996). The loans are then used for micro-enterprise initiatives, and this approach has successfully alleviated poverty in Asia and other parts of the world: Household income increased by 50% in villages where the Grameen Bank operates, and beneficiaries were primarily women, the landless, and marginal landowners (Srinivas, 1999). Other examples of banks that successfully work against poverty are the Village Banks of Bank Rakyat (BRI-UD) in Indonesia, which had great success in loans and savings in low-income rural communities; the Badan Kredit Kecamatan (BKK), also in Indonesia, which targets the poorest rural populations; and the Bank for Agriculture and Agricultural Co-operatives (BAAC), in Thailand. Like the Grameen Bank, they operate joint liability loans and group savings programs. Repayment rates of 97% are usual among populations it was thought would not repay. The key to the banks' success has been linking the social and the economic: The support given to the loan groups and to individuals by the bank officers might be likened to a case management approach.

These programs have been only slowly translated to the United States, and social work has been slow to take the economic dimension on board. However, Counts (1996) records a succesful micro-lending project in Chicago, based on the Grameen Bank model.

The following case studies from four continents, Eastern Europe, Africa, Asia, and South America, represent some examples of the human face of micro finance. They were presented as case studies at the Microcredit Summit in 1997 (Srinivas, 1999).

> Katayana Strzelinska, a 24-year-old former factory worker from Lodz, Poland, received a loan from Fundusz Mikro. She set up her own successful business making pantyhose.

> Daba Fall's family in Senegal, Africa, fell victim to the country's economic crisis when her husband lost his job. The family had no income, so Daba made stew of calves' feet and vegetables and sold it at the bus station. She received loans from the micro-lending program, Femme Developpement Enterprise en Afrique (FDEA), and eventually opened her own restaurant and built her family a house.

> The family of Mrs. Thay from the Mekong Delta in Vietnam was one of many forcibly repatriated from the city after the war. They were city dwellers with no means of earning a living. Mrs. Thay received a loan from The Friendship Bridge and began a pig-raising and basket-making business.

> Lastenia Lozano Flores had little education and married at the age of 15. She and her husband worked as farm laborers. They obtained a loan from Asociación Beneficia Prisma, planted rice, which they sold, and with the proceeds opened a general store. They have been able to install electricity in their house and pay for medical care.

There could be many parallels to these case studies among the rural and urban poor in the United States.

Sherraden's (1991) work on asset-based policies for the poor breaks new ground for social workers in the United States and offers a policy rationale for the development of micro-finance programs here. An asset-based policies approach represents a human investment strategy:

Individuals in poverty receive access to individual development accounts (IDAs), which may be subsidized or matched at different levels depending on the program. This may open new opportunities for education, housing, or use of banking facilities that were previously closed to this population. Some banks have been willing to participate to fulfill their obligations under the Community Reinvestment Act. Microlending programs such as Family Services America's Family Loan program in conjunction with the McKnight Foundation, established in 1994, are based on human investment and equal opportunity for economic participation. Cooperation between banks, foundations, and social welfare services has made such programs possible. The Family Services America Family Loan Program in Fort Worth, Texas, offers loans for employment-related needs such as tool purchase and transportation, including buying and repairing of cars, enabling an individual to remain in the labor market in areas with limited or no public transportation. Financial counseling and case management are offered with the loan.

Often, the poor are marginalized as a result of dual labor markets: The core labor market, operated by large corporations and federal and state governments, offers attractive employment options, such as retirement and health benefits and paid leave. The secondary labor market employs people at minimum wage, offers no benefits, and provides employment that may be part-time or temporary (Piore, 1997). Other causes of economic marginalization may be lack of access to property or land ownership. These are challenges to U.S. social work in the new century: Established, successful models of micro-finance programs are available in the developing world if the paradigm in the United States can be shifted and the profession is will-

ing to learn and adapt from these challenges to serve local and national populations.

Political empowerment. Many people who are the clients of social work agencies are disaffected and alienated. They often do not participate in political processes such as elections because they lack either transportation or motivation, through feeling disempowered. They believe that their vote or voice does not count. Political disaffection occurs through experiences of discrimination, unequal opportunity, and poor treatment by social agents such as police, immigration officials, and welfare officials.

Strategies for empowerment in social work are important in the profession's current thinking. Empowerment has both an individual personal component and an institutional component. Social work advocacy programs that address social justice and equal access to resources and promote human and citizenship rights are key components of a social development approach. We can learn from international approaches, such as this example from India.

In 1993, the reservationist policy of the Indian government toppled the centuries-old traditional barrier of caste by setting aside a third of all seats in the Panchayats, village governance councils, for women, including women of the lowest caste. This empowerment strategy, enabling low caste female participation in local politics, has resulted in remarkable leadership from women who less than a decade ago were enveloped in the institution of traditional servility. As a result of this momentous action, Rani, a washerwoman of the lower caste, has been appointed chief in Chijaras in North India. (Dugger, 1999)

Similar reservationist policies in favor of women political candidates are being experimented with in Peru and Argentina and in the industrialized countries of Germany and Belgium. In the United States, inviting the participation of women on welfare in housing planning committees, for example, which often are predominantly middle class and may not see the need for affordable housing, would change the nature of housing policies to better serve a disempowered population.

Human investment. This system represents the individual and family-based approach to social work practice. In a social development approach, however, emphasis is on human investment through strengths-based practice, empowerment, ecosystems, and person-inenvironment approaches (Allen-Meares & Lane, 1987; Germain & Gitterman, 1980; Gutiérrez, Delois, & Glenmaye, 1995; Saleeby, 1992; Simon, 1994). In their review of processes of change common to a range of currently used psychotherapies, Prochaska and Diclemente (1992) include consciousness-raising, self-liberation, and social liberation. Ivey's (1995) multicultural counseling and therapy model focuses on psychotherapy as liberation from phobias, fears, and anxieties. Wakefield (1988b) states the importance of individual psychotherapy goals such as self-esteem, self-confidence, self-awareness, self-knowledge, problem-solving skills, and assertiveness in personal empowerment. Thus, the new approach builds on the old.

In assessment, a social development approach requires a broader approach to clinical assessment than checking off a category in the *Diagnostic and Statistical Manual of Mental Disorders* (*DSM-IV*; American Psychiatric Association, 1994). For instance, a model such as that proposed by Cowger (1992) more closely approximates a social development perspective on assessment. The authors have discussed else-

where, in more detail than can be offered here, social development issues relating to social work clinical and group work practice. Issues raised are the role of household economics in the decision of women to stay in violent relationships; the role played by corporations in influencing the incidence of a diagnosis, such as ADHD, and prescriptions for drugs such as Ritalin; and the role played by the mental health insurance industry in *DSM-IV* diagnoses (Elliott, 1993; Elliott & Mayadas, 1996; Mayadas & Elliott, 1995). The change of usage when describing victims of crime, physical or sexual abuse, mental or physical illness—as *survivors* instead of *victims*—symbolizes well the changes that can be brought about by a social development model of social work practice. An example from rural Thailand illustrates how restructuring an issue changes the nature of the problem.

> The commercial sex industry has developed rapidly in Thailand, where poverty-stricken families have encouraged their daughters into prostitution. To free the girls from this entrapment, Thailand's NGOs, in collaboration with the government, have restructured the situation from personal immorality to an individual empowerment issue. Thus, interventions have been aimed at personal empowerment and enhancement of self-esteem through psychoeducation and vocational training. In addition, girls are briefed on the health risks of commercial sex. Vocational training provides an alternative lifestyle. With both alternatives at hand, the social work principle of self-determination ensures that the girls are free to select their own future course. The results of a 1995 survey demonstrated that using empowerment techniques lowered servitude in commercial sex; 94% of the adolescents attributed this change to receiving information on health risks in commercial sex. (Sacks, 1997)

Sullivan (1994) offers useful insights into links between strengths-based and empowerment practice and social development at micro, mezzo, and macro levels of practice through a review of individual and collective empowerment concepts. He takes the position that individual empowerment falls within the social development paradigm.

CONCLUSION

It would seem helpful to further the development of social work theory by articulating the commonalities between nations more clearly and by addressing the links with social work practice in a global model. This can be done while at the same time accommodating the social construction of social work and the need for social work to reflect as well as influence and change social and economic norms. Such a model would lead to greater recognition that social development is needed in industrialized countries and would facilitate international dialogues and discussions. At present, there is greater emphasis on global and regional differences and a lack of recognition of common needs. Midgley (1990) refers to the preoccupation of Western countries with poverty and social problems in developing countries, while not taking into account the parallels between those conditions and inner cities in industrialized countries. Social development values and interventions, as discussed in this chapter, offer equal benefits for meeting needs in both developing and industrialized worlds. Furthermore, a common intervention model supports the global approach to practice where knowledge and skills can be exchanged across national boundaries and used selectively as appropriate to local needs. The model promotes a unified applicability of assessment and change across

countries; diminishes the focus on regional, national, and international differences; and strengthens international understanding through emphasis on global social work practice. The model that we have proposed incorporates current thinking in social work such as the empowerment and strengths-based approaches. It addresses diversity and includes issues important for powerless groups such as women and minorities. It follows the systems-based integrative tradition in that it incorporates both the micro and the macro perspectives.

REFERENCES

Ankrah, E. M. (1992). Social work in Uganda: Survival in the midst of turbulence. In M. C. Hokenstad, S. K. Khinduka, & J. Midgley (Eds.), *Profiles in international social work* (pp. 145-162). Washington, DC: NASW Press.

Allen-Meares, P., & Lane, B. A. (1987). Grounding social work practice in theory: Ecosystems. *Social Casework, 68,* 515-521.

Asamoah, Y. (1997). Africa. In N. S. Mayadas, T. D. Watts, & D. Elliott (Eds.), *International handbook on social work practice and theory* (pp. 303-319). Westport, CT: Greenwood.

Barber, J. G. (1995). Politically progressive casework. *Families in Society: Journal of Contemporary Human Services, 76,* 30-37.

Billups, J. (1994a). Conceptualizing a partnership model between social work and social development. *Social Development Issues, 16,* 91-99.

Billups, J. (1994b). The social development model as an organizing framework for social work practice. In R. G. Meinert, J. T. Pardeck, & W. P. Sullivan (Eds.), *Issues in social work: A critical analysis* (pp. 22-37). Westport, CT: Auburn House.

Billups, J. O., & Juliá, M. C. (1996). Technology transfer and integrated social development: International issues and possibilities for social work. *Journal of Sociology and Social Welfare, 23,* 175-188.

Bose, A. B. (1992). Social work in India: Developmental roles for a helping profession. In M. C. Hokenstad, S. K. Khinduka, & J. Midgley (Eds.), *Profiles in international social work* (pp. 71-84). Washington, DC: NASW Press.

Counts, A. (1996). *Give us credit*. New York: Random House.

Cowger, C. D. (1992). Assessment of client strengths. In D. Saleebey (Ed.), *The strengths perspective in social work practice* (pp. 139-147). White Plains, NY: Longman.

Cox, D. (1995). Social development and social work education: The USA's continuing leadership in a changing world. *Social Development Issues, 17*(2/3) 1-17.

Dugger, C. A. (1999). A woman's place: In India lower-caste women turn village rule upside down. In *Bharati* (pp. 13-19). Dallas, TX: India Association of North Texas.

Elliott, D. (1993). Social work and social development: Toward an integrative model for social work practice. *International Social Work, 36*, 21-36.

Elliott D. (1997). Conclusion. In N. S. Mayadas, T. D. Watts, & D. Elliott (Eds.), *International handbook on social work practice and theory* (pp. 441-449). Westport, CT: Greenwood.

Elliott, D., & Mayadas, N. S. (1996). Social development and clinical practice in social work. *Journal of Applied Social Sciences, 21,* 61-68.

Elliott, D., & Mayadas, N. S. (1999). Infusing global perspectives into social work practice. In C. S. Ramanatham & R. Link (Eds.), *All our futures: Principles and resources for social work practice in a global era* (pp. 52-68). Belmont, CA: Wadsworth.

Elliott, D., & Walton, R. (1995). United Kingdom. In T. D. Watts, D. Elliott, & N. S. Mayadas (Eds.), *Handbook of social work education* (pp. 123-144). Westport, CT: Greenwood.

Estes, R. (1994). Education for social development: Curricular issues and models. *Social Development Issues, 16,* 69-89.

Finkelhor, D., & Korbin, J. (1988). Child abuse as an international issue. *Child Abuse and Neglect, 12,* 3-23.

Frumkin, M., & O'Connor, G. (1985). Where has the profession gone? Where is it going? Social work's search for identity. *Urban and Social Change Review, 18,* 13-18.

Germain, C., & Gitterman, A. (1980). *The life model of social work practice*. New York: Columbia University Press.

Gutiérrez, L. M., Delois, K. A., & Glenmaye, L. (1995). Understanding empowerment practice: Building on practitioner-based knowledge. *Families in Society: Journal of Contemporary Human Services, 76,* 534-542.

Guttmann, D., & Cohen, B. Z. (1995). Israel. In T. D. Watts, D. Elliott, & N. S. Mayadas (Eds.), *International handbook of social work education* (pp. 305-320). Westport, CT: Greenwood.

Hampson, J. (1995). Zimbabwe. In T. D. Watts, D. Elliott, & N. S. Mayadas (Eds.), *International handbook on social work education* (pp. 241-260). Westport, CT: Greenwood.

Harris, R. (1997). Internationalizing social work: Some themes and issues. In N. S. Mayadas, T. D. Watts, & D. Elliott (Eds.), *International handbook on social work practice and theory* (pp. 429-440). Westport, CT: Greenwood.

Healy, L. (1995). Overview. In T. D. Watts, D. Elliott, & N. S. Mayadas (Eds.), *International handbook on social work education* (pp. 421-440). Westport, CT: Greenwood.

Ivey, A. E. (1995). Psychotherapy as liberation: Towards specific skills and strategies in multicultural counseling and psychotherapy. In J. G. Ponterotto, J. M. Casa, L. A. Suzuli, & C. M. Alexander (Eds.), *Handbook of multicultural counseling and therapy* (pp. 53-72). Thousand Oaks, CA: Sage.

Lee, P. C. Y. (1992). Social work in Hong Kong, Singapore, South Korea and Taiwan: Asia's four little dragons. In M. C. Hokenstad, S. K. Khinduka, & J. Midgley (Eds.), *Profiles in international social work* (pp. 99-114). Washington, DC: NASW Press.

Leung, J. E. B. (1995). China. In T. D. Watts, D. Elliott, & N. S. Mayadas (Eds.), *International handbook of social work education* (pp. 403-420). Westport, CT: Greenwood.

Livermore, M. (1996). Social work, social development, and micro-enterprises: Techniques and issues for implementation. *Journal of Applied Social Sciences, 21,* 37-44.

Maeda, K. K. (1995). Japan. In T. D. Watts, D. Elliott, & N. S. Mayadas (Eds.), *International handbook of social work education* (pp. 389-402). Westport, CT: Greenwood.

Mandal, K. S. (1995). India. In T. D. Watts, D. Elliott, & N. S. Mayadas (Eds.), *International handbook of social work education* (pp. 355-366). Westport, CT: Greenwood.

Matsubara, Y. (1992). Social work in Japan: Responding to demographic dilemmas. In M. C. Hokenstad, S. K. Khinduka, & J. Midgley (Eds.), *Profiles in international social work* (pp. 85-98). Washington, DC: NASW Press.

Mayadas, N. S., & Elliott, D. (1995). Developing professional identity through social groupwork: A social development model for education. In M. D. Feit, J. H. Ramey, J. S. Wodarski, & A. R. Mann (Eds.), *Capturing the power of diversity* (pp. 89-107). New York: Haworth.

Mayadas, N. S., & Elliott, D. (1997). Lessons from international social work: Policies and practices. In M. Reisch & E. Gambrill (Eds.), *Social work in the 21st century* (pp. 175-185). Thousand Oaks, CA: Pine Forge.

Meinert, R., & Kohn, E. (1987). Toward operationalization of social development concepts. *Social Development Issues, 10,* 4-18.

Meinert, R., Kohn, E., & Strickler, G. (1984). International survey of social development concepts. *Social Development Issues, 8,* 70-88.

Melton, G. (1991). Preserving the dignity of children around the world: The UN Convention on the Rights of the Child. *Child Abuse and Neglect, 15,* 343-350.

Midgley, J. (1981). *Professional imperialism: Social work in the third world.* London: Heinemann.

Midgley, J. (1990). International social work: Learning from the third world. *Social Work, 35,* 295-301.

Midgley, J. (1995). *Social development: The developmental perspective in social welfare.* Thousand Oaks, CA: Sage.

Midgley, J. (1997a). *Social welfare in global context.* Thousand Oaks, CA: Sage.

Midgley, J. (1997b). Social work and international social development. In M. C. Hockenstad & J. Midgley (Eds.), *Issues in international social work* (pp. 11-26). Washington, DC: NASW Press.

Midgley, J., & Toors, M. (1992). Is international social work a one-way transfer of ideas and practice methods from the United States to other countries. In E. Gambrill & R. Pruger (Eds.), *Controversial issues in social work* (pp. 92-106). Boston: Allyn & Bacon.

Ntusi, T. (1997). South Africa. In T. D. Watts, D. Elliott, & N. S. Mayadas (Eds.), *International handbook of social work education* (pp. 261-280). Westport, CT: Greenwood.

Piore, M. (1997). The dual labor market. In D. Gordon (Ed.), *Problems in political economy.* Lexington, MA: Heath.

Prochaska, J. O., & Diclemente, C. C. (1992). The transtheoretical approach. In J. C. Norcross & M. R. Goldfried (Eds.), *Handbook of psychotherapy integration* (pp. 300-334). New York: Basic Books.

Queiro-Tajalli, I. (1997). Argentina. In T. D. Watts, D. Elliott, & N. S. Mayadas (Eds.), *International handbook of social work education* (pp. 87-102). Westport, CT: Greenwood.

Ragab, I. (1995). Middle East and Egypt. In T. D. Watts, D. Elliott, & N. S. Mayadas (Eds.), *International handbook of social work education* (pp. 281-304). Westport, CT: Greenwood.

Reinders, R. (1982). Toynbee Hall and the American settlement movement. *Social Service Review, 56,* 39-54.

Resnick, R. P. (1995). South America. In T. D. Watts, D. Elliott, & N. S. Mayadas (Eds.), *International handbook of social work education* (pp. 65-85). Westport, CT: Greenwood.

Rogge, M. E., & Darkwa, O. A. (1996). Poverty and the environment: An international perspective for social work. *International Social Work, 39,* 395-409.

Sacks, R. G. (1997). Commercial sex and the single girl: Women's empowerment through economic development in Thailand. *Development in Practice, 7,* 424-427.

Saleebey, D. (Ed.). (1992). *The strengths perspective in social work practice.* White Plains, NY: Longman.

Sarri, R. (1997). International social work at the millenium. In M. Reisch & E. Gambrill (Eds.), *Social work in the 21st century* (pp. 387-395). Thousand Oaks, CA: Pine Forge.

Segal, U. A., & Ashtekar, A. (1994). Detection of intrafamilial child abuse: Children at intake at a children's observation home in India. *Child Abuse and Neglect, 18,* 957-967.

Seidman, E. (1983). *A handbook of social intervention.* Beverly Hills, CA: Sage.

Sherraden, M. (1991). *Assets and the poor: A new American welfare policy.* New York: M. E. Sharpe.

Siddiqui, H. Y. (1997). *Working with communities.* New Delhi, India: Hira.

Simon, B. L. (1994). *The empowerment tradition in American social work: A history.* New York: Columbia University Press.

Specht, H., & Courtney, M. (1994). *Fallen angels: How social work has abandoned its mission.* New York: Free Press.

Srinivas, H. (1999). *Virtual library of micro-cedit* [On-line]. Available: www.soc.titech.ac.jp

Sullivan, W. P. (1994). The tie that binds: A strengths/empowerment model for social development. *Social Development Issues, 16,* 101-111.

United Nations. (1997). UN briefing papers. In *The world conferences: Developing priorities for the 21st century.* New York: United Nations, Department of Public Information.

United Nations Development Program & United Nations Department for Development Support and Management Services (UNDP/UNDDSMS). (1997). *Preventing and eradicating poverty: Main elements of a strategy to eradicate poverty in the Arab states.* New York: United Nations Development Program, Regional Bureau for Arab States.

UNHCR. (1998). *UNHCR 1997 statistical overview* [On-line]. Available: http://www.unicef/org/pon96/cotrnsl.htm

UNICEF. (1998a). *Child rights. About the convention* [On-line]. Available: http://www.unicef.org/crc/conven.htm

UNICEF. (1998b). *The CRC. Translating principles into law* [On-line]. Available: http://www.unicef/org/pon96/cotrnsl.htm

UNICEF. (1998c). *How to help the U.S. ratify* [On-line]. Available: http://www.unicef.org/crc/updates/us-how.htm

U.S. Bureau of the Census. (1996). *Projected number of households by type, race, and Hispanic origin: 1995-2010.* Available: www.census.gov/population/projections/nation/hhfam/table4n.txtp

Wakefield, J. C. (1988a). Psychotherapy, distributive justice, and social work: Part I. Distributive justice as a conceptual framework for social work. *Social Service Review, 62,* 187-210.

Wakefield, J. C. (1988b). Psychotherapy, distributive justice, and social work: Part II. Psychotherapy and the pursuit of justice. *Social Service Review, 62,* 354-382.

Walton, R., & Abo El Nasr, M. M. (1988). Indigenization and authentization in terms of social work in Egypt. *International Social Work, 31,* 135-144.

CHAPTER THIRTY-ONE

Fund-Raising for the Direct Services

ARMAND LAUFFER

It is no longer sufficient for direct service providers to be good at tutoring, counseling, or caregiving. Surviving and thriving in the first decade of the 21st century requires that they generate financial and other resources in support of what they do. Fund-raising is about maintaining and growing the services, improving and expanding them, and, paradoxically, increasing the independence of direct service providers from their supporters.

In this chapter, we address (a) elements of the funding environment that affect all direct services, (b) the most common mechanisms available for raising the needed cash and other resources, (c) the sources of supply, (d) who should be involved in fund-raising and what they should be doing, and (e) changes in the

funding environment that will take place over the next 10 years.

GOOD NEWS AND BAD NEWS ABOUT THE FUND-RAISING ENVIRONMENT

Direct services are funded though public and charitable sources and through fees for services paid by consumers or third parties. Although the resource base for many direct service enterprises has expanded over the past few decades, it tends to be an unsteady base, with the sources of income for specific services changing rapidly. There's good news here and bad.

Public funding. The bad news is that government cutbacks have put the squeeze on many providers. The good news is that, although there's been an aggregate reduction of funds for social programs, there have been some increases in public funds available for many direct services and many of these services—paid for in part by government agencies—are actually performed by nonprofit agencies and for-profit organizations. Governments, at all levels, use such mechanisms as grants and contracting work out to engage the private and voluntary sectors in supporting direct practice. Although the total amount of government money available for direct (social) services has declined since the 1970s, the sums transferred to nongovernment organizations appear to have increased, and the American appetite for using nongovernment organizations (NGOs) to conduct public business appears unabated. In effect, although the government may be spending less, it is conducting more and more of its business through the voluntary and private sectors.

Charitable giving. On the philanthropic front, the good news is that charitable giving by individual Americans appears to have risen 10% or more a year since 1995, reaching a record $135 billion in 1998. The bad news is that this percentage compares poorly with the 27% rise in the *Standard & Poor's* index of 500 stocks. At least some Americans are finding other than charitable uses for the gains associated with a booming market.

On the other hand, an increasing number of wealthy individuals appear to be deferring gifts through trusts and bequests ($13.6 billion in 1998, up 30% over the previous year), which are likely to generate huge sources of new philanthropic dollars in only a few years. And foundations added $17 billion in new gifts to their endowments (about $10 out of every $100 in charitable gifts). The same year, they gave $16.1 billion to the human services (up 27% over the previous year). American corporations donated more than $9 billion in cash gifts, mostly to nonprofit organizations, plus a similar amount via in-kind services and other noncash gifts.

Implications for the direct services. The good news is that a robust American economy has made this largesse possible. The bad news is there is no guarantee that the economy will continue growing at the current rate. And even if it does, new capital has created a very competitive environment in which the direct services are not the assured beneficiaries. Political and cause-oriented campaigns siphon billions away from philanthropy, and although a booming market may explain part of the rise in the absolute number of philanthropic dollars, investment firms are likely to induce donors to keep their funds heavily invested so long as the market keeps rising.

Some firms, such as Fidelity Investments, have created charitable gifts funds that permit donors to keep fully invested while realizing a tax benefit, allowing them to designate where their charitable gifts are to go. The good news is that this may increase the funds available to direct services in the future. The bad news is that it reduces the dollars currently available.

Competition for philanthropic dollars, state agency contracts, United Way allocations, and consumer or third-party fees for service has become increasingly fierce. Some organizations have developed competitive skills and contacts that give them an edge over others regardless of the quality of their programs. Others have added sales and royalties and investments and income-generating strategies.

FUNDING MECHANISMS

Readers may find it useful to review the kinds of mechanisms used to generate revenue before examining where money comes from and how to find out.

Allocations. Allocations are distributions from a central source to a program unit, usually on an annual basis. The source can be external or internal. An example of the former is a county social service department that allocates funds to a domestic violence shelter. An internal allocation is exemplified by a community center board allocating its annual budget to various direct service units, such as the day camp, senior citizens drop-in center, or latch-key program. Until recently, many direct service programs could assume annual allocations with minor adjustments for rising costs or changes in client demand from year to year. Today, this is less likely. For example, some United Way organizations have substituted competitive grants open to all qualifying nonprofits for the traditional annual allocations to member agencies.

Grants. Grants permit recipients to pursue activities of their own design within a set of guidelines provided by the funder. *Block* grants are the principal mechanism by which the federal government reallocates tax income to states and local government units for domestic programs such as housing and welfare reform. In turn, these dollars may be turned into either contracts or categorical grants that are intended for specific services to targeted populations. A

limited number of categorical grants are also available from federal agencies. Grants are also the primary mechanism used by foundations to make philanthropic awards to individuals, organizations, or collaborative enterprises.

Contracts. A contract is a legal agreement between a contractor and a vendor in which the former specifies what is to be done, by whom, to whom or to what, within what time frame, following what standards. The vendor agrees to do the work in return for a specified remuneration. *Purchase-of-service contracts* (POSCs) are used by governments to buy the services of both voluntary (nonprofit) or proprietary (private, for-profit) organizations. But contracts can move in any direction. For example, one state may purchase the services of a proprietary firm to build and manage prisons. But that firm, temporarily tight on space, may then contract with another public agency (such as a county jail) to house its wards.

Fees-for-service and tuition. Some direct services are paid all or in part through fees and tuition payments. Some fee schedules cover the full cost of service, whereas others use sliding scales to accommodate user capacities to pay. Fees paid on behalf of users by other organizations are called third-party payments. In the health field, this mechanism is used extensively by both private insurers and public programs such as Medicare and Medicaid. In education, third-party payments are also possible, when, for example, an employer, government body, or philanthropic organization covers the tuition of a staff member or another beneficiary.

Charitable gifts. Cash and in-kind charitable gifts are contributions made to a nonprofit or public body by individuals, other nonprofits (such as foundations and civic associations), or for-profit businesses. They can be given in the present or deferred (as when a pledge has a long-term payoff schedule or a bequest is payable only when the donor's estate is settled). Gifts can also be in-kind, for example, equipment or volunteer time that has some cash value. If it has no anticipated programmatic value (such as some real estate or art work), a non-cash gift might be sold to generate income for current use or investment.

Reserve funds, investments, sales, and royalties. Reserve funds are dollars set aside for use in the future. They may be banked to address emerging needs perhaps designated for specific purposes, such as reducing fees for clients-in-need, or invested in income-generating instruments such as a stock portfolio or some other commodity that can be sold or may generate royalties.[1] For example, a school might sell educational materials or earn royalties on the sale of booster items such as T-shirts. With some limitations, nonprofit organizations are permitted to sponsor commercial enterprises without paying taxes on income if the activity meets the "test of relatedness." This means that the activity must contribute in an important way to the performance of the organization's tax-exempt purpose.

SOURCES OF SUPPLY: GOVERNMENT, BUSINESS, AND THE VOLUNTARY SECTOR

Understanding these mechanisms is not very helpful unless one knows where and how to find the sources of supply of both cash and non-cash support.

Seeking government funds—the bucks start here. For the foreseeable future, government will continue to be the largest source of support for non-proprietary (nonprofit) direct services. Government agencies routinely fund others to provide services that prior to the 1970s might have been conducted by their own agencies. For example, whereas state mental hospitals once housed thousands of patients, today, the mentally ill may be served by clinics, halfway houses, and other facilities. Since the early 1960s, a wide range of direct service agencies, for-profit and not-for-profit, have been created expressly to take advantage of the government's interests in encouraging or contracting for the provision of services to specific populations. Recent examples include job training and child care programs that are funded to accommodate the requirements of welfare reform.

POSCs and third-party payments have become the preferred means of government funding because of the belief that both mechanisms lead to (a) cost cutting and improved efficiency, (b) better quality of service, and (c) improved fiscal accountability. Contractor and vendor are likely to understand the contracting process a bit differently. From the government's side, it includes four steps: (a) recruiting potential bidders; (b) rating, ranking, and selecting bids; (c) negotiating the contract; (d) monitoring and evaluating performance, which may lead to renewal or termination of the contract. The vendor is generally concerned about (a) finding out what is available, (b) submitting a winning bid, (c) negotiating reasonable terms, and (d) providing acceptable service.

When a government agency wants to initiate a program, expand services to new populations, and replace or expand the number of current providers, it will seek new bidders. First, a Request for Proposal (RFP) or Request for Quote (RFQ) is published and distributed to a list of potential bidders. If the program and its requirements are new—like the job training and child care programs that accompanied welfare reform—the agency may conduct one or more regionally based bidders' conferences at which the program and its requirements are explained and interested parties may be given consultation on how to prepare acceptable proposals. Direct service agencies can apply to become bidders by contacting the appropriate local or state government purchasing office. Those unsure of where to apply might contact the governor's or mayor's office or seek assistance from a state representative or from local officials. The RFPs[2] and vendor application materials are often available via state, county, or municipal web sites.

After proposals are submitted, their components (such as program goals, geographic area or population served, staffing, costs, local support) are scored by reviewers according to predetermined selection criteria. Proposals are then ranked, and vendors are notified if their proposals/bids were selected. Unlike grants, in which the notification of an award may be followed directly by a dollar transfer to the recipient agency, contracts are legal documents that require detailed specification. For example, when a state agency contracts with a direct service provider to open and manage a new group home for abused teens, the contractor and vendor are expected to work out specific price and payment procedures, client eligibility criteria, staff qualifications, location, monitoring and evaluation schedules, and so on. To avoid delays and future misunderstandings, the government's legal department and the vendor's attorney negotiate contract details. Once the project is in operation, regular reporting by the vendor may be required.

The contractor may make routine or spot checks to assure compliance with the terms of the agreement. If agreed-to standards are not met, funders may offer a carrot—for example, consultation, training, and even new resources—to help the vendor improve or use a stick by withholding payments until performance is improved or terminating the contract. If vendor performance is adequate or if the cost of generating new bids is too high, chances are that the contract will receive continuation funding the following year. However, funding may be cut when governmental priorities shift, and even successful programs may have to reapply when new competitors enter the scene.

Building on a strong foundation. Although, in the aggregate, foundation funding is not likely to provide more than 5% of what government agencies allocate to direct services, their dollars may be just what is needed to initiate new services, carry agencies through hard times, or provide supplemental support for activities that might not otherwise survive. Unfortunately, those unfamiliar with how foundations operate and how they differ from each other may discourage some direct service providers for applying and encourage unrealistic expectations in others.[3] So what are foundations, and what do they do?

Philanthropic foundations support charitable, educational, and other activities that serve the common welfare, primarily by making grants to other nonprofit organizations. By

2001, about 39,000 American foundations, with combined assets of over $300 billion, are expected to award grants totaling more than $20 billion (or about 6 cents of every charitable dollar). Eight out of 10 identify themselves as independent foundations, a term that indicates that its trustees are elected independently, that is, not appointed by any corporate or government entity. These account for three of every four foundation dollars expended. Company-sponsored foundations make up only 8% of the total number but account for $17 or $18 of every $100 awarded. And community foundations, under 3% of the total number, account for 6% of the grant dollars awarded.

Community foundations serve geographic areas as small as rural townships or as large as an entire state. Throughout the 1990s, their number increased at the rate of 10% per year, with endowments expanding at the rate of 20% to 30%. Most actively seek new funds from individuals and corporations, and they often manage trusts on behalf of specific donors. The largest among them have assets ranging from $500 million to $2 billion. Many collaborate with other local foundations to cofinance projects that would be too large or risky for a single institution to undertake or to attract new funds to the region. Some have initiated broad-based community programs that commingle funds from many sources.

For example, the Cleveland Foundation orchestrated a consortium of citizen's groups, corporations, and banks that received a $90 million Federal Empowerment Zone grant, which in turn generated over $2 billion in projects over 5 years. Such efforts require community foundation boards to be broadly representative. In Oakland, California, the community foundation, working closely with the public schools,

developed a family-centered approach to education and then recruited additional cash and non-cash contributions from private sector organizations such as Lukas Films.

In contrast, the trustees of company-sponsored foundations are generally officers of the sponsoring corporation whose task is to oversee the policies governing the company's philanthropic giving. In general, grants are made that benefit the company's employees, stockholders, and others with which it does business and are limited to locales where the company's headquarters, plants, or retail outlets are found. Although many companies manage grant-making activities at their headquarters, others—like the Dayton-Hudson Company, which has retail outlets throughout the country—may decentralize authority for grant making. For example, mangers of affiliated Target stores have considerable discretion in awarding grants to local nonprofits. Despite their generally more narrow focus, some corporate foundations sometimes do initiate collaborative efforts. For example, in many communities, company foundations often provide the leadership of informal "2 percent clubs" in which corporate givers are encouraged to contribute up to 2% of their annual profits to philanthropy and sometimes to coordinate gifts so as to increase their aggregate impact.

Most of the foundations that remain independent of either community or corporate authority are relatively small and locally oriented. However, a few, such as Ford, Kellogg, Hewlett-Packard, and Pew, have assets of $5 billion to $10 billion each, allowing them to fund projects nationally and internationally. In 1999, education received one of every four independent foundation dollars, health-related programs received 15 cents on the dollar (slight drop over the decade), and the human services inched up from 12 cents in 1990 to 14 or 15 cents by 1999. A small but growing number of foundations have focused their grant giving on women and minority services and causes. For example, the Ms. Foundation, founded in 1977, led the way for emergence of more than 100 foundations, now affiliated with the National Network of Women's Funds. African American foundations have long supported scholarships and the growth of black colleges and are now focusing on a broader range of educational initiatives. The Seventh Generation Foundation and the new casino-supported tribal foundations support economic and social development projects for Native Americans.[4]

Many foundations leverage their awards by issuing challenge grants, in effect enlisting potential recipients in attracting additional dollars from other sources. Foundations also partner with government and corporate sources in the creation of new funding programs. For example, as early as the 1970s, the Edna McConnel Clark Foundation joined with federal agencies to fund a number of youth initiatives. More recently, the Casey Foundation initiated collaboration on a youth initiative that coordinates funding with a dozen or so other national foundations. Concerned that some grantees have become dependent on specific foundations for annual support, some foundations use common application forms and procedures, teaming up to up teach grant seekers better methods of fiscal management and fund-raising.

The business of business is business. Corporate philanthropy is almost always limited to the places where companies do business and to charities that are likely to enhance their images. Sometimes, corporations work together on projects. An example of a non-cash gift is illustrative. Because of a personal contact between a state official and an industrialist, the Texas Department of Human Services received technical assistance from a public-private partnership of 16 corporations that included IBM Southwestern Bell, Humana, and others. Corporate executives provided expertise on telecommunications, site planning, purchasing, and automation.

Elsewhere, corporations make both cash and non-cash donations, such as computers and office equipment. Several websites serve as matchmakers between donors and petitioners. Corporations receive tax write-offs for their gifts, and the recipients get much-needed material goods. Some business entrepreneurs whose social consciousness was incubated in the 1960s and '70s use their creativity and drive to develop either service and non-service solutions to social problems. In an example of the latter, the owner of New Hampshire's Yogurt Works created his business to enable local dairy farmers to keep operating. By initiating an "adopt-a-cow" program and other marketing innovations, he helped reverse the region's economic and population decline. In contrast, service-oriented activities are often conducted in collaboration with existing direct service providers. For example, employees at Zingerman's Deli in Ann Arbor, Michigan, created a food-gatherers' consortium of restaurants that collects and distributes food to the homeless in collaboration with local agencies.

The United Way and its competitors. The more than 1,900 community-based United Way agencies in the United States provide support for 50,000 local service agencies and chapters of national organizations. Together, they involve about a million volunteers who serve on boards, work on campaign drives, set community funding priorities, determine allocations, and perform a variety of other tasks associated with fund-raising, planning, and volunteer development. Classic United Way fund-raising is centered on the annual payroll deduction drive through which employees contribute their "fair share" to support a complex of voluntary community services. Developed in the mid-20th century, this model appears to be changing in response to new conditions.

To begin with, campaign income is rarely sufficient to meet the expanding demand generated by government cutbacks and rising expectations. More worrisome, many local campaigns remain flat or actually shrink when measured against local economic growth. Structural changes in the U.S. economy may help explain this. In the last quarter of the 20th century, unions—traditional supporters of the United Way—have lost both members and influence. Corporate downsizing leads to hiring temporary workers who are not likely to identify with the company and its campaign targets. The United Way also faces new competition from alternative funds featured in the federally designated combined discretionary campaign.

Today, all federal payroll deduction programs allow employees to designate the portions of their gifts, if any, that go to the United Way and to any of several other federated funds, including the International Service Agencies, Combined Health Appeals and National Voluntary Health Agencies, United Arts Funds, Environmental Federation of America, National Network of Women's Funds, and other minority and/or social action funds. Local and state governments are signing on to the combined discretionary campaign, as are a number of large corporations. To cope with these pressures, United Way organizations have developed their own approaches to donor choice: designated giving to the campaign and endowment giving outside the campaign. The most common is to permit local donors to designate, on their pledge cards, how much of their gifts should go to specific communities or neighborhoods, types of service (such as counseling, camping), populations (children and youth, the elderly), and named agencies.

However, because income from local payroll deduction drives is almost always short of the need, many United Way agencies now seek major gifts outside of the annual campaign. The funds generated are not likely to be part of the annual allocation process. Often, they are managed by a local United Way foundation, which performs much the way a community foundation might—investing the gift and using the proceeds to seed innovations, supplement other sources of income, or make project grants to non-United Way agencies.[5] Some United Way communities, like those in Washington, D.C., and Lansing, Michigan, even use competitive grants to distribute dollars generated by the annual drive.

Many local communities are also graced by the presence of sectarian federations that use direct appeals and/or tithing to generate annual campaign dollars. Examples include Jewish Federations, Catholic Charities, Lutheran Social Services, Protestant Community Services, and so on.

Civic and mutual benefit organizations, religious associations and congregations. The potential for financial and other assistance from civic and religious organizations tends to be poorly understood by direct service providers.

Civic associations, such as the Rotary and Lions Clubs, Ruritarians, and Junior League chapters, are dedicated to the general good. In concrete terms, this often includes support for national endeavors as well as for local services. For example, in addition their international agenda of eradicating polio, local Rotary Clubs often recruit professional and business women and men to provide pro bono assistance to area charities. Although Lions Club International supports a global vision program, local chapters are free to support services for the sight- and hearing-impaired and others in their own communities.

Mutual benefit organizations were founded a hundred or more years ago to provide social and economic assistance to their own members but, today, they are more apt to function like civic associations responding to broader community needs. Among them are such familiar names as the Kiwanis, Variety Clubs, Knights of Columbus, B'nai B'rith, Shriners, Masons, Elks, Moose, Oddfellows, and Foresters. For example, the Shriners support a network of hospitals, and Masons support local cultural programs. The Kiwanis Clubs run thrift stores in support of local agencies. Although these efforts may not yield large sums, their grants often provide program support for which other funding is unavailable.

The 300,000 or so religious congregations and related organizations in the United States generated revenues of $79 billion in 1999, about 44% of all charitable donations. About $12 billion was transferred to denominational charities, such as Lutheran Social Services and Catholic Charities, or distributed to overseas agencies engaged in rescue and relief. However, $67 billion remained in local congregations to cover operating and programmatic expenses. Of this sum, about 9% ($6 billion) was used to support human service programs, 6% to 7% ($4 billion) went to health services, and 3% ($2 billion) went to community development and social justice programs.

About half this amount was linked to congregation and denominational charities. But that left up to $6 billion for other causes. Add volunteer involvement and in-kind support in the form of food, clothing, and housing, and this makes for a significant resource pool that is potentially available to non- or interdenominational direct services. Unfortunately, many direct service providers are unfamiliar with the way in which churches support social services or are fearful that sectarian purposes will be attached to the funds given. That is not necessarily the case. Consider the nonsectarian nature of Habitat for Humanity and various shelter programs for the homeless or victims of domestic violence. Although the funding sources may be sectarian, the services need not be.

Gifts from individuals: Grassroots fundraising, campaigns, and planned giving. Grassroots fund-raising collects money for two purposes, a program or service and organizational development. By engaging staff and volunteers in the effort, it can increase involvement, educate the participants and broader public about a need or problem, and build leadership for other activities. Some grassroots efforts generate big dollars, whereas others generate modest gifts from donors. Some include direct appeals, whereas others generate income in return for goods or services to the contributor. Examples include sales (for example, community-wide garage sales and thrift shops, bake sales, bazaars and auctions, and commercial goods and services), social/cultural activities (like potlucks and prepared dinners, dances, bingo and casino nights, trips, picnics, holiday celebrations, concerts and theater parties), or third-party contributions (e.g., supermarket donations of a percentage of all sales on a given day to a designated charity).

Campaigns use a more direct appeal to generate support. Campaigns are time-limited events. They can be one-time, such as a brick and mortar campaign intended to raise money to build or improve a facility, or ongoing, such as telephone, direct mail, and door-to-door canvassing that takes place each year in the same time period. Campaigns almost always require creation of a structure, with people assigned to the roles of solicitors, coordinators, event managers, publicists, and so on. Mass appeal campaigns—like door-to-door or letter campaigns—use a single message, although it may be modified for different demographic or geographic population groups. More targeted campaigns tend to use a highly differentiated structure. They begin by targeting a particular population, such as an ethnic group or alumni of a university, and then proceed to subdivide it into specific segments. These might be grouped by neighborhood, occupation, gender, or income (or size of previous gift). For example, doctors will solicit doctors, and potentially big givers will be approached by others who have made substantial contributions.

Like the United Way's annual payroll deduction drive, most campaigns are aimed at securing funds for current operations. However, a number of organizations, such as community foundations, Jewish federations, and universities, have discovered that planned giving approaches can yield greater payoff in the long run. Gifts may be made in the present, but their use is deferred to some time in the future. Examples include (a) bequests; (b) charitable gift annuities, which are contracts between a donor and recipient organization in which the latter agrees to pay the donor a monthly income for life, in return for the donated property; and (c) trusts, which are legal documents that specify what percentage of the income generated can be used in any given period. Because planned giving is relatively new and often includes complex legal instruments, it is not likely to be well understood by many potential donors. Yet, because of its great potential for providing long-term program continuity, it is rapidly becoming a significant component of agency fundraising.

THE WHAT, HOW, AND WHO OF SUCCESSFUL FUND-RAISING

Because fund-raising takes both time and a great deal of expertise, direct service agencies sometimes employ specialists to do the work. However, because specialists in fund-raising are not necessarily specialists in direct services, this is sometimes a poor decision.

Everyone's business. Successful fund-raising is rarely a sometime activity—or a one-person task. The day of the "Lone Ranger" fund-raiser who rides in on his white horse, cleans up the mess, locates and delivers the treasure, and rides off is long behind us, if it ever existed. Successful fund-raising is not measured by a one-time contract or grant or by a single major gift. It is an ongoing process that requires creative leadership and people willing to perform a variety of essential tasks.

Many of those tasks are associated with specific fund-raising approaches, such as planning and managing campaigns, locating potential

TABLE 31.1   Fund-Raising Inventory

How much current operating income is generated through each of these mechanisms?

     Allocations
     Grants
     Contracts
     Fees-for-service and tuition (including third-party payments)
     Charitable gifts
     Reserve funds, sales and royalties, and investments

Have the amounts changed significantly over the last 3 years? How?

What proportions would be more desirable in the future, say, 3 years from now?

What are the current sources of supply? How much from each?

     Government (federal, state, county, municipal)
     Foundations (national/local, independent/community/company)
     Business (in-cash or in-kind)
     United Way (and other federations)
     Civic, mutual benefit, and religious organizations
     Individuals (through gifts for current operations or planned giving)

Have the amounts changed significantly over the last 3 years? If so, how?

Should these proportions change over the next 3 years? How? To what potential advantage?

Who should be involved in making the decisions and taking responsibility for leading the change?

funders, writing grant or contract applications, and coordinating grassroots fund-raising activities. These often require involving many agency staffers, board members, and volunteers in a year-round process that uses proven fund-raising methods. Sometimes, it is necessary to contracting with or hire grant writers, planned giving experts, and other fund-raising specialists. The list in Table 31.1 is typical of the inventories used by fund-raising consultants to help direct service providers assess their fund-raising practices and to consider other possibilities.

Sources of information. In addition to sorting out the range of fund-raising options available to an organization and helping decision makers determine which ones are appropriate or likely to succeed at any given time, experienced fund-raisers in the direct services also know where to locate potential donors and funders. Generally, the first place to look is in the network of relationships between those who are engaged in the enterprise and other stakeholders. In addition to professional colleagues and volunteers associated with one's own agency, these include (a) colleagues in other settings who have had successes in grant getting, contracting, or some other fund-raising activity; (b) community specialists whose job it is to be helpful (such as community foundation and United Way staffers, planners in a government human services agency or coordinating council, such as an Area Agency on Aging); and (c) professionals and lay leaders in one's own

TABLE 31.2   Source Materials in Print

Federal government—available through the Government Printing Office, General Services Building, 300 7th Street SW, Washington, D.C. 21407 or on-line via GRANTS, ETC.

    Catalogue of Federal Domestic Assistance. The major source information on all federal agencies and grant-making programs of domestic relevance

    The Federal Register. A daily newsletter with updates on pending legislation, program regulations, and special grant opportunities

Foundations and corporations—available from the Foundation Center, 79 5th Avenue, New York, New York 10003

    Guide to U.S. Foundations, Their Trustees, Officers and Donors. A two-volume set that describes more than 35,000 national and local foundations, with information on where you can find more information

    Foundation Grants Index. Covers grant-making programs of the 1,000 largest foundations, with abstracts of more than 60,000 grants of $10,000 or more made each year. Quarterly updates and periodic web-based reports

    National Directory of Corporate Giving. Detailed portraits of 2,300 corporate foundations and direct giving programs

agency, who may have their own relationships with donors, funders, or colleagues in the know.

A systematic search for appropriate sources of supply for both cash and non-cash contributions may also require spending some time at the library or on the Internet, both of which provide quick and relatively easy access to data on foundations, state and local government agencies, churches and civic associations, the United Way and other federated funding bodies, and individual donors. Table 31.2 includes a number of useful sourcebooks on foundation, corporate, and government funding sources.

Web advantage. Every federal government agency and publication that is relevant to direct service fund-raising has its own website. Through the web, for example, one can access current and recent issues of the *Federal Register* and the *Catalogue of Federal Domestic Assistance.* Most major foundations have websites that describe

their funding priorities and may include application forms and guidelines. Many state government sites post RFPs and RFQs and provide instructions on how direct service agencies can be listed as potential vendors. Local government agencies, United Way organizations, civic associations, and other potential funding sources may also have websites with similar information.

Some websites guide users through the program design, budgeting, and proposal writing process and provide information about grant writing and fund-raising training programs. The Internet also includes a number of *listservs* and electronic newsletters that address a wide variety of issues relevant to those interested in fund-raising. An easy way to access these and other sites is via the GRANTS, ETC. site. It can be accessed through any web browser. The URL is: http://www.ssw.umich.edu/grantsetc

A start-up list of other websites is found in Table 31.3.

TABLE 31.3 Internet Fund-Raising Resources

Source	Web Address
GOVERNMENT INFORMATION	
Catalog of Federal Domestic Assistance	http://www.gsa.gov/fdac/
Federal Information Exchange	http://wwww.fie.com
GrantsNet	http://www.os.dhhs.gov/progorg/grantsnet/
NonProfit Gateway	http://www.nonprofit.gov/
State Government Links	http://www.law.indiana.edu/law/v-lib/states.html
FOUNDATION INFORMATION	
Community Foundations	http://fundsnetservices.com/commfoun.htm
Community Foundation Locator	http://www.cof.org/community/
Foundations, Grants, and Trusts	http://people.delphi.com/mickjyoung/money.html
Grantmaking Foundations	http://www.tgci.com/foundations/typefdn.htm
Private Foundations in the United States	http://w3.uwyo.edu/~Prospect/found-us.html
StateSearch	http://www.nasire.org/ss/index.html
The Foundation Center	http://fdncenter.org
The Council on Foundations	http://www.cof.org/
CORPORATE GIVING	
Corporate Giving	http://w3.uwyo.edu/~prospect/corp-giv.html
Corporate Grantmakers on the Internet	http://fdncenter.org/grantmaker/corp.html
Directory of Corporate Community	
* Involvement*	.charitynet.org/noframes/main.html linkages.
VOLUNTARY SECTOR FUNDING	
Catholic Charities USA	http://www.catholiccharitiesusa.org/
Charities USA	http://www.charitiesusa.com/
Independent Charities of America ICA	http://www.independentcharities.org/
Lions International	http://www.lions.org
Mennonite Central Committee	http://www.mennonitecc.ca/mcc/index.html
Nonprofit Sector Research Fund	http://www.aspeninst.org/dir/polpro/NSRF/NSRF1.html
Presbyterian Church U.S.A. Foundation	http://www.fdn.pcusa.org/fdn/index.html
United Jewish Appeal	http://www.uja.org/
United Way of America	http://www.unitedway.org/
HOW-TO AND RELATED INFORMATION	
Charitable Planning	http://www.netplanning.com/ch3.htm
A Proposal Writing Short Course	http://fdncenter.org/fundproc/prop.html
Funding Opportunities in the Behavioral	
* and Social Sciences*	http://cos.gdb.org/repos/fund/disc/behavioral.html
The Social Statistics Briefing Room	http://www.whitehouse.gov/fsbr/ssbr.html
Society for Nonprofit Organizations	
* Funding Alert*	http://danenet.wicip.org/snpo/funding.html
ON-LINE JOURNALS & NEWSLETTERS	
Chronicle of Philanthropy	http://philanthropy.com
Foundation News and Commentary	http://www.cof.org/fnc/fncindex.html
Fund$Raiser Cyberzine	http://www.fundsraiser.com
Grantmanship Center Magazine	http://www.tgci.com/publications/pub.htm

THE FIRST TEN YEARS

Although the past may be prologue, it is not always a good predictor of what is to come. What is clear, however, is that the funding environment during the first decade of the 21st century is likely to consolidate some of the trends identified during the 1980s and 1990s. This is good news for those who can gear up to the challenges, but bad news for those who remain fixed in the last decade.

Competition, collaboration, and consolidation. The competition for resources over the next decade is not likely to abate, nor is the increasing complexity of the funding environment. Funders, attempting to minimize risk and optimize benefits, will use both leveraging and targeting methods, insisting that providers collaborate wherever this may lead to cost-cutting and improved services. Although the government cutbacks in some human service settings may be offset by increased funding in others, that's small compensation for providers whose direct services are the ones being decimated. Nor is philanthropy likely to grow at anywhere the rate necessary to pick up the slack. Still, the growth of voluntary sector funding does present a hopeful picture. So long as the American economy remains robust, so will the grant-making and gifting capacities of foundations, federations, corporations, civic associations, religious organizations, and well-to-do individuals.

However, direct service providers will have to change the ways in which they do business to deal with the changing environment. They will have to become both more entrepreneurial and more adept at collaborating with others. Some will adapt or even transform their service programs to accommodate funder or donor priori-

ties. Many service providers will consolidate their efforts, joining forces into larger conglomerates that save money through economies of scale and "earn" dollars by underbidding other providers or increasing the quality of service. Some formerly public or voluntary programs will privatize and become regional or even national in scope. In so doing, they will follow the examples of the hospital and nursing home conglomerates that emerged in the 1980s and '90s. The process is already under way for group homes that serve vulnerable children and the elderly. If one is to extrapolate from the health field, such consolidation will, initially at least, leave some clients under- or unserved.

Broadening the base and tailoring the message. Virtually all direct service providers will have to broaden their funding bases to survive and thrive. And that may mean having to respond to a wider network of resource suppliers in the government, corporate, and voluntary sectors. To do so will require many direct service providers to expand the range of funding mechanisms used—from fees-for-services and/or allocations to a mix that also includes grant seeking, contracting, and fund-raising from individuals. It may also require developing new kinds of relationships with what would formerly have been unlikely partners—like the managers of charitable mutual fund accounts, financial planners, and trust officers. Finally, broadening the bases also means securing other than cash gifts: volunteered services, equipment and supplies, and goods that can substitute for or be converted into cash.

Broadening the base not only provides some added stability to the enterprise, it also reduces dependency on specific suppliers. If one source dries up, another may be available to pick up the slack. The capacity to tap the interests of multiple suppliers also requires being able to tailor one's message appropriately. For example, a proposal to fund the same AIDS education program for African American youth may look very different if pitched to foundations focusing on the gay community, on public health, or on the needs of specific minority communities. The issue is not to say what the donors want to hear but, rather, to find a common cause and to participate in a shared effort that furthers the enterprise's direct service mission.

REVIEW

Over the next decade, an increasingly competitive funding environment is likely to cause a shake-out of weaker programs and to require collaboration and consolidation among others. Dollars are a major resource for any agency, but non-cash gifts, like equipment and expertise, can round out any development effort. The sources of supply are multiple. They include individual donors, government, the business community, federated funding agencies, and other elements of the voluntary sector. Although three distribution mechanisms—gifts, contracts, and grants—were highlighted, these should be considered components of an integrated fund-raising approach that complements or, if need be, substitutes for the more traditional acquisition of funds through fees and allocations.

NOTES

1. Some income suppliers will not permit recipients to bank or invest funds received or even to carry dollars beyond the grant period. For example, it is unlikely that a government agency would permit vendors to use awards for any purposes other than those specified in the contract.

2. An RFP generally specifies what is expected of the potential vendor but permits applicants some latitude in the program design. In contrast, an RFQ fully spells out the program components, asking applicants only to specify what they would charge to do the work and to justify those charges.

3. In 1989, Brian O'Connel, then president of the *Independent Sector,* inferred from their respective economic sizes that the funding capacity of all domestically oriented government agencies in the United States is about 10 times that of the entire voluntary sector.

4. The development of minority foundations was boosted in the 1980s by the Council on Foundation's *Pluralism in Philanthropy Project.* The council is a national umbrella organization that advocates and conducts training programs and conferences for member foundations and affiliates.

5. In some communities, United Way Foundations, like community foundations, serve as matchmakers between potential donors and recipient organizations.

SUGGESTIONS FOR FURTHER READING

American Association of Fund-Raising Council. (1999). *Giving USA.* New York: AAFRC Trust for Philanthropy.

Allocating United Way money: A painstaking, often controversial process. (1993, January 12). *Chronicle of Philanthropy, 5*(6).

Diamond, H. (1998, Fall). A perfect union: Public-private partnerships can provide valuable services. *National Parks Forum, 40*(4).

Dobrof, R. (Fall 1998). Philanthropy and government: Partners in the community of caring. *Journal of Gerntological Social Work, 29*(3/4).

Doyle, W. L. (1995). *Fund-raising ideas for all nonprofits: charities, churches, clubs.* New York: American Fund Raising Institute.

Edwards, R. L., & Benefied, E. A. S. (1997). *Building a strong foundation: Fund-raising for nonprofits.* Washington, DC: NASW Press.

Grace, K. S. (1997). *Beyond fund-raising: New strategies for non-profit innovation and investment.* New York: John Wiley.

Hall, H. (1998, November). Campaigns with appeal. *The Chronicle of Philanthropy, 11*(3).

Joseph, J. A. (1993). *Black philanthropy: The potential and limits of private generosity in a civil society.* Washington, DC: Association of Black Foundation Executives.

Joyaux, S. P. (1997). *Strategic fund development: Building profitable relationships that last.* Gaithersburg, MD: Aspen.

Klein, K. (1997, January). Practical ways to build relationships with donors. *Grassroots Fund-Raising Journal, 16*(1).

Kling, P. F. (1993, December). Planned giving and annual giving can cooperate. *Fund Raising Management, 22*(12).

Kniffel, A. (1995, November). Corporate sponsorship: The new direction in fund-raising. *American Libraries, 26*(10).

Lauffer, A. (1997). *GRANTS, ETC—Grant getting, contracting and fund-raising for nonprofits.* Thousand Oaks, CA: Sage.

Marx, J. D. (1998, January). Corporate strategic philanthropy: Implications for social work. *Social Work, 43*(1).

Mount, J. (1998, Fall). Why donors give. *Nonprofit Management and Leadership, 7*(1).

Netting, F. E., & Williams, F. G. (1997, Fall). Is there an afterlife? How to move towards self-sufficiency when foundation dollars end. *Nonprofit Management & Leadership, 7*(3).

O'Connel, B. (1989, September/October). What voluntary activity can and cannot do for America. *Public Administration Review, 34*(4).

O'Neil, M. (1994, Spring). Philanthropic dimensions of mutual benefit organizations. *Nonprofit and Voluntary Sector Quarterly, 23*(1).

Practical guide to planned giving. (1996). Rockville, MD: The Taft Group.

Rose, M. S. (1994, Fall). Philanthropy in a different voice: The women's funds, *Nonprofit and Voluntary Sector Quarterly, 23*(3).

Rothblatt, D., & Robinson, R. (1996, Fall). A unity of purpose: A practical approach to integrating annual campaigns and planned giving fund-raising efforts. *Journal of Jewish Communal Service, 72*(1).

Saidel, J. R. (1991, August). Resource interdependence: The relationship between state agencies and nonprofit organizations. *Public Administration Review, 51*(6).

Seltzer, M., & Cunningham, M. (1991, July/August). General support vs. project support: A 77-year old debate. *Nonprofit World, 9*(4).

Shaw, S. C., & Taylor, M. A. (1995). *Reinventing fund-raising: Realizing the potential of women's philanthropy.* San Francisco: Jossey-Bass.

Wineburg, R. J. (1994, Summer). A longitudinal case study of religious congregations in local human services. *Nonprofit and Voluntary Sector Quarterly, 23*(2).

Conclusion

We began this book with a section on what we called "contextual issues," which included material on conditions in the larger society that have salience for social work as well as content in more specific institutional contexts such as the legal system. We stressed in this section that systemic thinking was essential for a contextualized practice, especially when used in a rigorous and thoughtful manner. We recognize that much systemic thinking is abstract and not adequately linked to research and to practice, and this linkage is a major task for the future. In reviewing the rest of the book, we were pleased that all of the authors in one way or another addressed the contexts of practice that were most relevant to the purposes of the chapters.

We then presented a series of chapters that we believe provide the frameworks that should guide the development of social work practice in the coming years. The authors of the chapters in this section argued for preventing dysfunc-tion as well as rehabilitating those who have succumbed to the stresses to which they have been exposed. Practices were also introduced that enhance life's quality and the power of people to promote their own welfare. Multicultural and feminist ideas increasingly are being integrated with each other and were presented as particularly compatible with the evolution of social work ideas and of heuristic value in this process. We see that social workers face a serious challenge to create a consensus about the choice of practice frameworks that further attainment of our mission and fulfillment of our practice roles.

In the section devoted to the activities of social workers in promoting change in individuals, groups, families, and their social circumstances, we intentionally abandoned the traditional way of dealing with these topics, which is to set off one theory against another. We urged the authors to present their ideas in ways that transcend a single theory approach; as we reviewed this section, however, we concluded that a great deal of work must be done to clarify the theoretical bases of practice and the linkages among various theoretical traditions.

Our contextualized view of practice led to the next section of the book, in which the authors examined practice in relationship to a variety of social problem configurations, such as mental health, corrections, the workplace, and the circumstances facing gay male and lesbian consumers of social services. It is not difficult to locate texts that organize chapters in this manner. Although we have not created a conceptual framework for comparing social work practices in different social contexts, we hope that the content and organization of this section will point us in this direction. This will help us to create situation-oriented practice theories in which underlying social and structural factors are used in constructing such theories.

Although we asked all the authors to consider relevant research and empirical issues, we sought to present these issues in their own right in the next section. We recognize that there are serious divisions between researchers and practitioners and that research and practice do not feed into each other as much as we would desire. This represents another major challenge to the profession, and we hope that this section moves us in the right direction.

In the last section, we asked a series of authors to consider major challenges to the profession. One of these arises from philosophy, particularly ethics. Another stems from the fact that the solutions to social problems are ultimately global in nature. A third is the need for better ideas about the education of social workers. A fourth is the need to enhance our resource base. All the ideas presented earlier in the book will remain only ideas and not actions unless supported through adequate resources and excellent training and education. Finally, the ethical issues might be summarized, as Charlotte Towle, a social work pioneer, once did when she declared social work's role to be the "conscience of the community."

The authors in this volume convey a sense of excitement and hope. We face serious problems, yet, we have a wealth of knowledge, directions for creating new knowledge, and a strong investment in carrying out our mission.

Author Index

Abbott, R., 575
Abel, E. M., 291
Abell, M. D., 289, 572
Abell, N., 538
Abelson, J. A., 236
Abo El Nasr, M. M., 636
Abraham, C., 360
Abramovitz, M., 15, 154, 524
Abramson, M., 593, 604
Acierno, R., 204
Ackerman, N., 311, 312
Ackley, D. C., 613
Adams, J., 462
Addams, J., 375, 376, 395
Ademek, M. E., 342
Affleck, G., 246, 340
Agnew, R., 96
Aguirre, A., 456
Aguirre, L. M., 417
Agyei, Y., 482
Ahmed, M., 572
Ainsworth, B., 570
Ainsworth, M., 274
Airaksinen, T., 591
Akabas, S., 360, 499, 501, 504, 506, 511, 512
Albee, G., 503
Albelda, R., 265
Albers, E., 341
Alcabes, A., 24

Aldwin, C. M., 344
Alexander, E., 246
Alexander, J. F., 101, 313, 317
Allen, D., 340
Allen, K. D., 206
Allen, S., 206
Allen-Meares, P., 137, 385, 415, 416, 559, 560, 605, 646
Allman, W. F., 619
Almeida, R., 320
Alonso, A., 617
Alperin, R. M., 613
Altepeter, T., 276
Alter, C., 376
Altheide, D. L., 614
Altpeter, M. A., 392
Altschuler, D. M., 461, 462
Alvarez, A. R., 396, 421
Amanto, P., 359
Ambert, A.-M., 524
Ames, D., 570
Amin, S., 17
Ammerman, R. T., 218
Anastasiades, P., 230
Andersen, T., 320
Anderson, A. L., 486, 488, 489
Anderson, B., 431
Anderson, C., 303
Anderson, C. M., 313, 319

669

Anderson, H., 313, 318
Anderson, J. R., 352
Anderson, K., 356
Anderson, M. L., 134
Anderson, N. B., 360, 524
Anderson, R. E., 66, 67, 68
Andreoli, A., 337, 343
Andrews, B., 344
Andrews, D., 569
Andrews, G., 250
Aneshensel, C., 350
Ankrah, E. M., 636
Anson, Y., 214
Anthony, D., 337, 341, 343
Anthony, E. J., 317
Anthony, J., 267
Antle, B., 34
Antonucci, T. C., 116
Aponte, H., 191, 306
Appelbaum, P. S., 34
Applebaum, P. S., 292
Apte, R. Z., 66
Arendt, H., 8
Armstead, C. A., 360, 524
Armstrong, K. J., 208
Armstrong, T. L., 461
Arnold, S., 590
Aronson, J., 613
Arroyo, C. G., 95
Artelt, T., 202
Arthur, M., 93, 94, 98, 100
Arzin, N. H., 252
Asamoah, Y., 134, 636
Aschan, H., 116
Ashtekar, A., 639
Aspinwall, L. G., 354, 356, 359, 361, 362, 363, 367(n5)
Atkin, J., 503, 511
Atlas, J., 11
Attkisson, C., 445
Austad, C. S., 618
Austin, D. M., 545, 546, 606
Austin, J. J., 392
Austin, K. M., 600
Austin, M. J., 395
Austrian, S., 158
Axelrad, S., 456
Axinn, J., 113
Axline, V., 275, 276
Ayers, C. D., 93
Azrin, N. H., 206

Babb, B. A., 26
Babbie, E., 606
Babcock, J., 317
Babcock, M., 158
Baca Zinn, M., 137
Baer, D. M., 54, 200, 213
Baer, L., 572
Bagley, C., 275
Baier, M., 253
Bailey, D., 398
Bailey, M. J., 482, 483
Baines, D., 137
Baird, S. C., 467
Baker, D., 456
Balas, A., 569
Balazs, K., 508, 509, 510
Ballou, M., 158, 159, 165
Bandura, A., 116, 246
Banerjee, M., 398
Bangert-Drowns, R., 245
Banks, J. A., 133
Banks, S. M., 245
Baptist, W., 168(n22), 404
Barber, J. G., 636
Bargh, J. A., 187, 290, 352
Barker, R., 33, 197, 601
Barkley, R., 276
Barlow, D. H., 224, 226, 227, 230, 233
Barnard, P. J., 180, 184, 185, 186, 188
Barnet, R. J., 12
Baron, N. S., 567
Barrett, M. J., 307, 320
Barry, P., 398
Barry, V., 595
Barth, R., 335, 340
Barthel, J., 270
Bartlett, H. M., 152, 377, 590
Barton, C., 101
Barton, K., 339
Barton, W., 463
Bass, D. M., 571
Bastian, L. D., 455
Bateman, A., 615
Bateson, G., 302, 308
Bath, H., 339
Batten, C., 621
Baucom, D., 252, 317
Baum, A. S., 522
Baumeister, R. F., 243, 244, 357
Baumoel, J., 30
Bayog, F., 572
Bazron, B. M., 388

Bearison, D. J., 289
Beaver, M. I., 415, 422
Beavers, W. R., 306, 307
Beavin, J., 302
Becerra, R., 133, 134, 137
Beck, A., 180, 181, 230, 232, 234, 343, 456, 555
Beck, J. S., 230, 231
Beck, R., 235
Becker, J., 276, 344
Becker, R. E., 235
Beckett, J., 420
Becnel, J., 569
Bednar, R. L., 252
Bedrosian, R. C., 234
Beehr, T. A., 366
Behrman, R., 264
Belar, C. D., 573
Belknap, J., 455, 469
Bell, A. P., 487
Bell, W. J., 288
Bellack, A. S., 201, 235
Bellah, R., 7, 8, 11, 13, 398
Bellos, N. S., 416
Bennis, W., 392
Bentelspacher, C. E., 291
Berg, I., 313, 318, 525
Bergan, J. R., 51
Berger, R. L., 415, 416, 419
Berger, R. M., 421, 422, 493
Berglund, L., 100
Bergman, A., 267
Berk, R. A., 56
Berkowitz, M. W., 253
Berlin, S. B., 183, 194, 243
Berliner, A. K., 600
Berliner, L., 275, 276, 356
Berman, M., 8
Berman, P. C., 615
Berman-Rossi, T., 283
Bernard, J. M., 621
Bernard, T., 452
Bernstein, A. D., 229
Bernstein, B., 600
Bernstein, B. E., 486
Bernstein, J., 501
Bernstein, S., 590
Bero, L., 60
Berrill, K., 487, 488
Berry, J. W., Jr., 247
Berry, M., 252, 253
Bertalanffy, L., 302
Bertcher, H. J., 284

Besa, D., 544
Besharov, D. S., 601
Besharov, S. H., 601
Best, C., 340
Best, K. M., 94
Betten, N., 395
Bettinger, M., 491
Beutler, L. E., 193, 254
Biernacki, P., 243, 245
Biestek, F. P., 590, 592
Bijou, S., 200
Bilchik, S., 465
Bilides, D. G., 283
Billingsley, A., 388
Billups, J., 606, 637, 638, 641
Binik, Y. M., 567, 570, 573
Birtle, J., 571
Bishop, D., 308, 456
Bissell, L., 603, 625
Bistline, J. L., 287
Black, P. N., 604
Blais, L. M., 243
Blakeslee, S., 179
Blanchard, E. B., 228
Blank, M. J., 393, 394, 402
Blank, R. M., 383, 398
Blazer, D. G., 222
Blechman, E. A., 464
Bloch, F., 30
Block, F., 292
Bloom, B. L., 570, 574
Bloom, B. W., 579
Bloom, J. R., 437, 438
Bloom, M., 95, 535, 536, 537, 540
Bloomquist, M., 276
Blumstein, A., 452, 456, 457, 465
Blumstein, P., 490, 491
Blythe, B., 552, 559
Boat, B., 275
Boback, H. B., 30
Bodin, A., 315
Boekaerts, M., 350
Boesen, M. B., 123
Bograd, M., 320
Bohart, A. C., 185
Boiney, L. G., 290
Boisvert, C. M., 572
Bok, S., 591
Bollas, C., 29
Bolton, B., 124
Bombyk, M., 376
Bonczar, R., 456

Bond, G. R., 291
Bond, J., 506
Boninger, D. S., 361
Bonner, B., 276
Bookwala, J., 350
Booraem, C. D., 288
Booth, A., 359, 454
Booth, C., 338, 388
Borden, W., 418, 419, 428, 431
Bordia, P., 290
Bordnick, P. S., 203
Borduin, C. M., 92, 101
Borkovec, T. D., 229, 234
Borman, L. D., 385
Bortner, M. A., 456
Boscolo, L., 315, 316
Bose, A. B., 636
Boss, P., 321
Bostwick, G. R., Jr., 551
Boszormenyi-Nagy, I., 311, 312
Bouhoutsos, J., 603
Bowen, G. L., 398
Bowen, M., 307, 311, 312
Bowlby, J., 183, 190, 267, 274
Bowman, J. A., 569
Bowman, P. J., 95, 136
Boxer, A., 485
Boyd, J., 319
Boyd-Franklin, N., 137, 321
Boyer, R., 222
Boykin, A., 116
Boyle, E. S., 290
Boyle, M., 52
Boyte, H., 9
Bradford, J. B., 487
Braga, A. A., 104
Brager, G., 392, 397, 402, 509
Brannon, B. R., 104
Branson, D. M., 601
Braverman, D. L., 353
Brawley, L., 116
Brecher, J., 12, 17
Breen, M., 276
Breggin, P. R., 44
Brehm, J. W., 245
Brehm, K., 101
Brehm, S., 245
Brennan, F., 283
Brennan, P. F., 289, 571
Brent, D., 92, 340
Breslau, N., 222
Breton, M., 117, 122, 283

Breunlin, D., 320
Brewin, C. R., 344
Breznitz, S., 349, 350, 361
Briar, S., 559
Briar-Lawson, K., 417, 529
Brice-Baker, J., 621
Bricker-Jenkins, M., 116, 136, 153, 156, 160, 162,
    163, 164, 167(n1), 167(n2), 167(n4), 168(n6),
    168(n15), 404, 492
Bridge, J., 340
Brieland, D., 590
Broadhurst, D., 266
Brodsky, A., 152
Bromberg, P. M., 617
Bromet, E., 222
Bronfenbrenner, U., 379
Bronner, E., 510
Bronson, D., 245, 541
Brookfield, S. D., 24
Brookings, J., 124
Brower, A. M., 285, 286, 293, 294, 352
Brown, D. R., 220
Brown, G. W., 223
Brown, J., 388, 613
Brown, J. D., 353, 354
Brown, L., 482
Brown, L. N., 284
Brown, L. S., 36
Brown, M. T., 621
Brown, P., 117
Brown, R. A., 431
Brown, T. A., 230
Browning, B. J., 613
Browning, C. H., 613
Bruch, M. A., 226
Bruck, M., 51
Bruni, F., 37
Brunner, J., 419
Buchanan, A., 592
Buckingham, C. D., 571
Buckley, W., 67
Buckner, J. C., 90
Budenz, D., 234
Budman, S. H., 287, 288
Buetow, S. A., 574
Bulger, J., 570
Bull, R., 356
Bullis, R. K., 595
Bumagin, V. E., 416
Burack, R. C., 575
Burden, D., 399, 502
Burford, G., 388, 390

Burghardt, S., 10, 15, 17, 125, 376, 392, 400
Burgoon, J. K., 290, 567
Burkhart, B., 345
Burland, J. C., 284
Burman, S., 332, 345
Burnam, A., 446
Burnes, D. W., 522
Burnett, J. W., 246
Burns, B. J., 101, 106
Burns, D. D., 230
Burt, M., 467
Burtless, G., 383
Burton, D., 93
Butcher, J. N., 254, 570
Butler, G., 229, 234
Butler, S., 283
Butler, T., 275
Butts, J., 463
Byng-Hall, J., 305, 311
Bynum, T., 457
Bystrintsky, A., 233

Cahn, E. S., 528
Cain, A. C., 90
Calhoun, C., 290
Caligor, L., 617
Callahan, D., 591
Callero, P. L., 356
Cameron, O. G., 219
Campbell, D., 544
Campbell, E., 575
Campbell, T., 320
Canetto, S. S., 340
Canobbio, R., 340
Canot, J., 567
Cantor, N., 188
Caplan, G., 89, 90, 95, 333, 340, 343
Carley, G., 417, 419, 432
Carlson, B. T., 137
Carlsson, S. G., 570
Carnetto, S., 340
Carpenter, B., 349
Carpenter, E., 134
Carr, J. E., 344
Carroll, D., 116
Carroll, K. M., 251
Carstensen, L., 116
Carter, B., 158, 303, 309, 310, 312, 314
Carter, G. W., 416
Carter, I., 66, 67, 68
Carter, P., 307

Carter, R., 592
Carver, C. S., 354, 355, 363, 364, 367(n4), 367(n5)
Cash, S., 252, 253
Cashwell, C. S., 621
Cass, V. C., 484, 485
Castelloe, P. E., 384, 395, 402
Castex, G. M., 137
Catalano, R., 98, 360, 467, 469
Catalano, R. F., 100, 101, 103
Catalano, R. F., Jr., 96, 103
Catania, A. C., 201
Cattanach, A., 275
Caughey, A., 596
Causby, V., 491
Cavalier, A. R., 290
C'deBaca, J., 244, 248
Cecchin, G., 315, 316
Ceci, S. J., 51
Cernovich, S. A., 469
Cerny, J. A., 227, 230, 233
Chalmers, D. J., 568
Chalmers, I., 60
Chamberlain, R., 432, 507
Chamberlin, J., 124
Chambers, A., 229
Chambers, C., 15
Chambless, D. L., 226, 232
Champion, D., 467
Chan, C. S., 480
Chance, P., 201
Chandler, M. K., 70
Chang, A., 290
Chapin, R. K., 27
Charng, H.-W., 356
Charping, J. W., 288
Chau, K., 134
Chau, K. L., 134, 136, 137, 293
Checkoway, B., 118, 395, 400, 401
Cheetham, J., 431
Cheng, L. C., 284
Cherlin, A., 266
Chernoff, S. N., 33
Chesney-Lind, M., 455, 469, 470
Chess, W. A., 218
Chetkow-Yanoov, B., 621
Chevron, E., 234, 343
Chiesa, J., 99, 463
Chiesa, M., 198
Childress, A., 203, 204
Childs, J., 17
Chilman, C., 505, 512
Chitwood, S., 503

Chiu, C., 356
Chodorow, N., 116
Christensen, A., 317
Christensen, H., 250
Christie, B., 567
Cialdini, R. B., 58
Cioci, M., 465
Clark, D. M., 227, 230, 232, 233
Clark, E. G., 95
Clark, J., 283
Clark, L. F., 362
Clark, S., 264
Clevenger, J. E., 292
Cloward, R., 11, 114, 116, 455
Clum, G. A., 248
Cluse-Tolar, T., 337, 340, 341, 343, 344
Coble, J. R., 567
Cohen, A., 455
Cohen, B. Z., 636
Cohen, C. B., 598
Cohen, H., 137, 138
Cohen, J., 276, 277, 337
Cohen, M. B., 283
Cohen, N. H., 100
Cohen, R. J., 600
Cohler, B., 267
Coie, J., 90, 95, 96, 99, 342
Colapinto, J., 315
Cole, R., 341, 342
Coleman, E., 484
Coleman, H. L. K., 622
Coleman, V. E., 491
Coley, S., 420
Collier, C., 417
Collins, A., 387
Collins, A. H., 387
Collins, B., 158
Collins, B. G., 158, 168(n13)
Collins, M. E., 276
Collins, P. H., 154
Collins, R. L., 360
Colon, Y., 289
Colten, M. E., 360
Comas-Díaz, L., 136, 138
Combs, G., 318, 418
Compas, B. E., 350
Compton, B., 14, 552
Conger, R., 317
Congress, E., 40, 292, 340
Connelly, H., 467
Connolly, T., 290
Connor, J., 350

Connors, G.-J., 251
Conrad, A. P., 598
Consoli, A., 570, 572
Conte, J., 276
Cook, D. A., 621
Cook, T., 544
Cooley, S., 288
Coontz, S., 305
Cooper, C. R., 441
Cooper, L., 390, 396, 399
Copeland, P., 483
Corbett, R., Jr., 471
Corcoran, J., 336
Corcoran, K., 35, 39, 556, 560, 561, 596
Corley, C., 457
Corpt, E. A., 619
Corrigan, P., 248, 249, 256
Costa, F. M., 93
Costa, P. T., 364
Costello, E., 234
Costello, T., 12, 17
Costin, L. B., 590
Cottler, J. M., 432
Coulton, C., 379, 512, 513
Counts, A., 634, 644
Courtney, M., 11, 13, 17, 266, 270, 391, 606, 612, 636
Cowan, C. P., 95
Cowan, P. A., 95, 225, 229
Cowger, C. D., 646
Cox, B. J., 236
Cox, D., 641
Cox, E., 116, 117, 118, 119, 122, 124, 125, 165
Cox, E. O., 159
Cox, E. V., 416, 420
Cox, F. M., 75, 395, 399
Cox, T. H., 293
Coyne, J. C., 218
Craig, J., 290
Cranford, R. E., 598
Craske, M. G., 230, 233
Cressey, D., 455
Crick, N. R., 106
Crits-Christoph, P., 250, 256
Crolley, J., 203
Crosbie-Burnett, M., 491
Crosby, G., 287
Cross, S., 189, 190, 191
Cross, T. L., 388
Croxton, T., 593
Croze, C., 596
Crump, S., 141

Cruzen, D., 355
Cue, K. L., 356
Cuffel, B., 440
Culnan, M. J., 567
Cunningham, P. B., 92
Currie, E., 452, 456
Curtis, G. C., 219, 225, 606
Curtis, P. A., 338
Cutler, J., 17, 595

Daguio, E. R., 29, 600, 601
Daiuto, A. D., 252
Dalaker, J., 521, 522
Dalton, E., 288
Danaher, K., 625
D'Andrade, R. G., 189
Danis, F., 331
Darkwa, O. A., 643
Darley, J. M., 352
Daro, D., 270
Darwin, K. M., 291
D'Augelli, A. R., 486
Davey, J. D., 124
David, P., 617
Davidson, B., 510
Davidson, J. R., 596
Davidson, R., 289
Davidson, T., 596
Davis, A., 15
Davis, A. F., 523
Davis, L., 509, 512
Davis, L. E., 283, 284, 293
Davis, M., 9
Davis, N., 472
Davis, R., 336
Dawes, R. M., 45, 51, 57
Day, P. J., 113, 615
Dazord, A., 341
Deal, A., 118, 376
Deblinger, E., 276, 277
DeFriese, G. H., 116
Deguchi, H., 213
Deitz, P., 613
DeJong, P., 525
de Jong, T. L., 288
Delgado, G., 17
Delgado, M., 136, 146, 378, 417, 422
DeLois, K., 126, 139
Delois, K. A., 646
DeLongis, A., 344, 350
del Pinal, J., 441

Deluty, R. H., 487
Delworth, U., 617
Demby, A., 288
Denner, J., 441
Dennis, K. W., 388
Dent, C. W., 93
de Ridder, D. T. D., 357, 366(n1)
Dermigny, R., 569
DeRoos, Y., 605
Derryberry, D., 362
Dertouzos, M. L., 576, 577, 579
DeRubeis, R. J., 250, 256
Deschenes, E., 462
deShazer, S., 313, 318
DeSilva, E., 291
Despard, M., 289, 293
de Tocqueville, A., 7, 387
Deutelbaum, W., 338
Deutsch, C., 603
Devine, J. A., 522, 526
DeVoe, E., 275
Devore, W., 136
de Vries, N. K., 355
Dewey, J., 43
Dhooper, S. S., 246
Diamond, G. S., 252
Diamond, S., 164
DiBello, L. W., 569
Dickey, M., 252
Dickson, D. T., 29, 30, 592, 601
DiClemente, C., 241, 243, 251, 254, 646
Dietzen, L., 291
DiFonzo, N., 290
Dimeff, L., 356
Dittmar, K., 338
Ditto, P. H., 352
Dodge, K. A., 106
Doernberger, C. H., 94
Doherty, H., 320
Doherty, W., 321
Dolezal-Wood, S., 573
Dolgoff, R., 292, 591, 596
Doll, B., 95
Donahue, J. D., 615
Donohue, B., 204
Donovan, D. M., 251
Dooley, D., 398
Doubleday, E., 283, 291
Doudera, E., 598
Douglas, M. A. D., 621
Douglas, R. M., 574
Downes, D., 283

Downey, E., 123
Downey, G., 95, 218
Downs, G., 472(n3)
Doyal, L., 14, 20
Drabman, R. S., 208
Draine, J., 291
Drake, R. E., 445
Drilea, S. K., 443
Drisko, J. W., 138
Dromi, P., 375
Drucker, P. F., 392
Drum, J., 133
Dryman, A., 219
DuBois, B., 117
Dubrovsky, V., 290
Duby, P., 283
Dugger, C. A., 645
Dunnett, G., 285
Dunst, C., 118, 376, 385, 388
Dupper, D. R., 398
Durkheim, E., 455
Durkin, T., 320
Durlak, J., 95, 97, 98, 99, 105, 106
Dworkin, G., 593
Dwyer, J. H., 104
Dyckman, J. M., 225, 229
Dyer, J. F. P., 243
Dziegielewski, S., 327, 438, 444

Earley, P. C., 360
Earls, F. J., 467
Early, B. P., 208
East, J., 116, 123
Eaton, W. W., 219, 220
Ebben, M., 158
Ebenstein, H., 288
Ebrahimi, S., 229
Eckenrode, J., 265, 349
Eddy, D. M., 56
Edelman, G. M., 178, 180
Edelstein, S., 247
Edgar, M., 361
Edinbergh, G. M., 432
Edinburg, G., 512
Edwards, C. S., 361
Edwards, R. L., 392, 402
Eggert, L., 342
Ehrenreich, B., 19
Ehrman, R., 203, 204
Ekman, P., 356
El-Bassel, N., 507

Eldridge, G. D., 213
Eldridge, K., 570
Elkin, I., 234, 235, 343
Ell, K., 245
Elliott, D., 635, 636, 639, 640, 641, 644, 646
Elliott, L. J., 590
Elliott, R., 181
Ellis, A., 181
Ellul, J., 57
Elshtain, J., 17
Emery, G., 180, 230
Emmet, D., 590
Endler, N. S., 349, 361, 366(n2)
Engi, S., 568
Enkin, M. W., 53
Ennis, R. H., 43
Entwistle, V. A., 49
Ephross, P. H., 284
Epstein, I., 536, 612
Epstein, L., 288, 536, 612
Epstein, N., 308, 317
Epston, D., 313, 318, 421
Erdman, H. P., 570
Erickson, A. G., 523
Erlich, J., 18, 67, 75, 547
Eron, L., 101
Esley, C. L., 33
Estes, R., 400, 636, 638, 641
Estrada, M., 340
Etzioni, A., 11, 17
Evans, D., 283
Evans, G. W., 358
Evans, I. N., 50
Evans, R. L., 289
Evans, T. W., 353
Evans, W., 341, 342
Evenson, R., 570
Everett, J. E., 420
Everson, M., 275
Ewalt, P. L., 398, 402
Ewart, C. K., 125

Fabricant, M., 10, 15, 17, 125, 376, 392, 400
Fagan, J., 283, 455
Fahlberg, V., 275
Fair, C., 289
Falicov, C., 306, 321
Faller, K. C., 272, 274, 275
Falloon, I., 313, 319
Fals-Stewart, W., 228
Fanshel, D., 249

Fanurik, D., 105
Farmer, F., 457
Farrington, D., 93, 101, 103, 452
Faul, A. C., 214, 538
Faust, D., 51
Favorini, A., 158
Fawcett, S. B., 547
Feagin, J. R., 116
Febbraro, A. R., 248
Feld, B. C., 453
Feldman, J. L., 613, 615
Feldman, L. H., 339
Feldman, S., 188
Fellenius, J., 226
Fellin, P., 83, 395
Fennell, M., 229
Fernandez, E., 235
Ferreira, J., 490
Ferris, P., 565
Feske, U., 226, 232
Fetzer, B. K., 354
Fewell, L., 603
Feyerherm, W. H., 456
Fifield, J., 246
Figlio, R., 455
Figueira-McDonough, J., 136, 137, 168(n21), 399
Figueroa, R., 209
Finch, W. A., 388
Finkelhor, D., 275, 276, 639
Finley, N. J., 164
Finn, E., 329, 330
Finn, J., 289, 572, 574
Fisch, R., 315
Fischer, D. J., 221
Fischer, J., 140, 201, 202, 207, 212, 540, 556, 560, 561
Fish, M. C., 491
Fisher, J., 114
Fisher, R., 5(n), 6, 16, 19, 374, 398, 400
Fisher, R. H., 246
Fisher, W. H., 615
Fishman, C., 315
Fishman, M., 289
Fiske, S. T., 359
Fitchen, J. M., 398
Fitzpatrick, R. J., 613, 615
Flacks, D., 398
Flatt, V., 477
Flay, B. R., 93
Fleming, J., 124
Fletcher, J., 598
Flowers, J. V., 288

Flynn, J., 27
Flynn, L. M., 446
Flynn, M. L., 569
Foa, E. B., 227, 228
Folbre, N., 265
Folkman, S., 249, 344, 349, 351, 353, 361
Fong, L., 510
Fong, M. L., 621
Ford, B., 283, 570, 579
Forgarty, L., 276
Forgas, J. P., 353
Forst, M., 455
Forsythe, P., 270
Forthofer, M. S., 236
Foster, D. A., 291
Foster, S., 341
Foucault, M., 318
Fowers, B., 320
Fox, H. R., 289
Fox, R. C., 487
Fox, S. W., 492
Framo, J., 311, 312
Frank, M. G., 356
Frank, R. G., 236
Franke, R., 487
Frankel, C., 590
Frankena, W. K., 597
Franklin, A. J., 283
Franklin, C., 181, 285, 291, 415, 416, 555, 556, 557, 558, 559
Fraser, M., 92, 400, 402
Fraser, M. W., 93, 101, 106, 291, 338, 339, 377, 378, 388, 389, 545
Frazier, C., 456
Frazier, P. A., 246
Fredriksen, K. I., 486
Freedman, D., 356
Freedman, J., 318, 418
Freedy, J. R., 357
Freeman, E. M., 398, 415, 417, 420, 422, 426, 430, 431
Freeman, L., 481
Freire, P., 115, 116, 138, 377, 384, 396, 420, 432, 525
Freitas, A. L., 95
French, J., 507
French, T. M., 244
Freud, A., 274
Freud, S., 481, 499
Frey, H., 471
Frieder, R., 116
Friedland, N., 354

Friedlander, W. A., 66
Friedman, J., 391, 400
Friedman, R. C., 482
Friedmann, J., 381
Friedrich, W., 277
Friesen, B., 393
Frieze, I., 343, 350
Frijda, N. H., 353, 367(n4)
Frisman, P., 39
Fromer, J., 320
Frumkin, M., 636
Fuchs, R., 116
Fujino, D. C., 141
Fuqua, W., 207
Furrey, J., 356
Furstenberg, F., 266
Futrell, J., 320

Gagnon, J. H., 359
Galaway, B., 14, 552
Galbraith, M. E., 355
Galbraith, M. W., 100
Galinsky, E., 506
Galinsky, M., 92, 378, 572
Galinsky, M. J., 281, 282, 283, 285, 286, 288, 289,
    291, 292, 293, 572
Gallant, J. P., 200
Gallegos, J., 134, 136
Galper, J., 114, 116, 376
Gambe, R., 283
Gamble, D., 374, 376, 377, 395, 396, 397, 398, 399,
    400, 401, 402
Gambrill, E., 39, 45, 47(n), 48(n), 50, 51, 57, 58,
    538
Garbarino, J., 200, 265, 388, 389, 466
Garbarino, K., 376
Garcia, A. O., 134
Gardner, H., 179
Gardner, R., 491
Garfield, S., 172
Garland, A. F., 342
Garland, J. A., 285
Garloch, J. L., 290
Garmezy, N., 94, 304
Garrett, J. A., 245
Garrison, R., 396, 398
Garvin, C., 65(n), 138, 281, 282, 284, 286, 376,
    384, 385
Garvin, C. D., 251, 252, 256, 283, 285, 288, 293,
    294, 340, 341, 395, 399, 552
Garvin, D. A., 392

Gaschke, Y. N., 353
Gaston, L., 251
Gates, L., 511, 512
Gaylord, J., 355, 357
Gechtman, L., 603
Geertz, C., 318
Gehrig, C. C., 590
Gelder, M., 229, 230
Gelman, S. R., 39, 579
Gendreau, P., 464
Gentry, J. H., 101
Genuis, M., 275
George, L. K., 222
George, W. H., 356
Gerard, R. W., 72
Gergen, K. J., 318, 572
Germain, C., 152, 200, 416, 420, 646
Gerson, R., 309
Getzel, G. S., 283
Ghannam, J., 243
Ghosh, A., 224
Gibbs, J., 510
Gibbs, L., 45, 47(n), 48(n), 58
Gibelman, M., 453, 615
Giddens, A., 479
Giebelhausen, P. N., 593
Giffords, E. D., 572
Gifis, S. H., 600
Gil, D., 19
Gil, D. G., 375, 377, 606
Gil, E., 275
Gilbert, N., 66
Gill, D., 284
Gillespie, J., 213
Gilovich, T., 58
Gimotty, P. A., 575
Ginsberg, C., 103
Ginsburg, L., 6
Giordano, J., 136, 306
Giordano, P., 308, 469
Giovannoni, J., 388
Girard, J., 320
Gittens, J., 451
Gitterman, A., 282, 420, 621, 646
Giuliano, T. A., 367(n5)
Gladstone, J., 288
Glasser, I., 283
Glasser, P., 285
Glassman, U., 283, 285
Gleicher, F., 361
Glenmaye, L., 139, 646
Glenmaye, W., 126

Gochros, H., 201, 202
Goetz, K., 385, 388
Goh, T. L. C., 291
Gold, S. N., 36
Goldberg, G., 376
Goldberger, L., 349, 350
Goldiamond, I., 50
Golding, J. M., 221
Goldner, V., 307, 320
Goldstein, A. P., 172
Goldstein, H., 595
Goldstein, J., 116
Goldstein, M., 313, 319
Gollwitzer, P. M., 187, 188, 352
Golombok, S., 491
Gomory, T., 57
Gonsiorek, J., 485, 486
Gonzalez, J., 291
Gonzalez, J. J., 291
Gonzalez-Reigosa, F., 142
Goodman, M., 613, 614
Googins, B., 502, 510
Goolishian, H., 313
Gopaul-McNicol, S. A., 621
Gordon, M. M., 396, 441
Gordon, R., 97
Gordon, W. E., 590
Gore, S., 360
Gorenberg, C., 30
Gorey, K., 213, 288
Gorovitz, S., 597
Gottlieb, B. H., 359, 385, 387, 388
Gottlieb, N., 136, 390, 399
Gottman, J., 308
Gottschalk, S., 182
Gough, I., 14, 20
Gould, K., 158
Graetz, K. A., 290
Graham, M., 340
Graham, T. L., 355, 357
Granello, P. F., 25, 34, 35
Grant, J. A., 103
Grawe, K., 251
Gray, J. A. M., 46, 53, 56
Grayson, J. B., 228
Green, B. L., 357
Green, J., 133, 137
Green, R. J., 307, 321
Green, V., 134
Greenberg, D. F., 484
Greenberg, L. S., 181, 182, 243
Greene, B., 137, 138

Greene, G., 335
Greene, L., 470
Greene, R. J., 206, 491
Greenspan, S., 274
Greenwood, P., 99, 274, 462
Greer, A., 292
Greist, J. H., 570, 572
Griffin, J., 569
Griffin, P., 451
Griffith, D., 385
Griffith, E. E. H., 136
Grimley, D., 243, 254
Grinnell, R. M., Jr., 606
Grossman, J. B., 100
Grossman, S. F., 243
Grosswald, B., 100
Gruen, R. J., 344
Grundy, J. F., 249
Guarino-Ghezzi, S., 453, 472
Guerin-Gonzales, C., 134
Guerney, B., 314, 315
Guerra, N. G., 102
Guidano, V. F., 181, 190, 191
Gummer, B., 510
Gurman, A., 320
Gustafson, D., 569
Guthrie, C. A., 356
Gutiérrez, L., 116, 118, 119, 121, 125, 126, 133,
    134, 137, 138, 139, 159, 165, 283, 378, 381,
    396, 399, 420, 421, 422, 646
Guttag, J. V., 579
Guttmann, D., 636
Guyatt, G. H., 52

Haaken, J., 158
Haapala, D. A., 338, 339
Haardman, D. G., 591
Haberman, P. W., 603
Habermas, J., 7
Hackmann, A., 230
Hadley, S. W., 242
Hadzi-Pavlovic, D., 250
Hage, J., 376
Hagen, J., 505, 509, 512
Haggerty, R., 95, 97, 99
Haley, J., 307, 313, 315
Halgin, R. P., 622
Hall, B. L., 122, 123
Hall, E., 252
Hall, L. K., 590
Hall, S. S., 178

Halstead, T. S., 256
Halter, A., 502, 505, 512
Hamer, D., 483
Hamilton, G., 590
Hammer, A. L., 350
Hammersmith, S. K., 487
Hammons, K., 289
Hampson, J., 636
Hampson, R., 306, 307
Hancock, R. N., 597
Hand, I., 235
Handy, C., 615, 616
Hanisch, C., 116, 117
Hanna, G. L., 221
Hannerz, U., 189
Hanrahan, P., 212
Hardcastle, D. A., 376, 377, 395, 396, 401
Harden, S. L., 439
Hardman, D. G., 595
Hardy, J., 288
Hare-Mustin, R., 307
Harnad, S., 201
Harrington, M., 523
Harris, P., 574
Harris, P. B., 289
Harris, P. W., 460
Harris, R., 639
Harrison, W. D., 421
Hartford, M., 384
Hartley, E. K., 604
Hartman, A., 387, 415, 420, 431
Harvey, A., 100
Hasenfeld, Y., 392
Hatfield, A., 319
Havassy, B. E., 252
Haveman, R., 520
Hawkins, D., 467, 469
Hawkins, J. D., 94, 96, 97, 98, 100, 102, 103, 104,
     466, 469
Hayek, F. A., 181
Hayes, S., 201
Haynes, K., 15
Haynes, K. N., 351
Haynes, K. S., 27
Haynes, R. B., 46
Hays, C., 392
Hays, J. R., 600
Healy, L., 634
Hearn, G., 66
Heatherton, T., 243, 244, 245
Hedlund, J., 290
Heflin, A., 276, 277

Heiman, R. J., 189
Heimberg, R. G., 226, 235
Heller, K., 96
Hellstroem, K., 225
Hellstrom, K., 229
Helmbrecht, L., 491
Helms, J. E., 621
Hendricks, C. O., 134, 622
Henggeler, S. W., 92, 101
Henretta, J., 456
Henry, W. P., 251
Hepworth, J., 320
Heraclitis, 168(n14)
Herdt, G., 480, 483, 485, 487
Herek, G. M., 487, 488
Hernandez, M., 393, 394, 402
Hernandez, S., 117, 291, 513
Herrnstein, R. J., 455
Hersen, M., 201, 218
Hershberger, S. L., 486
Herting, J., 342
Herzog, C., 592
Hetherington, M., 304
Hibbs, E., 92
Hickling, E. J., 228
Higgins, E. T., 182, 183
Hill, C. E., 242
Hill, G., 341
Hill, M., 154, 158, 159, 165, 167
Hill, P. L., 100
Hill-Collins, P., 134, 138
Hiltz, S. R., 565
Himle, J., 202, 219, 221, 228, 236
Hinkely, R. C., 569
Hipp, J. L., 622
Hirky, A. E., 366(n1)
Hirn, K., 416
Hiroko, A., 116
Hirschi, T., 455
Hoagwood, K., 92, 101
Hoats, D. L., 206
Hobfoll, S. E., 344, 357, 359, 361, 366(n2)
Hobgood, M. E., 164
Hodges, V. G., 385
Hoffman, L., 304, 316, 318
Hogan, D. B., 600
Hogarty, G., 252, 291, 319
Holahan, C. J., 361, 364
Holden, G., 289
Holland, T. P., 392
Holle, M. C., 394, 396
Hollenbeck, J. R., 290

Holliman, S., 570
Hollingshead, A. B., 290
Hollon, S. D., 234
Holloway, S., 392, 509
Holton, B., 352
Homan, M. S., 376, 392, 395, 396, 397
Hong, Y., 356
Hoover, B., 290
Hooyman, N., 136, 153, 156, 160, 162, 163, 167(n1), 167(n2)
Hope, D. A., 226, 232
Hopkins, K., 503, 510
Horning, C. D., 220
Horowitz, M. J., 180, 183, 366(n3)
House, J., 507, 509, 511
Housley, W. F., 621
Houston, B. K., 350
Houston-Vega, M. K., 29, 31, 38, 600, 601
Howard, C., 95
Howard, G., 133
Howard, K. I., 254
Howell, J., 104, 468
Howitt, D., 52, 56
Hu, L., 141
Huba, G., 568
Hudson, B., 208
Hudson, W. W., 198, 214, 536, 538, 540, 541, 549, 563
Huesmann, L. R., 102
Huggins, S. L., 491
Hughes, D., 222
Huling, T., 456
Hunter, J., 276, 422, 426
Hunter, W., 265
Hurley, K., 362
Hyde, C., 16, 19, 399, 402

Iadicola, P., 163
Icard, L., 357, 360, 480, 486
Iglehart, A., 133, 134, 137
Ilgen, D. R., 290
Imber-Black, E., 303, 306
Ingelby, D., 117
Irvine, M. J., 357
Irvine, S., 204
Isaac, A., 491
Isaacs, M. R., 388, 393, 394, 402
Israel, B. A., 118
Ivanoff, A., 552
Iversen, R., 512
Ivey, A. E., 646

Iwamasa, G. Y., 235

Jack, D., 223
Jackson, D., 302
Jackson, J. S., 136
Jackson, M., 357
Jacob, L., 304
Jacobs, D., 617
Jacobs, S. E., 480
Jacobs, W. J., 180
Jacobson, J. W., 47
Jacobson, N., 317
Jaffe, L., 253
James, B., 275
Jameson, L. B., 547
Janoff-Bulman, R., 343, 344, 345, 350, 360
Jansen, G. G., 399, 529
Jansson, B. S., 402
Jarvis, W. T., 57
Jaureguy, B. M., 289
Jayaratne, S., 211, 593, 603
Jayasuriya, L., 137
Jehu, D., 210
Jemmott, J. B., III, 352
Jenkins, P. H., 460
Jenkins, W., 512
Jensen, C., 256
Jensen, M. A. C., 285
Jensen, P., 92
Jenson, J. M., 545
Jerremalm, A., 229
Jessor, R., 93
Jessup, L. M., 290
Jivanjee, P. R., 621
Johannsson, V., 570
Johansson, J., 229
Johnson, A., 590
Johnson, A. K., 283
Johnson, H., 75
Johnson, H. C., 420
Johnson, J., 220
Johnson, K. W., 360
Johnson, P., 510
Johnsrud, L. K., 138
Jones, D. M., 283
Jones, E. E., 243, 247
Jones, H. E., 285
Jones, J. A., 24
Jones, L., 502, 512
Jones, M., 253
Jones, R., 603

Jones, R. R., 317
Jones, S., 419
Jonsen, A. R., 598
Jordan, C., 291, 555, 556, 557, 558, 559
Jordan, D., 108(n)
Jordan, K. M., 487
Jorgensen, J., 117, 513
Joseph, A., 417
Joseph, B., 116, 125
Joseph, M. V., 590, 596
Juliá, M. C., 637, 638

Kacen, L., 294
Kachele, H., 575
Kadushin, A., 617
Kaeser, R., 285
Kagan, S., 320, 385, 388
Kagle, J. D., 29, 33, 592, 593
Kahn, S., 396, 400, 402
Kaiser, G., 235
Kanfer, F. H., 172
Kaniasty, K., 336, 341, 343
Kant, I., 180-181, 597
Kaplan, E., 574
Kaplan, H. B., 349
Kaplan, L., 320
Kaplan, M., 342
Karger, H., 5(n), 6, 124, 374, 398, 400, 568
Karls, J., 218, 402, 617
Karno, M., 221
Karp, C., 275
Karpel, M., 322
Karrer, B., 320
Kasper, B., 151(n)
Kates, L., 283, 285
Katz, J., 357
Katz-Porterfield, S. L., 153, 159, 163
Kaufman, J., 304
Kaul, T. K., 252
Kazdin, A., 544, 545, 560
Kazi, M., 560
Keanau, E. J., 134
Keatinge, C., 617
Kegan, R., 191
Keinan, G., 354
Keirse, M. J. N. C., 53
Keith, D., 312, 314
Keith-Lucas, A., 590, 606
Keitner, G. I., 247
Keitnor, G., 308
Kelley, M. L., 209

Kelly, J. J., 421, 422
Kelly, R. J., 203
Kemp, S. P., 189, 525
Kempf, K., 455
Kempf-Leonard, K., 456
Kenardy, J., 572
Kennard, W. W., 289
Kennedy, D. M., 104
Kennedy, J. F., 89
Kenney, S. J., 154
Kent, M. M., 441
Kessler, R. C., 217, 218, 219, 220, 222, 223, 236, 237, 442, 621
Ketner, P. M., 376
Kets De Vries, M., 508, 509, 510
Kiam, R., 291
Kieffer, C., 118, 122
Kiesler, S., 290, 567
Kihlstrom, J. F., 182
Kilpatrick, D., 340, 357
Kim, W., 508, 509, 510
Kimberly, J. R., 392
Kimble, C. E., 290
Kimboko, P., 118, 123
King, C., 341, 342
King, S. A., 568, 574
Kinney, J., 338, 388
Kinsella, H., 154
Kipke, M., 568
Kirby, K. C., 567
Kirby, L. D., 93, 106
Kirk, B., 456
Kirk, S. A., 52, 535, 536, 538
Kirk-Sharp, C., 604
Kirsch, N., 360
Kisthardt, W., 122
Kitayama, S., 189
Klawitter, M. M., 477
Klein, A. R., 466
Klein, F., 487
Klein, J. G., 292
Klein, M. H., 570
Klein, W., 537
Klein, W. M., 354
Kleinman, A., 189
Klerman, G., 234, 343
Kline, A., 360
Kling, J., 16
Klingemann, H. K., 243, 244, 245, 250
Klinger, E., 178
Klosko, J. S., 233
Knapp, S., 592

Knee, R., 512
Knesper, D., 439
Knight, E., 265
Kochman, A., 492, 493
Koepke, J. M., 210
Kogan, E., 204
Kohn, E., 641
Kohner, K., 291
Kolko, D., 276, 277
Kolodny, R. L., 285
Kondrat, M. E., 125
Koney, K., 398
Kopels, S., 29, 592
Koptka, S. M., 254
Korbin, J., 639
Koss, M., 254, 345
Kostelny, K., 466
Kotch, J. B., 274
Kotlowitz, A., 267, 274
Kozloff, M. A., 51
Kramer, R., 374, 376
Kratochwill, T. R., 51
Krause, M. E., 254
Kretmann, J. P., 526
Kretzmann, J., 69, 376, 378, 395
Krishna, S., 569
Kristol, W., 11
Krone, K., 228
Krtezman, J., 398
Kubisch, A. C., 398
Kuch, K., 236
Kuipers, P., 353
Kunda, Z., 352
Kurdek, L. A., 491
Kurland, R., 282
Kurtz, L. F., 251, 252
Kurzman, P., 500, 506, 600
Kutchins, H., 52
Kyte, N. S., 551

Lago, C., 622
Laird, J., 158, 318, 321, 387
Lamb, D. H., 603
Lambert, M. J., 242
Lambert, S., 503
Lamison-White, L., 521
Land, H., 134, 154, 158, 480
Landis, E. R., 600
Landrum-Brown, J., 621
Landsman, M. J., 338
Lane, B., 559, 560

Lane, B. A., 646
Lane, R. C., 617
Lang, S., 57, 480
Langer, E. J., 352
La Puma, J., 598
LaRocco, J., 507
LaRossa, R., 321
LaRowe, K. D., 291
Larrow, L. D., 207
Larsson, B., 100
Lasch, C., 8, 13, 614
Last, C. G., 218, 233
Latane, B., 290
Latimer, P. R., 228
Laumann, E. O., 359
Launier, R., 359
Lauria, R., 566, 573
Laux, L., 357
Lavin, J., 344
Lavitt, M., 289, 572
Lavrakas, P. J., 360
Law, T., 304
Lawson, H. A., 417
Layfield, D. A., 105
Lazarus, R. S., 249, 344, 349, 351, 353, 359, 361, 364, 366
Lazere, E., 520
Leary, M. R., 357, 487
Lease, S. H., 621
Leavell, H. R., 95
Leavitt, S., 400, 402
Lebow, J., 320
Lechner, V., 509
Ledvinka, J., 504
Lee, J., 116, 119, 120, 121, 134
Lee, J. A. B., 283, 374, 376, 379, 380, 384, 385, 392, 394, 396, 400
Lee, M., 335
Lee, P., 375, 401
Lee, P. C. Y., 636
Lee, P. R., 590
Lefcourt, H. M., 359
Lefley, H., 319
Lehman, D., 246
Leiber, M. J., 456
Leiby, J., 589
Lemert, E., 455
Lentz, R. J., 205
Lepore, S. J., 350, 358
Lerman, P., 463, 464
Lerner, M., 612
Lester, D., 337

Letellier, P., 491
Leung, J. E. B., 636
Leutz, W. N., 387
LeVay, S., 482, 483
Leventhal, H., 357, 366(n1)
Levin, H., 113
Levine, C., 598
Levine, J., 568
Levine, J. M., 285
Levy, C. S., 590, 595
Levy, D., 45
Lewellen, A., 291
Lewin, K., 507, 509
Lewis, C., 288
Lewis, C. M., 331
Lewis, D. A., 103
Lewis, E., 133, 137, 138, 139, 146, 283, 396
Lewis, E. A., 421
Lewis, G. A., 108(n)
Lewis, H., 590
Lewis, R. E., 339, 545
Lewis, V. G., 482
Lewitt, E., 264, 265, 266
Lidz, C. W., 34
Lieberman, M. A., 385, 387
Liebman, M. C., 615
Liebowitz, M. R., 220
Lightburn, A., 596
Lindsay, B., 103
Lindsey, D., 340
Link, B. G., 524
Linville, P. W., 183
Liotti, G., 181, 190, 191
Lippmann, J., 276, 277
Lipschitz, A., 342
Lipsey, M., 99, 454, 466, 468
Lipsky, M., 82
Littell, J. H., 92
Litwak, E., 77
Livanou, M., 228
Livermore, M., 644
Llewelyn, S., 285
Lobel, S. A., 293
Locke, B., 396, 398
Lockett, P. W., 153, 167(n4), 168(n15)
Lockhart, L., 491
Loeber, R., 93, 96, 97, 101, 103
Loewenberg, F., 591, 596
Loffredo, L., 103
Loiben, T., 206
Loneck, B., 245
Long, D. D., 394, 396

Long, S., 264, 266
Longabaugh, R., 251
Longres, J., 14, 16, 137, 374, 396
Looby, E. J., 621
Lopez, J., 283
Lorde, A., 137
Loughran, E. J., 453, 472
Lovegrove, A., 467
Lovell, K., 228
Lovell, M., 361
Lowry, J. L., 254
Lubove, R., 589, 590
Luczak, R., 486
Ludwig, A. M., 244
Luiselli, J. K., 51
Lukes, A. C., 480
Lum, D., 133, 137, 138, 396, 442
Lunblad, K. S., 612
Lurie, H., 375
Lustman, P. J., 234
Luthar, S. S., 94
Luther, S. S., 317
Lynn, M., 292
Lyon, M. A., 95

Macbeth, J. E., 627
MacDonald, G., 213
Macdonald, G., 47
Mace, D., 341
Macgowan, M. J., 294
Machado, D. E., 193
MacIntosh, R., 95
MacKenzie, K. R., 288
Mackie, S. A., 35
Macy, R., 357
Madanes, C., 313, 315
Madden, R. G., 27, 30, 34, 36, 600, 601
Maddox, K., 211
Maddux, J. E., 116
Madrick, J., 614
Madsen, R., 7, 398
Maeda, K. K., 636
Maes, S., 357, 366(n1)
Magee, W. J., 220
Magen, R. H., 293, 294
Mahalik, J. R., 141
Mahler, M., 267
Mahoney, A., 455
Mahoney, M. J., 180, 181
Maidenberg, E., 233
Maier, S. F., 115

Mailick, M. D., 288
Maiuro, R. D., 344
Maki, K. M., 233
Malekoff, A., 283
Malin, M., 490
Mallinckrodt, B., 253, 256
Mallon, G., 283, 484
Malott, M., 201
Malott, R., 201
Maluccio, A. N., 387
Mancuso, A., 158
Mandal, K. S., 636
Mankiller, W., 134
Mann, C. R., 456
Mann, K. B., 243
Mann, T. L., 441
Mannarino, A., 276, 277
Manning, S. S., 123
Mannion, E., 291
Manstead, A. S. R., 367(n4)
Mantell, J. E., 360
Maple, F., 284
Maramba, G., 141
Marcus, L. A., 615
Marcuse, H., 115
Marger, M. N., 136
Margraf, J., 227
Mariano, W. E., 600
Markam, S., 353
Markowitz, J. C., 234, 235
Marks, A. P., 228
Marks, I. M., 224, 226, 228
Markus, H., 183, 189, 190, 191, 353
Markus, M. L., 567
Marlow, C., 502
Marrow, J., 307
Marsh, J. C., 194
Martin, M. A., 283
Martin, P., 8, 374
Martinez, A., 291
Marx, J., 500, 506, 510
Mash, E., 276
Masi, D. A., 399
Masland, M., 440
Mason, M. A., 40
Masten, A. S., 94
Mathews, A. M., 229
Matson, J. L., 51
Matsubara, Y., 636
Mattaini, M. A., 538
Matthews, G., 352
Mattick, R. P., 250

Mattison, D., 593
Maturana, H., 318
Matza, D., 455
Mauborgne, R., 508, 509, 510
Mauer, M., 456
Mauney, R., 399
Mayadas, N. S., 635, 636, 639, 640, 641, 644, 646
Mayer, G. R., 51
Mayer, J. D., 353
Mayeux, D. M., 284
Mazade, N. A., 446
McAdoo, H. P., 388
McBreen, J. T., 415
McCadam, K., 291
McCallion, P., 283
McCann, C. W., 595
McCarthy, C., 571
McClendon, M. J., 571
McCloyd, V. C., 189
McConatha, D., 569
McConatha, J. T., 569
McCorkle, B. H., 228
McCormick, J., 45
McCrae, R. R., 364
McCroskey, J., 388, 402
McCubbin, A., 320
McCubbin, H., 304, 317, 320
McCubbin, M., 320
McCulloch, C., 574
McDaniel, S., 320
McDermott, F. E., 590, 592, 593
McDonald, S. M., 283
McFarlane, W., 319
McGill, C., 319
McGillis, D., 103
McGlynn, E. A., 445
McGoldrick, M., 136, 158, 303, 304, 306, 307, 308, 309, 310, 312, 314, 320, 428
McGonagle, K. A., 220, 621
McGowan, B. G., 591
McGrade, B., 340
McGrath, J. E., 290, 366
McGrew, J. H., 291
McGuire, T. W., 290, 567
McIntosh, J., 336, 342
McIntosh, M., 116
McKay, C., 158
McKay, H., 455
McKay, M. M., 291
McKee, J., 571
McKenna, F. P., 354
McKenna, K. Y. A., 290

McKnight, J., 25, 69, 376, 378, 395, 398, 526
McLellan, A., 204
McLellan, T., 203, 204
McLennan, J., 569
McLeod, D., 591
McLeod, E., 14, 16
McLeod, P. L., 293
McLoyd, V. C., 524
McLuhan, E., 566
McLuhan, M., 566
McMahon, A., 137
McMillen, J. C., 246
McMillen, R., 245
McMurtry, S. L., 214, 376, 538
McNeil, B., 617
McNeil, J. S., 291
McPhail, B., 158, 168(n13)
McPhee, K., 219
McQueeney, M., 340
McRoy, R., 331, 384, 422, 426
Mead, D. E., 617
Mead, M., 483
Meana, M., 567
Mechanic, D., 443
Mederos, F., 320
Meehl, P. E., 51
Meezan, W., 388, 402
Meglin, D., 288
Mehr, J., 66
Meichenbaum, D. H., 235
Meier, A., 289
Meinert, R., 641
Meisel, A., 34
Meisel, M., 291
Melaville, A. I., 393, 394, 402
Melchior, L., 568
Melton, G., 32, 101, 639
Meltzer, J. D., 617
Menditto, A. A., 205
Mendola, M., 490
Meredith, L. S., 445
Mergenthaler, E., 575
Merry, J., 288
Merton, R., 71, 455
Meyer, C. H., 200, 536
Meyer, D. J., 617
Meyer, H., 591
Meyer, H. J., 77
Meyer, L. A., 569
Meyer, L. H., 50
Meyer, R. G., 600

Michael, R. T., 359
Mickelson, J., 15, 27
Mickelson, K. D., 290
Middleman, R. R., 283, 374, 376, 384, 394, 401, 402
Middleton, H., 230
Midgley, J., 137, 400, 633, 634, 636, 637, 641, 643, 647
Mihalic, S. F., 100
Miles, R. H., 392
Miley, K., 117
Miller, D., 95
Miller, D. A., 415, 422
Miller, D. C., 154
Miller, G., 158
Miller, G. E., 101
Miller, H., 66
Miller, I., 308
Miller, I. W., 247
Miller, J., 456, 472
Miller, J. B., 193, 396
Miller, J. G., 67, 75
Miller, J. K., 572
Miller, L. S., 99, 101, 102
Miller, S. M., 356, 360, 362
Miller, T. E., 288
Miller, W., 455
Miller, W. R., 247, 255
Miller, W. T., 244, 248
Millman, H., 276, 277
Mills, C. W., 525
Minahan, A., 152
Mindel, C., 134
Minuchin, P., 315
Minuchin, S., 313, 314, 315
Mirowsky, J., 189
Mischel, W., 188, 193, 356
Mishel, L., 501
Mishne, J., 276
Mitchum, C., 566
Mizahi, T., 394
Mize, J., 346(n)
Mizio, E., 138
Model, K., 99, 463
Mogane, M., 466
Mohr, D., 193
Molidar, C. E., 293
Moline, M. E., 600
Monat, A., 366
Mondros, J. B., 117, 400
Money, J., 482

Monheit, A. C., 443
Montalvo, B., 315
Montgomery, D., 12
Moore, R. F., 30, 292
Moore, S. M., 289
Moore, V. L., 402
Moos, R., 243, 246, 350, 361
Moote, G. T., 211
Morales, A., 134, 138
Mor-Barak, M., 506, 510
Moreau, M., 116
Moreland, R. L., 285
Morell, C., 158, 168(n13)
Morelli, P. T., 133
Morgan, R. T., 204
Moritz, G., 340
Morris, J. F., 484, 485
Morris, S., 452
Morrison, J. D., 398
Moskowitz, G. B., 187, 188
Mosteller, F., 46
Motenko, A. K., 615
Motley, S., 378
Mrazek, P., 95, 97, 98, 101
Mueser, K. T., 249, 252
Mulder, C., 569
Mulick, J. A., 47
Mulroy, E. A., 378, 379
Munroe, E., 45, 56
Munson, C. E., 612, 613, 614, 615, 616, 617, 620,
    622, 623, 624, 625, 627
Murdrick, N., 506
Murphy, G. E., 234
Murphy, J., 567
Murphy, T. F., 478, 481
Murray, G., 154
Murray, P. J., 565
Murray, R. B., 253
Murray, S. O., 484
Murrell, L., 570
Muzzonigro, P. G., 485, 486, 489
Myers, L., 27, 198, 200, 606

Nadel, L., 180
Nadler, S., 283
Nagda, B., 133
Naifeh, M., 521, 522
Naisbitt, J., 616
Nakanishi, M., 289
Nanus, B., 392

Naparstek, A. J., 398
Nash, J. K., 291
Nayowirth, S., 283
Neal, A. M., 219
Neal-Barnett, A. M., 225
Neale, M. C., 482
Nehs, R., 207
Neighbors, H. W., 219
Neilson, J. P., 53
Neisser, U., 367(n4)
Nelsen, J., 560
Nelson, C. B., 222
Nelson, G., 123
Nelson, K. E., 101, 338, 388
Nemon, H., 396, 421
Nes, J., 163
Nesse, R. M., 217, 236
Nesse, R. N., 228
Netting, F. E., 136, 376, 392, 395, 396, 399, 402
Neufeld, J., 341
Newman, B. S., 485, 486, 489
Newman, M. G., 570, 572
Newman, P., 146
Newmark, L., 467
Nezu, A. M., 249
Nezu, C. M., 249
Nicholas, L., 342
Nichols, M., 302
Nichols, P., 243, 244, 245
Nichols-Casebolt, A., 136, 399
Nicholson, J., 615
Nicolosi, J., 481
Nigg, J. T., 243
Ninacs, W. A., 399, 400
Nisbet, P., 341
Nisbett, R., 45, 51
Nishimoto, R., 134
Noponen, H., 400
Norcross, J. C., 243, 254
Nord, D., 492
Norlin, J. M., 218
Norman, E., 158
Norman, W. H., 247
Normoyle, J., 360
Norquist, G. S., 446
Norris, F., 336, 341, 343
Norris, J., 355, 356, 357
North, C. S., 283, 291
North, M. M., 567
North, S. M., 567
Northen, H., 200, 283, 291, 388

Noshirvani, H., 228
Novaco, R. W., 235
Nowak, B., 19
Ntusi, T., 636
Nudelman, R., 291
Nuehring, E. M., 29, 600, 601
Nugent, W. R., 536, 546, 547, 548, 549
Nurius, P. S., 183, 285, 352, 353, 354, 355, 356,
    357, 361, 541, 549
Nye, J., 285

O'Brien, C., 203, 204
O'Brien, G. T., 233
O'Brien, R. A., 100
O'Brien, T. B., 350
Ochoa, E., 292
Ochs, E., 567, 573
O'Connel, B., 665(n3)
O'Connor, G., 636
O'Connor, J., 8, 374
O'Connor, K. M., 290
O'Connor, L., 247
O'Connor, P., 569
O'Connor, T., 304
O'Dell, K., 420
Odencrantz, L. C., 23
O'Donnell, J., 490
O'Donohue, W., 200
Ofshe, R., 44, 51
Ogburn, W. F., 68
O'Hanlon, W., 318
O'Hare, W. P., 441
Ohlin, L., 455
Olbrich, R., 572
Olds, D., 100
Olenick, C., 283
Olin, J. T., 617
Olsen, M., 68
Olson, D., 306, 320
Olson, J. J., 100
Olson, K., 264
O'Melia, M., 117
Onek, J. N., 627
Oran-Sabia, V., 511
Orlandi, M. A., 136, 137
Orlinsky, D. E., 251, 254
Orme, J. G., 540
Orshansky, M., 520
Ortega, R., 283, 420

Ortiz de Mantellano, B., 49
Ory, M., 116, 569
Osgood, D. W., 454
Osowiechki, D., 350
Ost, L., 224, 225, 226, 229, 230
O'Sullivan, M., 356
Ottaviani, R., 232
Otto, M. W., 233
Ouchi, W., 503
Overton, A., 388
Oxman, A. D., 52
Oyserman, D., 189, 245
Ozawa, M., 39, 500, 526, 620, 621

Paine, A. L., 547
Paine, R. T., Jr., 590
Palmer, S. E., 180
Pancost, D. L., 387
Papp, P., 158, 307
Parad, H. J., 340, 343
Pardeck, J. T., 567
Parker, J., 292, 361, 366(n2)
Parkinson, B., 367(n4)
Parkinson, C. N., 625
Parks, B. K., 251
Parody, M., 36
Parsons, B., 101, 317
Parsons, R., 165, 513
Parsons, R. J., 116, 117, 118, 119, 123, 124, 159,
    416, 420
Pato, M., 228
Pattatucci, A. M. L., 483
Patterson, C. J., 491
Patterson, D., 480
Patterson, G. R., 93, 106, 313, 317
Patterson, J., 304, 317, 320
Patti, R., 392
Paul, B., 311, 312
Paul, G. L., 205, 229
Paul, N., 311, 312
Paul, R., 44
Paulo, P. P., 193
Paulson, R., 123, 124
Pawluck, A., 213
Payne, M., 115
Pear, J. J., 213
Pearce, D., 521
Pearce, J., 136, 276, 306
Pearce, P., 308

Pearlin, L. I., 350, 359, 360, 365
Peck, S., 385, 388
Pecora, P., 338, 339, 387, 388
Penava, S. J., 233
Penn, D. L., 249
Penn, P., 316, 318
Pennekamp, M., 417, 430, 433
Pennell, J., 388, 390
Penner, W., 465
Pentz, M. A., 104
Pepper, C., 46
Perlman, H. H., 590, 592, 612
Perlmutter, F. D., 402
Perloff, L. S., 354
Perper, J., 340
Perri, M. G., 249
Peterkin, D., 575
Peters, A. J., 283
Peters, S., 470
Peters, T., 503
Petersilia, J., 467, 471
Peterson, A. J., 256
Peterson, B. D., 439
Peterson, K. J., 492
Peterson, L., 570
Petit, M. R., 338
Pezzot-Pearce, T., 276
Pfeiffer, C., 246
Pham, L. B., 362
Phelan, J., 524
Phillips, D., 613, 627
Piaget, J. P., 190
Piccagli, G., 440
Piehl, A. M., 104
Pierce, G. R., 359, 367(n7)
Pigott, H. E., 575
Piliavin, J. A., 356
Pillard, R. C., 482
Pincus, A., 152
Pinderhughes, E., 138, 139, 308
Pine, F., 267
Pinker, S., 179
Pinsof, W., 243, 320
Piore, M., 645
Pippard, J. L., 399, 529
Piven, F., 11, 114, 116
Plant, R., 590
Plato, 59
Platt, A., 454
Plotnick, R., 265

Poertner, J., 393, 398
Polansky, N. A., 546
Polemis, B. W., 246
Pollack, C., 567
Pollack, D., 579
Pollack, M. H., 233
Pollard, J. A., 94, 107
Pollard, K. M., 441
Pollio, D. E., 283, 291
Pollock, D., 39
Pollock, E. J., 612
Polowy, C. I., 30
Pomeroy, E. C., 291
Poole, D. L., 398
Pope, C. E., 456
Pope, K. S., 603
Pope, L. K., 351
Pope-Davis, D. B., 622
Popper, K. R., 48, 59
Popple, P., 590, 606
Potocky, M., 502
Pottick, K. J., 463, 464
Poules, S. T., 568
Powell, D. R., 385, 387
Powell, J., 206
Powell, T. J., 284
Powers, P. R., 376
Prata, J., 315
Price, R., 465
Priest, R., 622
Pritzl, D. O., 289
Proch, K., 28
Prochaska, J. O., 241, 243, 254, 255, 646
Proctor, E., 214, 284, 293, 545
Prohaska, T., 125
Prothrow-Stith, D., 465
Pryor, K., 201
Pugh, C., 317
Pumphrey, M. W., 590
Pumphrey, R. E., 401
Punamaki, R., 116
Purdon, S., 292
Putnam, R., 8, 11
Pyant, C. T., 137
Pyszczynski, T., 352

Quam, J. K., 493
Queiro-Tajalli, I., 636
Quinney, R., 455

Quist, N., 598

Radabaugh, C., 360
Ragab, I., 636
Rakowski, W., 125
Ramey, C. T., 179
Ramey, J. H., 283
Ramey, S. L., 179
Ramsey, P. W., 251, 252
Rankin, L., 317
Rapoport, A., 67, 71
Rapp, C. A., 122
Rappaport, J., 117, 118, 122, 123
Rassi, S., 236
Ratcliffe, C., 264
Rauch, J., 100
Rave, E. J., 621
Rawlings, L., 521
Rawls, J., 375
Read, S. J., 361
Reamer, F. G., 34, 589, 590, 591, 592, 593, 595,
    596, 597, 598, 599, 600, 601, 603, 604, 606
Reed, B., 138, 146
Reed, M. A., 362
Rees, S., 15
Reeser, J. C., 612
Regehr, C., 34
Regev, Y., 354
Regier, D. A., 444, 445
Reid, E. M., 567
Reid, J. B., 317
Reid, P. N., 590, 606
Reid, W., 212, 249, 288, 557, 560
Reid, W. J., 243, 255, 537, 543, 544, 612
Reilly, L., 467
Reinders, R., 635
Reisch, M., 39, 134
Reisenzein, R., 353
Reishl, T. M., 123
Reison, M., 619
Reiss, A. J., Jr., 467
Reiss, D., 305, 319
Remer, P., 158
Renfrew, M. J., 53
Rennie, D., 60
Resch, N. L., 100
Resnick, G., 467
Resnick, H., 357, 392
Resnick, R. P., 636
Revenson, T. A., 344
Reynolds, B. C., 375, 401

Reynolds, L. K., 209
Reynolds, M. M., 590
Reynolds, T., 288
Rheinchild, J., 335
Rheingold, H., 566
Rhodes, M., 591
Rhodes, R., 291
Rice, L. N., 181
Rice, R. E., 567
Richard, R., 355
Richardson, W. S., 46
Richey, C. A., 339, 367(n7)
Richman, J. M., 398
Richmond, M., 90, 523, 612
Riffe, H. A., 125
Rifkin, M. J., 415
Ripple, L., 246
Rittner, B., 289
Ritvo, P., 357
Rivard, J. C., 101
Rivas, R. F., 251, 282, 384
Rivera, F., 18
Roach, W. H., 33
Roback, H. B., 292
Roberts, A. R., 327, 328, 329, 330, 331-335, 345
Roberts, J., 306
Roberts, L. D., 567
Roberts, M. C., 105
Robinson, J. G., 575
Robson, P., 229
Rock, B., 40
Rock, M. H., 617
Rode, D. C., 289
Rodriquez, F. I., 480
Roffman, R. A., 289, 291, 292
Rogers, C., 206
Rogers, J., 575
Rogge, M. E., 643
Rogler, L., 142
Rohde, P., 341, 342
Rojek, C., 115
Rolland, J. S., 319, 320
Rollin, J., 457, 466
Rollnick, S., 255
Romanelli, E., 392
Rooney, B. J., 383
Rooney, R., 245
Roscoe, W., 484
Rose, S. D., 210, 211, 283, 288, 291, 293, 431
Rose, S. M., 402
Rosen, A., 545, 549
Rosenbaum, D. P., 103

Rosenberg, G., 289
Rosenberg, S. A., 287
Rosenberg, W., 46
Rosenfield, M., 566
Rosenthal, B. R., 394
Rosman, B., 315
Ross, C. E., 189
Ross, E. C., 596
Ross, L., 45, 51
Rossi, J. S., 241
Rossi, P., 56, 270
Rothbaum, B. O., 567
Rothman, B., 289
Rothman, J., 67, 374, 376, 381, 395, 401, 546, 547
Rothspan, S., 361
Rounds, K. A., 289, 388, 402
Rounsaville, B., 234, 343
Roussi, P., 356
Rowland, M. D., 92
Roys, D., 203
Rozovski, U., 294
Ruark, J., 70
Rubey, C., 336
Rubin, A., 213, 291, 538, 606
Rubin, B. A., 522, 526
Rubin, H. J., 374, 376, 395, 396, 397, 398, 400,
    401, 402
Rubin, I. S., 374, 376, 395, 396, 397, 400, 401
Rudolph, J., 485
Ruesch, J., 302, 308
Ruffolo, M. C., 416
Rumsey, E., 100
Ruscio, J., 51
Rush, A. J., 180, 230
Russo, J., 344
Rutter, M., 93, 94, 317
Ryan, A. S., 622
Ryan, C., 308, 487
Ryan, D., 283, 291
Ryan, M., 6, 8
Rydell, C. P., 99, 463
Ryland, D., 291
Rzepnicki, T. L., 92

Sabin, J., 287, 596, 626
Sachs, J., 283
Sack, T., 158
Sackett, D., 46, 47(n), 60
Sacks, R. G., 646
Sadan, I., 119, 120
Sadao, K. C., 138

Safran, J. D., 181
Sakinofsky, I., 340
Saklofske, D., 364
Saladin, M. E., 357
Saleebey, D., 117, 159, 395, 419, 420, 422, 507,
    509, 525, 646
Salkovskis, P. M., 230
Salmon, R., 282
Salmon-Davis, S., 283
Saltzman, A., 28
Salyers, M., 291
Sampson, R., 456
Sandell, K. S., 153, 163
Sanders, P., 566
Sanderson, W. C., 35
Sanson-Fischer, R. W., 569
Santa, C., 204, 245
Saracho, O. N., 569
Sarason, B. R., 359, 367(n7)
Sarason, I. G., 359, 367(n7)
Sarri, R., 285, 457, 458(n), 460, 461, 466, 468, 637
Satir, V., 312, 314
Sato, K., 353
Saulnier, C. F., 163, 168(n10)
Saunders, B., 276, 340, 357
Savin-Williams, R. C., 489
Sayles, L. R., 70
Scannapieco, M., 339
Scarpello, V., 504
Schacht, T. E., 251
Schaecher, T., 422, 426
Schaefer, C., 275, 276, 277
Schaefer, J., 243, 246, 350, 361
Schamess, G., 596, 615
Scharff, D., 311
Scharff, J., 311
Scharlach, A., 100
Scheer, D. A., 336
Schefft, B. K., 172
Scheier, M. F., 355, 363, 364, 367(n4), 367(n5)
Schein, E., 75, 392
Schelling, T., 67
Scherer, K. R., 367(n4)
Schervish, P., 453
Schiavo, R. S., 101
Schiedermayer, D. L., 598
Schiele, J. H., 138, 139
Schiller, L. Y., 285
Schilling, R. F., 546, 547
Schinke, S., 97, 360, 468
Schlegel, P., 101
Schlesinger, E., 136

Schmale, J., 289, 572
Schmitt, J., 501
Schneider, S. K., 362
Schneier, F. R., 220
Schneir, A., 568
Schoech, D., 290
Schoenwald, S. K., 92
Schön, D., 158, 165, 192
Schooler, C., 359
Schopler, J., 281, 282, 283, 285, 286, 289, 290, 292,
    293, 572, 574
Schore, L., 503, 511
Schorr, J. B., 624
Schorr, L. B., 381, 398, 402
Schram, P., 10
Schreter, C. A., 596
Schreter, R. K., 596
Schriver, J. M., 375
Schroeder, C., 339
Schroeder, L. O., 26
Schroeder-Hartwig, K., 235
Schuemie, M., 567, 573, 574
Schuerman, J. R., 92
Schult, A., 118
Schulz, M. S., 95
Schumer, F., 315
Schumm, W., 321
Schutz, B. M., 600
Schwankovsky, L., 355
Schwartz, A. A., 47
Schwartz, I. M., 40
Schwartz, I. S., 54
Schwartz, M., 482
Schwartz, P., 490, 491
Schwartz, R., 302, 320
Schwartz, W., 507, 509
Schwartzman, P., 341, 342
Schwarzer, C., 366
Schwarzer, R., 116, 366
Scott, J., 136
Scott, W. R., 392
Seabury, B. A., 251, 252, 256, 552
Sedlak, A., 266
Seeley, J., 341
Seeman, M., 115
Segal, E. A., 521
Segal, S. P., 118, 123, 124, 212
Segal, U. A., 639
Segal, Z. V., 181
Segall, A., 116
Seidman, E., 641
Seidman, S., 483, 484

Self, D. J., 598
Seligman, M., 115
Sellin, T., 455
Selvini Palazzoli, M., 315, 316
Semin, G. R., 356
Sennett, R., 8, 9, 13
Serrano, A. C., 252
Shade, L. R., 577
Shadish, W., 252
Shafer, J., 228
Shakeshaft, A. P., 569
Shapiro, B. Z., 283
Shapiro, F., 228
Sharfstein, S. S., 596
Sharon, M., 252
Shaw, B. F., 180, 230
Shaw, C., 455
Shaw, G. B., 454
Shaw, W., 283
Shay, S., 378, 379
Shea, S. C., 624
Sheeran, P., 360
Sheldon, B., 213
Sheldon, T. A., 49
Shellenbeger, S., 309
Shelton, M., 30, 292
Sher, K. J., 241, 243, 244
Shera, W., 122, 126
Sherbourne, C. D., 445
Sheridan, S., 287
Sherman, H. J., 115
Sherman, J., 292
Shernoff, M., 492
Sherraden, M., 526, 644
Sherraden, M. S., 399, 400
Sherraden, M. W., 189
Shiffman, R., 378
Shilman, R. P., 289
Shoda, Y., 356, 357, 362
Shoemaker, D., 454
Shoham, V., 252
Shore, B., 178-179, 188
Shore, R., 179, 190
Shorkey, C. T., 384
Short, J., 567
Shulman, L., 283, 617
Sickmund, M., 451
Siddiqui, H. Y., 636
Sidel, R., 521
Siegel, D. H., 595
Siegel, J., 290, 567
Siemer, M., 353

Sieppert, J., 536
Silagy, C., 60
Silverman, C., 118
Silverman, W. A., 60
Silverstein, O., 158, 307
Simeonsson, R., 100
Simmons, K. P., 158
Simon, B., 14, 113
Simon, B. L., 139, 159, 165, 374, 376, 646
Simon, L., 615
Simon, R. I., 33
Simons, A. D., 234
Simons, J., 304
Singer, A., 441
Singer, S., 466
Singh, N. H., 51
Siporin, M., 251, 252, 590
Sisson, R. W., 252
Sither, J. W., 627
Skeel, J. D., 598
Skidmore, R. A., 66
Skinner, B. F., 197, 198, 200, 201
Skinner, E. A., 362, 446
Skogan, W., 336
Skolnick, A., 305
Skolnick, L., 292
Skorka, D., 36
Skrabanek, P., 45
Slack, W., 569
Sloan, K. A., 570
Slonim-Nevo, V., 214
Sluckin, A., 210
Smart, J. J. C., 597
Smith, A. D., 537
Smith, C., 506, 510
Smith, C. A., 351, 353
Smith, G. R., 446
Smith, H. B., 35
Smith, J., 225
Smith, K. M. S., 289
Smith, L. A., 101
Smith, L. M., 567
Smith, M., 341
Smith, N., 288
Smith, R., 97
Smyth, K. A., 289
Smyth, N. J., 211
Snibbe, J., 573
Snowden, L. R., 440, 442, 444
Snyder, H., 451, 452
Sobolew-Shubin, A., 355
Soderstrom, P., 615

Sohng, L., 122, 124
Soldz, S., 288
Solomon, B., 138, 139, 165, 420
Solomon, B. B., 114, 116, 119, 374, 376, 378, 388
Solomon, P., 291
Solomon, S., 357
Sonis, W. S., 252
Sonnega, A., 222
Sontheimer, H., 456
Sotomayor, M., 388
Soulios, C., 236
Sovreign, R. G., 247
Sowden, A., 49
Sparks, P., 356
Specht, H., 11, 13, 17, 66, 374, 376, 391, 397, 606, 612, 636
Spencer, D., 569
Spencer, E. D., 289
Spencer, M. S., 133, 360
Spender, D., 577
Spergel, I., 455, 465
Spilton-Koretz, D., 97
Spitzer, A., 116
Spradley, J., 419
Sproull, L., 290
Srinivas, H., 644
Stack, C., 388
Stacy, A. W., 93
Stall, R., 243, 245
Stalley, R. F., 590, 592
Stanley, R. T., 206
Stanton, M., 252, 320
Starr, P., 11
Starret, R., 134
Staudt, M., 538, 545
Steele, B., 274
Steenbarger, B. N., 35, 254, 287
Steer, R., 276, 277
Stehno, S., 134
Stein, D. J., 180
Stein, K. F., 183
Stein, L., 289
Steinberg, D. M., 283
Steinberg, R., 416
Steiner, C. M., 117
Steinglass, P., 320
Steinmetz, S., 321
Steinwachs, D. M., 446
Steketee, G., 228
Stern, D. N., 190
Sterner, U., 226
Stevens, P., Jr., 58

Stevenson, H., 283
Steward, M. S., 275
Stinson, C. H., 180, 366(n3)
Stoesz, D., 124
Stolle, D. P., 26, 27
Stoltenberg, C. D., 617
Stone, S., 291
Stoops, C., 291
Storrs, G. M., 467
Stout, K. D., 158, 168(n13)
Stouthamer-Loeber, M., 93
Strathman, A., 361
Strauman, T. J., 182, 183
Strauser, D., 512
Strecher, V., 246
Strecker, J. B., 288
Strickler, G., 641
Strickler, J., 360
Stroebe, M. S., 367(n7)
Stroebe, W., 367(n7)
Strom, K., 211
Stromberg, C., 31
Strom-Gottfried, K., 596
Stromwall, L. K., 525
Stroul, B., 393
Strube, M. J., 284
Struckman-Johnson, D. L., 339
Strupp, H. H., 242, 251
Stucker, J. R., 525
Sturm, R., 445
Suarez, Z., 146, 283
Suarez-Balcazar, Y., 547
Subramanian, K., 288, 291
Sue, S., 141
Suire, B., 123
Suler, J., 567
Sullivan, W., 7
Sullivan, W. M., 398, 614, 617
Sullivan, W. P., 646
Sulzer-Azaroff, B., 51
Sumerfield, M. R., 364
Summers, A. B., 598
Sundel, M., 285
Sundelson, D., 29
Sunderland, M. L., 456
Suroviak, J., 283
Sussman, L., 220
Sussman, S., 93
Sutherland, E., 455
Swan, J., 356
Swanberg, J., 506
Swartz, M., 222

Swidler, A., 7, 398
Swinson, R. P., 236
Szasz, T. S., 44, 52
Szymanski, L., 451

Taffe, L., 400
Takeuchi, D. T., 141
Tallent, N., 55
Tannenbaum, J., 283
Tasker, F., 491
Tatara, T., 420
Tataryn, D., 180
Tatum, B., 137
Taylor, B. M., 455
Taylor, C. B., 570
Taylor, S., 228
Taylor, S. E., 350, 352, 353, 354, 356, 359, 361, 362, 363, 367(n5)
Taylor, S. H., 388
Teague, G. B., 445
Teasdale, J. D., 180, 184, 185, 186, 187, 188
Teel, K., 598
Teicher, M., 590
Telch, M. J., 227
Temkin, T., 118
Tennen, J., 246
Teresa, J. G., 547
Terkel, S., 499
Terman, D., 264
ter Schure, E., 353
Test, M. A., 443
Thackeray, M. G., 66
Thoits, P. A., 359, 364
Thomas, E., 77
Thomas, E. J., 245, 381, 537, 546, 547
Thomas, R., 503
Thomas, R. M., 200
Thomas, T., 289
Thomas, W., 480
Thompson, A., 274
Thompson, E., 320, 342
Thompson, J., 622
Thompson, P., 290
Thompson, S., 340
Thompson, S. C., 355, 356
Thrasher, S., 228
Thyer, B. A., 27, 198, 200, 201, 202, 203, 204, 209, 210, 211, 212, 213, 225, 535, 538, 540, 606
Thyer, K. B., 209
Tierney, J. P., 100
Timms, N., 590

Tinker, K., 388
Tipton, S., 7, 398
Todd, L. H., 290
Todd, T., 320
Tolman, R. M., 293
Tomm, K., 243
Tonry, M., 455, 456
Toors, M., 636
Torbet, P., 451
Torczyner, J., 397
Torre, D., 114, 118, 124
Toseland, R. W., 251, 252, 282, 283, 384
Towle, C., 152, 377, 590, 668
Tracy, E., 189, 339, 388, 511, 525, 552
Trepper, T., 307, 320
Triandis, H. C., 441
Trickett, E. J., 92
Tripodi, T., 552, 559
Trivette, C., 118, 376, 385
Troiden, R. R., 484
Tropman, J., 65(n), 67, 75, 79(n), 83, 340, 341
Truax, C. B., 206
Tuchfeld, B. S., 244
Tucker, M. B., 136
Tuckman, B. W., 285
Turbin, M. S., 93
Turing, A., 179
Turkle, S., 566, 567, 577
Turnball, J. E., 288
Turner, R. M., 228
Turner, S., 219, 467
Turoff, M., 565
Tutty, L. M., 283
Tynan, M., 506
Tyre, P., 103

Uehara, E., 141, 142
Uken, J., 289, 572
Underwood, L., 208
Unger, D. G., 387
Urbano, J., 289

Vaihinger, H., 181
Valacich, J. S., 290
Valencia-Weber, G., 134
Valenstein, E. S., 44
Valentich, M., 158, 168(n13)
VandeCreek, L., 592
Van den Berg, N., 390, 396, 399
Van Den Bos, J., 93

van der Plight, J., 354, 355
Vanderryn, J., 93
Vandiver, S. T., 153
Vandiver, V., 35, 39, 291, 596
VanEtten, M. L., 228
Van Hook, M., 398
Van Kammen, W. B., 93
Van Laningham, L., 291
Van Noppen, B., 228
Van Soest, D., 133, 138, 140
Van Winkle, J., 292
Varela, F., 318
Varley, B. K., 591
Vassil, T. V., 284
Velez-Diaz, A., 142
Velicer, W. F., 241, 243
Veronen, L., 340
Vico, G., 180
Victor, S. B., 491
Vigilante, J., 590
Vinter, R., 77, 282, 285
Visher, E., 304
Visher, J. S., 304
Vistnes, J. P., 443
Vitaliano, P. P., 344
Vitelli, R., 570
Vivona, T. S., 455
Von, J., 340
Vourlekis, B., 512
Vrij, A., 356

Wachtel, P. L., 186, 249
Wagar, J., 283
Wagner, B., 341, 342
Wagner, D., 15, 16, 283, 374, 375
Wagner, F., 359
Wakefield, J., 200, 536, 538, 636, 646
Waldfogel, J., 502
Walker, C. E., 276
Walker, J., 134
Walker, R. J., 291
Wallerstein, J. S., 246
Walsh, F., 303, 304, 305, 306, 307, 308, 309, 310,
    317, 319, 320, 321, 322
Walters, E. E., 236
Walters, G. a. W. T., 455
Walters, M., 158, 307
Walther, J. B., 290, 567
Walton, E., 339
Walton, R., 636
Walton, W. K., 339

Wandrei, K. E., 218, 617
Wang, C.-T., 270
Ward, D., 124
Ward, G., 457
Warner, S., 7
Warren, J., 510
Warren, K. S., 46
Warren, R. L., 395
Warren, S. R., 445
Warres, N. E., 615
Washington, R., 138, 385
Wasserman, D. A., 252
Wasserman, G. A., 99, 101, 102
Waterman, R., 503
Waters, J., 329, 330
Watkins, S., 29, 500, 512
Watson, A. L., 241, 243, 244
Watson, J., 197
Watt, I. S., 49
Watters, E., 44, 51
Watts-Jones, D., 138
Watzlawick, P., 302, 303, 315
Waxman, R., 253
We, G., 577
Weakland, J., 315
Weber, H., 357
Webster, Y. O., 49
Weick, A., 153, 159, 507
Weick, K., 81
Weidner, G., 360
Weil, M., 374, 375, 376, 377, 385, 388, 393, 395,
     396, 397, 398, 399, 400, 401, 402
Weil, M. O., 388, 392, 393, 394, 402
Weinberg, H., 572
Weinberg, M. S., 487
Weinberg, N., 289, 572
Weinberger, A., 343
Weiner, A., 39, 579
Weiner-Davis, M., 318
Weinick, R. M., 443
Weinstein, N. D., 354
Weintraub, J. K., 363, 364
Weiss, J., Jr., 247
Weissbourd, B., 320, 385
Weissbourd, R., 266, 267
Weissman, H. H., 387, 388, 392
Weissman, M., 219, 220, 234, 343
Welch, A., 350
Wellman, B., 290
Wells, A., 95, 99, 106, 233, 352
Wells, J. D., 344
Wells, K. B., 445

Wells-Parker, E., 245
Welsh, B. L., 385
Welsh, W. N., 460
Wenocur, S., 134, 376
Werkhoven, W. S., 289
Werner, E., 97, 317
Wessel, K., 289, 572
West, J., 504
Westin, A., 595
Westling, B. E., 229
Weston, T., 283
Wetzel, J. W., 158
Wetzel, R. D., 234
Wexler, D. B., 26, 27
Whaley, D., 201
Wheaton, B., 359
Wheelan, S., 285
Wheeler, A. M., 627
Whelley, J., 604
Whisman, M. A., 247
Whitaker, C., 312, 314
White, B. W., 491
White, M., 313, 318, 421
Whitehouse, S., 101
Whiteman, M., 249
Whitford, G. S., 493
Whiting, R., 306
Whitmore, E., 122
Whittaker, J., 189, 200, 376, 387, 388, 389, 511,
     525, 552
Whittington, C., 590
Widom, C. S., 274
Wiebe, D. J., 363
Wiener, L. S., 289
Wier, K. R., 575
Wiers, R., 353
Wilk, R., 504, 510
Williams, B., 597
Williams, E., 399, 567
Williams, E. S., 392, 396
Williams, G. C., 217
Williams, G. T., 600
Williams, J. H., 93
Williams, M., 245
Williams, P. G., 363
Williams, S., 622
Williams, W., 480
Wills, T. A., 366(n1)
Wilner, M. E., 288
Wilson, D. R., 105
Wilson, G., 521
Wilson, J. Q., 455

Wilson, L., 524
Wilson, S. J., 590
Wilson, S. M., 117, 400
Wilson, W. J., 266, 398, 455
Winegar, N., 287
Winkler, E. R., 591
Winn, R., 456
Winship, J., 396, 398
Wintram, C., 283
Withorn, A., 15, 16, 19, 374, 376, 392, 400
Witkin, S., 182, 535, 536, 556
Witmer, J. M., 25, 34, 35
Wittchen, H. U., 220
Wlazlo, Z., 235
Wodarski, J. S., 198, 211, 538, 540, 545, 547
Wolf, M. M., 54
Wolf, S., 627
Wolfgang, M., 455
Wolfson, C., 457
Wolozin, D., 288
Wolpe, J., 229
Wolpert, J., 10
Wong, S. W., 207, 208, 209
Wood, G. C., 283
Wood, G. G., 374, 376, 384, 394, 401, 402
Wood, S., 339
Woody, J., 560
Worchel, S., 285
Wordes, M., 457
Worell, J., 158
Worthington, R. L., 141
Wright, J. D., 522, 526
Wright, R., 134
Wrong, D. H., 374, 376
Wu, B., 456
Wycoff, M., 336
Wyer, R. S., Jr., 352
Wynne, L., 320

Yankey, J. A., 392
Yarom, N., 246
Yeh, M., 141
Yonekura, S., 340
Yoram, B., 116
Young, D., 357
Young, G. C., 204
Young, J., 343
Young, J. E., 180, 234
Young, M., 335
Young, S. D., 615
Young, V. D., 470
Younghusband, E., 590
Youngren, J. N., 36
Yuan, Y. Y., 339

Zacks, E., 307, 491
Zajonc, R. B., 367(n4)
Zamora-Hernandez, C. E., 360, 480
Zeidner, M., 349, 350, 364
Zhao, S., 621
Zibalese-Crawford, M., 123
Zich, J. M., 445
Ziegler, E., 304, 317
Zigler, E., 94, 95, 342, 385
Zimet, C. N., 287
Zimmerman, M., 118, 123, 124
Zimmerman, P., 571
Zippay, A., 506
Zipper, I. N., 100, 388, 392, 393, 394, 402
Ziv, L., 116
Znoj, H. J., 366(n3)
Zue, V., 579
Zuvekas, S. H., 443

Subject Index

Abandonment, client, 38
Abuse. *See* Child abuse and neglect; Domestic
    violence; Sexual abuse
Accessibility of services, 418-419. *See also* Life-span
    perspective
Accommodation, and work issues, 504, 508, 510
Accountability, 52, 53, 140, 303, 311, 536, 574
Acculturation, 441
Action strategies for change, 248-250
Activity therapy, 204-205
ADA. *See* Americans with Disabilities Act
Adaptive behavior, 95, 304, 306. *See also* Prevention;
    Resilience
Addams, Jane, 523
ADHD. *See* Attention deficit-hyperactivity disorder
Adjustment problems, 342-343. *See also* Depressive
    disorders
Administration, evidence-based, 55-57. *See also*
    Supervision
Adolescence:
    criminal justice and. *See* Juvenile justice system
    sexual orientation and, 488-490
Adoption, 270, 271, 634-635
Adoption Assistance and Child Welfare Act, 270, 271
Adoption Assistance and Family Support Act, 270
Adoption Assistance and Safe Families Act, 271

Adult change, 241-256
    activities in, 247-254
    motivators for, 241, 244-247, 255
    principles of practice for, 255-256
    research on, 242-243
    stages of, 254, 255
    theoretical framework for, 243-254
    theory development in, 243
    value and, 242
Advocacy, 615, 620-621
AFDC. *See* Aid to Families with Dependent Children
Affective change:
    anger management strategies for, 235-236, 249
    cognitive therapy for, 230-234
    empirical treatment for, 223-236
    graded exposure therapy for, 223-228
    interpersonal psychotherapy for, 234-235
    relaxation therapies for, 224, 229-230
    social skills training for, 235
    systematic desensitization for, 228-229
Affective disorders, 201(table), 217-223
    anger, 217-218, 235-236
    anxiety disorders, 217-218, 219-222
    depressive disorders, 217-218, 222-223
    future directions and, 236-237
Affirmation, and positive punishment, 207

Affirmative action, 146, 505-506, 510, 513, 530
Aftercare programs, in juvenile justice system, 462-463
AGECAT, 570
Age Discrimination in Employment Act of 1967, 504
Agoraphobia, 220, 224, 226-227, 250, 333
Agreements, and informed consent, 34
AIDS. *See* HIV/AIDS
Aid to Families with Dependent Children (AFDC), 265, 524, 530. *See also* Temporary Aid to Needy Families
Aid to Victims of Domestic Abuse (AVDA), 18
Alcoholics Anonymous, 284
Alliance, therapeutic, 251, 254-255, 267
Allocations of funds, 653
Alzheimer's disease, 571
American Association of Social Workers (AASW), 590. *See also* National Association of Social Workers
American Association of State Social Work Boards, 604
American Association of Suicidology, 328, 336
Americans with Disabilities Act (ADA) of 1990, 504, 508, 530
Amplification effect, 456
Anecdotal reports, 46
Anger, 217-218, 235-236, 249
Anomie, 455
Anonymity, 570. *See also* Confidentiality; Privacy
Anxiety disorders, 217-218
    descriptions of, 219-222
    technology and, 572, 573
    treatment of, 202, 223-234
Applied and professional ethics, field of, 591. *See also* Ethical issues
Applied relaxation, 229-230
Appraisal, in coping, 351-357, 361-362. *See also* Assessment; Evaluation
Archival data, 558
Aristotle, 596
Arrests, 451-452, 456. *See also* Juvenile justice system
Assertive Community Treatment, 443
Assessment, 47(table), 551-563
    client-worker relationships and, 554-555, 560-561
    data collection problems in, 560-561
    ethnicity and, 561-562
    evidence-based, 49-52

future directions for, 562-563
gender and, 561-562
goals and, 555
in cognitive-integrative approach, 192, 194
in crisis intervention, 331-334
in family therapy, 303, 304-310, 322
in group work practice, 286
language used in, 145
measurement tools for, 555-560
monitoring and, 553-554, 557, 559, 560-561
purposes of, 552-554
supervision and, 617-618
system perspectives in, 73
technology and, 570-571
See also Appraisal; Evaluation
Association for the Advancement of Social Work with Groups, 572
Association for Women in Social Work (AWSW), 154, 155
Attachment framework, 274-275
Attention deficit-hyperactivity disorder (ADHD), 386
Attenuation versus potentiation of stress, 358
Attribution error, 45
Autistic disorder, 208
Automated therapy, 574. *See also* Computer-mediated communications
Automatic thoughts, 230
Autonomy, 613-614, 617
AVDA. *See* Aid to Victims of Domestic Abuse
AWSW. *See* Association for Women in Social Work

Badan Kredit Kecamatan, 644
Bank for Agriculture and Agricultural Co-operatives, 644
Banks, 399, 643-644
Beck Depression Inventory, 555, 556, 570
Behavior:
    definitions of, 197-198
    typology of, 172
Behavioral change, 197-214
    contemporary approaches to, 211-213
    coping and, 353
    diversity and, 211-212
    empowerment/structural approach to, 386, 400
    evaluation research in, 212-213, 214
    foundations for, empirical, 212-213
    foundations for, philosophical, 198-199

foundations for, theoretical, 199-201
future directions in, 213-214
modeling in, 201(table), 210-211, 249
negative punishment in, 208-209
negative reinforcement in, 206-207
operant conditioning in, 200-201, 201(table), 204-210, 213
operant extinction in, 209
operant shaping in, 209-210
positive punishment in, 207-208
positive reinforcement in, 204-206
practice procedures in, 201-202
principles governing, 202(table)
respondent conditioning in, 200, 201(table), 204
respondent extinction in, 202-204
respondent learning in, 202-204, 213
See also Cognitive-behavioral orientation
Behavioral confirmation bias, 45
Behavioral framework:
    change in children and, 276-277
    life-span perspective and, 419-423
Behavioral health organizations, 613. *See also* Health maintenance organizations; Managed care organizations
Behaviorism, foundations of, 197-201. *See also* Behavioral change
Belief systems, 61, 305-306, 309(table), 421. *See also* Critical thinking; Value(s)
Bell-and-pad conditioning treatment, 204
Bereavement, 492
Best practices approach, 35, 69
Biases:
    assessment and, 561-562
    coping appraisals and, 352, 354
    decision making and, 45, 51
    multiculturalism and, 141, 144
    research design and, 538, 543
    technology and, 575
Biological theories:
    delinquent behavior and, 454-455
    life-span perspective and, 419
    sexual orientation and, 482-483
Biopsychosocial orientation, 303
Bisexual orientation, 478, 479, 481
    coming out and, 484, 486-487
    families and, 490
    See also Sexual orientation
Black power movement, 116
Body state subsystem, 185

Boston Gun Project, 104
Boston Violence Prevention Project, 466
Boundary issues, 36, 593-594, 601, 602, 603
Bowen model, in family therapy, 311, 314
Brain, the mind as, 178-179
Breast cancer, 572
Breathing techniques, 229-230
Brief models, in group work, 287-288
Bullying, 209

Cancer-survivor support groups, 386
Capitalism:
    global, 11-13
    poverty and, 529
    privatization and, 7, 10, 11-13
Capitation, 438, 440. *See also* Managed care
CARES project, 378, 379
Car-safety devices (CSD), 105
Case rates, and MCOs, 612
Causes:
    behavioral change and, 198
    family therapy and, 303
    prevention science and, 91-92, 95-96
    research methodologies and, 538-539, 544
Center for Prevention Research (CPR), 96
Certification, 28
Change:
    activities in, 247-254
    affective, 217-237
    approaches to, 171-410
    behavioral, 197-214
    cognitive-integrative approach to, 175-194
    communications technology and, 568
    coping for, 349-367
    crisis intervention and, 327-345
    empowerment/structural approach to, 373-404
    feminist practice and, 162-167
    frameworks for, 274-277
    generators of, 242
    in adults, 241-256
    in children, 261-278
    in families, 301-322
    intentional, 241
    maintenance of, 254, 255
    managed care and, 439-441
    motivators for, 241, 244-247, 255
    multiculturalism and, 134-139, 143-144
    organizational, 391-395

readiness for, 255
safety and, 508-509
schematic, 186-188, 191
social, and context, 5-21
social, and legal issues, 23, 26, 39-40
stages of, 254, 255
stress in all, 310
systems and, 68-69
technological, 23, 39-40
theory of, need for, 243
work and, 507-510
See also Restructuring
Change agents, practitioners as, xi-xii
Charitable gifts, 652, 653-660
Charity Organization Societies (COS), 523, 590, 635
Chat rooms, 565
Child abuse and neglect, 270, 337-339, 377-379,
    390, 403
Childhood Immunization Initiative, 99, 100
Children:
    as clients, 268
    behavioral change in, 204, 206-207, 208-209,
        210
    brain development in, 179
    cognition, family life, and, 190-191
    confidentiality for, 30
    cooperation of, 206-207
    crisis intervention for, 337-339, 342
    empowerment/structural approach and, 377-379,
        388, 390, 393-394, 403
    international issues and, 634-635, 638-639, 643
    life-span perspective and, 417
    poverty and, 264-265, 266, 521, 523, 524
    prevention and, 99-103, 104, 105, 270
    risk and protective factors for, 93-94
    risk in placement of, 338(box), 338-339
    sexual abuse of, 36
    See also Juvenile justice system; School-based
        programs
Children, change in, 261-278
    case example on, 262-264
    direct practice roles and, 261, 268-269
    direct practice settings and, 269-274
    frameworks for, 274-277
    future issues for, 278
    philosophical issues and, 264-268
    value and, 264-268
Child welfare services, 270-272
CI approach. See Cognitive-integrative approach

Circular causality, in families, 303
Circular reasoning, 199(table)
Civic organizations, 658, 659
Civil Rights Act of 1964, 504, 505
Civil Rights Movements, 19, 114, 590
Class:
    delinquent behavior and, 455
    families and, 305-306, 314
    feminist practice and, 156
    multiculturalism and, 138-139
    See also Culture; Diversity
Classroom contingency training, 102
Client-centered services, 418-419. See also Life-span
    perspective
Clinical standards, 35. See also Standards
CMHCs. See Community mental health centers
Cochrane Collaboration, 60
Code of Ethics for Child Welfare Professionals, 55-56
Code of Ethics of AASW, 590
Code of Ethics of NASW, 591, 599-600
    critical thinking and, 43, 49, 52, 54, 55, 59
    empowerment and, 115
    ethical decision making and, 599
    ethical dilemmas and, 592, 593, 594
    ethics agenda and, 604, 606
    ethics education and, 604
    legal issues and, 24-25, 29
    multiculturalism and, 146
    poverty and, 522-523
    risk management and, 600
    supervision and, 625, 626, 627
Codes, in ICS model, 184-185
Cognition, social, 285. See also Constructivism
Cognitive approach:
    to change in children, 276-277
    to coping, 352-353, 356-357
    to crisis intervention, 334-335
Cognitive-behavioral orientation, 211, 213, 247
    crisis intervention and, 343
    family therapy and, 316-317
    group work and, 283
    juvenile justice system and, 464
    technology and, 572
    See also Behavioral change
Cognitive distortions, 230-231, 334
Cognitive-emotional system:
    change and, 244, 247-248
    crisis intervention and, 344, 345
Cognitive-integrative (CI) approach, 175-194

assumptions in, 177(table)
in practice, 191-194
interacting cognitive subsystems model and, 184-188
meaning, mind, and, 178-182
meaning, schemas, and, 182-188
meaning, social sources, and, 177, 188-191
options and opportunities in, 186-188, 192-194
schemas and, 176-177, 180, 182-188
Cognitive mastery, 334-335
Cognitive phenomena, and behavior, 201(table)
Cognitive restructuring, 230-234
Cognitive therapies, 230-234, 247
Cognitive triad of depression, 234
Cognitivism, 199(table)
Collaboration:
change and, 225, 230, 251, 391-395
family therapy and, 321, 322
feminist practice and, 146, 161
fund-raising and, 663
juvenile justice system and, 472
life-span perspective and, 415-416, 425, 433
multiculturalism and, 144
organizational change and, 391-395
research designs and, 547
supervision and, 620
See also Community; Empowerment; Integrated practice
Collaborative empiricism, 230, 234
Collectivization, and contextualized practice, 16-17
Color, people of, and multiculturalism, 134-139. *See also* Race and ethnicity
Coming out, and sexual orientation, 481, 484-488
Commitment, in relationships, 73-74
Common good, 19-20
Communications technology, 289, 327, 328-331. *See also* Computer-mediated communications
Communitarian movement, 17
Communities That Care (CTC), 103
Community:
behavioral phenomena in, 213
change in adults and, 253
change in children and, 265
cognition and, 176
contextualized practice and, 17-18
empowerment and, 121, 124
empowerment/structural approach and, 377-381, 387-390, 395-404
families and, 303, 307, 321

feminist practice and, 161
fund-raising and, 656, 657-658
group work and, 283, 290, 291
juvenile justice system and, 462-466, 467, 469
life-span perspective and, 421
multiculturalism and, 142, 144, 145, 146
poverty and, 529
practice models for, 397
prevention in, 96, 103-105
systems, levels, and, 74, 75
technology and, 575
work and, 513
Community building, 398-401
Community development theory, 421
Community Mental Health Center Act of 1963, 330
Community mental health centers (CMHCs), 437-438
Community Reinvestment Act, 645
Community-school-family-youth model, 467
Comorbidity, 444
Competency-based approaches, 55, 117
Complaints:
critical thinking and, 60-61
ethical issues and, 600-601
legal issues and, 28-29
Compositional elements, of systems, 76-80
Compositional intervention strategies, 81
Comprehensive Employment Training Act, 524
Compulsions. *See* Obsessive-compulsive disorder
Computer and the mind, 179-180
Computer Assisted Assessment Package, 563
Computer conferencing, 574, 579
Computer-mediated communications, 565-580
definition of, 565
practice applications of, 568-575
social inequality and, 575-578
theoretical issues in, 566-568
See also Technology
Conditioning. *See* Operant conditioning; Respondent conditioning
Confidentiality:
ethics of, 29, 32, 592, 602
in group work, 291-292
legal issues and, 29-30, 31-32, 39-40
technology and, 39-40, 570, 616-617
See also Privacy
Confirmation bias, 45, 51
Conflict resolution, 466, 472
Conflicts of interest, 594-595

Conflict theory, 115
Connectionism, 180
Connective work:
    families and, 306-307
    social support networks and, 389
    supportive/empowerment work and, 384-387
    See also Collaboration; Empowerment/structural
        approach
Consciousness raising, 116, 119, 121, 159, 384-385
Consent:
    for release of information, 31, 32
    informed, on treatment decisions, 34, 49, 602
Consequentialist theories, 597
Constructionism, social, 181, 285, 304, 421
Constructivism, 180-181, 285
Consultations, 55, 602. See also Referrals
Consumer-driven empowerment programs, 123
Content validity, 140
Contexts, of systems, 76-81
Contextual dependence, 95-96
Contextual forces, xii, 1-3. See also Contextualized
        practice; Critical thinking; Legal issues;
        Systems
Contextual interventions, 80-81
Contextualized practice, xii, 5-6, 667-668
    contemporary context and, 7-13, 21
    core elements of, 13-18
    in PIVOT Project, 18-19
    need for, 3
    public good and, 19-20
Contingencies, definition of, 50
Contingency analysis, 50
Continuous quality improvement, 446
Contracting, in groups, 286
Contracts, and funds, 653, 654
Control, 354, 358, 363. See also Empowerment;
        Power
Control theories, and delinquent behavior, 455, 461
Convention on Rights of the Child (CRC), 638-639
Coordination. See Collaboration
Coping, 349-367
    appraisal in, 351-357, 361-362
    complexity of, 354-357
    contextual versus dispositional view of, 351
    crisis intervention and, 333-334, 344-345
    emotions and, 353-354
    future research in, 364-366
    in adult change, 249-250
    in families, 304, 319. See also Family therapy
    information, knowledge, and, 352-353, 356-357

meaning of, 349-351
multiple aspects of, 357, 358
proactive, 360-364
psychological functioning and, 354-357
resources for, 357, 358-359, 361
situational variability and, 357-360, 364, 365-366
social structural factors in, 359-360
    See also Prevention; Stress
Core values, 24-25
Corporate philanthropy, 657
Correlational studies, 544
COS. See Charity Organization Societies
Cost-benefit analysis, in cognitive therapy, 231-232
Cost-effectiveness, and prevention, 99. See also
        Effectiveness
Council on Social Work Education, 133, 134, 136,
        137, 211, 523, 604, 629
Counterproductivity, paradoxical, 71
Counter-transference, 36
Courts, 30, 31-32. See also Legal issues
CPR. See Center for Prevention Research
CRC. See Convention on Rights of the Child
Crime victimization, 335-336, 341-342, 343
Criminal behavior. See Juvenile justice system
Crises:
    as motivator for change, 245-246
    definition of, 327
    in families, 304, 306
    in ICS model, 186
    in social casework, 212
    prevention and, 454
    vulnerability to, 339-343
Crisis intervention, 327-345
    coping responses and, 344-345
    definition of, 327
    empirical support for, 335-339
    for adjustment problems, 342-343
    for child abuse, 337-339
    for crime victimization, 335-336, 341-342, 343
    for domestic violence, 330-331, 344-345
    for psychiatric emergencies, 337
    for suicide, 329(box), 330, 336-337, 340, 341,
        342
    future research for, 345
    practices in, 331-334
    primary objective of, 329
    seven-stage model of, 328, 331-334
    social support and, 341-342
    solution-based therapy for, 328, 335
    strengths-based approach to, 328, 335

system-level, 339-343
    telephone hotlines for, 327, 328-331
    vulnerability factors and, 339-343
Critical consciousness:
    empowerment/structural approach and, 377, 384-
        385
    multiculturalism and, 141-142, 146
    See also Ethnoconscious approach
Critical constructivism, 181
Critical theory, 15, 16
Critical thinking, 43-61
    barriers to, 57-59
    barriers to, remedies for, 59-60
    benefits of, 45-49
    consultation and, 55
    empowerment and, 120
    ethics and, 43, 46, 49, 52, 54, 55-56, 59
    evaluation and, 54, 56
    evidence-based approached and, 49-57
    fallacies and, 48(table); 50, 55
    importance of, 44-49
    lifelong learning and, 57
    nature of, 43-44
    practice-related claims and, 47-48
    record keeping and, 55
    research methods and, 46-47
    theme of, xiii
    See also Evidence-based practice; Systems
Crystallization of discontent, 244
CSD. See Car-safety devices
CSWE. See Council on Social Work Education
CTC. See Communities That Care
Cue exposure, 203
Cultural competence, 137, 146, 394, 441-442
Cultural lag, 68
Culturally bound tools, 145
Cultural maintenance, 422
Cultural system, 68-69
Culture:
    affective change and, 218-219, 225
    as component of environment, xii
    behavioral change and, 212
    change in children and, 266
    cognition and, 176, 188-189
    contextualized practice and, 17-18
    delinquent behavior and, 455
    diversity in. See Diversity
    families and, 305-306, 307, 314
    feminist practice and, 161
    generators of change and, 242

international issues and, 633-636
    life-span perspective and, 421-422
    of silence, 115
    privatization and, 8-9
    sexual orientation and, 478, 480, 483-484
    social skills training and, 235
    supervision and, 621-622
    systems and, 68-69, 71
    work and, 503, 507-511
    See also Multiculturalism
Curriculum-based group work, 290-291
Curriculum Policy Statement of CSWE, 133
Cybertherapy, 573, 578, 579

Data collection and analysis, xii-xiii, 49-52. See also
        Measurement
Decision making:
    electronically mediated, 580
    ethics and, 596-600
    importance of, 44-49, 161-162
    See also Critical thinking
Defamation of character, 602
Deficits, and poverty, 526-530
Delinking, 203
Delinquency, 273-274, 454-455, 468-469. See also
        Juvenile justice system
Democracy, 11, 13
Demographics:
    change in children and, 278
    cultural competence and, 441-442
    feminist practice and, 162, 163
    group work and, 292-293
    legal issues and, 39
    mental illness and, 443
    multiculturalism and, 136, 140, 143
    of poverty, 520-522
    technology and, 576
Deontology, 597
Depressive disorders:
    assessment of, 555-556, 570
    cognitive triad of, 234
    crisis intervention and, 337, 342-343
    description of, 217-218, 222-223
    treatment of, 230-232, 234-235
Description questions, 47(table)
Determinism, 199(table)
Developmental framework:
    change and, 275-276, 284-286, 303-304

for international issues, 640-647
for risk analysis, 467
for sexual orientation, 481
multiculturalism and, 132-133
Developmental tasks, 415-433
Diagnosis, 617-618, 620, 646. *See also* Assessment
*Diagnostic and Statistical Manual of Mental
        Disorders*:
    DSM III-R, 570
    DSM-IV, 52, 218-222, 494-495, 617, 646
Dilemmas, ethical, 591-596. *See also* Ethical issues
Direct interventions, and systems, 77, 80, 81
Direct practice:
    broad concept of, xi-xii
    traditional definition of, xi
Disabilities, people with:
    empowerment/structural approach for, 386, 390-
        391
    severe mental illness and, 442
    technology and, 569
    work and, 502, 504
Discontent, crystallization of, 244
Discrepancies, in ICS model, 186-188, 189
Discrimination:
    empowerment and, 115, 399
    families and, 314
    international issues and, 637
    justice and, xii
    life-span perspective and, 424
    multiculturalism and, 133, 137
    poverty and, 530
    values and, 24-25
    work and, 504
    See also Oppression, 399
Discriminative facility, in coping, 356
Distributed processing, 180
Distributive justice, 375
Diversity:
    affective disorders and, 218-219, 236
    behavioral change and, 211-212
    cognition and, 189
    coping and, 357-360, 364, 365-366
    critical thinking and, 49
    cultural competence and, 441-442
    demographic trends and, 39
    empowerment and, 114-115, 119, 125, 396
    ethics and, 606
    families and, 304-305, 306, 320, 321
    feminist practice and, 154, 160, 162-164, 166

fund-raising and, 663, 665
group work and, 292-293
juvenile justice system and, 455-460
legal issues and, 39
life-span perspective and, 421-423
multiculturalism and, 134-139, 141
organization of, 189
sexual orientation and, 478-480, 490
supervision and, 621-622
systems and, 72, 82-83
theme of, xii
work and, 510-511
See also Culture; Multiculturalism
Divided loyalties, 594-595
Documentation. *See* Record keeping
Domains, in prevention programs, 97-105
Domestic violence, 18, 151, 330-331, 344-345,
        403
Drug abuse. *See* Substance abuse
*DSM. See Diagnostic and Statistical Manual of
        Mental Disorders*
Dual diagnosis, 444
Dualism, 199(table)
Dual relationships, 593-594
Dysthymic disorder, 222-223, 234

EAPs. *See* Employee Assistance Programs
Ecological theory, 14
Ecology:
    children's, 264-268
    life-span perspective and, 420
    See also Environment
Economic participation, 643-645
Economics:
    children and, 264-265
    crisis vulnerability and, 340
    family belief systems and, 306
    feminist practice and, 155, 156, 165
    global, 10, 11-13, 19
    health care services and, 443-444
    international issues and, 637, 639, 643-645
    life-span perspective and, 433
    poverty and. *See* Poverty
    privatization and, 10, 11-13
    restructuring and, 614
    work and, 501-502, 504, 511-514
    See also Fund-raising; Restructuring

Education:
    children and, 269
    poverty and, 526-528
    technology and, 569
Education for social work:
    behavioral change and, 211
    contextualized practice and, 14-15
    critical thinking and, 43, 57
    empowerment and, 115, 117, 126
    ethics and, 523, 604
    international issues and, 635
    multiculturalism and, 133, 134, 137, 139-140,
        142, 145
    poverty and, 523
    specific versus broad, 447
    See also Training
EEOC. *See* Equal Employment Opportunity
    Commission
Effectiveness:
    behavioral change and, 212-213
    compared to efficacy, 446
    ethics and, 606
    group designs and, 544-546, 548-549
    methodological debate and, 536-538
    multiculturalism and, 140-141
    number of sessions and, 288
    prevention science and, 91
    questions on, 47(table)
    single-systems designs and, 538-544, 547, 548-
        549
    See also Evaluation; Research
Efficacy, compared to effectiveness, 446
Efficacy testing, 91
Elderly, 400-401
    assessment of, 570
    life-span perspective and, 418-419, 428-432, 492-
        493
    poverty and, 521, 524
    sexual orientation and, 492-493
    supervision practice and, 620
Electronic information, 60
ELIZA, 578
E-mail, 565, 571, 579
EMDR. *See* Eye-movement desensitization and
    reprocessing
Emotions:
    affect and, 217. *See also* Affective change
    commitment and, 74
    communications technology and, 567-568

coping and, 249, 344, 353-354, 364
    families and, 311, 314
    in ICS model, 185
Empirical practice, 47. *See also* Evidence-based
    practice
Empiricism, 199(table)
Employee Assistance Programs (EAPs), 506, 509,
    510
Employment. *See* Work
Empowerment, 113-126
    challenges for, 125-126
    change in children and, 269
    contextualized practice and, 14-15, 16
    definitions of, 113-114, 146
    diversity and, 114-115, 119, 125, 396
    ethics and, 115, 606
    evaluation and, 122-124
    families and, 322
    feminism and, 115-116, 122-123, 165, 396
    future potential and, 124-125
    group medium and, 116-117, 121-122
    groups focused on, 283
    international issues and, 645-646
    legal issues and, 27
    life-span perspective and, 420
    multiculturalism and, 124, 138-139, 146, 396
    multidimensional approach and, 118
    politics and, 14-15, 114-121, 124, 126, 139, 645-
        646
    practice-based theory and, 116-118
    practice models for, 119-126
    principles for, 120, 121-122, 124
    process elements in, 119
    social/psychological theory and, 115-116
    theoretical base for, 114-118
    therapeutic jurisprudence and, 27
    See also Control; Power
Empowerment/structural approach, 373-404
    community building and, 398-401
    community practice and, 395-404
    examples of practice for, 383-384
    group work and, 384-387, 397
    importance of, 373-375
    macro interventions and, 373-374, 401-404
    model for, 376-383
    natural helping systems and, 387-391
    organizational work and, 391-395
    social networks and, 387-391
    supportive/empowerment aspect of, 384-387

Ending stage, legal issues in, 38-39
Enuresis, 204
Environment:
    affective change and, 218
    assessment and, 552-553, 559-560
    behavior and, 199-200
    change agents and, xi-xii
    change in adults and, 243-244, 252
    change in children and, 264-268, 277-278
    cognition and, 175-178, 182, 188-191, 192
    communications technology and, 566-567
    components of, xii
    coping and, 349-360, 364, 365-366
    crisis vulnerability and, 339-343
    critical thinking about, 44
    empowerment and, 119, 124, 373-404
    feminist practice and, 153
    fund-raising and, 651-653, 663, 665
    international, 633-647
    juvenile justice system and, 454-455
    life-span perspective and, 420
    prevention, risk, resilience, and, 92, 93, 94-96,
        107
    public and private, 8
    research designs and, 535-536
    supervision and, 617
    workplace culture and, 503, 507-511
    See also Person-in-environment
Environmentalism, 199(table)
Epidemiologic Catchment Area Survey, 220
Epidemiology, and prevention science, 90-91, 92
Equal Employment Opportunity Commission
        (EEOC), 501, 505
Equal Pay Act of 1963, 504
ERP. See Exposure and response prevention
Ethical issues, 589-606
    as component of environment, xii
    Code on. See Code of Ethics
    confidentiality and, 29, 32, 592, 602
    critical thinking and, 43, 46, 49, 52, 54, 55-56,
        59
    decision making and, 596-600
    dilemmas in, 591-596
    empowerment and, 115, 606
    evolution of, 589-591
    family therapy and, 322
    future agenda on, 603-606
    group work and, 292
    multiculturalism and, 146
    overview of, 589-591

peer review and, 29
poverty and, 522-523, 606
research designs and, 540, 541, 546
risk management in, 600-603
standards, 590, 599-601
supervision and, 602, 625-627
technology and, 578-579, 616-617
work and, 500
See also Legal issues
Ethical theory, 596-597
Ethics committees, 598
Ethnicity and race. See Multiculturalism; Race and
        ethnicity
Ethnic matching, 141
Ethnic sensitive practice, 136, 137, 138. See also
        Multiculturalism
Ethnocentrism, 134
Ethnoconscious approach, 138-139, 146. See also
        Critical consciousness
Ethnographic methods, 321
Etiology, and prevention science, 91-92
Evaluation:
    behavioral change and, 212-213, 214
    critical thinking about, 54, 56
    empowerment and, 122-124
    group designs in, 544-546, 548-549
    in family treatment, 543-544
    in group work, 286, 293-294
    in mental health services, 446
    intervention research designs for, 546-548, 549
    juvenile justice system and, 460-466
    methodological debates in, 535, 536-538
    prevention science and, 91
    report cards for, 446
    self-, 248-249, 541, 548-549
    single-systems designs in, 538-544, 547, 548-549
    technology for, 574-575
    See also Assessment; Appraisal; Critical thinking
Evidence-based practice:
    administration/supervision and, 55-57
    assessment and, 49-52, 552-554. See also
        Measurement
    barriers to, 57-59
    barriers to, remedies for, 59-60
    behavioral change and, 213-214, 247, 256
    clinical standards and, 35
    critical thinking and, 43-61
    definition of, 46
    ethics and, 606
    evaluation and, 54

family therapy and, 321
mental health services and, 446
methodology and, 46-47, 536-538
multiculturalism and, 140-141
research methods and, 46-47
service methods in, 52-54
Evidence, legal, 32, 601
Executive system, 69
Expectations, legal, 24, 25
in beginning stage, 29, 30
in treatment stage, 34, 35, 36
See also Legal issues
Experimental studies, 46-47, 544-545
Expert opinion, 33
Expert systems, 573, 575
Exploitation:
as component of environment, xii
ethics and, 603
feminist practice and, 164
international issues and, 639
See also Oppression
Exposure and response prevention (ERP), 228
Exposure therapy, 223-228, 250
Extinction, operant, 209
Eye-movement desensitization and reprocessing
(EMDR), 228

Face validity, 140
Fair Labor Standards Act of 1938, 504
Fallacies, 48(table); 50, 55. *See also* Critical thinking
Falsifiability, 48
Families:
behavioral phenomena in, 213
belief systems in, 305-306, 309(table)
change and, 301-322
change in adults and, 252
change in children and, 266-267, 269-271
change motivators and, 245
cognition, meaning, and, 190-191
communication in, 308-309, 309(table)
continuity in, 270-271
crisis intervention and, 337-339
empowerment/structural approach and, 379-384,
387-390, 393-394
functioning of, 304-310
juvenile justice system and, 463-464, 467
legal issues and, 26

life-span perspective and, 417-418, 420
multigenerational system in, 305, 307, 309-310
organizational patterns in, 306-308, 309(table)
preservation programs for, 337-339
prevention and, 100-101
processes in, 305-309, 309(table)
resilience in, 304, 306, 308, 309(table), 317, 321,
322
sexual orientation and, 314, 321, 489, 490-492,
495
structure of, 266-267
technology and, 576-577
time and, 309-310, 314, 509
work and, 502, 503, 504, 506, 509-510
See also Children; Domestic violence; Parenting
Family and Medical Leave Act of 1993 (FMLA), 100,
504, 506
Family developmental view, 303-304
Family group conferencing, 389-390, 403
Family network theory, 420
Family Service America Family Loan Program, 645
Family systems, 302-304
Family therapy, 301-322
approaches to, 310-320, 312-313(table)
assessment in, 303, 304-310
Bowen model in, 311, 314
challenges for, 320-321
cognitive-behavioral approaches to, 316-317
diversity in, 320, 321
evolution of field of, 301-302
experiential approaches to, 314
intergenerational approaches to, 310-314
postmodern approaches to, 317-319
problem-solving approaches to, 314-320
psychodynamics in, 310-311
psychoeducational approaches to, 319-320
resilience and, 304, 306, 308, 309(table), 317,
321, 322
single-system studies of, 543-544
strategic-systemic models in, 315-316
strength-based approaches to, 316-317, 320,
322
structural model in, 314-315
systems orientation in, 302-306, 311, 320-322
Fear. *See* Phobias
Feedback:
computer generated, 575
in assessment, 560-561
in proactive coping, 362-363
Fees-for-service, and funding, 653

Feminism:
    contextualized practice and, 18
    delinquent behavior and, 455
    empowerment and, 115-116, 122-123, 165, 396
    evaluation and, 122-123
    family therapy and, 303
    multiculturalism and, 136
    stated purpose of, 160
Feminist practice, 151-168
    activism and, 152-154
    as identity, 157, 163-164
    as metatheory, 157-159, 164-165
    as method, 159-160
    changes in, 162-167
    defining of, 157-162
    economic issues and, 155, 156, 165
    FP98 Reprise study of, 154-163
    FPP and, 153, 154, 158
    gap between theory and, 165-167
    goals of, 156-157
    group work and, 283
    historical overview for, 151-152
    lesbians and gay men and, 155, 482
    nonfeminist practitioners and, 159
    political forces and, 152, 153, 155, 156, 159-167
    principles and, 153-154, 158, 163
    shifts in, 155-156
    transformation and, 156, 159, 162, 165-167
    variations of, 162-163
Feminist Practice Project (FPP):
    launching of, 153
    metatheory and, 158
    Pilot Reprise by, 154-163
    Pilot Study by, 153, 154
Feminist therapy, 165
FFT. See Functional Family Therapy
Flexibility, in families, 306
FMLA. See Family and Medical Leave Act
Food, and poverty, 520
Force field analysis, 507-508, 509
Foster care, 270
Foundation funding, 655-657
FPP. See Feminist Practice Project
Fraud, 602
Functional Family Therapy (FFT), 101
Fundamental attribution error, 45
Fund-raising, 651-665
    environment of, 651-653, 663, 665
    information sources on, 661-662

    mechanisms for, 653-654
    sources for, 654-660
    specialists for, 660-661
    See also Resources
Fuzzy logic, 579

GAD. See Generalized anxiety disorder
Gandhi, 114
Gay and lesbian community. See Lesbians and gay
    men
Gender:
    anxiety disorders and, 219, 220, 221, 222
    assessment and, 561-562
    coping and, 360
    crisis vulnerability and, 340-341
    empowerment/structural approach and, 396
    families and, 306, 307-308
    feminist practice and, 156, 158, 159, 162
    group work and, 284, 292-293
    juvenile justice system and, 455, 456, 469-471
    life-span perspective and, 426
    mental illness and, 442
    multiculturalism and, 131, 136-139
    suicide crisis intervention and, 337
    technology and, 566, 577
    work and, 501, 504, 510
    See also Feminism; Feminist practice; Men;
        Women
Generalist models of practice, 117
Generalization, critical thinking about, 53-54
Generalized anxiety disorder (GAD), 222, 233-234
Generalized representations of interactions, 190
General knowledge, and self-knowledge, 356
General systems approach, 66. See also Systems
Generations. See Intergenerational approaches;
        Multigenerational system
Genograms, 309, 314
Geographic information systems (GIS), 575
Geriatrics. See Elderly
Gifting. See Charitable gifts
GIS. See Geographic information systems
Global issues, xii
    contextualized practice and, 13-14
    demographic trends and, 39
    grassroots organizations and, 17-18
    legal issues and, 39

practice issues and, 634-635, 636-640
privatization and, 10, 11-13, 19
See also Internationalism
Globalization, definition of, 633-634
Goal displacement, 455
Goals, 424, 429, 431, 455, 555
Government, role of, 7, 19
funding and, 652, 654-655
privatization and, 10-11
restructuring and, 615-616
Graded exposure therapy, 223-228
Grameen Bank, 399, 643-644
Grants, 653, 657. *See also* Fund-raising
Grassroots organizations, 17-18, 146, 328, 659-660.
See also Community
Grievances, peer review of, 29. *See also* Complaints
Group designs for research, 544-546, 548-549
Group work practice, 281-294
adults in, 250-251
children in, 266-267, 269
critical issues in, 291-294
current trends in, 286-291
curriculum-based, 290-291
development in, 284-286
empowerment/structural approach and, 384-387,
397
generalizability in, 291
intervention processes in, 286
life-span perspective and, 417
managed care and, 287
poverty and, 525
purposes for, 282-283
structure for, 283-284
technology-based, 289-290, 572, 574
time-limited models in, 287-288
treatment integrity in, 291
work group and, 511

Health maintenance organizations (HMOs), 39, 287,
438, 439, 575. *See also* Managed care;
Managed care organizations
Helping networks, natural, 387-391
Helplessness, 115, 116, 118
Heterosexism, 479, 485
Heterosexual orientation, 478, 479, 480
coming out and, 481, 484-486

origins of, 481-484
See also Sexual orientation
Hierarchical linear model (HLM), 547-548, 549
Historical perspectives:
on ethics, 589-591
on family therapy, 301-302
on feminist practice, 151-152
on internationalism, 635-636
on poverty, 523-524
on sexual orientation, 477
HIV/AIDS:
contextualized practice and, 19
coping and, 360
empowerment/structural approach and, 394, 400
life-span perspective and, 423-424
uniqueness of, 492
HLM. *See* Hierarchical linear model
HMOs. *See* Health maintenance organizations
Holistic healing, 207. *See also* Wholistic perspective
Home-based family preservation services, 101
Homebuilders program, 338
Homelessness, 394, 403, 522. *See also* Poverty
Homophobia, 155. *See also* Lesbians and gay men;
Sexual orientation
Homosexual orientation, 478, 479
coming out and, 481, 484-486
origins of, 481-484
See also Lesbians and gay men; Sexual orientation
Hotlines:
for crisis intervention, 327, 328-331
for ethical decision making, 598
Housing, and social investment, 642-643
Human investment, 646-647
Human rights, 404, 494, 500, 590, 638
Hypotheses, and critical thinking, 49

ICS. *See* Interacting cognitive subsystems
IDAs. *See* Individual development accounts
Identity:
communications technology and, 568
ethnic or cultural, 441
feminist practice as, 157, 163-164
intersectionality of, 138, 145
life-span perspective and, 426-427
sexual orientation and, 478, 479, 480, 482, 484-
486

work and, 510
Ideology, 16, 58, 158, 164
Idiographic research, 537
IECs. *See* Institutional ethics committees
Imaginal exposure, 229
Immersive virtual reality, 573
Immigration Control and Reform Act of 1967, 504
Immunization programs, 99, 100
Impaired practitioners, 603
Imperialism, professional, 636
Implicational subsystem, 184-185
INAH. *See* Interstitial nuclei, anterior hypothalamus
Incarceration, 451-452, 456. *See also* Juvenile justice
    system
Incentives, as motivator for change, 246
Inclusion, in life-span perspective, 417
Incorrigibility, 470
Indicated prevention, 107(n2)
Indirect interventions, and systems, 77, 80-81
Individual deficit theory, 526-528
Individual development accounts (IDAs), 644-645
Individual intervention:
    contextualized practice and, 13-14, 16-17
    empowerment and, 118, 119-121
    groups for, 283
    prevention programs and, 99-100
Individualism, and privatization, 8-9, 13
Individuals with Disabilities Education Act, 273
Information:
    assessment, feedback, and, 561
    cognition, schemas, and, 176-177, 180, 184-188
    dissemination of, about programs, 92-93
    release of, 30-31, 32, 59
    right to know and, 59
    technology and, 565-580, 614, 616
    See also Informed consent; Knowledge; Record
        keeping
Information processing:
    by the mind, 179-180
    in coping, 352, 356-357
    in ICS model, 184-188
Informed consent, 34, 49, 602
Injustice, 375. *See also* Social justice
Input subsystem, 69
Institutional ethics committees (IECs), 598
Institutional review boards (IRBs), 598-599
Instrumental behaviors, change in, 197-214
Insurance benefits, absence of, 38-39, 501

Insurance-driven services, 287, 443. *See also*
    Managed care
Intake systems, 569-570
Integrated practice, 13-14
    empowerment/structural approach to, 373-404
    life-span perspective and, 416-417, 433
    physical and mental health and, 437-448
Interacting cognitive subsystems, 184-188
Interactional view:
    families and, 190-191, 302-303
    group work and, 283, 284-286
Interdisciplinariness, xiii
    coping and, 349
    education, training, and, 447-448
    empowerment and, 125
    family therapy and, 321
    feminist practice and, 154
    legal issues and, 23, 26
    mental health services and, 443
    prevention science and, 89
    supervision and, 620
Intergenerational approaches, to family therapy, 310-
    314. *See also* Multigenerational system
International Association of Schools of Social Work,
    635
International Commission of the Council of Social
    Work Education, 635
International Committee of NASW, 635
International Council on Social Welfare, 635
International Federation of Social Workers, 635
Internationalism, 633-647
    benefits of, 636-640
    phases of, 635-636
    scope of, 633-635
    social development and, 640-647
Internet:
    communications and, 565, 568, 569-570, 576,
        579
    critical thinking and, 60
    fund-raising and, 662
    restructuring and, 614
    See also Computer-mediated communications
Interorganizational work, and collaboration, 391-
    395
Interpersonal context:
    adult change and, 250-252
    communications technology and, 566-567
    crisis intervention and, 343
    delinquent behavior and, 455

empowerment and, 118, 119-121, 124
families and, 190-191
Interpersonal psychotherapy (IPT), 234-235
Intersectionality, 138, 145. *See also* Diversity;
    Multiculturalism
Interstitial nuclei, anterior hypothalamus (INAH),
    482, 483
Inter University Consortium for International Social
    Development, 635
Intervention research designs, 546-548, 549
Interviews, assessment, 559
Intuition, 47-48
Invalidity, social, 54. *See also* Validity
Investments:
    for fund-raising, 654
    human, 646-647
    social, 642-643
IPT. *See* Interpersonal psychotherapy
IRBs. *See* Institutional review boards

Johnson Intervention, 245
Joint Training and Partnership Act (JTPA), 505
JTPA. *See* Joint Training and Partnership Act
Justice:
    distributive, 375
    social. *See* Social justice
Juvenile justice system, 40, 273-274, 451-472
    adult system and, 451, 456
    community and, 462-466, 467, 469
    diversity and, 455-460
    gender and, 455, 456, 469-471
    philosophies in, 453-454
    practice issues and, 460-471
    practice principles for, 471-472
    prevention and, 454, 465-466, 468-469, 472
    punitive legislation and, 451-452
    recidivism in, 461
    reintegration services and, 461-464
    structured decision making in, 467-468
    theoretical issues and, 454-455
    values and, 453-454

Kant, Immanuel, 180-181, 597
Keystone risk and protective factors, 94, 97

Knowledge:
    coping and, 352-353, 356
    critical thinking and, 48, 55-56, 57
    empowerment and, 119
    ethics and, 604-606
    expert, of clients, 417
    feminist practice and, 166
    group work and, 282-288
    interdisciplinary, xiii, 23, 90, 447-448
    of multiculturalism, 134-139, 144-146
    of self, 182-183
    prevention science and, 90-93
    rational thought and, 181
    single-systems methodologies and, 538-543
    See also Information

Labeling theory, 455
Labor force, 501-502. *See also* Work
Language:
    communications technology and, 568, 575
    family therapy and, 318
    feminist practice and, 163
    international issues and, 639
    multiculturalism and, 141, 142, 145, 146
    professional, 619-620
    schemas, memory, and, 185
Latent function, 71-72
Law. *See* Legal issues
Lawsuits, 28, 600-601. *See also* Legal issues
Leadership:
    in families, 306
    in groups, 283, 284, 285
Learned behavior, 201(table). *See also* Behavioral
    change; Social learning theory
Learned helplessness, 115
Learned hopefulness, 78
Legal issues, 23-41
    children and, 264
    confidentiality and, 29-30, 31-32, 39-40
    direct impact of, 24
    emerging, 39-40
    ethics, risk, and, 600-601
    group work and, 292
    privilege and, 30, 31-32
    record keeping and, 32-34, 39-40
    regulation of practice in, 28-29
    release of information and, 30-31, 32

risk and, 27, 34, 35-38
    stages of practice and, 27-39
    subpoenas and, 31-32, 33
    therapeutic jurisprudence in, 26-27, 41
    treatment issues and, 27-39
    values and, 24-25
    See also Ethical issues; Juvenile justice system
Lesbians and gay men, 477-496
    coming out and, 481, 484-486
    diversity and, 478-480, 490
    empowerment/structural approach and, 399
    feminism and, 155, 482
    identity and, 479, 480, 482, 484-486
    pivotal, historical events for, 477
    See also Homosexual orientation; Sexual
        orientation
Lesbians and gay men, services to:
    across the life span, 423-428, 488-493
    future issues for, 493-494
    principles for, 494-496
Levels, 65-84
    composition, context, and, 76-80
    definition of, 66
    emergent properties in, 72
    empowerment practice models and, 119-120
    importance of, 65-67, 83-84
    multiculturalism and, 144, 146
    relationship intensity and, 73-75
    social development and, 642-647
    See also Systems
Liability, legal, 25, 35, 37-38, 39. See also Legal
        issues
Licensing, 28-29
Life-course, 419
Life-cycle models, 310, 416
Lifelong learning, 57
Life-span development theory, 132-133
Life-span perspective:
    developmental tasks and, 415-433
    goal setting and, 424, 429, 431
    managed care and, 432-433
    organizational analysis and, 421, 423-432
    practice principles and, 427-428, 430-432
    practice roles and, 424-427
    sexual orientation and, 423-428, 488-493
    theoretical issues in, 419-423
    values and, 416-423, 426-427
Loan programs, 529, 643-645

LONGSCAN, 265
Loyalties, divided, 594-595

Macro and micro contextualizations, 13-20, 67, 117,
        253, 256, 402, 638-640
Macro-oriented interventions, 373-374, 401-404,
        529. See also Empowerment/structural
        approach
Macro practitioners, compared to direct
        practitioners, xi-xii
MACS. See Metropolitan Area Child Study
Maintenance programs, 53-54
Major depressive disorder, 222, 234
Managed care, 38-39, 146, 155, 214
    characteristics of, 439-440
    education, training, and, 447-448
    ethics and, 596, 606
    evaluation research and, 536
    group work and, 287
    life-span perspective and, 432-433
    mental health services under, 438
Managed care organizations (MCOs), 611-615, 618-
        621, 623, 626-627. See also Health
        maintenance organizations
Manifest function, 71-72
MAPs. See Membership Assistance Programs
Marxian theory, 115
Mastery:
    cognitive, 334-335
    in coping, 354, 358
Masturbation, 202-203, 208-209
MCOs. See Managed care organizations
Meaning:
    culture and, 188-189
    group work and, 285-286
    mind and, 178-182
    schemas and, 182-188
    search for, 175-176
    social sources of, 177, 188-191
    social structures and, 189-190
    See also Cognitive-integrative approach
Measurement:
    client participation in, 560-561
    data collection problems in, 560-561
    definition of, 551
    ethnicity and, 561-562
    gender and, 561-562

qualitative, 558-559, 562
quantitative, 555-558
supervision and, 618
technology and, 570-571
tool selection for, 555-560
See also Assessment; Evaluation
Media, the:
    as component of environment, xii
    demographic trends and, 39
    legal issues and, 39
    prevention programs and, 105
    See also Internet
Medicaid, 437, 438, 439, 524, 529
Medically indigent, 443-444. *See also* Poverty
Membership Assistance Programs (MAPs), 506
Memory models, 176, 177, 184-188. *See also*
    Cognitive-integrative approach; Schemas
Memory, recovered, 36
Men:
    crisis intervention for, 341
    juvenile justice system and, 456, 469
    See also Gender
Mental ability, and multiculturalism, 138-139
Mental health, and coming out, 487-488
Mental Health Assessment and Service Agencies
    (MHASAs), 438
Mental health services:
    education and training in, 447-448
    performance assessment in, 446-447
    physical health and, 445
    research-practice relationship in, 445-447
    substance abuse and, 444-445, 446
    therapeutic jurisprudence and, 26
    transformation of, 438-439
Mental illness:
    comorbidity in, 444-445
    crisis intervention and, 337
    family therapy and, 319-320
    negative reinforcement and, 206-207
    positive reinforcement and, 204-206
    poverty and, 524
    prescriptive treatments for, 218
    severe and persistent, 442-443
    See also Affective change
Mentalism, 199(table)
Mental simulations, 362
Mentoring, 100, 425, 431, 464
Metaethics, 597

Meta worry, 233
Methodist Home for Children, 392-393
Metropolitan Area Child Study (MACS), 102
MHASAs. *See* Mental Health Assessment and Service
    Agencies
Micro and macro contextualizations, 13-20, 67, 117,
    253, 256, 402, 638-640. *See also* Macro-
    oriented interventions
Micro finance, 529, 643-645
Midwestern Prevention Project, 104
Migration, human, 639-640
Mind:
    as brain, 178-179
    behavior and, 199
    information processing by, 179-180
    reality construction by, 180-182
    See also Cognitive-integrative approach
Minimum wage, 504-505
Minority populations. *See* Race and ethnicity
Misconduct, 595, 600. *See also* Complaints
Misdiagnosis, 35
Mistakes, and critical thinking, 56, 59
MMPI, 571
Modeling, in behavioral change, 201(table), 210-211,
    249, 464
Monism, 199(table)
Monitoring:
    assessment and, 553-554, 557, 559, 560-561
    supervision and, 613
    See also Assessment; Evaluation
Morality, 589-590. *See also* Ethical issues
Moral philosophy, 596-597
Motivations for coping, 350
Motivators for change, 241, 244-247
MST. *See* Multisystemic therapy
Multiculturalism, 131-147
    as meta-theory, 132-133
    contextualized practice and, 18
    critical thinking and, 49
    definitions of, 132, 133, 139, 146
    empowerment and, 124, 138-139, 146, 396
    foundation for, 141-142
    group work and, 292-293
    life-span perspective and, 132-133, 421-422
    principles and methods for, 143-146
    research in, agenda for, 141, 142
    research in, critique of, 139-141
    sexual orientation and, 131, 136-139, 478

waves of change and, 134-139, 144-145
  See also Culture; Diversity
Multidisciplinary issues. See Interdisciplinariness
Multigenerational system, in families, 305, 307, 309-
  310. See also Intergenerational approaches
Multiple relationships, 593-594
Multisystemic therapy (MST), 101
Multi-user domains, 565
Muscle relaxation, 229
Mutism, 210
Mutual aid groups, 525
Mutual benefit organizations, 659
Myers, Toby, 18

NAMI. See National Alliance for the Mentally Ill
Narratives:
  in assessment, 558
  in family therapy, 318, 544
  life-span perspective and, 419, 421-422
  poverty and, 525-526
NASW. See National Association of Social Workers
National Alliance for the Mentally Ill (NAMI), 442,
  443, 448
National Association of Black Social Workers, 136
National Association of Social Workers (NASW):
  ethics and, 598. See also Code of Ethics
  International Committee, 635
  legal issues and, 24-25, 26, 28, 29
  multiculturalism and, 136
  National Committee on Women's Issues
    (NCOWI), 153
  on impaired practitioners, 603
National Comorbidity Study, 220
National Domestic Violence Hotline, 330
National Institute of Mental Health (NIMH), 330,
  546
National Labor Relations Act (NLRA) of 1935, 504-
  505
National Save-a-Life League, 330
Native American people, 480
Natural helping systems, 387-391
Naturalistic studies, 544
NCOWI. See National Association of Social Workers,
  National Committee on Women's Issues
Negative automatic thoughts, 230
Negative consequences, as motivator for change, 245
Negative punishment, 208-209

Negative reinforcement, 206-207
Neglect, child. See Child abuse and neglect
Negligence claims, and supervisors, 37
Neighborhoods. See Community
Neighborhood Watch programs, 103
Neoconservatives, 12, 19
Networks:
  computer, 571-572
  natural helping, 387-391
  social. See Social networks
Neuroscience, 178
New Deal, 523
New horizons, as motivator for change, 246-247
NGOs. See Nongovernment organizations
Nihilism, 199(table)
NIMH. See National Institute of Mental Health
NLRA. See National Labor Relations Act
Nomothetic research, 537
Nongovernment organizations (NGOs), funding for,
  652. See also Fund raising
Normative ethics, 597
Notes, personal, 33

Observational measures, 557-558
Obsessive-compulsive disorder (OCD), 220-221,
  228, 236, 332-333, 572
OCD. See Obsessive-compulsive disorder
One-on-one interaction, 250-251, 254. See also
  Interpersonal context
Operant conditioning, 200-201, 201(table), 204-210,
  213
Operant extinction, 209
Operation Cease-Fire, 104
Operationism, 199(table)
Operation Nightlife, 104
Opportunities, in cognitive-integrative approach,
  186-188, 192-194
Opportunity theory, 455
Oppression:
  as component of environment, xii
  definition of, 375
  empowerment and, 115-116, 120, 124
  empowerment/structural approach and, 375, 396,
    399, 401
  ethics and, 606
  feminist practice and, 152, 156, 157
  life-span perspective and, 421-423

multiculturalism and, 137, 142, 144
 poverty and, 526
 See also Exploitation
Options, in cognitive-integrative approach, 186-188,
 192-194
Organizational issues:
 collaboration and, 391-395
 life-span perspective and, 421, 423-432
 work and, 507-508, 509-511
Outcomes:
 behavioral change and, 212-213, 214
 clinical standards and, 35
 coping and, 358
 critical thinking and, 53, 54, 59
 empowerment and, 116, 124, 126
 expert systems and, 575
 family therapy and, 303-304
 group work and, 293-294
 mental health services and, 446
 performance assessment and, 446
 prevention programs and, 91
 supervision and, 618, 620
 work and, 500
 See also Evidence-based practice
Output subsystem, 69
Outreach, technology for, 568
Overt action, as change activity, 248-250

PACT. *See* Program of Assertive Community
 Treatment
Panic attacks, 220, 226, 227, 229, 232-233
Panic disorder, 220, 227, 229, 230, 232-233, 572
Paradoxical counterproductivity, 71
Parallel versus serial processing, 180
Parenting, 102, 210-211, 491-492. *See also* Children;
 Families
Parsimony, 199(table)
Participatory education, 384
Participatory evaluation, 122
Passive-observational studies, 544
Paternalism, ethics of, 593
Pathology of systems, 71
Patient compliance, 206-207
Peace, world, 634, 637, 638
Pedophiles, treatment of, 202-203, 204
Peer interactions, 251. *See also* Group work practice;
 Interpersonal context

Peer review, 29
Performance assessment, 446-447. *See also*
 Evaluation
Perkins, Frances, 523
Personal empowerment, 118, 119-121, 124. *See also*
 Empowerment
Personality disorders, 337
Personal notes, 33
Personal Responsibility and Work Opportunity
 Reconciliation Act, 643
Person-in-environment (PIE), 14, 199-200, 218, 617
 family therapy and, 301, 302
 international issues and, 643
 See also Behavioral change; Environment
Phases of practice. *See* Stages of practice
Phenylketonuria (PKU) testing, 99-100
Philanthropy, 655-657. *See also* Charitable gifts
Phobias, 219-220, 224, 225-226, 232, 235, 250, 572
Physical ability, and multiculturalism, 138-
 139
Physical environment, xii, 7, 9. *See also* Environment
PIE. *See* Person-in-environment
PIVOT Project, 18-19
PKU testing. *See* Phenylketonuria testing
Placement, risk of, 337-339, 338(box)
Placement services, 270-271
Play therapy, 275
Poison Prevention Packaging Act of 1970, 105
Politics:
 as component of environment, xii
 children and, 264, 265
 empowerment and, 14-15, 114-121, 124, 126,
  139, 645-646
 empowerment/structural approach and, 379-381,
  392
 feminist practice and, 152, 153, 155, 156, 159-
  167
 international issues and, 639-640, 645-646
 life-span perspective and, 424
 multiculturalism and, 139
 nature of social work and, 15-16
 organizational change and, 392
 privatization and, 7, 10, 11-13
 restructuring and, 614
 sexual orientation and, 479
Poor People's Summit, 403-404
POSCs. *See* Purchase-of-service contracts
Positive punishment, 207-208
Positive reinforcement, 204-206, 248

Positivism, 199(table)
Positivity bias, 354-355
Possible selves, 183, 192
Postmodernism, 317-319, 421
Postpositivist research, 321
Post-traumatic stress disorder (PTSD), 221-222, 223,
    227-228
Potentiation versus attenuation of stress, 358
Poverty, 519-531
    children in, 264-265, 266, 521, 523, 524
    coping and, 360
    defining of, 519-520
    demographics of, 520-522
    empowerment and, 115, 122, 381, 403-404
    ethics and, 522-523, 606
    feminist practice and, 155, 156
    future challenges and, 530
    global capitalism and, 12
    health care services and, 443-444
    history of involvement in, 523-524
    international issues and, 637, 644
    intervention issues for, 524-530
    juvenile justice system and, 459
    supervision practice and, 620
    theoretical issues and, 526-528
    women in, 521, 530
    work and, 501, 504, 512, 514
Power:
    contextualized practice and, 14-15, 17, 18
    definitions of, 396
    delinquent behavior and, 455
    families and, 303, 307-308
    feminist practice and, 153, 160, 161, 162, 165
    global capitalism and, 11-13, 19
    life-span perspective and, 424
    multiculturalism and, 137, 138
    social, types of, 381
    See also Empowerment
Powerlessness, 115-116, 264, 612. See also
    Empowerment; Power
Practice guidelines, 620. See also Standards
Pragmatism, 199(table)
Praxis, 144
Preferred practice approaches, 35
Preferred provider organizations (PPOs), 439. See
    also Managed care
Pregnancy Discrimination Act of 1978, 504
Prenatal and Early Childhood Nurse Home Visitation
    Program, 100

Prescriptive treatment, 218
Prevention, 89-108
    assumptions for success in, 95-96
    challenges for, 106-107
    children and, 99-103, 104, 105, 270
    classification of interventions in, 97-98
    exemplary programs in, 99-105
    juvenile justice system and, 454, 465-466, 468-
        469, 472
    legal issues and, 40
    of affective disorders, 236
    of placement, 337-339
    of poverty, 528
    of privatization, 13
    primary, 378-379
    proactive coping and, 360-364
    process of, 106
    punishment versus, 40
    risk chain interruption in, 96-97
    secondary, 379
    supervision and, 623
    tertiary, xiii, 379
    theme of, xiii
    See also Coping; Crisis intervention; Exposure
        and response prevention
Prevention questions, 47(table)
Prevention science, 90-108
    focus of, 96
    growth of, 96-97
    practice knowledge and, 90-93
    resilience and, 93-95
    risk and, 91-94, 95-107
    status of, 95-96
Privacy, 25, 33, 592, 602. See also Confidentiality
Privatization, 6-7, 19, 440, 615
    causal factors in, 11-13
    central features of, 7
    contemporary context and, 7-13
    feminist practice and, 155
    individuals and, 8-9
    institutions and, 10-11
    See also Contextualized practice; Restructuring
Privilege:
    in families, 307-308
    in group work, 291-292
    legal concept of, 30, 31-32
Proactive coping, 360-364
Problem definition, 57. See also Critical thinking
Problem-focused coping, 249, 344, 364

Problem solving:
  as framework, 277
  empowerment/structural approach and, 396
  importance of, 44-45
  in families, 308
  See also Critical thinking
Procedural fidelity, 53
Professional imperialism, 636
Professional issues. *See* Ethical issues; Fund-raising;
      Internationalism; Supervision
Professional judgment rule, 37
Prognosis questions, 47(table)
Program of Assertive Community Treatment (PACT),
      291, 443
Progressive Era, 523
Progressive muscle relaxation, 229
Progressive practice, xii
Propaganda, 46, 57
Propositional subsystem, 184-186
Protection, and duty to warn, 36-37, 624
Protective factors, 93-97, 99, 106. *See also*
      Prevention
Protective services, 270
Pseudoscience, 46, 57-58
Psychiatric emergencies, 337
Psychodynamics:
  as framework, 276
  cognitive-emotional change and, 247
  family therapy and, 310-311
  sexual orientation and, 480-481
Psychoeducational approaches, to family therapy,
      319-320
Psychotherapy:
  feminist influence on, 152
  for depression, 234-235
  number of sessions in, 288
  privatization and, 8, 11, 13
PTSD. *See* Post-traumatic stress disorder
Public child welfare services, 270-272
Public good, 19-20
Public world, 6-7
  privatization and, 8-13, 440
  rebuilding of, 13-18
Punishment versus prevention, 40. *See also* Negative
      punishment; Positive punishment
Purchase-of-service contracts (POSCs), 653, 654

Quackery, 46, 57-58

Qualitative methods:
  assessment and, 558-559, 562
  behavioral change and, 213-214
  empowerment evaluation and, 123-124
  family therapy and, 321
  methodology and, 544, 545, 547, 548
  multiculturalism research and, 145
Quality of services, and critical thinking, 56
Quantitative methods:
  assessment and, 555-558
  family therapy and, 321
  methodology and, 544, 548
Quantum changers, 248
Quasi-experimental studies, 544, 545
Questions, research methods for, 46-47. *See also*
      Critical thinking; Research
Quinlan, Karen Ann, 598

Race and ethnicity:
  anxiety disorders and, 219, 220, 221, 222, 225
  assessment and, 561-562
  children and, 266, 278
  coping and, 359
  cultural competence and, 441-442
  depressive disorders and, 223
  empowerment/structural approach and, 395
  families and, 305-306, 314
  feminist practice and, 156
  grant giving and, 657
  group work and, 284, 292-293
  juvenile justice system and, 455-460, 469-470
  life-span perspective and, 422
  multiculturalism and, 131, 133, 134-139
  poverty and, 521-522, 530
  social investment and, 642-643
  social skills training and, 235
  technology and, 576-578
  work and, 501, 502
  See also Culture; Diversity
Radical practice:
  contextualized practice and, 15
  empowerment and, 116
  feminist practice and, 156, 163, 164
Radical theory, 455
RAIs. *See* Rapid assessment instruments
RAP. *See* Recognize, Anticipate, Problem-solve model

Rapid assessment instruments (RAIs), 539
Rating scales, 556-557
Rationalism, 199(table)
Reactance theory, 245
Readiness:
    for change, 255
    for coping, 353, 363
Realism, 199(table)
Reality construction, 180-182
Reasoning, 44. *See also* Critical thinking
Recidivism, 461
Reciprocal causation, in prevention programs, 95-96
Recognize, Anticipate, Problem-solve (RAP) model,
        293
Record keeping:
    assessment and, 558, 559
    cognitive-integrative approach and, 194
    critical thinking and, 55
    ethics, risk, and, 602
    language of, 619-620
    legal issues and, 32-34, 39-40
    See also Information, release of
Recovered memory cases, 36
Reductionism, 72-73
Referrals, 38, 55, 602
Refugee services, 394-395
Regulation of practice, 28-29
Rehearsal strategies, 362
Reification, 199(table)
Reinforcement:
    adult change activities and, 248-249
    crisis intervention and, 332
    negative, 206-207
    positive, 204-206, 248
Reintegration services, 461-464
Relapse prevention, 107(n2). *See also* Recidivism
Relationships:
    assessment and, 554-555, 560-561
    boundary issues and, 36, 593-594, 601, 602, 603
    divided loyalties and, 594-595
    ethics and, 593-595
    systems levels and, 73-75
    technology and, 616
Relaxation therapies, 224, 229-230
Release of information, legal requirements for, 30-
        31, 32. *See also* Informed consent; Record
        keeping
Reliability:
    assessment measures and, 556, 559

critical thinking and, 49, 51
Religious congregations, 659. *See also* Spirituality
Reminders, computer generated, 575
Replication, and research design, 543
Representations of interactions, generalized, 190
Request for proposal (RFP), 655
Request for quote (RFQ), 655
Research:
    clinical standards and, 35
    comparative, 637
    critical thinking and, 46-47
    empowerment tools and, 124
    group designs in, 544-546, 548-549
    international issues and, 637
    intervention designs in, 546-548, 549
    methodological debates in, 535, 536-538
    prevention program design and, 91
    single-systems designs in, 538-544, 547, 548-549
    validity in, 140
    See also Assessment; Evidence-based practice;
        Measurement
Resemblance criteria, 45
Reserve funds, 654
Residential programs, in juvenile justice system, 462-
        463
Resilience:
    in children, 378
    in crises, 335
    in families, 304, 306, 308, 309(table), 317, 321,
        322
    life-span perspective and, 418
    prevention, risk, and, 93, 94-107
Resources:
    for coping, 357, 358-359, 361
    life-span perspective and, 433
    scarce, 56-57, 125, 268
Respect, 161-162
Respondeat superior, 38, 602
Respondent conditioning, 200, 201(table), 204
Respondent extinction, 202-204
Respondent learning, 202-204, 213
Response cost, 208-209
Response prevention, exposure and (ERP), 228
Restorative justice programs, 466, 472
Restructuring, 611-629
    government role and, 615-616
    services and, 614-615
    supervision and, 613-614, 616, 617-629
    technology and, 614, 615, 616-617

See also Privatization
RFP. *See* Request for proposal
RFQ. *See* Request for quote
Richmond, Mary, 523
Right to know, 59. *See also* Information; Informed
      consent
Risk:
      ambiguity in, 355-356
      crisis intervention and, 331-332
      critical thinking and, 46
      ethics and, 600-603
      juvenile justice system and, 467-468
      legal issues and, 27, 34, 35-38
      medically indigent and, 444
      placement and, 338(box), 338-339
      prevention and, 91-107
      social stress and, 189-190
      structured decision making and, 467-468
      supervision and, 623-624
      See also Coping
Risk chains, 93, 96-97, 106
Risk factors, 93-97, 99, 106, 339-343. *See also*
      Prevention; Risk
Risk questions, 47(table)
Romantic relationships. *See* Sexual relationships with
      clients
Roosevelt, Franklin D., 523
Royalties, and fund-raising, 654
Rules, legal, 24. *See also* Legal issues

Safety, and change, 508-509
SAGE. *See* Senior Action in a Gay Environment
Sales, for fund-raising, 654
Salvation Army, 330
Scales, assessment, 556-557
Scarce resources, 56-57, 125, 268
Schemas, 176-177, 180
      as memory patterns, 182
      change in, mechanisms of, 186-188, 191
      cognitive subsystems and, 184-188
      cognitive therapy and, 231-232, 233-234
      for coping, 356-357
      multiple selves and, 183, 187
      self-, 182-183, 190
Schizophrenia, 386, 390, 445, 573
School-based programs:
      change in children and, 272-273

crisis intervention and, 342
juvenile justice system and, 467
life-span perspective and, 417, 423-428
multiculturalism and, 133
prevention and, 101-103
sexual orientation and, 489
School-linked services, 273
Science, misuses of, 58
Scientific evidence, theme of, xii-xiii. *See also*
      Evidence-based practice
Scientific method, 58, 212
Scientific practice, 620
Scientific skepticism, 199(table)
Scientist-practitioner model, 541, 548
Screening, 552-553. *See also* Assessment
Seattle Social Development Project (SSDP), 102
Self-anchored scales, 556-557
Self-awareness, 120, 144, 176
Self-blame, 344-345
Self-care behaviors, 116
Self-determination, 592-593
Self-efficacy, 116, 117, 118, 120, 125, 246
Self-evaluation, in adult change, 248-249
Self-evaluative practitioners, 541, 548-549
Self-help groups, 525, 572. *See also* Social support
Self-injury, 208
Self-knowledge, 356
Self-monitoring, 248, 557
Self-reflection, 144
Self-schemas, 182-183, 190
Self-stimulation, 208
Selves:
      multiple, 183, 187
      possible, 183, 192
Senior Action in a Gay Environment (SAGE), 493
Seniors. *See* Elderly
Serial versus parallel processing, 180
Service methods, evidence-based, 52-54
Service providers, 53
Settlement Movement, 395, 523, 635
Seven-stage model of crisis intervention, 328, 331-
      334
Sexism, 156, 160, 162, 314. *See also* Gender;
      Heterosexism; Homophobia
Sex offenders, treatment of, 202-203, 204
Sexpert system, 573
Sexual abuse, 26, 36, 152, 336, 390, 470, 639
Sexual orientation:
      biological research on, 482-483

coming out and, 481, 484-488
culture and, 478, 480, 483-484
diversity and, 478-480, 490
empowerment/structural approach and, 399
families and, 314, 321, 489, 490-492, 495
feminist practice and, 155
group work and, 292-293
identity and, 478, 479, 480, 482, 484-486
juvenile justice system and, 460
life-span perspective and, 423-428, 488-493
multiculturalism and, 131, 136-139, 478
origins of, 481-484
psychodynamic theories of, 480-481
See also Diversity
Sexual relationships with clients, 36, 593, 601, 602, 603
Shaping, operant, 209-210
Shrink-Link, 578
Simulations, 362, 573
Single-systems research designs, 538-544, 547, 548-549
Situational context:
coping and, 357-360, 364, 365-366
delinquent behavior and, 455
Skillman Intensive Aftercare Program, 462
Skills, 57, 235, 249. *See also* Education; Training
Skills modeling, 210-211
Slavery, 314
Social bond theory, 455
Social capital, 265
Social change:
contextualized practice and, 13-21
empowerment/structural approach to, 373-404
legal issues and, 23, 26, 39-40
See also Change
Social cognition, 285, 360. *See also* Constructivism
Social competence training, 102
Social constructionism, 181, 285, 304, 421
Social development, 640-647
Social disorganization, 455
Social environment, empowerment/structural approach to, 373-404. *See also* Environment
Social groups:
as component of environment, xii
critical thinking and, 49
intersectionality and, 138
systems, levels, and, 73-75
See also Culture; Multiculturalism; Race and ethnicity

Social identities, intersectionality of, 138, 145
Social investment, 642-643
Social justice:
demographics and, 39
empowerment and, 114-115, 124, 126
empowerment/structural approach and, 375, 381
ethics and, 590
family therapy and, 322
frameworks for, 85
international issues and, 637
legal system trends and, 40
life-span perspective and, 422
mission of, 20
multiculturalism and, 138, 142, 146
theme of, xii
values and, 24-25
See also Juvenile justice system; Legal issues
Social learning theory, 200-201
modeling in, 201(table), 210-211
operant conditioning in, 201(table), 204-210
respondent learning in, 201(table), 202-204
See also Behavioral change
Social networks:
adult change and, 252-253
coping and, 356-357
empowerment/structural approach and, 387-391
life-span perspective and, 420
mapping process and, 511
poverty and, 525
work and, 511
Social phobia, 219-220, 224, 226, 232, 235
Social power, types of, 381
Social pressure, for change, 244-245
Social reform mission, 401
Social Security Act, 504, 523, 524
Social Security Administration (SSA), 520
Social skills training, 235, 249
Social stress, 189-190
Social-structural theories, 419-421
Social support:
computer mediated, 571-572
coping and, 359
crisis vulnerability and, 341-342
empowerment/structural approach and, 387-391
work issues and, 507, 511
Social systems, xiii, 68-69. *See also* Systems
Social validity data, 54. *See also* Validity
Social work:

contextualized practice in. *See* Contextualized practice
contributions of, 611-613
core values of, 24-25
political nature of, 15-16
Social Workers Helping Social Workers, 603
Social Work Research Development Centers, 546
Societal prevention programs, 105
Societal restructuring. *See* Restructuring
Socioeconomic status, 340, 359-360, 637. *See also* Class; Economics
Sociological propaganda, 57
Sociopolitical empowerment, 119, 124. *See also* Empowerment; Politics
Socrates, 59-60, 596
Solution-based therapy, 328, 335, 525
Spaces, public and private, 8-9. *See also* Environment
Specialization, 82
Specific phobia, 219, 224, 225-226, 232
Speech recognition systems, 579
Spirituality, 164, 306, 321
SSA. *See* Social Security Administration
SSDP. *See* Seattle Social Development Project
SSI. *See* Supplemental Security Income
Stability, in families, 306
Stages of group development, 285
Stages of practice:
    beginning stage, 27-34
    ending stage, 38-39
    legal issues and, 27-39
    phase model for, 552
    treatment stage, 34-38
Standardized measures, 555-556, 562, 563
Standards, 23, 25, 27
    ethical, 590, 599-601. *See also Code of Ethics*
    in beginning stage, 28, 33
    in treatment stage, 34-35, 36, 37
    practice versus clinical, 34-35
    supervision practice and, 627-629
    See also Legal issues; Practice guidelines
Stereotypes:
    critical thinking and, 49
    in coping, 358
    multiculturalism and, 134, 137, 141
    systems and, 82
Stimulus control, 250
Stories. *See* Narratives
Strategic-systemic models, in family therapy, 315-316
Strengths-based approaches, 117, 159, 162

empowerment/structural approach and, 381
life-span perspective and, 420
social development and, 646-647
to crisis intervention, 328, 335
to family therapy, 316-317, 320, 322
to poverty, 524-525
work issues and, 507
Stress:
    coping with. *See* Coping
    families and, 310, 319. *See also* Family therapy
    potentiation versus attenuation of, 358
    poverty and, 524
    social, 189-190
    supervision and, 624-625
    technology and, 571
Stress-inoculation therapy, 235-236
Stressors, 351-358, 361-364. *See also* Coping
Structural change. *See* Empowerment/structural approach
Structural family therapy, 314-315
Structures, legal, 24. *See also* Legal issues
Subpoenas, 31-32, 33
Substance abuse:
    mental health and, 444-445, 446
    prevention of, 104
    treatment of, 203-204
Subsystems, 69, 184-188
Suicide, 445, 489
    crisis intervention and, 329(box), 330, 336-337, 340-342
Supervision:
    advocacy and, 620-621
    assessment and, 617-618
    business models and, 618-619
    culture and, 621-622
    ethics and, 602, 625-627
    evidence-based, 55-57
    language and, 619-620
    measurement and, 618
    relationship models and, 618-619
    restructuring and, 613-614, 616, 617-629
    risk management and, 623-624
    standards for, 627-629
    stress and, 624-625
    technology and, 616-617
Supervisor liability, 37-38, 602
Supplemental Security Income (SSI), 529
Supportive/empowerment group work, 384-387

Support networks. *See* Social networks; Social
    support; Supportive/empowerment group
    work
Survivors, victims as, 646
Swallowing problems, 207-208, 209-210
Swearing, treatment for, 207
Systematic desensitization, 228-229
Systemic models. *See* Strategic-systemic models
Systems, 65-84
    adult change and, 243, 244, 245
    aspects of, 68-69
    behavior and, 200
    cognition and, 176, 184-188
    components of, 67
    composition, context, and, 76-80
    contradictory nature of, 82-83
    crisis intervention and, 339-343
    definition of, 66
    empowerment and, 115
    environment and, 373-404
    family therapy and, 302-306, 311, 320-322
    functioning of, 69-72
    history and future of, 67, 72
    importance of, 65-67, 83-84
    interventions and, 72-83
    juvenile justice and, 451-472
    life-span perspective and, 416
    performance assessment and, 446-447
    power and, 14
    relationship intensity and, 73-75
    social development and, 641-647
    subsystems of, 69, 184-188
    theme of, xiii
    workplace intervention and, 506
    See also Critical thinking; Schemas

TANF. *See* Temporary Aid to Needy Families
*Tarasoff v. Board of Regents of the University of
    California*, 592-593
Technology:
    assessment and, 563
    communications, 289, 327, 328-331. *See also*
        Computer-mediated communications
    definition of, 566
    ethics and, 578-579, 616-617
    group work and, 289-290
    international issues and, 637-638

legal issues and, 23, 39-40
    restructuring and, 614, 615, 616-617
    work and, 514
Teleology, 199(table), 597
Telephone conferencing, 289
Telephone hotlines, 327, 328-331, 598
Telephone therapy, 574
Television, 9, 11, 579
Temporary Aid to Needy Families (TANF), 262, 265,
        529, 530. *See also* Aid to Families with
        Dependent Children
Termination of services, 38-39, 552, 602
Tertiary prevention, xiii. *See also* Prevention
Testimony, 30, 31
Textual analysis, computerized, 575
Theories, assessment of, 48-49. *See also* Research
Therapeutic alliance, 251, 254-255, 267
Therapeutic jurisprudence, 26-27, 41
Threats, 349-357. *See also* Coping; Risk
"Three-strikes" law, 99
Throughput subsystem, 69
Time dependence:
    in assessment, 552-553, 554
    in families, 309-310, 314, 509
    in prevention programs, 96
Time-limited models, 287-288, 440
Token economies, 248
Trade unions, 502-503, 506
Training:
    critical thinking and, 55
    empowerment and, 115
    ethics and, 604
    for jobs, 505, 524
    for research, 545
    in adult change, 249
    in new world of practice, 447-448
    in public child welfare services, 272
    in school-based prevention, 102
    multiculturalism and, 140, 142
    systems and, 82
    See also Education for social work
Transdisciplinary fields, 154. *See also*
        Interdisciplinariness
Transference, management of, 36
Transformation:
    empowerment and, 381
    feminist practice and, 156, 159, 162, 165-167
    ICS model and, 185, 186
    mental health services and, 438-439

Traumatic events. *See* Crises; Crisis intervention; Post-traumatic stress disorder
Treatment stage, legal issues in, 34-38
Trial testimony, 30, 31
Triangulation, and family organization, 307
Trust, 27, 567
Tuition, 653
Turing, Alan, 179
Twelve Step groups, 284
Two-person system, for adult change, 250-251, 253
Two-spirited Native American people, 480

Uncertainty, 59
Unemployment, 459, 501, 505
UNICEF. *See* United Nations Children's International Education Fund
Unions, 502-503, 506. *See also* Work
United Nations, 404, 634, 636, 638-639, 640
United Nations Children's International Education Fund (UNICEF), 634, 638-639
United Way, 652, 657-658
Utilitarianism, 597

Validity:
    assessment measures and, 556, 559
    critical thinking and, 49, 51, 54
    multicultural research and, 140
Value(s):
    change and, 242, 264-268
    core, 24-25
    critical thinking and, 43, 44
    empowerment and, 114-115, 119, 120, 124-125
    ethics and, 590-591, 592-596
    injustice, oppression, and, 375-376
    internationalism and, 633
    juvenile justice system and, 453-454
    life-span perspective and, 416-423, 426-427
    mental health services and, 439
    multiculturalism and, 134, 140
    organizational, 392
    poverty and, 522-523
    sexual orientation and, 479, 480
    systems and, 68
    work and, 502, 503, 510-511
    See also Belief systems

Victim assistance programs, 335-336, 341-342, 343, 466. *See also* Juvenile justice system
Victims, as survivors, 646
Videotaping, 616
Village Banks of Bank Rakyat, 644
Violence:
    domestic. *See* Domestic violence
    duty to warn and, 36-37, 624
    international issues and, 637
    juvenile, 452, 465-466. *See also* Juvenile justice system
    prevention of, 103, 104-105, 465-466
    supervision practice and, 623-624
Virtual reality, 573, 580
Vitalism, 199(table)
Voice mail, in group work, 290
Vulnerability:
    supervision practice and, 621
    to crises, 339-343
    to poverty, 522
    to threats, 354, 356. *See also* Coping

Wage gap, 501, 504
Warnings, about clients, 36-37, 624
War on Poverty, 523-524
Warren, Harry M., Jr., 330
Wealth, 11-12. *See also* Economics
Web sites. *See* Internet
Welfare reform, 10, 146, 152, 643
    adult change and, 253
    children and, 264-265
    empowerment/structural approach and, 383
    feminist practice and, 155
    poverty and, 530
Whistle-blowing, 595-596
Wholistic perspective, 162, 164. *See also* Holistic healing
Women:
    anxiety disorders and, 219, 220, 221, 222
    communications technology and, 566
    coping and, 360
    crisis vulnerability and, 340-341, 344
    depressive disorders and, 223
    empowerment and, 115, 116, 122, 123
    empowerment/structural approach and, 390, 399, 403
    grant giving and, 657

identity and, 157
juvenile justice system and, 469-471
mental illness and, 442
multiculturalism and, 136, 137
NASW National Committee on, 153
poverty and, 521, 530
supervision practice and, 620-621
work and, 504, 506, 512-513
See also Feminism; Feminist practice; Gender
Women's movement, 151-152, 158. *See also*
          Feminism; Feminist practice
Work, 499-515
          diversity and, 510-511

economic self-sufficiency and, 501-502, 504, 511-514
family needs and, 502, 503, 504, 506, 509-510
importance of, 499-502, 514-515
legislation and, 503-506
practice applications for, 509-514
theoretical issues and, 506-509
workplace issues and, 501-503, 507-511
Workers Compensation Act, 504

Youth Violence Strike Force (YVSF), 104
YVSF. *See* Youth Violence Strike Force

About the Editors

Paula Allen-Meares (MSW, Child Welfare, 1971, University of Illinois, Urbana; Ph.D., Social Work and Educational Administration, 1975, University of Illinois, Urbana; Management Development Program, Harvard University Graduate School of Education, 1990) is currently Dean and Professor of Social Work at the University of Michigan School of Social Work. Her research interests include the tasks and functions of social workers employed in educational settings; psychopathology in children, adolescents, and families; adolescent sexuality; premature parenthood; and various aspects of social work practice. She is principal investigator of a W. K. Kellogg Foundation Grant, co-principal investigator of the National Institute of Mental Health (NIMH) Social Work Research Center on Poverty, Risk, and Mental Health; and co-investigator on an NIMH research grant. She serves on several editorial boards and on national professional and

scientific committees promoting the intellectual and empirical advancement of the profession. She is a member of the Board of Trustees of the William T. Grant Foundation. She also serves on numerous committees at the University of Michigan that promote interdisciplinary research, development, and diversity. She is the recipient of a Management Institute Certificate from Harvard University and a Management of Managers Certificate from the University of Michigan.

Charles Garvin is Professor of Social Work at the School of Social Work of the University of Michigan, where he has been a faculty member for almost 35 years. He holds a master's degree and Ph.D. from the School of Social Service Administration of the University of Chicago. He is the author of *Contemporary Group Work* and coauthor of *Interpersonal Practice in Social Work, Social Work in Contemporary Society* and *Generalist Practice.* He is also the coeditor of the journal *Small Group Research.* In addition, he has written many articles on social work practice. He is former chair of the Group for the Advancement of Doctoral Education in Social Work. He has provided many consulta- tions outside of the United States, most recently in several countries in Eastern Europe. He is currently doing research on services for people who suffer from mental illness and alcoholism and on approaches in different societies to re- duction of conflict among youth groups.

About the Contributors

Neil Abell is Associate Professor and was formerly the doctoral program director at the School of Social Work, Florida State University. His research and teaching center on psychometrics, practice evaluation, HIV/AIDS, and family stress and coping.

Sheila H. Akabas is Professor of Social Work and Director of the Center for Social Policy and Practice in the Workplace at Columbia University School of Social Work. As chair of the World of Work field of practice, she has developed curricula and taught courses in social policy, research, delivery of services to workers, and human resource management and supervision.

Jane E. Barden is a doctoral student in the School of Social Service Administration at the University of Chicago.

M. Daniel Bennett, is a third-year doctoral student at the School of Social Work, University of North Carolina at Chapel Hill. He works with the Carolina Children's Initiative, for children with aggressive, antisocial behavior, and the Triangle Night Flight Basketball League, designed to combat the problems of drugs and crime in economically distressed communities.

Sharon B. Berlin is Helen Ross Professor in the School of Social Service Administration at the University of Chicago.

Betty Blythe is Professor of Social Work at the Boston College Graduate School of Social Work. She conducts research on programs for children and families in the United States and other countries and is a board member of the International Initiative for Children, Youth, and Families.

Mary Bricker-Jenkins is a mother, farmer, writer, and social worker in public practice. She teaches social work at Temple University and works as an ally of the Kensington Welfare Rights Union in the growing movement to end poverty.

Aaron M. Brower is Harold C. Bradley Faculty Fellow and Professor of Social Work and Integrated Liberal Studies and Associate Director at the University of Wisconsin, Madison, School of Social Work. His work focuses on the development and evaluation of educational innovations and learning communities.

Jacqui Corcoran is Assistant Professor and Co-Director of the Community Service Clinic at the University of Texas–Arlington School of Social Work. She has published in the areas of family therapy, solution-focused therapy, and adolescent pregnancy and is the author of *Evidence-Based Social Work Practice With Families: A Lifespan Approach.*

Enid O. Cox is Professor of Social Work and Director of the Institute of Gerontology at the University of Denver. She has more than 30 years experience in direct practice, program development, administration, research, and teaching in social work, with an emphasis in gerontology.

Carmen Crosser is a doctoral student in the School of Social Service Administration at the University of Chicago and a licensed clinical social worker, specifically in family therapy.

Doreen Elliott is Professor of Social Work at the University of Texas–Arlington. Her published work has focussed on social work in the residential setting, juvenile delinquency, field practice in social work education, comparative international approaches to policy and social work education, and most recently, theory building and an international approach in social work through social development.

Kathleen Coulborn Faller is Professor of Social Work, Director of the Family Assessment Clinic, faculty coordinator of the Civitas Child and Family Programs, and principal investigator for the Interdisciplinary Child Welfare Training Program (at the University of Michigan). She is also involved in clinical work, teaching, training, and writing in the area of child maltreatment.

Robert Fisher is Professor and Chair of Political Social Work at the Graduate School of Social Work, University of Houston. He has been active in various community organizing efforts since the early 1970s. He is the recipient of two Fulbright fellowships to Austria and currently holds the Henry and Lucy Moses Distinguished Professorship at Hunter College School of Social Work.

Marilyn Flynn is Dean of the School of Social Work at the University of Southern California in Los Angeles. She currently serves as a commissioner for the Council on Social Work Accreditation and is an elected member of the National Nominating Committee for the Council on Social Work Education.

Mark W. Fraser holds the John A. Tate Distinguished Professorship for Children in Need at the School of Social Work, University of North Carolina at Chapel Hill. In addition, he directs the Carolina Children's Initiative, an early intervention research project for children with aggressive, antisocial behavior.

Karen I. Fredriksen is Associate Professor in the School of Social Work, University of Washington. She is Director of the AIDS and Caregiving Project and has served as a consultant on numerous family care projects.

Edith M. Freeman is Professor in the School of Social Welfare at the University of Kansas. She has practiced as a school social worker, medical social worker, and in public child welfare. She also provides consultation to public schools and to community organizations.

Maeda J. Galinsky is a Kenan Professor at the School of Social Work, University of North Carolina at Chapel Hill. She is currently involved in research on teaching about technology-based groups and in the development and evaluation of interventions for aggressive children and their families.

Eileen Gambrill is Professor in the School of Social Welfare at the University of California, Berkeley. Her research interests include professional education and decision making, behavioral methods, evaluation of practice, and social skills training.

Lorraine Gutiérrez teaches in the School of Social Work and Department of Psychology at the University of Michigan. She is also co-coordinator of the Detroit Initiative in Psychology, a program of scholarship, teaching, and service with community-based organizations in Detroit.

Joseph A. Himle is Clinical Assistant Professor and Director of Education in ambulatory psychiatry at the University of Michigan, Department of Psychiatry. He is also associate director of the Anxiety Disorders Program at the Department of Psychiatry. He holds an adjunct faculty appointment at the University of Michigan School of Social Work.

Walter W. Hudson (deceased) was Professor in the School of Social Work, Florida State University. Emphasizing the development of scales and indexes for practice and research, he did innovative work on the use of computers in human service assessment and was the first recipient of the Society for Social Work and Research's Lifetime Achievement Award.

Howard Jacob Karger is Professor and Director of the doctoral program at the Graduate School of Social Work, University of Houston. The recipient of two Fulbright fellowships, he has published widely in national and international journals.

Armand Lauffer is Professor of Social Work at the University of Michigan. He is the designer of the Grants, Etc. website, which provides a gateway to the world of grants, contracts, and funding sources. He is also director of Project Star, which is a professional leadership training program in Jewish Communal Service.

Edith Lewis is Associate Professor of Social Work and Women's Studies at the University of Michigan. She teaches in the areas of culturally competent social work practice, family relationships, group process, and behavioral theory and interventions.

John F. Longres is Professor of Social Work at the University of Washington in Seattle. He has published extensively in the areas of human behavior and the social environment, ethnic and race relations, mental health, juvenile delinquency, and gerontology.

Robert G. Madden is Professor of Social Work at Saint Joseph College in West Hartford, Connecticut. He currently maintains a private practice that provides representation, consultation, and training regarding legal issues to the social work community. He also serves on the board of directors of the Children's Law Center of Connecticut.

Nazneen S. Mayadas is Professor of Social Work at the University of Texas at Arlington. She served as Chief of Social Services with the United Nations' High Commissioner for Refugees.

Elizabeth Misener is a doctoral student at the School of Social Welfare, University at Albany, State University of New York. Her practice experience includes work with youths in the correctional system, with individuals diagnosed as mentally ill, and with families.

Carlton E. Munson is Professor and Director of the doctoral program at the University of Maryland School of Social Work. He also directs the Washington Area Supervision Institute at Woodstock Forest. He is a clinician-scientist whose practice and research activity focus on trauma and loss in children.

Laura L. Myers is Adjunct Instructor of Social Work at the University of Georgia. She is also managing editor of the *College Student Administration Journal*.

Paula S. Nurius is Professor of Social Work at the University of Washington School of Social Work, where she also directs the doctoral program and an NIMH Predoctoral Prevention Research Training Program. Her current research focuses on women's appraisal of and coping responses to acquaintance sexual aggression and on prevention interventions designed to strengthen anticipatory and proactive coping.

Ruth J. Parsons is Professor of Social Work and Director of the doctoral program at the Graduate School of Social Work at the University of Denver. Her contributions to social work are in integrated social work practice and empowerment, which has included development of measurement scales and evaluations of empowerment projects for the elderly and mental health.

David E. Pollio is Associate Professor at the George Warren Brown School of Social Work, Washington University, St. Louis, Missouri. He is also on the faculty of the Center for Mental Health Services Research. Currently, he is principal investigator on an NIMH-funded grant testing the effectiveness of "family-responsive" psychoeducation groups.

Karen A. Randolph is Assistant Professor at the School of Social Work, University at Buffalo, State University of New York. Her current work includes the application of quantitative methods in understanding risk and resilience in adolescence.

Frederic G. Reamer is Professor in the graduate program of the School of Social Work, Rhode Island College. He has served as a social worker in mental health, correctional, and housing agencies and in a governor's office. He was chair of the committee that wrote the current *National Association of Social Workers' Code of Ethics*.

William J. Reid is Distinguished Professor at the School of Social Welfare, University at Albany, State University of New York, where he teaches research methods and clinical practice.

Anita Reithoffer is a doctoral student at Boston College, where she is conducting research on family preservation services. She is interested in using adventure-based programs to develop behavioral, social, and cognitive skills in children and adolescents.

Katherine E. Richards-Schuster is a doctoral student in social work and sociology at the University of Michigan. Her work focuses on youth development and participation in organizations, organizational change and collaborations, the impacts of organizational change on community development, and the structure of human service organizations.

Albert R. Roberts is Professor of Social Work and Administration of Justice at Rutgers, the State University of New Jersey, Piscataway. He is editor-in-chief of *Crisis Intervention and Time-Limited Treatment,* a peer-reviewed international journal. He is also the series editor of the Springer Series on Social Work and the Springer Series on Family Violence.

Rosemary C. Sarri is Professor Emerita of Social Work and Faculty Associate in the Institute for Social Research at the University of Michigan. Her research interests have included studies of child and youth welfare, juvenile justice systems, women in poverty and in the criminal justice system, and the effects of social policy and administration on the delivery of human services.

Elizabeth A. Segal is Professor of Social Work and Director of the School of Social Work at Arizona State University in Tempe. She is a cofounder and coeditor of *The Journal of Poverty,* a quarterly dedicated to exploring the social, economic, and political aspects of poverty and inequality.

Lonnie R. Snowden is Professor in the School of Social Welfare at the University of California, Berkeley. He also serves as Director of the Center for Mental Health Services Research at Berkeley, an organization bringing together an interdisciplinary group of researchers from Berkeley and from the University of California at San Francisco.

Michael Spencer is Assistant Professor of Social Work and Faculty Associate of the Social Work Research Development Center on Poverty, Risk, and Mental Health. He teaches courses that focus on human behavior in the social environment, cultural diversity, and social justice.

Layne K. Stromwall is Assistant Professor in the School of Social Work at Arizona State University, Tempe. Her research interests include poverty and welfare reform, especially as they affect native populations. She also serves as an editorial reviewer for the *Journal of Poverty.*

Bruce A. Thyer is Research Professor of Social Work at the University of Georgia. He is the founding and current editor of the bimonthly journal *Research on Social Work Practice.*

John E. Tropman is Professor of Social Work at the University of Michigan. His research focuses on the structure of social problems, executive leadership, policy development, nonprofit management, and values and ethics in decision making. He also teaches courses at the University of Michigan Business School, the Executive Leadership program, and the Honors College.

Froma Walsh is Professor in the School of Social Service Administration and Department of Psychiatry and Codirector of Center for Family Health, at the University of Chicago. She is the editor of *Journal of Marital & Family Therapy.*

Marie Weil is Berg-Beach Distinguished Professor of Community Practice at the School of Social Work, University of North Carolina, Chapel Hill. She is Director of the Community Social Work Program and Associate Director of the Jordan Institute for Families. She edits the *Journal of Community Practice.*